Psychology and Life

Psychology and Life

Fourteenth Edition

Philip G. Zimbardo
Stanford University

Richard J. Gerrig
State University of New York at Stony Brook

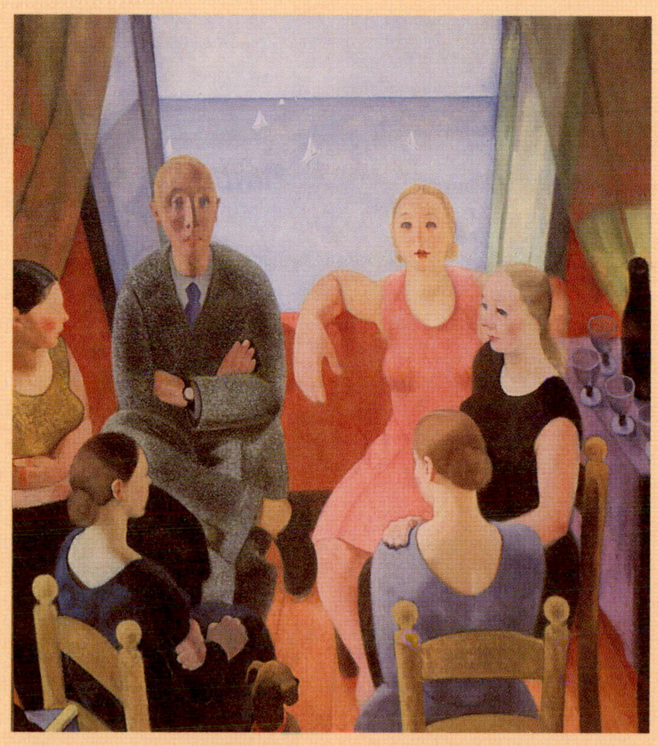

HarperCollins*CollegePublishers*

Acquisitions Editor: Catherine Woods
Developmental Editor: Elaine Silverstein
Project Editor: Shuli Traub
Text and Cover Designer: John Sparks
Cover Images: Top left, Scala/Art Resource, New York; top center, Tate Gallery, London/Art Resource, New York; top right, Giraudon/Art Resource, New York; middle left, Victoria & Albert Museum, London/Art Resource, New York; middle center, Alinari/Art Resource, New York; middle right, National Museum of American Art, Washington, DC/Art Resource, New York; lower left, Erich Lessing/Art Resource, New York; lower center, National Museum of American Art, Washington, DC/Art Resource, New York; lower right, Scala/Art Resource, New York
Art Studio: Electragraphics/Bob Supina/Hilda Muinos
Photo Researcher: Elsa Peterson
Electronic Production Manager: Alexandra Odulak
Desktop Administrator/Electronic Page Makeup: Joanne Del Ben
Manufacturing Manager: Hilda Koparanian
Printer and Binder: R. R. Donnelley & Sons Company
Cover Printer: New England Book Components

For permission to use copyrighted material, grateful acknowledgment is made to the copyright holders on pp. C-1–C-8, which are hereby made part of this copyright page.

Psychology and Life, Fourteenth Edition

Library of Congress Cataloging-in-Publication Data

Zimbardo, Philip G
Psychology and life / Philip G. Zimbardo, Richard J. Gerrig. — 14th ed.
p. cm.
Includes bibliographical references and indexes.
ISBN 0-673-99007-9
1. Psychology. I. Gerrig, Richard J. II. Title
BF121.Z54 1995 95–21566
150—dc20 CIP

96 97 98 9 8 7 6 5 4 3 2

To Adam, Zara, and Tanya—the joys of my life, and hopes for the future—P.G.Z.

To Alex—for filling my life with love and laughter—R.J.G.

Brief Contents

Detailed Contents

Preface

Our Goals and Objectives

Teaching Introductory Psychology well is one of the greatest challenges facing any academic psychologist. Indeed, because of the range of our subject matter, it is probably the most difficult course to teach effectively in all of academia. We must cover both the micro-level analyses of nerve cell processes and the macro-level analyses of cultural systems; both the vitality of health psychology and the tragedy of lives blighted by mental illness. Our challenge in writing this text—like your challenge in teaching—is to give form and substance to all this information: to bring it to life for our students.

More often than not, students come into our course filled with misconceptions about psychology that they have picked up from faulty mass media accounts and from the infusion of "pop psychology" into our society. They also bring with them high expectations about what they want to get out of a course in psychology—they want to learn much that will be personally valuable, that will help them improve their everyday lives. Now that is a tall order for any teacher to fill! But we believe that *Psychology and Life* can help you to fill it. At every stage in the development of this new edition of our text, we have tried to create the most relevant, correct, and up-to-date platform from which you can launch your teaching efforts.

Our goal has been to design a text that students will enjoy reading as they learn what is so exciting and special about the many fields of psychology. In every chapter, in every sentence, we have tried to make sure that students will want to go on reading. At the same time, we have focused on how our text will work within the syllabi of instructors who value a research-centered, applications-relevant approach to psychology.

History of a Groundbreaking Text

Psychology and Life, and this new edition in particular, is special in several ways. *Psychology and Life* is the oldest continuously selling textbook in all of psychology. Having begun back in 1937, it will celebrate its sixtieth birthday during this edition. This classic, under the stewardship of its original author, Floyd Ruch, changed the way psychology was taught in the United States. It was the first text written for students rather than primarily for professional psychologists, and it was the first to present a theoretically unbiased, eclectic overview of all the major fields of psychology. Virtually every major introductory text since then has followed the path started and shaped by *Psychology and Life,* a path we continue to forge with this fourteenth edition.

I took over authorship of this popular text in 1969 and have written the last six editions. With each revision, I have faced the challenge of integrating new theories and research with the classic knowledge, while at the same time balancing scientific rigor with psychology's relevance to contemporary life concerns. This fourteenth edition is now co-authored by Richard J. Gerrig, and eventually he will become its senior and sole author. After teaching the introductory psychology course for nearly 40 years and writing this text for more than 25 years, I felt that the time had come to bring in new vision and energy to continue *Psychology and Life's* tradition of excellence.

We have worked closely together on this major revision to create a seamless presentation of new ideas, research, and examples, both by blending our writing styles so they are indistinguishable, and by speaking to our readers in a common author's voice. Richard is also an award-winning teacher of introductory psychology, and thus he brings to his writing the same concerns I have: that a good text must make the course experience better for both the student who reads it and for the teacher who adopts it.

What's New and Improved

The first thing you will notice about this new edition is its length. The primary criticism of previous editions (and one that I could never quite get a handle on by myself!) was that I often added more material than I cut. This time around, Richard has streamlined the text, cutting it by about 25 percent without harming its integrity, currency, or lively writing style. As a result, the fourteenth edition retains the essence of what was best in the previous editions, while adding much that is new in each of our 18 chapters. This remarkable accomplishment now allows *Psychology and Life* to be published in a single-column format, which in turn gives it a more open, accessible look, and enables us to have more visual graphic elements to enrich our text.

Updated Content The addition of Richard J. Gerrig, an outstanding cognitive psychologist, to the *Psychology and Life* team will be most evident in sections of the book that present new research and theories about language, memory, and cognitive processes. For example, we have expanded the sections on language development in Chapter 5 and on thought and language in Chapter 11. We have also completely rewritten the chapters on memory (Chapter 10) and on cognitive processes (Chapter 11). They are now both state-of-the-art treatments of these vital areas in contemporary psychology.

Another major content change will be found in the expanded coverage of adolescence and adulthood in the two chapters on life-span development (Chapters 5 and 6). You will find this new edition of *Psychology and Life* to have the most thorough coverage of life-span development, and the most balanced and accurate coverage of adulthood and aging, of any text available today.

Instructors who are familiar with prior editions of *Psychology and Life* will find new material incorporated into almost every paragraph of the text, but the following are a few of the most important additions you will find:

- Coverage of *heredity and behavior* and of the *biological basis of behavior* has been updated and integrated more thoroughly throughout the text than ever before. You will find major emphasis on evolution and the biology of behavior in Chapters 1, 3, 5, 9, 12, and 13.

- Material on *life-span development* has been reorganized to allow us to present more fully than ever before the enormous amount of new research on adolescent and adult development. We now cover physical and cognitive development in Chapter 5 and social and moral development in Chapter 6. Chapter 6 in particular emphasizes the cultural context of development, with special attention to the effects of **contemporary lifestyle and family changes.** We also devote new sections to recent **research into moral development** after childhood and to aspects of **successful aging.**

- Chapter 8, on perception, adds a new survey of **historical and contemporary approaches** to the study of perception to provide students with an intellectual context for this potentially difficult, yet fascinating topic. And in our effort to shorten and tighten these chapters, we have not forgotten to include much new research or to present the many **perceptual puzzles and illusions** that so fascinate students!
- You will find that Chapters 10 and 11 present the most current, interesting, and up-to-date coverage of **cognitive psychology** in any introductory textbook. We tell the story of the emergence and contemporary state of cognitive science. We show how cognitive psychologists work to produce new insights into the nature of language, thought, and problem solving. Along the way, we ask and answer some fascinating questions about the nature of language, memory, and thought. We think that you will find these chapters to be timely, lively, and approachable.
- Chapter 12, on motivation, now includes much new information on the physiology and psychology of eating and on **eating disorders.** We have incorporated fascinating recent research on the psychology and physiology of eating and attempted to answer the question of whether diets can work. We have also enhanced our coverage of sexual motivation and homosexuality.
- Chapter 15, on assessment, adds a new section on **creativity**—what it is and how it is measured. We also address in some detail the controversy over the uses of **intelligence scores,** elucidating the debates students are familiar with from the nightly news by providing historical context on the measurement of intelligence and racial issues.
- Chapter 16, on social processes, includes a new section on interpersonal relations, covering both **prejudice** and **interpersonal attraction.** Thorough, up-to-date coverage of these topics puts *Psychology and Life*'s respected historical survey of social psychology into a more contemporary context for students.
- Chapters 17 and 18, on psychological disorders and therapies for personal change, have been completely revised to reflect the categories and definitions used in *DSM-IV.* In addition, we have increased our coverage of depression, teen suicide, and psychoactive drugs, topics that are very much in the news and of great interest to students.

Accuracy and Currency We have made these and all other changes in response to detailed feedback from the many reviewers of the previous edition and of early drafts of this edition. Much of our revision plan has been shaped by this extensive feedback from colleagues who are experts in given areas, from instructors, from *Psychology and Life* users, and even from those who have preferred the texts of our competitors—in the past. Each chapter of the fourteenth edition has been reviewed in detail by experts in the appropriate fields.

Revision has also been influenced by new information and approaches to various aspects of psychology that we have been adding to our teaching in recent years. Those of you who are familiar with *Psychology and Life* will find something new and interesting on every page. Those of you who are new to it will, we think, be impressed by its freshness and accuracy. The more than 700 new references added in this edition attest to the extent of our commitment to sustain the scientific integrity, accuracy, and currency of *Psychology and Life.* Simply stated, our goal is to be the most current, most accurate, and most accessible treatment of our discipline today.

Special Features

The following pedagogical features have been added to enhance the acquisition of psychological knowledge, or have been modified from the last edition to make them more serviceable for our students.

- Each chapter now opens with an intellectual puzzle to be solved, an everyday event that does not seem to make sense, or a problem that needs a solution. Why do people go to horror movies? What happens in your brain when you commit even the simplest fact to memory? Why do seemingly ordinary statements have multiple meanings? Why do you get up when the alarm clock rings instead of lolling in bed all day? We use these everyday puzzles to present complex ideas in the context of everyday events, thus showing students the relevance of psychological knowledge to their daily lives.

- A distinguishing feature of *Psychology and Life* has always been its detailed presentation of empirical research. In this edition, we have highlighted these summaries under the logo **"How We Know."**

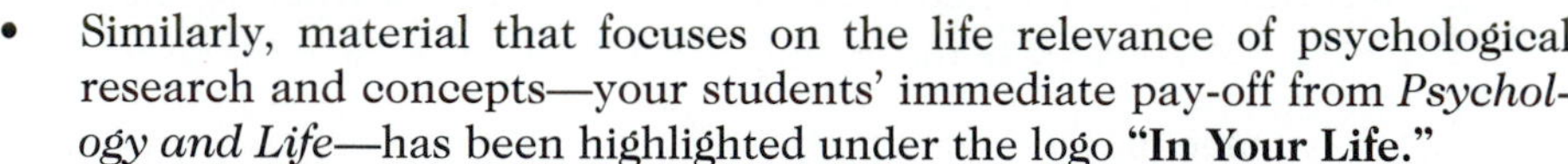

- Similarly, material that focuses on the life relevance of psychological research and concepts—your students' immediate pay-off from *Psychology and Life*—has been highlighted under the logo **"In Your Life."**
- **Close-up** boxes focus in detail on the process of discovery in psychology. Is day care harmful to small children? Why do some people love to eat hot peppers? Are the conclusions drawn in *The Bell Curve* valid? What effects does Prozac have on personality? What is the insanity defense, and is there any psychological basis for the legal definition of insanity? Close-up boxes show how psychologists go about answering these and a host of other intriguing questions about the human mind.
- Throughout each chapter, **summaries of key points** are placed strategically in the margins. These provide students with an overview of the main points as they read, and help students locate key ideas in later review.
- In addition to our popular and information-rich chapter summaries, under the heading **Recapping Main Points,** each chapter now ends with a **Resources** list of current additional references. In selecting the items included on this list, we have used criteria of timeliness, scientific rigor, and accessibility. Our aim is to give students a starting point for term papers in later courses, both inside and outside of the psychology department.
- You will find a greatly improved and enlarged program of **art, graphics, and photos** in this edition. Much time and creative effort have gone into coordinating the visual and text elements of *Psychology and Life* so that they compliment each other and contribute to better understanding of key concepts in every chapter. In this edition, we have added new photo captions that expand upon the text discussion and often pose additional questions for the student to consider.

- Our **Glossary**, which is really a mini psychology dictionary, has been expanded with new terms and the clarification and updating of many others. This should provide students with a comprehensive resource in later courses.

THE ABC'S: ACCESSIBILITY, BALANCE, AND COMPREHENSIVENESS

The goals of this revision can be captured in three words: accessibility, balance, and comprehensiveness. Throughout each chapter, we have sought to provide an even balance between what we know and how we know it, making the material relevant to students' lives without sacrificing scientific magic.

Accessibility In addition to the organizational and pedagogical improvements we have already noted, many other features make the information in this text **accessible** to the widest possible range of student abilities. These features include many direct questions and personal examples in the authors' voices; student exercises; demonstrations; critical thinking exercises; lists of special resources for students; and personal, student-focused information about topics such as psychological testing, health and wellness, sleep disorders, eating disorders, coping with stress, date rape, AIDS, and ways to maintain one's mental health.

Accessibility also includes a student-oriented writing style that blends readability and high interest level. Maintaining this writing style consistently throughout the book has been a major priority in our revision of *Psychology and Life.*

Balance **Balance** means many things in an introductory psychology text. A *balance of conceptual and theoretical viewpoints* is achieved by presenting the five major approaches that guide most psychological thought and practice—cognitive, behavioral, psychodynamic, biopsychological, and humanistic—along with a new approach that is gaining many supporters: evolutionary psychology. These differing perspectives are outlined in Chapter 1 and then reintroduced as organizing themes in subsequent chapters. In line with the history and tradition of *Psychology and Life,* our presentation remains eclectic and unbiased in its theoretical orientation by arguing for what is best in each of these approaches while critically evaluating their relevance to various topics and applications.

Balance also means *combining the best of the old with the cutting edge of the new.* To this end, we have retained those classic studies that form the foundation of much of our knowledge of psychology and joined them with the newest evidence and emerging research paradigms. The addition of so many new references is one indication that we have worked hard at continuing the tradition of scientific rigor and depth of coverage that has been a hallmark of *Psychology and Life.* At the same time, our text always tries to give students the historical context they need to appreciate the intellectual origins of important ideas and controversies in psychology.

Balance also refers to the merging of scientifically rigorous research and lofty theories with practical applications and life-relevant issues. We have highlighted descriptions of research in the text for two reasons: to provide a continual emphasis on the process of scientific inquiry, and to help students distinguish procedure and results from the generalizations that proceed from them. At the same time, as our title and our "In Your Life" sections imply, we have continuously connected psychology with life: the abstract *and* the pragmatic, the scientific *and* the applied.

Comprehensiveness *Psychology and Life* is comprehensive enough to satisfy the most discriminating and demanding instructor, without overwhelming the beginning student with excessive detail. The text explains and illustrates critical processes and phenomena, rather than merely describing them. Our goal is for students to understand important psychological concepts and principles, not merely to name them on examinations, so we have foregone superficial coverage for more in-depth analysis. The breadth of our text materials, combined with your class presentations, will prepare your students for any psychology courses in your department and allow them to appreciate what modern psychology and the process of scientific inquiry are about.

THE TOTAL *PSYCHOLOGY AND LIFE* TEACHING PROGRAM

A good textbook is only one part of the package of educational materials that makes an introductory psychology course valuable for students and effective for instructors. To make the difficult task of teaching introductory psychology easier for you and more interesting for your students, we have prepared a number of valuable ancillary materials.

Instructor's Resource Kit For new teachers and others interested in improving their teaching effectiveness, this unique instructor's manual offers both general teaching strategies and specific tactics that have been class tested and are known to succeed. For each chapter of the text, you will find a detailed learning objectives and outlines; innovative lecture ideas and discussion topics; biographical profiles; comprehensive timelines; suggestions for further reading; and a complete media resource section. As a special bonus, adopters will be offered a three-ring binder with tabs, especially designed for the instructor's customized storage and organization of these resource materials. This new edition of the Instructor's Resource Kit (ISBN 0-673-55806-1) is co-authored by Melissa Frost-Weston and Rose McDermott, in consultation with Phil Zimbardo.

Test Bank I Expertly authored by John Caruso at the University of Massachusetts–Darmouth, and completely revised and reviewed by the parent text authors, Test Bank I includes more than 2000 multiple-choice and essay items. Each question is page referenced; keyed according to chapter, type, topic, and skill level (factual, applied, or conceptual); and crossed-referenced to the Study Guide. Thorough and authoritative, this Test Bank is a must for adopters. An additional Test Bank will also be available.

TestMaster Computerized Test Bank A powerful test-generation system, TestMaster allows instructors to construct test files with multiple-choice and essay questions from the test banks. Questions can be exchanged between the TestMaster program and the instructor's word-processing software. TestMaster is available for IBM (ISBN 0-673-55808-8), most compatibles, and Macintosh computers (ISBN 0-673-55807-X).

Transparency Resource Package Class lectures can be enhanced by this set of approximately 200 overhead transparencies that accompanies *Psychology and Life* (ISBN 0-673-55811-1). These transparencies include color graphs, tables, diagrams, and illustrations.

Discovering Psychology Videos This set of 26 half-hour videos is available for class use from the Annenberg/CPB collection. Written, designed, and hosted by Philip Zimbardo, this course supplement has won numerous prizes and is widely used in the United States and internationally. A free preview cassette with four programs can be obtained by calling 1-800-LEARNER; in Canada, the number is 416-383-6060.

Discovering Psychology Telecourse Guides In consultation with Phil Zimbardo, author Rose McDermott of Stanford University authors the fully revised telecourse Faculty Guide and Study Guide. Designed to coordinate the video programs with *Psychology and Life,* these guides are available to adopters by calling 1-800-LEARNER.

Student Study Guide and Practice Tests Authored by Richard Gerrig and John Caruso, this innovative workbook (ISBN 0-673-99385-X) provides students with a variety of dynamic activities designed to strengthen the learning experience. Each chapter begins with a chapter outline and "what you need to know" questions for each major topic. Next, a *Guided Study* section directs the students' learning by providing a variety of questions and exercises. Each chapter also makes suggestions *For Group Study* in which students are encouraged to master and extend course material with the help of their classmates. Finally, the Study Guide provides students with two practice multiple-choice tests and answers.

PsychInteractive (Mac/Windows Hybrid CD-ROM) *PsychInteractive* is a digital presentation of *Psychology and Life.* It contains the entire book, laid out just as it appears in the printed version. Easy to navigate, read, and search, it includes a *"find"* feature that quickly locates words or phrases anywhere in the text, a *"zoom"* feature that allows you to adjust the appearance of the text page on screen, and an extensive *Pronunciation Glossary.* The Glossary defines key terms and provides audio pronunciations. In addition, *PsychInteractive* features interactive activities, animations, and full-motion video clips. Accessible at a mouseclick, these multimedia annotations extend and reinforce major concepts in the text. *PsychInteractive* also features *QuizInteractive,* an interactive version of the Student Study Guide by Richard Gerrig and John Caruso. Incorrectly answered questions automatically display the textbook page and paragraph containing the correct answer.

MediaPortfolio (Mac/Windows Hybrid CD-ROM) Designed as a digital alternative to overhead transparencies, *MediaPortfolio* is a compilation on CD-ROM of line art from *Discovering Psychology* and other HarperCollins Introductory Psychology texts. All imagery is in standard graphic file format that can be imported into commonly used presentation software programs. *MediaPortfolio* also features the *LectureActive*™ presentation software, a tool to link imagery to class lecture notes for custom presentations. *LectureActive* is preprogrammed with the caption and book-reference information for *Laserdisc* and *MediaPortfolio* CD-ROM. Still and motion imagery can be played back on a TV monitor, LCD panel, or computer screen.

Psychology Encyclopedia IV Laserdisc The *Laserdisc* will include approximately 60 minutes of video and animation from *PsychInteractive*, the modified textbook art from *MediaPortfolio,* plus selected other still images. *LectureActive* software will be packaged with the *Laserdisc* on 3½-inch diskettes for Macintosh and Windows.

SuperShell II: Computerized Tutorial Complete with diagnostic and feedback capabilities, the computerized tutorial SuperShell II provides immediate correct answers and references the text page on which each topic is presented. When students miss a question, the question appears on screen more frequently. A flash-card feature drills students on important terms and concepts. Prepared by Michael J. Caruso, SuperShell II is available for IBM compatible (ISBN 0-673-55810-X) and Macintosh (ISBN 0-673-97482-0) computers.

Journey II Interactive Software This unique software provides students with full-color graphic modules on experimental research, the nervous system, learning, development, and psychological assessment. It is available for IBM and Macintosh computers.

For more information on our unique media supplements package, please contact your local HarperCollins sales representative. A full array of student and instructor presentation media items is available to qualified adopters.

Personal Acknowledgments

Although the Beatles may have gotten by with a little help from their friends, we have survived the revision and production of this edition of *Psychology and Life* only with a great deal of help from many colleagues and friends. We especially thank Arthur Aron, Linda Bartoshuk, Theodore Beauchaine, Susan Brennan, Robert Crowder, Nancy Franklin, Ronald Friend, Joseph Gordon, Jonathan Holmes, Lee Jussim, Donna Kat, Barbara Lento, Diane Levitan, Alexandra Logue, Suzanne Lovett, Letitia Naigles, John Neale, Rahul Pandit, Timothy Peterson, Elizabeth Phelps, Deborah Prentice, John Robinson, Arthur Samuel, Michael Schober, Nancy Squires, Zvi Strassberg, Michael Tarr, and Jeremy Wolfe.

The following content specialists provided valuable feedback on particular chapters. The authors extend grateful thanks for these experts' detailed comments at several stages of manuscript development. They are listed here in alphabetical order: Robin M. Akert, Wellesley College (Social Psychology); Bernard Barrs, The Wright Institute (Mind, Consciousness, and Alternative States); Joseph Brown, Stanford University (Assessment); Lisa D. Butler, Stanford University (Abnormal Psychology); Progga Choudhury, Stanford University (Assessment); Robert A. Emmons, University of California–Davis (Personality); Michela Gallagher, University of North Carolina–Chapel Hill (Biopsychology and Neuroscience); Randolph C. Grace, University of New Hampshire (Learning); Steven Greene, Princeton University (Cognitive Processes); Bert Hayslip, University of North Texas (Developmental Psychology); David E. Irwin, University of Illinois (Sensation and Perception); Alan Monat, California State University–Hayward (Emotion, Stress, and Health); Ian Neath, Purdue University (Memory); Monisha Pasaputhi, Stanford University (Developmental Psychology); Suparna Rajaram, SUNY at Stony Brook (Memory); Brian Ross, Beckman Institute, University of Illinois (Cognitive Processes); Richard Snow, Stanford University (Assessment); Peter J. Urcuioli, Purdue University (Motivation); Edward A. Wasserman, University of Iowa (Learning); Susan Krauss Whitbourne, University of Massachusetts–Amherst (Developmental Psychology); Jennifer J. Wilson, Duke University Medical Center (Assessment).

In addition, the following instructors (also listed in alphabetical order) read drafts of the manuscript and provided extremely valuable feedback: Mark D. Alicke, Ohio University; Christi Antillou, Northeast Mississippi Community College; Elaine Baker, Marshall University; James H. Butler, James Madison University; David Christian, University of Idaho; Paul L. DeVito,

Saint Joseph's University; Michael E. Enzle, University of Alberta; Melissa B. Frost-Weston, University of Houston; Charles R. Grah, Austin Peay State University; Justin M. Joffe, University of Vermont; Joel Morgovsky, Brookdale Community College; Jane O'Brien, Felician College; Marites F. Pinon, Southwest Texas State University; Marvin Schwartz, University of Cincinnati; David Shavalia, College of DuPage; Alexander Skavenski, Northeastern University; Don Sprague, North Idaho College; Karen L. St. Clair, Shaw University; Holly R. Straub, University of South Dakota; Robert Weiskopf, Indiana University; Catherine E. Wright, Mitchell College.

The enormous task of writing a book of this scope was possible only with the expert assistance of all these friends and colleagues, and that of the editorial staff of HarperCollins. Richard Gerrig and I gratefully acknowledge their invaluable contributions at every stage of this project, collectively and, now, individually. We thank the following people at HarperCollins: Catherine Woods, Acquisitions Editor; Diane Wansing, Supplements Editor; Priscilla McGeehon, Editor-in-Chief; Marcus Boggs, Editorial Director; Elaine Silverstein, Development Editor; Mark Paluch, Marketing Manager; Art Pomponio, Managing Editor; Lisa Pinto, Director of Development; Shuli Traub, Project Editor; Elsa Peterson, Photo Researcher; and John Sparks and Alice Fernandes-Brown, Designers.

To the Student

You are about to embark with us on an intellectual journey through the many areas of modern psychology. Before we start, we want to share with you some important information that will help guide your adventures. "The journey" is a metaphor used throughout *Psychology and Life;* your teacher serves as the tour director, the text as your tour book, and we, your authors, as your personal tour guides. The goal of this journey is for you to discover what is known about the most incredible phenomena in the entire universe: the brain, the human mind, and the behavior of all living creatures. *Psychology is about understanding the seemingly mysterious processes that give rise to your thoughts, feelings, and actions.*

This Preface offers general strategies and specific suggestions about how to use this book to get the quality grade you deserve for your performance and to get the most from your introduction to psychology.

Study Strategies

1. **Set aside sufficient time** for your reading assignments and review of class notes. This text contains much new technical information, many principles to learn, and a new glossary of terms to memorize. To master this material, you will need at least three hours reading time per chapter.
2. **Keep a record of your study time** for this course. Plot the number of hours (in half-hour intervals) you study at each reading session. Chart your time investment on a cumulative graph. Add each new study time to the previous total on the left-hand axis of the graph and each study session on the base line axis. The chart will provide visual feedback of your progress and show you when you have not been hitting the books as you should.
3. **Be an active participant.** Optimal learning occurs when you are actively involved with the learning materials. That means reading attentively, listening to lectures mindfully, paraphrasing in your own words what you are reading or hearing, and taking good notes. In the text, underline key sections, write notes to yourself in the margins, and summarize points that you think might be included on class tests.
4. Research in psychology tells us that it is best to **space out your studying,** doing it regularly rather than cramming just before tests. If you let yourself fall behind, it will be difficult to catch up with all the information included in Introductory Psychology at last-minute panic time.

5. **Get study-centered.** Find a place with minimal distractions for studying. Reserve that place for studying, reading, and writing course assignments—and do nothing else there. The place will come to be associated with study activities, and you will find it easier to work whenever you are seated at your study center.
6. **Encode reading for future testing.** Unlike reading magazines and watching television (which you do usually for their immediate impact), reading textbooks demands that you process the material in a special way. You must continually put the information into a suitable form (encode it) that will enable you to retrieve it when you are asked about it later on class examinations. Encoding means that you summarize key points, rehearse sections (sometimes aloud), and ask questions you want to be able to answer about the contents of a given section of a chapter as you read.

You should also take the teacher's perspective, anticipating the kinds of questions she or he is likely to ask, and then making sure you can answer them. Find out what kind of tests you will be given in this course—essay, fill-in, multiple choice, or true-false. That form will affect the extent to which you focus on the big ideas and/or on details. Essays and fill-ins ask for recall-type memory, while multiple-choice and true-false tests ask for recognition-type memory. (Ask the teacher for a sample test to give you a better idea of the kinds of questions for which you need to prepare.)

Study Tactics

1. Review the **outline of the chapter.** It shows you the main topics to be covered, their sequence, and their relationship, giving you an overview of what is to come. The outline at the start of each chapter contains first-level and second-level headings of the major topics. The section headings indicate the structure of the chapter, and they are also convenient break points, or time-outs, for each of your study periods.
2. Jump to the end of the chapter to read the **Recapping Main Points** section. There you will find the main ideas of the chapter organized under each of the first-level headings, which will give you a clear sense of what the chapter will be covering.
3. Skim through the chapter to get the gist of its contents. Don't stop, don't take notes, and read as quickly as you can (one hour maximum time allowed).
4. Finally, dig in and master the material by actively reading, underlining, taking notes, questioning, rehearsing, and paraphrasing as you go (two hours minimum time expected). Pay particular attention to the **marginal summaries** in this detailed reading, since they serve as an outline of the entire chapter.

Special Features

1. Each chapter opens with **a problem to be solved,** a puzzle, something that does not seem to make sense. These openings have two purposes: to grab and focus your attention, and to show you the practical, everyday relevance of the material to be covered. These openings underscore a basic theme of the chapter. Be especially alert when we refer back to them, because we often use them to tie together the loose ends of the chapter.

2. **Marginal summaries** encapsulate the key points that you should know before going ahead to the next section. Review the summaries as you finish your in-depth reading of each main section. If you don't understand a summary point, plunge back into the text and reread the appropriate material until you feel confident that you understand. Similarly, use the marginal summaries as a starting point for your studying before tests.
3. **Key terms and major contributors** are highlighted within the chapter in **boldface type** so they will stand out for you to notice. When you study for a test, be sure you can define each term and identify each major researcher. In addition, all key terms are listed alphabetically and defined in the Glossary at the end of the book.
4. Throughout this book, you'll notice two repeating logos, **"How We Know"** and **"In Your Life."** Their common purpose is to link *what psychologists do*—How We Know what we know about psychology—with *everyday life experiences*—the things that happen In Your Life. When you see these symbols, you'll know that we want you to focus on a concrete example of the linkage between psychology and life. That's what our book is all about.

5. The list of **Resources** at the end of every chapter is designed to help you find out more about topics that particularly interest you. The lists includes, well-researched, well-written books and articles on topics covered in the chapter. You will find them to be useful starting points when you need to write a term paper in this or a later psychology course.
6. The **Glossary,** to be found at the end of the text, provides formal definitions of all key terms that appear in the text, and the page numbers on which they appear. Use it to refresh your memory while studying for tests.
7. The **References,** also at the end of the text, present bibliographic information on every book, journal article, or media source cited in the text. It is a valuable resource in case you wish to find out more about some topic for a term paper in this or another course, or just for your personal interest. A name and date set off by parentheses in the text—(Freud, 1923)—identifies the source and publication date of the citation. You will then find the full source information in the References section. Citations with more than two authors list the senior author followed by the notation *et al.,* which means "with others."
8. The **Name Index** and **Subject Index,** also at the end of the text, provide you with alphabetized listings of all terms, topics, and individuals that were covered in the text, along with their page citations.
9. Finally, your study and test performance is likely to be enhanced by using the **Student Study Guide and Practice Tests** (ISBN 0-673-99385-X) that accompanies *Psychology and Life.* It was prepared to give students a boost in studying more efficiently and taking tests more effectively. The Study Guide contains helpful tips for mastering each chapter, sample practice tests and answers, and interesting experiments and demonstrations (especially valuable if your course has sections or a laboratory component). To order, please contact your bookstore or call 1-800-782-2665.

So, there you have it—some helpful hints to increase your enjoyment of this special course and to help you get the most out of it. Our text will demand concentrated attention when you are studying to master its wealth of information. Other texts may seem to be easier because they do not give you as much depth as *Psychology and Life,* but then less in means less out.

We value the opportunity your teacher has provided in selecting *Psychology and Life.* You will find it a source of valuable knowledge about a wide range of topics. Many students have reported that *Psychology and Life* has proven to be an excellent reference manual for term papers and projects in other courses as well. You might consider keeping it in your personal library of valuable resources. However, we must begin at the beginning, with the first steps in our journey.

A Final Request

Throughout this book, and through many previous editions, we have tried to make *Psychology and Life* interesting and relevant to you. We have done our best to show you the link between psychological research and your daily life—to show you that what happens in a psychologist's laboratory or clinic explains and elucidates the everyday mysteries of your mind. To do this, we have described why people react the way they do to horror movies, why some people like to eat hot peppers, and why many messages have multiple meanings. As you read, we would like you to think of relevant and interesting examples from your own life, and to **send them to us** (use the tear-out student feedback form at the back of this book, or write us a letter). We might even ask to **publish your examples in future editions of this book!**

We invite you to become part of *Psychology and Life* with us. And we can't wait to start on our journey with you.

Philip G. Zimbardo
Richard J. Gerrig

About the Authors

Philip G. Zimbardo is professor of psychology at Stanford University, where he has taught since 1968, after earlier teaching at Yale University, New York University, and Columbia University. His dedication to both undergraduate and graduate teaching, as well as his charismatic teaching style, has earned him awards for distinguished teaching from NYU, the American Psychological Association, the Western Psychological Association, and Stanford. Zimbardo has been a prolific, innovative researcher across a number of fields in social psychology, with more than 100 professional articles, chapters, and books to his credit. In addition, he has "crossed over" into the popular realm to introduce psychology to the general public through his best-selling trade books on shyness and mass media articles, his appearances on talk shows, and his *Discovering Psychology* video series.

Zimbardo is currently doing research in three areas of long-term interest: how normal people first begin to develop symptoms of madness, how good people are recruited or seduced into engaging in evil, and how one's time perspective framework influences thoughts, feelings, and actions.

Zimbardo is the proud father of Adam, who is training to be a psychotherapist; Zara, a Swarthmore College student interested in religious studies and world travel; and Tanya, a high school student who enjoys historical analysis, dance, and creative writing. His wife, Christina Maslach, is a professor of psychology at the University of California, Berkeley.

Richard J. Gerrig is an associate professor of psychology at the State University of New York at Stony Brook. Before joining the Stony Brook faculty, Gerrig taught for ten years at Yale University, where he was awarded the Lex Hixon Prize for teaching excellence in the social sciences. A series of psychology lectures that Gerrig gave for Associates of the Smithsonian Institution, titled "The Life of the Mind," were videotaped and became bestsellers for The Teaching Company (a company that makes courses by top-rated college and university professors available to the general public).

Gerrig's research on cognitive psychological aspects of language use has been widely published. One line of work examines the mental processes that underlie efficient communication. A second research program considers the cognitive and emotional changes readers experience when they are transported to the worlds of stories. His book *Experiencing Narrative Worlds* appeared in 1993.

Gerrig is the proud father of Alexandra, who at age 4 provides substantial and valuable advice about computer use. Life on Long Island is greatly enhanced by the company of Timothy Peterson.

A Visual Guide To:

PSYCHOLOGY and LIFE

Fourteenth Edition

Philip Zimbardo
Stanford University

Richard Gerrig
State University of New York at Stony Brook

ISBN 0-673-99007-9

The classic text in the field, the fourteenth edition of *Psychology and Life* continues to offer a rigorous, research-centered, authoritative introduction to the discipline. The first book written for students of psychology rather than psychologists, *Psychology and Life, 14/e* offers today's student a most comprehensive and accessible introduction to the discipline. Together, Phil Zimbardo and new co-author Richard Gerrig (SUNY, Stony Brook; Ph. D., Stanford) have streamlined the text, cutting its word count by approximately 25 percent. *Psychology and Life, 14/e,* continues to feature impartial treatment of the various psychological perspectives (psychodynamic, behavioral, cognitive, humanistic, biological, and evolutionary), superior and engaging writing, and a direct approach that applies psychology to issues of everyday concern. Additions include increased coverage of contemporary issues, such as eating disorders and the controversy over the uses of intelligence scores, and advancements in research on the biological basis of behavior, life-span development, and cognitive psychology. The pedagogical program has been improved to engage the reader fully, provide detailed descriptions of empirical research, and promote review of key concepts and terms.

NEW CO-AUTHOR

In this new edition, Phil Zimbardo welcomes dynamic new co-author, Richard Gerrig, a respected cognitive psychologist and an award-winning teacher of introductory psychology. Together, the authors have worked hard to integrate new theories and research with classic knowledge, while at the same time balancing scientific rigor with psychology's relevance to contemporary life.

LATEST RESEARCH AND THEORIES ABOUT COGNITIVE PROCESSES

New sections of the book present the latest research and theories about language, memory, and cognitive processes. Chapter 11 on Cognitive Processes has been completely rewritten for this edition to present the most current, interesting, and up-to-date coverage of cognitive psychology in any introductory textbook.

0079.ZIMB.341.la.Fig.11.9

A

B

Figure 11.9 Are Both of These Cats on the Mat?

Allan Paivio suggests that concrete words are mentally represented by both verbal and imaginal codes, a concept referred to as dual-coding theory.

work a listener does to figure out exactly what the speaker meant. You usually aren't aware of all this work! Does this give you a greater appreciation for the elegant design of your cognitive processes?

Let's turn now from circumstances in which meaning is communicated through words to those in which meaning relies also on pictures.

VISUAL COGNITION

In **Figure 11.9**, we give you two choices for visual representations of the sentence "The cat is on the mat." Which one seems right? If you think in terms of language-based propositions, each alternative captures the right meaning—the cat *is* on the mat. Even so, you're probably happy only with option A, because it matches the scene you likely called to mind when you first read the sentence (Searle, 1979b). How about option B? It probably makes you somewhat nervous because it seems as if the cat is going to tip right over. This anxious feeling must arise because you can think with pictures. In a sense, you can *see* exactly what's going to happen. In this section, we will explore some of the ways in which visual images and visual processes contribute to the way you think.

Visual Representations

Let's begin our discussion with the issue of mental representations. Research on language processing suggests that important categories of mental representations are language based. But what other types of representations might you have? Because, as we explained earlier, science is guided by the rule of parsimony, some researchers resisted the idea that mental representations take more than one form (Pylyshyn, 1981). The burden correctly rested on the shoulders of those who wished to champion a belief in two (or more) types of representations to provide definitive proof. A variety of evidence now supports the existence of multiple forms of representation. Let's see how.

To begin, consider a fact of your mental life: you find concrete words (like *table*) easier to remember than abstract words (like *justice*). Why should that be so? As part of his *dual-coding theory,* **Allan Paivio** (1986) proposed that concrete words are mentally represented in two different codes—verbal and imaginal. Abstract words are coded only verbally. The advantage concrete words have over abstract words is explained by the extra code, which leads to more elaborate representations. Paivio's theory, thus, makes a strong claim for two types of representation.

Researchers used an event-related potential (ERP) technique to find evidence in brain activity for Paivio's two codes. While measurements were being taken from scalp electrodes, subjects judged words presented on a computer monitor as *abstract* or *concrete.* As in past experiments, subjects were faster to respond to concrete words. Furthermore, distinct patterns of brain activity were found for each type of word. The difference was particularly pronounced over the right hemisphere—exactly what you would expect if the concrete words, but not the abstract words, involved imaginal processing (Kounios & Holcomb, 1994; see Chapter 3 for a discussion of hemispheric differences).

These results provide strong evidence that this classic performance difference—the advantage of concrete words over abstract—has its roots in representations in the brain.

Other ERP research has revealed that when people generate visual imagery, they use the same brain structures as when they are involved in an act of visual perception (Farah, 1988; Ishai & Sagi, 1995; Miyashita, 1995). For example, when people are asked to imagine a cat, there is disproportion

- *Physical copresence.* Physical copresence exists when a speaker and a listener are directly in the physical presence of objects or situations. This includes both the setting of the conversation and all the people around the conservationalists.

Thus your use of *Alex* in "I'm having lunch with Alex" might succeed because your friend and you are part of a small community (e.g., roommates) that includes only one Alex (community membership). Or it might succeed because you've introduced the existence of Alex earlier in the conversation (linguistic copresence). Or Alex might be standing right there in the room (physical copresence).

Let's focus a bit more on community membership. Suppose you are meeting someone for the first time. If you want to be a cooperative conversationalist, one of the first things you must do is to determine the communities to which that individual belongs.

Researchers created circumstances in which unacquainted students were asked to perform a matching task. The *director* had an array of 16 New York postcards in front of her. She had to describe the sights pictured in the postcards so that the *matcher* could recreate the correct 4-by-4 ordering of the pictures. Although the director and the matcher couldn't see each other, they could converse freely. As a consequence, the directors were quickly able to determine whether their matchers were "experts" or "novices" about New York. When they discovered that they were talking to a fellow New Yorker, they were much more likely to use a proper name to pinpoint a postcard—"It's the Citicorp building"—than to give a roundabout description—"It's the tall building with a triangular top" (Isaacs & Clark, 1987).

Among ichthyologists, this is a Choerodon fasciatus. *What would you call it if you were talking or writing about it to a friend?*

Thus speakers adjusted their utterances based on their expectations about what the listener would be able to understand. On the whole, people are pretty accurate at guessing what members of their own communities are likely to know—although they tend to err in the direction of believing other people know the same things they do (Fussell & Krauss, 1992). The accurate guesses make possible appropriate adjustments in language production.

Our discussion so far has focused on language production at the level of the message: how you shape what you wish to say will depend on the audience to whom you are speaking. Let's turn now to a discussion of the mental processes that allow you to produce these messages.

Speech Execution and Speech Errors

Would you like to be famous for tripping over your tongue? Consider the Reverend W. A. Spooner of Oxford University, who lent his name to the *spoonerism:* an exchange of the initial sounds of two or more words in a phrase or sentence. Reverend Spooner came by this honor honestly. When, for example, he was tongue-lashing a lazy student for wasting the term, Reverend Spooner said, "You have tasted the whole worm!" A spoonerism is one of the limited types of speech errors that language producers make. These errors give researchers insight into the *planning* that goes on as speakers produce utterances. As you can see in **Table 11.3**, you need to plan an utterance at a number of different levels, and speech errors give evidence for each of those levels (Fromkin, 1971, 1973; Garrett, 1975). What should impress you about all these examples of errors is that they are not just random—they make sense given the structure of spoken English. Thus a speaker might exchange initial consonants—"tips of the slung" for "slips of the tongue"—but would never say, "tlips of the sung," which would violate the rule of English that "tl" does not occur as an initial sound (Fromkin, 1980).

LATEST RESEARCH AND THEORIES ABOUT LANGUAGE

This fourteenth edition presents the most current and cutting-edge knowledge and theories on language. The text includes expanded sections on Language Development (in Chapter 5) and on Language Use (Chapter 11).

LATEST RESEARCH AND THEORIES ON MEMORY

A completely rewritten chapter on memory (Chapter 10) provides a state-of-the-art treatment on the subject.

syllables. This research was based on the assumption that there was only one kind of remembering. By studying memory in as "pure" a form as possible, uncontaminated by meaning, researchers hoped to find basic principles that would shed light on more complex examples of remembering. Researchers still aspire to discover those basic principles, but they have also turned to the study of memory for meaningful material. As we will now see, expanding the range of material in memory experiments has led researchers to understand that humans possess several different types of memory.

Types of Memory

When you think about memory, what is most likely to come to mind at first are situations in which you use your memory to recall (or try to recall) specific events or information: your favorite movie, the dates of World War II, or your student ID number. In fact, one of the important functions of memory is to allow you to have conscious access to the personal and collective past. But memory does much more for you than that. It also enables you to have effortless continuity of experience from one day to the next. When you drive in a car, for example, it is this second type of memory that makes the stores along the roadside seem familiar. In defining types of memory, we will make plain to you how hard your memory works, often outside of conscious awareness.

Implicit and Explicit Memory

Consider **Figure 10.2**. What's wrong with this picture? It probably strikes you as unusual that there's a bunny rabbit in the kitchen. But where does this feeling come from? You didn't have any sense of going through the objects in the picture one by one and asking yourself, "Does the refrigerator belong?" "Do the cabinets belong?" Rather—in some way—the rabbit jumps out at you as being out of place.

This simple example allows you to understand the difference between **explicit** and **implicit uses of memory.** Your discovery of the rabbit is implicit, because your memory processes brought past knowledge of kitchens to bear on your interpretation of the picture without any particular effort on your part. Suppose now we asked you, "What's missing from the picture?" To answer this second question, you probably have to put explicit memory to

Figure 10.2 What's Wrong with This Picture?

It appears that disuse, rather than decay, may be responsible for isolated deficits in intellectual performance. Further research has shown that "many older individuals have a sizeable reserve capacity of intelligence" that makes possible the reactivation of old knowledge or skills or the acquisition of new knowledge and skills (P. Baltes & Lindenberger, 1988, p. 290). As promised, we have again arrived at the conclusion that "Use it or lose it (or seek training to get it back)" is an appropriate motto for the wise older adult.

How can older adults cope successfully with whatever changes inevitably accompany increasing age? Successful aging might consist of making the most of gains while minimizing the impact of the normal losses that accompany aging. This strategy for successful aging, proposed by psychologists **Paul Baltes** and **Margaret Baltes**, is called **selective optimization with compensation** (M. Baltes, 1986; P. Baltes, 1987; P. Baltes et al., 1992). *Selective* means that people scale down the number and extent of their goals for themselves. *Optimization* refers to people exercising or training themselves in areas that are of highest priority to them. *Compensation* means that people use alternative ways to deal with losses—for example, choosing age-friendly environments. Let's consider an example:

> When the concert pianist [Arthur] Rubinstein was asked, in a television interview, how he managed to remain such a successful pianist in his old age, he mentioned three strategies: (1) In old age he performed fewer pieces, (2) he now practiced each piece more frequently, and (3) he produced more ritardandos [slowings of the tempo] in his playing before fast segments, so that the playing speed sounded faster than it was in reality. These are examples of selection (fewer pieces), optimization (more practice), and compensation (increased use of contrast in speed). (P. Baltes, 1993, p. 590)

Virtuoso pianist Arthur Rubinstein used strategic techniques that enabled him to continue giving successful performances until he was over 90.

Memory

A common complaint among the elderly is the feeling that their ability to remember things is not as good as it used to be. On a number of tests of memory, adults over 60 *do* perform worse than young adults in their 20s (Baltes & Kliegl, 1992; Craik, 1994). People experience memory deficits with advancing age, even when they have been highly educated and otherwise have good intellectual skills (Zelinski et al., 1993). But not all memory systems show deficits with age. For example, aging does not seem to diminish elderly individuals' ability to access their general knowledge store and personal information about events that occurred long ago. In a study of name and face recognition, middle-aged adults could identify 90 percent of their high school classmates in yearbooks 35 years after graduation, while older adults were still able to recognize 70 to 80 percent of their classmates some 50 years later (Bahrick et al., 1975). What is more problematic, however, is the ability of older adults to acquire new information. Age-related changes affect the processes that allow new information to be effectively organized, stored, and retrieved (Craik, 1994; Giambra & Arenberg, 1993). For example, individuals' use of consciously controlled memory processes declines with age. Do you recall the "false fame" experiment we described in Chapter 4? That experiment demonstrated the influence of unconscious memories on fame judgments. Because elderly individuals have more difficulty controlling memory processes than do younger adults, they are even more prone to making judgments of false fame (Jennings & Jacoby, 1993).

As yet, researchers have been unable to develop a wholly adequate description of the mechanisms that underlie memory impairment in older adults (Light, 1991). Some theories focus on differences between older and younger

The memory problems of older adults seem to occur in the area of acquiring new information rather than in remembering people or events from their distant past.

EXPANDED COVERAGE OF ADOLESCENCE AND ADULTHOOD

Expanded coverage of adolescence and adulthood is found in the two chapters on Life-span Development (Chapters 5 and 6).

"HOW WE KNOW" SECTIONS

Several "How We Know" sections throughout each chapter provide detailed presentations of empirical research, including discussions of a study investigating hardiness and stress (Wiebe, 1991) in Chapter 13, and a report on the consequences of dissatisfying marriages (Levenson et al, 1993, pictured here) in Chapter 6.

nest" (Lowenthal & Chiriboga, 1972). Parents may enjoy their children most when they are no longer under the same roof (Levenson et al., 1993). Have we discouraged you from having children? We certainly hope not! Our goal, as always, is to make you aware of research that can help you anticipate and interpret the patterns in your own life. You might think about the steps you could take to ensure that a much-awaited child doesn't undermine marital satisfaction.

If marriages are, on the whole, happier when the spouses reach late adulthood, should everyone try to stay married late into life? Researchers would like to be able to determine which couples are fundamentally mismatched—with respect, for example, to their patterns of interactions—and which couples could avoid being among the approximately two thirds of marriages that now end in divorce (Gottman, 1994). It is clear, however, that the consequences of staying in an unsatisfying marriage are more unfortunate for women than for men:

Researchers studied 82 middle-aged couples (older spouse between the age of 40 and 50) who had been married for at least 15 years and 74 older couples (older spouse between 60 and 70) who had been married for at least 35 years. Each group of couples was divided into those who were satisfied with their marriages and those who were dissatisfied. The researchers measured the mental and physical health of all the participants. Results revealed that satisfaction with the marriage did not have much of an impact on the men. For women, however, both physical and mental health was impaired when they were in a dissatisfying marriage (Levenson et al., 1993).

Another way of thinking about this result is that men almost always receive a benefit from being married, whereas women suffer in a bad marriage. Women are also more likely to outlive their husbands. Often this means that they pass from a period in which they must care for an unhealthy elderly husband to a period of mourning and financial insecurity (Carstensen & Pasupathi, 1993). Once again, we are not trying to discourage anyone, or women in particular, from getting married. Our best advice is to plan for the future by understanding what might take place.

CURRENCY

Influenced by new information and approaches to various aspects of psychology, this updated revision is filled with new and interesting material on each page. More than 700 new references have been added to this edition, making *Psychology and Life, 14/e,* the most current, accurate, and accessible treatment of psychology available today.

The theory of restrained eating suggests why it might be difficult for people to lose weight once they have become overweight. Many overweight people report themselves as constantly on diets—they are often restrained eaters. If stressful life events occur that cause these eaters to become disinhibited, binge eating can easily lead to weight gain. Thus the psychological consequences of being constantly on a diet can create circumstances that are more likely to lead to weight *gain* than to weight *loss*. In the next section, we will see how these same psychological forces can lead to health- and life-threatening eating disorders.

Eating Disorders

We began this section on psychological aspects of eating by noting that the group of people who believe themselves to be overweight is larger than the group of people who are actually overweight. When the disparity between people's perceptions of their body image and their actual size becomes too large, they may be at risk for *eating disorders*. **Anorexia nervosa** is diagnosed when an individual weighs less than 85 percent of her or his expected weight, but still expresses an intense fear of becoming fat (DSM-IV, 1994). The behavior of people diagnosed with **bulimia nervosa** is characterized by binges—periods of intense, out-of-control eating—followed by measures to purge the body of the excess calories—self-induced vomiting, misuse of laxatives, fasting, and so on (DSM-IV, 1994). Sufferers from anorexia nervosa may also be bulimic. They may binge and then purge as a way of minimizing calories absorbed. Because the body is being systematically starved, both of these syndromes have serious medical consequences. In the long run, sufferers may starve to death.

In Chapter 5, we noted that adolescent girls are at particular risk for eating disorders (Rolls et al., 1991; Striegel-Moore et al., 1993). The prevalence of anorexia among women in late adolescence and early adulthood is about 0.5 to 1.0 percent (DSM-IV, 1994). From 1 to 3 percent of the women in this same age group suffer from bulimia (DSM-IV, 1994; Rand & Kuldau, 1992). Women suffer from both diseases at approximately ten times the rate of men.

Why do people begin to starve themselves to death, and why are most of those people women? There is some evidence that a predilection toward eating disorders may be genetically transmitted (Strober, 1992). Much research attention, however, has focused on women's expectations for their ideal weight as generated by society and the media. For example, many of the magazines that are marketed specifically to women put great emphasis on weight loss; the same is not true for the magazines that men read (Andersen & DiDomenico, 1992). Thus women may get more cultural support for their belief that they are overweight than do men. Culturally driven misperception may initiate the types of behavior associated with eating disorders. We already have described how restrained eaters may become binge eaters when threats to self-esteem lead to disinhibition. Because people with eating disorders try to enforce extreme restraint, this pattern of bingeing may become even more exaggerated (Polivy & Herman, 1993).

Right now, you're likely to be part of a particular culture that promotes eating disorders. Women in college tend to suffer from anorexia or bulimia more than do nonstudents. In college settings, women may solve the tension between wanting to look attractive and wanting to eat and drink with their friends by bingeing—enjoying the party—and then purging—eliminating the calories (Rand & Kaldau, 1992). You should be aware that college life provides this dangerous potential.

By now you are probably wary of the very idea of dieting. In the close-up, we consider whether dieters can ever achieve their goals.

Models who conform to an unrealistically thin stereotype may lead other women to think of themselves as overweight.

and turnover, impaired job performance, poor relations with coworkers, family problems, and poor personal health (Leiter & Maslach, 1988; Maslach, 1982; Maslach & Florian, 1988; Schaufeli et al., 1993).

What recommendations can be made? Several social and situational factors affect the occurrence and level of burnout and, by implication, suggest ways of preventing or minimizing it. For example, the quality of the patient-practitioner interaction is greatly influenced by the number of patients for whom a practitioner is providing care—the greater the number, the greater the cognitive, sensory, and emotional overload. Another factor in the quality of that interaction is the amount of direct contact with patients. Longer work hours in continuous direct contact with patients are correlated with greater burnout. This is especially true when the nature of the contact is difficult and upsetting, such as contact with patients who are dying or who are verbally abusive. The emotional strain of such prolonged contact can be eased by a number of means. For example, practitioners can modify their work schedules in order to withdraw temporarily from such high-stress situations. They can use teams rather than only individual contact. They can arrange opportunities to get positive feedback for their efforts.

A Toast to Your Health

It's time for some final advice. Instead of waiting for stress or illness to come and then reacting to it, you should set goals and structure your life in ways that are most likely to forge a healthy foundation. The following nine steps to greater happiness and better mental health are presented as guidelines to encourage you to take a more active role in your own life and to create a more positive psychological environment for yourself and others. Think of the steps as *year-round resolutions.*

1. Never say bad things about yourself. Look for sources of your unhappiness in elements that can be modified by future actions. Give yourself and others only *constructive criticism*—what can be done differently next time to get what you want?
2. Compare your reactions, thoughts, and feelings with those of friends, coworkers, family members, and others so that you can gauge the appropriateness and relevance of your responses against a suitable social norm.
3. Have several close friends with whom you can share feelings, joys, and worries. Work at developing, maintaining, and expanding your social support networks.
4. Develop a sense of *balanced time perspective* in which you can flexibly focus on the demands of the task, the situation, and your needs; be future oriented when there is work to be done, present oriented when the goal is achieved and pleasure is at hand, and past oriented to keep you in touch with your roots.
5. Always take full credit for your successes and happiness (and share your positive feelings with other people). Keep an inventory of all the qualities that make you special and unique—those qualities you can offer others. For example, a shy person can provide a talkative person with the gift of attentive listening. Know your sources of personal strength and available coping resources.
6. When you feel you are losing control over your emotions, distance yourself from the situation by physically leaving it, role-playing the position of another person in the situation or conflict, projecting your imagination into the future to gain perspective on what seems an overwhelming problem now, or talking to a sympathetic listener. Allow yourself to feel and express your emotions.
7. Remember that failure and disappointment are sometimes blessings in disguise. They may tell you that your goals are not right for you or may

"IN YOUR LIFE" SECTIONS

These sections highlight the importance and applicability of psychological findings to everyday life. The example depicted here, "A Toast to Your Health," appears in Chapter 13.

The Bell Curve

In 1994, a book burst onto the scene that brought all the issues we have been considering about the nature and nurture of intelligence directly into the public forum. In *The Bell Curve*, **Richard Herrnstein** and **Charles Murray** argued that the United States is in danger of becoming a country stratified into an IQ elite versus the unintelligent masses. Most controversially, they suggested that the majority of members of minority groups, African Americans and Latinos, are genetically doomed to reside in the unintelligent mass. Herrnstein and Murray assume their place in a long line of writers who have clothed their personal biases in the mantle of science to draw conclusions that many have called racist. For example, there was extensive media coverage in the 1960s and 70s of the allegation by William Shockley, a Stanford University professor and Nobel Prize winner in physics, that the low IQ test scores of African Americans in the United States were genetically based and nothing could, or should, be done to change their destiny. He concluded, after examining IQ data collected by some psychologists, "that the major deficit in Negro intellectual performance must be primarily of hereditary origin and thus relatively irremediable by practical improvements in environment" (Shockley, 1968, p. 87). Herrnstein and Murray arrive at much the same conclusion. Their science is equally suspect, as is the logic that environmental changes cannot remedy heredity-based defects—glasses, for example, do improve poor vision. (For a fuller presentation of these issues see Fraser, 1995; Tucker, 1994; and Pearson, 1992.)

The argument of *The Bell Curve* rests on four assumptions. As Stephen Jay Gould put it, "Intelligence, in [Hernnstein and Murray's] formulation, must be depictable as a single number, capable of ranking people in linear order, genetically based, and effectively immutable [unchangeable by intervention]" (1994, p. 139). In our discussion of intelligence, we have already provided evidence that should allow you to challenge each of these assumptions. Let's review.

- Is intelligence depictable by a single number? Certainly, if you administer IQ tests, it is possible to produce a single number for any individual (and that single number makes it possible to rank individuals in a way in which everyone is compared with everyone else, and viewed as better or worse on this continuum). As we have seen, however, contemporary scholars of intelligence almost universally reject the equating of IQ with intelligence—of a single test score to measure the complex set of processes that constitute intellectual functioning. This change in theory is not just a matter of broadening a definition. It reflects equally the fact that no test is a perfect measure of a complex construct—and that few tests measure a construct well for all people.
- Is intelligence genetically based? We have reviewed evidence that clearly shows genetic inheritance makes a contribution to IQ. Recall, however, that heritability *within* groups does not permit conclusions to be drawn about the differences *between* groups. Although Herrnstein and Murray acknowledge this problem, they then go on largely to ignore it. Also, whatever percentage of the variation in IQ is accountable for by genes, there is much left over that is accounted for only by environmental factors and by interactions of nature and nurture.
- Is intelligence effectively immutable, not modifiable by environmental interventions? Herrnstein and Murray examine much of the same evidence we have presented to you—but they dismiss it. For example, they conclude that Head Start has provided no evidence of success, which is simply false. They note the short-term increase in IQ scores but then focus on how quickly these differences faded away. But shouldn't it be a great difficulty for any theory of immutability if IQ scores could increase 10 points, even in the short term? Overall, research shows "massive gains" in intelligence levels in 14 nations since World War II (Flynn, 1987). Furthermore, contemporary theories of intelligence are concerned not just with numbers (IQ = 98; IQ = 113) but with the

"CLOSE-UP" BOXES

Found in every chapter, these boxes focus in detail on the process of discovery in psychology.

CHAPTER-OPENERS ENGAGE STUDENTS' INTUITIONS

These chapter openers engage students in considering puzzles, events from their lives, and problems in need of solutions, including "What Makes You a Unique Individual?" and "Why Do People Respond the Way They Do to Horror Movies?"

The alarm clock rang this morning. You would have loved to hit the snooze button, to get a few extra minutes of sleep, but you dragged yourself right out of bed. Why? Were you desperately hungry? Did you have important studying to do? Did you need to rush to a job to make some extra money? Had you made a date with someone you wished to woo? When you consider the question "Why did I get out of bed this morning?" you have arrived directly at the core issue of motivation: What makes you act as you do? What makes you persistently try to attain some goals despite the high effort, pain, and financial costs involved? Why do you procrastinate too long before attempting to achieve other goals or give in and quit too soon?

Your day-to-day life is filled with circumstances in which people invoke motivational factors to explain events that do and do not take place. You'll hear a sports announcer proclaim, "This team came here to win!" Your friend will reveal that she failed an exam because the professor never got her motivated enough. You'll read a mystery story and try to figure out the motive for a crime—and by doing so, satisfy your own goal of beating the detective to the identity of the murderer. Like millions of other viewers worldwide, you'll glue yourself to soap operas each day to peer into the cauldrons of seething motives like greed, power, and lust.

It is the task of psychological researchers to bring theoretical rigor to such examples of motivation. How might motivational states affect the outcome of a sports competition or an exam? Why do some people become overweight and others starve themselves to death? Are our sexual practices determined by our genetic heritage? In this chapter, you will learn that human actions are motivated by a variety of needs—from fundamental physiological needs like hunger and thirst to psychological needs like personal achievement. But you will see that physiology and psychology are often not easy to separate. Even a seemingly biological drive such as hunger competes with an individual's need for personal control and social acceptance to determine patterns of eating.

What accounts for the popularity of television series that focus on basic—or base—human motivations?

We begin the chapter by providing you with a framework to understand general issues about the nature and study of motivation. In the second part of the chapter, we will look in depth at three types of motivation, each important in a different way and each varying in the extent to which biological and psychological factors operate. These three are hunger, sex, and personal achievement.

UNDERSTANDING MOTIVATION

Motivation is the general term for all the processes involved in starting, directing, and maintaining physical and psychological activities. The word *motivation* comes from the Latin *movere,* which means "to move." All organisms move toward some stimuli and activities and away from others, as dictated by their appetites and aversions. We want theories of motivation to explain both the general patterns of "movement" of each animal species, including humans, and the personal preferences and performances of the

suffer from language disorders (*aphasias*) following injury to their left hemispheres then are women. Why might that be true? One hypothesis would be that women tend to have language functions represented *bilaterally*—that is, in both sides of the brain. If speech, let's say, were present in both hemispheres, then an injury to just one hemisphere would be less likely to cause disruptions. But that can't be right—men are, in fact, more likely to be left-handers than are women, which means that men, not women, are more likely to have language represented in the right hemisphere or bilaterally. What, then, explains the difference in the incidence of aphasias? Kimura's data suggest that speech is organized differently *within* the left hemispheres of men and women. For men, aphasias may result from damage to virtually all major cortical speech areas. For women, aphasias result from damage only to a subset of those. Comparable damage, therefore, will cause an aphasia in a man but not in a woman. Why the left hemisphere is organized differently for men and women is not exactly clear, although Kimura believes that hormonal influences during brain development may play a role. Whatever the origin of the differences, we have seen that the brains of males and females are identical neither at birth nor later in life.

The research of Grattan and of Kimura suggests that there are differences in the way male and female brains are organised with regard to speech.

Individual Styles in Lateralization

Even against this background of general differences between the brains of men and women, there is still room for further variation: each individual has some distinctive pattern for distributing functions across the two hemispheres. To make this point, we turn to consideration of *face recognition.* It will not surprise you to learn that faces can be quite hard to recognize. They consist of pretty much the same basic parts in the same basic arrangement—to discriminate among faces, you must attend to much smaller details than just the presence of a couple of eyes, a nose, a mouth, and so on (Diamond & Carey, 1986). Because face recognition seems so difficult, researchers at first wondered whether there was neural architecture specially devoted to carrying out this function. Evidence suggests, however, that face recognition requires a general ability to make distinctions between configurations of features—you might, for example, recognize one friend because her eyes are particularly close together or another because he has a large distance between his nose and mouth.

Researchers have developed a method to show that normal individuals most often show an asymmetry across hemispheres for this type of configural processing (Levy et al., 1983). **Figure 3.26** gives an example of a pair of *chimeric faces.* Each face is made up of the identical smiling and neutral halves; they are just mirror reversed. The question is, Which composite do you think looks happier? If you are like most viewers, you will choose the face for which the happy side is on the left. Because information from the left side of the picture ends up in the right hemisphere, this is evidence that the right hemisphere plays a stronger role in recognition of facial expression—for most viewers. But you need not be in the category of "most viewers"—some people do not show this right hemisphere preference. This simple task, therefore, can be used to demonstrate individual differences—for intact individuals—in the lateralization of function.

We can demonstrate the importance of individual differences with a second method. **Figure 3.27** shows an experimental paradigm in which two different stimuli are projected simultaneously to the right and left visual fields. A subject's task is to recognize or report accurately everything that was presented. For faces, once again, most people are more accurate overall in recognizing the stimuli presented to the left visual field—which are processed first in the right hemisphere. (Recall that because the corpus callosum is intact, information will be shared, after a very brief interval, between both

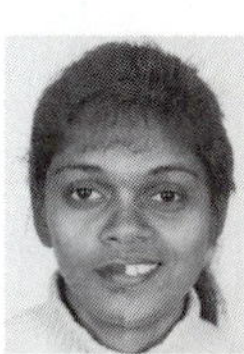

Figure 3.26 An Item Modeled on the Chimeric Faces Task
Which of these faces looks happier?

NEW! ATTRACTIVE DESIGN

The text's new one-column design makes material more readable and engaging for students.

MARGINAL SUMMARIES

These marginal summaries encapsulate the key points students should know before going ahead to the next section. Students who do not understand a summary point can go back and reread the appropriate material until they feel more confident about what they've read.

A drawback of cross-sectional research is the cohort effect. What differences might exist between these two groups of children (above) and of women (below) as a result of the era through which they have lived?

In order to discover age-related differences, researchers also use cross-sectional designs, studying groups of subjects of different chronological ages.

who grew up in the 1970s, in ways related to their different eras as well as to their developmental stages.

The best features of cross-sectional and longitudinal approaches are combined in **sequential designs.** The various types of sequential designs all involve studying, over time, individuals from different birth cohorts. For example, researchers might choose to undertake a *cohort-sequential* study. In this method, subjects would span a certain age range. They are grouped according to the years of their births, and the groups are observed repeatedly over several years. For example, a sequential study might start in 1994 with four birth cohorts of children ages 5 (1989), 4 (1990), 3 (1991), and 2 (1992), tested each year for three years. By choosing cohorts whose ages will overlap during the course of the study, a researcher can capture the benefits of both the cross-sectional and the longitudinal approaches.

Each of these techniques gives researchers the opportunity to document change from one age to another. But how do we determine what forces brought about the changes? We will seek an initial answer to this question by considering in turn what is shared and what is unique about each person's development.

Explaining Shared Aspects of Development

Most children will learn to use language, but each child does so at a slightly different rate. Most adolescents reason more efficiently than their younger siblings, but some reason better than others. To explain development, we have to consider both universal, shared aspects of change and the unique aspects of change that characterize each individual. We will begin by discussing shared aspects of change and describe the potential of *nature* and *nurture* to shape development.

Recapping Main Points

The Nature of Psychological Disorders

Abnormality is judged by the degree to which a person's actions resemble a set of indicators that include distress, maladaptiveness, irrationality, unpredictability, unconventionality, observer discomfort, and violation of standards. There are a number of approaches to studying the etiology of psychopathology. The biological approach concentrates on abnormalities in the brain, biochemical processes, and genetic influences. Psychological approaches include psychodynamic, behavioral, and cognitive models.

Classifying Psychological Disorders

Classification systems for psychological disorders should provide a common shorthand for communicating about general types of psychopathology and specific cases. The most widely accepted diagnostic and classification system is *DSM-IV.* It emphasizes descriptions of symptom patterns and uses a multidimensional system of five axes that encourages mental health professionals to consider psychological, physical, and social factors that might be relevant to a specific disorder.

Major Types of Psychological Disorders

Personality disorders are patterns of perception, thinking, or behavior that are long-standing and inflexible and that impair an individual's functioning. Dissociative disorders involve a disruption of the integrated functioning of memory, consciousness, or personal identity. The five major types of anxiety disorders are generalized, panic, phobic, obsessive-compulsive, and posttraumatic stress. Mood disorders involve disturbances of emotion. Unipolar depression is the most common affective disorder, while bipolar disorder is much rarer. Suicides are most frequent among people suffering from depression. Biological and psychological explanations account for different facets of the etiology of anxiety and mood disorders.

Schizophrenic Disorders

Schizophrenia is a severe form of psychopathology that is a universal human phenomenon. It is characterized by extreme distortions in perception, thinking, emotion, behavior, and language. The five subtypes of schizophrenia are disorganized, catatonic, paranoid, undifferentiated, and residual. Evidence for the causes of schizophrenia has been found in a variety of factors including genetics, brain abnormalities, family environment and communication, and faulty cognitive processes.

Judging People as Abnormal

The task of labeling someone as psychologically or mentally disordered is ultimately a matter of human judgment. Judgments can be influenced by context and biased by prejudice. Those with psychological disorders are often stigmatized in ways that most physically ill people are not.

Resources

Beck, A. T. (1985). *Anxiety disorders and phobias.* New York: Basic Books. Explains anxiety disorders as disturbances in cognition that cause problems in feeling and behavior.

PEDAGOGICAL REINFORCEMENTS

A number of pedagogical features have been added or improved to enhance students, grasp of psychology, including *Recapping Main Points.* These popular and information-rich chapter summaries provide an overview of the main ideas of the chapter.

1

Probing the Mysteries of Mind and Behavior

- *Parents worry that they will harm their children's psychological development by putting them in day care. How can they determine what is in the best interest of their children?*

- *A young man has been assigned to a facility for criminal psychiatric patients because he was found insane when attempting to assassinate the president of the United States. Is it possible that he will ever be sufficiently "cured" to allow him his freedom?*

- *Thousands of Americans live with VCRs permanently flashing* 12:00, 12:00, 12:00. *How can engineers design such devices so that ordinary individuals can understand and use them?*

- *A terrorist blows himself up in the course of bombing 241 U.S. marines, members of an international peacekeeping force. What explains such suicidal devotion to a cause?*

- *Some surgical patients believe that they can remember what their doctors said when they were under anesthesia. How can you evaluate this claim?*

Some of these questions may be familiar to you from the experiences you have had in your own life. What they all have in common is the relevance of psychological expertise. In each case, the type of knowledge psychologists possess about the regularities of human behavior contributes to a complete understanding of and answer to the question.

The first objective of Psychology and Life *is to give you the power to participate fully in these issues: we will enhance your psychological expertise by providing a comprehensive survey of what psychologists have discovered about the workings of the brain, mind, and behavior. Psychology holds the key to a general understanding of how human beings function. Many of the urgent issues of these times—global ecological destruction, drug addiction, urban crime, prejudice—benefit from a psychological perspective. At the same time, you can apply your growing expertise to change your own behavior for the better. As* Psychology and Life *unfolds, you should begin to appreciate more fully how remarkably gifted you are in having at your command so many abilities and skills, and you can begin to take even greater control over aspects of your life. Our second goal, therefore, is to show how psychological knowledge can be applied in your everyday life, and how it can be used wisely to enhance the human condition.*

We welcome you to the start of this exciting journey into the realms of the human mind. There are many paths that you must travel to understand human nature. You will journey through the inner spaces of brain and mind and the outer dimensions of human behavior. Between those extremes, we will investigate things that you take for granted, such as how you perceive your world, communicate, learn, think, remember, and even sleep. But we will also detour to try to understand how and why you dream, fall in love, feel shy, act aggressively, and become mentally ill.

As authors of Psychology and Life, *we believe in the power of psychological expertise. The appeal of psychology has grown personally for us over our careers as educators and researchers. In recent years there has been a virtual explosion of new information about the basic mechanisms that govern mental and behavioral processes. As new ideas replace or modify old ideas, we are continually intrigued and challenged by the many fascinating pieces of the puzzle of human nature. We hope that by the end of this journey, if you put in the necessary time and effort, you too will cherish your store of psychological knowledge.*

Foremost in the journey will be a scientific quest for understanding. We shall inquire about the how, what, when, *and* why *of human behavior and about the causes and consequences of behaviors you observe in yourself, in other people, and in animals. We will explain why you think, feel, and behave as you do. What makes you uniquely different from all other people? Yet why do you often behave so much like others in some situations? Are you molded by heredity, or are you shaped more by personal experiences? How can aggression and altruism, love and hate, and madness and creativity exist side by side in this complex creature—the human animal?*

PSYCHOLOGY: DEFINITIONS AND GOALS

This section will look at some formal definitions of psychology and establish what psychology is all about. We will see how psychology compares with other disciplines that analyze behavior, the brain, and the mind. Then we will preview the five general goals that guide the research and practice of professional psychologists.

DEFINITIONS

Psychology is formally defined as the scientific study of the behavior of individuals and their mental processes. Many psychologists seek answers to the fundamental question: What is human nature? Psychology answers this

Psychologists try to understand both groups and individuals.

question by looking at processes that occur within individuals as well as the forces that arise within the physical and social environment. After we examine each part of the definition of psychology—*scientific, behavior, individual, mental*—we will draw comparisons with other fields. By doing so, we will help to pinpoint the unique perspective of psychology.

Psychologists use the scientific method to draw conclusions about the behavior and mental processes of individuals.

The *scientific* aspect of psychology requires psychological conclusions to be based on evidence collected according to the principles of the scientific method. The **scientific method** consists of a set of orderly steps used to analyze and solve problems. This method also uses objectively collected information as the factual basis for drawing conclusions. Authority and personal beliefs should never determine whether something is true or accepted. Researchers rely on unbiased methods to make observations, collect data, and formulate conclusions. We will elaborate the features of the scientific method more fully in the next chapter when we consider how psychologists conduct their research.

Behavior is the means by which organisms adjust to their environment. Behavior is action. The subject matter of psychology is largely the observable behavior of humans and other species of animals. Smiling, crying, running, hitting, talking, and touching are some obvious examples of behavior you can observe. Psychologists observe how an individual functions, what the individual does, and how the individual goes about doing it within a given behavioral setting and social context.

Most psychological study focuses on individuals—usually human ones, but sometimes those of other species.

The subject of psychological analysis is most often an individual—a newborn infant, a teenage athlete, a college student adjusting to life in a dormitory, a man in midlife crisis, or a woman coping with the stress of her husband's deterioration from Alzheimer's disease. However, the subject might also be a chimpanzee learning to use symbols to communicate, a white rat navigating a maze, a hungry pigeon learning to peck a button to deliver food, or a sea slug responding to a danger signal. An individual might be studied in its natural habitat or in the controlled conditions of a research laboratory.

Many researchers in psychology also recognize that they cannot understand human actions without also understanding *mental processes,* the workings of the human mind. Much human activity takes place as private, internal events—thinking, planning, reasoning, creating, and dreaming. Many psychologists believe that mental processes represent the most important aspect of psychological inquiry. Psychological investigators have devised new techniques to study such mental events and processes, as you shall soon see.

The combination of these concerns defines psychology as a unique field. As you have seen, psychologists focus largely on behavior in individuals, whereas sociologists study the behavior of people in groups or institutions, and anthropologists focus on the broader context of behavior in different cultures. Even so, psychologists sample broadly from the insights of other scholars. As one of the *social sciences,* psychology draws from economics, political science, sociology, and cultural anthropology. Because it systematically analyzes behavior, along with its causes and consequences, psychology is a *behavioral science.* Psychologists share many interests with researchers in *biological sciences,* especially with those who study brain processes and the biochemical bases of behavior. As part of the emerging area of *cognitive science,* psychologists' questions about how the human mind works are related to research and theory in computer science, artificial intelligence, and applied mathematics. As a *health science*—with links to medicine, education, law, and environmental studies—psychology seeks to improve the quality of each individual's and the collective's well-being. Psychology also retains ties to philosophy and areas in the humanities and the arts, such as literature, drama, and religion.

While the remarkable breadth and depth of modern psychology are a source of delight to those who become psychologists, it is often what makes the field a challenge to the student exploring it for the first time. There is so much more to the study of psychology than one expects initially, and there will be so much of value that you can take away from this introduction to psychology. The best way to learn about the field is to learn to share the goals of practicing psychologists. We turn now to those goals.

The Goals of Psychology

The goals of the psychologist conducting basic research are to describe, explain, predict, and control behavior. The applied psychologist has a fifth goal—to improve the quality of human life. These goals form the basis of the psychological enterprise. What is involved in trying to achieve each of them?

Through basic research, a psychologist seeks to describe, explain, predict, and control behavior.

Describing What Happens

The first task in psychology is to make accurate observations about behavior. Psychologists typically refer to such observations as their *data* (*data* is the plural, *datum* the singular). **Behavioral data** are reports of observations about the behavior of organisms and the conditions under which the behavior occurs or changes. When researchers undertake data collection, they must choose an appropriate *level of analysis* and devise measures of behavior that ensure *objectivity.*

Figure 1.1 Levels of Analysis
Psychological analysis can be conducted on various levels, from macro to micro.

Researchers analyze data at three levels: macro, molecular, and micro.

In order to investigate an individual's behavior, researchers may use different *levels of analysis*—from the broadest, most global level down to the most minute, specific level. We can compare the broad level to a photograph of a family (see **Figure 1.1**). In the photograph, you can focus on one individual within the group setting or even on one feature of that person. Then you can examine even finer details of that feature—for example, you can focus on the pupil of an eye. Similarly, at the broadest level of psychological analysis, researchers investigate the behavior of the whole person within complex social and cultural contexts. This level is the macroscopic or *macro level of analysis.* At the macro level, for example, researchers may study cross-cultural differences in violence, the origins of prejudice, and the symptoms of mental illness. At the next level, the *molecular level,* many psychologists focus on narrower, finer units of behavior, such as speed of reaction to a stimulus, eye movements during reading, and grammatical errors made by children acquiring language. Researchers can study even smaller units of behavior. At this third level, the microscopic or *micro level,* researchers work to discover the biological bases of behavior by identifying the places in the brain where different types of memories are stored, the biochemical changes that occur during learning, and the sensory paths responsible for vision or hearing. Each level of analysis yields information essential to the final composite portrait of human nature that psychologists hope ultimately to develop.

However tight the focus of the observation, psychologists strive to describe behavior *objectively.* Collecting the facts as they exist, and not as one would expect or personally hope they would be, is of utmost importance. This

Figure 1.2 Objective Definitions
Suppose you were interested in quantifying how happy each individual is, based only on these photographs. What factors would you take into consideration?

method sounds easy, but because every observer has personal biases, prejudices, and expectations, it is difficult to prevent subjectivity from creeping in and distorting the data. As you will see in Chapter 2, psychological researchers have developed a variety of techniques to avoid the "sin of creeping subjectivity." These techniques emphasize clear definitions of the behaviors that are being reported and careful descriptions of the conditions under which the observations were made.

Psychologists strive for objectivity in gathering and analyzing data.

To see how the choice of level of analysis and the need for objectivity interact, consider the individuals pictured in **Figure 1.2**. Suppose you were interested in quantifying how happy each individual is, based only on these photographs. At one level of analysis, you might be content simply to note your impression of each facial expression: is the individual smiling or not? At a somewhat finer level of analysis, you might perform more precise measurements of the shape of each individual's mouth: To what extent does the mouth approximate a curve rather than a straight line? For both types of observations, you must assure yourself of objectivity: How could you ensure that observers do not always assume women to be happier than men? How could you ensure that some individuals' mouths do not show more curvature, irrespective of the mood they are in?

Explaining What Happens

While *descriptions* must stick to perceivable information, *explanations* deliberately go beyond what can be observed. In many areas of psychology, the central goal is to find regular patterns in behavioral and mental processes. Psychologists want to discover *how* behavior works. Why do you laugh at situations that differ from your expectations of what is coming next? What conditions could lead someone to attempt suicide or commit rape?

Psychologists often begin to forge answers to such questions by establishing relationships between stimuli and responses. The specific behavior that can be measured objectively is termed the *response.* Attempts to explain a particular behavior are anchored in the belief that responses are triggered by environmental conditions known as *stimuli* (the singular of *stimuli* is *stimulus*). Imagine, for example, that you are collecting behavioral data on a baby. You might observe that the baby exhibits a particular response, crying, to the stimulus of a loud noise. Some stimuli originate in the external environment as patterns of physical energy that are detected and responded to by your sense receptors. Other stimuli, such as hormonal changes, creative thoughts, and vivid dreams, come from within the organism.

Psychologists seek explanations for behavior by looking for consistent stimulus-response relationships.

Psychologists look for consistent, reliable relationships between stimuli and responses—for example, noise level and study habits. They also look for relationships between sets of particular responses, such as having the personality trait of generosity and contributing to charity. Psychologists identify and study these relationships to understand something about the person or organism making the response or about the underlying process that causes or relates responses and stimuli.

Often a psychologist's goal is to explain a wide variety of stimulus-response pairings in terms of one underlying cause. Consider a situation in which your teacher says that to earn a good grade, each student must participate regularly in class discussions. Your roommate, who is always well prepared for class, never raises his hand to answer questions or volunteer information. The teacher chides him for being unmotivated and assumes he is not bright. That same roommate also goes to parties but never asks anyone to dance, doesn't openly defend his point of view when it is challenged by someone less informed, and rarely engages in small talk at the dinner table. What is your diagnosis? What underlying cause might account for this range of responses to this variety of stimuli? How about *shyness?* Like many other people who suffer from intense feelings of shyness, your roommate is unable to behave in desired ways (Cheek, 1989; Zimbardo, 1990). We can use the concept of shyness to explain the full pattern of your roommate's behavior.

To forge such causal explanations, researchers must often engage in a creative process of examining a diverse system of stimuli and responses. Master detective Sherlock Holmes made shrewd deductions from scraps of evidence, and Sigmund Freud brilliantly explained irrational behaviors, such as slips of the tongue, after carefully observing many details and their behavioral context. In a similar fashion, every researcher must put forth an *informed imagination,* which creatively synthesizes what is known and what is not yet known. A well-trained psychologist can explain observations by using her or his insight into the human experience, along with the facts previous researchers have uncovered about the phenomenon in question.

Sometimes researchers make an *inference*—a reasonable judgment not based on direct observation—about a process that is happening inside an organism. That inferred process helps to make the observed behavior more understandable. Psychologists make inferences about **intervening variables**—inner, unseen conditions that are assumed to function within organisms. These variables may be physiological conditions, such as hunger, or psychological processes, such as fear or creativity. Any proposed intervening variable needs to be validated through the systematic collection of data. You will learn that much psychological research attempts to determine which of several explanations most accurately accounts for a given behavioral pattern.

Researchers make inferences that increase the understanding of observed behavior.

A psychological prediction.

Predicting What Will Happen

Predictions in psychology are statements about the likelihood that a certain behavior will occur or that a given relationship will be found. Often an accurate explanation of the causes underlying some form of behavior will allow a researcher to make accurate predictions about future behavior. Thus, if we believe your roommate to be shy, we could confidently predict that he would be uncomfortable when asked to have a conversation with a stranger. When different explanations are put forward to account for some behavior or relationship, they are usually judged by how well they can make accurate and comprehensive predictions. If your roommate were to blossom in contact with a stranger, we would be forced to rethink our diagnosis.

Just as observations must be made objectively, scientific predictions must be worded precisely enough to enable them to be tested, and rejected if the evidence is not supportive. A *scientific prediction* is based upon an understanding of the ways events relate to one another, and it suggests what mechanisms link those events to certain predictors. Scientific predictions can then account for changes in situations. Predictions in psychology usually recognize that most behavior is influenced by a combination of factors. Some factors operate within the individual, such as genetic makeup, motivation, intelligence level, or self-esteem. These inner determinants of behavior are called **organismic variables.** They tell something special about the organism. In the case of humans, these determinants are known as **dispositional variables.** Some factors, however, operate externally. Suppose, for example, that someone starts taking drugs because of the pressure of gang members, or that a child tries to please a teacher in order to win a prize, or that a motorist trapped in a traffic jam gets frustrated and hostile. These behaviors are largely influenced by events outside the person. External influences on behavior are known as **environmental** or **situational variables.**

In order to make scientific predictions, a psychologist must consider both dispositional and situational variables.

A *causal prediction* in psychology specifies that some behavior will be changed by the influence of a given stimulus variable. For example, the presence of a stranger is a stimulus that reliably causes human and monkey babies, beyond a certain age, to respond with signs of anxiety. Changes in the observed behavior, then, depend on variations in the nature of the stimulus, such as the extent of strangeness. Would there be fewer signs of anxiety in a human or a monkey baby if the stranger was also a baby rather than an adult, or if the stranger was of the same rather than of a different species? A researcher could manipulate such variations in stimulus conditions and observe their influence on the subject's response.

A causal prediction suggests a cause-effect relationship between a given stimulus and response.

Note that psychologists can often make successful predictions even when they cannot frame a causal explanation: knowing how people or groups of people behaved in the past—if their behavior was consistent—is a good indicator of how they will continue to behave in the future. This type of prediction is known as a base rate prediction. A **base rate** is a statistic that identifies the typical frequency, or probability, of a given event. Auto insurance companies use statistical probability to make predictions about how likely it is for members of a certain age group to have accidents. Statistics also help opinion pollsters predict election results. Although researchers *may* have a causal explanation to link an observed statistical relationship, such an explanation is not always critical for successful prediction.

Base rate predictions, based on statistical probabilities, can be made even in the absence of causal explanations.

The use of base rates also allows psychologists to generalize from the small group of subjects who participated in their experiments to greater populations. Suppose, for example, we wanted to predict what you, as a typical college student, would do if an authority figure ordered you to deliver an intense electric shock to a nice middle-aged man. What is your intuition about your likely behavior? Now suppose you found out that in an experiment in which this situation actually occurred, two thirds of the participants blindly complied with the instructions (Milgram, 1974)? Now what is your prediction about your own behavior? Although you may be reluctant to acknowledge it, you probably would respond to the special pressures in that situation just as the majority did. Throughout *Psychology and Life,* our predictions about the psychological forces that influence *your life* will be anchored in similar applications of base rates. If you disagree with our predictions, you should try to examine why you believe yourself to be atypical: What causal factor explains the divergence between our prediction and your belief about your likely behavior?

Controlling What Happens

For many psychologists, control is the central, most powerful goal. Control means making behavior happen or not happen—starting it, maintaining it, stopping it, and influencing its form, strength, or rate of occurrence. A causal explanation of behavior is convincing if it can create conditions under which the behavior can be controlled.

Consider smoking as an example. Smoking is a major risk factor in heart disease, cancer, and other illnesses. How does a smoker who wants to live a long, healthy life go about the behavioral task of quitting? Surveys show that the majority of adult smokers in the United States would like to quit and that many have tried but failed to kick their addiction. Are they suffering from a lack of willpower? Is the nicotine so addictive that withdrawing from it is painful enough to overcome the best of intentions to quit? These explanations are countered by evidence, from the Stanford Heart Disease Prevention Program, that outlines a plan for smokers to take self-directed control of their smoking behavior (Farquhar, 1978, 1991). The plan acknowledges that smoking is a complex behavior controlled by oral satisfaction and nicotine effects. However, the plan also recognizes that, from pleasurable experiences or from exposure to tobacco ads, people might develop the attitude that smoking is macho or sexy—and that attitude contributes to the habit. Each factor that contributes to smoking must then be recognized and met by an opposing factor in order for the individual to overcome the habit.

The ability to control behavior is important not only because it validates scientific explanations but also because it gives psychologists ways of helping people improve their lives. In this respect, psychologists are a rather optimistic group; many believe that virtually any undesired behavior pattern can be modified by the proper *intervention.* Such attempts at control are at the heart of all programs of psychological treatment or therapy.

Controlling behavior is important because it validates scientific explanations and helps improve people's lives.

What causes people to smoke? Can psychologists create conditions under which people will be less likely to engage in this behavior?

Serious *ethical issues* can arise, however, when anyone tries to control another person's behavior. Not too long ago, psychotherapists attempted to "cure" homosexual men of their alleged sickness by applying extreme forms of aversive behavior modification. That "treatment" stopped once the scientifically accepted conception of homosexuality was changed from one of sexual *deviance* to one of sexual *preference.* The point is that, until recently, therapists, with the best of intentions, were intervening in the lives of gay men in ways that now would be considered unethical, if not illegal.

It is interesting to note that understanding—rather than control—tends to be the ultimate goal of psychologists in many Asian and African countries (Nobles, 1980; Triandis, 1990). Critics have argued that the focus on control in Western psychology represents a cultural bias that emerged from industrialization and colonialism by Europeans and from the mentality of conquest of the frontier in the United States. The control focus of Western psychology has also been depicted as more typically a male perspective that might not have dominated if women had been more prominent in the development of psychology (Bornstein & Quina, 1988; Riger, 1992).

Improving the Quality of Life

Many of the findings of psychology are applied to solve human problems. Using psychological knowledge to improve the quality of people's lives and enable society to function more effectively is the final goal of psychology. Psychology enriches life in profound ways that shape many fundamental ideas and perspectives underlying so-called commonsense knowledge. For example, teachers now routinely use positive rewards and incentives rather than punishment and ridicule to motivate their students. In fact, the principle of reinforcement to produce desirable behavioral consequences came from laboratory research on animal learning! Today's parents are more likely to touch, provide intellectual stimulation, and encourage playfulness in their children than parents of earlier generations. The long-term positive effects of such modes of parenting have been documented by psychologists studying human development. Social psychologists in the United States who established principles of group dynamics have contributed to the success of Japanese industry. By allowing employees to participate in small supportive groups, the Japanese workplace has been designed to recognize workers' needs for experiencing self-esteem, sharing in decision making with management, and taking pride in the product of their labors. Ironically, the Japanese are now

Education, parenting, and business have all benefited from psychologists' efforts to improve the quality of life through applied research.

How might the quality of life be measured?

exporting those ideas back to American businesses, which have traditionally been organized on a model that stresses individual achievement (Lincoln & Kalleberg, 1990).

THE EVOLUTION OF MODERN PSYCHOLOGY

In the 1990s, it is relatively easy for us to define psychology and to state the goals of psychological research. As you begin to study psychology, however, it is important to understand the many forces that led to the emergence of modern psychology. At the core of this historical review is one simple principle: *ideas matter.* Much of the history of psychology has been characterized by heated debates about what constitutes the appropriate subject matter for a science of behavior and what types of behaviors can be studied rigorously. If you see how psychology penetrates directly to the heart of human nature, you will understand the passion that scholars brought to these debates.

Our historical review will be carried out at two levels of analysis. In the first section, we will consider the period of history in which some of the critical groundwork for modern psychology was laid down. This tight focus will enable you to witness at close range the battle of ideas. In the second section, we describe in a broader fashion six perspectives that have emerged in the modern day. For both levels of focus, you should allow yourself to imagine the intellectual passion with which the theories evolved.

Psychology's Historical Foundations

"Psychology has a long past, but only a short history," wrote one of the first experimental psychologists, **Hermann Ebbinghaus** (1908). Scholars had long asked important questions about human nature—about how people perceive reality, the nature of consciousness, and the origins of madness—but they did not possess the means to answer them. Consider the fundamental questions posed in the fourth and fifth centuries B.C. by the classical Greek philosophers Socrates, Plato, and Aristotle. Although forms of psychology existed in ancient Indian Yogic traditions, Western psychology traces its origin to these great thinkers' dialogues about how the mind works, the nature of free will, and the relationship of individual citizens to their community or state. While these philosophers and their followers posed fundamental questions about

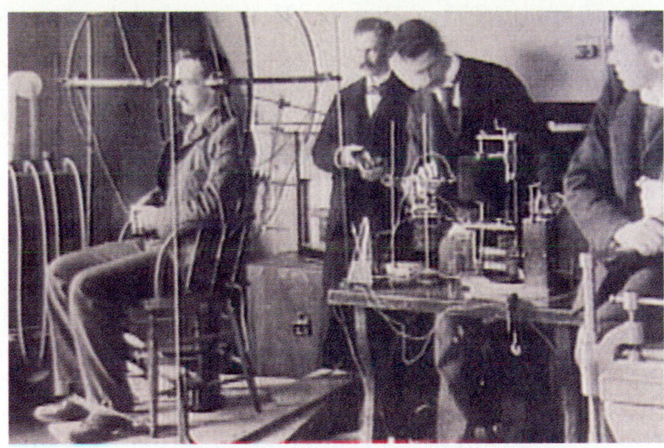

In 1879, Wilhelm Wundt founded the first formal laboratory devoted to experimental psychology.

human nature, the proof for their theories was limited to the power of logic. Even this form of speculation, however, contradicted the doctrine of the Roman Catholic church. Theologians taught that the mind and soul had free will (God's gift to humans) and were not subject to the natural laws and principles that determined the actions of other creatures. There could be no scientific psychology until this assumption was challenged.

The roots of psychology can be traced to philosophy and natural science.

Modern psychology can be traced back only a little over a century. In 1879, in Leipzig, Germany, **Wilhelm Wundt,** who was probably the first person to refer to himself as a psychologist, founded the first formal laboratory devoted to experimental psychology. Soon afterward, psychological laboratories appeared in universities throughout North America, the first at Johns Hopkins University in 1883. By 1900 there were more than 40 such laboratories (Hilgard, 1986).

Perhaps as a continuing legacy of the Protestant rebellion against the church of Rome, in the late 1880s German physicists, physiologists, and philosophers began to challenge the notion that the human organism is special in the "great chain of being." They did this by demonstrating that natural laws determine human actions. **Hermann von Helmholtz**, trained as a physicist, conducted simple but revealing experiments on perception and the nervous system. He was the first to measure the speed of a nerve impulse. At about the same time, another German, **Gustav Fechner**, studied how physical stimulation is translated into sensations that are experienced psychologically. Like Wundt, von Helmholtz and Fechner operated on the assumption that psychological processes could be studied objectively by using experimental methods adapted from the natural sciences, such as physics and physiology. They believed in **determinism,** the doctrine that physical, behavioral, and mental events are determined by specific causal factors.

Early psychologists demonstrated that human behavior is determined by natural laws.

Wundt wrote extensively about the new psychology and trained many young researchers, who, in turn, went out to spread the new gospel of scientific psychology. Among his disciples was **Edward Titchener,** who, with his new laboratory at Cornell University, became one of the first psychologists in the United States.

Ideas and intellectual traditions from both philosophy and natural science converged to give rise to the development of psychology. On this side of the Atlantic, in 1890, a young Harvard philosophy professor who had studied medicine and had strong interests in literature and religion developed a uniquely American perspective. **William James,** brother of the great novelist Henry James, wrote a two-volume work, *The Principles of Psychology* (1890), which many experts consider to be the most important psychology text ever written. Shortly after, in 1892, G. Stanley Hall founded the American Psychological Association.

Almost as soon as psychology emerged, a debate arose as to the proper subject matter and methods for the new discipline. This debate isolated some of the issues that still loom large in psychology. We will describe, specifically, the tension between structuralism and functionalism.

Structuralism: The Contents of the Mind

Psychology's potential to make a unique contribution to knowledge became established when psychology became a laboratory science organized around experiments. In Wundt's laboratory, subjects made simple responses (saying yes or no, pressing a button) to stimuli they perceived under conditions varied by laboratory instruments. Because the data were collected through systematic, objective procedures, independent observers could replicate the results of these experiments. Emphasis on the scientific method, concern for precise measurement, and statistical analysis of data characterized Wundt's psychological tradition.

Edward Titchener believed that psychology should focus on the elements of the conscious mind, an approach called structuralism.

When Titchener brought Wundt's psychology to the United States, he advocated that such scientific methods be used to study consciousness. His method for examining the elements of conscious mental life was *introspection,* the systematic examination by individuals of their own thoughts and feelings about specific sensory experiences. Titchener emphasized the "what" of mental contents rather than the "why" or "how" of thinking. His approach came to be known as **structuralism,** the study of the structure of mind and behavior.

Structuralism was criticized for being reductionistic, elemental, and mentalistic.

Structuralism was based on the presumption that all human mental experience could be understood as the combination of simple events or elements. The goal of this approach was to reveal the underlying structure of the human mind by analyzing the basic elements of sensation and other experience that form an individual's mental life. Many psychologists attacked structuralism on three fronts: (1) it was *reductionistic* because it reduced all complex human experience to simple sensations; (2) it was *elemental* because it sought to combine parts into a whole rather than study the variety of behaviors directly; and (3) it was *mentalistic* because it studied only verbal reports of human conscious awareness, ignoring the study of subjects who could not describe their introspections, including animals, children, and the mentally disturbed. The major opposition to structuralism came under the banner of *functionalism.*

Functionalism: Minds with a Purpose

William James agreed with Titchener that consciousness was central to the study of psychology, but for James, the study of consciousness was not reduced to elements, contents, and structures. Instead, consciousness was an ongoing stream, a property of mind in continual interaction with the environment. Human consciousness facilitated one's adjustment to the environment; thus the acts and *functions* of mental processes were of significance, not the contents of the mind.

John Dewey and William James believed that psychology should focus on the functions of mental processes, not on the elements or structure of the mind. This approach came to be known as functionalism.

Functionalism gave primary importance to learned habits that enable organisms to adapt to their environment and to function effectively. For functionalists, the key question to be answered by research was "What is the function or purpose of any behavioral act?" The founder of the school of functionalism was the American philosopher **John Dewey.** His concern for the practical uses of mental processes led to important advances in education.

Although James believed in the importance of careful observation, he put little value on the rigorous laboratory methods of Wundt. In James's psychology there was a place for emotions, self, will, values, and even religious and mystical experience. His "warm-blooded" psychology recognized a unique-

Among John Dewey's achievements was an innovative approach to education that applied learning to practical tasks. In this 1904 photo, students at his Laboratory School in Chicago are planting a garden.

ness in each individual that could not be reduced to formulas or numbers from test results. For James, explanation rather than experimental control was the goal of psychology (Arkin, 1990).

The Legacy of These Approaches

Despite their differences, the insights of the practitioners of both structuralism and functionalism created an intellectual context in which modern psychology could flourish. Psychologists currently examine *both* the structure and the function of behavior. They employ a great variety of methodologies to study the general forces that apply to all humans as well as unique aspects of each individual.

Current Psychological Perspectives

This section outlines the perspectives, or conceptual approaches, that dominate contemporary psychology. Each perspective—biological, psychodynamic, behavioristic, humanistic, cognitive, and evolutionary—defines a different area that is important in the study of psychology. The six perspectives can be understood as *broad conceptual models*—simplified ways of thinking about the basic components of and relationships among phenomena in an area of knowledge. A **model** represents a pattern of relationships found in data or in nature, and it attempts to duplicate or imitate that pattern.

The six broad conceptual perspectives in psychology are the biological, psychodynamic, behavioristic, humanistic, cognitive, and evolutionary.

These six conceptual models define points of view and assumptions that influence both what will be studied and how it will be investigated: Are humans inherently good or evil? Do people have free will, or do they simply act out a script imposed by their heredity (biological determinism) or their environment (environmental determinism)? Are organisms basically active and creative or reactive and mechanical? Can psychological and social phenomena be explained in terms of physiological processes? Is complex behavior simply the sum of many smaller components, or does it have new and different qualities? A psychologist's point of view determines what to look for, where to look, what methods to employ, and what level of analysis to use.

As you read each of the sections that follow, note how each perspective carves out the domain of behavior to which it applies. Observe the precision with which each perspective defines its target behaviors and how much each relies on empirical research findings. Be aware of the level at which each perspective habitually analyzes behavior.

Finally, although each perspective represents a different approach to the central issues of psychology, you should come to appreciate why most psychologists borrow and blend concepts from more than one of these perspectives. Each perspective enhances your understanding of the entirety of human experience. In the chapters that follow, we will elaborate in some detail on the contributions of each approach, because, taken together, they represent what modern psychology is all about.

Biological Approach

The **biological approach** guides psychologists who search for the causes of behavior in the functioning of genes, the brain, the nervous system, and the endocrine system (controlling hormones). An organism's functioning is explained in terms of underlying physical structures and biochemical processes. Experience and behaviors are largely understood as the result of chemical and electrical activities taking place within and between nerve cells.

The four assumptions of this approach are that (1) psychological and social phenomena can be understood in terms of biochemical processes; (2) complex phenomena can be understood by analysis, or reduction, into ever smaller, more specific units; (3) behavior—or behavior potential—is determined by physical structures and hereditary processes; and (4) experience can modify behavior by altering these underlying biological structures and processes. The task of researchers is to understand behavior at the most precise microscopic level of analysis.

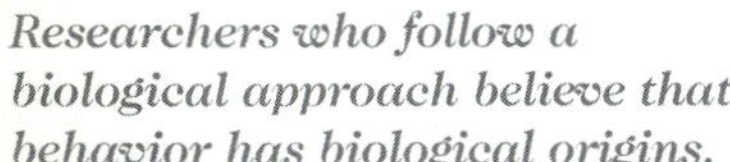
Researchers who follow a biological approach believe that behavior has biological origins.

While many such researchers work in university and medical school laboratories, others work in clinical settings. The former might study whether memory in elderly rats can be improved by grafting tissue from the brains of rat fetuses. The latter might study patients suffering a memory loss following an accident or disease. The unifying concern of these researchers is the aspects of behavior that originate from biological forces.

Psychodynamic Approach

According to the **psychodynamic approach**, behavior is driven, or motivated, by powerful inner forces. In this view, human actions stem from inherited instincts, biological drives, and attempts to resolve conflicts between personal needs and society's demands to act appropriately—action is the product of inner tension, but the main purpose of your actions is to reduce tension. Motivation is the key concept in the psychodynamic model. Deprivation states, physiological arousal, conflicts, and frustrations provide the power for behavior just as coal fuels a steam locomotive. In this model, the organism stops reacting when its needs are satisfied and its drives reduced.

Sigmund Freud, photographed with his daughter, Anna, on a trip to the Italian Alps in 1913.

Psychodynamic principles of motivation were most fully developed by the Viennese physician **Sigmund Freud** in the late nineteenth and early twentieth centuries. Freud's ideas grew out of his work with mentally disturbed patients, but he believed that the principles he observed applied to both normal and abnormal behavior. Freud's psychodynamic theory adopts a macro level of analysis, viewing a person as pulled and pushed by a complex network of inner and outer forces. Freud's model was the first to recognize that human nature is not always rational, that actions may be driven by motives that are not in conscious awareness. Many psychologists since Freud have taken the psychodynamic model in new directions. Freud himself emphasized early childhood as the stage in which personality is formed. Neo-Freudian theorists have broadened Freud's theory to include social influences and interactions that occur over the individual's entire lifetime.

Freud's ideas have had a greater influence on more areas of psychology than those of any other person. You will encounter different aspects of his contributions as you read about child development, dreaming, forgetting, unconscious motivation, personality, and psychoanalytic therapy. But you may be surprised to discover that his ideas were never the result of systematic scientific research. Instead, they were the product of an exceptionally creative mind obsessed with unraveling the deeper mysteries of human thoughts, feelings, and actions. Freud closely observed people—his patients and, most of all, himself.

Behavioristic Approach

Those who follow the **behavioristic approach** are interested in overt behaviors that can be objectively recorded. These researchers are not concerned with biochemical processes or inner motivations—that is, inferred psychic phenomena. Behaviorally oriented psychologists look to specific, measurable responses—blinking an eye, pressing a lever, or saying yes following an identifiable stimulus (a light or a bell)—for their data.

The main objective of behavioristic analysis is to understand how particular environmental stimuli control particular kinds of behavior. First, behaviorists analyze the *antecedent* environmental conditions—those that precede the behavior and set the stage for a response or the withholding of a response. Next, they look at the *behavioral response,* which is the main object of study—the action to be understood, predicted, and controlled. Finally, they examine the observable *consequences* that follow from the response—its impact on the environment.

The behavioristic approach centers on the relationship between behavior and environmental stimuli.

Behaviorists typically collect their data from controlled laboratory experiments; they may use electronic apparatuses and computers to introduce stimuli and record responses. They insist on precise definitions of the phenomena studied and on rigorous standards of evidence, usually in quantifiable form. Often they study animal subjects because, with animals, researchers can control the conditions much more completely than with human subjects. Behavorists assume that the basic processes they investigate with their animal subjects represent general principles that hold true for different species.

For much of the twentieth century, the behavioristic model dominated American psychology. Its influence is still provocative, however, because critics have rightly argued that the behaviorist approach excluded the study of many of the fullest expressions of the human species—language, thought, and consciousness. Still, **behaviorism** has yielded a critical practical legacy. Its emphasis on the need for rigorous experimentation and carefully defined variables has influenced most areas of psychology. Although early behaviorists conducted their basic research with animal subjects (mostly pigeons and rats), the principles of behaviorism have been widely applied to human problems. Behaviorist principles have yielded a more humane approach to educating children (through the use of positive reinforcements rather than punishment), new therapies for modifying behavior disorders, and guidelines to create model utopian communities.

Humanistic Approach

Humanistic psychology emerged in the 1950s as an alternative to the pessimism and determinism of the psychodynamic and the behavioristic models. In the humanistic view, people are neither driven by the powerful, instinctive forces postulated by the Freudians nor manipulated by their environments, as proposed by the behaviorists. Instead, people are active creatures who are innately good and capable of choice. According to the **humanistic approach,** the main task for humans is to strive for growth and development of their potential.

Humanism views people as innately good, capable of choice, and filled with desire to reach their potential.

Humanistic psychologists study behavior, but not by reducing it to components, elements, and variables in laboratory experiments. Instead, they look for patterns in life histories of people. In sharp contrast to the behaviorists, humanistic psychologists focus on the subjective world experienced by the individual, rather than on the objective world seen by external observers and researchers. To that extent, they are also considered to be *phenomenologists,* those who study the individual actor's personal view of events. Humanistic psychologists also try to deal with the whole person, practicing a *holistic* approach to human psychology. They believe that true understanding requires integrating knowledge of the individual's mind, body, and behavior with an awareness of social and cultural forces.

The humanistic approach expands the realm of psychology beyond the confines of science to include valuable lessons from the study of literature, history, and the arts. In this manner, psychology becomes a more complete discipline that balances the empiricism of the sciences with the nonempirical, imaginative approaches of the humanities (Korn, 1985). Many critics of this view see humanism as unscientific, feel-good, pop psychology. Some humanists respond by advocating a more rigorous application of the concepts, definitions, and principles central to the humanistic approach (Rychlak, 1979). Others argue that their view is the yeast that will help psychology rise above its focus on negative forces and on the animal-like aspects of humanity.

Cognitive Approach

Cognitive psychologists believe that behavior is partly determined by preceding stimuli but that it also results from novel ways of thinking.

The cognitive revolution in psychology emerged over the past three decades as another challenge to the limits of behaviorism. The centerpiece of the **cognitive approach** is human thought and all the processes of knowing—attending, thinking, remembering, expecting, solving problems, fantasizing, and consciousness. From the cognitive perspective, people act because they think, and people think because they are human beings uniquely equipped to do so.

In the cognitive model, behavior is only partly determined by preceding stimulus events and past behavioral consequences, as behaviorists believe. Some of the most significant behavior emerges from totally novel ways of thinking, not from predictable ways used in the past. The ability to imagine options and alternatives that are totally different from what is or was enables people to work toward futures that transcend current circumstances. An individual responds to reality not as it is in the objective world of matter but as it is in the *subjective reality* of the individual's inner world of thoughts and imagination.

Cognitive psychologists view thoughts as both results and causes of overt actions. Feeling regret when you've hurt someone is an example of thought as a result. But apologizing for your actions after feeling regret is an example of thought as a cause. Cognitive psychologists study thought processes at both the micro and the macro levels. They may examine patterns of blood flow in the brain during different types of cognitive tasks (micro) or a student's recollection of an early childhood event (macro). Many researchers see the new cognitive orientation as the dominant one in psychology today.

What mental abilities were needed by the Australopithecus afarensis *of 4 million years ago, and how might these abilities have evolved to the present day?*

Evolutionary Approach

The evolutionary approach is one of the newest perspectives in the study of psychology. This approach seeks to connect modern psychology to the oldest and most central idea of the life sciences, Charles Darwin's theory of evolution by natural selection. The idea of natural selection is quite simple: those organisms that are better suited to their environments tend to produce offspring (and pass on their genes) more successfully than do those organisms with poorer adaptations to changes in the environment. Over many generations, more of the better-suited organisms survive, and their numbers gradually increase.

The **evolutionary approach** in psychology begins with the idea that mental abilities evolved over millions of years to serve particular adaptive purposes, just as physical abilities did. The approach assumes that animals' brains evolve just as other organs do: natural selection shapes their internal structure and functioning to the requirements of their physical and social environment. Brains that generate more adaptive behavior get selected and proliferate. Brains that generate maladaptive behavior die out.

The evolutionary approach suggests that through natural selection, those people whose brains generate adaptive behavior will survive and thrive.

To practice evolutionary psychology, researchers focus on the environmental conditions in which the human brain evolved. Humans spent 99 percent of their evolutionary history as hunter-gatherers living in small groups during the Pleistocene era (the roughly 2 million-year period ending 10,000 years ago). Evolutionary psychology uses the rich theoretical framework of evolutionary biology to identify the central adaptive problems that faced this species: avoiding predators and parasites, gathering and exchanging food, finding and retaining mates, and raising healthy children. After identifying the adaptive problems that these early humans faced, evolutionary psychologists generate inferences about the sorts of mental mechanisms, or psychological adaptations, that might have evolved to solve those problems.

Evolutionary psychology differs from other perspectives most fundamentally in its temporal focus on the extremely long process of evolution as a central explanatory principle. Psychological adaptations cannot really be characterized as good or evil—they are only designs that happened to have been selected in particular environments. As you will see in later chapters, evolution seems sometimes to have left humans with inclinations that may now be valued negatively. Research in this field has identified, for example, the male tendency to seek sexual variety, the female tendency to seek wealthy mates, and the tendency of stepparents to assault their stepchildren sexually while favoring their natural children. The applied side of the evolutionary perspective uses knowledge about evolved tendencies to help people choose their actions rather than be directed by evolved tendencies they are unaware of or do not understand (Cosmides & Tooby, 1987).

The fundamental difference between the evolutionary approach and the five other major perspectives is its focus on the long history of human development.

Comparing Perspectives: Focus on Aggression

Each of the six approaches just discussed rests on a different set of assumptions and leads to a different way of looking for answers to questions about behavior. **Table 1.1** summarizes the approaches. As an example, let's briefly compare how psychologists using these models might deal with the question of why people act aggressively. All of the following approaches have been used in the effort to understand the nature of aggression and violence:

Biological. Studies the role of specific brain systems in aggression by stimulating different regions and then recording any destructive actions that are elicited. Also analyzes the brains of mass murderers for abnormalities; examines female aggression as related to phases of the menstrual cycle.

Psychodynamic. Analyzes aggression as a reaction to frustrations caused by barriers to pleasure, such as unjust authority. Views aggression as an adult's displacement of hostility originally felt as a child against his or her parents.

Behavioristic. Identifies reinforcements of past aggressive responses, such as extra attention given to a child who hit classmates or siblings. Asserts that children learn from physically abusive parents to be abusive with their own children.

Humanistic. Looks for personal values and social conditions that foster self-limiting, aggressive perspectives instead of growth-enhancing, shared experiences.

Table 1.1 Comparison of Six Approaches to Modern Psychology

Approach	View of Human Nature	Determinants of Behavior	Focus of Study	Primary Research Approach Studied
Biological	Passive Mechanistic	Heredity Biochemical processes	Brain and nervous system processes	Biochemical basis of behavior and mental processes
Psychodynamic	Instinct-driven	Heredity Early experiences	Unconscious drives Conflicts	Behavior as overt expression of unconscious motives
Behavioristic	Reactive to stimulation Modifiable	Environment Stimulus conditions	Specific overt responses	Behavior and its stimulus causes and consequences
Humanistic	Active Unlimited in potential	Potentially self-directed	Human experience and potentials	Life pattern Values Goals
Cognitive	Creatively active Stimulus reactive	Stimulus conditions Mental processes	Mental processes Language	Inferred mental processes through behavioral indicators
Evolutionary	Adapted to solving problems of the Pleistocene era	Adaptations and environmental cues for survival	Evolved psychological adaptations	Mental mechanisms in terms of evolved adaptative functions

Cognitive. Explores the hostile thoughts and fantasies people experience while witnessing violent acts, noting both aggressive imagery and intentions to harm others. Studies the impact of violence in films and videos, including pornographic violence, on attitudes toward gun control, rape, and war.

Evolutionary. Considers what conditions would have made aggression an adaptive behavior for early humans. Then identifies psychological mechanisms capable of selectively generating aggressive behavior under those conditions.

It is not only professional psychologists who have theories about why people do what they do. You probably have some convictions about whether behavior is influenced more by heredity or by environment, whether people are basically good or evil, and whether or not humans have free will. As you read about the findings based on these formal models, keep checking psychologists' conclusions against your own views. Examine where your personal convictions come from and think about some ways you might want to broaden or modify them.

WHAT PSYCHOLOGISTS DO

You now know enough about psychology to begin to formulate questions that span the full range of psychological practice and research. If we asked you to prepare such a list of questions, you would likely touch on the areas of expertise of the great variety of individuals who call themselves psychologists. To give you a sense of the diversity of the field, we will present our own version of these questions. In this chapter, we will only indicate what sort of psychologist might address each question. You should look forward to full answers to these questions as you journey through *Psychology and Life.*

- *How are psychologists able to treat mental illness?*

  The sort of psychologist who could answer this question is probably familiar to you based on what you have seen on television or read in the media—your image of a typical psychologist may well be a therapist who works in his or her private office treating patients with mental problems. You may label that person a *psychiatrist,* a *psychologist,* or even a *shrink.* Members of this group differ with respect to the type of training they have received and treatments they can offer. A *psychiatrist* is a medical specialist, with an M.D. degree. Of the many professionals concerned with helping those suffering from mental problems, only psychiatrists can prescribe medication or treatments involving physical-biological methods, such as the use of electroshock therapy for extreme forms of depression. Individuals who call themselves psychologists have most often had graduate-level training in psychology that earned them a Ph.D. degree. They usually have a broader background in research psychology than psychiatrists do; like psychiatrists, they concentrate on the diagnosis and treatment of severe emotional and behavioral problems. *Clinical psychologists* tackle not only mental illness but also juvenile delinquency, drug addiction, criminal behavior, mental retardation, and marital and family conflict. *Counseling psychologists* are similar to clinical psychologists, but they often work on problems of a less severe nature, and the treatment they provide is usually shorter in duration. *Community psychologists* work in community settings delivering social and psychological services to the poor, minorities, immigrants, and the growing number of homeless people in U.S. cities.

- *How do memories get stored in the brain?*

  The scientist who could answer this question would most likely be interested in *biological psychology.* Researchers in this specialization study the biological bases of behavior, feelings, and mental processes. They seek to discover how the nervous system and the endocrine system (which controls the flow of hormones) affect learning, memory, emotions, sexual arousal, and other basic processes vital to human and animal functioning. In recent years, the explosion of interest in and research on the brain has created a new area of study for researchers from many disciplines. *Neuroscience* is the study of the mechanisms that link the brain to the reactions it influences or controls. *Psychopharmacology* is the branch of psychology that investigates the effects of drugs on behavior. Psychopharmacologists study, often in applied settings such as pharmaceutical companies, the effect of drugs on some biological system and the consequent changes in responses. Researchers interested in how heredity contributes to various patterns of behavior and mental functioning work in the area of *behavioral genetics.*

- *How can I get my dog to fetch the newspaper?*

  The answer to this question would most often fall within the expertise of an *experimental psychologist.* Originally, experimental psychology was restricted to basic experimental research on issues such as learning and conditioning, sensation and perception, motivation and emotion. Experimental psychologists currently do laboratory studies on animals, as well as on humans, in the hopes of discovering laws of psychology that apply to more than one species. The goal of their approach is to identify the stimulus conditions under which different individuals behave similarly.

This use of the term *experimental,* however, is outdated. As we shall see in the next chapter, it now refers to all researchers who use experimental methods.

- *Why do I forget telephone numbers so quickly?*

  An expert in *cognitive psychology* would best be able to answer this question. The research of cognitive psychologists focuses on consciousness and on mental processes, such as remembering and forgetting, thinking and communicating, judgment and decision making, reasoning and problem solving. To the extent that human nature is shaped by the processes and products of the mind, cognitive psychologists contribute to a fuller understanding of the human species. In this way, cognitive psychologists share the interests of scholars of philosophy, linguistics, anthropology, and artificial intelligence, who also seek to understand how information is represented and processed in the mind. Taken together, these interrelated interests have formed the core of a flourishing area called *cognitive science.*

- *Why do I sometimes feel as if my personality changes depending on what situation I am in?*

  A *personality psychologist* could explain to you how to interpret your unique identity—the distinctive characteristics that help determine the individual ways in which you and others respond to the same stimulus situation. Personality psychologists use psychological tests and inventories to assess unique traits and individual differences. These psychologists also advance theories about the origins of personality and the factors that influence the development of personality.

- *How does "peer pressure" work?*

  Social psychologists would draw on their knowledge about conformity and compliance to answer this question. To understand how individuals are influenced by other people, the social psychologists study how behavior and thought are affected by the social context in which stimuli are experienced. These researchers emphasize the power of situational variables in influencing behavior. This approach enables them to explore topics as diverse as persuasion, aggression, and altruism.

- *What do babies know about the world?*

  If you were a *developmental psychologist,* you could answer this question and then go on to explain how knowledge changes over the full course of an individual's lifetime. The developmental psychologist focuses on identifying the factors that shape behavior from birth through childhood into adulthood. Developmental psychologists typically specialize in change in one aspect of experience. They might, for example, be interested in how children acquire language—a cognitive issue—or in how newborns become attached to their parents—a social issue.

- *Why does my job make me feel so depressed?*

  To obtain a greater understanding of the experiences you have in the workplace, you might talk to a scientist who specializes in *industrial psychology* or *organizational behavior.* Such psychologists work on problems related to employee selection, morale, productivity, job enrichment, management effectiveness, and job stresses. *Human factors psychologists* investigate the interaction between worker, machines, and working environment. Human factors psychologists study how to make equipment, such as computers, user friendly, as well as how to design

Developmental psychologists may use puppets or other toys in their study of how children behave, think, or feel.

airplane cockpits and automobile display panels for optimal effectiveness by a human operator.

- *Why does psychology matter for everyday life?*

  Most psychologists seek to demonstrate the ways in which psychological knowledge can be brought to bear on real-world problems. Some of those practitioners work specifically as *applied psychologists* in a variety of settings. *Educational* and *school psychologists* study how to improve all aspects of the learning process, with the former working in colleges and universities and the latter working in elementary and secondary schools. These psychologists help design school curricula, teacher-training programs, and child-care programs. *Environmental psychologists* may work with architects and urban planners to design housing projects, offices, and shopping centers that meet the needs of the residents and the community. Some environmental psychologists are studying ways to promote behaviors that will conserve energy to help free the United States from reliance on imported oil. *Health psychologists* collaborate with medical researchers to understand how different lifestyles affect physical health and how to manage or prevent stress. *Forensic psychologists* apply psychological knowledge to human problems in the field of law enforcement. They may work with the courts to determine the mental competence of defendants, counsel inmates in prison rehabilitation programs, or help lawyers with jury selection and with problems such as the unreliability of eyewitness testimony. *Sports psychologists* analyze the performance of athletes and use motivational, cognitive, and behavioral principles to help them achieve peak performance levels.

A forensic psychologist may be called as an expert witness in a trial in which emotional traumas or other complex motives are central to the defense or prosecution.

This review may have left you wondering exactly how many practicing psychologists there are in the world. Surveys from around 1992 suggest that the number is well over 500,000 (Rosenzweig, 1992). Of that number, approximately 62,000 to 82,000 work at psychological research (see **Figure 1.3**). Although the percentage of psychologists in the population is greatest in Western industrialized nations, there is currently a revival of or new interest in psychology in many countries—notably in Eastern Europe and China (Rosenzweig, 1984a). The American Psychological Association (APA), an organization that includes psychologists from all over the world, had 118,200 members at the end of 1992 (Fowler, 1993). A second international

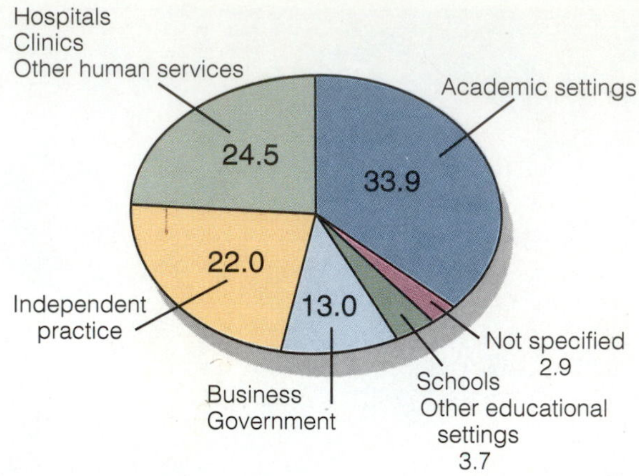

Figure 1.3 Work Settings of Psychologists
Shown are percentages of psychologists working in particular settings, according to a survey of American Psychological Association (APA) members holding doctorate degrees in psychology.

organization, the American Psychological Society, focuses more on scientific aspects of psychology and less on the clinical, or treatment, side. As psychology continues to contribute to the scientific and human enterprise, more people—men and women, and members of all segments of society—are being drawn to it as a career.

LOOKING AHEAD

This opening chapter has provided an overview of the entire field of scientific and professional psychology. You have seen that psychologists are interested in understanding the behavioral and mental functioning of individuals as well as using their knowledge to help people. Following Chapter 2, each chapter will focus on one area of contemporary psychology. The researchers, theorists, and practitioners in these areas will share what they are discovering about the relationships among brain, mind, and behavior. Their work seeks to illuminate both what is basic and what is special about human nature.

Before we examine in detail what researchers have found in each of the major areas of psychology, we need to find out the ways that psychologists gather knowledge about behavior and mental processes. Chapter 2 describes briefly the methods used in research and psychological testing. It also will help you think more critically about research and what it proves. We believe that you will become a wiser consumer of research-based conclusions after reading the next chapter.

A unique feature of this edition of *Psychology and Life* is the inclusion of special **Close-ups** that feature instances in which psychological research has immediate applications to important issues of everyday experience. We emphasize with this feature the personal relevance and social significance of psychological expertise. Think back to the questions with which we began this chapter. We hope you found them to be thought-provoking. The answers to these types of questions will be provided in each close-up. In this opening chapter, we presented a general discussion of circumstances in which psychologists offer their expertise in public settings.

You're on your way. We hope it will be a worthwhile journey. Be forewarned that, at times, the going will be a little rough and require that you extend yourself. If you do, the journey will become as rewarding as reaching the destination. Let's go, or, as the Italians say, "Andiamo!"

Psychological Expertise in the Public Forum

In 1969, George Miller delivered a presidential address to the American Psychological Association entitled "Psychology as a Means of Promoting Human Welfare." Miller reached the celebrated conclusion that the responsibility of professional psychologists "is less to assume the role of experts and try to apply psychology ourselves than to give it away to the people who really need it—and that includes everyone" (p. 1071):

> Our scientific results will have to be instilled in the public consciousness in a practical and usable form so that what we know can be applied by ordinary people. There simply are not enough psychologists... to meet every need for psychological services. The people at large will have to be their own psychologists, and make their own applications of the principles we establish. (pp. 1070–1071)

We have written *Psychology and Life,* in part, to fulfill Miller's vision. Our goal will be to communicate important insights of modern psychology in "a practical and usable form," with the hope that you can apply those insights immediately and directly to your own lives.

In a variety of other settings, psychologists regularly "give away" their knowledge. Because psychological expertise spans such a large range of human experience, serious journalism on public-policy issues almost always includes comments by psychologists. The assumption is widely shared that for any pressing problem, psychologists will have undertaken appropriate research. That assumption is often warranted. In the last decade, for example, many researchers have turned their attention to new topics such as the psychological ramifications of the AIDS crisis (Backer et al., 1988) and homelessness (Jones et al., 1991). Journalists regularly attend the major conventions of psychological organizations and write articles about the novel research findings that are presented.

Psychologists become even more visible to the public when they testify at congressional hearings or become expert witnesses in legal settings. Within the psychological community there has been active debate about what circumstances are appropriate for psychologists to present research findings "under oath" (McCloskey et al., 1986). Unfortunately, there is no automatic way to gauge the general acceptance of ideas. Researchers often disagree sharply over what theoretical claims are sufficiently solid to bear scrutiny in court (Elliott, 1991a, 1991b; Ellsworth, 1991). One solution is to do research about research—to survey experts' beliefs on particular topics, such as the unreliability of eyewitness testimony, and see if a strong consensus emerges (Kassin et al., 1989). Another approach would be to eliminate the need for direct testimony by psychologists by incorporating generally accepted principles of psychology directly into the legal decision-making process (Monahan & Walker, 1988).

On some occasions the American Psychological Association itself participates as an institution to affect a legal decision. The APA, for example, has filed several *amicus curiae* (literally, "friend of the court") briefs to provide social science data relevant to cases appearing before the Supreme Court. These briefs demonstrate that psychological expertise can be applied to some of the most pressing societal concerns. Thus, in a broad range of forums, psychologists, as individuals and as a group, "give away" their expertise to help public causes—to help you.

Recapping Main Points

Psychology: Definitions and Goals

Psychology is the scientific study of the behavior and the mental processes of individuals. The goals of psychology are to describe, explain, predict, and help control behavior. An applied goal is to help improve human functioning. The objective data that psychology uses are observable stimuli and responses.

The Evolution of Modern Psychology

Structuralism emerged from the work of Wundt and Titchener. It emphasized the structure of the mind, and behavior built from elemental sensations. Functionalism, developed by Dewey and James, emphasized the purpose behind behavior. Taken together, these theories created the agenda for modern psychology.

Each of the six contemporary approaches to studying psychology differs in its view of human nature, the determinants of behavior, the focus of study, and the primary research approach. The biological perspective studies relationships between behavior and brain mechanisms. The psychodynamic perspective looks at behavior as driven by instinctive forces, inner conflicts, and conscious and unconscious motivations. The behavioristic perspective views behavior as determined by external stimulus conditions. The humanistic perspective emphasizes an individual's inherent capacity to make rational choices. The cognitive perspective stresses mental processes that intervene between stimulus input and response initiation. Finally, the evolutionary perspective looks at behavior as having evolved as an adaptation for survival in the environment.

What Psychologists Do

Psychologists work in a variety of settings and draw on expertise from a range of specialty areas. Almost any question that can be generated about real-life experiences is addressed by some member of the psychological profession.

Resources

Dennett, D. C. (1995). *Darwin's dangerous idea: Evolution and the meanings of life.* New York: Simon and Schuster. Understanding the evolutionary perspective on psychology requires a knowledge and appreciation of Darwin's remarkable theory and his initial data regarding evolution and natural selection. Dennett, a philosopher, argues that Darwin's idea is the best single idea anyone has ever had because it unifies the realms of life with those of space and time, cause and effect, mechanism and natural law.

Hunt, M. (1993). *The story of psychology.* New York: Doubleday. An interesting history of psychology from ancient philosophy to modern research.

Kimble, G. A., Wertheimer, M. & White, C. (Eds.). (1991). *Portraits of pioneers in psychology.* Washington, DC: American Psychological Association; Hillsdale, NJ: Erlbaum.

Leahey, T. (1992). *A history of psychology: Main currents in psychological thought.* Englewood Cliffs, NJ: Prentice-Hall. Leahey notes that most definitions of psychology assert that psychology is a science but vary in what psychology is a science of. Some definitions restrict psychology to the study of behavior, whereas others include mind or mental processes. Leahey's answer to whether psychology qualifies as a science is a qualified yes.

Schultz, D. P., & Schultz, S. E. (Eds.). (1992). *A history of modern psychology* (5th ed.). Fort Worth: Harcourt Brace Jovanovich.

Watson, R. I., & Evans, R. B. (1991). *The great psychologists: A history of psychological thought* (5th ed.). New York: HarperCollins.

2

Psychological Research

In Chapter 1 we emphasized that psychological knowledge must *be directly relevant to your everyday experience. Bertrand Russell, one of the most influential philosophers of our time, proclaimed that "psychology is the most important of the sciences.... all the data upon which our inferences should be based are psychological in character... " (1948, p. 53). Because we expect you to make immediate use of the data of psychology, it is critical for you to understand the methods by which researchers produce those data. Chapter 2 will reveal those methods.*

We will focus on the kinds of evidence psychological investigators seek, as well as on the special procedures they use to gather that evidence. Recall that psychology is the scientific study *of the behavioral and mental functioning of individuals. In this chapter you will discover what is special about the way psychology applies the* scientific method *to its domain of knowledge. How do psychologists measure behavior and design their research? What are the special features of a psychological experiment? How can solid conclusions ever be drawn from the complex and often fuzzy phenomena that psychologists study—how you think, feel, and behave?*

Even if you never do any scientific research in your life, mastering the information in this chapter will be useful. The underlying purpose here is to help improve your critical thinking skills *by teaching you how to ask the right questions and evaluate the answers about the causes, consequences, and correlates of behavior and psychological phenomena. The mass media constantly release stories that begin with, "Research shows that... " The stories often end with direct or implied calls for some citizen action based on that research. By sharpening your intelligent skepticism, we will help you become a more sophisticated consumer of the research-based conclusions that confront you in everyday life. We will show you how to settle arguments with "facts rather than polemics" (Miller, 1992).*

The study of methods of psychological research can make you a more wary consumer of research-based conclusions.

THE CONTEXT OF DISCOVERY

The first step in the research process is to use observations, beliefs, information, and general knowledge to formulate a new idea.

The research process in psychology, as in all empirical sciences, can be divided into two major categories that usually occur in sequence: getting an idea (*discovery*) and then testing it (*justification*). The **context of discovery** is the initial phase of research during which observations, beliefs, information, and general knowledge lead someone to come up with a new idea or a different way of thinking about phenomena.

Where do researchers' questions and theories about physical reality and human nature originate? Some come from direct observations of the events, animals, people, and things in the environment. In line with the goals we described in Chapter 1, psychologists perceive that new aspects of human experience can be studied and explained. Other research questions and theories are traditional parts of the field: some issues are considered to be "great unanswered questions"; some theories are thought to offer sufficiently important insights to be worthy of further test. Often researchers combine old ideas in unique ways that offer an original perspective. The hallmark of the

"We plan to determine once and for all if there really ARE any cultural differences between them."

Scientific research may confirm or negate beliefs that have been commonly accepted for generations.

truly creative thinker is the discovery of a new truth that moves society and science in a better direction.

Psychological theories, in general, attempt to understand how brain, mind, behavior, and environment function and how they may be related. Any particular theory focuses on a specific aspect of this broad conception, using a body of interrelated principles to explain or predict some psychological phenomenon. At the common core of most psychological theories is the assumption of **determinism**, the idea that all events—physical, mental, and behavioral—are the result of, or determined by, specific causal factors. These causal factors are limited to those in the individual's environment or within the person. Researchers also assume that behavior and mental processes follow *lawful patterns* of relationships, patterns that can be discovered and revealed through research. Psychological theories are typically claims about the causal forces that underlie such lawful patterns.

Psychological theories are attempts to understand the deterministic relationships among the brain, mind, behavior, and the environment.

When a theory is proposed in psychology, it is generally expected both to account for known facts and to generate new ideas and hypotheses. A **hypothesis** is a tentative and testable explanation of the relationship between causes and consequences. Hypotheses are often stated as if–then predictions, specifying certain outcomes from specific conditions. We might predict, for example, that *if* children view a lot of violence on television, *then* they will engage in more aggressive acts toward their peers. Sometimes hypotheses are hunches about what ideas go together, based not on formal theories but on a psychologist's observations, introspection, creative intuition, or analysis of a pattern of available evidence. In addition, new *technologies* and new *models* also stimulate psychological discoveries. For example, the scientific study of sleeping and dreaming opened up only after the development of a technology for recording changes in brain wave patterns that vary as consciousness is altered.

The understanding of a complex process is also aided by using the correct paradigm. In psychological research, a **paradigm** is a model of the behavior, mental processes, or physiological processes under study. Sigmund Freud, for example, developed a paradigm for understanding irrational behavior by relating it to unconscious motives or conflicts. Entire fields of knowledge, including psychology, can change directions when new paradigms challenge existing ones. When paradigms shift, revolutions of knowledge usually follow (Kuhn, 1970). However, before a new theory, hypothesis, or paradigm makes

Technological advances and paradigm shifts stimulate new psychological discoveries.

Scientific theories undergo rigorous testing, whose results must be replicated by independent investigators before the theories are recognized as proven.

a difference in science, it has to undergo an ordeal of proof by the scientific community. It then moves into the public eye, where ideas are tested and proven—or discarded as false.

Another important part of the context of discovery is the special attitudes and values required for participation in research. Science demands an *open-minded—critical* and *skeptical*—attitude toward any conclusion until it has been duplicated repeatedly by independent investigators. Open-mindedness serves two purposes. First, it makes truth provisional, ever ready to be modified by new data. Second, an open-minded orientation makes researchers willing to evaluate seriously claims for phenomena that they may not personally believe or accept, such as extrasensory perception (Bem & Honorton, 1994).

Scientific knowledge is based on respect for empirical evidence obtained through controlled observation and careful measurement. In the realms of science, when good data clash with the opinions of experts, data win. Data must be collected by special methods that eliminate or correct the subjective influences and biases of researchers. Secrecy is banned from the research procedure because all data and methods must eventually be open for *public verifiability;* that is, other researchers must have the opportunity to inspect, criticize, replicate, or disprove the data and methods. Descriptions of the data, results, and the methods for collecting the data are kept separate from any inferences and conclusions about the meaning of the evidence. In scientific publications, each part of an investigation is reported in a distinct section, to allow readers to distinguish the objective features of the data from subjective interpretation by the researchers. Finally, there is a demand that research be published, to add to the cumulative body of knowledge about the topic studied, as well as to enable other investigators to replicate the findings.

THE CONTEXT OF JUSTIFICATION: SAFEGUARDS FOR OBJECTIVITY

Psychologists face a difficult challenge when they try to get accurate data and reliable evidence that will generate valid conclusions. They rely on one ally to make success possible: **the scientific method.** As we explained in Chapter 1, the scientific method is a general set of procedures for gathering and interpreting evidence in ways that limit sources of errors and yield dependable conclusions. Psychology is considered a science to the extent that it follows the rules established by the scientific method.

The second step in the research process is justification. For this, psychologists rely on the scientific method and the critical factor of objectivity.

Since subjectivity must be minimized in the data collection and analysis phases of scientific research, procedural safeguards are used to increase objectivity. One of these safeguards needs no explanation: researchers must keep complete records of observations and data analyses in a form that other researchers can understand and evaluate. For other aspects of the scientific method, we wish to make vivid to you why a particular procedure is so critical. Accordingly, each of the next two sections begins with a challenge to objectivity and then describes the remedy prescribed by the scientific method.

Observer Biases and Operational Definitions

The Challenge to Objectivity

An **observer bias** is an error in observation that distorts perceptual evidence and that is due to the personal motives and expectations of the viewer. At times, people see and hear what they expect rather than what is. This bias explains how the same evidence can lead different observers to different conclusions. The biases of the observers act as *filters* through which some things are noticed as relevant and significant, while others are ignored as irrelevant and not meaningful. Observational biases come from sources of influence on perceptions, such as culture, gender, age, social class, and education.

Around the beginning of the twentieth century, a leading psychologist, **Hugo Munsterberg,** gave a speech on peace to a large audience that included many reporters. He summarized the news accounts of what they heard and saw in this way:

> The reporters sat immediately in front of the platform. One man wrote that the audience was so surprised by my speech that it received it in complete silence; another wrote that I was constantly interrupted by loud applause and that at the end of my address the applause continued for minutes. The one wrote that during my opponent's speech I was constantly smiling; the other noticed that my face remained grave and without a smile. The one said that I grew purple-red from excitement; and the other found that I grew chalk-white. The one told us that my critic, while speaking, walked up and down the large stage; and the other, that he stood all the while at my side and patted me in a fatherly way on the shoulder. (1908, pp. 35–36)

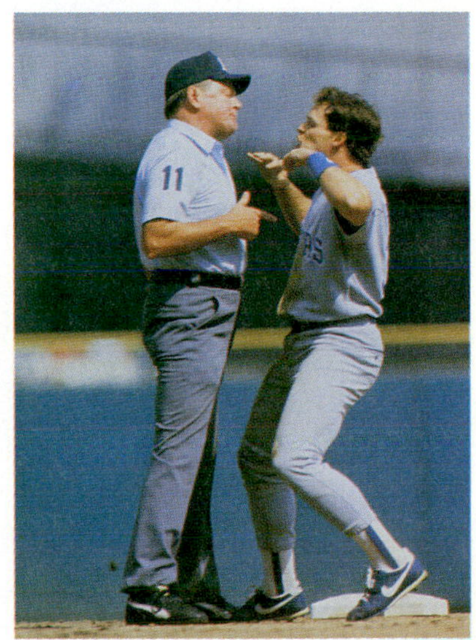

Participants, as well as spectators and broadcast viewers, are subject to observer bias.

Even scientists can be guilty of this error when their beliefs get in the way of their observations. On one occasion, a team of French researchers declared they had made a remarkable discovery: a substance remained biologically active even when it was so diluted that it disappeared! This strange finding contradicted a basic law of chemistry. It also supported the notion of *homeopathic medicine,* which contends that a person can be cured of a disease by taking minute doses of substances that cause its symptoms. However, an investigative team from the science journal *Nature* failed to replicate the findings even in the same French laboratory and with the original researchers' notes and data. The results of the original study are suspicious because the salaries of some of the researchers were paid by a French maker of homeopathic medicines; there may have been bias to find favorable results (Revkin, 1989).

Figure 2.1 Observer Bias
Is the glass in the center half empty or half full?

Let's take a demonstration break to illustrate how easy it is to create an observer bias in you. Look at the glass in the center of **Figure 2.1**. How would you answer the classic question: Is the glass half empty or half full? Suppose you watched the sequence in the top panel, in which water is poured into the glass. Wouldn't you be likely to describe the glass as half full? Suppose you watched the sequence in the bottom panel. Now doesn't the glass seem half empty? If such a brief experience could predispose you to see the same glass differently, you can readily imagine how the lifelong effects of cultural experiences or learned prejudices can create major observer biases—and sometimes major disagreements and social conflicts.

The Remedy

Objectivity is preserved by standardizing procedures for data collection and by using operational definitions for concepts.

To eliminate observer biases, researchers rely on *standardization* and *operational definitions.* **Standardization** means using uniform, consistent procedures in all phases of data collection. Instructions must be delivered in the same way to each person each time the test, interview, or experiment is conducted. Having results printed or recorded helps ensure their comparability in different times and places and with different subjects and researchers. All features of the test or experimental situation should be sufficiently standardized so that all research participants experience exactly the same experimental conditions. Standardization means asking questions in the same way and scoring responses according to preestablished rules.

Observations themselves must also be standardized: scientists must solve the problem of how to translate concepts that have meaning for them into concepts that have a commonly accepted meaning for anyone using them. The strategy for standardizing the meaning of concepts is called *operationalization.* An **operational definition** standardizes meaning by defining a concept in terms of specific operations or procedures used to measure it or to determine its presence. All the variables in an experiment must be given operational definitions. A **variable** is any factor that varies in amount or kind. In experimental settings, the stimulus condition whose values are free to vary independently of any other variable in the situation is known as the

independent variable. Any variable whose values are the results of changes in one or more independent variables is known as a **dependent variable.**

Imagine, for example, that you wished to test the hypothesis we mentioned earlier: that children who view a lot of violence on television will engage in more aggressive acts toward their peers. You could devise an experiment in which you manipulated the amount of violence each subject viewed (the independent variable) and then assessed how much aggression he or she displayed (the dependent variable). An important part of your experimental design would be to operationalize both the amount of violence contained in various television programs and the amount of aggression the subjects in your experiments displayed. You should think for a moment about what procedures you could develop to make both of these measures precise.

Is violent behavior caused by viewing violence on television?

Psychologists are often faced with the problem of operationalizing variables that are really quite complex. For constructs "like weight or speed it's clear what you measure, but what would you measure if you wanted to understand political instability? Somehow, you would have to design a series of actual operations that yield a suitable measurement" (Diamond, 1987, p. 35). All researchers might not agree that you have operationalized the variable successfully—they might believe that you have failed to capture the essence of political instability—but if you have offered a precise operational definition, they will know how to judge and replicate your work.

Experimental Methods: Alternative Explanations and the Need for Controls

The Challenge to Objectivity

When psychologists test a hypothesis, they most often have in mind an explanation for why change in the independent variable should affect the dependent variable in a particular way. For example, you might predict, and demonstrate experimentally, that the viewing of television violence leads to high levels of aggression. But how can you know that it was *exactly* the viewing of violence that produced aggression? To make the strongest possible case for their hypotheses, psychologists must be very sensitive to the existence of possible **alternative explanations.** The more alternative explanations there might be for a given result, the less confidence we have in our initial hypothesis. When something other than what an experimenter purposely introduces into a research setting changes a subject's behavior and adds confusion to the interpretation of the data, it is called a **confounding variable.** When the real cause of some observed behavioral effect is *confounded,* the experimenter's interpretation of the data is put at risk.

Although each different experimental method potentially gives rise to a unique set of alternative explanations, we can identify two types of confounds that apply to almost all experiments, which we will call *expectancy effects* and *placebo effects.* Unintentional **expectancy effects** occur when a researcher or observer subtly communicates to the subjects the behaviors he or she expects to find—thereby producing the desired reaction in the subjects. Under these circumstances, the "experimenter's expectations" actually help trigger the observed reactions rather than the independent variable hypothesized.

Robert Rosenthal has studied the phenomenon of expectancy bias and how it can distort research results:

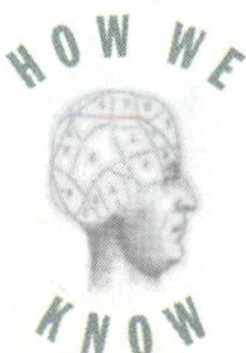

College students were hired to be "experimental assistants" in a research project supposedly designed to study if research subjects could accurately rate the success or failure of target people just by looking at their photographs. Subjects were to rate expressions in the photographs on a scale from +10 (extreme success) to −10 (extreme failure). Actually, all the photos had earlier been rated as

> neutral by other students. The real study manipulated what the research assistants were told about the kind of ratings to expect. Half of them were led to believe that the subjects they observed would give ratings that averaged about +5 across all the photos. The other half of the experimental assistants were told to expect average ratings of –5. Both groups of assistants then read the same instructions to their subjects.
>
> Both sets of assistants achieved the results they were expecting. In some subtle, nonverbal way, even though they had read standard instructions and had only watched while the photos were being judged, they had communicated their expectations to their subjects. In turn, the subjects reacted as expected, giving ratings of moderate success or moderate failure according to what their experimental assistant believed was true (Rosenthal, 1966).

An expectation bias distorts the content of discovery. It makes us "discover" only what is already on our minds and not how minds and behavior truly function.

A **placebo effect** occurs when subjects change their behavior in the *absence* of any kind of experimental manipulation. This concept originated in medicine to account for cases in which a patient's health improved after he or she had received medication that was chemically inert or a treatment that was nonspecific. The placebo effect refers to an improvement in health or well-being due to the individual's *belief* that the treatment will be effective. Some treatments with no genuine medical effects have been shown, even so, to produce good or excellent outcomes for 70 percent of the patients on whom they were used (Roberts et al., 1993).

In a psychological research setting, a placebo effect has occurred whenever a behavioral response is influenced by a person's expectation of what to do or how to feel, rather than by the specific intervention or procedures employed to produce that response. Recall your experiment relating television viewing to later aggression. Suppose we discovered that subjects who

"Well, you don't look like an experimental psychologist to <u>me</u>"

In subtle, nonverbal ways, experimenters may influence how subjects perform.

hadn't watched any television at all also showed high levels of aggression. We might conclude that these subjects, by virtue of being put in a situation that allowed them to display aggression, would expect that they were *supposed* to behave aggressively and would go on to do so. Experimenters must always worry that subjects change the way they behave simply because they are aware of being observed or tested. For example, subjects may feel special about being chosen to participate in a study and thus act differently than they would ordinarily. Such effects can compromise an experiment's results.

The Remedy

Because human and animal behaviors are complex and often have multiple causes, good research design involves anticipating possible confounds and devising strategies for eliminating them. Similar to defensive strategies in sports, good research designs anticipate what the other team might do and set plans to counteract it. Researchers' strategies are called **control procedures**—methods that attempt to hold constant all variables and conditions other than those related to the hypothesis being tested. In an experiment, instructions, room temperature, tasks, the way the researcher is dressed, time allotted, the way the responses are recorded, and many other details of the situation must be similar for all subjects, to ensure that their experience is the same. The only differences in subjects' experiences should be those introduced by the independent variable. Let us look at remedies for the specific confounding variables, expectancy and placebo effects.

Imagine, for example, that we enriched the aggression experiment to include a treatment group that watched comedy programs. We'd want to be careful not to treat our comedy and violence subjects in different ways based on our expectations. Such bias can be eliminated by keeping both subjects and experimental assistants unaware of, or blind to, which subjects get which treatment. This technique is called a **double-blind control** condition. In the experiment, we would want the research assistant who greeted the subjects and later assessed their aggression to be unaware whether they had watched a violent program or a comedy. For other sorts of research designs—such as the one in which Rosenthal originally demonstrated expectancy effects—we could simply not allow the researcher to enter the testing room during data collection!

Researchers use double-blind controls and placebo control procedures to preserve objectivity.

To account for placebo effects, researchers generally include an experimental condition in which the treatment is not administered. We call this a **placebo control.** Placebo controls fall into the general category of controls by which experimenters assure themselves that they are making appropriate comparisons. Consider the story of a young girl who, when asked if she loved her older sister, replied, "Compared to what?" That question is one that must be asked—and satisfactorily answered—before you can really understand what a research finding means. The data from control conditions often serve as the comparison or baseline against which the experimental effect is evaluated.

In some research designs, which are referred to as **between-subjects designs,** different groups of subjects are *randomly assigned,* by chance procedures, to an **experimental condition** (exposed to the independent variable or treatment) or to a **control condition** (not exposed to the experimental treatment). This is the design we had in mind for the aggression experiment. The random assignment to experimental and control conditions makes the two groups similar in important ways at the start of an experiment, because each subject has the same probability of being in the treatment condition as in the control condition. If outcome differences are found between the two conditions, the researcher can be more confident that the differences were caused by treatment or intervention rather than by already existing differences.

Random assignment is an important means of control that produces similarity between the control and experimental groups.

Sometimes in a between-subjects design there is no formal control group. Instead, comparisons might be made with a group that received a different *level* of the experimental treatment. Thus we might have one experimental group watch one hour of violence on television and a second experimental group watch six hours of such programs. Our prediction might be that the second group would display more aggression than the first.

In an A-B-A experimental design, subjects are used as their own controls.

Another type of experimental design—a **within-subjects design**—uses each subject as his or her own control. For example, the behavior of an experimental subject before getting the treatment might be compared with his behavior after. In what is known as an **A-B-A design**, subjects first experience the baseline, or control, condition (A), then experience the experimental treatment (B), and then go back to the baseline (A):

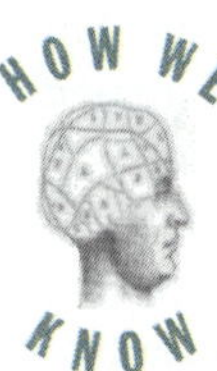

This A-B-A design was used by an investigator who wanted to test the hypothesis that making children feel anonymous would increase their level of aggression when the situation provided an opportunity. Grade-school children were invited to a Halloween party where a variety of games were available, both those that invited aggressive and non-aggressive play. In the baseline condition (A), the children played without wearing Halloween costumes. Then in the treatment condition (B), they put on costumes and continued to play the games of their choice. Finally, in a return to the baseline condition (A), they were told the costumes had to be returned but they could continue playing without them. The results supported the experimenter's hypothesis, as you can see in **Figure 2.2**. Across the three conditions that were otherwise constant, the same children were much more aggressive when they were anonymous than when they were identifiable (Fraser, 1974).

When schoolchildren attended a Halloween party (that was also an experiment), they engaged in significantly more aggressive play when they were anonymous than when they were identifiable.

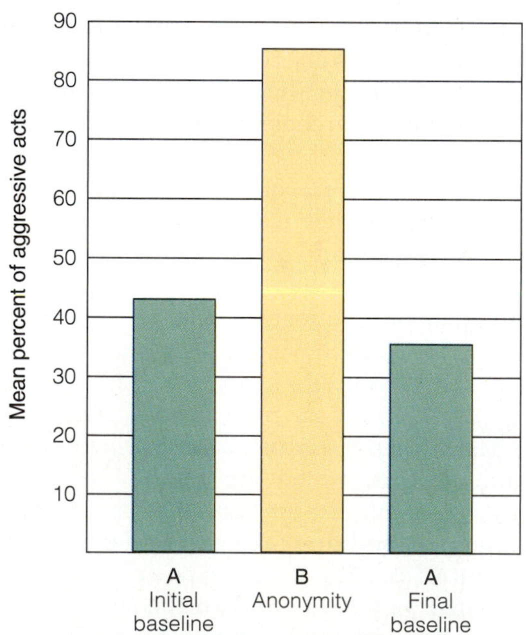

Figure 2.2 Anonymity-Induced Aggression
The effects of being anonymous are dramatic: aggression is much higher in the anonymous condition than for the same children before and again after they put on Halloween costumes.

So what is the first question you should ask when you read that a study shows that "more than three-quarters of a group of people trying to quit smoking were able to win with the help of nicotine patches" (Andrews, 1990)? Compared to what? What about the control group? In this study's placebo control group, which wore nicotine-free patches, a full 39 percent also stopped smoking! Moreover, the longer they wore those medically useless patches, the more likely they were to quit smoking (Abelin et al., 1989). So the nicotine patch was an effective treatment, but more than half of its effectiveness was due to the placebo effect of expecting that it would work. When we report experimental results in the chapters to come, we will take great care in answering the question *Compared to what?* This is the essence of the scientific method.

The research methodologies we have described so far all involve the creation of a treatment to look for an effect—the manipulation of an independent variable to look for an effect on a dependent variable. This approach is called the **experimental method.** Although the experimental method often allows researchers to make the strongest claims about causal relations among variables, it is not always desirable to use it. First, during an experiment, behavior is frequently studied in an artificial environment, one in which the situational factors are controlled so heavily that the environment may distort the behavior from the way it would occur naturally. Critics claim that much of the richness and complexity of natural behavior patterns is lost in controlled experiments, sacrificed to the simplicity of dealing with only one or a few variables and responses. Second, research subjects typically know they are in an experiment and are being tested and measured. They may react to this awareness by trying to please the researcher, attempting to "psych out" the research purpose, or changing their behavior from what it would be if they were unaware of being monitored. Third, there are some important research problems that are not amenable to ethical experimental treatment. We could not, for example, try to discover whether the tendency toward child abuse is transmitted from generation to generation by creating an experimental group of children who would be abused and a control group of children who would not be. In the next section, we turn to a type of research methodology that often addresses all these concerns.

The experimental method allows researchers to make claims about cause-effect relationships.

CORRELATIONAL METHODS

Is intelligence associated with creativity? Are optimistic people healthier than pessimists? What is the link between social isolation and madness? Is there a relationship between being easily hypnotized and being conforming? All these questions involve variables that a psychologist could not easily or ethically manipulate. To answer these questions, as we will in later chapters, requires research based on **correlational methods.** Psychologists use correlational methods when they want to determine to what extent two variables, traits, or attributes are related.

Researchers use correlational methods to determine the extent to which two variables are related.

To determine the precise degree of correlation that exists between two variables, psychologists compute a statistical measure known as the **correlation coefficient** (r). This value can vary between +1.0 and –1.0, where +1.0 is a perfect positive correlation, –1.0 is a perfect negative correlation, and 0.0 indicates there is no correlation at all. A positive correlation coefficient means that as one set of scores increases, a second set also increases. The reverse is true with negative correlations; the second set of scores goes in the opposite direction to the values of the first scores (see **Figure 2.3**). Correlations that are closer to zero mean that there is a weak relationship or no

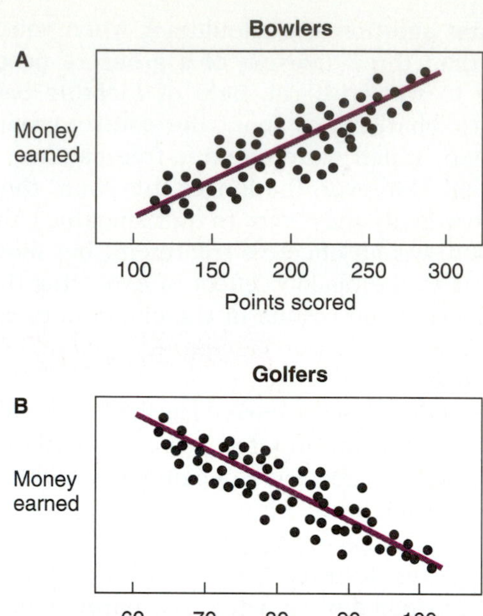

Figure 2.3 Positive and Negative Correlations
These imaginary data display the difference between positive and negative correlations. Each point represents a single bowler or golfer. (A) In general, the more *points a professional bowler scores, the* more *money he or she will earn. Thus there is a positive correlation between those two variables. (B) The correlation for golf is negative because golfers earn* more *money when they score* fewer *points.*

relationship between scores on two measures. As the correlation coefficient gets stronger, closer to the +/–1.0 maximum, predictions about one variable based upon information about the other variable become increasingly more accurate.

For example, a researcher exploring the relationship between worker productivity and stress might measure how much stress people are experiencing in their lives and how well they are performing at work. *Stress* might be operationally defined as a particular score on a stress questionnaire. *Job productivity* might be defined as the number of units of a given product a worker produces each day. The researcher could then measure each variable for many different workers and compute the correlation coefficient between them. A strongly negative score would mean that as stress goes up, productivity goes down. Knowing someone's life stress score would then allow the researcher to make a reasonable prediction about that person's productivity.

The researcher might want to take the next step and say that the way to increase productivity would be to lower stress. This assessment is incorrect. A strong correlation indicates only that two sets of data covary in a systematic way; the correlation does not ensure that one causes the other. *Correlation does not imply causation.* The correlation could reflect any one of several cause-and-effect possibilities, or none.

An important limitation of correlation is that it does not imply causation.

For example, a negative stress and productivity correlation might mean that (1) stress at home carries over to cause people to do poorly at work, (2) poor job productivity makes people experience more stress, or (3) those with a certain personality style are more likely to experience stress and also to perform poorly on the job. (Note that in the last case, a third variable is caus-

The constant demand for vigilance and the high costs of human error put air traffic controllers at risk for chronic stress reactions. To study the relationship between stress and job performance, a researcher must devise methods of measuring both factors.

ing the other two to vary.) Consider another example: there is a strong correlation between contraceptive use in Taiwan and the number of electrical appliances in Taiwanese homes. Given this finding, would you expect contraceptive use to increase if the government gave away radios and popcorn machines? The answer would be yes only if the two variables are related causally. In actuality, a third set of variables—education and social class—is responsible for both phenomena (Li, 1975). Can you see how?

Correlations may also be spurious because researchers did not make the appropriate control comparisons. Consider the supposed connection between the power blackout in New York City in 1965 and the reported jump in the birthrate nine months later. "New Yorkers are very romantic. It was the candlelight," said one new father. An official for a planned parenthood group offered the explanation that, because of the blackout, "all the substitutes for sex—meetings, lectures, card parties, theaters, saloons—were eliminated that night. What else could they do?" (*The New York Times,* 8/11/1966). The same kind of correlation is often reported after major blizzards and other disasters in many parts of the world. "Quake May Have Caused Baby Boom in Bay Area" was a more recent headline in the *San Francisco Chronicle* (Chen, 1990). However, when anyone takes the time to compare these apparently dramatic birthrate increases with the ordinary seasonal variations, the correlation turns out to be coincidence masquerading as causation. That is, there is a *real* correlation between season and birthrate—this is the control comparison for the coincidental "disaster" correlation. Clearly we must apply the same caution to correlational results as we apply to research results that emerge from experimental methods.

We don't want to leave you with the impression that correlational methods aren't valuable research tools. Throughout *Psychology and Life* we will see many correlational studies that have led to important insights. We offer here the example of **cross-cultural research** to reinforce this claim. Cross-cultural research is used to discover whether behavior found in one culture also occurs in other cultures. To examine the influence of culture on behavior, psychologists cannot manipulate cultures experimentally. Rather, they must look for patterns of correlation. In this type of research, the unit of analysis is

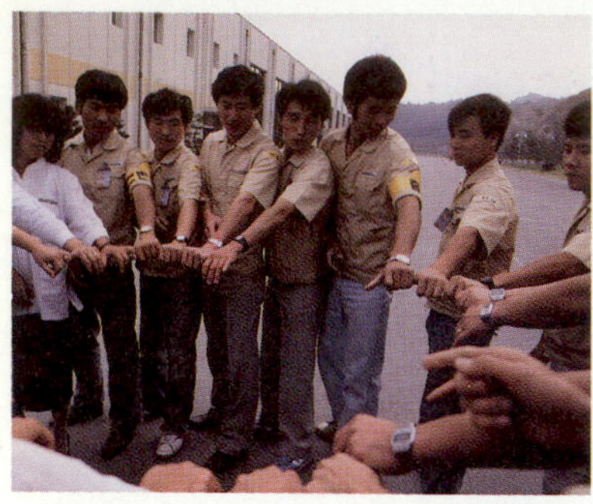

People in collectivist societies are rewarded for cooperation and loyalty to the group.

a whole culture or society rather than an individual. However, the data still consist of observations of individuals' behaviors. The cross-cultural method has been used to compare diverse sexual practices, perceptual differences in reactions to illusions, and cultural factors that influence productivity.

A survey of more than 100 cross-cultural studies points to a basic distinction between societies throughout the world—namely, whether they are *individualistic* or *collectivist* (Triandis, 1990). Individualistic societies stress the individual as the most important unit; they value competition, individual achievement, and personal fulfillment. In contrast, collectivist societies place the greatest value on social group, family, community, or tribe. Cooperation, sharing, altruism, and the social good are the main values that guide collectivist societies. These two fundamentally different orientations influence a wide range of behavioral patterns. For example, in one study, a researcher tested his hypothesis about the relationship between societal lifestyles and conformity by comparing people from a hunting society (the Inuit) with people from an agricultural society (the Temne in Africa). He found a tendency toward conformity on a standardized test in the agricultural society, whose members had learned to cooperate and depended on each other for their food. Conformity scores were lower in the hunting society, where food gathering was an individual activity and required independence and self-reliance (Berry, 1967). Around the world, individualistic or collectivist societies are unequally distributed; 70 percent of societies are collectivist and only 30 percent are individualistic. Because most of modern psychology is based on research conducted in individualistic societies in North America and Europe, it becomes questionable how far the conclusions of this research can be generalized to other cultures.

Cross-cultural research reveals a basic distinction between individualistic and collectivist cultures.

Subliminal Influence?

To close out this section on the context of justification, we offer one real-life example of how psychological research has been used to assess the vigorous claims of advertisers anxious to make you believe in their products. You almost certainly have been subjected to commercials for audiotapes that promise to change your life with messages outside conscious awareness—*subliminal* messages: it's cassette magic! One tape guarantees a better sex life; another provides a quick cure for low self-esteem; a third promises safe and effective weight loss. How? All you have to do is *listen*—in bed, while jogging, when doing your homework—to the "restful splash of ocean waves breaking on sandy shores."

Do subliminal messages influence the attitudes and behavior of those who hear them?

"Subliminal" influence has a long history. Although it was almost certainly a hoax (Rogers, 1993), a 1957 study made headlines when the "inventor" of subliminal advertising claimed that the message "Buy Popcorn" flashed on the screen during a movie yielded a 58 percent increase in popcorn sales! *The Wall Street Journal* reported in 1980 that a New Orleans supermarket significantly decreased stealing and cashier shortages after piping the following subliminal message into its Muzak system: "If I steal, I will go to jail." In 1989, the heavy metal band Judas Priest was indicted for recording disguised messages on its albums. The group was sued by the parents of two teenagers who had committed suicide after listening to one of their tapes. A telephone survey in Toledo, Ohio, showed that nearly 75 percent of the 400 adults surveyed were familiar with subliminal advertising (Rogers & Smith, 1993). Of that group, again nearly 75 percent believed that subliminal advertising was used successfully by marketers. And, in general, the better educated the respondents were, the more likely they were to believe in the effectiveness of subliminal advertising!

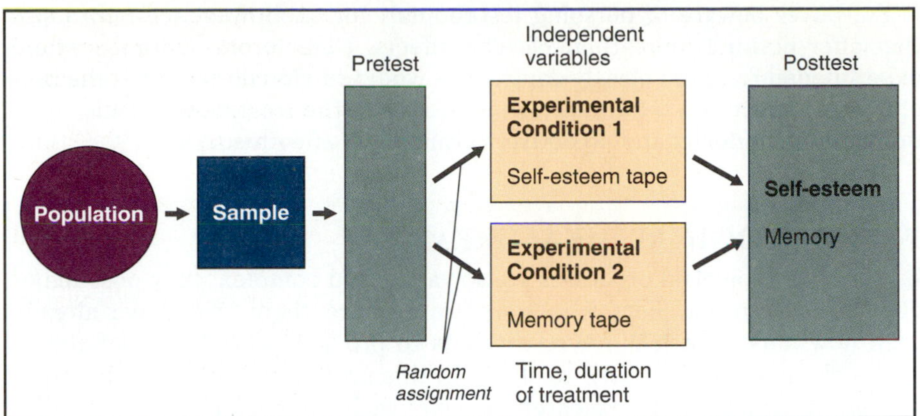

Figure 2.4 Experimental Design for Testing Hypotheses About the Effectiveness of Subliminal Audiotapes
In this simplified version of the experiment, a sample of people is drawn from a larger, general population. They are given a series of pretest measures and randomly assigned to receive subliminal tapes with either memory or self-esteem messages. They are then given posttests that objectively assess any changes in the dependent variables: memory and self-esteem. The study found no significant effects of subliminal persuasion.

You now have the knowledge to address the critical question. Do the subliminal audiotapes really influence mental states and behavior as their advocates claim? Our answer comes from the experimental methods we have described (see **Figure 2.4**):

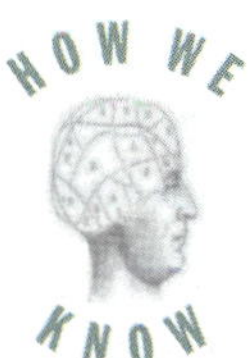

A team of experimenters set out to determine the effectiveness of listening to commercially available audiotapes designed to improve self-esteem or memory. The subjects were 237 men and women volunteers, ranging from 18 to 60 years of age. After a pretest session in which their initial self-esteem and memory were measured on standard psychological tests and questionnaires, the subjects were randomly assigned to two conditions. Half of them received subliminal memory tapes, while the others received subliminal self-esteem tapes. They listened regularly to the tapes for a five-week period and then returned to the laboratory for a posttest session to evaluate their memories (using four memory tests) and self-esteem (using three self-esteem scales). The researchers were blind to which subjects received which treatment (Greenwald et al., 1991).

Did the tapes boost self-esteem and enhance memory? The results from this controlled experiment indicate that there was *no significant improvement* shown on any of the objective measures of either self-esteem or memory. However, one very powerful effect did emerge: the placebo effect of expecting to be helped. Anticipating this effect, the researchers had added another independent variable. Half the subjects in each group received memory tapes that were mismarked "self-esteem" and the others received self-esteem tapes in "memory boxes." Subjects believed their self-esteem improved if they received tapes with that label or felt that their memory improved if their tapes were labeled "memory"—even when they had been listening to the other tape! The findings are best described by researcher **Anthony Greenwald** as "what you expect is what you believe but not necessarily what you get."

So, buyer beware of personal testimonials for subliminal self-help tapes that offer nothing more than placebo effects. Here is one instance where experimental research clearly contradicts what individuals believe is the psychological effect of a treatment—they believe in the treatment because they do not systematically and objectively evaluate its effectiveness.

PSYCHOLOGICAL MEASUREMENT

Psychological researchers are challenged by the tasks of operationally defining and quantifying the phenomena they wish to study.

Because psychological processes are so varied and complex, they pose major challenges to researchers who want to measure them. You have already seen how important it is for researchers to provide operational definitions of the phenomena they wish to study. In this section we consider the range of options available to researchers who wish to perform psychological measurements.

The researcher's first challenge is to access the psychological phenomenon he or she wishes to understand. Although some actions and processes are easily seen, many, such as anxiety or dreaming, are not. Thus one task for a psychological researcher is to make the unseen visible, to make internal events and processes external, and to make private experiences public. Many methods are available for accomplishing this task, each with its particular advantages and disadvantages. A second challenge is to find the right measure—the best *outcome variable*—to assess the psychological phenomenon described in the theory or hypothesis.

All attempts at measurement use some procedure for assigning numbers to, or *quantifying,* different levels, sizes, intensities, or amounts of a variable. Some measures are physical, such as the speed at which a subject reacts to a red light, while others are scaled along a continuum that orders the variable in some systematic way: "How often do you feel shy when you are alone with someone of the opposite sex? Always? Almost always? Sometimes? Hardly ever? Never?" Other measures take qualitative answers, such as statements of the subject's feelings, and code them into categories that can be quantified. Assigning numbers to variables increases the precision of scientific communication of procedures and results.

Our review of psychological measurement begins with a discussion of the distinction between two ways of gauging the accuracy of a measure. We then review three important methods of measurement that are part of the descriptive research techniques psychologists use: self-reports, behavior analysis, and physiological measures.

Once a psychological phenomenon has been quantified, the resulting data must be subjected to statistical analysis.

By whatever means psychologists collect their data, they must use appropriate statistical methods to verify their hypotheses. A full description of how psychologists analyze their data is given in the Statistical Appendix. You should read it in conjunction with this chapter.

ACHIEVING RELIABILITY AND VALIDITY

Psychological measurement must produce findings that are both reliable and valid.

The goal of psychological measurement is to generate findings that are both reliable and valid. **Reliability** refers to the consistency or dependability of behavioral data resulting from psychological testing or experimental research. A reliable result is one that will be repeated under similar conditions of testing at different times. A reliable measuring instrument or device yields comparable scores when employed repeatedly (and when the thing being measured does not change). As we will see in Chapter 15, there are a number of ways to assess just how reliable a psychological test is.

Reliability is enhanced when (1) the research, test, or measurement conditions are standardized; (2) enough observations are made or responses are measured so that atypical ones do not distort the overall effect; and (3) factors that might cause the data to vary in unsystematic ways are anticipated and controlled.

Validity means that the information produced by research or testing accurately measures the psychological variable or quality it is intended to measure. A valid test enables the investigator to make predictions from the test scores about performance in other situations. For example, SAT scores are a fairly valid predictor of early college grades, in general (assuming the student's level of academic motivation does not change dramatically between high school and college). But SAT scores are *not* valid for predicting how creative, popular, or healthy a student will be.

Serious misuse of psychological information occurs when test results that are valid for one group or one type of prediction are used as the basis for evaluating another group's performance. This misuse has been found in some tests of intelligence and achievement developed only on subjects who were white, male, or native speakers but then used to assess nonwhites, females, and the foreign-born (see Chapter 15). As we describe three types of measures in this section—self-reports, behavior analysis, and physiological measures—and throughout *Psychology and Life,* we will try to make you aware of psychologists' ongoing concerns about reliability and validity.

Self-report Measures

Often researchers are interested in obtaining data about experiences they cannot directly observe. Sometimes these experiences are internal psychological processes such as daydreams or insights. At other times these experiences are external behaviors but—like sexual activities or criminal acts—not generally appropriate for psychologists to witness. In these cases, investigations rely on verbal reports. **Self-report measures** are verbal answers, either written or spoken, to questions the researcher poses. Researchers devise reliable ways to quantify these self-reports so they can make meaningful comparisons between different individuals' responses.

Self-reports are the primary method for getting information about beliefs, attitudes, feelings, motives, and personality. However, there are limits to their usefulness, and there are problems with their validation. Obviously, self-reports cannot be used with preverbal children, illiterate adults, speakers of other languages, some mentally disturbed people, and animals. Even when verbal reports can be used, they may not be accurate. Subjects may misunderstand the questions or not remember clearly what they actually experienced. One confounding variable in the use of verbal reports is social desirability—people may give false or misleading answers to create a favorable impression of themselves. They may be embarrassed to report their true experiences or feelings.

Self-reports include responses made on questionnaires and surveys and during interviews. A *questionnaire* is a written set of questions, ranging in content from questions of fact ("Are you a registered voter?"), to questions about past or present behavior ("How much do you smoke?"), to questions about attitudes and feelings ("How satisfied are you with your present job?"). *Open-ended* questions allow respondents to answer freely in their own words. Questions may also have a number of *fixed alternatives* such as *yes, no,* and *undecided.*

Self-report measures are obtained through questionnaires, surveys, and interviews.

Questionnaires are used in *survey research,* which is a way to gather information efficiently from a large number of people. In a *survey,* a standardized set of questions is given to a large number of participants, either by mail, telephone, or face-to-face. Unlike a census, which tries to survey the

Open-ended questions can yield some surprising responses.

entire population, a sample survey collects information from a carefully selected group of people who are believed to have attributes that are representative of the entire population from which the sample is drawn. One example of a sample survey is a public opinion poll; its conclusions about national opinions are often based on a sample of about 1500 people.

There is always the risk of error in sampling a population. Most polls carry a standard warning label about the margins for error. Often the margin of error is about 3 percent, which means that the data are accurate within 3 percent, plus or minus, of the values presented. (A value reported at 30 percent with a margin of error of 3 could actually be as high as 33 percent or as low as 27 percent.)

An *interview* is a face-to-face dialogue between a researcher and an individual for the purpose of obtaining detailed information. Instead of being completely standardized, as a questionnaire is, an interview is *interactive.* An interviewer may vary the questioning to follow up on something the respondent said. Good interviewers are also sensitive to the process of the social interaction as well as to the information revealed. They are trained to establish *rapport,* a positive social relationship with the respondent that encourages trust and the sharing of personal information.

Interviews can sometimes generate invalid data. Respondents who are aware of the interviewer's purpose may lie or alter the truth to get a job, to get discharged from a mental hospital, or to accomplish any other goal. The interview situation also allows personal biases and prejudices to affect how the interviewer asks questions and how the respondent answers them.

Behavioral Measures

Although psychological researchers are interested in behavior, the kind of behavior they are interested in varies dramatically. They may study a rat running a maze, a child drawing a picture, a student memorizing a poem, or a worker repeatedly performing a task. **Behavioral measures** are ways to study overt actions and observable and recordable reactions.

One of the primary ways to study what people do is *observation*. Researchers use observation in a planned, precise, and systematic manner. Observations focus on either the *process* or the *products* of behavior. In an experiment on learning, for instance, a researcher might observe how many times a subject rehearsed a list of words (process) and then how many words the subject remembered on a final test (product). Or the researcher might observe behavioral products that were generated in the past or made for purposes other than research. Personal documents, such as autobiographies, letters, diaries, drawings, and speeches can yield other valuable background information.

For *direct observations,* the behavior under investigation must be clearly visible and overt and easily recorded. For example, in a study of communication patterns, a researcher might ask a group of students to discuss a controversial issue while he or she makes direct observations about who starts the discussion, who changes the topic, turn-taking patterns, and so forth. In a laboratory experiment on emotions, a researcher could observe a subject's facial expressions as the subject looked at emotionally arousing stimuli.

A researcher's direct observations are often augmented by technology. For example, psychologists employ stop-action photography to document rapidly changing behavior. Among other things, stop-action photography has been used in studies of the way subtle changes in facial expressions of mothers and their babies become synchronized and similar over time. Other researchers rely on computers to provide very precise measures of the time it takes for subjects to perform various tasks, such as reading a sentence or solving a problem. Although some forms of exact measurement were available before the computer age, computers now provide extraordinary flexibility in collecting and analyzing precise information.

Depending on the behavior of interest, a psychologist might investigate using behavioral measures such as direct observation or naturalistic observation.

In *naturalistic observations,* some naturally occurring behavior is viewed by a researcher, who makes no attempt to change or interfere with it. For example, a researcher behind a one-way mirror might observe the play of children who are not aware of being observed. From observations about each child's interaction patterns, the researcher might make inferences about

By watching from behind a one-way mirror, a researcher can record observations of a child at play without influencing or interfering with the child's behavior. These photos are from the laboratory of Jerome Kagan at Harvard University.

Jane Goodall has spent most of her adult life making naturalistic observations of chimpanzees.

sociability or relationships with adults. Some kinds of human behavior can be studied only through naturalistic observation, because it would be unethical or impractical to do otherwise. For example, it would be unethical to experiment with severe deprivation in early life to see its effects on a child's later development.

When studying behavior in a laboratory setting, a researcher is unable to observe the long-term effects that one's natural habitat has in shaping complex patterns of behavior. One of the most valuable examples of naturalistic observation conducted in the field is the work of **Jane Goodall** (1986, 1990; Peterson & Goodall, 1993). Goodall has spent many years studying patterns of behavior among chimpanzees in Gombe, on Lake Tanganyika in Africa. The focus of her research is the insight chimpanzee behavior might shed on the evolutionary development of certain forms of human behavior, especially aggression. Goodall's exhaustive observational analysis of every aspect of chimpanzee behavior began over 30 years ago and continues today, even though it was originally scheduled to last for only 10 years. Goodall notes that had she ended her research after 10 years, she would not have drawn the correct conclusions:

> We would have observed many similarities in their behavior and ours, but we would have been left with the impression that chimpanzees were far more peaceable than humans. Because we were able to continue beyond the first decade, we could document the division of a social group and observe the violent aggression that broke out between newly separated factions. We discovered that in certain circumstances the chimpanzees may kill and even cannibalize individuals of their own kind. On the other side of the coin, we have learned of the extraordinarily enduring affectionate bonds between family members... advanced cognitive abilities, [and the development of] cultural traditions... (Goodall, 1986, pp. 3–4)

In the early stages of an investigation, naturalistic observation is especially useful. It helps researchers to discover the extent of a phenomenon or to get an idea of what the important variables and relationships might be.

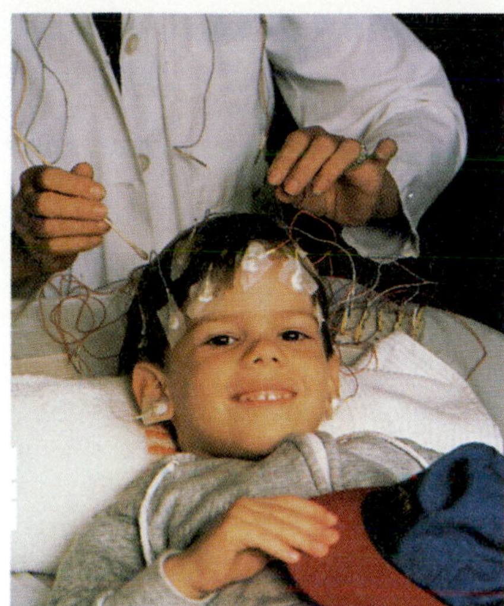
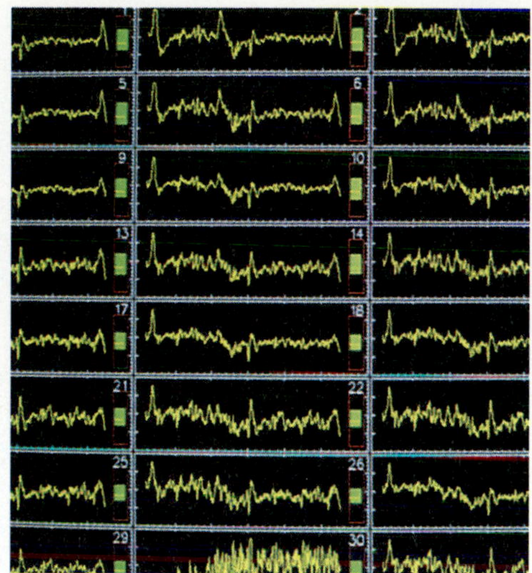

By connecting subjects to an EEG, scientists can study the activity of the brain.

The data from naturalistic observation often provide clues for an investigator to use in formulating a specific hypothesis to be tested or new research methods.

Physiological Measures

How does a researcher know what the brain is doing when someone is asleep or solving a problem? Special instruments are available to show these internal reactions in a measurable form. For example, researchers can collect information about brain activity by attaching a series of electrodes to different locations on a subject's scalp. A graphic representation of the pattern of the brain's electrical signals is known as an *electroencephalogram* (EEG). Researchers use the patterns of activity in the EEG to draw inferences about various psychological processes. It is possible, for example, to demonstrate that readers produce different patterns of brain activity when they encounter an unexpected word in a sentence than when they encounter an unusual grammatical construction (Osterhout & Holcomb, 1992). From such patterns of response, researchers can begin to infer the structure of psychological processes.

Technological advances have greatly improved researchers' ability to "see" areas of the brain at work. Techniques such as *positron-emission tomography* (PET) and *magnetic resonance imaging* (MRI) were originally developed to improve diagnoses in medical settings. With assistance from sophisticated computer software, these techniques provide images of the structure and activity of brain tissue. Psychologists have quickly adapted these techniques to answer a wide range of questions. For example, MRI and PET techniques enable researchers to demonstrate differences in the brain activity of mentally ill versus normal individuals (Resnick, 1992).

Physiological measures may be taken through the use of EEGs, PET scans, and MRIs.

At a more precise level of analysis, researchers interested in discovering how information is processed in specialized cells in the brain can do so by implanting minute electrodes into specific brain areas, or even single brain cells, and recording their pattern of activity. They test hypotheses about the role of specific brain structures in psychological processes by observing the effect that different external stimuli, or relationships among external stimuli, have on the activities of single brain cells or small collections of cells.

ETHICAL ISSUES IN HUMAN AND ANIMAL RESEARCH

In the study that tested the effectiveness of subliminal messages, the researchers deceived the participants by mislabeling the tapes. They did so to see if the subjects' expectations would lead them to believe that the messages were helpful even if objective measures of memory and self-esteem showed no improvement. Deception is always ethically suspect, but in this case, how else could researchers assess the placebo effect of false beliefs held by the subjects? How would you weigh the *potential gains* of a research project against the *costs* it incurs to those who are subjected to procedures that are risky, painful, stressful, or deceptive?

Respect for the basic rights of humans and animals is a fundamental obligation of all researchers. To guarantee that these rights are honored, special committees oversee every research proposal, imposing strict guidelines issued by the U.S. Department of Health and Human Services. Psychology departments at universities and colleges, hospitals, and research institutes each have review panels that approve and reject proposals for human and animal research. In a sense, these institutional review boards try to adjust the balance of power between experimenters and research participants. The American Psychological Association (1982) has established detailed guidelines for ethical standards for researchers. What are some of those guidelines and ethical concerns?

Informed Consent

Typically all laboratory research on human subjects starts with a full description of the procedures, potential risks, and expected benefits that subjects will experience. Before beginning the research, subjects are given this information and asked to sign statements indicating that they give their *informed consent* to participate. The subjects are assured in advance that they may leave an experiment anytime they wish, without penalty, and are given the names and phone numbers of officials to contact if they have any grievances.

Risk/Gain Assessment

Most psychology experiments carry little risk to the subjects, especially where participants are merely asked to perform routine tasks. However, some experiments that study more personal aspects of human nature—such as emotional reactions, self-images, conformity, stress, or aggression—can be upsetting or psychologically disturbing. Therefore, whenever a researcher conducts such a study, he or she should include, as a basic feature of the research design, procedures intended to protect the subjects' physical and psychological well-being (Diener & Crandall, 1978). Risks must be minimized, subjects must be informed of the risks, and suitable precautions must be taken to deal with strong reactions by the subjects. Where any risk is involved, it is carefully weighed by each institutional review panel in terms of its necessity for achieving the benefits to the participants of the study, to science, and to society. Similar precautions are exercised in animal research, where the humane and considerate treatment of all animal subjects is now clearly recognized as essential.

Intentional Deception

For some kinds of research, it is not possible to tell the subjects the whole story in advance without biasing the results. If you were studying the effects on aggression of violence on television, for example, you would not want your subjects to know your purpose in advance. But is your hypothesis enough to justify the deception? Some researchers have argued that any type of deception is incompatible with the basic right of informed consent (Korn, 1987). Others assert that the immorality of any deception does harm to the subjects, the profession of psychology, and to society (Baumrind, 1985). Users of deception address these concerns by citing follow-up studies that typically reveal that most subjects enjoyed participating in the experiments and report having acquired important self-knowledge.

Perhaps the most controversial study in psychology was one in which subjects were made to think they should follow the orders of an authority figure who instructed them to deliver painful shocks to another subject. In fact, they were not actually hurting the victim, although they did not know this. In this study of blind obedience to authority, the subjects were torn between honoring their research commitment by doing as they were told and quitting the experiment (Milgram, 1974). Even so, the researcher reported that over 80 percent of the subjects were "very glad" or "glad" to have been in the study, that only 1 percent said they were "sorry" or "very sorry," and that the rest were neither glad nor sorry to have participated (Milgram, 1977).

Yet if even one subject feels harmed by participating in a deceptive experiment, doesn't that make it unethical? Alternatives to deception research are being put into practice wherever possible, and safeguards are instituted to reduce the potential risks. In risky experiments, the review committee may impose constraints, insist on monitoring initial demonstrations of the procedure, or deny approval (Steininger et al., 1984).

Debriefing

Participation in psychological research should always be a mutual exchange of information between researcher and subject. The researcher may learn something new about a behavioral phenomenon from the subject's reactions, while the subject should be informed of the purpose, hypothesis, anticipated results, and expected benefits of the study. At the end of an experiment, each subject must be given a careful **debriefing**, in which the researcher provides as much information about the study as possible and makes sure that no one leaves feeling confused, upset, or embarrassed. If it was necessary to mislead the subjects during any stage of the research, the experimenter carefully explains the reasons for the deception. In addition, the privacy of subjects is protected: all records of their behavior are kept strictly confidential; any public sharing of them must be approved by the subjects. Finally, subjects have the right to withdraw their data if they feel they have been misused or their rights abused in any way.

Important ethical issues in human research include informed consent, an assessment of the risks and benefits of the research, the use of intentional deception, and the necessity for debriefing.

Issues in Animal Research: Science, Ethics, Politics

Should animals be used in psychological and medical research? Before we consider the pros and cons of this heated issue, let's first outline some reasons that psychologists use animals in their research. First, with animals bred and reared under controlled conditions, it is more possible to tease apart hereditary and environmental factors that influence performance than it ever could be in humans. Second, since many species breed more rapidly than do humans, studies of developmental processes that occur over many generations are possible. Third, in some species, basic processes—such as sensation, learning, memory, and even social interaction—are comparable to those in humans. Because they may occur in animals in less complex forms that can be more readily investigated, animal models of these processes shed light on human functioning. Fourth, psychologists often study animal behavior not to gain more information about humans but to learn about a given animal species or to better understand general laws of behavior that are true across species.

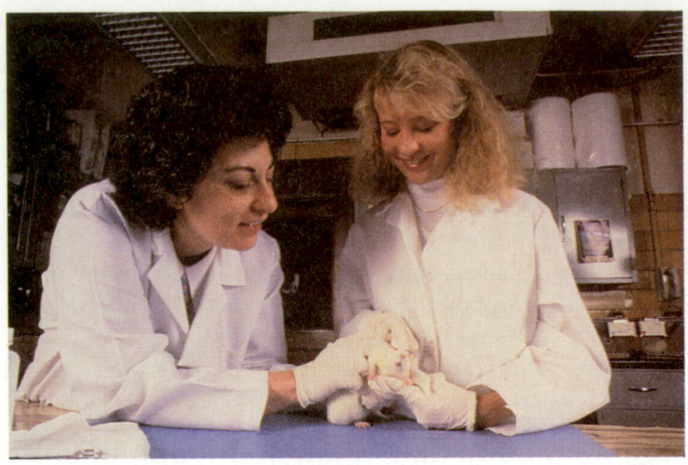

Researchers who use animal subjects are required to provide a humane environment.

Defenders of the use of animals most often cite the contributions that scientific research with animals, and with humans, makes daily to the health and well-being of humans and animals alike. The benefits of animal research have included discovery and testing of drugs that treat anxiety, mental illnesses, and Parkinson's disease; new knowledge about drug addiction; rehabilitation of neuromuscular disorders; and work on the desperately sought cure for AIDS (Miller, 1985).

Research with animal subjects has resulted in significant contributions to the welfare of animals and humans.

A different perspective on the debate comes from a catalog of benefits that animal research has made to animals. On a worldwide basis, immunizations for various animal diseases, such as rabies, distemper, and anthrax, are preventing suffering and untimely deaths in billions of domestic animals. Psychological researchers have shown how to alleviate the stresses of confinement experienced by zoo animals. Their studies of animal learning and social organization have led to the improved design of enclosures and animal facilities that promote good health (Nicoll et al., 1988).

In recent years, concern over the care and treatment of animals used in psychological and biomedical research has led to strict guidelines that researchers must follow in order to receive funds and conduct their research (Baldwin, 1993). Laboratory facilities must have adequate space, be well maintained, and use qualified staff to care for the animals. The health of the animals and their general well-being also are monitored. Every effort must be made to minimize pain and discomfort and to seek alternative procedures that are not stressful.

To defenders of animal rights, these precautions and procedures do not undercut the deep error of believing that there is a "morally relevant difference separating *Homo sapiens* from other creatures" (Bowd & Shapiro, 1993, p. 136). Such an analysis on the part of animal rights advocates rejects the notion that benefits to humans can be used to justify animal research. Taken to its limit, the views held by these advocates can lead to violent action: the Animal Liberation Front takes credit for "liberating" research animals from many laboratories and for breaking into the labs, trashing them, and even burning some to the ground (*U.S. News & World Report,* 8/31/87). Many animal rights activists, however, believe such actions to be inconsistent with their basic moral stance (Herzog, 1993). More careful thinkers argue for "a shift from laboratory-based invasive research to minimally manipulative research conducted in naturalistic and semi-naturalistic settings" (Bowd &

Evaluating Drug Prevention

Imagine that you are a research psychologist with a critical objective: you must provide sound scientific feedback to government officials about the relative success of programs intended to prevent drug use in our society. You want to help the government spend its money wisely. Let us look at drug prevention programs that have been implemented in the United States and see how they have been—or should be—evaluated using the scientific method.

One of the most dramatic drug prevention programs initiated since the mid-1980s was President George Bush's "war on drugs." The U.S. government conducted a one-year, $9.5 billion experiment in which more than 70 percent of the funds were earmarked for "get-tough" law enforcement. The premise was that tougher law enforcement would reduce drug use. Did it? In fact, both those who believed the program worked and those who did not were able to cite statistics to support their point of view. President Bush and antidrug czar William Bennett cited studies that found decreases in cocaine and marijuana use and reductions in the number of hospital emergency room records that mentioned cocaine or heroin. At the same time, the Drug Policy Foundation, an international group seeking alternatives to the "war on drugs," cited increases in drug-related crimes, an overloaded criminal justice system, a heroin comeback, and underfunded treatment programs. These competing statistics should suggest to you that the program was not effectively evaluated. How might you do better?

You could first operationally define a set of dependent variables that measure, for example, the harm posed to society by drug abuse. You might come up with some of the following: incidence of new drug addicts, rates of needle-transmitted AIDS and HIV infection, incidence of newborns showing opiate withdrawal symptoms at birth, incidence of drug-related homicides, and the cost of imprisoning drug addicts and pushers. Without specific definitions like these, the "drug problem" remains so vaguely defined and multifaceted that, through careful selection and emphasis, you might find strong empirical support for any position. You would also consider the appropriateness of the study's time span. Many of the important questions about drugs and behavior—or any major social-economic problem—cannot be answered by a short-term study. While you can tell almost immediately if flea-bombing your cat worked, the effects of government and health policies (educational programs, antidrug legislation, methadone maintenance) may not become evident for years or even decades. As government research czar, you would insist on appropriate research designs.

You might also be called upon to evaluate prevention programs for elementary school students. The best known of these programs is *DARE* (Drug Abuse Resistance Education). DARE's objective is to reach children at an early age and to decrease their likelihood of drug use by instilling both negative attitudes toward drugs and positive coping strategies for avoiding situational pressure toward drug use. Once again, those who support DARE and those who believe it is ineffective both cite statistics in favor of their point of view. Why is this so?

When evaluating DARE, researchers find important differences between the way the program changes attitudes and the way it changes behaviors. In studies that compare students who have participated in DARE with those who haven't, DARE students consistently show stronger attitudes against substance abuse (Harmon, 1993). What is less consistent, unfortunately, is the evidence for actual changes in behavior. DARE participation does not regularly lead to decreased abuse of alcohol, marijuana, or cigarettes. This does not necessarily mean that DARE is a failure: the implication is that the program must be reworked so that it improves its emphasis on the link between attitudes and behavior. Even so, you have learned an important lesson. When we describe research, we cannot report isolated facts or statistics. We must always try to consider the whole phenomenon—and explain how all the pieces fit together.

Shapiro, 1993, p. 140). Reasoned proponents of animal rights create a moral context in which each animal researcher must judge his or her work with heightened scrutiny.

Citizens must inform themselves with accurate information about the total context of animal research before deciding to take political, legal, or destructive actions to stop it. In a democracy, as in scientific endeavors, rational information should guide decisions. As you read *Psychology and Life,* you may encounter descriptions of experiments that you consider to be ethically suspect—with either humans or nonhuman animals as subjects. Although it is not at all our goal to cause you discomfort, we welcome those moments as opportunities for you to explore your own personal sense of which experimental methods are justified by the need for particular types of psychological knowledge or psychological treatments.

BECOMING A WISER RESEARCH CONSUMER

This chapter has emphasized an appreciation of the methods, approaches, and values that form the scientific foundation of psychology. It has also highlighted the need to be critically aware of sources of error in conclusions that are reported to be based on research. In this final section, we will focus on the kinds of critical thinking skills you need in order to become a wiser consumer of psychological knowledge.

Honing these thinking tools is essential for any responsible person in a dynamic society such as ours—one so filled with claims of truth, with false "commonsense" myths, and with biased conclusions that serve special interests. Analytical skills enable the individual to begin to assess the plausibility of claims made about "what research shows." They encourage an open-minded skepticism about proofs and conclusions based solely on the opinions of "experts." They provide means for monitoring the confidence one has in personal testimonials and eyewitness observations—even one's own. To be a critical thinker is to go beyond the information as given and to delve beneath slick appearances, with the goal of understanding the substance without being seduced solely by style and image.

Critical-thinking skills help you make informed appraisals of the many psychological claims that are part of your daily life.

Because psychology is so much a part of your everyday life and is often misrepresented in the media, professional psychologists want to communicate accurate information to the public about what is known and about how one can evaluate its validity. Much information on psychology in the public domain does not come from the books, articles, and reports of accredited practitioners. Rather, this information comes from newspaper and magazine articles, TV and radio shows, pop psychology and self-help books, and the "pseudosciences industry" (astrology, psychic surgery, and "New Age" gimmicks). Return to the idea of subliminal mind control. Although it began as a hoax propagated by profit-minded marketing consultant James M. Vicary (Rogers, 1993)—and, as we have seen, has been rigorously discredited in the laboratory—the idea of subliminal influences on overt behavior continues to exert a pull on people's beliefs—and their wallets!

A news interview with an expert may include misleading sound bites taken out of context, or oversimplified "nutshell" descriptions of research conclusions.

Studying psychology will help you make wiser decisions based on evidence gathered either by you or by others. Psychological claims are an unavoidable aspect of the daily life of any thinking, feeling, and acting person in this psychologically sophisticated society. You should always try to apply the insights you derive from your formal study of psychology to the informal psychology that surrounds you: ask questions about your own behavior or that of other people, seek answers to these questions with respect to rational psychological theories, check out the answers against the evidence available to you.

Here are some general rules to keep in mind in order to be a more sophisticated shopper as you travel through the supermarket of knowledge:

- Avoid the inference that correlation is causation.
- Ask that critical terms and key concepts be defined operationally so that there can be consensus about their meanings.
- Consider first how to disprove a theory, hypothesis, or belief before seeking confirming evidence, which is easy to find when you're looking for a justification.
- Don't buy into personal testimonials and case studies that omit objective data on how typical they are, their comparative base rates, and any special conditions associated with their success and failure.
- Always search for alternative explanations to the obvious ones proposed, especially when the explanations benefit the proposer.
- Recognize how personal biases can distort perceptions of reality.
- Be suspicious of simple answers to complex questions or single causes and cures for complex effects and problems.
- Question any statement about the effectiveness of some treatment, intervention, or product by finding the comparative basis for the effect: compared to what?
- Be open-minded yet skeptical: recognize that most conclusions are tentative and not certain; seek new evidence that decreases your uncertainty while keeping yourself open to change and revision.
- Be sensitive to the fallacy of explaining social and psychological problems, such as poverty, in terms of the special features (dispositions) of *people* alleged to cause them rather than in terms of the *situations* that influence the people's behavior.
- Challenge authority that is unjust, uses personal opinion in place of evidence for conclusions, and is not open to constructive criticism.

We want you to apply open-minded skepticism while you read *Psychology and Life.* We don't want you to view your study of psychology as the acquisition of a list of facts. Instead, we hope you will participate in the joy of observing and discovering and putting ideas to the test.

Recapping Main Points

The Context of Discovery

In the discovery phase of research, observations, beliefs, information, and general knowledge lead to a new way of thinking about a phenomenon. The researcher verbalizes an idea to be tested as a theory, hypothesis, or paradigm. Scientific knowledge is based on respect for empirical evidence.

The Context of Justification: Safeguards for Objectivity

Justification is the phase in which ideas are tested and proven or disproven to some degree of certainty. To test their ideas, researchers use the scientific method, a set of procedures for gathering and interpreting evidence in ways that limit errors. Researchers combat observer biases by standardizing procedures and using operational definitions. They rule out alternative explanations by using appropriate control procedures. Experimental research methods determine whether causal relationships exist between variables specified by the hypothesis being tested. Correlational research methods determine if and how much two variables are related. Correlations do not imply causation.

Psychological Measurement

Researchers strive to produce measures that are both reliable and valid. Descriptive research techniques include self-reports, behavior analysis, and physiological measures.

Ethical Issues in Human and Animal Research

Respect for the basic rights of human and animal subjects is the obligation of all researchers. A variety of safeguards have been enacted to guarantee ethical and humane treatment.

Becoming a Wiser Research Consumer

Becoming a wise research consumer involves learning how to think critically and knowing how to evaluate claims about what research shows.

Resources

Bordens, K. S., & Abbott, B. B. (1988). *Research design and methods: A process approach.* Mountain View, CA: Mayfield. Applies the research process to both theoretical and practical problems.

Brannigan, G. G., & Merrens, M. R. (Eds.). (1992). *The undaunted psychologist: Adventures in research.* New York: McGraw-Hill. Narrative descriptions of their research by 15 psychologists. Brings research to life in a warm, practical way.

Korn, J. H. (1988). Students' roles, rights, and responsibilities as research participants. *Teaching of Psychology, 15,* 74–78.

McCain, G., & Segal, E. M. (1982). *The game of science* (4th ed.). Monterey, CA: Brooks/Cole. A brief, clever presentation of the general characteristics of science and the scientific method.

Stanovich, K. E. (1996). *How to think straight about psychology.* (4th ed.). New York: HarperCollins. Scholarly yet entertaining account of the necessity of using the scientific method in psychology.

3

The Biological Bases of Behavior

What makes you a unique individual? Psychology and Life *provides many answers to this question, but in this chapter our focus will be on the biological aspects of your individuality. To give you an understanding of what makes you different from the people around you, we will describe the role that heredity plays in shaping your life and in forming the brain that controls your experiences. Of course, you can only appreciate these differences against the background of what you have in common with all other people. You might, therefore, think of this as a chapter about biological* potential: *What possibilities for behavior define the human species, and how do those possibilities emerge for particular members of that species?*

In a way, this chapter stands as proof of one remarkable aspect of your biological potential: *your brain is sufficiently complex to carry out a systematic examination of its own functions. Why is this so remarkable? You are accustomed to computers that can perform thousands of operations in a fraction of a second—but even the world's mightiest computer is incapable of reflecting on the rules that guide its own operation. Your brain is sometimes likened to a spectacular computer: at only three pounds, your brain contains more cells than there are stars in our entire galaxy—over 100 billion cells—designed to communicate and store information. Like the fastest computers, your brain is capable of carrying out vast numbers of operations in a second. You are more than a computer, however, because your consciousness allows you to put that computational power to work trying to determine your species' own set of rules for operation. All the research we describe in this chapter arose from the special human desire for self-understanding.*

For many students this chapter will pose a greater challenge than the rest of Psychology and Life. *It requires that you learn some anatomy and many new terms that seem far removed from the information you may have expected to get from an introduction to psychology. However, understanding your biological nature will enable you to appreciate more fully the complex interplay among the brain, mind, behavior, and environment that creates the unique experience of being human. And that experience is what your journey in life is all about.*

Studying your biological nature will help you understand the complex interaction among the brain, mind, and environment as they influence behavior.

Recall that the goal of this chapter is to allow you to understand how biology contributes to the creation of unique individuals against a shared background potential. To approach this goal, we will first describe how evolution and heredity determine your biology and behavior. We will then see how laboratory and clinical research provides a view into the workings of the brain, the nervous system, and the endocrine system. We will examine some intriguing relationships between these biological functions and some aspects of life experiences. Finally, we will consider differences among individuals in the relationship of brain to behavior.

HEREDITY AND BEHAVIOR

In Chapter 1, we defined one of the major goals of psychology to be the discovery of the causes underlying the variety of human behavior. An important dimension of causal explanation within psychology is defined by the end points of **nature** versus **nurture**, or **heredity** versus **environment**. Consider, as we did in Chapter 1, the question of the roots of aggressive behavior. You might imagine that individuals are aggressive by virtue of some aspect of their biological makeup: they may have inherited a tendency toward violence from one of their parents. Alternatively, you might imagine that all humans are about equally predisposed to aggression—as members, that is, of the human species—and that the degree of aggression individuals will display arises in response to features of the environment in which they are raised. The correct answer to this question has a profound impact on how society treats individuals who are overly aggressive—by focusing resources on changing certain environments or on changing aspects of the people themselves. You need to be able to discriminate the forces of heredity from the forces of environment.

Because the features of environments can be directly observed, it is often easier to understand how they affect people's behavior. You can, for example, actually watch a parent acting aggressively toward a child and wonder what consequences such treatment might have on the child's later tendency toward aggression. The biological forces that shape behavior, by comparison, are never plainly visible to the naked eye. To make the biology of behavior more comprehensible to you, we will begin by exposing some of the basic principles that shape a species' potential repertory of behaviors—the theory of **evolution**—and then describe how *behavioral variation* is passed from generation to generation.

The effects of environment on behavior are often directly observable; the effects of heredity are more difficult to discern.

EVOLUTION

In 1831, **Charles Darwin**, fresh out of college with a degree in theology, set sail from England on the HMS *Beagle*, an ocean research vessel, for a five-year cruise to survey the coast of South America. During the trip, Darwin collected everything that crossed his path: marine animals, birds, insects,

The physical characteristics determined by heredity are often relatively easy to observe.

Finches were one of the early inspirations for Darwin's development of the theory of evolution.

In 1859, Charles Darwin published his theory of evolution based on the concept of natural selection.

plants, fossils, seashells, and rocks. His extensive notes became the foundation for his books on topics ranging from geology to emotion to zoology. The book for which he is most remembered is *The Origin of Species*, published in 1859. In this work, Darwin set forth science's grandest theory: the evolution of life on planet earth.

Natural Selection

Darwin developed his theory of evolution by closely examining the species of animals he had encountered while on his voyage. One of the many places the *Beagle* visited was the Galápagos Islands, a volcanic archipelago off the west coast of South America. These islands are a haven for diverse forms of wildlife, including 13 species of finches, now known as *Darwin's finches.* Darwin wondered how so many different species of finches could have come to inhabit the islands. He reasoned that they couldn't have migrated from the mainland, because those species didn't exist there. He suggested, therefore, that the variety of species reflected the operation of a process he came to call **natural selection.**

Apparently, long ago, a small flock of finches found their way to one of the islands; they mated among themselves and eventually their number multiplied. Food resources and living conditions—*habitats*—vary considerably from island to island. Some of the islands are lush with berries and seeds, others are covered with cacti, and others have plenty of insects. Over time, some finches migrated to different islands in the archipelago. What happened next is the process of natural selection. At first, there was *variation* among the groups of finches on *each* island. Over time, however, birds that migrated to islands rich in berries and seeds were more likely to surive and reproduce if they had thick beaks. On those islands, birds with thinner, more pointed beaks, unsuitable for crushing or breaking open seeds, died. Birds that migrated to insect-rich islands were more likely to survive and reproduce if they had thinner, more pointed beaks. There, birds with thick beaks, not useful for eating insects, died. The environment of each island determined which among the originally variable finches would live and reproduce and which would more likely perish, leaving no offspring. The diversity of habitats on these islands permitted the different species of Darwin's finches to evolve from the original ancestral group.

In general, the theory of natural selection—as proposed at much the same time by Darwin and by Alfred Russel Wallace (Huxley, 1958)—suggests that organisms well adapted to their environment, whatever it happens to be, will produce more offspring than those less well adapted. Over time, those organisms possessing traits more favorable for survival will become more numerous than those not possessing those traits. In evolutionary terms, an individual's success is measured by the number of offspring he or she produces.

Recent research has shown that natural selection can have dramatic effects, even in the short run. In a series of studies by **Peter Grant** (1986), involving one species of Darwin's finches, records were kept of rainfall, food supply, and the population size of these finches on one of the Galápagos Islands. In 1976, the population numbered well over 1000 birds. The following year brought a murderous drought that wiped out most of the food supply. The smallest seeds were the first to be depleted, leaving only larger and tougher seeds. That year the finch population decreased by more than 80 percent. However, smaller finches with smaller beaks died at a higher frequency than larger finches with thicker beaks. Consequently, and as Darwin would have predicted, the larger birds became more numerous in the following years. Why? Because only they, with their larger bodies and thicker beaks, were fit enough to respond to the environmental change caused by the drought. Interestingly, in 1983, rain was plentiful, and seeds, especially the smaller ones, became abundant. As a result, smaller birds outsurvived larger birds, probably because their beaks were better suited for pecking the smaller seeds. As Grant's study shows, while evolutionary effects occur over a very long time frame, natural selection can have noticeable effects even over short periods.

Recent short-term investigations, such as Peter Grant's study of birds, support Darwin's theory of natural selection.

Genotypes and Phenotypes

The example of the ebb and flow of finch populations demonstrates why Darwin characterized the course of evolution as *survival of the fittest.* Imagine that each environment poses some range of difficulties for each species of living beings. Those members of the species who possess the range of physical and psychological attributes best adapted to the environment are most likely to survive. To the extent that the attributes that foster survival can be passed from one generation to another—and stresses in the environment endure over time—the species is likely to evolve.

To unpack this process, we must introduce some of the vocabulary of evolutionary theory. Let us focus on an individual finch. At birth, that finch inherited a **genotype,** or genetic structure, from its parents. In the context of a particular environment, this genotype determined the finch's development and behavior. The outward appearance and characteristics of the finch are known as its **phenotype.** For our finch, its genotype may have interacted with the environment to yield the phenotype of *small beak* and *able to peck smaller seeds.* If seeds of all type were plentiful, this phenotype would have no particular bearing on the finch's survival. If, however, only small seeds were available, our finch would be at a *selective advantage* with respect to finches with large beaks. If only large seeds were available, our finch would be at a disadvantage.

Only finches that survive can reproduce. Only those animals that reproduce can pass on their genotypes. Therefore, if the environment continued to provide only small seeds, over several generations the finches would probably come to have almost exclusively small beaks—with the consequence that they would be almost exclusively capable of eating only small seeds. In this way, forces in the environment can shape a species's repertory of possible behaviors. **Figure 3.1** provides a simplified model of the process of natural selection. Let us now apply these ideas to human evolution.

HUMAN EVOLUTION

By looking backward to the circumstances in which the human species evolved, you can begin to understand why certain physical and behavioral features are part of the biological endowment of the entire human species. Through the combined efforts of hundreds of naturalists, biologists, anthropologists, and geneticists, we now know that, in the evolution of our species, natural selection favored two adaptations—bipedalism and encephalization. Together, they made possible the rise of human civilization. **Bipedalism** refers to the ability to walk upright, and **encephalization** refers to increases in brain size. These two adaptations are responsible for most, if not all, of the other major advances in human evolution, including cultural development (see **Figure 3.2**). As our ancestors evolved the ability to walk upright, they were able to explore new environments and exploit new resources. As brain size increased, our ancestors became more intelligent and developed capacities for complex thinking, reasoning, remembering, and planning. (However, the evolution of a bigger brain did not guarantee that humans would become more intelligent—what was important was the kind of tissue that developed

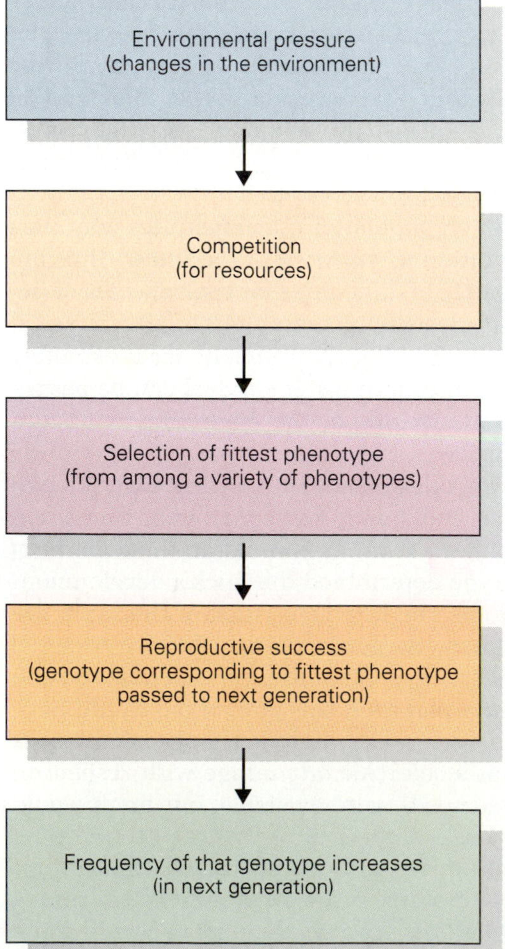

Figure 3.1 How Natural Selection Works
Environmental changes create competition for resources among species members. Only those individuals possessing characteristics instrumental in coping with these changes will survive and reproduce. The next generation will have a greater number of individuals possessing these genetically based traits.

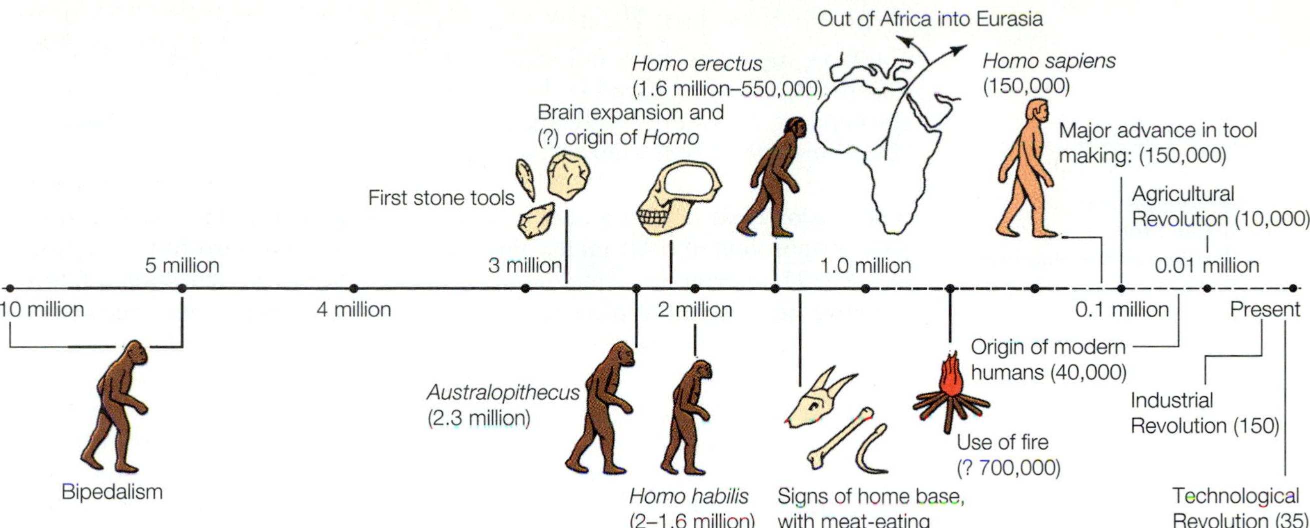

Figure 3.2 Approximate Time Line for the Major Events in Human Evolution
Bipedalism freed the hands for grasping and tool use. Encephalization provided the capacity for higher cognitive processes such as abstract thinking and reasoning. These two adaptations probably led to the other major advances in human evolution.

and expanded within the brain, as we shall soon describe.) The genotype coding for intelligent and mobile phenotypes slowly squeezed out other, less well adapted genotypes from the human gene pool, affording only intelligent bipeds the opportunity to reproduce.

The two most important adaptations in the evolution of humans are bipedalism and encephalization.

After bipedalism and encephalization, perhaps the most important evolutionary milestone for our species was the advent of *language* (see Bickerton, 1990). Language is the tool by which cultures are fashioned and refashioned. Think of the tremendous adaptive advantages that language conferred upon early humans. Simple instructions for making tools, finding a good hunting or fishing spot, and avoiding danger would save time, effort, and lives. Instead of learning every one of life's lessons firsthand, by trial and error, humans could benefit from experiences shared by others. Conversation, even humor, would strengthen the social bonds among members of a naturally gregarious species. Most important, the advent of language would provide for the transmission of accumulated wisdom, from one generation to future generations. Language is the basis for *cultural evolution,* which is the tendency of cultures to respond adaptively, through learning, to environmental change. Cultural evolution has given rise to major advances in toolmaking, to improved agricultural practices, and to the development and refinement of industry and technology. In short, cultural evolution is critical to the development and maintenance of the kinds of lifestyles enjoyed by our species today.

The development of language is important to human evolution because language allows for cultural evolution.

In contrast to biological evolution, cultural evolution allows our species to make very rapid adjustments to changes in environmental conditions. Instead of taking thousands, even millions, of years, as biological adaptation does, cultural adaptations may appear within a single generation. Adaptations to the use of personal computers, for example, have arisen in only the last ten to fifteen years. Even so, cultural evolution could not occur without genotype coding for the capacities to learn and to think abstractly. Culture—including art, literature, music, scientific knowledge, and philanthropic activities—is possible only because of the human genotype.

Variation in the Human Genotype

Bipedalism and the capacity for thought and language demonstrate the shared potential in the human genotype, but heredity influences the tremendous variation that exists within that shared potential.

You have seen that the conditions in which humans evolved favored the evolution of important shared biological potential: for example, bipedalism, and the capacity for thought and language. There remains, however, considerable variation within that shared potential. It is that genotypic variation that determines the impact of heredity on your behavior. Your mother and father have endowed you with a part of what their parents, grandparents, and all past generations of their family lines have given them, resulting in a unique biological blueprint and timetable for your development. The study of heredity—the inheritance of physical and psychological traits from ancestors—is called **genetics.**

Basic Genetics

Your basic appearance and many of your behaviors are determined by the instructions in your DNA.

In the nucleus of each of your cells is genetic material called DNA (deoxyribonucleic acid). DNA contains the instructions for the production of proteins. These proteins regulate the body's physiological processes and the expression of phenotypic traits: body build, physical strength, intelligence, and many behavior patterns. DNA is organized into tiny units, called **genes,** that are found on rodlike structures, known as *chromosomes.*

At the very instant you were conceived, you inherited from your parents 46 chromosomes—23 from your mother and 23 from your father. Each of these chromosomes contains thousands of genes—the union of a sperm and an egg results in only one of many billion possible gene combinations. The **sex chromosomes** are those that contain genes coding for development of male or female physical characteristics. You inherited an X chromosome from your mother and either an X or a Y chromosome from your father. An XX combination codes for development of female characteristics; an XY combination codes for development of male characteristics.

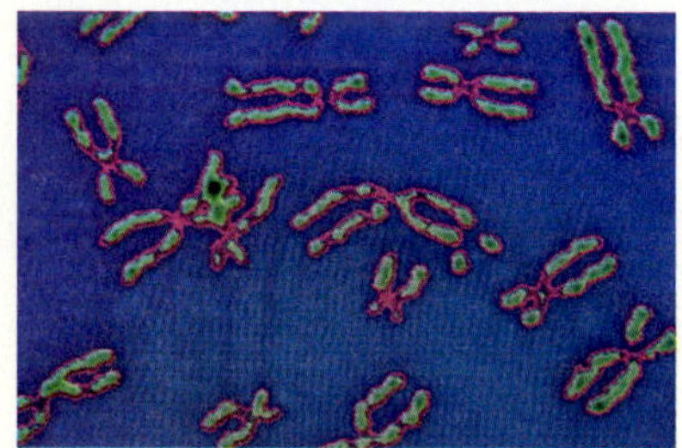

Human chromosomes

Although, on average, you have 50 percent of your genes in common with your brothers or sisters, your set of genes is unique unless you have an identical twin. The difference in your genes is one reason why you differ, physically and behaviorally, from your brothers and sisters. The other reason is that you do not live in exactly the same environment as they do. An important goal of psychology, once again, is to understand the balance between these two sources of influence.

Genes and Behavior

You have reached a point at which you can understand why there *might* be genetic influences on behavior: evolution has allowed a considerable amount of variation to remain in human genotypes; the interactions of these genotypes with particular environments produces variation in human phenotypes. The next step is to demonstrate that genetic factors *do* play a measurable causal role. Researchers in the field of **human behavior genetics** unite genetics and psychology to provide such demonstrations for behavioral traits and functioning, including intelligence, mental disorders, and altruism (Fuller, 1982; Plomin & Rende, 1991; Plomin et al., 1994).

To explore the logic of behavioral genetics, we will describe one surprising finding: the amount of television that 3- to 5-year-old children prefer to view is determined, in part, by genetic forces:

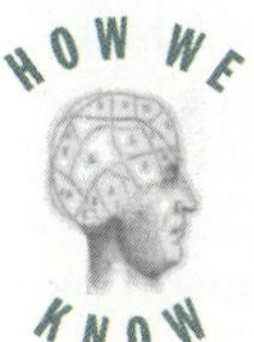

A team of researchers compared the television viewing preferences of several groups of children and adults. We focus on three groups: a group of children who had been separated from their biological mothers and placed in adoptive homes by the end of their first month of life; one group of adults who were the biological parents (mostly mothers) of the children who were given up

> for adoption; and a second group of adults who were the adoptive parents of those children. For each individual, the researchers obtained a measure of the *amount* of television he or she watched. With this measure, they could discriminate the effects of nature and nurture. A positive correlation (see Chapter 2) for television viewing between the adopted-away children and their adoptive parents would suggest a role for environment. A positive correlation for the adopted-away children and their biological parents would suggest a role for heredity. The researchers found reliable correlations between the children and *both* sets of parents, arguing for both environmental and genetic influences on television viewing (Plomin et al., 1990b).

You are probably not surprised that children's television viewing is influenced by the environment: it is likely that adults in the environment in which you grew up tried to influence the amount of television you watched. However, you might be surprised, as we were, that there is a genetic influence. The researchers were able to make this claim because the biological parents had no contact with their adopted-away children later in life. Any influence—and the investigators demonstrated that there was a measurable relationship—could be attributed only to the activity of genes.

If you are wondering how this could be true, you are now thinking like a behavioral geneticist. After all, television is a recent invention. It couldn't be the case that you have information encoded in your genotype that is directly relevant to television viewing. Instead, researchers must try to discover what other aspects of children's behavior—which could have evolved over a suitable time course—mediate the genetic influence on television viewing. Meanwhile, the existence of this genetic relationship, and others like it, suggests that the genes you receive from your parents have much broader effects than just determining your eye color or height.

Remember, though, that genes do not code for *destinies;* they code for *potential.* Just because you're tall doesn't mean you will play basketball. Just because you're a woman doesn't mean you will bear children. Also keep in mind that genotypes are expressed in particular contexts. Physical size, for example, is determined jointly by genetic factors and nutritional environ-

To what extent do genes determine the course of your life?

ment. Physical strength can be developed in both males and females through special exercise programs. Intellectual growth is determined by both genetic potential and educational experiences. Neither genes nor the environment alone determines who you are or what kind of person you ultimately become. Genes control only the range of effects that the environment can have in shaping your phenotype and your behavioral patterns.

The kind of person you ultimately become will be influenced by both your genes and your environment.

BIOLOGY AND BEHAVIOR

We turn our attention now to the remarkable products of the human genotype: the biological systems that make possible the full range of thought and performance. Long before Darwin made preparations for his trip aboard the *Beagle,* scientists, philosophers, and others debated the role that biological processes play in everyday life. One of the most important figures in the history of brain studies was the French philosopher **René Descartes** (1596–1650). Descartes proposed what at that time was a very new and very radical idea: the human body is an "animal machine" that can be understood scientifically—by discovering natural laws through empirical observation. He raised purely *physiological* questions, questions about body mechanics and motion that led him to speculate about the forces that control human action.

René Descartes posed physiological questions about behavior. Because he viewed the human body as a machine, he theorized that human behavior consists of reflex responses to environmental stimuli.

Basically, Descartes argued that human action is a mechanical reflex to environmental stimulation. He explained that physical energy excites a sense organ. When stimulated, the sense organ transmits the excitation to the brain in the form of "animal spirits." The brain then transmits the animal spirits to the appropriate set of muscles, setting in motion a reflex. Today the idea of reflexive behavior is something that most people, especially psychologists, take for granted. In the seventeenth century, the idea had serious implications that could have angered religious leaders. At the time, the prevailing religious dogma taught that humans were special, endowed by a higher agency with the power of free will. Descartes's idea of reflexive behavior, however, implied that humans had much in common with other animals.

Descartes's notion of the reflex did not have valid scientific support until 1906, when **Sir Charles Sherrington** discovered that reflexes are composed of direct connections between sensory and motor nerve fibers at the level of the spinal cord. Sherrington also developed the idea that the nervous system involves both *excitatory* (increasing neural activity) and *inhibitory* (decreasing neural activity) processes. And it was also not until the twentieth century that scientists knew anything at all about the basic unit of the nervous system, the *neuron.* Also near the turn of the century, **Santiago Ramón y Cajal** theorized that the nervous system is composed of neurons. Fifty years later, with the aid of the electron microscope, other scientists proved his ideas. In 1948, **Donald Hebb** proposed that the brain is not merely a mass of tissue but a highly integrated series of structures, or "cell assemblies," that perform specific functions.

Researchers in the tradition we have traced back to Descartes now call themselves *neuroscientists.* Today **neuroscience** is one of the most rapidly growing areas of research. Important discoveries come with astonishing regularity. What is permitting such rapid advances in neuroscience? Broadly speaking, the answer to that question is *cultural evolution.* Knowledge and wisdom acquired over hundreds of years of science, in combination with advances in research technology, have given today's neuroscientists both the intellectual resources and the technological wizardry necessary to uncover the biology of behavior.

Our discussion of neuroscience begins with an overview of the techniques researchers use to hasten new discoveries. We then offer a general description of the structure of the nervous system, followed by a more detailed look at the brain itself. Finally, we discuss the activity of the endocrine system, a second biological control system that works in cooperation with your nervous system and brain.

Eavesdropping on the Brain

Neuroscientists have developed five major ways to uncover the nervous system's secrets: studying patients suffering from brain damage, producing lesions at specific brain sites, stimulating the brain, recording brain activity, and using computer-driven scanning devices to "image" the brain. Each of these techniques serves a dual purpose: first, to produce knowledge about the structure, organization, and biochemical basis of normal brain functions; and second, to diagnose brain disease and dysfunctions and then evaluate the effects of treatments designed to improve the patient's functioning.

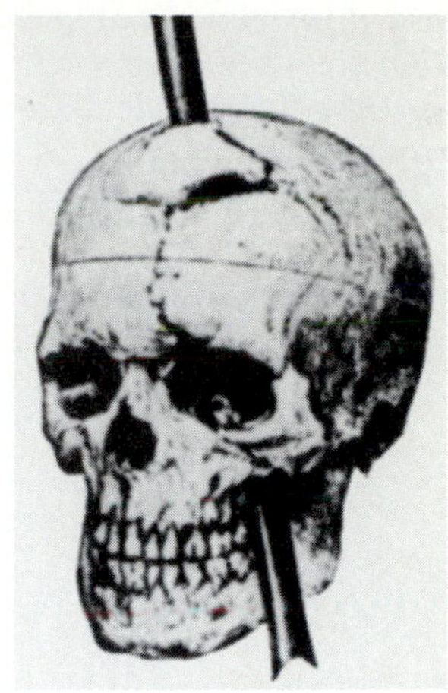

Phineas Gage's skull is preserved in the collections of the Warren Anatomical Museum, Harvard University Medical School.

Brain Damage

Researchers frequently study individuals who have suffered accidental injuries to their brains, to test hypotheses about the functions of particular brain structures. Consider the famous case of railroad worker *Phineas Gage,* who in September 1848 suffered an accident in which a 3-foot-long pole was blown, as the result of an unexpected explosion, clear through his head. Gage's physical impairment was remarkably slight: he lost vision in his left eye, and the left side of his face was partially paralyzed, but his posture, movement, and speech were all unimpaired. Yet, psychologically, he was a changed man, as his doctor's account makes clear:

Researchers may test theories about brain function by studying individuals with brain damage.

> He is fitful, irreverent, indulging at times in the grossest profanity (which was not previously his custom). . . . Previous to his injury . . . he possessed a well-balanced mind, and was looked upon by those who knew him as a shrewd, smart businessman, very energetic and persistent in executing all his plans of operation. In this regard his mind was radically changed, so decidedly that his friends and acquaintances said he was "no longer Gage." (Bigelow, 1850, pp. 13–22)

Researchers were able to document the location of the brain tissue destroyed by Gage's accident. This enabled them to start to develop hypotheses about the brain "location" of personality.

At about the same time that Gage was convalescing from his injury, **Paul Broca** was studying the brain's role in language. His first research in this area involved an autopsy of a man whose name was derived from the only word he had been able to speak, "Tan." Broca found that the left front portion of Tan's brain had been severely damaged. This finding led Broca to study the brains of other persons who suffered from language impairments. In each case, Broca's work revealed similar damage to the same area of the brain. He concluded that language ability depends on the functioning of structures in a specific region of the brain, a region now known as **Broca's area.**

Lesions

The problem with studying accidentally damaged brains, of course, is that researchers have no control over the location, extent of the damage, or related complications (infection, blood loss, traumas). If science was to produce a well-founded understanding of the brain and its relationship to behavioral and cognitive functioning, Broca's colleagues needed a better method. Instead of waiting for patients with brain damage to show up in hospital emergency rooms, researchers asked, "Why not deliberately produce carefully placed **lesions** in the brains of research subjects?" Researchers have developed a variety of techniques to produce highly localized brain injuries: they surgically remove specific brain areas, cut the neural connections to those areas, or destroy those areas through application of intense heat, cold,

The use of lesions to study brain function gives the researcher control over the specific area to be examined.

electricity, or laser surgery. As you would guess, experimental work with lesions is carried out exclusively with nonhuman animals. (Recall our discussion in Chapter 2 that the ethics of this type of animal research has now come under heightened scrutiny.)

Our conception of the brain has been radically changed as researchers have repeatedly compared and coordinated the results of lesioning experiments on animals with the growing body of clinical findings on the effects of brain damage on human behavior. Knowledge of brain functions gained from laboratory studies has also been supplemented by observation of the effects of lesions used for medical therapy. For example, a type of lesion used widely with epileptic patients involves severing the nerve fibers connecting the two hemispheres, or sides, of the brain. In addition to easing the suffering of patients, these types of studies have also revealed important information about the brain's role in everyday conscious experience, a topic we will take up at the end of this chapter.

Electrical Stimulation

Under some circumstances, neuroscientists can learn about the function of brain regions by directly stimulating them. Pioneering work on this technique was done in the 1940s by the Canadian neurosurgeon **Wilder Penfield.** Before Penfield operated on the brain of a patient suffering from epileptic seizures, he tried to localize the origin of the seizures so that he could leave unharmed other areas vital to the patient's functioning. His major tool was an **electrode,** a thin wire through which small amounts of precisely regulated electrical current could pass. As Penfield touched different regions of the brain, the conscious patient (under local anesthesia only, since there are no pain receptors in the brain itself) reacted in various ways. When stimulating some sites, Penfield observed motor reactions of hand clenching and arm raising; when touching others, he witnessed "experiential responses" as the patient vividly recalled past events or had sudden feelings such as fear, loneliness, or elation—Penfield "touched" memories stored silently for years in the recesses of his patient's brain (Penfield & Baldwin, 1952).

In the mid-1950s, **Walter Hess** pioneered the use of electrical stimulation to probe structures deeper in the brain than the surface of the cortex. For example, Hess put electrodes into the brains of freely moving cats. By pressing a button, he could then send a small electrical current to the point of the electrode. Hess carefully recorded the behavioral consequences of stimulating each of 4500 brain sites in nearly 500 cats. Hess discovered that sleep, sexual arousal, anxiety, or terror could be provoked by the flick of the switch—and turned off just as abruptly. Electrical stimulation of certain regions of the brain led the otherwise gentle cats to bristle with rage and hurl themselves upon a nearby object.

Wilder Penfield and Walter Hess pioneered the technique of direct brain stimulation using electrodes.

Recording Brain Activity

Other neuroscientists map brain function by using electrodes to record the electrical activity of the brain in response to environmental stimulation. The brain's electrical output can be monitored at different levels of precision. At the most specific, researchers can insert ultrasensitive microelectrodes into the brain to record the electrical activity of a single brain cell. Such recordings can illuminate the mechanisms by which individual cells change in response to the environment—to form lasting memories.

For human subjects, researchers often place a number of electrodes on the surface of the scalp to record larger, integrated patterns of electrical activity. These electrodes provide the data for an **electroencephalogram (EEG),** or an amplified tracing of the brain activity. EEGs can be used to study the relationship between psychological activities and brain response.

For example, in one experiment, changing aspects of human thought were detected by 124 EEG sensors applied to the scalp of each subject. In the split second *before* they were to respond behaviorally, the subjects' brains showed activity in brain areas that would be activated during execution of the task—suggesting mental rehearsal prior to acting (Barinaga, 1990; Givens, 1989).

Brain Scans

The most exciting technological innovations for studying the brain are machines originally developed to help neurosurgeons detect brain abnormalities, such as damage caused by strokes or diseases. These devices produce images of the living brain without invasive procedures that risk damaging brain tissue. Brain imaging is a promising tool for achieving a better understanding of both normal and abnormal brain function (Posner, 1993).

In research with the positron-emission tomography scanner, or **PET scanner,** subjects are given different kinds of radioactive (but safe) substances that eventually travel to the brain, where they are taken up by brain cells. Recording instruments outside the skull can detect the radioactivity emitted by cells that are active during different cognitive or behavioral activities. This information is then fed into a computer that constructs a dynamic portrait of the brain, showing where different types of psychological activity are actually occurring.

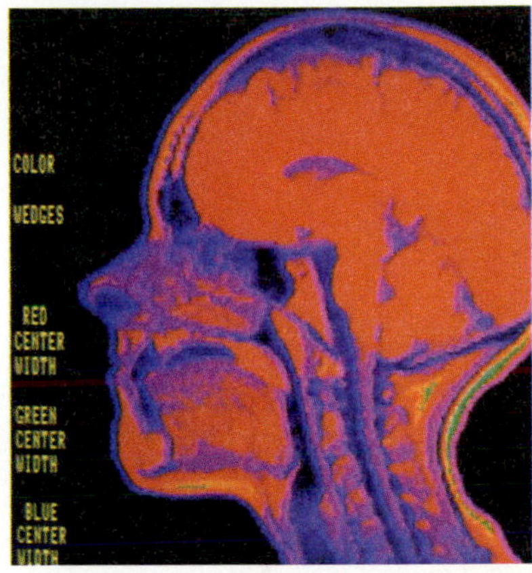

Magnetic resonance imaging (MRI) produces this color-enhanced profile of a normal brain. MRI uses a combination of radio waves and a strong magnetic field to view soft tissue.

Magnetic resonance imaging, or **MRI,** uses magnetic fields and radio waves to generate pulses of energy within the brain. As the pulse is tuned to different frequencies, some atoms line up with the magnetic field. When the magnetic pulse is turned off, the atoms vibrate (resonate) as they return to their original positions. These vibrations are picked up by special radio

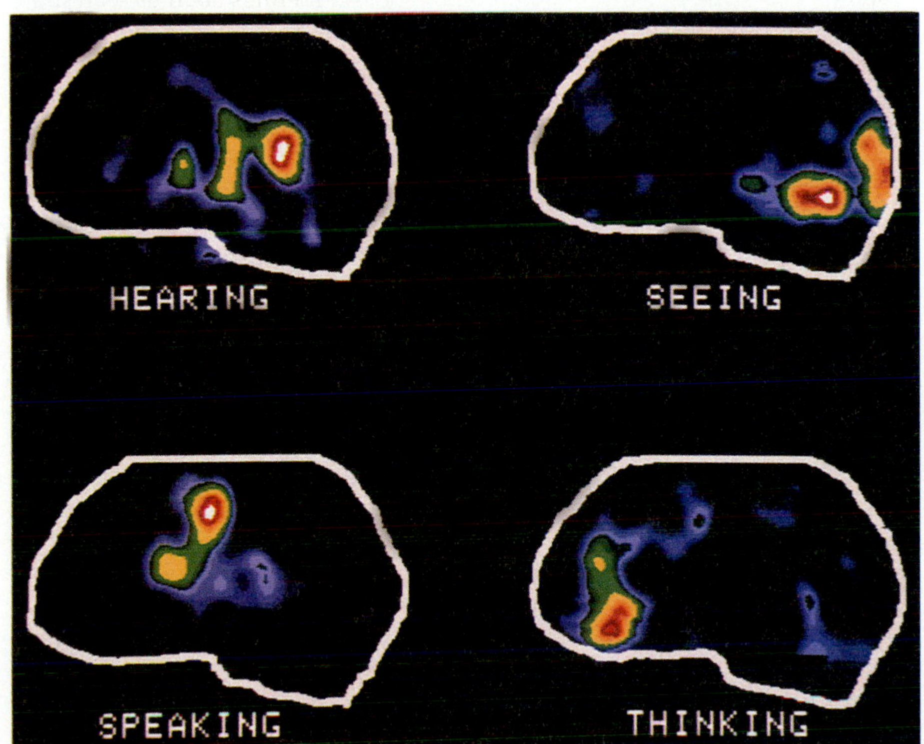

These PET scans show that different tasks stimulate neural activity in distinct regions of the brain.

receivers that channel information about the vibrations into a computer. In turn, the computer generates images of the locations of different atoms in areas of the brain. By looking at the image, researchers can locate abnormalities in brain tissue, which permits them to link brain structure to the psychological symptoms exhibited by the individual. An even newer technique, **echo-planar MRI**, produces high-resolution MRI images, but swiftly enough to study the functioning brain and body (Alper, 1993).

More than 300 years have passed since Descartes sat in his candlelit study and mused about the brain; over 100 years have passed since Broca discovered that brain regions seem to be linked to specific functions. In the time since these developments, cultural evolution has provided neuroscientists with the technology necessary to reveal some of your body's most important secrets. The remainder of this chapter describes some of those secrets—and why it is important to know about them.

The Nervous System

The nervous system is composed of billions of highly specialized nerve cells, or *neurons,* that are organized either into densely packed clusters, called *nuclei,* or into pathways (some of which are very extensive), called *nerve fibers.* The major task of the nuclei is to process information; the chief job of nerve fibers is to relay information to and from the nuclei. We will soon discuss the nuclei in detail—most of them make up the brain. To a lesser degree, nuclei are found outside the brain, mainly along the spinal cord, where they receive and relay sensory and motor information to and from the brain.

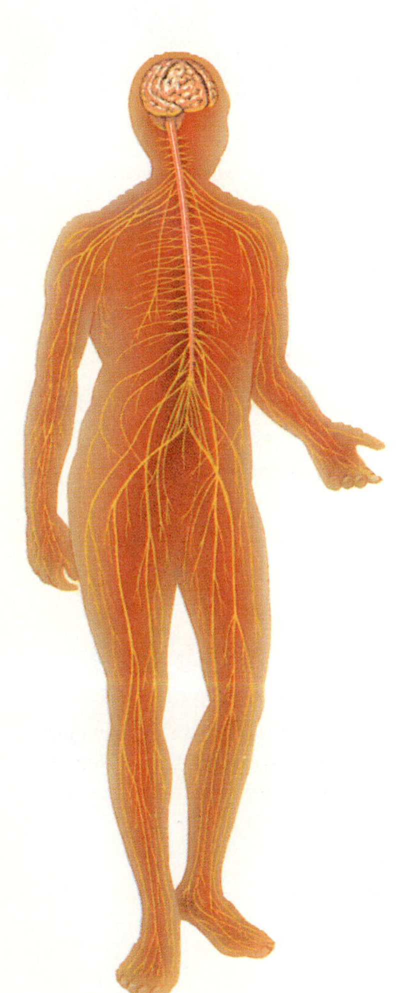

Figure 3.3 Physical Organization of the Human Nervous System

The sensory and motor nerve fibers that constitute the peripheral nervous system are linked to the brain by the spinal cord.

The brain and the nerve fibers that are found throughout the body constitute the nervous system. The nervous system is subdivided into two major divisions: the **central nervous system** (CNS) and the **peripheral nervous system** (PNS). The CNS is composed of all the neurons in the brain and spinal cord; the PNS is made up of all the neurons forming the nerve fibers that connect the CNS to the body. **Figures 3.3** and **3.4** show the relationship of the CNS to the PNS.

The job of the CNS is to integrate and coordinate all bodily functions, process all incoming neural messages, and send out commands to different parts of the body. The CNS sends and receives neural messages through the *spinal cord,* a trunk line of neurons that connects the brain to the PNS. The trunk line itself is housed in a hollow portion of the vertebral column, called the spinal column. Spinal nerves branch out from the spinal cord between each pair of vertebrae in the spinal column, eventually connecting with sensory receptors throughout the body and with muscles and glands. The spinal cord also coordinates the activity of the left and right sides of the body and is responsible for simple, fast action reflexes that do not involve the brain. For example, an organism whose spinal cord has been severed from its brain can still withdraw its limb from a painful stimulus. Though an intact brain would normally be notified of such action, the organism can complete the action without directions from above. Damage to the nerves of the spinal cord can result in paralysis of the legs or trunk, as seen in paraplegic individuals. The extent of paralysis depends on how high up on the spinal cord the damage occurred; greater paralysis results from higher damage.

Despite its commanding position, the CNS is isolated from any direct contact with the outside world. It is the role of the PNS to provide the CNS with information from sensory receptors, such as those found in the eyes and ears, and to relay commands from the brain to the body's organs and muscles. The PNS is actually composed of two subdivisions of nerve fibers (see Figure 3.4). The **somatic nervous system** regulates the actions of the body's

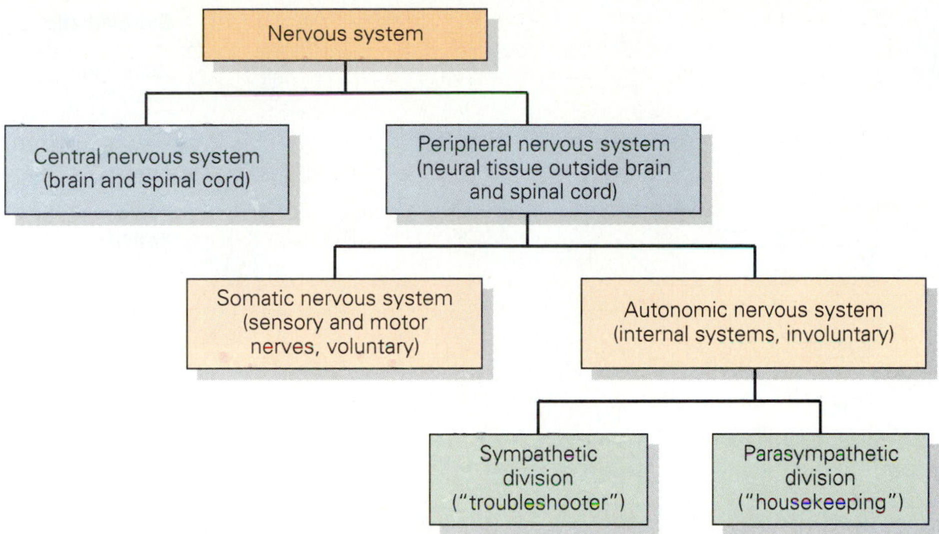

Figure 3.4 Hierarchical Organization of the Human Nervous System
The central nervous system is composed of the brain and the spinal cord. The peripheral nervous system is divided according to function: the somatic nervous system controls voluntary actions, and the autonomic nervous system regulates internal processes. The autonomic nervous system is subdivided into two systems: the sympathetic nervous system governs behavior in emergency situations, and the parasympathetic nervous system regulates behavior and internal processes in routine circumstances.

skeletal muscles. For example, imagine you are typing a letter. The movement of your fingers over the keyboard is managed by your somatic nervous system. As you decide what to say, your brain sends commands to your fingers to press certain keys. Simultaneously, the fingers send feedback about their position and movement to the brain. If you strike the wrong key (thw), the somatic nervous system informs the brain, which then issues the necessary correction, and, in a fraction of a second, you delete the mistake and hit the right key (the).

The other subdivision of the PNS is the **autonomic nervous system** (ANS), which sustains basic life processes. This system is on the job 24 hours a day, regulating bodily functions that you usually don't consciously control, such as respiration, digestion, and arousal. The ANS must work even when the individual is asleep, and it sustains life processes during anesthesia and prolonged coma states. The autonomic nervous system deals with survival matters of two kinds: those involving threats to the organism and those involving bodily maintenance. To carry out these complex functions, the autonomic nervous system is further subdivided into the sympathetic and parasympathetic nervous system (see Figure 3.4). These divisions work in opposition to accomplish their tasks. The **sympathetic division** governs responses to emergency situations, when large amounts of energy must be mobilized and behavior initiated with split-second timing. The **parasympathetic division** monitors the routine operation of the body's internal functions. The sympathetic division can be regarded as a troubleshooter—in an emergency or stressful situation, it arouses the brain structures for "fight or flight." Digestion stops, blood flows away from internal organs to the muscles, oxygen transfer increases, and heart rate increases. After the danger is over, the parasympathetic division takes charge to decelerate these processes, and the

The autonomic nervous system sustains basic life processes such as respiration, digestion, and arousal.

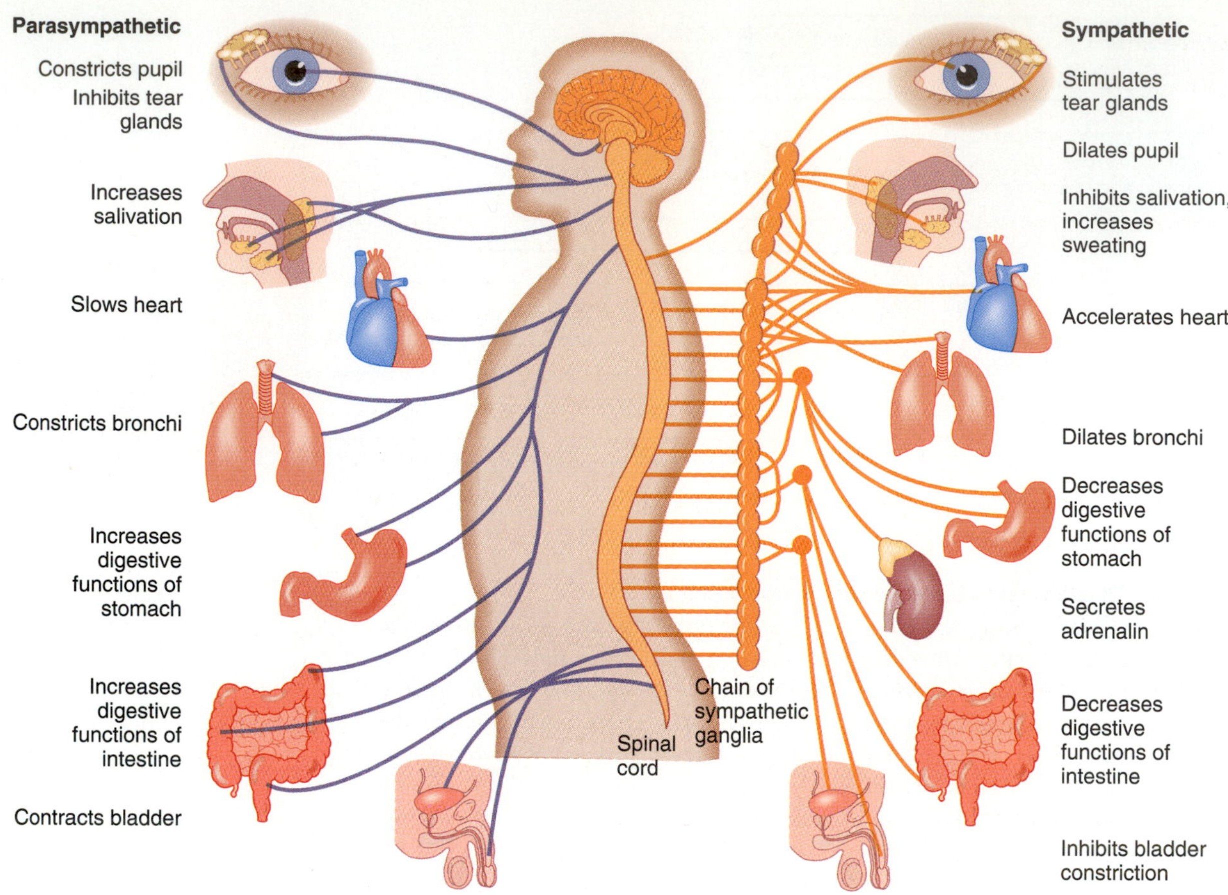

Figure 3.5 The Autonomic Nervous System

The parasympathetic nervous system, which regulates day-to-day internal processes and behavior, is shown on the left. The sympathetic nervous system, which regulates internal processes and behavior in stressful situations, is shown on the right. Note that on their way to and from the spinal cord, the nerve fibers of the sympathetic nervous system innervate, or make connections with, ganglia, which are specialized clusters of neuron chains.

individual begins to calm down. Digestion resumes, heartbeat slows, and breathing is relaxed. Basically, the parasympathetic division carries out the body's nonemergency housekeeping chores, such as elimination of bodily wastes, protection of the visual system (through tears and pupil constriction), and long-term conservation of body energy. The separate duties of the sympathetic and parasympathetic nervous systems are illustrated in **Figure 3.5.**

Brain Structures and Their Functions

The brain is the most important component of your central nervous system. The brains of human beings have three interconnected layers. In the deepest recesses of the brain, in a region called the *brain stem,* are structures involved primarily with autonomic processes such as heart rate, breathing, swallowing, and digestion. Enveloping this central core is the *limbic system,* which is involved with motivation, emotion, and memory processes. Wrapped around these two regions is the *cerebrum.* The universe of the human mind exists in this region. The cerebrum, and its surface layer, the

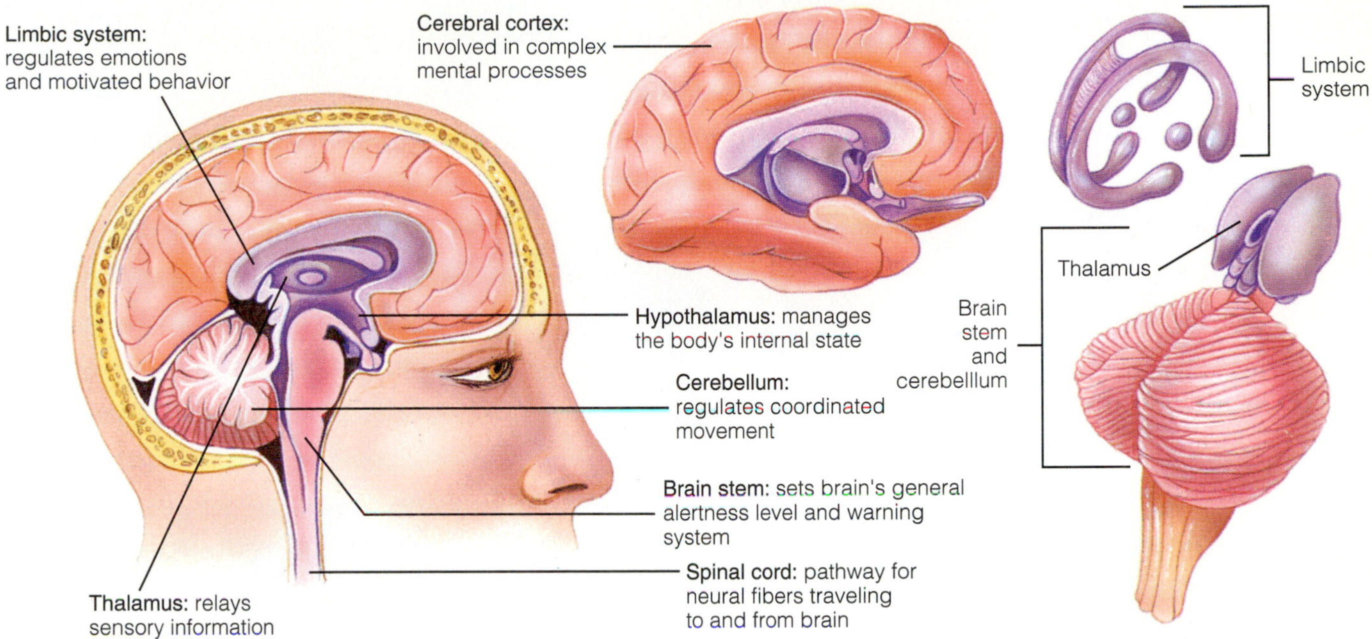

Figure 3.6 Brain Structures

cerebral cortex, integrates sensory information, coordinates your movements, and facilitates abstract thinking and reasoning (see **Figure 3.6**).

The structures of the brain perform specific activities that can be divided into five general categories: (1) internal regulation, (2) reproduction, (3) sensation, (4) motion, and (5) adaptation to changing environmental conditions. The first two are the brain's way of controlling bodily processes that keep you alive, well, and prepared to produce and nourish offspring. The third activity enables the brain to make contact with the outside world by processing sensory information from receptors located throughout the body. The brain also monitors internal sensations that provide information about balance, gravity, movements of limbs, and orientation. The fourth activity allows the brain to get muscles to move so that an organism can effect desired changes in its environment. The final function—adapting to the environment—involves the brain's remarkable ability to modify itself as it learns, store what it has experienced, and direct new actions based on feedback from the consequences of its previous actions. Let's look more closely at the three major brain regions that regulate these numerous activities, beginning with the brain stem and cerebellum.

The Brain Stem and Cerebellum

The **brain stem** is found in all vertebrate species. It contains four structures that collectively regulate the internal state of the body (see **Figure 3.7**). The **medulla,** located at the very top of the spinal cord, is the center for breathing, blood pressure, and the beating of the heart. Because these processes are essential for life, damage to the medulla can be fatal. Nerve fibers ascending from the body and descending from the brain cross over at the medulla, which means that the left side of the body is linked to the right side of the brain and the right side of the body is connected to the left side of the brain. Directly above the medulla is the **pons,** which provides inputs to other structures in the brain stem and to the cerebellum (*pons* is the Latin word for bridge). The **reticular formation** is a dense network of nerve cells that serves as the brain's sentinel. It arouses the cerebral cortex to attend to new stimu-

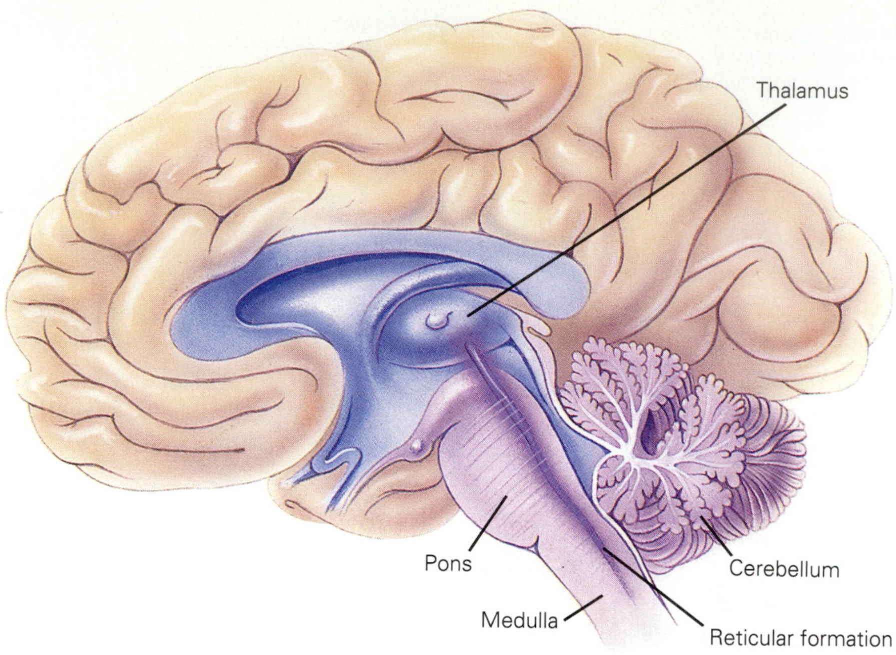

Figure 3.7 The Brain Stem and Cerebellum
These structures are primarily involved in basic life processes: breathing, pulse, arousal, movement, balance, and rudimentary processing of sensory information.

lation and keeps the brain alert even during sleep. Massive damage to this area often results in a coma. The reticular formation has long tracts of fibers that run to the **thalamus,** which channels incoming sensory information to the appropriate area of the cerebral cortex, where that information is processed. For example, the thalamus relays information from the eyes to cortical areas for vision. The **cerebellum,** attached to the brain stem at the base of the skull, coordinates bodily movements, controls posture, maintains equilibrium, and plays a role in some forms of learning. Damage to the cerebellum interrupts the flow of otherwise smooth movement, causing it to appear uncoordinated and jerky.

The brain stem, which regulates the body's internal state, consists of the medulla, the pons, the reticular formation, and the thalamus.

The Limbic System

The **limbic system** mediates motivated behaviors, emotional states, and memory processes. It also regulates body temperature, blood pressure, and blood-sugar level and performs other housekeeping activities. The limbic system comprises three structures: the hippocampus, amygdala, and hypothalamus (see **Figure 3.8**).

The limbic system plays an important role in motivation, emotion, and memory.

The **hippocampus,** which is the largest of the limbic system structures, plays an important role in the acquisition of *explicit* memories (Squire, 1992). (Explicit memories are memories that you are aware of retrieving; see Chapter 10.) There is considerable clinical evidence to support this view, notably from studies of a patient, H. M., perhaps psychology's most famous subject:

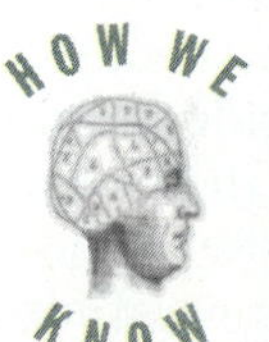

When he was 27, H. M. underwent surgery in an attempt to reduce the frequency and severity of his epileptic seizures. During the operation, parts of his hippocampus were removed. As a result, H. M. could only recall the very distant past; his ability to put new information into long-term memory was gone. Long after his surgery, he continued to believe he was living in 1953, which was the year the operation was performed.

Damage to the hippocampus does not, on the other hand, impair the abil-

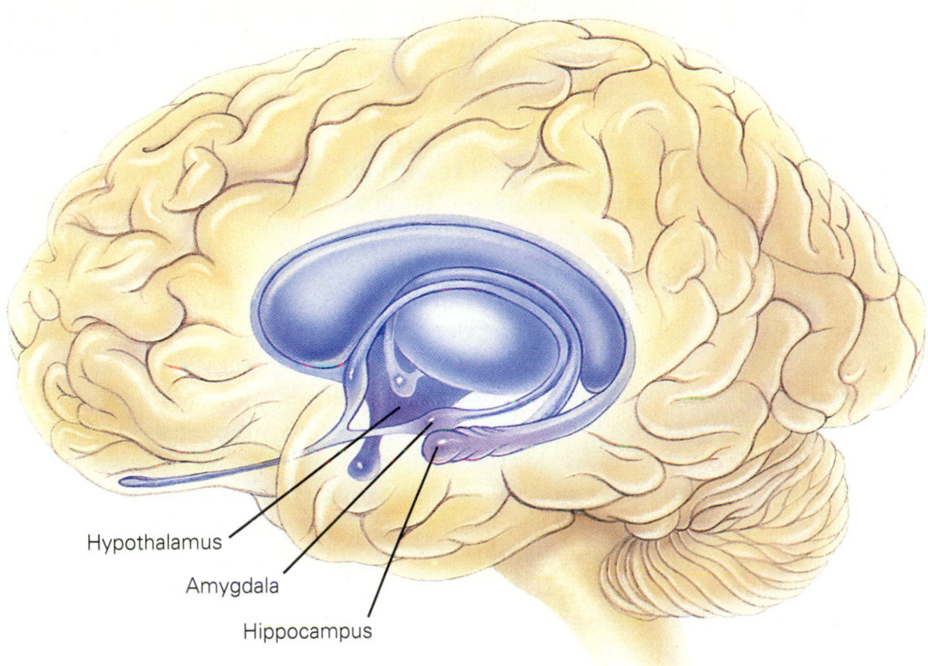

Figure 3.8 The Limbic System
The structures of the limbic system, which are present only in mammals, are involved in motivated behavior, emotional states, and memory processes.

ity to acquire *implicit* memories, outside of conscious awareness. Thus, H. M. was able to acquire new skills. If you were in an accident and sustained damage to your hippocampus, you would still be able to learn some new tasks, but you would not be able to remember having done so! (We will return to the brain bases of memory in Chapter 10.)

The **amygdala** plays a role in emotional control and the formation of emotional memories. Because of this control function, damage to the amygdala may have a calming effect on otherwise mean-spirited individuals. (We discuss psychosurgery in Chapter 18.) Also, because the amygdala participates in memory for appropriate emotional responses, animals who have undergone amygdalectomies (surgical removal of the amygdala) will show bizarre sexual behavior, attempting to copulate with just about any available partner.

The **hypothalamus** is one of the smallest structures in the brain, yet it plays a vital role in many of your most important daily actions. It is actually composed of several nuclei, small bundles of neurons that regulate physiological processes involved in motivated behavior (including eating, drinking, temperature regulation, and sexual arousal). The hypothalamus maintains the body's internal equilibrium, or **homeostasis.** When the body's energy reserves are low, the hypothalamus is involved in stimulating the organism to find food and to eat. When body temperature drops, the hypothalamus causes blood-vessel constriction, or minute involuntary movements you commonly refer to as the "shivers." The hypothalamus also regulates the activities of the endocrine system.

The Cerebrum

In humans, the **cerebrum** dwarfs the rest of the brain, occupying two thirds of its total mass. Its role is to regulate the brain's higher cognitive and emotional functions. The outer surface of the cerebrum, made up of billions of cells in a layer about a tenth of an inch thick, is called the **cerebral cortex.** The cerebrum is also divided into two almost symmetrical halves, the **cerebral hemispheres,** each mediating different mental functions (as we will

The cerebrum is responsible for higher thought processes and emotional functions.

describe in a later section of this chapter). The two hemispheres are connected by a thick mass of nerve fibers, collectively referred to as the **corpus callosum.** This pathway sends messages back and forth between the hemispheres.

Neuroscientists have mapped each hemisphere, using two important landmarks as their guides. One groove, called the *central sulcus,* divides each hemisphere vertically, and a second similar groove, called the *lateral fissure,* divides each hemisphere horizontally (see **Figure 3.9**). These vertical and horizontal divisions help to define four areas, or brain lobes, in each hemisphere. The *frontal lobe,* which is involved in motor control and cognitive activities, such as planning, making decisions, and setting goals, is located above the lateral fissure and in front of the central sulcus. Accidents that damage the frontal lobes can have devastating effects on human action and personality. This was the location of the injury that brought about such a dramatic change in Phineas Gage (Damasio et al., 1994). The *parietal lobe* is involved in controlling incoming sensory information and is located directly behind the central sulcus. The *occipital lobe,* the final destination for visual information, is located at the back of the head. The *temporal lobe,* where auditory information is processed, is found below the lateral fissure, on the sides of each cerebral hemisphere.

Although scientists are interested in localizing various functions in specific regions of the brain, you should remember that the brain functions as a whole, with the various structures working in concert.

It would be misleading to say that any lobe alone controls any one specific function. The structures of the brain perform their duties in concert, working smoothly as an integrated unit, similar to a symphony orchestra. Whether you are doing the dishes, solving a calculus problem, or carrying on a conversation with a friend, your brain works as a unified whole, each lobe interacting and cooperating with the others. Nevertheless, neuroscientists can identify areas of the four lobes of the cerebrum that are necessary for specific functions, such as vision, hearing, language, and memory. When they are damaged, their functions are disrupted or lost entirely.

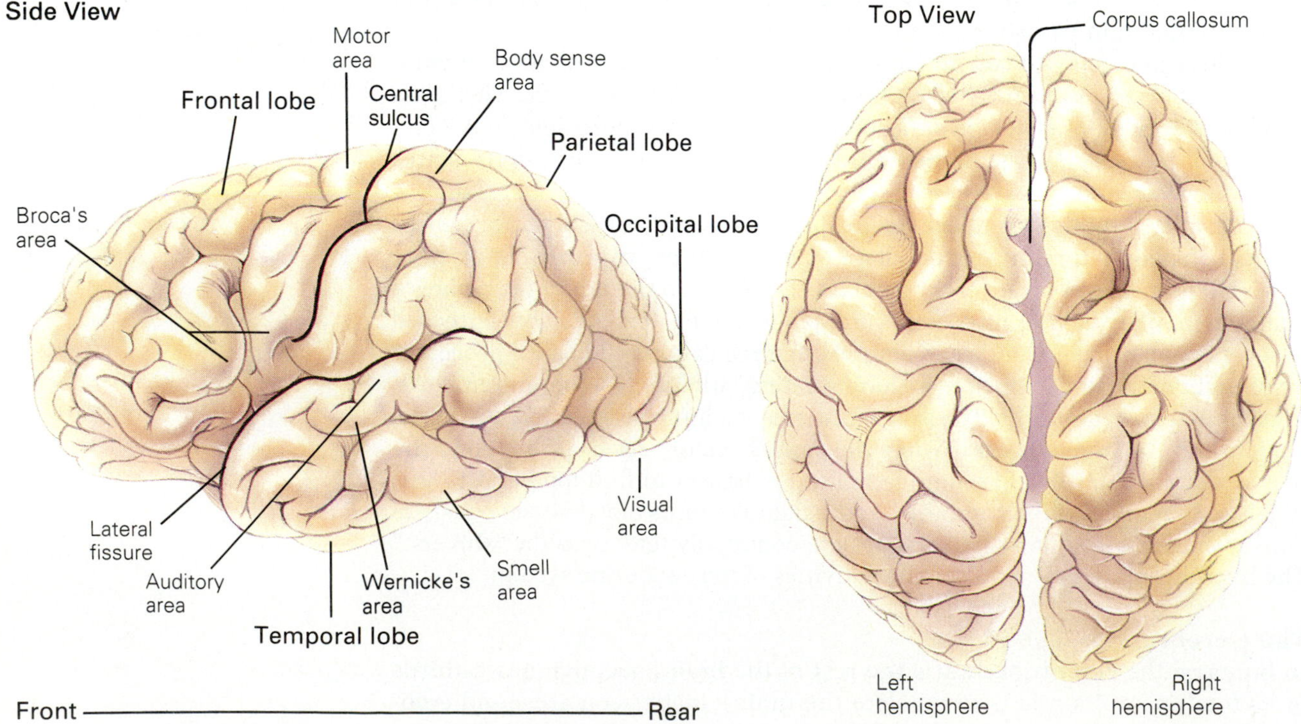

Figure 3.9 The Cerebral Cortex
Each of the two hemispheres of the cerebral cortex has four lobes. Different sensory and motor functions have been associated with specific parts of each lobe.

The actions of the body's voluntary muscles, of which there are more than 600, are controlled by the **motor cortex,** located just in front of the central sulcus in the frontal lobes. Recall that commands from one side of the brain are directed to muscles on the opposite side of the body. Also, muscles in the lower part of the body—for example, the toes—are controlled by neurons in the top part of the motor cortex. Muscles in the upper part of the body, such as the throat, are controlled by neurons in the lower part of the motor cortex. As you can see in **Figure 3.10**, the upper parts of the body receive far more detailed motor instructions than the lower parts. In fact, the two largest areas of the motor cortex are devoted to the fingers—especially the thumb—and to the muscles involved in speech. Their greater brain area reflects the importance in human activity of manipulating objects, using tools, eating, and talking.

Movement of voluntary muscles is controlled by the motor cortex.

The **somatosensory cortex** is located just behind the central sulcus in the left and right parietal lobes. This part of the cortex processes information about temperature, touch, body position, and pain. Similar to the motor cortex, the upper part of the sensory cortex relates to the lower parts of the body, and the lower part to the upper parts of the body. Most of the area of the sensory cortex is devoted to the lips, tongue, thumb, and index fingers—the parts of the body that provide the most important sensory input (see **Figure 3.10**). And like the motor cortex, the right half of the somatosensory cor-

The somatosensory cortex is responsible for processing information about the body such as temperature, sense of touch, position, and pain.

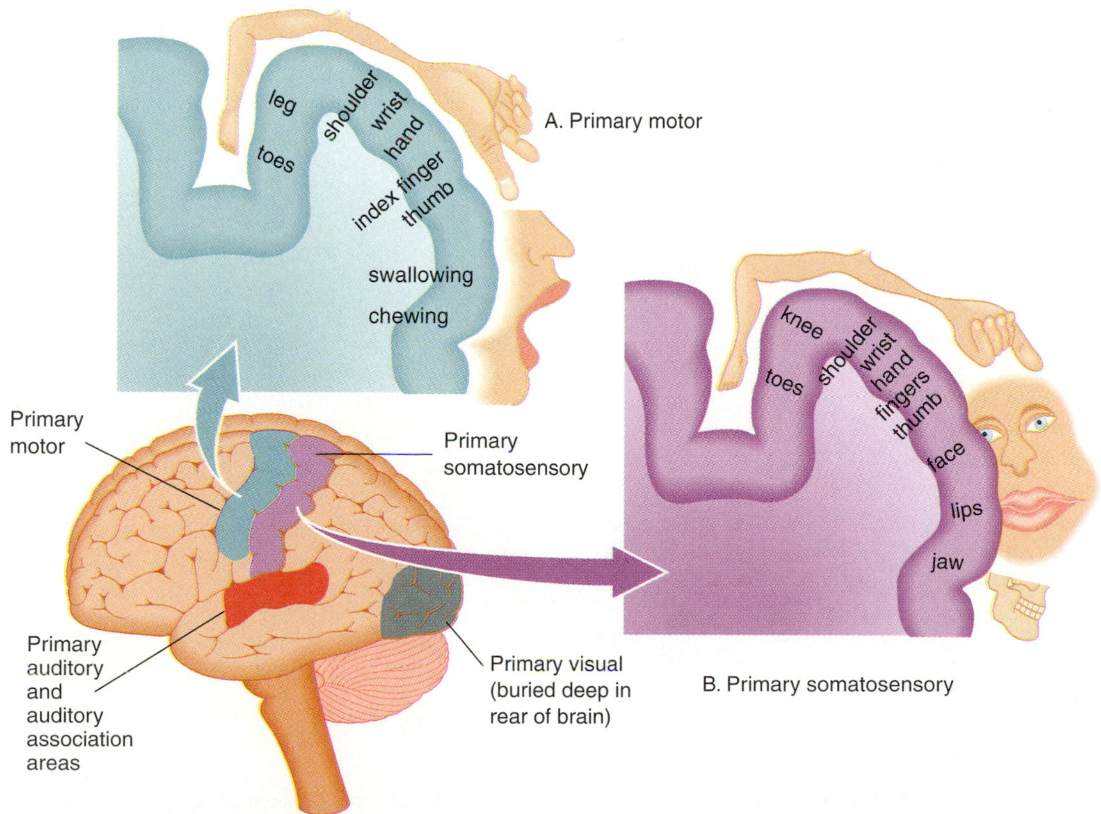

Figure 3.10 Motor and Somatosensory Cortex
Different parts of the body are more or less sensitive to environmental stimulation and brain control. Sensitivity in a particular region of the body is related to the amount of space in the cerebral cortex devoted to that region. In this figure, the body is drawn so that size of body parts is relative to the cortical space devoted to them. The larger the body part in the drawing, the greater its sensitivity to environmental stimulation and the greater the brain's control over its movement.

tex communicates with the left side of the body, and the left half communicates with the right side of the body.

Auditory information is processed in the **auditory cortex,** which is in the two temporal lobes. The auditory cortex in *each* hemisphere receives information from *both* ears. One area of the auditory cortex is involved in the production of language, and a different area is involved in language comprehension. Visual input is processed at the back of the brain in the **visual cortex,** located in the occipital lobes. Here the greatest area is devoted to input from the center part of the retina, at the back of the eye, the area that transmits the most detailed visual information.

Information is gathered from the environment by the somatosensory cortex and relayed to the association cortex, which integrates and interprets the information and allows you to formulate a response.

Not all of the cerebral cortex is devoted to processing sensory information and commanding the muscles to action. In fact, the majority of it is involved in *interpreting* and *integrating* information. Processes such as planning and decision making are believed to occur in the **association cortex**—all the areas of the cortex *not* labeled in Figure 3.9. Your association cortex allows you to combine information from various sensory modalities to plan appropriate responses to stimuli in the environment.

How do these different areas of the brain work in unison? Consider, as an example, the biology of speaking a written word (see **Figure 3.11**). Imagine that your psychology instructor hands you a piece of paper with the word *chocolate* written on it and asks you to say the word aloud. The biological processes involved in this action are surprisingly subtle and complex. Neuroscience can break down your verbal behavior into numerous steps. First, the visual stimulus (the written word *chocolate*) is detected by the nerve cells in the retinas of your eyes, which send nerve impulses to the visual cortex (via the thalamus). The visual cortex then sends nerve impulses to an area in the rear of the temporal lobe (called the angular gyrus) where visual coding for the word is compared with its acoustical coding. Once the proper acoustical

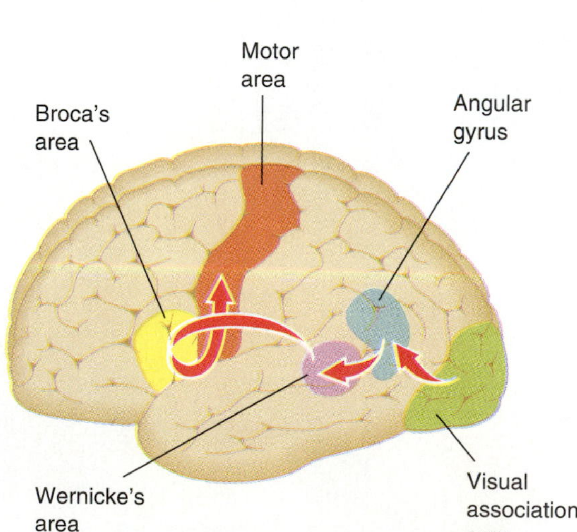

Figure 3.11 How a Written Word Is Spoken
Nerve impulses, laden with information about the written word, are sent by the retinas to the visual cortex via the thalamus. The visual cortex sends the nerve impulses to an area in the rear of the temporal lobe, the angular gyrus, where visual coding for the word (the arrangements of letters and their shapes, etc.) is compared with its acoustical coding (the way it sounds). Once the proper acoustical code is found, it is relayed to an area of the auditory cortex known as Wernicke's area. Here it is encoded and interpreted. Nerve impulses are sent to Broca's area, which sends the message to the motor cortex. The motor cortex puts the word in your mouth by stimulating the lips, tongue, and larynx to act in synchrony.

code is located, it is relayed to an area of the auditory cortex known as *Wernicke's area,* where it is decoded and interpreted: "Ah! Chocolate! I'd like some now." Nerve impulses are then sent to Broca's area, which, in turn, sends a message to the motor cortex, stimulating the lips, tongue, and larynx to produce the word *chocolate.*

That's a lot of mental effort for just one word. Now imagine what you require of your brain every time you read aloud a book or even a billboard. The truly amazing thing is that your brain responds effortlessly and intelligently, translating thousands of marks on paper into a neurological code, informing other brain areas about what's going on, and, finally, putting words in your mouth (Montgomery, 1990).

The Endocrine System

The human genotype specifies a second highly complex communication system, the **endocrine system,** to supplement the work of the nervous system. The endocrine system is a network of glands that manufacture and secrete chemical messengers called **hormones** into the bloodstream (see **Figure 3.12**). Hormones are important in everyday functioning, although they are more vital at some stages of life and in some situations than others. Hormones influence your body growth. They initiate, maintain, and stop development of primary and secondary sexual characteristics; influence levels of arousal and awareness; serve as the basis for mood changes; and regulate metabolism, the rate at which the body uses its energy stores. The endocrine system promotes the survival of an *organism* by helping fight infections and

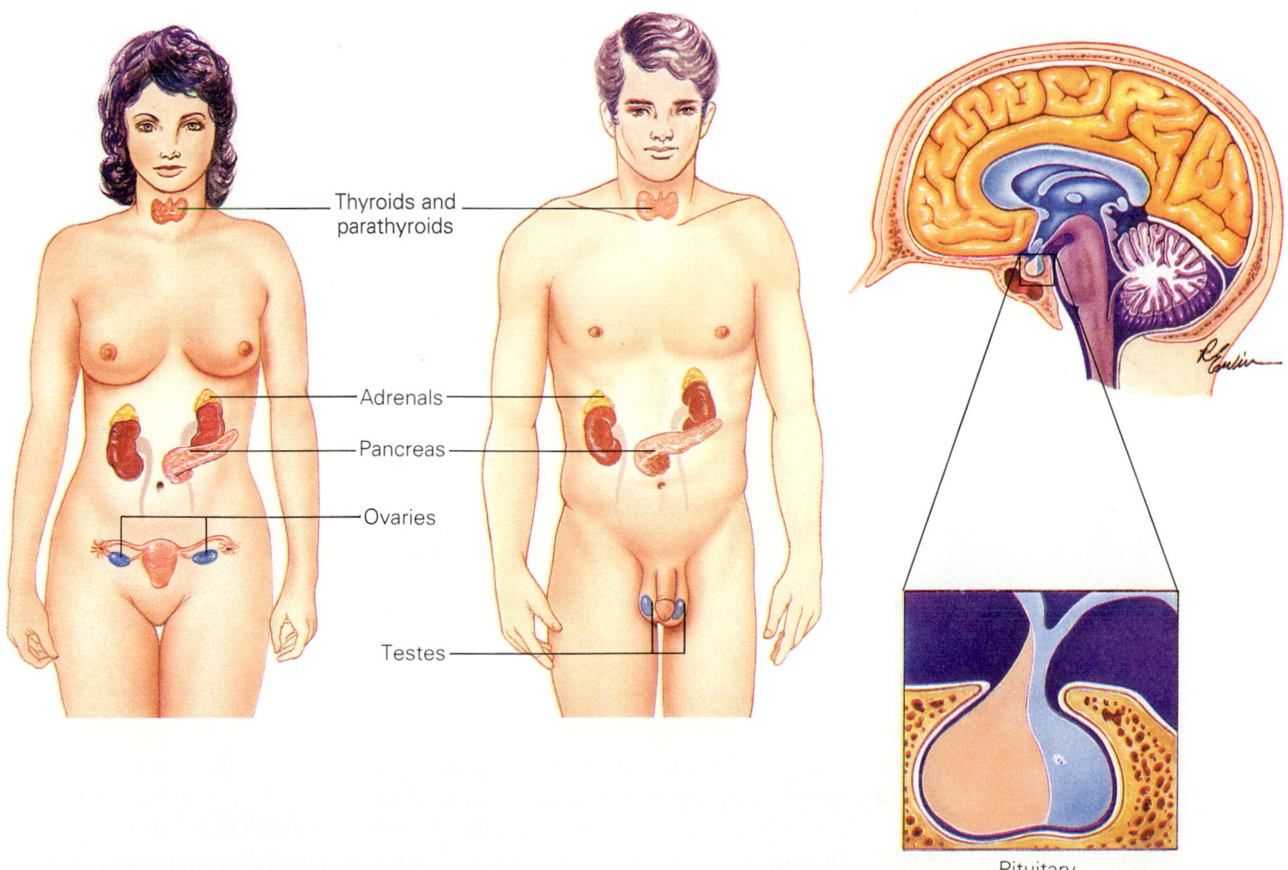

Figure 3.12 Endocrine Glands in Females and Males
The pituitary gland is shown at the far right; it is the master gland that regulates the glands shown at the left. The pituitary gland is under the control of the hypothalamus, an important structure in the limbic system.

The endocrine system is a network of glands that produce and secrete hormones, or chemical messages, into the bloodstream.

disease. It advances the survival of the *species* through regulation of sexual arousal, production of reproductive cells, and production of milk in nursing mothers. Thus you could not survive without an effective endocrine system.

Endocrine glands respond to the levels of chemicals in the bloodstream or are stimulated by other hormones or by nerve impulses from the brain. Hormones are then secreted into the blood and travel to distant target cells that have specific receptors; hormones exert their influence on the body's program of chemical regulation only at the places that are genetically predetermined to respond to them. In influencing diverse, but specific, target organs or tissue, hormones can regulate such an enormous range of biochemical processes that they have been called "the messengers of life" (Crapo, 1985). This multiple-action communication system allows for control of slow, continuous processes such as maintenance of blood-sugar levels and calcium levels, metabolism of carbohydrates, and general body growth. But what happens during crises? The endocrine system also releases the hormone adrenaline into the bloodstream; adrenaline energizes your body so that you can respond quickly to challenges.

The hypothalamus relays messages between the central nervous system and the endocrine system.

As we mentioned earlier, the brain structure known as the *hypothalamus* serves as a relay station between the endocrine system and the central nervous system. Specialized cells in the hypothalamus receive messages from other brain cells commanding it to release a number of different hormones to the pituitary gland, where they either stimulate or inhibit the release of other hormones. Hormones are produced in several different regions of the body. These "factories" make a variety of hormones, each of which regulates different bodily processes, as outlined in **Table 3.1**. Let's examine the most significant of these processes.

The **pituitary gland** is often called the "master gland," because it produces about ten different kinds of hormones that influence the secretions of all the other endocrine glands, as well as a hormone that influences growth. The absence of this growth hormone results in dwarfism; its excess results in

Table 3.1 Major Endocrine Glands and the Functions of the Hormones They Produce

These Glands:	Produce Hormones That Regulate:
Hypothalamus	Release of pituitary hormones
Anterior pituitary	Testes and ovaries Breast milk production Metabolism Reactions to stress
Posterior pituitary	Water conservation Breast milk excretion Uterus contraction
Thyroid	Metabolism Growth and development
Parathyroid	Calcium levels
Gut	Digestion
Pancreas	Glucose metabolism
Adrenals	Fight or flight responses Metabolism Sexual desire in women
Ovaries	Development of female sexual traits Ova production
Testes	Development of male sexual traits Sperm production Sexual desire in men

gigantic growth. In males, pituitary secretions activate the testes to secrete **testosterone,** which stimulates production of sperm. The pituitary gland is also involved in the development of male secondary sexual characteristics, such as facial hair, voice change, and physical maturation. Testosterone may even increase aggression and sexual desire. In females, a pituitary hormone stimulates production of **estrogen,** which is essential to the hormonal chain reaction that triggers the release of ova from a woman's ovaries, making her fertile. Certain birth-control pills work by blocking the mechanism in the pituitary gland that controls this hormone flow, thus preventing the ova from being released.

The pituitary gland produces growth hormones and other hormones that in turn influence the secretions of all the other glands in the endocrine system.

THE NERVOUS SYSTEM IN ACTION

To interact with the world, you depend more on the nervous system than you do on the endocrine system. Although both systems are critical to your ability to live the way you do, the nervous system allows you to sense and to respond to the outside world. For that reason, one of the major goals of early physiologists was to understand better how the nervous system operates. In large measure, modern neuroscientists have accomplished this goal, although they continue to work on solving smaller pieces of the puzzle. Our objective in this section is to analyze and understand how the information available to your senses is ultimately communicated throughout your body and brain by nerve impulses. We begin by discussing the properties of the basic unit of the nervous system, the neuron.

The Neuron

A **neuron** is a cell specialized to receive, process, and/or transmit information to other cells within the body. Neurons vary in shape, size, chemical composition, and function—over 200 different types have been identified in mammal brains—but all neurons have the same basic structure (see **Figure 3.13**).

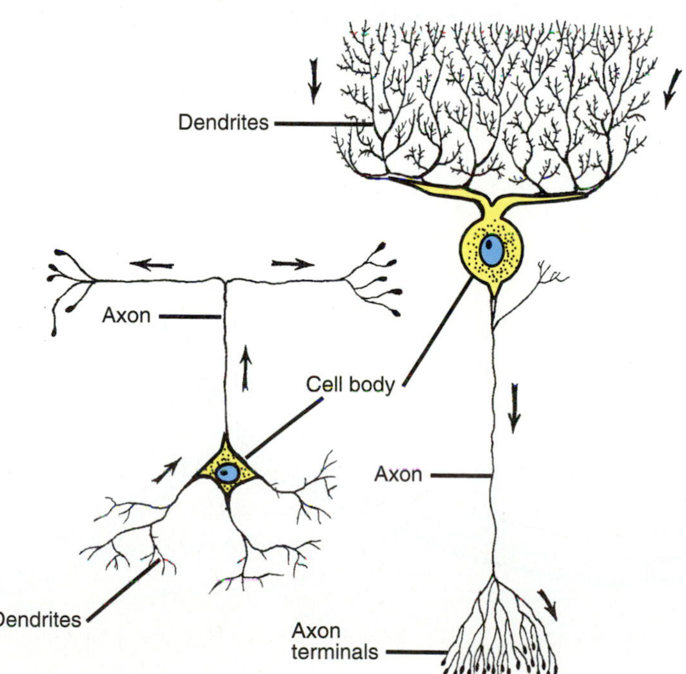

Figure 3.13 Two Types of Neurons

Note the differences in shape and dendritic branching. Arrows indicate directions in which information flows. Both cells are types of interneurons.

Your brain starts out with between 100 billion and 1 trillion neurons. Those neurons die out in astonishing numbers—somewhere in the neighborhood of 200,000 each and every day of your life (Dowling, 1992)! Fortunately, because you start out with so many neurons and because some types of neurons are replenished, you would lose only about 7 percent of your original supply in 100 years. The deteriorated brain functioning that sometimes occurs in old age is usually not a result of the decrease in the number of neurons but an effect of destructive changes within the neurons themselves or in the chemical substances that carry signals between neurons.

Neurons receive incoming messages through their dendrites and send the messages on to the next neuron through their axons.

Neurons typically take in information at one end and send out messages from the other. The part of the cell that receives incoming signals is a set of branched fibers called **dendrites,** which extend outward from the cell body. The basic job of the dendrites is to receive stimulation from sense receptors or other neurons. The cell body, or **soma,** contains the nucleus of the cell and the cytoplasm that sustains its life. The soma integrates information about the stimulation received from the dendrites (or in some cases received directly from another neuron) and passes it on to a single, extended fiber, the **axon.** In turn, the axon conducts this information along its length—which, in the spinal cord, can be several feet and, in the brain, less than a millimeter. At the other end of axons are swollen, bulblike structures called **terminal buttons,** through which the neuron is able to stimulate nearby glands, muscles, or other neurons. Neurons generally transmit information in only one direction: from the dendrites through the soma to the axon to the terminal buttons (see **Figure 3.14**).

Three major types of neurons are sensory neurons, motor neurons, and interneurons. Most of the neurons in the brain are interneurons.

There are three major classes of neurons. **Sensory neurons** carry messages from sense receptor cells *toward* the central nervous system. Receptor cells are highly specialized cells that are sensitive to light, sound, and body position. **Motor neurons** carry messages *away* from the central nervous system toward the muscles and glands. The bulk of the neurons in the brain are **interneurons,** which relay messages from sensory neurons to other interneurons or to motor neurons. For every motor neuron in the body there are as many as 5000 interneurons in the great intermediate network that forms the computational system of the brain (Nauta & Feirtag, 1979).

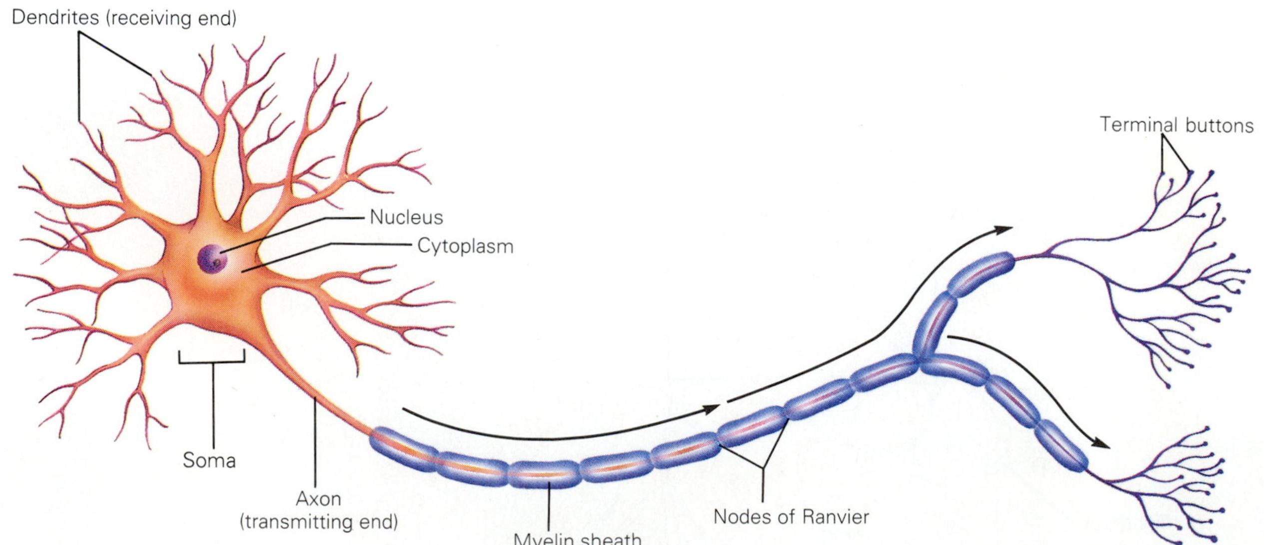

Figure 3.14 The Major Structures of the Neuron
The neuron receives nerve impulses through its dendrites. It then sends the nerve impulses through its axon to the terminal buttons, where neurotransmitters are released to stimulate other neurons.

As an example of how these three kinds of neurons work together, consider once again the pain withdrawal reflex (see **Figure 3.15**). When pain receptors near the skin's surface are stimulated by a sharp object, they send messages via sensory neurons to an interneuron in the spinal cord. The interneuron responds by stimulating motor neurons, which, in turn, excite muscles in the appropriate area of the body to pull away from the pain-producing object. It is only *after* this sequence of neuronal events has taken place, and the body has been moved away from the stimulating object, that the brain is informed of the situation. In cases such as this, where survival depends on swift action, your perception of pain often occurs after you have physically responded to the danger. Of course, then the information from the incident is stored in the brain's memory system so that the next time you will avoid the potentially dangerous object altogether before it can hurt you.

Interspersed among the brain's vast web of neurons are about five to ten times as many glial cells **(glia).** The word *glia* is derived from the Greek word for *glue,* which gives you a hint of one of the major duties performed by these cells: they hold neurons in place. In vertebrates, glial cells have several other important functions. Their first function is housekeeping. When neurons are damaged and die, glial cells in the area multiply and clean up the cellular junk left behind; they can also take up excess chemical substances at the gaps between neurons. Their second function is insulation. Glial cells form

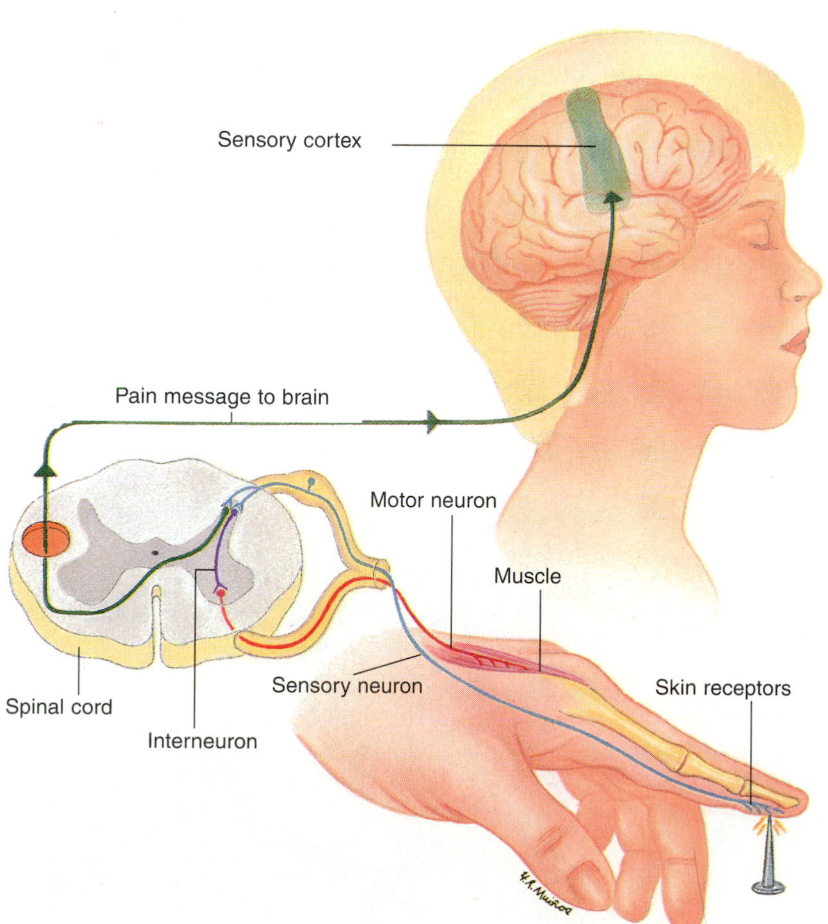

Figure 3.15 The Pain Withdrawal Reflex
The pain withdrawal reflex shown here involves only three neurons: a sensory neuron, a motor neuron, and an interneuron.

an insulating cover, called a *myelin sheath*, around some types of axons. This fatty insulation greatly increases the speed of nerve signal conduction. The third function of glial cells is to prevent toxic substances in the blood from reaching the delicate cells of the brain. Specialized glial cells, called astrocytes, make up a *blood-brain barrier,* forming a continuous envelope of fatty material around the blood vessels in the brain. Substances that are not soluble in fat do not dissolve through this barrier, and since many poisons and other harmful substances are not fat-soluble, they cannot penetrate the barrier to reach the brain.

The glial cells, interspersed among the neurons, clean up after damaged neurons, help insulate neurons, and form a barrier to prevent toxic substances from reaching the brain.

Graded and Action Potentials

So far, we have spoken loosely about neurons "sending messages" or "stimulating" each other. The time has come to describe more formally the kinds of electrochemical signals used by the nervous system to process and transmit information. It is these signals that are the basis of all you know, feel, desire, and create. The basic question asked of each neuron is: Should it or should it not *fire*—produce a response—at some given time? In loose terms, neurons make this decision by summing the information arriving at their dendrites and soma (cell body) and determining whether those inputs are predominantly saying "fire" or "don't fire." More formally, each neuron will receive a balance of **excitatory**—fire!—and **inhibitory**—don't fire!—**inputs**. **Graded potentials** are generated by the excitatory inputs. These potentials are called "graded" because they vary in size according to the magnitude of stimulation. For example, in sensory receptors, such as the retina of the eye, light is converted, or transduced, into a graded potential (often called a receptor potential). The size of this potential depends upon how intense or bright the light is. This makes sense: the brighter the light, the more important it is to pass information about it deeper into the brain; the brain should "know" about it.

Neurons will fire when they receive the right balance of excitatory and inhibitory inputs.

Graded potentials are only useful as short-term, local signals within the neuron, because they weaken over long distances. It is frequently the case that no one graded potential is sufficient to cause a neuron to fire (particularly in the presence of opposing inhibitory signals). Neurons will often reach their thresholds for firing by virtue of **temporal summation**—several small

THE MELANCHOLY NEURON

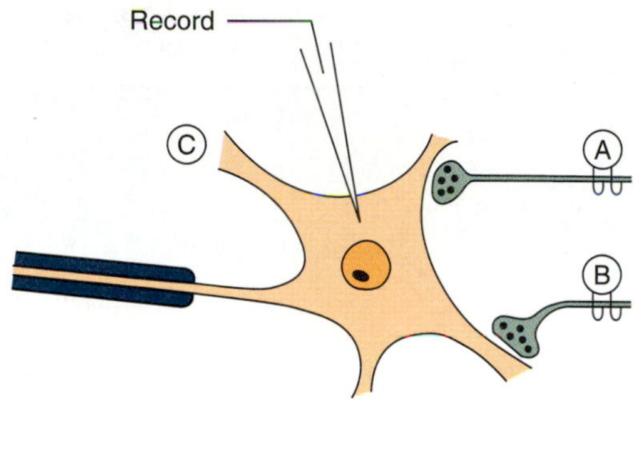

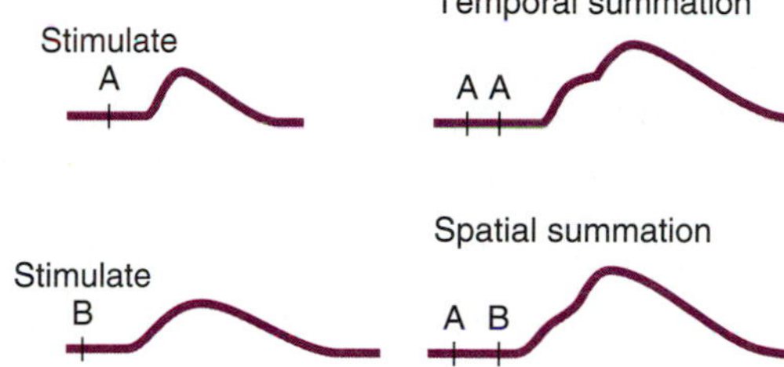

Figure 3.16 Temporal and Spatial Summation
Two neurons (A and B) both form connections with a third neuron (C). An input from either A or B will cause an excitatory potential in C. However, if either A or B provides an input twice in short succession (temporal summation), or both cells provide excitatory inputs close together (spatial summation), a larger response is produced in C.

excitatory or inhibitory inputs from the same source summate over time—or **spatial summation**—several small excitatory and inhibitory inputs from different sources occur at the same time (see **Figure 3.16**). You experience conscious versions of temporal and spatial summation nearly every day. Suppose you have to decide whether to ask someone out on a date. If the same friend encourages you repeatedly, you should be more likely to do so—that's temporal summation. If several friends all encourage you at the same time, that's spatial summation. In neurons, the right pattern of excitatory inputs over time or space will lead to the production of an action potential.

The Biochemical Basis of Action Potentials

To explain how an **action potential** works, we need to describe the biochemical environment in which neurons summate incoming information. All neural communication is produced by the flow of electrically charged particles, called *ions,* through the neuron's membrane, a thin "skin" separating the cell's internal and external environments. Think of a nerve fiber as a macaroni, filled with salt water, floating in a salty soup. The soup and the fluid in the macaroni both contain ions—atoms of sodium (NA^+), chloride (CL^-), calcium (CA^+), and potassium (K^+)—that have either positive (+) or negative (–) charges (see **Figure 3.17**). The membrane, or the surface of the macaroni, plays a critical role in keeping the ingredients of the two fluids in an appropriate balance. When a cell is inactive, or in a *resting* state, there are about ten times as many potassium ions inside as there are sodium ions outside. The membrane is not a perfect barrier; it "leaks" a little, allowing some sodium ions to slip in while some potassium ions slip out. To correct for this, nature has provided transport mechanisms within the membrane that pump out sodium and pump in potassium. Successful operation of these pumps leaves the fluid inside a neuron with a slightly negative voltage (70/1000 of a volt) relative to the fluid outside. This means that the cellular fluid is *polarized* with respect to the extracellular fluid. This slight polarization is called the **resting potential.** It provides the electrochemical context in which a nerve cell can produce an action potential.

A resting potential exists when the cellular fluid of a neuron is slightly polarized with respect to the extracellular fluid.

The nerve cell begins the transition from a resting potential to an action potential in response to the pattern of inhibitory and excitatory inputs. Each

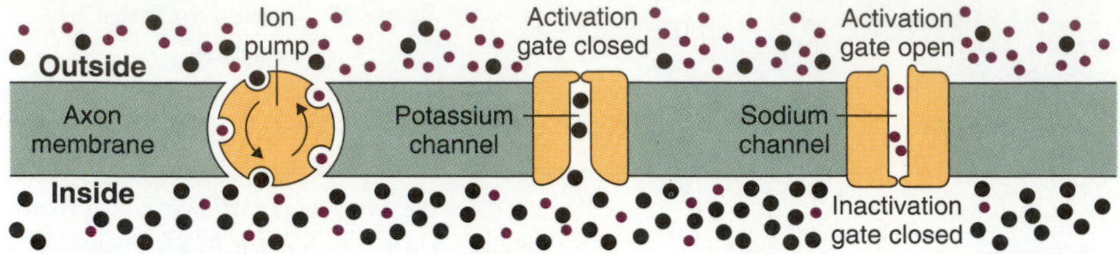

Figure 3.17 The Biochemical Basis of Action Potentials
The axon membrane separates fluids that differ greatly in their content of sodium ions (colored dots) *and potassium ions* (black dots). *The exterior fluid is about 10 times richer in sodium ions than in potassium ions; in the interior fluid, the ratio is the reverse. The membrane is penetrated by proteins that act as selective channels for preferentially passing either sodium or potassium ions. In the resting state, when no nerve impulse is being transmitted, the two types of channel are closed and an ion pump maintains the ionic disequilibrium by pumping out sodium ions in exchange for potassium ions. The interior of the axon is normally about 70 millivolts negative with respect to the exterior. If this voltage difference is reduced by the arrival of a nerve impulse, the sodium channel opens, allowing sodium ions to flow into the axon. An instant later, the sodium channel closes and the potassium channel opens, allowing an outflow of potassium ions. The sequential opening and closing of the two kinds of channels effects the propagation of the nerve impulse.*

kind of input affects the likelihood that the balance of ions from the inside to the outside of the cell will change. They cause changes in the function of **ion channels,** excitable portions of the cell membrane that selectively permit certain ions to flow in and out. Inhibitory inputs cause the ion channels to work harder to keep the inside of the cell negatively charged—this will keep the cell from firing. Excitatory inputs cause the ion channels to begin to allow sodium ions to flow in—this will allow the cell to fire. Because sodium ions have a positive charge, their influx can begin to change the relative balance of positive and negative charges across the cell membrane. An action potential begins when the excitatory inputs are sufficiently strong with respect to inhibitory inputs to *depolarize* the cell from −70 millivolts to −55 millivolts: sufficient sodium has entered the cell to effect this change.

Once the action potential begins, sodium rushes into the neuron. As a result, the inside of the neuron becomes positive relative to the outside, meaning the neuron has become fully depolarized. A domino effect now propels the action potential down the axon. The leading edge of depolarization causes ion channels in the adjacent region of the axon to open and allow sodium to rush in. In this way—through successive depolarization—the signal passes down the axon (see **Figure 3.18**).

How does the neuron return to its original resting state of polarization after it fires? When the inside of the neuron becomes positive, the channels that allow sodium to flow in close and channels that allow potassium to flow out open. The outflow of potassium ions restores the negative charge of the neuron. Thus, even while the signal is reaching the far end of the axon, the portions of the cell in which the action potential originated are being returned to their resting balance, so that they can be ready for their next stimulation.

Properties of the Action Potential

The biochemical manner in which the action potential is propagated leads to several important properties. Unlike the graded potential, whose intensity is directly proportional to the intensity of the stimulus, the action potential is unaffected by properties of the stimulus. The action potential obeys the **all-or-none law:** The size of the action potential is unaffected by increases in the intensity of stimulation beyond the threshold level. Once excitatory inputs

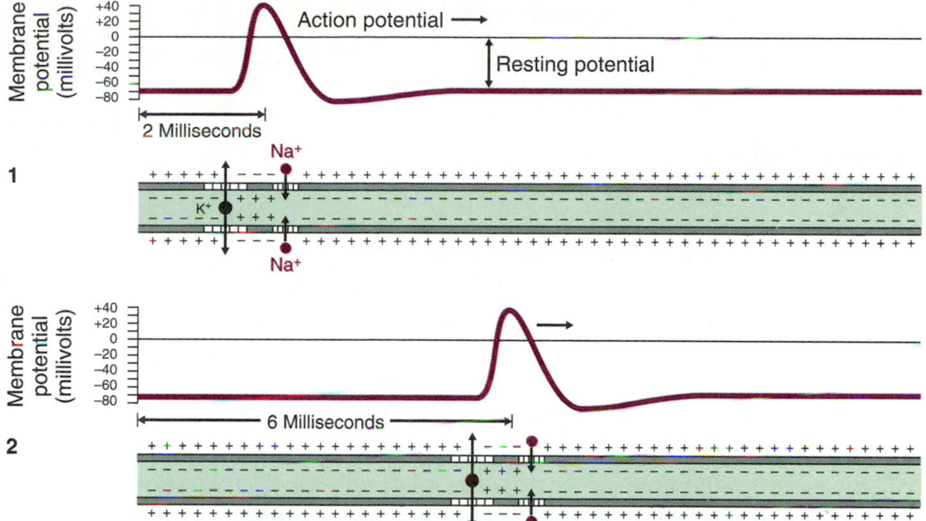

Figure 3.18 Propagation of a Nerve Impulse

The propagation of a nerve impulse along the axon coincides with a localized inflow of sodium ions (Na^+) followed by an outflow of potassium ions (K^+). The action potential propagates itself down the axon. After a brief refractory period, a second impulse can follow. The impulse-propagation speed is that measured in the giant axon of the squid.

sum to reach the threshold level, a uniform action potential is generated. If the threshold is not reached, no action potential occurs. An added consequence of the all-or-none property is that the size of the action potential does not diminish along the length of the axon. In this sense, the action potential is said to be *self-propagating;* once started, it needs no outside stimulation to keep itself moving. It's similar to a lit fuse on a firecracker.

Action potentials operate according to the all-or-none law: the size of the action potential is unaffected by the intensity of the stimulus.

Different neurons conduct action potentials along their axons at different speeds; the fastest have signals that move at the rate of 200 meters per second, the slowest plod along at 10 centimeters per second. The axons of the faster neurons are covered with a tightly wrapped myelin sheath—consisting, as we explained earlier, of glial cells—making this part of the neuron resemble short tubes on a string. The tiny breaks between the tubes are called *nodes of Ranvier* (see Figure 3.14). In neurons having myelinated axons, the action potential literally skips along from one node to the next—saving the time and energy required to open and close ion channels at every location on the axon. Damage to the myelin sheath throws off the delicate timing of the action potential and causes serious problems. Multiple sclerosis (MS) is a devastating disorder caused by deterioration of the myelin sheath. It is characterized by double vision, tremors, and eventually paralysis. In MS, specialized cells from the body's immune system actually attack myelinated neurons, exposing the axon and disrupting normal synaptic transmission (Joyce, 1990a).

After an action potential has passed down a segment of the axon, that region of the neuron enters a **refractory period** for 0.5 to 2 milliseconds: further stimulation, no matter how intense, cannot cause another action potential to be generated (see **Figure 3.19**). Have you ever tried to flush the toilet while it is filling back up with water? There must be a critical level of water for the toilet to flush again. Similarly, in order for a neuron to be able to generate another action potential, it must "reset" itself and await simulation beyond its threshold. The refractory period ensures, in part, that the action potential will only travel in one direction down the axon: it cannot move backward, because "earlier" parts of the axon are in a refractory state.

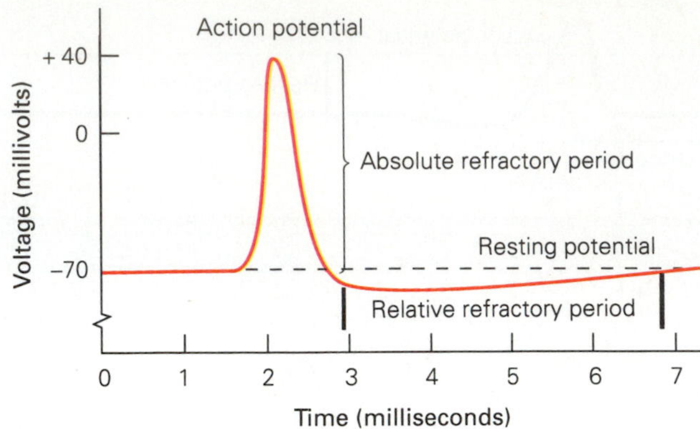

Figure 3.19 Timetable for Electrical Changes in the Neuron During an Action Potential
Sodium ions entering the neuron cause its electrical potential to change from slightly negative during its polarized, or resting, state to slightly positive during depolarization. Once the neuron is depolarized, it enters a brief refractory period during which further stimulation will not produce another action potential. Another action potential can occur only after the ionic balance between the inside and the outside of the cell is restored.

Synaptic Transmission

Neurons don't touch: they are joined at a small gap called a synapse. Thus information must be relayed from one neuron to the next across the synaptic gap.

When the action potential completes its leapfrog journey down the axon to a terminal button, it must pass its information along to the next neuron. But no two neurons ever touch: they are joined at a **synapse**, with a small gap between the *presynaptic membrane* (the terminal button of the sending neuron) and the *postsynaptic membrane* (the surface of a dendrite or soma of a receiving neuron). When the action potential reaches the terminal button, it sets in motion a series of events called **synaptic transmission**, which is the relaying of information from one neuron to another across the synaptic gap (see **Figure 3.20**). Synaptic transmission begins when the arrival of the action potential at the terminal button causes small round packets, called *synaptic vesicles,* to move toward and affix themselves to the interior membrane of the terminal button. Inside each vesicle are **neurotransmitters**, biochemical substances that stimulate other neurons. The action potential also causes ion channels to open that admit calcium ions into the terminal button. The influx of calcium ions causes the rupture of the synaptic vesicles and the release of whatever neurotransmitters they contain (Zucker & Lando, 1986). Once the synaptic vesicles rupture, the neurotransmitters are dispersed rapidly across the *synaptic cleft* to the postsynaptic membrane. To complete synaptic transmission, the neurotransmitters attach to *receptor molecules* embedded in the postsynaptic membrane.

Neurotransmitters are chemicals that aid the transmission of neural impulses across the synaptic gap.

The neurotransmitters will bind to the receptor molecules under two conditions. First, no other neurotransmitters or other chemical substances can be attached to the receptor molecule. Second, the shape of the neurotransmitter must match the shape of the receptor molecule—as precisely as a key fits into a keyhole. If neither condition is met, the neurotransmitter will not attach to the receptor molecule. This means that it will not be able to stimulate the postsynaptic membrane. If the neurotransmitter does become attached to the receptor molecule, then it may provide "fire" or "don't fire" information to this next neuron. Once the neurotransmitter has completed its job, it detaches from the receptor molecule and drifts back into the synaptic gap. There it is either decomposed through the action of enzymes or reabsorbed into the presynaptic terminal button for quick reuse.

Depending on the receptor molecule, a neurotransmitter will have either an excitatory or an inhibitory effect. That is, the same neurotransmitter may

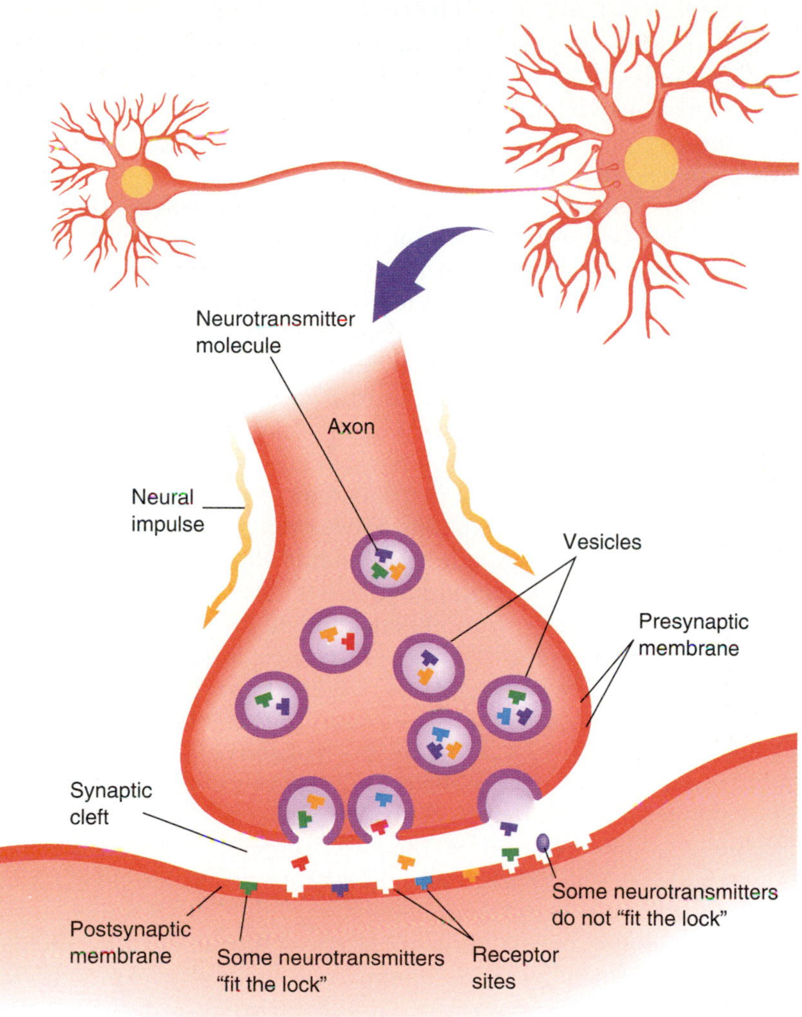

Figure 3.20 Synaptic Transmission

The action potential in the presynaptic neuron causes neurotransmitters to be released into the synaptic gap. Once across the gap, they stimulate receptor molecules embedded in the membrane of the postsynaptic neuron. Multiple neurotransmitters can exist within the same cell.

be excitatory at one synapse but inhibitory at another. Excitatory inputs produce graded potentials; inhibitory inputs dampen them—and we are back to where we began! Each neuron integrates the information it obtains at synapses with between 1,000 and 10,000 other neurons to decide whether it ought to initiate another action potential. It is the integration of these thousands of inhibitory and excitatory inputs that allows all-or-none action potentials to provide the foundation for all human experience.

Neurotransmitters may have either an excitatory or an inhibitory effect.

You may be wondering why we have taken you so deep into the nervous system. After all, this is a psychology course, and psychology is supposed to be about behavior and thinking and emotion. In fact, synapses are the biological medium in which all of these activities occur. If you change the normal activity of the synapse, you change how people behave, how they think, and how they feel. Understanding the functioning of the synapse has led to tremendous advances in the understanding of learning and memory, emotion, psychological disorders, drug addiction, and, in general, the chemical formula for mental health. You will use the knowledge you have acquired in this chapter throughout *Psychology and Life.*

The biopsychology of the brain plays an important role in the understanding of psychological concerns such as learning and memory, emotion, psychological disorders, and drug addiction.

Neurotransmitters and their Functions

More than 60 different chemical substances are known or suspected to function as neurotransmitters in the brain. The neurotransmitters that have been studied most intensively meet a set of technical criteria. Each is manufactured in the presynaptic terminal button and is released when an action potential reaches that terminal. The neurotransmitter's presence in the synaptic cleft produces a biological response in the postsynaptic membrane, and, if its release is prevented, no subsequent responses can occur. To give you a sense of the effects different neurotransmitters have on the regulation of behavior, we will review a set that has been found to play an important role in the daily functioning of the brain. This brief review will also enable you to understand many of the ways in which neural transmission can go awry.

Acetylcholine is found in both the central and peripheral nervous systems. Memory loss among patients suffering from Alzheimer's disease, a degenerative disease that is increasingly common among older persons, is believed to be caused by the deterioration of neurons that secrete acetylcholine. Acetylcholine is also excitatory at junctions between nerves and muscles, where it causes muscles to contract. A number of toxins affect the synaptic actions of acetylcholine. For example, botulinum toxin, often found in food that has been preserved incorrectly, poisons an individual by preventing release of acetylcholine in the respiratory system. This poisoning, known as *botulism,* can cause death by suffocation. Curare, a poison Amazon Indians use on the tips of their blowgun darts, paralyzes lung muscles by occupying critical acetylcholine receptors, preventing the normal activity of the transmitter.

Acetylcholine is a neurotransmitter implicated in the memory loss suffered by Alzheimer's patients.

GABA (gamma-amino butyric acid) is affected by a variety of depressants, chemical compounds that reduce central nervous system activity. For example, barbiturates are believed to bind to receptor molecules sensitive to GABA, causing sedation. This effect implies that low levels of GABA may be responsible for anxiety (Paul et al., 1986).

The *catecholamines* are a class of chemical substances that include two important neurotransmitters, *dopamine* and *norepinephrine.* Both have been shown to play prominent roles in psychological disorders, such as mood disturbances and schizophrenia. Norepinephrine appears to be involved in some forms of depression: drugs that increase brain levels of this neurotransmitter elevate mood and relieve depression. Conversely, higher than normal levels of dopamine have been found in persons with schizophrenia. As you might expect, one way to treat people with this disorder is to give them a drug that decreases brain levels of dopamine. In the early days of drug therapy, an interesting but unfortunate problem arose. High doses of the drug used to treat schizophrenia produced symptoms of Parkinson's disease, a progressive and ultimately fatal disorder involving disruption of motor functioning. (Parkinson's disease is caused by deterioration of neurons that manufacture most of the brain's dopamine.) This finding led to research that improved drug therapy for schizophrenia and to research that focused on drugs that could be used in the treatment of Parkinson's disease.

Dopamine and norepinephrine are two neurotransmitters believed to play a role in psychological disorders such as mood disturbances and schizophrenia.

All the neurons that produce *serotonin* are located in the brain stem, which is involved in arousal and many autonomic processes. The hallucinogenic drug LSD (lysergic acid diethylamide) appears to produce its effects by suppressing the effects of serotonin neurons. These serotonin neurons normally inhibit other neurons: the lack of inhibition produced by LSD creates vivid and bizarre sensory experiences, some of which last for hours. Many antidepressant drugs, such as Prozac, enhance the action of serotonin by preventing it from being removed from the synaptic cleft (Barondes, 1994).

The *endorphins* are a group of chemicals that are usually classified as neuromodulators. A **neuromodulator** is any substance that modifies or modulates the activities of the postsynaptic neuron. Endorphins (short for *endogenous morphines*) play an important role in the control of emotional

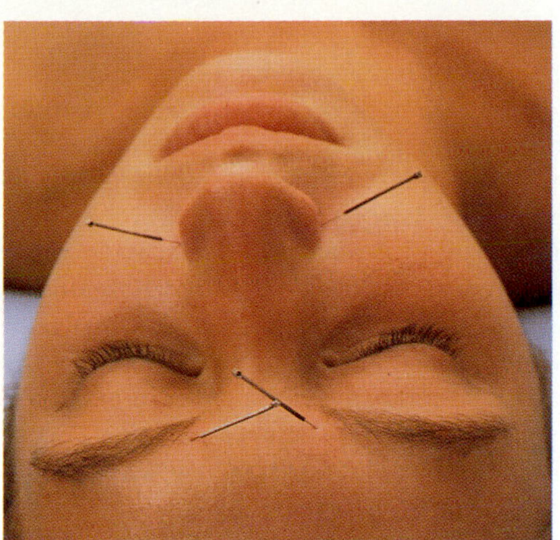

Why do patients experience pain relief from acupuncture?

behaviors (anxiety, fear, tension, pleasure) and pain—drugs like opium and morphine bind to the same receptor sites in the brain. Endorphins have been called the "keys to paradise" because of their pleasure–pain controlling properties. Researchers have examined the possibility that endorphins are at least partially responsible for the pain-reducing effects of acupuncture (Watkins & Mayer, 1982) and placebos (Fields & Levine, 1984). Such tests rely on the drug *naloxone,* whose only known effect is to block morphine and endorphins from binding to receptors (Hopson, 1988). Any procedure that reduces pain by stimulating release of endorphins becomes ineffective when naloxone is administered. With the injection of naloxone, acupuncture and placebos do, in fact, lose their power—suggesting that, ordinarily, endorphins help them do their work.

Endorphins, classified as neuromodulators, are important in the control of emotions and pain.

In recent years, researchers have discovered that gases like *carbon monoxide* and *nitric oxide* can function as neurotransmitters (Barinaga, 1993). What is most surprising about this new class of neurotransmitters is that they violate many of the normal expectations about synaptic transmission. For example, rather than binding to receptor molecules, as do the other neurotransmitters we have discussed, these gaseous transmitters appear to pass directly through the receptor cell's outer membrane. This surprising discovery should reinforce your impression that the brain possesses many secrets yet to be revealed.

Neural Networks

You are now acquainted with the basic elements that give rise to the complex range of human thought, feeling, and action: graded potentials and action potentials; inhibitory and excitatory inputs; the variety of neurotransmitters; the actions of the endocrine system. To complete the journey toward a basic understanding of the biological foundations of behavior, we need only introduce the concept of **neural networks.** These circuits or systems of neurons function together to perform tasks that individual cells cannot carry out alone. The principle by which the brain operates is that a large number of simple devices acting as a unit—recall that you have over 100 billion neurons—can produce extremely complex behavior. As a simple analogy, imagine the members of a chorus singing the different notes of a chord. Each section of the group sings a simple note, but the product of their combined effort can be dazzlingly beautiful. So it is with neural networks.

Complex tasks that cannot be performed by single cells are completed by neural networks.

Neural networks follow a basic principle of nature: all life processes are organized *hierarchically.* In other words, simpler units, structures, and processes are organized into levels of ever greater complexity, with higher ones exercising some control over lower ones. At each level of complexity there are limits and constraints that can be overcome only by a more complex system (Jacob, 1977). Just as new capabilities become available at each level, from molecule to cell to organ to organism, new potential for information processing becomes available with increasingly complex neural networks.

We have already looked at one of the simplest neural networks, the pain withdrawal reflex. If you review Figure 3.15, you can see how different neurons play different roles. Because human neural networks are usually more complex, scientists usually study the neural networks of simple organisms such as invertebrates. A favorite subject has been the sea slug *Aplysia.* Because it has relatively few, large neurons—some can be seen with the naked eye—"wiring diagrams" can be worked out for given types of behavior. For example, *Aplysia*'s heart rate is controlled by a simple neural network involving only a few cells: some excite it to pump and others inhibit it. These critical cells control other cells and, thus, trigger entire behavioral sequences.

Because it has relatively few, large neurons, the sea slug Aplysia *has been a key organism in the study of neural networks.*

A more complex neural network is found in *Aplysia*'s gill withdrawal reflex, a defensive response that protects organs vital to its survival. Tactile stimuli applied to the siphon of *Aplysia* at first elicit gill withdrawal. With repeated stimulation, however, the withdrawal response *habituates:* it becomes weaker and weaker until it may not be made at all. Habituation is the simplest form of memory for a specific stimulus.

Eric Kandel and his associates have studied habituation of the gill withdrawal reflex extensively and derived the wiring diagram shown in **Figure 3.21** (Kandel, 1979, 1989). The sensory neurons encode information about

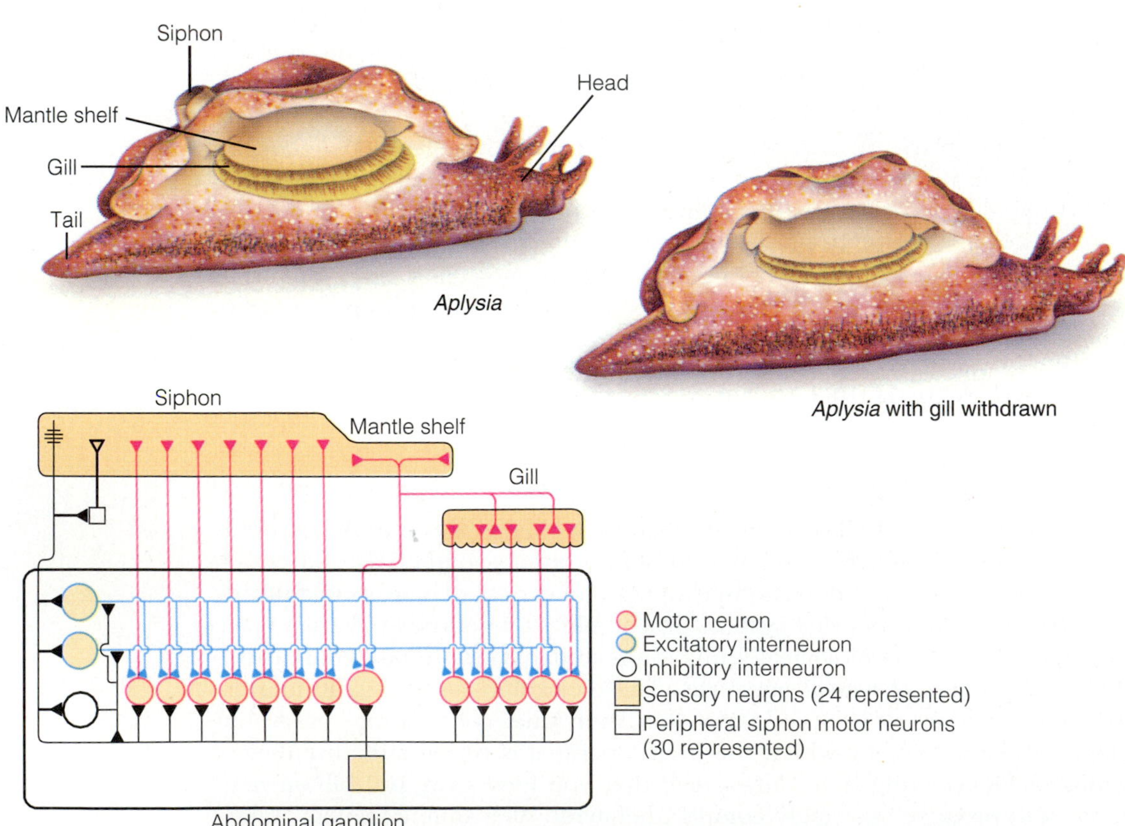

Figure 3.21 Neural Network for the Gill Withdrawal Reflex in *Aplysia*
The top left drawing shows the sea slug in its normal state. The top right drawing shows it with the gill withdrawn. The schematic diagram represents the neural network controlling the reflex. The sensory neurons involved are indicated by a single line, but each of the motor and interneurons is shown.

the tactile stimulation; this information is processed through the network by interneurons that stimulate the motor neurons to withdraw the gill. The network stores information about the match between old and new stimuli. If a stimulus is repeated, the gill response is damped down; a new stimulus leads to renewed activity. By examining the separate neurons in the network, Kandel and his colleagues were able not only to determine the precise synapses at which habituation takes place but also to observe the actual biochemical changes that mediate habituation. With this knowledge in hand, neuroscientists can start the search for the biological bases of the more profound types of memory that guide human experience.

HEMISPHERIC SPECIALIZATION AND INDIVIDUAL DIFFERENCES

At the chapter's outset, we posed the question, What makes you a unique individual? In our review of heredity we gave part of that answer: you have inherited a unique collection of genes from your parents. In this final section we will provide more of the answer: You have some habitual, individualistic way of distributing responsibility for the tasks of living to the left and right hemispheres of your brain. We will begin by describing the "average" specialization of the hemispheres and then discuss individual differences against that background. This section should enable you to consider how your unique approach to life may be defined, in part, by the structure of your brain.

Cerebral Dominance: Two Brains or One?

You are already in possession of information that might lead you to wonder whether there are differences in the functions of the two hemispheres of your brain. Recall that when Paul Broca carried out his autopsy on Tan, he discovered damage in the left hemisphere. As he followed up this original discovery, Broca found that other patients who showed similar disruption of their language abilities—a pattern now known as *Broca's aphasia*—also had damage on the *left* side of their brains. Damage to the same areas on the *right* side of the brain did not have the same effect. What should one conclude?

The left-hemisphere activity that makes sign language possible is similar to that for vocal speech.

We now know that for most people, many language-related functions are *dominated* by the left hemisphere. The phrase **cerebral dominance** applies when one cerebral hemisphere plays the primary role in directing some bodily or mental function; researchers also say that a function is *lateralized* to one hemisphere or the other. Speech—the ability to produce coherent spoken language—is perhaps the most highly lateralized of all functions. Neuroscientists have found that only about 5 percent of right-handers and 15 percent of left-handers have speech controlled by the right hemisphere, while another 15 percent of left-handers have language functions occurring in both sides of the brain. For most people, therefore, speech is a left hemisphere function. As a consequence, damage to the left side of most people's brains can cause speech disorders. What is interesting is that for users of languages like American Sign Language—which use systems of intricate hand positions and gestures to convey meaning—left-brain damage is similarly disruptive (Poizner et al., 1991). What is lateralized, therefore, is not speech as such but, rather, the ability to produce motor gestures—either vocal or manual—that encode communicative meaning.

For most people, language functions are dominated by the left hemisphere, supporting the notion of cerebral dominance or lateralization.

The strong lateralization of such language functions led researchers to wonder what other differences might be found across the two hemispheres. The chance to investigate further differences first arose in the context of a treatment for severe epilepsy in which surgeons sever the corpus callosum—

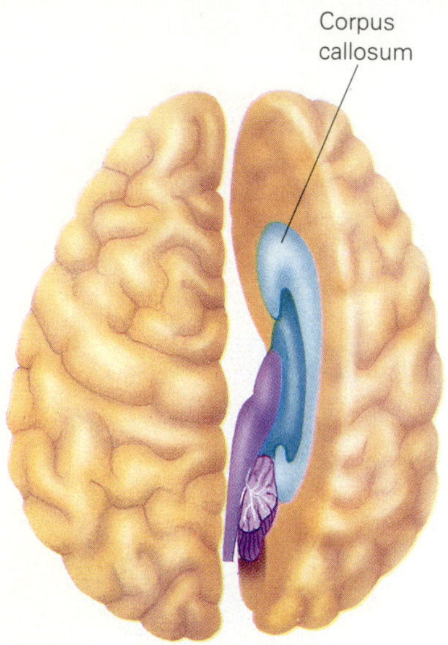

Figure 3.22 The Corpus Callosum
The corpus callosum is a massive network of nerve fibers that channels information between the two hemispheres. Severing the corpus callosum impairs this communication process.

the bundle of about 200 million nerve fibers that transfers information back and forth between the two hemispheres (see **Figure 3.22**). The goal of this surgery is to prevent the violent electrical rhythms that accompany epileptic seizures from crossing between the hemispheres (Wilson et al., 1977). The operation is usually successful, and a patient's subsequent behavior in most circumstances appears normal. Patients who undergo this type of surgery are often referred to as *split-brain* patients.

To test the capabilities of the separated hemispheres of epileptic patients, **Roger Sperry** (1968) and **Michael Gazzaniga** (1970) devised situations that could allow visual information to be presented separately to each hemisphere. Sperry and Gazzaniga's methodology relies on the anatomy of the visual system (see **Figure 3.23**). For each eye, information from the *right visual field* goes to the left hemisphere, and information from the *left visual field* goes to the right hemisphere. Ordinarily, information arriving from both hemispheres is shared very quickly across the corpus callosum. But because

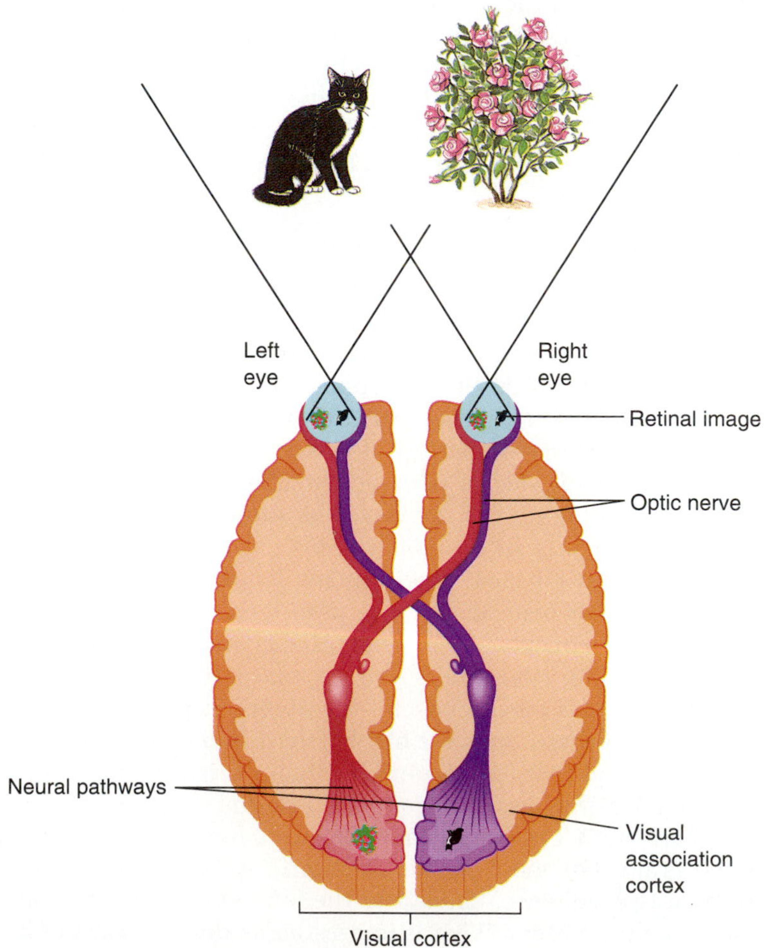

Figure 3.23 The Neural Pathways for Visual Information
The neural pathways for visual information coming from the inside portions of each eye cross from one side of the brain to the other at the corpus callosum. The pathways carrying information from the outside portions of each eye do not cross over. The ultimate destination of all visual information is the visual cortex. Severing the corpus callosum prevents information selectively displayed in the right visual field from entering the left hemisphere, and left visual field information cannot enter the right hemisphere.

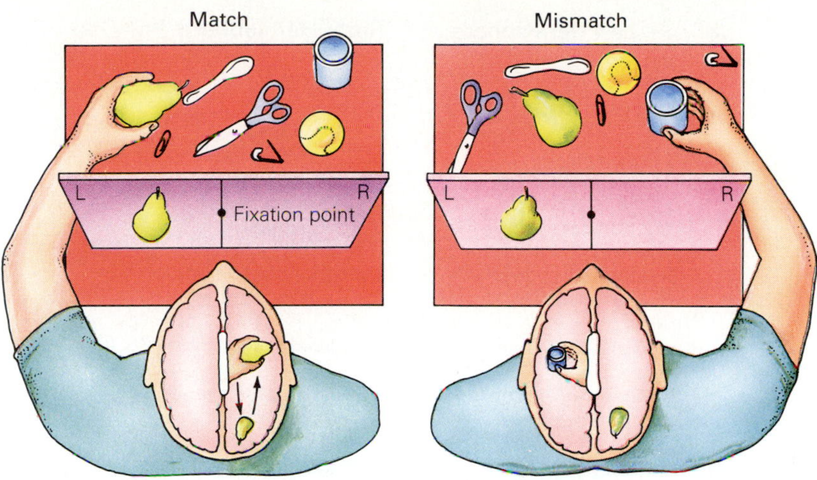

Figure 3.24 Coordination Between Eye and Hand

Coordination between eye and hand is normal if a split-brain patient uses the left hand to find and match an object that appears in the left visual field, because both are registered in the right hemisphere. However, when asked to use the right hand to match an object seen in the left visual field, the patient cannot do so, because sensory messages from the right hand are going to the left cerebral hemisphere, and there is no longer a connection between the two hemispheres. Here the cup is misperceived as matching the pear.

these pathways have been severed in split-brain patients, information presented to the right or left visual field may remain only in the left or right hemisphere (see **Figure 3.24**).

The researchers found that the left hemisphere was superior to the right hemisphere in problems involving language or requiring logic and sequential or analytic processing of concepts (see **Figure 3.25**). The left hemisphere could "talk back" to the researchers, while the right hemisphere could not. Communication with the right hemisphere was achieved by confronting it with manual tasks involving identification, matching, or assembly of objects—tasks that did not require the use of words. The right hemisphere turned out to be better than the left at solving problems involving spatial relationships and at pattern recognition. However, it could only add up to 10 and was about at the level of a 2-year-old in the use and comprehension of word combinations.

Sperry and Gazzaniga found that the brain's left hemisphere was superior to the right in solving problems involving language, logic, and sequential or analytic processing of concepts.

The two hemispheres also seemed to have different "styles" for processing the same information. For example, on matching tasks, the left hemisphere matched objects *analytically* and verbally—by similarity in function. The right hemisphere matched things *holistically*—because they looked alike or fit together to form a whole pattern. Thus, when pictures of a hat, a knife, and a fork were presented only to the left hemisphere, a split-brain subject who was asked to match the correct one with a picture of cake on a plate would report, "You eat cake with a fork and knife." When the test stimuli were presented to the right hemisphere, the same patient might match the hat with the cake, since the items were similar in shape (Levy & Trevarthen, 1976).

The brain is designed to function as a whole with a vast, precise communication network integrating both hemispheres. When the hemispheres are disconnected, the result is two separate brains and a *duality of consciousness.* Consider the following demonstration of a split-brain subject using his

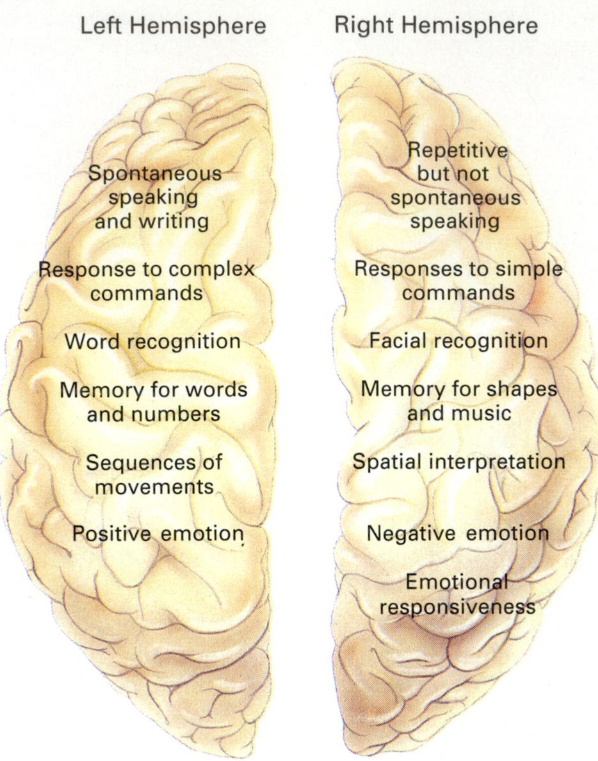

Figure 3.25 Specialization of the Cerebral Hemispheres

left half brain to account for the activity of his left hand, which was being guided by his right half brain:

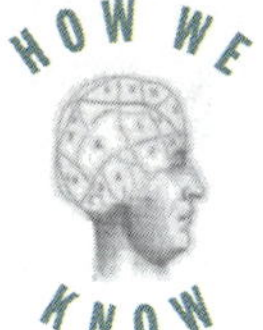

> A snow scene was presented to the right hemisphere and a picture of a chicken claw was simultaneously presented to the left hemisphere. The subject selected, from an array of objects, those that "went with" each of the two scenes. With his right hand, the patient pointed to a chicken head; with his left hand he pointed to a shovel. The patient reported that the shovel was needed to clean out the chicken shed (rather than to shovel snow). Since the left brain was not privy to what the right brain "saw" because of the severed corpus callosum, it needed to explain why the left hand was pointing at a shovel when the only picture the left hemisphere was aware of seeing was a chicken claw. The left brain's cognitive system provided a theory to make sense of the behavior of different parts of its body. It appears that the dominant left hemisphere interprets the meaning of overt behaviors, emotional responses, and the experiences of the right hemisphere (Gazzaniga, 1985).

We must be cautious, however, about generalizing such findings from split-brain patients into a basic view of the way that normal brains function. We can never be sure, first of all, that the severe epilepsy that made the split-brain operation necessary did not disrupt other normal patterns of function within the brain. It is important to verify some of the same patterns with individuals whose brains are intact. Secondly, we must not confuse what a hemisphere might "prefer" to do—for example, process analytically or holistically—and what the hemisphere has the potential to do (Trope et al., 1992). Finally, we must acknowledge that, even for split-brain patients, there are large individual differences in the extent and patterning of lateralization (Gazzaniga, 1987; Trope et al., 1992). In the next section we will describe such individual differences—and in individuals who, like most of you, have not undergone split-brain surgery.

Individual Differences in the Lateralization of Function

When we introduced the lateralization of speech, we also introduced a first individual difference: left-handers are somewhat more likely to have speech dominated by their right hemisphere, or equally present in both hemispheres. In this section we explore other individual differences. We can make some predictions about lateralization depending on whether you are male or female; other differences appear to relate more purely to individual style.

Although each hemisphere generally specializes in certain functions, individual differences in the lateralization of function are also significant.

Sex Differences

We know from the section on heredity that there are genetic differences between males and females. Are there also general differences in the way that male and female brains carry out their functions (Breedlove, 1994)? We can begin to answer such a question by measuring the performance of newborn girls and boys on tests that enable us to detect a left- or right-hemisphere advantage. **Mary Grattan** and her colleagues (1992) performed a number of such tests on children who were roughly two days old. The reflexes of each child—the child's reflex response, for example, to close his or her hand over the experimenter's finger—was measured on both the left and the right side of the body. The experimenters' logic was that a stronger or more coordinated response on one side or the other would reflect an innate asymmetry in the potential of the two hemispheres. In general, Grattan and her associate found that children were right-biased, suggesting an advantage for the left hemisphere. This general conclusion, however, was modified somewhat by evidence of sex differences. For one particular class of reflexes—those that involve the legs and feet—the girls remained right-biased but many of the boys were left-biased. Why might this be? The researchers acknowledge the possibility that this difference might be short-lived—because, on average, boys are neurologically less developed at birth than girls. The researchers were more inclined, however, to believe that this difference is an early sign of the sorts of asymmetries that have been documented for adult males and females.

Let us focus on one such asymmetry described by Canadian psychologist **Doreen Kimura.** Kimura (1983, 1987) reported that men are more likely to

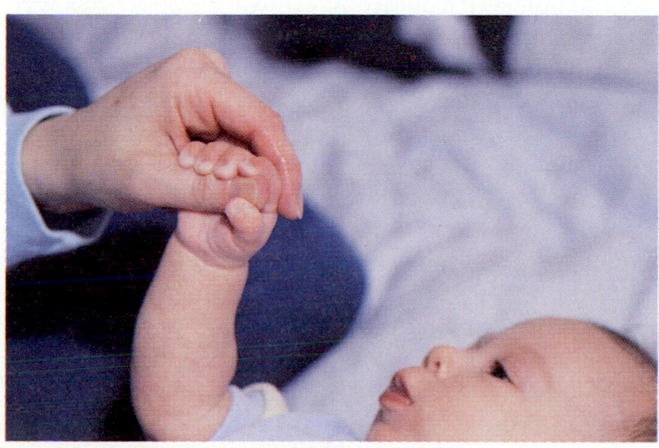

Do most babies show hemispheric asymmetries from birth?

suffer from language disorders (*aphasias*) following injury to their left hemispheres then are women. Why might that be true? One hypothesis would be that women tend to have language functions represented *bilaterally*—that is, in both sides of the brain. If speech, let's say, were present in both hemispheres, then an injury to just one hemisphere would be less likely to cause disruptions. But that can't be right—men are, in fact, more likely to be left-handers than are women, which means that men, not women, are more likely to have language represented in the right hemisphere or bilaterally. What, then, explains the difference in the incidence of aphasias? Kimura's data suggest that speech is organized differently *within* the left hemispheres of men and women. For men, aphasias may result from damage to virtually all major cortical speech areas. For women, aphasias result from damage only to a subset of those. Comparable damage, therefore, will cause an aphasia in a man but not in a woman. Why the left hemisphere is organized differently for men and women is not exactly clear, although Kimura believes that hormonal influences during brain development may play a role. Whatever the origin of the differences, we have seen that the brains of males and females are identical neither at birth nor later in life.

The research of Grattan and of Kimura suggests that there are differences in the way male and female brains are organized with regard to speech.

Individual Styles in Lateralization

Even against this background of general differences between the brains of men and women, there is still room for further variation: each individual has some distinctive pattern for distributing functions across the two hemispheres. To make this point, we turn to consideration of *face recognition.* It will not surprise you to learn that faces can be quite hard to recognize. They consist of pretty much the same basic parts in the same basic arrangement—to discriminate among faces, you must attend to much smaller details than just the presence of a couple of eyes, a nose, a mouth, and so on (Diamond & Carey, 1986). Because face recognition seems so difficult, researchers at first wondered whether there was neural architecture specially devoted to carrying out this function. Evidence suggests, however, that face recognition requires a general ability to make distinctions between configurations of features—you might, for example, recognize one friend because her eyes are particularly close together or another because he has a large distance between his nose and mouth.

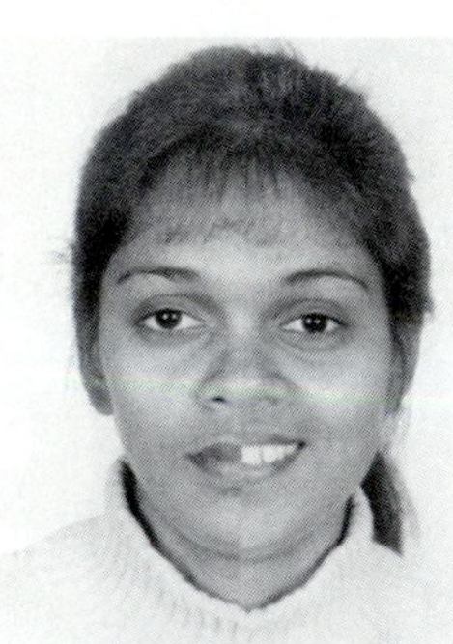

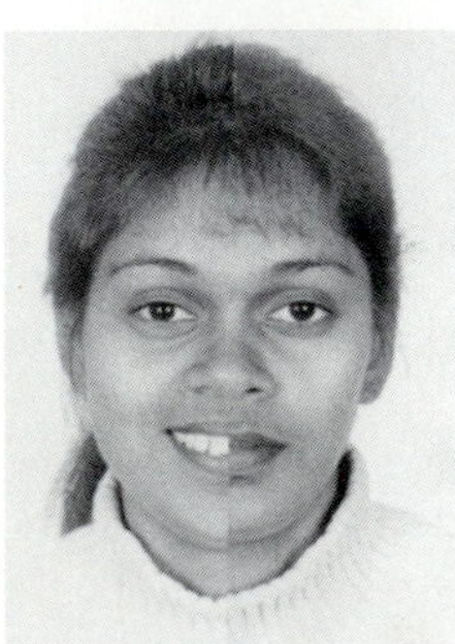

Figure 3.26 An Item Modeled on the Chimeric Faces Task
Which of these faces looks happier?

Researchers have developed a method to show that normal individuals most often show an asymmetry across hemispheres for this type of configural processing (Levy et al., 1983). **Figure 3.26** gives an example of a pair of *chimeric faces.* Each face is made up of the identical smiling and neutral halves; they are just mirror reversed. The question is, Which composite do you think looks happier? If you are like most viewers, you will choose the face for which the happy side is on the left. Because information from the left side of the picture ends up in the right hemisphere, this is evidence that the right hemisphere plays a stronger role in recognition of facial expression—for most viewers. But you need not be in the category of "most viewers"—some people do not show this right hemisphere preference. This simple task, therefore, can be used to demonstrate individual differences—for intact individuals—in the lateralization of function.

We can demonstrate the importance of individual differences with a second method. **Figure 3.27** shows an experimental paradigm in which two different stimuli are projected simultaneously to the right and left visual fields. A subject's task is to recognize or report accurately everything that was presented. For faces, once again, most people are more accurate overall in recognizing the stimuli presented to the left visual field—which are processed first in the right hemisphere. (Recall that because the corpus callosum is intact, information will be shared, after a very brief interval, between both

A. Presentation

B. Test Array

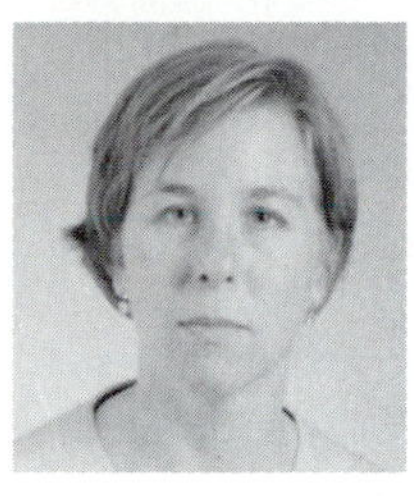

Figure 3.27 Test for Hemispheric Asymmetries in Face Recognition
*(A) Subjects must report the fixation symbol (in this case the *) and then try to recognize the faces in the test array.*
(B) Subjects use this array to indicate which faces they saw in the initial presentation. The average *subject gives more correct responses for faces that were initially localized to the right hemisphere (based on Kim & Levine, 1992).*

hemispheres.) Against this norm, however, there are subjects who fail to show a left visual field advantage, or who even show an advantage for the right visual field. Whatever the preference—left, neutral, or right—it tends to generalize to other types of mental tasks: individuals possess "characteristic perceptual asymmetries" such that their brains have a characteristic, consistent way of distributing tasks to the two hemispheres (Kim & Levine, 1992). It is quite possible, therefore, that you and your best friend would use different patterns of brain activity to recognize each other's faces! This is strong evidence for biological roots for your uniqueness.

Research with tasks requiring face recognition indicates that there are individual differences in cerebral lateralization.

YOUR RESPONSIVE BRAIN

In this chapter we have peeked at a small bit of the marvelous 3-pound universe that is your brain. It is one thing to recognize that the brain controls behavior and your mental processes, but quite another to understand *how* the brain serves all those functions that you take for granted when it operates normally—and what happens when it doesn't. Neuroscientists are engaged in the fascinating quest to understand the interplay between brain, hormones, behavior, experience, and environment.

Much new research, across a wide range of species, is demonstrating that the brain is a *dynamic* system capable of changing itself—both its functions and its physical structure—in response to various kinds of stimulation and

The Biological Roots of Sexuality

In this chapter we have emphasized that individual differences may arise by virtue of nature rather than nurture. In the domain of human sexuality, this claim has sparked controversy centering on one question: Are there genetic or brain differences that *cause* individuals to be heterosexual or homosexual? We will refer to some of your new knowledge to begin to answer this question.

How can we tease apart the genetic and environmental contributions to the determination of sexual orientation? One approach is to compare the concordance rates of sexual preference in *monozygotic* (*MZ*) twins (those who are genetically identical) and *dizygotic* (*DZ*) twins (those who, like siblings, share only half their genes). When both members of a pair of twins have the same orientation—homosexual or heterosexual—they are concordant. If one twin is homosexual and the other is heterosexual, they are discordant. Studies of both gay men and lesbians have demonstrated considerably higher concordance rates for MZ than for DZ twins (Bailey & Pillard, 1991; Bailey et al., 1993). In these studies, the experimenters searched out individual gay or lesbian twins and then obtained information from them about the sexual orientation of their co-twins or other siblings. The results were startling. Among women, 48 percent of MZ twins were both lesbians, compared with 16 percent of DZ twins (Bailey et al., 1993). Among men, 52 percent of MZ twins were both gay, compared with 22 percent DZ twins (Bailey & Pillard, 1991). Although MZ twins may also be reared in more similar environments than DZ twins—they may be treated more similarly by their parents—this pattern strongly suggests that sexuality may, in part, be genetically determined.

With this knowledge in hand, researchers have started to search for the gene sequences that might control the emergence of homosexuality or heterosexuality. Recall that males receive an X chromosome from their mothers and a Y chromosome from their fathers. Dean Hamer and his colleagues have demonstrated that gay men are likely to have more gay relatives in their mother's family tree than in their father's—implicating the X chromosome as a likely site for genetic material related to sexual orientation (Hamer et al., 1993). These researchers were able to identify a region of the chromosome that was common for the majority of pairs of gay brothers.

A different approach to the search for the biological roots of sexuality is to compare the actual brain structures relevant to the expression of sexuality in homosexuals and in heterosexuals. Simon LeVay (1991, 1993) focused his attention on the hypothalamus. You have already learned that the hypothalamus is a part of the limbic system that regulates sexual arousal. LeVay performed autopsies on the brains of homosexual men and heterosexual men and women. He prepared slices of brain tissue in such a way that he was able to measure the size of relevant nuclei (small bundles of neurons) in the hypothalamus. LeVay discovered that one nucleus, known as *INAH 3,* was two to three times bigger in heterosexual men than in heterosexual women. This area was also two to three times bigger in heterosexual men than in homosexual men. Homosexual men and heterosexual women did not differ. LeVay acknowledged that "correlation is not causation" (see Chapter 2), but he argued, even so, that the similar size of INAH 3 in gay men and straight women could explain the similarity in their choices of sexual partners. Does your hypothalamus determine your sexual destiny? Further research may strengthen or weaken the case, but it seems clear that some aspects of homosexuality and heterosexuality emerge in response to purely biological forces (Gladue, 1994).

environmental challenges (Fernald, 1984; R. Sapolsky, 1990). We are thus led to a new perspective about the nature of the brain. In addition to the well-known *behaving brain,* which controls behavior, there is the *responsive brain,* which is changed by the behavior it generates and by environmental stimulation. This capacity for its own internal modification makes the complex human brain the most dynamic, responsive system of all (Rosenzweig, 1984b).

Recapping Main Points

Heredity and Behavior

Species originate and change over time because of natural selection. In the evolution of humans, bipedalism and encephalization were responsible for subsequent advances, including language and culture. The basic unit of heredity is the gene. Genes determine the range of effects that environmental factors can have in influencing the expression of phenotypic traits.

Biology and Behavior

Neuroscientists use five methods to research the relation between brain and behavior: studying brain-damaged patients, producing lesions at specific brain sites, electrically stimulating the brain, recording brain activity, and scanning the brain with computerized devices.

The brain and the spinal cord make up the central nervous system (CNS). The peripheral nervous system (PNS) is composed of all neurons connecting the CNS to the body. The PNS consists of the somatic nervous system, which regulates the body's skeletal muscles, and the autonomic nervous system (ANS), which regulates life-support processes. The sympathetic division of the ANS is active during stress. The parasympathetic division operates under routine circumstances. The brain consists of three integrated layers: central core, limbic system, and cerebral cortex. The central core is responsible for breathing, digestion, and heart rate. The limbic system is involved in long-term memory, aggression, eating, drinking, and sexual behavior. The cerebral cortex controls higher mental functions.

The endocrine system produces and secretes hormones into the bloodstream. Hormones help regulate growth, primary and secondary sexual characteristics, metabolism, digestion, and arousal. The hypothalamus controls the endocrine system by stimulating the pituitary gland. The pituitary gland then secretes the appropriate hormone to stimulate one or more of the other endocrine glands.

The Nervous System in Action

The neuron, the basic unit of the nervous system, receives, processes, and relays information to other cells, glands, and muscles. Neurons relay information in a fixed direction from the dendrites through the cell body (soma) to the axon to the terminal buttons. Sensory neurons receive messages from specialized receptor cells and send them toward the CNS. Motor neurons channel messages away from the CNS to muscles and glands. Interneurons relay information from sensory neurons to other interneurons or to motor neurons.

Information passes from dendrites to the soma in the form of graded potentials. Once the summation of graded potentials exceeds a specific threshold, an action potential is sent along the axon to the terminal buttons. Action potentials are created when the opening of ion channels allows an exchange of positive and negative ions across the cell membrane. Neurotransmitters are released into the synaptic gap between neurons. Once across the gap, they lodge in the receptor molecules of the postsynaptic membrane. Whether these neurotransmitters excite or inhibit the membrane depends on the nature of the receptor molecule.

Hemispheric Specialization and Individual Differences

The two hemispheres of the brain are specialized for different functions. For example, most individuals have speech localized in the left hemisphere and face recognition localized in the right hemisphere. However, individual differences can modify these general conclusions. Males and females have somewhat different patterns of lateralization. Individuals also have different characteristic distributions of functions to their two hemispheres.

The behaving brain initiates and controls behavior. The responsive brain's functions and structure are changed by stimulation from the environment and from its own behavior.

Resources

Carlson, N. R. (1992). *Foundations of physiological psychology* (2nd ed.). Boston: Allyn and Bacon. A well-written introduction to the field of physiological psychology.

Coren, S. (1990). *Left-handedness: Behavioral implications and anomalies.* New York: Elsevier.

Epstein, A. N., & Morrison, A. (Eds.). (1992). *Progress in psychobiology and physiological psychology.* San Diego: Academic Press.

Gazzaniga, M. S. (1985). *The social brain.* New York: Basic Books. A personalized account of research on split-brain patients by a leading researcher in the field.

Sacks, O. (1985). *The man who mistook his wife for a hat and other clinical tales.* New York: Harper & Row. A fascinating book about individuals with various neurological and neuropsychological problems.

4

Mind, Consciousness, and Alternate States

We'd like you to take a moment to pick a number between one and ten. Now take a moment to reflect on where that number came from *and where it* arrived. *Although you obviously have information about the numbers one to ten stored in your brain, it is very unlikely that you had a number "in mind" just as you were sitting down to read your psychology text. Therefore, you might feel comfortable saying that the number arrived in your* consciousness*—and that it came from some part of your brain that was not then conscious. But* how *did your particular number come to mind? Did you actually consider several different numbers? That is, were you consciously aware of making a choice? Or did a single number somehow just emerge—by virtue of some set of unconscious operations—into your consciousness?*

If you have introspected carefully about the simple act of picking a number between one and ten, you already have an intuitive grasp of the major topics of Chapter 4. We will address a series of questions: What is ordinary conscious awareness? What determines the contents of your consciousness? Why do you need consciousness? Can unconscious *mental events really influence your thoughts, emotions, and behavior? How does consciousness change over the course of a day–night cycle, and how can you intentionally alter your state of consciousness? The budding psychologist in you should also want to know how aspects of mind can be studied scientifically. How can you externalize the internal, make public the private, and measure precisely subjective experiences?*

Our analysis will begin with an exploration of the content and function of consciousness. Along the way, we will turn our spotlight on the human mind. *We will help you understand an age-old problem for philosophers, psychologists, and neuroscientists: What is the relationship between brain and mind? Then we will shift to the regular mental changes you all experience during daydreaming, fantasizing, sleeping, and night dreaming. Finally, we will look at how consciousness is altered dramatically by hypnosis, meditation, religious rituals, and drugs.*

THE CONTENTS OF CONSCIOUSNESS

We must start by admitting that the term **consciousness** is ambiguous. We can use the term to refer to a general state of mind *or* to its specific contents: sometimes you say you were "conscious" in contrast to being "unconscious" (for example, being under anesthesia or asleep); at other times, you say you were conscious—*aware*—of certain information or actions. There is, in fact, a certain consistency here—to be conscious of any particular information, you must be conscious. (To be aware, you must be awake!) In this chapter, when we speak of the *contents* of consciousness, we mean exactly that body of information at the intersection of the two types of consciousness.

Awareness and Consciousness

Some of the earliest research in psychology concerned the contents of consciousness. As psychology gradually diverged from philosophy in the 1800s, it became the science of the mind. Wundt and Titchener used introspection to explore the contents of the conscious mind, and William James observed his own stream of consciousness (see Chapter 1). In fact, James asserted on the very first page of his 1890 classic text that "psychology [is] the description and explanation of 'consciousness' as such."

Ordinary waking consciousness includes your perceptions, thoughts, feelings, images, and desires at a given moment—all the mental activity on which you are focusing your attention. You are conscious of both what you are doing and also of the fact that you are doing it. At times, you are conscious of the realization that others are observing, evaluating, and reacting to what you are doing. A *sense of self* comes out of the experience of watching yourself from this privileged "insider" position. Taken together, these various mental activities form the contents of consciousness—all the experiences you are consciously aware of at a particular time.

Consciousness involves all the activity of the mind, the monitoring of this activity, and having a sense of self.

We can define, more formally, three different levels of consciousness. They correspond roughly to (1) a basic level, an awareness of the inner and outer world; (2) a second level, a reflection on what you are aware of; and (3) a top level, an awareness of yourself as a conscious, reflective individual (Hilgard, 1980; Natsoulas, 1981; Tulving, 1985). At the basic level, consciousness is the awareness that you are perceiving and reacting to available perceptual information. At the second level, consciousness relies on symbolic knowledge to free you from the constraints of real objects and present events. At this level, you can contemplate and manipulate objects in their absence; visualize new forms and uses for the familiar; plan utopias; and invent new products. The top level of consciousness is **self-awareness**, cognizance (or awareness) that personally experienced events have an *autobiographical* character. Self-awareness gives you your sense of personal history and identity. At this level of consciousness, if you have personally experienced a fairly orderly, predictable world, you come to expect it, and this expectation equips you to choose the best present actions and plans for the future (Lachman & Naus, 1984).

Personal history and identity are experienced through self-awareness.

A fascinating illustration of the *absence* of self-awareness is the case of patient N. N., who suffered a head injury to the frontal lobes of his cortex. Recall from Chapter 3 that the frontal lobes are essential for planning and thus for your sense of time perspective:

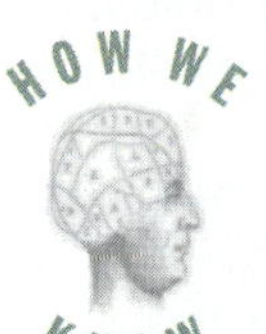

> N. N. is conscious, remembers many things about the world, can solve problems in a flexible, symbolic way, has good language skills and general knowledge. Although he has a sense of clock time, he has no sense of personal time perspective—no awareness of his own autobiography over time. He does not know what he did yesterday or what he will do tomorrow. When asked questions about his activities, he reports his mind is blank—he feels as if he is looking for a piece of furniture in an empty room. He lives in a state of "permanent present" without any anxiety over his inability to experience an awareness of his relationship to past and future events (Tulving, 1985).

Accessibility to Consciousness

We have defined the general types of information that *might* be conscious, but what determines what *is* conscious right now? Were you, for example, aware of your heartbeat just now? Probably not; its control is part of *nonconscious processes.* Were you thinking about your last vacation, or about the author of *Hamlet*? Again, probably not; control of such thoughts are part of *preconscious memories.* Were you aware of background noises, such as a clock ticking, traffic, and a fluorescent light buzzing? You couldn't be and still pay full

Certain material, such as nonconscious processes, preconscious memories, and unattended information, is not conscious but can be brought to consciousness.

attention to the meaning of the material in this chapter, because awareness of nonrelevant stimuli is part of *unattended information.* Finally, there may be types of information that are *unconscious*—not readily accessible to conscious awareness—such as the set of grammatical rules that enable you to understand this sentence. Let's examine each of these types of awareness.

Nonconscious Processes

There is a range of **nonconscious** bodily activities that rarely, if ever, impinge on consciousness. An example of nonconscious processes at work is the regulation of blood pressure. Your nervous system monitors physiological information to detect and act on changes continually, without your awareness. At certain times, some ordinarily nonconscious activities can be made conscious: you can, for example, choose to exercise conscious control over your pattern of breathing. Even so, your nervous system takes care of many important functions without requiring conscious resources.

Preconscious Memories

Memories accessible to consciousness only after something calls your attention to them are known as **preconscious memories.** The storehouse of memory is filled with an incredible amount of information, such as your general knowledge of language, sports, or geography and recollections of your personally experienced events. Preconscious memories function silently in the background of your mind until a situation arises in which they are consciously necessary (as when we asked you to pick a number between one and ten).

Unattended Information

At any given time, you are surrounded by a vast amount of stimulation. You can focus your *attention* only on a small part of it; and what you focus on, in combination with the memories it evokes, will determine, to a large extent, what is in consciousness. Nevertheless, you often have an *unconscious representation* of the information that is not in the focus of your attention. For example, at a noisy party, you might focus attention on your attractive date and remain seemingly oblivious to a nearby conversation—until you overhear your name mentioned. Suddenly you are aware that you must have been monitoring the conversation—in some unconscious way—to detect that special signal amid the noise. (We will discuss attention further in Chapter 8.)

At any given time, thoughts about your job, your parents, or your hungry pet may flow below the level of consciousness until something occurs to focus your attention on one of these topics.

The Unconscious

You typically recognize the existence of *unconscious* information when you cannot explain all your behaviors by virtue of forces that can be made conscious. An initial theory of unconscious forces was developed by **Sigmund Freud,** who argued that certain life experiences—traumatic memories and taboo desires—are sufficiently threatening that your psychological apparatus permanently banishes them from consciousness. Freud believed that when the content of original, unacceptable ideas or motives is *repressed*—put out of consciousness—the strong feelings associated with the thoughts still remain and influence behavior. We will revisit this idea when we discuss the origin of your unique personality in Chapter 14.

Sigmund Freud suggested that repressed memories of traumatic events or taboo desires become part of the unconscious, but many psychologists believe the unconscious also includes thoughts that are not of such negative origin.

Many psychologists now use the term *unconscious* to refer to information and processes that are more benign than the types of thoughts Freud suggested must be repressed (Greenwald, 1992; Kihlstrom et al., 1992). Consider this sentence (Baars, 1988):

> The ship sailed past the harbor sank.

Did you find that difficult to understand? It's likely that the unconscious processes that enable you to recover the grammatical structure of the sentence initially interpreted "sailed" as the main verb of the sentence rather than as the start of a reduced relative clause. Now consider the same sentence in a longer context:

> A small part of Napoleon's fleet tried to run the English blockade at the entrance to the harbor. Two ships, a sloop and a frigate, ran straight for the harbor while a third ship tried to sail *past* the harbor in order to draw enemy fire. The ship sailed past the harbor sank.

Did you find the sentence easier to understand in this context? If you did, it's because unconscious adjustments were made in your language comprehension processes.

With this example, we demonstrate that information that *cannot* be conscious, such as your expectations for the structure of a sentence, can affect your behavior—in this case, the ease with which you understood the sentence. We have, thus, shifted subtly from discussing the contents of consciousness to discussing the function of consciousness. Before we take up that topic in detail, however, we will briefly describe two ways in which just the contents of consciousness can be studied.

Studying the Contents of Consciousness

To study consciousness, researchers have had to devise methodologies to make deeply private experiences overtly measurable. One method is a new variation on Wundt and Titchener's practice of *introspection.* Subjects are asked to speak aloud as they work through a variety of complex tasks. They report, in as much detail as possible, the sequence of thoughts they experience while they complete the tasks. The subjects' reports, called **think-aloud protocols,** are used to document the mental strategies and representations of knowledge that the subjects employ to do the task. These protocols also allow researchers to analyze the discrepancies between task performance and awareness of how it is carried out (Ericsson & Simon, 1993; Newell & Simon, 1972).

In the **experience-sampling** method, subjects wearing electronic pagers are asked to write down or describe to a portable tape recorder what they are feeling and thinking whenever the pager signals. A radio transmitter activates the pager at various random times each day for a week or more (Hurlburt, 1979). Whenever the pager signals, subjects may also be asked to respond to questions, such as "How well were you concentrating?" In this way, researchers can keep a running record of subjects' thoughts, awareness, and focuses of attention as they go about their everyday lives (Csikszentmihalyi, 1990). From such reports, researchers can piece together a descriptive account of the typical contents of consciousness.

Psychologists use think-aloud protocols and experience sampling to study the contents of consciousness.

THE FUNCTIONS OF CONSCIOUSNESS

To understand the functions of consciousness, you must understand the forces that control your behavior. Early human ancestors traced the causes of their actions to their *anima,* or inner life force, and the operation of outer spiritual forces, both divine and demonic, that they believed existed in nature. In these *animistic* explanations of behavior, the same kinds of spiritual forces guided all creatures of nature. An individual's spirit, or soul, was assumed to be separate from the body, doing all those things that make people human: seeing, talking, remembering, and feeling. In modern times, philosophers have replaced the concept of spirit with the concepts of consciousness and mind. Before you can begin to understand these modern concepts, however, we still need to define the relationship between the body and the mind.

THE MIND-BODY PROBLEM

Classical Conceptions of Body and Mind

The problem of the relationship between the mind and the brain has long perplexed serious thinkers and defied easy solutions. In the Western tradition, Plato was one of the first Greek philosophers to try to distinguish between notions of mind and body. In his view, the mind and its mental processes were absolutely distinct from the physical aspects of body and brain. Plato believed that the mind went beyond the directly sensed physical world to consider abstractions and "ideal realities," and he speculated that the mind survived the death of the body. Plato's view became known as dualism. **Dualism** proposes that the mind is fundamentally different from and independent of the brain: the mind and brain are dual aspects of human nature.

With the rise of the Roman Empire, consideration of such matters lay dormant for several hundred years. It was not until the Renaissance that a renewed appreciation for scientific, rational inquiry sparked efforts to understand the nature of the mind. As we explained in Chapter 3, it was in the 1600s that the French philosopher René Descartes advanced the radical new theory that the body was an "animal machine." In this *mechanistic approach,* animal behaviors and some basic human behaviors are seen as reflex reactions to physical energies impinging on the senses. It follows from Descartes's theory that, as a machine, the body can't be subject to moral principles. Therefore, other human behaviors—reasoning, decision making, and thinking about oneself, for example—must be based on the operation of the soul, or mind. Descartes's dualistic view enabled him to resolve the dilemmas he faced as a devoutly religious Catholic (who believed in the immortal soul), a rational thinker (who believed in the mortal mind), and a scientific observer (who believed in the mechanistic view of perception and reflex actions).

The relationship of body to mind has also been an active part of the philosophy of non-Western cultures. Some ancient Chinese philosophers, for example, did not believe in a mind–body dualism; there was no mind, only the organic body. Mental and physical activities were attributed to the actions of the internal organs, just as mental disorders and physical ailments were the products of imbalances in these organs. Treatment for all ailments consisted of herbal drugs and acupuncture to alter the functioning of specific internal organs and return the person to a holistic balance. This organic outlook is deeply ingrained in Chinese thought and in the thinking of many other East Asian cultures.

Buddhism distinguishes between thinking, or human reasoning, and mind, or universal wisdom. Individuals may experience mind through the regular practice of silent, motionless meditation.

Indian views of the mind are diametrically different. According to the teachings of Buddhism, the visible universe is an illusion of the senses; the world is nothing but mind; and the mind of the individual is part of the collective, universal mind. Excessive mental activity distracts one from focusing on inner experience and allowing the mind to rise above sensory experience. Meditation is a lifelong exercise in learning how to remove the mind from distractions and illusions, allowing it to roam freely and discover wisdom. To become an enlightened being requires controlling bodily yearnings, stopping the ordinary experiences of the senses and mind, and discovering how to see things in their true light.

The Emergence of Modern Theories

Scholars in the modern era have sought to bring research to bear on these different philosophies of mind. There is now a reasonable consensus in favor of the philosophical opponent to dualism, **monism,** which proposes that mind and brain are one—that mental phenomena are nothing but the products of the brain. Monists contend that mind and its mental states are reducible, in principle, to brain states—that is, all thought and action have a physical, material base (Churchland, 1986; Dennett, 1991).

Our discussion of the brain in Chapter 3 was intended, in part, to provide evidence in favor of a monist position. Recall, for example, that Wilder Penfield was able to touch his electrode to portions of his patients' brains and bring memories into consciousness. Recall, similarly, that the patient H. M. suffered brain damage that impaired his conscious access to new information: he can learn certain new skills, but he is not aware that he has learned those skills. Both of these types of evidence support the belief that the experience of consciousness resides in the brain.

Both Western and non-Western philosophers have pondered the relationship between the mind and the body, producing the competing theories of dualism and monism.

The triumph of monism has not, however, eliminated the mystery of the everyday experience of consciousness: What motivated the dualists, after all, was the discontinuity they perceived between physical acts and thoughts—and, in particular, between the mental capabilities of nonhuman animals and those of humans. To fully endorse a monist position, it is necessary to know what is unique about human consciousness and how it evolved.

The mind's ultimate evolutionary breakthrough was the ability of animals to have *symbolic representations* of the outer world and of their own actions—enabling them to remember, plan, predict, and anticipate (Craik, 1943). Instead of merely reacting to stimuli in the physical present or to biological needs, *Homo sapiens* can model the world and imagine how present realities could be transformed into alternative scenarios. The capacity to deal with objective reality in the here and now was expanded by the capacity to bring back lessons from the past (memory) and to imagine future options (foresight). A brain that can deal with both objective and subjective realities needs a mechanism to keep track of the focus of attention. That part of the brain is the *conscious mind.*

Symbolic representation allows you to have conscious awareness of the past, present, and future, and to consider such questions as "Do animals have consciousness?"

But do other animals have consciousness? To answer this question, researchers have begun to study the properties of the "minds" of nonhuman primates. Vervet monkeys, for example, can communicate with each other in

What do chimpanzees know and when do they know it?

a variety of ways (Cheney & Seyfarth, 1990). They make distinct vocalizations to signal the presence of different dangers, such as leopards, eagles, and snakes. These monkeys are able to understand that two acoustically different calls have the same meaning—a *wrr* and a *chutter* both signal the same predator. Even so, vervets appear not to be able to attribute mental states to other vervets: they are not capable of reasoning about what other monkeys might or might not know. This capability appears only in primates a step closer to humans, chimpanzees (Povinelli, 1993). Chimps, unlike monkeys, can modify their behavior when they believe that someone else is in possession of knowledge. For example, chimps experienced a situation in which only one of a pair of experimenters knew under which inverted cup some food was hidden. The second experimenter could only guess where the food was. When the "knowing" and "guessing" experimenters pointed to different cups to indicate the location of the food, the chimps were very likely to choose the same cup as the "knowing" experimenter. Thus researchers are able to see evolution from monkey to chimpanzee to human in the functions of consciousness made possible through evolution of the physical brain.

What forces may have given *mind* survival value? The prominence of *Homo sapiens* among all other creatures may be attributed to the development of human consciousness forged in the crucible of competition with the most hostile force in its evolutionary environment—other humans. The human mind may have evolved as a consequence of the extreme *sociability* of human ancestors, which was perhaps originally a group defense against predators and a means to exploit resources more efficiently. However, close group living then created new demands for cooperative as well as competitive abilities with other humans. Natural selection favored those who could think, plan, and imagine alternative realities that could promote both bonding with kin and victory over adversaries. Those who developed language and tools won the grand prize of survival of the fittest mind—and, fortunately, passed it on (Lewin, 1987).

The Uses of Consciousness

Because consciousness evolved, you should not be surprised that it provides a range of functions that aid in the survival of the species (Baars & McGovern, 1994; Cheney & Seyfarth, 1990; Ornstein, 1991). Consciousness also plays an important role in allowing for the construction of both personal and culturally shared realities.

Aiding Survival

From a biological perspective, consciousness probably evolved because it helped individuals to make sense of environmental information and to use that information in planning the most appropriate and effective actions. Usually you are faced with a sensory-information overload. William James described the massive amount of information that strikes the sensory receptors as a "blooming, buzzing confusion" assailing you from all sides. Consciousness helps you adapt to your environment by making sense of this profusion of confusion in three ways.

First, it reduces the flow of stimulus input by restricting what you notice and what you pay attention to. This *restrictive function* of consciousness tunes out much of the information that is not relevant to your immediate goals and purposes. All that is evaluated as "irrelevant" becomes background *noise* to be ignored while you focus conscious awareness on "relevant" input, the *signal* you wish to process and respond to.

Second, consciousness performs a *selective storage function*. After the stream of all sensory input is perceptually processed into a smaller number of recognizable patterns and categories, consciousness provides a mental storage for those special stimuli you want to analyze, interpret, and act upon (Duncan & Humphreys, 1989; Marcel, 1983).

The third function of consciousness is to make you stop, think, consider alternatives based on past knowledge, and imagine various consequences. This *planning or executive control function* enables you to suppress strong desires when they conflict with moral, ethical, or practical concerns. Without this kind of consciousness, you might try to steal an apple if you were hungry and it was the first food you saw. Because consciousness gives you a broad *time perspective* in which to frame potential actions, you can call upon abstract representations of the past and the future to influence your current decisions. For all these reasons, consciousness gives you great potential for flexible, appropriate responses to the changing demands in your life (Ornstein, 1986b; Rozin, 1976).

Consciousness reduces the flow of stimulus input, determines which stimuli will be stored, and allows you to plan actions in consideration of their consequences.

Personal and Cultural Constructions of Reality

No two people interpret a situation in exactly the same way. Your *personal construction of reality* is your unique interpretation of a current situation based on a broader scheme or model that includes your general knowledge, memories of past experiences, current needs, values, beliefs, and future goals. Each person attends more to certain features of the stimulus environment than to others precisely because his or her personal construction of reality has been formed from a selection of unique inputs. When your personal construction of reality remains relatively stable, your *sense of self*—your consciousness of your self—has continuity over time.

Individual differences in personal constructions of reality are even greater when people have grown up in different cultures, lived in different environments within a culture, or faced different survival tasks. The opposite is also true—because the people of a given culture share many of the same experiences, they often have similar constructions of reality. *Cultural constructions of reality* are ways of thinking about the world that are shared by most members of a particular group of people. When a member of a society develops a personal construction of reality that fits in with the cultural construction, it is affirmed by the culture and, at the same time, it affirms the cultural construction. This mutual affirmation of conscious constructions of reality is known as **consensual validation** (Natsoulas, 1978; Rozin & Fallon, 1987).

What is your unique way of viewing the world around you? Artist David Hockney created this collage entitled George, Blanche, Celia, Albert and Percy, London, Jan. 1983 *from Polaroid photographs.*

Thus you come to accept some interpretations of reality as "true" because most people agree about how to interpret them.

Studying the Functions of Consciousness

Many of the functions of consciousness include implicit comparisons with what remains unconscious. That is, conscious processes often affect or are affected by unconscious processes. To study the functions of consciousness, researchers often study the relationship between conscious and unconscious influences on behavior. Note, once again, that Freud intended the concept of the unconscious to mean something more specific—and less benign—than its usual meaning in experimental psychology. Freud's "discovery" of the unconscious contradicted a long tradition of Western thought. From the time the English philosopher John Locke (1690) wrote his classic text on the mind, *An Essay Concerning Human Understanding,* most thinkers firmly believed that rational beings had access to all the activities of their own minds. Freud's initial hypothesis about the existence of unconscious mental processes was considered outrageous by his contemporaries (Dennett, 1987). Researchers have now developed a variety of ways to demonstrate that Freud was correct in believing that unconscious processes can affect conscious behavior (Greenwald, 1992; Kihlstrom et al., 1992).

For example, researchers have used the *SLIP* (*S*poonerisms of *L*aboratory-*I*nduced *P*redisposition) technique to determine the way in which unconscious forces affect the probability of making a speech error (Baars et al., 1992). The SLIP procedure enables an experimenter to induce slips of the tongue by setting up expectations for certain patterns of sound. Thus, after pronouncing a series of word pairs like *ball doze, bell dark,* and *bean deck,* a subject might read out *barn door* rather than the pair as written, *darn bore.* Experimenters can assess conscious or unconscious influences on the probability of such sound exchanges by altering circumstances external to the task. For instance, male subjects were more likely to make the error *bad shock* (from *shad bock*) when they believed they might receive a painful electric shock sometime during an experiment (Motley & Baars, 1979). Similarly, male subjects who performed the SLIP task in the presence of a provocative female experimenter were more likely to err in producing *good legs* (from *lood gegs*). These results suggest an unconscious contribution to the production of speech errors.

Researchers study the functions of consciousness by inducing speech errors and by putting conscious and unconscious processes in opposition.

Another way to study the relationship between conscious and unconscious processes is by putting them in *opposition* (Kelley & Jacoby, 1993). Consider the experiment presented in **Figure 4.1.** In this situation, subjects are asked to judge a name such as "Adrian Marr" as famous or nonfamous (Jacoby et al., 1989). Prior to making these judgments, subjects read a long list of names aloud (including "Adrian Marr") in circumstances that did not allow them to concentrate all their attention on the names. When they performed the fame judgments, the subjects were warned that all of the names they had read on the earlier list were *not* famous—thus if they came upon a name that they recognized from the list, they should say that the person wasn't famous. Suppose, now, that subjects get to the name "Adrian Marr." If subjects are able to find a conscious memory for this name, they will know that it appeared on the earlier list—and, therefore, they will say that "Adrian Marr" *is not* famous. If they can't find a conscious memory, they might instead have the general feeling that "they've heard this name before" and say that "Adrian Marr" *is* famous. This phenomenon is an opposition between conscious ("Say no!") and unconscious ("Say yes!") processes. In fact, subjects are likely to say that "Adrian Marr" *is* famous, providing evidence that an unconscious memory influences their judgments.

We have seen how the contents and functions of consciousness are defined and studied. We turn now to ordinary and then extraordinary alterations in consciousness.

— 6 5 19 28 11 17 41 12 . . .

ADRIAN MARR

ADRIAN MARR

Phase 1:

The subjects read out loud a computer-presented list of nonfamous names, while at the same time trying to detect sequences of three odd numbers within a list of numbers presented auditorily.

Phase 2:

Subjects are asked to judge a list of names as famous or nonfamous.

They are told that all the names they read previously were nonfamous.

Therefore, if they remember that a name was on the list, they should say **nonfamous:** If they have a conscious memory of the name, they will know it couldn't be famous.

When they say **famous** to a name that was on the list, that must be because the unconscious memory of the name makes it seem familiar.

Subjects often will say **famous,** demonstrating the influence of unconscious memories.

Figure 4.1 The Influence of Unconscious Memories on "Fame" Judgments

EVERYDAY CHANGES IN CONSCIOUSNESS

Watch children stand on their heads or spin around in order to make themselves dizzy and then ask them why they do it. "So everything looks funny." "It feels weird." "To see things tumble around in my head." Answers such as these support the belief that "human beings are born with a drive to experience modes of awareness other than the normal waking one; from very young ages, children experiment with techniques to change consciousness" (Weil, 1977, p. 37). In this section we will look at everyday changes in conscious-

Why do children like to play on merry-go-rounds, swings, and monkey bars?

Consciousness and Memory

What is your idea of what it means to be unconscious? If you have ever had the experience of going under general anesthesia, you probably remember something like "100, 99, 98, 97. . . " and then darkness. When you wake up minutes or hours later, you can't remember anything of the experience—or perhaps you can? Accumulating evidence indicates that many patients who are anesthetized and have no conscious recall of their operation may still hear what is going on during their surgery (Bitner, 1983; Guerra & Aldrete, 1980; Millar & Watkinson, 1983). Your hearing sensitivity appears to remain on alert even under adequate anesthesia. The reasons for this auditory alertness may be deeply rooted in evolutionary history—animals in the open had to respond swiftly to possible danger sounds even when asleep. Whatever the reason, highly specialized cells in the auditory nerve make signals passing along it exceptionally clear and hard to block out with anesthetics. Because of this sensitivity, even casual remarks in the operating room can be dangerous. "I think they can kill people, if you want to know the truth," said a researcher in the department of anesthesiology at a California medical center. "I've seen cardiac arrests during surgery that can't be explained except by comments made around the operating table."

Researchers have explored the possibility that there may be a match between the consciousness of the subject and the consciousness of the memory. John Kihlstrom and his colleagues (1990) recruited 30 patients, who were about to undergo surgery, to participate in a memory study. The patients were told that, while they were under anesthesia, a message would be played to them over a tape recorder. In fact, the tape contained a series of pairs of associated words. In memory experiments, subjects are often given the first word, the *cue word,* of such a pair and asked to produce the second word, the *target word.* In this case, the experimenters wished to see if patients under anesthesia could learn such associations. The subjects were tested both immediately following surgery (after about 90 minutes in the recovery room), and again about two weeks after surgery. Their memory performance on word pairs from the list they had heard was compared with their performance on word pairs from a matched control list.

The first way Kihlstrom et al. assessed learning under anesthesia was by asking the subjects for *explicit*—conscious—memories of the appropriate cue-target pairs. In one test of explicit memory, subjects were given the cue words from both their experimental and control lists and asked to reproduce the targets. In a second test, subjects were shown the full list of cue–target pairs for their experimental and control lists and asked to indicate which of those pairs they had heard while under anesthesia. For these two measures, subjects showed *no differences* on either the immediate or delayed test. Unconscious subjects had failed to create conscious memories.

Performance was different, however, on a test of *implicit* memory. On this third test, subjects were given each cue word (once again from their experimental list or the matched control) and asked simply to report the first word that came to mind. Under these circumstances, on both the immediate and delayed tests, subjects produced reliably more correct responses to the experimental cues than to the neutral cues. Thus only when the subjects were not consciously trying to evoke memories were they able to do so. Unconscious subjects had successfully created unconscious memories.

This study suggests that there can be a dissociation between information that you are aware that you know—explicit memories—and information that you might actually know—implicit memories. It also can provide further clues about the biology of consciousness. Different anesthesias act on different parts of the central nervous system. By charting which types of anesthesias do and do not preserve implicit memory, researchers can develop a detailed model of where memory and consciousness reside in the brain. Note also that subjects can acquire neither explicit nor implicit memories while they are in deep sleep (Wood et al., 1992). In some states of unconsciousness, you are relatively safe from any external information!

ness that are unavoidable, occur naturally, and play important functions in your life.

DAYDREAMING AND FANTASY

Imagine that you have just won millions of dollars in the lottery. What will you do with all your money? Or imagine that it's finals time, and you ace exam after exam—ending up with straight A's and praise from everyone. Or, while we're playing mind games, imagine that the person you find most desirable in the whole world says, "Yes, of course" to your request for lifelong companionship.

You will recognize these suggestions as exercises in **daydreaming**, a mild form of consciousness alteration that involves a shift of attention—spontaneously or intentionally—away from the immediate situation or task to "stimulus independent" thoughts (Singer, 1975). Daydreams may be focused on current concerns or may be more purely fantasy. Daydreaming occurs when people are alone, relaxed, engaged in a boring or routine task, or just about to fall asleep. If you daydream regularly, you are in very good company. In one sample of 240 respondents with some college education, ages 18 to 50, 96 percent reported daydreaming daily. Young adults, ages 18 to 29, reported the most daydreaming; there was a significant decline with age (Singer & McCraven, 1961).

A daydream questionnaire, the Imaginal Processes Inventory, is used to study differences in the kinds of daydreamers. This inventory was developed by **Jerome Singer**, a pioneer in daydreaming research, and his colleague, John Antrobus. It reveals that daydreamers vary in how many vivid, enjoyable daydreams they have regularly, how many of their daydreams are ridden with guilt or fear, and how easily they are distracted from or can maintain attention toward their daydreams (Singer & Antrobus, 1966).

While the daydreaming of a Little Leaguer may serve different functions from that of a major league baseball player, daydreaming is more valuable than previous generations believed.

Surprisingly, sexual and violent fantasies account for only a small percentage of all daydreams. The combined results from many studies show that explicitly sexual daydreams average only about 5 percent of the total, while violent fantasies are even less frequent. In fact, sexual fantasies are most typical *during* sexual activity. The most common fantasy is having sex with someone other than the actual partner. Others include having sex in a more romantic setting, having sex with more than one partner, and forcing a partner to have sex or being forced into sex (Pelletier & Herold, 1983). Men tend to have more reality-based sexual daydreams, whereas women tend more toward purely imaginative situations. In general, sexually explicit fantasies enhance sexual pleasure.

What triggers daydreams? Usually the trigger is a cue from the environment or your own thoughts in the form of words or pictures. The cue automatically activates a mental association with current concerns. Emotionally tinged cues are the most effective in sparking daydreams. However, you may also deliberately initiate daydreams to relieve the tedium of a boring lecture or job or to prepare yourself for a particular task. One study revealed that more than 80 percent of lifeguards and truck drivers daydream at times to ease their boredom at work (Klinger, 1987).

Although most people daydream, experts once considered it to be a bad habit—a sign of laziness, infantile wish fulfillment, or mental failure to separate reality from fantasy. As recently as the middle of the twentieth century, educational psychologists cautioned that children who were permitted to daydream could develop neuroses and even schizophrenia! Today experts believe that daydreaming serves valuable functions and that it is often healthy for children and adults alike (Klinger, 1987). Current research using the experience-sampling method suggests that most daydreams dwell on practical and current concerns, everyday tasks, future goals (trivial or significant), and interpersonal relationships. Daydreaming reminds you to plan for things to come, helps you solve problems, and gives you creative time-outs

Psychologists today view daydreaming as valuable. Earlier, daydreams were thought of as bad habits indulged in by lazy individuals.

from routine mental activities. Sports psychologists often have athletes deliberately daydream as part of visualization training, and soldiers going into battle may prepare themselves by daydreaming about the hated enemy (Keen, 1986). When you fantasize about what might be, you are confronting the complexities of life and working through actual difficulties.

To Sleep, Perchance to Dream

Although daydreams sometimes seem within your conscious control, nighttime dreams are solidly outside ordinary waking consciousness. Every day of your life, you ride on a consciousness roller coaster that careens through alert wakefulness to drowsiness, light sleep, deep sleep, dreaming (which sometimes includes nightmares), light sleep again, near awakeness, and, finally, full alertness once more. A third of your life is spent sleeping, when your muscles are in a state of "benign paralysis" and your brain is humming with varied activity. We begin this section by considering the general biological rhythms of wakefulness and sleeping. We then focus more directly on the physiology of sleeping. Finally, we examine the major mental activity that accompanies sleep—dreaming—and explore the role dreams play in human psychology.

Circadian Rhythms

All creatures are influenced by nature's rhythms of day and night. Humans are attuned to a time cycle known as a **circadian rhythm:** your arousal levels, metabolism, heart rate, body temperature, and hormonal activity ebb and flow according to the ticking of your internal clock (Moore-Ede et al., 1982). For the most part, these human activities reach their peak during the day—usually during the afternoon—and hit their low point at night while you sleep. However, the clock the body uses to measure time is not the same clock you use to keep your daily appointments. Studies of persons who have no access to timekeeping devices suggest that your biological clock tends to run on a schedule closer to 25 hours than to 24.

Changes that cause a mismatch between your biological clock and environmental clocks affect how you feel and act (Moore-Ede, 1993). Perhaps the most dramatic example of how such mismatches arise comes from long-distance air travel. When people fly across time zones, they may experience *jet lag,* a condition whose symptoms include fatigue, irresistible sleepiness, and subsequent unusual sleep-wake schedules. Jet lag occurs because the internal circadian rhythm is out of phase with the normal temporal environment. For example, your body says it's 2 A.M.—and thus is at a low point on many phys-

When does peak productivity occur for you?

iological measures—when local time requires you to act as if it is noon. Jet lag, a special problem for flight crews, is responsible for pilot errors that cause airplane accidents (Coleman, 1986).

What variables influence jet lag? The direction of travel and the number of time zones passed through are the most important variables. Traveling eastbound creates greater jet lag than does westbound flight, since your biological clock can be more readily extended than shortened, as required on eastbound trips (it is easier to stay awake longer than it is to fall asleep sooner). When healthy volunteer subjects were flown back and forth between Europe and the United States, their peak performance on standard tasks was reached within two to four days after westbound flights but nine days after eastbound travel (Klein & Wegmann, 1974).

The Technology of Sleep and Dreams

About a third of your circadian rhythm is devoted to that period of quiescence called sleep. Most of what is known about sleep concerns the electrical activities of the brain. The methodological breakthrough for the study of sleep came in 1937 with the application of a technology that records brain wave activity of the sleeper in the form of an electroencephalogram (EEG). The EEG provided an objective, ongoing measure of the way brain activity varies when people are awake or asleep. With the EEG, researchers discovered that brain waves change in form at the onset of sleep and show further systematic, predictable changes during the entire sleep period (Loomis et al., 1937).

The next significant discovery in sleep research was that bursts of **rapid eye movement** (REM) occur at periodic intervals during sleep (Aserinsky & Kleitman, 1953). The time when a sleeper is not showing REM is known as **non-REM sleep** (NREM). During a study, sleepers were awakened and asked to describe their mental activity during REM sleep or NREM sleep. The NREM reports were filled with brief descriptions of ordinary activities, similar to waking thoughts. But the REM reports were qualitatively different; they were vivid, fanciful, bizarre scenes from incomplete plots—in essence, dreams. Adult subjects in sleep laboratories were found to have four or five distinct dreams every night. Thus rapid eye movement is a reliable behavioral sign that a sleeper's mental activity is centered on dreaming. Many investigators were excited by this new objective pathway into a previously hidden side of human activity (Dement & Kleitman, 1957). Since then, researchers in sleep laboratories throughout the world have been adding to the understanding of this nightly alteration of human consciousness.

The Sleep Cycle

Let us track your brain waves through the night. As you prepare to go to bed, an EEG records that your brain waves are moving along at a rate of about 14 cycles per second (cps). Once you are comfortably in bed, you begin to relax and your brain waves slow down to a rate of about 8 to 12 cps. When you fall asleep, you enter your *sleep cycle,* each of whose stages shows a distinct EEG pattern. In Stage 1 sleep, the EEG shows brain waves of about 3 to 7 cps. During Stage 2, the EEG is characterized by *sleep spindles,* minute bursts of electrical activity of 12 to 16 cps. In the next two stages (3 and 4) of sleep, you enter into a very deep state of relaxed sleep. Your brain waves slow to about 1 to 2 cps, and your breathing and heart rate decrease. In a final stage, the electrical activity of your brain increases; your EEG looks very similar to those recorded during stages 1 and 2. It is during this stage that you will experience REM sleep, and you will begin to dream (see **Figure 4.2**). (Because the EEG pattern during REM sleep resembles that of an awake person, REM sleep was originally termed *paradoxical sleep.*)

Patterns of brain activity change dramatically over the course of a night's sleep.

Cycling through the first four stages of sleep, which are NREM sleep,

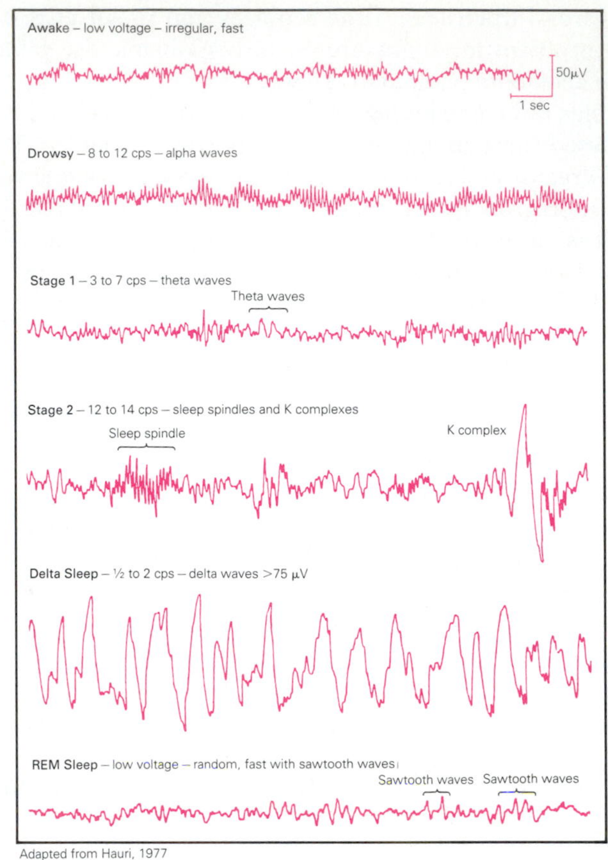

Adapted from Hauri, 1977

Figure 4.2 **EEG Patterns Reflecting the Stages of a Regular Night's Sleep**

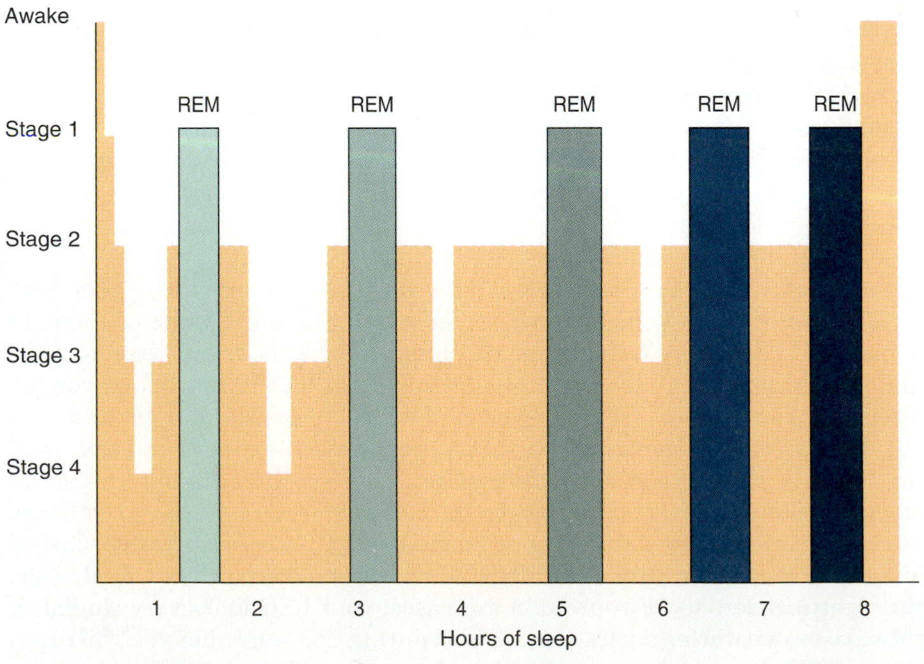

Figure 4.3 **Stages of Sleep**

A typical pattern of the stages of sleep during a single night includes deeper sleep in the early cycles but more time in REM in the later cycles.

requires about 90 minutes. REM sleep lasts for about 10 minutes. Over the course of a night's sleep, you pass through this 100-minute cycle four to six times (see **Figure 4.3**). With each cycle, the amount of time you spend in deep sleep (stages 3 and 4) decreases, and the amount of time you spend in REM sleep increases. During the last cycle, you may spend as much time as an hour in REM sleep. NREM sleep accounts for 75 to 80 percent of total sleep time, while REM sleep makes up 20 to 25 percent of sleep time (Carskadon & Dement, 1989).

Researchers have begun to study the bodily systems that regulate the rhythms of sleep (see **Figure 4.4**). Like humans, many animals have regular sleep-wake cycles, orderly stages of sleep, and a standard ratio of REM to NREM sleep. The sleep-wake cycle has been found to correspond to activity in specific areas of the brain, such as certain brain stem neurons and cells in the thalamus—the principal gateway to the cerebral cortex (Steriade & McCarley, 1990). Researchers have also identified some of the chemicals that affect sleep-wake cycles (Maugh, 1982). For instance, sleep is promoted when large amounts of the hormone melatonin are released from the pineal gland (Binkley, 1979), and the neurotransmitter serotonin seems to be involved in changes in arousal levels.

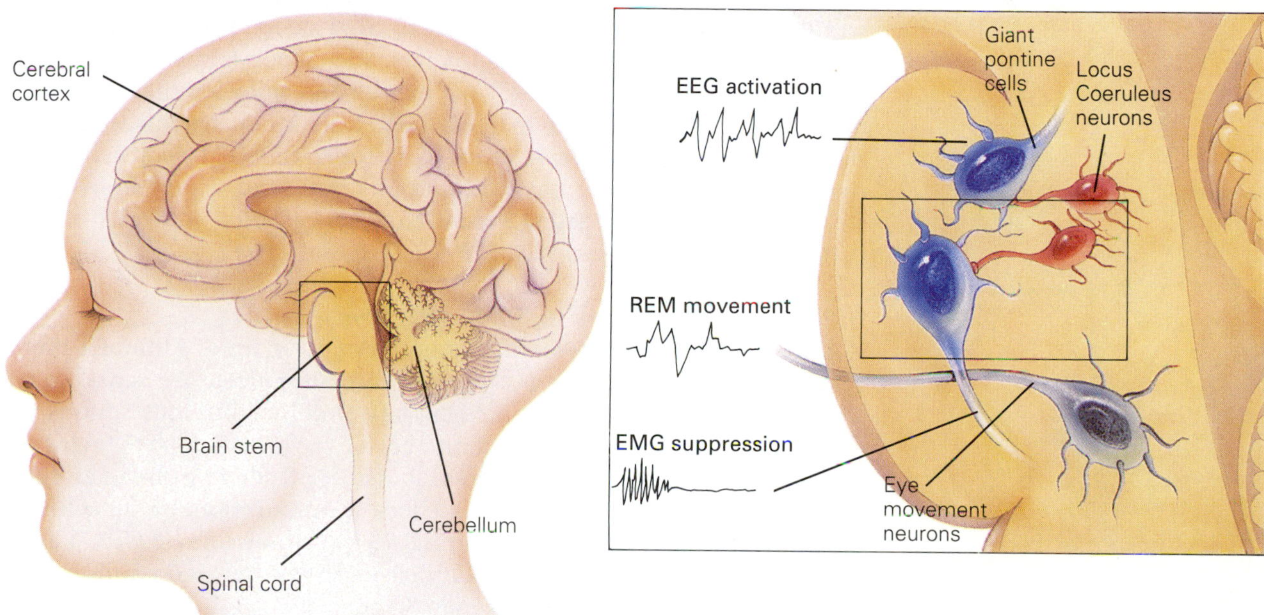

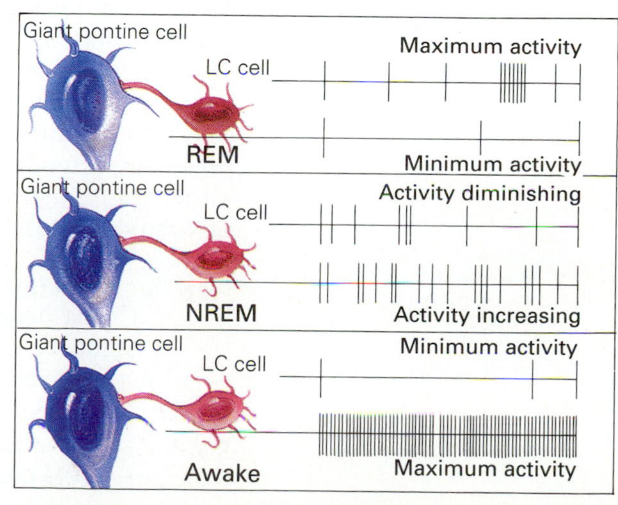

Figure 4.4 Sleep and Dream Cycles
*In the brain stem, a group of giant cells called the pontine reticular formation is involved in the generation of REM sleep. Just prior to and during REM sleep, the activity of these pontine cells greatly increases and excites eye movement neurons. Activity now diminishes in the region adjacent to another nearby group of cells—*locus coeruleus, or LC cells*—that affects muscle tone via the cerebral cortex. During NREM sleep and wakefulness, the LC cells inhibit the pontines, suggesting that the two cell groups act reciprocally.*

Why Sleep?

The orderly progression of stages of sleep in humans and other animals suggests that there is an evolutionary basis and a biological need for sleep. Why do humans sleep so much and what functions do types of sleep—NREM and REM—serve?

The two most general functions for NREM sleep may be *conservation* and *restoration.* Sleep may have evolved because it enabled animals to *conserve* energy at times when there was no need to forage for food, search for mates, or work (Allison & Cicchetti, 1976; Cartwright, 1982; Webb, 1974). On the other hand, sleep also enables the body to engage in housekeeping functions and to *restore* itself in any of several ways. During sleep, neurotransmitters may be synthesized to compensate for the quantities used in daily activities, and postsynaptic receptors may be returned to their optimal level of sensitivity (Stern & Morgane, 1974). A different function is proposed by Francis Crick (Nobel Prize winner for unraveling the structure of DNA) and mathematician Graeme Mitchison, who believe that sleep and dreams help the brain to flush out the day's accumulation of unwanted and useless information (Crick & Mitchison, 1983).

If you were to be deprived of REM sleep for a night, you would have more REM sleep than usual the next night, suggesting that REM sleep also serves some necessary functions. A number of interesting, but not yet fully demonstrated, benefits have been attributed to REM sleep (Moffitt et al., 1993). For example, it appears that, during infancy, REM sleep is responsible for establishing the pathways between your nerves and muscles that enable you to move your eyes. REM sleep may establish functional structures in the brain, such as those involving the learning of motor skills. REM sleep can also play a role in the maintenance of mood and emotion, and it may be required for storing memories and fitting recent experiences into networks of previous beliefs or memories (Cartwright, 1978; Dement, 1976).

Individual Differences in Sleep Patterns

Not all individuals sleep for the same amount of time. Although there is a genetic *sleep need* programmed into the human species, the actual amount of sleep each individual obtains is highly affected by conscious actions. People actively control sleep length in a number of ways, such as by staying up late or using alarm clocks. Sleep duration is also controlled by circadian rhythms; that is, *when* one goes to sleep influences sleep duration, because REM sleep increases with length of sleep. Getting adequate amounts of NREM and REM sleep is only likely when you standardize your bedtime and rising time across the entire week, including weekends. In that way the time you spend in bed is likely to correspond closely to the sleepy phase of your circadian rhythm.

What accounts for variations in amount of sleep? Individuals who sleep longer than average are found to be more nervous and worrisome, artistic, creative, and nonconforming. Short sleepers tend to be more energetic and extroverted (Hartmann, 1973). Strenuous physical activity during the day increases the amount of time spent in the slow-wave sleep of Stage 4, but it doesn't affect REM time (Horne, 1988). Mental problems seem to have a great effect on extending REM sleep—severe psychological depression exerts a variety of influences on sleep patterns, according to research from the sleep laboratory of **Rosalind Cartwright,** a leader in the field:

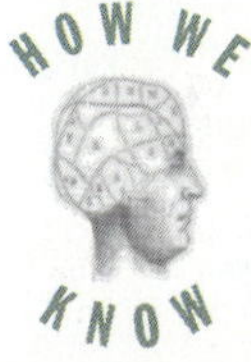

The researcher compared sleep and dream patterns among divorcing people who were depressed, divorcing people who were not depressed, and happily married people. The depressed divorcing subjects showed sleep abnormalities typical for severely depressed people: an initial REM period that is unusually early (20 to 65 minutes instead of the norm of about 90 minutes after sleep onset); REM that lasts unusually long (20 to 30 minutes instead of 5 to 10 minutes); and REM periods that vary more in their duration and that contain more than the usual amount of rapid eye movements. The content of their dreams also differed in unhealthy ways from those not so troubled. The dreams of the depressed people studied were "stuck in the past," allowing no working through of problems nor exploration of new roles and future possibilities, as occurred in the dreams of the happier people (Cartwright, 1984).

Of further interest is the dramatic change in patterns of sleep that occurs over an individual's lifetime (shown in **Figure 4.5**). You started out in this world sleeping for about 16 hours a day, with nearly half of that time spent in REM sleep. By age 50 you may sleep only 6 hours and spend only about 20 percent of the time in REM sleep. Young adults typically sleep 7 to 8 hours, with about 20 percent REM.

Variations in amount of sleep can be attributed to differences in personality characteristics, differences in amount of physical activity, and state of mental health.

Sleep Disorders

It is estimated that more than 100 million Americans get insufficient sleep, posing a serious burden to their personal lives and careers. Disordered sleep can also have societal consequences. Of those individuals whose work schedules include night shifts, more than half nod off at least once a week on the job. Some of the world's most serious industrial accidents—Three Mile Island, Chernobyl, Bhopal, and the *Exxon Valdez* disaster—have occurred during late evening hours. People have speculated that these accidents occurred because key personnel failed to function optimally as a result of insufficient sleep. Because sleep disorders are important in many students' lives, we will review them here. As you read, remember that sleep disorders vary in severity. Similarly, their origins vary between biological and psychological forces.

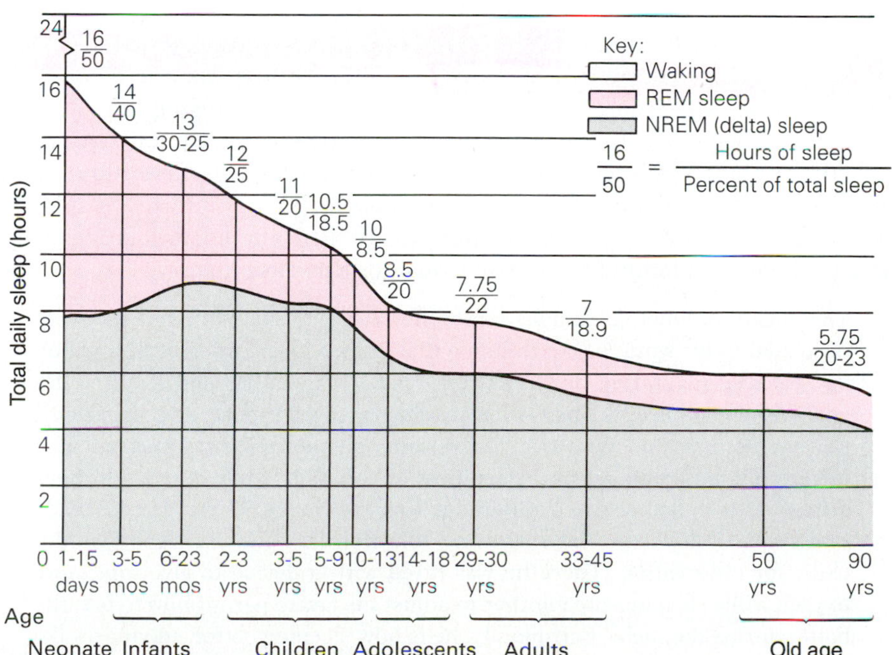

Figure 4.5 Patterns of Human Sleep Over a Lifetime

The graph shows changes with age in total amounts of daily REM and NREM sleep and percentage of REM sleep. Note that the amount of REM sleep decreases considerably over the years, while NREM diminishes less sharply.

Insomnia. When people are dissatisfied with their amount or quality of sleep, they are suffering from **insomnia.** This chronic failure to get adequate sleep is characterized by an inability to fall asleep quickly, frequent arousals during sleep, or early morning awakening (Bootzin & Nicasio, 1978). Insomnia is a complex disorder caused by a variety of psychological, environmental, and biological factors (Borkovec, 1982). However, when insomniacs are studied in sleep laboratories, the objective quantity and quality of their actual sleep varies considerably, from disturbed sleep to normal sleep. Research has revealed that many insomniacs who complain of lack of sleep actually show completely normal patterns of sleep—a condition described as *subjective insomnia.* Equally curious is the finding that some people who show detectable sleep disturbances report no complaints of insomnia (Trinder, 1988). The discrepancies may result from differences in the way people recall and interpret a state of light sleep. For example, they may recall light sleep as much more frequent and distressing than it was and have no memory of having slept deeply.

Narcolepsy. **Narcolepsy** is a sleep disorder characterized by a periodic compulsion to sleep during the daytime. It is often combined with *cataplexy,* a total loss of muscle control brought on by emotional excitement (such as laughing, anger, fear, surprise, or hunger) that causes the afflicted person to fall down suddenly. When they fall asleep, narcoleptics enter REM sleep almost immediately. This rush to REM causes them to experience—and be consciously aware of—vivid dream images or hallucinations. In the United States, about 1 of every 1000 individuals is afflicted with the disease, but many of these people remain undiagnosed long after they first notice its symptoms (Guilleminault et al., 1976; Joyce, 1990b). Because narcolepsy runs in families, scientists assume the disease has a genetic basis. The search is under way for drugs that can control the symptoms of the disorder without undesirable side effects, but none has yet been discovered. In the meantime, narcoleptics can benefit from recognizing the nature of their disease and belonging to a social support group.

Sleep Apnea. **Sleep apnea** is an upper respiratory sleep disorder in which the person stops breathing while asleep. When this happens, the blood's oxygen level drops and emergency hormones are secreted, causing the sleeper to awaken and begin breathing again. While most people have a few such apnea episodes a night, someone with sleep apnea disorder can have hundreds of such cycles every night. Sometimes apnea episodes frighten the sleeper, but often they are so brief that the sleeper fails to attribute accumulating sleepiness to them (Guilleminault, 1989). Consider this case history:

> This highly productive, famous researcher, who is usually intense and very dedicated to his work, began thinking that he was losing interest in psychology because he started dozing during research meetings and lectures. He could not keep his eyes open when reading research reports and, especially, student dissertations. He was suffering from undetected sleep apnea and mistakenly attributed his daytime sleepiness to boredom (while others may have attributed it to laziness or indifference to their work). When his wife made him aware of his disturbing nighttime behavior, he went to a sleep disorder clinic for observation. There he was fitted with a device to give him more oxygen while sleeping and another to adjust his jaw to permit him to breathe better during the night. Fortunately, he is now sleeping better, staying awake during meetings and lectures, and keeping his students active doing research. His case illustrates how a biologically based sleep disorder can have negative psychological and social effects in many areas of life. In other similar cases, people have lost their jobs, friends, and even spouses because their daytime behavior was so disrupted by their nighttime disorder. (Zimbardo, personal communication, 1991)

Apnea during sleep is also frequent in premature infants, who sometimes need physical stimulation to start breathing again. Because of their underdeveloped respiratory system, these infants must remain attached to monitors in intensive care nurseries as long as the problem continues.

Daytime Sleepiness. The major complaint of the majority of patients evaluated at U.S. sleep disorder centers is excessive **daytime sleepiness** (Roth et al., 1989). About 4 to 5 percent of the general population surveyed reports this disorder. Excessive sleepiness causes diminished alertness, delayed reaction times, and impaired performance on motor and cognitive tasks. Nearly half the patients with excessive sleepiness report having been involved in automobile accidents, and more than half have had job accidents, some serious.

In preparing *Sleep Alert,* a documentary film on this sleep deprivation disorder, psychologist **James Maas** reported that "there are some people who are literally walking zombies." He learned of airline pilots who told of falling asleep on the job for short naps, only to find the rest of the crew napping when they awoke. High school and college students also typically suffer from excessive sleepiness. They get an average of only six hours of sleep a night, when they need about ten hours to function optimally. According to Maas, as many as 30 percent of high school students fall asleep in class once a week. Some degree of sleepiness is to be expected when individuals' lifestyles or job requirements prohibit them from getting sufficient nocturnal sleep. Excessive sleepiness, however, often has physiological roots, and sufferers should seek medical attention (Roth et al., 1989).

Millions of people suffer from sleep disorders such as insomnia, narcolepsy, sleep apnea, and daytime sleepiness.

Need help with a chronic sleep disorder? The following organizations offer assistance to individuals who suffer from persistent sleep problems:

National Sleep Foundation, 1367 Connecticut Ave., NW, Suite 200, Washington, DC 20036

American Sleep Disorders Association, 685 2nd Street, SW, Rochester, Minnesota 55902

Stanford Medical School, Sleep Disorders Clinic, 401 Quarry Rd., Stanford, CA 94305

Dreams: Theater of the Mind

During every ordinary night of your life, you enter into the complex world of dreams. Vivid, colorful, often nonsensical images overtake your mind; surrealistic plots transform time, sequence, and place. Amid all this "theater of the absurd," the dreamer may recognize representations of life problems or solutions to those problems. Once only the province of prophets, psychics, and psychoanalysts, dreams have become a vital area of study for scientific researchers. Much dream research begins in sleep laboratories, where experimenters can monitor sleepers for REM and NREM sleep. Although dreams are primarily REM phenomena, some dreaming (of a different quality) also takes place during NREM periods. Dreaming associated with NREM states is less likely to contain dramatic story content. It is full of specific thoughts but has little sensory imagery. Subjects recall a much higher percentage of REM dreams than NREM dreams (Freeman, 1972). NREM dreaming is enhanced in those with sleep disorders and in normal sleepers during the very late morning hours (Kondo et al., 1989).

Enough individuals have had their sleep interrupted—in the name of science—for us to begin to detect stable patterns of developmental and individual differences. There seems to be a developmental timetable for dreaming that follows the same timetable as the development of general cognitive abilities. This conclusion emerges from studies in which children between the ages of 3 and 9 were awakened from sleep on successive nights and asked what they remembered. The youngest children reported frozen scenes of static, storybook-like images. By the age of 5 or 6, children have dreams that are stories with action and movement. But not until age 7 or 8 do children star in their dreams, and not until age 8 or 9 do they begin dreaming as adults do. Some developmental researchers believe that this sequence depends on the maturation of the brain, which makes it possible for children to use symbols and to analyze concepts and weave them into novel patterns.

Dream research also reveals that men and women tend to have different dream content—as a function, perhaps, of cultural roles. Men's dreams are generally more active and include more fighting, male antagonists, mechanical images, traveling, and explicit sex. Men dream more often than women do about being naked in public places and about finding money. Women's dreams feature more conversations, emotions, interior scenes, and plots in which they are pursued or endangered. However, the sexual revolution is showing up in women's dreams in the form of more outdoor activity and torrid sex (Begley, 1989).

The Origins of Dream Content

Alongside these group differences in dream content, it is certainly the case that each individual has unique dreams. Do these dreams have significance? Virtually every culture has provided a mechanism for interpreting the content of dreams. The most prominent theory in modern Western culture was originated by Sigmund Freud. We will describe his theory and contrast it with an account of the origins of unique dreams that is more anchored in physiology.

Freudian Dream Analysis. Freud called dreams "transient psychoses" and models of "everynight madness." He also called them "the royal road to the unconscious." He made the analysis of dreams the cornerstone of psychoanalysis with his classic book *The Interpretation of Dreams* (1900). Freud saw dream images as symbolic expressions of powerful, unconscious, repressed wishes. These wishes appear in disguised form because they harbor forbidden desires, such as sexual yearning for the parent of the opposite sex. The two dynamic forces operating in dreams are, thus, the *wish* and the *censorship,* a defense against the wish. The censor transforms the hidden mean-

Fantastic or grotesque visions often occur in dreams. This image is the work of famed photographer Man Ray.

ing, or **latent content**, of the dream into **manifest content**, which appears to the dreamer after a distortion process that Freud referred to as **dream work.** The manifest content is the acceptable version of the story; the latent content represents the socially or personally unacceptable version but also the true, "uncut" one.

Dreams have a psychological interpretation, most notably provided by Sigmund Freud.

The interpretation of dreams requires working backward from the manifest content to the latent content. To the therapist who uses dream analysis to understand and treat a patient's problems, dreams reveal the patient's unconscious wishes, the fears attached to those wishes, and the characteristic defenses the patient employs to handle the resulting psychic conflict between the wishes and the fears. Freud believed in both idiosyncratic and universal meanings—many of a sexual nature—for the symbols and metaphors in dreams:

> Boxes, cases, chests, cupboards and ovens represent the uterus, and also hollow objects, ships, and vessels of all kinds. Rooms in dreams are usually women; if the various ways in and out of them are represented, this interpretation is scarcely open to doubt. . . . A dream of going through a suite of rooms is a brothel or harem dream. . . . It is highly probable that all complicated machinery and apparatus occurring in dreams stand for the genitals (and as a rule male ones). . . . (Freud, 1900, pp. 354–356)

Systems of dream interpretation predate Freud by thousands of years. Freud, however, was the first scholar to forcefully relate dream symbols to an explicit theory of human psychology.

A Physiological Theory of Dreaming. The cornerstone of the Freudian view—and other theories that take Freud as a touchstone—is that manifest or latent dream images provide a "royal road" to the dreamer's psychological functioning. This view is facing its severest challenge from biologically based theories that assert that all dreams begin with random electrical discharges from deep within the brain. The proponents of this theory, **J. Allan Hobson** and **Robert McCarley** (1977), suggest that signals emerge from the brain stem and then stimulate areas of the brain's cortex. These electrical discharges occur automatically about every 90 minutes and stay activated for 30 minutes or so—a time period equivalent to REM sleep periods. They are sent to the forebrain and association areas of the cortex, where they trigger memories and connections with the dreamer's past experiences. According to Hobson and McCarley's view, there are no logical connections, no intrinsic meaning, and no coherent patterns to these random bursts of electrical signals.

A contrasting physiological theory of dreams is supported by researchers J. Allan Hobson and Robert McCarley.

Note that this view does not say the content of dreams is meaningless, only that their source is random stimulation and not unconscious wishes. Hobson (1988) claims that the meaning is added as a kind of brainstorm afterthought. He writes that because the brain is so "inexorably bent upon the quest for meaning," it makes sense out of totally random signals by investing them with meaning. That meaning comes from the dreamer's current needs and concerns, past experiences, and expectations. Using this idiosyncratic material, the brain imposes order on chaos, and creates what you recognize as dreams by synthesizing the separate bursts of electrical stimulation into a coherent story.

You can gain a further understanding of the origin of dreams with respect to neurotransmitters and structures in the brain. The "stuff" of dreams may be *acetylcholine,* which is turned on by one set of neurons in the brain stem during REM. Those neurons are "on" only when others, which trigger the release of *serotonin* and *norepinephrine,* are "off." (Recall our discussion of

Examination of the role of neurotransmitters, such as acetylcholine, serotonin, and norepinephrine, adds credibility to Hobson and McCarley's physiological theory of dreaming.

neurotransmitters in Chapter 3.) Furthermore, your eyes move during REM—but your other muscles do not—because of the action of groups of cells in the brain stem that make up the pontine reticular system (see Figure 4.4). With this model, you can see how a common set of processing systems in the brain produces both dreaming and waking perceptions (Hobson, 1992; Steriade & McCarley, 1990). By better understanding the mechanisms of dreaming, you can enhance your knowledge of waking aspects of imagery and conscious thought processes (Antrobus, 1991).

Nightmares

When a dream frightens you by making you feel helpless or out of control, you are having a nightmare. Although they are relatively infrequent (occurring only a few times a year), nightmares can be terrifying, especially for children. Typically, nightmares are triggered by stress, especially fear of harm and of desertion. Being stabbed, shot, hurled off a cliff, and chased by a predator are some of the feared events appearing in nightmares. People who have experienced traumatic events, such as rape or war, may have repetitive nightmares that force them to relive some aspects of their trauma. Although the distinguishing feature of most nightmares is the dreamer's sense of being endangered, the nightmares of new parents often involve their babies.

We can consider nightmares to be at the outer limit of everyday changes in consciousness. We turn now to circumstances in which individuals deliberately seek to go beyond those everyday experiences.

EXTENDED STATES OF CONSCIOUSNESS

Sleep and dreaming are considered ordinary transformations of consciousness, with nightmares being the extreme form. But individuals in every culture seek other means of altering their consciousness.

In every society, people have been dissatisfied with ordinary transformations of their waking consciousness. They have developed practices that take them beyond familiar forms of consciousness to experiences of extended states of consciousness. Some of these practices are individual, such as taking recreational drugs. Others, such as certain religious practices, are shared attempts to transcend the normal boundaries of conscious experience. We survey the full range of such practices.

Lucid Dreaming

Is it possible to be aware that you are dreaming while you are dreaming? Proponents of the theory of **lucid dreaming** have demonstrated that being consciously aware that one is dreaming is a learnable skill—perfected with regular practice—that enables dreamers to control the direction of their dreams (Gackenbach & LaBerge, 1988; Garfield, 1975; LaBerge, 1986). In lucid dreaming research, sleepers wear specially designed goggles that flash a red light when they detect REM sleep. The subjects have learned previously that the red light is a cue for becoming consciously aware that they are dreaming. Once aware of dreaming, yet still not awake, sleepers move into a state of lucid dreaming in which they can take control of their dreams, directing them according to their personal goals and making their outcomes fit their current needs. The ability to have lucid dreams reportedly increases when sleepers firmly believe that such dreams are possible and regularly practice the induction techniques (LaBerge & Rheingold, 1990). Researchers such as **Stephen LaBerge** argue that gaining control over the "uncontrollable" events of dreams is healthy because it enhances self-confidence and generates positive experiences for the individual. However, some therapists who use dream analysis as

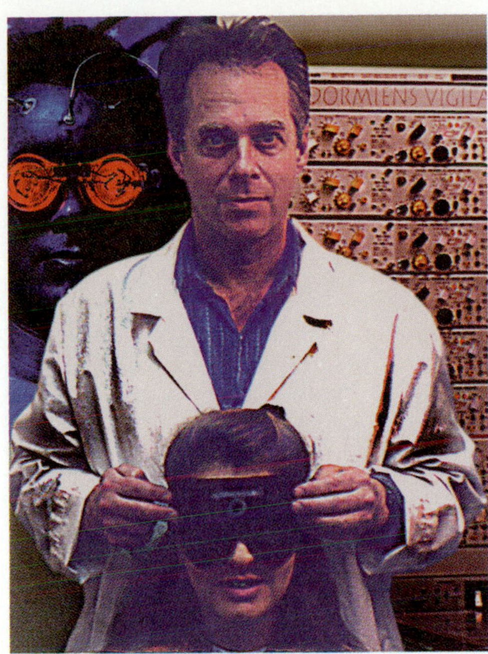

Researcher Steven LaBerge adjusts the special goggles that will alert the sleeping subject that REM sleep is occurring. The subject is trained to enter a state of lucid dreaming, being aware of the process and content of dream activity.

part of their understanding of a patient's problems oppose such procedures because they feel that they distort the natural process of dreaming.

HYPNOSIS

As portrayed in popular culture, hypnotists wield vast power over their witting or unwitting subjects. Is this view of hypnotists accurate? What is hypnosis, what are its important features, and what are some of its valid psychological uses? The term **hypnosis** is derived from Hypnos, the name of the Greek god of sleep. Sleep, however, plays no part in hypnosis, except that subjects may in some cases give the *appearance* of being in a deeply relaxed, sleeplike state. (If subjects were really asleep, they could not respond to hypnosis.) A broad definition of hypnosis is that it is an alternative state of awareness characterized by the special ability some people have of responding to suggestion with changes in perception, memory, motivation, and sense of self-control (Orne, 1980). In the hypnotic state, subjects experience heightened responsiveness to the hypnotist's suggestions—they often feel that their behavior is performed without intention or any conscious effort.

Researchers disagree about the psychological mechanisms involved in hypnosis. Some argue that hypnosis is nothing more than heightened motivation, and others believe it is only social role playing, a kind of *placebo response* of trying to please the hypnotist (see Chapter 2). However, as we will describe shortly, research has shown that the specific effects hypnosis produces in deeply hypnotized subjects can be distinguished both from the expectancy effects of placebo response and from general suggestibility effects (Evans, 1989). A reliable body of empirical evidence, bolstered by expert opinion, strongly suggests that hypnosis can exert a powerful influence on many psychological and bodily functions (Bowers, 1976; Burrows & Dennerstein, 1980; E. Hilgard, 1968, 1973).

There is reliable evidence that hypnosis can influence both psychological and physiological functions.

Induction of Hypnosis

Hypnosis begins with a *hypnotic induction,* a preliminary set of activities that minimizes external distractions and encourages subjects to concentrate

This 1960 film, entitled The Hypnotic Eye, *perpetuated a common fallacy that subjects will commit horrific acts under posthypnotic suggestion.*

only on suggested stimuli and believe that they are about to enter a special state of consciousness. Induction activities involve suggestions to imagine certain experiences or to visualize events and reactions. When practiced repeatedly, the induction procedure functions as a learned signal so that subjects can quickly enter the hypnotic state.

The typical induction procedure uses suggestions for deep relaxation, but some people can become hypnotized with an active, alert induction—such as imagining that they are jogging or riding a bicycle. A child in the dentist's chair can be hypnotized while his or her attention is directed to vivid stories or to imagining the exciting adventures of a favorite TV character. Meanwhile, the dentist drills and fills cavities, using no anesthesia, but the child feels no pain (Banyai & E. Hilgard, 1976).

Hypnotizability

Stage performances of hypnosis give the impression that the power of hypnosis lies with the hypnotist. However, the single most important factor in hypnosis is a participant's ability or "talent" to become hypnotized. **Hypnotizability** represents the degree to which an individual is responsive to standardized suggestions to experience hypnotic reactions. There are wide individual differences in susceptibility, varying from a complete lack of responsiveness to total responsiveness.

Figure 4.6 shows the percentage of college-age subjects at various levels of hypnotizability the first time they were given a hypnotic induction test. What does it mean to have scored "high" or "very high" on this scale? When the test is administered, the hypnotist makes a series of posthypnotic suggestions, dictating the experiences each subject might have. When the hypnotist suggested that their extended arms had turned into bars of iron, highly hypnotizable subjects were likely to find themselves unable to bend those arms. With the appropriate suggestion, they were likely to brush away a nonexistent fly. As a third example, highly hypnotizable subjects probably couldn't nod their heads "no" when the hypnotist suggested they had lost that ability. Students who scored "low" on the hypnotizability scale experienced few if any of these reactions.

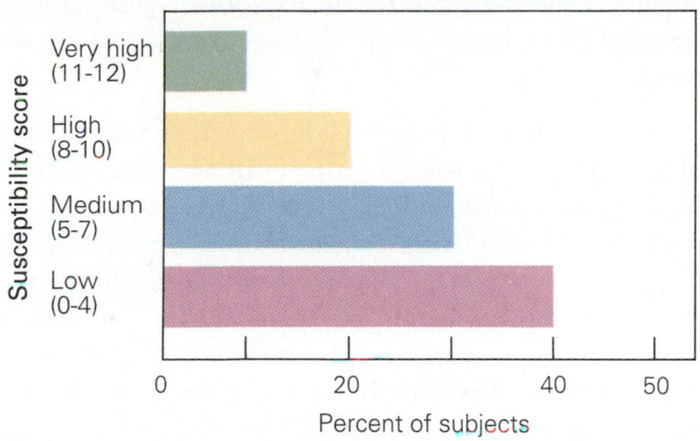

Figure 4.6 Level of Hypnosis at First Induction

The graph shows the results for 533 subjects hypnotized for the first time. Hypnotizability was measured on the Stanford Hypnotic Susceptibility Scale, which consists of 12 items.

Hypnotizability is a relatively stable attribute. An adult's scores remain about the same when measured various times over a 10-year period (Morgan et al., 1974). In fact, when 50 men and women were retested 25 years after their college hypnotizability assessment, the results indicated a remarkably high correlation coefficient of .71 (Piccione et al., 1989). Children tend to be more suggestible than adults; hypnotic responsiveness peaks just before adolescence and declines thereafter. There is some evidence for genetic determinants of hypnotizability, because the scores of identical twins are more similar than are those of fraternal twins (Morgan et al., 1970).

Although hypnotizability is relatively stable, it is not correlated with any personality trait like gullibility or conformity (Fromm & Shor, 1979). Rather, hypnotizability reflects a unique cognitive ability—which develops early in life—to become completely absorbed in an experience. A hypnotizable person is capable of deep involvement in the imaginative-feeling areas of experience, such as reading novels or listening to music. Hypnotizability may also involve a willingness to suspend ordinary reality. Under hypnosis, highly hypnotizable subjects can so vividly imagine a scene suggested to them that it seems to be happening at that moment (J. R. Hilgard, 1970, 1979). A hypnotizable person can be hypnotized by anyone he or she is willing to respond to, while someone who is unhypnotizable will not respond to the tactics of the most skilled hypnotist.

Pain Control

An undisputed value of hypnosis is its ability to reduce pain (*hypnotic analgesia*). Your mind can amplify pain stimuli through anticipation and fear; you can diminish this psychological effect with hypnosis. Pain control is accomplished through a variety of hypnotic suggestions: imagining the part of the body in pain as nonorganic (made of wood or plastic) or as separate from the rest of the body, taking one's mind on a vacation from the body, and distorting time in various ways. Hypnosis has proven especially valuable to surgery patients who cannot tolerate anesthesia, to mothers in natural childbirth, and to cancer patients learning to endure the pain associated with the disease and its treatment. Self-hypnosis (*autohypnosis*) is the best approach to controlling pain because patients can then exert control whenever pain arises. In a study of 86 women with metastatic cancer, those using self-hypnosis for pain control reported having only half as much pain as others (Spiegel et al., 1989).

Researchers have used pain reduction to demonstrate that hypnosis produces effects beyond the willingness of subjects to play along with what they or the experimenter expects:

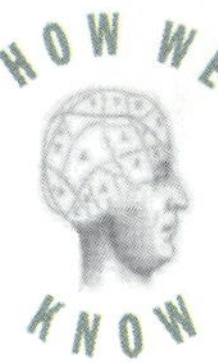

Excruciating muscle pain was delivered to volunteer subjects. The subjects' ability to tolerate the pain was measured during three experimental sessions: (1) with highly motivating instructions; (2) following the induction of hypnotic analgesia; and (3) after ingesting a placebo capsule described as painkilling medication. The contrast between (1) and (2) allows for an assessment of the effects of hypnosis beyond the subjects' desire to do well in the experiment. The contrast between (2) and (3) allows for a demonstration that hypnosis is more than a placebo effect. The experimenter who actually tested the subjects did not know which had ingested the placebo pill and was misled to believe that hypnotic analgesia worked for all of them. In fact, 12 subjects were highly hypnotizable and 12 scored low on the scale. These measures eliminated the possibility that the experimenter brought about differential results.

The placebo pill significantly reduced pain in all subjects, beyond the level of the motivating instructions. In addition, *expecting* hypnosis to reduce pain also had a significant effect on all subjects—a placebo expectancy effect. However, pain tolerance for the highly hypnotizable subjects during the hypnotic analgesia induction period was significantly greater than for the low hypnotizables and for any of the other conditions—hypnosis is not just a placebo (McGlashan et al., 1978).

The reduction of pain through hypnosis is not merely a placebo effect. Subjects who are highly hypnotizable experience greater pain reduction through hypnosis than through other pain reduction techniques.

For highly hypnotizable subjects, pain reduction is achieved more efficiently through hypnotic suggestion than through other pain reduction techniques (Miller & Bowers, 1993).

The Hidden Observer

Research on pain reduction has also revealed how hypnosis interacts with consciousness. A pioneering researcher in hypnosis, **Ernest Hilgard,** made the startling discovery that subjects under hypnosis who had banished pain from consciousness nonetheless could produce evidence that they retained nonconscious knowledge of the pain. In these experiments, subjects reported feeling no pain when given the hypnotic suggestion that a painful stimulus would evoke no feeling. They were then told that a hidden part of them knew what was going on in their bodies and could report it accurately. Some of these subjects were able to access this hidden source—what Hilgard (1977) called the *hidden observer*—and report pain intensity levels closer to those of individuals not hypnotized (Kihlstrom, 1985).

This experience is captured in a college student's remarks:

> The hidden observer and the hypnotized part are both all of me, but the hidden observer is more aware and reported honestly what was there. The hypnotized part of me just wasn't aware of the pain. In hypnosis I kept my mind and body separate, and my mind was wandering to other places—I was not aware of the pain in my arm. When the hidden observer was called up, the hypnotized part had to step back for a minute and let the hidden part tell the truth. (Knox et al., 1974, p. 845, 846)

Such individuals function at two levels of consciousness while they are in the hypnotic trance state: (1) a full, but hypnotic, consciousness of the suggested experience and (2) a concealed, nonconscious awareness. Such highly hypnotizable subjects can sometimes reveal this hidden level of their consciousness if they are instructed to engage in *automatic writing* or *automatic talking,* processes in which a person writes or speaks meaningful messages without conscious awareness.

Meditation

Many religions and traditional psychologies of the East work to direct consciousness away from immediate worldly concerns. They seek to achieve an inner focus on the mental and spiritual self. **Meditation** is a form of consciousness change designed to enhance self-knowledge and well-being by reducing self-awareness. During meditation, a person may focus on and regulate breathing, assume certain bodily positions (yogic positions), minimize external stimulation, generate specific mental images, or free the mind of all thought.

There is some controversy over the measurable effects of meditation. Critics have suggested that there are few physiological differences between a normal "eyes-closed" resting state and the special procedures of meditation (Holmes, 1984). However, advocates of meditation suggest that the true physiology of meditation can be characterized as *restful alertness,* a state of lower bodily arousal but heightened awareness (Dillbeck & Orme-Johnson, 1987; Morrell, 1986). Thus meditation will at least reduce anxiety, especially in those who function in stress-filled environments (Benson, 1975; Shapiro, 1985). The goal, however, is for meditative practices to be more than just time-outs from tension. When practiced regularly, some forms of meditation can heighten consciousness, help achieve *enlightenment* by enabling the individual to see familiar things in new ways, and free perception and thought from the restrictions of automatic, well-learned patterns. A foremost Buddhist teacher of meditation, Nhat Hanh (1991), recommends awareness of breathing and simple appreciation of your surroundings and minute daily acts as a path to psychological equilibrium.

The goal of meditation is to reduce stress and heighten awareness.

Hallucinations

Under unusual circumstances, a distortion in consciousness occurs during which an individual sees or hears things that are not actually present. **Hallucinations** are vivid perceptions that occur in the absence of objective stimulation; they are a mental construction of an individual's altered reality. They differ from *illusions,* which are perceptual distortions of real stimuli. Consider **Figure 4.7.** Most people see a triangle in this figure, although it is not "really" there. However, we would not want to call this a hallucination, because, as we shall explain in Chapter 8, the triangle "appears" because of the normal processes you use to perceive the world. Unlike a hallucination, you could not make this illusory triangle disappear by reminding yourself that it is not real. If individuals can swiftly demonstrate to themselves the unreality of a hallucination—by evaluating it against reality—the experience will be short-lived. In some cases, however, individuals cannot dispel the "reality" of their hallucinations, and the hallucinations wield an influence on their lives (Siegel, 1992).

Hallucinations are fostered by heightened arousal, states of intense need, or the inability to suppress threatening thoughts. They also occur when the brain experiences an unusual type of stimulation—during, for example, high fevers, epileptic seizures, and migraine headaches—or in patients with severe mental disorders, who respond to private mental events as if they were external sensory stimuli. Hallucinations are also frequently induced by psychoactive drugs, such as LSD and peyote, as well as by withdrawal from alcohol in

Figure 4.7 An Illusion, Not a Hallucination!

severe cases of alcoholism (these hallucinations are known as *delirium tremens,* "the DTs"). These chemically induced hallucinations are prompted by direct effects of the drugs on the brain.

Some psychologists wonder why people do not hallucinate all the time. They believe that the ability to hallucinate is always present but normally inhibited by interaction with sensory input, by continual reality checks, and by feedback from the environment. Because the complex functioning of the brain requires some continuous level of external stimulation, when it is lacking, the brain manufactures its own. Some subjects, when kept in a special environment that minimizes all sensory stimulation, show a tendency to hallucinate. *Sensory isolation* "destructures the environment" and may force subjects to try to restore meaning and stable orientation to a situation. Hallucinations may be a way of reconstructing a reality in accordance with one's personality, past experiences, and the demands of the present experimental setting (Suedfeld, 1980; Zubeck et al., 1961).

Sleep, hypnosis, and meditation are altered states of consciousness that are viewed as valuable, but hallucinations may be seen as signs of mental illness.

In some cultural or religious settings, hallucinations are a desirable and important occurrence (Siegel, 1992). In these circumstances, hallucinations are interpreted as mystical insights that confer special status on the visionary. So, in different settings, the same vivid perception of direct contact with spiritual forces may be deprecated as a sign of mental illness or respected as a sign of special gifts. Evaluation of such mental states often depends as much on the judgment of observers as on the content of the perceptual experience itself.

Religious Ecstasy

Meditation, prayer, fasting, and spiritual communication all contribute to intense *religious experiences.* For William James (1902), religious experiences constituted unique psychological experiences characterized by a sense of oneness and relatedness of events, of realness and vividness of experiences, and an inability to communicate, in ordinary language, the nature of the whole experience. For many people, religious experiences are clearly not part of their ordinary consciousness.

Some people have religious experiences that are not part of ordinary consciousness.

There are few religious experiences more intense than those of the Holy Ghost people of Appalachia. Their beliefs and practices create a unique form of consciousness that enables them to do some remarkable things. At church services they handle deadly poisonous snakes, drink strychnine poison, and handle fire. To prepare for these experiences, they listen to long sermons and participate in loud, insistent singing and wild spinning and dancing:

> The enthusiasm may verge on violence. . . . Members wail and shake and lapse into the unintelligible, ecstatic "new tongues" of glossolalia [artificial speech with no linguistic content]. . . . The ecstasy spreads like contagion. . . . Their hands are definitely cold, even after handling fire. This would correspond with research in trance states involved in other religious cultures. It would also account for the vagueness of memory, almost sensory amnesia, that researchers have reported in serpent handlers as well as fire handlers. (Watterlond, 1983, pp. 53, 55)

Psychological research on serpent-handling religious-group members has found them to be generally well-adjusted people who receive powerful social and psychological support from being part of the group. Participating in the "signs of the spirits" gives them a "personal reward equaled in no other aspect of their lives" (Watterlond, 1983).

The Holy Ghost people of Appalachia and other religious sects engage in such practices as snake handling to prove faith and achieve changes in consciousness. Rayford Dunn was bitten on the hand by this cottonmouth moments after this picture was taken in Kingston, Georgia. Although he behaved normally afterward—going out to eat, and returning to church the next day to handle snakes again—some believers have died from poisonous snake bites.

MIND-ALTERING DRUGS

Since ancient times, people have taken drugs to alter their perception of reality. There is archaeological evidence for the uninterrupted use of sophora seed (mescal bean) for over 10,000 years in the southwestern United States and Mexico, from the ninth millennium B.C. to the nineteenth century A.D. Ancient Americans smoked sophora to bring about ecstatic hallucinatory visions. Sophora was later replaced by the more benign peyote cactus, which is still used in the sacred rituals of many Native American tribes.

Today, drugs are associated less with sacred communal rituals than with recreation. Individuals throughout the world take various drugs to relax, cope with stress, avoid facing the unpleasantness of current realities, feel comfortable in social situations, or experience an alternate state of consciousness. Using drugs to alter consciousness was popularized by the publication of *The Doors of Perception* by Aldous Huxley (1954). Huxley took mescaline as an experiment on his own consciousness. A few decades after Huxley's book appeared, nearly 55 percent of American high school seniors (in annual surveys of over 16,000 students) reported using one or more illegal drugs in their senior year. Although this figure has declined steadily since 1982 (to about 38 percent in 1987), the number of adolescents addicted to drugs has reached epidemic proportions (Johnston et al., 1989).

Dependence and Addiction

Psychoactive drugs are chemicals that affect mental processes and behavior by temporarily changing conscious awareness. Once in the brain, they attach themselves to synaptic receptors, blocking or stimulating certain reactions. By doing so, they profoundly alter the brain's communication system, affecting perception, memory, mood, and behavior. However, continued use of a given drug creates **tolerance**—greater dosages are required to achieve the same effect. (We describe some of the psychological roots of tolerance in Chapter 9.) Hand in hand with tolerance is **physiological dependence,** a process in which the body becomes adjusted to and dependent on the sub-

The use of drugs as an extraordinary means of altering consciousness is a dangerous act that can lead to addiction and even death.

stance, in part because neurotransmitters are depleted by the frequent presence of the drug. The tragic outcome of tolerance and dependence is **addiction.** A person who is addicted requires the drug in his or her body and suffers painful **withdrawal symptoms** (shakes, sweats, nausea, and, in the case of alcohol withdrawal, even death) if the drug is not present.

When an individual finds the use of a drug so desirable or pleasurable that a *craving* develops, with or without addiction, the condition is known as **psychological dependence.** Psychological dependence can occur with any drug. The result of drug dependence is that a person's lifestyle comes to revolve around drug use so wholly that his or her capacity to function is limited or impaired. In addition, the expense involved in maintaining a drug habit of daily—and increasing—amounts often drives an addict to robbery, assault, prostitution, or drug peddling. One of the gravest dangers currently facing addicts is the threat of getting AIDS by sharing hypodermic needles—intravenous drug users can unknowingly share bodily fluids with those who have this deadly immune deficiency disease.

Teenagers who use drugs to relieve emotional distress and to cope with daily stressors suffer long-term negative consequences.

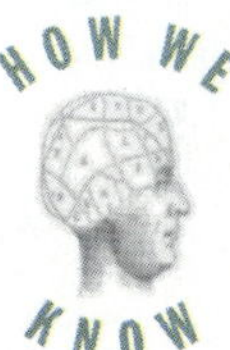

An eight-year study of teenage drug use starting in 1976, with 1634 junior high school students from Los Angeles, collected complete annual data on 739 subjects. While fewer than 10 percent of those studied were regular or chronic drug users, fewer than 10 percent reported not using any drugs. The results can be grouped into four major findings (Newcomb & Bentler, 1988; Stacy et al., 1991).

- Daily drug use had a negative impact on personal and social adjustment, disrupting relationships, reducing educational potential, increasing nonviolent crime, and encouraging disorganized thinking.
- Hard drugs, such as stimulants and narcotics, increased suicidal and self-destructive thoughts while reducing social support, thereby promoting loneliness.
- Drug effects varied with type of drug and mixed use of drugs, so that cocaine increased confrontations and weakened close relationships, but the combination of hard drugs and cigarettes was most damaging to psychological and physical health.
- Surprisingly, teenagers who used alcohol moderately and no other drugs showed increased social integration and increased self-esteem. These students may have been better adjusted to begin with than their peers.

Varieties of Psychoactive Drugs

Drugs affect the central nervous system by stimulating, depressing, or altering neurotransmission.

Common psychoactive drugs are listed in **Table 4.1.** We noted in Chapter 3 how drugs have differing effects on the central nervous system: they may stimulate, depress, or alter neurotransmission. Here we will summarize some of the major psychological experiences created by these drugs and examine the conditions under which they are taken.

The most dramatic changes in consciousness are produced by drugs known as *hallucinogens* or *psychedelics;* these drugs alter both perceptions of the external environment and inner awareness. As the name implies, these drugs often create hallucinations and a loss of the boundary between self and nonself. The four most commonly known hallucinogens are *mescaline* (from cactus plants), *psilocybin* (from a mushroom), and *LSD* and *PCP,* which are synthesized in laboratories. PCP, or *angel dust,* produces a particularly strange dissociative reaction in which the user becomes insensitive to pain, becomes confused, and feels apart from his or her surroundings. Hallucinogenic drugs act in the brain at specific receptor sites for the chemical neurotransmitter serotonin (Jacobs, 1987).

Table 4.1 Psychoactive Drugs: Uses, Duration, and Dependencies

	Medical Uses	Duration of Effect (Hours)	Dependence	
			Psychological	Physiological
Opiates (Narcotics)				
Morphine	Painkiller, cough suppressant	3–6	High	High
Heroin	Under investigation	3–6	High	High
Codeine	Painkiller, cough suppressant	3–6	Moderate	Moderate
Hallucinogens				
LSD	None	8–12	None	Unknown
PCP (Phencyclidine)	Veterinary anesthetic	Varies	Unknown	High
Mescaline (Peyote)	None	8–12	None	Unknown
Psilocybin	None	4–6	Unknown	Unknown
Cannabis (Marijuana)	Nausea associated with chemotherapy	2–4	Unknown	Moderate
Depressants				
Barbiturates (e.g., Seconal)	Sedative, sleeping pill, anesthetic, anticonvulsant	1–16	Moderate–High	Moderate–High
Benzodiazepines (e.g., Valium)	Antianxiety, sedative, sleeping pill, anticonvulsant	4–8	Low–Moderate	Low–Moderate
Alcohol	Antiseptic	1–5	Moderate	Moderate
Stimulants				
Amphetamines	Hyperkinesis, narcolepsy, weight control	2–4	High	High
Cocaine	Local anesthetic	1–2	High	High
Nicotine	Nicotine gum for cessation of smoking habit	Varies	Low–High	Low–High
Caffeine	Weight control, stimulant in acute respiratory failure, analgesic	4–6	Unknown	Unknown

Cannabis is a plant with psychoactive effects. Its active ingredient is *THC,* found in both *hashish* (the solidified resin of the plant) and *marijuana* (the dried leaves and flowers of the plant). The experience derived from inhaling THC depends on its dose—small doses create mild, pleasurable highs, and large doses result in long hallucinogenic reactions. Regular users report euphoria, feelings of well-being, distortions of space and time, and, occasionally, out-of-body experiences. However, depending on the context, the effects may be negative—fear, anxiety, and confusion. Because motor coordination is impaired with marijuana use, those who work or drive under its influence may suffer industrial and auto accidents (Jones & Lovinger, 1985). Cannabinoids, the active chemicals in marijuana, work by binding to specific receptors in the brain that are designed to be activated only by that chemical. These cannabinoid receptors are particularly common in the hippocampus, the brain region involved in memory.

Opiates, such as *heroin,* suppress physical sensation and response to stimulation. The initial effect of an intravenous injection of heroin is a rush of pleasure—feelings of euphoria supplant all worries and awareness of bodily needs. Serious addiction is likely once a person begins to inject heroin.

The *depressants* include *barbiturates* and, most notably, *alcohol.* These drugs tend to depress (slow down) the mental and physical activity of the body by inhibiting or decreasing the transmission of nerve impulses in the

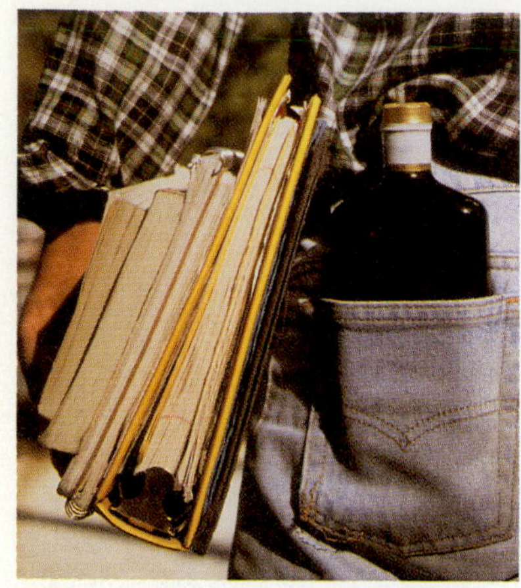

Excess consumption of alcohol is a major cause of problems in schools and colleges, ranging from impaired academic performance to fatal accidents.

central nervous system. High dosages of barbiturates induce sleep but reduce the time spent in REM sleep. After withdrawal from prolonged periods of barbiturate use, extended REM periods are punctuated by nightmares. More deaths are caused by overdoses of barbiturates, taken either accidentally or with suicidal intent, than by any other poison (Kolb, 1973). One of the most subtly addictive depressants is *Valium,* which is prescribed as a tranquilizer to reduce temporary anxiety. Valium often becomes a permanent habit that is very difficult to kick.

Alcohol was apparently one of the first psychoactive substances used extensively by early humans. Under its influence, some people become silly, boisterous, friendly, and talkative; others become abusive and violent; still others become quietly depressed. Researchers still do not understand the exact way in which alcohol wields its effects on the brain. At small dosages, alcohol can induce relaxation and slightly improve an adult's speed of reaction. However, the body can break down alcohol at only a slow rate, and large amounts consumed in a short time period overtax the central nervous system. Driving accidents and fatalities occur six times more often to individuals with 0.10 percent alcohol in their bloodstream than to those with half that amount. Another way alcohol intoxication contributes to accidents is by dilating the pupils of the eyes, thereby causing night vision problems. When the level of alcohol in the blood reaches 0.15 percent, there are gross negative effects on thinking, memory, and judgment, along with emotional instability and loss of motor coordination.

The opiates, barbiturates, and alcohol are all depressants that suppress mental and physical activity.

Excess consumption of alcohol is a major social problem in the United States. Alcohol-related automobile accidents are the leading cause of death among people between the ages of 15 and 25. When the amount and frequency of drinking interferes with job performance, impairs social and family relationships, and creates serious health problems, the diagnosis of *alcoholism* is appropriate. Physical dependence, tolerance, and addiction all develop with prolonged heavy drinking. For some individuals, alcoholism is associated with an inability to abstain from drinking. For others, alcoholism manifests itself as an inability to stop drinking once the person takes a few drinks (Cloninger, 1987).

Stimulants, such as *amphetamines* and *cocaine,* keep the drug user aroused by mimicking the effects of the sympathetic nervous system (see Chapter 3). They have three major effects that users seek: increased self-confidence, greater energy and hyperalertness, and mood alterations approaching euphoria. Heavy users experience frightening hallucinations and develop beliefs that others are out to harm them. These beliefs are known as *paranoid delusions.* A special danger with cocaine use is the contrast between euphoric highs and very depressive lows. This leads users to increase uncontrollably the frequency of drug use and the dosage. One survey of 1212 cocaine users who went to the hospital for a variety of reasons found that about 20 percent had severe seizures and impaired psychological functioning. A particularly destructive street drug is *crack,* a highly purified form of cocaine. It produces a swift high that wears off quickly. Because it is sold in small, cheap quantities that are readily available to the young and the poor, crack is destroying many social communities.

Stimulants are used by people who wish to increase self-confidence, have greater energy and hyperalertness, and experience euphoria.

Two stimulants that you may often overlook as psychoactive drugs are *caffeine* and *nicotine.* As you may know from experience, two cups of strong coffee or tea administer enough caffeine to have a profound effect on heart, blood, and circulatory functions and make it difficult for you to sleep. Nicotine, a chemical found in tobacco, is a sufficiently strong stimulant to have been used in high concentrations by Native American shamans to attain mystical states or trances. Unlike some modern users, however, the shamans knew that nicotine is addictive, and they carefully chose when to be under its influence. Like all addictive drugs, nicotine mimics natural chemicals released by the brain. These chemicals stimulate receptors that make you feel good whenever you have done something right—a phenomenon that aids survival. Unfortunately, nicotine teases those same brain receptors into responding as if it were good for you to be smoking. It's not. The total negative impact of nicotine on health is greater than that of all other psychoactive drugs combined, including heroin, cocaine, and alcohol. The U.S. Public Health Service attributes 400,000 deaths annually to cigarettes. While smoking is the leading cause of preventable sickness and death, it is both legal and actively promoted—billions are spent annually on advertising. Although anti-smoking campaigns have been somewhat effective in reducing the overall level of smoking in the United States, some 54 million Americans still smoke. Of the million people who start smoking each year, many of them now are under 14, female, and members of a racial minority (Goodkind, 1989). In part, this trend can be traced to targeted advertising that focuses on youth, women, and minorities.

The leading cause of preventable illness and death is nicotine, a drug that is both legal and aggressively advertised.

We began this chapter by asking you to pick a number between one and ten. We chose that as an example of an entirely ordinary event that nonetheless allowed us to pose some interesting questions about consciousness: Where did your number come from? How did it emerge? Where did it arrive? You've now learned some of the theories that apply to these questions, and how it has been possible to test those theories. You've seen that consciousness ultimately allows you to have the full range of experiences that define you as human.

We also asked you to consider some increasingly less ordinary uses of consciousness. Why, we asked, do people become dissatisfied with their everyday working minds and seek to alter their consciousness in so many ways? Ordinarily, your primary focus is on meeting the immediate demands of tasks and situations facing you. However, you are aware of these reality-based constraints on your consciousness. You realize they limit the range and depth of your experience and do not allow you to fulfill your potential. Perhaps, at times, you long to reach beyond the confines of ordinary reality (Targ & Harary, 1984). You seek—with known or unknown danger—the uncertainty of freedom instead of settling for the security of the ordinary.

Recapping Main Points

The Contents of Consciousness

Consciousness is an awareness of the mind's contents. Three levels of consciousness are (1) a basic awareness of the world, (2) a reflection on what you are aware of, and (3) self-awareness. The contents of waking consciousness contrast with nonconscious processes, preconscious memories, unattended information, the unconscious, and conscious awareness. Different research techniques, including think-aloud protocols and experience sampling, are used to study the contents of consciousness.

The Functions of Consciousness

A continuing debate in psychology and philosophy has centered on the relationship between mind and brain. Dualism considers them separate; monism postulates they are one. Modern neuroscience supports the monist position. Researchers make comparisons across animal species to explain how the mind's capabilities evolved. Consciousness aids your survival and enables you to construct both personal and culturally shared realities. Researchers have studied the relationship between conscious and unconscious processes.

Everyday Changes in Consciousness

Ordinary alterations of consciousness include daydreaming, fantasy, sleep, and dreams. Daydreaming is a useful, common experience when attention is shifted from the immediate situation. Both biological—such as circadian rhythms—and volitional factors determine the length of sleep for humans. The amount of sleep, and relative proportion of REM to NREM sleep, change with age. REM sleep is signaled by rapid eye movements and accompanied by vivid dreaming. About one fourth of sleep is REM, coming in four or five separate dream episodes. Sleep disorders are more common than usually recognized, especially among overactive people. Insomnia, narcolepsy, and sleep apnea can be modified with medical and psychological therapy. Daytime sleepiness is a widespread, serious problem.

Freud proposed that the content of dreams is unconscious material slipped by a sleeping censor. Recent dream theories challenge Freud's psychodynamic approach with purely biological explanations.

Extended States of Consciousness

Lucid dreaming is an awareness that one is dreaming, in an attempt to control the dream. Hypnosis is an alternate state of consciousness characterized by the ability of hypnotizable people to change perception, motivation, memory, and self-control in response to suggestions. Pain control is one of the major benefits of hypnosis. Meditation changes conscious functioning by ritual practices that focus attention away from external concerns to inner experience. Hallucinations are vivid perceptions that occur in the absence of objective stimulation. Psychoactive drugs affect mental processes by temporarily changing consciousness as they modify nervous system activity. Among psychoactive drugs that alter consciousness are hallucinogens, stimulants, opiates, and depressants.

Resources

Bowers, K.S. (1983). *Hypnosis for the seriously curious*. New York: Norton.

Brown, J. W. (1991). *Self and process: Brain states and the conscious present.* New York: Springer-Verlag.

Dement, W. C. (1992). *The sleepwatchers.* Stanford, CA: Stanford Alumni Press.

Farthing, G. W. (1992). *The psychology of consciousness.* Englewood Cliffs, NJ: Prentice-Hall.

Gackenbach, J., & LaBerge, S. (Eds.). (1988). *Conscious mind, sleeping brain: Perspectives on lucid dreaming.* New York: Plenum Press.

Herzog, P. S. (1991). *Conscious and unconscious: Freud's dynamic distinction reconsidered.* Madison, CT: International Universities Press.

Ward, C. A. (Ed.). (1989). *Altered states of consciousness and mental health: A cross-cultural perspective.* Newbury Park, CA.: Sage Publications. Volume 12 of cross-cultural research and methodology series.

5

Cognitive Aspects of Life-span Development

Imagine you are holding a newborn baby. How might you predict what this child will be like as a 1-year-old? At 5 years? At 15? At 50? At 70? Your predictions would almost certainly consist of a mixture of the general and the specific—the child is extremely likely to learn a language but might or might not be a gifted author. Your predictions would also rely on considerations of heredity and of environment—if both of the child's parents were gifted authors, you might be willing to guess that the child would also show literary talent; if the child was educated in an enriched environment, you might predict that the child's accomplishments would exceed those of the parents. In this chapter and the next, we describe the theories of developmental psychology that enable us to think systematically about the types of predictions we can make for the life course of a newborn child.

Developmental psychology *is the branch of psychology that is concerned with changes in physical and psychological functioning that occur from conception across the entire life span. The task of developmental psychologists is to find out* how *and* why *organisms change over time. Investigators study the time periods in which different abilities and functions first appear and observe how they are modified. In this chapter and the next, we will examine different aspects of* **life-span development.** *Our basic premise is that mental functioning, social relationships, and other vital aspects of human nature continue to develop and change throughout the entire life cycle. You are always in the process of becoming. Table 5.1 presents a rough guide to the major periods of the life span.*

Developmental psychologists propose theories to explain how and why organisms change over time.

In this chapter we will provide a general account of how researchers document development and the theories they use to explain change over time. We will then divide your life experiences into different domains, and trace development in each domain. In this chapter, we focus on physical, cognitive, and language development. In Chapter 6, we will discuss the changing nature of social relationships over the life span as well as the specific tasks individuals face at different moments in their lives. Let's begin now with the question of what it means to study development.

STUDYING AND EXPLAINING DEVELOPMENT

Suppose we ask you to make a list of all the ways in which you believe you have changed in the last year. What sorts of things would you put on the list? Have you undertaken a new physical fitness program? Or have you let an injury heal? Have you developed a range of new hobbies? Or have you decided to focus on just one interest? Have you developed a new circle of friends? Or have you become particularly close to one individual? When we describe development, we will conceptualize it in terms of *change*. We have asked you to perform this exercise of thinking about your own changes to make the point that change almost always involves trade-offs. Often people conceptualize the life span as mostly *gains*—changes for the better—in childhood and mostly *losses*—changes for the worse—over the course of adulthood. However, the perspective on development we will take here emphasizes that options, and therefore gains and losses, are features of all development (Uttal

Table 5.1 Stages in Life-span Development

Stage	Age Period
Prenatal	Conception to birth
Infancy	Birth at full term to about 18 months
Early childhood	About 18 months to about 6 years
Late childhood	About 6 years to about 13 years
Adolescence	About 13 years to about 20 years
Early adulthood	About 20 years to about 30 years
Middle adulthood	About 30 years to about 65 years
Late adulthood	About 65 years and older

& Perlmutter, 1989). When, for example, people choose a lifetime companion, they give up variety but gain security. When people retire, they give up status but gain leisure time. It is also important that you not think of development as a *passive* process. You will see that many developmental changes require an individual's *active* engagement with his or her environment (Bronfenbrenner & Ceci, 1994; Thompson, 1988).

In this first section, we will describe some of the methodologies researchers use to document developmental change. We then explore the general theoretical constructs that explain how these changes come about.

Development requires an individual's active engagement with the environment.

Documenting Development

To think critically about developmental research, you must learn to differentiate between research that documents *age changes*—the way people change as they grow older—and research that documents *age differences*—the way people of different ages differ from one another. Consider an imaginary study on computer literacy. You sit people of varying ages in front of computers and ask them to perform basic word processing tasks. You discover that the older a subject is, the worse he or she performs the task. Should you conclude that, as people age, they lose their abilities to use computers? Certainly not. Members of older generations did not have access to such technology until they were well into their adult years, if ever. You, by contrast, are more than likely computer literate. The critical difference is experience, not age—and just wait to see how your children's skills will surpass your own as they learn to navigate the information superhighway. Although there are, of course, individual differences that are of interest to psychologists, our primary concern here will be with documenting actual age changes. Let's consider some techniques researchers use to do this.

Normative investigations seek to describe a characteristic of a specific age or developmental stage. By systematically testing individuals of different ages, researchers can determine developmental landmarks, such as those listed in **Table 5.2**. These data provide *norms,* standard patterns of development or achievement, based on observation of many children. The data indicate the average age at which the behaviors were performed. Thus a child's performance can be diagnosed in terms of its position relative to the standard for the typical individual at the same age. Norms allow psychologists to make a distinction between **chronological age**—for example, the number of months or years since the birth of a child—and **developmental age**—for example, the chronological age at which most children show the particular level of physical or mental development demonstrated by that child. A 3-year-old child who has verbal skills typical of most 5-year-olds is said to have

Researchers use normative investigations to describe a particular characteristic of a specific age or developmental stage.

Table 5.2 Norms for Infant Mental and Motor Development (Based on the Bayley Scales)

One month
- Responds to sound
- Becomes quiet when picked up
- Follows a moving person with eyes
- Retains a large, easily grasped object placed in hand
- Vocalizes occasionally

Two months
- Smiles socially
- Engages in anticipatory excitement (to feeding, being held)
- Recognizes mother
- Inspects surroundings
- Blinks to objects or shadows (flinches)
- Lifts head and holds it erect and steady

Three months
- Vocalizes to the smiles and talk of an adult
- Searches for sound
- Makes anticipatory adjustments to lifting
- Reacts to disappearance of adult's face
- Sits with support, head steady

Four months
- Head follows dangling ring, vanishing spoon, and ball moved across table
- Inspects and fingers own hands
- Shows awareness of strange situations
- Picks up cube with palm grasp
- Sits with slight support

Five months
- Discriminates strange from familiar persons
- Makes distinctive vocalizations (e.g., pleasure, eagerness, satisfaction)
- Makes effort to sit independently
- Turns from back to side
- Has partial use of thumb in grasp

Six months
- Reaches persistently, picks up cube deftly
- Transfers objects hand to hand
- Lifts cup and bangs it
- Smiles at mirror image and likes frolicking
- Reaches unilaterally for small object

Seven months
- Makes playful responses to mirror
- Retains two of three cubes offered
- Sits alone steadily and well
- Shows clear thumb opposition in grasp
- Scoops up pellet from table

Eight months
- Vocalizes four different syllables (such as *da-da*, *me*, *no*)
- Listens selectively to familiar words
- Rings bell purposively
- Attempts to obtain three presented cubes
- Shows early stepping movements (prewalking progression)

This table shows the average age at which each behavior is performed up to 8 months. Individual differences in rate of development are considerable, but most infants follow this sequence.

a developmental age of 5 for verbal skills. Norms provide a standard basis for comparison both between individuals and between groups.

Developmental psychologists use several other types of research designs to understand possible mechanisms of change and causal influences on behavior. In a **longitudinal design,** the same individuals are repeatedly observed and tested over time, often for many years. An advantage of longitudinal research is that, because the subjects have lived through the same socioeconomic period, age-related changes cannot be confused with variations in differing societal circumstances (Schaie, 1989). But there are several disadvantages. The results can be generalized only to a very limited group: those born in the same time period as the subjects. Also, longitudinal design is costly because it is difficult to keep track of the subjects over extended time periods in a society that is so highly mobile, and data are easily lost due to subjects' quitting or disappearing.

The advantage of a longitudinal design is that observed changes cannot be attributed to societal circumstances.

In a longitudinal design, observations are made of the same individual at different ages, often for many years. This well-known woman might be part of a longitudinal study of British children born in 1926.

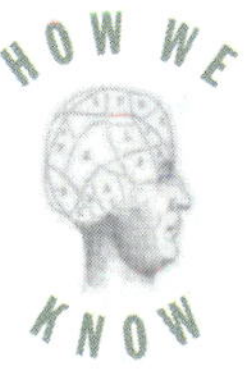

One of the most ambitious longitudinal designs is the study of geniuses, begun by Lewis Terman soon after World War I and still going on 60 years later through the work of psychologists at Stanford University. Over 1500 boys and girls, in grades three through eight (born about 1910), were selected on the basis of high intelligence scores (in the genius range). They have been tested at regular intervals ever since—first, to see how they compared with youngsters in general, later to see if their intellectual superiority would be maintained over the years, and then to discover the conditions and experiences that contributed to life satisfaction and to different styles of handling important life problems (Terman, 1925; Terman & Oden, 1947, 1959). Those still living continue to provide data to researchers (Shneidman, 1989).

Most research on development uses a **cross-sectional design,** in which groups of subjects, of different chronological ages, are observed and compared at one and the same time. A researcher can then draw conclusions about behavioral differences that may be related to those age differences. Using a cross-sectional design, researchers can investigate an entire age range at one time. The disadvantage of cross-sectional designs comes from comparing individuals who differ by year of birth as well as by chronological age differences. Age-related changes are confounded by differences in the social or political conditions experienced by different *birth cohorts* (people born in the same time period). Thus a study comparing samples of 10- and 18-year-olds now might find that the subjects differ from 10- and 18-year-olds

A drawback of cross-sectional research is the cohort effect. What differences might exist between these two groups of children (above) and of women (below) as a result of the era through which they have lived?

In order to discover age-related differences, researchers also use cross-sectional designs, studying groups of subjects of different chronological ages.

who grew up in the 1970s, in ways related to their different eras as well as to their developmental stages.

The best features of cross-sectional and longitudinal approaches are combined in **sequential designs.** The various types of sequential designs all involve studying, over time, individuals from different birth cohorts. For example, researchers might choose to undertake a *cohort-sequential* study. In this method, subjects would span a certain age range. They are grouped according to the years of their births, and the groups are observed repeatedly over several years. For example, a sequential study might start in 1994 with four birth cohorts of children ages 5 (1989), 4 (1990), 3 (1991), and 2 (1992), tested each year for three years. By choosing cohorts whose ages will overlap during the course of the study, a researcher can capture the benefits of both the cross-sectional and the longitudinal approaches.

Each of these techniques gives researchers the opportunity to document change from one age to another. But how do we determine what forces brought about the changes? We will seek an initial answer to this question by considering in turn what is shared and what is unique about each person's development.

Explaining Shared Aspects of Development

To explain development, psychologists must consider both universal aspects of change and the unique changes that characterize each individual.

Most children will learn to use language, but each child does so at a slightly different rate. Most adolescents reason more efficiently than their younger siblings, but some reason better than others. To explain development, we have to consider both universal, shared aspects of change and the unique aspects of change that characterize each individual. We will begin by discussing shared aspects of change and describe the potential of *nature* and *nurture* to shape development.

Nature and Nurture

The sharpest contrast among theories of development has most often been applied to childhood aspects of change. The question is how best to account for the profound differences between a newborn and, for example, a 10-year-old: To what extent is such development determined by heredity (nature), and to what extent is it a product of learned experiences (nurture)? The **nature–nurture controversy** is a long-standing debate among philosophers, psychologists, and educators over the relative importance of heredity and learning. On one side of this debate are those who believe that the human infant is born without knowledge or skills and that experience, in the form of human learning, etches messages on the blank tablet (in Latin, the *tabula rasa*) of the infant's unformed mind. This view, originally proposed by British philosopher **John Locke,** is known as *empiricism.* It credits human development to experience. Empiricists believe that what directs human development is the stimulation people receive as they are *nurtured.* Among the scholars opposing empiricism was French philosopher **Jean-Jacques Rousseau.** He argued the *nativist* view that *nature,* or the evolutionary legacy that each child brings into the world, is the mold that shapes development. People are, at birth, "noble savages," he argued, likely to be spoiled or corrupted by contact with society (Cranston, 1991).

Psychologists have long debated the relative importance of heredity versus experience in producing individual differences.

The nature–nurture debate reached a fever pitch toward the end of the eighteenth century. At this time, "mental medicine," an early version of modern psychology, had begun to capture the interest of learned people. Scholars debated the true nature of the human species, the influences of the mind on behavior, and the differences between humans and animals. The struggle between the empiricists and the nativists was intensified by the discovery, in 1798, of a boy who had apparently been raised by animals in the forests around the village of Aveyron, France. This 12-year-old *feral* (wild) child, who became known as the Wild Boy of Aveyron, was thought to hold the answers to profound questions about human nature: Could he, having survived the absence of human contact as a child, become fully human?

Victor, the Wild Boy of Aveyron.

A young doctor, **Jean Marc Itard,** accepted the challenge of trying to civilize and educate the Wild Boy of Aveyron, whom he named Victor. At first, Itard's intensive training program seemed to be working; Victor became affectionate and well mannered and learned to follow instructions. After five years, however, progress stopped, and the teacher reluctantly called an end to the experiment (Itard, reprinted 1962). Did nature or nurture fail? Perhaps Victor had been abandoned as an infant because he was developmentally disabled. If that was the case, any training could have had only limited success. If not, would modern training procedures have helped the boy develop more fully than Itard's methods? One authority on Victor's story, Harlan Lane (1976, 1986), believes that the case shows clearly the vital role of early social contact on communication and mental growth. Outside of society, says Lane, humans are nothing more than "ignoble savages."

Researchers have now developed a range of techniques to study the effects of nature and nurture without requiring unfortunate *experiments of nature* like Victor's case. We know that the extreme positions of Locke and Rousseau do injustice to the richness of human behavior. Almost any complex action is shaped both by an individual's biological inheritance and by personal experience, including learning. Heredity and environment have a continuing mutual influence on each other. As we shall illustrate shortly, heredity provides potential; experience determines the way in which the potential will be fulfilled (Bronfenbrenner & Ceci, 1994).

Researchers now believe that any complex behavior is influenced by the interaction of heredity and environment.

The Shared Human Inheritance

In Chapter 3, we introduced you to the evolution of the human genotype. Certain aspects of the development of all humans, no matter what the environment, are consistent because those aspects of development are standard elements of the human genetic inheritance. For example, children begin by uttering isolated words and progress to full sentences. Adolescents experience growth spurts and sexual maturation. Older adults encounter changes in their memory abilities. To explain the equivalence of developmental changes across individuals, researchers often point to the shared human inheritance.

Even when researchers believe that certain changes are dictated by the human genotype, there are still different ways to describe the overall sequence of changes. Some theorists believe that development is characterized by **developmental stages** that progress toward an expected end state (Cairns & Valsinger, 1984). Developmental stages are assumed to occur always in the same sequence; each stage is a necessary building block for the next. People may go through the stages at different rates, but not in different orders. In this view, development is *discontinuous,* a series of discrete stages rather than a smooth transformation. Change is seen as a succession of reorganizations—behavior is *qualitatively* different in different age-specific life periods.

Theorists disagree as to whether development is discontinuous—occurring in a sequence of orderly stages representing qualitative differences—or continuous—occurring through the gradual accumulation of quantitative differences.

Other psychologists take the position that development is essentially *continuous;* they believe it occurs gradually through the accumulation of *quantitative* changes. According to this view, you become more skillful in thinking, talking, or using your muscles in much the same way that you become taller—through the cumulative action of the same continuing processes. In this view, particular aspects of development are discontinuous, although development, as a whole, is a continuous process.

As with many theoretical oppositions, we will see cases that fit both points of view. The brain itself provides evidence that some development is continuous while other development is discontinuous. A study of the activity of the cerebral hemispheres revealed different patterns of development on the two sides of the brain (Thatcher et al., 1987). Patterns of electrical activity in the right and left hemispheres were studied in more than 500 subjects, ranging in age from 2 months to early adulthood. As can be seen in **Figure 5.1**, the left hemisphere develops in sudden growth spurts, while the right hemisphere

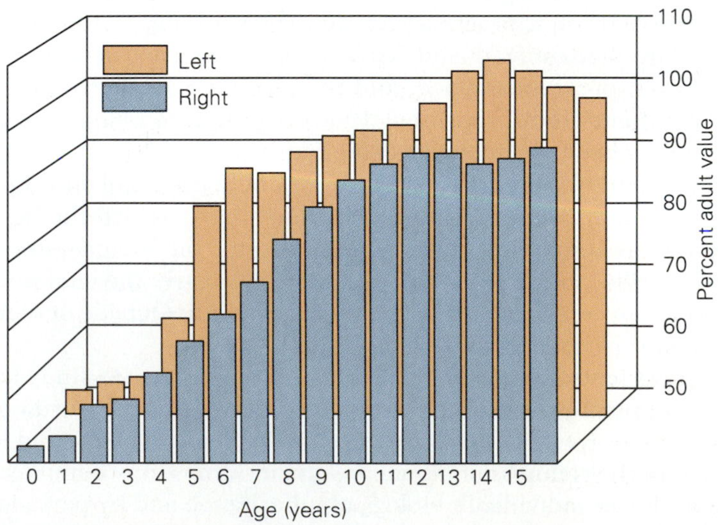

Figure 5.1 EEG Activity in the Cerebral Hemispheres

The graph shows the findings of research on 577 children, ages 2 months to early adulthood. The electrical activity in the right (front, blue) and left (rear, brown) hemispheres at each age period is compared to an adult level. While the development shown in the right hemisphere is continuous, there are growth spurts and discontinuities in the left hemisphere at early ages that correspond to Piaget's cognitive development stages (to be presented shortly).

changes gradually and continuously. Such results contribute toward the belief that you are biologically prepared to experience different domains of development with and without distinct stages.

The Impact of Environments

However development occurs—by qualitative or quantitative change—researchers can try to determine what, if any, information is necessary from the environment for development to take place. Thus, although children are biologically prepared to learn *any* language, they can acquire some particular language only by experiencing it in the world around them. When we turn, later in the chapter, to the study of language acquisition, you will see that much theoretical debate surrounds the question of how input—the types of things parents say to their children—affects the rate at which children learn to communicate effectively. You will see that children use expectations they bring into the world with them to make sense of the input in the environment (Pinker, 1994).

In some cases, the genotype might specify that certain types of environmental input must be present during critical periods. A **critical period** is a sensitive time when an organism is optimally ready to acquire a particular behavior if certain experiences occur. If those experiences do not occur, the organism does not develop the behavior at that time. When the critical period has passed, the organism will have a difficult time ever acquiring the behavior.

Experimental evidence supports the existence of critical periods in the development of both humans and animals.

Experimental evidence supports the idea that critical periods for certain functions occur in animals. For example, salamander tadpoles usually start swimming immediately upon birth. If they are prevented from swimming during their first eight days (by being kept in an anesthetizing solution), they swim normally as soon as they are released. However, if they are kept in the solution four or five days longer, they are never able to swim; the critical period has passed (Carmichael, 1926). Likewise, dogs and monkeys raised in isolation for a few months after birth behave in bizarre ways throughout their lives, even if they are later reared with other normal animals (Scott, 1963). This suggests that there is a critical period for developing social relationships.

Because it would be unethical to deprive human infants of normal experiences, information on critical periods generally comes from tragic experiments of nature, such as the Wild Boy of Aveyron. For example, malnutrition can impair mental capacities if it occurs shortly before birth and for a few months thereafter (when the brain is growing rapidly), but not when it occurs later in life (Wurtman, 1982). Children raised in institutions with minimal social attachments to adult caretakers show attentional and social problems in school, even when they are adopted after the age of 4 into caring families (Tizard & Hodges, 1978). However, some domains of development are not subject to critical periods. Although, for example, children's intellectual development is sensitive to environmental change, deprivation in early years does not necessarily cause permanent handicaps (Rutter, 1979).

When researchers discuss the forces of nature and nurture, it's easiest to focus on the earliest phases of the life span. Children, in a sense, seem closer to "nature" than do adolescents and adults, who have experienced more "nurture." The changes that characterize life from the teen years onward also provide fewer dramatic starting points and end points. The physical changes between a 31- and a 41-year-old, for example, are not nearly as startling as the physical changes between a 1- and an 11-year-old. Even so, we can still view important aspects of development beyond childhood as processes in which environmental input allows shared genetic potential to unfold.

Errors of the Genotype

Some physical and psychological disorders arise directly from errors in the genotype. Consider *Down syndrome,* a condition caused by an extra chromosome in the twenty-first pair (resulting in three chromosomes instead of two in the pair). Down syndrome is characterized by impaired psychomotor and physical development as well as mental retardation. Without intervention from psychologists and other skilled professionals, people with this disorder depend almost wholly on others to fulfill their basic needs. However, psychologists generally strive to use the resources of the environment to alleviate as much disability as possible. Special educational programs can teach persons with Down syndrome to care for themselves, hold simple jobs, and establish a small degree of personal independence that would otherwise be impossible.

Understanding the gene-environment-behavior pathway has led to a remarkably simple treatment for another kind of mental deficiency, *phenylketonuria,* or *PKU.* A PKU infant lacks the genetic material to produce an enzyme that metabolizes the amino acid *phenylalanine.* Because of this deficiency, phenylalanine accumulates in the infant's nervous system and interferes with normal growth and brain development. Changing the infant's diet to eliminate or greatly reduce food substances containing phenylalanine (such as lettuce) counteracts the negative genetic predisposition, and intellectual development moves into the normal range (Koch et al., 1963). Here, once again, you see why neither nature nor nurture alone can predict a child's accomplishments.

Down syndrome and PKU are examples of errors in the human genotype.

Let's turn now to aspects of the interaction of nature and nurture that make each individual unique.

Individual Genotypes and Environments

Important aspects of your body build, behavior, and development were all determined at the moment the genetic material in sperm and egg cells of your parents united. The meeting of sperm and egg determined many of the basic **constitutional factors** that will remain fairly consistent throughout your lifetime. Constitutional factors are apparent in a newborn child's characteristic physiological functioning and basic reaction tendencies. For example, some babies are more sensitive to stimulation than others—some have a high energy level and some are placid and not easily upset. Basic reaction tendencies such as these may affect the way children interact with their environment and, thus, what they will experience and how they will develop (Miyake et al., 1985). Let's see how genes may determine constitutional factors.

The Role of Genes

Recall from Chapter 3 that all normal human body cells have 46 chromosomes, half of which come from the mother and half from the father. One pair of chromosomes differs between males and females: males have one X chromosome and one smaller Y chromosome (an XY pair); females have two X chromosomes (an XX pair). **Genes** are segments along the chromosome strands that contain the blueprints or instructions for the development of physical characteristics and even of some psychological attributes.

Many human characteristics are polygenic, determined by a combination of genes.

Research in behavior genetics has determined that most human characteristics in which heredity plays a role are *polygenic,* or dependent on a combination of genes. The mere presence of a gene may or may not indicate that a certain human characteristic will develop. Genes that are always expressed when they are present in an individual, regardless of their combination with another gene, are called *dominant genes.* Genes that are expressed only when paired with a similar gene are called *recessive genes.* For example, an individual who has a gene for brown eyes, a dominant gene, will always have brown eyes, whether that gene pairs with a blue-eye gene or a brown-eye gene. However, an individual who has a gene for blue eyes, a recessive gene, will have blue eyes only if that gene pairs with another blue-eye gene. All-or-nothing characteristics, such as eye color, are controlled by either a single gene or by a pair of genes, depending on whether the characteristic is dominant or recessive. Characteristics that vary in degree, such as height, are thought to be controlled by several genes. Complex characteristics, including some psychological attributes such as emotionality, are surely controlled or influenced by the interaction of many groups of genes.

Genes that are always expressed are said to be dominant. Those that are expressed only when paired with a similar gene are recessive.

Only about 10 percent of the genes you inherit will be used in the course of your life. The unused *genetic potential* in your genotype is similar to a trust fund, available only if your usually constant environment changes in significant ways. If that environment does change, those who possess a genetic trust fund with the "right stuff" will be able to adapt to the change and pass on these environmentally appropriate genes to the next generation.

The Impact of Environments

Although the environment may have very little effect on your eye color, for more complex physical and psychological attributes your genotype specifies a potential that may or may not be realized in a particular environment. For example, your heredity determines how tall you can grow; how tall you actually become depends partly on nutrition, an environmental factor. **Figure 5.2** illustrates the interaction of height and favorableness of environment for groups of children with different genotypes for height. Similarly, your level of mental ability seems to depend on genetic potential, early stimulation, and environmental opportunity. In almost every instance we examine, nature and nurture interact. Nature provides the raw materials, and environment affects how genes play out their potential.

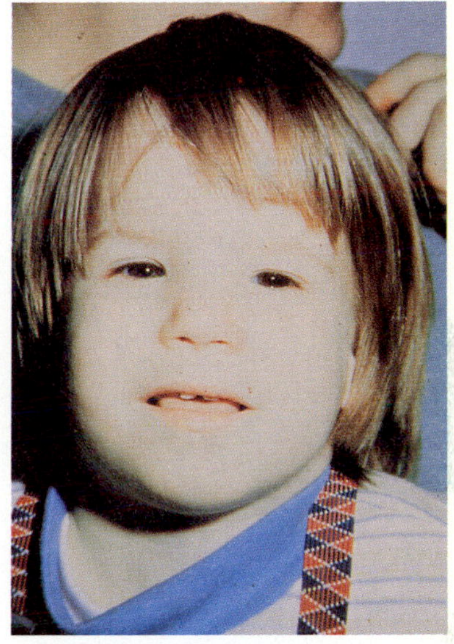

Exposure to alcohol during the critical prenatal period can result in mental retardation, behavioral disturbances, heart defects, and facial deformities—a cluster of abnormalities referred to as fetal alcohol syndrome.

The environment relevant to the fulfillment of genetic potential includes the chemical environment the child encounters while still in the mother's womb. During the first months of pregnancy, environmental factors such as malnutrition, infection, radiation, or drugs can prevent the normal formation of organs and body structures. Mothers who consume certain substances like alcohol put their unborn children at risk (Jacobson et al., 1993). Illegal substances may bring about even greater damage. Cocaine, for example, travels through the placenta and can affect fetal development directly. In adults, cocaine causes blood vessels to constrict; in pregnant women, cocaine

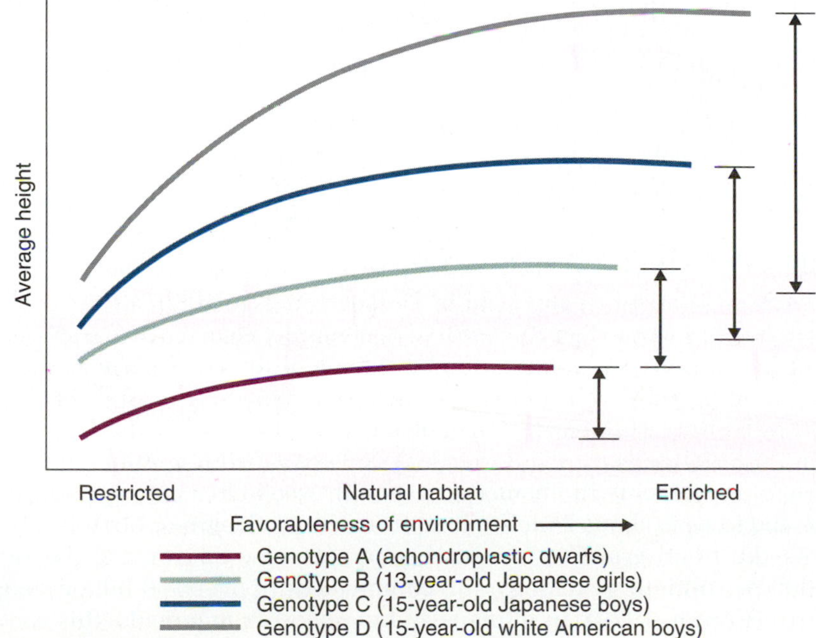

Figure 5.2 Reaction Ranges for Height as a Function of Environment

restricts placental blood flow and oxygen supply to the fetus. If severe oxygen deprivation results, blood vessels in the fetus's brain may burst. Such prenatal strokes can lead to lifelong physical and mental handicaps (Chasnoff, 1989; Chasnoff et al., 1985, 1989). Addicts often give birth to drug-dependent babies. For a cocaine-addicted newborn, the first two to three weeks of life are spent in the agony of drug withdrawal. Some of these babies are sluggish and depressed, while others are jittery and easily excitable. Once provoked, they are almost impossible to calm. Later, the child may experience such symptoms as hyperactivity, mental retardation, impaired motor and cognitive skills, short attention span, speech problems, apathy, aggression, and emotional flattening (Hamilton, 1990; Quindlen, 1990). Costly educational programs can only begin to undo the damage that occurs in the prenatal environment.

Early in the prenatal period, environmental factors such as nutrition or drugs can prevent normal development.

The environments that individuals experience after they are born, of course, vary enormously. Many of those differences play an important causal role in individual development (Dannefer & Perlmutter, 1990). For example, in Chapter 6 you will learn that parents have different expectations for boys and girls almost from birth. How does that environmental reality influence boys' and girls' development? We will also discuss there some of the cultural forces that shape the life outcomes for members of socially and, particularly, economically deprived groups. If you consider the profound differences among environments, it might not surprise you to learn that the older people become, the more different from each other they also become (Nelson & Dannefer, 1992). Often developmentalists try to characterize members of a particular cohort by describing the average member. Each individual's departure from that average tends to become relatively larger with increasing age. The explanation may be that the longer experience of differing environments successively weakens the influence of the shared genetic inheritance.

The older people become, the more different they become, possibly because the longer experience in the environment weakens the influence of shared genetic potential.

Let's turn now to our first particular domain of development, physical changes across the life span.

PHYSICAL DEVELOPMENT ACROSS THE LIFE SPAN

Many of the types of development we describe in this chapter and the next require some special knowledge to detect. For example, you might not notice landmarks in moral development until you read Chapter 6. We will begin, however, with a realm of development in which changes are often plainly visible to the untrained eye: **physical development.** There is no doubt that you have undergone enormous physical changes since you were born. Changes will continue until the end of your life. Because physical changes are so numerous, we will focus on the types of changes that have an impact on other realms of psychological development.

BABIES PREWIRED FOR SURVIVAL

The earliest behavior of any kind is the heartbeat. It begins in the *prenatal period,* before birth, when the embryo is about 3 weeks old and a sixth of an inch long. Responses to stimulation have been observed as early as the sixth week, when the embryo is not yet an inch long. Spontaneous movements are observed by the eighth week (Carmichael, 1970; Humphrey, 1970).

After the eighth week, the developing embryo is called a *fetus.* The mother feels fetal movements in about the sixteenth week after conception. At this point, the fetus is about 7 inches long (the average length at birth is 20 inches). As the brain grows in utero, it generates new neurons at the rate of 250,000 per minute, reaching a full complement of over 100 billion neurons by birth (Cowan, 1979). In humans and many other mammals, this cell proliferation and migration of neurons to their correct locations takes place prenatally, while the development of the branching processes of axons and dendrites largely occurs after birth (Kolb, 1989). The sequence of brain development, from 25 days to 9 months, is shown in **Figure 5.3**.

What capabilities are programmed into this brain at birth? William James, the foremost American psychologist at the beginning of the twentieth century, believed that the human infant was a totally helpless and confused organism. After experiencing the tranquillity of life in the womb, the infant was assailed on all sides by sudden bursts of stimulation—the world was "one great blooming, buzzing confusion." In 1928, John Watson, the founder of behaviorism, described the human infant as "a lively, squirming bit of flesh, capable of making a few simple responses." As recently as 1964, the author of a medical textbook proclaimed that the newborn could not focus its eyes or respond to sounds and did not possess consciousness.

These observers were more wrong than they could imagine. Moments out of the womb, infants reveal that they are precocious, sophisticated, and friendly: babies start life equipped with remarkable abilities to take information in through their senses and react to it. They might be thought of as *prewired for survival,* well suited to respond to adult caregivers and to influence their social environments. Newborns appear to come equipped to accomplish three basic tasks: (1) sustenance (feeding), (2) defense against

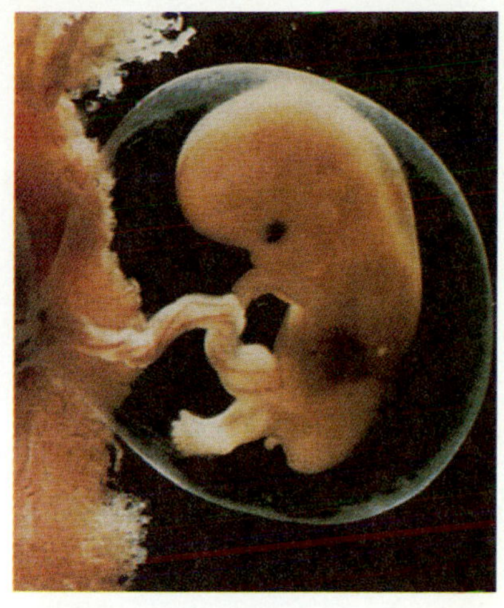

As the brain grows in the developing fetus, it generates 250,000 new neurons per minute.

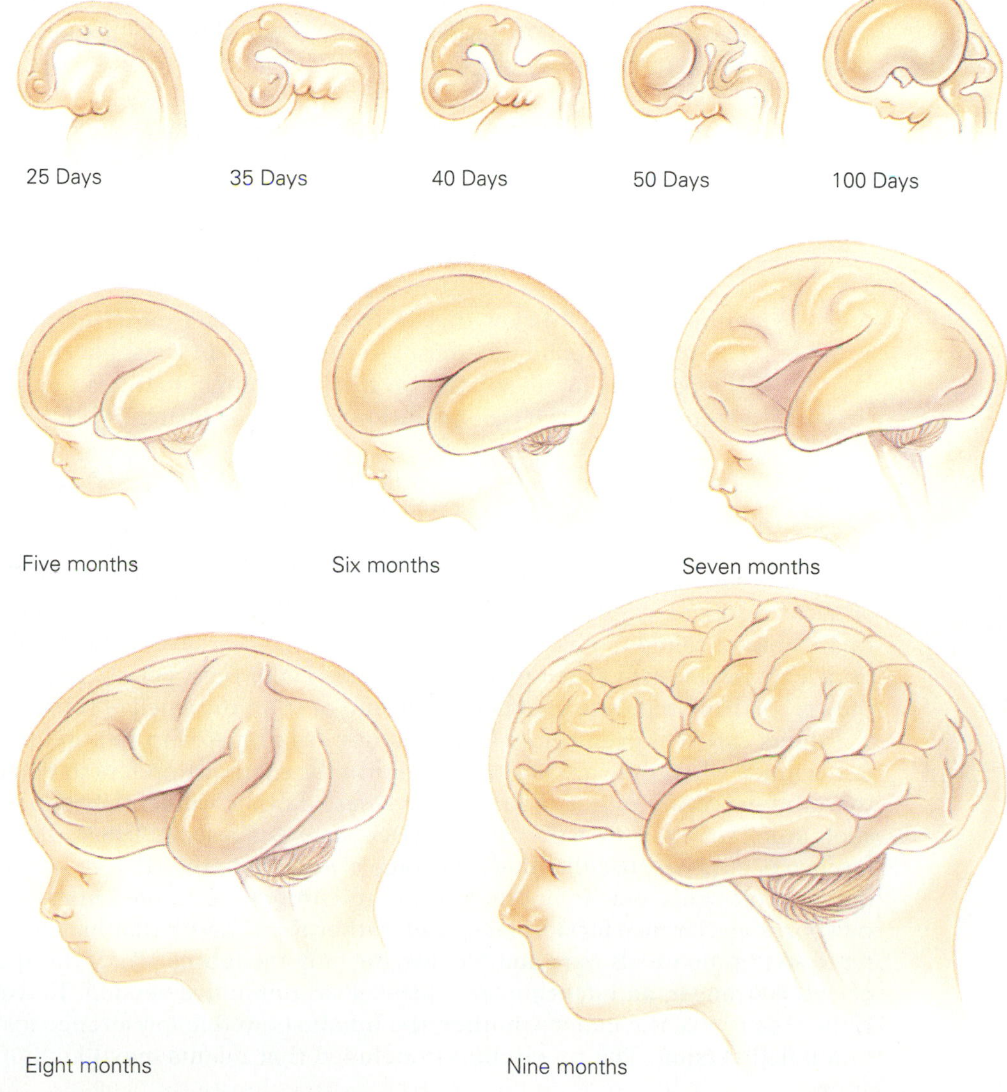

Figure 5.3 The Development of the Human Brain

harmful stimuli (withdrawing from pain or threat), and (3) maintenance of contact with people (for protection and care). These tasks require some ability to understand experiences with people and objects and some basic thinking skills, such as the capacity to combine information from different senses (von Hofsten & Lindhagen, 1979). We now examine some of the evidence that infants have sophisticated capabilities.

Sensory Abilities and Preferences

Even within the first few hours of life, a newborn infant, given an appropriate stimulus, is capable of a variety of responses. If placed upon the mother's abdomen, the baby will usually make crawling motions. The baby will also turn its head toward anything that strokes its cheek—a nipple or a finger—and root around with its mouth for something to suck. *Suckling* is the only behavior that is common among all mammals (Blass & Teicher, 1980). Suckling is an exceedingly complex, highly developed behavior pattern involving intricate coordination of tongue and swallowing movements and synchronization of the baby's breathing with the suckling and swallowing sequence. Yet most babies know how to do it from the start. Suckling is an adaptable behavior that can be changed by its *consequences.* The rapidity of suckling, for example, depends on the sweetness of the fluid being received. The sweeter the fluid, the more continuously—and also the more forcefully—an infant will suckle (Lipsitt et al., 1976). In fact, the suckling rate even depends on the *pattern* of sweetness over time, rather than simply on the absolute amount of sweetness at the moment:

Suckling is a complex behavior pattern present in the newborn, allowing the baby to eat.

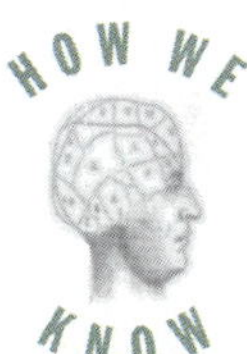

A group of newborns who were given a sucrose-sweetened solution through an automated nipple apparatus responded at the average rate of 55 sucks per minute, compared with 46 sucks per minute for a group that received water. A third group, which had sucrose first and then water, matched the rate of the first group while it was getting sucrose; but when the sucrose changed to water, the group's rate fell below that of the water-only group. Not only did this group respond differently to the different tastes, but the experience of the sweet solution in the preceding 5 minutes weakened its response to the water solution (Kobre & Lipsitt, 1972).

Infants apparently come into the world programmed to like and seek pleasurable sensations, such as sweetness, and to avoid or escape unpleasant stimulation, such as loud noises, bright lights, strong odors, and painful stimuli. As early as 12 hours after birth, they show distinct signs of pleasure at the taste of sugar water or vanilla, and they smile when they smell banana essence. Infants prefer salted to unsalted cereal, even when they have had virtually no prior experience with salted foods (Bernstein, 1990; Harris et al., 1990). But they recoil from the taste of lemon or shrimp or from the smell of rotten eggs.

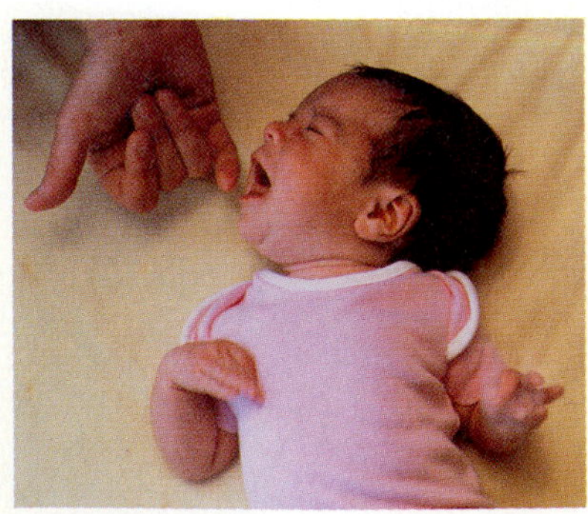

The rooting reflex.

Infants can hear even before birth, so they are prepared to respond to certain sounds when they are born. A newborn, for example, prefers to listen to the mother's voice rather than to the voices of other women but shows no such preference for the father's voice (DeCasper & Prescott, 1983). This difference occurs because the mother's voice is audible to the fetus in utero but outside voices are not. In another study, researchers examined instances of newborns' preference for normal speech rather than speech that had been filtered so that no words were audible, leaving only the intonation. If the speaker was a stranger, an infant preferred the clear, unmuffled version. However, if the tape was of the infant's mother, the infant showed no preference for the unmuffled version. The researchers concluded that infants may like muffled maternal speech equally well early on because it sounds similar to what they heard in utero (Spence & DeCasper, 1987).

Infants prefer the mother's voice, indicating that they can hear before they are born.

Children also put their visual systems to work almost immediately: a few minutes after birth, a newborn's eyes are alert, turning in the direction of a voice and searching inquisitively for the source of certain sounds. Even so, vision is less well developed than the other senses at birth; indeed, babies are born "legally blind," with a visual acuity of about 20/500. Good vision—sensitivity to contrast, visual acuity, and color discrimination—requires that a great many photoreceptor cells function in the center of the eye's receptive area and that the optics of the eye develop appropriately (see Chapter 7). Front-end information losses are due to the immaturity of these components of the infant's visual system. On the back end, good vision requires numerous connections between the neurons in the visual cortex of the brain. At birth, not enough of these connections are laid down.

At birth, vision is less well developed than the other senses.

These immature systems develop very rapidly, however, and as they do, the baby's visual capacities become evident (Banks & Bennett, 1988). Early on, infants can perceive large objects that display a great deal of contrast. A 1-month-old child can detect contours of a head at close distances; at 7 weeks, the baby can scan the features of the mother's face, and as the mother talks, the baby can scan her eyes. As early as 2 months of age, the baby begins to see a world of color, differentiating patterns of white, red, orange, and blue. At 3 months, the baby can perceive depth and is well on the way to enjoying the visual abilities of adults. Even without perfect vision, however, children have visual preferences. Pioneering researcher **Robert Fantz** (1963) observed that babies as young as 4 months old preferred looking at objects with contours rather than those that were plain, complex ones rather than simple ones, and whole faces rather than faces with features in disarray.

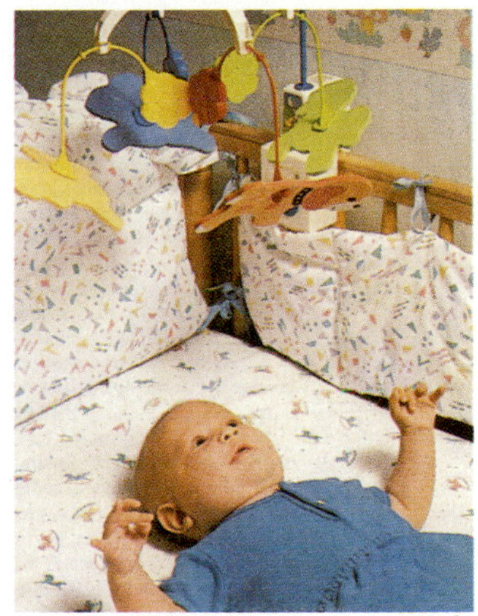

Early on, infants can perceive large objects that display a great deal of contrast.

Generating Expectations

Rather than being passive recipients of sensory stimulation, newborns possess an innate cognitive ability to extract cause-and-effect relationships in the world. The infant's responses imply that a simple memory system must be operating and, further, that expectations and inferences are being formed. **Elliott Blass** (1990) and his research team demonstrated such innate memory abilities by teaching newborns only 1 to 2 days old to *anticipate* the pleasurable sensation of the sweet taste of sucrose.

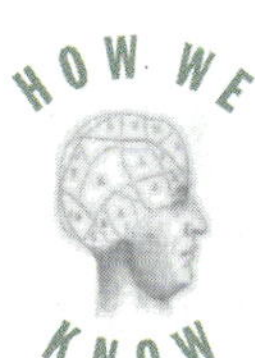

The researchers played the click of a castanet for a 10-second period before they gave infants sugar water. Soon the sound of the click would cause the baby to turn its head in the direction the sweet fluid was delivered—in anticipation of good times past. What do you predict happened when the click was not followed by sucrose? The babies got upset. Almost all (6 of 8) newborns cried when the sweets failed to show up. It is as if the babies were responding emotionally to a violation of a reliable relationship that had been established. Surprisingly, the click was the only sound the researchers found that was effective in this role. The babies ignored a *psst* sound and the *ting* of a triangle; they became calm and inactive when they heard a *shhh* sound. The explanation for this finding might be that clicks are similar to the types of kissing and clucking sounds that caregivers ordinarily make (Blass, 1990).

It seems that babies start to build up their knowledge of the world by extracting relationships between sensory events. Through interactions of inherited response tendencies and learned experiences, babies, in time, become competent to acquire vast amounts of information. Let's turn now from innate capacities to early physical changes.

Patterns of Physical Growth and Maturation

Newborn infants change at an astonishing rate but, as shown in **Figure 5.4**, physical growth is not equal across all physical structures. You've probably noticed that babies seem to be all head. At birth, a baby's head is already about 60 percent of its adult size and measures a quarter of the whole body length (Bayley, 1956). Disproportionate early growth takes place *within* the head. By virtue of the development of axons and dendrites, the total mass of brain cells grows at an astonishing rate, increasing by 50 percent in the first two years and continuing to grow rapidly before leveling off by about 11 years of age. An infant's body weight doubles in the first six months and triples by the first birthday; by the age of 2, a child's trunk is about half of its adult length. Genital tissue shows little change until the teenage years and then develops rapidly to adult proportions.

Research suggests that early growth takes place in concentrated bursts.

With what pattern do these changes occur? You may believe that this growth goes on fairly smoothly and continuously, but research suggests that much early growth takes place in concentrated bursts:

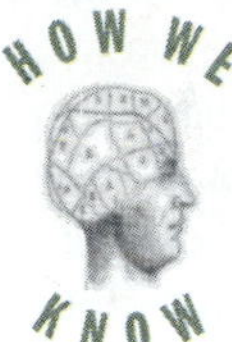

A team of researchers visited 3-day- to 21-month-old children in their homes to measure their length, weight, and head circumference. Some children were measured every day. Others were measured once or twice a week. The researchers discovered that much of the time no growth took place from one measurement to the next. In fact, almost all the growth appeared to take place during concentrated 24-hour periods. For example, the average time between days of growth in length was about 12 days. On growth days, the babies would, on average, all at once become about 0.4 inches longer (Lampl et al., 1992).

These results suggest that the majority of your young life was spent *not* growing—but when the time came, growth happened in quite a burst.

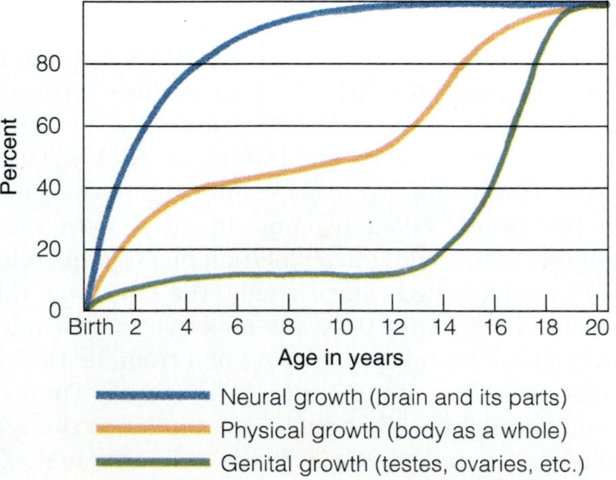

Figure 5.4 Growth Patterns Across the First Two Decades of Life
Neural growth occurs very rapidly in the first year of life. It is much faster than overall physical growth. By contrast, genital maturation does not occur until adolescence.

For most children, physical growth is accompanied by the maturation of motor ability. The characteristic maturational sequences newborns experience are determined by the interaction of inherited biological boundaries and environmental inputs. **Maturation** refers to the process of growth typical of all members of a species who are reared in the species' usual habitat. Maturation describes the systematic changes occurring over time in bodily functioning and behavior. These changes are influenced by genetic factors, chemical factors in the prenatal and postnatal environments (nutritive or toxic influences), and sensory factors that are *constant* for all members of the species—such as the force of gravity or basic social contacts (Hebb, 1966).

Physical growth is usually accompanied by maturation of motor ability.

For example, in the sequence for locomotion, as shown in **Figure 5.5**, a child learns to walk without special training. Development of walking follows a fixed, time-ordered sequence that is typical of all physically capable members of the human species. However, in cultures in which there is less physical stimulation, children begin to walk later. The Native American practice of carrying babies in tightly bound back cradles retards walking, but once released, the child goes through the same sequence. Therefore, you can think of all unimpaired newborn children as possessing the same potential for physical maturation.

If you look again at Figure 5.4, you'll observe that physical changes progress slowly from about age 4 until adolescence (Bee, 1994). For most of that period of time, children average a 2- to 3-inch increase in length each year and a 6-pound increase in weight. By age 6 or 7, most basic motor skills

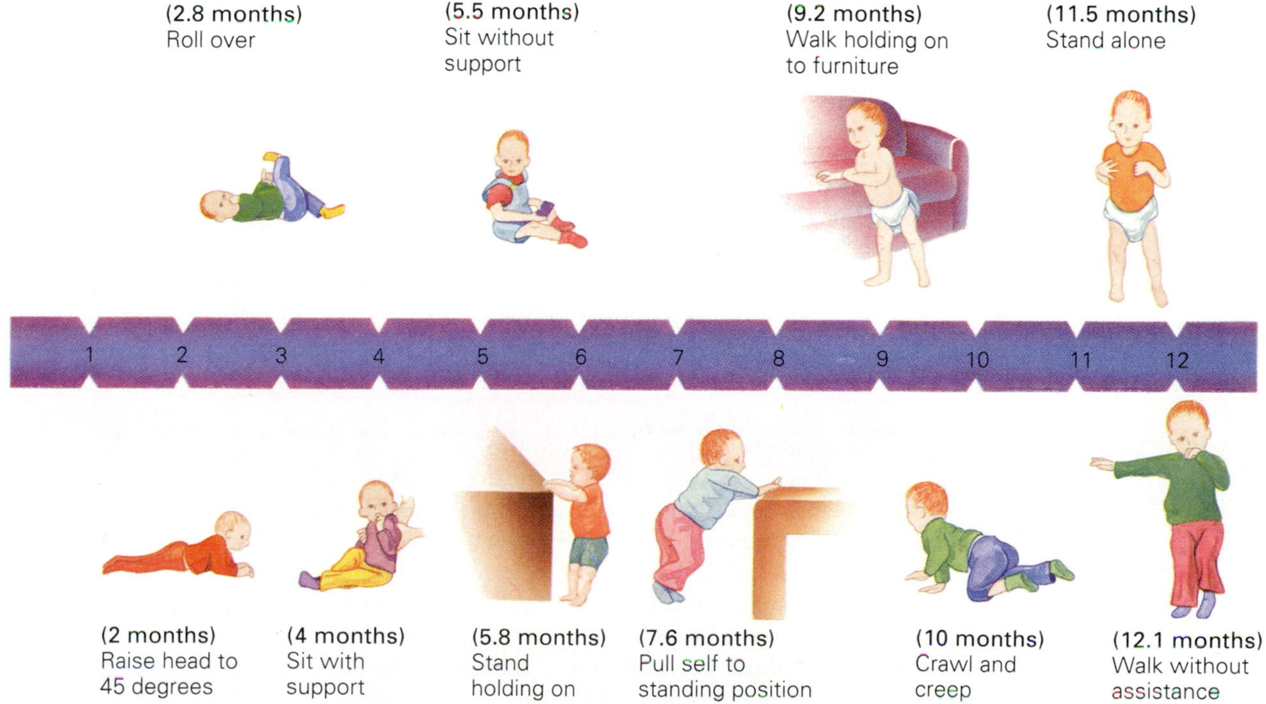

Figure 5.5 Maturational Timetable for Locomotion

The development of walking requires no special teaching. It follows a fixed, time-ordered sequence that is typical of all physically capable members of our species. In cultures that provide stimulation for very young children, youngsters begin to walk sooner (Shirley, 1931).

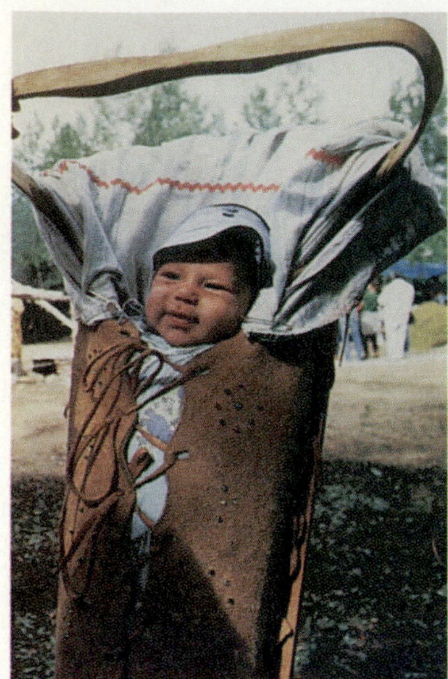

What effect does a cradle board have on the infant's ability to learn to walk?

are in place. Late childhood is spent improving those skills. The next period of rapid change is adolescence, to which we now turn.

Physical Development in Adolescence

The first concrete indicator of the end of childhood is the *pubescent growth spurt.* At around age 10 for girls and age 12 for boys, growth hormones flow into the bloodstream. For several years, the adolescent may grow three to six inches a year and gain weight rapidly as well. The adolescent's body does not reach adult proportions all at once (Bee, 1994). Hands and feet grow to full adult size first. The arms and legs come next, with the torso developing most slowly. Thus an individual's overall shape changes several times over the teenage years.

Two to three years after the onset of the growth spurt, **puberty,** or sexual maturity, is reached. (The Latin word *pubertas* means *covered with hair* and signifies the growth of hair on the arms and legs, under the arms, and in the genital area.) Puberty for males begins with the production of live sperm, while for girls it begins at **menarche,** the onset of menstruation. In the United States, the average time for menarche is between the ages of 12 and 13, although the normal range extends from 11 to 15. For boys, the production of live sperm first occurs, on average, between the ages of 12 and 14, but again there is considerable variation in this timing. These physical changes often bring about an awareness of sexual feelings. In Chapter 12, we will discuss the onset of sexual motivation.

While menarche marks the beginning of puberty in females, puberty begins in males with the production of live sperm.

The physical changes of puberty have an impact on other aspects of the adolescent's psychological development. These changes often cause adolescents to focus considerable attention on their physical appearance. Attractiveness has been found to have an influence on the way people view each other at all ages (Hatfield & Sprecher, 1986), but the forces of adolescence—dramatic physical changes and heightened emphasis on peer acceptance (especially peers of the opposite sex)—exaggerate individuals' concern with their **body image**—their subjective view of their appearance. This image depends not only on measurable features, such as height and weight, but also on other people's assessments and on cultural standards of physical beauty. In adolescent populations, girls appear, on average, to have even less confidence in their physical attractiveness than do boys (Wade, 1991). In data averaged across adolescents from ten countries (including the United States, Bangladesh, Turkey, and Taiwan), 38 percent of the girls and 27 percent of the boys reported feeling ugly and unattractive (Offer et al., 1988). When exaggerated, girls' preoccupation with body image and other aspects of their *social self* can lead to self-destructive behavior (Rolls et al., 1991; Striegel-Moore et al., 1993). To achieve their misperceived perfection, adolescent females may develop serious eating disorders, such as *anorexia,* which involves self-starvation, and *bulimia,* which involves binging and purging. (We will discuss eating disorders more fully in Chapter 12.) Fortunately, early adolescence appears to be the peak period for this preoccupation. Over time, adolescents become more accepting of their appearances.

Adolescents tend to place exaggerated emphasis on body image.

With the passing of adolescence, your body once again reaches a period of the life span in which biological change is comparatively minimal. You may affect your body in a variety of ways—by diet and exercise, for example—but the next striking set of changes that are consistent consequences of aging occur in middle and late adulthood.

Physical Changes in Adulthood

Some of the most obvious changes that occur with age concern people's physical appearances and abilities. As you grow older, you can expect your skin to

A significant percentage of adolescents in a variety of cultures report feeling unhappy with their looks.

wrinkle, your hair to thin and gray, and your height to decrease an inch or two. You can also expect some of your senses to become less acute. These changes do not appear suddenly at age 65. They occur gradually, beginning as soon as early adulthood. However, before we describe some common age-related changes, we want to make a more general point: many physical changes arise not from aging but from *disuse.* Researchers have supported this assertion by comparing the physical changes in older adults with physical changes in younger individuals who, for one reason or another, are required to have periods of inactivity (Bortz, 1982). For example, individuals who need extended bed rest experience the same decline in heart and lung efficiency as older adults. These results support a general belief in the maxim "Use it or lose it." Older adults who maintain (or renew) a program of physical fitness may experience fewer of the difficulties that are often thought to be inevitable consequences of aging. (Note that we will reach exactly the same conclusion when we discuss cognitive and social aspects of middle and late adulthood.) Let's now look, however, at some changes that are largely unavoidable and frequently have an impact on the way adults think about their lives.

Many of the physical changes associated with age result not from age itself but from disuse.

Vision

The vast majority of people over 65 experience some loss of visual function (Carter, 1982; Pitts, 1982). With age, the lenses of people's eyes become yellowed and less flexible. The yellowing of the lens is thought to be responsible for diminished color vision experienced by some older people. Colors of lower wavelengths—violets, blues, and greens—are particularly hard for some older adults to discriminate. The rigidity of the lens can make seeing objects at close range difficult. Lens rigidity also affects dark adaptation,

Older adults can and do enjoy the many benefits of intimacy and sexual relationships.

making night vision a problem for older people. Most normal visual changes can be aided with corrective lenses.

Hearing

Hearing loss is common among those 60 and older. The average older adult has difficulty hearing high frequency sounds (Corso, 1977). This impairment is usually greater for men than for women. Older people can have a hard time understanding speech—particularly that spoken by high-pitched voices. (Oddly enough, with age, people's speaking voices increase in pitch due to stiffening of the vocal cords.) Deficits in hearing can be gradual and hard for an individual to notice until they are extreme. In addition, even when individuals become aware of hearing loss, they may deny it, because it is perceived as an undesirable sign of aging. Some of the physiological aspects of hearing loss can be overcome with the help of hearing aids. You should also be aware, as you grow older or interact with older adults, that it helps to speak in low tones, enunciate clearly, and reduce background noise.

By age 65, most people experience some loss in visual function, and hearing loss is common in adults age 60 and older.

Reproductive and Sexual Functioning

We saw that puberty marks the onset of reproductive functioning. In middle and late adulthood, reproductive capacity diminishes (Bee, 1994). Around age 50, most women experience *menopause,* the cessation of menstruation and ovulation. For men, changes are less abrupt, but the quantity of viable sperm falls off after age 40 and the volume of seminal fluid declines after age 60. Of course, these changes are relevant primarily to reproduction. Increasing age and physical change do not necessarily impair other aspects of sexual experience (Turner & Adams, 1988). Indeed, sex is one of life's healthy pleasures that can enhance successful aging since it is arousing, provides aerobic exercise, stimulates fantasy, and is a vital form of social interaction (Ornstein & Sobel, 1989).

You have had a brief review of the landmarks of physical development. Against that background, let's turn now to the ways in which you developed an understanding of the world around you.

EARLY COGNITIVE DEVELOPMENT

How does an individual's understanding of physical and social reality change across the life span? **Cognitive development** is the study of the processes and products of the mind as they emerge and change over time. In this section, we will focus on the earliest stages of cognitive development, in childhood through early adolescence. In the next section, we trace cognitive development across the adult years.

As we consider the cognitive development of children, we address the question, How and when do children begin to reason, think, plan strategies, and solve problems? We will also consider the way in which children's perceptions of their physical and social worlds mature. Finally, we will explore questions concerned with the child's theory of mind. Do children know that objects still exist even when they can't see them? Do they know that it is possible to believe in ideas that aren't true and that people, but not objects, have desires and dreams? Cognitive developmentalists want to know how and what children think.

We begin our overview by describing the pioneering work of the late Swiss psychologist **Jean Piaget.** We then see how Piaget's work has been amended and incorporated into modern views of perceptual and cognitive development. Along the way, you will have to work hard to reexperience the types of thoughts you had as a 2-, 4-, 6-, or 10-year-old.

Piaget's Insights into Mental Growth

For nearly 50 years, Jean Piaget developed theories about the ways that children think, reason, and solve problems. Perhaps Piaget's interest in cognitive development grew out of his own intellectually active youth: Piaget published his first article at age 10 and turned down an offer to become a museum curator while still in high school (Flavell, 1963). His early training in biology and biological observation helped him investigate human cognition. Piaget saw the human mind as an active biological system that seeks, selects, interprets, and reorganizes environmental information to fit with or adjust to its own existing mental structures.

Piaget began his quest to understand the nature of the child's mind by carefully observing the behavior of his own three children. He would pose problems to them, observe their responses, slightly alter the situations, and once again observe their responses. Piaget used simple demonstrations and sensitive interviews with his own children and with other children to generate complex theories about early mental development. His interest was not in the amount of information children possessed but in the ways their thinking and inner representations of outer physical reality changed at different stages in their development. We now review the major components of Piaget's approach to cognitive development.

Schemes

Piaget gave the name **schemes** to the mental structures that enable individuals to interpret the world. Schemes are the building blocks of developmental change. Piaget characterized the infant's initial schemes as *sensorimotor intelligence*—mental structures or programs that guide sensorimotor sequences, such as suckling, looking, grasping, and pushing. Schemes are enduring abilities and dispositions to carry out specific kinds of action sequences that aid the child's adaptation to its environment. With practice, elementary schemes are combined, integrated, and differentiated into ever-more-complex, diverse action patterns, as when a child pushes away undesired objects to seize a desired one behind them. At first, these sensorimotor sequences depend on the physical presence of objects that, for example, can be sucked, or watched, or grasped. But thereafter, mental structures increasingly incorporate *symbolic representations* of outer reality. As they do, the child performs more complex mental operations (Gallagher & Reid, 1981; Piaget, 1977).

Piaget suggested that children use schemes to adapt to changes in their environment.

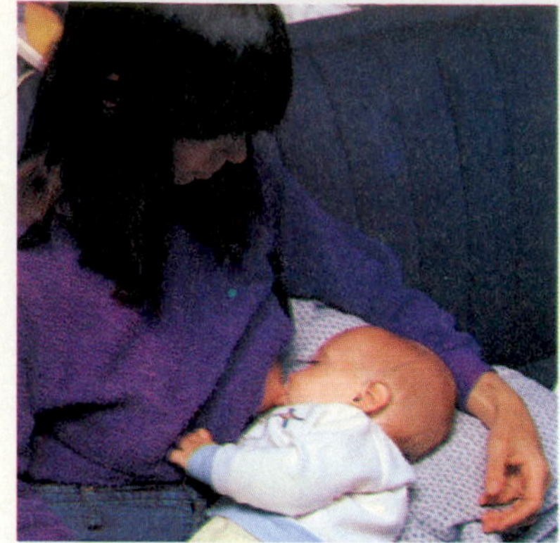

Although an infant begins to suck a bottle just the way he or she sucked a breast (assimilation), the infant soon discovers that some changes are necessary (accommodation). The child will make an even greater accommodation in the transitions from bottle to straw to cup.

Assimilation and Accommodation

According to Piaget, two basic processes work in tandem to achieve cognitive growth—assimilation and accommodation. **Assimilation** modifies new environmental information to fit into what is already known. The child accesses existing schemes to structure incoming sensory data. **Accommodation** restructures or modifies the child's existing schemes so that new information is accounted for more completely. Consider the transitions a baby must make from suckling at a mother's breast, to suckling the nipple of a bottle, to sipping through a straw, and then to drinking from a cup. The initial suckling response is a reflex action present at birth, but it must be modified somewhat so that the child's mouth fits the shape and size of the mother's nipple. In adapting to a bottle, an infant still uses many parts of the sequence unchanged (assimilation) but must grasp and draw on the rubber nipple somewhat differently from before and learn to hold the bottle at an appropriate angle (accommodation). The steps from bottle to straw to cup require more accommodation but continue to rely on earlier skills.

Piaget saw cognitive development as the result of exactly this sort of interweaving of assimilation and accommodation. Assimilation keeps and adds to what exists, thereby connecting the present with the past. Accommodation results from new problems posed by the environment. Discrepancies between the child's old ideas and new experiences force a child to develop more adaptive inner structures and processes that, in turn, permit creative and appropriate action to meet future challenges. The balanced application of assimilation and accommodation permits children's behavior and knowledge to become less dependent on concrete external reality, relying more on abstract thought. Mental growth follows a path from reliance on *appearances* to reliance on *rules.* It also progresses from reliance on the *concrete* and *physical* to reliance on the *abstract* and *symbolic.*

Stages in Cognitive Development

Piaget strongly believed that children's cognitive development could be divided into a series of ordered, discontinuous stages. He proposed four qualitatively different stages of cognitive growth: the *sensorimotor stage* (infancy), the *preoperational stage* (early childhood), the *concrete operational stage* (middle childhood), and the *formal operational stage* (adolescence). Distinct cognitive styles emerge at each step of this progression. All children are assumed to progress through these stages in the same sequence, although one child may take longer to pass through a given stage than another.

Sensorimotor Stage. The period extends roughly from birth to age 2. In the early months, much of an infant's behavior is based on a limited array of inborn schemes, like suckling, looking, grasping, and pushing. During the first year, sensorimotor sequences are improved, combined, coordinated, and integrated (suckling and grasping, looking and manipulating, for example). They become more varied as the infant tests different aspects of the environment, discovers that her actions have an effect on external events, and begins to perform what appear to be intentional, directed behaviors toward clear goals. But in the sensorimotor period, the child is tied to her immediate environment and motor-action schemes, because she lacks the cognitive ability to represent objects symbolically.

The most important cognitive acquisition of the infancy period is the ability to form mental representations of absent objects—those with which the child is not in direct sensorimotor contact. By the end of the second year, the child has developed this ability. **Object permanence** refers to a child's perceptions that objects exist and behave independently of her actions or awareness. In the first months of life, children follow objects with their eyes, but when the objects disappear from view, they turn away as if the objects had also disappeared from their minds. Around 3 months of age, however, they keep looking at the place where the objects had disappeared. Between 8 and 12 months, children begin to search for those disappearing objects. Not until about 2 years, however, are children capable of displaying object permanence in all the situations Piaget invented (Flavell, 1985).

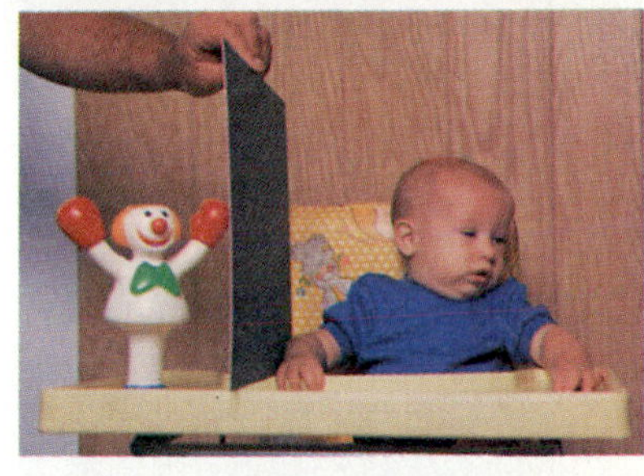

Piaget observed that the typical 6-month-old will attend to an attractive toy (top photo) but will quickly lose interest if a screen blocks the toy from view (bottom photo).

Preoperational Stage. This period extends roughly from 2 to 7 years of age. The big cognitive advance in this developmental stage is an improved ability to represent mentally objects that are not physically present. Although representational thought begins in the sensorimotor period, it becomes fully functioning in the preoperational stage. Except for this development, Piaget characterizes the preoperational stage according to what the child *cannot* do. We describe three aspects of preoperational thought.

At the preoperational stage, young children's thought is marked by **egocentrism:** an inability to take the perspective of another person or to imagine a scene from any perspective other than one's own. You have probably noticed egocentrism if you've heard a 2-year-old's conversations with other children. Children at this age often seem to be talking to themselves rather than interacting. To demonstrate more general egocentrism, Piaget showed children a three-dimensional, three-mountain scene and asked them to describe what a teddy bear standing on the far side would see; his subjects could not describe this scene from that other perspective accurately until about age 7 (Piaget & Inhelder, 1967).

Preoperational children also have difficulty distinguishing the mental world from the physical world. You can see this in their tendency to physicalize mental phenomena, such as when they say that dreams are pictures on the walls that everyone can see. Parents are familiar with this phenomenon: consider a 3½-year-old boy who appeared in his parents' room at 2 A.M. to tell them there was a bad giraffe in his room. You can also see this in their *animistic thinking*—attributing life and mental processes to physical, inanimate objects and events. Thus, for example, clouds cover the sun "on purpose" because "we ought to go to sleep" (Piaget, 1929).

Finally, preoperational children typically experience **centration**—the tendency to be captivated by the more perceptually striking features of objects. Centration is illustrated by Piaget's classic demonstration of a child's inability to understand that the amount of a substance does not change as a function of the size or shape of its container.

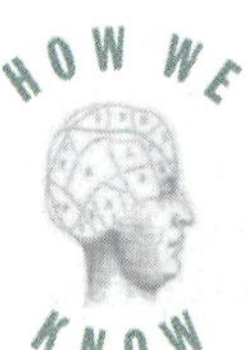

When an equal amount of lemonade is poured into two identical glasses, children of ages 5 and 7 report that the glasses contain the same amount. When, however, the lemonade from one glass is poured into a tall, thin glass, their opinions diverge. The 5-year-olds know that the lemonade in the tall glass is the same lemonade (qualitative identity), but they believe that somehow it has become more. The 7-year-olds correctly assert that there is no difference between the amounts. The younger children still rely on appearance; the older ones rely on a rule. The younger children center on a single, perceptually salient dimension—the height of the lemonade in the glass; the older ones take into account both height and width.

Egocentrism and centration are primary characteristics of a child's thinking during the preoperational stage.

Concrete Operational Stage. The period goes roughly from 7 to 11 years of age. The 7-year-olds in the lemonade study have mastered what Piaget called **conservation:** they know that the physical properties of objects do not change when nothing is added or taken away, even though the objects'

This 5-year-old girl is aware that the two containers have the same amount of colored liquid. However, when the liquid from one is poured into a taller container, she indicates that there is more liquid in the taller one. She has not yet grasped the concept of conservation, which she will understand by age 6 or 7.

appearance changes. The ability to conserve is one of the hallmarks of the concrete operational stage. Now the child is capable of *mental operations.* The deficiencies of the earlier stages no longer operate as long as the child is dealing with concrete, perceptually visible objects. For example, if a child sees that Adam is taller than Zara and, later, that Zara is taller than Tanya, the child can reason that Adam is the tallest of the three. But if the information about their relative heights is presented to the child verbally and he is not permitted to observe their height directly, he cannot draw the correct conclusion.

The child's inability to solve the relative height problem without direct observation suggests that abstract thought is still in the offing in the period of concrete operations. The symbols children of this age use in reasoning are still symbols for concrete objects and events, and not abstractions. The limitations of their thinking are shown in the familiar game of Twenty Questions, the goal of which is to determine the identity of an object by asking the fewest possible questions of the person who thinks up the object. A child of 7 or 8 usually sticks to very specific questions, such as "Is it a bird?" or "Is it a cat?" Children at the concrete operational stage usually don't ask abstract questions, such as "Does it fly?" or "Does it hunt?"

Formal Operational Stage. This covers a span roughly from age 11 on. In this final stage of cognitive growth, thinking becomes abstract. Adolescents can see how their particular reality is only one of several imaginable realities, and they begin to ponder deep questions of truth, justice, and existence. Most young adolescents have acquired all the mental structures needed to go from being naive thinkers to experts. The approach of adolescents and adults to the Twenty Questions game demonstrates their ability to use abstractions and to adopt an information-processing strategy that is not merely random guesswork. They impose their own structures on the task, starting with broad categories and then formulating and testing hypotheses in the light of their knowledge of categories and relationships. Their questioning moves from general categories ("Is it an animal?") to subcategories ("Does it fly?") and then to specific guesses ("Is it a bird?") (Bruner et al., 1966).

Contemporary Perspectives on Early Cognitive Development

Piaget's theory of the dynamic interplay of assimilation and accommodation is the model many developmental psychologists rely on to understand how other mental and behavioral processes develop. However, contemporary researchers have come up with more flexible ways of studying the development of the child's cognitive abilities. Their research has shown that there is a greater degree of order, organization, and coherence in the perceptual and cognitive experience of the infant and young child than Piaget realized.

Many of the modifications of Piaget's theory have arisen because researchers have improved on his original tasks. In developing his ideas, Piaget did not distinguish between *performance* (doing) and *competence* (knowing). Therefore, he assumed that failure to perform correctly showed a lack of underlying cognitive competence. However, on some of his tasks, the young child may not have understood his verbal instructions or may not have had sufficient motivation to carry out the complex routine required. For example, research shows that the difference in conceptual understanding between preoperational and concrete operational children may actually be a difference in immediate memory (Case, 1985). Children at the preoperational stage are unable to perform tasks that overload their limited memory system, even when they understand the basic concepts involved in the task. We will now see how a variety of creative new techniques have refined Piaget's conclusions about children's competence.

The Sensorimotor Child Revisited

Piaget suggested that the development of object permanence is the major accomplishment of the 2-year-old child. However, new research techniques suggest that infants as young as 3 months old, and perhaps younger, have already developed this concept. They apparently understand the basic principle that solid objects cannot pass through other solid objects. This important finding has been shown with different tasks devised by researcher **Renée Baillargeon** (Buy-ay-zhon) (1987a, 1987b). During one task, infants demonstrated surprise when observing sequences of events that were impossible.

Research demonstrating that infants are surprised at impossible events suggests the development of object permanence at a much earlier age than Piaget theorized.

The infants sat in front of a large display box. Directly before them was a small screen; to the left of the screen was a long ramp. The infants watched the following event: the screen was raised (so the infants could see there was nothing behind it) and then lowered; a toy car was pushed onto the ramp; the car rolled down the ramp and across the display box, disappearing as it shot behind the screen, reappearing at the end of the screen, and finally exiting the display box to the right (see **Figure 5.6**).

After the infants habituated to this event, they saw two test events. In both test events, a box was revealed when the screen was raised, but the location of the box differed. In the *possible event,* the box was placed at the back of the display box, behind the tracks of the car, so the car could roll freely through the display. In the *impossible event,* the box was placed on top of the tracks so that it blocked the car's path. Even so, during the event, the car appeared to roll freely across the display. The infants showed more surprise and looked longer at the "impossible" event.

In another experiment, a stick was moved repeatedly back and forth behind a block of wood until habituation occurred. Then the subjects were shown two displays of sticks moving as before but missing the block. One dis-

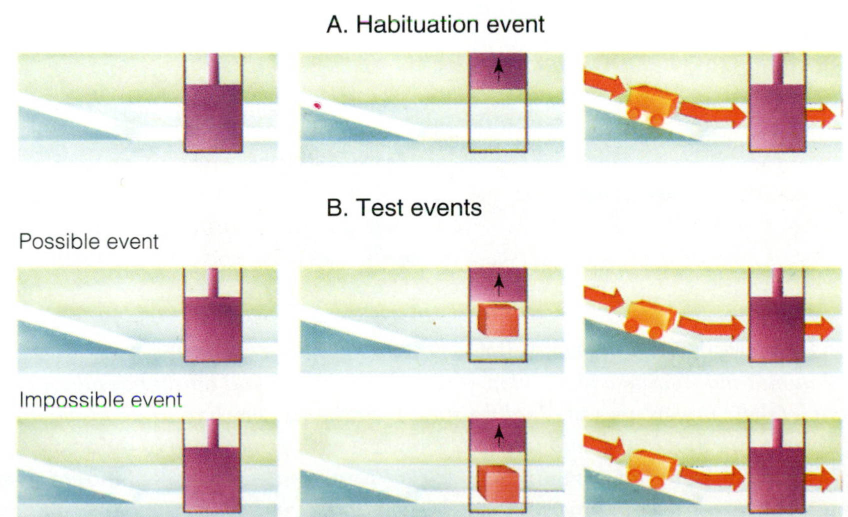

Figure 5.6 A Schematic Representation of Habituation and Test Events
In the habituation phase, infants' interest in the event diminished over time. In the test phase, their interest was recaptured by the impossible event.

play consisted of a solid stick; the other display consisted of two sticks, one above and one below where the solid block used to be (see **Figure 5.7**). Which display did the babies prefer? They preferred the broken rod to the more familiar, habituated, whole stick. Thus they could determine object boundaries by perceiving relative motion (Kellman & Spelke, 1983; Spelke, 1988, 1991).

Infants also show signs of being able to integrate information across sensory domains. In one study, 1-month-old infants were habituated to sucking on pacifiers with either bumpy or smooth surfaces, but they weren't allowed to see them. When the pacifiers were removed and the infants were shown both kinds of pacifiers, they looked longer at the type of pacifier they had felt tactually in their mouths (Meltzoff & Borton, 1979). This is clear evidence for very early sensory coordination and visual recognition of objects felt but never seen.

The Preoperational Child Revisited

Researchers have also provided cause to question the ongoing egocentrism of preoperational children. Children can take the perspective of others if the task is simple. When shown a card with a horse on one side and an elephant on the other, they can say that the experimenter sitting across from them sees the elephant while they are seeing the horse (Masangkay et al., 1974). Children can also adapt their communication to different types of listeners. When a 4-year-old tells a 2-year-old about a toy, she uses shorter, simpler utterances than she does when telling a peer or adult about that toy (Shatz & Gelman, 1973).

Research with preoperational children indicates that they may be able to see another's point of view, if the task is simple.

Children in this stage can also differentiate mental and physical worlds if the right questions are asked of them. Researchers showed 3- to 5-year-old

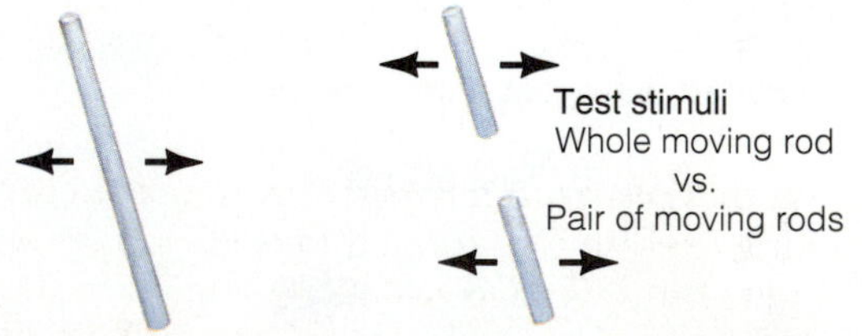

Figure 5.7 Task Stimuli Used to Demonstrate That Infants Perceive Objects and Boundaries
Three-month-old infants can develop concepts of objects and object boundaries, as shown by their preferences in a habituation paradigm. They habituate to the top display of a rod moving behind a block. They are tested with each of the two lower displays: the moving rod without the block in front, and two pieces of moving rods that appear as parts of the rod previously seen above and below the block. The infants continue to habituate to the whole rod, instead preferring to look at the "novel" broken rod. They show no preference for either kind of stationary rod after seeing a stationary rod behind the block. Can you explain what this preference means in terms of forming concepts of objects at this age?

children drawings of two characters. One character was described as really possessing something ("This boy . . . is hungry, so his mother *gave* him a cookie"); the other character was described as just thinking about something ("This boy . . . is hungry, so he is *thinking* about a cookie"). Children at all three ages were able to say that only the first boy could actually eat the cookie (Wellman & Estes, 1986). A related study showed that preoperational children are not exclusively captured by the physical features of stimuli (Lillard & Flavell, 1990). Three-year-old children were shown three differently colored photocopies of the same picture. The experimenter described one in terms of a behavior ("He's wiping up his spilled milk") and a second in terms of a mental state ("He's feeling sad about his spilled milk"). The children were then shown a third version of the picture and asked to tell a puppet, George, about the boy. Despite the perceptual salience of the boy's behavior (wiping up the milk), these preoperational children were likely to describe this scene, and others like it, in terms of the character's mental state.

Children's Theories of Mind and World

Piaget's theory is built around stages in which landmark changes take place in children's ways of thinking. More recently, researchers have explored the idea that changes occur separately, in each of several major domains, as children develop **foundational theories**—frameworks for initial understanding—to explain their experiences of the world (Carey, 1985; Wellman & Gelman, 1992; Wellman, 1990). For example, children accumulate their experiences of the properties of mental states into a *theory of mind,* or naive psychology. By doing so, they are better able to understand the thought processes of themselves and others. Children must "discover" a surprising array of truths about mental lives. Three-year-olds, for example, do not yet understand the correlation between knowledge and perceptual modality:

Children develop foundational theories—frameworks for understanding their world.

Three- and four-year-old children were asked to advise a puppet about how to acquire information about different properties of a hidden toy. For example, if the puppet was "interested" in the color of the toy, the children were asked whether he should look at the toy or listen to the toy. Although the 4-year-olds performed somewhat better than the 3-year-olds, neither age group had a really solid grasp of the connection between the particular dimension of perceptual information and the required perceptual activity. These children did, however, know that the puppet had to perform *some* perceptual action. They did quite well when asked to decide whether to have the puppet acquire knowledge by looking in the container or just standing on it (Pillow, 1993).

You can see from this research how aspects of the theory of mind fall into place with continuing experience—the child understands some but not all of the links between perception and knowledge.

To build a theory of mind, children must perform the functions of psychologists. They must also be neophyte practitioners of other disciplines—such as physics and biology—to perfect their understanding of other aspects of the world. Although children's early theories may be incorrect, given the way the world really works, you can see them working hard to form generalizations. One 2½-year-old, for example, watched gardeners bag fallen leaves in November. He then pointed to the bare branches and explained that the gardeners would come and put the leaves back on the trees.

Children form generalizations about the world based on what they have experienced and observed.

Researchers have formally studied the development of scientific concepts, such as the way in which children project biological properties from one species to another. When asked which of a series of animals breathe or have

Your Earliest Memories

What's the first thing from your life you can remember? If you are like most people, you will be able to cite some event from around the time you were 3½ years old. What's your next memory after that? Most people report sparse memories for a few years even beyond that 3½-year mark. Have you ever wondered why this is so? You might be thinking, "Well, little kids just have bad memories," but is that really true? Have you ever baby-sat for a 1-year-old? Did that child remember you from one visit to the next? The answer is very likely to be yes. You may have played a major role in that child's life for a full year. But if your contact ended by age 2, you've probably faded forever from the child's memory. The real puzzle, thus, is why a child's accurate day-to-day memories don't turn into the types of memories that can be called back to mind for years to come. This phenomenon has been called *childhood* (or *infantile*) *amnesia.*

Try to think a bit more about your own earliest memory. Does it concern an event? A scene? Was it emotionally charged? Was the emotion positive or negative? How sure are you that the memory is accurate? Sigmund Freud (1905/1953), who offered the earliest discussion of childhood amnesia, believed that only events with strong negative emotion could overcome the innate weakness of infants' memory systems. Even then, Freud believed that the memories were likely to be stored in a distorted form. To test these ideas, you would need to ask a large sample of people to provide their earliest memories and see what properties those memories have. Then, as far as possible, you would want to find other individuals who can confirm or disconfirm the accuracy of the information. A team of researchers followed this procedure with 300 undergraduate subjects and uncovered several patterns (Howes et al., 1993):

- Most of the memories came from the ages of 3 to 5 years.
- The memories were largely accurate. For some of them, no one was able to provide confirmation or disconfirmation (because, for example, a parent could not remember the event). For the group of memories for which feedback was available, 80 percent were at least partially verified. Thus there was no evidence that early memories involve systematic distortions.
- More of the memories involved negative emotion (55 percent) than positive emotion (19 percent). However, the accuracy of recall was nearly identical in both these circumstances. Thus early negative events, like falling off your bicycle, may be more memorable overall than positive events, like getting a great toy as a birthday gift, but the negative emotion isn't necessary to form an accurate memory.
- Many of the memories weren't very dramatic. They were small moments like looking for pieces of broken china in a garden or tying one's shoelaces for the first time.

What happens that allows children to emerge from the period of childhood amnesia? As we observed earlier, the problem is not that children don't have any sort of memory—they regularly remember what happens from one day to the next—but that those memories don't become the sort of *autobiographical* memories that last for a lifetime. What changes? One type of theory focuses on the development of children's ability to use language in a particular way (Nelson, 1992, 1993). The suggestion is that only when children are comfortable using language to compare their own experiences with the experiences of others can they have memories that are specifically autobiographical. Other theorists have made the somewhat more general proposal that autobiographical memory relies on the overall development of a cognitive *sense of self* (Howe & Courage, 1993). Consider it this way: until you begin to think of yourself as a wholly separate individual, you can't begin to preserve the details of your autobiography. Your development of a sense of self—and the memories that preserve that sense of self—was a major breakthrough of your young life.

bones, 4-year-old children were inclined to make their judgments based on their perceptions of the similarity of the animal to humans (Carey, 1985). Over time, children must replace this theory with one that acknowledges more structure in the animal kingdom. Similarly, 3- and 4-year-old children understand that what is inside objects affects their functions—although they have no clear idea what those insides are (Gelman & Wellman, 1991). Thus, although 3- and 4-year-olds aren't entirely sure what kinds of things are inside dogs, they are quite certain that a dog would cease to be a dog if you removed whatever *is* inside. In each domain, you see that children begin to develop a general theory and then use a range of new experiences to provide successive refinements.

The developmental changes we have documented so far are very dramatic. It's easy to tell that a 12-year-old has all sorts of cognitive capabilities unknown to a 1-year-old. In the Close-up, we look at another dramatic change—in your ability to preserve memories about your own life. Then we turn to the more subtle changes that take place through adolescence into adulthood.

COGNITIVE DEVELOPMENT IN ADOLESCENCE AND ADULTHOOD

Our description of cognitive development in childhood focused largely on the way in which each individual's repertory of thought processes expands over time. In our review of adulthood, you will see more expansion—a change from formal thought to *postformal thought*. You will also see that the transition to late adulthood brings some trade-offs. Although older adults lose some cognitive flexibility, they can compensate by virtue of the *wisdom* they have acquired over their life span.

POSTFORMAL THOUGHT

Recall that, according to Piaget, the final stage of cognitive development is that of formal operational thought, achieved in adolescence through maturation and educational experience. Formal thinking enables people to reason logically, use abstract thought to solve general problems, and consider hypothetical possibilities in given types of structured systems. But most everyday, practical problems for adults occur in ambiguous, unstructured social and work relationships. How should you decide who pays for a date? How should you ask your boss for a raise? Dealing with these situations with formal thought is too limiting and rigid. What adult life requires is a more dynamic, less abstract, and less absolute way of thinking that can deal with inconsistencies, contradictions, and ambiguities. This pragmatic, world-wise cognitive style is referred to as **postformal thought** (Basseches, 1984; Labouvie-Vief, 1985).

Postformal thought refers to a style of adult thinking that is more dynamic, less abstract, and less absolute than Piaget's notion of formal thought.

A clear contrast between formal and postformal thought arises when adolescents and adults are asked to reason about situations that are emotionally charged.

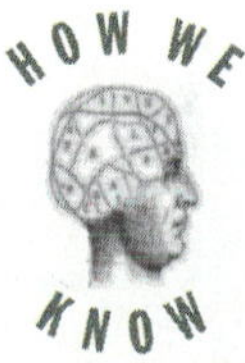

In one experiment, adolescents (ages 14 to 16½), young adults (ages 20 to 25), and middle adults (ages 30 to 46) were asked to read two conflicting accounts of an adolescent's visit with his parents to his grandparents. One account took the perspective of the adolescent: "Even though I was being as polite as I could, it was boring. I felt forced into everything." The other account took the parents' perspective: "Even though he was reluctant to go with us at first, he seemed to have a good time, to enjoy the family close-

> ness." The three groups of subjects were asked to interpret the conflict in their own words and to judge, for example, who was at fault and who was victorious in the situation. The adolescents' responses were largely concerned with strict judgments of right and wrong. They found it difficult, on average, to consider the situation from more than one perspective. The young adults, by contrast, were somewhat more able to appreciate that different points of view could be taken on the conflict. The middle adults continued this trend. Their responses attempted to separate facts from interpretive bias (Blanchard-Fields, 1986).

This experiment demonstrates cognitive change still at work well into the adult years. An important part of the circumstances, however, is the emotional content. When adolescents and young adults interpreted a situation that was relatively free of emotional content (conflicting accounts of a fictional war), no differences in their reasoning styles emerged. This result reinforces the claim that the transition from formal to postformal thought reflects an improved ability to accommodate the emotional ambiguities of day-to-day experience (Labouvie-Vief et al., 1989).

Cognitive Changes in Late Adulthood

As we have traced cognitive development through middle adulthood, it has seemed that "change" meant "change for the better." When we arrive at the period of late adulthood, though, cultural stereotypes suggest that "change" means "change for the worse" (Parr & Siegert, 1993). However, even when people believe that the course of adulthood brings with it general decline, they still anticipate certain types of gains very late into life (Heckhausen et al., 1989). We will look at intelligence and memory to see the interplay of losses and gains.

Intelligence

There is little evidence to support the notion that general cognitive abilities decline among the healthy elderly. Only about 5 percent of the population experiences major losses in cognitive functioning. When age-related decline in cognitive functioning occurs, it is usually limited to only some abilities. The majority of people experience more difficulty in forming new associations, and you can expect to acquire new information more slowly by the time you are in your 70s or 80s. IQ test scores do decline with age, but only

Does intellectual performance decline in late adulthood? Many prominent figures, such as the late Justice Thurgood Marshall, continue to make important professional contributions through their 70s and beyond.

Table 5.3 Features of Wisdom

- Rich factual knowledge: General and specific knowledge about the conditions of life and its variations
- Rich procedural knowledge: General and specific knowledge about strategies of judgment and advice concerning life matters
- Life-span contextualism: Knowledge about the contexts of life and their temporal (developmental) relationships
- Relativism: Knowledge about differences in values, goals, and priorities
- Uncertainty: Knowledge about the relative indeterminacy and unpredictability of life and ways to manage

because education influences IQ scores and each successive generation is better educated—the historical cohort effect mentioned before. When intelligence is separated into the components that make up your verbal abilities (*crystallized intelligence*) and those that are part of your ability to learn quickly and thoroughly (*fluid intelligence*), only fluid intelligence shows slight decline with age (Botwinick, 1977). There is even evidence that some aspects of intellectual functioning may be superior in older people. For instance, psychologists are now exploring age-related gains in **wisdom**—expertise in the fundamental pragmatics of life (P. Baltes, 1990, 1993). **Table 5.3** presents some of the types of knowledge that define wisdom (Smith & Baltes, 1990). You can see that each type of knowledge is best acquired over a long and thoughtful life.

There is little evidence to support the notion of general cognitive decline among the elderly.

While crystallized intelligence is generally maintained in later adulthood, the slight decline in fluid intelligence may be offset by gains in wisdom.

Because older individuals' cognitive abilities are so diverse, psychologists reject claims that cognitive decline in old age is caused by inevitable physiological decay of the central nervous system. Individuals vary greatly in their later-life intellectual performance. Some people, such as Supreme Court justices and important contributors to cultural life, do not show any decline until their 80s or later. Research indicates that elderly people who pursue high levels of environmental stimulation, including both formal and informal education, tend to maintain high levels of cognitive abilities:

Research indicates that high levels of environmental stimulation tend to promote high levels of cognitive abilities.

HOW WE KNOW

The cognitive functioning of 229 community-dwelling elderly people in good health (aged 64 to 95) was assessed over a 14-year period. Individuals were classified into two groups: those who had declined (122) and those who had remained stable (107) in inductive reasoning and spatial orientation abilities. Subjects were then assigned to 5-hour training programs on one ability or the other. The study employed a pretest-treatment-posttest design: All subjects took pretests and posttests for both inductive reasoning and spatial abilities, and each training group served as a treatment control for the ability on which they had not received new training. Results showed that (1) cognitive training reversed documented decline in a substantial number of older adults (up to 50 percent of subjects experienced complete remediation of their decline in ability); (2) reversals were documented for both inductive reasoning and spatial orientation; and (3) training procedures also enhanced the performance of many older people who had remained stable in their abilities (Schaie & Willis, 1986).

It appears that disuse, rather than decay, may be responsible for isolated deficits in intellectual performance. Further research has shown that "many older individuals have a sizeable reserve capacity of intelligence" that makes possible the reactivation of old knowledge or skills or the acquisition of new knowledge and skills (P. Baltes & Lindenberger, 1988, p. 290). As promised, we have again arrived at the conclusion that "Use it or lose it (or seek training to get it back)" is an appropriate motto for the wise older adult.

How can older adults cope successfully with whatever changes inevitably accompany increasing age? Successful aging might consist of making the most of gains while minimizing the impact of the normal losses that accompany aging. This strategy for successful aging, proposed by psychologists **Paul Baltes** and **Margaret Baltes,** is called **selective optimization with compensation** (M. Baltes, 1986; P. Baltes, 1987; P. Baltes et al., 1992). *Selective* means that people scale down the number and extent of their goals for themselves. *Optimization* refers to people exercising or training themselves in areas that are of highest priority to them. *Compensation* means that people use alternative ways to deal with losses—for example, choosing age-friendly environments. Let's consider an example:

Virtuoso pianist Arthur Rubinstein used strategic techniques that enabled him to continue giving successful performances until he was over 90.

> When the concert pianist [Arthur] Rubinstein was asked, in a television interview, how he managed to remain such a successful pianist in his old age, he mentioned three strategies: (1) In old age he performed fewer pieces, (2) he now practiced each piece more frequently, and (3) he produced more ritardandos [slowings of the tempo] in his playing before fast segments, so that the playing speed sounded faster than it was in reality. These are examples of selection (fewer pieces), optimization (more practice), and compensation (increased use of contrast in speed). (P. Baltes, 1993, p. 590)

Memory

A common complaint among the elderly is the feeling that their ability to remember things is not as good as it used to be. On a number of tests of memory, adults over 60 *do* perform worse than young adults in their 20s (Baltes & Kliegl, 1992; Craik, 1994). People experience memory deficits with advancing age, even when they have been highly educated and otherwise have good intellectual skills (Zelinski et al., 1993). But not all memory systems show deficits with age. For example, aging does not seem to diminish elderly individuals' ability to access their general knowledge store and personal information about events that occurred long ago. In a study of name and face recognition, middle-aged adults could identify 90 percent of their high school classmates in yearbooks 35 years after graduation, while older adults were still able to recognize 70 to 80 percent of their classmates some 50 years later (Bahrick et al., 1975). What is more problematic, however, is the ability of older adults to acquire new information. Age-related changes affect the processes that allow new information to be effectively organized, stored, and retrieved (Craik, 1994; Giambra & Arenberg, 1993). For example, individuals' use of consciously controlled memory processes declines with age. Do you recall the "false fame" experiment we described in Chapter 4? That experiment demonstrated the influence of unconscious memories on fame judgments. Because elderly individuals have more difficulty controlling memory processes than do younger adults, they are even more prone to making judgments of false fame (Jennings & Jacoby, 1993).

The memory problems of older adults seem to occur in the area of acquiring new information rather than in remembering people or events from their distant past.

As yet, researchers have been unable to develop a wholly adequate description of the mechanisms that underlie memory impairment in older adults (Light, 1991). Some theories focus on differences between older and younger people in their efforts to organize and process information. Other theories point to the elderly people's reduced ability to pay attention to information. Still others suggest that elderly individuals' performance may be impaired by their very belief that their memory will be poor (Hertzog et al., 1990; Levy & Langer, 1994). Researchers continue to evaluate each of these claims.

Other theories look to differences in the brain. There are two general ways in which age-related, neurobiological changes might result in impaired memory. The first is cell loss or decay in the brain itself. The second is deficiencies in the biochemicals, or neurotransmitters, that flow through the brain. If the brain mechanisms responsible for memory are intact in older people but are not optimally fueled, then memory impairment might be lessened by increasing neurotransmitter levels.

Some forms of memory impairment are clearly biological. Older adults who suffer from **Alzheimer's disease** experience a gradual loss of memory and deterioration of personality. This disease afflicts about 5 percent of Americans over 65 and 20 percent of those over 80, including, as he made public in November 1994, former president Ronald Reagan. Alzheimer's disease onset is deceptively mild—in early stages the only observable symptom may be memory impairment. However, its course is one of steady deterioration: victims may show gradual personality changes, such as apathy, lack of spontaneity, and withdrawal from social interactions. In advanced stages, people with Alzheimer's disease may become completely mute and inattentive, even forgetting the names of their spouse and children. In these final stages, Alzheimer patients can become incapable of caring for themselves, lose memory of who they are, and eventually die. Clearly, this form of memory impairment is more profound and tragic than the ordinary memory impairment of late adulthood.

Some theoretical attempts at explaining age-related differences in memory focus on neurobiological changes in the brain. Alzheimer's disease is an example of memory loss related to neurobiology.

Both cognitive theories and neurobiological theories of memory changes related to aging are being vigorously investigated at this time. The hope is not only to achieve a general understanding of the nature of human memory and the aging process but to develop strategies and procedures for overcoming memory impairment (Craik, 1994).

Let's now narrow our focus from general cognitive development to the more specific topic of the acquisition of language.

ACQUIRING LANGUAGE

Imagine that you lived in a country where no one could translate for you or teach you the language. Would you be able to learn this foreign language—let's call it language Z—on your own? How would you figure out what stretches of sound represented words in language Z? How would you figure out what the words meant or what grammatical rules organized the words into larger meanings? Could you learn the norms for proper conversation?

When you let yourself reflect on these questions, you can see how hard it must be to learn a new language—and yet, in the span of only a few years and with little explicit assistance, young children do just that. By the time they are 6 years old, children can analyze language into its minimal, separable units of sound and meaning, use the rules they have discovered to combine sounds into words and words into meaningful sentences, and take an active part in coherent conversations. Children's remarkable language accomplishments have prompted most researchers to agree that the ability to learn language is biologically based—that you are born with an innate language capacity. Even so, depending on where a child happens to be born, he or she may end up as a native speaker of any one of the world's 4000 different languages. In addition, children are prepared to learn both spoken languages and gestur-

Table 5.4 The Structure of Language

Grammar is the field of study that seeks to describe the way language is structured and used. It includes several domains:

Phonology—the study of the way sounds are put together to form words.

A **phoneme** is the smallest unit of speech that distinguishes between any two utterances. For example, *b* and *p* distinguish *bin* from *pin*.

Phonetics is the study and classification of speech sounds.

Syntax—the way in which words are strung together to form sentences. For example, subject (*I*) + verb (*like*) + object (*you*) is a standard English word order.

A **morpheme** is the minimum distinctive unit of grammar that cannot be divided without losing its meaning. The word *bins* has two morphemes, *bin* and *s*, indicating the plural.

Semantics—the study of the meanings of words and their changes over time. **Lexical meaning** is the dictionary meaning of a word. Meaning is sometimes conveyed by the *context* of a word in a sentence ("Run *fast*" versus "Make the knot *fast*") or the *inflection* with which it is spoken (try emphasizing different words in a *white house cat*).

Pragmatics—rules for participating in conversations; social conventions for communicating, sequencing sentences, and responding appropriately to others.

Researchers agree that children are born with a biologically based ability to learn language.

al languages, like American Sign Language. This means that the innate predisposition to learn language must be both quite strong and quite flexible (Meier, 1991).

To explain how it is that infants are such expert language learners, we will describe the evidence that supports the claim of an innate language capacity. We will, however, also discuss the role that the environment plays—after all, children learn the particular languages that are being used in the world around them. **Table 5.4** outlines the various types of knowledge children must acquire for their particular signed or spoken language. We first describe the general context of acquisition and then turn to particular areas of accomplishment.

The Context of Acquisition

Probably without realizing it, parents work to introduce their infants to language by engaging them in *proto-dialogues*. Parents talk and pause at certain points to let infants respond. Parents will accept as valid responses anything the babies do, even burping or sneezing. Given this bit of help, babies communicate long before they begin to speak or sign. Infants use gestures (pointing) and nonverbal vocalizations (crying) to communicate their desires and interests. Thus, although babies are able to comprehend the language of others before they can produce the appropriate words and grammatical structures themselves, they have gained experience at communicating in their nonverbal days. As babies grow older, parents become more demanding conversational partners, requiring at first that babies verbalize, later that they use actual words, and later still that they use words relevant to the topic at hand.

Parents work to keep their infants' interest and to introduce them to language. When adults speak to infants and young children, they use a special form that differs from adult speech: an exaggerated, high-pitched intonation

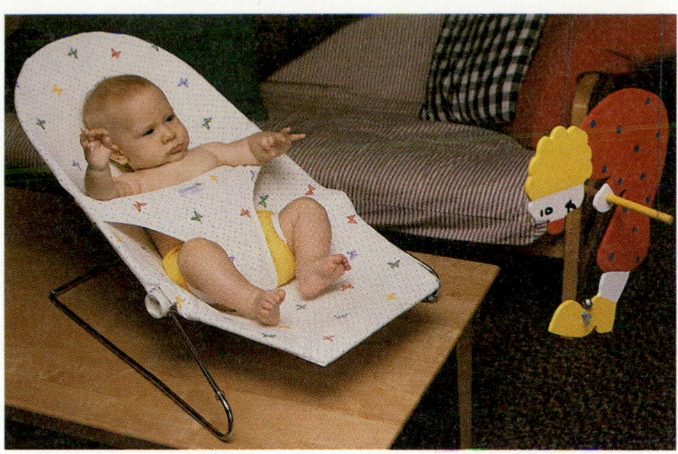

Before they begin to talk, infants are already proficient at communicating by means of gestures and crying.

known colloquially as **motherese,** or more formally as **child-directed speech.** This way of speaking appears to serve a number of functions, among them to get and hold the infants' attention, communicate affect (feelings), and mark turn taking in parent–infant dialogues. Research suggests that infants prefer motherese to other kinds of speech:

Motherese, or child-directed speech, serves the functions of getting and holding the infant's attention, communicating feelings, and teaching turn taking.

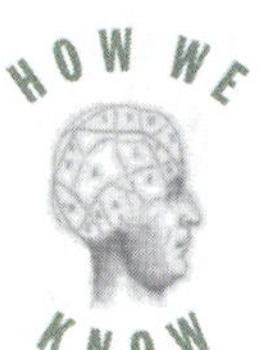

A sample of 48 4-month-old infants listened to tape-recorded speech samples of other mothers talking to their babies, and these infants also heard adult-directed speech by the same women. The infants' preferences were measured by the number of times they turned their heads in the direction of one of these types of speech stimuli. The majority of infants revealed a clear preference for motherese (Fernald, 1985).

So one way that motherese helps infants to acquire language is by keeping them interested in and attentive to the things that their parents say to them. Furthermore, motherese intonations contain affective messages without words. Parents use rising intonation to engage babies' attention, falling intonation to comfort them, and short staccato bursts as prohibitions. Research by **Anne Fernald** and her colleagues shows that parents in many different cultures use these patterns and that babies understand them, even in languages other than their native tongue (Fernald et al., 1989). We will return to the functions of motherese when we describe the acquisition of grammar.

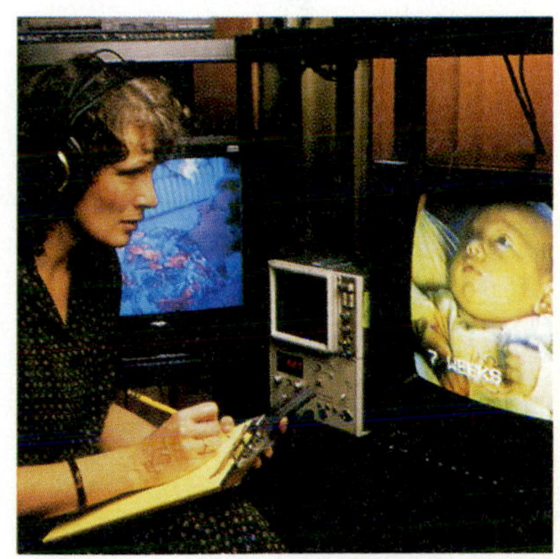

Anne Fernald studies infants' responses to motherese.

Speech Perception Abilities

A child's first step in acquiring a particular language is to make note of the sound contrasts that are used meaningfully in that language. (For signed languages, the child must attend to contrasts in, for example, hand positions.) Each spoken language samples from the set of possible distinctions that can be produced by the vocal tract; no language uses all of the speech-sound contrasts that can be made. The minimal, meaningful units are known as **phonemes.** There are about 45 distinct phonemes in English. Imagine you heard someone speak the words *right* and *light.* If you are a native speaker of English, you would have no trouble hearing the difference—/r/ and /l/ are different phonemes in English. If, however, your only language experience was with Japanese, you would not be able to hear the difference between these two words! Why not? Do English speakers acquire the ability to make this distinction or do Japanese speakers lose it?

To answer this type of question, researchers needed to develop methods to obtain linguistic information from prelinguistic children. Early research relied on the finding that children show **habituation** (see Chapter 3) to repeated presentations of the same stimulus:

One- to 4-month-old infants were given special pacifier nipples that electronically recorded their rate of spontaneous sucking (babies this age will suck, even when they are not being fed). Then the infants heard synthetic speech sounds, for example *ba ba ba ba ba,* which were *contingent* on their sucking; that is, every time an infant sucked, he or she heard a *ba.* After a while, babies became bored with the sound (became habituated to it), and their rate of sucking decreased. Then the researchers played the infants a test stimulus: either a *ba ba ba* sound or a *pa pa pa* sound. Infants who heard *pa pa pa* dishabituated—they started sucking more rapidly, presumably to hear the new sound more. Infants who continued to hear *ba ba ba,* however, did not increase their rate of sucking. Thus, newborns showed sensitivity to the change in phoneme (Eimas et al., 1971).

We know from this research that infants can make *some* language-relevant sound distinctions. But what about those distinctions that never become relevant in their own language, like /r/ and /l/ for children acquiring Japanese? To address this question, **Janet Werker** turned to sound distinctions that are used in Hindi, but not in English—distinctions that make it difficult for adult English speakers to learn Hindi. Werker and her colleagues measured the ability of infants learning English and Hindi, as well as adults who spoke English and Hindi, to hear the differences between the Hindi phonemes. She found that all the infants, regardless of which language they were learning, could hear the differences until the age of 8 months. However, of the infants older than 8 months and of the adults, only the Hindi speakers or speakers-to-be could hear the Hindi contrasts. Thus infants start out with sensitivities to sounds that they lose if these contrasts are not used in their language (Werker, 1991; Werker & Lalond, 1988). It seems that you had a biological head start with respect to the sound contrasts that will be important for acquiring a language.

Research suggests that infants start out with sensitivity to many phonemic distinctions and lose the sensitivity to those that are not present in the language they learn.

Learning Word Meanings

There is no denying that children are excellent word learners. At around 18 months, children's word learning often takes off at an amazing rate. At this age, a child might point to every object in a room and ask, "What's that?" Researchers have called this phase the *naming explosion* because children begin to acquire new words, especially names for objects, at a rapidly increasing rate (see **Figure 5.8**). By the age of 6, the average child is estimated to understand 14,000 words (Templin, 1957). Assuming that most of these words are learned between the ages of 18 months and 6 years, this works out to about nine new words a day, or almost one word per waking hour (Carey, 1978). How is this possible?

At about age 18 months, children experience the naming explosion, rapidly increasing the rate at which they learn new words, especially the names of things.

Imagine a straightforward situation in which a child and her father are walking through a park and the father points and says, "That's a doggie." The

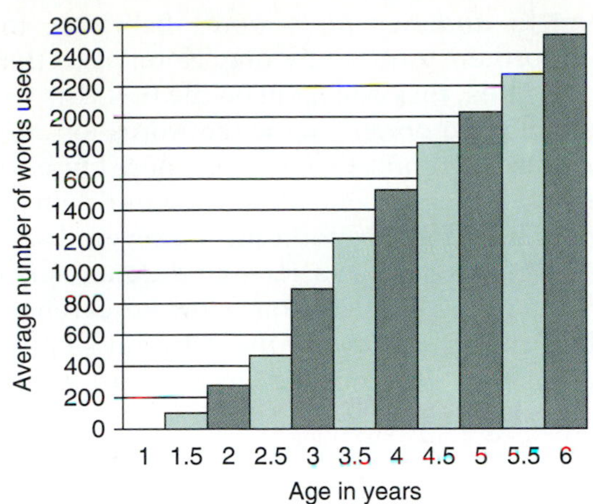

Figure 5.8 Children's Growth in Vocabulary

The number of words a child can use increases rapidly between the ages of 18 months and 6 years. This study shows children's average vocabularies at intervals of six months. (Source: B. A. Moskowitz. 1978. The acquisition of language. Scientific American, *Inc. All rights reserved. Reprinted by permission.)*

child must decide to which piece of the world *doggie* applies. This is no easy feat (Quine, 1960). Perhaps *doggie* means "any creature with four legs" or "the animal's fur" or "the animal's bark" or any of the other large set of meanings that will be true each time someone points toward a dog. Given all the possibilities, how are children able to fix the meanings of individual words?

We suggest that children act like scientists—developing *hypotheses* about what each new word might mean. You can, for example, see children's scientific minds actively at work when they *overextend* words, using them incorrectly to cover a wide range of objects: they may use the word *doggie* to refer to all animals, or the word *moon* to refer to all round objects, including clocks and coins. You can see how a child might form these hypotheses. Other

How do children learn the characteristics that are true of all dogs and that differentiate dogs from all other four-legged animals?

times, children might *underextend* a word—believing, for example, that *doggie* refers only to their own family dog. Note, also, that when children wish to refer to something, they will often do the best they can with their limited vocabularies. If a child doesn't know the words for *cow* or *pig,* he may use *doggie,* not because he thinks that cows are dogs but because it's the closest word he has for a four-legged animal; it fits better than *table.*

The view that children form hypotheses, however, does not explain why children are vastly more likely to imagine that *doggie* refers to the whole animal and not, for example, to its left front paw. Researchers have suggested that children's hypotheses are *constrained* by possibly innate principles (Clark, 1987; Markman, 1989). Consider, for example, the principle of *mutual exclusivity,* which suggests that children act as if each object *must* have only one label. How does this principle constrain children's hypotheses? Under normal circumstances, children have a bias toward hypothesizing that a new word applies to a whole object. However, when they already know the name for a whole object, like *telephone,* they apply mutual exclusivity and develop the hypothesis that a word unknown to them, like *receiver,* must label some part of the object (Markman & Wachtel, 1988). The child's hypothesis will most often be correct. Mutual exclusivity also explains why a 2-year-old might become irate when his mother calls his fire *engine* a fire *truck.*

Researchers believe that children learn new word meanings by forming and revising hypotheses that are constrained by innate principles such as mutual exclusivity.

Also like good scientists, children use what they've already learned about their language to help them acquire more new meanings (Landau & Gleitman, 1985; Pinker, 1987). Researchers call this process *bootstrapping,* from the idiom "to pull oneself up by one's bootstraps." For example, in English, there is a strong association between the grammatical structures in which verbs appear and the causal nature of the verb. Thus, if you were to hear a sentence with a novel verb like "The duck is *gorping* the bunny" and then look at a scene involving a duck and a bunny, you would most likely try to associate *gorping* with some causal action that the duck was performing on the bunny. When 2-year-olds were shown a pair of videos, one of which displayed a causal action and one of which displayed a noncausal action, they preferred to look at the causal video. The children's viewing preference was an indication of their understanding (Naigles, 1990; Naigles & Kako, 1993). These very young children use their incomplete knowledge of English grammar to help pin down the meanings of unfamiliar words.

Children are able to use their early successes at word learning to acquire more complex concepts. As children grow older, they go beyond talking about their physical world and begin to talk about their psychological world. For example, around the age of 2, children begin to use words such as *dream, pretend, believe,* and *hope* (Shatz et al., 1983). They also refer to emotional states with words such as *happy, sad,* and *angry.* Finally, after the cognitive advances that occur later in childhood, they understand and use abstract words such as *truth, justice,* and *idea.*

Acquiring Grammar

To explain how children acquire meanings, we characterized children as scientists whose hypotheses are constrained by innate principles. We can use the same analogy to describe how children acquire the rules by which units of meaning are combined into larger units—in other words, grammar. The challenge for the child is that different languages follow different rules. For example, in English the typical ordering of units in a sentence is subject–verb–object, but in Japanese the ordering is subject–object–verb.

Children must discover what order is present in the language being used around them. How do they do that?

The Role of Input

You saw the important role that adults play for meaning acquisition: if parents, or other proficient speakers, did not point to objects and label them, children would be hard-pressed to learn new words; the teaching of vocabulary is explicit. Grammar, however, is a very different case. It would be unusual for a parent *explicitly* to teach an infant rules of grammar. Most adults don't even have explicit knowledge of those rules. You may, for example, have gotten to be a skilled English speaker without ever reflecting on the standard order of subject, verb, and object. Furthermore, when children use words with the wrong meanings, parents will often correct them—"No, honey, that's a cow, not a doggie"—but parents rarely, if ever, directly correct a child's grammar (Brown & Hanlon, 1970).

Considerations like these led theorists to believe that motherese might play quite a small role in the acquisition of grammar. Linguist **Noam Chomsky** (1965, 1975), for example, argued that children are born with mental structures that facilitate the comprehension and production of language. Some of the best evidence for such a biological basis for grammar comes from children who acquire complete grammatical structure in the absence of well-formed input. For example, researchers have studied deaf children whose hearing loss was sufficiently severe that they could not acquire spoken language but whose parents did not expose them to full-fledged signed languages such as American Sign Language (Goldin-Meadow & Mylander, 1990). These children began to invent signing systems of their own and—despite the lack of environmental support for these invented languages—the gestural systems came to have regular, grammatical structure: "With or without an established language as a guide, children appear to be 'ready' to seek structure at least at word and sentence levels when developing systems for communication" (Goldin-Meadow & Mylander, p. 351).

According to Noam Chomsky, children learn grammar without explicit instruction because they are biologically predisposed to do so.

Thus the child's biological preparedness takes much of the pressure off adults to teach grammar explicitly. We can, however, look at individual differences in the way that adults speak to children to explain the particular time

Children develop linguistic fluency by listening to the speech patterns of those around them.

courses with which different children acquire grammar (Newport et al., 1977). For example, early in life some children are *referential*—their vocabularies consist largely of common nouns such as *doggie* and *ball*. Other children are *expressive*—their vocabularies consist largely of formulaic expressions such as "I want it" (Nelson, 1973). These two types of children seem to believe, early on, in different functions for language. Consequently, they follow different routes to the acquisition of grammar. Researchers have demonstrated that differences in parental input contribute to the development of these styles (Hampson & Nelson, 1993). The mothers of expressive children, for example, used fewer nouns when talking to their children than did other mothers. Furthermore, differences in the match between adults' and children's styles predicted how efficiently the children were acquiring language. Therefore, although parents need not do anything special for their children to acquire grammar, some of their language practices can affect the style and rate of acquisition.

The Language-making Capacity

Cross-linguistic studies help researchers determine what aspects of grammar are most likely supported by innate predispositions.

Theorists now firmly believe that important aspects of the acquisition of grammar are biologically predetermined. But how can researchers go about specifying exactly what knowledge is innately given? The most productive approach to this question is to study language acquisition across many languages—*cross-linguistically*. By examining what is hard and what is easy for children to acquire across the world's many languages, researchers can determine what aspects of grammar are most likely to be supported by innate predispositions.

Here we arrive back at the child as scientist. For grammar, there are two ways in which the child's hypotheses are constrained. First, there are general constraints on the possible forms of human languages (Wexler, 1982). All languages sample from the same repertory of grammatical "tricks." Children appear to be innately predisposed to hypothesize that they are learning languages drawn only from this appropriate class (Pinker, 1994). All children believe, for example, that different words play different roles in sentences. Second, there are innate guidelines that children bring to the task of learning a particular language. **Dan Slobin** has defined these guidelines as a set of *operating principles* that together constitute the child's **language-making capacity.**

Dan Slobin theorized that children acquire their knowledge of grammar through a set of operating principles.

In Slobin's (1985) theory, the operating principles take the form of directives to the child. Here, for example, is an operating principle that helps children discover the words that go together to form a grammatical unit: "store together ordered sequences of word classes and functor classes that co-occur in the expression of a particular proposition type, along with a designation of the proposition type" (p. 1252). Did you follow all of that? We didn't really expect you to: we just wanted to give you an example of the surprising amount of linguistic sophistication Slobin's operating principles require. Fortunately, because these principles are encoded as part of the human genome, you were born to be a great intuitive linguist! (The gist of this operating principle, by the way, is that children must keep track of the relationship between the order in which words appear and the meanings they express.) Slobin derived the operating principles by summarizing across the data provided by a large number of other researchers, who examined a variety of different languages. We will, however, use English examples to demonstrate the principles at work.

Consider what English-speaking children can do when they begin, at about age 2, to use combinations of words—the *two-word stage*. Children's speech at this point has been characterized as *telegraphic* because it is filled with short, simple sequences using mostly nouns and verbs. Telegraphic speech lacks function words, such as *the, and,* and *of,* which help express the relationships between words and ideas. For example, "Allgone milk" is a telegraphic message.

For adults to understand two-word utterances, they must know the context in which the words are spoken. "Tanya ball," for example, could mean, among other things, "Tanya wants the ball" or "Tanya throws the ball." Even so, children at the two-word stage show evidence that they have already acquired some knowledge of the grammar of English. Operating principles allow them to discover that word order is important in English and that the three critical elements are actor–action–object (subject–verb–object), arranged in that order. Evidence for this "discovery" comes when children misinterpret a sentence such as "Mary was followed by her little lamb to school" as *Mary* (actor) *followed* (action) *her lamb* (object) (see **Figure 5.9**). Over time, children must apply other operating principles to discover that there are exceptions to the actor–action–object rule.

Consider now an operating principle, which Slobin calls *extension,* that requires children to try, in all cases, to use the same unit of meaning, or *morpheme,* to mark the same concept. Examples of such concepts are possession, past tense, and continuing action. In English, each of these concepts is expressed by adding a grammatical morpheme to a content word, such as *-'s* (e.g., Maria*'s*), *-ed* (e.g., call*ed*), and *-ing* (e.g., laugh*ing*). Note how the addition of each of these sounds to a noun or verb changes its meaning.

Children use operating principles like extension to form hypotheses about how these morphemes work. Because, however, this principle requires that the child try to mark all cases in the same way, the error of **overregularization** often results. For example, once children learn the past-tense rule (adding *-ed* to the verb), they add *-ed* to all verbs, forming words such as

Figure 5.9 Acquiring Grammar

Many toddlers would interpret "Mary was followed by the lamb" and "Mary followed the lamb" to have identical meanings.

doed and *breaked.* As children learn the rule for plurals (adding the sound -*s* or -*z* to the end of a word), they again overextend the rule, creating words such as *foots* and *mouses.* Overregularization is an especially interesting error, because it usually appears *after* children have learned and used the correct forms of verbs and nouns. The children first use the correct verb forms (for example, *came* and *went*), apparently because they learned them as separate vocabulary items; but when they learn the general rule for the past tense, they immediately extend it to all verbs, even to words that are exceptions to the rule—words that they previously used correctly. Once again, children will have to use other operating principles to overcome this momentary overapplication.

Critical Periods

Operating principles work quite efficiently for young children. However, the ability to learn grammar appears to diminish with age. Many aspects of language emerge and evolve at particular periods—critical acquisition periods—that correspond more closely to physical and cognitive maturation than to particular learning experiences (Lenneberg, 1969). A study of people whose first language is American Sign Language (ASL) supports this point. ASL, one language used by the hearing-impaired community in the United States, has an intricate grammar that is as different from English grammar as is the grammar of any other language. ASL permits as broad a range of expression as any spoken language. Even so, the hearing impaired do not uniformly learn ASL—many are taught to lip-read and use vocal speech instead. Also, many hearing-impaired children are born to hearing parents who do not know ASL. Researchers have used the fact that signers learn ASL at vastly different ages to study critical periods for language acquisition:

Individuals who learn ASL at an early age seem to have a lifelong advantage in using the full complexity of the language.

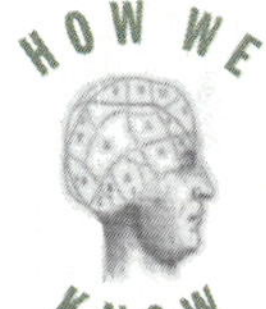

Researchers identified hearing-impaired adults who had been fluent signers of ASL for many years. Some of these signers had been exposed to ASL since birth, others did not encounter it until they started school at 5, and still others hadn't encountered ASL until they were teenagers. Even though all of the signers were able to use ASL quite fluently, there were differences in their abilities to use its full potential. Adults who had used ASL since birth or early childhood were much better at complex language tasks than adults who had started learning ASL later, even though all of the adults studied had been signers for 30 years or more (Newport, 1990).

In a follow-up study, the researchers did a similar analysis of people who learned English as a second language. In second-language learning, there was a clear advantage for those who had started learning English at a young age. Thus it seems that infancy and early childhood are the peak years for learning language, whether it be a first or second language (Newport, 1990). That is why you will have more difficulty learning a new language than a 2-year-old will in the same context!

In this chapter, we have given you general theories of the causes of changes across the life span and how they might be studied. We described how individual differences might arise in the context of biologically determined changes. We have also looked at the particular domains of physical, cognitive, and language development. Thus we have provided you with the beginning of an answer to our question about the predictions you might make for the life course of a newborn baby. For age 1, you might say something about the types of word meanings the child will have acquired. For age 15, you might say something about the preoccupation the adolescent will have with body image. For age 70, you might say something about the steps the older adult will take to maintain memory performance. To make your predictions complete, however, you will want to include social aspects of the ongoing experience of life-span changes. In Chapter 6, we turn to the domain of social development.

Recapping Main Points

Studying and Explaining Development

Researchers collect normative, longitudinal, cross-sectional, and sequential data to document change. Life-span development depends on both genetic factors—nature—and environmental inputs—nurture. These forces apply at the levels of the species and of the individual.

Physical Development Across the Life Span

Newborns and infants possess a remarkable range of capabilities: they are prewired for survival. At puberty, adolescents may become overly concerned with their body image. Some physical changes in late adulthood are consequences of disuse, not inevitable deterioration.

Early Cognitive Development

Piaget's key ideas about cognitive development include development of schemes, assimilation, accommodation, and the four-stage theory of discontinuous development. The four stages are sensorimotor, preoperational, concrete operational, and formal operational. Many of Piaget's theories are now being challenged by ingenious research paradigms that reveal infants and young children to be more precocious than Piaget had thought. Researchers suggest that children develop foundational theories, which change over time, in different psychological and physical domains.

Cognitive Development in Adolescence and Adulthood

Adult thought shows the emergence of postformal thinking. Age-related declines in cognitive functioning are typically evident in only some abilities. Declines in performance can often be reversed with educational training. This suggests that isolated cognitive deficits are caused by disuse rather than by decay of the central nervous system. Successful aging can be defined by people optimizing their functioning in select domains that are of highest priority to them and compensating for losses by using substitute behaviors.

Acquiring Language

Children are master language learners. Many researchers believe that humans have an inborn language-making capacity. Culture and parental interaction are essential parts of the language acquisition process. Like scientists, children develop hypotheses about the meanings and grammar of their language. These hypotheses are often constrained by innate principles.

Resources

Ault, R. L. (1983). *Children's cognitive development: Piaget's theory and the process approach.* New York: Oxford University Press.

Bee, H. (1994). *Lifespan development.* New York: HarperCollins.

Bloom, L. (1991). *Language development from two to three.* New York: Cambridge University Press.

Cox, M. V. (1991). *The child's point of view* (2nd ed.). New York: Harvester Wheatsheaf.

Neubauer, P. (1990). *Nature's thumbprint: The role of genetics in human development.* Boston: Addison-Wesley.

Pinker, S. (1994). *The language instinct: How the mind creates language.* New York: Morrow.

Plomin, R., & McClearn, G. E. (1993). *Nature, nurture, and psychology.* Washington, DC: American Psychological Association.

Rosser, R. A. (1993). *Cognitive development: Psychological and biological perspectives.* Boston: Allyn & Bacon.

6

Social Aspects of Life-span Development

Life-Span Theories
- Erikson's Psychosocial Stages
- Jung's Outward and Inward Directedness
- Neugarten's Changes in Adulthood

The Cultural Context of Development
- Changing Conceptions of Childhood
- Families and Youth at Risk

Social Development in Childhood
- Social Capabilities of Newborns
- Attachment and Social Support
- *Close-up: Children in Day Care*
- The Costs of Deprivation
- Gender Roles

Adolescence
- The Experience of Adolescence
- Identity Formation in Adolescence

Adulthood
- Intimacy
- Generativity
- The Cultural Construction of Late Adulthood
- At Life's End

Moral Development
- Kohlberg's Stages of Moral Reasoning
- Moral Reasoning in Adolescents and Adults
- Moral Action

Learning to Age Successfully

Who hasn't had this experience: you go away from home for a few months, perhaps to college, and when you come back, people start to say, "You've changed!" In Chapter 5, we suggested that the claim "You've changed!" is almost certainly true, all across your life span. There, we examined the types of development that occur in physical and cognitive aspects of your life. In Chapter 6, we will consider social aspects: How do your interactions with other people change over time? What are the consequences of these changes?

We will see that the social and cultural environment interacts with biological aging to provide each period of the life span with its own special challenges and rewards. Children must create trusting relationships with their caretakers and begin to understand their gender identities. Adolescents must develop a sense of personal identity and separateness from their parents. Adults must make the transition from dependence on their parents and institutions, such as college, to responsibility for their own well-being and that of others who may come to depend on them. They must also deal with intimate relationships that change over time, with loneliness and the death of loved ones, and, in many cases, with divorce. With late adulthood comes either the opportunity for self-exploration and reflection, guided by a sense of wisdom and resulting in feelings of contentment, or a time to lament unrealized potential, illness, and loss. In this chapter we expand on these themes.

We begin with a discussion of Erik Erikson's psychosocial approach to life-span development. We then put the concept of life stages into a cultural perspective and consider the crises facing many modern families, especially those that must survive below the poverty level. We next expand our analysis to explore the major developmental tasks in the social sphere facing children, adolescents, and adults. We conclude by considering what it means to experience successful change across the life span.

Erik Erikson's psychosocial stage model is a widely used tool for understanding human development over the life cycle.

LIFE-SPAN THEORIES

Theories of life-span development must satisfy two goals: they must explain both the *discontinuities* that occur between the different periods of each individual's life and the *continuities* that enable us to recognize each individual as unique across the life course. The life-span theories we review here attempt to explain both what is special to each period of life and how the psychological challenges of each period lead from one to the next. We begin with the life-span theory of Erik Erikson, which outlines the full slate of life's challenges, from birth to late adulthood. Erikson's theory allows you to see the continuity of human lives. We round out Erikson's account with complementary ideas from the work of Carl Jung and Bernice Neugarten.

ERIKSON'S PSYCHOSOCIAL STAGES

Erik Erikson, who was trained by Sigmund Freud's daughter Anna Freud, focused on each individual's experience within the broader context provided by the person's culture. Erikson's insights about successive crises of the life

Table 6.1 Erikson's Psychosocial Stages

Approximate Age	Crisis	Adequate Resolution	Inadequate Resolution
0–1½	Trust vs. mistrust	Basic sense of safety	Insecurity, anxiety
1½–3	Autonomy vs. self-doubt	Perception of self as agent capable of controlling own body and making things happen	Feelings of inadequacy to control events
3–6	Initiative vs. guilt	Confidence in oneself as initiator, creator	Feelings of lack of self-worth
6–puberty	Competence vs. inferiority	Adequacy in basic social and intellectual skills	Lack of self-confidence, feelings of failure
Adolescent	Identity vs. role confusion	Comfortable sense of self as a person	Sense of self as fragmented; shifting, unclear sense of self
Early adult	Intimacy vs. isolation	Capacity for closeness and commitment to another	Feeling of aloneness, separation; denial of need for closeness
Middle adult	Generativity vs. stagnation	Focus of concern beyond oneself to family, society, future generations	Self-indulgent concerns; lack of future orientation
Later adult	Ego-integrity vs. despair	Sense of wholeness, basic satisfaction with life	Feelings of futility, disappointment

span arose from his own immigrant experience of U.S. society and were refined by his work with Native Americans and returning World War II veterans. Erikson identified eight **psychosocial stages** in the life cycle. At each stage, a particular conflict comes into focus, as shown in **Table 6.1**. Although each conflict never completely disappears, it needs to be sufficiently resolved at a given stage if an individual is to cope successfully with the conflicts of later stages. Each stage requires a new level of social interaction; success or failure in achieving it can change the course of subsequent development in a positive or negative direction.

Erik Erikson identified eight psychosocial stages. During each stage, the individual must resolve a conflict in order to successfully cope with later stages.

For example, in the first stage, an infant needs to develop a basic sense of *trust* in the environment through interaction with caregivers. Trust is a natural accompaniment to a strong attachment relationship with a parent who provides food, warmth, and the comfort of physical closeness. But a child whose basic needs are not met, who experiences inconsistent handling, lack of physical closeness and warmth, and the frequent absence of a caring adult, may develop a pervasive sense of mistrust, insecurity, and anxiety. This child will not be prepared for the second stage, which requires the individual to be adventurous.

The task of Erikson's first stage is to develop a basic sense of trust.

With the development of walking and the beginnings of language, there is an expansion of a child's exploration and manipulation of objects (and sometimes people). With these activities should come a comfortable sense of *autonomy* and of being a capable and worthy person. Excessive restriction or criticism at this second stage may lead instead to self-doubts, while demands beyond the child's ability, as in too-early or too-severe toilet training, can discourage the child's efforts to persevere in mastering new tasks. Excessive demands can also lead to stormy scenes of confrontation, disrupting the close, supportive parent–child relationship that is needed to encourage the child to accept risks and meet new challenges. The 2-year-old who insists that a particular ritual be followed or demands the right to do something without help is acting out of a need to affirm his or her autonomy and adequacy.

In the second stage, the child's need to develop a sense of autonomy may be thwarted by excessive restriction or criticism.

Toward the end of the preschool period, a child who has developed a basic sense of trust, first in the immediate environment and then in himself or herself, can now *initiate* both intellectual and motor activities. The ways that parents respond to the child's self-initiated activities either encourage the sense of freedom and self-confidence needed for the next stage or produce guilt and feelings of being an inept intruder in an adult world.

During the third stage, the child has the opportunity to develop competencies, usually in school activities and sports.

During the elementary school years, the child who has successfully resolved the crises of the earlier stages is ready to go beyond random exploring and testing to the systematic development of *competencies.* School and sports offer arenas for learning intellectual and motor skills, and interaction with peers offers an arena for developing social skills. Other opportunities develop through special lessons, organized group activities, and perseverance of individual interests. Successful efforts in these pursuits lead to feelings of competence. Some youngsters, however, become spectators rather than performers or experience enough failure to give them a sense of inferiority, leaving them unable to meet the demands of the next life stages.

In adolescence, the challenge is to develop a sense of identity.

The conflict to be resolved by the young adult is intimacy versus isolation, while in middle adulthood the goal is generativity.

Erikson believed that the essential crisis of adolescence is discovering one's true *identity* amid the confusion created by playing many different roles for the different audiences in an expanding social world. Resolving this crisis helps the individual develop a sense of a coherent self; failing to do so adequately may result in a self-image that lacks a central, stable core. The essential crisis for the young adult is to resolve the conflict between *intimacy* and *isolation*—to develop the capacity to make full emotional, moral, and sexual commitments to other people. Making that kind of commitment requires that the individual compromise some personal preferences, accept some responsibilities, and yield some degree of privacy and independence. Failure to resolve this crisis adequately leads to isolation and the inability to connect to others in psychologically meaningful ways. (We will see throughout *Psychology and Life* that anything that *isolates* you from sources of social support—from a reliable network of friends and family—puts you at risk for a host of physical ills, mental problems, and even social pathologies. That is one of our most important "take-home" lessons for you to act on in your own life.)

The next major opportunity for growth, which occurs during adult midlife, is known as *generativity.* People in their 30s and 40s move beyond a focus on self and partner to broaden their commitments to family, work, society, and future generations. Those who haven't resolved earlier developmental tasks may, however, experience a midlife crisis. These people are still self-indulgent, question past decisions and goals, want to give up commitments for one last fling, and pursue freedom at the expense of security.

In late adulthood, the individual reviews life and the resolution of the earlier stages and faces the crises of integrity versus despair.

Awareness of one's mortality and changes in body, behavior, and social roles are the foundation for Erikson's final stage: later adulthood. The crisis at this stage is the conflict between *ego-integrity* and *despair.* Resolving the crises at each of the earlier stages prepares the older adult to look back without regrets and to enjoy a sense of wholeness. When previous crises are left unresolved, aspirations remain unfulfilled, and the individual experiences futility, despair, and self-depreciation. The result is that the individual fails to solve this final crisis as well.

Erikson's stage model emerged from his study of biographies, in-depth interviews, and personal experiences. In later sections, we will examine other sources of evidence for the validity of his model of adult development. It is important to note here, however, that Erikson's formulation most accurately describes life-span experiences in Western societies that prize individuality and autonomy. It describes less well the lives of people in societies that are based on principles of *collective organization,* and that minimize individual initiative and self-focus (Triandis, 1990, 1994). Similarly, cultures

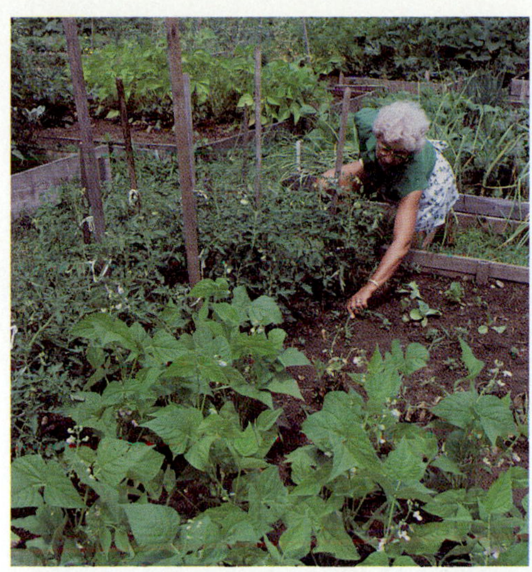

Late adulthood can be a fulfilling period in which the individual finds a sense of wholeness and connection with other living things.

with strong religious values that severely limit women's experiences, such as some Muslim or Hindu societies, force women to confront a different set of developmental crises from males (see Bond, 1988; Dhruvarajan, 1990; Shweder & Bourne, 1982).

Jung's Outward and Inward Directedness

Carl Jung challenged his mentor Sigmund Freud with the hypothesis that adulthood, not childhood, represents the most significant phase of psychological growth. Jung believed that a sense of self does not even become established until adolescence. At that time, societal prohibitions and limitations are imposed, challenged, obeyed, and internalized (Jung, 1953). Jung identified two major periods for self-development: youth (puberty to about age 35) and adulthood (ages 35–40 to old age).

In youth, values expand in an *outward direction.* Individuals must focus outward to confront issues of sexuality, make connections with others, and establish a place in the world. With adulthood, values are focused in an *inward direction.* Adults develop a more refined sense of spirituality, as well as commitments to life and to a smaller circle of loved ones. They must contemplate their values, culture, and even death. Jung believed that the changes in adulthood, although they are not as obvious, are broader and more profound than the swift changes of infancy and early childhood.

Carl Jung turned the focus of development away from childhood, identifying two periods for self-development: outward-directed youth and inner-directed adulthood.

Neugarten's Changes in Adulthood

Bernice Neugarten (1973, 1977; Neugarten & Neugarten, 1986) has focused attention on differences between *chronological age* and *social age.* When you count the number of years from the day you were born, that's your chronological age. At the same time, society marks different stages of life that may have more psychological bearing than your chronological age. Thus your life stage may be marked more by whether you are in a long-term relationship or whether you have children than by your age of 30, 40, or 50. Because social age is correlated with life experiences, people reach the social criteria for the various life stages—for example, the transition from adolescence to adulthood—at different chronological ages. Thus chronological age will often not be the most accurate index of an individual's success at meeting life's tasks.

According to Neugarten, life stages may be identified by social situations rather than by chronological age.

Neugarten's research also provided data consistent with Jung's idea that aging brings with it a shift in focus from the outer to the inner world. Older adults become more individualistic in their responses to the external environment; they become less sensitive to the reactions of others. Against this background, however, Neugarten identified some important sex differences. Compared with younger men, older men are more open to playing a passive, nurturant role. Compared with younger women, older women tend to be more aggressive in social interactions. This pattern has been confirmed across a variety of cultures (Gutmann, 1977). These changes can be interpreted, in part, as a release from the responsibilities of early adulthood. Historically, women have been primarily responsible for nurturing children and men have been primarily responsible for channeling their aggressiveness toward activities that support a family. As aging brings with it a release from these responsibilities, men and women may change to become more alike.

Neugarten confirmed Jung's notion of an age-produced shift in focus from the outer world to the inner world.

We have reviewed these three bodies of work to provide a framework for a more detailed analysis of the major features of each period of the life span. As you read the remainder of this chapter, you should keep in mind how the tasks of life are jointly determined by a biological accumulation of years and a social accumulation of cultural experiences. However, before we move formally to our consideration of life stages, we will explore in more detail the role that culture plays in the shaping of social developmental outcomes.

THE CULTURAL CONTEXT OF DEVELOPMENT

In Chapter 5, we described the interactions of nature and nurture that give rise to developmental change. In this chapter, you have already seen life-span theories that make predictions about relationships between age and experiences. As always, researchers would like to determine which experiences are inevitable consequences of a biological program of aging and which experiences are brought about by the environment. When we look at social development, it becomes particularly clear that each of life's tasks is played out against a background of ever-changing cultural patterns. In the United States, for example, the extreme conformity and conservatism of the 1950s sowed the seeds of the adolescent revolution of the 1960s and early 1970s. The resulting sexual freedom was bolstered by the development of birth-control technology; but that freedom has been challenged in the 1990s by the fear of widespread sexually transmitted diseases, especially AIDS. An array of social ills—for example, drug use, crime, teenage pregnancy, and homelessness—seem to have sparked a conservative backlash to the free-thinking, experimental mood of the 1960s and 1970s (Shinn & Weitzman, 1990). You can understand that the way in which you might experience different periods of your life would depend, in part, on the expectations of the culture surrounding you.

The study of social development must include some emphasis on the cultural context.

For many individuals, culture actively shapes the environment in which they develop. In Chapter 5, we acknowledged that each individual experiences a different environment, and those different environments affect developmental outcomes. When we turn to social development, the effect of different environments is particularly easy to observe. For example, people who live in circumstances of economic hardship undergo types of stress that are absent from the "normal" course of development (Conger et al., 1994; Duncan et al., 1994). Our culture also enforces different outcomes for men and for women and for individuals who belong to minority groups. For example, elderly women are more often economically disadvantaged than elderly men; elderly African-American women are worse off even than elderly white women (Carstensen & Pasupathi, 1993). These differences are direct products of structural inequities in our society. When we draw conclusions about the "average" life course, you should keep in mind that culture dictates that some individuals will depart from this average.

Let's take a closer look at cultural influences on the course of development. We will begin with the way in which childhood has been conceived over time.

Changing Conceptions of Childhood

Prior to the sixteenth century, most children older than 6 years of age were considered small adults and were expected to perform as adults whenever their competencies allowed it. During this period of history, parents and employers had virtually unlimited power to abuse or enslave children (McCoy, 1988; Pappas, 1983). Although parents formed loving relationships with some of their children, no stigma attached to abandoning other children—and social structures existed to make abandonment easy (Boswell, 1988).

From the sixteenth through the eighteenth centuries, children were considered property, useful for doing family work and for supporting parents. In those times of high infant and child mortality, children's individual identities were imperfectly acknowledged. Children were expected to assume adult responsibilities as soon as they were physically able. Not until the nineteenth-century industrial revolution reduced the need for children as cheap sources of labor was adolescence "invented," and then the concept was developed only to keep young people out of a competitive job market (Kett, 1977). Eventually, children began to be treated as valuable and also as vulnerable property by parents, schools, and society. During the 1800s, people perceived that many conditions associated with industrialization, urbanization, and immigration were threatening to children. These concerns led to child labor laws and compulsory education.

During the first half of the twentieth century, child-oriented family life emerged, along with external sources of influence on child care, such as developmental psychology and juvenile courts. But the child's status as a person did not receive societal acknowledgment until the second half of the twentieth century. The emerging status of *child as person* afforded children legal rights, including protection from abuse and neglect, due process in juvenile courts, and self-determination. Children are now recognized as competent persons worthy of considerable freedom (Horowitz, 1984). However, at this point in history, further advances in securing the person status of children will require greater contribution by psychologists. As a science, psychology can provide empirical evidence of children's capacities for self-determination and develop the best practices for achieving self-determination within a context of nurturing support and protection. "As a human service profession, psychology is capable of translating its knowledge base into support for a positive ideology of children that involves them in establishing their rights. Psychology has a preeminent responsibility to assist persons toward higher levels of self-determination and personhood" (Hart, 1991, pp. 57–58).

The recent view of children as persons with legal rights is a significant change from earlier views of children as property or as miniature adults.

Families and Youth at Risk

Current trends in the United States and in other countries throughout the world make it imperative for developmental psychologists to consider the exceptional circumstances in which many children, adolescents, and adults are forced to live—circumstances that continually put their sanity, safety, and survival at risk (Dryfoss, 1990; Huston et al., 1994). Numerous indicators suggest that the 1980s were terrible for many families, and that conditions are worsening in the 1990s. More American children in the mid-1990s than at the start of the last decade are likely to be poor, pregnant, in jail, hungry, homeless, suffering from psychological problems, or dead from violence and preventable diseases. These conclusions emerge from a number of nationwide surveys (National Center for Health Statistics, 1990; National Association of Children's Hospitals, 1991; Carnegie Foundation, 1990; *The Health of America's Children,* 1991).

IN YOUR LIFE

Consider the following evidence for the decline in the quality of life of America's youth and their families:

- Low birth weight, affecting 270,000 infants annually, doubles or triples the risk of chronic handicap, such as mental retardation, deafness, and blindness. The major cause of low birth weight is lack of or delayed prenatal care.

- Nationwide, 68 percent of teachers report the existence of undernourished children in their schools; 69 percent have said that the poor health of their students poses a problem in the classroom; and 89 percent report that there are abused or neglected children in their schools.

- Census figures show that over 20 percent of children in the United States live in families with incomes below the poverty line. Family poverty is an extension of the social and economic changes affecting families in all income classes (Bane & Ellwood, 1989).

- The teenage suicide rate has doubled in the past two decades. Teenage violent deaths increased by 12 percent between 1984 and 1988; juvenile incarceration rates increased by 41 percent between 1979 and 1987; and more than 50,000 juveniles are currently serving time in some kind of penal institution.

- It is estimated that one third of the growing population of homeless people in cities throughout the United States consists of families who live in shelters or on the streets. There may be as many as 750,000 homeless children in this country. Today's homeless are not only more numerous than in the past; they are also much younger and include more women, minorities, veterans, and former mental patients (Shinn & Weitzman, 1990). Homeless children suffer specific physical, psychological, academic, and emotional damage due to the unstable, hostile circumstances accompanying homelessness (Molnar et al., 1990).

As many as 20 percent of American children live in families with incomes below the poverty line. The cabin in which this girl lives with her mother and sister has no electricity or running water.

As we describe the psychological challenges facing the "ordinary" individual, you must bear in mind that many individuals face extraordinary challenges. It is the role of researchers to document the impact of contemporary problems—and to design interventions to alleviate their harshest consequences. Major reforms are clearly needed to institute and coordinate better health care, welfare programs, and social policy. Psychologists will play a role in helping to define what is in the best interest of families and their children (Scarr & Eisenberg, 1993).

Let's turn next to the origins of social relationships.

SOCIAL DEVELOPMENT IN CHILDHOOD

We now begin our review of the tasks and accomplishments of the different periods of the life span. We will discover that one of most important accomplishments of childhood is to form stable, trusting bonds with adults in the environment. Children's basic survival depends on forming meaningful, effective relationships with other people. **Socialization** is the lifelong process through which an individual's behavior patterns, values, standards, skills, attitudes, and motives are shaped to conform to those regarded as desirable in a particular society (Hetherington & Parke, 1975). This process involves many people—relatives, friends, teachers—and institutions—schools, houses of worship—that exert pressure on the individual to adopt socially approved values and standards of conduct. The family, however, is the most influential shaper and regulator of socialization. The concept of family itself is being transformed to recognize that many children grow up in circumstances that include either less (a single parent) or more (an extended household) than a mother, father, and siblings. Whatever the configuration, though, the family helps the individual form basic patterns of responsiveness to others—and these patterns, in turn, become the basis of the individual's lifelong style of relating to other people.

Of all the institutions and individuals that influence social development, the family is the most significant.

Parents' socialization goals for their children range from behavioral compliance with specific social rules—saying "please" and "thank you" and not talking with a mouth full of food—to internalization of general social values—being cooperative, honest, and responsible. Overall, parents are interested in fostering the optimal development of their children so that as adults they will be able to function within the framework of their particular culture and time. Western culture, for example, values the ability to form bonds of intimacy and stability with others (Maccoby & Martin, 1983). Other cultures give top priority to different social functions, such as group cooperation.

We will begin our discussion of socialization with a theme that will be familiar from Chapter 5. In our review of physical and cognitive development, we suggested that each child is "prewired for survival." We make the same claim here with respect to social development.

Social Capabilities of Newborns

Babies are designed to be sociable. They prefer looking at human faces to most other patterns (Fantz, 1963). When only a week old, some babies can distinguish their mother's voice from the voices of other women. In another week, babies can perceive their mother's voice and face as part of a total unit and will get upset when experimenters pair the mother's face with the voices of strangers (Carpenter, 1973).

Babies not only respond to but also interact with their caregivers. High-speed film studies of this interaction reveal a remarkable degree of *synchronicity*—the gazing, vocalizing, touching, and smiling of mothers and infants are closely coordinated (Martin, 1981; Murray & Trevarthen, 1986). Babies respond and learn, but they also send out messages to those willing to listen to and love them. Not only are the behaviors of mothers and infants linked in a socially dynamic fashion, but their feelings are also matched (Fogel, 1991). A 3-month-old infant may laugh when its mother laughs and frown or cry when she is sad (Tronick et al., 1980). This social ability is essential for survival—it serves to ensure that adult caretakers will respond to the infant's needs.

Human infants are prewired for social development, displaying responses to and interaction with caregivers in the form of synchronized touching, smiling, and vocalizing.

We have described, thus far, the social abilities that newborns share. Given our discussion of individual differences in Chapter 5, it will probably not surprise you that, even at birth, there are some constitutional differences

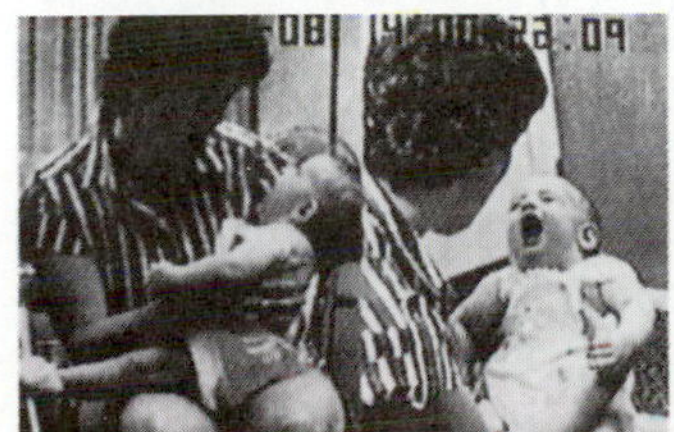
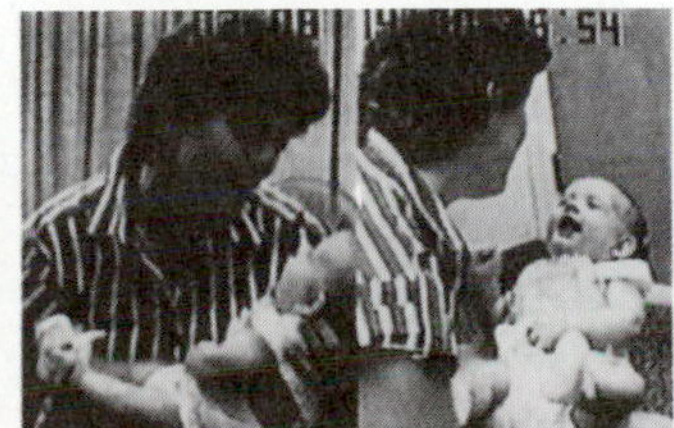

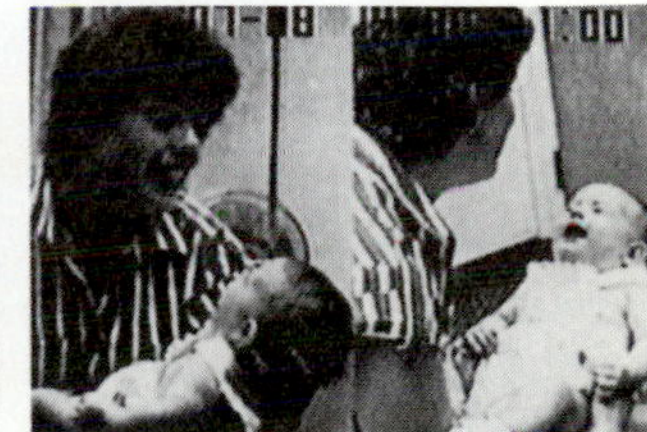

Researcher Alan Fogel has shown that an infant can match its mother's emotions.

in social preferences. Researcher **Jerome Kagan** has shown that about 10 to 15 percent of infants are "born shy" or "born bold" (Kagan & Snidman, 1991; Kagan et al., 1988). They differ in sensitivity to physical and social stimulation—the shy or timid baby is more easily frightened and less socially responsive. People are less likely to interact and be playful with the shy baby, accentuating the child's initial disposition. However, constitution need not always be destiny. Experience and special training can modify the way a constitutional factor is expressed.

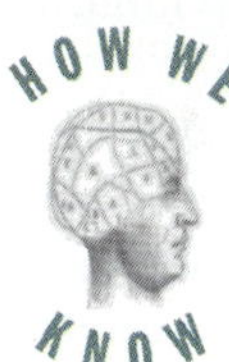

Genetically shy monkey temperament has been studied by researcher **Steven Suomi** (1990), who sees many parallels with shy children. When faced with challenges, these monkeys exhibit consistent behavior patterns; they cling to their mothers, do not explore, are easily frightened by strangers, and are tense in posture, very cautious, and very vigilant. They seem to have brain alarm systems that are easily triggered to release hormones into the bloodstream, causing respiration and heart rate to accelerate and pupils to dilate. Blood testing established that the shy trait was inherited, and it was apparent that shy mothers tended to have shy babies. To modify the behavior pattern, the research team arranged for foster parenting by nonshy, supportive, calm mothers and nurturing grandmothers, which worked to help shy youngsters handle social threats with greater confidence.

Suomi's research with shy monkeys reinforces the idea that environmental influence can strengthen or undo genetic differences.

This research with shy monkeys reinforces one central theme of this chapter: environments can function to strengthen or undo differences in genetic constitutional factors.

We turn now to the close attachments children form with their caretakers as an important consequence of their innate social skills.

Attachment and Social Support

Social development begins with the establishment of a close emotional relationship between a child and a mother, father, or other regular caregiver. This intense, enduring, social-emotional relationship is called **attachment.** Because children are incapable of feeding or protecting themselves, the earliest function of attachment is to ensure survival. Accordingly, in many nonhuman species, biology conspires to bring about attachment. Among rats, for example, the mother's licking of the newborn or eating of the placenta activates hormones that prime her to provide care and protection for her young (Pedersen et al., 1982). In other species, the infant automatically becomes **imprinted** on the first moving object it sees or hears (Johnson & Gottlieb, 1981). Imprinting occurs rapidly during a critical period of development and cannot easily be modified. The automaticity of imprinting can sometimes be problematic. Ethologist **Konrad Lorenz** demonstrated that young geese raised by a human will imprint on the human instead of on one of their own kind. A monkey raised by a dog will become more strongly attached to its foster canine mother than to other monkeys (Mason & Kenney, 1974). In nature, fortunately, young geese mostly see other geese first and monkeys other monkeys.

Human infants rely less on instinctive attachment behaviors. Although many hospitals try to foster attachment by placing newborn babies on the mother's stomach, humans rely on more complex signals to solidify adult–child bonding. Infants' *proximity-promoting signals*—such as smiling, crying, and vocalizing—appear to be behaviors built in to signal others to respond to them (Campos et al., 1983). Ten-month-old infants, for example, use smiles selectively to produce an effect on their audience:

While animals form attachments through instinctive behaviors, human infants rely on signals such as smiling, crying, and vocalizing to encourage responses in caregivers.

Konrad Lorenz, the researcher who pioneered the study of imprinting, graphically demonstrates what can happen when young animals become imprinted on someone other than their mother.

Videotapes were analyzed of infants playing with toys in a laboratory while their mothers either watched them attentively or were inattentive (reading magazines), according to a prearranged sequence. The mother's attentiveness predicted the rate at which the child smiled. If she looked at the baby when the infant glanced at her, the baby smiled, but if she was inattentive, the baby usually turned back to the toys without smiling. Thus the 10-month-olds did not smile just because they were happy; they could already control their facial expressions to serve social goals: "Smiling is partially dependent on the infant's appraisal of the social context and partially independent of emotion at this early point in development" (Jones et al., 1991, p. 49).

When imprinting studies go awry.

Successful attachment, of course, depends not only on an infant's ability to emit signals such as smiles but also on an adult's tendency to respond to the signals. Who can resist a baby's smile? According to **John Bowlby** (1973), an influential theorist on human attachment, infants will form attachments to individuals who consistently and appropriately respond to their signals.

Assessing the Quality and Consequences of Attachment

Researchers generally believe that secure attachment has powerful, lasting, beneficial effects: it provides a psychological home base from which an individual can explore the physical and social environment. Secure attachment to adults who offer dependable social support enables the child to learn a variety of prosocial behaviors, to take risks, to venture into novel situations, and to seek and accept intimacy in personal relationships. To verify these claims, researchers have had to develop techniques for determining the quality of a parent–child bond.

One of the most widely used research procedures for assessing attachment is the Strange Situation Test, developed by **Mary Ainsworth** and her colleagues (Ainsworth et al., 1978).

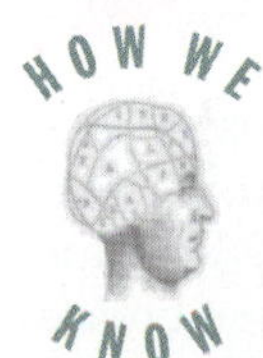

In the first of several standard episodes, the child is brought into an unfamiliar room filled with toys. With the mother present, the child is encouraged to explore the room and to play. After several minutes, a stranger comes in, talks to the mother, and approaches the child. Next, the mother exits the room. After this brief separation, the mother returns, there is a reunion with her child, and the stranger leaves. The researchers record the child's behaviors at separation and reunion.

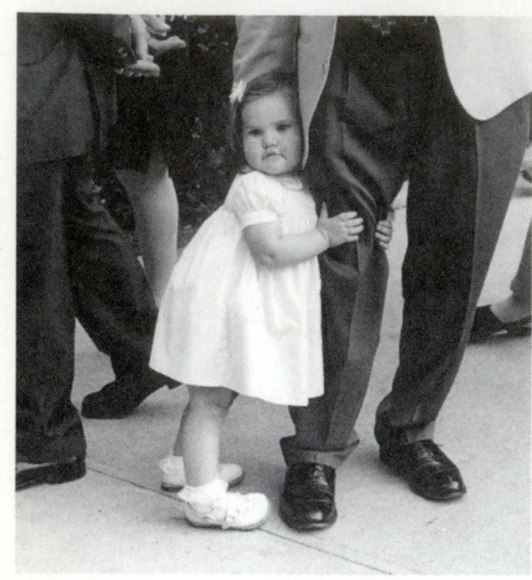

A child needs to develop a secure attachment to a parent or other caregiver before feeling ready to venture into new situations.

Researchers have found that children's responses on this test fall into four general categories (Ainsworth et al., 1978; Main et al., 1985):

- *Securely attached* children show some distress when the parent leaves the room; seek proximity, comfort, and contact upon reunion; and then gradually return to play.
- *Insecurely attached–avoidant* children seem aloof and may actively avoid and ignore the parent upon her return.
- *Insecurely attached–ambivalent* children become quite upset and anxious when the parent leaves; at reunion they cannot be comforted and they show anger and resistance to the parent but, at the same time, express a desire for contact.
- *Insecurely attached–disorganized* children act dazed and confused upon reunion. After the parent's return, they may stop moving completely or show contradictory behavior patterns, such as gazing away while in contact with the parent.

Categorizations based on the Strange Situation Test have proven to be highly predictive of a child's later behavior in a wider variety of settings—particularly the overall division between children who are securely and insecurely attached. For example, longitudinal research has revealed that children who showed secure or insecure behavior in the Strange Situation at 15 months differed widely in their preschool behavior at age 3½ (Waters et al., 1979). Observers, who were unaware of the children's previously assessed quality of attachment, rated the securely attached children as considerably more competent on dimensions like "suggests activities," "other children seek his [or her] company," and "likes to learn new cognitive skills." Similar continuity from the quality of attachment to later years has been demonstrated in 4- and 5-year-olds (LaFreniere & Sroufe, 1985) and 10-year-olds (Urban et al., 1991). This suggests that the quality of attachment, as revealed in the Strange Situation, really does have long-term importance. What can parents do to help bring about these critical secure attachments?

Parenting Styles and Parenting Practices

Researchers have located the most beneficial **parenting style** at the intersection of the two dimensions of *demandingness* and *responsiveness* (Maccoby & Martin, 1983): "Demandingness refers to the parent's willingness to act as a socializing agent, whereas responsiveness refers to the parent's recognition of the child's individuality" (Darling & Steinberg, 1993, p. 492). As shown in **Figure 6.1**, *authoritative* parents make appropriate demands on their children—they demand that their children conform to appropriate rules of behavior—but are also responsive to their children—they keep channels of communication open to foster their children's ability to regulate themselves (Baumrind, 1967, 1973). This authoritative style is most likely to produce an effective parent–child bond. The contrast, as seen in Figure 6.1, is to parenting styles that, for example, may be either *authoritarian*—parents apply discipline with little attention to the child's autonomy—or *indulgent*—parents fail to help children learn about the structure of social rules in which they must live.

The authoritative parenting style is most likely to produce an effective parent–child bond.

Even parents with the same overall styles put different priorities on the *socialization goals* they consider important for the children. **Parenting practices** arise in response to particular goals (Darling & Steinberg, 1993). Thus authoritative parents who wish their children to do well in school may create a home environment in which the children come to understand why their parents value that as a goal—and may strive to do well in school because

	Accepting Responsive Child-centered	*Rejecting Unresponsive Parent-centered*
Demanding, controlling	Authoritative-reciprocal High in bidirectional communication	Authoritarian Power assertive
Undemanding, low in control attempts	Indulgent	Neglecting, ignoring, indifferent, uninvolved

Figure 6.1 A Classification of Parenting Patterns

they are effectively socialized toward that goal. However, because not all authoritative parents value school success, you could not predict children's school performance based only on their parents' style (Steinberg et al., 1992). Parents' general attitudes and specific behaviors are both important for charting their children's life course.

We can see the dramatic effect of parenting style in a longitudinal study that spanned 35 years.

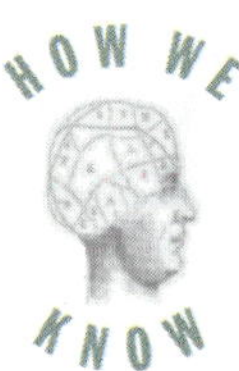

The study began in 1951 with interviews of 379 mothers about the child-rearing practices they were using with their 5-year-olds. Additional data about the social and personal adjustment of each child (202 boys and 177 girls from both working-class and middle-class backgrounds) were collected from their kindergarten teachers. Until the children turned 18, researchers made measures of sources of family stress including divorce, death, hospitalization, and moving. When these subjects turned 41, those who could be contacted completed questionnaires and interviews. The final sample consisted of 76 married or previously married white subjects—33 men and 43 women—primarily from middle-class backgrounds.

The key finding in this study was that the mothers' treatment of their 5-year-old children was significantly associated with social adjustment more than three decades later. Adults with warm, affectionate mothers or fathers were able to sustain long and relatively happy marriages, raise children, and be involved with friends at midlife. The socially accomplished adults were emotionally stable, active, reliable, and self-disciplined. In addition, those whose marriages and family lives were working best were also more committed to and involved with their life work (Franz et al., 1991).

A close interactive relationship with loving adults is a child's first step toward healthy physical growth and normal socialization. As the original attachment to the primary caregiver extends to other family members, they too become models for new ways of thinking and behaving. From these early attachments, children develop the ability to respond to their own needs and to the needs of others.

A close interactive relationship with loving adults is a child's first step toward normal socialization.

Children in Day Care

When psychologists first began to study social development, many of the infants on whom they based their conclusions stayed home full time with their mothers. However, societal constraints have shifted over the last few decades, making it necessary for much larger numbers of mothers to work outside the home. As a consequence, many children spend long hours of even the earliest part of their lives outside the influence of their parents. Researchers have reacted to this shift by addressing a pair of questions: In what ways is day care better or worse for the developing child? What is the optimal form of day care?

We have already provided the context in which you can interpret the first question: If the attachments between children and mothers are so critical, shouldn't anything that disrupts the formation of those attachments—such as day care—be necessarily bad for the children? The answer to this question is, "On balance, *no.*" To arrive at this answer, researchers typically made comparisons between children who stayed at home and those who were placed in day care, on measures of both intellectual and social development. Researchers have found that children placed in day care are often at an *advantage* with respect to these measures, primarily because day care provides more opportunities (Clarke-Stewart, 1991, 1993). Intellectual development can benefit from a greater range of educational and play activities; social development can benefit from a wider variety of social interactions than would be available in the home.

There are two reasons, however, that the answer is "*On balance,* no." One is that there are individual differences in the way children respond to care outside the home. The second is that day care takes many forms. Researchers, therefore, have turned their attention away from the "better or worse" question toward the issue of what constitutes quality care for particular children (Zaslow, 1991).

Alison Clarke-Stewart (1993), an expert on day care, has summarized the research literature to provide a series of guidelines for quality day care. Some of her recommendations relate to the physical comfort of the children:

- The day-care center should be physically comfortable and safe.
- There should be at least one caretaker for every six or seven children (more for children under 3).

Other recommendations cover educational and psychological aspects of the day-care curriculum:

- Children should have a free choice of activities intermixed with explicit lessons.
- Children should be taught social problem-solving skills.

Clarke-Stewart has also suggested that day-care providers should share the qualities of good parents:

- Caregivers should be responsive to the children's needs and actively involved in their activities.
- Caregivers should not put undue restrictions on the children.
- Caregivers should have sufficient flexibility to recognize differences among the needs of individual children.

If these guidelines are followed, quality day care can be provided to all children whose parents work outside the home. For day care to be truly effective, however, there will have to be changes in the general attitudes of society. First, people must accept the reality that increasing numbers of children will be experiencing day care—and society must direct its resources toward the goal of making all day care be quality day care (Scarr et al., 1990). Second, people must work to eliminate the stigma associated with "working motherhood" and day care itself (Hoffman, 1989). As psychologists spread the message that day care does not harm, and may even enhance, children's development, parents should feel less stress about the necessity of a dual-career family. Such a reduction in stress could only improve the child's overall psychological environment.

The Costs of Deprivation

What happens when children have no possibility of attachment to individuals in their environment? Because researchers would never purposefully endanger human children, experiments on deprivation have involved nonhuman animals. Human societies, however, often conspire to produce tragic circumstances of deprivation outside the laboratory.

Contact Comfort and Social Experience

What do children obtain from the attachment bond? Sigmund Freud and other psychologists argued that babies become attached to their parents because the parents provide them with food—their most basic physical need. This view is called the *cupboard theory* of attachment. If the cupboard theory were correct, children should thrive as long as they are adequately fed. Does this seem right?

Harry Harlow (1965) did not believe that the cupboard theory explained the importance of attachment. He set out to test the cupboard theory against his own hypothesis that infants might also attach to those who provide **contact comfort** (Harlow & Zimmerman, 1958). Harlow separated macaque monkeys from their mothers at birth and placed them in cages, where they had access to two artificial "mothers": a wire one and a terry cloth one. Harlow found that the baby monkeys nestled close to the terry cloth mother and spent little time on the wire one. They did this even when only the wire mother gave milk! The baby monkeys also used the cloth mother as a source of comfort when frightened and as a base of operations when exploring new stimuli. When a fear stimulus (for example, a toy bear beating a drum) was introduced, the baby monkeys would run to the cloth mother. When novel and intriguing stimuli were introduced, the baby monkeys would gradually venture out to explore and then return to the terry cloth mother before exploring further.

One of Harlow's monkeys and its artificial terry cloth mother. Harlow found that the contact comfort mothers provide is essential for normal social development.

Further studies by Harlow and his colleagues found that the monkeys' formation of a strong attachment to the mother substitute was not sufficient for healthy social development. At first, the experimenters thought the young monkeys with terry cloth mothers were developing normally, but a very different picture emerged when it was time for the female monkeys who had been raised in this way to become mothers. Monkeys who had been deprived of chances to interact with other responsive monkeys in their early lives had trouble forming normal social and sexual relationships in adulthood.

When the "motherless" monkeys had children, most were either indifferent or unresponsive to their babies or brutalized them, biting off their fingers or toes, pounding them, and nearly killing them, until human caretakers intervened. One of the most interesting findings was that, despite the consistent punishment, the babies persisted in their attempts to make maternal contact. In the end, "it was a case of the baby adopting the mother, not the mother adopting the baby" (Harlow, 1965, p. 259). Fortunately, with successive pregnancies, the maternal behavior of these mothers improved, so that this brutal behavior was no longer the norm.

What these "motherless" monkeys seemed chiefly to lack was any sort of social experience. In subsequent studies, researchers found that the monkeys who had had only terry cloth mothers showed adequate, but considerably delayed, adjustment if they were given ample opportunity to interact with other infant monkeys as they were growing up (Harlow & Harlow, 1966). Younger, normally reared monkeys served as "peer therapists" when paired with the unattached, socially deprived monkeys, helping them to attain a more normal mode of social functioning (Suomi & Harlow, 1972).

Harlow's motherless monkeys proved to be lacking in social skills and knowledge of basic mothering behaviors.

Primate researcher Stephen Suomi (1987, 1990) has shown that putting emotionally vulnerable infant monkeys in the foster care of supportive mothers virtually turns their lives around. Suomi notes that monkeys put in the care of mothers known to be particularly loving and attentive are transformed from marginal members of the monkey troop into bold, outgoing young males who are among the first to leave the troop at puberty to work their way into a new troop. This *cross-fostering* gives them coping skills and information essential for recruiting support from other monkeys and for maintaining a high social status in the group. Let's see now what lessons research with monkeys holds for human deprivation.

Human Deprivation

Tragically, human societies have sometimes created circumstances in which children are deprived of contact comfort. Consider institutions in Romania where as many as 40,000 homeless infants and children were kept under the worst possible conditions. Totalitarian dictator Nicolae Ceauşescu (overthrown in 1990) started a campaign to increase Romania's population, at any cost. The country's extremely poor economic conditions caused such hardships that many mothers abandoned the babies they had conceived in response to Ceauşescu 's campaign. Many of these children who were left in state institutions "appear to suffer chiefly from isolation and neglect." Western relief workers found "children tied to their beds, starving and filthy. Often, the children have never been touched or held. No one has talked to them. They rock back and forth, staring blankly, or cower in the presence of strangers" (Sachs, 1990).

Lack of close, loving relationships in infancy affects physical growth and even survival.

Many studies have shown that a lack of close, loving relationships in infancy affects physical growth and even survival. In 1915, a doctor at Johns Hopkins Hospital reported that, despite adequate physical care, 90 percent of the infants admitted to orphanages in Baltimore died within the first year. Studies of hospitalized infants over the next 30 years found that, despite adequate nutrition, the children often developed respiratory infections and fevers of unknown origin, failed to gain weight, and showed general signs of physiological deterioration (Bowlby, 1969; Sherrod et al., 1978). Another study of infants in foundling homes in the United States and Canada reported evidence of severe emotional and physical disorders as well as high mortality rates, despite good food and medical care (Spitz & Wolf, 1946).

The negative effects of early institutionalization hold true for high-stress, hostile family environments. In family environments marked by emotional detachment and hostility, children are found to weigh less and to have retarded bone development. They begin to grow when they are removed from the hostile environment, but their growth again becomes stunted if they are returned to it—a phenomenon that is known as **psychosocial dwarfism** (Gardner, 1972). Negative environments also affect social development. In one study of ten abused toddlers, ages 1 to 3 years, researchers found that the children did not respond appropriately when a peer was in distress. When another child is upset and crying, toddlers will normally show concern, empathy, or sadness. By contrast, the abused children were more likely to respond with fear, anger, or physical attacks (Main & George, 1985).

Although hostile environments may impede physical growth and social development, psychologists are working to develop interventions to help individuals overcome early deprivation.

What can be done for these children? The research with monkeys provides a glimmer of hope that early deprivation can be overcome. Studies with children have also suggested that the early proximity of the child to the biological mother is *not* necessary for attachment and healthy social development (Rutter, 1981). Positive bonds can be formed with any caregiver who is comforting, interacts actively, and is responsive to a baby's signals (Ainsworth, 1973). But some such responsive adult *is* necessary. A critical goal of psychology is to develop interventions that help overcome early deprivation.

Gender Roles

Children who are securely attached to their caretakers have developed a ready link for acquiring information about their social world. One type of information most children acquire early on is that there are two categories of people in that social world, males and females. Note that, at first, the differences children perceive are entirely social: they begin to sense sex differences well before they understand anything about anatomy. As an adult who both knows about anatomy and understands that sex differences are more than just physical, you can begin to consider why these differences arise. Which differences are indirect consequences of biology? Which are products of socialization? How do boys and girls learn the different expectations their culture has of them?

How do children form the belief that kitchen work is women's work?

Biologically based characteristics that distinguish males and females are referred to as **sex differences.** These characteristics include different reproductive functions and differences in hormones and anatomy. These differences are universal, biologically determined, and unchanged by social influence. Over time, they have also led to the development of some traditional social roles—for example, since women can breastfeed their babies, prehistoric peoples may have determined that women should also remain close to home, caring for children, while the men hunted for food (Rossi, 1984).

Sex differences may also explain the finding that, after infancy, boys are more physically active and aggressive than girls. All over the world, boys are more likely than girls to engage in rough play. This difference is partly related to sex hormones—biological factors can create behavioral dispositions (Maccoby, 1980). Researchers know that sex hormones affect social play, because observations of young male and female rats and monkeys reveal the same behavioral differences found in humans (Meany et al., 1988). Male animals engage in vigorous forms of physical play that require gross motor activity. Female animals engage in activities that require precise motor skills.

In contrast to biological sex, **gender** is a psychological phenomenon referring to learned, sex-related behaviors and attitudes. Cultures vary in how strongly gender is linked to daily activities and in the amount of tolerance for what is perceived as cross-gender behavior. **Gender identity** is an individual's

Source: CATHY by Cathy Guisewite. Copyright, 1986, Universal Press Syndicate. Reprinted with permission. All rights reserved.

sense of maleness or femaleness; it includes awareness and acceptance of one's sex. This awareness develops at quite a young age: 10- to 14-month-old children already demonstrate a preference for a video showing the abstract movements of a child of the same sex (Kujawski & Bower, 1993). A sense of gender identity is important to a child's psychological well-being. Some theorists believe that children inherently value what is similar to them and, therefore, seek out sex-appropriate activities (Kohlberg, 1966).

Gender identity is evident in 10- to 14-month-old children, who indicate a preference for videos showing same-sex children.

Gender roles are patterns of behavior regarded as appropriate for males and females in a particular society. They provide the basic definitions of *masculinity* and *femininity.* Much of what people consider masculine or feminine is shaped by culture (Williams, 1983). Gender-role socialization begins at birth. In one study, parents described their newborn daughters, using words such as *little, delicate, beautiful,* and *weak.* By contrast, parents described their newborn sons as *firm, alert, strong,* and *coordinated.* The babies actually showed no differences in height, weight, or health (Rubin et al., 1974). The differences in the responses of these parents seem to be based on *gender-role stereotypes.* Parents dress their sons and daughters differently, give them different kinds of toys to play with, and communicate with them differently (Rheingold & Cook, 1974). For example, parents hold their sons more often, give them more physical stimulation, and pay more attention to their vocalizations and signals for food (Parke & Sawin, 1976; Yarrow, 1975). Later in life, adults reward children for gender-appropriate behavior and punish them for actions that are gender-inappropriate. Boys, in particular, receive strong negative responses from their fathers for engaging in cross-gender behavior (Langlois & Downs, 1980). And parents have different expectations for their sons and daughters. **Jeanne Block** (1983) concludes that parents give their girls "roots" to build homes and families, but they give their boys "wings" to soar to new adventures.

Parents are not, however, the only socializers of gender roles. **Eleanor Maccoby** (1988) argues, for example, that parents do not merely stamp in gender roles. She has found evidence that play styles and toy preferences are not, in fact, highly correlated with parental preferences or roles. Young children are segregationists—they seek out peers of the same sex even when adults are not supervising them or in spite of adult encouragement for mixed-group play. Maccoby believes that many of the differences in gender behavior among children are the results of peer relationships. Because of gender-role socialization, boys and girls grow up in different psychological environments that shape their views of the world and their ways of dealing with problems. Boys' groups, for example, are more concerned with dominance—who has power over whom—than are girls' groups; girls' groups are typically more interested in consensus than power.

Eleanor Maccoby believes that peer relationships can influence gender roles as much as parental actions can.

Children between the ages of 2 and 6 seem to have more extreme and inflexible perceptions of gender than do adults (Stern & Karraker, 1989). When shown infants dressed in neutral clothing, children of this age are much more consistently affected in their judgments about the infant by an arbitrary label of "male" or "female" than are adults. Younger children's extreme reactions may be linked to the fact that they are at an age when they are trying to establish their own gender identity. They appear, on the whole, to be much more attuned to the "scripts" for gender-appropriate behavior than are their older siblings (Levy & Fivush, 1993).

Our discussion so far has focused on development in childhood. You have seen how important it is that each child develop secure attachments with adult caretakers. You have also seen that children's identities as girls and boys have roots both in nature and in nurture. In the next section, on adolescence, we will see that people's social interactions continue to change as life provides a new set of challenges.

ADOLESCENCE

In Chapter 5, we defined adolescence by physical and cognitive changes. In this section, we will take those changes as background. Because the individual has reached a certain level of physical and mental maturity, new social and personal challenges present themselves. We will first consider the general experience of adolescence and then turn to the individual's changing social world.

The Experience of Adolescence

Many cultures have strong expectations about the psychological consequences of the transition from childhood to adulthood. We will examine how those expectations affect the way in which individuals experience adolescence.

Transition Markers and Initiation Rites

Can you identify a time when you were aware that you had emerged from childhood? Most nonindustrial societies do not identify a stage of adolescence between childhood and adulthood. Instead, many such societies have *rites of passage,* or **initiation rites.** These rituals usually take place around puberty and serve as a public acknowledgment of the transition from childhood to adulthood. The rites themselves vary widely, from instruction in sexual and cultural practices to periods of seclusion involving survival ordeals. Rites involving genital operations or forms of physical scarring or tattooing give initiates permanent physical markers of adult status. Separate rites are carried out for males and females, reflecting the clear separation of gender roles in these cultures. In many traditional societies, then, the period of adolescence as a transition between childhood and adulthood lasts for only the few hours or the few months of the rite of passage. Once individuals have passed through that period, they are adults, and the ties to their childhood have been severed.

In modern society, there are few transition rituals to help children clearly mark changes of status. Even those religious rituals that share content with other initiation rites, such as Christian confirmations or Jewish bar mitzvahs (for males) and bat mitzvahs (for females), do not accord full adult status. In the United States, adolescence has no clearly defined beginning or

Many cultures have initiation rites that signal a child's passage into adulthood. Shown at top left is a bar mitzvah, a Jewish ceremony marking a boy's thirteenth birthday. The top right photo records the puberty rites of the White Mountain Apaches of Arizona. At bottom is the initiation ceremony of a young Lamaist monk.

end. It can extend for more than a decade, through the teens to the mid-20s, until adult roles begin. The legal system defines adult status according to age; but different legal ages exist for "adult" activities, such as drinking alcohol in public, driving, marrying without parental consent, and voting. In many cases, only social events—such as graduation from high school (or college, or graduate school), moving out of the family home, the establishment of financial independence, and marriage—mark the beginning of adulthood.

In our society, adulthood is likely to begin with social markers, such as graduation from high school or moving away from home.

The period of adolescence, thus, is defined in part by cultural norms. Cultural expectations also prescribe some aspects of the psychological experience of adolescence.

The Myth of Adolescent "Storm and Stress"

The traditional view of adolescence predicts a uniquely tumultuous period of life, characterized by extreme mood swings and unpredictable, difficult behavior: "storm and stress." This view can be traced back to Romantic writers of the late eighteenth and early nineteenth centuries, such as Goethe. The storm and stress conception of adolescence was strongly propounded by **G. Stanley Hall,** the first psychologist of the modern era to write at length about adolescent development (1904). Following Hall, the major proponents of this view have been psychoanalytic theorists working within the Freudian tradition (for example, Blos, 1965; A. Freud, 1946, 1958). Some of them have argued that not only is extreme turmoil a normal part of adolescence but that failure to exhibit such turmoil is a sign of arrested development. **Anna Freud** wrote that "to be normal during the adolescent period is by itself abnormal" (1958, p. 275).

G. Stanley Hall and Anna Freud were strong proponents of the storm-and-stress view of adolescence.

Two early pioneers in cultural anthropology, **Margaret Mead** (1928) and **Ruth Benedict** (1938), argued that the storm and stress theory is not applicable to many non-Western cultures. They described cultures in which children gradually take on more and more adult responsibilities without any sudden stressful transition or period of indecision and turmoil. It was not until large studies were undertaken of representative adolescents in Western society, however, that the turmoil theory finally began to be widely questioned within psychology. The results of such studies have been consistent: few adolescents experience the inner turmoil and unpredictable behavior ascribed to them (Offer et al., 1981a, b, 1988; Oldham, 1978a, b). **Table 6.2** summarizes key findings from a study of the psychological adjustment of over 20,000 adolescents (Offer et al., 1981a).

Margaret Mead and Ruth Benedict argued that many non-Western cultures do not experience the storm and stress of adolescence.

Unfortunately, those few adolescents who experience serious maladjustment are likely to continue doing so as they move into adulthood (Bachman

Table 6.2 The Psychological Self of the Normal Adolescent

Item	Percentage of Adolescents Endorsing Each Item
I feel relaxed under normal circumstances.	91
I enjoy life.	90
Usually I control myself.	90
I feel strong and healthy.	86
Most of the time I am happy.	85
Even when I am sad I can enjoy a good joke.	83

et al., 1979; Offer & Offer, 1975; Vaillant, 1977). Consider the following research that points to a strong link between adolescent conduct problems and subsequent adult criminality.

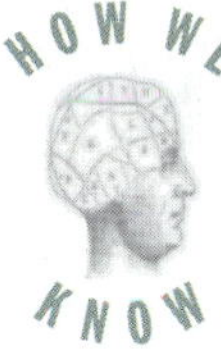

A large-scale longitudinal study of adolescents (ages 10–13) attending school in a typical Swedish town compared their conduct status (from teachers' reports) and biological functioning with the likelihood of their having criminal records or other adjustment problems as young adults (ages 18–26). Among the boys, those who showed early aggressiveness and restlessness (hyperactivity) were significantly more likely to develop into adults who would commit registered criminal offenses. In addition, a more severe pattern of early maladjustment was correlated with other adult adjustment problems as well, such as alcohol abuse and being under psychiatric care. **Figure 6.2** shows the extent to which early aggressiveness is linked to adult criminality (Magnusson, 1987; Magnusson & Bergman, 1990).

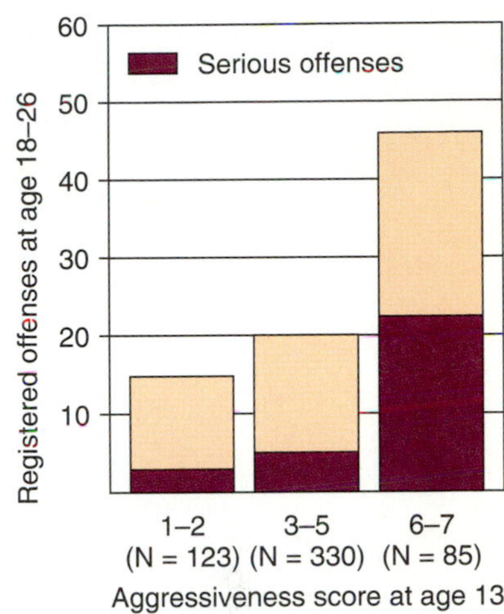

Figure 6.2 Adolescent Aggression and Adult Criminality
This chart shows percentages of individuals who achieved various ratings of aggressiveness at the age of 13 and who were registered for criminal offenses at the ages of 18 to 26.

Adolescent problems should not, therefore, be incorrectly attributed to the myth of "storm and stress." Particularly because adolescents are at high risk for suicide (Garland & Zigler, 1993), signs of disturbance should be treated with sincere attention by all those in contact with such adolescents.

Let's turn now to aspects of identity formation in adolescence.

Identity Formation in Adolescence

In Erikson's description of the life span, the essential task of adolescence is to discover one's true *identity.* We will see now the roles that social relationships and future goals play in the formation of this sense of identity.

Social Relationships

Much of the study of social development in adolescence focuses on the changing roles of family (or adult caretakers) and friends (Laursen, 1993; Paikoff, 1991). We have already seen that attachments to adults form soon after birth. Children also begin to have friends at very young ages. Adolescence, however, marks the first period in which peers appear to compete with parents to shape a person's attitudes and behaviors. With peers, adolescents refine their social skills and try out different social roles and behaviors. Adolescents report spending more than four times as much time talking to peers as to adults and also admit a preference for talking to their peers (Csikszentmihalyi et al., 1977). Through interaction with peers, adolescents gradually define the social component of their developing identities, determining the kind of people they choose to be and the kind of relationships they choose to pursue (Berndt, 1992). For this reason, adolescents and their friends are often tightly clustered—for example, with respect to their patterns of drug use (Dinges & Oetting, 1993).

Because peers become an increasingly important source of social support, there is also an increase in anxiety associated with being rejected. As a consequence, conformity to peer values and behaviors—the *peer pressure* that parents fear—rises to a peak around ages 12 and 13 (Brown, 1989). Concerns with acceptance and popularity are particularly strong for females, who appear to be more focused on social relations than their male counterparts, but females are less likely to conform to group pressures to engage in antisocial behaviors than are males (Berndt, 1979).

In adolescence, the influence of peers begins to compete with adult (parental) influence for the first time as peer pressure peaks at about age 12 or 13.

Because of the possibility of peer pressure, parents often worry that they must compete for influence with their children's friends to keep their chil-

Friends are a vital source of social support beginning in adolescence; teens will go to great lengths to fit in with their peers.

dren from developing harmful attitudes or behaviors. What may be more true, however, is that adolescents generally communicate with their parents and peers about different categories of life experiences. For example, adolescents indicate that they are very likely to discuss with their parents, but not their friends, how well they are doing in school. With their friends, but not their parents, they are likely to discuss their views on dating behavior and sex (Youniss & Smollar, 1985). Thus parents who wish to "compete" with their children's friends in certain domains may have to develop ways to get their adolescents to discuss "friends" topics.

Parents and their adolescent children must also weather a transition in their relationship from one in which a parent has unquestioned authority to one in which the adolescent is granted reasonable independence, or *autonomy*, to make important decisions (Holmbeck & O'Donnell, 1991; Youniss & Smollar, 1985). This transition can be difficult for parents who wish to acknowledge an adolescent's progress toward adulthood by allowing dissent—without allowing improper choices to compromise his or her future. Although friendships change somewhat over the adolescent years (Shulman, 1993), these changes reflect greater mutual dependence rather than changes in the equality of the relationship. Parent–child relationships, thus, may have more built-in potential for conflict than peer relationships.

Identity development ultimately requires the adolescent to establish independent commitments that are sensitive to parental *and* peer environments but are not mere reflections of either. What is important is that adolescents find some consistent sources of social support in their environment (Carnegie Foundation, 1990). Such social support will enable the adolescent to plan for the future, the topic to which we now move.

Future Goals

Adolescence is the period in which individuals are expected to begin to answer seriously the ubiquitous question "What are you going to be when you grow up?" The question itself reflects the common assumption that individuals' identities are fixed, in part, by their goals. The selection, for example, of a future occupation involves tasks central to identity formation: appraisal of one's abilities and interests, awareness of realistic alternatives, and the ability to make and follow through on a choice. Adolescents have concerns about the future at both the personal and societal levels: they worry about their occupations and families as well as global threats of economic collapse or nuclear war (Nurmi, 1991). They also have a keen sense of how their futures should unfold with age. First, educational goals must be met, followed by occupational goals, and finally family goals. At each juncture, goals are shaped by the constraints of gender roles and family context and resources.

Adolescents worry about their futures at both the personal level and the societal level.

Choices about educational and occupational goals made in later adolescence can have a profound effect on future options. But, as with all aspects of identity, goal formation is best conceived of in the context of the whole life cycle. The key is a flexibility and a willingness to explore new directions based on a sense of self-confidence developed during successful negotiation through the demands of adolescence. These successes in adolescence set the stage for adult development.

ADULTHOOD

Erikson defined two tasks of adulthood to be intimacy and generativity. Freud identified the needs of adulthood to be *Lieben und Arbeiten,* or love and work. Abraham Maslow (1968, 1970) described the needs of this period of life as love and belonging, which, when satisfied, develop into the needs for success and esteem. Other theorists label these needs as affiliation or social acceptance and achievement or competence needs. The shared core of these theories is that adulthood is a time in which both relationships and accomplishments take on special priority. In this section, we track these themes across the breadth of adulthood.

Many theorists share the idea that adulthood is a time of concern for both relationships and accomplishments.

INTIMACY

Erikson described **intimacy** as the capacity to make a full commitment—sexual, emotional, and moral—to another person. Intimacy, which can occur in both friendships and romantic relationships, requires openness, courage, ethical strength, and usually some compromise of one's personal preferences. Research has consistently confirmed Erikson's supposition that social intimacy is a prerequisite for a sense of psychological well-being across the adult life stages (Ishii-Kuntz, 1990). **Figure 6.3** demonstrates that interactions with family and friends tradeoff over this long span of years to provide a fairly constant level in people's reports of their own well-being. The changes

The early adulthood task of forming intimate relationships requires openness, courage, ethical strength, and compromise.

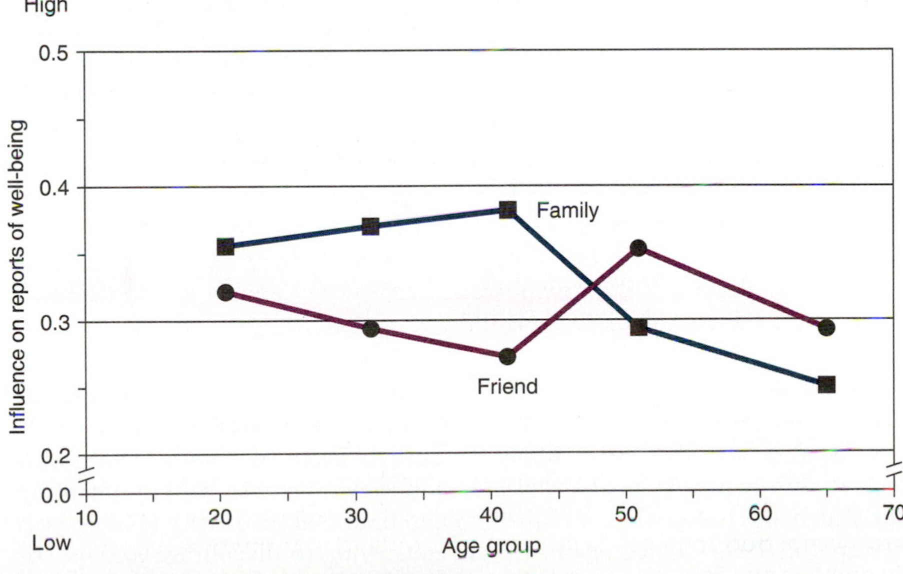

Figure 6.3 The Effects of Social Interaction on Well-Being
Across the life span, social interactions with family and friends trade off to provide a fairly constant level of individuals' reports of well-being.

in these sources of support reflect, in part, the life events that are typically correlated with each age. Let's examine these correlations.

Young adulthood is the period in which many people enter into marriage or other stable relationships. The group that counts as family, thus, will ordinarily grow larger. Families also grow when individuals decide to include children in their lives. What may surprise you, however, is that the birth of children can often pose a threat to the overall happiness of a marriage. Why might that be? Researchers have focused on differences in the way that men and women make the transition to parenthood (Cowan et al., 1985). In contemporary society, marriages are more often founded on notions of equality between men and women than was true in the past. However, children's births can have the effect of pushing husbands and wives in the direction of more traditional sex roles. The wife may feel too much of the burden of child care; the husband may feel too much pressure to support a family. The net effect may be that, following the birth of a child, the marriage changes in ways that both spouses find to be negative (Cowan et al., 1985).

For many couples, satisfaction with the marriage continues to decline because of conflicts as the child or children pass through their adolescent years. Contrary to the cultural stereotype, many parents look forward to the time when their youngest child leaves home and leaves them with an "empty nest" (Lowenthal & Chiriboga, 1972). Parents may enjoy their children most when they are no longer under the same roof (Levenson et al., 1993). Have we discouraged you from having children? We certainly hope not! Our goal, as always, is to make you aware of research that can help you anticipate and interpret the patterns in your own life. You might think about the steps you could take to ensure that a much-awaited child doesn't undermine marital satisfaction.

If marriages are, on the whole, happier when the spouses reach late adulthood, should everyone try to stay married late into life? Researchers would like to be able to determine which couples are fundamentally mismatched—with respect, for example, to their patterns of interactions—and which couples could avoid being among the approximately two thirds of marriages that now end in divorce (Gottman, 1994). It is clear, however, that the consequences of staying in an unsatisfying marriage are more unfortunate for women than for men:

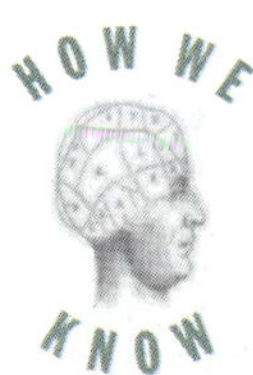

Researchers studied 82 middle-aged couples (older spouse between the age of 40 and 50) who had been married for at least 15 years and 74 older couples (older spouse between 60 and 70) who had been married for at least 35 years. Each group of couples was divided into those who were satisfied with their marriages and those who were dissatisfied. The researchers measured the mental and physical health of all the participants. Results revealed that satisfaction with the marriage did not have much of an impact on the men. For women, however, both physical and mental health was impaired when they were in a dissatisfying marriage (Levenson et al., 1993).

Research suggests that the consequences of staying in an unsatisfying marriage are more unfortunate for women than for men.

Another way of thinking about this result is that men almost always receive a benefit from being married, whereas women suffer in a bad marriage. Women are also more likely to outlive their husbands. Often this means that they pass from a period in which they must care for an unhealthy elderly husband to a period of mourning and financial insecurity (Carstensen & Pasupathi, 1993). Once again, we are not trying to discourage anyone, or women in particular, from getting married. Our best advice is to plan for the future by understanding what might take place.

When we contemplate the death of a spouse, we have come back to one reason that the balance of social interactions shifts somewhat from family to friends late in life (see Figure 6.3). A stereotype about late adulthood is that individuals become more socially isolated. While it is true that older individuals may interact socially with fewer people, the nature of those interactions changes so that intimacy needs continue to be met. This trade-off is captured by the **selective social interaction** theory. This view suggests that, as people age, they become more selective in choosing social partners who satisfy their emotional needs. According to **Laura Carstensen** (1987, 1991; Lang & Carstensen, 1994), selective interaction may be a practical means by which people can regulate their emotional experiences and conserve their physical energy. Older adults remain vitally involved with some people—particularly family members and longtime friends.

Statistically speaking, which spouse is likely to outlive the other? What effect might the quality of the marriage have on this outcome?

Let's conclude this section where we began, with the idea that social intimacy is a prerequisite for psychological well-being. What matters most, however, is not the quantity of social interaction but the quality (particularly, in our culture, for women). As you grow into older adulthood, you will begin to protect your need for intimacy by selecting those individuals who provide the most direct emotional support.

Let's turn now to a second aspect of adult development, generativity.

GENERATIVITY

Those people who have established an appropriate foundation of intimate relationships are most often able to turn their focus to issues of **generativity.** This is a commitment beyond oneself to family, work, society, or future generations—typically a crucial step in development in one's 30s and 40s (McAdams et al., 1993). An orientation toward the greater good allows adults to establish a sense of psychological well-being that offsets any longing for youth.

Generativity, a commitment to family, work, society, or future generations, usually becomes important to people in their 30s or 40s.

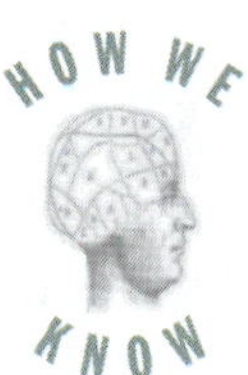

George Vaillant studied the personality development of 95 highly intelligent men through interviews and observations over a 30-year period following their graduation from college in the mid-1930s. Many of the men showed great changes over time, and their later behavior was often quite different from their behavior in college. The interviews covered the topics of physical health, social relationships, and career achievement. At the end of the 30-year period, the 30 men with the best outcomes and the 30 with the worst outcomes were identified and compared (see **Table 6.3**). By middle life, the best-outcome men were carrying out generativity tasks, assuming responsibility for others, and contributing in some way to the world. Their maturity even seemed to be associated with the adjustment of their children—the more mature fathers were better able to give children the help they needed in adjusting to the world (Vaillant, 1977).

When asked what it means to be well-adjusted, middle-aged adults (average age 52) and older adults (average age 74) gave the same response as their most frequent answer. Both groups suggested that adjustment relies on being "others oriented"—on being a caring, compassionate person and having good relationships (Ryff, 1989). This is the essence of generativity.

Let us also note that most older adults looking back on their lives do so with a degree of well-being that is unchanged from earlier years of adulthood (Carstensen & Freund, 1994). As we have seen with respect to social relationships, late adulthood is a time when goals are shifted; priorities change when the future does not apparently flow as freely. Across that change in priorities, however, older adults preserve their sense of the value of their lives.

Table 6.3 Differences Between Best- and Worst-Outcome Subjects on Factors Related to Psychosocial Maturity

	Best Outcomes (30 Men)	Worst Outcomes (30 Men)
Childhood environment poor	17%	47%
Pessimism, self-doubt, passivity, and fear of sex at 50	3%	50%
Personality integration rated in bottom fifth percentile during college	0	33%
Dominated by mother in adult life	0	40%
Failure to marry by 30	3%	37%
Bleak friendship patterns at 50	0	57%
Current job has little supervisory responsibility	20%	93%
Children's outcome described as good or excellent	66%	23%
Subjects whose career choice reflected identification with father	60%	27%

Data suggest that most adults look back over their lives with a feeling of integrity.

Erikson defined the last crisis of adulthood to be the conflict between *ego-integrity* and *despair*. The data suggest that few adults look back over their lives with despair. Most older adults review their lives—and look to the future—with a sense of wholeness and satisfaction.

The Cultural Construction of Late Adulthood

Our review of research on the long period of adulthood has emphasized continuities rather than discontinuities: there is no moment at which an individual suddenly becomes *old.* Even so, it is clear that there are strong cultural beliefs and expectations about the last periods of life. Researchers have documented these expectations by gathering evidence of the stereotypes college-age adults have about the members of their grandparents' generation. These studies suggest that young adults have more than one stereotype of older adults (Brewer et al., 1981; Brewer & Lui, 1989). Attitudes toward older adults vary with these stereotypes. Young adults have relatively positive attitudes toward a "perfect grandparent" and relatively negative attitudes toward a "despondent" older person (Schmidt & Boland, 1986). Even so, the overall stereotype is negative, particularly with respect to declines in physical attractiveness and mental competence (Kite & Johnson, 1988). Our concern here is that the existence of these negative stereotypes might actually change the experience of older adults for the worse. Let's explore this concern.

Overall, college-age adults have a negative stereotype of the elderly that may have a harmful impact on the experience of older adults.

Recall from Chapter 5 that certain aspects of memory performance are impaired with increasing age. Researchers have explored the possibility that elements of this decline can be explained by negative attitudes toward the capabilities of older adults.

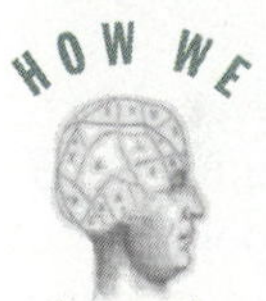

The members of both American Deaf culture and mainland Chinese culture have more positive attitudes toward older adults than do members of mainstream hearing American culture. Is memory performance affected by these attitudes? To test this possibility, the performance of groups of older adults from each population (average age 70) was compared with the performance of younger adults (average age 22). Although there was no effect of culture

> among the younger subjects—memory performance was very similar—among the older subjects, hearing Americans were by far the most impaired. In fact, the difference between the older Chinese and the older hearing Americans was considerably larger than the difference between the older and younger Chinese (Levy & Langer, 1994).

The negative attitude toward their memory abilities apparently affects the way the older hearing Americans approach memory situations. Not surprisingly, negative expectations lead to impaired performance. Here you can see that the way mainstream culture thinks about late adulthood can change actual experiences.

Researchers observe the same type of cause and effect when they see caretakers artificially bringing about patterns of increased dependence. Caretakers behave according to a *dependency-support script:* they rush to give support to behaviors that make older adults more, rather than less, dependent (Baltes & Wahl, 1992). For example, rather than encouraging older adults to dress themselves, caretakers might react to any hesitation with swift assistance. There is no doubt that the caretakers mean to be useful. Unfortunately, if they are continually put in the position of being helped, older adults may come to believe that they cannot get by without that aid. Thus an initial expectation of dependence can bring about dependence.

These results strongly suggest that members of our society should work to combat the particular prejudice against older people, called **ageism.** Ageism leads to discrimination against the elderly that limits their opportunities, isolates them, and fosters negative self-images. Psychologists themselves are often guilty of ageism in the language they use (Schaie, 1993). A survey of 139 undergraduate texts written over the past 40 years revealed that many failed to cover late adulthood or presented stereotypical views of the elderly (Whitbourne & Hulicka, 1990). But a more dramatic instance of ageism is shown in the personal experiences of a reporter who deliberately "turned old" for a while.

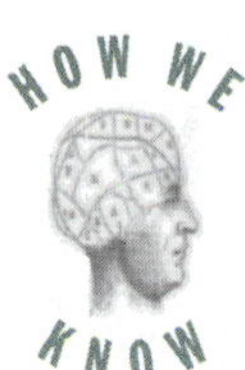

Pat Moore disguised herself as an 85-year-old woman and wandered the streets of over 100 American cities to discover what it means to be old in the United States. Clouded contact lenses and earplugs diminished her vision and hearing; bindings on her legs made walking difficult; and taped fingers had the dexterity of arthritic ones. This "little old lady" struggled to survive in a world designed for the young, strong, and agile. She couldn't open jars, hold pens, read labels, or climb up bus steps. The world of speed, noise, and shadows frightened her. When she needed assistance, few ever offered it. She was often ridiculed for being old and vulnerable and was even violently attacked by a gang of adolescents (Moore, 1990).

The top photo is of Pat Moore; in the photo on the bottom, she is disguised as an elderly woman (Discovering Psychology, *1990, Program 18).*

Moore's experience reinforces the idea that society, in both the physical and social sense, conspires against the elderly. As you contemplate the changes that accompany aging—and as you experience more of them yourself—you must fight the effects of the stereotype. You must learn to distinguish between genuine physiological and psychological changes of aging and those consequences of aging that are just the result of societal ageism.

At Life's End

It is almost impossible to think about old age without considering the approach of death. People, however, do not die of "old age." Most people die in this period of their life simply because they did not die earlier—so dying in old age is the only remaining possibility. In fact, you must grapple with the concept of death all through your life span. This is particularly true in modern times, when medical advances have changed the manner of dying. Chronic illnesses now constitute the major causes of death. When dying becomes a lengthy process, people have time to prepare psychologically for death. Let's consider both how people anticipate their own deaths and how they respond to the deaths of others.

Anticipating Death

How old were you when you first became aware of the concept of death? Were you prepared to understand the finality that death brings with it? What do you anticipate about your own death? We have chosen to discuss death in the context of adulthood, but experiences of death come throughout the life span. As a consequence, researchers have studied the way that *death anxiety*—people's fearfulness about death—changes with age. The peak for death anxiety is not, as many people expect, in old age. Typically, adolescents and young adults are more anxious about death than are older adults (Kastenbaum, 1992)—perhaps because older adults have had more experience with the deaths of people around them. There is also quite a bit of individual variation in what, specifically, makes people anxious about death. It may be, for example, a fear of extinction or a fear of the actual process of dying.

Older adults exhibit less death anxiety than adolescents and young adults.

What happens when an individual comes to believe that his or her own death is imminent? Early theories of coping with death, notably that of **Elisabeth Kübler-Ross** (1969, 1975), suggested that all dying patients go through the same series of emotional stages. However, research on the dying indicates that reactions are highly individualistic (Corr, 1993; Kastenbaum, 1986). There are a number of potential responses to impending death. People may, for example, respond with denial, anger, depression, acceptance, or any combination. Different responses may appear or reappear at different times during the dying process, depending on what the context of the death is and whether an illness such as cancer or AIDS is involved (Kastenbaum, 1986). The emotional reactions vary according to the perceived stigma of the illness, the social support received during treatment, and the pattern of decline or improvement over time. It is important to note that all of these responses are those of a *living* individual (Corr, 1993). People must take care not to treat someone who is dying as if he or she is already dead.

Elisabeth Kübler-Ross proposed a theory of coping with death that has since been refuted by research. It appears that there are many responses to advanced knowledge of death, not a fixed set of sequential reactions.

Research on the anticipation of death makes it clear that dying people, as well as their families and friends, have a number of social and emotional needs that must be acknowledged. The need to maintain a sense of dignity and self-worth can be met, in part, by allowing dying people control over the course of their treatments. Needs for social closeness and emotional support can be satisfied by involving family members in the treatment process and by allowing dying people ample private time with their loved ones. Often the needs of the chronically ill can be better met in hospices, which create homelike atmospheres, than in hospitals. The primary goal of the **hospice approach** is to make the process of dying more humane than it can be in institutional settings (Mor, 1987; Mor et al., 1988).

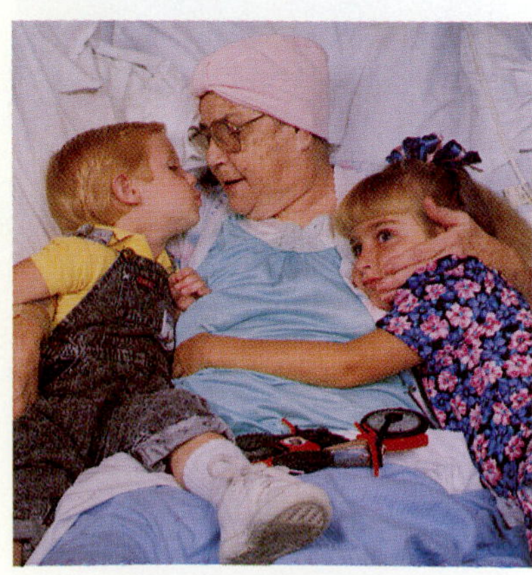

Private time with loved ones is an important way of meeting the terminally ill patient's need for closeness and social support.

Bereavement

The impact of death does not end when a person dies. Family and friends cope with their own feelings of grief and bereavement for months or even years after the death of someone close to them. Loss of a spouse after decades of marriage can be particularly traumatic. It substantially increases illness and mortality rates. Compared with the general population, widows and widowers have twice as many diseases as do those of the same age who are single or married (Stroebe et al., 1982). Intense grief may actually alter the immune system.

One effect of bereavement is that intense grief may alter the immune system.

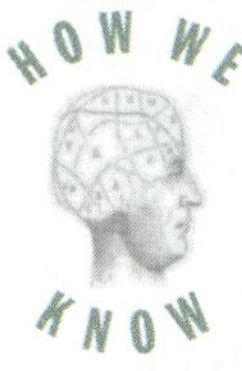

The immune-system functioning of 15 healthy men (age 33 to 76) whose wives were diagnosed with terminal cancer was examined over the course of bereavement. Lymphocyte function was assessed while their wives were still alive, and again at 2 and at 14 months after their wives had died. As predicted, compared with the prebereavement period, each man showed suppressed lymphocyte function, especially during the two months following his wife's death. These findings are consistent with a hypothesis that changes in the immune system following bereavement are related to the increased mortality of bereaved widowers (Schleifer et al., 1983).

Because women typically marry men older than themselves and live longer than men, losing a spouse is much more common for women than for men. For widows, feelings of bereavement are often compounded by economic distress and lack of societal supports (Carstensen & Pasupathi, 1993).

Some investigators have identified distinct stages of mourning (Kalish, 1985). The first stage, *shock,* is followed by the *longing* phase, characterized by desire to be with the deceased. The third major reaction is the *depression* stage, with despair at the loss, sometimes combined with irrational anger and confusion. Finally, the last stage of mourning is the *recovery* phase, when the death is put into a meaningful perspective.

The distinct stages of mourning are shock, longing, depression, and recovery.

With anticipated deaths (as opposed to sudden, accidental deaths), people have time to prepare for the inevitable endings of their important relationships with others and work through *anticipatory grief.* Preparing for such endings might entail sharing innermost feelings and spending quality time together. These last interactions represent an important part of what a survivor remembers about his or her relationship with the deceased (Fredrickson, 1991).

We have worked our way through the life span by considering social and personal aspects of childhood, adolescence, and adulthood. To close out the chapter, we will trace one last domain in which experience changes over time, the domain of *moral development.*

MORAL DEVELOPMENT

So far we have seen how important it is, across the life span, that you develop close social relationships. Let's now consider another aspect of what it means to live as part of a social group: on many occasions you must judge your behavior according to the needs of society, rather than just according to your own needs. This is the basis of *moral behavior.* **Morality** is a system of beliefs, values, and underlying judgments about the rightness or wrongness of human acts. Society needs children to become adults who accept a moral value system and whose behavior is guided by moral principles. As you know, however, what constitutes moral and immoral behavior in particular situations can become a matter of heated public debate. Perhaps it is no coincidence, therefore, that the study of moral development has also proved to be controversial. The controversy begins with the foundational research of Lawrence Kohlberg.

The basis of moral behavior is a consideration of society's needs rather than just your own needs.

KOHLBERG'S STAGES OF MORAL REASONING

Lawrence Kohlberg (1964, 1981) founded his study of moral development on the study of *moral reasoning*—the judgments people make about what courses of action are correct or incorrect in particular situations. Kohlberg's theory was shaped by the earlier insights of Jean Piaget (1965), who sought to tie the development of moral judgment to a child's general cognitive development. In Piaget's view, as the child progresses through the stages of cognitive growth, he or she assigns differing relative weights to the *consequences* of an act and to the actor's *intentions.* For example, to the *preoperational* child, someone who breaks ten cups accidentally is "naughtier" than someone who breaks one cup intentionally. As the child gets older, the actor's intentions weigh more heavily in the judgment of morality. Kohlberg expanded Piaget's view to define stages of moral development. Each stage is characterized by a different basis for making moral judgments (see **Table 6.4**). The lowest level of moral reasoning is based on self-interest, while higher levels center on social good, regardless of personal gain.

Kohlberg developed a stage theory of moral development by studying moral reasoning.

To document these stages, Kohlberg used a series of dilemmas that pit different moral principles against one another:

> In one dilemma, a man named Heinz is trying to help his wife obtain a certain drug needed to treat her cancer. An unscrupulous druggist will only sell it to Heinz for ten times more than what the druggist paid. This is much more money than Heinz has and more than he can raise. Heinz becomes desperate, breaks into the druggist's store, and steals the drug for his wife. Should Heinz have done that? Why? An interviewer probes the subject for the reasons for the decision and then scores the answers.

The scoring is based on the reasons the person gives for the decision, not on the decision itself. For example, someone who says that the man should steal the drug because of his obligation to his dying wife or that he should not steal the drug because of his obligation to uphold the law (despite his personal feelings) is expressing concern about meeting established obligations and is scored at Stage 4.

Four principles govern Kohlberg's stage model: (1) an individual can be at only one stage at a given time; (2) everyone goes through the stages in a fixed

Table 6.4 Kohlberg's Stages of Moral Reasoning

Levels and Stages		Reasons for Moral Behavior
I Preconventional morality		
Stage 1	Pleasure/pain orientation	To avoid pain or not to get caught
Stage 2	Cost-benefit orientation; reciprocity—an eye for an eye	To get rewards
II Conventional morality		
Stage 3	Good-child orientation	To gain acceptance and avoid disapproval
Stage 4	Law and order orientation	To follow rules, avoid censure by authorities
III Principled morality		
Stage 5	Social contract orientation	To promote the society's welfare
Stage 6	Ethical principle orientation	To achieve justice and avoid self-condemnation
Stage 7	Cosmic orientation	To be true to universal principles and feel oneself part of a cosmic direction that transcends social norms

order; (3) each stage is more comprehensive and complex than the preceding; and (4) the same stages occur in every culture. Kohlberg inherited much of this stage philosophy from Piaget, and, in fact, the progression from Stages 1 to 3 appears to match the course of normal cognitive development. The stages proceed in order, and each can be seen to be more cognitively sophisticated than the preceding. Almost all children reach Stage 3 by the age of 13. Much of the controversy with Kohlberg's theory occurs beyond Stage 3. Let's see why.

Moral Reasoning in Adolescents and Adults

In Kohlberg's original view, people would continue their moral development in a steady progression beyond level 3. However, not all people attain Stages 4 to 7. In fact, many adults never reach Stage 5, and only a few go beyond it. In addition, the higher stages are not found in all cultures and appear to be associated, in Western culture, with more education and greater verbal ability. These features should not be prerequisites for moral achievement (Rest & Thoma, 1976).

Kohlberg originally believed that people would continue their moral development in a steady progression, but in fact only a few people reach Stage 5 or beyond.

Kohlberg's failure to predict moral reasoning beyond childhood has prompted contemporary theorists to examine more closely the content of his later stages. The content of these stages appears to be subjective, and it is hard to understand each successive stage as more comprehensive and sophisticated than the preceding. For example, "avoiding self-condemnation," the basis for moral judgments at Stage 6, does not seem obviously more sophisticated than "promoting society's welfare," the basis for Stage 5.

Kohlberg's later stages have also been criticized because they fail to recognize that adult moral judgments may reflect different, but equally moral, principles. In a well-known critique, **Carol Gilligan** (1982) pointed out that Kohlberg's original work was developed from observations only of boys. She argued that this research approach overlooked potential differences between the habitual moral judgments of men and women. Gilligan proposed that women's moral development is based on a standard of *caring for others* and progresses to a stage of self-realization, whereas men base their reasoning on a standard of *justice*. Thus Gilligan's theory broadens Kohlberg's ideas about the range of considerations that may be relevant to moral judgments beyond childhood. Although we can value this contribution, research has suggested that she is incorrect to identify unique styles of moral reasoning for men and women. Let's examine the evidence.

Gilligan argued that Kohlberg's research overlooked basic differences between the moral judgments of men and women.

Some studies have indicated that women mold their moral decisions to maintain harmony in their social relationships, whereas men refer more to fairness (Lyons, 1983). Even so, researchers continue to dispute whether gender differences in moral reasoning really exist at all (Baumrind, 1986; Pratt et al., 1988; Walker, 1984, 1986). Although men and women may arrive at their adult levels of moral development through different processes, the actual judgments they make as adults are highly similar (Boldizar et al., 1989). One possibility is that the gender differences are really consequences of the different types of social situations that arise in the lives of men and women. When asked to reason about the same moral dilemmas, men and women gave highly similar patterns of care and justice responses (Clopton & Sorell, 1993). Furthermore, studies of gender differences in prosocial or moral behaviors have found no consistent gender differences (Eisenberg & Mussen, 1989; Radke-Yarrow et al., 1983).

We can, thus, characterize adult reasoning about moral dilemmas as a mix between considerations of justice and considerations of caring. This mix will remain in place over most of the life span. However, as you might expect, moral judgments are affected by general changes in adult cognition (see

Moral reasoning in adulthood appears to be a mix between considerations of justice and considerations of caring, not merely a product of gender differences.

Chapter 5). One relevant change of late adulthood is that individuals shift the grounds for their judgments away from the details of specific situations toward the use of general principles. Consequently, moral judgments come to be based more on general societal concerns—for example, What is the law?—than on particular dilemmas—for example, Should an exception be made in this case? (Pratt et al., 1988) Let's turn now from the realm of moral judgment to that of moral action.

Moral Action

Moral action appears to be related more closely to the demands of the situation than to the level of moral understanding.

We have focused so far on aspects of moral reasoning. However, if you want to understand moral development more completely, you must consider what motivates people to *behave* honestly, cooperatively, or altruistically. One's level of moral understanding may have little to do with one's display of moral action:

In the 1920s, a team of Yale University behaviorists set out to study moral knowledge and its relation to moral behavior in children ages 6 to 14. They administered tests of moral knowledge to large numbers of children and observed their behavior in situations where there was a chance to be either honest or dishonest. The data were unexpected. Most children were honest in some situations and dishonest in others. Instead of being guided by a general trait of honesty or dishonesty, behavior seemed to depend more on the situation—how attractive the reward was and how likely the children were to get caught. Also, moral or immoral behavior showed little relation to moral knowledge, which was generally high, and there was no evidence of greater moral development with age. These experimenters concluded that, although moral knowledge may be stable, moral behavior is not a stable quality in people; rather, it is a response that varies with the *demands of the situation* (Hartshorne & May, 1928).

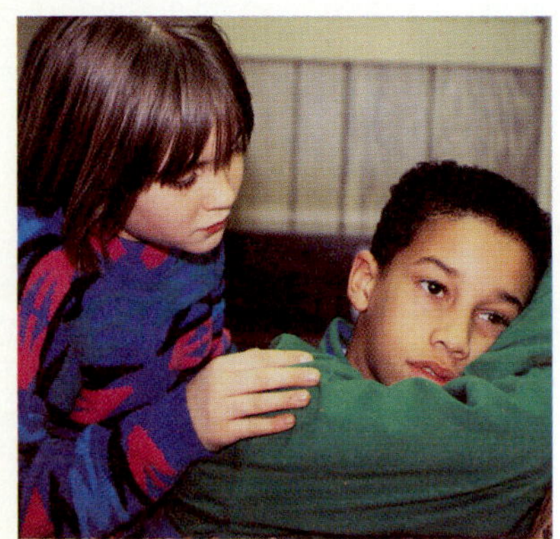

Empathy, which is present from very early childhood, may be a building block for future moral behavior patterns.

Psychologists have begun to investigate the emotional and social roots of morality. **Martin Hoffman** (1987) argued that emotions within the child, especially empathy, may provide the motivation for moral behavior. **Empathy** is the condition of feeling someone else's emotion. Young children are capable of positive social behaviors designed to help or comfort others in apparent distress. First, children feel distress with, and then sorrow for, another individual. Children may want to reduce these unpleasant feelings, and they discover that acting positively toward the distressed person helps accomplish this. Observational studies reveal that children experience empathy at very young ages, and some researchers believe that empathy may actually be an innate response, much like sucking or crying. Empathy may represent part of the foundation for future moral behavior.

LEARNING TO AGE SUCCESSFULLY

Let us now review some of the themes of these last two chapters, to form a prescription for successful aging. In Chapter 5, we encouraged you to think of development as a type of change that always brings with it gains and losses. In this light, the trick to prospering across the life span is to solidify one's gains and minimize one's losses. We saw in Chapter 5 that the rule "use it or lose it" applies in both physical and cognitive domains of life. Many of the changes that are stereotypically associated with aging are functions of disuse rather than decay. Our first line of advice is straightforward: Keep at it!

In Chapter 5, we also suggested that part of successful aging means to employ *selective optimization with compensation* (M. Baltes, 1986; P. Baltes, 1987; P. Baltes et al., 1992). As you may recall, *selective* means that people choose the most appropriate goals for themselves. *Optimization* indicates that people exercise or train themselves in areas that are of highest priority to them. *Compensation* refers to the alternative ways that people use to deal with losses. In this chapter, we saw another good example of this process when we considered the way in which social relationships change during adulthood. Older adults select the goal of having friends who provide optimal levels of emotional support; the choice of friends must change over time to compensate for deaths or other disruptions (Lang & Carstensen, 1994). Although the selective optimization perspective originated in research on the aging process, it is a good way to characterize the choices you must make throughout your life span. You should always try to select the goals most important to you, optimize your performance with respect to those goals, and compensate when progress toward those goals is blocked. That's our final bit of advice about life-span development. We hope you will age wisely and well.

Recapping Main Points

Life-Span Theories

Three psychologists who have contributed theories about development over the life course are Erikson, Jung, and Neugarten. The theories define the crises and general trends of development.

The Cultural Context of Development

Social development takes place in a particular cultural context. Departures from the typical course of developmental change are often products of culturally determined environments. Many youths now face a hostile economic and social environment that puts them at risk for psychological and social problems.

Social Development in Childhood

Socialization is the process whereby children acquire values and attitudes that conform to those considered desirable in our society. Socialization begins with an infant's attachment to a caregiver. Failure to make this attachment leads to numerous physical and psychological problems. Gender is a psychological phenomenon referring to learned, sex-related behavior and attitudes. Gender-role socialization begins at birth. A variety of socializing agents reinforce gender stereotypes.

Adolescence

Adolescence is defined by transition rites or by other social markers. Research shows that most adolescents are satisfied with their lives. Adolescents must develop a personal identity by forming comfortable social relationships with parents and peers and by choosing future goals.

Adulthood

The central concerns of adulthood are organized around the needs of intimacy and generativity. The quality of social relationships helps to predict feelings of well-being. Child rearing puts a strain on many marriages. Women are more affected by dissatisfying marriages than are men. People become less socially active as they grow older because they selectively maintain only those relationships that matter most to them emotionally. People assess their lives, in part, by their ability to contribute positively to the lives of others. Negative stereotypes of older adults lead to ageism. As people approach old age, they anticipate and respond to death in different ways.

Moral Development

Kohlberg defined stages of moral development. The stages are controversial because they don't represent the full range of considerations that affect moral judgments, nor do they capture moral action.

Resources

Adler, L. L. (Ed.). (1989). *Cross-cultural research in human development: A lifespan perspective.* Westport, CT: Greenwood.

Gross, F. L., Jr. (1986). *Introducing Erik Erikson: An invitation to his thinking.* Lanham, MD: University Press of America.

Kastenbaum, R. (1992). *The psychology of death* (2nd ed.). New York: Springer.

Kohlberg, L. (1984). *Essays on moral development: Vol. 2. The psychology of moral development.* San Francisco: Harper & Row.

Matteo, S. (Ed.). (1993). *American women in the nineties: Today's critical issues.* Boston: Northeastern University Press.

Merriam, S. B. (1991). *Lifelines: Patterns of work, love, and learning in adulthood.* San Francisco: Jossey-Bass. The Jossey-Bass social and behavioral science series.

7

Sensation

Consider the sensory world around you. How does your brain—locked in the dark, silent chamber of the skull—experience the blaze of color in a Van Gogh painting, the driving rhythms and melodies of rock 'n' roll, the refreshing taste of watermelon on a hot day, the soft touch of a lover's lips, or the fragrance of a field of wildflowers in the springtime? Our task in this chapter is to explain how your brain and body make sense of the buzz of stimulation—sights, sounds, and so on—constantly around you. You will see how evolution has equipped you with the capability to detect many different dimensions of experience. You will discover that the senses you most often take for granted involve a remarkably intricate set of processes.

This chapter deals with sensory processes, *the sense organs and peripheral aspects of the nervous system that put you in direct contact with sources of environmental stimulation. Sensation involves the basic biological elements of experience:* sensation *is the process by which a stimulated sensory receptor gives rise to neural impulses that result in an elementary experience of feeling, or awareness, of conditions inside or outside the body. Chapter 8 deals with the processes associated with higher level activity of the central nervous system, the* perceptual processes—*the identification, interpretation, integration, and classification of sensory experiences. In Chapter 7, you will learn how each sensory system separates out different types of information from the external world. By the end of the next chapter, you should understand how your brain ultimately recombines those different types of information to give you a coherent experience of that world.*

We begin this chapter with a discussion of those features of sensory processing that are common to all your senses. We also examine how psychological researchers measure and quantify your sensory experiences. Then we consider the functioning of specific sensory modalities, *such as vision and hearing.*

However, before starting this journey into the world of sensation, let's pause to reflect on the dual functions of your senses: survival *and* sensuality. *Your senses help you survive by sounding alarms of danger, priming you to take swift action to ward off hazards, and directing you toward agreeable sensations. Your senses also provide you with sensuality. Sensuality is the quality of being devoted to the gratification of the senses; it entails enjoying the experiences that appeal to the senses of sight, sound, touch, taste, and smell. As you read this chapter, you might consider how knowledge of the mechanisms of sensation can help you discover the healthy pleasures of sensuality and teach you to take new delight in the world of sounds, colors, smells, tastes, and touch (Ornstein & Sobel, 1989).*

Sensuality is the enjoyment of sensory experiences.

SENSORY KNOWLEDGE OF THE WORLD

Your experience of external reality must be relatively accurate and error-free; if not, you couldn't survive. You need food to sustain you, shelter to protect you, interactions with other people to fulfill social needs, and awareness of danger to keep out of harm's way. To meet these needs, you must get reliable information about the world. All species have developed some kinds of specialized *information-gathering apparatuses.* The human species does not specialize in one particular sensory domain: you lack the acute vision of hawks, hearing of bats, and sense of smell of rodents. Instead, humans are equipped with sensory apparatuses that enable them to process a wider variety of complex sensory input than any other creature.

The study of sensation has had a prominent place since the earliest history of experimental psychology. We saw in Chapter 1 that Wundt (1907) proposed that sensations and feelings are the elementary processes from which complex experiences are built. Titchener (1898) brought this view to the United States, giving sensation a central place in his introspective examination of the contents of consciousness.

Sensory psychologists now work along with physiologists, biologists, geneticists, and neurologists to map the process by which physical energy from the external world is transformed into sensations that result in your nine senses: vision, hearing, smell, taste, touch, temperature, vestibular sense, kinesthesis, and pain. Later in this chapter, we will discuss the mechanisms underlying some of these senses, but first let's consider how sensory psychologists study sensation.

From Physical Energy to Mental Events

At the heart of sensation lies a profound mystery: How do physical energies give rise to psychological experiences? How, for example, do the various physical wavelengths of light give rise to your experience of a rainbow? Information from the external world arrives at your sensory receptors as physical stimuli of some kind: waves of light or sound, complex chemicals, and so on. The special cells in your eyes, ears, nose, mouth, and skin convert physical stimuli into electrochemical signals that the nervous system can transmit. When a signal reaches the appropriate regions of your cerebral cortex, you have sensations as diverse as sights, sounds, tastes, and smells.

Sensory physiology is the study of the way biological mechanisms convert physical events into neural events. The goal of this field is to discover what happens at a neural level in the chain of events from physical energy to sensory experience. The conversion of one form of physical energy, such as light, to another form, such as neural impulses, is called **transduction.** Sensory psychologists try to discover how the transduction of physical energy into the electrochemical activity of the nervous system gives rise to sensations of different quality (red rather than green) and different quantity (loud rather than soft).

A goal of sensory physiology is to discover what happens in the brain when physical energy is converted into neural events by means of transduction.

Because all sensory information is transduced into identical types of neural impulses, your brain differentiates sensory experiences by devoting special areas of cortex to each sense domain. This fact of biology was first proposed in 1826 by **Johannes Müller** as the *doctrine of specific nerve energies.* Different sensory experiences, such as sight or taste, do not produce different types of neural activity; they produce the same types of activity in different, specific, places. The coding for *sensory qualities* of your different sense modalities takes place according to brain codes in the specific neural pathways activated by each sense.

Johannes Müller was the first to propose the doctrine of specific nerve energies, which suggests that different sensory experiences occur in different areas of the brain.

Within each sensory domain, you can differentiate not only different qualities—sweet versus sour—but also the *intensity* of a particular quality: Which is sweeter, dark chocolate or milk chocolate? The primary way stimulus *intensity* is coded across all sensations is in terms of the *rate of neural impulses.* For example, a light touch on the skin will generate a series of electrical impulses in nerve fibers at that point. As the pressure is increased,

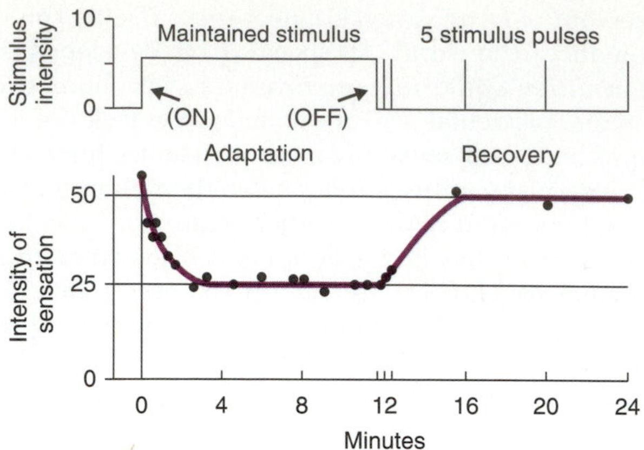

Figure 7.1 Sensory Adaptation
Initial response to the onset of a stimulus is vigorous, but as the stimulus is maintained, the receptor adapts to it. This adaptation is reflected by the diminishing activity in the nerve fiber over time. The low level of activity (of which you are not usually aware) is immediately modified with the offset of the maintained stimulus. Brief, periodic stimuli cause the receptor to respond fully each time without any adaptation.

the impulses increase in their *frequency* of firing but do not change their basic form. A second way that intensity is coded is by the regularity in the *temporal patterning* of these nerve impulses. At weak intensities, the firing is spaced and irregular, but as the intensity increases, the patterning becomes not only more closely spaced but more constant.

The process of sensory adaptation causes you to respond more rapidly to new sensory stimuli than to steady states.

Your sensory systems are also more sensitive to *changes* in the sensory environment than to steady states. The systems have evolved so that they favor new environmental inputs over old through a process called *adaptation*. **Sensory adaptation** is the diminishing responsiveness of sensory systems to prolonged stimulus input. (Adaptation is similar to the process of habituation we described in Chapter 3.) **Figure 7.1** illustrates a typical adaptation to a maintained stimulus. Your environment is always full of a great diversity of sensory stimulation. The mechanism of adaptation allows you to notice, and react, more quickly to the challenges of new sources of information.

We have been describing the abstract properties that all your various sensory processes share. Sensory systems also share the same basic flow of information. The trigger for any sensing system is the detection of an environmental event, or *stimulus*. Environmental stimuli are detected by *stimulus detector units*—specialized sensory receptor neurons. The stimulus detector converts the physical form of the sensory signal into cellular signals that can be processed by the nervous system. These cellular signals contribute information to higher level neurons that integrate information across different detector units. At this stage, neurons extract information about the basic qualities of the stimulus, such as its size, intensity, shape, and distance. Deeper into the sensory systems, information is combined into even more complex codes that are passed on to specific areas of the sensory and association cortex of the brain. **Table 7.1** summarizes the stimuli and receptors for each of the human senses.

We have described the shared biological aspects of your sensory systems. We turn now to the methods researchers have developed to link physical sensations to psychological experiences.

Table 7.1 Human Sensory System: Fundamental Features

Sense	Stimulus	Sense Organ	Receptor	Sensation
Sight	Light waves	Eye	Rods and cones of retina	Colors, patterns textures
Hearing	Sound waves	Ear	Hair cells of the basilar membrane	Noises, tones
Skin sensations	External contact	Skin	Nerve endings in skin (Ruffini corpuscles, Merkel disks, Pacinian corpuscles)	Touch, pain, warmth, cold
Smell	Volatile substances	Nose	Hair cells of olfactory epithelium	Odors (musky, flowery, burnt, minty)
Taste	Soluble substances	Tongue	Taste buds of tongue	Flavors (sweet, sour, salty, bitter)
Vestibular sense	Mechanical and gravitational forces	Inner ear	Hair cells of semicircular canals and vestibule	Spatial movement, gravitational pull
Kinesthesis	Body movement	Muscles, tendons, and joints	Nerve fibers in muscles, tendons, and joints	Movement and position of body parts

Psychophysics

How loud must a fire alarm at a factory be in order for workers to hear it over the din of the machinery? How bright does a warning light on a pilot's control panel have to be to appear twice as bright as the other lights? How loud can a motorcycle be before its driver should be cited for noise pollution? To answer these questions, we must be able to measure the intensity of sensory experiences. This is the central task of **psychophysics**, the study of lawful correlations between physical stimuli and the behavior or mental experiences the stimuli evoke. Psychophysics represents the oldest field of the science of psychology (Levine & Shefner, 1981).

The most significant figure in the history of psychophysics was the German physicist **Gustav Fechner** (1801–1887). Fechner coined the term *psychophysics* and provided a set of procedures to relate the intensity of a physical stimulus—measured in physical units—to the magnitude of the sensory experience—measured in psychological units (Fechner, *Elements of Psychophysics,* 1860). Fechner's techniques are the same whether the stimuli are for light, sound, taste, odor, or touch: researchers determine thresholds and construct psychophysical scales relating strength of sensation to strength of stimuli. Two kinds of thresholds can be measured by these techniques: absolute thresholds and difference thresholds.

Can you hear the tone? Hearing evaluation is usually done with an absolute threshold test.

Absolute Thresholds

What is the smallest, weakest stimulus energy that an organism can detect? How soft can a tone be, for instance, and still be heard? These questions refer to the **absolute threshold** for stimulation—the minimum amount of physical energy needed to produce a sensory experience. Researchers measure absolute thresholds by asking vigilant observers to perform detection tasks, such as trying to see a dim light in a dark room or trying to hear a soft sound in a quiet room. During a series of many trials, the stimulus is presented at varying intensities, and on each trial the observers indicate whether they were aware of it. (If you've ever had your hearing evaluated, you participated in an absolute threshold test.)

The results of an absolute threshold study can be summarized in a **psychometric function:** a graph that shows the percentage of detections (plotted on the vertical axis) at each stimulus intensity (plotted on the hori-

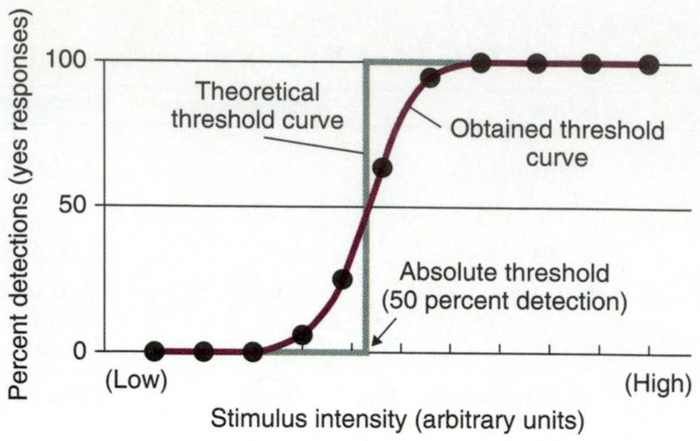

Figure 7.2 Calculation of Absolute Thresholds
Because a stimulus does not become suddenly detectable at a certain point, absolute threshold is defined as the intensity at which the stimulus is detected half of the time over many trials.

Absolute threshold is determined by the strength of the stimulus and the condition of the viewer.

zontal axis). A typical psychometric function is shown in **Figure 7.2.** For very dim lights, detection is at 0 percent; for bright lights, detection is at 100 percent. If there were a single, true absolute threshold, you would expect the transition from 0 to 100 percent detection to be very sharp, occurring right at the point where the intensity reached the threshold. But this does not happen, in part because viewers themselves change slightly each time they try to detect a stimulus (because of changes in attention, fatigue, and so on). Thus the psychometric curve is usually a smooth S-shaped curve, in which there is a region of transition from no detection to occasional detection to detection all the time.

Because a stimulus does not suddenly become clearly detectable at all times at a specific intensity, the operational definition of absolute threshold is *the stimulus level at which a sensory signal is detected half the time.* Thresholds for different sense modalities can be measured using the same procedure, simply by changing the stimulus dimension. **Table 7.2** shows absolute threshold levels for several familiar natural stimuli.

Response Bias

Threshold measurements can be affected by a **response bias,** the systematic tendency for an observer to favor responding in a particular way because of factors unrelated to the sensory features of the stimulus. For example, someone could overrespond *yes* in a detection task because she wanted to be selected for a job requiring acute sensitivity, while someone else might favor

Table 7.2 Approximate Thresholds of Familiar Events

Sense Modality	Detection Threshold
Light	A candle flame seen at 30 miles on a dark, clear night
Sound	The tick of a watch under quiet conditions at 20 feet
Taste	One teaspoon of sugar in 2 gallons of water
Smell	One drop of perfume diffused into the entire volume of a 3-room apartment
Touch	The wing of a bee falling on your cheek from a distance of 1 centimeter

no if he thought that poor acuity would get him out of a dangerous assignment.

Why does someone's detection threshold become distorted by response bias? At least three sources for bias have been identified: desire, expectation, and habit. When you want a particular outcome, you are more likely to give whatever response will achieve that desired objective—"I didn't see anything, officer" is likely if you want to avoid getting involved; "Yes, I'm sure he's the one" is a more probable response if you want to be in line for a reward. Your expectations, or knowledge, of stimulus probabilities may also influence your readiness to report a sensory event. You would, for example, be more likely to detect and report as a submarine a weak blip on a sonar scope if you are on a cruiser during wartime than if you are on a yacht during peacetime. Finally, people develop habits of responding—some people chronically answer yes and some no. This learned habit of biased response means that under conditions of uncertainty, some people will overreport the presence of a stimulus event while others will consistently underreport it.

How might you detect such biases during tests of absolute thresholds? One procedure researchers use is *catch trials:* on a few of the trials, they present no stimulus at all, to catch subjects with biases to respond yes. The researchers then adjust the threshold estimate according to how often such *false alarms* occur. But how might you catch a subject who overuses no when there is a stimulus present? To address all types of response biases, researchers turn to signal detection theory.

Signal Detection Theory

Signal detection theory (SDT) is a systematic approach to the problem of response bias (Green & Swets, 1966). Instead of focusing strictly on sensory processes, signal detection theory emphasizes the process of making a *judgment* about the presence or absence of stimulus events. Whereas classical psychophysics conceptualized a single absolute threshold, SDT identifies two distinct processes in sensory detection: (1) an initial *sensory process,* which reflects the subject's sensitivity to the strength of the stimulus and (2) a subsequent separate *decision process,* which reflects the subject's response biases.

SDT offers a procedure for evaluating both the sensory process and the decision processes at once. The measurement procedure is actually just an extension of the idea of catch trials. The basic design is given in **Figure 7.3.**

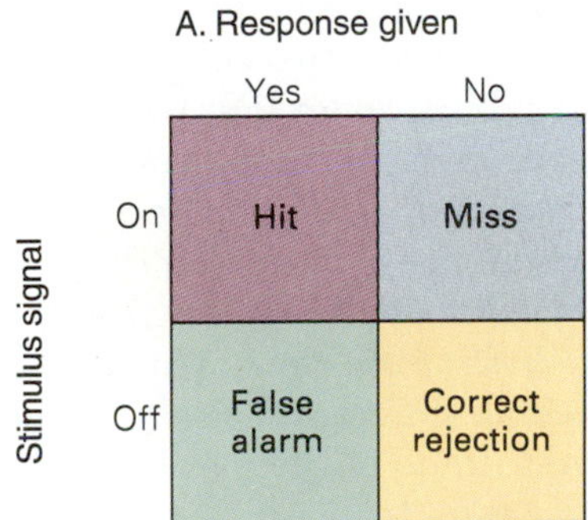

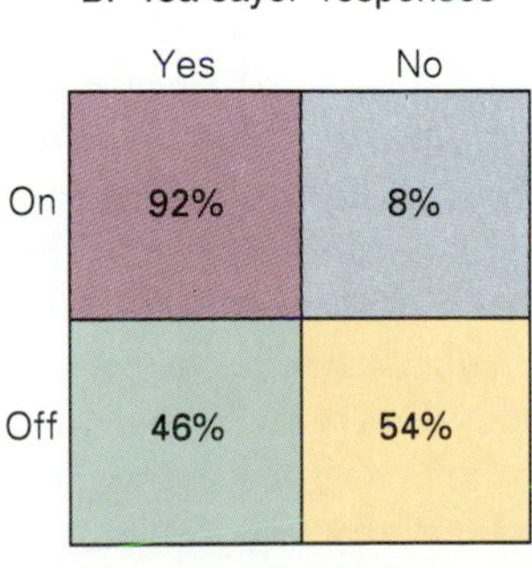

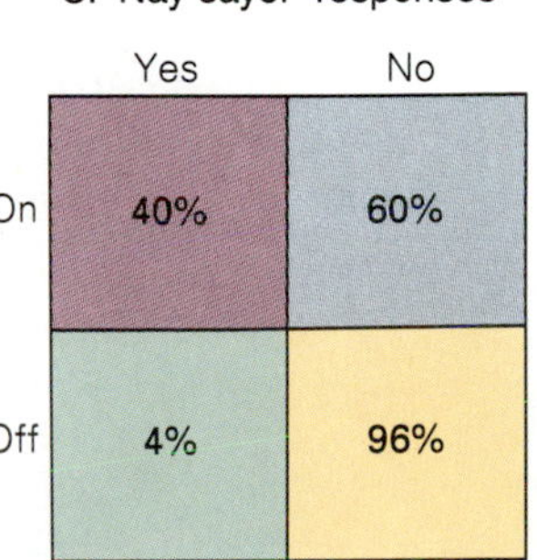

Figure 7.3 The Theory of Signal Detection
Matrix A shows the possible outcomes when a subject is asked if a target stimulus occurred on a given trial. Matrixes B and C show the typical responses of a yea sayer *(biased toward saying yes) and a* nay sayer *(biased toward saying no).*

A weak stimulus is presented in half the trials; no stimulus is presented in the other half. In each trial, subjects respond by saying yes if they think the signal was present and no if they think it wasn't. As shown in matrix A of the figure, each response is scored as a hit, a miss, a false alarm, or a correct rejection, depending on whether a signal was, in fact, presented and whether the observer responded accurately.

An observer who is a *yea sayer* (chronically answers yes) will give a high number of hits but will also have a high number of false alarms, as shown in matrix B. One who is a *nay sayer* (chronically answers no) will give a lower number of hits but also a lower number of false alarms, as shown in matrix C. Combining the percentages of hits and false alarms creates a mathematical relationship that differentiates sensory responses from response biases. This procedure makes it possible to find out whether two observers have the same sensitivity despite large differences in response criterion. By providing a way of separating sensory process from response bias, the theory of signal detection allows an experimenter to identify and separate the roles of the sensory stimulus and the individual's criterion level in producing the final response.

The SDT approach provides a model of decision making that can be used in other contexts as well. Many everyday decisions involve different rewards for every hit and correct rejection and penalties for every miss and false alarm. For example, if you decline an invitation to the movies, will you be avoiding a dull evening (a correct rejection) or eliminating the chance for a lifetime of love (a miss)? Your decisions are likely to be biased by the schedule of anticipated gains and losses. Such a detection matrix is called a *payoff matrix.* If, for example, saying no when a stimulus is present (a miss) is more costly than saying yes when it is absent (a false alarm), a yes bias will rule. Surgeons are often in this situation. They usually prefer to operate when they are not entirely certain a tumor is malignant, thereby risking a false alarm, rather than risking a missed malignancy—and failing to prevent a death. In general, decision makers must consider the available evidence, the relative costs of each type of error, and the relative gains from each type of correct decision. Signal detection theory provides an important tool for organizing decisions.

The principles of signal detection theory provide a framework for evaluating other types of decisions.

Difference Thresholds

Imagine you have been employed by a beverage company that wants to produce a cola product that tastes noticeably sweeter than existing colas, but (to save money) the firm wants to put as little extra sugar in the cola as possible. You are being asked to measure a **difference threshold,** the smallest physical difference between two stimuli that can still be recognized as a difference. To measure a difference threshold, you use pairs of stimuli and ask your subjects whether they believe the two stimuli to be the same or different.

For the beverage problem, you would give your subjects two colas on each trial, one of some standard recipe and one just a bit sweeter. For each pair, the observer would say *same* or *different.* After many such trials, you would plot a psychometric function by graphing the percent of *different* responses on the vertical axis as a function of the actual differences, plotted on the horizontal axis. The difference threshold is operationally defined as *the point at which the stimuli are recognized as different half of the time.* This difference threshold value is known as a **just noticeable difference,** or JND. The JND is a quantitative unit for measuring the magnitude of the psychological difference between any two sensations.

In 1834, **Ernst Weber** pioneered the study of JNDs and discovered the important relationship that we illustrate in **Figure 7.4.** Suppose you perform a difference threshold experiment with a standard bar length of 10 millimeters, using increases of varying amounts. You find the difference threshold to

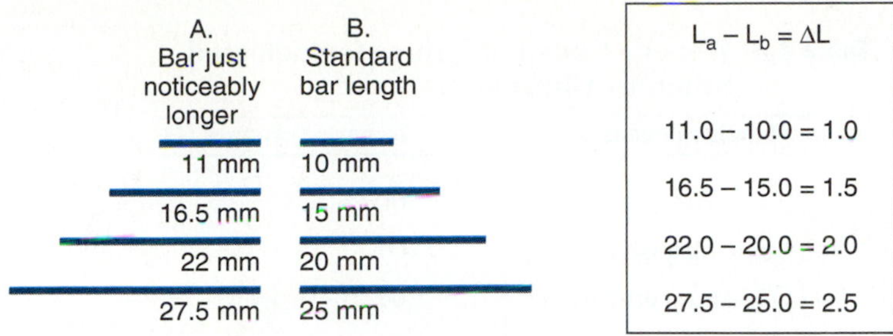

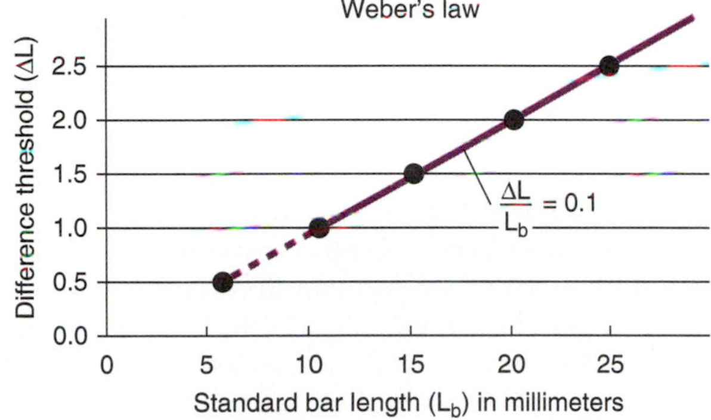

Figure 7.4 Just Noticeable Differences and Weber's Law
The longer the standard bar, the greater the amount you must add (Δ L) to see a just noticeable difference. The difference threshold is the added length detected on half the trials. When these increments are plotted against standard bars of increasing length, the proportions stay the same—the amount added is always one-tenth of the standard length. The relationship is linear, producing a straight line on the graph. We can predict that the Δ L for a bar length of 5 will be 0.5.

be about 1 millimeter—you know that a 10-millimeter bar will be detected as different from an 11-millimeter bar 50 percent of the time. With a 20-millimeter standard bar, however, a 1 millimeter increment is not enough. To get a just noticeable difference, you need to add about 2 millimeters. With a bar of 40 millimeters, you would need to add 4 millimeters. Figure 7.4 shows that JNDs increase steadily as the length of the standard bar increases.

What remains the same for both long and short bars is the *ratio* of the size of the increase that produces a just noticeable difference to the length of the standard bar. For example, *1 mm/10 mm = 0.1; 2 mm/20 mm = 0.1.* This relationship is summarized as **Weber's law:** *the JND between stimuli is a constant fraction of the intensity of the standard stimulus.* Thus the bigger or more intense the standard stimulus, the larger the increment needed to get a just noticeable difference. This is a very general property of all sensory systems. The formula for Weber's law is $\Delta I/I = k$, where I is the intensity of the standard; ΔI, or Delta I, is the size of the increase that produces a JND. Weber found that each stimulus dimension has a characteristic value for this ratio. In this formula, k is that ratio, or *Weber's constant,* for the particular stimulus dimension. (Work through the bar length example plotted in Figure 7.4 to be sure you understand what a JND is, what Weber's law is, and how they are related.) Weber's law provides a good approximation, but not a perfect fit to experimental data, of how the size of JND increases with intensity (most problems with the law arise when stimulus intensities become extremely high).

Ernst Weber discovered that the just noticeable difference increased as the intensity of the standard stimulus increased. He described the relationship in Weber's law.

Table 7.3 Weber's Constant Values for Selected Stimulus Dimensions

Stimulus Dimension	Weber's Constant (*k*)
Sound frequency	.003
Light intensity	.01
Odor concentration	.07
Pressure intensity	.14
Sound intensity	.15
Taste concentration	.20

You see in **Table 7.3** that Weber's constant (k) has different values for different sensory dimensions—there is greater sensitivity as the value becomes smaller. So this table tells you that you can differentiate two sound frequencies more precisely than light intensities, which, in turn, are detectable with a smaller JND than odor or taste differences are. Your beverage company would need a relatively large amount of extra sugar!

Constructing Psychophysical Scales

You are already familiar with physical scales—the metric scale for lengths and the Fahrenheit and Celsius scales for temperature, to name just a few. Could such scales be used directly for measuring psychological sensations? According to Weber's law, they couldn't, because psychological differences are not directly equivalent to physical differences. So, for example, while a person would be able to detect the difference between 1° C and 2° C much more easily than the difference between 22° C and 23° C, the actual difference in both cases is the same: 1° C.

A hundred years after Fechner's pioneering work in psychophysics, **S. S. Stevens** devised a general method for constructing psychophysical scales. Using a method called **magnitude estimation,** Stevens asked observers to assign numbers to their sensations. Observers were presented with an initial stimulus—for instance, a light of some known intensity—and asked to assign a value to it—say, 10. They were then presented with another light at a different magnitude and told that if they perceived it as twice as bright, they should call it 20. If it were half as bright, they should call it 5, and so on. When Stevens constructed psychological scales in this manner, he found that the results could be described by a mathematical equation known as a *power function:* $S = kI^b$, where S is the magnitude of the sensory experience, I is the physical intensity of the stimulus, k is a constant, and b is an exponent that varies for different sensory dimensions.

S. S. Stevens's power function relates sensory experience to the physical intensity of a stimulus.

Figure 7.5 shows psychophysical curves for brightness and electric shock, where the exponents are very different. Doubling the physical intensity of a light less than doubles the sensation of brightness. That is why a 100-watt lightbulb does not appear to you to be twice as bright as a 50-watt lightbulb. As you might guess, however, doubling the magnitude of an electric shock much more than doubles its corresponding sensation. Your body is protecting itself—this scaling up of the sensation of pain allows you to react strongly before a painful stimulus has done you harm. Stevens's approach has proved to be very useful, because almost any psychological dimension can be readily scaled in this way. Psychologists have used magnitude estima-

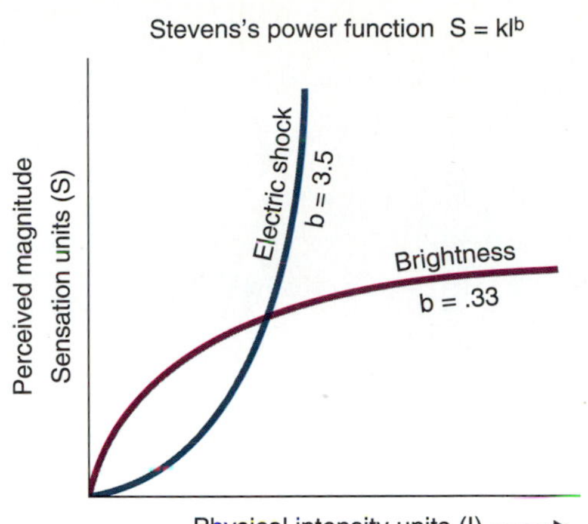

Figure 7.5 Stevens's Power Law
According to Stevens's equation, which is based on direct judgments of sensory magnitude, the psychophysical curve is different for different stimuli.

tion to construct psychological scales for everything from pitch and length, to beauty, the seriousness of crimes, and the goodness of Swedish monarchs (Stevens, 1961, 1962, 1975).

You are now acquainted with general biological and psychological features of the design of your sensory systems. We next examine how these general principles apply to each of your specific sensory domains. We focus most on vision and hearing, but you will also learn critical facts about smell, taste, touch, and your other senses.

THE VISUAL SYSTEM

Vision is the most complex, highly developed, and important sense for humans and most other mobile creatures. Animals with good vision have an enormous evolutionary advantage. Good vision helps animals detect their prey or predators from a distance. Vision enables humans to be aware of changing features in the physical environment and to adapt their behavior accordingly. Vision is the most studied of all the sense modalities.

Visual acuity enables predatory animals to detect potential prey from a distance.

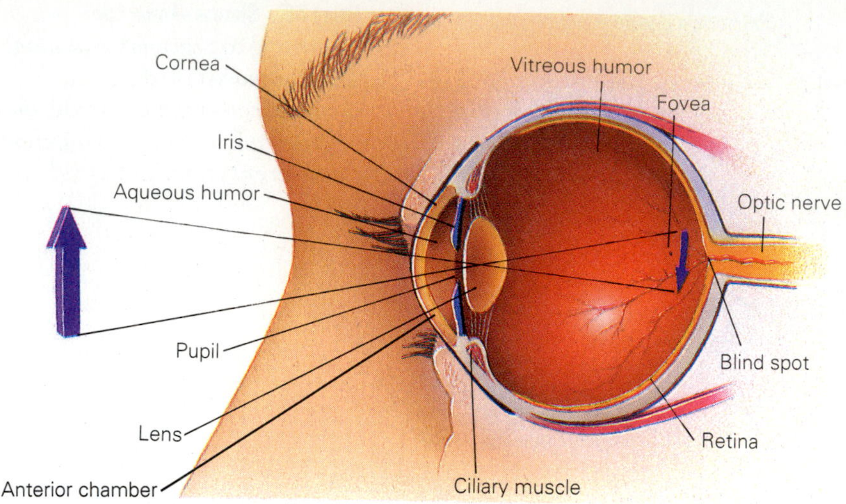

Figure 7.6 Structure of the Human Eye

The Human Eye

The eye is the camera for the brain's motion pictures of the world (see **Figure 7.6**). A camera views the world through a lens that gathers and focuses light. The eye also gathers and focuses light—light enters the *cornea,* a transparent bulge on the front of the eye. Next it passes through the *anterior chamber,* which is filled with a clear liquid called the *aqueous humor.* The light then passes through the *pupil,* an opening in the opaque *iris.* To focus a camera, you move its lens closer to or further from the object viewed. To focus light in the eye, a bean-shaped crystalline *lens* changes its shape, thinning to focus on distant objects and thickening to focus on near ones. To control the amount of light coming into a camera, you vary the opening of the lens. In the eye, the muscular disk of the iris changes the size of the pupil, the aperture through which light passes into the eyeball. At the back of a camera body is the photosensitive film that records the variations in light that have come through the lens. Similarly, in the eye, light travels through the *vitreous humor,* finally striking the *retina,* a thin sheet that lines the rear wall of the eyeball.

The functions of a camera provide a good analogy for study of the human eye.

As you can see, the features of a camera and the eye are very similar. Now let's examine the components of the vision process in more detail.

The Pupil and the Lens

The pupil is the opening in the iris through which light passes. The iris makes the pupil dilate or constrict to control the amount of light entering the eyeball. Light passing through the pupil is focused by the lens on the retina; the lens reverses and inverts the light pattern as it does so. The lens is particularly important because of its variable focusing ability for near and far objects. The ciliary muscles can change the thickness of the lens and, hence, its optical properties in a process called **accommodation.**

The variable focusing of the lens is particularly important in the ability to see both far and near objects.

Many people suffer from accommodation problems. For example, people who are nearsighted cannot focus on distant objects properly, while those who are farsighted cannot focus on nearby objects. The lens starts off as clear, transparent, and convex. As people age, however, the lens becomes more amber tinted, opaque, and flattened, and it loses its elasticity. The effect of some of these changes is that the lens cannot become thick enough for close vision. When people age past the 45-year mark, the blur point—the closest point at which they can focus clearly—gets progressively farther away.

The Retina

You look with your eyes but see with your brain. The eye gathers light, focuses it, and starts a neural signal on its way toward the brain. The eye's critical function, therefore, is to convert information about the world from light waves into neural signals. This happens in the **retina,** at the back of the eye. Under the microscope, you see that the retina has several highly organized layers of different types of neurons.

The basic conversion from light energy to neural responses is performed in your retina by *rods* and *cones*—receptor cells sensitive to light. These **photoreceptors** are uniquely placed in the visual system between the outer world, ablaze with light, and the inner world of neural processing and visual sensation. Because you sometimes operate in near darkness and sometimes in bright light, nature has provided two ways of processing light. The 120 million thin **rods** operate best in near darkness. The 7 million fat **cones** are specialized for the bright, color-filled day. When the rods and cones are functioning in tandem, you get information about the size, shape, edges, boundaries, and color of whatever is in your focus of vision (see **Figure 7.7**). In the very center of the retina is a small region called the **fovea,** which contains nothing but densely packed cones—it is rod-free. The fovea is the area of your sharpest vision—both color and spatial detail are most accurately detected there.

The basic conversion of light energy to neural energy occurs in the retina, where the rods specialize in vision in near darkness and the cones respond best to bright, colorful stimuli.

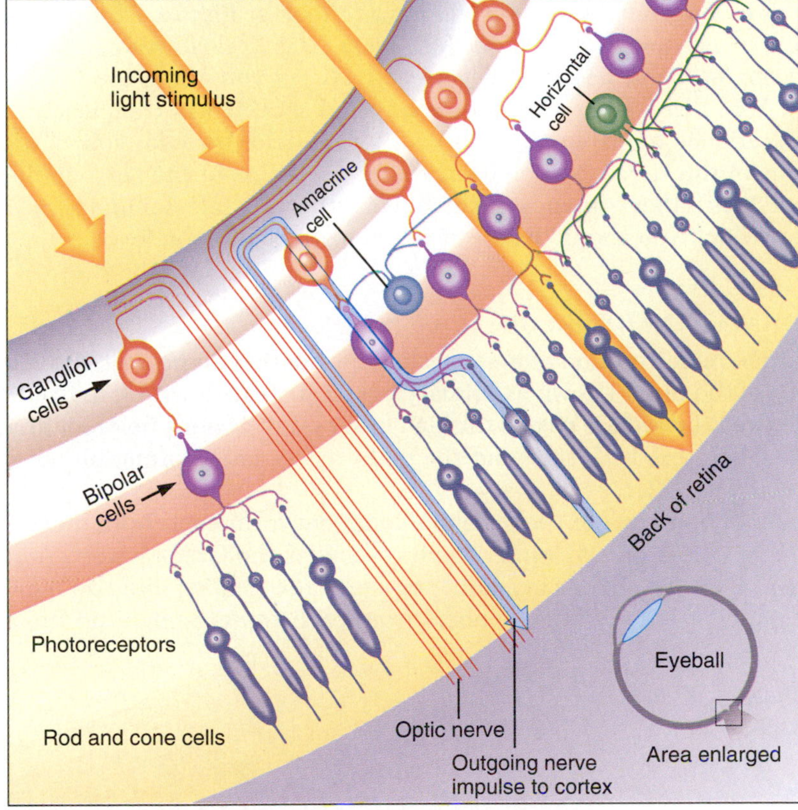

Figure 7.7 Retinal Pathways

This is a stylized and greatly simplified diagram showing the pathways that connect three of the layers of nerve cells in the retina. Incoming light passes through all these layers to reach the receptors, at the back of the eyeball, that are pointed away from the source of light. Note that the bipolar cells gather impulses from more than one receptor cell and send the results to ganglion cells. Nerve impulses (blue arrow) from the ganglion cells leave the eye via the optic nerve and travel to the next relay point.

Other cells in your retina are responsible for integrating information across regions of rods and cones. The **bipolar cells** are nerve cells that combine impulses from many receptors and send the results to ganglion cells. Each **ganglion cell** then integrates the impulses from one or more bipolar cells into a single firing rate. The cones in the central fovea send their impulses to the ganglion cells in that region while, further out on the periphery of the retina, rods and cones converge on the same bipolar and ganglion cells. The axons of the ganglion cells make up the optic nerve, which carries this visual information out of the eye and back toward the brain.

Your **horizontal cells** and **amacrine cells** integrate information across the retina. Rather than send signals toward the brain, horizontal cells connect receptors to each other, while amacrine cells link bipolar cells to other bipolar cells and ganglion cells to other ganglion cells. These cells restrict the spread of the signal within the retina, and thus improve the precision of your visual system.

An interesting curiosity in the anatomical design of the retina exists where the optic nerve leaves each eye. This region, called the optic disk, or *blind spot,* contains no receptor cells at all. You do not experience blindness there, except under very special circumstances, because (1) the blind spots of the two eyes are positioned so that receptors in each eye register what is missed in the other, and (2) the brain "fills in" this region with appropriate sensory information from the surrounding area.

To find your blind spot, you will have to look at **Figure 7.8** under special viewing conditions. Hold this book at arm's length, close your right eye, and fixate on the bank figure with your left eye as you bring the book slowly closer. When the dollar sign is in your blind spot, it will disappear, but you will experience no gaping hole in your visual field. Instead, your visual system fills in this area with the background whiteness of the surrounding area so you "see" the whiteness, which isn't there, while failing to see your money, which you should have put in the bank before you lost it!

Pathways to the Brain

The ultimate destination of much visual information is the part of the occipital lobe of the brain known as primary **visual cortex.** However, most information leaving the retinas passes through other brain regions before it arrives at the visual cortex. Let's trace out the pathways visual information takes (Van Essen et al., 1992).

The million axons of the ganglion cells that form each **optic nerve** come together in the *optic chiasma,* which resembles the Greek letter χ (*chi,* pronounced *kye*). The axons in each optic nerve are divided into two bundles at the optic chiasma. Half of the fibers from each retina remain on the side of

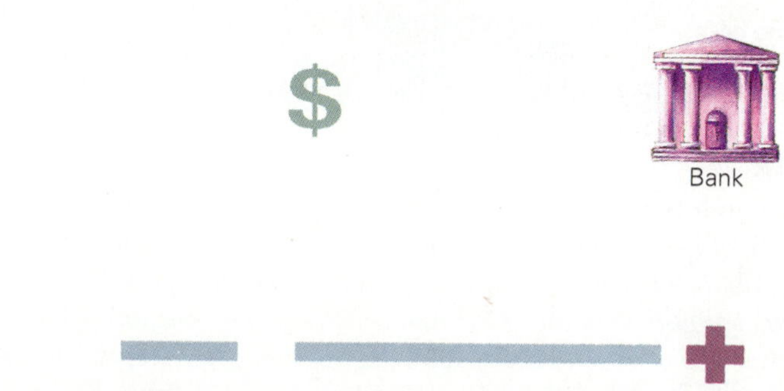

Figure 7.8 Find Your Blind Spot

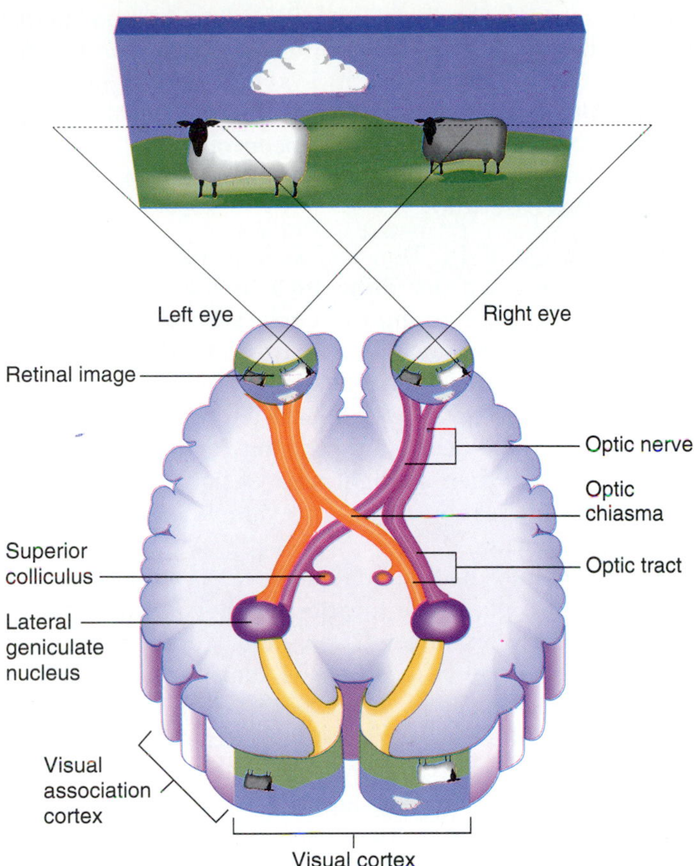

Figure 7.9 Pathways in the Human Visual System
The diagram shows the way light from the visual field projects onto the two retinas and shows the routes by which neural messages from the retina are sent to the two visual centers of each hemisphere.

the body from which they originated. The axons from the inner half of each eye cross over the midline as they continue their journey toward the back of the brain (see **Figure 7.9**). These two bundles of fibers, which now contain axons from both eyes, are renamed *optic tracts.* The optic tracts deliver information to two clusters of cells in the brain: 80 percent of the nerve fibers project to the lateral geniculate nucleus; the bulk of the remainder project to the superior colliculus.

Of these two brain structures, the **superior colliculus** is evolutionarily older. In less developed animals, like the frog, it is the major area for visual processing. In humans, the superior colliculus gives the organism flexibility in orienting to environmental stimulation across multiple senses. The nerve cells of the superior colliculus integrate light and sound to help guide the motor responses that orient the eyes, ears, and head toward a wide variety of environmental cues (Meredith & Stein, 1985).

The more evolutionarily advanced **lateral geniculate nucleus** is required to perform detailed visual analysis. This region both sends information to and receives information from the primary visual cortex. The lateral geniculate nucleus also integrates information from the *reticular activating system,* in the brain stem, which controls an organism's general level of arousal (see Chapter 3). The brain's interpretation of visual information is sensitive, therefore, to the overall arousal state of the animal. Distinct layers

Vision is separated into pathways for pattern recognition and place recognition.

of cells in the lateral geniculate nucleus encode information about color and other aspects of the visual world. Research also supports the theory that visual analysis is separated into pathways for *pattern recognition*—how things look—and *place recognition*—where things are (Wilson et al., 1993).

The separation of visual functions has been observed most dramatically when individuals have lost portions of their visual cortex through injury or surgery. Consider this case study.

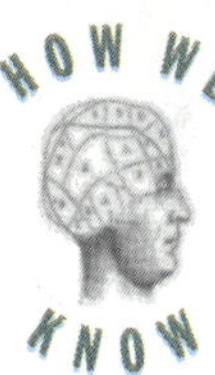

From the age of 14, Don had severe, prolonged headaches and incapacitating sensory difficulties in his left visual field. When Don was 34, in an attempt to correct the problem, he decided to have an operation in which a neurosurgeon would remove a small portion of his right occipital cortex. The surgery permanently cured Don's headaches, but he was left totally blind in the left half of his visual field because the region removed contained primary visual cortex. When a bright spot of light was shown directly to the left of his fixation point, for example, he was simply unaware of its presence.

On an informed hunch, however, a group of psychologists asked Don to guess the location of the spot of light by pointing with his left index finger. The results were remarkable. Don was nearly as accurate at locating the spot in this "blind" left field as he was at locating spots in the "sighted" right visual field! Further experiments showed that he could also guess whether a line in his "blind" field was vertical or horizontal and whether a figure presented there was an *X* or an *O*. Throughout the tests, Don was completely unaware of the presence of the spots, lines, or figures. He claimed he was merely guessing. When shown videotapes of his testing, Don was openly astonished to see himself pointing to lights he hadn't seen (Weiskrantz et al., 1974).

Don's "vision" was aptly dubbed *blindsight:* his behavior was visually guided in the absence of conscious visual awareness of an object. Comparable results have been found in tests on several other patients with similar damage in the visual cortex (Perenin & Jeannerod, 1975). This pattern of performance has been interpreted as evidence that subcortical structures that remain intact even when cortex is destroyed provide a level of visual analysis appropriate for these tasks—but outside of awareness. This conclusion, however, remains controversial, in large part because of the multiple pathways the brain uses to encode visual information (Fendrich et al., 1992, 1993; Stoerig, 1993; Weiskrantz, 1993). Whatever the neural mechanisms, however, blindsight demonstrates that accurate visual performance can occur outside of consciousness.

The phenomenon called blindsight demonstrates that visual performance can occur outside of consciousness.

You have now learned how visual information is distributed from the eyes to various parts of the brain. We next turn to your experiences of particular aspects of the visual world. One of the most remarkable features of the human visual system is that your experiences of form, color, position, and depth are based on processing the same sensory information in different ways. How do the transformations in processing occur that enable you to see these different features of the visual world?

Seeing Color

Physical objects seem to have the marvelous property of being painted with color. You most often have the impression of brightly colored objects at a distance—red valentines, green fir trees, or blue robins' eggs—but your vivid experience of color relies on the rays of light these objects reflect onto your sensory receptors. One of the first to argue this view was **Sir Isaac Newton** in 1671:

> For the rays [of light], to speak properly, are not colored. In them there is nothing else than a certain power and disposition to stir up a sensation of this or that color. For as sound, in a bell or musical string or other sounding body, is nothing but a trembling motion, and in the air nothing but that motion propagated from the object,... so colors in the object are nothing but a disposition to reflect this or that sort of ray more copiously than the rest....

Color is created when your brain processes the information coded in the light source.

As Sir Isaac Newton was the first to explain, color is not in the object but is created when the brain processes the light reflected from the object.

Wavelengths and Hues

The light you see is just a small portion of a physical dimension called the *electromagnetic spectrum* (see **Figure 7.10**). Your visual system is not equipped to detect other types of waves in this spectrum, such as X rays, microwaves, and radio waves. The physical property that distinguishes types of electromagnetic energy, including light, is *wavelength,* the distance between the crests of two adjacent waves. Wavelengths of visible light are measured in *nanometers* (billionths of a meter). What you see as light is the range of wavelengths from 400 to about 700 nanometers. Each color you see is the result of experiencing light rays of a particular physical wavelength—for example, violet-blue at the lower level and red-orange at the higher level. Thus light is described physically in terms of wavelengths, not colors; colors exist only in your sensory system's interpretation of the wavelengths.

All experiences of color can be described in terms of three basic dimensions: hue, saturation, and brightness. **Hue** is the dimension that captures the qualitative experience of the color of a light. In pure lights that contain only one wavelength (such as a laser beam), the psychological experience of

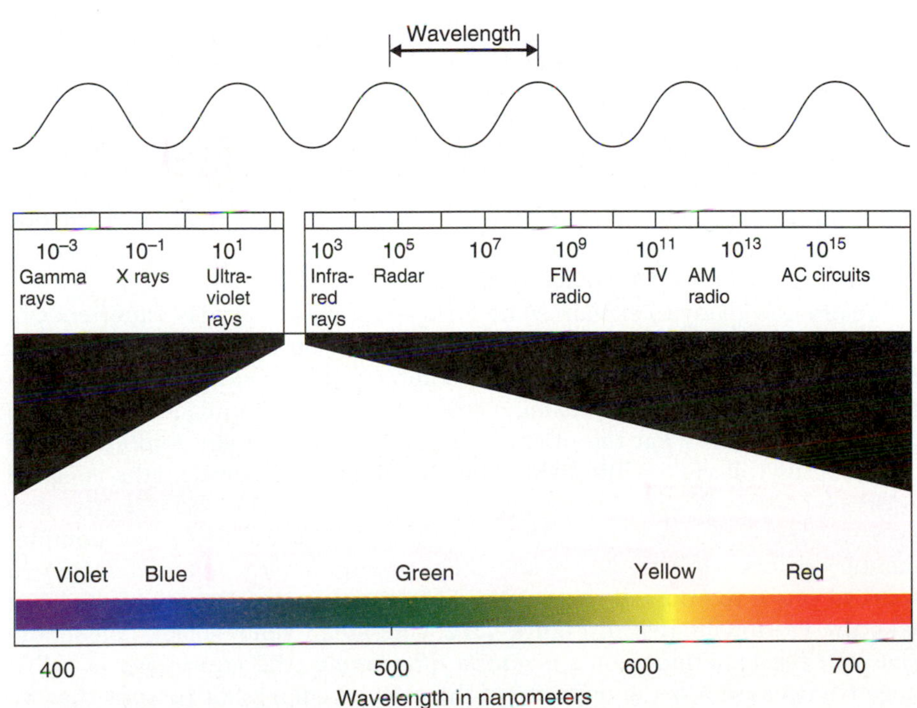

Figure 7.10 The Electromagnetic Spectrum

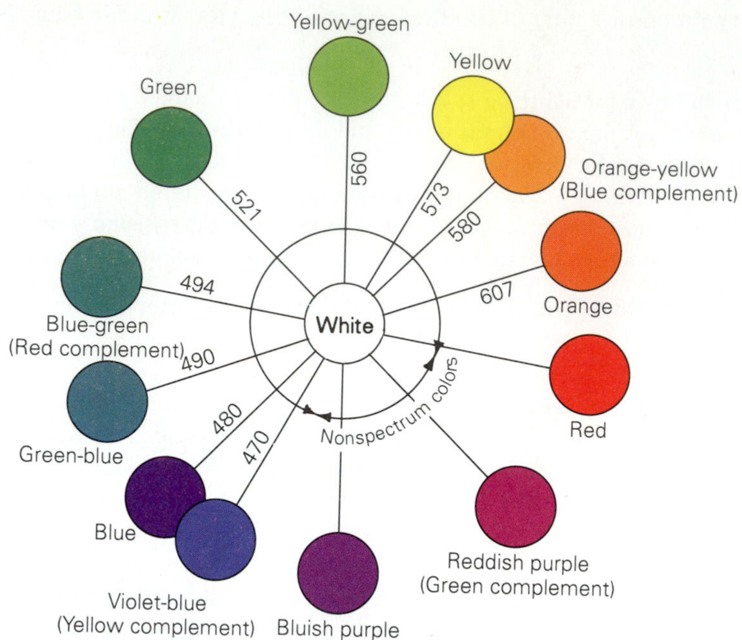

Figure 7.11 The Color Circle

Colors are arranged by their similarity. Complementary colors are placed directly opposite each other. Mixing complementary colors yields a neutral gray or white light at the center. The numbers next to each hue are the wavelength values for spectral colors, those colors within the region of visual sensitivity. Nonspectral hues are obtained by mixing short and long spectral wavelengths.

hue corresponds directly to the physical dimension of the light's wavelength. **Figure 7.11** presents the hues arranged in a *color circle.* Those hues perceived to be most similar are in adjacent positions. This order mirrors the order of hues in the spectrum. **Saturation** is the psychological dimension that captures the purity and vividness of color sensations. Undiluted colors have the most saturation; muted, muddy, and pastel colors have intermediate amounts of saturation; and grays have zero saturation. **Brightness** is the dimension of color experience that captures the intensity of light. White has the most brightness; black has the least. When colors are analyzed along these three dimensions, a remarkable finding emerges: humans are capable of visually discriminating about 7 million different colors! However, most people can label only 150 to 200 of those.

The experience of color can be described by three dimensions: hue, the actual color; saturation, the purity of the color; and brightness, the intensity of the color.

We are now ready to explain some facts about your everyday experience of color. At some point in your science education, you may have repeated Sir Isaac Newton's discovery that sunlight combines all wavelengths of light: you repeated Newton's proof by using a prism to separate sunlight into the full rainbow of colors. What the prism tells you is that the right combination of wavelengths will yield white light. The combination of wavelengths is called *additive color mixture*. Take a look back at Figure 7.11. Wavelengths that appear directly across from each other on the color circle—called **complementary colors**—will create the sensation of white light when mixed. Do you want to prove to yourself the existence of complementary colors? You can take the Patriotism Test in **Figure 7.12**. The green-yellow-black flag should give you the experience of a *negative afterimage* (the afterimage is called negative because it is the opposite of the original color). For reasons that we will explain when we consider theories of color vision, when you stare at any color long enough to partially fatigue your photoreceptors, looking at a white surface will allow you to experience the complement of the original color.

Any two unique hues yield the complement of a third color, but the combination of the three wavelengths produces white light.

Figure 7.12 Color Afterimages: The Patriotism Test
Stare at the dot in the center of the green, black, and yellow flag for at least 30 seconds. Then fixate on the center of a sheet of white paper or a blank wall. Try this aftereffect illusion on your friends.

You have probably noticed afterimages from time to time in your everyday exposure to colors. Most of your experience with colors, however, does not come from complementary lights. Instead, you have probably spent your time at play with colors combining crayons or paints of different hues. The colors you see when you look at a crayon mark, or any other colored surface, are the wavelengths of light that are *not* absorbed by the surface. Although yellow crayon looks mostly yellow, it lets some green wavelengths escape. Similarly, blue crayon lets both blue and some green wavelengths escape. When yellow and blue crayon are combined, yellow absorbs blue and blue absorbs yellow—the only wavelengths that are not absorbed look green! This phenomenon is called *subtractive color mixture.* The remaining wavelengths that are not absorbed—the wavelengths that are *reflected*—give the crayon mixture the color you perceive.

All these rules about the experience of color do not apply to those people born with a color deficiency. *Color blindness* is the partial or total inability to distinguish colors. The negative afterimage effect of viewing the green, yellow, and black flag will not work if you are color-blind. Color blindness is usually a sex-linked hereditary defect associated with a gene on the X chromosome. Because males have a single X chromosome, they are more likely to show this recessive trait than females. Females would need to have a defective gene on both X chromosomes to be color-blind. An estimate for color blindness among Caucasian males is about 10 percent, but less than 0.5 percent among females.

Men are considerably more likely than women to be color-blind, because color blindness is a sex-linked hereditary defect.

Most color blindness involves difficulty distinguishing red from green, especially at weak saturations. More rare are people who confuse yellows and blues. Rarest of all are those who see no color at all, only variations in brightness. To see whether you have a color deficiency, look at **Figure 7.13**. If you see the numbers 1 and 5 in the pattern of dots, your color vision is probably normal. If you see something else, you may be at least partially color-blind. (Try the test on others as well—particularly people you know who are color-blind—to find out what they see.) Let's now see how scientists have explained such facts about color vision as complementary colors and color blindness.

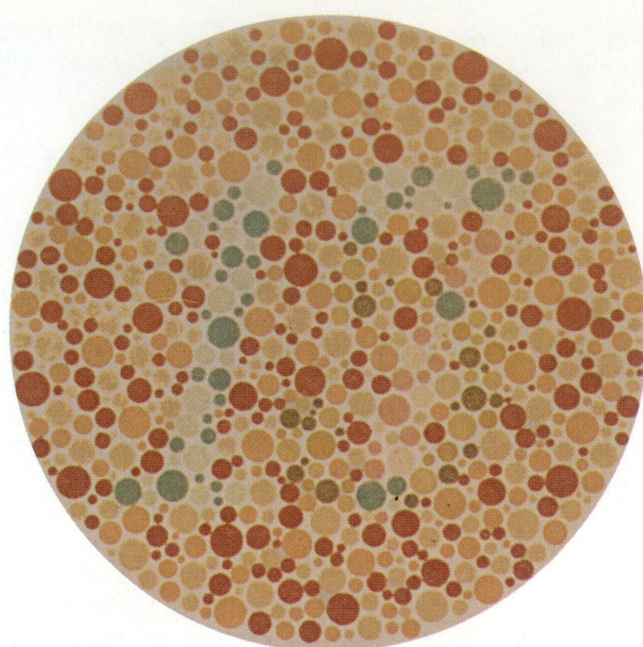

Figure 7.13 A Color Blindness Test
A person who cannot discriminate between red and green colors will not be able to identify the number hidden in the figure. What do you see? If you see the number 15 in the dot pattern, your color vision is probably normal.

Theories of Color Vision

The trichromatic theory of color vision was first proposed by Thomas Young and later revised by Hermann von Helmholtz.

The first scientific theory of color vision was proposed by **Sir Thomas Young** around 1800. He suggested that there were three types of color receptors in the normal human eye that produced psychologically primary sensations: red, green, and blue. All other colors, he believed, were additive or subtractive combinations of these three primaries. Young's theory was later refined and extended by **Hermann von Helmholtz** and came to be known as the Young-Helmholtz **trichromatic theory.**

Trichromatic theory provided a plausible explanation for people's color sensations and for color blindness (according to the theory, color-blind people had only one or two kinds of receptors). However, other facts and observations were not as well explained by the theory. Why did adaptation to one color produce color afterimages that had the complementary hue? Why did color-blind people always fail to distinguish *pairs* of colors: red and green or blue and yellow?

Questions unanswered by the trichromatic color theory gave rise to Ewald Hering's opponent-process theory of color vision.

Answers to these questions became the cornerstones for a second theory of color vision proposed by **Ewald Hering** in the late 1800s. According to his **opponent-process theory,** all color experiences arise from three underlying systems, each of which includes two opponent elements: red versus green, blue versus yellow, or black (no color) versus white (all colors). Hering theorized that colors produced complementary afterimages because one element of the system became fatigued (from overstimulation) and, thus, increased the relative contribution of its opponent element. In Hering's theory, types of color blindness came in pairs because the color system was actually built from pairs of opposites, not from single primary colors.

For many years, scientists argued about which theory was correct. Eventually, scientists recognized that the theories were not really in conflict; they simply described two different stages of processing that corresponded to successive physiological structures in the visual system (Hurvich & Jameson, 1974). We now know, first, that there are, indeed, three types of cones—each of which is most sensitive to light at a particular wavelength.

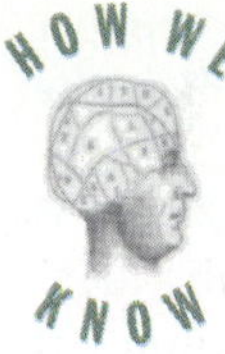

Vision researchers have developed a technique for analyzing the electrical activity of a single cone. Single cone cells from macaque monkeys were "sucked up" into a special hollow glass tube that is less than 1/25th the diameter of a human hair. Light of various wavelengths was shone on the tube, and the strength of electrical signals emitted from the cone cell was amplified and measured. Using this technique, the researchers found that some cells were tuned to respond maximally to light wavelengths of 435 nanometers (blue cells), others to 535 nm (green cells), and others to 570 nm (red cells). Now researchers are trying to identify the biochemical activities of these cells that start the process of transduction of external energy into neural energy that underlies your visual sensation (Baylor, 1987).

The responses of these cone types correspond to the three primary colors in the Young-Helmholtz theory. People who are color-blind lack one or more of these three types of receptor cones.

Second, we now know that the retinal ganglion cells combine the outputs of these three cone types in accordance with Hering's opponent-process theory (R. De Valois & Jacobs, 1968). According to the modern version of opponent-process theory, as supported by **Leo Hurvich** and **Dorothea Jameson** (1974), the two members of each color pair work in opposition (are opponents) by means of neural inhibition. Some ganglion cells receive excitatory input from lights that appear red and inhibitory input from lights that appear green. Other cells in the system have the opposite arrangement of excitation and inhibition. Together, these two types of ganglion cells form the physiological basis of the red/green opponent-process system. Other ganglion cells make up the blue/yellow opponent system. The black/white system contributes to your perception of color saturation and brightness.

Leo Hurvich and Dorothea Jameson's modern version of the opponent-process theory suggests that color pairs become opponents through patterns of excitation and inhibition in the ganglion cells.

Seeing Form, Depth, and Movement

Seeing the world of color is only a small part of the complex task facing your visual system. If you want to catch a football or avoid a hornet's nest, you must also detect the form or shape of objects, their depth or distance, and their movement in space. Your visual system consists of several separate and independent subsystems that analyze different aspects of the same retinal image. Distinct sets of neurons have unique properties that generate the perceptions of color, form, contrast, movement, and texture (Livingstone & Hubel, 1988). Although your final perception is of a unified visual scene, your vision of it is accompanied by a host of channels in your visual system that, under normal conditions, are exquisitely coordinated (Merigan & Maunsell, 1993).

Much of the evidence for subdivisions in the visual system has come from patients with various types of brain damage. You might recall our description of blindsight, which showed that recognition is divided from consciousness. Other patients have shown a loss of color discrimination but not of form perception, a loss of motion perception but not of color and form perception, or a loss of the ability to recognize familiar faces but not of other visual abilities. These clinical cases constrain theories of the mechanisms of visual processing. Let's see what we have learned about the building blocks of visual processing.

Receptive Fields and Contrast Effects

You can start to understand how vision works by knowing a single fact: The cells at each level in the visual pathway respond *selectively* only to a particular part of the visual field. For example, we noted earlier that each retinal ganglion cell integrates information about light patterns from many receptor cells. The receptors that contribute information to each ganglion cell make up the **receptive field** of that cell.

Receptive fields of retinal ganglion cells are of two types (see parts A and B of **Figure 7.14**): (1) those in which stimulation in the center of the field excites the cell, while stimulation in the surrounding part inhibits it; and (2) those with the opposite organization—an inhibitory center and an excitatory surround. Ganglion cells respond to the *differences* in stimulation coming from their center and the surround. They are most excited by *stimulus contrast;* those with *on* centers fire most strongly to a bright spot surrounded by a dark border, while those with *off* centers fire most vigorously to a dark spot surrounded by a light border. Uniform illumination causes the center and surround to cancel each other's activity—the cell is not as excited by uniform illumination as it is by a spot or bar of light.

A ganglion cell responds to the differences in stimulation coming from its center and the receptive field.

Let's use this information to consider a pair of *contrast effects.* In **Figure 7.15**, you can see that a patch of gray appears lighter against a dark background than it does against a light background. Why is this so? You should be able to understand how a subset of your ganglion cells would respond more or less vigorously as the pattern of light in the center and surround changes.

To explain **Figure 7.16**, we need a bit more physiology. First, let's see how the contrast effect works. Rectangle A and rectangle B seem similar—they both have dark right halves and light left halves. To prove that the right half of rectangle A is darker than the left half, place a pencil along the center of the rectangle. Note the brightness difference on either side of the pencil. Now try rectangle B. Visual magic! The difference between the left and right halves has vanished. A light meter moved across rectangle A records the sharp change in light intensity at the midpoint of the rectangle; but the bottom rectangle is shown to have the same light intensity throughout except at the midpoint between the two halves, where there is a gradual shift toward brighter on the left side and darker on the right. The midpoint border creates a false impression of contrast that fools your visual system into seeing a difference where there is none. (We will often see that the best way to demon-

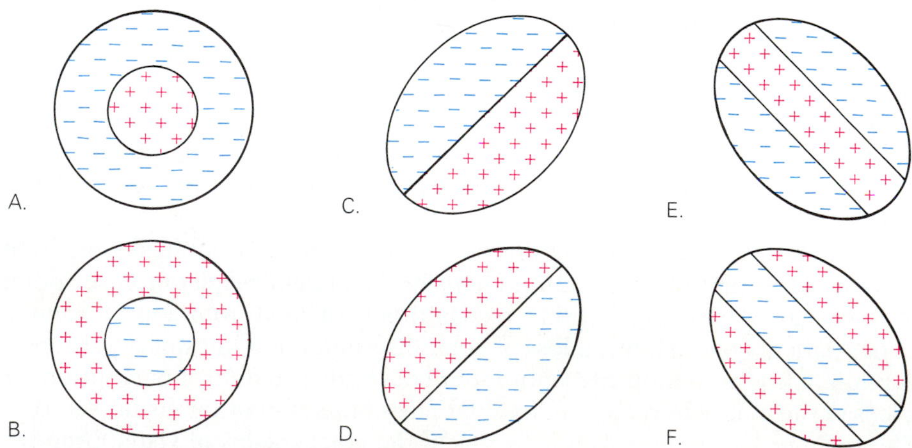

Figure 7.14 Receptive Fields of Ganglion and Cortical Cells
The receptive field of a cell in the visual pathway is the area in the visual field from which it receives stimulation. The receptive fields of the ganglion cells in the retina are circular (A, B); those of the simplest cells in the visual cortex are elongated in a particular orientation (C, D, E, F). In both cases, the cell responding to the receptive field is excited by light in the regions marked with plus signs and inhibited by light in the regions marked with minus signs.

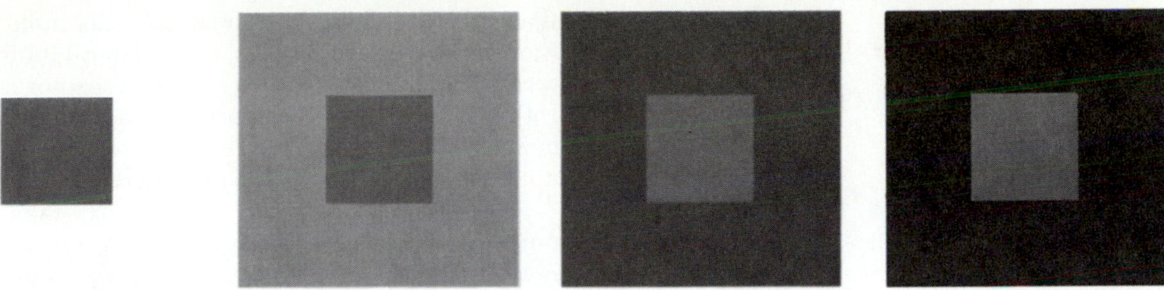

Figure 7.15 Brightness Contrast
These four (objectively) identical gray squares are set on different backgrounds. As you can see, the lighter the background, the darker the gray squares appear.

strate the normal—successful—operations of your sensory and perceptual systems is to explore when and why they break down.)

An explanation of Figure 7.16 begins back at your retina. When a receptor cell is stimulated by light, information is transmitted in two directions: upward to the brain and sideways to neighboring receptor cells. The

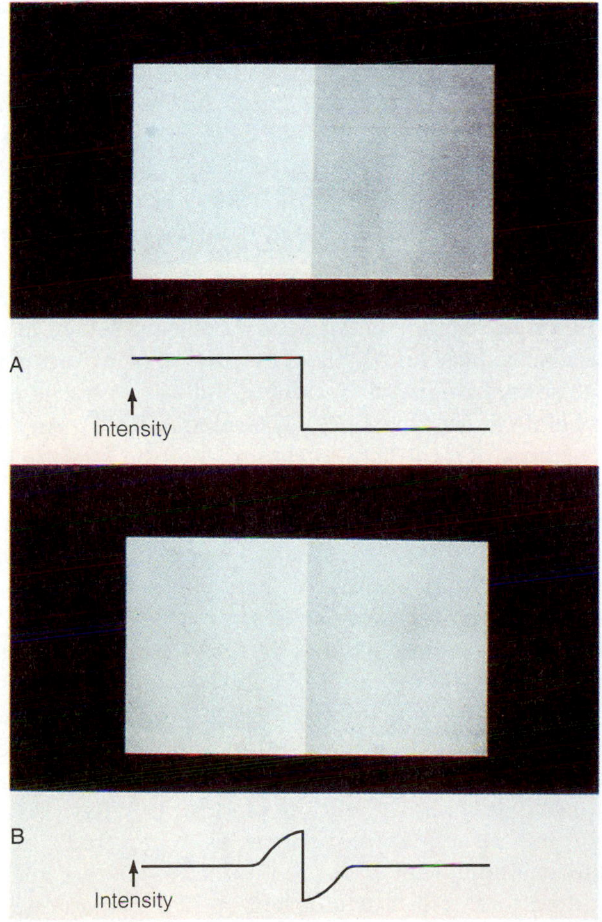

Figure 7.16 The Illusion of Contour
Put a pencil or a straightedge down the center divide between the left and right sections of A. Then do the same for B. What happens to the difference between the left and right segments of each?

impulses sent out to adjacent cells *inhibit* those adjacent cells' ability to fire. This sideways suppression of other receptor cells, called **lateral inhibition**, is the basis for many aspects of brightness contrast. As one receptor is excited by an intense amount of light, it inhibits neighboring cells from producing a response to the stimulus. Lateral inhibition exaggerates the difference between them, generating messages to the brain that there is more contrast than actually exists.

Contrast allows you to detect boundaries and distinct edges, giving objects shape, size, and orientation in space.

In the visual environment, contrasts in brightness often provide indications of the boundaries and distinct edges that give objects shape, size, and orientation in space. Lateral inhibition and receptive fields help accentuate these contrasts, to get visual analysis under way. However, not all the details of brightness illusions can be explained by these simple mechanisms (Adelson, 1993). The visual system also undertakes more sophisticated visual analyses.

Complex Visual Analysis

You have now learned some of the properties of visual processing at your receptor and ganglion cells. What happens at higher levels in your visual system? Pioneering work on this question was done by **David Hubel** and **Torsten Wiesel**, sensory physiologists who won a Nobel Prize in 1981 for their studies of receptive fields of cells in the visual cortex. Hubel and Wiesel recorded the firing rates from single cells in the visual cortex of cats in response to moving spots and bars in the visual field. When Hubel and Wiesel mapped out the receptive fields of these cortical cells, they found an organization of cells that had successively more narrow constraints on the visual stimuli that were most likely to cause them to fire (Hubel & Wiesel, 1962, 1979). One type of cortical cell, *simple* cells, responded most strongly to bars of light in their "favorite" orientation (see Figure 7.14). *Complex* cells also each have a "favorite" orientation, but they require as well that the bar be moving. *Hypercomplex* cells require moving bars of a particular length, or moving corners or angles.

Your visual system does more, however, than just extract orientations and motion from the visual signal. Many cortical cells are sensitive to successive, *contrasting* bands of dark and light. This property of brain response has given rise to the **spatial-frequency model** of the way patterns and shapes are perceived (De Valois & De Valois, 1990; Graham, 1992). Any image that is composed of patterns of dark-light variations can be analyzed according to the number of its dark-light cycles over a given distance of visual space. These *spatial frequencies* can be recovered mathematically by a procedure called Fourier analysis. Research evidence suggests that the human visual system may analyze visual scenes by actually performing some kind of Fourier analysis on the patterns of dark-light cycles it detects (Blakemore & Campbell, 1969). Any two-dimensional pattern—from an American flag to a photograph of Groucho Marx—can be analyzed mathematically and broken down into its many spatial frequencies. **Figure 7.17** reveals what you would see of Groucho Marx with only low spatial frequencies—the overall shape in the blurry picture, A. The high spatial frequencies are responsible for the sharp edges and fine detail in the outline picture, B. What you ordinarily see is the combination of all spatial frequencies, as in picture C.

Sets of cortical cells are organized into channels that respond to different spatial frequencies. Combining channels allows you to sense the full range of spatial frequencies and thus see a clear picture of a visual stimulus.

Just as in this example, sets of cortical cells may be organized into channels that are tuned to respond to different spatial frequencies. Some channels, specific to low frequencies, pick up blobs of light, others detect high frequencies, and still others are specific for frequencies in between. Together, they provide all the information needed to represent a visual scene by combining the range of spatial frequencies that define its dark-light pattern.

A

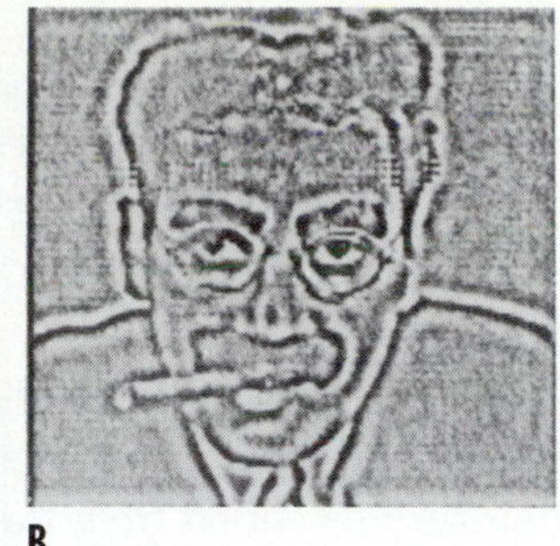
B

C

Figure 7.17 High and Low Spatial Frequencies

Do not attempt to adjust your television set. Detection of only low spatial frequencies would give you the blurry view in A. Detection of only the high spatial frequencies would give you the outline view in B. Normal detection of all frequencies gives you the full view in C.

What Neurons "See," the Brain Perceives

We close out the section on vision by reminding you that what you see in the world (as well as what you hear, smell, and so on) depends on the pattern of activity that is created in your brain. Researchers can make this point effectively by exciting brain cells independent of environmental inputs. Stimulating distinct circuits of receptive fields of neurons in the visual cortex not only excites the neurons but also causes certain perceptions to occur (Newsome & Pare, 1988).

Stimulating certain areas in the brain demonstrates that sensation is really created in the brain.

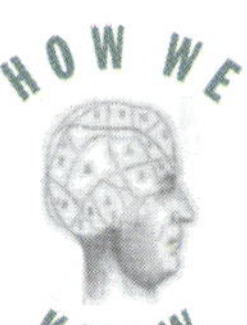

Rhesus monkeys were trained to make a specific response to a visual display of dots moving in a certain direction on a television screen. If they correctly identified the direction of movement—as up or down, for example—they were rewarded. During the experiment, researchers directly stimulated those cortical neurons that were sensitive to a given direction of motion in the visual field. Thus, when cells sensitive to upward movement were electrically stimulated, the monkeys would often "report" upward movement of the random dots—even when the actual movement of the dots was downward (Salzman et al., 1990).

In these experiments, the researchers provided artificial stimulation to compete with the information coming in from the external environment. In Chapter 8, we will see that people's perceptions of the world often represent combinations of external information—the sort of visual analysis we have focused on in this chapter—with internal sources of competing information—knowledge already stored in the brain. We turn now from the world of sight to the world of sound.

HEARING

Hearing and vision play complementary functions in your experience of the world. You often hear stimuli before you see them, particularly if they take place behind you or on the other side of opaque objects such as walls. Although vision is better than hearing for identifying an object once it is in the field of view, you often see the object only because you have used your ears to point your eyes in the right direction.

Hearing is also the principal sensory modality for human communication. People who lack the capacity to hear are excluded from much human interaction and may suffer psychological problems associated with feelings of frustration, rejection, and isolation. People can usually tell right away that someone is visually impaired, so they are able to make adjustments in their behavior (i.e., verbally describing an incident to a visually impaired person; a hearing impairment, however, may go unrecognized even by the individual who is experiencing the impairment, if the onset is gradual. Depression and paranoid disorders may accompany undetected loss of hearing (Post, 1980; Zimbardo et al., 1981). The importance of hearing and the tragedy of its loss is captured in this eloquent description:

> The world will still make sense to someone who is blind or armless or minus a nose. But if you lose your sense of hearing, a crucial thread dissolves and you lose track of life's logic. You become cut off from the daily commerce of the world, as if you were a root buried beneath the soil. (Ackerman, 1990, p. 175)

The Physics of Sound

Clap your hands together. Whistle. Tap your pencil on the table. Why do these actions create sounds? The reason is that they cause objects to vibrate. The vibrational energy is transmitted to the surrounding medium—usually air—as the vibrating objects push molecules of the medium back and forth. The resulting slight changes in pressure spread outward from the vibrating objects in the form of a combination of *sine waves* traveling at a rate of about 1100 feet per second (see **Figure 7.18**). Sound cannot be created in a true vacuum (such as outer space) because there are no air molecules in a vacuum for vibrating objects to move.

The quality of a sound is determined by the frequency and amplitude of the sine wave.

A sine wave has two basic physical properties that determine how it sounds to you: frequency and amplitude. *Frequency* measures the number of cycles the wave completes in a given amount of time. A cycle, as indicated in Figure 7.18, is the left-to-right distance from the peak in one wave to the peak in the next wave. Sound frequency is usually expressed in **Hertz** (Hz), which measures cycles per second. *Amplitude* measures the physical property of strength of the sound wave, as shown in its peak-to-valley height. Amplitude is defined in units of sound pressure or energy.

Psychological Dimensions of Sound

The physical properties of frequency and amplitude give rise to the three psychological dimensions of sound: pitch, loudness, and timbre. Let's see how this phenomenon works.

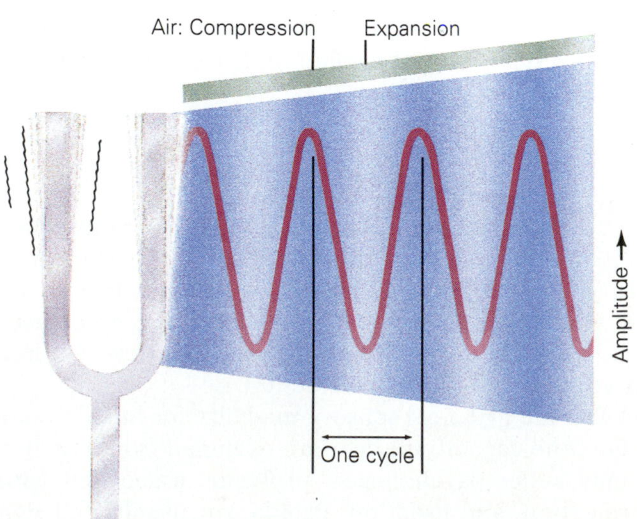

Figure 7.18 An Idealized Sine Wave

Pitch

Pitch is the highness or lowness of a sound determined by the sound's frequency; high frequencies produce high pitch, and low frequencies produce low pitch. The full range of human sensitivity to pure tones extends from frequencies as low as 20 Hz to frequencies as high as 20,000 Hz. (Frequencies below 20 Hz may be experienced through touch as vibrations rather than as sound.) You can get a sense of how big this range is by noting that the 88 keys on a piano cover only the range from about 30 Hz to 4000 Hz.

As you might expect from our earlier discussion of psychophysics, the relationship between frequency (the physical reality) and pitch (the psychological effect) is not a linear one. At the low end of the frequency scale, increasing the frequency by just a few Hz raises the pitch quite noticeably. At the high end of frequency, you require a much bigger increase in order to hear the difference in pitch. For example, the two lowest notes on a piano differ by only 1.6 Hz, whereas the two highest ones differ by 235 Hz. This is another example of the psychophysics of just noticeable differences.

Loudness

The **loudness,** or physical intensity, of a sound is determined by its amplitude; sound waves with large amplitudes are experienced as loud and those with small amplitudes as soft. The human auditory system is sensitive to an enormous range of physical intensities. At one limit, you can hear the tick of a wristwatch at 20 feet. This is the system's absolute threshold—if it were more sensitive, you would hear the blood flowing in your ears. At the other extreme, a jetliner taking off 100 yards away is so loud that the sound is painful. In terms of physical units of sound pressure, the jet produces a sound wave with more than a billion times the energy of the ticking watch.

The pitch and loudness of a sound are determined respectively by the frequency and amplitude of the sound wave.

Because the range of hearing is so great, physical intensities of sound are usually expressed in ratios rather than absolute amounts; loudness is measured in units called **decibels** (dB). **Figure 7.19** shows the loudness of some representative natural sounds in decibel units. It also shows the correspond-

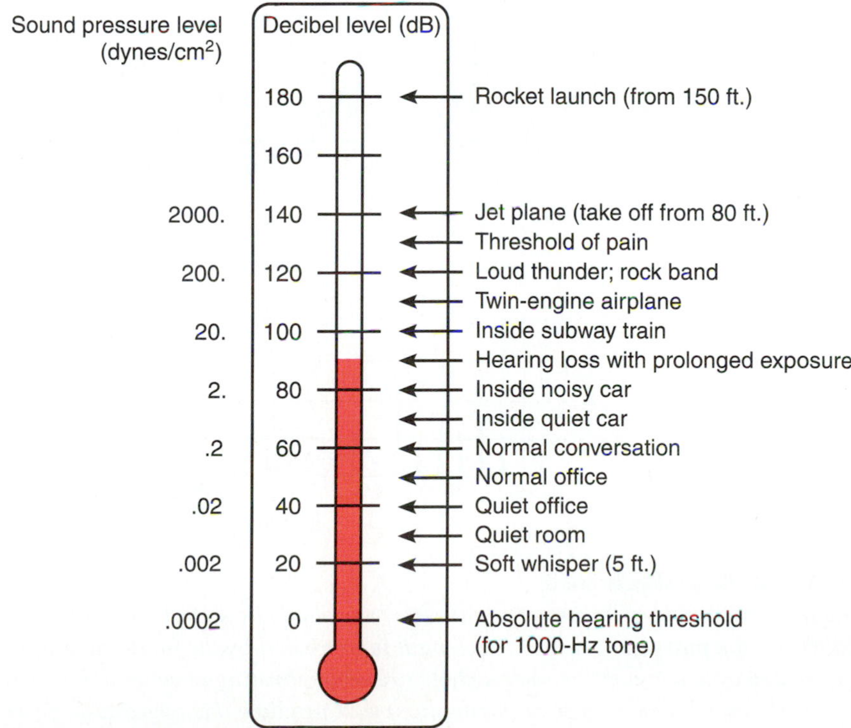

Figure 7.19 Loudness of Familiar Sounds

ing sound pressures for comparison. Note that sounds louder than about 90 dB can produce hearing loss, depending on how long you are exposed to them.

Timbre

The **timbre** of a sound reflects the components of its complex sound wave. Timbre is what sets apart, for example, the sound of a piano and the sound of a flute. A small number of physical stimuli, such as a tuning fork, produce *pure tones* consisting of a single sine wave. A pure tone has only one frequency and one amplitude. Most sounds in the real world are not pure tones. They are complex waves, containing a combination of frequencies and amplitudes. **Figure 7.20** displays the complex waveforms that correspond to several familiar sounds. The graph in the figure shows the sound spectrum for middle C on a piano—the range of all the frequencies actually present in that note and their amplitudes.

In a complex tone such as middle C, the lowest frequency (about 256 Hz) is responsible for the pitch you hear; it is called the *fundamental.* The higher frequencies are called *harmonics,* or overtones, and are simple multiples of the fundamental. The complete sound you hear is produced by the total effect of the fundamental and the harmonics shown in the spectrum. If pure tones at these frequencies and intensities were added together, the result would sound the same to you as middle C on a piano.

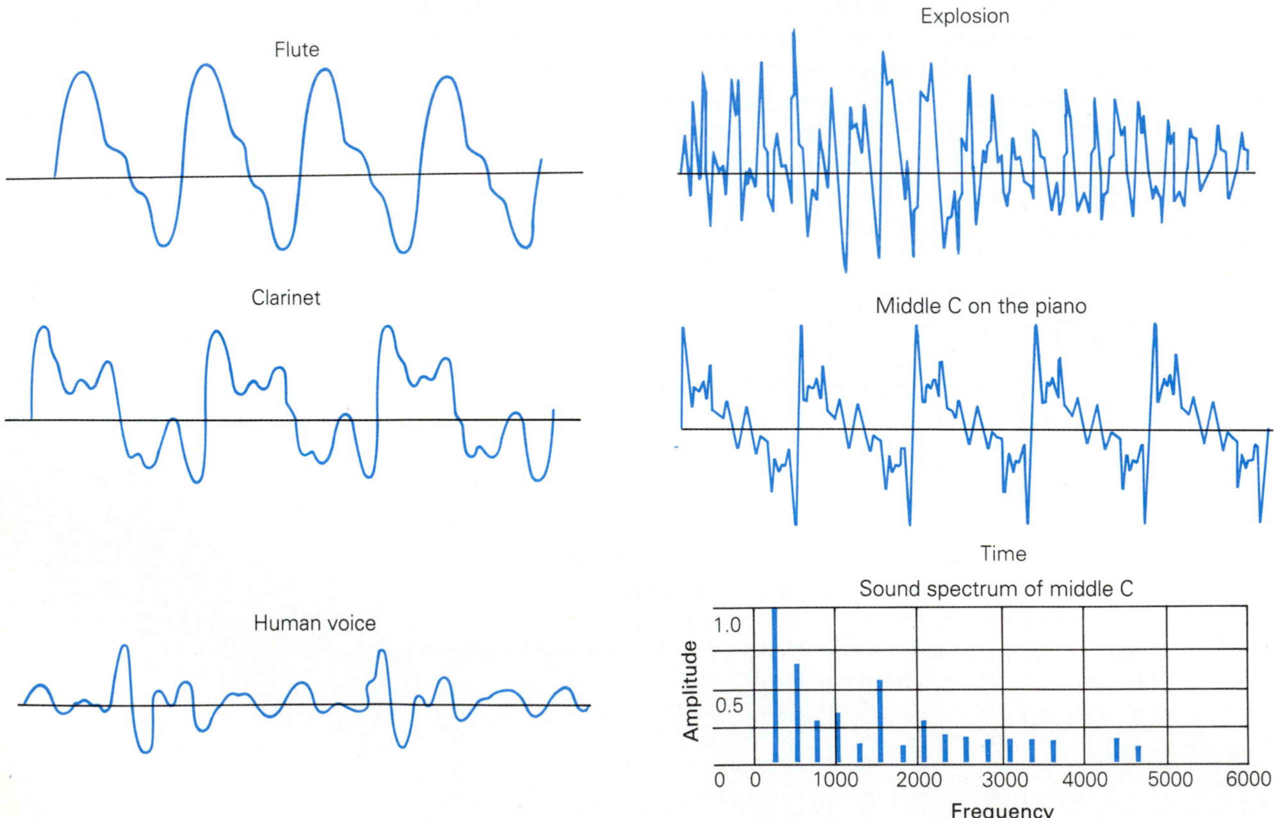

Figure 7.20 Waveforms of Familiar Sounds
Below the complex waveforms of five familiar sounds is the sound spectrum for middle C on the piano. The basic wavelength is produced by the fundamental, in this case 256 cycles, but the piano's strings are also vibrating at several higher frequencies (known as overtones, or harmonics) that produce the jaggedness of the wave pattern. These additional frequencies are identified in the sound spectrum.

The sounds that you call *noise* do not have the clear, simple structures of fundamental frequencies and harmonics. Noise contains many frequencies that are not systematically related to each other. For instance, the static noise you hear between radio stations contains energy at all audible frequencies; you perceive it as having no pitch because it has no fundamental frequency.

Humans hear the characteristic tone colors, or timbres, of various instruments by distinguishing the way harmonics resonate.

The Physiology of Hearing

Now that you know something about the physical bases of your psychological experiences of sound, let's see how those experiences arise from physiological activity in the auditory system. First we will look at the way the ear works. Then we will consider some theories about how pitch experiences are coded in the auditory system and how sounds are localized.

The Auditory System

You have already learned that sensory processes transform forms of external energy into forms of energy within your brain. For you to hear, as shown in **Figure 7.21**, four basic energy transformations must take place: (1) airborne sound waves must get translated into *fluid* waves within the *cochlea* of the ear, (2) the fluid waves must then stimulate mechanical vibrations of the *basilar membrane,* (3) these vibrations must be converted into electrical impulses, and (4) the impulses must travel to the *auditory cortex.* Let's examine each of these transformations in detail.

Hearing depends on four basic energy transformations: sound waves are translated to fluid waves in the cochlea, the fluid waves vibrate the basilar membrane, the vibrations are converted to electrical impulses, and the impulses travel to the auditory cortex.

In the first transformation, vibrating air molecules enter the ears (see Figure 7.21). Some sound enters the external canal of the ear directly and some enters after having been reflected off the *external ear,* or *pinna.* The sound wave travels along the canal through the outer ear until it reaches the end of the canal. There it encounters a thin membrane called the eardrum, or *tympanic membrane.* The sound wave's pressure variations set the eardrum into motion. The eardrum transmits the vibrations from the outer ear into the middle ear, a chamber that contains the three smallest bones in the human body: the *hammer,* the *anvil,* and the *stirrup.* These bones form a mechanical chain that transmits and concentrates the vibrations from the eardrum to the primary organ of hearing, the *cochlea,* which is located in the *inner ear.*

In the second transformation, which occurs in the cochlea, the airborne sound wave becomes "seaborne." The **cochlea** is a fluid-filled, coiled tube that has a membrane, known as the **basilar membrane,** running down its middle along its length. When the stirrup vibrates against the *oval window* at the base of the cochlea, the fluid in the cochlea causes the basilar membrane to move in a wavelike motion.

In the third transformation, the wavelike motion of the basilar membrane bends the tiny hair cells connected to the membrane. The hair cells are the receptor cells for the auditory system. As the hair cells bend, they stimulate nerve endings, transforming the mechanical vibrations of the basilar membrane into neural activity.

Finally, in the fourth transformation, nerve impulses leave the cochlea in a bundle of fibers called the **auditory nerve.** These fibers meet in the *cochlear nucleus* of the brain stem. Similar to the crossing over of nerves in the visual system, stimulation from one ear goes to both sides of the brain. Auditory signals pass through a series of other nuclei on their way to the **auditory cortex,** in the temporal lobes of the cerebral hemispheres. Higher order processing of these signals begins in the auditory cortex. (As you will see shortly, other parts of the ear labeled in Figure 7.21 play roles in your other senses.)

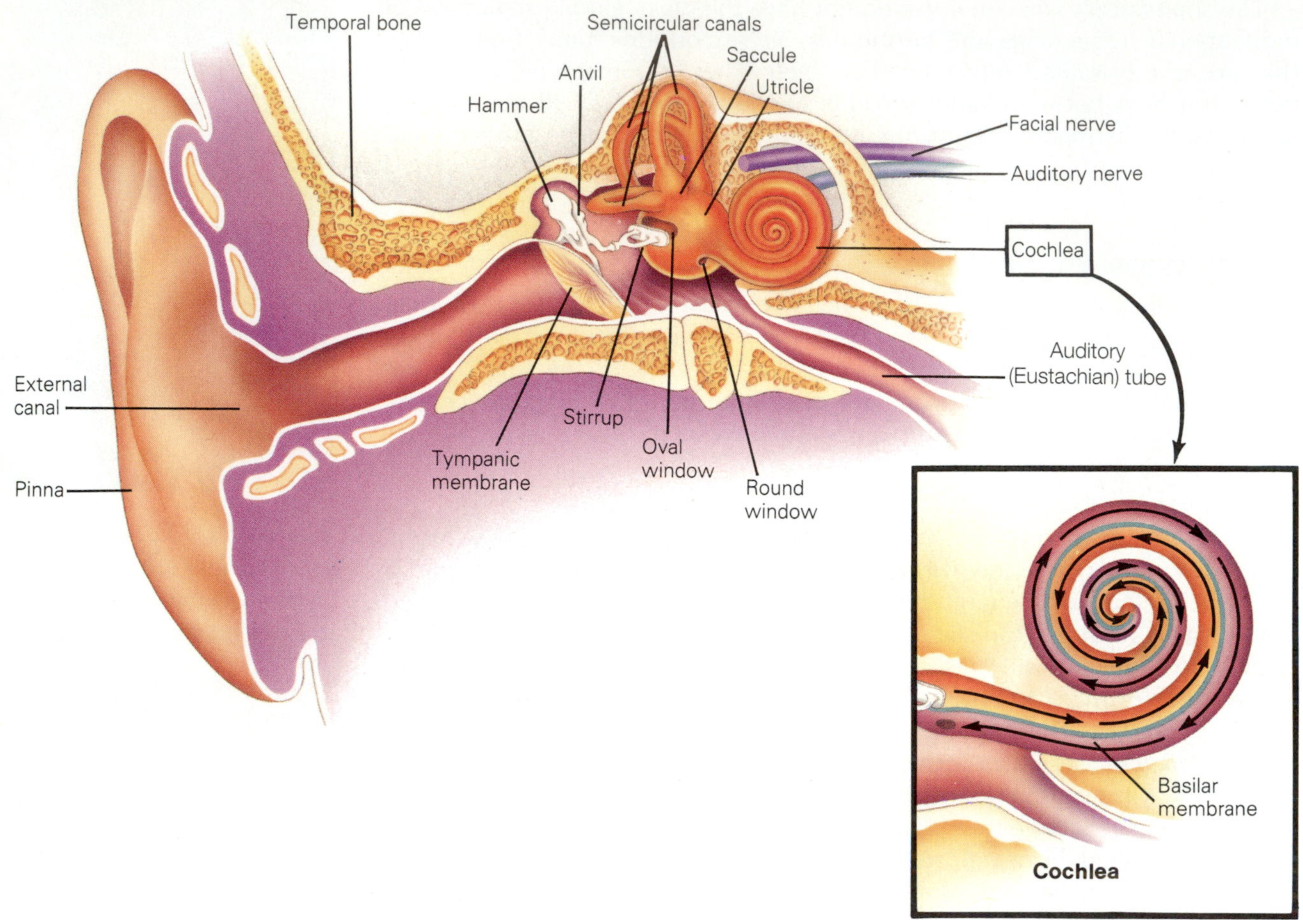

Figure 7.21 Structure of the Human Ear
Sound waves are channeled by the external ear, or pinna, through the external canal, causing the tympanic membrane to vibrate. This vibration activates the tiny bones of the inner ear—the hammer, anvil, and stirrup. Their mechanical vibrations are passed along from the oval window to the cochlea, where they set in motion the fluid in its canal. Tiny hair cells lining the coiled basilar membrane within the cochlea bend as the fluid moves, stimulating nerve endings attached to them. The mechanical energy is then transformed into neural energy and sent to the brain via the auditory nerve.

The four transformations occur in fully functioning auditory systems. However, millions of people suffer from some form of hearing impairment. There are two general types of hearing impairment, each caused by a defect in one or more of the components of the auditory system. The less serious type of impairment is *conduction deafness,* a problem in the conduction of the air vibrations to the cochlea. Often in this type of impairment, the bones in the middle ear are not functioning properly, a problem that may be corrected in microsurgery by insertion of an artificial anvil or stirrup. The more serious type of impairment is *nerve deafness,* a defect in the neural mechanisms that create nerve impulses in the ear or relay them to the auditory cortex. Damage to the auditory cortex can also create nerve deafness. Researchers have explored techniques for alleviating hearing loss by prompting damaged or destroyed cochlear hair cells to regenerate (Forge et al., 1993; Warchol et al., 1993).

Theories of Pitch Perception

To explain how the auditory system converts sound waves into sensations of pitch, researchers have outlined two distinct theories: place theory and frequency theory.

Place theory was initially proposed by Hermann von Helmholtz in the 1800s and was later modified, elaborated, and tested by **Georg von Békésy,** who won a Nobel Prize for this work in 1961. Place theory is based on the fact that the basilar membrane moves when sound waves are conducted through the inner ear. Different frequencies produce their most movement at particular locations along the basilar membrane. For high-frequency tones, the wave motion is greatest at the base of the cochlea, where the oval and round windows are located. For low-frequency tones, the greatest wave motion of the basilar membrane is at the opposite end. So place theory states that perception of pitch depends upon the specific location on the basilar membrane at which the greatest stimulation occurs.

Place theory suggests that pitch corresponds to the location of greatest stimulation along the basilar membrane.

The second theory, **frequency theory,** explains pitch by the rate of vibration of the basilar membrane. This theory predicts that a sound wave with a frequency of 100 Hz will set the basilar membrane vibrating 100 times per second. The frequency theory also predicts that the vibrations of the basilar membrane will cause neurons to fire at the same rate, so that rate of firing is the neural code for pitch. One problem with this theory is that individual neurons cannot fire rapidly enough to represent high-pitched sounds, because none of them can fire more than 1000 times per second. This limitation makes it impossible for one neuron to distinguish sounds above 1000 Hz—which, of course, your auditory system can do quite well. The limitation might be overcome by the **volley principle,** which explains what might happen at such high frequencies. As shown in **Figure 7.22**, several neurons in a combined action, or volley, could fire at the frequency that matched a stimulus tone of 2000 Hz, 3000 Hz, and so on (Wever, 1949).

Frequency theory suggests that pitch corresponds to the rate of vibrations along the basilar membrane.

As with the trichromatic and opponent-process theories of color vision, the place and frequency theories each successfully accounts for different aspects of your experience of pitch. Frequency theory accounts well for coding frequencies below about 5000 Hz. At higher frequencies, neurons cannot fire quickly and precisely enough to code a signal adequately, even in volley.

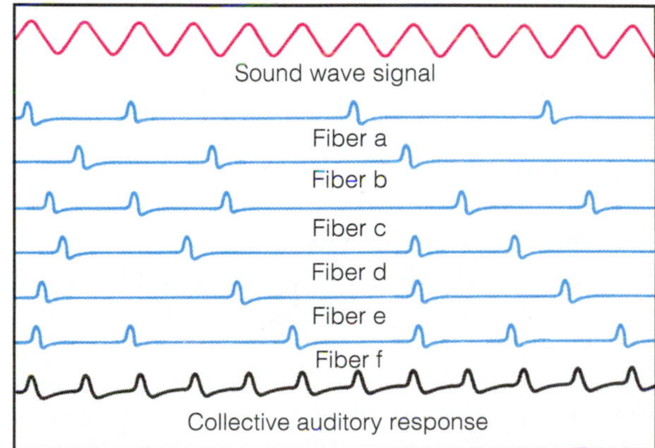

Figure 7.22 The Volley Principle
The total collective activity of the auditory (black) nerve cells has a pattern that corresponds to the input sound wave (red) even though each individual fiber may not be firing fast enough to follow the sound wave pattern.

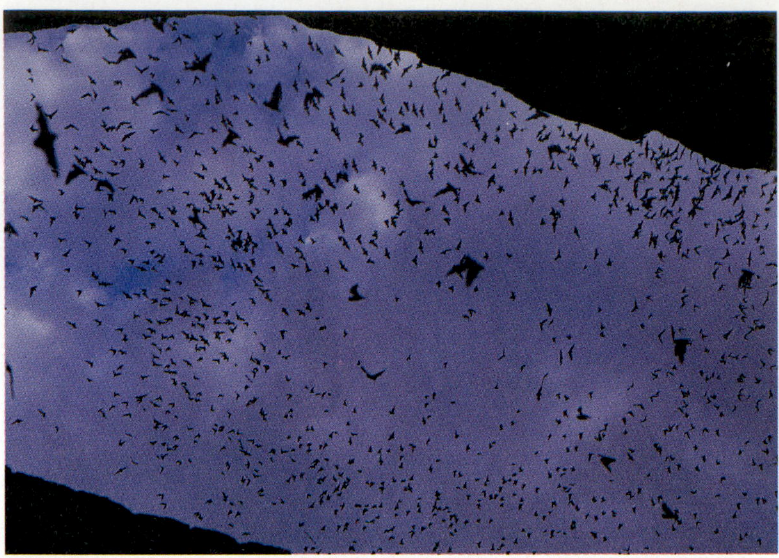

Bats are one of the few species that navigate by echolocation instead of vision.

Place theory accounts well for perception of pitch at frequencies above 1000 Hz. Below 1000 Hz, the entire basilar membrane vibrates so broadly that it cannot provide a signal distinctive enough for the neural receptors to use as a means of distinguishing pitch. Between 1000 and 5000 Hz, both mechanisms can operate. A complex sensory task is divided between two systems that, together, offer greater sensory precision than either system alone could provide. We will next see that you also possess two converging neural systems to help you localize sounds in the environment.

Sound Localization

Porpoises and bats do not use vision to locate objects in dark waters or dark caves. Instead, they use *echolocation*—they emit high-pitched sounds that bounce off objects, giving them feedback about the objects' distances, locations, sizes, textures, and movements. Although humans lack this special ability, you do use sounds to determine the location of objects in space, especially when seeing them is difficult. You do so through two mechanisms: assessments of the relative timing and relative intensity of the sounds that arrive at each ear (Middlebrooks & Green, 1991; Phillips, 1993).

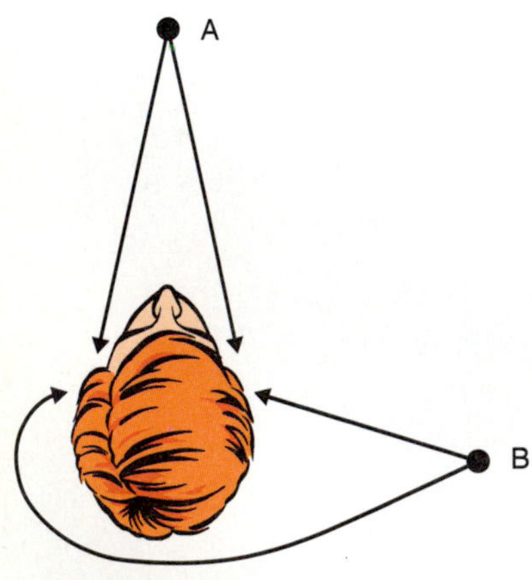

Figure 7.23 Time Disparity and Sound Localization
The brain uses differences in the time course with which sounds arrive at the two ears to localize the sounds in space.

The first mechanism involves neurons that compare the relative times when incoming sound reaches each ear. A sound off to your right side, for example, reaches your right ear before your left (see point B in **Figure 7.23**). Neurons in your auditory system are specialized to fire most actively for specific time delays between the two ears. Your brain uses this information about disparities in arrival time to make precise estimates for the likely origins of a sound in space.

The second mechanism relies on the principle that a sound has a slightly greater intensity in the first ear at which it arrives—because your head itself casts a *sound shadow* that weakens the signal. These intensity differences depend on the relative size of the wavelength of a tone with respect to your head. Large-wavelength, low-frequency tones show virtually no intensity differences, whereas small-wavelength, high-frequency tones show measurable intensity differences. Your brain, once again, has specialized cells that detect intensity differences in the signals arriving at your two ears.

But what happens when a sound creates neither a timing nor an intensity difference? In Figure 7.23, a sound originating at point A would have this property. With your eyes closed, you cannot tell its exact location. So you must move your head—to reposition your ears—to break the symmetry and provide the necessary information for sound localization.

YOUR OTHER SENSES

We have devoted the most attention to vision and hearing because scientists have studied them most thoroughly. However, your ability both to survive in and to enjoy the external environment relies on your full repertory of senses. We will close our discussion of sensation with brief analyses of several of your other senses.

Smell

You can probably imagine circumstances in which you'd be just as happy to give up your sense of smell: Did you ever have a family dog who lost a battle with a skunk? But to avoid that skunk experience, you'd also have to give up the smells of fresh roses, hot buttered popcorn, and sea breezes. Odors—both good and bad—first make their presence known by interacting with receptor proteins on the membranes of tiny hairs in your nose (*olfactory cilia*). It takes only eight molecules of a substance to initiate one of these nerve impulses, but at least 40 nerve endings must be stimulated before you can smell the substance. Once initiated, these nerve impulses convey odor information to the **olfactory bulb,** located just above the receptors and just below the frontal lobes of the cerebrum (see **Figure 7.24**). Odor stimuli start the process of smell by stimulating an influx of chemical substances into ion channels in olfactory neurons, an event that, as you may recall from Chapter 3, triggers an action potential (Restrepo et al., 1990). Your sense of smell is one of very few neural systems in which you acquire new neurons on an ongoing

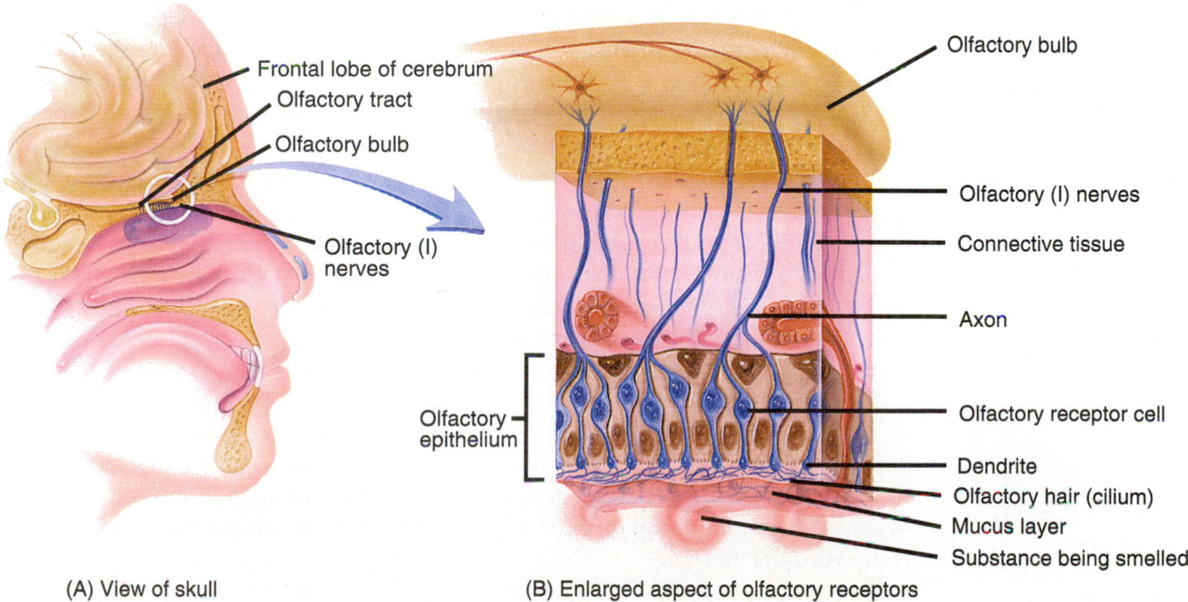

Figure 7.24 Receptors for Smell

basis. When your olfactory neurons age and die, they are replaced by new cells that form their own connections to the olfactory bulb (Farbman, 1992).

Smell presumably evolved as a system for detecting and locating food (Moncrieff, 1951). For many species, smell is also used to detect potential sources of danger. It serves this function well because organisms do not have to come into direct contact with other organisms in order to smell them. In addition, smell can be a powerful form of active communication. Members of some species communicate with each other by secreting and detecting chemical signals called pheromones. **Pheromones** are chemical substances used within a given species to signal sexual receptivity, danger, territorial boundaries, and food sources. For example, worker ants and bees use pheromone signals to let others in their colonies or hives know where they found a food source (Marler & Hamilton, 1966).

The significance of the sense of smell varies greatly across species. Dogs, rats, insects, and many other creatures for whom smell is central to survival have a far keener sense of smell than humans do. Relatively more of their brain area is devoted to smell. Humans seem to use the sense of smell primarily in conjunction with taste to seek and sample food, but there is some evidence that humans may also secrete and sense sexual pheromones. Suggestive evidence comes, for example, from the fact that, over time, menstrual cycles of close friends in women's dormitories have been shown to fall into a pattern of synchrony (McClintock, 1971). This synchronization has been attributed to chemical signals carried through the sense of smell (Cutler et al., 1986; Preti et al., 1986). Further evidence that smell retains, for humans, some of its evolutionary function comes from the fact that about a fourth of the people with smell disorders find that their sex drive disappears (Henkin, in Ackerman, 1990).

Why would a man with chronic sinus trouble be ill-advised to take up wine tasting?

Taste

Although food and wine gourmets are capable of making remarkably subtle and complex taste distinctions, many of their sensations are really smells and not tastes. Taste and smell work together closely when you eat. In fact, when you have a cold, food seems tasteless, because your nasal passages are blocked and you can't smell the food. Demonstrate this principle for yourself: hold your nose and try to tell the difference between foods of similar texture but different tastes, such as pieces of apple and raw potato. Some students living in dormitories with notoriously bad food have reported that wearing nose plugs to meals makes everything taste uniformly bland—which is better than the usual taste!

The surface of your tongue is covered with *papillae,* which give it a bumpy appearance. Many of these papillae contain clusters of taste receptor cells called the **taste buds** (see **Figure 7.25**). Single-cell recordings of taste receptors show that individual receptor cells respond best to one of the four primary taste qualities: sweet, sour, bitter, and saline (salty) (Frank & Nowlis, 1989). Although the receptor cells may produce small responses to other tastes, the "best" response most directly encodes quality.

Taste receptors can be damaged by many things you put in your mouth, such as alcohol, cigarette smoke, and acids. Fortunately, your taste receptors get replaced every few days—even more frequently than smell receptors. Indeed, the taste system is the most resistant to damage of all your sensory systems; it is extremely rare for anyone to suffer a total, permanent taste loss (Bartoshuk, 1990).

Touch and Skin Senses

The skin is a remarkably versatile organ. In addition to protecting you against surface injury, holding in body fluids, and helping regulate body tem-

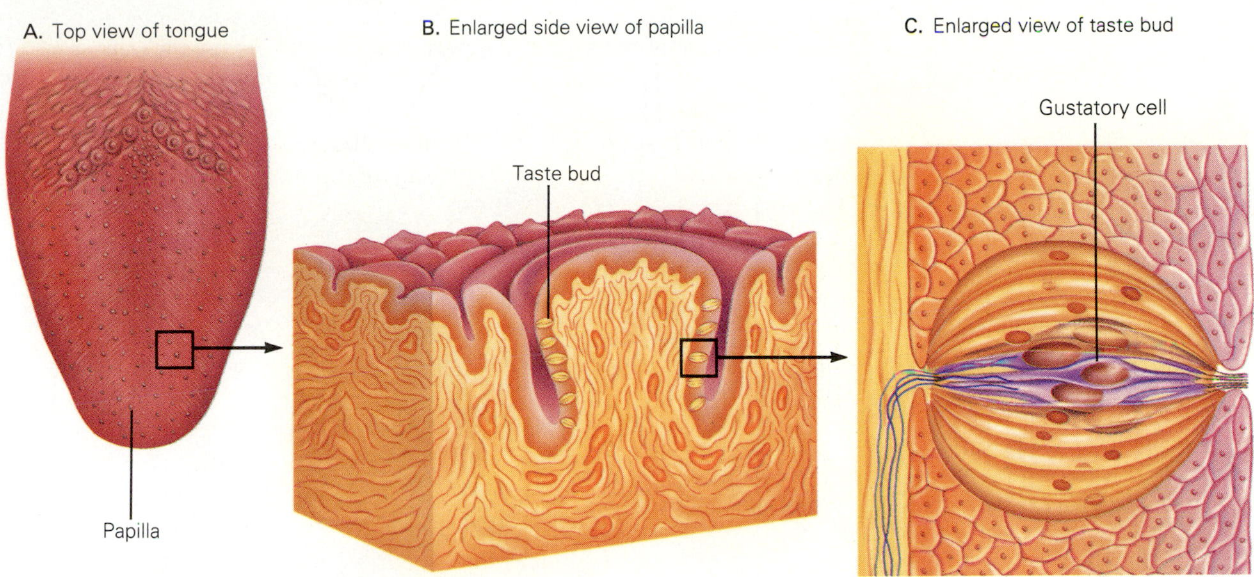

Figure 7.25 Receptors for Taste
Part A shows the distribution of the papillae on the upper side of the tongue. Part B shows a single papilla enlarged so that the individual taste buds are visible. Part C shows one of the taste buds enlarged.

perature, it contains nerve endings that produce sensations of pressure, warmth, and cold. These sensations are called the **cutaneous senses** (skin senses).

The skin senses include sensitivity to pressure, warmth, and cold.

Because you receive so much sensory information through your skin, many different types of receptor cells operate close to the surface of the body (see **Figure 7.26**). Each of the types of receptors pictured respond to somewhat different patterns of contact with the skin (Sekuler & Blake, 1994). As two examples, *Meissner corpuscles* respond best when something rubs against the skin, while *Merkel disks* are most active when a small object exerts steady pressure against the skin. You may be surprised to learn that you have separate receptors for warmth and coolness. Rather than having one type of receptor that works like a thermometer, your brain integrates separate warm and cool signals to monitor changes in environmental temperature.

The skin's sensitivity to pressure varies tremendously over the body. For example, you are ten times more accurate in sensing the position of stimulation on your fingertips than on your back. The variation in sensitivity of different body regions is shown by the greater density of nerve endings in these regions and also by the greater amount of sensory cortex devoted to them. In Chapter 3, you learned that your sensitivity is greatest where you need it most—on your face, tongue, and hands. Precise sensory feedback from these parts of the body permits effective eating, speaking, and grasping.

One aspect of cutaneous sensitivity plays a central role in human relationships: *touch*. Through touch, you communicate to others your desire to give or receive comfort, support, love, and passion. However, where you get touched or touch someone else makes a difference; those areas of the skin surface that give rise to erotic, or sexual, sensations are called **erogenous zones.** Other touch-sensitive erotic areas vary in their arousal potential for different individuals, depending on learned associations and the concentration of sensory receptors in the areas.

Touch may also play a role in survival. For example, premature babies who were massaged for 45 minutes a day during their hospital stays not only grew faster than untouched preemies, but their mental development was also

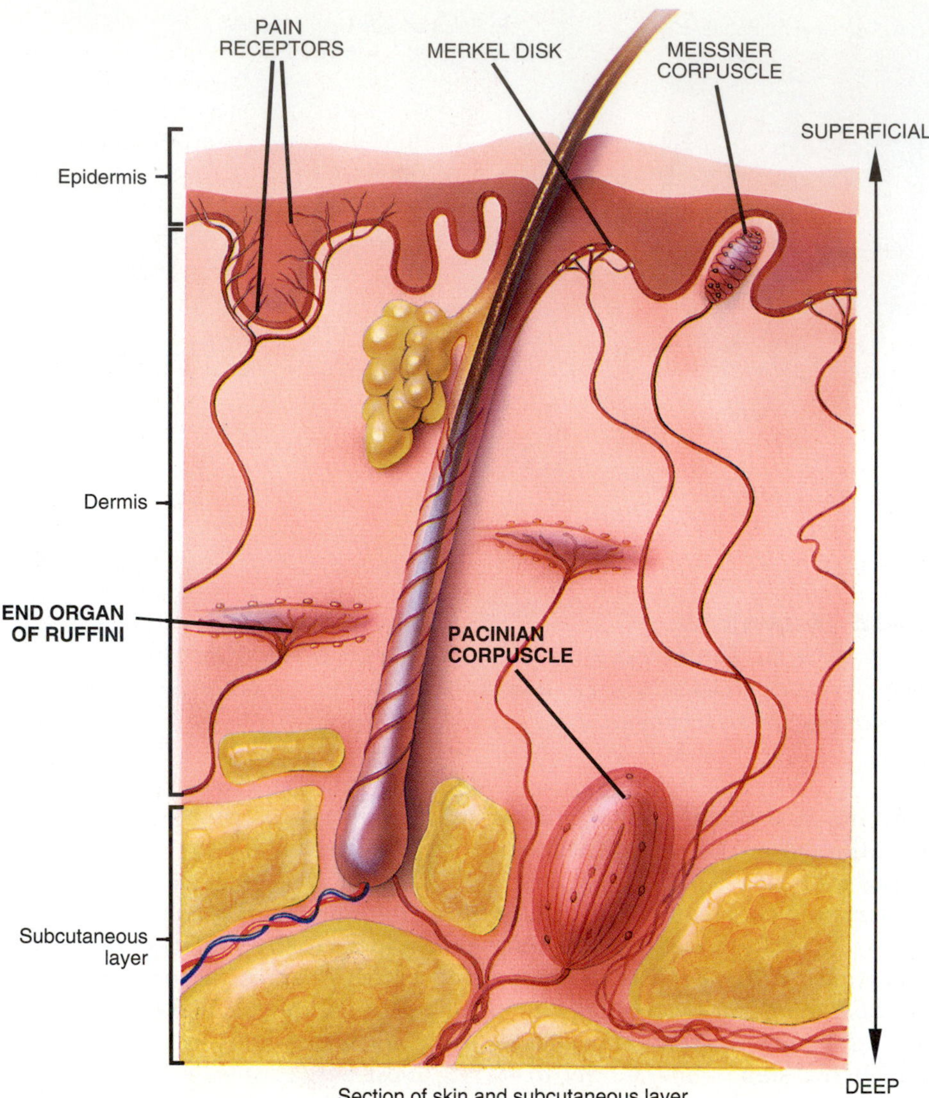

Figure 7.26 Receptors for the Cutaneous Senses

enhanced by the touch (Field & Schanberg, 1990). Comparable research with rats shows that vigorous stimulation releases growth hormones and activates the growth enzyme ODC (onithine decarboxylase) in the brain and other vital organs. Rat pups that were handled daily in their early lives showed a lifelong enhancement of many aspects of their health. Compared to control animals, the stimulated pups were more resistant to stress and grew old more gracefully, sustaining more brain cells and better memory than unstimulated pups (Meany et al., 1988). The practical message is clear: touch those you care about often and encourage others to touch you—it not only feels good, it's healthy for you and for them (Lynch, 1979; Montague, 1986).

Research with both human and animal infants indicates that touch may promote physical growth and mental development.

The Vestibular and Kinesthetic Senses

The next pair of senses we will describe may be entirely new to you, since they do not have receptors you can see directly, like eyes, ears, or noses. Your **vestibular sense** tells you how your body—especially your head—is oriented in the world with respect to gravity. The receptors for this information are tiny hairs in fluid-filled sacs and canals in the inner ear. The hairs bend when the fluid moves and presses on them, which is what happens when you turn your head quickly. The *saccule* and *utricle* (shown in Figure 7.21) tell you about acceleration or deceleration. The three canals, called the *semicircular canals,* are at right angles to each other and, thus, can tell you about motion in any direction. They inform you how your head is moving when you turn, nod, or tilt it.

People who lose their vestibular sense because of accidents or disease are initially quite disoriented and prone to falls and dizziness. However, most of these people eventually compensate by relying more heavily on visual information. *Motion sickness* can occur when the signals from the visual system conflict with those from the vestibular system. People feel nauseated when reading in a moving car because the visual signal is of a stationary object, while the vestibular signal is of movement. Drivers rarely get motion sickness because they are both seeing and feeling motion.

Why would riding in the front seat of a roller coaster be less likely to make you nauseated than riding in the rear?

Whether you are standing erect, drawing pictures, or making love, your brain needs to have accurate information about the current positions and movement of your body parts relative to each other. The **kinesthetic sense** (also called kinesthesis) provides constant sensory feedback about what the body is doing during motor activities. Without it, you would be unable to coordinate most voluntary movements.

You have two sources of kinesthetic information: receptors in the joints and receptors in the muscles and tendons. Receptors that lie in the joints respond to pressures that accompany different positions of the limbs and to pressure changes that accompany movements of the joints. Receptors in the muscles and tendons respond to changes in tension that accompany muscle shortening and lengthening.

Receptors for the vestibular sense are located in the inner ear, while the receptors for the kinesthetic sense are in the joints, muscles, and tendons.

The brain often integrates information from your kinesthetic sense with information from touch senses. Your brain, for example, can't grasp the full meaning of the signals coming from each of your fingers if it doesn't know exactly where your fingers are in relation to each other. Imagine that you pick up an object with your eyes closed. Your sense of touch may allow you to guess that the object is a stone, but your kinesthetic sense will enable you to know how large it is.

PAIN

Earlier we reviewed the beneficial aspects of touch. You know, however, that certain forms of physical contact can lead to pain. **Pain** is the body's response to stimulation from noxious stimuli—those that are intense enough to cause tissue damage or threaten to do so. Are you entirely happy that you have such a well-developed pain sense? Your answer probably should be "yes and no." On the "yes" side, your pain sense is critical for survival. People born with congenital insensitivity to pain feel no hurt, but their bodies often become scarred and their limbs deformed from injuries that they could have avoided had their brains been able to warn them of danger. In fact, because of their failure to notice and respond to tissue-damaging stimuli, they tend to die young (Manfredi et al., 1981). Their experience makes you aware that pain serves as an essential defense signal—it warns you of potential harm.

On the "no" side, there are certainly times when you would be happy to be able to turn your pain sense off. About one third of Americans suffer from persistent or recurring pain (Wallis, 1984). Some 100 million Americans experience back pain, 90 million are debilitated by arthritic pain, and more than 40 million suffer annually from headaches. Medical treatment for pain and the workdays lost because of pain are estimated to cost more than

$55 billion annually in the United States (Kraus, 1990). Depression and even suicide can result from the seemingly endless nagging of chronic pain.

Researchers generally wish to understand the mechanisms that produce sensations of pain so that they can find more efficient techniques for alleviating suffering. *Acute pain* is studied experimentally in laboratories with paid volunteers who experience varying degrees of a precisely regulated stimulus, such as heat applied briefly to a small area of the skin. This procedure can test a subject's *tolerance* for pain as well as measure the sensory and subjective responses to it—without causing any damage to the skin tissue. In some cases, a human subject's nerve impulses are monitored by passing a slender recording sensor through the skin into the nerve fiber itself. This enables the researcher to listen to signals being sent by cells in the peripheral nervous system to the brain. *Chronic pain* is typically studied in hospital research clinics as part of a treatment program to find new ways to alleviate it.

Pain Mechanisms

Almost all animals are born with some type of pain defense system that triggers automatic withdrawal reflexes to certain stimulus events. When the stimulus intensity reaches threshold, organisms respond by escaping—if they can. In addition, they quickly learn to identify painful stimulus situations, avoiding them whenever possible.

People can suffer from two kinds of pain: *nociceptive* and *neuropathic.* **Nociceptive pain** is the negative feeling induced by a noxious external stimulus; for example, the feeling you have when you touch a hot stove with your hand. Specialized nerve endings in the skin send the pain message up your arm, through the spinal cord, and into your brain, which issues the "pull away" command. By withdrawing, you can make this type of pain stop. **Neuropathic pain** is caused by the abnormal functioning or overactivity of nerves. It comes from injury or disease of nerves caused by accidents or cancer, for example. Drugs and other therapies that calm the nerves can relieve much of this type of pain.

Nociceptive pain is induced by contact with an external stimulus, whereas neuropathic pain is the result of abnormal functioning or overactivity of nerves caused by injury or diseases.

Scientists have begun to identify the specific sets of receptors that respond to pain-producing stimuli. They have learned that some receptors respond only to temperature, others to chemicals, others to mechanical stimuli, and still others to combinations of pain-producing stimuli. This network of pain fibers is a fine meshwork that covers your entire body. Peripheral nerve fibers send pain signals to the central nervous system by two pathways: a fast-conducting set of nerve fibers that are covered with myelin and slower, smaller nerve fibers without any myelin coating. Starting at the spinal cord, the impulses are relayed to the thalamus and then to the cerebral cortex, where the location and intensity of the pain are identified, the significance of the injury is evaluated, and action plans are formulated (McKean, 1986).

Researchers have used both PET scans and magnetic resonance imaging to discover where pain is represented in the brain. In experimental studies with healthy, awake volunteers subjected to nociceptive heat pain, the researchers found that pain information is not distributed over large areas of the cortex. Instead, signals of pain intensity are processed by specific sites in the parietal and frontal cortical areas. Emotional reactions to pain are processed in a different region—by the limbic system (Talbot et al., 1991).

The Psychology of Pain

Your emotional responses, context factors, and your interpretation of the situation can be as important as actual physical stimuli in determining how much pain you experience (Turk, 1994). The importance of psychological processes in the experience of pain is shown in two extreme cases—one in which there is pain but there is no physical stimulus for it and another in

The sensation of pain may not be directly related to the intensity of the stimulus. Individuals taking part in religious rituals, such as walking on a bed of hot coals, are able to block out pain.

which there is no pain but there is an intensely painful stimulus. For example, up to 10 percent of people who have limbs amputated report extreme or chronic pain in the limb that is no longer there—the **phantom limb phenomenon** (Melzack, 1989). In contrast, some individuals who take part in religious rituals are able to block out pain while participating in activities involving intense stimulation, such as walking on a bed of hot coals or having their bodies pierced with needles.

Your experience of pain is influenced not only by the actual physical stimuli but also by your emotional response, context factors, and your interpretation of the situation.

Much research points to the conclusion that the pain one feels is affected by the context in which it occurs and by learned habits of response (Weisenberg, 1977). Because pain is in part a psychological response, it can be modified by treatments that make use of mental processes, such as hypnosis, deep relaxation, and thought-distraction procedures. For example, the Lamaze method of preparation for childbirth without anesthetics attempts to reduce the woman's intense labor pains by combining several of these methods. Lamaze breathing exercises aid relaxation and focus attention away from the pain area. The use of distracting, pleasant images, massage that creates gentle counterstimulation, and social support from a coaching spouse or friend all work to give the prospective mother a greater sense of control over this painful situation. Research has shown that such techniques increase the subject's pain tolerance in other experiences as well. For example, pregnant women who have received Lamaze training are able to keep their hands immersed in ice water longer than they were before the training (Worthington et al., 1983).

One of the most potent of all treatments for pain is *placebo therapy* (Fish, 1973). Pain can be relieved by drugs expected to be painkillers that are, in fact, inert substances with no medicinal value. Believing that a particular treatment will lead to pain reduction is sufficient to bring about major psychological and physiological relief in many people. Research evidence suggests that the one third of the population who are positive placebo responders may have higher concentrations of endorphins—the body's natural painkillers—than other people do (Levine et al., 1974).

How are pain sensations affected by the psychological context? One theory about the way pain may be modulated is known as the **gate-control theory,** developed by **Ronald Melzack** (1973, 1980). This theory suggests that certain cells in the spinal cord act as neurological gates, interrupting and

Taste and Pain

Have you ever had this experience? You are eating a very "hot" dish in a Chinese or Mexican restaurant and you accidentally bite directly into a chili pepper. In just moments you go from enjoyment to intense pain. If this *has* happened, then you know that, in the realm of taste, there is a fine line between what gives pleasure and what gives pain. Let's explore this relationship.

Physiologically, it's easy to explain why hot pepper can cause you pain. On your tongue, your taste buds have associated with them nociceptive pain fibers (Bartoshuk, 1993). Thus the very same chemical that can stimulate the receptors in your taste buds can stimulate the closely allied pain fibers. In the case of hot pepper, this chemical is *capsaicin.* If you want to enjoy a spicy meal, you have to keep the concentration of capsaicin in your meal sufficiently low, so that your taste receptors are more active than your pain receptors.

But why, you might wonder, do different people have such obvious differences in their preferences for hot food? People often find it very difficult to understand how their friends can or cannot eat food that is very spicy. Again, we can look to physiology to explain these differences. **Figure 7.27** shows photographs of tongues from two individuals studied by **Linda Bartoshuk** and her colleagues. You can see that one tongue has considerably more taste buds than the other. If there are more taste buds, there will be more pain receptors. Therefore, people with more taste buds are more likely to get a strong pain response from capsaicin. The group of individuals who have more taste buds have been dubbed *supertasters* (Bartoshuk, 1993). They form a sharp contrast, in the extremes of their sensory experiences, to *nontasters.* For many taste sensations, these two groups are equivalent—you wouldn't know at most times whether you were a supertaster, a nontaster, or somewhere in between. The differences arise only for certain chemicals—capsaicin is an important example.

The variations in the density of taste buds on different people's tongues appear to be genetic (Bartoshuk et al., 1994). Women are much more likely to be supertasters than are men. Supertasters generally have more sensitivity to bitter chemicals—a sensory quality shared by most poisons. You can imagine that, if women generally were responsible for nurturing and feeding offspring over the course of evolution, the children of women with greater taste sensitivity would be more likely to survive. Because taster status is genetic, you can find preference differences among children at very young ages (Anliker et al., 1991). Five- to 7-year-old supertasters preferred milk to cheddar cheese. This

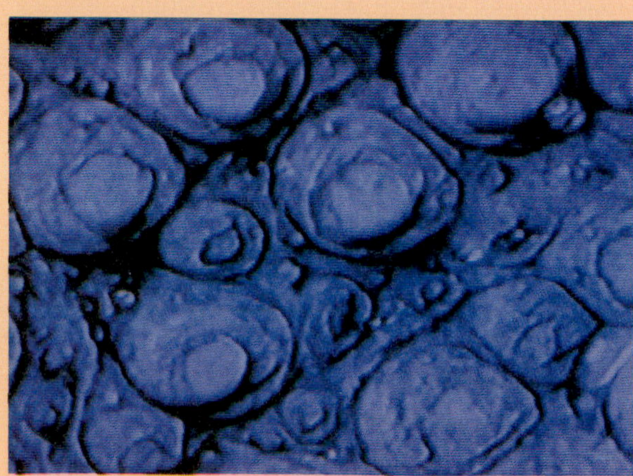

Figure 7.27 (A) The tongue of a supertaster

(B) The tongue of a nontaster

preference was reversed for nontasters. Why? The supertasters may perceive the milk as sweeter and the cheese as more bitter than do the nontasters. Thus genetic differences may help explain why some young children have such strong (and vocal) taste preferences.

But let's return to the restaurant meal at which you have had your painful accident. What you might have noticed is that the sensation of pain fades over time. In this respect, the pain receptors in your mouth act like other sensory receptors: over time, you adapt (or habituate) to a constant stimulus. Medical researchers have explored the possibility of using such adaptation as a treatment to help alleviate oral pain. The basic idea is that you can use capsaicin to fatigue the mouth's pain receptors and thereby mute their response to other sources of pain. Ann Berger and her colleagues (1995) have given cancer patients suffering from painful oral sores taffy laced with cayenne pepper. Although the candy itself provided an initial burning sensation, it reliably helped to alleviate pain once the burn had faded. These researchers hope to increase their knowledge about the sensation of taste and pain to perfect this innovative treatment.

blocking some pain signals and letting others get through to the brain. Small fibers in the spine open these gates when signals from injured tissues are received, while the large fibers of the spine close the gates, shutting down the pain response. Treatment for chronic pain sometimes involves electrical stimulation designed to activate the gate-closing function of the large neural fibers.

The gate-control theory of pain suggests that certain cells in the spinal cord act as neurological gates, allowing some pain signals to reach the brain and blocking others.

The way you perceive your pain, what you communicate about it to others, and even the way you respond to pain-relieving treatments may reveal more about your psychological state—about the psychological context in which you interpret the pain—than about the intensity of the pain stimulus. What you perceive may be different from, and even independent of, what you sense—as you will see in Chapter 8, in our study of the psychology of perception.

Recapping Main Points

Sensory Knowledge of the World

Sensation is the first stage in the process of perception; it translates the physical energy of stimuli into neural codes via transduction. During sensory coding, the rate of neural firing and the pattern of neural impulses conveys information about stimulus intensity. Sensory quality is coded by specific neurons that are activated in sense receptors and by patterns of neural impulses in sensory pathways to the cortex. Adaptation enables sensory fibers to favor new stimulus signals. Psychophysics investigates psychological responses to physical stimuli. To study sensation, researchers measure absolute thresholds and just noticeable differences between stimuli. Signal detection corrects for response biases that affect the measurement of thresholds.

The Visual System

Photoreceptors in the retina, called rods and cones, convert light energy into neural impulses. Ganglion cells in the retina integrate input from receptors and bipolar cells. Their axons form the optic nerves that meet at the optic chiasma. Some information about the stimulus location is processed in the superior colliculus. Information about color and detail is processed in the visual cortex.

The wavelength of light is the stimulus for color. Color sensations differ in hue, saturation, and brightness. Color vision theory combines the trichromatic theory of three color receptors with the opponent-process theory of color systems composed of opponent elements.

Detection of stimulus features occurs through the action of feature detection cells in the retina and higher visual centers and the analysis of spatial frequencies of dark-light cycles. Contrasts in brightness form boundaries and distinct edges that give objects size, shape, and spatial orientation.

Hearing

Hearing is produced by sound waves that vary in frequency, amplitude, and complexity. In the cochlea, sound waves are transformed into fluid waves that move the basilar membrane. Hairs on the basilar membrane stimulate neural impulses that are sent to the auditory cortex. Place theory best explains the coding of high frequencies, and frequency theory best explains the coding of low frequencies. Two pairs of neural mechanisms compute the relative intensity and timing of sounds coming to each ear.

Your Other Senses

Smell and taste respond to the chemical properties of substances and work together when people are seeking and sampling food. Olfaction is accomplished by odor-sensitive cells deep in the nasal passages. Pheromones are chemical signals detected by smell. Taste receptors are taste buds embedded in papillae, mostly in the tongue. The cutaneous (skin) senses give sensations of pressure and temperature. The vestibular sense gives information about the direction and rate of body motion. The kinesthetic sense gives information about the position of body parts and helps coordinate motion. Pain is the body's response to potentially harmful stimuli. The physiological response to pain involves chemical reactions at the site of the pain stimulus and nerve impulses moving between the brain and the spinal cord. Pain is in part a psychological response that can be modified by treatments that emphasize mental processes and thought distraction.

Resources

Ackerman, D. (1990). *A natural history of the senses*. New York: Random House.

Agosta, W.C. (1992). *Chemical communication: The language of pheromones.* New York: W. H. Freeman.

Fletcher, R., & Voke, J. (1985). *Defective color vision.* New York: Taylor & Francis.

Melzack, R., & Wall, P. D. (1989). *The challenge of pain.* New York: Penguin. These prominent researchers describe topics of interest such as phantom limb pain and the psychological issues in pain relief.

Sacks, O. (1995). *An anthropologist on Mars: Seven paradoxical tales*. New York: Knopf.

Sekular, R., & Blake, R. (1994). *Perception* (3rd ed.). New York: McGraw-Hill.

Yost, W. A., Poppet, A. N., & Fay, R. R. (Eds.). (1993). *Human psychophysics.* New York: Springer-Verlag.

8

Perception

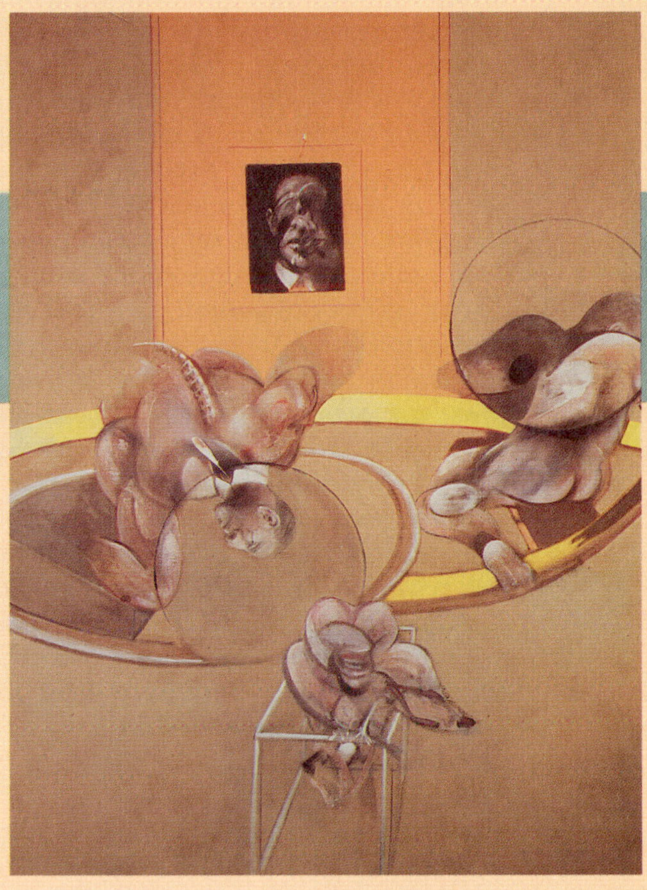

Sensing, Organizing, Identifying, and Recognizing
- The Proximal and Distal Stimulus
- Reality, Ambiguity, and Illusions
- Approaches to the Study of Perception
- *Close-up: Ambiguity in Art*

Attentional Processes
- Selective Attention
- Attention and Objects in the Environment

Organizational Processes in Perception
- Region Segregation
- Figure, Ground, and Closure
- Shape: Figural Goodness and Reference Frames
- Principles of Perceptual Grouping
- Spatial and Temporal Integration
- Motion Perception
- Depth Perception
- Perceptual Constancies

Identification and Recognition Processes
- Bottom-up and Top-down Processes
- Object Recognition
- The Influence of Contexts and Expectations
- Creatively Playful Perception
- Final Lessons

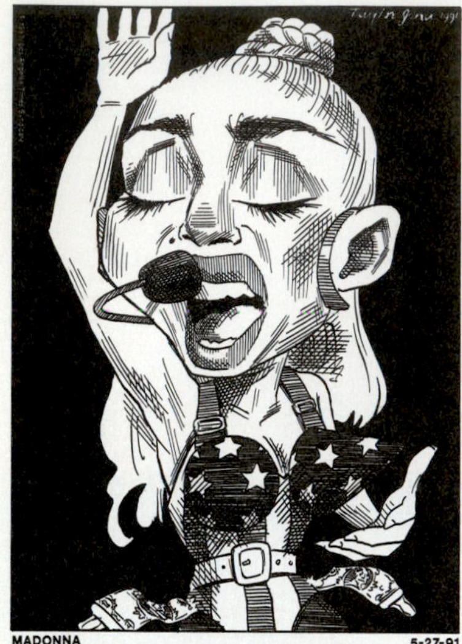

Figure 8.1 **What Enables You to Recognize These Celebrities?**

Who are the people in Figure 8.1? If their fame has not been too fleeting, you should be able to recognize each of these individuals. But is this what they really look like? Probably not, at least on their good days. Your skill at identifying each of these caricatures suggests that your perception *of the world relies on more than just the information arriving at your sensory receptors. Your ability to transform and interpret sensory information—your ability to have what you know interact with what you see—allows you to recognize Madonna, Oprah Winfrey, and Bill Clinton from these exaggerated portraits.*

In Chapter 7, we tried to convince you that your environment is filled with waves of light and sound—and it is—but that's not the way in which you experience the world. You don't "see" waves of light; you see a poster on the wall. You don't "hear" waves of sound; you hear music from a nearby radio. Sensation is what gets the show started, but something more is needed to make a stimulus meaningful and interesting and, most important, to make it possible for you to respond to it effectively. The processes of perception *provide the extra layers of interpretation that enable you to navigate successfully through your environment.*

We can offer a simple demonstration to help you think about the relationship between sensation and perception. Hold your hand as far as you can in front of your face. Now move it toward you. As you move your hand toward your eyes, it will take up more and more of your visual field. You may no longer be able to see the poster on the wall in back of your hand. How can your hand block out the poster? Has your hand gotten bigger? Has the poster gotten smaller? Your answer must be "Of course not!" This demonstration tells you something about the difference between sensation and perception. Your hand can block out the poster because, as it comes closer to your face, the hand projects an increasingly larger image on your retina. It is your perceptual processes that allow you to understand that despite the change in the size of the projection on your retina, your hand—and the poster behind it—do not change in actual size.

We might say that the role of perception is to make sense of sensation. Perceptual processes extract meaning from the continuously changing, often chaotic, sensory input from external energy sources and organize it into stable, orderly percepts. A percept *is what is perceived—the phenomenological, or experienced, outcome of the process of perception. It is* not *a physical object or its image in a receptor but, rather, the psychological product of perceptual activity. Thus your percept of your hand remains stable over changes in the size of the image because your interpretation is governed by stable perceptual activities. Most of the time, sensing and perceiving occur so effortlessly, continuously, and automatically that you take them for granted. It is our goal in this chapter to allow you to understand and appreciate the processes that afford you a suitable account of the world, with such apparent ease. We begin with an overview of perceptual processes in the visual domain.*

SENSING, ORGANIZING, IDENTIFYING, AND RECOGNIZING

The term *perception,* in its broad usage, refers to the overall process of *apprehending* objects and events in the external environment—to sense them, understand them, identify and label them, and prepare to react to them. The process of perception is best understood when we divide it into three stages: sensation, perceptual organization, and identification/recognition of objects.

The three stages of perception are sensation, perceptual organization, and identification/recognition.

As we saw in Chapter 7, **sensation** refers to conversion of physical energy into the neural codes recognized by the brain. Sensation provides a first-pass representation of the basic facts of the visual field. Your retinal cells are organized to emphasize edges and contrasts while reacting only weakly to unchanging, constant stimulation. Cells in your brain's cortex extract features and spatial frequency information from this retinal input.

Perceptual organization refers to the next stage, in which an internal representation of an object is formed and a percept of the external stimulus is developed. The representation provides a working description of the perceiver's external environment. Perceptual processes provide estimates of an object's likely size, shape, movement, distance, and orientation. Those estimates are based on mental computations that integrate your past knowledge with the present evidence received from your senses and with the stimulus within its perceptual context. Perception involves *synthesis* (integration and combination) of simple sensory features, such as colors, edges, and lines, into the percept of an object that can be recognized later. These mental activities most often occur swiftly and efficiently, without conscious awareness.

To understand the difference between these first two stages more clearly, consider the case study of Dr. Richard, whose brain damage left his sensation intact but altered his perceptual processes.

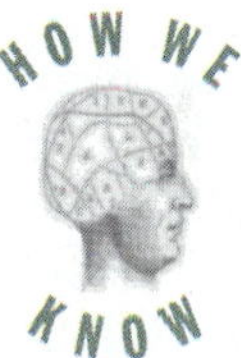

Dr. Richard was a psychologist with considerable training and experience in introspection. This special skill enabled him to make a unique and valuable contribution to psychology. However, tragically, he suffered brain damage that altered his visual experience of the world. Fortunately, the damage did not affect the centers of his brain responsible for speech, so he was able to describe quite clearly his subsequent unusual visual experiences. In general terms, the brain damage seemed to have affected his ability to put sensory data together properly. For example, Dr. Richard reported that if he saw a complex object, such as a person, and there were several other people nearby in his visual field, he sometimes saw the different parts of the person as separate parts, not belonging together in a single form. He also had difficulty combining the sound and sight of the same event. When someone was singing, he might see a mouth move and hear a song, but it was as if the sound had been dubbed with the wrong tape in a foreign movie.

To see the parts of an event as a whole, Dr. Richard needed some common factor to serve as "glue." For example, if the fragmented person moved, so that all parts went in the same direction, Dr. Richard would then perceive the parts reunited into a complete person. Even then, the perceptual "glue" would sometimes result in absurd configurations. Dr. Richard would frequently see objects of the same color, such as a banana, a lemon, and a canary, going together even if they were separated in space. People in crowds would seem to merge if they were wearing the same colored clothing. Dr. Richard's experiences of his environment were disjointed, fragmented, and bizarre—quite unlike what he had been used to before his problems began (Marcel, 1983).

There was nothing wrong with Dr. Richard's eyes or with his ability to *analyze* the properties of stimulus objects—he saw the parts and qualities of objects accurately. Rather, his problem lay in synthesis—putting the bits and pieces of sensory information together properly to form a unified, coherent perception of a single event in the visual scene. His case makes salient the distinction between sensory and perceptual processes. It also serves to remind you that both sensory analysis and perceptual organization must be going on all the time even though you are unaware of the way they are working or even that they are happening.

Identification and recognition, the third stage in this sequence, assigns meaning to percepts. Circular objects "become" baseballs, coins, clocks, oranges, and moons; people may be identified as male or female, friend or foe, movie star or rock star. At this stage, the perceptual question "What does the object look like?" changes to a question of identification—"What is this object?"—and to a question of recognition—"What is the object's function?" To identify and recognize what something is, what it is called, and how best to respond to it involves higher level cognitive processes, which include your theories, memories, values, beliefs, and attitudes concerning the object.

We have now given you a brief introduction to the stages of processing that enable you to arrive at a meaningful understanding of the perceptual world around you. Because Chapter 7 focused on sensation, we will devote the bulk of our attention here to aspects of perception beyond the initial transduction of physical energy. In everyday life, perception seems to be entirely effortless. We will try, beginning in the next section, to convince you that you actually do quite a bit of sophisticated processing, a lot of mental work, to arrive at this "illusion of ease."

The Proximal and Distal Stimulus

Imagine you are the person in **Figure 8.2**, surveying a room from an easy chair. Some of the light reflected from the objects in the room enters your eyes and forms images on your retinas. Figure 8.2 shows what would appear to your left eye as you sat in the room. (The bump on the right is your nose, and the hand and knee at the bottom are your own.) How does this retinal image compare with the environment that produced it?

One very important difference is that the retinal image is *two-dimensional,* whereas the environment is *three-dimensional.* This difference has many consequences. For instance, compare the shapes of the physical objects in Figure 8.2 with the shapes of their corresponding retinal images. The table, rug, window, and picture in the real-world scene are all rectangular, but only the image of the window actually produces a rectangle in your retinal image. The image of the picture is a trapezoid, the image of the table top is an irregular four-sided figure, and the image of the rug is actually three separate regions with more than 20 different sides! Here's our first perceptual puzzle: How do you manage to perceive all of these objects as simple, standard rectangles?

How can one person's thumb wipe out the Empire State Building?

The situation is, however, even a bit more complicated. You can also notice that many parts of what you perceive in the room are not actually present in your retinal image. For instance, you perceive the vertical edge between the two walls as going all the way to the floor, but your retinal image of that edge stops at the table top. Similarly, in your retinal image parts of the rug are hidden behind the table; yet this does not keep you from correctly perceiving the rug as a single, unbroken rectangle. In fact, when you consider all the differences between the environmental objects and the images of them on your retina, you may be surprised that you perceive the scene as well as you do.

The differences between a physical object in the world and its optical image on your retina are so profound and important that psychologists

A. Physical object (distal stimulus)

B. Optical image (proximal stimulus)

Figure 8.2 Interpreting Retinal Images

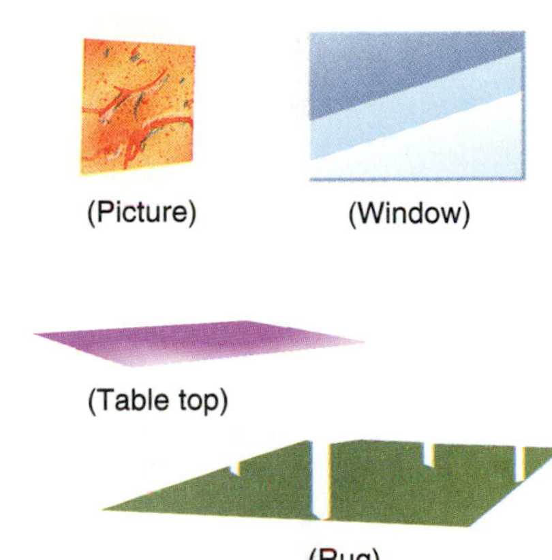

distinguish carefully between them as two different stimuli for perception. The physical object in the world is called the **distal stimulus** (distant from the observer) and the optical image on the retina is called the **proximal stimulus** (proximate, or near, to the observer), as shown **in Figure 8.3**.

The critical point of our discussion can now be restated more concisely: what you *perceive* corresponds to the *distal stimulus*—the "real" object in the environment—whereas the stimulus from which you must derive your information is the *proximal stimulus*—the image on the retina. The major computational task of perception can be thought of as the process of determining the distal stimulus from information contained in the proximal stimulus. This is true across perceptual domains. For hearing, touch, taste, and so on, perception involves processes that use information in the proximal stimulus to tell you about properties of the distal stimulus.

To show you how the distal stimulus and proximal stimulus fit with the three stages in perceiving, let's examine one of the objects in the scene from Figure 8.2: the picture hanging on the wall. In the sensory stage, this picture corresponds to a two-dimensional trapezoid in your retinal image; the top and bottom sides converge toward the right, and the left and right sides are different in length. This is the proximal stimulus. In the perceptual organization stage, you see this trapezoid as a rectangle turned away from you in three-dimensional space. You perceive the top and bottom sides as parallel,

The major task of visual perception is to interpret or identify the distal stimulus, the actual object in the environment, using the information from the proximal stimulus, the retinal image produced by the object.

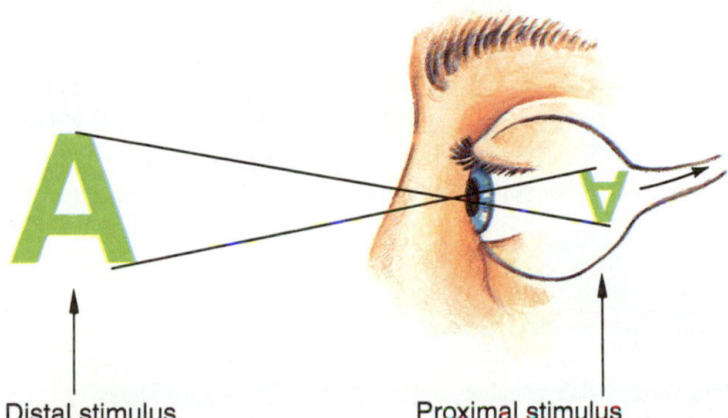

Figure 8.3 Distal and Proximal Stimulus

The distal stimulus is the pattern or external condition that is sensed and perceived. The proximal stimulus is the pattern of sensory activity that is determined by the distal stimulus. As illustrated here, the proximal stimulus may resemble the distal stimulus, but they are separate events.

but receding into the distance toward the right; you perceive the left and right sides as equal in length. Your perceptual processes have developed a strong *hypothesis* about the physical properties of the distal stimulus; now it needs an identity. In the recognition stage, you identify this rectangular object as a picture. **Figure 8.4** is a flowchart illustrating this sequence of events. The processes that take information from one stage to the next are shown as arrows between the boxes. By the end of this chapter, we will explain all the interactions represented in this figure.

Reality, Ambiguity, and Illusions

We have defined the task of perception as the identification of the distal stimulus from the proximal stimulus. Before we turn to some of the perceptual mechanisms that make this task successful, we want to discuss a bit more some other aspects of stimuli in the environment that make perception complex. Once again, you should look forward to learning how your perceptual processes deal with these complexities. We will discuss *ambiguous* stimuli and perceptual *illusions.*

Ambiguity

A primary goal of perception is to get an accurate "fix" on the world. Survival depends on accurate perceptions of objects and events in your environ-

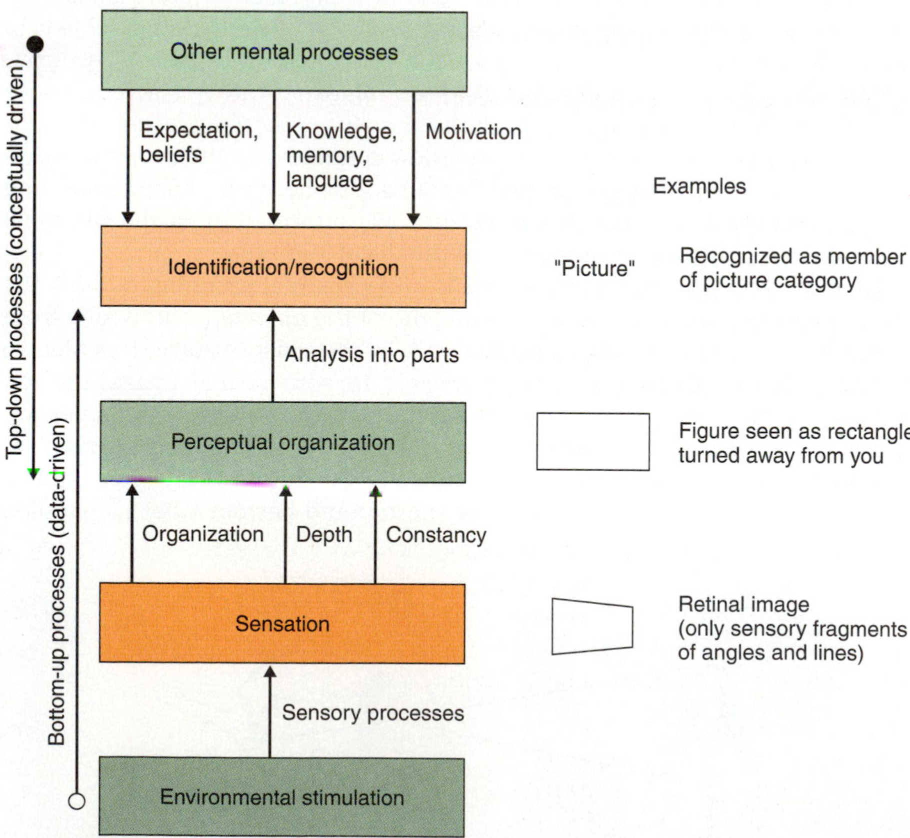

Figure 8.4 Sensation, Perceptual Organization, and Identification/Recognition Stages

The diagram outlines the processes that give rise to the transformation of incoming information at the stages of sensation, perceptual organization, and identification/ recognition. Bottom-up processing occurs when the perceptual representation is derived from the information available in the sensory input. Top-down processing occurs when the perceptual representation is affected by an individual's prior knowledge, motivations, expectations, and other aspects of higher mental functioning.

Figure 8.5 Ambiguous Picture

ment—Is that motion in the trees a tiger?—but the environment is not always easy to read. Take a look at the photo of black-and-white splotches in **Figure 8.5**. What is it? Try to extract the stimulus figure from the background. Try to see a dalmatian taking a walk. The dog is hard to find because it blends with the background, so its boundaries are not clear. (Hint: the dog is on the right side of the figure, with its head pointed toward the center.) This figure is *ambiguous* in the sense that critical information is missing, elements are in unexpected relationships, and usual patterns are not apparent. **Ambiguity** is an important concept in understanding perception because it shows that a *single image* at the sensory level can result in *multiple interpretations* at the perceptual and identification levels.

Ambiguous figures are confusing because they represent a single image at the sensory level that may have multiple interpretations at the perceptual organization and identification levels.

Figure 8.6 shows three examples of ambiguous figures. Each example permits two unambiguous but conflicting interpretations. Look at each image until you can see the two alternative interpretations. Notice that once you have seen both of them, your perception flips back and forth between them as you look at the ambiguous figure. This perceptual *instability* of ambiguous figures is one of their most important characteristics.

The vase/faces and the Necker cube are examples of ambiguity in the perceptual organization stage. You have two different perceptions of the same objects in the environment. The vase/faces can be seen as either a central white object on a black background or as two black objects with a white area between them. The Necker cube can be seen as a three-dimensional hollow cube either below you and angled to your left or above you and angled toward your right. With both vase and cube, the ambiguous alternatives are different physical arrangements of objects in three-dimensional space, both resulting from the same stimulus image.

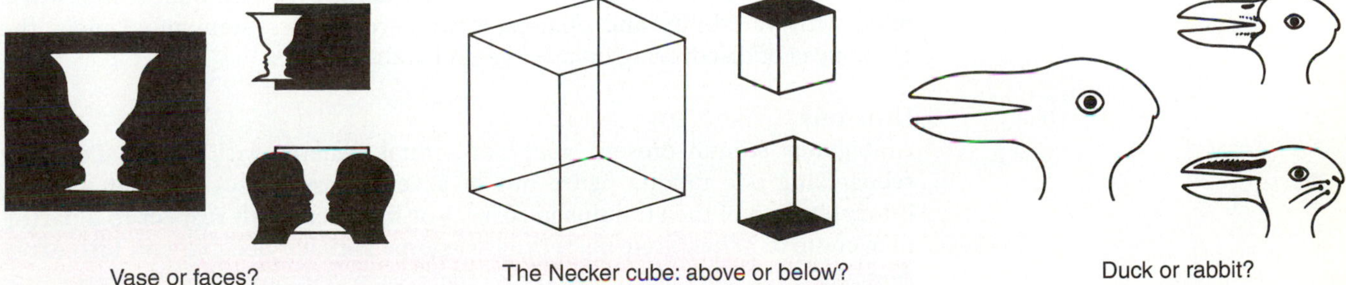

Vase or faces?
The Necker cube: above or below?
Duck or rabbit?

Figure 8.6 Perceptual Ambiguities

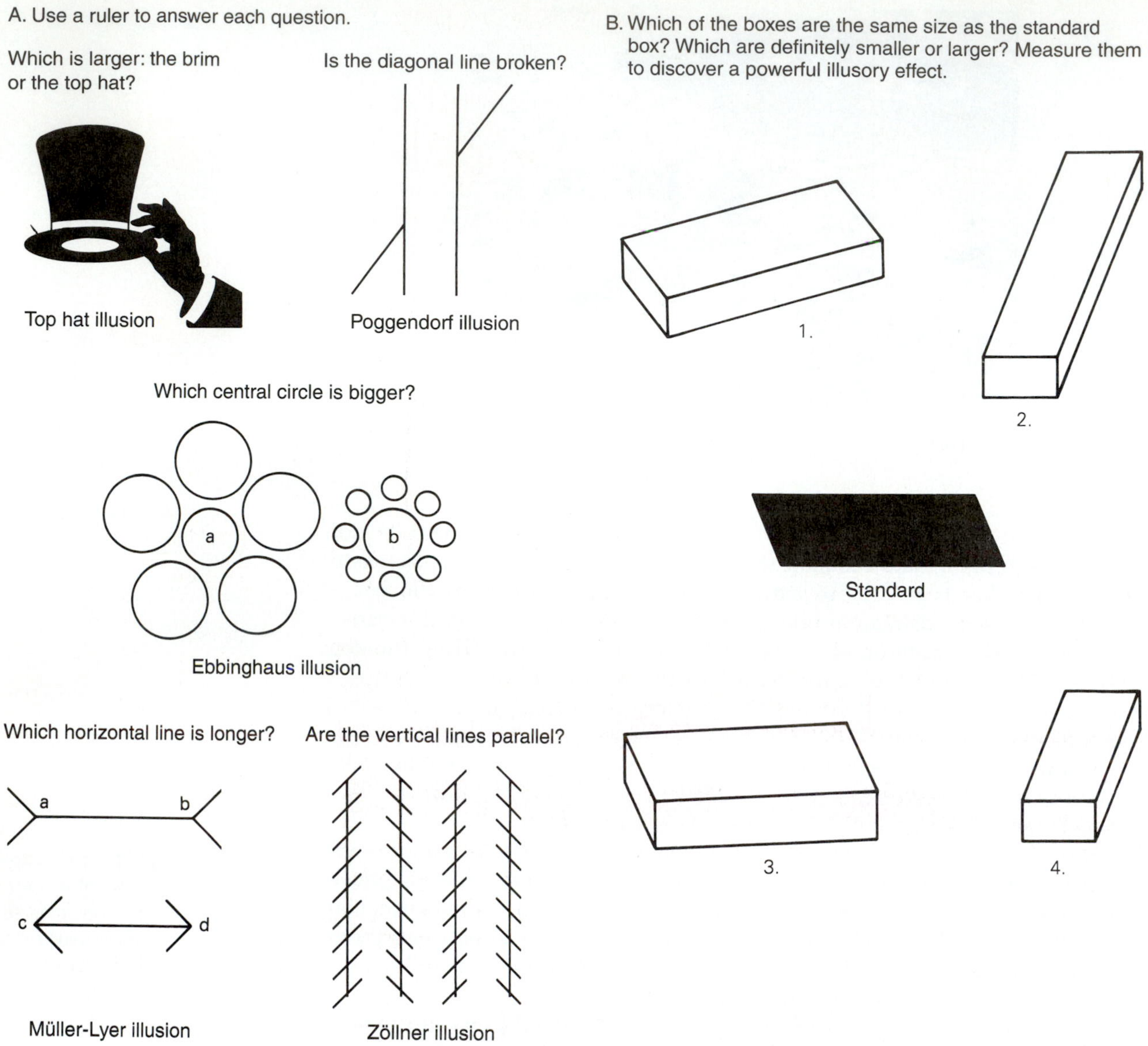

A. Use a ruler to answer each question.

Which is larger: the brim or the top hat?

Top hat illusion

Is the diagonal line broken?

Poggendorf illusion

Which central circle is bigger?

a

b

Ebbinghaus illusion

Which horizontal line is longer?

a b

c d

Müller-Lyer illusion

Are the vertical lines parallel?

Zöllner illusion

B. Which of the boxes are the same size as the standard box? Which are definitely smaller or larger? Measure them to discover a powerful illusory effect.

1.

2.

Standard

3.

4.

Figure 8.7 Six Illusions to Tease Your Brain

The duck/rabbit figure is an example of ambiguity in the recognition stage. It is perceived as the same physical shape in both interpretations. The ambiguity arises in determining the kind of object it represents and in how best to classify it, given the mixed set of information available.

One of the most fundamental properties of normal human perception is the tendency to transform ambiguity and uncertainty about the environment into a clear interpretation that you can act upon with confidence. In a world filled with variability and change, your perceptual system must meet the challenges of discovering invariance and stability.

Illusions

Ambiguous stimuli present your perceptual systems with the challenge of recognizing one unique figure out of several possibilities. One or another interpretation of the stimulus is correct or incorrect with respect to a particular context. When your perceptual systems actually deceive you into experiencing a stimulus pattern in a manner that is demonstrably incorrect, you are experiencing an **illusion.** The word *illusion* shares the same root as *ludicrous*—both stem from the Latin *illudere,* which means "to mock at." Illusions are shared by most people in the same perceptual situation because of shared physiology in sensory systems and overlapping experiences of the world. (As we explained in Chapter 4, this sets illusions apart from *hallucinations.* Hallucinations are nonshared perceptual distortions that individuals experience as a result of unusual physical or mental states.) Examine the classic illusions in **Figure 8.7**. Although it is most convenient for us to present you with visual illusions, illusions also exist abundantly in other sensory modalities such as hearing (Bregman, 1981; Shepard & Jordan, 1984) and taste (Todrank & Bartoshuk, 1991).

Since the first scientific analysis of illusions was published by J. J. Oppel in 1854–1855, thousands of articles have been written about illusions in nature, sensation, perception, and art. Oppel's modest contribution to the study of illusions was a simple array of lines that appeared longer when divided into segments than when only its end lines were present:

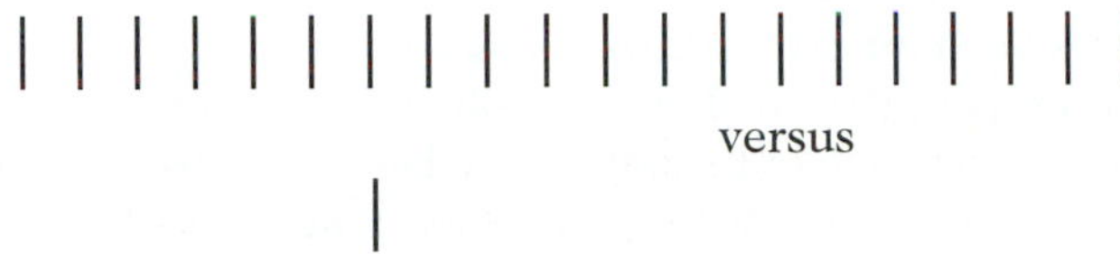

Oppel called his work the study of *geometrical optical illusions.* Illusions point out the discrepancy between percept and reality. They can demonstrate the abstract conceptual distinctions between sensation, perceptual organization, and identification and can help you understand some fundamental properties of perception (Cohen & Girgus, 1973).

Let's examine an illusion that works at the sensation level: the *Hermann grid,* in **Figure 8.8.** As you stare at the center of the grid, dark, fuzzy spots appear at the intersections of the white bars. How does that happen? The answer lies in something you read about in the last chapter—*lateral inhibition.* Assume the stimulus is registered by ganglion retinal cells, two of which have their receptive fields drawn in the lower corner of the grid. The receptive field at the center of the intersection has two white bars projecting through its surround, while the neighboring receptive field has only one. The

Figure 8.8 The Hermann Grid
Two ganglion-cell receptive fields are projected on this grid; it is an example of an illusion at the sensory stage.

Illusions at the sensation level generally occur because receptor processes have been stimulated in a way that generates a distorted image.

cell at the center, therefore, receives more light and can respond at a lower level because of the greater lateral inhibition by the surround. Its reduced response shows up as a dark spot in its center. Illusions at this level generally occur because the arrangement of a stimulus array sets off receptor processes in an unusual way that generates a distorted image.

Illusions in Reality

Are illusions just peculiar arrangements of lines, colors, and shapes used by artists and psychologists to plague unsuspecting people? Hardly. Illusions are a basic part of your everyday life. They are an inescapable aspect of the subjective reality you construct. And even though you may recognize an illusion, it can continue to occur and fool you again and again.

Consider your day-to-day experience of your home planet, the earth. You've seen the sun "rise" and "set" even though you know that the sun is sitting out there in the center of the solar system as decisively as ever. You can appreciate why it was such an extraordinary feat of courage for Christopher Columbus and other voyagers to deny the obvious illusion that the earth was flat and sail off toward one of its apparent edges. Similarly, when a full moon is overhead, it seems to follow you wherever you go even though you know the moon isn't chasing you. What you are experiencing is an illusion created by the great distance of the moon from your eye. When they reach the earth, the moon's light rays are essentially parallel and perpendicular to your direction of travel, no matter where you go.

Illusions have practical application in the real world, producing such desirable effects as making a small room look larger or making a technical workspace more appealing to the senses.

People can control illusions to achieve desired effects. Architects and interior designers use principles of perception to create objects in space that seem larger or smaller than they really are. A small apartment becomes more spacious when it is painted with light colors and sparsely furnished with low, small couches, chairs, and tables in the center of the room instead of against the walls. Psychologists working with NASA in the U.S. space program have researched the effects of environment on perception in order to design space capsules that have pleasant sensory qualities. Set and lighting directors of movies and theatrical productions purposely create illusions on film and on stage.

Despite all of these illusions—some more useful than others—you generally do pretty well getting around the environment. That is why researchers typically study illusions to help explain why perception ordinarily works so well. The illusions themselves suggest, however, that your perceptual systems cannot perfectly carry out the task of recovering the distal stimulus from the proximal stimulus.

Approaches to the Study of Perception

You now are acquainted with some of the major questions of perception: How does the perceptual system recover the structure of the environment? How is ambiguity resolved? Why do illusions arise? Before we move on to answer these questions, we need to give you more of a background in the types of theories that have dominated research on perception.

Many of the differences between these theories can be captured by the distinction between *nature* and *nurture* we introduced in Chapter 3. At issue is how much of a head start you have in dealing with the perceptual world by virtue of your possession of the human genotype. Do you, as a *nativist* might argue, come into the world with some types of innate knowledge or brain structures that aid your interpretation of the environment? Or do you, as an *empiricist* might assert, come into the world with a relatively blank slate, ready to learn what there is to learn about the perceptual world? Most modern theorists agree that your experience of the world consists of a combination of

Ambiguity in Art

The ambiguous figures that psychologists developed served as catalysts for several prominent modern artists who became fascinated with the complex, dynamic visual experiences the figures created for the viewers. These artists have used perceptual ambiguity as the central creative device in many of their works. On this page, you will find three examples. The first, by *Victor Vasarely,* at bottom left, produces depth reversals similar to the Necker cube. The corners of the surfaces can be seen either as coming out toward you or going away from you. The next, by *M. C. Escher,* is based on figure/ground reversals similar to the vase/faces. In *Sky and Water,* at top right, Escher has created an ambiguous mosaic of interweaving fish and birds at the center, where you tend to see the fish or the birds but not both. Toward the top and bottom of the work, the figures become gradually less ambiguous. Notice that after you look at the unambiguous birds at the top, you tend to see birds rather than fish in the ambiguous center section; but after you look at the unambiguous fish at the bottom, you tend to see fish rather than birds in the center section. This tendency demonstrates the influence of context on your perception, a topic we will discuss later in more detail.

The final example is *Slave Market with the Disappearing Bust of Voltaire,* by *Salvador Dali,* shown at bottom right. This work reveals a more complex ambiguity in which a whole section of the picture must be radically reorganized and reinterpreted to allow perception of the "hidden" bust of the French philosopher-writer Voltaire. The white sky under the lower arch is Voltaire's forehead and hair; the white portions of the two ladies' dresses are his cheeks, nose, and chin. (If you have trouble seeing him, try squinting, holding the book at arm's length, or taking off your glasses.) Once you have seen the bust of Voltaire in this picture, however, you will never be able to look at it without knowing where this Frenchman is hiding.

Most modern theorists agree that perceptual abilities are the products of both nature and nurture, but disagree on the size of the portion that should be attributed to each.

nature and nurture. We will see, however, that these theorists disagree on the size of the portions that make up this combination.

Helmholtz's Classical Theory

Hermann von Helmholtz argued for the importance of nurture, or experience, in perception.

In 1866, **Hermann von Helmholtz** argued for the importance of *experience*—or nurture—in perception. His theory emphasized the role of mental processes in interpreting the often ambiguous stimulus arrays that excite the nervous system. By using prior knowledge of the environment, an observer makes hypotheses, or inferences, about the way things really are. For instance, you would be likely to interpret your brief view of a four-legged creature moving through the woods as a dog rather than as a wolf. Perception is thus an *inductive* process, moving from specific images to inferences (reasonable hunches) about the general class of objects or events that the images might represent. Since this process takes place out of your conscious awareness, Helmholtz termed it **unconscious inference.** Ordinarily, these inferential processes work well. However, perceptual illusions can result when unusual circumstances allow multiple interpretations of the same stimulus or favor an old, familiar interpretation when a new one is required.

Helmholtz's theory broke perception down into two stages. In the first, *analytic* stage, the sense organs analyze the physical world into fundamental sensations. In the second, *synthetic* stage, you integrate and synthesize these sensory elements into perceptions of objects and their properties. Helmholtz's theory proposes that you learn how to interpret sensations on the basis of your experience with the world. Your interpretations are, in effect, informed guesses about your perceptions.

The Gestalt Approach

The Gestalt approach emphasized that a perceptual phenomenon must be viewed as a whole in order to be understood, and favored the role of nature, or innate processes, in perception.

Gestalt psychology, founded in Germany in the second decade of the twentieth century, put greater emphasis on the role of innate structures—nature—in perceptual experience. The main exponents of Gestalt psychology, like **Kurt Koffka** (1935), **Wolfgang Köhler** (1947), and **Max Wertheimer** (1923), maintained that psychological phenomena could be understood only when viewed as organized, structured *wholes* and not when broken down into primitive perceptual elements. The term *Gestalt* roughly means "form," "whole," "configuration," or "essence." Gestalt psychology challenged atomistic views of psychology by arguing that the whole is more than the sum of its parts. For example, when you listen to music, you perceive whole melodies even though they are composed of separate notes. Gestalt psychologists argued that the holistic perception of the world arises because the cortex is organized to function that way. You organize sensory information the way you do because it is the most economical, simple way to organize the sensory input, given the structure and physiology of the brain. (Many of the examples of perceptual organization we will discuss in a later section were originated by the Gestaltists.)

Gibson's Ecological Optics

James Gibson (1966, 1979) proposed a very influential nativist approach to perception. Instead of trying to understand perception as a result of an organism's structure, Gibson suggested that it could be better understood through an analysis of the immediately surrounding environment (or its ecology). As one writer put it, Gibson's approach was, "Ask not what's inside your head, but what your head's inside of" (Mace, 1977). In effect, Gibson's **theory of ecological optics** was concerned with the perceived stimuli rather than with the mechanisms by which you perceive the stimuli. This approach was a radical departure from all previous theories. Gibson's ideas emphasized perceiving as *active exploration* of the environment. When an observer is *moving* in the world, the pattern of stimulation on the retina is constantly

The theory of ecological optics deals with invariant properties of the visual world. What information might a nature guide obtain from this view of a herd of wildebeests?

changing over time as well as over space. The theory of ecological optics tried to specify the information about the environment that was available to the eyes of a moving observer. Theorists in Gibson's tradition agree that perceptual systems evolved in organisms who were active—seeking food, water, mates, and shelter—in a complex and changing environment (Gibson, 1979; Pittenger, 1988; Shaw & Turvey, 1981; Shepard, 1984).

According to Gibson, the answer to the question "How do you learn about your world?" is simple. You directly pick up information about the *invariant,* or stable, properties of the environment. There is no need to take raw sensations into account or to look for higher level systems of perceptual inference—perception is direct. While the retinal size and shape of each environmental object changes, depending on the object's distance and on the viewing angle, these changes are not random. The changes are systematic, and certain properties of objects remain invariant under all such changes of viewing angles and viewing distances. Your visual system is tuned to detect such invariances because humans evolved in the environment in which perception of invariances was important for survival (Palmer, 1981).

James Gibson's nativist approach to perception emphasized the role of the observer as an active explorer who moves through the environment and focuses on the invariant patterns in the observed stimuli.

Toward a Unified Theory of Perception

These diverse theories can be unified to set the agenda for successful research on perception. (You will see repeatedly in *Psychology and Life* that competing theories can often be reconciled to provide a deeper understanding of the topic at hand.) You can recognize that the different perspectives contribute different insights to the three levels of analysis a theory of perception must address (Banks & Krajicek, 1991):

- *What are the physiological mechanisms involved in perception?*

  Chapter 7 was largely an answer to this question.

- *What is the process of perceiving?*

  This question is usually tackled by researchers who follow in the tradition originated by Helmholtz and the Gestaltists. Modern researchers often try to understand how sources of information are combined to arrive at a perceptual interpretation of the world. These researchers compare the process of perception to conceptual problem solving (Beck, 1982; Kanizsa, 1979; Pomerantz & Kubovy, 1986; Rock, 1983, 1986; Shepp & Ballisteros, 1989). We will see some of their insights in the remaining sections of this chapter.

- *What are the properties of the physical world that allow you to perceive?*

  This question makes contact with Gibson's theory. His central insight was that the world makes available certain types of information—and your perceptual apparatus is innately prepared to recover that information. Gibson's research made it clear that theories of perception must be constrained by accurate understandings of the environment in which people perceive.

We now begin our discussion of perceptual processes by considering what it means to select, or attend to, only a small subset of the information the world makes available.

ATTENTIONAL PROCESSES

We'd like you to take a moment now to find ten things in your environment that had not been, so far, in your immediate awareness. Had you noticed a spot on the wall? Had you noticed the ticking of a clock? If you start to examine your surroundings very carefully, you will discover that there are literally thousands of things on which you could focus your **attention.** Generally, the more closely you attend to some object or event in the environment, the more you can perceive and learn about it. That's why attention is an important topic in the study of perception: your focus of attention determines the types of information that will be most readily available to your perceptual processes. As you will now see, researchers have tried to understand what types of environmental stimuli require your attention and how attention contributes to your experience of those stimuli. We will start by considering how attention functions to selectively highlight objects and events in your environment.

Selective Attention

We began this section by asking that you try to find—to bring into attention—several things that had, up to that point, escaped your notice. This thought experiment illustrated an important function of attention: to select some part of the sensory input for further processing. Let us see how you make decisions about the subset of the world to which you will attend, and what consequences those decisions have for the information readily available to you.

Determining the Focus of Attention

What forces determine the objects that become the focus of your attention? The answer to this question has two components, which we will call goal-directed selection and stimulus-driven capture (Yantis, 1993). **Goal-directed selection** reflects the choices that you make about the objects to which you'd like to attend, as a function of your own goals. You are probably already comfortable with the idea that you can explicitly choose objects for particular scrutiny. **Stimulus-driven capture** occurs when features of the stimuli—objects in the environment—themselves automatically *capture* your attention, independent of your local goals as a perceiver. Research suggests, for example, that new objects in a perceptual display automatically capture attention.

You attend to stimuli in the environment either because you choose to—goal-directed selection—or because something about the stimulus captures your attention—stimulus-driven capture.

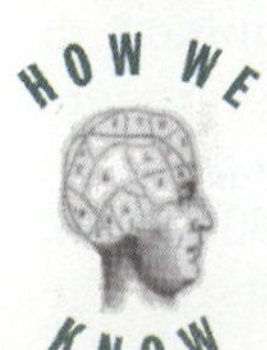

Consider the figure shown in part A of **Figure 8.9**. How hard do you think it would be for you to identify the overall, global figure as an H? The answer will depend on the extent to which you have to attend to the local letters that make up the global figure. Parts B and C of the figure show how researchers manipulated attention.

In each condition of the experiment, subjects were given a preview display that consisted of a figure 8 made of 8s. In the control condition, the figure 8 was complete. But, as you can see, in the novel object condition, there was a gap in the figure. What will happen if the next display you see fills in that gap? The researchers predicted that the object filling the gap (the novel object) would capture your attention—you couldn't help looking at it. And if your attention is focused on the letter S, you should find it harder than you ordinarily would to say that the global letter is an H.

That is exactly the result the researchers obtained. If you compare the two test displays in Figure 8.9, you'll see that they are identical. In each case an S helps to make up the global H. However, it was only in the case when the S appeared in a space that was previously unoccupied that subjects' performance—the speed with which they could name the global letter—was impaired (Hillstrom & Yantis, 1994).

You can recognize this phenomenon as stimulus-driven capture, because it works in the opposite direction of the perceiver's goals. Because, that is, the subjects would perform the task better if they ignored the small S, they must be unable to ignore it (since subjects almost always prefer to perform as well as possible on the tasks researchers assign them). The important general conclusion is that your perceptual system is organized so that your attention is automatically drawn to objects that are new to an environment.

The Fate of Unattended Information

If you have selectively attended to some subset of a perceptual display—by virtue of your own goals or of properties of the stimuli—what is the fate of the information to which you did not attend? Imagine listening to a lecture while people on both sides of you are engaged in conversations. How

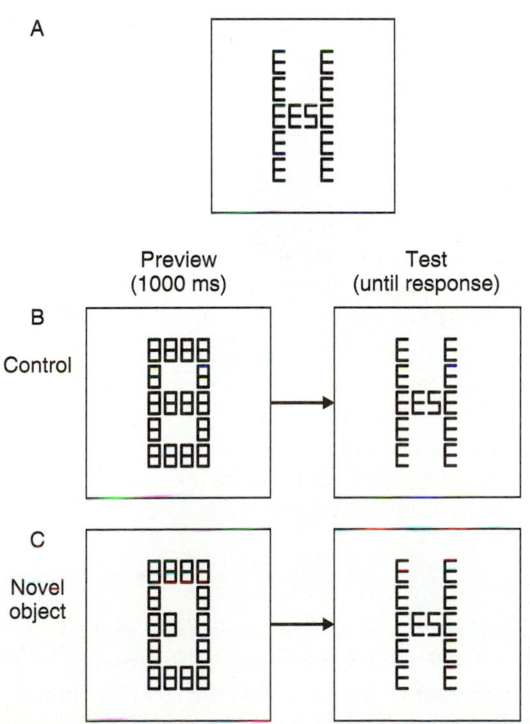

Figure 8.9 Stimulus-Driven Capture *How hard is it to recognize that the figure in (A) is an H? When the S fills a prior gap in the display (C), subjects find it more difficult to see that the overall figure is an H than they do in the control condition (B).*

are you able to keep track of the lecture? What do you notice about the conversations? Could anything appear in the content of one or the other conversation to divert your attention from the lecture?

This constellation of questions was first explored by **Donald Broadbent** (1958), who conceived of the mind as a *communications channel*—similar to a telephone line or a computer link—that actively processes and transmits information. Broadbent re-created the real-life situation of multiple sources of input in his laboratory with a technique called **dichotic listening.**

A subject wearing earphones listens to two tape-recorded messages played at the same time—a different message is played into each ear. The subject is instructed to repeat only one of the two messages to the experimenter, while ignoring whatever is presented to the other ear. This procedure is called *shadowing* the attended message (see **Figure 8.10**).

Subjects in shadowing experiments remember the attended message and do not remember the ignored message. Subjects usually do not even notice major alterations in the ignored message, such as changing the language from English to German or playing the tape backward. However, they do notice marked physical changes as, for example, when the pitch is raised substantially by changing the speaker's voice from male to female (Cherry, 1953). Thus gross physical features of the unattended message receive perceptual analysis, apparently below the level of consciousness, but most meaning does not get through.

According to Broadbent, the mind has limited capacity for acting as a communications channel. Therefore, you use attention to regulate the flow of information.

According to Broadbent's theory, as a communications channel the mind has only *limited capacity* to carry out complete processing. This limit requires that attention strictly regulate the flow of information from sensory input to consciousness. Attention creates a bottleneck in the flow of information through the cognitive system, filtering out some information and allowing other information to continue. The *filter theory* of attention asserted that the selection occurs early on in the process, before the input's meaning is accessed.

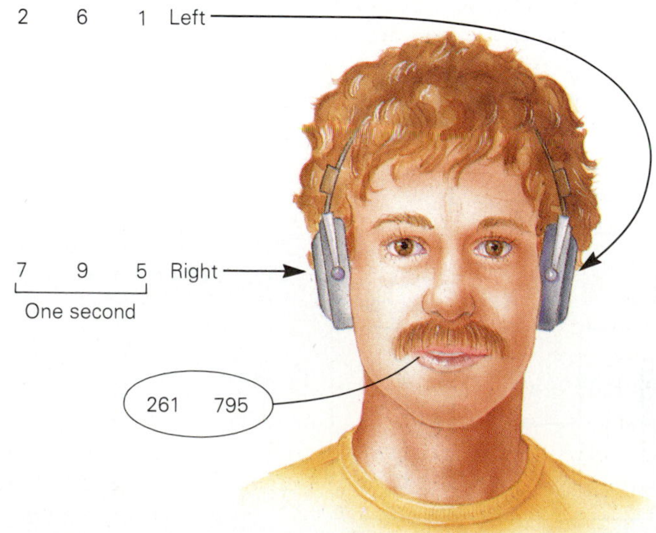

Figure 8.10 Dichotic Listening Task
A subject hears different digits presented simultaneously to each ear: 2 (left), 7 (right), 6 (left), 9 (right), 1 (left), and 5 (right). He reports hearing the correct sets—261 and 795. However, when instructed to attend only to the right-ear input, the subject reports hearing only 795.

The strongest form of filter theory was challenged when it was discovered that some subjects were perceiving things they would not have been able to if attention had been totally filtering all ignored material. In dichotic listening tasks, subjects sometimes noticed their own names and other personally meaningful information contained in the message they were instructed to ignore (Cherry, 1953). When a story being shadowed in one ear was switched to the unattended ear and replaced by a new story, some subjects continued to report words from the original story, even though it was now entering the supposedly ignored ear. The subjects did so even though they had been accurately following the instruction about which ear to shadow (Treisman, 1960). Apparently, subjects were intrigued by the meaning and continuity of the particular message they had been shadowing, which momentarily distracted them from the attended channel. Some meaningful analysis of the ignored channel must have been taking place—otherwise, subjects would not have known that the message on that channel was the continuation of the message they had been shadowing. Therefore, attention does not function as an absolute filter. But then how does it function?

Research now suggests, in fact, that unattended objects are sufficiently processed by your perceptual system so that those objects become less available for later use (Tipper et al., 1991; Treisman, 1992).

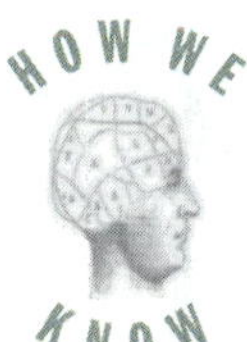

Look at **Figure 8.11**. Try to read the red letters in each column. Disregard the overlapping green letters. Did you notice that one of the columns is harder to read? Which one? Now look carefully at the green letters. In the first column, there is no relationship between the green letters and the red letters. However, in the second list, beginning with the second red letter, each red letter is the same as the green letter above it. A number of experiments show that subjects take longer to read the second list (Driver & Tipper, 1989; Tipper & Driver, 1988).

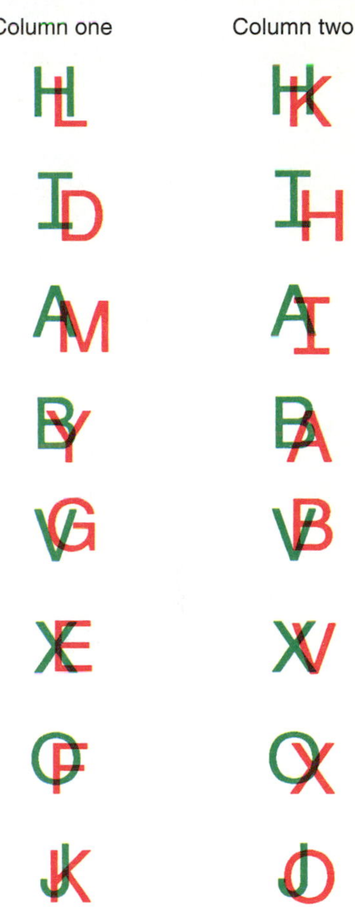

Figure 8.11 A Test of Your Attentional Mechanisms
First, read aloud the red letters in Column One as quickly as possible, disregarding the green. Next, quickly read the red letters in Column Two, also disregarding the green. Which took longer?

According to the authors of such experiments, subjects take longer to read the second column because they actually process the green letters unconsciously and have to inhibit or prevent themselves from responding to them. When, after having inhibited a particular letter, subjects are asked to respond to it, they are slowed down because they have to unblock or disinhibit the letter and make it available for response. For example, when you read the first red letter in the second row, you had to ignore, or inhibit, a green H. The second red letter in the row happens to be the letter H. Thus, when you try to read the red H, you have to unblock, or disinhibit, the letter H. Nothing similar to this happens when you read the first row of letters; the red letters in this row never appear as green letters.

Phenomena like this one suggest that selective attention works in two ways. First, your internal representations of the stimuli on which you have focused attention become highlighted in memory. Second, your internal representations of the unattended stimuli are somewhat suppressed. You can see how these processes of highlighting and suppression will make the attended objects specifically prominent in your consciousness. You can also see why it's dangerous to let yourself become distracted from your immediate task or goal. If you fail to pay attention to some body of information—your professor's lecture, perhaps—you may find it extra hard to catch up later. Let's turn now to the role attention plays in allowing you to find and correctly identify objects in your environment.

Selective attention works in two ways: first, to highlight stimuli on which you have focused, and second, to suppress unattended stimuli.

Attention and Objects in the Environment

One of the main functions of attention is to help you find particular objects in a noisy visual environment. To get a sense of how this works, you can carry out a very simple experiment. Put your book down for a minute and look for two things: a red object and a red object in the shape of a circle. Did it seem to you that you could find a red object almost instantly—without having to look at each part of the room—while finding the red circle required you to look around the room object by object? You have just discovered the difference between *preattentive processing* and processing that requires attention. We will now expand on these differences.

Preattentive Processing and Guided Search

Even though conscious memory and recognition of objects require attention, quite complex processing of information goes on without attention and without awareness. This earlier stage of processing is called **preattentive processing** because it operates on sensory inputs before you attend to them, as they first come into the brain from the sensory receptors. The simple demonstration in **Figure 8.12** gives you a rough idea of what can and cannot be processed without attention (adapted from Rock & Gutman, 1981). Your memory for the attended (red) shapes in the figure is much better than memory for the unattended shapes. However, you remember some basic features

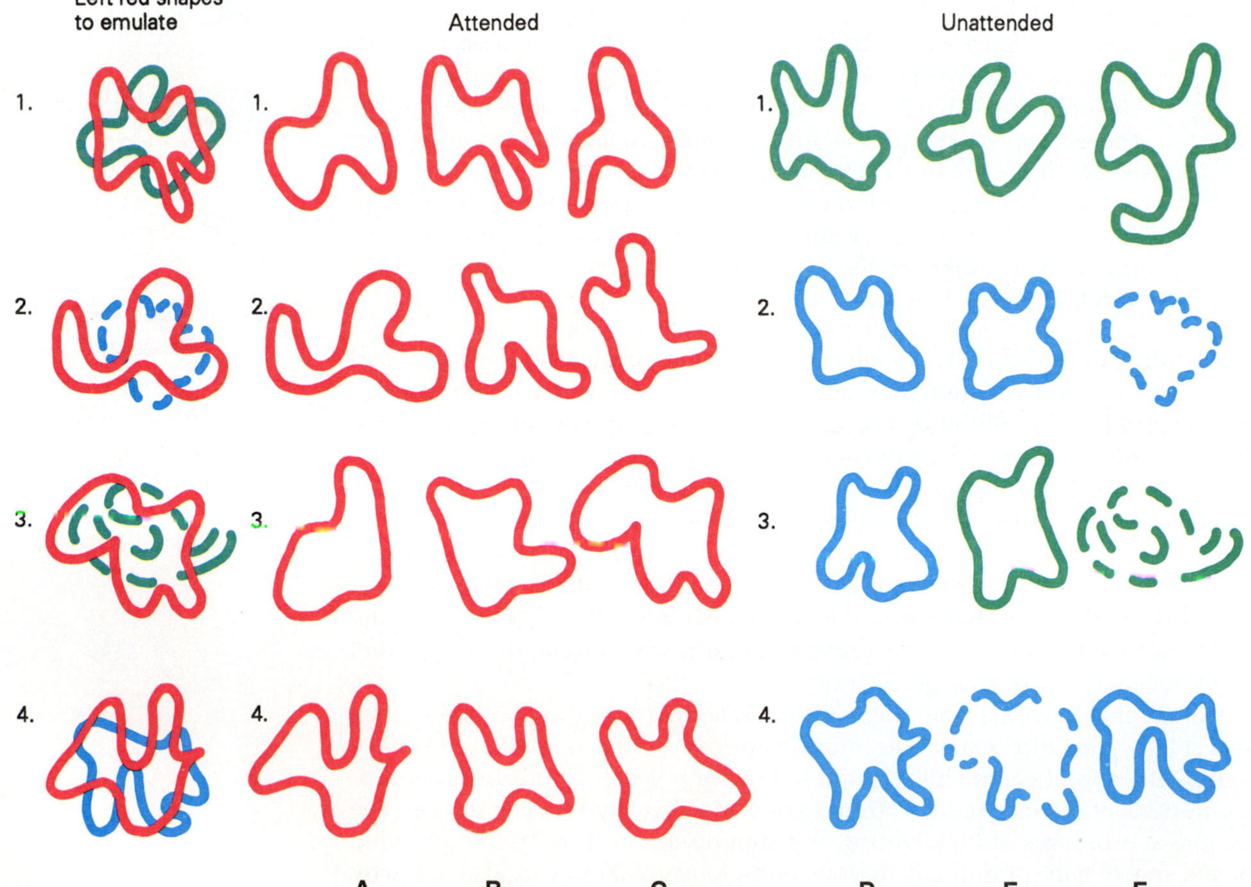

Figure 8.12 An Example of Overlapping Figures

Cover the right part of the figure with a piece of paper. Look at the pictures of overlapping colored shapes on the left side of the figure. Try to attend to the red shapes only and rate them according to how appealing they seem to you. Next, cover the left side of the figure and uncover the right side. Now test your memory for the red (attended) figures and the blue and green (unattended) figures. Put a check mark next to each figure on the left you definitely recall seeing. How well do you remember the attended versus the unattended shapes?

of the unattended shapes, such as their color and whether they were drawn continuously or had gaps. It is as though your visual system extracted some of the simple features of the unattended objects but never quite managed to put them together to form whole percepts.

Preattentive processing is quite skilled at finding objects in the environment that can be defined by single features (Treisman & Sato, 1990; Wolfe, 1992). Look at part A of **Figure 8.13**. Can you find the white T? This is a comparable exercise to finding a red object in the room around you. Preattentive processing allows you to search the environment in *parallel* for a single salient feature. This means that you can search all locations in the display at the same time: as a product of this parallel search, your attention is directed to the one correct object.

Now consider part B of Figure 8.13. Try, once again, to find the white T. Didn't it feel harder? In this case, your attentional system is not equipped to differentiate white T's from white L's in a parallel search. You can still use your capability for parallel search to ignore all the black T's, but you must then consider each white symbol one by one, or *serially*. This experience is comparable to finding something in your environment that is both red and a circle. Preattentive processing allows you swiftly to find things that are red or things that are circles—preattentive processing allows a **guided search** of your environment (Wolfe, 1992). At that point, however, you need to attend

You use preattentive processing to find objects in the environment that can be identified by a single feature by means of a guided search.

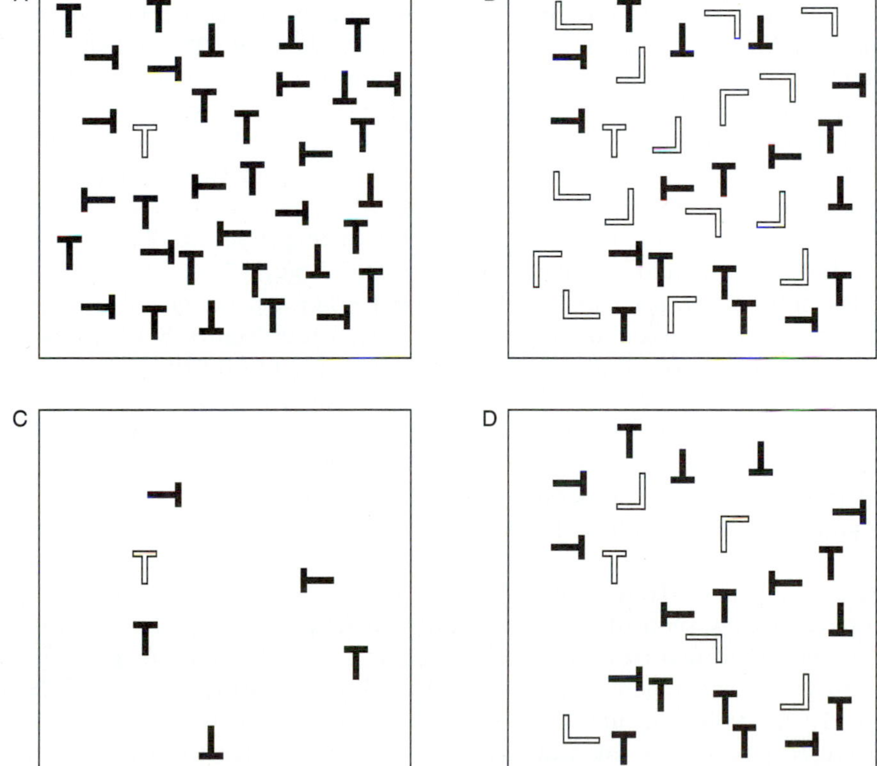

Figure 8.13 Attention and Visual Search

(A) To find an object that differs on one salient feature, you can use parallel search.
(B) To find an object based on the conjunction of features, you must use serial search.
(C) Because parallel search is used, there is no difference in search time for this small array of distractors, as compared with the large array in part A.
(D) With serial search, the size of the array of distractors does make a difference. Search in D is faster than search in B.

Suppose you were driving on this street and discovered you had passed your destination and needed to turn around. What feature of this visually noisy environment would your attention seek out?

to each object individually to determine whether it fits the *conjunction* of the two features round and red.

Humans search for environmental stimuli in two ways: in parallel (scanning many locations or stimuli at once) or serially (examining stimuli one by one).

Researchers recognize the difference between a parallel and a serial search by determining how hard it is to find a target as a function of the number of distractors. Suppose we ask you to find a white T in a display with five black T's (as in part C of Figure 8.13) versus a display with 34 black T's (as in part A). Because you can carry out this task in parallel, it will take you roughly the same amount of time to find the white T in each case. On the other hand, when you move from part B to part D of this figure, you can sense that you're much quicker to find the white T in D. You have to attend to each white element serially, so each white element you look at (until you find the right one) adds a separate increment of time.

Researchers can use this logic to discover other aspects of the perceptual world that can be processed preattentively. Consider **Figure 8.14**. In part A, try to find the yellow-and-blue item. In part B, try to find the yellow house with blue windows. Wasn't this second task much easier? Performance is much less affected by extra distractors when the two colors are organized into *parts* and *wholes* (Wolfe et al., 1994). Demonstrations of this sort suggest that preattentive processing provides you with relatively sophisticated assistance in finding objects in your environment.

Putting Features Together

We have already seen that serially focused attention is often needed to find conjunctions of features. Researchers believe that, in general, putting the features of objects together into a complete percept requires attention (Treisman, 1986, 1988; Treisman & Gelade, 1980). To demonstrate that attention is necessary to feature integration, researchers often divert or overload their subjects' attention. Under such circumstances, errors in feature combinations may occur, known as **illusory conjunctions.**

HOW WE KNOW

Researchers have produced illusory conjunctions by briefly flashing (for less than one-fifth of a second) three colored letters with digits on both sides of them.

5XOT7

The subjects' task is to report the digits first and then to report all of the color-letter combinations. On a third of the trials,

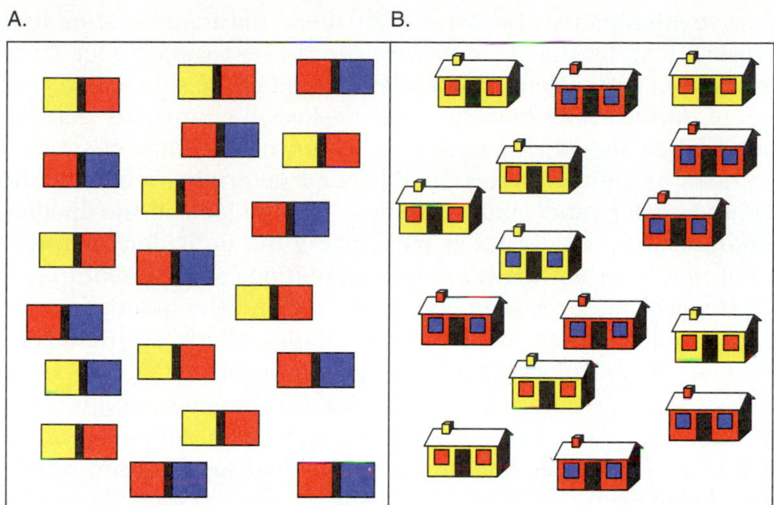

Figure 8.14 Search for the Conjunction of Two Colors
(A) Find the yellow-and-blue item.
(B) Find the yellow house with blue windows.
(A) Search is very inefficient when the conjunction is between the colors of two parts of a target. (B) However, search is much easier when the conjunction is between the color of the whole item and the color of one of its parts.

subjects report seeing the wrong color-letter combination. For example, they report a yellow X instead of a blue X or a yellow O. They rarely make the mistake of reporting any colors or letters that were not present in the display, such as a red X or a blue Z.

Subjects were also likely to report that they saw a dollar sign ($) in the briefly flashed display containing S's and line segments shown in **Figure 8.15**. The same effect was obtained even when the display contained S's and triangles. This result demonstrates that the subjects did not combine the lines of the triangles right away; the lines were floating unattached at some stage of perceptual processing, and one of the lines could be borrowed by the visual system to form the vertical bar in the dollar sign (Treisman & Gelade, 1980).

These results suggest that preattentive processing may allow perceivers to get individual features correct but, without focused attention, they are at risk for creating illusory conjunctions.

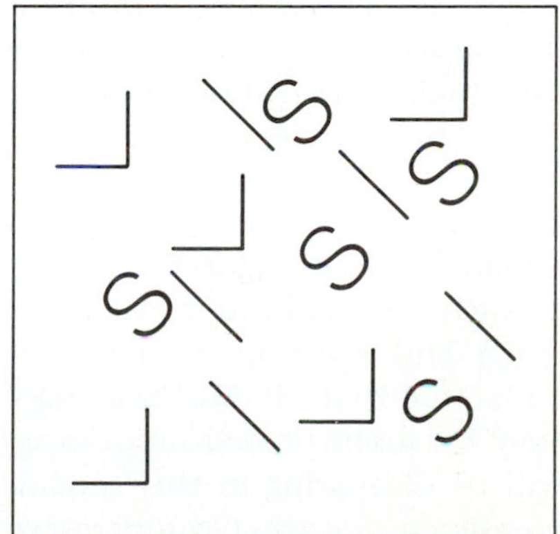

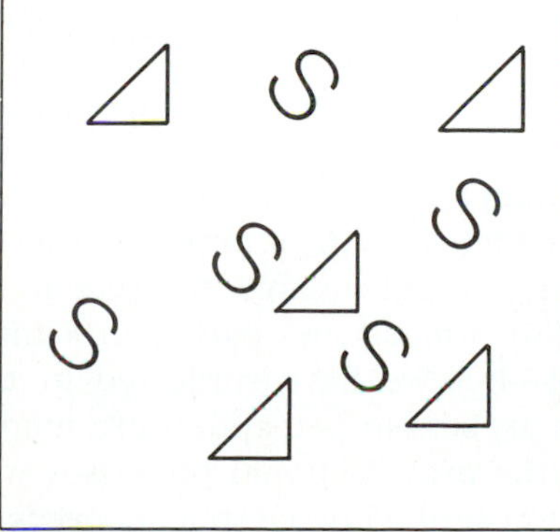

Actually observed

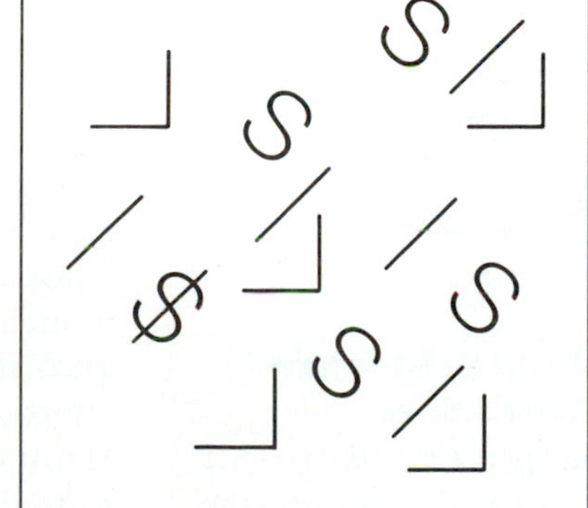

Reported with illusory $

Figure 8.15 Combinations of Features

Illusory conjunctions also arise with more naturalistic stimuli. In one study, researchers used a slide projector to present subjects for 10 seconds with drawings of faces (Reinitz et al., 1994). Half of the subjects were put in a situation of *divided attention:* they were asked to count dots that appeared superimposed on the slide of each face. Later, both groups of subjects were asked to look at another series of slides and determine which of the faces they had seen before and which were new. The subjects in the divided attention condition were successful at recognizing the individual features of the faces—but they were inattentive to recombinations of those features. Thus, if a "new" face had the eyes from one "old" face and the mouth from another, they were as likely to say "old" as if the relations between the features had stayed intact. This results suggests that extracting facial features requires little or no attention, whereas extracting relationships between features *does* require attention. As a consequence, subjects who suffered from divided attention could remember what features they had seen but not which whole faces they belonged to!

If you make so many mistakes when putting the features together without attention in the laboratory, why don't you notice mistakes of this type when your attention is diverted or overloaded in the real world? Part of the answer is that you just might notice such mistakes if you start to look for them. It is common, for example, for eyewitnesses to give different accounts of the way the features of a crime situation combined to make the whole. Two witnesses might agree that *someone* was brandishing a gun but disagree on which of a team of bank robbers it was. Another part of the answer is provided by a leading researcher on attention, **Anne Treisman.** Treisman argues that most stimuli you process are familiar and sufficiently different from one another so that there are a limited number of sensible ways to combine their various features. Even when you have not attended as carefully as necessary for accurate integration of features, your knowledge of familiar perceptual stimuli allows you to guess how their features ought to be combined. These guesses, or perceptual hypotheses, are usually correct, which means that you construct some of your percepts by combining preattentive perception of single stimulus features with memory for familiar, similar whole figures.

We are now ready to make the transition from attention to individual features to the perception of whole objects and scenes.

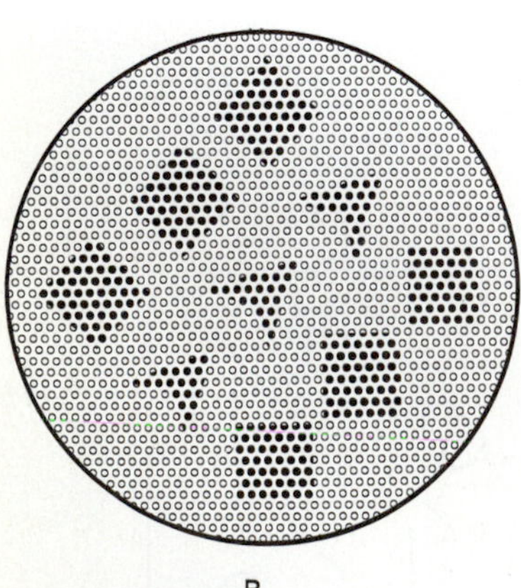

Figure 8.16 Percept of a Two-dimensional Geometric Design

What is your percept of the geometrical design in A? B represents the mosaic pattern that stimulus A makes on your retina.

ORGANIZATIONAL PROCESSES IN PERCEPTION

Imagine how confusing the world would be if you were unable to put together and organize the information available from the output of your millions of retinal receptors. You would experience a kaleidoscope of disconnected bits of color moving and swirling before your eyes. The processes that put sensory information together to give you the perception of coherence are referred to collectively as processes of **perceptual organization.** You have seen that what a person experiences as a result of such perceptual processing is called a *percept*.

For example, your percept of the two-dimensional geometric design in part A of **Figure 8.16** is probably three diagonal rows of figures, the first being composed of squares, the second of arrowheads, and the third of diamonds. (We will discuss part B in a moment.) This probably seems unremarkable—but we have suggested in this chapter that all the seemingly effortless aspects of perception are made easy by sophisticated processing. Many of the organizational processes we will be discussing in this section were first described by Gestalt theorists who argued that what you perceive depends on laws of organization, or simple rules by which you perceive shapes and forms.

Region Segregation

Consider your initial sensory response to Figure 8.16. Because your retina is composed of many separate receptors, your eye responds to this stimulus pattern with a mosaic of millions of independent neural responses coding the amount of light falling on tiny areas of your retina (see part B of Figure 8.16). The first task of perceptual organization is to find coherent regions within this mosaic of responses. In other words, your perceptual system must combine the outputs of the separate receptors into appropriate larger units. The primary information for this region-segregating process comes from color and texture. An abrupt change in color (hue, saturation, or brightness) signifies the presence of a boundary between two regions. Abrupt changes in texture can also mark boundaries between visibly different regions.

Perceptual organization is facilitated by region segregation.

Researchers now believe that the feature-detector cells in the visual cortex, discovered by Hubel and Wiesel (see Chapter 7), are involved in these region-segregating processes (Marr, 1982). Some cells have elongated receptive fields that are ideally suited for detecting boundaries between regions that differ in color. Others have receptive fields that seem to detect bars or lines—of the sort that occur in grassy fields, wood grains, and woven fabrics. These cortical line-detector cells may be responsible for your ability to discriminate between regions with different textures (Beck, 1972, 1982; Julesz, 1981a, b).

Figure, Ground, and Closure

As a result of region segregation, the stimulus in Figure 8.16 has now been divided into ten regions: nine small dark ones and a single large light one. You can think of each of these regions as a part of a unified entity, such as nine separate pieces of glass combined in a stained-glass window. Another organizational process divides the regions into figures and background. A **figure** is seen as an objectlike region in the forefront, and **ground** is seen as the backdrop against which the figures stand out. In Figure 8.16, you probably see the dark regions as figures and the light region as ground. However, you can also see this stimulus pattern differently by reversing figure and ground, much as you did with the ambiguous vase/faces drawing and the Escher art. To do this, try to see the white region as a large white sheet of paper that has nine holes cut in it through which you can see a black background.

The tendency to perceive a figure as being in *front* of a ground is very strong. In fact, you can even get this effect in a stimulus when the perceived figure doesn't actually exist! In the first image of **Figure 8.17**, you probably perceive a fir tree set against a ground containing several red circles on a

Figure 8.17 Subjective Contours That Fit the Angles of Your Mind

The human tendency to perceive a figure as being in front of a ground is so strong that the effect can be perceived even in instances where the figure does not actually exist.

white surface. Notice, however, that there is no fir tree shape; the figure consists only of three solid red figures and a base of lines. You see the illusory white triangle in front because the straight edges of the red shapes are aligned in a way that suggests a solid white triangle. The other image in Figure 8.17 gives you the illusion of one complete triangle superimposed on another, although neither is really there.

In this example, there seem to be three levels of figure/ground organization: the white fir tree, the red circles, and the larger white surface behind everything else. Notice that, perceptually, you divide the white area in the stimulus into two different regions: the white triangle and the white ground. Where this division occurs, you perceive illusory **subjective contours** that, in fact, exist not in the distal stimulus but only in your subjective experience.

Your perception of the white triangle in these figures also demonstrates another powerful organizing process: closure. **Closure** makes you see incomplete figures as complete. Though the stimulus gives you only the angles, your perceptual system supplies the edges in between that make the figure a complete fir tree. Closure processes account for your tendency to perceive stimuli as complete, balanced, and symmetrical, even when there are gaps, imbalance, or asymmetry.

Shape: Figural Goodness and Reference Frames

Once a given region has been segregated and selected as a figure against a ground, the boundaries must be further organized into specific *shapes.* You might think that this task would require nothing more than perceiving all the edges of a figure, but the Gestaltists showed that visual organization is more complex. If a whole shape were merely the sum of its edges, then all shapes having the same number of edges would be equally easy to perceive. In reality, organizational processes in shape perception are also sensitive to something the Gestaltists called **figural goodness,** a concept that includes perceived simplicity, symmetry, and regularity. **Figure 8.18** shows several figures that exhibit a range of figural goodness even though each has the same number of sides. Do you agree that figure A is the "best" figure and figure E the "worst"?

You perceive and remember good figures more readily than bad ones.

Experiments have shown that good figures are more easily and accurately perceived, remembered, and described than bad ones (Garner, 1974). Such results suggest that shapes of good figures can be coded more rapidly and economically by the visual system. In fact, the visual system sometimes tends to see a single bad figure as being composed of two overlapping good ones, as shown in **Figure 8.19**.

Your perceptual system also relies on **reference frames** to identify a figure's shape. Consider **Figure 8.20**. If you saw the left-hand image in A by itself, it would resemble a diamond, whereas the right-hand image would resemble a square. When you see these images as parts of diagonal rows, as shown in B, the shapes reverse: the line composed of diamonds resembles a tilted column of squares, and the line composed of squares resembles a tilted column of diamonds. The shapes look different because the orientation of

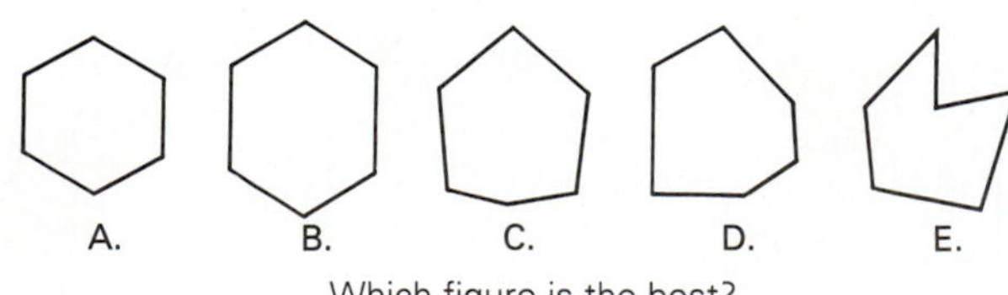

Figure 8.18 Figural Goodness—1

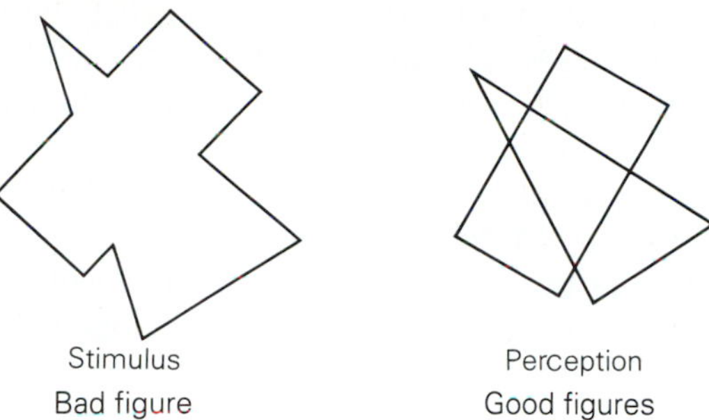

Figure 8.19 Figural Goodness—2

each image is seen in relation to the reference frame established by the whole row (Palmer, 1984, 1989). In effect, you see the shapes of the images as you would if the rows were vertical instead of diagonal (turn the book 45 degrees clockwise to see this phenomenon).

There are other ways to establish a contextual reference frame that has the same effect. These same images appear inside rectangular frames tilted 45 degrees in C of Figure 8.20. If you cover the frames, the left image resembles a diamond and the right one a square. When you uncover the frames, the left one changes into a square and the right one into a diamond.

Principles of Perceptual Grouping

In Figure 8.16, you perceived the nine figural regions as being grouped together in three distinct rows, each composed of three identical shapes placed along a diagonal line. How does your visual system accomplish this **perceptual grouping,** and what factors control it?

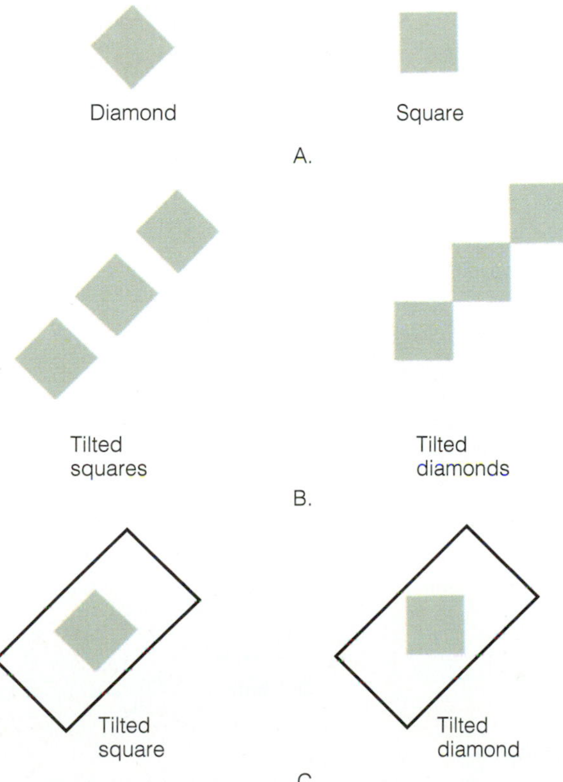

Figure 8.20 Reference Frames

The problem of grouping was first studied extensively by Gestalt psychologist Max Wertheimer (1923). Wertheimer presented subjects with arrays of simple geometric figures. By varying a single factor and observing how it affected the way people perceived the structure of the array, he was able to formulate a set of laws of grouping. Several of these laws are illustrated in **Figure 8.21**. In section A, there is an array of equally spaced circles that is ambiguous in its grouping—you can see it equally well as either rows or columns of dots. However, when the spacing is changed slightly so that the horizontal distances between adjacent dots are less than the vertical distances, as shown in B, you see the array unambiguously as organized into horizontal rows; when the spacing is changed so that the vertical distances are less, as shown in C, you see the array as organized into vertical columns. Together, these three groupings illustrate Wertheimer's **law of proximity:** all else being equal, the nearest (most proximal) elements are grouped together. The Gestaltists interpreted such results to mean that the whole stimulus pattern is somehow determining the organization of its own parts; in other words, the *whole percept* is different from the mere collection of its *parts.*

In D, the color of the dots instead of their spacing has been varied. Although there is equal spacing between the dots, your visual system automatically organizes this stimulus into rows because of their *similar color.* You see the dots in E as being organized into columns because of *similar size,* and you see the dots in F as being organized into rows because of *similar shape* and *orientation.* These grouping effects can be summarized by the **law of similarity:** all else being equal, the most similar elements are grouped together.

When elements in the visual field are moving, similarity of motion also produces a powerful grouping. The **law of common fate** states that, all else being equal, elements moving in the same direction and at the same rate are grouped together. If the dots in every other column of G were moving upward, as indicated by the blurring, you would group the image into columns because of their similarity in motion. You get this effect at a ballet when several dancers move in a pattern different from the others. Remember Dr. Richard's observation that an object in his visual field became organized properly when it moved as a whole. His experience was evidence of the powerful organizing effect of common fate.

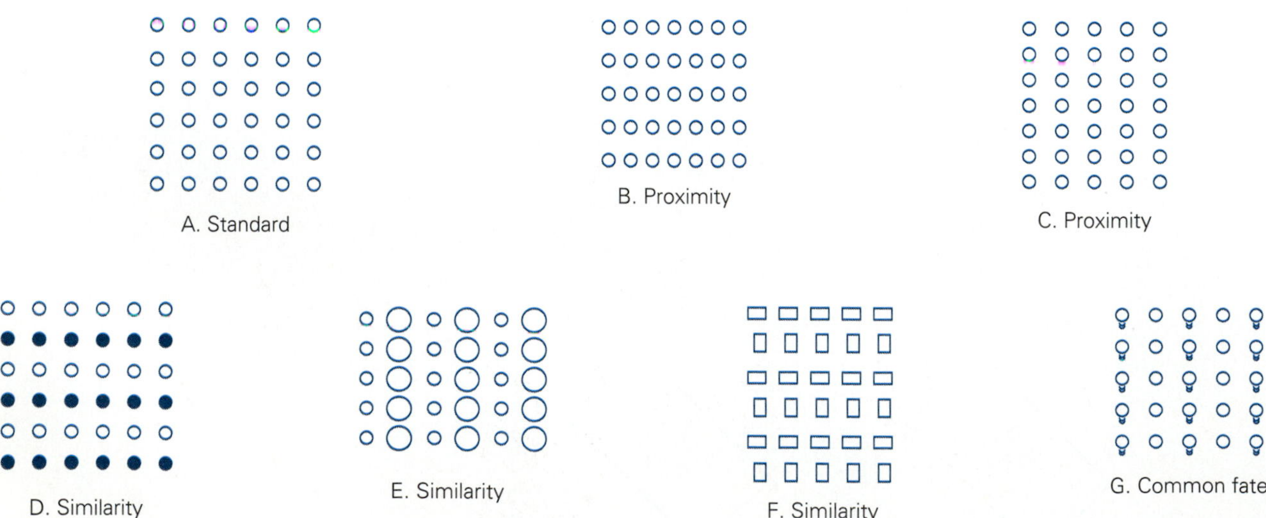

Figure 8.21 Grouping Phenomena
We perceive each array from B through G as being organized in a particular way, according to different Gestalt principles of grouping.

Is there a more general way of stating the various grouping laws we have just discussed? We have mentioned the law of proximity, the law of similarity, the law of common fate, and the law of symmetry, or figural goodness. Gestalt psychologists believed that all of these laws are just particular examples of a general principle, the **law of pragnanz** (*pragnanz* translates roughly to "good figure"): you perceive the simplest organization that fits the stimulus pattern.

According to the Gestalt psychologists, the various grouping laws are all examples of a more general law, the law of pragnanz, which states that you perceive the simplest organization that fits the stimulus pattern.

Spatial and Temporal Integration

All the Gestalt laws we have presented to you so far should have convinced you that a lot of perception consists of putting the pieces of your world together in the "right way." Often, however, you can't perceive an entire scene in one glance, or *fixation* (recall our discussion of attention). What you perceive at a given time is often a restricted glimpse of a large visual world extending in all directions to unseen areas of the environment. What may surprise you is that your visual system does not work very hard to create a moment-by-moment, integrated picture of the environment. Research suggests that your visual memory for each fixation on the world does not preserve precise details (Irwin, 1991). Why is that so? Part of the answer might be that the world itself is generally a stable source of information (O'Regan, 1992). It is simply unnecessary to commit to memory information that remains steadily available in the external environment.

One interesting consequence of the way you treat the information from different fixations is that you are taken in by illusions called "impossible" objects, such as those in **Figure 8.22**. For example, each fixation of corners and sides provides an interpretation that is consistent with an object that seems to be a three-dimensional triangle (image A); but when you try to integrate them into a coherent whole, the pieces just don't fit together properly

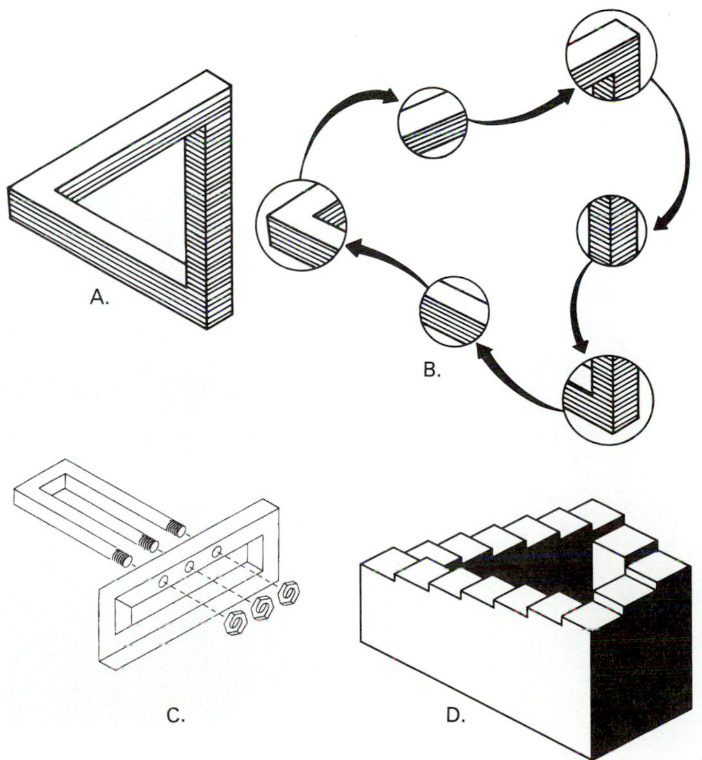

Figure 8.22 Impossible Figures

(image B). Image C has two arms that somehow turn into three prongs right before your vigilant gaze, and the perpetual staircase in image D forever ascends or descends.

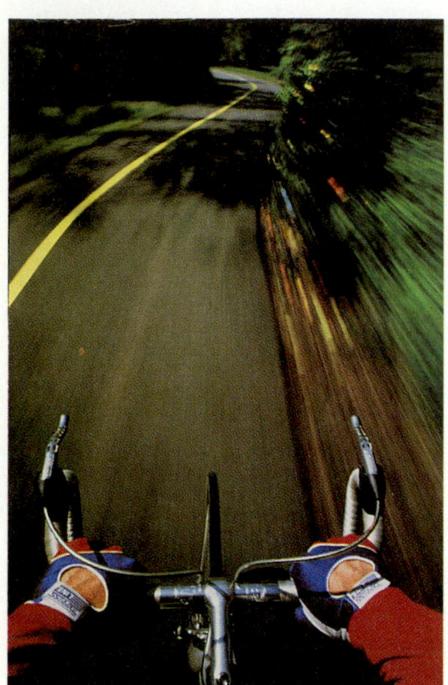

What makes you aware that the "protagonist" in this photo is moving—and in what direction is the motion?

Motion Perception

One type of perception that does require you to compare across different glimpses of the world is motion perception. Consider the two images given in **Figure 8.23**. Suppose that this individual has stood still while you have walked toward him. The size of his image on your retina has expanded as you have drawn near. The rate at which this image has expanded gives you a sense of how quickly you have been approaching (Gibson, 1979). You use this type of information to navigate effectively in your world.

Suppose, however, you are still but other objects are in motion. The perception of motion, like the perception of shape and orientation, often depends on a reference frame. If you sit in a darkened room and fixate on a stationary spot of light inside a lighted rectangle that is moving very slowly back and forth, you will perceive instead a *moving* dot going back and forth within a *stationary* rectangle. This illusion, called **induced motion,** occurs even when your eyes are quite still and fixated on the dot. Your motion-detector cells are not firing at all in response to the stationary dot but presumably are firing in response to the moving lines of the rectangle. To see the dot as moving requires some higher level of perceptual organization in which the dot and its supposed motion are perceived within the reference frame provided by the rectangle.

There seems to be a strong tendency for the visual system to take a larger, surrounding figure as the reference frame for a smaller figure inside it. You have probably experienced induced motion many times without knowing it. The moon (which is nearly stationary) frequently looks as if it is moving through a cloud, when, in fact, it is the cloud that is moving past the moon. The surrounding cloud induces perceived movement in the moon just as the rectangle does in the dot (Rock, 1983, 1986). Have you ever been in a train

Figure 8.23 Approaching a Man

The size of an image expands on your retina as you draw nearer to the stimulus.

that started moving very slowly? Didn't it seem as if the pillars on the station platform or a stationary train next to you might be moving backward instead?

The illusion of induced motion is influenced by a strong tendency for the visual systems to take a larger, surrounding figure as the reference frame for a smaller figure inside it.

Another movement illusion that demonstrates the existence of higher level organizing processes for motion perception is called **apparent motion.** The simplest form of apparent motion, the **phi phenomenon,** occurs when two stationary spots of light in different positions in the visual field are turned on and off alternately at a rate of about 4 to 5 times per second. This effect occurs on outdoor advertising signs and in disco light displays. Even at this relatively slow rate of alternation, it appears that a single light is moving back and forth between the two spots. There are multiple ways to conceive of the path that leads from the location of the first dot to the location of the second dot. Yet human observers normally see only the simplest path, a straight line (Cutting & Proffitt, 1982; Shepard, 1984). This straight-line rule is violated, however, when subjects are shown alternating views of a human body in motion. Then the visual system fills in the paths of normal biological motion (Shiffrar, 1994).

Depth Perception

Until now, we have considered only two-dimensional patterns on flat surfaces. Everyday perceiving, however, involves objects in three-dimensional space. Perceiving all three spatial dimensions is absolutely vital for you to approach what you want, such as interesting people and good food, and avoid what is dangerous, such as speeding cars and falling comets. This perception requires accurate information about *depth* (the distance from you to an object) as well as about its *direction* from you. Your ears can help in determining direction, but they are not much help in determining depth.

When you think about depth perception, keep in mind that the visual system must rely on retinal images that have only two spatial dimensions—vertical and horizontal. To illustrate the problem of having a 2-D retina doing a 3-D job, consider the situation shown in **Figure 8.24**. When a spot of light stimulates the retina at point a, how do you know whether it came from position a_1 or a_2? In fact, it could have come from *anywhere* along line A, because light from any point on that line projects onto the same retinal cell. Similarly, all points on line B project onto the single retinal point b. To make matters worse, a straight line connecting any point on line A to any point on line B (a_1 to b_2 or a_2 to b_1, for example) would produce the same image on the retina. The net result is that the image on your retina is ambiguous in depth: it could have been produced by objects at any one of several different distances.

The two possible views of the Necker cube from Figure 8.6 result from this ambiguity in depth. The fact that you can be fooled under certain circumstances shows that depth perception requires an *interpretation* of sensory input and that this interpretation can be wrong. (You already know this if you've ever swung at a tennis ball and come up only with air.) Your interpre-

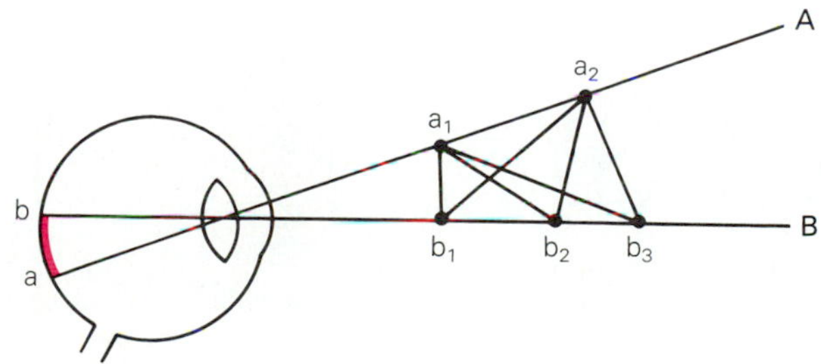

Figure 8.24 Depth Ambiguity

tation of depth relies on many different information sources about distance (often called *depth cues*)—among them binocular cues, motion cues, and pictorial cues.

Binocular and Motion Cues

Have you ever wondered why you have two eyes instead of just one? The second eye is more than just a spare—it provides some of the best, most compelling information about depth. The two sources of binocular depth information are *binocular disparity* and *convergence.*

Because the eyes are about two to three inches apart horizontally, they receive slightly different views of the world. To convince yourself of this, try the following experiment. First, close your left eye and use the right one to line up your two index fingers with some small object in the distance, holding one finger at arm's length and the other about a foot in front of your face. Now, keeping your fingers stationary, close your right eye and open the left one while continuing to fixate on the distant object. What happened to the position of your two fingers? The second eye does not see them lined up with the distant object because it gets a slightly different view.

Binocular disparity and convergence are binocular depth cues resulting from the horizontal positioning of the eyes.

This displacement between the horizontal positions of corresponding images in your two eyes is called *binocular disparity.* It provides depth information because the amount of disparity, or difference, depends on the relative distance of objects from you (see **Figure 8.25**). For instance, when you switched eyes, the closer finger was displaced farther to the side than was the distant finger.

When you look at the world with both eyes open, most objects that you see stimulate different positions on your two retinas. If the disparity between corresponding images in the two retinas is small enough, the visual system is able to fuse them into a perception of a single object in depth. (However, if the images are too far apart, as when you cross your eyes, you actually see the double images.) When you stop to think about it, what your visual system does is pretty amazing: it takes two different retinal images, compares them for horizontal displacement of corresponding parts (binocular disparity), and produces a unitary perception of a single object in depth. In effect, the visual system interprets horizontal displacement between the two images as depth in the three-dimensional world.

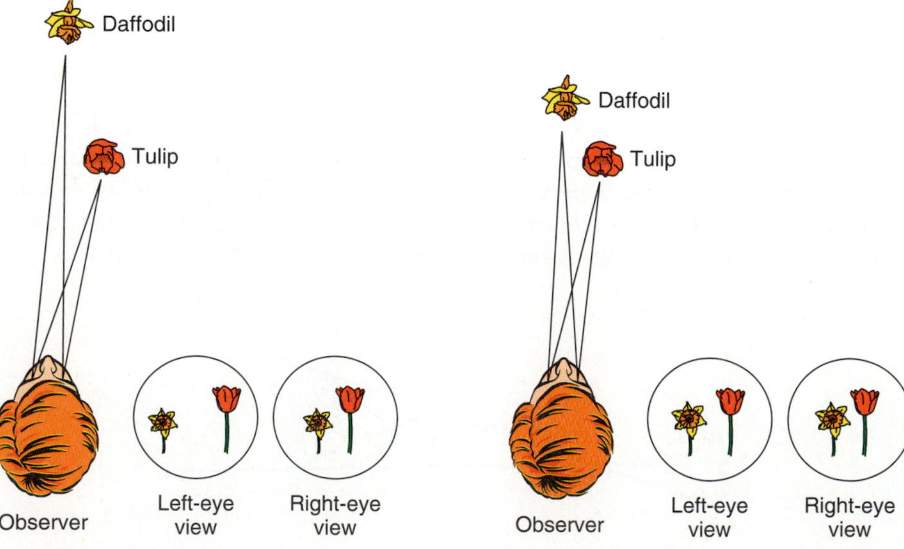

Figure 8.25 Retinal Disparity

Retinal disparity increases with the distance, in depth, between two objects.

Other binocular information about depth comes from *convergence.* The two eyes turn inward to some extent whenever they are fixated on an object (see **Figure 8.26**). When the object is very close—a few inches in front of your face—the eyes must turn toward each other quite a bit for the same image to fall on both foveae. You can actually see the eyes converge if you watch a friend focus first on a distant object and then on one a foot or so away. Your brain uses information from your eye muscles to make judgments about depth. However, convergence information from the eye muscles is useful for depth perception only up to about 10 feet. At greater distances, the angular differences are too small to detect, because the eyes are nearly parallel when you fixate on a distant object.

IN YOUR LIFE

To see how *motion* is another source for depth information, try the following demonstration. As you did before, close one eye and line up your two index fingers with some distant object. Then move your head to the side while fixating on the distant object and keeping your fingers still. As you move your head, you see both your fingers move, but the close finger seems to move farther and faster than the more distant one. The fixated object does not move at all. This source of information about depth is called **relative motion parallax.** Motion parallax provides information about depth because, as you move, the relative distances of objects in the world determine the amount and direction of their relative motion in your retinal image of the scene. Next time you are a passenger on a car trip, you should keep a watch out the window for motion parallax at work. Objects at a distance from the moving car will appear much more stationary than those closer to you.

Pictorial Cues

But suppose you had vision in only one eye. Would you not be able to perceive depth? In fact, further information about depth is available from just one eye. These sources are called *pictorial cues,* because they include the kinds of depth information found in pictures. Artists who create images in what appear to be three dimensions (on the two dimensions of a piece of paper or canvas) make skilled use of pictorial cues.

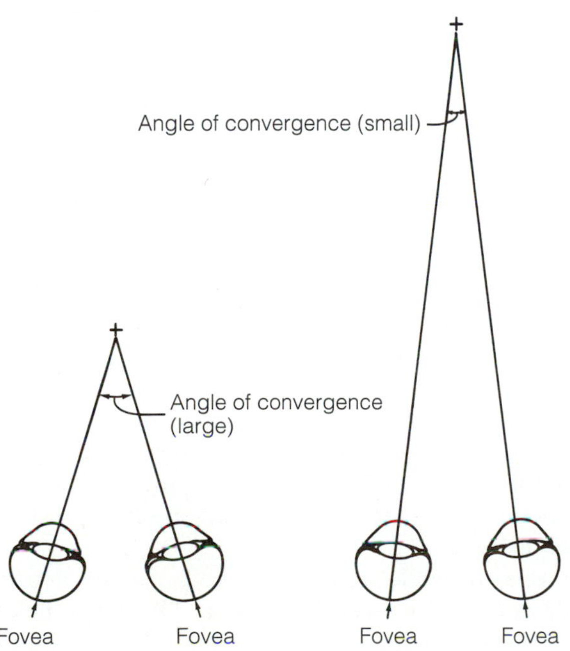

Figure 8.26 Convergence Cues to Depth

Figure 8.27 Interposition Cues to Depth *What are the visual cues that tell you whether or not this woman is behind the bars?*

Artists use pictorial depth cues, such as interposition, linear perspective, and texture gradients, to create the appearance of a third dimension in two-dimensional drawings and paintings.

Interposition, or *occlusion,* arises when an opaque object blocks out part of a second object (see **Figure 8.27**). Interposition gives you depth information indicating that the occluded object is farther away than the occluding one. Occluding surfaces also block out light, creating shadows that can be used as an additional source of depth information.

Three more sources of pictorial information are all related to the way light projects from a three-dimensional world onto a two-dimensional surface such as the retina: relative size, linear perspective, and texture gradients. *Relative size* involves a basic rule of light projection: objects of the same size at different distances project images of different sizes on the retina. The closest one projects the largest image and the farthest one the smallest image. This rule is called the *size/distance relation.* As you can see in **Figure 8.28**, if you look at an array with identical objects, you interpret the smaller ones to be further away.

Linear perspective is a depth cue that also depends on the size/distance relation. When parallel lines (by definition separated along their lengths by the same distance) recede into the distance, they converge toward a point on the horizon in your retinal image (see **Figure 8.29**). This important fact was discovered around 1400 by Italian Renaissance artists, who were then able to paint depth compellingly for the first time (Vasari, 1967). Prior to their discovery, artists had incorporated in their paintings information from interposition, shadows, and relative size, but they had been unable to depict realistic scenes that showed objects at various depths.

Your visual system's interpretation of converging lines gives rise to the *Ponzo illusion* (also shown in Figure 8.29). The upper line looks longer because you interpret the converging sides according to linear perspective as parallel lines receding into the distance. In this context, you interpret the upper line as though it were farther away, so you see it as longer—a farther object would have to be longer than a nearer one for both to produce retinal images of the same size.

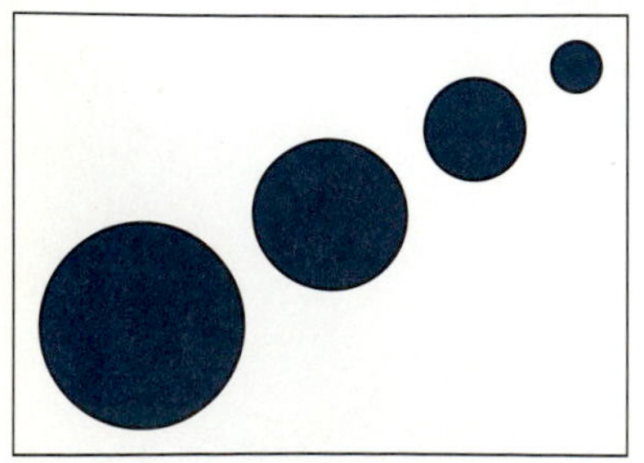

Figure 8.28 Relative Size as a Depth Cue

Texture gradients provide depth cues because the density of a texture becomes greater as a surface recedes in depth. The wheat field in **Figure 8.30** is an example of the way texture is used as a depth cue. You can think of this as another consequence of the size/distance relation. In this case, the units that make up the texture become smaller as they recede into the distance, and your visual system interprets this diminishing grain as greater distance

How convincing is the perspective in each of these frescoes? Note the difference in the dates when they were created (Left: Duccio, Maesta: Christ Before Anna and the Denial of St. Peter. *1308–11. Right: Perugino,* Delivering the Keys of the Kingdom to St. Peter. *1481–83. Both: Scala/Art Resource, New York.)*

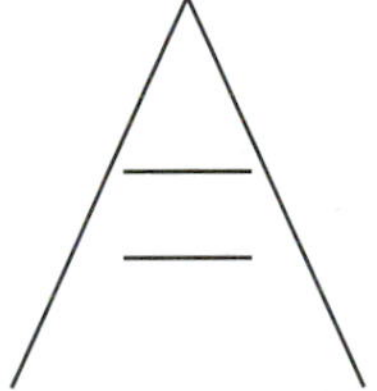

Figure 8.29 The Ponzo Illusion
The converging lines add a dimension of depth, and, therefore, the distance cue makes the top line appear larger than the bottom line, even though they are actually the same length.

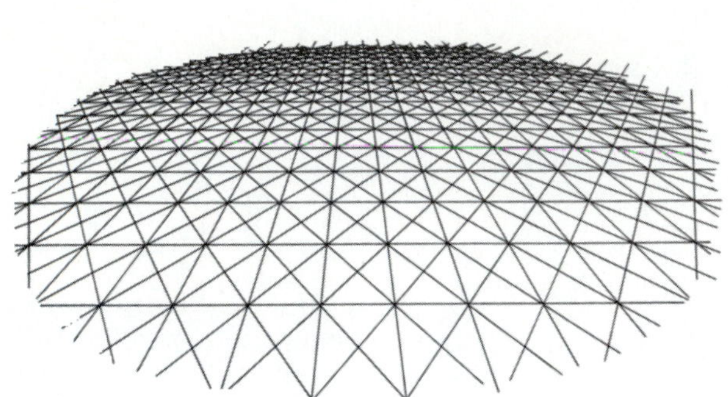

Figure 8.30 Examples of Texture as a Depth Cue
The wheat field is a natural example of the way texture is used as a depth cue. Notice the way wheat slants. The geometric design uses the same principles.

in three-dimensional space. Gibson (1966, 1979) suggested that the relationship between texture and depth is one of the invariants available in the perceptual environment.

By now, it should be clear that there are many sources of depth information. Under normal viewing conditions, however, information from these sources comes together in a single, coherent three-dimensional interpretation of the environment. You experience depth, not the different cues to depth that existed in the proximal stimulus. In other words, your visual system uses cues like differential motion, interposition, and relative size automatically, without your conscious awareness, to make the complex computations that give you a perception of depth in the three-dimensional environment.

Perceptual Constancies

To help you discover another important property of visual perception, we are going to ask you to play a bit with your textbook. Put your book down on a table, then move your head closer to it so that it's just a few inches away. Then move your head back to a normal reading distance. Although the book stimulated a much larger part of your retina when it was up close than when it was far away, didn't you perceive the book's size to remain the same? Now set the book upright and try tilting your head clockwise. When you do this, the image of the book rotates counterclockwise on your retina, but didn't you still perceive the book to be upright?

In general, you see the world as *invariant, constant,* and *stable* despite changes in the stimulation of your sensory receptors. Psychologists refer to this phenomenon as **perceptual constancy.** Roughly speaking, it means that you perceive the properties of the distal stimuli, which are usually constant, rather than the properties of proximal stimuli, which change every time you move your eyes or head. For survival, it is critical that you perceive constant and stable properties of objects in the world despite the enormous variations in the properties of the light patterns that stimulate your eyes. The critical task of perception is to discover *invariant* properties of your environment despite the *variations* in your retinal impressions of them. We will see how this works for size, shape, and orientation.

Perceptual constancy helps you to survive in an environment that presents you with many challenging variations of sensory input.

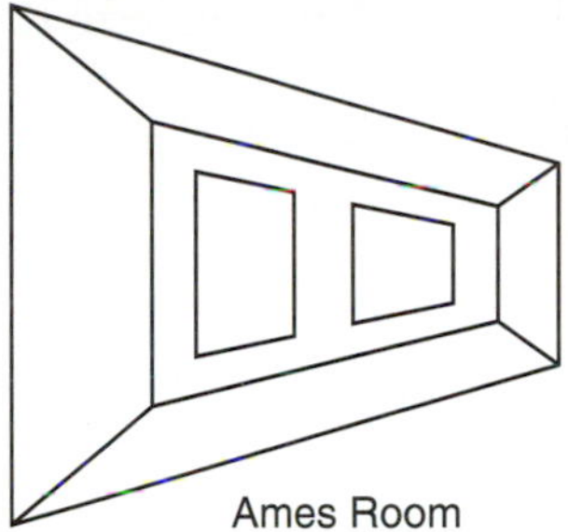

1
2
Viewer

Figure 8.31 **The Ames Room**

Size and Shape Constancy

What determines your perception of the size of an object? In part, you perceive an object's actual size on the basis of the size of its retinal image. However, the demonstration with your book shows that the size of the retinal image depends on both the actual size of the book and its *distance* from the eye. As you now know, information about distance is available from a variety of depth cues. Your visual system combines that information with retinal information about image size to yield a perception of an object size that usually corresponds to the actual size of the distal stimulus. **Size constancy** refers to your ability to perceive the true size of an object despite variations in the size of its retinal image.

You perceive size constancy by using distance cues and prior knowledge about the size of similar objects.

If the size of an object is perceived by taking distance cues into account, then you should be fooled about size whenever you are fooled about distance. One such illusion occurs in the Ames room shown in **Figure 8.31**. In comparison to his 4-foot daughter, Tanya Zimbardo, your 6-foot-tall author looks quite short in the left corner of this room, but he looks enormous in the right corner. The reason for this illusion is that you perceive the room to be rectangular, with the two back corners equally distant from you. Thus you perceive Tanya's actual size as being consistent with the size of the images on your retina in both cases. In fact, Tanya is not at the same distance, because the Ames room creates a clever illusion. It appears to be a rectangular room, but it is actually made from nonrectangular surfaces at odd angles in depth and height, as you can see in the drawings that accompany the photos. Any person on the right will make a larger retinal image, because he or she is twice as close to the observer.

Another way that the perceptual system can infer objective size is by using prior knowledge about the characteristic size of similarly shaped objects. For instance, once you recognize the shape of a house, a tree, or a dog, you have a pretty good idea of how big each is, even without knowing its distance from you. Universal Studios in Hollywood uses your expectations about the normal sizes of doors to make its actors in westerns look bigger or smaller to you. The doors on one side of the street on a western set are made to be smaller than the doors on the other side of the street. When shooting the scenes of the westerns, directors position male actors on the side of the street with small doors. This makes them look bigger. Female actors, on the other hand, get filmed on the other side of the street, against the background of large doors, which makes them look petite.

When past experience does not give you knowledge of what familiar objects look like at extreme distances, size constancy may break down. You have experienced this problem if you have looked down at people from the top of a skyscraper and thought that they resembled ants. Consider, also, the experience of a man named Kenge of the equatorial Africa Pygmy culture. Kenge had lived in dense tropical forests all his life. He had occasion, one day, to travel by car for the first time across an open plain with anthropologist Colin Turnbull. Later, Turnbull described Kenge's reactions.

> Kenge looked over the plains and down to where a herd of about a hundred buffalo were grazing some miles away. He asked me what kind of *insects* they were, and I told him they were buffalo, twice as big as the forest buffalo known to him. He laughed loudly and told me not to tell such stupid stories, and asked me again what kind of insects they were. He then talked to himself, for want of more intelligent company, and tried to liken the buffalo to the various beetles and ants with which he was familiar.
>
> He was still doing this when we got into the car and drove down to where the animals were grazing. He watched them getting larger and larger, and though he was as courageous as any Pygmy, he moved over and sat close to me and muttered that it was witchcraft.... Finally, when he realized that they were real buffalo he was no longer afraid, but what puzzled him still was why they had been so small, and whether they *really* had been small and had so suddenly grown larger, or whether it had been some kind of trickery. (Turnbull, 1961, p. 305)

In this unfamiliar perceptual environment, Kenge first tried to fit his novel perceptions into a familiar context, by assuming the tiny, distant specks he saw were insects. With no previous experience seeing buffalo at a distance, he had no basis for size constancy, and as the fast-moving car approached them and Kenge's retinal images got larger and larger, he had the frightening illusion that the animals were changing in size. We can assume that, over time, Kenge would have come to see them as Turnbull did. The knowledge he acquired would allow him to arrive at an appropriate perceptual interpretation for his sensory experience.

Shape constancy is closely related to size constancy. You perceive an object's actual shape correctly even when the object is slanted away from you, making the shape of the retinal image substantially different from that of the object itself. For instance, a rectangle tipped away projects a trapezoidal image onto your retina; a circle tipped away from you projects an elliptical image (see **Figure 8.32**). Yet you usually perceive the shapes accurately as a circle and a rectangle slanted away in space. When there is good depth information available, your visual system can determine an object's true shape simply by taking into account your distance from its different parts.

Shape constancy is aided by good depth information.

Figure 8.32 Shape Constancy
As a coin is rotated, its image becomes an ellipse that grows narrower and narrower until it becomes a thin rectangle, an ellipse again, and then a circle. At each orientation, however, it is still perceived as a circular coin.

Orientation Constancy

When you tilted your head to the side in viewing your book, the world did not seem to tilt; only your own head did. **Orientation constancy** is your ability to recognize the true orientation of the figure in the real world, even though its orientation in the retinal image is changed. Orientation constancy relies on output from the vestibular system in your inner ear (discussed in Chapter 7)—which makes available information about the way in which your head is tilted. By combining the output of the vestibular system with retinal orientation, your visual system is usually able to give you an accurate perception of the orientation of an object in the environment.

Orientation constancy relies on the vestibular sense and prior knowledge about the objective orientation of the observed object.

In familiar environments, prior knowledge provides additional information about objective orientation. However, you may not be good at recognizing complex and unfamiliar figures when they are seen in unusual orientations. Can you recognize the shape in **Figure 8.33**? When a figure is complex and consists of subparts, you must adjust for the orientation of each part separately (Rock, 1986). So, while you rotate one part to its proper orientation, other parts are still perceived as unrotated. Look at the two upside-down pictures of Russian leader Boris Yeltsin. You can probably tell that one of them has been altered slightly around the eyes and mouth, but the two pictures look pretty similar. Now turn the book upside down and look again. The same

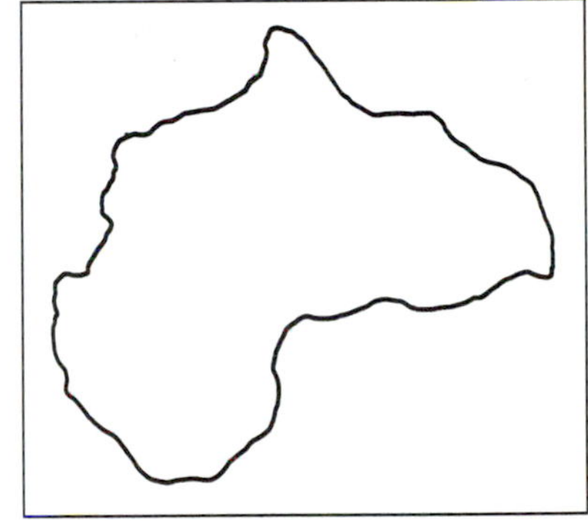

Figure 8.33 Africa Rotated 90 Degrees

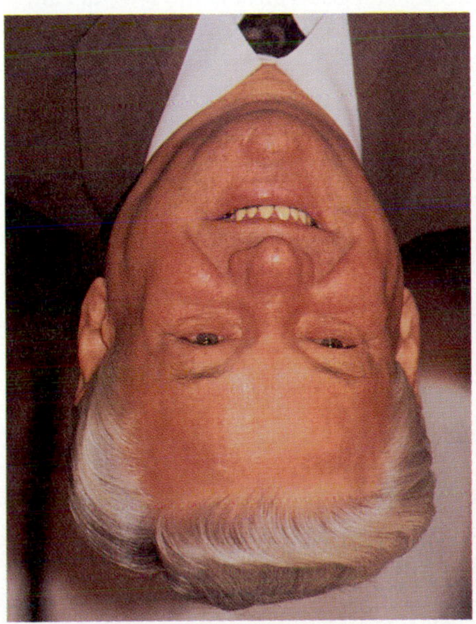
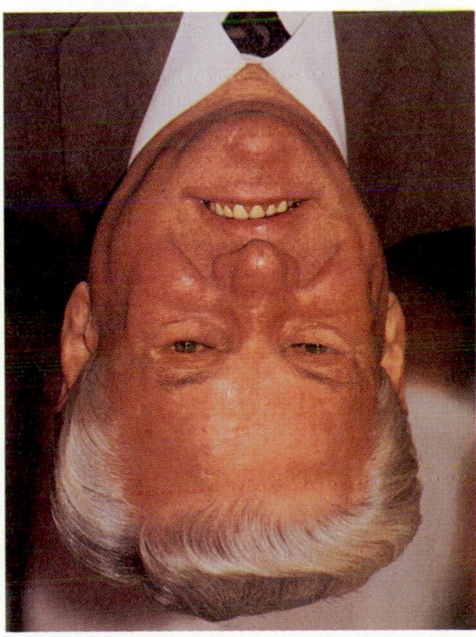

Which of these portraits might express Boris Yeltsin's feelings after hearing bad news about the Russian economy?

pictures look extraordinarily different now. One is still Boris Yeltsin, but the other is a ghoulish monster that not even his mother could love! Your failure to see that obvious difference before turning the book upside down may be due to your inability to rotate all of the parts of the face at the same time. It is also a function of years of perceptual training to see the world right side up and to perceive faces in their usual orientation.

IDENTIFICATION AND RECOGNITION PROCESSES

You can think of all the perceptual processes described so far as providing reasonably accurate knowledge about physical properties of the distal stimulus—the position, size, shape, texture, and color of objects in a three-dimensional environment. With just this knowledge and some basic motor skills, you would be able to walk around without bumping into anything and manipulate objects that were small and light enough to move. However, you would not know what the objects were or whether you had seen them before. Your experience would resemble a visit to an alien planet where everything was new to you; you wouldn't know what to eat, what to put on your head, what to run away from, or what to date. Your environment appears nonalien because you are able to recognize and identify most objects as things you have seen before and as members of the meaningful categories that you know about from experience. Identification and recognition attach meaning to percepts.

BOTTOM-UP AND TOP-DOWN PROCESSES

When you identify an object, you must match what you see against your stored knowledge. Taking sensory data into the system and sending it upward for extraction and analysis of relevant information is called bottom-up processing. **Bottom-up processing** is anchored in empirical reality and deals with bits of information and the transformation of concrete, physical features of stimuli into abstract representations. This type of processing is also called *data-driven* processing, because your starting point for identification is the sensory evidence you obtain from the environment—the data.

In many cases, however, you can use information you already have about the environment to help you make a perceptual identification. If you visit a zoo, for example, you might be a little more ready to recognize some types of animals than you otherwise would be. You are more likely to hypothesize that you are seeing a tiger than you would be in your own back yard. When your expectations affect perception, the phenomenon is called top-down processing. **Top-down processing** involves your past experiences, knowledge, motivations, and cultural background in perceiving the world. With top-down processing, higher mental functioning influences how you understand objects and events. Top-down processing is also known as *conceptually driven* (or hypothesis-driven) processing, because the concepts you have stored in memory are affecting your interpretation of the sensory data. The importance of top-down processing can be illustrated by drawings known as *droodles* (Price, 1953/1980). Without the labels, these drawings are meaningless. However, once the drawings are identified, you can easily find meaning in them (see **Figure 8.34**).

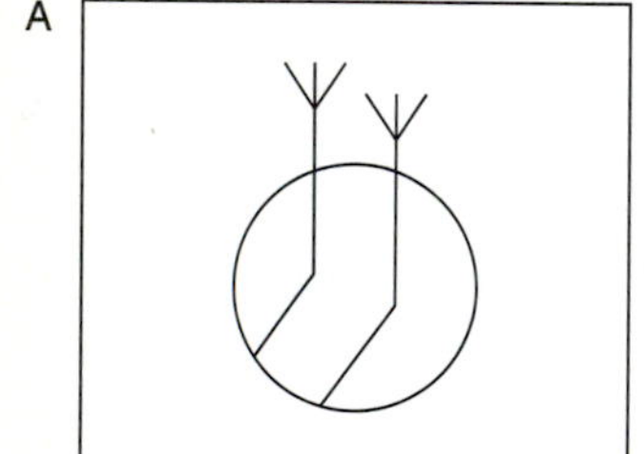

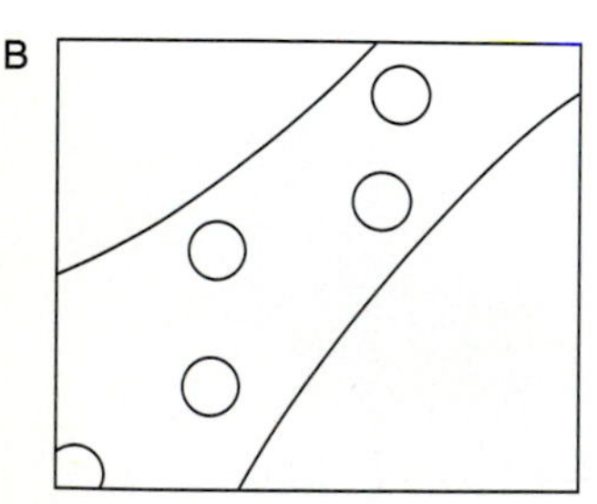

Figure 8.34 Droodles
What are these animals? Do you see in (A) an early bird who caught a very strong worm and in (B) a giraffe's neck? Each of these figures can be seen as representing something familiar to you, although this perceptual recognition usually does not occur until some identifying information is provided.

For a more detailed example of top-down versus bottom-up processing, we turn to the domain of speech perception. You have undoubtedly had the experience of trying to carry on a conversation at a very loud party. Under those circumstances, it's probably true that not all of the physical signal you are producing arrives unambiguously at your acquaintance's ears: some of what you had to say was almost certainly obscured by coughs, thumping music, or peals of laughter. Even so, people rarely realize that there are gaps in the physical signal they are experiencing. This phenomenon is known as

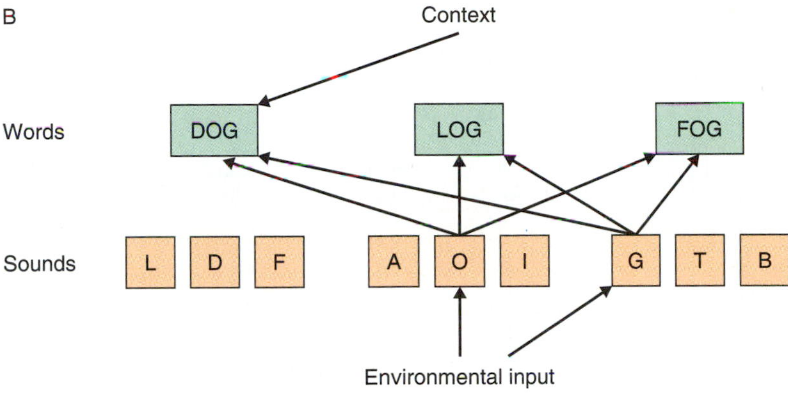

Figure 8.35 Phonemic Restoration

phonemic restoration (Warren, 1970). Samuel (1981, 1991) has shown that subjects often find it difficult to tell whether they are hearing a word that has a noise replacing part of the original speech signal or whether they are hearing a word with a noise just superimposed on the intact signal (see the top panel of **Figure 8.35**).

The bottom panel of Figure 8.35 shows how bottom-up and top-down processes could interact to produce phonemic restoration (McClelland & Elman, 1986). Suppose part of what your friend says at a noisy party is obscured so that the signal that arrives at your ears is "I have to go home to walk my (noise)og." If noise covers the /d/, you are likely to think that you actually heard the full word *dog*. But why? In Figure 8.35, you see two of the types of information relevant to speech perception. We have the individual sounds that make up words, and the words themselves. When the sounds /o/ and /g/ arrive in this system, they provide information—in a bottom-up fashion—to the word level (we have given only a subset of the words in English that end with /og/). This provides you with a range of candidates for what your friend might have said. Now top-down processes go to work—the context helps you select *dog* as the most likely word to appear in this utterance. When all of this happens swiftly enough—bottom-up identification of a set of candidate words and top-down selection of the likely correct candidate—you'll never know that the /d/ was missing. Your perceptual processes believe that the word was intact. (You may want to review Figure 8.4 to see how everything in this chapter fits together.)

Identification involves both bottom-up and top-down processing, which often works together to complete a perception, such as filling in a small gap in a conversation.

Object Recognition

From the example of speech perception, we can derive a general approach that researchers bring to the bottom-up study of recognition: they try to determine the building blocks that perceptual systems use to recognize whole percepts. For language, your speech perception processes combine environmental information about series of sounds to recognize individual words. What are the units from which you construct your representations of

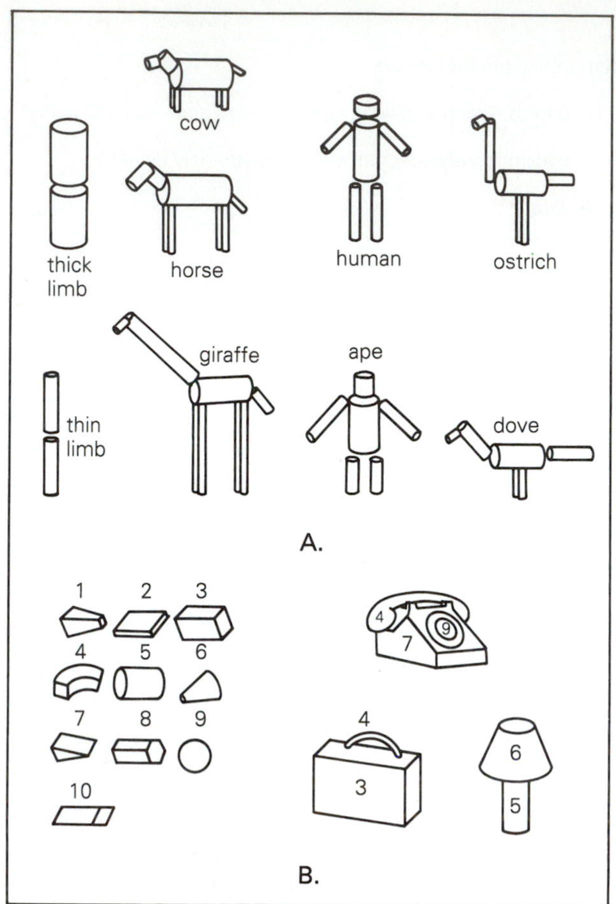

Figure 8.36 Recognition by Components

Suggested components of 3-dimensional objects and examples of how they may combine. In the top half of the figure, each 3-D object is constructed of cylinders of different sizes. In the bottom half of the figure, several different building blocks are combined to form familiar objects.

objects in the world? How, for example, do you decide that a gray, oddly shaped, medium-size, furry thing is actually a cat? Presumably, you have a memory representation of a cat. The identification process consists in matching the information in the percept to your memory representation of the cat. But how are these matches accomplished? One possibility is that the memory representations of various objects consist of components and information about the way these components are attached to each other (Marr & Nishihara, 1978). **Irving Biederman** (1985, 1987) has proposed that all objects can be assembled from a set of *geometrical ions,* or *geons.* Geons are not a large or arbitrary set of shapes. Biederman argued that a set of 36 geons can be defined by following the rule that each three-dimensional geon creates a unique pattern of stimulation on the two-dimensional retina. This uniqueness rule would allow you to work backward from a pattern of sensory stimulation to a strong guess at what the environmental object was like. **Figure 8.36** gives examples of the way in which objects can be assembled from this collection of standard parts.

Irving Biederman's theory of object recognition suggests that all objects can be assembled from a set of geometrical ions, or geons.

Researchers have shown that such parts do, in fact, play a role in object recognition. They have done so by presenting subjects with degraded pictures of objects that either do or do not leave parts intact (Biederman, 1987; Biederman & Cooper, 1991). The first column of **Figure 8.37** shows line drawings of common objects. The middle column shows those same objects

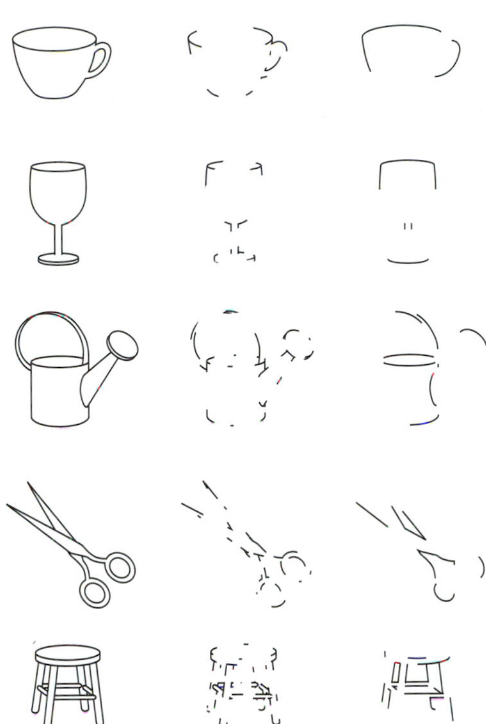

Figure 8.37 Role of Parts in Object Recognition *The deletions of visual information in the middle column leave the parts intact. In the right-hand column, the deletions disrupt the parts. Do you agree that the objects are easier to recognize in the middle versions?*

with only information deleted that still allows you to detect what the parts are and how they are combined. The right-hand column presents deletions that disrupt the identities of and relationships between the parts. Do you agree that it would be hard for you to recognize some of these objects based just on the drawings in the third column? The contrast here suggests that you can recognize objects with limited information (just as you can restore missing phonemes), but not if that information disrupts the critical parts.

Recovery of components alone, however, will not always be sufficient to recognize an object (Tarr, 1994). One difficulty, as shown in **Figure 8.38**, is that you often see objects from radically different perspectives. The appearance of the parts that make up the object may be quite different from each of these perspectives. As a hedge against this difficulty, you must store separate memory representations for each of the major perspectives from which you view standard objects (Tarr & Pinker, 1989). When you encounter an object in the environment, you may have to mentally transform the percept to determine if it correctly matches one of those views. Thus to recognize a gray, oddly shaped, medium-size, furry thing as a cat, you must recognize it both as an appropriate combination of geons and as that appropriate combination of geons from a specific viewpoint.

Although research supports Biederman's theory of a set of standard parts, object recognition also depends on the perspective from which the parts are seen.

The Influence of Contexts and Expectations

What also might help you recognize the cat, however, is to find that gray, oddly shaped, medium-size, furry thing in its accustomed place in your home. This is the top-down aspect of perception: expectations can influence your hypotheses about what is out there in the world. Have you ever had the experience of seeing people you knew in places where you didn't expect to see them, such as in the wrong city or the wrong social group? It takes much longer to recognize them in such situations, and sometimes you aren't even sure that you really know them. The problem is not that they look any different but that the *context* is wrong; you didn't *expect* them to be there. The spatial and temporal context in which objects are recognized provides an

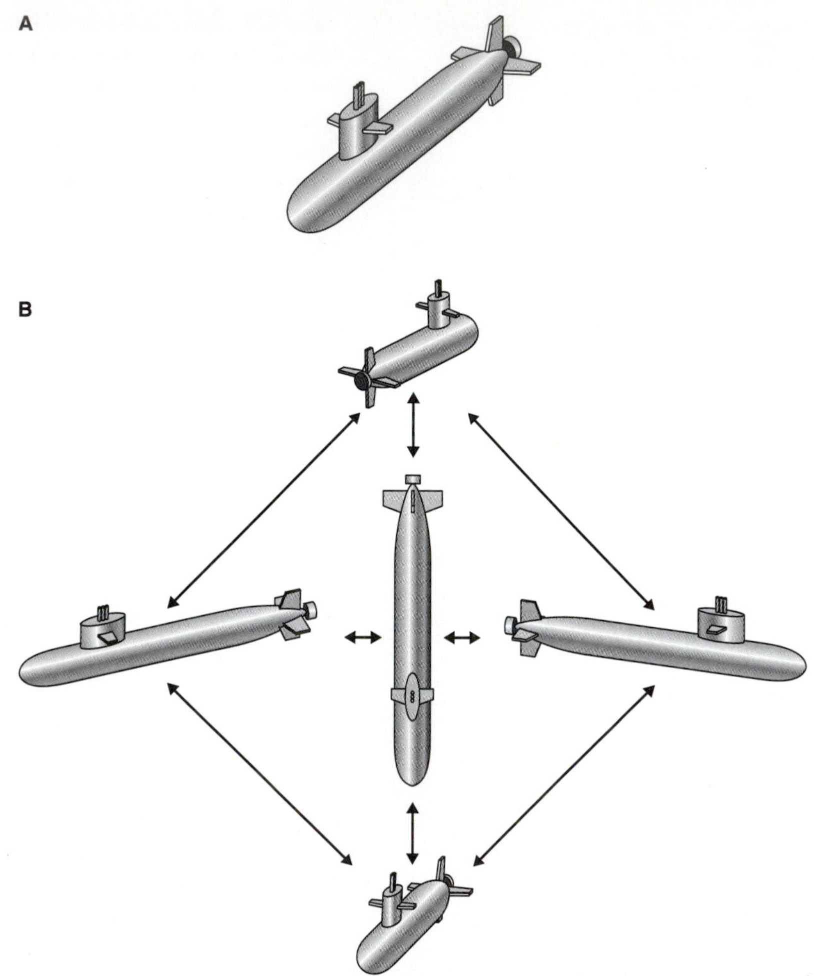

Figure 8.38 Looking at the Same Object From Different Perspectives
You see different parts of an object when you view it from different perspectives. To overcome this difficulty, you store multiple views of complex objects in memory.

The spatial and temporal context in which an object is seen creates expectations that influence your ability to recognize the object.

important source of information, because from the context you generate expectations about what objects you are and are not likely to see nearby (Biederman, 1989).

Perceptual identification depends on your expectations as well as on the physical properties of the objects you see—*object identification is a constructive, interpretive process.* Depending on what you already know, where you are, and what else you see around you, your identification may vary. Read the following words:

THE CAT

They say *THE CAT,* right? Now look again at the middle letter of each word. Physically, these two letters are exactly the same, yet you perceived the first as an H and the second as an A. Why? Clearly, your perception was affected by what you know about words in English. The context provided by T_E makes an H highly likely and an A unlikely, whereas the reverse is true of the context of C_T (Selfridge, 1955).

Researchers have often documented the effects of context and expectation on your perception (and response) by studying set. **Set** is a temporary readiness to perceive or react to a stimulus in a particular way. There are three types of set: motor, mental, and perceptual. A *motor set* is a readiness to make a quick, prepared response. A runner trains by perfecting a motor set to come out of the blocks as fast as possible at the sound of the starting gun. A *mental set* is a readiness to deal with a situation, such as a problem-solving task or a game, in a way determined by learned rules, instructions, expectations, or habitual tendencies. A mental set can actually prevent you from solving a problem when the old rules don't seem to fit the new situation, as we'll see when we study problem solving in a later chapter. A *perceptual set* is a readiness to detect a particular stimulus in a given context. A new mother, for example, is perceptually set to hear the cries of her child.

Figure 8.39
(A) A Young Beauty

Often a set leads you to change your interpretation of an ambiguous stimulus. Consider these two series of words:

FOX; OWL; SNAKE; TURKEY; SWAN; D?CK

BOB; RAY; DAVE; BILL; HENRY; D?CK

Did you read through the lists? What word came to mind for D?CK in each case? If you thought DUCK and DICK, it's because the list of words created a set that directed your search of memory in a particular way.

Labels can provide a context that gives a perceptual set for an ambiguous figure. You have seen how meaningless droodles turn into meaningful objects. Look carefully at the picture of the woman in **Figure 8.39A** on this page; have a friend (but not you) examine **Figure 8.39B** on page 301. Next, together look at **Figure 8.39C** on page 302—what does each of you see? Did the prior exposure to the unambiguous pictures with their labels have any effect on perception of the ambiguous image? This demonstration shows how easy it is for people to develop different views of the same person or object, based on prior conditions that create different sets.

Researchers have documented the effects of context on perception by studying the phenomena of motor set, mental set, and perceptual set.

All the effects of context on perception clearly require that your memory be organized in such a fashion that information relevant to particular situations becomes available at the right times. In other words, to generate appropriate (or inappropriate) expectations, you must be able to make use of prior knowledge stored in memory. Sometimes you "see" with your memory as much as you see with your eyes. In Chapter 10, we will discuss the properties of memory that make context effects on perception possible.

Creatively Playful Perception

Because of your ability to go beyond the sensory gifts that evolution has bestowed on the human species, you can become more creative in the way you perceive the world. Your role model is not a perfectly programmed computerized robot with exceptional sensory acuity. Instead, it is a great artist like Pablo Picasso. Picasso's genius was, in part, attributable to his enormous talent for "playful perception." This artist could free himself from the bonds of perceptual and mental sets to see not the old in the new but the new in the old, the novel in the familiar, and the unusual figure concealed within the familiar ground.

Perceptual creativity involves experiencing the world in ways that are imaginative, personally enriching, and fun (Leff, 1984). You can accomplish perceptual creativity by consciously directing your attention and full awareness to the objects and activities around you. Your goal should be to become more flexible in what you allow yourself to perceive and think, remaining open to alternative responses to situations.

We can think of no better way to conclude this formal presentation of the psychology of perception than by proposing ten suggestions for playfully enhancing your powers of perception:

- Imagine that everyone you meet is really a machine designed to look humanoid, and all machines are really people designed to look inanimate.
- Notice all wholes as ready to come apart into separately functioning pieces that can make it on their own.
- Imagine that your mental clock is hooked up to a video recorder that can rewind, fast-forward, and freeze time.
- Recognize that most objects around you have a "family resemblance" to other objects.
- View the world as if you were an animal or a home appliance.
- Consider one new use for each object you view (use a tennis racket to drain cooked spaghetti).
- Suspend the law of causality so that events just happen, while coincidence and chance rule over causes and effects.
- Dream up alternative meanings for the objects and events in your life.
- Discover something really interesting about activities and people you used to find boring.
- Violate some of the assumptions that you and others have about what you would and wouldn't do (without engaging in a dangerous activity).

Final Lessons

The important lesson to be learned from the study of perception is that a perceptual experience in response to a stimulus event is a response of the whole person. In addition to the information provided when your sensory receptors are stimulated, your final perception depends on who you are, whom you are with, and what you expect, want, and value. A perceiver often plays two different roles that we can compare to gambling and interior design. As a gambler, a perceiver is willing to bet that the present input can be understood in terms of past knowledge and personal theories. As a compulsive interior decorator, a perceiver is constantly rearranging the stimuli so that they fit better and are more coherent. Incongruity and messy perceptions are rejected in favor of those with clear, clean, consistent lines.

If perceiving were completely bottom-up, you would be bound to the same mundane, concrete reality of the here and now. You could register experience but not profit from it on later occasions, nor would you see the world differently under different circumstances. If perceptual processing were completely top-down, however, you could become lost in your own fantasy world of what you expect and hope to perceive. A proper balance between the two extremes achieves the basic goal of perception: to experience what is out there in a way that maximally serves your needs as a biological and social being moving about and adapting to your physical and social environment.

Figure 8.39
(B) An Old Woman

Recapping Main Points

Sensing, Organizing, Identifying, and Recognizing

Your perceptual systems do not simply record information about the external world but actively organize and interpret information as well. Perception is a three-stage process consisting of a sensory stage, a perceptual organization stage, and an identification and recognition stage. At the sensory level of processing, physical energy is detected and transformed into neural energy and sensory experience. At the organizational level, brain processes organize sensations into coherent images and give you perception of objects and patterns. At the level of identification, percepts of objects are compared with memory representations in order to be recognized as familiar and meaningful objects. The task of perception is to determine what the distal (external) stimulus is from the information contained in the proximal (sensory) stimulus. Ambiguity may arise when the same sensory information can be organized into different percepts. Knowledge about perceptual illusions can give you clues about normal organizing processes.

Attentional Processes

Attention refers to your ability to select part of the sensory input and disregard the rest. Both your personal goals and the properties of objects in the world determine where you will focus your attention. Attention accomplishes its tasks by both facilitating the processing of the relevant, attended stimuli and suppressing the processing of irrelevant, unattended stimuli. Preattentive processing enables you to search the visual environment efficiently, although focused attention is required in many cases to find combinations of features. Attention also allows simple physical properties of objects to be combined correctly.

Organizational Processes in Perception

Organizational processes provide percepts consistent with the sensory data. These processes segregate your percepts into regions and organize them into

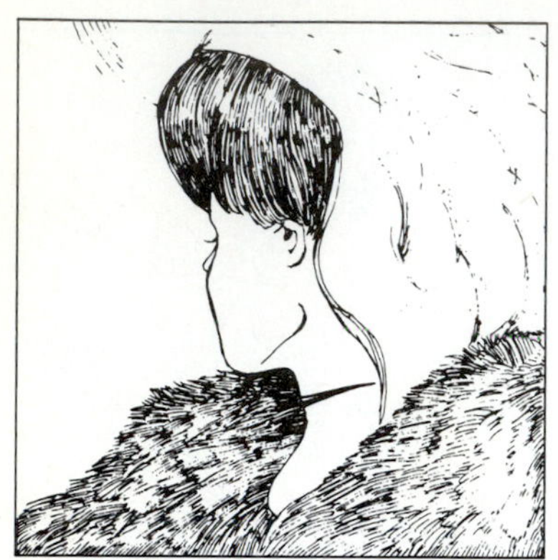

Figure 8.39
(C) Now What Do You See?

You: ______________________

Friend: ______________________

figures that stand out against the ground. You tend to see incomplete figures as wholes; group items by similarity; and see "good" figures more readily. You tend to organize and interpret parts in relation to the spatial and temporal context in which you experience them. You also tend to see a reference frame as stationary and the parts within it as moving, regardless of the actual sensory stimulus. In converting the two-dimensional information on the retina to a perception of three-dimensional space, the visual system gauges object size and distance: distance is interpreted on the basis of known size, and size is interpreted on the basis of various distance cues. You tend to perceive objects as having stable size, shape, and orientation. Prior knowledge normally reinforces these and other constancies in perception; under extreme conditions, perceptual constancy may break down.

Identification and Recognition Processes

During the final stage of perceptual processing—identification and recognition of objects—percepts are given meaning through processes that combine bottom-up and top-down influences. Context, expectations, and perceptual sets may guide recognition of incomplete or ambiguous data in one direction rather than another, equally possible one. Perception thus depends on what you know and expect as well as on the sensory stimulus.

Resources

Berkley, M. A., & Stebbins, W. C. (Eds.). (1991). *Comparative perception.* New York: Wiley.

Gibson, E. J. (1991). *An odyssey in learning and perception.* Cambridge, MA: MIT Press.

Rock, I. (1983). *The logic of perception.* Cambridge, MA: MIT Press. This book considers theories of perception and perception as problem solving.

Sekuler, R., & Blake, R. (1994). *Perception.* (3rd ed.). New York: McGraw-Hill.

Shepard, R. N. (1990). *Mind sights: Original visual illusions, ambiguities, and other anomalies.* New York: Freeman.

9

Learning and Behavior Analysis

Imagine that you are in a movie theater watching a horror film. As the hero approaches a closed door, the music on the movie's sound track grows dark and menacing. You suddenly feel the urge to yell, "Don't go through that door!" Meanwhile, you find that your heart is racing and you're sweating all over the theater's upholstery. But why? If you think about this question formally, you might come to the answer, "I have learned an association between movie music and movie events—and that's what's making me nervous!" But had you ever thought about this relationship before? Probably not. Somehow, by virtue of sitting in enough movie theaters, you have learned the association without any particular thought. The main topic of Chapter 9 is the type of associations that you acquire effortlessly in your day-to-day experience.

Psychologists have long been interested in **conditioning**, *or the ways in which events and behavior become associated with one another. In this chapter, we will examine two basic types of conditioning: classical conditioning and operant conditioning. As you shall see, each of these types of conditioning represents a different way in which organisms acquire and use information about the structure of their environments. For each of these forms of conditioning, we will describe both the basic mechanisms that govern its operation in the laboratory and applications to real-life situations. Finally, we will discuss how researchers have begun to create formal models of the* how *of conditioning.*

Before we begin our study in earnest, let's consider the significance of learning from an evolutionary perspective. *Learning is as much a product of your genetic endowment as any other aspect of your experience. Humans, like other organisms, inherit a particular* capacity *for learning. The capacity for learning varies among animal species according to their genetic blueprint (Mayr, 1974). Some creatures, such as reptiles and amphibians, learn little from interactions with the environment. Their survival depends on living in a relatively constant habitat, in which their innate responses to specific environmental events bring them to what they need or take them away from what they must avoid. For other animals, genes play much less of a role in determining specific behavior-environment interactions and allow for greater* plasticity, *or variability, in learning. These animals are able to learn according to the ways in which their behavior produces changes in their environment. You should always bear in mind, however, that you have inherited only a capacity to learn. Whether that capacity is realized—and to what extent—depends on the individual's personal experiences.*

THE STUDY OF LEARNING

To begin our exploration of learning, we will first define learning itself and then offer a brief sketch of the history of research on the topic.

What Is Learning?

Learning is a process that results in a relatively consistent change in behavior or behavior potential and is based on experience. Let's look more closely at the three critical parts of this definition.

A Change in Behavior or Behavior Potential

It is obvious that learning has taken place when you are able to demonstrate the results, such as drive a car or use a microwave oven. You can't directly observe learning itself—you can't ordinarily see the changes in your brain—but learning is apparent from improvements in your **performance.** Often, however, your performance doesn't show everything that you have learned. Sometimes, too, you have acquired general attitudes, such as an *appreciation* of modern art or an *understanding* of Eastern philosophy, that may not be apparent in your measurable actions. In such instances, you have achieved a *potential for behavior change,* because you have learned attitudes and values that can influence the kind of books you read or the way you spend your leisure time. This is an example of the **learning–performance distinction**—the difference between what has been learned and what is expressed, or performed, in overt behavior.

A Relatively Consistent Change

To qualify as learned, a change in behavior or behavior potential must be relatively consistent over different occasions. Thus once you learn to swim, you will probably always be able to do so. Note that consistent changes are not always permanent changes. You may, for example, have become quite a consistent dart thrower when you practiced every day. If you gave up the sport, however, your skills might have deteriorated toward their original level. (But if you have learned once to be a championship dart thrower, it ought to be easier for you to learn a second time. In that sense the change may be permanent.)

As every athlete knows, constant practice (in psychological terms, learning through repetition) is a vital ingredient in the ability to perform consistently.

A Process Based on Experience

Learning can take place only through experience. Experience includes taking in information (and evaluating and transforming it) and making responses that affect the environment. Learning consists of a response influenced by the lessons of memory. We won't count as learned behavior changes that come about because of physical maturation or brain development as the organism ages, nor those caused by illness or brain damage. Some lasting changes in behavior require a combination of experience and maturational readiness. For example, consider the timetable that determines when an infant is ready to crawl, stand, walk, run, and be toilet trained. No amount of training or practice will produce those behaviors before the child has matured sufficiently. Psychologists are especially interested in discovering what aspects of behavior can be changed through experience and how such changes come about.

Behaviorism and Behavior Analysis

John B. Watson is known as the founder of behaviorism.

It will be important, as you read this chapter, to ask yourself the question How much of human behavior can be explained by virtue of simple forms of learning? Or, to put the question somewhat differently, Are there any forms of behavior that *cannot* be explained in these terms? The most prominent answer to this question, a position known as *radical behaviorism,* was formulated by **B. F. Skinner** (1904–1990). In his writing, most famously in the popular book *Beyond Freedom and Dignity* (1972), Skinner argued that all behavior could be understood as interactions of an organism's genetic inheritance with simple forms of learning. We will briefly trace how Skinner arrived at this position.

Much of modern psychology's view of learning finds its roots in the work of **John Watson** (1878–1958), who founded the school of psychology known as *behaviorism.* For nearly 50 years, American psychology was dominated by the behaviorist tradition expressed in Watson's 1919 book, *Psychology from the Standpoint of a Behaviorist.* Watson argued that introspection—subjects' verbal reports of sensations, images, and feelings—was *not* an acceptable means of studying behavior because it was too subjective. How could scientists verify the accuracy of such private experiences? But once introspection has been rejected, what should the subject matter of psychology be? Watson's answer was *observable behavior.* In Watson's words, "States of consciousness, like the so-called phenomena of spiritualism, are not objectively verifiable and for that reason can never become data for science" (Watson, 1919, p. 1). Watson also defined the chief goal of psychology as "the prediction and control of behavior" (Watson, 1913, p. 158).

B. F. Skinner expanded upon Watson's ideas and applied them to a wide spectrum of behavior.

B. F. Skinner began his graduate study in psychology at Harvard after reading Watson's 1924 book, *Behaviorism.* Skinner embraced Watson's cause and expanded his agenda: Skinner's complaint against internal states and mental events dealt not so much with their legitimacy as data as with their legitimacy as *causes of behavior* (Skinner, 1990). In Skinner's view, mental events, such as thinking and imagining, do not cause behavior. Rather, they are examples of behavior that are caused by environmental stimuli. Suppose that we deprive a pigeon of food for 24 hours, place it in an apparatus where it can obtain food by pecking a small disk, and find that it soon does so. Skinner would argue that the animal's behavior can be fully explained by environmental events—deprivation and the use of food as reinforcement. The subjective feeling of hunger, which cannot be directly observed or measured, is not a cause of the behavior but the result of deprivation. It adds nothing to our account to say that the bird pecked the disk because it was hungry or because it wanted to get the food. To explain what the bird does, you need not understand anything about its inner psychological states. This is the essence of Skinner's brand of behaviorism (Delprato & Midgley, 1992).

This same brand of behaviorism served as the original philosophical cornerstone of **behavior analysis**, the area of psychology that focuses on discovering environmental determinants of learning and behavior (Grant & Evans, 1994). In general, behavior analysts argue that human nature can be understood by using extensions of the methods and principles of natural science. The task is to discover regularities in learning that are universal, occurring in all types of animal species, including humans, under comparable situations. These researchers generally assume that elementary processes of learning are *conserved across species*—that is, across all animal species, these processes are comparable in their basic features. That is why studies with nonhuman animals have been so critical to progress in this area. Complex forms of learning represent combinations and elaborations of simpler processes, and not qualitatively different phenomena. Behavior analysis seeks to identify the orderly principles that underlie changes in people's actions in response to their experience. It is, once again, the relationship between behavior and environmental events and not the relationship between behavior and mental events that is of primary concern.

Behavior analysis focuses on discovering the environmental determinants of learning and behavior.

Although this behavioristic position has yielded many valuable explanations of human performance, we will see that its strongest form has been challenged by psychologists who insist on keeping a thinking brain in control of the behaving body. As you read Chapter 9, you will be able to weigh the evidence for and against the radical behaviorist position.

CLASSICAL CONDITIONING: LEARNING PREDICTABLE SIGNALS

Imagine once more that you are watching that horror movie. Why do you start to sweat when the sound track signals trouble for the hero? Somehow your body has learned to produce a physiological response when one environmental event (for instance, scary music) is associated with another (scary visual events). This type of learning is known as **classical conditioning**, a basic form of learning in which one stimulus or event predicts the occurrence of another stimulus or event. The organism learns a new *association* between two stimuli—a stimulus that did not previously elicit the response and one that naturally elicited the response. As you shall see, the innate capacity to quickly associate pairs of events in your environment has profound behavioral implications.

PAVLOV'S SURPRISING OBSERVATION

The first rigorous study of classical conditioning was the result of what may well be psychology's most famous accident. The Russian physiologist **Ivan Pavlov** (1849–1936) did not set out to study classical conditioning or any other psychological phenomenon. He happened upon classical conditioning while conducting research on digestion, research for which he won a Nobel Prize in 1904.

Pavlov had devised a technique to study digestive processes in dogs by implanting tubes in their glands and digestive organs to divert bodily secretions to containers outside their bodies so that the secretions could be measured and analyzed. To produce these secretions, Pavlov's assistants put meat powder into the dogs' mouths. After repeating this procedure a number of times, Pavlov observed an unexpected behavior in his dogs—they salivated *before* the powder was put in their mouths! They would start salivating at the mere sight of the food and, later, at the sight of the assistant who brought the food or even at the sound of the assistant's footsteps. Indeed, any stimulus that regularly preceded the presentation of food came to elicit salivation.

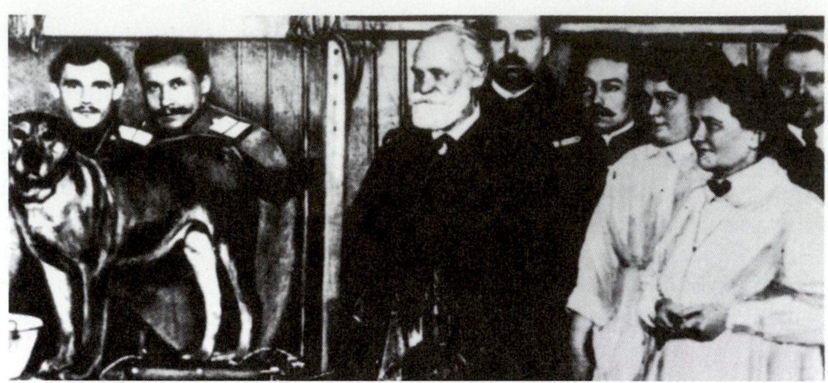

Physiologist Ivan Pavlov (shown here with his research team) observed classical conditioning while conducting research on digestion.

Quite by accident, Pavlov had observed that learning may result from two stimuli becoming associated with each other.

After observing the basic principles of classical conditioning by accident, Pavlov devoted the remainder of his career to determining the specific variables that influence conditioning.

Fortunately, Pavlov had the scientific skills and curiosity to begin a rigorous attack on this surprising phenomenon. He ignored the advice of the great physiologist of the time, Sir Charles Sherrington, that he should give up his foolish investigation of "psychic" secretions. Instead, Pavlov abandoned his work on digestion and, in so doing, changed the course of psychology forever (Pavlov, 1928). For the remainder of Pavlov's life, he continued to search for the variables that influence classically conditioned behavior. Classical conditioning is also called *Pavlovian conditioning* because of Pavlov's discovery of the major phenomena of conditioning and his dedication to tracking down the variables that influence it.

Pavlov's considerable research experience allowed him to follow a simple and elegant strategy to discover the conditions necessary for his dogs to be conditioned to salivate. Dogs in his experiments were first placed in a restraining harness. At regular intervals, a stimulus like a tone was presented and a dog was given a bit of food. Importantly, the tone had no prior meaning for the dog with respect to food or salivation. As you might imagine, the dog's first reaction to the tone was only an *orienting response*—the dog pricked its ears and moved its head to locate the source of the sound. However, with *repeated pairings* of the tone and the food, the orienting response stopped and salivation began. What Pavlov had observed in his earlier research was no accident: the phenomenon could be replicated under controlled conditions. Pavlov demonstrated the generality of this effect by using a variety of other stimuli ordinarily neutral with respect to salivation, such as lights and ticking metronomes.

The main features of Pavlov's classical conditioning procedure are illustrated in **Figure 9.1**. At the core of classical conditioning are reflex responses. A **reflex** is an unlearned response—such as salivation, pupil contraction, knee jerks, or eye blinking—that is naturally elicited by specific stimuli that are biologically relevant for the organism. Any stimulus, such as food, that naturally elicits a reflexive behavior is called an **unconditional stimulus** (UCS), because learning is not a necessary condition for the stimulus to control the behavior. The behavior elicited by the unconditional stimulus is called the **unconditional response** (UCR).

In a typical classical conditioning experiment, a *neutral stimulus*—a stimulus, such as a light or a tone, that ordinarily has no meaning in the context of the UCS-UCR reflex—is repeatedly paired with the unconditional stimulus so that the UCS predictably follows the neutral stimulus. The neutral stimulus paired with the unconditional stimulus is called the **conditional stimulus** (CS), because its power to elicit behavior like the UCR is *condi-*

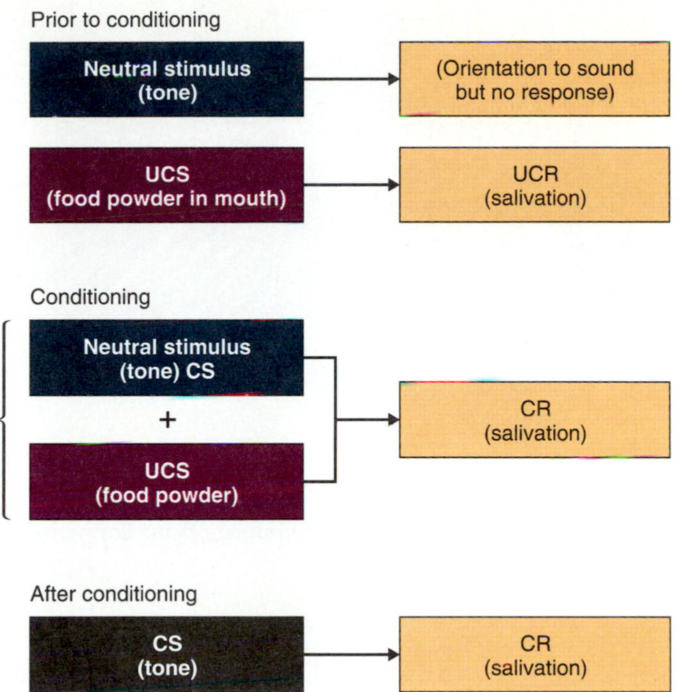

Figure 9.1 Basic Features of Classical Conditioning
Before conditioning, the unconditional stimulus (UCS) naturally elicits the unconditional response (UCR). A neutral stimulus, such as a tone, has no eliciting effect. During conditioning, the neutral stimulus is paired with the UCS. Through its association with the UCS, the neutral stimulus becomes a conditional stimulus (CS) and elicits a conditional response (CR) that is similar to the UCR.

tional upon its association with the UCS. After several trials, the CS is presented alone. Now it generally elicits a response similar to the unconditional response. The behavior elicited by the CS is called the **conditional response** (CR). In other words, nature provides the UCS-UCR connections, but the learning produced by classical conditioning creates the CS-CR connection. The conditional stimulus acquires some of the power to influence behavior that was originally limited to the unconditional stimulus. Let's now look in more detail at the optimal conditions for classical conditioning.

In classical conditioning, an unconditional stimulus naturally elicits a reflexive behavior called an unconditional response. After repeated pairings of the unconditional stimulus with a neutral stimulus, the neutral stimulus will elicit the response.

The Acquisition of Classically Conditioned Responses

So far, we have *described* classical conditioning, but we have not yet *explained* it. Pavlov believed that classical conditioning resulted from the mere pairing of the CS and the UCS. In his view, if a response is to be classically conditioned, the CS and the UCS must occur close together in time—that is, be *temporally contiguous*. As we shall now see, contemporary research has modified that view.

Contingency

Pavlov's theory dominated classical conditioning until the mid-1960s, when **Robert Rescorla** (1966) conducted a very telling experiment using dogs as subjects. Rescorla designed an experiment that contrasted circumstances in which a tone (the CS) and a shock (the UCS) were merely contiguous—which, if Pavlov was correct, would be sufficient to produce classical conditioning—versus circumstances in which, additionally, the tone reliably predicted the presence of the shock.

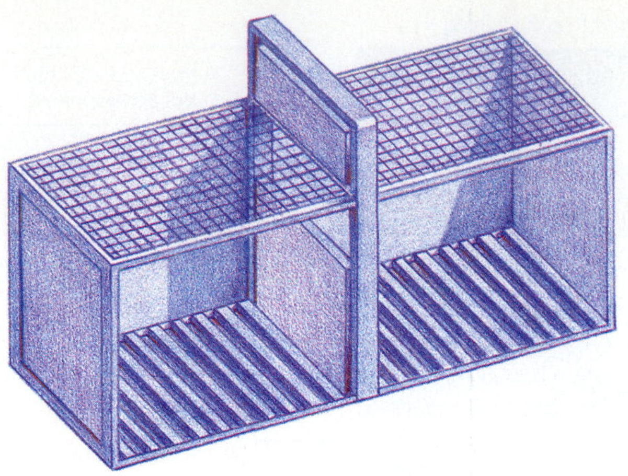

Figure 9.2 A Shuttlebox
Rescorla used the frequency with which dogs jumped over a barrier as a measure of fear conditioning.

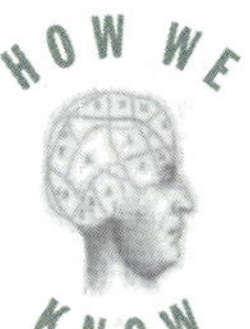

In the first phase of the experiment, Rescorla trained dogs to jump a barrier from one side of a shuttlebox to the other, to avoid an electric shock delivered through the grid floor (see **Figure 9.2**). If the dogs did not jump, they received a shock; if they did jump, the shock was postponed. Rescorla used the frequency with which dogs jumped the barrier as a measure of fear conditioning.

When the dogs were jumping across the barrier regularly, Rescorla divided his subjects into two groups and subjected them to another training procedure. To the random group, the UCS (the shock) was delivered randomly and independently of the CS (the tone) (see **Figure 9.3**). Although the CS and the UCS often occurred close together in time—they were, by chance, temporally contiguous—the UCS was as likely to be delivered in the

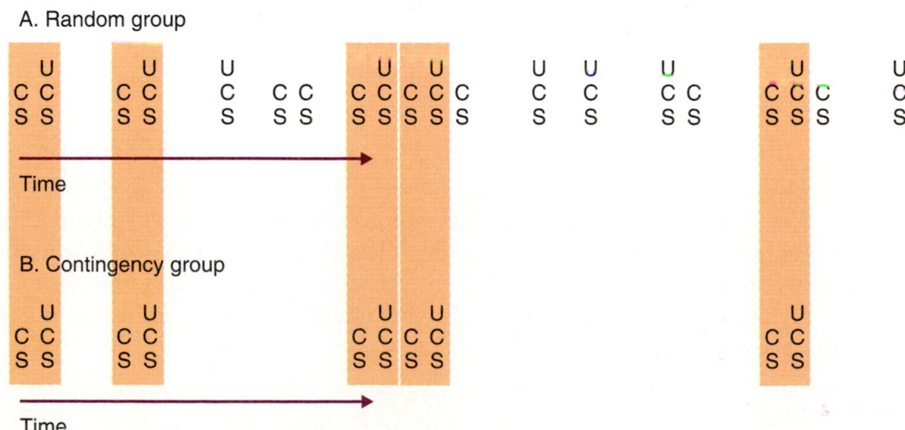

Figure 9.3 Rescorla's Procedure for Demonstrating the Importance of Contingency
For the Random group, 5-second tones (the CS) and 5-second shocks (the UCS) were distributed randomly through the experimental period. For the Contingency group, the dogs experienced only the subset of tones and shocks that occurred in a predictive relationship (the onset of the CS preceded the onset of the UCS by 30 seconds or less). Only the dogs in the Contingency group learned to associate the CS with the UCS.

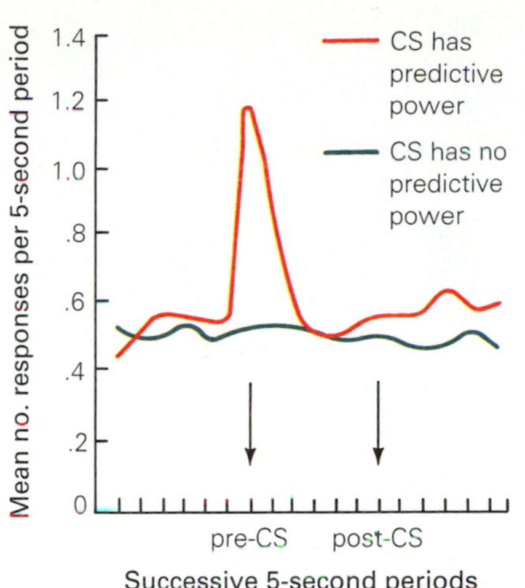

Figure 9.4 The Role of Contingency in Classical Conditioning
Rescorla demonstrated that dogs trained under the contingent CS-UCS relation showed more jumping (and thus conditioned fear) than did dogs trained under the contiguous but noncontingent CS-UCS relation. The arrows indicate the onset and offset of the CS tone.

absence of the CS as it was in its presence. Thus the CS had no predictive value. For the contingency group, however, the UCS always followed the CS. Thus for this group, the sounding of the tone was a reliable predictor of the delivery of the shock.

Once this training was complete, the dogs were put back into the shuttlebox, but this time with a twist. Now the tone used in the second training procedure occasionally sounded, signaling shock. What happened? **Figure 9.4** indicates that dogs exposed to the *contingent* (predictable) CS-UCS relation jumped more frequently in the presence of the tone than did dogs exposed only to the contiguous (associated) CS-UCS relation. Contingency was critical for the signal to serve the dogs as a successful cue for the shock.

Rescorla's research demonstrated that the UCS and the CS must be contingent as well as contiguous.

Thus, in addition to contiguity, it appears that the CS *must reliably predict* the occurrence of the UCS in order for classical conditioning to occur (Rescorla, 1988). This finding makes considerable sense. After all, in natural situations, where learning enables organisms to adapt to changes in their environment, stimuli come in clusters and not in neat, simple units, as they do in traditional laboratory experiments.

The need for a contingent, predictive relationship between the CS and UCS explains why, in conditioning, as in telling a good joke, *timing* is critical. The CS and UCS must be presented close enough in time to be perceived by the organism as being related. (We will describe an exception to this rule in a later section on *taste-aversion learning.*) Researchers have studied four temporal patterns between the two stimuli, as shown in **Figure 9.5** (Hearst, 1988). The most widely used type of conditioning is called *delayed conditioning,* in which the CS comes on prior to and stays on at least until the UCS is presented. In *trace conditioning,* the CS is turned off before the UCS is presented. *Trace* refers to the memory that the organism is assumed to have of the CS, which is no longer present when the UCS appears. In *simultaneous conditioning,* both the CS and UCS are presented at the same time. Finally, in the case of *backward conditioning,* the CS is presented after the UCS.

Conditioning is usually more effective with a short interval between the onsets of the CS and UCS. The range of time intervals between the CS and the UCS that will produce the best conditioning depends upon the response being conditioned. For skeletal responses, such as eye blinks, a short interval, of a second or less, is best. For visceral responses, such as heart rate and salivation, however, longer intervals, of 5 to 15 seconds, work best. Condi-

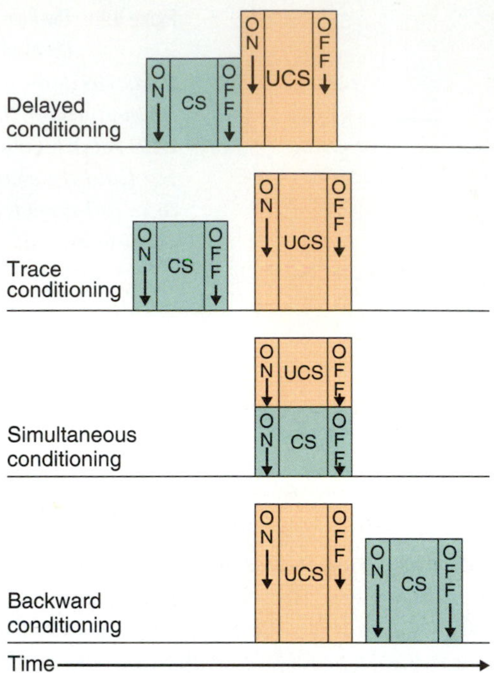

Figure 9.5 Four Variations of the CS-UCS Temporal Arrangement in Classical Conditioning

tioned fear usually requires a longer interval still, of many seconds or even minutes, to develop.

Conditioning is generally poor with a simultaneous procedure and very poor with a backward procedure. Evidence of backward conditioning may appear after a few pairings but disappear with extended training as the animal learns that the CS is followed by a period free of the UCS. In both cases, conditioning is weak because, as you have learned, the CS does not actually predict the onset of the UCS. So contingency is very important. But there's still more to classical conditioning.

Informativeness

Rescorla's work showed that contingency plays a crucial role in classical conditioning. **Leon Kamin** (1969) demonstrated that the CS must also be *informative* (see **Figure 9.6**).

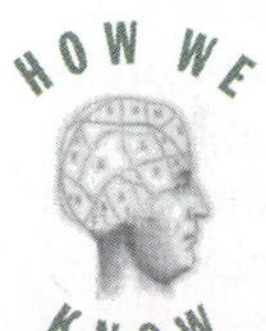

Kamin's study involved two groups of rats. The experimental group was first trained to press a lever in the presence of a tone (CS) to avoid shock (UCS). Next, a second CS—a light—was added; now the UCS was preceded by two CSs: the tone (CS_1) and the light (CS_2). The control group was exposed only to this sequence of tone-light-shock; it never experienced the tone alone as a predictor of shock delivery. Kamin then tested both groups of rats for fear conditioning to the light alone or to the tone alone. If contingency is sufficient to explain classical conditioning, then both groups of rats should have responded in equal amounts to the light and the tone. That is not what Kamin found. The experimental rats responded to the tone but not to the light, whereas control rats responded equally to both the tone and the light (Kamin, 1969).

Kamin explained his results in terms of the *informativeness* of the conditional stimuli. For experimental rats, the previous conditioning to the tone in the first phase of the experiment *blocked* any subsequent conditioning that could occur to the light. In other words, the previous experience with the

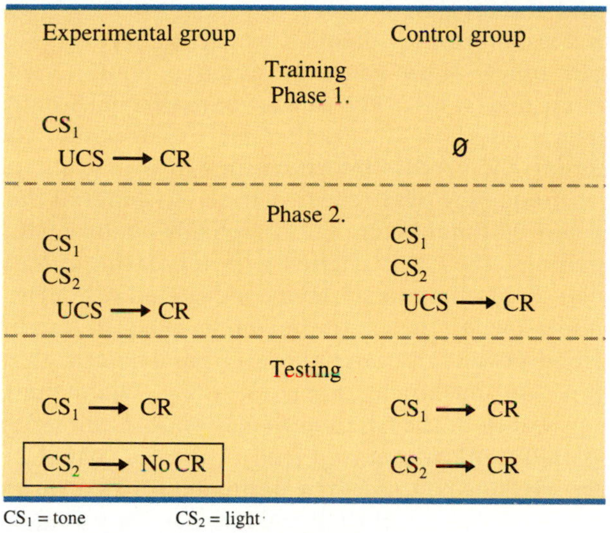

Experimental group		Control group
	Training Phase 1.	
CS_1 UCS → CR		Ø
	Phase 2.	
CS_1 CS_2 UCS → CR		CS_1 CS_2 UCS → CR
	Testing	
CS_1 → CR		CS_1 → CR
CS_2 → No CR		CS_2 → CR

CS_1 = tone CS_2 = light

Figure 9.6 Kamin's Procedure for Producing the Blocking Effect
Rats in the experimental group were first trained to respond to a tone (CS_1). Next, they were trained to respond to both a tone (CS_1) and a light (CS_2). Rats in the control group were trained only to the compound light and tone (CS). When tested for conditioning to a light alone and a tone alone, only the control rats responded to both stimuli. According to Kamin, experimental rats did not respond to the light because it contained no new information predicting the occurrence of the UCS: the tone's effect blocked the light's effect.

tone made the light irrelevant as a predictor of the UCS. From the rat's point of view, the light may as well not have existed; it provided no additional information beyond that already given by the tone. The ability of the first CS to reduce the informativeness of the second CS because of subjects' previous experience with the UCS is called **blocking.** For control rats, both the light and the tone were equally informative—the rats had no previous experience with either CS, so one did not reduce the informativeness of the other.

Kamin's research demonstrated that in addition to being contingent and contiguous to the UCS, a CS must be informative.

The requirement of informativeness explains why conditioning occurs most rapidly when the CS stands out against the many other stimuli that may also be present in an environment. A stimulus is more readily noticed the more *intense* it is and the more it *contrasts* with other stimuli. Either a strong, novel stimulus in an unfamiliar situation or a strong, familiar stimulus in a novel context leads to good conditioning (Kalat, 1974; Lubow et al., 1976). In real life, as in the conditioning laboratory, the key to developing a strong conditional response is to increase the signal-to-noise ratio of the CS by making it a stronger signal than all other competing events—background or irrelevant stimuli. If you want to get a date to start salivating, you'd better pick a conditional stimulus that you're sure will get noticed.

You can see that classical conditioning is more complex than even Pavlov originally realized. A neutral stimulus will only become an effective CS if it is both appropriately contingent and informative. But now let's shift your attention a bit. We have focused so far just on the **acquisition** of conditioned responses—how they get started. Let's turn to other aspects of the processes of classical conditioning.

Processes of Conditioning

What is the time course of classical conditioning? How precise are the associations? How fragile is the learning? In this section we review answers to these questions that have emerged from hundreds of different studies.

Acquisition and Extinction

Recall Pavlov's dogs: Were they doomed to salivate forever, every time they heard a certain tone? More generally, once a conditioned response is acquired, how long does it last? For an answer to this question, take a look at **Figure 9.7**, which displays a hypothetical experiment. The first panel reviews acquisition, the process by which the CR is first elicited and gradually increases in frequency over repeated trials. In general, the CS and UCS must be paired several times before the CS reliably elicits a CR. With systematic CS-UCS pairings, the CR is elicited with increasing frequency, and the organism may be said to have acquired a conditioned response.

But what happens when the CS (for example, the tone) no longer predicts the UCS (the food powder)? Under those circumstances, the CR becomes weaker over time and eventually stops occurring. When the CR no longer appears in the presence of the CS (and the absence of the UCS), the process of **extinction** is said to have occurred (see Figure 9.7, panel 2). Conditional responses, then, are not necessarily a permanent aspect of the organism's behavioral repertory. However, the CR will reappear in a weak form when the CS is presented alone again (see Figure 9.7, panel 3). Pavlov referred to this sudden reappearance of the CR after a rest period, or time-out, without further exposure to the UCS as **spontaneous recovery.**

The process of extinction demonstrates that conditional responses do not become permanent behaviors.

When the original pairing is renewed, postextinction, the CR gets rapidly stronger. This more rapid relearning is an instance of **savings:** less time is necessary to reacquire the response than to acquire it originally, so some of the original conditioning must be retained by the organism even after experimental extinction appears to have eliminated the CR. In other words, extinction has only weakened performance, not wiped out the original learning.

Stimulus Generalization

Suppose we have taught a dog that presentation of a tone of a certain frequency predicts food powder. Is the dog's response specific to only that stimulus? If you think about this question for a moment, you will probably not be surprised that the answer is no. In general, once a CR has been conditioned to a particular CS, similar stimuli may also elicit the response. For example, if conditioning was to a high-frequency tone, a slightly lower tone could also elicit the response. A child bitten by a big dog is likely to respond with fear even to smaller dogs. This automatic extension of responding to stimuli that

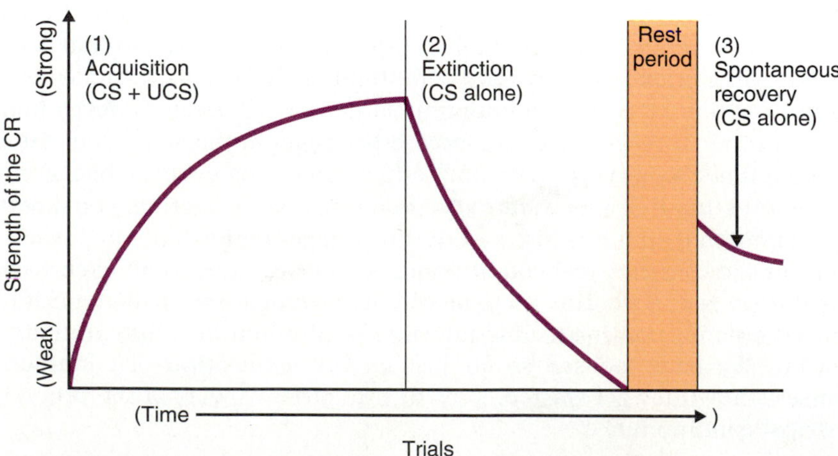

Figure 9.7 Acquisition, Extinction, and Spontaneous Recovery in Classical Conditioning
During acquisition (CS + UCS), the strength of the CR increases rapidly. During extinction, when the UCS no longer follows the CS, the strength of the CR drops to zero. The CR may reappear after a brief rest period, even when the UCS is still not presented. The reappearance of the CR is called spontaneous recovery.

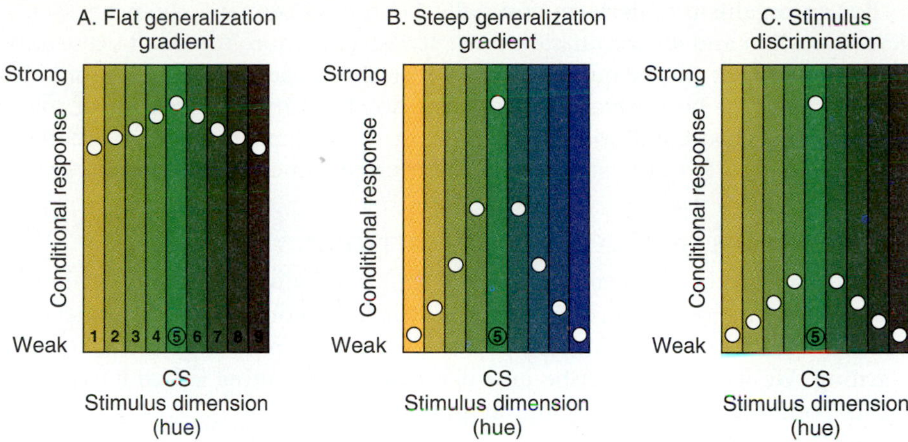

Figure 9.8 Stimulus Generalization Gradients
After conditioning to a medium green stimulus, the subject responds almost as strongly to stimuli of similar hues, as shown by the flat generalization gradient in panel A. When the subject is exposed to a broader range of colored stimuli, responses grow weaker as the color becomes increasingly dissimilar to the training stimulus. The generalization gradient becomes very steep, as shown in panel B. The experimenter could change the generalization gradient shown in panel A to resemble the one in panel C by giving the subject discrimination training. In this case, the medium green stimulus would be continually paired with the UCS, but stimuli of all other hues would not.

have never been paired with the original UCS is called **stimulus generalization.** The more similar the new stimulus is to the original CS, the stronger the response will be. When response strength is measured for each of a series of increasingly dissimilar stimuli along a given dimension, as shown in **Figure 9.8**, a *generalization gradient* is found.

The existence of generalization gradients should suggest to you the way classical conditioning serves its function in everyday experience. Because important stimuli rarely occur in exactly the same form every time in nature, stimulus generalization builds in a similarity safety factor by extending the range of learning beyond the original specific experience. With this feature, new but comparable events can be recognized as having the same meaning, or behavioral significance, despite apparent differences. For example, even when a predator makes a slightly different sound or is seen from a different angle, its prey can still recognize and respond to it quickly.

A child who has been frightened by one dog may develop a generalized fear response to all dogs.

Stimulus Discrimination

In some circumstances, however, it is important that a response be made to only a very small range of stimuli. An organism should not, for example, exhaust itself by fleeing too often from animals that are only superficially similar to its natural predators. **Stimulus discrimination** is the process by which an organism learns to respond differently to stimuli that are distinct from the CS on some dimension (for example, differences in hue or in pitch). An organism's discrimination among similar stimuli (tones of 1000, 1200, and 1500 Hz, for example) is sharpened with discrimination training in which only one of them (1200 Hz, for example) predicts the UCS and in which the others are repeatedly presented without it. Early in conditioning, stimuli similar to the CS will elicit a similar response, though not quite as strong. As discrimination training proceeds, the responses to the other, dissimilar stimuli weaken: the organism gradually learns which event-signal predicts the onset of the UCS and which signals do not.

Stimulus generalization and stimulus discrimination allow you to recognize and respond appropriately to new and slightly different features of the environment.

For an organism to perform optimally in an environment, the processes of generalization and discrimination must strike a balance. You don't want to be overselective—it can be quite costly to miss the presence of a predator—nor do you want to be overresponsive—you don't want to be fearful of every shadow. Classical conditioning provides a mechanism that allows creatures to react efficiently to the structure of their environments (Garcia, 1990).

Applications of Classical Conditioning

Your knowledge of classical conditioning can help you understand significant everyday behavior. In this section, we will help you recognize some real-world instances of emotions and preferences as the products of this form of learning. We will then describe how classical conditioning is being exploited for its potential to enhance immune function.

Emotions and Preferences

To get you started on classical conditioning, we asked you to think about your experience at a horror movie. In that case, you (unconsciously) learned an association between scary music (the CS) and certain likely events (the UCS—the kinds of things that happen in horror movies that cause reflexive revulsion). If you pay careful attention to events in your life, you will discover that there are many circumstances in which you can't quite explain why you are having such a strong emotional reaction or why you have such a strong preference about something. You might take a step back and ask yourself, Is this the product of classical conditioning?

Consider these situations (Rozin & Fallon, 1987; Rozin et al., 1986):

- Do you think you'd be willing to eat fudge that had been formed into the shape of dog feces?
- Do you think you'd be willing to drink a sugar-water solution if the sugar was drawn from a container that you knew was incorrectly labeled *poison*?
- Do you think you would be willing to drink apple juice into which a sterilized cockroach had been dipped?

Classically conditioned responses are difficult to eliminate through conscious reasoning because they are not acquired through conscious thought processes.

If each of these situations makes you feel uneasy, you are not alone. The classically conditioned response—"This is disgusting" or "This is dangerous"—wins out over the knowledge that the stimulus is really okay. Because classically conditioned responses are not built up through conscious thought, they are also hard to eliminate through conscious reasoning!

One of the most extensively studied real-world products of classical conditioning is *fear conditioning.* In the earliest days of behaviorism, John Watson and his colleague Rosalie Rayner sought to prove that many fear responses could be understood as the pairing of a neutral stimulus with something naturally fear-provoking. To test their idea, they experimented on an infant who came to be called Little Albert.

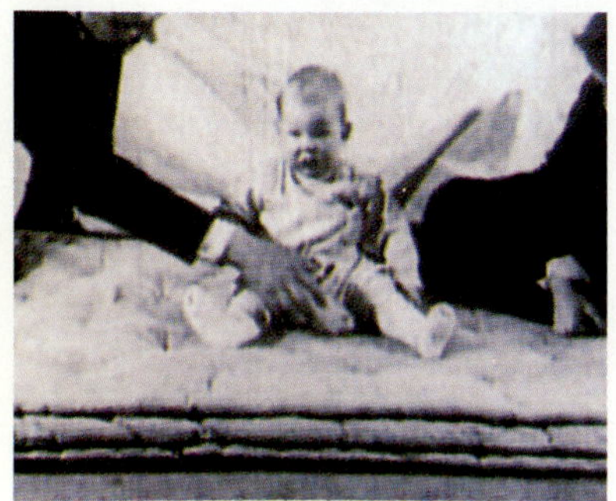

John Watson and Rosalie Rayner conditioned Little Albert to fear small, furry objects (Discovering Psychology, *1990).*

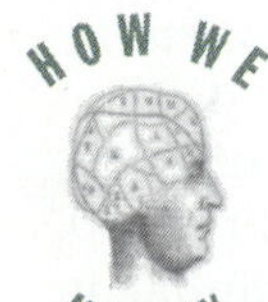

Watson and Rayner (1920) trained Albert to fear a white rat he had initially liked, by pairing its appearance with an aversive UCS—a loud gong struck just behind him. The unconditional startle response and the emotional distress to the noxious noise was the basis of Albert's learning to react with fear to the appearance of the white rat. His fear was developed in just seven conditioning trials. The emotional conditioning was then extended to behavioral conditioning when Albert learned to escape from the feared stimulus. The infant's learned fear then generalized to other furry objects, such as a rabbit, a dog, and even a Santa Claus mask! (In the early days of psychology, careful attention to possible harmful effects of experiments on subjects was sometimes lacking. In fact, Albert's mother, a wet nurse at the hospital where the study was conducted, took him away before the researchers could remove the experimentally conditioned fear. So we don't know whatever happened to Little Albert [Harris, 1979].)

We know now that conditioned fear is highly resistant to extinction. With the passage of time, an individual may be quite unaware of why a reaction is occurring. Conditional fear reactions may persist for years, even when the original frightening UCS is never again experienced. For example, researchers demonstrated that, 15 years after the end of World War II, navy veterans still produced a marked response to a "danger signal." During the war, sailors were called to battle stations with a gong that sounded at the rate of 100 rings a minute. That particular auditory pattern—which had been reliably predictive of danger—continued to elicit strong emotional arousal (Edwards & Acker, 1962).

Interestingly, when strong fear is involved, conditioning may take place after only *one* pairing of a neutral stimulus with the UCS. A single traumatic event can condition you to respond with strong physical, emotional, and cognitive reactions—perhaps for a lifetime. For example, one of our friends was in a bad car accident during a rainstorm. Now every time it begins to rain while he is driving, he becomes panic stricken, sometimes to the extent that he has to pull over and wait out the storm. On one occasion this rational, sensible man even crawled into the back seat and lay on the floor, face down, until the rain subsided. We will see in Chapter 18 that therapists have designed treatments, for these types of fears, that are intended to counter the effects of classical conditioning.

We don't want to leave you with the impression that only negative responses are classically conditioned. In fact, we suspect that you will also be able to interpret responses of happiness or excitement as instances of classical conditioning. Certainly toilers in the advertising industry hope that classical conditioning works as a positive force. They strive, for example, to create associations in your mind between their products (e.g., blue jeans, sports cars, and soda pop) and passion.

By associating a product with the euphoric feelings of passionate love, advertisers hope to profit from classical conditioning.

Fifteen years after the Second World War was over, navy veterans still responded as if to current danger signals when exposed to auditory stimuli resembling battleship gongs.

Harnessing Classical Conditioning

In the early 1980s, researchers made the rather startling discovery that the body's immune system can be affected by the processes of learning. Historically, it had been assumed that immunological reactions—rapid production of antibodies to counterattack substances that invade and damage the organism—were automatic, biological processes that occurred without any involvement of the central nervous system. Conditioning experiments proved that assumption to be incorrect.

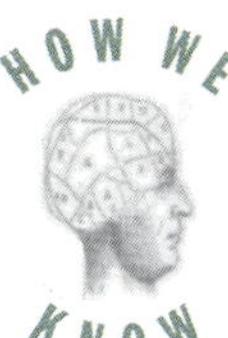

Groundbreaking researchers **Robert Ader** and **Nathan Cohen** (1981) taught one group of rats to associate sweet-tasting saccharin with cyclophosphamide (CY), a drug that weakens immune response. A control group received only the saccharin. Later, when both groups of rats were given only saccharin, the animals that had been conditioned to associate saccharin with CY produced significantly fewer antibodies to foreign cells than those rats in the control group. Thus the learned association alone was sufficient to elicit suppression of the immune system, making the experimental rats vulnerable to a range of diseases. The learning effect was so powerful that, later in the study, some of the rats died after drinking only the saccharin solution.

Results like this one hold out the promise that classical conditioning can be harnessed to modify the function of the immune system. A new field of study, **psychoneuroimmunology**, has emerged to explore these types of results that involve psychology, the nervous system, and the immune system (Ader & Cohen, 1993).

Researchers have demonstrated that learning can affect biological processes, such as the functioning of the immune system, and have also successfully applied conditioning principles in the treatment of high blood pressure.

One goal of this new field is to discover techniques that allow conditioning to replace high doses of medications—which often have serious side effects. Ader and his colleague Anthony Suchman, for example, found that patients with high blood pressure (hypertension) who were taken off medication while continuing to be treated with placebos maintained healthy blood pressures longer than patients who did not get placebos (Ader & Suchman, 1993; Suchman & Ader, 1989). How could an inert pill cure hypertension? Imagine the routine that develops when you take medication on a regular basis. The actual physical ritual involved in taking the drug can serve as the CS, so that when it comes to predict the UCS—the drug—the act can itself elicit the response of lowering blood pressure. In this way, a placebo—which re-creates the ritual without administering an active substance—can elicit the beneficial bodily reaction. To make this work as a treatment, of course, researchers must ensure that a drug's harsh side effects do not also survive as a product of conditioning. (You will see in the Close-up that the same conditioning mechanism can sometimes prove deadly.)

Researchers hope that classically conditioned immune responses might even be effective in the fight against cancer.

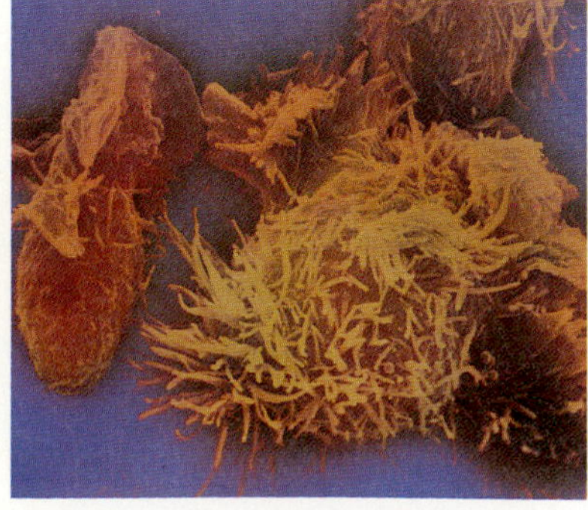

Researchers are studying the possible use of classical conditioning to increase resistance to cancer cells.

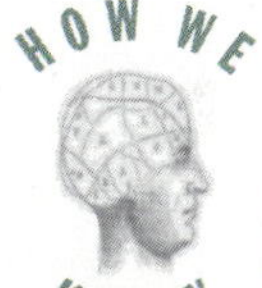

A team of scientists created a conditioning situation in which the smell of camphor (mothballs) was paired with an injection of poly I:C (polyinodinic:polycytidylic acid), which produces enhanced immune response. In this paradigm, camphor served as the CS and poly I:C as the UCS. After training was complete, the mice were injected with cells that would normally bring about tumor growth and death. At this point, half of the 20 mice were systematically reexposed to the camphor odor. Those 10 mice survived, on average, longer than the other group, who did not reexperience the camphor. In fact, 2 of the 10 mice were tumor-free at the end of the experiment. No other mice survived the injection of the tumor cells. The camphor odor alone, functioning as a conditional

Learning to Be a Drug Addict

A man's body lay in a Manhattan alley, a half-empty syringe dangling from his arm. Cause of death? The coroner called it an overdose, but the man had ordinarily shot up far greater doses than the one that had supposedly killed him. This sort of incident had happened before, and it baffled investigators. How could an addict with high drug tolerance die of an overdose when he didn't even get a full hit?

Psychologist **Shepard Siegel** thought something else might be happening. Studies of rats had convinced him that *tolerance*—decreased responsiveness to a drug after repeated use—involved more than just *physiological* changes in the brain. He thought that *learning*—an association of the drug with the physical setting and rituals normally associated with its use—also contributed to tolerance.

Some time ago, Pavlov (1927) and later his colleague Bykov (1957) pointed out that tolerance to opiates can develop when an individual anticipates the pharmacological action of a drug. Perhaps with advance notice—provided by the conditional stimulus associated with the ritual of injection—the body somehow learns to protect itself by preventing the drug from having its usual effect. In settings ordinarily associated with drug use, the body physiologically prepares itself for the drug's expected effects. Over time, larger doses are needed to achieve the desired effect.

In one study, Siegel classically conditioned rats to expect *heroin* injections (UCS) in one setting (CS_1) and *dextrose* (sweet sugar) solution injections in a different setting (CS_2) (Siegel et al., 1982). In the first phase of training, all rats developed heroin tolerance. On the test day, all subjects received a larger-than-usual dose of heroin—nearly twice the previous amount. Half of them received it in the setting where heroin had previously been administered; the other half received it in the setting where dextrose solutions had been given during conditioning. More than twice as many rats died in the dextrose-solution setting as in the usual heroin setting—82 percent versus 31 percent! Presumably, those receiving heroin in the usual setting were more prepared for this potentially dangerous situation, perhaps because they initiated a physiological response that countered the drug's typical effects (Poulos & Cappell, 1991).

To find out if a similar process might operate in humans, Siegel and a colleague interviewed heroin addicts who had come close to death from supposed overdoses. In seven out of ten cases, the addicts had been shooting up in a new and unfamiliar setting (Siegel, 1984). Although this natural experiment provides no conclusive data, it suggests that a dose for which an addict has developed tolerance in one setting may become an overdose in an unfamiliar setting. Classical conditioning thus increases the dangers of drug addiction.

stimulus, had succeeded in enhancing immune response (Ghanta et al., 1987).

We have come a long way with classical conditioning—from Pavlov's salivating dogs to fear conditioning to immune enhancement. We suggest, once again, that you be on the lookout for signs of classical conditioning in your own life.

OPERANT CONDITIONING: LEARNING ABOUT CONSEQUENCES

Let's return to the movie theater. The horror film is now over, and you peel yourself off your seat. The friend with whom you saw the movie asks you if you're hoping that a sequel will be made. You respond, "I've learned that I shouldn't go to horror films." You're probably right, but what kind of learning is this? Once again our answer begins around the turn of the twentieth century.

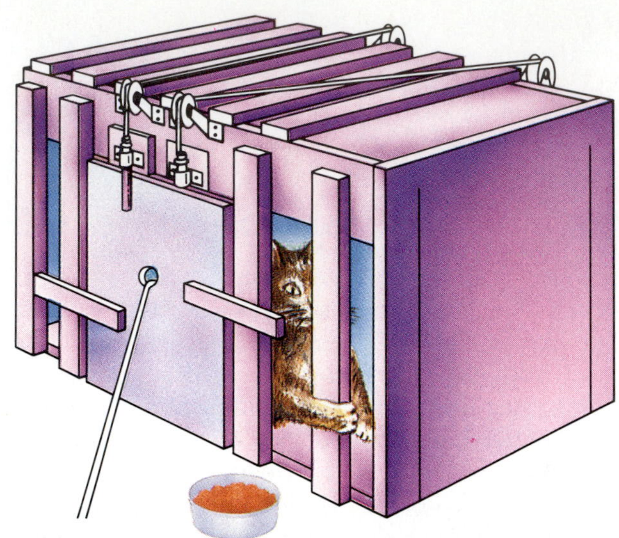

Figure 9.9 A Thorndike Puzzle Box
To get out of the puzzle box and obtain food, Thorndike's cat had to manipulate a mechanism to release a weight that would then pull the door open.

The Law of Effect

At about the same time that Pavlov was using classical conditioning to induce Russian dogs to salivate to the sound of a bell, **Edward L. Thorndike** (1898) was watching American cats trying to escape from puzzle boxes (see **Figure 9.9**). Thorndike reported his observations and inferences about the kind of learning he believed was taking place in his subjects:

> When put into the box, the cat shows evident signs of discomfort and develops an impulse to escape from confinement. . . . Whether the impulse to struggle [to escape] be due to an instinctive reaction to confinement or to an association, it is likely to succeed in letting the cat out of the box. The cat that is clawing all over the box in [its] impulsive struggle will probably claw the string or loop or button so as to open the door. And gradually all the other unsuccessful impulses will be *stamped out* and the particular impulse leading to the successful act will be *stamped in* by the resulting pleasure, until, after many trials, the cat will, when put in the box, immediately claw the button or loop in a definite way. (Thorndike, 1898, p. 13)

What had Thorndike's cats learned? According to Thorndike's analysis, learning was an association between stimuli in the situation and a response that a subject learned to make: a *stimulus-response* (S-R) *connection.* Thus the cats had learned to produce an appropriate response (for example, clawing at a button or loop) that in these stimulus circumstances (confinement in the puzzle box) led to a desired outcome (momentary freedom). Note that the learning of these S-R connections occurred gradually and automatically in a mechanistic way as the animal experienced the consequences of its actions through blind *trial and error.* Gradually, the behaviors that had satisfying consequences increased in frequency; they eventually become the dominant response when the animal was placed in the puzzle box. Thorndike referred to this relationship between behavior and its consequences as the **law of effect.**

Experimental Analysis of Behavior

B. F. Skinner embraced Thorndike's view that environmental consequences exert a powerful effect on behavior. Skinner outlined a program of research, called the **experimental analysis of behavior,** whose purpose was to discover, by systematic variation of stimulus conditions, the ways that various environmental conditions affect the likelihood that a given response will occur:

> A natural datum in a science of behavior is the probability that a given bit of behavior will occur at a given time. An experimental analysis deals with that probability in terms of frequency or rate of responding. . . . The task of an experimental analysis is to discover all the variables of which probability of response is a function. (Skinner, 1966, pp. 213–214)

Skinner's analysis was experimental rather than theoretical—theorists are guided by derivations and predictions about behavior from their theories, but empiricists, such as Skinner, advocate the bottom-up approach. They start with the collection and evaluation of data within the context of an experiment and are not theory driven.

To analyze behavior experimentally, Skinner developed **operant conditioning** procedures, in which he manipulated the *consequences* of an organism's behavior in order to see what effect they had on subsequent behavior. An **operant** is any behavior that is *emitted* by an organism and can be characterized in terms of the observable effects it has on the environment. Literally, *operant* means *affecting the environment,* or operating on it (Skinner, 1938). Operants are *not elicited* by specific stimuli, as classically conditioned behaviors are. Pigeons peck, rats search for food, babies cry and coo, some people gesture while talking, and others stutter. The probability of these behaviors occurring in the future can be increased or decreased by manipulating the effects they have on the environment. Operant conditioning, then, modifies the probability of different types of operant behavior as a function of the environmental consequences they produce.

Skinner developed operant conditioning techniques to manipulate the consequences of an organism's behavior in order to observe the effects on subsequent behavior.

To carry out his new experimental analysis, Skinner invented an apparatus that allowed him to manipulate the consequences of behavior, the *operant chamber.* **Figure 9.10** shows how the operant chamber works. In many

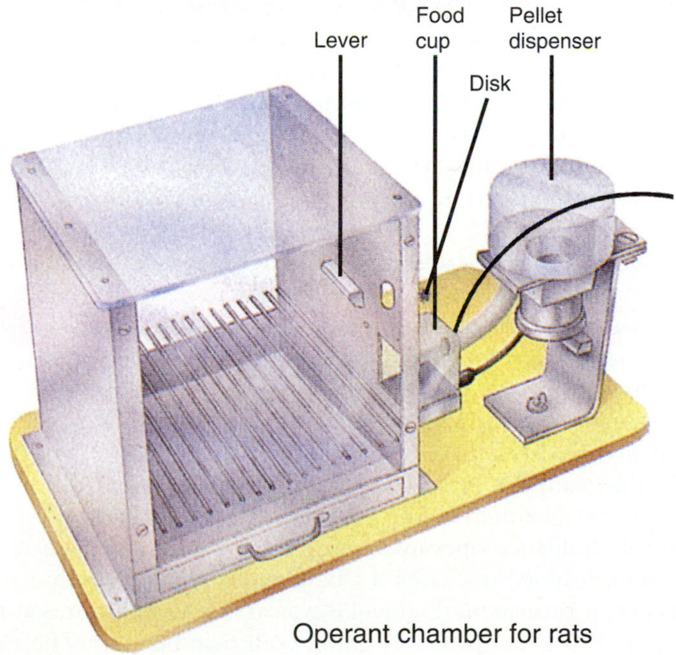

Figure 9.10 Operant Chamber
In the operant chamber typical of those used with rats, each press on the lever is followed by delivery of a food pellet.

operant experiments, the measure of interest is how much of a particular behavior an animal carries out in a period of time. Researchers record the pattern and total amount of behavior emitted in the course of an experiment. This methodology allowed Skinner to study the effect of reinforcement contingencies on animals' behavior.

Reinforcement Contingencies

A **reinforcement contingency** is a consistent relationship between a response and the changes in the environment that it produces. Imagine, for example, an experiment in which a pigeon's pecking (the response) is generally followed by the presentation of grain (the corresponding change in the environment). This consistent relationship, or reinforcement contingency, will usually be accompanied by an increase in the rate of pecking. For delivery of grain to increase *only* the probability of pecking, it must be contingent *only* on the pecking response—the delivery must occur regularly after that response but not after other responses, such as turning or bowing. Based on Skinner's work, modern behavior analysts seek to understand behavior in terms of reinforcement contingencies. Let's take a closer look at what has been discovered about these contingencies.

Positive and Negative Reinforcers

Events that can strengthen an organism's responses if they are contingently related are called *reinforcers.* Reinforcers are always defined empirically—in terms of their effects on changing the probability of a response. A **positive reinforcer** is any stimulus that—when made contingent upon a behavior—increases the probability of that behavior over time. The delivery of a positive reinforcer contingent upon a response is called *positive reinforcement.* A food pellet positively reinforces a rat's lever press. Laughter positively reinforces a human's joke telling. Your attention positively reinforces your professor's lecturing.

Both positive and negative reinforcers increase the probability of a behavior.

A **negative reinforcer** is any stimulus that, when removed, reduced, or prevented, increases the probability of a given response over time. The removal, reduction, or prevention of a negative reinforcer following a response is called *negative reinforcement.* Using an umbrella to prevent getting wet during a downpour is a common example of a behavior that is maintained by negative reinforcement. The negative reinforcer, getting wet, is avoided by using an umbrella. An automobile seat belt buzzer also serves a negative reinforcing function; its annoying sound is terminated when the driver buckles up.

Kicking a vending machine would be reinforced if candy or soda came out as a result.

To distinguish clearly between positive and negative reinforcement, try to remember the following: both positive reinforcement and negative reinforcement *increase* the probability of the response that precedes them. Positive reinforcement increases response probability by the presentation of a "positive" stimulus following a response; negative reinforcement does the same in reverse, through the removal, reduction, or prevention of a "negative" stimulus following a response.

You should recall that for classical conditioning, when the unconditional stimulus is no longer delivered, the conditional response suffers extinction. The same rule holds for operant conditioning—if reinforcement is withheld, **operant extinction** occurs. Thus if a behavior no longer produces predictable consequences, it returns to the level it was at before operant conditioning—it is *extinguished.* You can probably catch your own behaviors being reinforced and then extinguished. Have you ever had the experience of dropping a few coins into a soda machine and getting nothing in return? If you kicked the machine one time and your soda came out, kicking would be reinforced.

However, if the next few times your kicking produced no soda, kicking would quickly be extinguished.

Positive and Negative Punishment

You are probably familiar with another technique for decreasing the probability of a response—punishment. A **punisher** is any stimulus that—when it is made contingent upon a response—decreases the probability of that response over time. *Punishment* is the delivery of a punisher following a response. Just as we could identify positive and negative reinforcement, we can identify positive punishment and negative punishment. When a behavior is followed by the presentation of an aversive stimulus, the event is called **positive punishment** (you can remember *positive,* because something is added to the situation). Touching a hot stove, for example, produces pain that punishes the preceding response so that you are less likely next time to touch the stove. When a behavior is followed by the removal of a pleasant stimulus, the event is referred to as **negative punishment** (you can remember *negative,* because something is subtracted from the situation). Thus, when a parent withdraws a child's allowance after she hits her baby brother, the child learns not to hit her brother in the future. Which kind of punishment explains why you might stay away from horror movies?

Both positive and negative punishers decrease the probability of a response.

Although punishment and reinforcement are closely related operations, they differ in important ways. A good way to differentiate them is to think of each in terms of its effects on behavior. Punishment, by definition, always *reduces* the probability of a response occurring again; reinforcement, by definition, always *increases* the probability of a response recurring. For example, some people get severe headaches after drinking caffeinated beverages. The headache is the stimulus that *positively punishes* and reduces the behavior of drinking coffee. However, once the headache is present, people often will take aspirin or another pain reliever to eliminate the headache. The aspirin's analgesic effect is the stimulus that *negatively reinforces* the behavior of ingesting aspirin.

Discriminative Stimuli and Generalization

You are unlikely to want to change the probability of a certain behavior at all times. Rather, you may want to change the probability of the behavior in a particular context. Through their associations with reinforcement or punishment, certain stimuli that precede a particular response—**discriminative stimuli**—come to set the context for that behavior. Organisms learn that in the presence of some stimuli but not of others, their behavior is likely to have a particular effect on the environment. For example, in the presence of a green street light, the act of crossing an intersection in a motor vehicle is reinforced. When the light is red, however, such behavior may be punished—it may result in a traffic ticket or an accident. Skinner referred to the sequence of discriminative stimulus-behavior-consequence as the **three-term contingency** and believed that it could explain most human action (Skinner, 1953). **Table 9.1** describes how the three-term contingency might explain several different kinds of human behavior.

Under laboratory conditions, manipulating the consequences of behavior in the presence of discriminative stimuli can exert powerful control over that behavior. For example, a pigeon might be given grain after pecking a disk in the presence of a green light but not a red light. The green light is a discriminative stimulus that sets the occasion for pecking; the red is a discriminative stimulus that sets the occasion for *not* pecking. The green light is a *positive discriminative stimulus,* or S^D (pronounced ess *dee*). The red light is a *negative discriminative stimulus, or* S^Δ (pronounced ess *Delta*). Organisms learn quickly to discriminate between these conditions, respond-

B. F. Skinner believed that the three-term contingency, stimulus-behavior-consequence, could explain most human behavior.

Table 9.1 The Three-Term Contingency: Relationships Among Discriminative Stimuli, Behavior, and Consequences

	Discriminative Stimulus (S^D)	Emitted Response (R)	Stimulus Consequence (S)
1. **Positive reinforcement:** A response in the presence of an effective signal (S^D) produces the desired consequence. This response increases.	Soft-drink machine	Put coin in slot	Get drink
2. **Negative reinforcement** (escape): An unpleasant situation is escaped from by an operant response. This escape response increases.	Heat	Fan oneself	Escape from heat
3. **Extinction training:** An operant response is *not* followed by a reinforcer. It decreases in rate.	None or S^{Δ}	Clowning behavior	No one notices and response becomes less frequent
4. **Positive punishment:** A response is followed by an aversive stimulus. The response is eliminated or suppressed.	Attractive matchbox	Play with matches	Get burned or get caught and spanked
5. **Negative punishment:** A response is followed by the removal of a pleasant stimulus. The response is eliminated or suppressed.	Brussels sprouts	Refusal to eat them	No dessert

ing regularly in the presence of an S^D and not responding in the presence of an S^{Δ}. By manipulating the components of the three-term contingency, you can constrain a behavior to a particular context.

Organisms also *generalize* responses to other stimuli that resemble the S^D. Once a response has been reinforced in the presence of one discriminative stimulus, a similar stimulus can become a discriminative stimulus for that same response. For example, pigeons trained to peck a disk in the presence of a green light will also peck the disk in the presence of lights that are lighter or darker shades of green than the original discriminative stimulus.

Using Reinforcement Contingencies

Are you ready to put your new knowledge of reinforcement contingencies to work? Here are some considerations you might have:

- *How can you define the behavior that you would like to reinforce or eliminate?*

  You must always carefully target the specific behavior whose probability you would like to change. Reinforcement should be contingent on exactly that behavior. When reinforcers are presented noncontingently, their presence has little effect on behavior. For example, if a parent praises bad work as well as good efforts, a child will not learn to work harder in school—but, because of the positive reinforcement, other behaviors are likely to increase. (What might those be?)

- *How can you define the contexts in which a behavior is appropriate or inappropriate?*

  Remember that you rarely want to allow or disallow every instance of a behavior. You must define the discriminative stimuli and investigate how broadly the desired response will be generalized to similar stimuli.

Effective reinforcement must be contingent on a specific behavior in a well-defined set of circumstances.

- *Have you unknowingly been reinforcing some behaviors?*

  Suppose you want to eliminate a behavior. Before you turn to punishment as a way of reducing its probability (more on that in a moment), you should try to determine whether you can identify reinforcers for that behavior. If so, you can try to extinguish the behavior by eliminating those reinforcers. Imagine, for example, that a young boy throws a large number of tantrums. You might ask yourself, Have I been reinforcing those tantrums by paying the boy extra attention when he screams? If so, you can try to eliminate the tantrums by eliminating the reinforcement. Even better, you can combine extinction with positive reinforcement of more socially approved behaviors.

  Behavior analysts assume that any behavior that persists does so because it results in reinforcement. Any behavior, they argue—even irrational or bizarre behavior—can be understood by discovering what the reinforcement or payoff is. For example, symptoms of mental or physical disorders are sometimes maintained because the person gets attention and sympathy and is excused from normal responsibilities. These *secondary gains* reinforce irrational and sometimes self-destructive behavior. Can you see how shy behaviors can be maintained through reinforcement even though the shy person would prefer not to be shy? It is, of course, not always possible to know what reinforcers are at work in an environment. However, as a behavior becomes more or less probable, you might try to carry out a bit of behavior analysis.

According to behavior analysts, even bizarre or irrational behavior can be understood by discovering what reinforces it.

- *When is punishment appropriate?*

  The easiest answer to this question is "rarely, if ever." To eliminate undesired behaviors, it is almost always preferable to reinforce the alternative, desired behavior than it is to punish the undesired behavior. Consider a classic situation in which a parent spanks a child for being aggressive toward a playmate. The punishment may very well suppress the child's immediate behavior. Unfortunately, the child may also be learning the lesson that physical aggression is a good tool for controlling behavior in others—"Look, it worked on me!" Thus, outside of the immediate situation, a spanking might work opposite to the intended effect.

  In this situation, the parents would be better off rewarding the child when she engages in positive, friendly behaviors with other children. You should be aware that this often requires patience. The reason many parents use punishment is that it can stop a child's unwanted behavior immediately. Because the parents achieve their short-term goal, the children's immediate response reinforces the parents' punishing behavior (Grant & Evans, 1994). Parents must patiently forgo that immediate reinforcement to act in the better, long-term interest of their children.

  When parents' attempts at reinforcement are not possible or do not stop their children's undesirable actions swiftly enough, punishment may become the only alternative. Research shows that punishment should meet a number of conditions. It should be swift and brief, be administered right after the response occurs, be limited in intensity, be a response to behaviors and never to the person's character, be limited to the situation in which the response occurs, and consist of *penalties* instead of physical *pain* (Walters & Grusec, 1977).

A child who spanks her doll, shouting, "Mommy told you!" has no doubt learned that physical aggression is a good way to control smaller, weaker individuals.

  Serious long-term problems arise with the use of punishment because angry parents or emotional teachers rarely meet the conditions just mentioned. Children are punished often and hard—federal surveys reveal that corporal punishment is meted out three million times a year in our schools, mostly to elementary-school boys and disproportionately to African Americans (Schmidt, 1987). Punishment is often counterproductive, suppressing the punished response only in the presence of authority and causing physical harm, emotional scars, stigmatization (when given in public), and hatred for the institution in which it is experienced. Worst of all, the physically punished child learns that physical aggression is an acceptable means of controlling the behavior of others (Bongiovanni, 1977; Hyman, reported in Schmidt, 1987). Although some parents and school officials say corporal punishment is essential to maintain discipline and order, its presence means that these adults do not understand how to reinforce positive behaviors.

Effective punishment should be swift and brief, limited in intensity, specific to behavior and not personal character, limited to the situation where the response occurs, and should consist of penalties and not physical pain.

We have recommended that you use reinforcement exclusively, rather than punishment. Let's now take a look at which reinforcers work best.

Properties of Reinforcers

Reinforcers are the power brokers of operant conditioning—they change or maintain behavior. Reinforcers have a number of interesting and complex properties. They can start out as weak and become strong, can be learned through experience rather than be biologically determined, and can be activities rather than objects. In some situations, even ordinarily powerful reinforcers may not be enough to change a dominant behavior pattern (in this case, we would say that the consequences were not actually reinforcers).

Conditioned Reinforcers

When you came into the world, there were a handful of **primary reinforcers**, such as food and water, whose reinforcing properties were biologically determined. Over time, however, otherwise neutral stimuli have become associated with primary reinforcers and now function as **conditioned reinforcers** for operant responses. Conditioned reinforcers can come to serve as ends in themselves. In fact, a great deal of human behavior is influenced less by biologically significant primary reinforcers than by a wide variety of conditioned reinforcers. Money, grades, smiles of approval, gold stars, and various kinds of status symbols are among the many potent conditioned reinforcers that influence much of your behavior.

Conditioned reinforcers exert more influence than primary reinforcers on many human behaviors.

Virtually any stimulus can become a conditioned reinforcer by being paired with a primary reinforcer. In one experiment, simple tokens were used with animal learners.

With edible raisins as primary reinforcers, chimps were trained to solve problems. Then tokens were delivered along with the raisins. When only the tokens were presented, the chimps continued working for their "money" because they could later deposit the hard-earned tokens in a "chimp-o-mat" designed to exchange tokens for the raisins (Cowles, 1937).

Inedible tokens can be used as conditioned reinforcers. In one study, chimps deposited tokens in a "chimp-o-mat" in exchange for raisins.

Teachers and experimenters often find conditioned reinforcers more effective and easier to use than primary reinforcers because (1) few primary reinforcers are available in the classroom, whereas almost any stimulus event that is under control of a teacher can be used as a conditioned reinforcer; (2) they can be dispensed rapidly; (3) they are portable; and (4) their reinforcing effect may be more immediate, since it depends only on the perception of receiving them and not on biological processing, as in the case of primary reinforcers.

In some institutions, *token economies* have been set up based on these principles. Desired behaviors (grooming or taking medication, for example) are explicitly defined, and token payoffs are given by the staff when the behaviors are performed. These tokens can later be exchanged by the patients for a wide array of rewards and privileges (Ayllon & Azrin, 1965; Holden, 1978; Kazdin, 1994). These systems of reinforcement are especially effective in modifying patients' behaviors regarding self-care, upkeep of their environment, and, most important, frequency of their positive social interactions.

Probable Activities as Positive Reinforcers

Suppose you need to get a child to do something. You don't want to pay her or give her a gold star, so instead you strike this bargain: "When you finish your homework, you can play with your video game." Your use of "video game playing" in these circumstances is in keeping with the **Premack principle,** named after its discoverer, **David Premack** (1965). The Premack principle suggests that a more probable activity (that is, a behavior with a higher probability of occurring under ordinary circumstances) can be used to reinforce a less probable one. In his initial research, Premack found that water-deprived rats learned to increase their running in an exercise wheel when running was followed by an opportunity to drink. Conversely, exercise-deprived rats learned to increase their drinking when that response was followed by a chance to run. According to the Premack principle, a reinforcer may be any event or activity that is valued by the organism.

The Premack principle suggests that a more probable activity can be used to reinforce a less probable activity.

The Premack principle has powerful applications. Consider the challenging task of getting nursery-school children to sit quietly and listen to someone talk. Here was one inventive solution:

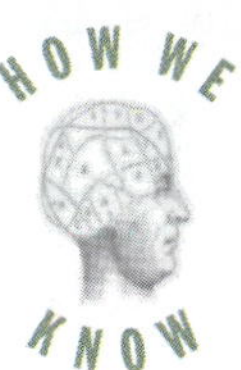

> Short periods during which the children sat quietly in their chairs facing the blackboard were occasionally followed by the sound of a bell and the instruction "Run and scream." The students immediately jumped out of their chairs and ran around the room screaming and having a good time. After a few minutes, another signal alerted them to stop and return to their chairs. Later in the study, the children were given the opportunity to earn tokens for engaging in low-probability behaviors, such as practicing arithmetic. The children could use the tokens to buy the opportunity to participate in high-probability activities, such as playing with toys. With this kind of procedure, control was virtually perfect after a few days (Homme et al., 1963).

Reprogramming classroom contingencies succeeded where pleas, punishment, and a bit of screaming by the teacher had failed.

You can see how you can apply the Premack principle to get children to engage in low-probability activities. For a socially outgoing child, playing with friends can reinforce the less pleasant task of finishing homework first. For a shy child, reading a new book can be used to reinforce the less preferred activity of playing with other children. You can also use this principle for self-management. If you are easily distracted from your studies, try promising yourself a half-hour break to engage in an activity you really want to do—but only after you have studied for a given period of time or have read a given number of pages. Whatever activity is valued can be used as a reinforcer and thus increase the probability of engaging in an activity that is not currently valued. Over time, there is the possibility that the less favored activities will come to be valued, as exposure to them leads to discovery of their intrinsic worth.

Schedules of Reinforcement

What happens when you cannot, or do not want to, reinforce an animal on every occasion when it performs a behavior? Consider a story about the young B. F. Skinner. It seems that one weekend he was secluded in his laboratory with not enough of a food-reward supply for his hard-working rats. He economized by giving the rats pellets only after a certain interval of time—no matter how many times they pressed in between, they couldn't get any more pellets. Even so, the rats responded as much with this *partial reinforcement schedule* as they had with continuous reinforcement. And what do you predict happened when these animals underwent extinction training and their responses were followed by no pellets at all? The rats whose lever pressing had been partially reinforced continued to respond longer and more vigorously than did the rats who had gotten payoffs after every response. Skinner was onto something important!

The discovery of the effectiveness of partial reinforcement led to extensive study of the effects of different **schedules of reinforcement** on behavior (see **Figure 9.11**). You have experienced different schedules of reinforcement in your daily life. When you raise your hand in class, the teacher sometimes calls on you and sometimes does not; some slot machine players continue to put coins in the one-armed bandits even though the reinforcers are delivered only rarely. In real life or in the laboratory, reinforcers can be delivered according to either a *ratio schedule,* after a certain number of responses, or an *interval schedule,* after the first response following a specified interval of time. In each case, there can be either a constant, or *fixed,* pattern of reinforcement or an irregular, or *variable,* pattern of reinforcement, making four major types of schedules in all. So far you've learned about the **partial reinforcement effect:** responses acquired under schedules of partial reinforcement are more resistant to extinction than those acquired with continuous reinforcement (Bitterman, 1975). Let's see what else researchers have discovered about different schedules of reinforcement.

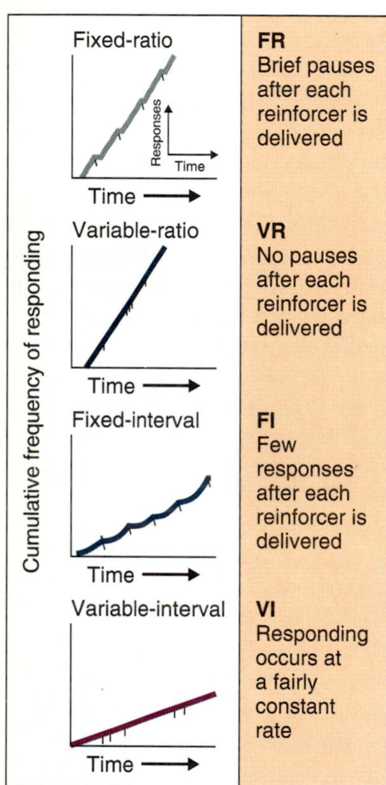

Figure 9.11 Reinforcement Schedules
These different patterns of behavior are produced by four simple schedules of reinforcement. The hash marks indicate when reinforcement is delivered.

Fixed-ratio (FR) Schedules

In *fixed-ratio schedules,* the reinforcer comes after the organism has emitted a fixed number of responses. When reinforcement follows one response, the schedule is called an FR-1 schedule (this is the original continuous reinforcement schedule). When reinforcement follows only every twenty-fifth response, the schedule is an FR-25 schedule. FR schedules generate high rates of responding because there is a direct correlation between responding and reinforcement—a pigeon can get as much food as it wants in a period of time if it pecks often enough. Figure 9.11 shows that FR schedules produce a pause after each reinforcer. The higher the ratio, the longer the pause after each reinforcement. Stretching the ratio too thin by requiring a great many responses for reinforcement without first training the organism to emit that many responses may lead to extinction. Many salespeople are on FR schedules: they must sell a certain number of units before they can get paid.

"FR 25! Pass it on!"

In reinforcement studies, animals have been shown to adjust their response rates according to the reward schedule.

Variable-ratio (VR) Schedules

In a *variable-ratio schedule,* the average number of responses between reinforcers is predetermined. A VR-10 schedule means that, on average, reinforcement follows every tenth response, but it might come after only 1 response or after 20 responses. Variable-ratio schedules generate the highest rate of responding and the greatest resistance to extinction, especially when the VR value is large. Suppose you start a pigeon with a low VR value (for example, VR-5) and then move it toward a higher value. A pigeon on a VR-110 schedule will respond with up to 12,000 pecks per hour and will continue responding for hours even with no reinforcement. Gambling would seem to be under the control of VR schedules. The response of dropping coins in slot machines is maintained at a high, steady level by the payoff, which is delivered only after an unknown, variable number of coins has been deposited. VR schedules leave you guessing when the reward will come—you gamble that it will be after the next response, not many responses later (Rachlin, 1990).

Fixed-interval (FI) Schedules

On a *fixed-interval schedule,* a reinforcer is delivered for the first response made after a fixed period of time. On an FI-10 schedule, the subject, after receiving reinforcement, will have to wait 10 seconds before another response can be reinforced—irrespective of the number of responses. Response rates under FI schedules show a scalloped pattern. Immediately after each reinforced response, the animal makes few if any responses. As the payoff time approaches, the animal responds more and more. A monthly paycheck puts you on a FI schedule.

Variable-interval (VI) Schedules

For *variable-interval schedules,* the average interval is predetermined. For example, on a VI-20 schedule, reinforcers are delivered at an average rate of 1 every 20 seconds. This schedule generates a moderate but very stable response rate. Extinction under VI schedules is gradual and much slower than under fixed-interval schedules. In one case, a pigeon pecked 18,000 times during the first 4 hours after reinforcement stopped and required 168 hours before its responding extinguished completely (Ferster & Skinner, 1957). You have experienced a VI schedule if you've taken a course with a professor who gave occasional, irregularly scheduled pop quizzes. Did you study your notes each day before class?

Shaping and Chaining

Suppose that you want to train a rat to press a lever in an operant chamber. You've settled on a reinforcer, food, and a schedule of reinforcement, FR-1, but you know that it's unlikely that the rat will ever press the lever spontaneously. The rat has learned to use its paws in many ways, but it probably has never pressed a lever before. To train new or complex behaviors, you will want to use a method called **shaping by successive approximations**—in which you reinforce any responses that successively approximate and ultimately match the desired response.

Here's how you'd do it. First, you deprive the rat of food for a day. (Without deprivation, food is not likely to serve as a reinforcer.) Then you systematically make food pellets available in the food hopper in an operant chamber so that the rat learns to look there for food. Now you can begin the actual shaping process by making delivery of food contingent upon specific aspects of the rat's behavior, such as orienting itself toward the lever. Next, food is delivered only as the rat moves closer and closer to the lever. Soon the requirement for reinforcement is actually to touch the lever. Finally, the rat

In order for shaping to work, it is necessary to define progress toward the target behavior and to use differential reinforcement to refine each step in the learning process.

must depress the lever for food to be delivered. In small increments, the rat has learned that a lever press will produce food. Thus, for *shaping* to work, you must define what constitutes progress toward the target behavior and use *differential reinforcement* to refine each step along the way.

Let's look at another example, in which shaping was used to improve the life of a young autistic child.

The patient was a 3-year-old boy who was diagnosed as autistic. He lacked normal social and verbal behavior and was given to ungovernable tantrums and self-destructive actions. After a cataract operation, he refused to wear the glasses that were essential for the development of normal vision. So, first, he was given a bit of candy or fruit at the clicking sound of a toy noisemaker; through its association with food, the sound became a conditioned reinforcer. Then training began with empty eyeglass frames. At first, the noisemaker was sounded after the child picked up the glasses. Soon, though, it sounded only when the child held the glasses and, later, only when he carried them. Slowly and through successive approximations, the boy was rewarded for bringing the frames closer to his eyes. After a few weeks, he was putting the empty frames on his head at odd angles, and, finally, he was wearing them in the proper manner. With further training, the child learned to wear his glasses up to 12 hours a day (Wolf et al., 1964).

Let's return to your rat. Suppose, now, that you'd like him to work a bit harder for a food pellet. You decide you'd like him to turn a wheel before he presses the lever—only in those circumstances will he get the food pellet. To teach this sequence of actions, you could use a technique called **chaining.** In chaining, the last response of the sequence is reinforced (with the primary reinforcer) first. You have already established this link between lever pressing and the delivery of a food pellet. This final response then becomes a conditioned reinforcer for the response that occurs just before it. Thus the rat will now learn another behavior to obtain the opportunity to press the lever (to get food). As the experimenter, you control reinforcement, so that only when the rat first turns the wheel will a press of the lever produce a food pellet. Working backward from the primary reinforcer, you can create quite long chains of behavior. Each link in the behavior chain serves as a *discriminative stimulus* for the next response

This woman, Sue Strong, was assisted by a monkey who had been operantly shaped to comb her hair, feed her, turn book pages, and make other responses she could not do for herself because of paralysis.

in line and as a *conditioned reinforcer* for the response that immediately precedes it.

You can probably find complex behaviors in your own life that you learned by chaining. (Though, since you are human, you don't always need a primary reinforcer at the end of the line.) Did a parent teach you to eat with a spoon? You probably started at the end—having food put in your mouth—and worked back toward the beginning—picking food up and bringing it yourself to your mouth. Can you tell what the middle steps might be?

The two forms of learning we have examined so far—classical conditioning and operant conditioning—have most often been studied with the assumption that processes of learning were consistent across all animals. In fact, we have cited examples from dogs, cats, rats, mice, pigeons, and humans to show exactly such consistency. However, researchers have come to understand that learning is modified in many situations by the particular biological and cognitive capabilities of individual species. We turn now to the processes that limit the generality of the laws of learning.

Animals can learn to do some surprising things, with a little help from their human friends and the application of operant conditioning techniques. Waterskiing, anyone?

BIOLOGY AND LEARNING

The contemporary view that a single, general account of the associationist principles of learning is common to humans and all animals was first proposed by English philosopher **David Hume** in 1748. Hume reasoned that any theory by which we explain the operations of the understanding, or the origin and connexion of the passions in man, will acquire additional authority, if we find that the same theory is requisite to explain the same phenomena in all other animals" (Hume, 1748/1951, p. 104).

The appealing simplicity of such a view has come under scrutiny since the 1960s as psychologists have discovered certain *constraints,* or limitations, on the generality of the findings regarding conditioning (Bailey & Bailey, 1993; Garcia, 1993; Todd & Morris, 1992, 1993). In Chapter 3, we familiarized you with the idea that animals have evolved in response to the need for survival: we can explain many of the differences among species as adaptations to the demands of their particular environmental niches. The same evolutionary perspective applies to a species' capacity for learning (Leger, 1992). **Biological constraints on learning** are any limitations on learning imposed by a species' genetic endowment. These constraints can apply to the animal's sensory, behavioral, and cognitive capacities. We will examine two areas of research that show how behavior-environment relations can be biased by an organism's genotype: instinctual drift and taste-aversion learning.

INSTINCTUAL DRIFT

You have no doubt seen animals performing tricks on television or in the circus. Some animals play baseball or Ping-Pong, and others drive tiny race cars. For years, **Keller Breland** and **Marion Breland** used operant conditioning techniques to train thousands of animals from many different species to perform a remarkable array of behaviors. The Brelands had believed that general principles derived from laboratory research using virtually any type of response or reward could be directly applied to the control of animal behavior outside the laboratory.

At some point after training, though, some of the animals began to "misbehave." For example, a raccoon was trained to pick up a coin, put it into a toy bank, and collect an edible reinforcer. The raccoon, however, would not immediately deposit the coin. Even worse, when there were two coins to be deposited, conditioning broke down completely—the raccoon would not give up the coins at all. Instead, it would rub the coins together, dip them into the bank, and then pull them back out. But is this really so strange? Raccoons often engage in rubbing and washing behaviors as they remove the outer shells of a favorite food, crayfish. Similarly, when pigs were given the task of putting their hard-earned tokens into a large piggy bank, they instead would drop the coins onto the floor, root (poke at) them with their snouts, and toss them into the air. Again, should you consider this strange? Pigs root and shake their food as a natural part of their inherited food-gathering repertory.

The Brelands discovered that operant responses learned by animals would drift toward instinctual behaviors, a process they called instinctual drift.

These experiences convinced the Brelands that, even when animals have learned to make operant responses perfectly, the "learned behavior drifts toward instinctual behavior" over time. They termed this tendency **instinctual drift** (Breland & Breland, 1951, 1961). The behavior of their animals is not explainable by ordinary operant principles, but it is understandable if you consider the species-specific tendencies imposed by an inherited genotype. These tendencies override the changes in behavior brought about by operant conditioning.

The bulk of traditional research on animal learning focused on arbitrarily chosen responses to conveniently available stimuli. The Brelands' theory and demonstration of instinctual drift makes it evident that not all aspects of learning are under the control of the experimenters' reinforcers. Behaviors will be more or less easy to change as a function of an animal's normal, genetically programmed responses in its environment. Conditioning will be particularly efficient when you can frame a target response as biologically relevant. For example, what change might you make to get the pigs to place their tokens in a bank? If the token was paired with a water reward for a thirsty pig, it would then not be rooted as food but would be deposited in the bank as a valuable commodity—dare we say a *liquid asset*?

Taste-Aversion Learning

Your authors have a pair of confessions to make: one of us still gets a bit queasy at the thought of eating pork and beans; the other has the same response, alas, to popcorn. Why? In each case, we became violently ill after eating one of these foods. Although it's very unlikely that it was the food itself that made us sick—and we have tried valiantly, particularly for the popcorn, to convince ourselves of that fact—we nonetheless have this queasy response. We can look to nonhuman animals for a clue to why this is so.

Suppose we asked you to devise a strategy for tasting a variety of unfamiliar substances. If you had the genetic endowment of rats, you would be very cautious in doing so. When presented with a new food or flavor, rats take only a very small sample. Only if it fails to make them sick will they go back for more. To flip that around, suppose we include a substance with the new flavor that does make the rats ill—they'll never consume that flavor again. This phenomenon is known as **taste-aversion learning.** You can see why having this genetic capacity to sample and learn which foods are safe and which are toxic could have great survival value.

Taste aversion is so powerful that it is permanently learned after only one pairing of a CS and its consequences.

In fact, taste-aversion learning is an enormously powerful mechanism. Unlike other instances of classical conditioning, taste aversion is learned with only one pairing of a CS (the novel flavor) and its consequences (the underlying UCS—the element that actually brings about the illness). This is true even with a long interval, 12 hours or more, between the time the rat consumes the substance and the time it becomes ill. Finally, unlike many classically conditioned associations that are quite fragile, this one is permanent after one experience. Again, to understand these violations of the norms of classical conditioning, you should consider how dramatically this mechanism aids survival.

John Garcia, the psychologist who first documented taste-aversion learning in the laboratory, and his colleague Robert Koelling used this phenomenon to demonstrate that, in general, animals are biologically prepared to learn certain associations. The researchers discovered that some CS-UCS combinations can and some cannot be classically conditioned in particular species of animals.

In phase 1 of their experiment, thirsty rats were first familiarized with the experimental situation in which licking a tube produced three CSs: saccharin-flavored water, noise, and bright light. In phase 2, when the rats licked the tube, half of them received only the sweet water and half received only the noise, light, and plain water. Each of these two groups was again divided: half of each group was given electric shocks that produced pain, and half was given X-ray radiation that produced nausea and illness.

The amount of water drunk by the rats in phase 1 was compared with the amount drunk in phase 2, when pain and illness were involved (see **Figure 9.12**). Big reductions in drinking occurred when flavor was associated with illness (taste aversion) and when noise and light were associated with pain. However, there was little change in behavior under the other two conditions—when flavor predicted pain or when the "bright-noisy water" predicted illness.

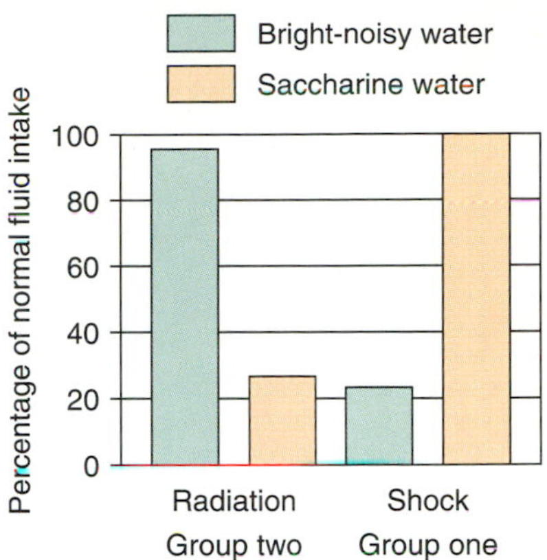

Figure 9.12 Inborn Bias
Results from Garcia and Koelling's study (1966) showed that rats possess an inborn bias to associate certain cues with certain outcomes. Rats avoided saccharin-flavored water when it predicted illness but not when it predicted shock. Conversely, rats avoided the "bright-noisy water" when it predicted shock but not when it predicted illness.

The pattern of results suggests that rats have an inborn bias to associate particular stimuli with particular consequences (Garcia & Koelling, 1966). Some instances of conditioning, then, depend not only on the relationship between stimuli and behavior but also on the way an organism is genetically predisposed toward stimuli in its environment (Barker et al., 1978). Animals appear to have encoded, within their genetic inheritance, the types of sensory cues—taste, smell, or appearance—that are most likely to signal dimensions of reward or danger. Experimenters who try arbitrarily to break these genetic links will look forward to little success.

Researchers have put knowledge of the mechanisms of taste-aversion learning to practical use. To stop coyotes from killing sheep (and sheep ranchers from shooting coyotes), John Garcia and colleagues have put toxic lamb burgers wrapped in sheep fur on the outskirts of fenced-in areas of sheep ranches. The coyotes who eat these lamb burgers get sick, vomit, and develop an instant distaste for lamb meat. Their subsequent disgust at the mere sight of sheep makes them back away from the animals instead of attacking.

One of the most serious instances of taste aversions in humans occurs when cancer patients become unable to tolerate normal foods in their diets—to such an extent that they become anorexic and malnourished. Their aversions are, in part, a consequence of their chemotherapy treatments, which often follow meals and which produce nausea. Researchers have devised means to counteract this effect (Bernstein, 1988, 1991). They have arranged, for example, for children with cancer not to be given meals just

The coyote is showing disgust responses to the carcass of prey after having been exposed to taste-aversion conditioning.

before chemotherapy. They've also created "scapegoat" aversions. The children are given candies or ice cream of unusual flavors to eat before the treatments so that the taste aversion becomes conditioned only to those special flavors. Extension of this practical solution may be a lifesaver for some cancer patients.

You have now seen why modern behavior analysts must be attentive to the types of responses each species is best suited to learn (Todd & Morris, 1992). If you want to teach an old dog new tricks, you're best off adapting the tricks to the dog's genetic behavioral repertory! Our survey of learning is not complete, however, because we have not yet dealt with types of learning that might require more complex cognitive processes. We turn now to those types of learning.

COGNITIVE INFLUENCES ON LEARNING

Our reviews of classical and operant conditioning have demonstrated that a wide variety of behaviors can be understood as the products of simple learning processes. You might wonder, however, if there are certain classes of learning that require more complex, more cognitive types of processes. **Cognition** is any mental activity involved in the representation and processing of knowledge, such as thinking, remembering, perceiving, and language use. In this section, we look at forms of learning in animals and humans that cannot be explained only by patterns of reinforcement in the environment. We suggest, therefore, that the behaviors are partially the product of cognitive processes.

ANIMAL COGNITION

"Stimulus, response. Stimulus, response! Don't you ever think?"

THE FAR SIDE, by Gary Larson. Copyright © 1986. Universal Press Syndicate. Reprinted with permission. All rights reserved.

In this chapter, we have emphasized that, species-specific constraints aside, rules of learning acquired from research on rats and pigeons apply as well to dogs, monkeys, and humans. Researchers who study **animal cognition** have demonstrated that it is not only classical and operant conditioning that generalizes across species (Wasserman, 1993, 1994). In his original formulation of the theory of evolution, Charles Darwin suggested that the mind evolved along with the physical forms of animals. In fact, we saw in Chapter 4 that studies with monkeys and chimpanzees have contributed to a theory of the continuous evolution of consciousness. In this section we will describe two impressive forms of animal performance that indicate further continuity in the cognitive capabilities of nonhuman and human animals.

Cognitive Maps

Edward C. Tolman (1886–1959) pioneered the study of cognitive processes in learning by inventing experimental circumstances in which mechanical, one-to-one associations between specific stimuli and responses could not explain animals' observed behavior. Consider the maze shown in **Figure 9.13**. Tolman and his students demonstrated that, when an original goal path is blocked in a maze, a rat will take the shortest detour around the barrier, even though that particular response was never previously reinforced (Tolman & Honzig, 1930). The rats, therefore, behaved as if they were responding to an internal **cognitive map**—a representation of the overall layout of the maze—rather than blindly exploring different parts of the maze through trial and error (Tolman, 1948). Tolman's results showed that conditioning involves more than the simple formation of associations between sets of stimuli or between responses and reinforcers. It includes learning and representing other facets of the total behavioral context (Balsam & Tomie, 1985).

Research in Tolman's tradition has consistently demonstrated an impressive capacity for spatial memory in rats and other animals (Olton, 1979,

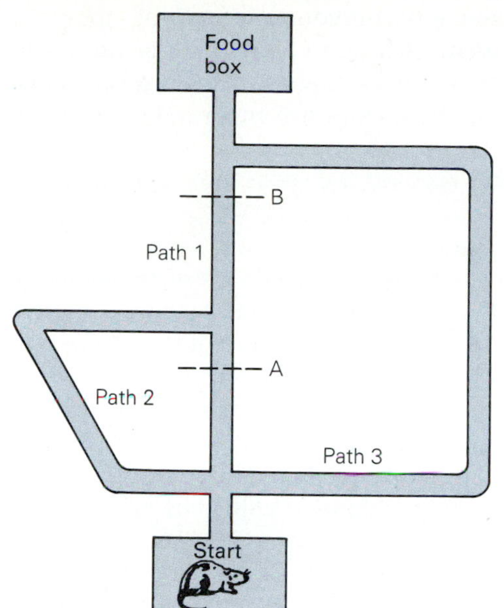

Figure 9.13 Use of Cognitive Maps in Maze Learning
Subjects preferred the direct path (Path 1) when it was open. With a block at A, they preferred Path 2. When a block was placed at B, the rats usually chose Path 3. Their behavior seemed to indicate that they had a cognitive map of the best way to get the food.

1992). To understand the efficiency of spatial cognitive maps, consider the functions they serve (Poucet, 1993):

Tolman's research with cognitive maps, and the behavior of bird species such as Clark's nutcracker, indicate the presence of a cognitive component of learning in animals.

- Animals use spatial memory to recognize and identify features of their environment.
- Animals use spatial memory to find important goal objects in their environments.
- Animals use spatial memory to plan their route through an environment.

You can see these different functions of cognitive maps at work in the many species of birds that store food over a dispersed area but are able to recover that food with great accuracy when they need it:

> Clark's nutcracker is the champion among food storers that have been studied. In the late summer, these birds bury up to 6,000 caches of pine seeds on mountainsides in the American Southwest. They recover the seeds as late as the next spring, when the cached food supports exceptionally early breeding. (Shettleworth, 1993, p. 180)

How do animals use spatial memory?

The birds are not just roaming their environment and coming upon the seeds through good fortune. They return, with up to 84 percent accuracy, to the thousands of locations at which they buried their seeds (Kamil & Balda, 1990). Note that these birds' "storing" behaviors are not reinforced when they initially bury their pine seeds. Only if their cognitive maps remained accurate over the winter can they later recover the seeds and reproduce.

Conceptual Behavior

We have seen that cognitive maps, in part, help animals preserve details of the spatial locations of objects in their environments. But what cognitive processes do animals use to preserve the category structure of those objects? In Chapter 5, we suggested that one of the challenges of language acquisition is for children to form generalizations about new *concepts* and *categories* they are learning, like the words *dog* and *tree*. Human children, however, are not the only animals capable of facing this challenge. Researchers have demonstrated that pigeons as well have the cognitive ability to make use of *conceptual* distinctions.

Researchers have also demonstrated that animals such as pigeons are capable of making conceptual distinctions.

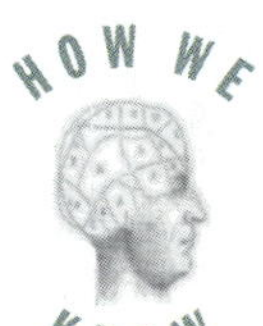

Edward Wasserman and his colleagues (1992) presented pigeons with color photographs of people, flowers, cars, and chairs. For each pigeon, the set of four concepts was divided into two larger categories (see **Figure 9.14**). For example, one pigeon might receive food if it pecked an orange key after viewing a person or a car and if it pecked a red key after viewing a flower or a chair. The pigeons learned to make the appropriate responses around 80 percent of the time or better. In a second training phase of the experiment, the pigeon was trained to provide a new response to only half the members—one smaller category—of each of these larger categories. Thus, the pigeon might be required to peck a green key when it saw a person and a white key when it saw a chair. Once again, performance on this task was about 80 percent accurate or better.

Now what happens when the pigeons are shown a flower or a car and must choose between the green and white keys? They have no history of reinforcement that links these stimuli to these responses, so we can't predict behavior based on simple learning processes. But what would you do if we put you in this situation?

	Stimulus	Reinforced response
Training Phase 1	People or Cars	Orange Key Press
	Flowers or Chairs	Red Key Press
Training Phase 2	People	Green Key Press
	Chairs	White Key Press
	Stimulus	Category response
Test Phase	Cars	Green Key Press
	Flowers	White Key Press

Figure 9.14 Concept Learning in Pigeons

The first training phase teaches the pigeons which concepts go together into the same larger category. The second training phase teaches a new response for half of the members of each category. The test phase demonstrates generalization to the other members of the newly acquired categories. (This is one example of the different combinations of stimuli and responses presented to different pigeons.)

> In the first phase of the experiment, you would have learned that, for example, flowers and chairs go together. In the second phase of the experiment, you would have learned that you should provide one of two responses to each photo of a flower. When confronted with a chair, and the same choice of responses, you would probably try the response that had applied to flowers. That is, in fact, what pigeons largely did as well. On 60 to 70 percent of test trials, they used "category" information to emit a previously unreinforced behavior.

We already saw that generalization occurs in classical and operant conditioning based on the perceptual similarity of stimuli. In the experiment by Wasserman and colleagues, the generalization did not involve perceptual similarity—cars and flowers, for example, don't look much alike. Instead, the grounds for generalization was the cognitive similarity brought about by the newly acquired conceptual structure.

We will devote Chapters 10 and 11 to an analysis of cognitive processes in humans. The experiments we have described here, however, should convince you that humans are not the only species with impressive and useful cognitive capabilities. Let's move now to another type of learning that requires cognitive processes.

Observational Learning

To introduce this further type of learning, we'd like you to return for a moment to the comparison of rats' and humans' approaches to sampling new foods. The rats are almost certainly more cautious than you are, but that's largely because they are missing an invaluable source of information—input from other rats. When you try a new food, it's almost always in a context in which you have good reason to believe that other people have eaten and enjoyed the food. The probability of your "food-eating behavior" is thus influenced by your knowledge of patterns of reinforcement for other individuals. This example illustrates your capacity to learn via *vicarious reinforcement* and *vicarious punishment.* You can use your cognitive capacities for memory and reasoning to change your own behaviors in light of the experience of others.

How likely would you be to try an unfamiliar food if you had no opportunity to see other people eating and enjoying it?

In fact, much *social learning* occurs in situations where learning would not be predicted by traditional conditioning theory, because a learner has made no active response and has received no tangible reinforcer. The individual, after simply watching another person exhibiting behavior that was reinforced or punished, later behaves in much the same way, or refrains from doing so. This is known as **observational learning.** Cognition often enters into observational learning in the form of expectations. In essence, after observing a model, you may think, If I do exactly what she does, I will get the same reinforcer or avoid the same punisher. A younger child may be better behaved than his older sister because he has learned from the sister's mistakes.

This capacity to learn from watching as well as from doing is extremely useful. It enables you to acquire large, integrated patterns of behavior without going through the tedious trial-and-error process of gradually eliminating wrong responses and acquiring the right ones. You can profit immediately from the mistakes and successes of others. Researchers have demonstrated that observational learning is not special to humans. Even octopuses are capable of changing their behavior after merely observing the performance of another member of their species (Fiorito & Scotto, 1992).

Observational learning allows you to profit immediately from the mistakes and successes of others.

A classic demonstration of human observational learning occurred in the laboratory of **Albert Bandura.** After watching adult models punching, hitting, and kicking a large plastic BoBo doll, the children in the experiment later

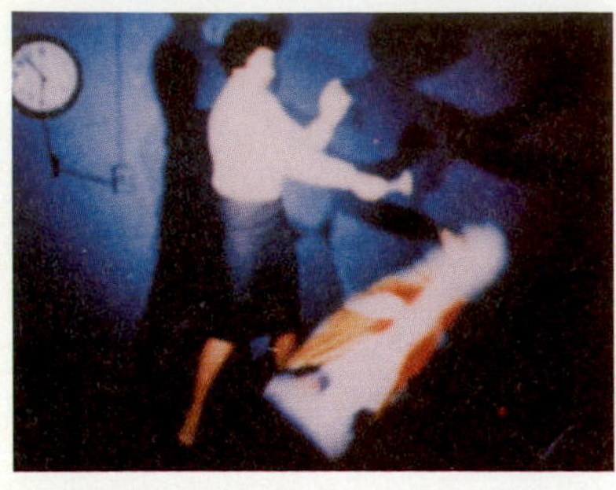

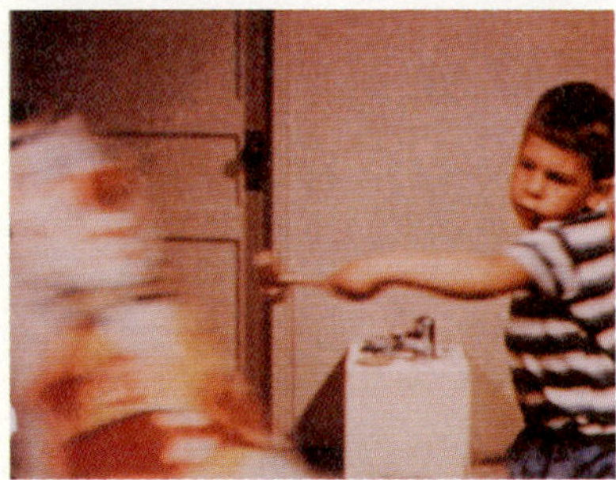

From top to bottom: Adult models aggression; boy imitates aggression; girl imitates aggression.

showed a greater frequency of the same behaviors than did children in control conditions who had not observed the aggressive models (Bandura et al., 1963). Subsequent studies showed that children imitated such behaviors just from watching filmed sequences of models, even when the models were cartoon characters.

There is little question now that we learn much—both prosocial (helping) and antisocial (hurting) behaviors—through observation of models, but what variables are important in determining which models will be most likely to influence you? Research has yielded the following general conclusions (Baldwin & Baldwin, 1973; Bandura, 1977a). A model's observed behavior will be most influential when (1) it is seen as having reinforcing consequences; (2) the model is perceived positively, liked, and respected; (3) there are perceived similarities between features and traits of the model and the observer; (4) the observer is rewarded for paying attention to the model's behavior; (5) the model's behavior is visible and salient—it stands out as a clear figure against the background of competing models; and (6) it is within the observer's range of competence to imitate the behavior. To understand this list of findings, you should imagine yourself in modeling situations and see how each item in the list would apply. Imagine, for example, you are watching someone who is learning how to parachute jump. Or consider how someone might learn to be a "good" gang member by observing his or her buddies.

Because people learn so efficiently from models, you can understand why a good deal of psychological research has been directed at the behavioral impact of television: Are viewers affected by what they see being rewarded and punished on TV? Attention has focused on the link between televised acts of violence—murder, rape, assault, robbery, terrorism, and suicide—and children's and adolescents' subsequent behavior. Does exposure to acts of violence foster imitation? The conclusion from psychological research is yes—it does for some people, and particularly in the United States (Comstock & Paik, 1991; Huesmann & Eron, 1986). In controlled laboratory studies, the two major effects of filmed violence were *psychic numbing,* a reduction in both emotional arousal and in distress at viewing violence, and an increase in the likelihood of engaging in aggressive behavior (Murray & Kippax, 1977). Research has shown that children can also learn prosocial, helping behaviors when they watch television programs that provide prosocial behavioral models (Friedrich & Stein, 1975; Singer & Singer, 1990). You should take seriously the idea that children learn from the television they watch. As a parent or caretaker, you may want to help children select appropriate televised models.

An analysis of observational learning acknowledges both that principles of reinforcement influence behavior and that humans have the capacity to use their cognitive processes to change behaviors with vicarious rewards and punishment. This approach to the understanding of human behavior has proven to be very powerful (Bandura, 1986). In Chapter 18 we will look at successful programs of therapy that have emerged from the cognitive modification of maladaptive patterns of behavior.

FORMAL MODELS OF LEARNING

Throughout this chapter, we have been focusing on the *what* and *when* of learning—the circumstances under which certain responses will become more or less probable. We turn now to *learning models,* hypothesized systems that try to describe rigorously the *how* of learning—the processes and structures that make learning possible. To show you that these are different concerns, we will ask you to imagine you are in a simple learning experiment. As shown in **Figure 9.15**, we will present you with numbers between

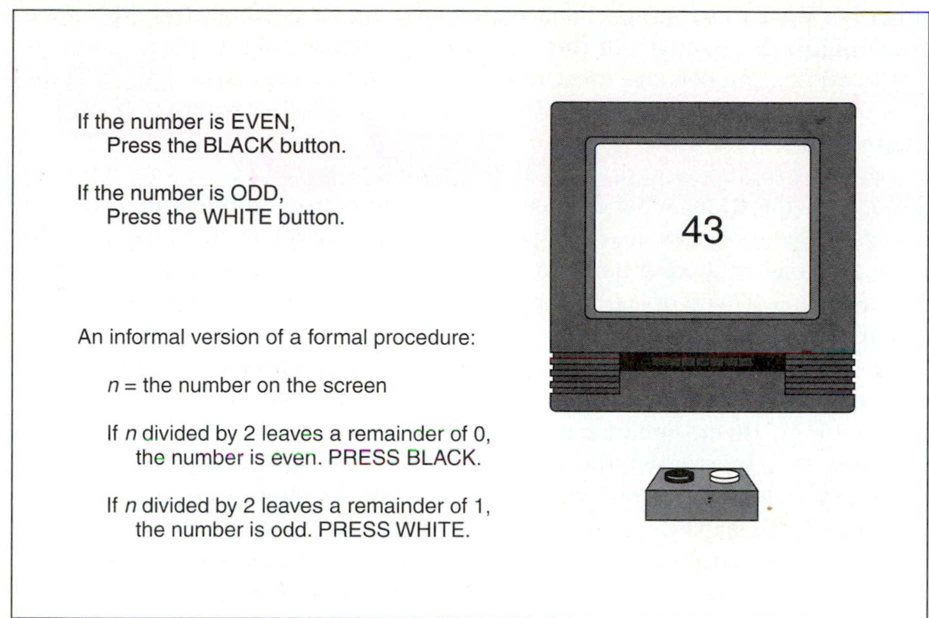

If the number is EVEN,
Press the BLACK button.
If the number is ODD,
Press the WHITE button.
43
An informal version of a formal procedure:
n = the number on the screen
If n divided by 2 leaves a remainder of 0,
the number is even. PRESS BLACK.
If n divided by 2 leaves a remainder of 1,
the number is odd. PRESS WHITE.

Figure 9.15 A Model for Even/Odd Judgments

10 and 99 on a computer screen. If the number is even, we want you to press the black button. If the number is odd, we want you to press the white button. Do you agree that you'd learn this task very efficiently? But how are you able to do it? Imagine that we asked you to write a computer program to carry out the task. Such a program would be a *formal model,* because you would have to specify exactly, formally, what each step of the procedure does: *How* you do it rather than just *what* you're doing.

In Figure 9.15, we've given an informal version of possible formal steps—a procedure for determining whether a number is odd or even. The procedure will work, but do you think it's what you're doing? To perform the task, are you dividing by two and checking the remainder? Probably not. Subjects appear to make odd and even judgments by focusing on the units (rightmost) digit and retrieving from memory whether that one digit is odd or even (Dehaene et al., 1993). Even so, a careful specification of the formal model for odd/even judgments allowed for a meaningful test of the theory.

A formal model is always just one hypothesis about what happens between inputs and outputs. The adequacy of the model can be tested, just like any other hypothesis. Researchers who propose such models must provide evidence that the model is consistent with the known facts of psychological processes. The best formal models are constrained by existing data and lead to predictions about new phenomena (Lewandowsky, 1993; Seidenberg, 1993).

Formal models of learning most often make claims about the computations—the mental steps—that relate conditions in the environment to behavioral responses. Their adequacy is tested much as we would test the odd/even rule in our simple learning task. Researchers ask, Does this set of computations (which are typically implemented as a series of equations on a high-speed computer) produce the correct relationships in a plausible fashion?

Formal models of learning are concerned with the mental steps that relate environmental conditions to behavioral responses.

One area of active research on learning models is known as **connectionism.** Connectionist models consist of a collection of units—representing concepts, parts of concepts, or sensations—and *connections* between these units—representing the relations between the various concepts and sensations. In a model of classical conditioning, the units might represent stimuli like bells, buzzers, food powder, and electric shock and responses like salivation and emotional arousal. The connections would represent the associa-

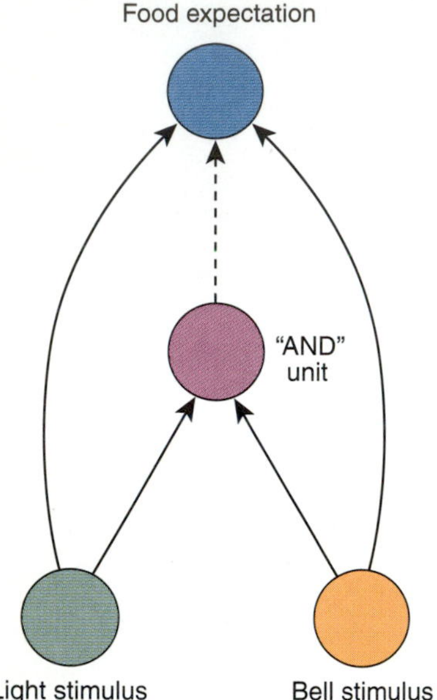

Figure 9.16 Connectionism *In a complex connectionist network, a subject can expect food in response to a light stimulus or a bell stimulus but not both. The complex network includes the "AND" unit in the center, which comes on when both the light and the bell are perceived, turning off the food expectation unit (hence the strong negative connection from it to the top unit). An extended version of error-correcting learning (the generalized delta rule) is necessary for learning the proper connections in such a network.*

tions between these units. Each connection has a certain strength, corresponding to the strength of the relationship between the units it connects. Connectionist models are most often defined by two features: (1) an *architecture*—the configuration of units and the connections between them (see **Figure 9.16**) and (2) a *learning rule*—the computations that adjust the strengths of the connections as a function of experience. Researchers seek to answer the question, What combination of architecture and learning rule can successfully model how learning takes place? Let's explore this question with respect to classical conditioning.

The simplest type of learning rule we might think of to change connection strengths between units would be purely associational. So, whenever two units are "on" simultaneously—that is, whenever their two concepts are both true at about the same time—you will positively strengthen the connection between them. For instance, whenever you have a shock and tone on together, you strengthen the connection between your representations of those external stimuli. Soon you may learn that the shock and tone regularly co-occur. Such learning is often called *Hebbian learning,* after **Donald Hebb,** who proposed it in a general form (Hebb, 1949). If you apply this type of learning model to the case of bells, buzzers, and shocks, you can easily model how an animal might build up associations between conditional stimuli (the bell or buzzer) and unconditional stimuli (the shock) and its unconditional response.

Although Hebbian learning is a useful beginning for modeling some forms of conditioning, it errs by building up associations between *any* conceptual units that happen to be "on" close together in time. For example, imagine that a tone and a shock are presented together. A learning model using a Hebbian rule will come to associate these two sensations with each other, as expected. Now imagine that a tone and a light are paired with the shock. Hebbian learning will continue to take place, this time also strengthening the association between the light and the shock, since they occur near in time to each other. Thus the model will predict that a tone implies the shock *and* a light implies the shock. As you saw in the blocking experiments, however, animals do not learn this second association; they pick up only the first association. The Hebbian model of animal learning fails in this case, and we need to find a new learning rule to explain this blocking situation.

The new learning rule comes from the notion of *informativeness* of the CS, which we saw was critical for classical conditioning. We will change the interpretation of the interaction of units in the model slightly. Now, instead of merely associating pairs of concepts or sensations, we will use the connections between units to *predict* some concept or sensation, given the presence of others. The connection between the tone unit and the shock unit represents the prediction about whether a tone will be followed by a shock. If there is a strong positive connection between the two, then a tone will predict a shock, but if there is a zero-strength connection between them, then hearing a tone neither implies a shock nor guarantees that there won't be one.

For example, imagine that the model begins with zero-strength connections between a tone unit and a shock unit, and between a light unit and the same shock unit. When we first present the model with a tone, the connection from the tone unit to the shock unit is still zero, and the model will not predict that a shock is about to happen. When we turn on the tone unit to correspond to a shock sensation, the model now realizes that it has been incorrect in its prediction—it should have predicted a shock—and the new learning rule will cause the strength of the connection between the tone unit and the shock unit to be increased. After we do this tone–shock pairing a few times, the connection between the two corresponding units will be strong enough that the next time we present the model with a tone, it will predict a shock.

In this model, learning takes place because at first there is a mismatch between what the model predicts in response to the tone and what takes place. Information about that mismatch is propagated back through the system to adjust connection strengths. However, what happens if we turn on the tone and the light together? The tone–shock connection will still predict a shock—so there will be no mismatch between what is predicted and what occurs. Without a mismatch, no learning about the relationship between the light and the shock can take place. In this way, we have achieved *blocking* with our new learning rule, and we've added another degree of realism to our learning model (Rescorla & Wagner, 1972).

Because this new learning rule causes a change in the connection strengths only when the model makes a mistake in its prediction about the world, it is known as *error-correcting,* or error-minimizing, learning. It is often called the *delta rule,* because it deals with the difference, or delta, between predictions and reality (Rumelhart & McClelland, 1986). The delta rule can model a variety of learning situations, but to achieve even greater sophistication, we must also appropriately adjust the architecture of our models. For instance, imagine that you want to train an animal to respond to expect food *either* when a light comes on *or* when a bell is rung but *not* when the light and the bell occur together. You cannot merely have a connectionist model, using the delta rule, that learns a positive connection from a light unit to a food unit and from a bell unit to the same food unit, because then food will be predicted for either stimulus *and* for both.

The delta rule describes error-correcting learning, in which changes in connection strengths occur as the result of mistakes in predictions about the world.

To solve this problem, you need *new conceptual units* that are not themselves inputs (such as lights and bells) nor outputs (such as expectations for foods). As shown in Figure 9.16, such a unit should come "on" only when both the bell and the light are on and have a strong negative connection to the food unit. Thus, by adjusting the architecture just a little, we can start to capture more complex behavior in our model. Many researchers consider connectionist models promising exactly because these models explain and predict sophisticated patterns of responses with a limited repertory of devices. Such formal models can extend our understanding and appreciation of the processes of learning and may suggest future directions for research.

Let's close out this chapter where we began, with your visit to a horror movie. How can behavior analysis explain your experiences? If you went to the movie because a friend who had seen it already recommended it to you, you have succumbed to vicarious reinforcement. If you made it to the theater, despite having to find your way around a new obstacle, you have shown evidence of a cognitive map. If the sound of scary music made you fear for the hero's well-being, you felt the effects of classical conditioning. If your failure to enjoy the film made you vow never to see a horror movie again, you have discovered the effect a punisher has on your subsequent behavior.

Are you ready to return to the theater?

What principles of behavior analysis might be applied to the experience of going to see a movie featuring a killer shark?

Recapping Main Points

The Study of Learning

Learning entails a relatively consistent change in behavior or behavior potential based on experience. Behaviorists believe that much behavior can be explained by simple learning processes. They also believe that many of the same principles of learning apply to all organisms.

Classical Conditioning: Learning Predictable Signals

In classical conditioning, investigated by Pavlov, an unconditional stimulus (UCS) elicits an unconditional response (UCR). A neutral stimulus paired with the UCS becomes a conditional stimulus (CS), which elicits a similar response, called the conditional response (CR). For classical conditioning to occur, there must be a contingent and informative relationship between the CS and UCS. Extinction occurs when the UCS no longer follows the CS. Stimulus generalization is the phenomenon whereby stimuli similar to the CS elicit the CR. Discrimination learning narrows the range of CSs to which an organism responds. Classical conditioning explains many emotional responses and has been used to change immune function.

Operant Conditioning: Learning About Consequences

Thorndike demonstrated that behaviors that bring about satisfying outcomes tend to be repeated. Skinner's behavior analytic approach centers on manipulating contingencies of reinforcement and observing the effects on behavior. Behaviors are made more likely by positive and negative reinforcement. They are made less likely by positive and negative punishment. Contextually appropriate behavior is explained by the three-term contingency of discriminative stimulus-behavior-consequence.

Primary reinforcers are stimuli that function as reinforcers even when an organism has not had previous experience with them. Conditioned reinforcers are acquired by association with primary reinforcers. Behavior is affected by schedules of reinforcement that may be varied or fixed and delivered in intervals or in ratios. Complex responses may be learned through chaining or shaping.

Biology and Learning

Research suggests that learning may be constrained by the species-specific repertoires of different organisms. Instinctual drift may overwhelm some response-reinforcement learning. Taste-aversion learning suggests that species are genetically prepared for some forms of CS-UCS associations.

Cognitive Influences on Learning

Cognitive influences on learning are demonstrated by cognitive maps, conceptual behavior, and observational learning. Animals develop cognitive maps to enable them to function in a complex environment. Behaviors can be vicariously reinforced or punished. Humans and other animals can learn through observation.

Formal Models of Learning

Formal models specify the "how" of psychological processes. Connectionist models specify the architecture and rules that underlie learning.

Resources

Axelrod, S., & Apsche, J. (Eds.). (1983). *The effects of punishment on human behavior.* San Diego: Academic Press.

Druckman, D., & Bjork, R. A. (Eds.). (1991). *In the mind's eye: Enhancing human performance.* Washington, DC: National Academy Press.

Grant, L., & Evans, A. (1994). *Principles of behavior analysis.* New York: HarperCollins.

Kazdin, A. E. (1994). *Behavior modification in applied settings* (5th ed.). Pacific Grove, CA: Brooks/Cole.

Watson, D. L., & Tharp, R. G. (1985). *Self-directed behavior: Self-modification for personal adjustment* (4th ed.). Monterey, CA: Brooks/Cole.

10

Memory

Because this is a chapter on memory, we're going to put your memory immediately to work. We'd like you to remember the number 34. Do whatever you need to do to remember 34. And yes, there will be a test!

Now, a slightly different exercise. We'd like you to imagine what it would be like if you suddenly acquired total amnesia and had no memory of your past—of the people you have known or of events that have happened to you. You wouldn't remember your mother's face, or your tenth birthday, or your senior prom. Without such "time anchors," how would you maintain a sense of who you are—of your self-identity? Or suppose you lost the ability to form any new memories. What would happen to your most recent experiences? Could you follow a conversation or untangle the plot of a TV show? Everything would vanish, as if events had never existed, as if you had never had any thoughts in mind. Is there any activity you can think of that is not influenced by memory?

If you have never given much thought to your memory, it's probably because it tends to do its job reasonably well—you take it for granted, alongside other bodily processes, like digestion or breathing. But as with stomach aches or allergies, the times you notice your memory are likely to be the times when something goes wrong: you forget your car keys, an important date, lines in a play, or the answer to an examination question that you know you "really knew." There's no reason you shouldn't find these occasions irritating, but you should also reflect for a moment on the estimate that the average human brain can store 100 trillion bits of information. The task of managing such a vast array of information is a formidable one. Perhaps you shouldn't be too surprised when an answer is sometimes not available when you need it!

Our goal in this chapter is to explain how you usually remember so much, and why you forget some of what you have known. We will explore how you get your everyday experiences into and out of memory. You will learn what psychology has discovered about different types of memory and about how those memories work. We hope that in the course of learning the many facts of memory, you will gain an appreciation for how wonderful a skill memory is.

Memorization—of movements and expressions as well as of words—is a key skill for actors and other performers.

WHAT IS MEMORY?

To begin, we will define **memory** as the capacity to store and retrieve information. In this chapter, we will describe memory as a type of *information processing*. The bulk of our attention, therefore, will be trained on the flow of information in and out of your memory systems. Our examination of the processes that guide the acquisition and retrieval of information will enable you to refine your sense of what *memory* means. Our discussion starts with the earliest formal body of research on memory, published in 1885. We will then introduce you to distinctions among types of memory, carved out by contemporary researchers.

EBBINGHAUS QUANTIFIES MEMORY

See if this statement rings true: "Facts crammed at examination time soon vanish, if they were not sufficiently grounded by other study and later subjected to a sufficient review." In other words, if you cram for a test, you're not likely to remember very much a few days later. This astute, and very modern, observation was made in 1885 by the German psychologist **Hermann Ebbinghaus,** who outlined a series of such phenomena to motivate his new science of memory. Ebbinghaus's observations added up to a convincing argument in favor of an empirical investigation of memory. What was needed was a methodology, and Ebbinghaus invented a brilliant one.

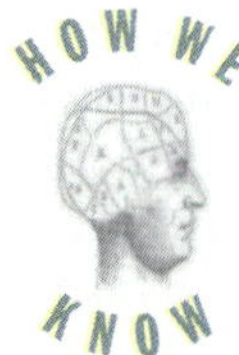

Ebbinghaus used nonsense syllables—meaningless three-letter units consisting of a vowel between two consonants, such as *CEG* or *DAX*. He used nonsense syllables, rather than meaningful words, like DOG, because he hoped to obtain a "pure" measure of memory—one uncontaminated by previous learning or associations that a person might bring to the experimental memory task.

Not only was Ebbinghaus the researcher, he was also his own subject. He performed the research tasks himself and measured his own performance. The task he assigned himself was memorization of lists of varying length. Ebbinghaus chose to use *rote learning,* memorization by mechanical repetition, to perform the task.

Ebbinghaus learned lists of nonsense syllables in order to gain a pure measure of memory uncontaminated by previous learning.

Ebbinghaus started his studies by reading through the items one at a time until he finished the list. Then he read through the list again in the same order, and again, until he could recite all the items in the correct order—the *criterion performance*. Then he distracted himself from rehearsing the original list by forcing himself to learn many other lists. After this interval, Ebbinghaus measured his memory by seeing how many trials it took him to *relearn* the original list. If he needed fewer trials to relearn it than he had needed to learn it, information had been *saved* from his original study. (This concept should be familiar from Chapter 9. Recall that there is often a savings when animals relearn a conditioned response.)

For example, if Ebbinghaus took 12 trials to learn a list and 9 trials to relearn it several days later, his savings score for that elapsed time would be 25 percent (12 trials − 9 trials = 3 trials; 3 trials ÷ 12 trials = 25 percent). Using this **savings method,** Ebbinghaus recorded the degree of memory retained after different time intervals. The curve he obtained is shown in **Figure 10.1**. As you can see, he found a rapid initial loss of memory, followed by a gradually declining rate of loss. Ebbinghaus's curve is typical of results from experiments on rote memory.

The learning curve that Ebbinghaus demonstrated showed a rapid initial loss of memory followed by a gradually declining rate of loss.

Following Ebbinghaus's lead, psychologists studied verbal learning for many decades by observing subjects attempting to learn and recall nonsense

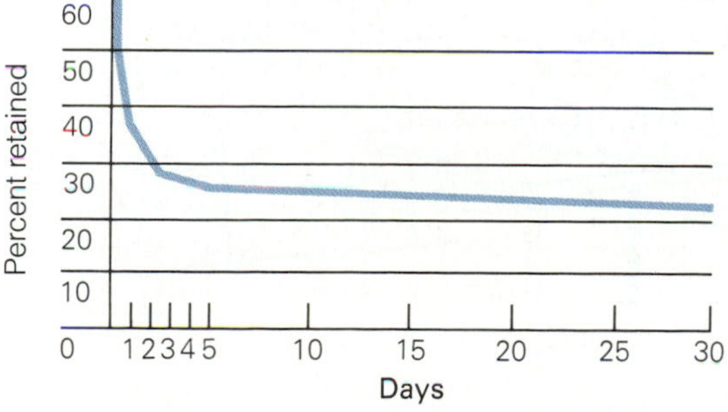

Figure 10.1 Ebbinghaus's Forgetting Curve

The curve shows how many nonsense syllables are remembered by individuals using the savings method when tested over a 30-day period. The curve decreases rapidly and then reaches a plateau.

syllables. This research was based on the assumption that there was only one kind of remembering. By studying memory in as "pure" a form as possible, uncontaminated by meaning, researchers hoped to find basic principles that would shed light on more complex examples of remembering. Researchers still aspire to discover those basic principles, but they have also turned to the study of memory for meaningful material. As we will now see, expanding the range of material in memory experiments has led researchers to understand that humans possess several different types of memory.

Types of Memory

When you think about memory, what is most likely to come to mind at first are situations in which you use your memory to recall (or try to recall) specific events or information: your favorite movie, the dates of World War II, or your student ID number. In fact, one of the important functions of memory is to allow you to have conscious access to the personal and collective past. But memory does much more for you than that. It also enables you to have effortless continuity of experience from one day to the next. When you drive in a car, for example, it is this second type of memory that makes the stores along the roadside seem familiar. In defining types of memory, we will make plain to you how hard your memory works, often outside of conscious awareness.

Implicit and Explicit Memory

Consider **Figure 10.2**. What's wrong with this picture? It probably strikes you as unusual that there's a bunny rabbit in the kitchen. But where does this feeling come from? You didn't have any sense of going through the objects in the picture one by one and asking yourself, "Does the refrigerator belong?" "Do the cabinets belong?" Rather—in some way—the rabbit jumps out at you as being out of place.

This simple example allows you to understand the difference between **explicit** and **implicit uses of memory.** Your discovery of the rabbit is implicit, because your memory processes brought past knowledge of kitchens to bear on your interpretation of the picture without any particular effort on your part. Suppose now we asked you, "What's missing from the picture?" To answer this second question, you probably have to put explicit memory to

Figure 10.2 What's Wrong with This Picture?

work. What appears in the typical kitchen? What's missing? (Did you think of the sink or the stove?) Thus, when it comes to using knowledge stored in memory, sometimes the use will be implicit—the information becomes available without any conscious effort—and sometimes it will be explicit—you make a conscious effort to recover the information.

We can make the same distinction when it comes to the initial acquisition of memories. How do you know what should appear in a kitchen? Did you ever memorize a list of what appears there and what the appropriate configuration should be? Probably not. Rather, it's likely that you acquired most of this knowledge through implicit memory processes. By contrast, you probably learned the names of many of the objects in the room explicitly. As we saw in Chapter 5, to learn the association between words and experiences, your younger self needed to engage in explicit memory processes. You learned the word *refrigerator* because someone called your explicit attention to the name of that object.

The explicit use of information stored in memory requires a conscious effort, whereas the implicit use of stored information does not.

The distinction between implicit and explicit memory greatly expands the range of questions researchers must address about memory processes (Graf & Schacter, 1985; Roediger, 1990; Seger, 1994). In the tradition established by Ebbinghaus, most research concerned the explicit acquisition of information. Experimenters most frequently provided subjects with new information to retain, and theories of memory were directed to explaining what subjects could and could not remember under those circumstances. However, as you will see in this chapter, researchers have now devised methods for studying implicit memory as well. Thus we can give you a more complete account of the variety of uses to which you put your memory. We can acknowledge that most circumstances in which you encode or retrieve information represent a mix of implicit and explicit uses of memory (Toth et al., 1994). Let's turn now to a second dimension along which memories are distributed.

Declarative and Procedural Memory

Can you whistle? Go ahead and try. Or if you can't whistle, try snapping your fingers. What kind of memory allows you to do these sorts of things? You probably remember having to learn these skills, but now they seem effortless. The examples we gave before of both implicit and explicit memories all involved the recollection of *facts* and *events,* which is called **declarative memory.** Now we see that you also have memories for *how to do things,* which is called **procedural memory.** Because the bulk of this chapter will be focused on how you acquire and use facts, let's take a moment now to consider how you acquire the ability to do things.

Procedural memory refers to the way you remember how things get done. It is used to acquire, retain, and employ perceptual, cognitive, and motor skills (Anderson, 1982; Tulving, 1983). Theories of procedural memory most often concern themselves with the time course of learning (Anderson, 1987, 1993): How do you go from a conscious list of facts about some activity to unconscious, automatic performance of that same activity? And why is it that after learning a skill, you often find it difficult to go back and talk about the component facts?

We can see these phenomena at work in even the very simple activity of dialing a phone number that, over time, has become highly familiar (Anderson, 1983). At first, you probably had to think your way through each digit, one at a time. You had to work through a list of declarative facts:

First, I must dial *2,*

Next, I must dial *0,*

Then I dial *7,*

and so on.

Does pretending to dial a phone number help you remember it? Thank your procedural memory!

However, when you began to dial the number often enough, you could start to produce it as one unit—a swift sequence of actions on the touch-tone pad. The process at work is called *knowledge compilation.* As a consequence of practice, you are able to carry out longer sequences of the activity without conscious intervention. But you also don't have conscious access to the *content* of these compiled units: back at the telephone, it's not uncommon to find someone who can't actually remember the phone number without pretending to dial it. In general, knowledge compilation makes it hard to share your procedural knowledge with others. You may have noticed this if your parents tried to teach you to drive. Although they may be good drivers themselves, they may not have been very good at communicating the content of compiled good-driving procedures.

You may also have noticed that knowledge compilation can lead to errors. If you are a skilled typist, you've probably suffered from the *the* problem: as soon as you hit the *t* and the *h* keys, your finger may fly to the *e,* even if you're really trying to type *throne* or *thistle.* Once you have sufficiently committed the execution of *the* to procedural memory, you can do little else but finish the sequence. Without procedural memory, life would be extremely laborious—you would be doomed to go step-by-step through every activity. However, each time you mistakenly type *the,* you can reflect on the trade-off between efficiency and potential error. Let's now turn to an overview of the basic processes that apply to all these different types of memory.

A procedural memory process called knowledge compilation *enables you to carry out long sequences of an activity but denies you the specific content of the compiled units.*

An Overview of Memory Processes

No matter what the category of memory, being able to use knowledge at some later time requires the operation of three mental processes: encoding, storage, and retrieval. **Encoding** is the initial processing of information that leads to a representation in memory. **Storage** is the retention over time of encoded material. **Retrieval** is the recovery at a later time of the stored information. Simply put, encoding gets information in, storage holds it until you need it, and retrieval gets it out. Let's now expand on these ideas.

All categories of memory involve the three basic processes of encoding, storage, and retrieval.

Encoding requires that you form *mental representations* of information from the external world. You can understand the idea of mental representations if we draw an analogy to representations outside your head. Imagine we wanted to know something about the best gift you got at your last birthday party. (Let's suppose it's not something you have with you.) What could you do to inform us about the gift? You might describe the properties of the object. Or you might draw us a picture. Or you might pretend that you're using the object. In each case, these are representations of the original object. Although none of the representations is likely to be quite as good as having the real thing present, they should allow us to acquire knowledge of the most important aspects of the gift. Mental representations work much the same way. They preserve the most important features of past experiences in a way that enables you to *re-present* those experiences to yourself. We will also refer to mental representations of individual memories as *memory traces.* The idea there is that what you store in your memory systems is the actual residue—a trace—of the original experience. (Because the encoding of memories requires biochemical changes in your brain, the notion of a memory trace is more than just a figure of speech.)

If information is properly encoded, it will be retained in *storage* over some period of time. Storage requires both short- and long-term changes in the structures of your brain. At the end of the chapter, we will see how researchers are attempting to locate the anatomical structures that are responsible for storing new and old memories. We will also see what happens in cases of extreme amnesia, where individuals become incapable of storing new memories.

Retrieval is the payoff for all your earlier effort. When it works, it enables you to gain access—often in a split second—to information you stored earlier. Can you remember what comes before storage: decoding or encoding? The answer is simple to retrieve now, but will you still be able to retrieve *encoding* as swiftly and with as much confidence when you are tested on this chapter's contents days or weeks from now? Discovering how you are able to retrieve one specific bit of information from the vast quantity of information in your memory storehouse is a challenge facing psychologists who want to know how memory works and how it can be improved.

Although it is easy to define encoding, storage, and retrieval as separate memory processes, the interaction among the three processes is quite complex. For example, to be able to encode the information that you have seen a tiger, you must first retrieve from memory the concept *tiger*. Similarly, to commit to memory the meaning of a sentence such as "He's as honest as Benedict Arnold," you must retrieve the meanings of each individual word, retrieve the rules of grammar that specify how word meanings should be combined in English, and retrieve cultural information that specifies exactly how honest Benedict Arnold—a famous Revolutionary War traitor—was.

The three basic processes of encoding, storage, and retrieval work together in a complex interaction to help you form and use new memories.

We are now ready to look in more detail at the encoding, storage, and retrieval of information. (**Figure 10.3** previews much of the information you will acquire about the workings of memory. You can refer back to it as you complete each section of the chapter.) Our discussion will start with short-lived types of memories, beginning with sensory memory, and then move to the more permanent forms of long-term memory. We will give you an account of how you remember and why you forget. Our plan is to make you forever self-conscious about all the ways in which you use your capacity for memory. We hope this will even allow you to improve some aspects of your memory skills.

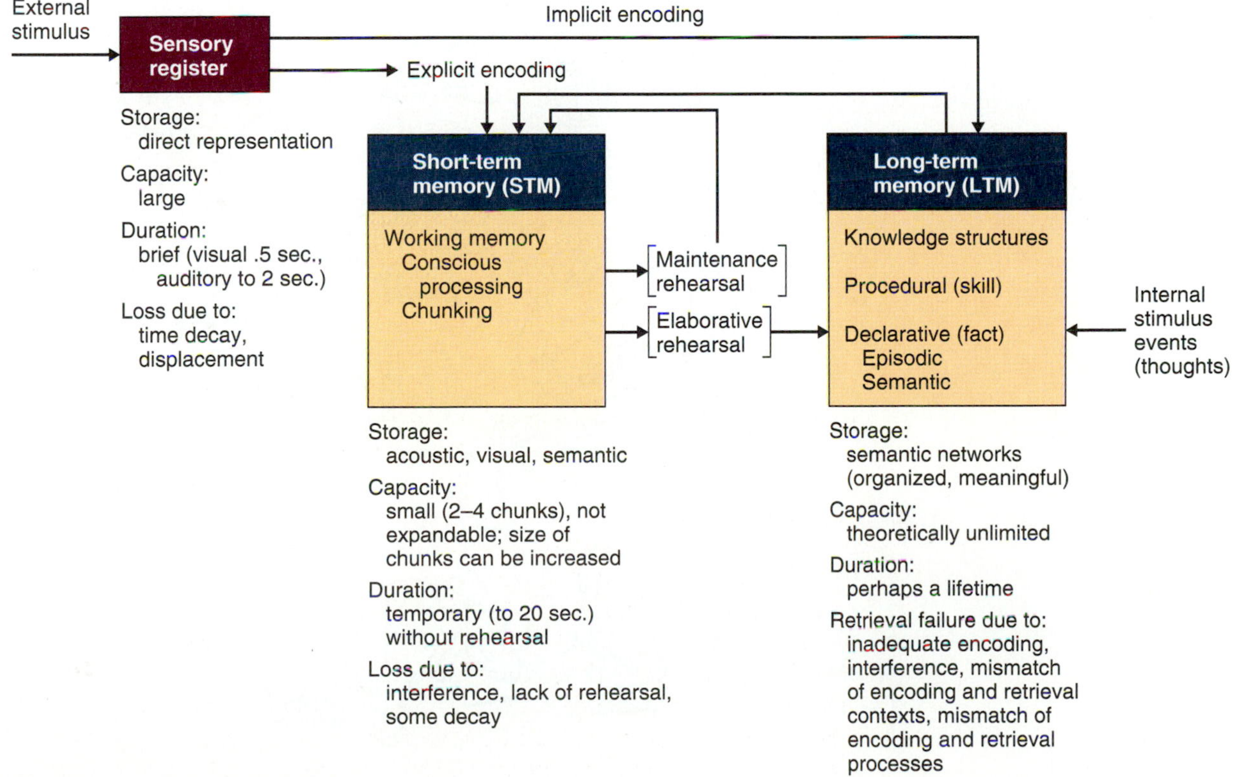

Figure 10.3 The Main Features of Memory

SENSORY MEMORY

Let's begin with a demonstration of the impermanence of some memories. In **Figure 10.4** we have provided you with a reasonably busy visual scene. We'd like you to take a quick look at it—about 10 seconds—and then cover it up. Suppose we now ask you a series of questions about the scene:

1. What tool is the little boy at the bottom holding?
2. What is the middle man at the top doing?
3. In the lower right-hand corner, does the woman's umbrella handle hook to the left or to the right?

To answer these questions, wouldn't you be more comfortable if you could go back and have an extra peek at the picture?

Fortunately, the opportunity to have an "extra peek" at the sensory world is built into your memory processes. Psychologists hypothesize that for each of your sensory modalities, you have a **sensory memory** or **sensory register** that extends the availability of information acquired from the environment. To make this idea more concrete for you, we will describe research on sensory memory in the visual and auditory modalities.

Sensory memory extends the availability of information acquired from the environment.

ICONIC MEMORY

Researchers have labeled sensory memory in the visual domain **iconic memory** (Neisser, 1967). Iconic memory allows very large amounts of infor-

Figure 10.4 How Much Can You Remember from This Scene?

mation to be stored for very brief durations. A visual memory, or *icon*, lasts about half a second. Iconic memory was first revealed in experiments that required subjects to retrieve information from visual displays that were exposed for only one-twentieth of a second.

HOW WE KNOW

George Sperling (1960, 1963) flashed all at once arrays of three rows of three consonants in front of subjects.

D J B
X H G
C L Y

Subjects were asked to perform two different tasks. In a *whole-report procedure,* they tried to recall as many of the letters in the display as possible. Typically, they could report only about four items of the nine they saw. Other subjects underwent a *partial-report procedure,* which required them to report only one row rather than the whole pattern. A signal of a high, medium, or low tone was sounded immediately after the presentation to indicate which row the subjects were to report. Sperling found that regardless of which row he asked for, the subjects' recall was nearly perfect.

Because subjects could accurately report any of the three rows in response to a tone, Sperling concluded that all of the information in the display must have gotten into iconic memory. That is evidence for its large capacity. At the same time, the difference between the whole- and partial-report procedures suggests that the information fades rapidly: the subjects in the whole-report procedure were unable to recall all the information present in the icon. This second point was reinforced by experiments in which the identification signal was slightly delayed. **Figure 10.5** shows that as the delay interval increases from zero seconds to one second, the number of items accurately reported declines steadily. Researchers have measured quite accurately the time course with which information must be transferred from

Iconic memory is a form of visual memory that allows you to store large amounts of information for very brief durations.

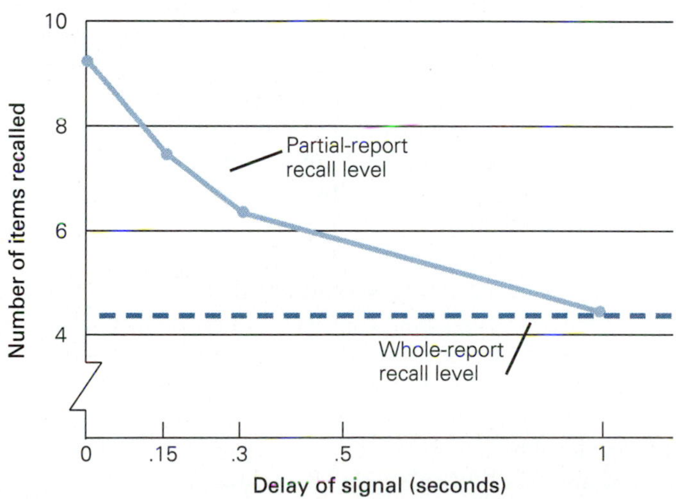

Figure 10.5 Recall by the Partial-report Method
The solid line shows the average number of items recalled using the partial-report method, both immediately after presentation and at four later times. For comparison, the dotted line shows the number of items recalled by the whole-report method. (Adapted from Sperling, 1960.)

the fading icon (Gegenfurtner & Sperling, 1993; Loftus et al., 1992). To take advantage of the "extra peek" at the visual world, your memory processes must very quickly transfer information to more durable stores.

Echoic Memory

Sensory memory for sounds is called **echoic memory.** Just like iconic memory, echoic memory briefly preserves more information than subjects can report before it fades away (Darwin et al., 1972). Research on echoic memory has illustrated another important property of sensory memories: they are easily displaced by new information that is similar to the sensory experience that gave rise to the memory. The *suffix effect* is an example of such displacement (Crowder & Morton, 1969).

The suffix effect in echoic memory demonstrates the fact that sensory memories are easily displaced by new information similar to the original stimulus.

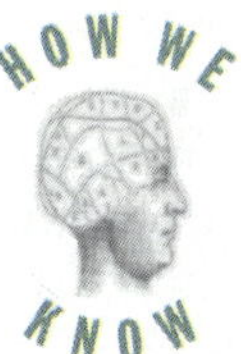

Subjects are asked to listen to a list of digits and told that they must try to recall all the digits in order. At the end of each list, the same extra stimulus—the suffix—occurs. For some subjects, it is the word "zero"; for others it is a buzzer. When the list is followed by the buzzer, subjects show almost perfect memory for the final item on the list. When, however, the list ends with "zero," memory for the final digit is only between 40 and 50 percent accurate (Crowder, 1976).

When subjects hear only the buzzer, their echoic memory for the last digit greatly aids their performance. The buzzer is insufficiently similar to the spoken digits to displace the echoic memory. However, when "zero" (or, for that matter, any other word) is the suffix, it replaces the final digit in echoic memory, so the potential memory benefit is lost.

Researchers originally believed that only the physical similarity of the sounds determined whether one stimulus would displace another in echoic memory. However, we now know that the way a subject categorizes an auditory stimulus also matters (Ayres et al., 1979).

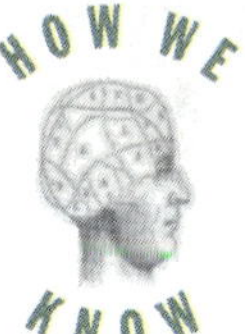

Subjects participated in a memory experiment in which lists of letters were followed by a suffix. The suffix was always the same physical stimulus—it sounded like a sheep's *baa.* However, in one case subjects were led to believe that it was genuinely an animal sound, while in another case subjects believed that it was a *baa* produced by a human trying to sound like a sheep (as it really was). The suffix served to displace information in echoic memory only when the subjects believed it to be produced by a human (Neath et al., 1993).

Remember that the actual physical sound was the same in both cases. But only when the subjects categorized the list (letters read by a human) and the *baa* (a noise produced by the human) in the same way, did a suffix effect occur. Thus, even at the earliest stages of the encoding and storage of memories, your *interpretation* of the world becomes important.

You might wonder why sensory memories have the two basic properties of being short-lived and easily displaced. The answer is that these properties fit the facts of your interactions with the environment. You are constantly experiencing new visual and auditory stimulation. This new information must also be processed. Sensory memories are durable enough to give you a sense of the continuity of your world but not sufficiently strong to interfere with new sensory impressions. We now turn to the types of memory processes that enable you to form more durable memories.

SHORT-TERM MEMORY (STM)

Before you began to read this chapter, you may not have been aware that you had iconic or echoic memory. It is very likely, however, that you were aware that there are some memories that you possess only for the short term. Consider the common occurrence of consulting a telephone book to find a friend's number and then remembering the number just long enough to dial it. If the number turns up busy, you often have to go right back to the phone book. When you consider this experience, it's easy to understand why researchers have explored a special type of memory called **short-term memory** (STM).

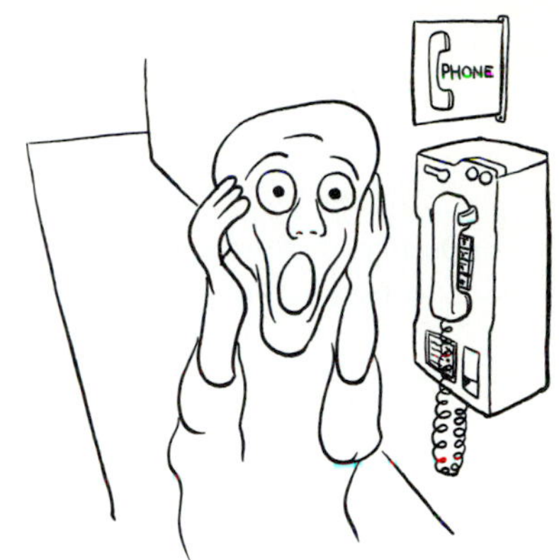

A main function of short-term memory is to provide initial encoding for the explicit acquisition of memories. As we have seen, you have acquired a vast inventory of implicit memories outside of conscious awareness. Short-term memory provides a temporary store only for the information you wish explicitly to remember. However, you shouldn't think of short-term memory as a particular place that memories go to, but rather as a built-in mechanism for focusing cognitive resources on some small set of mental representations (Cowan, 1993; Shiffrin, 1993). But the resources of STM are fickle. As even your experience with phone numbers shows, you have to take some special care to ensure that memories become encoded into more permanent forms. What properties of STM allow you to do this?

A primary function of short-term memory is to provide the initial encoding for the explicit acquisition of memories.

THE CAPACITY LIMITATIONS OF STM

The major features of short-term memories are an immediate consequence of the vast amount of information you could potentially make the focus of consciousness. There is always a great amount of new information available. In Chapter 8 we described how your attentional resources are devoted to selecting the objects and events in the external world on which you will expend your mental resources. Just as there are limits on your capacity to attend to more than a small sample of the available information, there are limits on your ability to keep more than a small sample of information active in STM. The limited capacity of STM enforces a sharp focus of mental attention.

To estimate the capacity of STM, researchers at first turned to tests of *memory span.* At some point in your life, you have probably been asked to carry out a task like this one:

> Read the following list of random numbers once, cover them, and write down as many as you can in the order they appear.
>
> 8 1 7 3 4 9 4 2 8 5
>
> How many did you get correct?
>
> Now read the next list of random letters and perform the same memory test.
>
> J M R S O F L P T Z B
>
> How many did you get correct?

If you are like most individuals, you probably could recall somewhere in the range of five to nine items. **George Miller** (1956) suggested that seven (plus or minus two) was the "magic number" that characterized people's memory performance on unrelated (that is, random lists) of familiar items: letters, words, numbers, or almost any kind of meaningful item.

Tests of memory span, however, overestimate the true capacity of STM because subjects are able to use other sources of information to carry out the task. Remember, for example, that echoic memory will help you to improve your recall on the last few items of a list that is read aloud (at least if there is no suffix). When other sources of memory are factored out, researchers have estimated the pure contribution of STM to your seven (or so) item memory span to be only between two and four items (Crowder, 1976). But if that's all the capacity you have to commence the acquisition of new memories, why don't you notice your limitations more often?

The capacity of short-term memory is two to four items.

Accommodating to STM Capacity

Despite the capacity limitations of STM, you function efficiently for at least two reasons. First, the encoding of information in STM can be enhanced—we will describe *rehearsal* and *chunking.* Second, the retrieval of information from STM is quite rapid.

Rehearsal

The length of time that information remains in short-term memory can be increased through maintenance rehearsal, often consisting of rote repetition.

One of the best ways to enhance memory of any type is to encode the information more diligently. You probably know that a good way to keep your friend's telephone number in mind is to keep repeating the digits in a cycle in your head. This memorization technique is called **maintenance rehearsal.** The fate of *un*rehearsed information was demonstrated in an ingenious experiment.

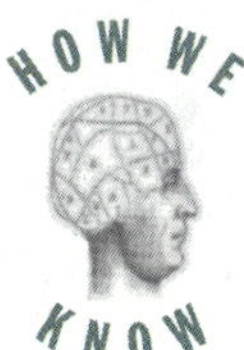

Subjects heard three consonants, such as F, C, and V. They had to recall those consonants when given a signal after a variable interval of time, ranging from 3 to 18 seconds. To prevent rehearsal, a *distractor task* was put between the stimulus input and the recall signal—the subjects were given a three-digit number and told to count backward from it by threes until the recall signal was presented. Many different consonant sets were given and several short delays were used over a series of trials with a number of subjects.

As shown in **Figure 10.6**, recall got increasingly poorer as the time required to retain the information got longer. After even 3 seconds, there was considerable memory loss, and by 18 seconds, loss was nearly total. In the absence of an opportunity to rehearse the information, short-term recall was impaired with the passage of time (Peterson & Peterson, 1959).

Performance suffered because information could not be rehearsed. It also suffered because of interference from the competing information of the distractor task. (Interference as a cause of forgetting will be discussed later in this chapter.) The conclusion so far is that rehearsal will help you to keep information from fading out of STM. But suppose the information you wish to acquire is, at least at first, too cumbersome to be rehearsed? You might turn to the strategy of chunking.

Chunking

A **chunk** is a meaningful unit of information. A chunk can be a single letter or number, a group of letters or other items, or even a group of words or an entire sentence. For example, the sequence 1–9–8–4 consists of four digits that could exhaust your STM capacity. However, if you see the digits as a year or the title of George Orwell's book *1984,* they constitute only one chunk, leaving you much more capacity for other chunks of information. **Chunking** is the process of reconfiguring items by grouping them on the basis of similarity or some other organizing principle, or by combining them into larger patterns based on information stored in long-term memory.

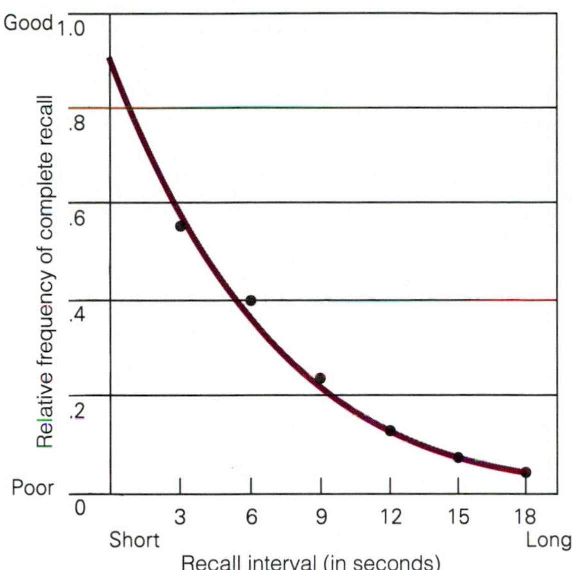

Figure 10.6 Short-term Memory Recall Without Rehearsal
When the interval between stimulus presentation and recall was filled with a distracting task, recall became poorer as the interval grew longer.

See how many chunks you find in this sequence of 20 numbers: 19411917186518121776. You can answer "20" if you see the sequence as a list of unrelated digits, or "5" if you break down the sequence into the dates of major wars in U.S. history. If you do the latter, it's easy for you to recall all the digits in proper sequence after one quick glance. It would be impossible for you to remember them all from a short exposure if you saw them as 20 unrelated items.

Students can put the process of chunking to good use while listening to a lecture.

Your memory span can always be greatly increased if you can discover ways to organize an available body of information into smaller chunks. A famous subject, S. F., was able to memorize 84 digits by grouping them as racing times (S. F. was an avid runner):

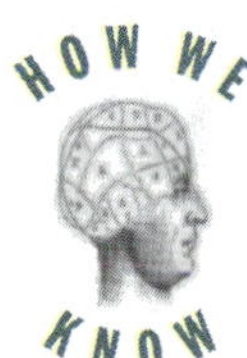

> S. F.'s memory protocols provided the key to his mental wizardry. Because he was a long-distance runner, S. F. noticed that many of the random numbers could be grouped into running times for different distances. For instance, he would recode the sequence 3, 4, 9, 2, 5, 6, 1, 4, 9, 3, 5 as 3:49.2, near record mile; 56:14, 10-mile time; 9:35, slow 2 miles. Later, S. F. also used ages, years of memorable events, and special numerical patterns to chunk the random digits. In this way, he was able to use his long-term memory to convert long strings of random input into manageable and meaningful chunks. S. F.'s memory for letters was still only seven, plus or minus two, because he had not developed any chunking strategies to recall alphabet strings (Chase & Ericsson, 1981; Ericsson & Chase, 1982).

S. F.'s use of running times to "chunk" a string of numbers illustrates the benefit of organization to improve memory.

Like S. F., you can structure incoming information according to its personal meaning to you (linking it to the ages of friends and relatives, for example); or you can match new stimuli with various codes that have been stored in your long-term memory. Even if you can't link new stimuli to rules, meanings, or codes in your long-term memory, you can still use chunking. You can simply *group* the items in a rhythmical pattern or temporal group (181379256460 could become 181, pause, 379, pause, 256, pause, 460). You know from everyday experience that this grouping principle works well for remembering telephone numbers.

Retrieval from STM

Rehearsal and chunking both relate to the way in which you encode information to enhance the probability that it will remain or fit in STM. Even without these strategic measures, however, it turns out that retrieval from STM is very efficient. In a series of classic studies, **Saul Sternberg** (1966, 1969) invented a task that enabled him to demonstrate the great speed with which subjects could assess which information was in short-term focus.

On each of many trials, subjects were given a memory set consisting of from one to six items—for instance, the digits 5, 2, 9, 4, and 6. From trial to trial, the list would vary in terms of which digits and how many were shown. After presenting each set, Sternberg immediately offered a single test "probe"—a digit that the subjects would determine either had or had not been a part of the memory set just shown. Subjects could easily perform the task without error. The dependent variable was, therefore, not accuracy but *speed of recognition.* How quickly could subjects press a *yes* button to indicate that they had seen the test item in the memory set or a *no* button to indicate they were sure that they had not seen it? Sternberg calculated that it took about 400 milliseconds to encode the test stimulus and make a response and then about 35 milliseconds more to compare the stimulus to each item in the memory set. In a single second, a person could make about 30 such comparisons. Retrieval from STM proved to be extremely efficient.

Sternberg's research demonstrates the efficiency of retrieval from short-term memory.

Although different theories have been offered to explain Sternberg's results (Ratcliff, 1978; Townsend, 1971, 1990), they all agree that retrieval from STM is very swift. Let's draw some conclusions from this finding by making an analogy to a vast research library. Given the abundance of volumes in the library (the abundance of sensory impressions available to you), you would probably be dismayed to discover that the library allowed you to borrow only three books at any given time (the limitations of STM). But suppose each patron could access the information in a book with lightning speed (the speed of retrieval from STM). With this high level of performance, you would use the library and only rarely become aware of the three-book rule. Your short-term memory provides the same trade-off between capacity and efficiency of processing.

STM as Working Memory

Our focus so far has been on the role STM plays in the explicit acquisition of new memories. STM, however, plays an equally important role in the retrieval of preexisting memories. For example, at the start of this chapter we asked you to commit a number to memory. Can you remember now what it was? If you *can* remember (if not, peek), you have made your mental representation of that memory active once more in STM. This is why short-term memory is often called **working memory** (Baddeley, 1986). In STM, material made available from either sensory or long-term memory—new or previously acquired information—can be worked over, thought about, and organized.

Short-term memory serves as a workbench where you can think about and organize information made available through either sensory or long-term memory.

The interpretation of short-term memory as working memory should help reinforce the idea that STM is not a place but a *process.* To do the work of cognition—to carry out cognitive activities like language processing or problem solving—you must bring a lot of different elements together in quick succession. You can think of STM as short-term special focus on the necessary elements. If you wish to get a better look at a physical object, you can shine a brighter light on it. STM shines a brighter mental light on your mental objects—your memory representations.

Short-term memory also helps maintain your psychological present. It is what sets a context for new events and links separate episodes together into a continuing story. It enables you to maintain and continually update your representation of a changing situation and to keep track of topics during a conversation. All of this is true because STM serves as a conduit for information coming and going to long-term memory. Let's turn our attention now to that durable form of memory.

LONG-TERM MEMORY (LTM): ENCODING AND RETRIEVAL

We'd like you to do a quick exercise. What is your earliest memory? How old were you when the events took place? How many years ago was that? For some of you reading this book, the answer will be about 15 years. For many others, it will be 20 years, or 40, or 60. How long can memories last? Consider the 90-year-old memories of a woman who vividly recalls the 1906 San Francisco earthquake and subsequent fire. She remembers exactly how she felt as she and the other children scrambled to fetch water from the bay to drench big burlap bags. Her father took the bags she soaked and draped them over the roof, hoping to save their home from the hungry flames. No subsequent memories have displaced the terror and excitement she felt as a young girl watching her city being leveled to the ground.

When psychologists speak of **long-term memory** (LTM), it is with the knowledge that memories will often last a lifetime. Therefore, whatever theory explains how memories are acquired for the long term must also explain how they can remain accessible over the life course. Long-term memory is the storehouse of all the experiences, events, information, emotions, skills, words, categories, rules, and judgments that have been acquired from sensory and short-term memories. LTM constitutes each person's total knowledge of the world and of the self.

A theory of long-term memory must explain how memories are acquired and how they are maintained for a lifetime.

Psychologists know that it is often easier to acquire new long-term information when an important conclusion is stated in advance. With that conclusion in place, you have a framework for understanding the incoming information. For memory, the conclusion we will reach is this: your ability to remember will be greatest when there is a good match between the circumstances in which you encoded information and the circumstances in which you attempt to retrieve it. We will see over the next several sections what it means to have a "good match."

RETRIEVAL CUES

We will begin our exploration of the match between encoding and retrieval by asking you to imagine you are involved in a classic memory experiment. Try to commit to memory the pairs of words in part A of **Table 10.1**. Keep working at it until you can go through the six pairs three times in a row without an error. (Do Part A now. Part B will come later.)

To make this memory test more interesting, we now need to do something to give you a *retention interval*—a period of time over which you must keep the information in memory. Let's spend a moment, therefore, discussing some of the procedures we might use to test your memory. You might assume that you either know something or you don't and that any method of testing what you know will give the same results. Not so. For example, we shall see that tests for implicit and explicit memory can give quite different results.

Table 10.1 Paired-Associate Learning

A. Try to learn these pairs:	B. Would it be harder for you to learn these new pairs?
Apple–Boat	Apple–Robe
Hat–Bone	Hat–Circle
Bicycle–Clock	Bicycle–Roof
Mouse–Tree	Mouse–Magazine
Ball–House	Ball–Baby
Ear–Blanket	Ear–Penny

For now, however, let's consider two tests for explicit memory, recall and recognition.

When you **recall,** you reproduce the information to which you were previously exposed. "What is the suffix effect?" is a recall question. **Recognition** refers to the realization that a certain stimulus event is one you have seen or heard before. "Which is the term for a visual sensory memory: (1) echo; (2) engram; (3) icon; or (4) abstract code?" is a recognition question. You can relate recall and recognition to your day-to-day experiences of explicit memory. When trying to identify a criminal, the police would be using a recall method if they asked the victim to describe, from memory, some of the perpetrator's distinguishing features: "Did you notice anything unusual about the attacker?" They would be using the recognition method if they showed the victim photos, one at a time, from a file of criminal suspects, or if they asked the victim to identify the perpetrator in a police lineup.

Let's now use these two procedures to test you on the word pairs you learned a few moments ago. What words finished the pairs?

Hat–? Bicycle–? Ear–?

Can you select the correct pair from these possibilities?

Apple–Baby	Mouse–Tree	Ball–House
Apple–Boat	Mouse–Tongue	Ball–Hill
Apple–Bottle	Mouse–Tent	Ball–Horn

Was the recognition test easier than the recall test? It should be. Let's try to explain this result with respect to retrieval cues.

Retrieval cues are the stimuli available as you search for a particular memory. These cues may be provided externally, such as questions on a quiz ("What memory principles do you associate with the research of Sternberg and Sperling?"), or generated internally ("Where have I met her before?"). Each time you attempt to retrieve an explicit memory, you do so for some purpose, and that purpose often supplies the retrieval cue. It won't surprise you that memories can be easier or harder to retrieve depending on the quality of the retrieval cue. If a friend asks you, "Who's the one emperor I can't remember?" you're likely to be involved in a guessing game. If she asks instead, "Who was the emperor after Claudius?" you can immediately respond "Nero."

Let's return to recall and recognition. Both memory tests require a search using cues. The cues for recognition, however, are much more useful. For recall, you have to hope that the cue alone will help you locate the information. For recognition, part of the work has been done for you. When you look at the pair "Mouse–Tree," you only have to answer yes or no to "Did I have this experience?" rather than, in response to "Mouse–?" "What was the experience I had?" In this light, you can see that we made the recognition test reasonably easy for you. Suppose we had given you, instead, recombinations of the original pairs. Which of these are correct?

Hat–Clock	Ear–Boat
Hat–Bone	Ear–Blanket

Now you must recognize not just that you saw the word before but that you saw it in a particular *context.* (We will return to the idea of context shortly.) If you are a veteran of difficult multiple-choice exams, you have come to learn how tough even recognition situations can be. However, in most cases your recognition performance will be better than your recall, because retrieval cues are more straightforward for recognition. Let's look at some other aspects of retrieval cues.

Performance is often better for recognition tasks than for recall tasks because retrieval cues for recognition provide more information.

Episodic and Semantic Memories

We have already made a pair of distinctions about types of memories. You have implicit and explicit memories and declarative and procedural memories. We can define another dimension along which declarative memories differ with respect to the cues that are necessary to retrieve them from memory. Canadian psychologist **Endel Tulving** (1972) first proposed the distinction between *episodic* and *semantic* types of declarative memory.

Episodic memories preserve, individually, the specific events that you have personally experienced. For example, memories of your happiest birthday or of your first kiss are stored in episodic memory. To recover such memories, you need retrieval cues that specify something about the time at which the event occurred and something about the content of the events. Depending on how the information has been encoded, you may or may not be able to produce a specific memory trace for an event. For example, do you have any specific memories to differentiate the tenth time ago you brushed your teeth from the eleventh time ago?

All the memories you have began their existence as episodic memories. Everything you know, you began to acquire in some particular context. However, there are large classes of information that you encounter in many different contexts. These classes of information come to be available for retrieval without reference to their multiple times and places of experience. These **semantic memories** are generic, categorical memories, such as the meanings of words and concepts. For most people, facts like the formula $E = MC^2$ and the capital of France don't require retrieval cues that make reference to the episodes, the original learning contexts, in which the memory was acquired.

Of course, this doesn't mean that your recall of facts that can be considered semantic memories is foolproof. You know perfectly well that you can forget many facts that have become dissociated from the contexts in which you learned them. A good strategy when you can't recover a semantic memory is to treat it like an episodic memory again. By thinking to yourself, "I know I learned the names of the Roman emperors in my Western civilization course," you may be able to provide the extra retrieval cues that will shake loose a memory.

Events of personal importance, like seeing a good friend for the first time after a year's separation, are retained in episodic memory.

Interference

When we asked you to learn the paired associates earlier, we were really asking you to acquire new episodic memories. Suppose, now, we asked you to learn the pairs of words given in part B of Table 10.1. Examine the list. You can see what we've done—each old prompt is paired with a new response. Do you think this would make it harder for you to learn these new pairs? If you learn these new pairs, do you think it would be harder for you to recall the old ones? The answer in both cases, as you probably could guess, is "absolutely yes." This brief thought experiment (if you want, you can learn the second set of pairs, or test a friend with both sets, to make it a real experiment) should give you a sense of another aspect of retrieval cues, interference. **Interference** occurs when retrieval cues do not point effectively to one specific memory. The greater the uncertainty about the proper response to a specific retrieval cue, the more memory is impaired (Bower et al., 1994).

We have already given you a real-life example of the problem of interference when we asked you to try to differentiate your recollections of your episodes of toothbrushing. All of the specific memories interfere with each other. *Proactive interference* (*proactive* means "forward acting") refers to circumstances in which information you have acquired in the past makes it more difficult to acquire new information. *Retroactive interference* (*retroactive* means "backward acting") occurs when the acquisition of new information makes it harder for you to remember older information. We asked you to think about both of these types of interference with respect to the lists in Table 10.1. You've also experienced both proactive and retroactive interference if you've ever moved and had to change your phone number. At first, you probably found it hard to remember the new number—the old one kept popping out (proactive interference). However, after finally being able to reliably reproduce the new one, you may have found yourself unable to remember the old number—even if you had used it for years (retroactive interference).

Interference can be proactive, where old information interferes with the recall of new information, or retroactive, where new learning interferes with old.

As with many other memory phenomena, Hermann Ebbinghaus was the first researcher to document interference rigorously through experiments. Ebbinghaus, after learning dozens of lists of nonsense syllables, found himself forgetting about 65 percent of the new ones he was learning. Fifty years later, students at Northwestern University who studied Ebbinghaus's lists had the same experience—after many trials with many lists, what the students had learned earlier interfered proactively with their recall of current lists (Underwood, 1948, 1949).

The most obvious prediction that emerges from interference theory is that information undisturbed by new material will be recalled best. Imagine that, rather than make you read the paragraphs about recall and recognition between memorizing the paired associates and displaying your memory for them, we had simply allowed you to hum to yourself. Don't you imagine your memory would have been better? A classic study by Jenkins and Dallenbach (1924) provides support for this hypothesis. Subjects who went to sleep immediately after learning new material recalled it better the next morning than a comparison group who spent the same amount of time after learning performing their usual activities. You probably can't spend all the time between studying for an exam and taking the exam sleeping. But you can keep the problem of interference in mind. You

should design your work schedule so that whatever else you must learn or do in that interval is different enough from the test material that it will not interfere.

Remember that the conclusion we are working toward is that the match between encoding and retrieval is critical. So far we have seen that effective retrieval cues are necessary to recover memories. In the next sections we will see that it is the close relationship between encoding and retrieval that makes these cues particularly effective.

Context and Encoding

Here's a phenomenon that you might call "context shock." You see someone across a crowded room and you know that you know the person but you just can't place her. Finally, after staring for longer than is absolutely polite, you remember who it is—and you realize that the difficulty is that the person is entirely in the wrong context. What is the woman who delivers your mail doing at your best friend's party? Whenever you have this type of experience, you have rediscovered the principle of **encoding specificity:** memories emerge most efficiently when the context of retrieval matches the context of encoding. Let's see how researchers have demonstrated that principle.

After receiving a traffic warning from this man, would you recognize him if you ran into him at a party?

Encoding Specificity

What are the consequences of learning information in a particular context? Endel Tulving and Donald Thomson (1973) first demonstrated the power of encoding specificity by reversing the usual performance relationship between recall and recognition.

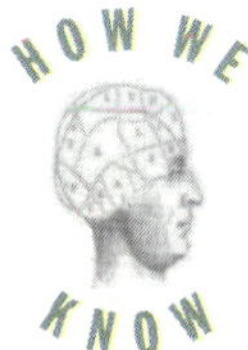

Subjects were asked to learn pairs of words like *train–black,* but they were told that they would be responsible for remembering only the second word of the pair. In a subsequent phase of the experiment, subjects were asked to generate four free associates to words like *white.* Those words were chosen so that it was likely that the original to-be-remembered words (like *black*) would be among the associates. The subjects were then asked to check off any words on their associates lists that they recognized as to-be-remembered words from the first phase of the experiment. They were able to do so 54 percent of the time. However, when the subjects were later given the first words of the pair, like *train,* and asked to recall the associate, they were 61 percent accurate.

Why was recall better than recognition? Tulving and Thomson suggested that what mattered was the change in context. After the subjects had studied the word *black* in the context of *train,* it was hard to recover the memory trace when the context was changed to *white.* Given the significant effect of even these minimal contexts, you can anticipate that richly organized real-life contexts would have an even greater effect on your memory.

Researchers have been able to demonstrate rather remarkable effects of context on memory. In one experiment, scuba divers learned lists of words either on a beach or underwater. They were then tested for retention of those words, again in one of those two contexts. Performance was nearly 50 percent better when the context at encoding and recall matched—even though the material had nothing at all to do with water or diving (Gooden & Baddeley, 1975). In another study, memory performance was much improved when the smell of chocolate was present at both time of encoding and time of recall (Schab, 1990). Do you see an application to your own life in school? You may want to study for an exam in the same room in which you will take it.

The principle of encoding specificity, however, can give you even stronger ideas about how best to study. Most often "context" will mean "the context of other information," rather than just the room you are in. If you always study material in the same context, you may find it difficult to retrieve it in a different context—so, if a professor's questions come at a topic in a slightly unusual way, you might be entirely at a loss. As a remedy, you should change contexts even while you study. Rearrange the order of your notes. Ask yourself questions that mix different topics together. Try to make your own novel combinations. But if you get stuck while you're taking an exam, try to generate as many retrieval cues as you can that reinstate the original context: "Let's see. We heard about this in the same lecture we learned about short-term memory. . . ."

The Serial Position Effect

We can also use changes in context to explain one of the classic effects in memory research: the **serial position effect.** Suppose we required you to learn a list of unrelated words. If we asked you to recall those words in order, your data would almost certainly conform to the pattern shown in **Figure 10.7**: you would do very well on the first few words (the *primacy* effect) and very well on the last few words (the *recency* effect) but rather poorly on the middle part of the list. We have confidence that you would perform in this way because researchers have found primacy and recency in a wide variety of test situations (Crowder, 1976; Neath, 1993). Do you believe, for example, that it would take you almost a second less to answer the question "What day is it today?" at the beginning or end of the week than in the middle (Koriat & Fischoff, 1974)?

The role context plays in producing the shape of the serial position curve has to do with the contextual distinctiveness of different items on a list, different experiences in your life, and so on. To understand **contextual distinctiveness,** you can ask the question, "How different were the contexts in which I learned this information from the context in which I will try to recall it?" Let's focus on recency. **Figure 10.8** is a visual representation of distinctiveness. Imagine, in part A, that you are looking at train tracks. What you can see is that they look as if they clump together at the horizon—even though they are equally spaced apart. We could say that the nearest tracks stand out most—are most distinctive—from your context. Imagine now that you are trying to remember the last ten movies you've seen. The movies are like the train tracks. Under most circumstances, you should remember the

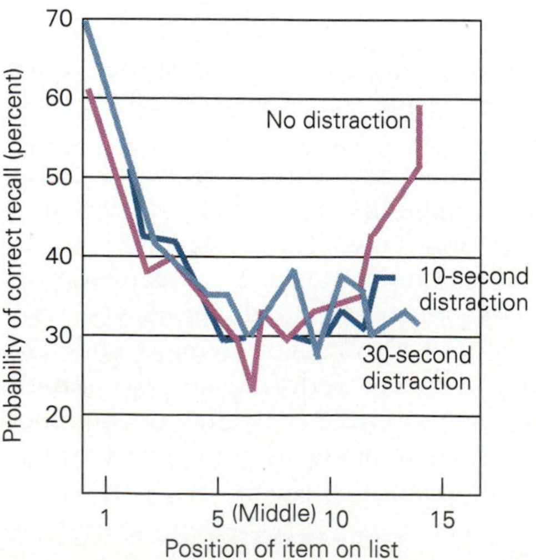

Figure 10.7 The Serial Position Effect
The graph shows the effects of a distracting task performed between the presentation of the list and the request for recall. The items at the beginning of the list are recalled best, regardless of the delay-distraction. The items at the end are recalled well without delay-distraction, but gradually worsen as the delay-distraction is lengthened. The poorer recall at the middle of the list reveals the serial position effect. (After Glanzer & Cunitz, 1966.)

A

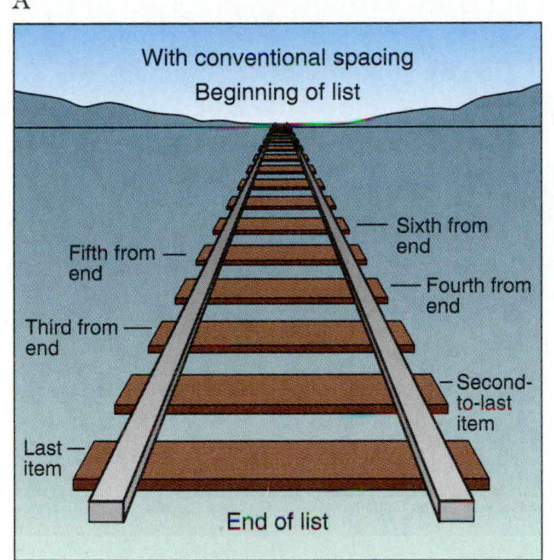

B

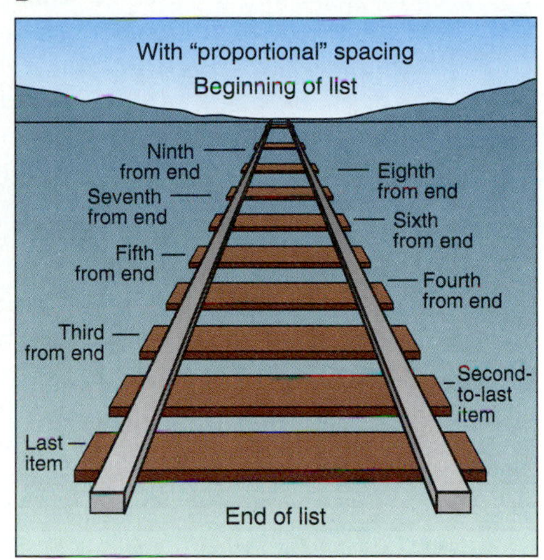

Figure 10.8 Contextual Distinctiveness

You can think of items you put into memory as train tracks. In part A, you can imagine that memories further back in time become blurred together, just like train tracks in the distance. In part B, you see that one way to combat this effect is to make the earlier tracks physically further apart, so the distances look proportional. Similarly, you can make early memories more distinctive by moving them apart psychologically.

last movie best, because you share the most overlapping context with the experience—it is "closest" to the context of your current experiences. This logic suggests that "middle" information will become more memorable if it is made more distinctive. The idea with respect to our analogy, as shown in part B of Figure 10.8, is to make the train tracks seem equally far apart.

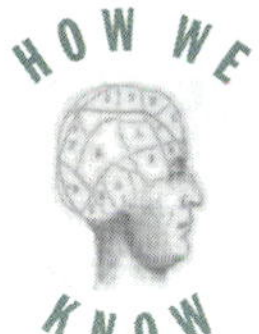

To make the train tracks seem evenly spaced, engineers would have to make the more distant ones actually be further apart. Researchers have used the same logic for a memory test, by exploiting the analogy between space and time. They had subjects try to learn lists of letters, but they manipulated how far apart in time the letters were made to seem. This manipulation was accomplished by asking subjects to read out some number of random digits that appeared on a computer screen between the letters. In the *conventional* condition (like part A of Figure 10.8), each pair of letters was separated by two digits. In the *proportional* condition (like part B), the first pair had four digits and the last pair zero digits—this should have the effect of making the early digits more distinctive, just like moving distant train tracks further apart. Subjects, in fact, showed better memory for early items on the list when those items had been made more separate (Neath & Crowder, 1990).

This experiment suggests that the standard recency effect arises because the last few items are almost automatically distinctive. The same principle may explain primacy—each time you begin something new, your activity establishes a new context. In that new context, the first few experiences are particularly distinctive. Thus you can think of primacy and recency as two views of the same set of train tracks—one from each end!

Once again, let's apply this information to your classroom setting. You now know that you must do something special to make "middle information"

memorable. In fact, college students fail more exam items on material from the middle of a lecture than on material from the start or end of the lecture (Holen & Oaster, 1976; Jensen, 1962). So you should devote some extra time and effort to that material. You might also take note that the chapter you're reading now is about at the middle of *Psychology and Life.* If you have a final examination that covers all the course material, you're going to want to make an especially careful review of this chapter.

The Processes of Encoding and Retrieval

We have seen so far that a match between the context of encoding and of retrieval is beneficial to good memory performance. We will now refine this conclusion somewhat by considering the actual processes that are used to get information to and from long-term memory. We will see that memory functions best when encoding and retrieval processes make a good match as well.

Levels of Processing

Let's begin with the idea that the type of processing you perform on information—the type of attention you pay to information at time of encoding—will have an influence on your memory for the information. **Levels-of-processing theory** suggests that the *deeper* the level at which information was processed, the more likely it is to be committed to memory (Craik & Lockhart, 1972; Lockhart & Craik, 1990). If processing involves more analysis, interpretation, comparison, and elaboration, it should result in better memory.

The depth of processing is often defined by the types of judgments subjects are required to make with respect to experimental materials. Consider the word *GRAPE.* We could ask you to make a physical judgment—is the word in capital letters? Or a rhyme judgment—does the word rhyme with *tape?* Or a meaning judgment—does the word represent a type of fruit? Do you see how each of these questions requires you to think a little bit more deeply about *GRAPE?* In fact, the deeper the original processing subjects carry out, the more words they remember (Lockhart & Craik, 1990).

A difficulty of the levels-of-processing theory, however, is that researchers have not always been able to specify exactly what makes certain processes "shallow" or "deep." Even so, results of this sort confirm that the way in which information is committed to memory—the mental processes that you use to encode information—has an effect on whether you can retrieve that information later. However, so far we have discussed only explicit memory. We will now see that the match between processes at encoding and retrieval is particularly critical for implicit memory.

Processes and Implicit Memory

Earlier, we defined the explicit versus implicit dimension for memories as a distinction that applies both at encoding and at retrieval (Roediger, 1990; Seger, 1994). Under many circumstances, for example, you will retrieve implicitly memories that you originally encoded explicitly. This is true when you greet your best friend by name without having to expend any particular mental effort. Even so, implicit memories are often most robust when there is a strong match between the processes at implicit encoding and the processes at implicit retrieval. To examine this effect, we will first describe some of the methodologies that are used to demonstrate implicit memories. Then we will show how the match between encoding and retrieval processes matters.

Let's consider a typical experiment in which implicit memory is assessed. The researchers presented subjects with lists of concrete nouns and asked them to judge the pleasantness of each word on a 1 (least pleasant) to 5 (most pleasant) scale (Rajaram & Roediger, 1993). The pleasantness ratings required subjects to think about the meaning of a word without explicitly committing it to memory. After this study phase, subjects' memory was assessed using one of four implicit memory tasks (suppose that a word on one list was *unicorn*):

- *Word fragment completion*—the subject is given fragments of a word, like *__ni__or__*, and asked to complete the fragments with the first word that comes to mind.
- *Word stem completion*—the subject is asked to complete a stem, like *uni*_______, with the first word that comes to mind.
- *Word identification*—words are flashed on a computer screen in such a fashion that subjects cannot see them clearly. They must try to guess each word that is flashed. In this case, one of the words would be *unicorn*.
- *Anagrams*—subjects are given a scrambled word, like *corunni*, and asked to give the first unscrambled word that comes to mind.

Just like our example with *unicorn,* correct responses to each of the tasks can be provided by words from the earlier lists. What is critical, however, is that the experimenters have not called attention to the relationship between the words on the earlier list and appropriate responses on these new tasks—that's why the use of memory is implicit.

To assess the degree of implicit memory, the researchers compared the performance of subjects who had seen a particular word, like *unicorn,* on the pleasantness lists with those who had not. **Figure 10.9** plots the improvement brought about by implicit memory for a word—percent correct when the word had appeared on the subject's list minus percent correct when it had not. (Different subjects experienced different word lists.) You can see that for each task there was an advantage to having seen a word before, even though subjects had been asked only to say whether the word had a pleasant meaning. This advantage is known as **priming,** because the first experience of the word *primes* memory for later experiences. For some memory tasks, like word fragment completion, researchers have found priming effects lasting a week and beyond (Sloman et al., 1988).

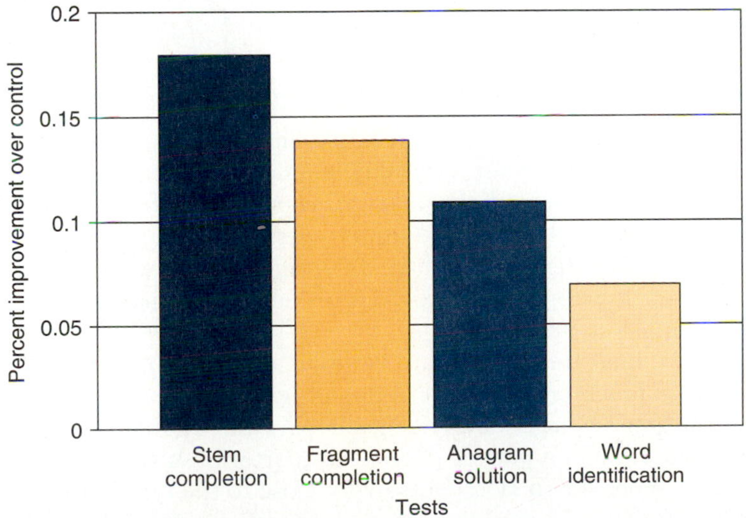

Figure 10.9 Priming on Implicit Memory Tests
Priming reflects improvement on the various tasks over performance on control words. Some implicit memory tests demonstrate that priming can last a week or more.

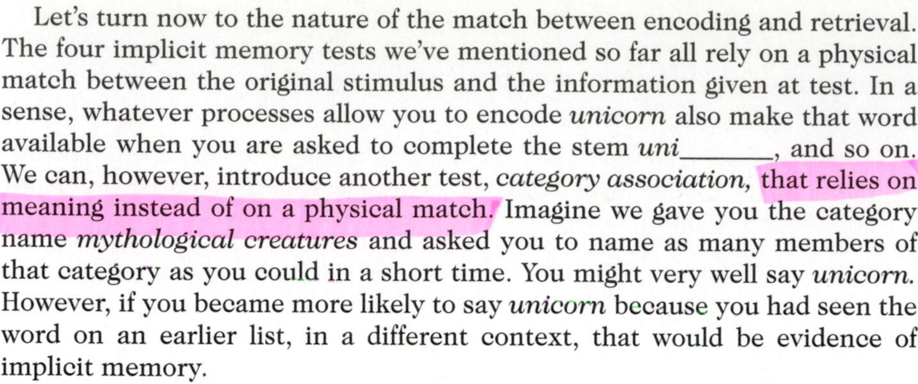

Let's turn now to the nature of the match between encoding and retrieval. The four implicit memory tests we've mentioned so far all rely on a physical match between the original stimulus and the information given at test. In a sense, whatever processes allow you to encode *unicorn* also make that word available when you are asked to complete the stem *uni*_______, and so on. We can, however, introduce another test, *category association,* that relies on meaning instead of on a physical match. Imagine we gave you the category name *mythological creatures* and asked you to name as many members of that category as you could in a short time. You might very well say *unicorn.* However, if you became more likely to say *unicorn* because you had seen the word on an earlier list, in a different context, that would be evidence of implicit memory.

Implicit memory research tasks may involve a physical match of exact words, or a match by meaning, as in category association.

With two different types of implicit memory tests based on priming—by physical features or by meaning—we can look for a relationship between encoding and retrieval.

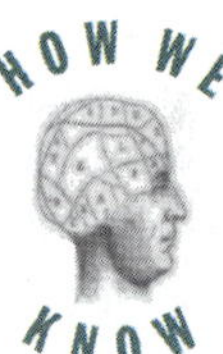

Memory researchers designed a levels-of-processing experiment to demonstrate that different implicit memories rely on different types of processes. Subjects were given lists of words and asked either to make a meaning judgment—how pleasant is the meaning of this word?—or a physical judgment—how many consonants does this word have? The researchers predicted that priming on the category association test would occur only when the implicit encoding required an analysis of meaning. The results confirmed their prediction. Similarly, physical judgments produced priming only on implicit memory tests that also relied on physical features (Srinivas & Roediger, 1990).

Remembering is enhanced when the processing of information at encoding matches the processing at retrieval.

The conclusion based on this research is that if you use a certain type of processing—for example, physical or meaning analysis—to encode information, you will retrieve that information most efficiently when the processing uses the same type of analysis. Several pages ago we made this assertion: your ability to remember will be greatest when there is a good match between the circumstances in which you encoded information and the circumstances in which you attempt to retrieve it. This section provided the research evidence for this assertion. Let's now see how we can put theories of encoding and retrieval further to work for you.

Improving Memory for Unstructured Information

After reading this whole section, you should have some concrete ideas about how you could improve your everyday memory performance. You know, especially, that you're best off trying to recover a piece of information in the same context, or by performing the same types of mental tasks, as when you first acquired it. But there's a slightly different problem with which we still must give you some help. It has to do with encoding unstructured or arbitrary collections of information.

For example, imagine that you are working as a clerk in a store. You must try to commit to memory the several items that each customer wants: "The woman in the green blouse wants hedge clippers and a garden hose. The man in the blue shirt wants a pair of pliers, six quarter-inch screws, and a paint scraper." This scenario, in fact, comes very close to the types of experiments in which researchers ask you to memorize paired associates. How did you go about learning the pairs in Table 10.1? The task probably was somewhat of a chore, because the pairs were not particularly *meaningful* for you—and information that isn't meaningful is hard to remember. To find a way to get the right items to the right customer, you need to make associations seem less arbitrary. Let's see how.

A general strategy for improving encoding is called *elaborative rehearsal.* The basic idea of this technique is that while you are rehearsing information—while you are first committing it to memory—you elaborate on the material to enrich the encoding. One way to do this is to invent a relationship that makes an association seem less arbitrary. For example, if you wanted to remember the pair *Mouse–Tree,* you might conjure up an image of a mouse scurrying up a tree to look for cheese. Recall is enhanced when you encode separate bits of information into this type of miniature story line (Bower, 1972). Can you imagine, in the clerk situation, swiftly making up a story to link each customer with the appropriate items? (It will work with practice.) You may have already guessed that it is also often helpful to supplement your story line with a mental picture—a *visual image*—of the scene you are trying to remember. Visual imagery can enhance your recall because it gives you codes for both verbal and visual memories simultaneously (Paivio, 1968).

Forming a visual image is a form of elaborative rehearsal, an encoding strategy that consists of elaborating on material when you first learn it so that the encoding is enriched.

To help yourself remember, you can also draw on special mental strategies called mnemonics (from the Greek word meaning "to remember"). **Mnemonics** are short, verbal devices that encode a long series of facts by associating them with familiar and previously encoded information. Many mnemonics work by giving you ready-made retrieval cues that help organize otherwise arbitrary information.

Consider the *method of loci,* first practiced by ancient Greek orators. The singular of *loci* is *locus,* and it means "place." The method of loci is a means of remembering the order of a list of names or objects—or, for the orators, the individual sections of a long speech—by associating them with some sequence of places with which you are familiar. To remember a list of people you are meeting, you might mentally put each one sequentially along the route you take to get from home to school. To remember their names later, you mentally go through your route and find the name associated with each spot.

Other mnemonic devices use organizational schemes that rely on word or sound associations to put items into a pattern that is easy to remember. In an *acrostic-like mnemonic,* the first letters of each word cue a response. For example, the familiar Every Good Boy Does Fine is an acrostic mnemonic for remembering the musical notes on the treble clef: E, G, B, D, F. In *acronym mnemonics,* each letter of a word stands for a name or other piece of infor-

What's your favorite memory technique?

mation. The colors of the spectrum in their proper sequence become a person's name: Roy G. Biv (red, orange, yellow, green, blue, indigo, violet). Similarly, HOMES serves as an acronym for the Great Lakes: Huron, Ontario, Michigan, Erie, Superior. You can mix these techniques together to remember the order of the lakes' locations, from west to east: Sergeant Major Hates Eating Onions. You can see that the key to learning arbitrary information is to encode the information in such a fashion that you provide yourself with efficient retrieval cues.

A benefit of mnemonics is that these little memory strategies provide additional retrieval cues for encoded information.

Metamemory

Suppose you're in a situation in which you'd really like to remember something. You're doing your best to use retrieval cues that reflect the circumstances of encoding, but you just can't get the bit of information to emerge. Part of the reason you're expending so much effort is that *you're sure* that you are in possession of the information. But are you correct to be so confident about the contents of your memory? Questions like this one—about how your memory works or how you know what information you possess—are questions of **metamemory.** One major question on metamemory has been when and why *feelings-of-knowing*—the subjective sensations that you *do* have information stored in memory—are accurate.

Research on feelings-of-knowing was pioneered by J. T. Hart (1965), who began his studies by asking students a series of general knowledge questions. Suppose, for example, we asked you, "What planet is the largest in our solar system?" Do you know the answer? If you don't, how would you respond to this question: "Even though I don't remember the answer now, do I know the answer to the extent that I could pick the correct answer from among several wrong answers?" This was the question Hart put to his subjects, and he allowed them to give ratings from 1, to say they were quite sure they wouldn't choose correctly on the multiple choice, to 6, to say they were quite sure they would choose correctly. What would your rating be? Now here are your alternatives:

a. Pluto b. Venus c. Earth d. Jupiter

If you made an accurate feeling-of-knowing judgment, you should have been less likely to get the correct answer, d, if you gave a 1 rating than if you gave a 6. (Of course, to have a fair test, we'd want to give you a long series of questions.) Hart found that when subjects gave 1 ratings, they answered the questions correctly only 30 percent of the time, whereas 6 ratings predicted 75 percent success. That's pretty impressive evidence that feelings-of-knowing are generally accurate.

Hart's research on metamemory indicates that feelings-of-knowing are generally accurate.

Research on metamemory has begun to focus on both the processes that give rise to feelings-of-knowing and on how their accuracy is ensured:

- The *cue familiarity hypothesis* suggests that people base their feelings-of-knowing on their familiarity with the retrieval cue. Thus, if you have prior familiarity with the concepts of "planet" and "solar system," you might think that you probably would be able to recognize the correct alternative (Metcalfe et al., 1993; Schwartz & Metcalfe, 1992).
- The *accessibility hypothesis* suggests that people base their judgments on the accessibility, or availability, of partial information from memory. Thus, if the question "What planet is the largest in our solar system?" calls quite easily to mind information you believe to be related to the correct answer, you are likely to think that you will be able to recognize the correct answer as well (Koriat, 1993).

Both of these theories have obtained empirical support—and both suggest that you can generally trust your instincts when you believe that you know something. (Later in the chapter, we will present a Close-up on repressed memories, which will provide an exception to this general rule.)

You have now learned quite a bit about how you get information in and out of memory. You know what we mean by a "good match" between the circumstances of encoding and of retrieval. In the next section we will shift our focus from your memory processes to the content of your memories.

STRUCTURES IN LONG-TERM MEMORY

In most of our examples so far, we have asked you to try to acquire and retrieve isolated or unrelated bits of information. What you mostly have represented in memory, however, are large bodies of *organized knowledge.* Recall, for example, that we asked you to consider whether *grape* is a fruit. You could say yes very quickly. How about *porcupine?* Is it a fruit? How about *tomato?* In this section, we will examine how the difficulty of these types of judgments relates to the way information is structured in memory. We will also discuss how memory organization allows you to make a best guess at the content of experiences you can't remember exactly.

MEMORY STRUCTURES

A primary function of memory is to draw together similar experiences so that you may find patterns in the environment.

An essential function of memory is to draw together similar experiences, to enable you to discover patterns in your interactions with the environment. (Recall a similar description, in Chapter 8, on the functions of perception.) You live in a world filled with countless individual events, from which you must continually extract information to combine them into a smaller, simpler set that you can manage mentally. But apparently you don't need to expend any particular conscious effort to find structure in the world. Just as we suggested when we defined the implicit acquisition of memories, it's unlikely that you ever formally thought to yourself something like, "Here's what belongs in a kitchen." It is through ordinary experience in the world that you have acquired mental structures to mirror environmental structures. Let's look at the types of memory structures you have formed in your moment-by-moment experience of the world.

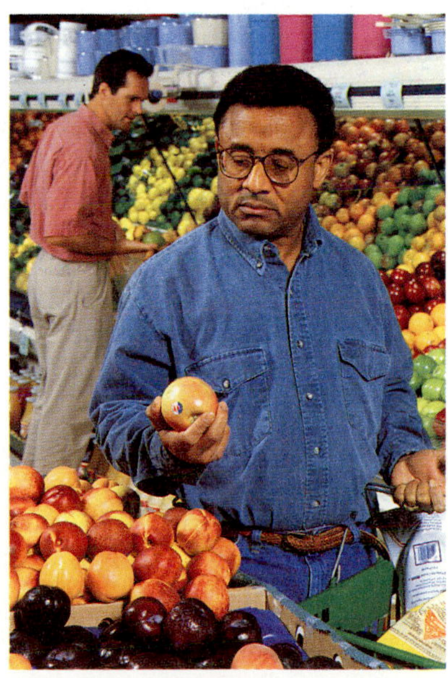

Most adults have formed categories—such as what constitutes a healthy head of lettuce, a sweet melon, or a flavorful tomato—to help with daily decisions like what to buy for dinner.

Concepts

Recall, from Chapter 5, the mental effort a child must go through to acquire the meaning of the word *doggie.* For this word to have meaning, the child must be able to store each instance in which the word *doggie* is used, as well as information about the context. In this way, the child finds out what common core experience—a furry creature with four legs—is meant by *doggie.* The child must acquire the knowledge that *doggie* applies not just to one particular animal but to a whole category of creatures. This ability to *categorize individual experiences*—to take the same action toward them or give them the same label—is one of the most basic abilities of thinking organisms (Mervis & Rosch, 1981).

The mental representations of the categories you form are called **concepts.** The concept *doggie,* for example, names the set of mental representations of experiences of dogs that a young child has gathered together in memory. (As we saw in Chapter 5, if the child hasn't yet refined his or her meaning for *doggie,* the concept might also include experiences that adults wouldn't consider to be appropriate.) You have acquired a vast array of concepts. You have categories for *objects* and *activities,* such as barns and baseball. Concepts may also represent *properties,* such as *red* or *large; abstract ideas,* such as *truth* or *love;* and *relations,* such as *smarter than* or *sister of.* Each concept represents a summary unit for your experience of the world.

Prototypes

Given the number of dogs you've seen in your life, what exactly do you think about when, for example, you read a sentence like, "The dog buried the bone"? Do you call to mind some particular dog? Or do you envision some typical dog, averaged across all the dogs you have experienced—your **prototype** for a dog? Let's look at an experiment that helps to address these questions.

Subjects were shown a set of *exemplar* faces that varied, to different degrees, from prototype faces (see **Figure 10.10**). Then they saw a second group of faces: some of the original exemplar faces, some new ones that were made to differ from the prototype, and the original prototype face, which they had never actually seen. The subjects' task was to rate their confidence in having seen each face before, during the first presentation.

Three results clearly emerged, as seen in the chart in Figure 10.10. Recall confidence was equally high for all the old items, even if they had only a 25 percent similarity to the prototype. The new items were confidently identified as unfamiliar to the extent that they differed from the prototype. Finally, the highest level of confidence was for the prototype face itself—although the subjects had never seen it before (Solso & McCarthy, 1981).

In this experiment, subjects acted as if they had averaged together all the exemplar faces they had seen to construct the prototypical face.

The prototypes you have for categories are derived from all your experiences with members of that category. For that reason, your prototype shifts subtly every time you encounter a new exemplar of a category. Conse-

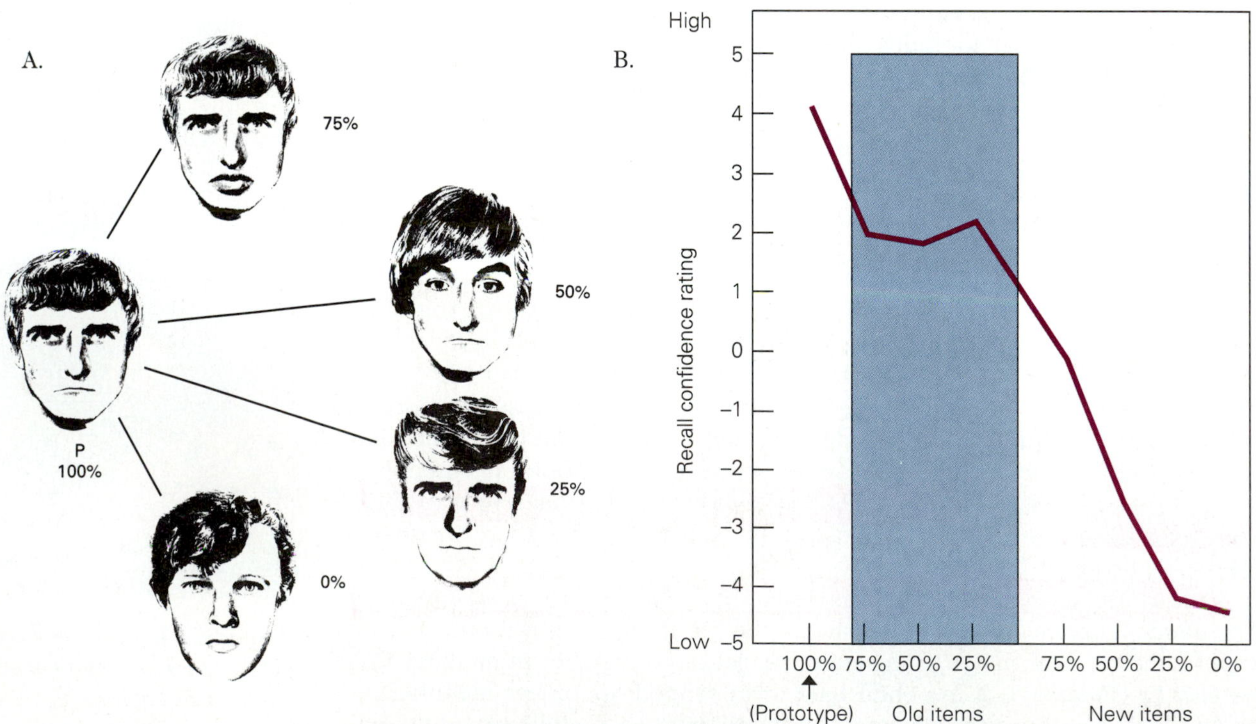

Figure 10.10 **(A) Prototype Face and Exemplar Faces**
(B) Confidence Ratings for Prototype, Old Items, and New Items

The 75-percent face has all the features of the prototype face except the mouth; the 50-percent face has different hair and eyes; the 25-percent face has only the eyes in common; and the 0-percent face has no features in common.

quently, researchers believe that you do not actually have a specific mental representation of the prototype for a particular category. Rather, the prototype emerges as an average across your pool of exemplars (Hintzman, 1986; Nosofsky et al., 1992). For example, all the dogs you have encountered to this moment contribute to your notion of the prototypical dog. Moreover, if you go for a walk today and see a dog or two, your prototype will change just the slightest bit.

A prototype is derived from all experiences with members of a category and will, therefore, shift subtly every time you encounter a new exemplar.

Being able to find the prototype for a category like *dog* also allows you to recognize some category members as more or less typical—the more features the members share with the prototypical member of the category, the more typical they are likely to be. You can develop this intuition if you think about a category like *bird.* What makes a robin a typical bird, but an ostrich or a penguin atypical? The answer has to do with the degree of match of these creatures to all the other entities that you have classified in memory as birds. The degree of typicality of a category member—the extent to which something matches your prototype—has real-life consequences. Research has shown, for example, that people respond more quickly to typical members of a category than to its more unusual ones. Your reaction time to determine that a robin is a bird would be quicker than your reaction time to determine that an ostrich is a bird (Rosch et al., 1976). This effect arises, once again, because you maintain in memory your history of experiences with the members of the category *bird.* It is easier to find robin experiences than ostrich experiences (unless, of course, you have spent your life among ostriches).

A last note on prototypes: in at least one important domain, people seem to find the average member of a category most pleasant.

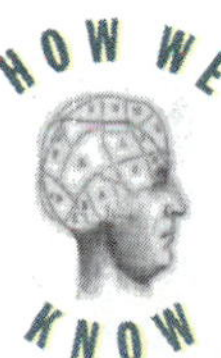

Researchers used computer processing to produce composite photographs of male and female college students. Their composites combined 2, 4, 8, 16, or 32 faces (see **Figure 10.11**). The individual photos and the composite photos were presented in random order to 300 college students of both sexes, who were asked to rate the photos on their physical attractiveness. The results were

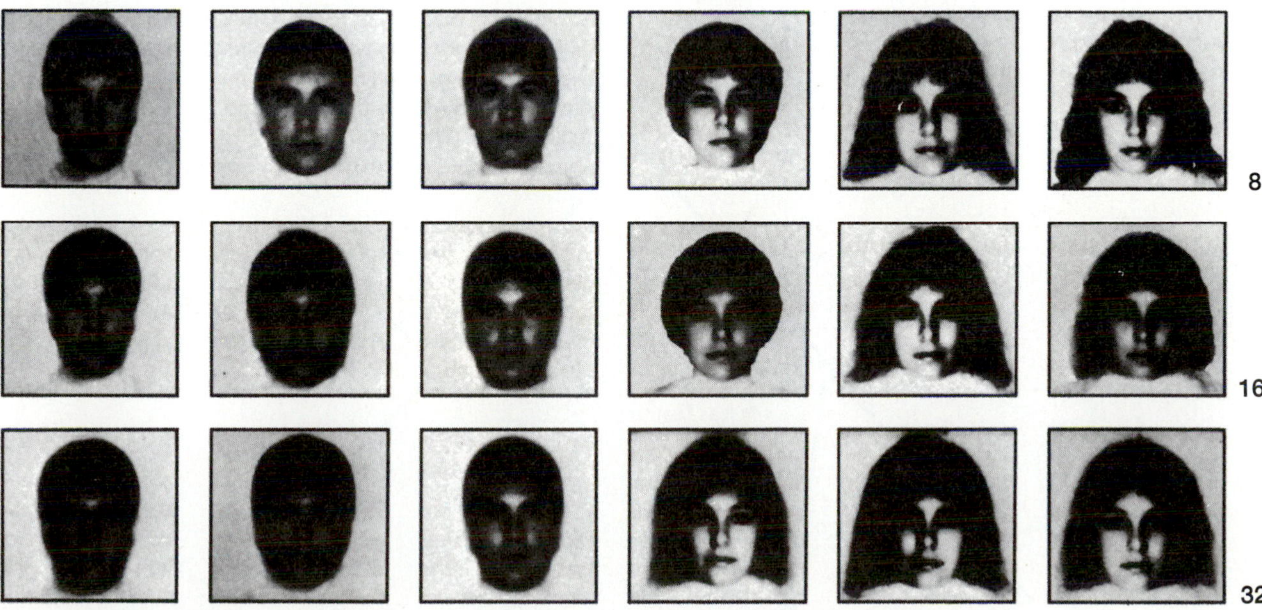

Figure 10.11 Composite Faces
The faces from left to right represent six different composite sets. Faces from top to bottom represent composite levels of 8 faces, 16 faces, and 32 faces.

> the same for both male and female faces and for male and female raters. When 16 or 32 faces contributed to the composites, they were judged as significantly more attractive than the individual faces. Only rarely was any individual face evaluated as more attractive than the composite (Langlois & Roggman, 1990; Langlois et al., 1994).

These researchers suggested that their findings have both a cognitive component—memory processes favor average category members—and an evolutionary component—people prefer individuals with average faces because they are less likely to produce "deviant" looking offspring. You can see, in any case, that when being average means being prototypical, it's really not such a bad thing.

Hierarchies and Basic Levels

Concepts, and their prototypes, do not exist in isolation. As shown in **Figure 10.12**, concepts can often be arranged into meaningful organizations. A broad category like *animal* has several subcategories, such as *bird* and *fish,* which in turn contain exemplars such as *canary, ostrich, shark,* and *salmon.* The animal category is itself a subcategory of the still larger category of *living beings.* Concepts are also linked to other types of information: you store the knowledge that some birds are *edible,* some are *endangered,* some are *national symbols.*

There appears to be a basic level at which people best categorize and think about objects.

There seems to be a level in such hierarchies at which people best categorize and think about objects. This has been called the **basic level** (Rosch, 1973, 1978). For example, when you buy an apple at the grocery store, you could think of it as a *piece of fruit*—but that seems imprecise—or a *Golden Delicious*—but that seems too specific or picayune. The basic level is just *apple.* If you were shown a picture of such an object, that's what you'd be likely to call it. You would also be faster to say that it was an apple than that it was a piece of fruit (Rosch, 1978). The basic level emerges pretty much through the same forces that give rise to the prototype. You have more experience with the term *apple* than with its more or less specific alternatives. If you became an apple grower, however, your basic level would probably shift lower in the hierarchy.

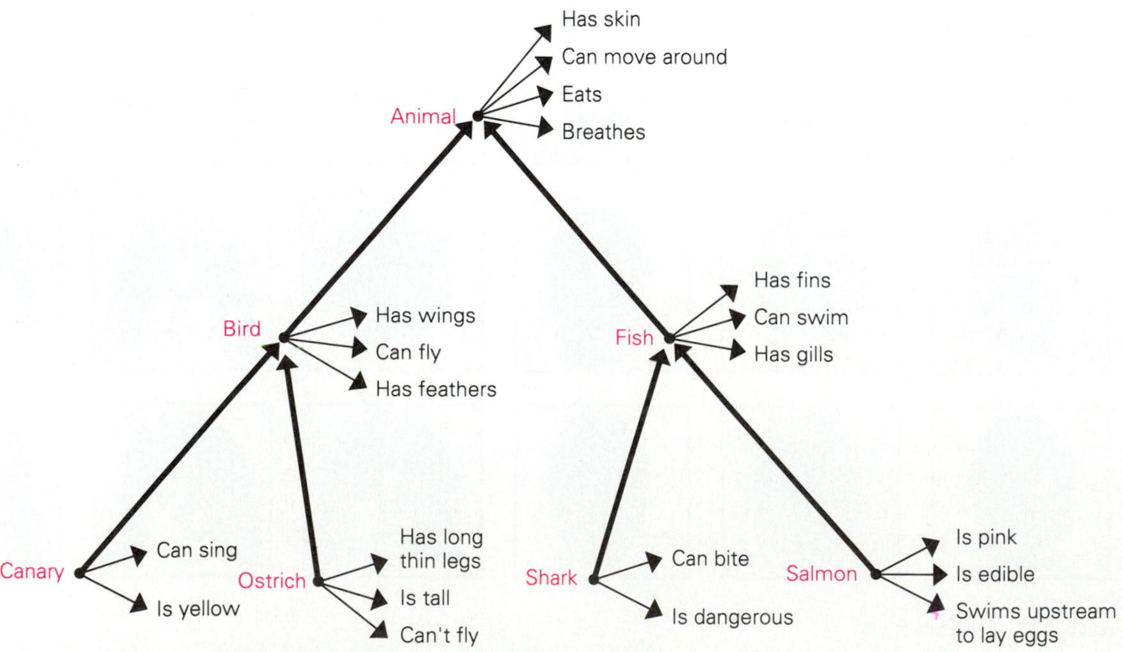

Figure 10.12 Hierarchically Organized Structure of Concepts

Schemas

We have seen that concepts are the building blocks of memory hierarchies. They also serve as building blocks for more complex mental structures. Recall Figure 10.2. Why did you instantly know that the rabbit didn't belong in the kitchen? We suggested earlier that this judgment relied on implicit memory—but we didn't say what type of memory structure you were using. Clearly, what you need is some representation in memory that combines the individual concepts of a kitchen—your knowledge about ovens, sinks, and refrigerators—into a larger unit. We call that larger unit a schema. **Schemas** are conceptual frameworks, or clusters of knowledge, regarding objects, people, and situations. Schemas are "knowledge packages" that encode complex generalizations about your experience of the structure of the environment. You have schemas for kitchens and bedrooms, race car drivers and professors, surprise parties and graduations. You should take a minute right now to think about the types of generalizations you would be willing to offer about each of these categories of experience.

One thing you may have guessed is that your schemas do not include all the individual details of all your varied experiences. Just as a prototype is the average of your experiences of a category, a schema represents your average experience of situations in the environment. Thus, also like prototypes, your schemas are not permanent but shift with your changing life events (Rumelhart et al., 1986). Your schemas also include only those details in the world to which you have devoted sufficient attention. For example, when asked to draw the information on the head sides of U.S. coins, college students virtually never filled in the word *Liberty,* although it appears on every coin (Rubin & Kontis, 1983). Thus your schemas provide an accurate reflection of what you've noticed about the world. Let's now look at all the ways in which you use your concepts and schemas.

Schemas are not permanent representations of conceptual frameworks: rather, they change as you experience new situations in the environment.

Using Memory Structures

Psychologists invoke memory structures with great frequency: anytime we wish to explain the effect of systematic knowledge on people's experiences, we suggest that concepts or schemas have come into play. We can identify five general functions for these types of memory structures (Medin & Ross, 1992):

- *Classification*—As we discussed in Chapter 8, memory structures enable you to classify objects and scenes in the perceptual environment as instances of familiar categories. For example, your past encounters with parades help you to understand that it is a parade you have accidentally wandered upon and not a mob of suburbanites marching, by coincidence, to military music.
- *Explanation*—Because memory structures encode past experiences, they can help you to explain current experiences. For example, because you have a schema for what happens at a restaurant, you will not be surprised when a server brings you a menu or offers you a cup of coffee. You have a ready explanation for those events (Schank & Abelson, 1977).
- *Prediction*—Memory structures also enable you to have accurate expectations about what sorts of things go together or what the future might hold. Once again, your schema for visiting a restaurant specifies that someone must pay for the meal. This expectation allows you to determine how much food you (or someone else) can afford to order.
- *Reasoning*—You also often use memory structures to make inferences that go beyond what is directly present in the world. You would, for example, almost certainly be willing to infer that your psychology

professor has a heart and a brain, though you are unlikely to have acquired any direct evidence in support of these assumptions.

- *Communication*—Memory structures enable you to communicate about many topics with reasonable confidence. Although it is unlikely that you and your best friend have experienced exactly the same set of dogs—on which you will have based your concept *dog*—you can communicate successfully about dogs because you are likely to have much the same average concept.

You use schemas and concepts to perform the functions of classification, explanation, prediction, reasoning, and communication.

Let's consider a couple of instances of memory structures in action. You already saw that your schema for *kitchen* enables you to determine that the bunny just doesn't belong. For a second example, think back to Chapter 8, where we discussed how prior knowledge has an effect on interpretations of ambiguous stimuli. Do you remember **Figure 10.13**? Do you see a duck or a rabbit? Let's suppose we give you the expectation that you're going to see a duck. If you match the features of the picture against your schematic expectations for the features of a duck, you're likely to be reasonably content. The same thing would happen if we told you to expect a rabbit. You use information from memory to generate—and confirm—expectations.

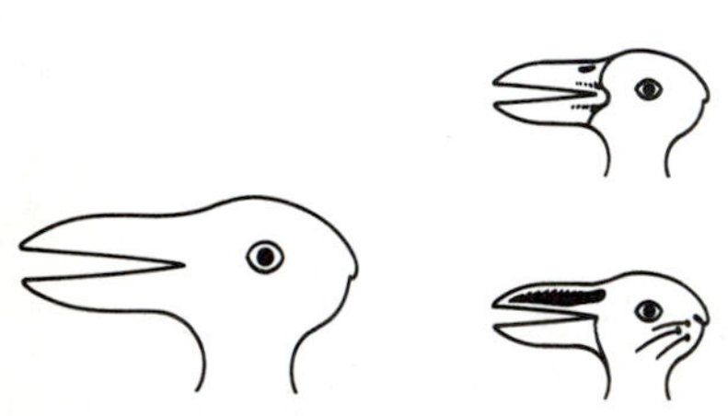

Figure 10.13 Recognition Illusion
Duck or rabbit?

You also have memory structures that influence what you perceive and remember about people (Cantor & Mischel, 1979). For example, you have probably acquired the concepts of dentists, cult leaders, environmentalists, and used-car salespeople. If a person you do not know is described as belonging to one of these categories, your *stereotypes* may lead you to assume that the person has particular personality characteristics or behaves in a particular way. Social psychologists have demonstrated that even the words a language makes available can influence this interpersonal use of concepts.

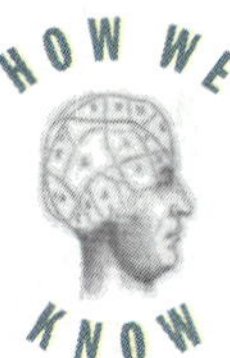

The researchers created descriptions of four individuals, two of whom could easily be labeled by personality-type terms in English, but not in Chinese, and two of whom could easily be labeled in Chinese, but not in English. Consider the term *shì gù*. In Chinese, this term captures an individual who is "worldly, experienced, socially skillful, devoted to his or her family, and somewhat reserved" (Hoffman et al., 1986, p. 1098). In English, no single term or phrase applies to this whole collection of traits. Similarly, no single phrase in Chinese captures the English stereotype of the *artistic type*.

Chinese-English bilinguals read the descriptions in either Chinese or English (half read each description in each language). The researchers predicted that the availability or unavailability of an organized concept in a language would determine whether subjects' reasoning was guided by their stereotypes. This expectation was borne out. The impressions subjects wrote down for each character were considerably more congruent with a stereotype when the language of processing matched the language in which a concept label was available (Hoffman et al., 1986).

This research demonstrates that the availability of memory structures can influence the way you think about the world: your past experiences color your present experiences and change your expectations for the future. You will see shortly that, for much the same reasons, concepts and schemas can sometimes work against accurate memory. But now let's take a last look at what we mean when we talk about mental "structures."

What "Structure" Means

Before we close out this section on memory structures, we want to provide a brief word of caution: when we talk about memory "structures," you should keep in mind that we are using that phrase only by analogy to physical structures. Consider again Figure 10.12. We would never expect to find the information arrayed just like this inside your brain. Instead, you behave, in your use of memory, *as if* your memories are organized in this fashion. For example, if we asked you to verify the assertion "a bird has wings," the task would take you less time than to verify "a canary has wings" (Collins & Quillian, 1969). This result is predicted because "has wings" is stored as information connected directly to *bird.* To verify that a canary has wings, you first have to work your way through the structure from *canary* to *bird.* That takes time. Psychologists often try to provide such pictures of the way in which memory is organized—to predict when memory will or will not work effectively. The pictures, however, are just figurative representations of the biological reality of memory (a topic we address at the end of the chapter).

Psychologists use the concept of memory structures to understand the ways in which memory is organized—to predict when memory will or will not work effectively.

Remembering as a Reconstructive Process

Let's turn now to another important way in which you use memory structures. In many cases when you are asked to remember a piece of information, you can't remember the information directly. Instead, you **reconstruct** the information based on more general types of stored knowledge. To experience reconstructive memory, consider this trio of questions:

When an exact memory cannot be retrieved, the memory is often reconstructed.

- Did Chapter 3 have the word *the* in it?
- Did 1991 contain the day *July 7*?
- Did you breathe yesterday between 2:05 and 2:10 P.M.?

You probably were willing to answer "Yes!" to each of these questions without much hesitation, but you almost certainly don't have specific, episodic memory traces to help you (unless, of course, something happened to fix these events in memory—perhaps July 7 is your birthday or you crossed out all the *the*'s in Chapter 3 to curb your boredom). To answer these questions, you must use more general memories to reconstruct what is likely to have happened. Let's examine this process of reconstruction in a bit more detail.

The Accuracy of Reconstructive Memory

If people reconstruct some memories, rather than recovering a specific memory representation for what happened, then you might expect that you could find occasions on which the reconstructed memory differed from the real occurrence—*distortions.* One of the most impressive demonstrations of memory distortions is also the oldest. In his classic book *Remembering: A Study in Experimental and Social Psychology* (1932), **Sir Frederic Bartlett** undertook a program of research to demonstrate how individuals' prior knowledge influenced the way they remembered new information. Bartlett studied the way British undergraduates remembered stories whose themes and wording were taken from another culture. His most famous story was "The War of the Ghosts," an American Indian tale.

Bartlett found that his readers' reproductions of the story were often greatly altered from the original. The distortions Bartlett found involved three kinds of reconstructive processes:

- *leveling*—simplifying the story.
- *sharpening*—highlighting and overemphasizing certain details.
- *assimilating*—changing the details to better fit the subject's own background or knowledge.

Thus readers reproduced the story with words familiar in their culture taking the place of those unfamiliar: *boat* might replace *canoe* and *go fishing* might replace *hunt seals.* Bartlett's subjects also often changed the story's plot to eliminate references to supernatural forces that were unfamiliar in their culture.

Following Bartlett's lead, modern researchers have demonstrated a variety of memory distortions that occur when people use constructive processes to reproduce memories (Bower et al., 1979; Brewer & Nakamura, 1984; Spiro, 1977). For example, one team of researchers produced what they called a "soap opera" effect in story recall (Owens et al., 1979). Here's an example of an episode from one of their stories:

> Nancy arrived at the cocktail party. She looked around the room to see who was there. She went to talk to her professor. She felt she had to talk to him but was a little nervous about just what to say. A group of people started to play charades. Nancy went over and had some refreshments. The hors d'oeuvres were good but she wasn't interested in talking to the rest of the people at the party. After a while she decided she'd had enough and left the party.

Suppose, while you were at this barbecue, someone told you the man on your left was a millionaire. How would this affect your memories of his actions at the barbecue?

Imagine how different it would have been to read that excerpt if you had been among the half of the subjects who read this extra introduction to the story:

> Nancy woke up feeling sick again and she wondered if she really were pregnant. How would she tell the professor she had been seeing? And the money was another problem.

You might go back now and reread the story excerpt. For the original subjects, the presence or absence of the introduction had a dramatic effect on memory performance. When asked to recall the story or to recognize statements from it, readers who had read the extra introductory material—and, thereby, called to mind a schema for an "unwanted pregnancy"—were much more likely to produce or recognize invented statements related to Nancy's pregnancy. The subjects' use of the schema led to predictable distortions.

It is important to keep in mind, however, that just as in Chapter 8, when we discussed perceptual illusions, psychologists often infer the normal operation of processes by demonstrating circumstances in which the processes lead to errors. Just as perceptual illusions don't cause you to walk into walls, memory "illusions" will rarely cause you serious day-to-day worry. You can think of these memory distortions as the consequences of processes that usually work pretty well. In fact, a lot of the time you don't need to remember the exact details of a particular episode. Reconstructing the gist of events will serve just fine.

Let's explore a bit further the idea that you don't always have to remember particular details. To see how you can reconstruct memories to suit your goal for a particular occasion of memory use, we can look to *quotation.* There are many situations in which you will pepper your own speech with quotations from others' speech. You might, for example, say, "Remember what our psych professor told us, 'Correlation is not causation.'" When you quote someone else's speech, you choose the aspects of that speech that you will reconstruct from memory (Clark & Gerrig, 1990). You may try to reproduce the exact words, or just the gist of what was said. You may try to reproduce an accent or a stutter, or just speak in your own way. You make these decisions based on your conversational goals. Researchers have demonstrated that the use of memory varies with such goals.

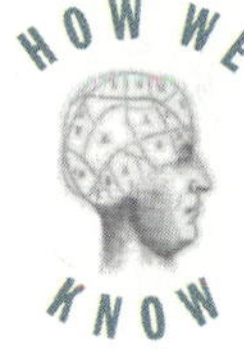

Subjects watched a videotape of a one-and-a-half minute scene from the movie *Breakfast at Tiffany's* and committed the dialogue to memory. The memorization took a bit of work—the subjects were allowed up to 45 minutes—but over time all the subjects were able to reproduce the conversation with near-perfect accuracy. The subjects were then divided into two groups. Each subject retold the dialogue to a second student, but half were asked to make the retelling as accurate as possible, while the other half were asked to make the retelling amusing or interesting. Subjects with accuracy instructions reproduced 99 percent of the original dialogue, word for word. Subjects with interestingness instructions reproduced only 62 percent of the original dialogue. Because both groups had memorized the conversation nearly perfectly, the interestingness group clearly chose not to reproduce all the dialogue (Wade & Clark, 1993).

This result suggests that the amount of care you take to produce a precise memory will depend on the circumstances. If you are held responsible for exactly what happened, you will produce a precise replica—or perhaps admit that you are unable to do so. In many real-life circumstances, however, it's enough to be able to reconstruct more or less what happened. That's your goal, so that's what you do. There is, however, at least one real-life domain in which you are always held responsible for *exactly* what happened. Let's turn now to eyewitness memory.

Researchers have demonstrated that the use of memory varies as communication goals vary.

Eyewitness Memory

A witness in a courtroom swears "to tell the truth and nothing but the truth." Throughout this chapter, however, we have seen that whether a memory is accurate or inaccurate depends on the care with which it was encoded and the match of the circumstances of encoding and retrieval. Because researchers understand that people may not be able to report "the truth," even when they genuinely wish to do so, they have focused a good deal of attention on the topic of *eyewitness memory.* The goal is to help the legal system discover the best methods for ensuring the accuracy of witnesses' memories.

Influential studies on eyewitness memory were carried out by **Elizabeth Loftus** (1979, 1992) and her colleagues. The general conclusion from their research was that eyewitnesses' memories for what they had seen were quite vulnerable to distortion from *postevent information.* For example, subjects in one study were shown a film of an automobile accident and were asked to estimate the speeds of the cars involved (Loftus & Palmer, 1974). However, some subjects were asked, "How fast were the cars going when they smashed into each other?" while others were asked, "How fast were the cars going when they contacted each other?" *Smash* subjects estimated the cars' speed to have been over 40 miles per hour; *contact* subjects estimated the speed at 30 miles per hour. About a week later, all the eyewitnesses were asked, "Did you see any broken glass?" In fact, no broken glass had appeared in the film. However, about a third of the *smash* subjects reported that there had been glass, while only 14 percent of the *contact* eyewitnesses did so. Thus postevent information had a substantial effect on what eyewitnesses reported they had experienced.

How well do eyewitnesses remember events?

Postevent information can impair eyewitness memories even when the witnesses are made explicitly aware that the experimenter has attempted to mislead them.

Repressed Memories

On September 22, 1969, 8-year-old Susan Nason vanished from her northern California neighborhood. In December 1969, her body was found. For 20 years, no one knew who had murdered her. Then, in 1989, Susan's friend Eileen Franklin-Lipsker contacted county investigators. Eileen told them that, with the help of psychotherapy, she had recalled a long-repressed, horrifying memory about what had happened to Susan. In the fall of 1990, Eileen testified that, over two decades earlier, she had witnessed her father, George Franklin, sexually assault Susan and then bludgeon her to death with a rock (Marcus, 1990; Workman, 1990). Eileen reported that her father had threatened to kill her if she ever told anyone. This testimony was sufficient to have George Franklin convicted of first-degree murder.

How, in theory, had these memories remained hidden for 20 years? The answer to this mystery finds its roots in Sigmund Freud's concept of **repressed memories.** As we shall see in Chapter 14, Freud (1923) theorized that some people's memories of life experiences become sufficiently threatening to their psychological well-being that the individuals banish the memories from consciousness. Freud gave the label **repression** to the mental process by which people protect themselves from such unacceptable or painful memories. Clinical psychologists are often able to help clients take control of their lives by interpreting disruptive life patterns as the consequences of repressed memories.

But not all experiences of repressed memories remain in the therapist's office. In recent years there has been an explosion of mass media claims for the dramatic recovery of repressed memories. After long intervals of time, individuals report sudden vivid recollections of horrifying events, such as murders or childhood sexual abuse. Could all these claims be real? Our review of memory research—particularly research on eyewitness memories—has provided you with grounds for skepticism (Loftus, 1993; Loftus & Ketcham, 1994). You know from this research that people will report as true memories information that was provided from an artificial source. They will do so even when, as witnesses, they have been specifically warned that they have been misled. Thus, being in confident possession of a memory provides no assurance of the ultimate source of that memory.

In practice, what memory research suggests is that even when witnesses are absolutely certain about the truth of an experience, there's no reliable method to determine what really took place—particularly after 20 or more years have passed for "postevent" information to accrue. You can even worry that media descriptions of repressed memories will lead some individuals to "recover" the same memories. What an individual saw on TV could be reborn as a personal memory if information about the TV as source somehow got lost. Basically, the individual has lost access to the *source* of the memory but held on to the *content* (Johnson et al., 1993).

Belief in the recovery of repressed memories may provide a measurable benefit for patients in psychotherapy. No doubt some portion of recovered memories may be genuine. However, as you have seen, the use of recovered memories in courtrooms poses a great risk to individuals like George Franklin, whose daughter's damning memories may have arisen from postevent sources (Loftus, 1993). Skepticism toward repressed memories is an appropriate research corollary to the legal requirement of "innocent until proven guilty."

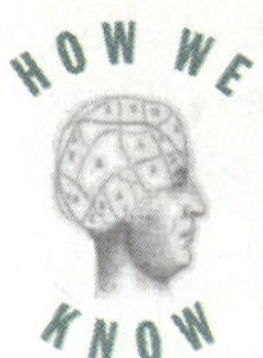

In one experiment, subjects viewed a slide show of an office theft. The slide show was accompanied by a tape recording of a woman's voice describing the sequence of events. Immediately after the slide show, the subjects heard the woman describe the events again. However, this postevent narrative contained misinformation. For example, for subjects who had seen *Glamour* magazine, the tape mentioned *Vogue* instead. Forty-eight hours later, the researcher tested his subjects' memory for the information pic-

> tured in the slides, but he explicitly informed them that there was no question on the memory test for which the correct answer was mentioned in the postevent narrative. Thus, if subjects were able to make a clear distinction in memory between the original events and the postevent information, they should have remained unaffected by that postevent information. That was not the case. Even with fair warning, subjects often recalled postevent information rather than real memories (Lindsay, 1990).

The subjects had been unable to discriminate between the original sources—event or postevent—of the memory traces (Johnson et al., 1993; Weingardt et al., 1995). Although some controversy still surrounds the psychological mechanisms that give rise to this memory performance (for reviews, see Lindsay, 1993; Loftus, 1992), the potential for eyewitnesses' reports to be altered in response to postevent information has now been firmly established. This research reinforces the idea that your memories are often collages, reconstructed from different elements of your past experiences. The Close-up applies this insight to the controversial topic of repressed memories.

The general conclusion of Loftus and her colleagues is that eyewitness testimony is vulnerable to distortion from postevent information.

BIOLOGICAL ASPECTS OF MEMORY

The time has come, once again, for us to ask you to recall the number you committed to memory at the beginning of the chapter. Can you still remember it? What was the point of this exercise? Think for a minute about biological aspects of your ability to look at an arbitrary piece of information and commit it instantly to memory. How can you do that? To encode a memory requires that you instantly change something inside your brain. If you wish to retain that memory for at least the length of a chapter, the change must have the potential to become permanent. Have you ever wondered how this is possible? Our excuse for having you recall an arbitrary number was so that we could ask you to reflect on how remarkable the biology of memory really is. Let's take a closer look inside the brain.

SEARCHING FOR THE ENGRAM

Let's consider your memory for the number 34 or, more specifically, your memory that the number 34 was the number we asked you to remember. How could we determine where in your brain that memory resides? **Karl Lashley** (1929, 1950), who performed pioneering work on the anatomy of memory, referred to this question as the search for the **engram**, the physical memory trace. Lashley devised a methodology to determine whether specific memories are localized in specific small regions of the cerebral cortex or distributed across broad areas. He trained rats to learn mazes, removed varying-size portions of their cortexes, and then retested their memories for the mazes. Lashley found that memory impairment from brain lesioning was proportional to the amount of tissue removed. The impairment grew worse as more of the cortex was damaged. However, memory was not affected by *where* in the cortex the tissue was removed. Lashley concluded that the elusive engram did not exist in any localized regions but was widely distributed throughout the entire brain.

In searching for the biological bases of memory, Karl Lashley found that memory impairment is proportional to the amount of brain tissue removed but that the specific location in the cortex is not significant.

Perhaps Lashley could not localize the engram partly because of the variety of types of memory that are called into play even in an apparently simple situation. Maze learning, in fact, involves complex interactions of spatial, visual, and olfactory signals. Neuroscientists now believe that memory for complex sets of information is distributed across many neural systems, even though discrete types of knowledge are separately processed and localized in limited regions of the brain (Petri & Mishkin, 1994; Squire et al., 1993).

Four major brain structures are involved in memory:

- The *cerebellum*—essential for procedural memory, memories acquired by repetition, and classically conditioned responses.
- The *striatum*—a complex of structures in the forebrain—the likely basis for habit formation and for stimulus-response connections.
- The *cerebral cortex*—responsible for sensory memories and associations between sensations.
- The *amygdala* and *hippocampus*—largely responsible for declarative memory of facts, dates, and names and also for memories of emotional significance.

Other parts of the brain, such as the thalamus, the basal forebrain, and the prefrontal cortex, are involved also as way stations for the formation of particular types of memory (see **Figure 10.14**).

In Chapter 3, we focused directly on brain anatomy. Here, let's take a look at the methods that neuroscientists use to draw conclusions about the role of specific brain structures for memory. Consider one prominent type of learning that we described in Chapter 9, classical conditioning. For the past 20 years, neuropsychologist **Richard Thompson** (1986) has been investigating the brain structures that allow rabbits to learn that a tone (the conditional stimulus) predicts an air puff to the eye (the unconditional stimulus). The air puff causes the rabbit to blink its eye (the unconditional response). Over time, the tone alone will cause the rabbit to blink. Where in the brain does this association reside? In recent research, Thompson and his colleagues have focused on the cerebellum (Lavond et al., 1993).

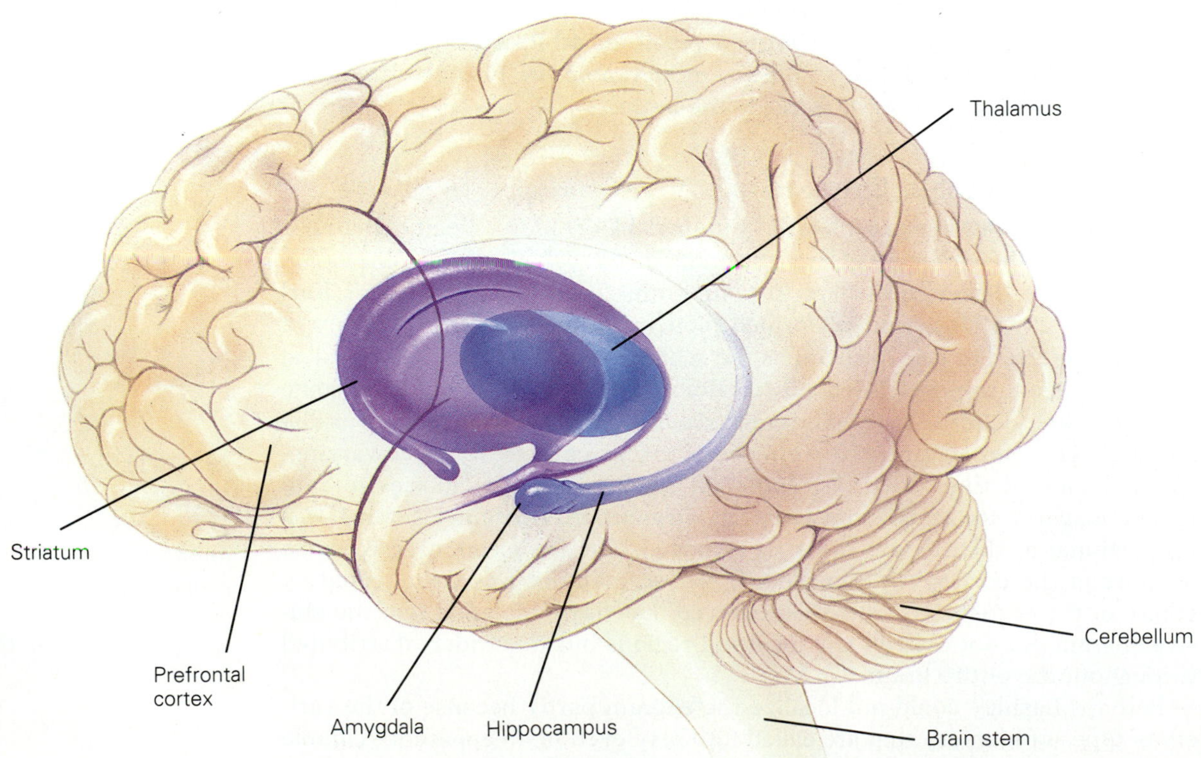

Figure 10.14 Brain Structures Involved in Memory
This simplified diagram shows some of the main structures of the brain that are involved in the formation, storage, and retrieval of memories.

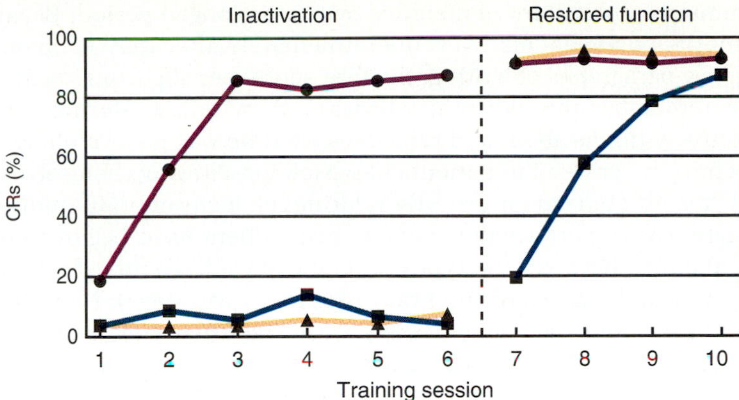

Figure 10.15 The Cerebellum and Classical Conditioning
Rabbits who have their red nucleus inactivated (trials 1 to 6) are only unable to express the motor aspects of a classically conditioned response, as shown when the nucleus is allowed to function again (trials 7 to 10). By contrast, when the cerebellum is inactivated, little or no learning takes place. This pattern of data suggests that the cerebellum is necessary for learning.

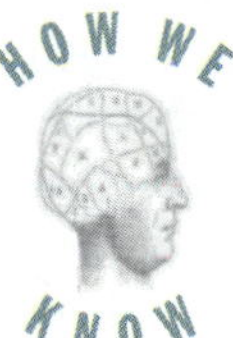

Because it inhibits the neurotransmitter GABA, the drug muscimol can be used to temporarily inactivate select regions of the brain. In one experiment, muscimol was used with rabbits to inactivate either the cerebellum—a structure that has been implicated in the types of memory that underlie aversive conditioning—or the *red nucleus*—a structure in the brain stem that controls motor activity. Both groups of rabbits were put through a series of trials to train them on the tone–air puff pairing. However, neither group showed any evidence of learning (see **Figure 10.15**). After six training sessions, the infusion of muscimol was discontinued. In the seventh training session, the rabbits whose cerebellums had been inactivated showed no signs of prior experience. However, the red nucleus rabbits displayed immediate knowledge of the association (Krupa et al., 1993).

From this pattern of data, we can conclude that the cerebellum is necessary for learning: when it is made inactive, the rabbit shows no learning. Inactivation of the red nucleus, by contrast, affects only motor aspects of classical conditioning. Even though the rabbit cannot demonstrate that it is acquiring the association, the conditional response is found to be fully present when the red nucleus once again becomes active. Through painstaking research of this sort, researchers are developing detailed analyses of the locations of different memory traces in the brain. As we shall see next, human "experiments of nature" have also contributed to the search for the engram.

Amnesia and Types of Memory

In 1960, Nick A., a young air force radar technician, experienced a freak injury that permanently changed his life. Nick had been sitting at his desk while his roommate played with a miniature fencing foil. Then, suddenly, Nick stood up and turned around—just as his buddy happened to lunge with the sword. The foil pierced Nick's right nostril and continued to cut into the left side of his brain. The accident left Nick seriously disoriented. His worst problem was **amnesia**, the failure of memory over a prolonged period. Because of Nick's amnesia, he forgets many events immediately after they happen. After he reads a few paragraphs of writing, the first sentences slip from his memory. He cannot remember the plot of a television show unless, during commercials, he actively thinks about and rehearses what he was just watching.

Researchers are grateful to patients like Nick for allowing themselves to be studied as "experiments of nature." By relating the locus of brain injuries like Nick's to patterns of performance deficit, researchers have begun to understand the mapping between the types of memory we have introduced you to in this chapter and regions of the brain (Squire et al., 1989). Nick, himself, still remembers *how* to do things—his procedural knowledge appears to be intact even in the absence of declarative knowledge. So, for example, he remembers how to mix, stir, and bake the ingredients in a recipe, but he forgets what the ingredients are. This selective impairment of procedural memory strongly suggests that different regions of the brain are specialized for the two types of knowledge.

The selective impairment in amnesia patients suggests that different regions in the brain are specialized for declarative knowledge and procedural knowledge.

Let's consider another memory distinction that may be related to different anatomical structures. Researchers have shown that damage to the hippocampus most often impairs explicit, but not implicit, memories (Squire, 1992).

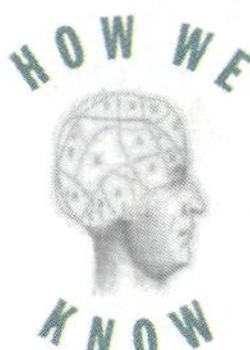

The subjects in one series of studies were patients who had suffered hippocampal damage as a consequence of *Korsakoff syndrome,* a product of chronic alcoholism. Both these amnesic patients and a nonamnesic control group were presented with a lists of words and asked to judge how much they liked or disliked each word. To test their memory, subjects were provided with word stems, like *uni*_______. In the *cued recall* task, they were told that the stem could be completed with a word that had appeared on the list and that they should try to provide the word. In the *completion* task, they were asked only to provide the first word that came to mind. For the cued recall task, amnesic subjects performed considerably less well than the unimpaired control subjects. However, their performance on the stem completion task was equivalent to that of the controls (Graf et al., 1984).

This result suggests that the brain damage caused by Korsakoff syndrome affects explicit memory but leaves implicit priming intact. Researchers have demonstrated that such implicit priming can be very long-lived.

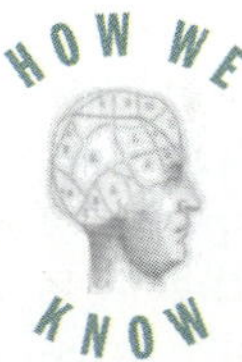

Groups of amnesic and unimpaired subjects were asked to name out loud line drawings of common items. Some of the drawings were repeated in subsequent sessions two and seven days after the initial session. At both delays, the amnesics were able to name the repeated drawings more quickly than the first time through—implicit priming—even when their recognition memory for the pictures—explicit memory—was impaired with respect to normal controls (Cave & Squire, 1992).

Again, you can see that implicit memory can be quite impressive even with substantial damage to the hippocampus.

Psychologists have gained a great deal of knowledge about the relationship between anatomy and memory from the amnesic patients who generously serve as subjects in these experiments. However, the advent of brain imaging techniques has enabled researchers to study memory processes in individuals without brain damage. (You may want to review the section on imaging techniques in Chapter 3.) For example, using *positron-emission tomography* (PET), Endel Tulving and his colleagues (1994) have identified a difference between the two brain hemispheres in the encoding and retrieval of episodic information. Their studies parallel standard memory studies, except that the subjects' cerebral blood flow is monitored through PET scans during encoding or retrieval. These researchers discovered disproportionately high brain activity in the left prefrontal cortex (see Figure 10.14) for encoding of episodic information and in the right prefrontal cortex for retrieval of episodic information. This pattern suggests that encoding and retrieval processes occur in different parts of the brain. Thus the processes are *anatomically* distinct—they are not just conceptual distinctions invented by cognitive psychologists.

Imaging techniques such as PET scans allow researchers to study memory processes in individuals without brain damage.

These results also suggest why researchers from different disciplines must work closely together in the quest for a full understanding of memory processes. Psychologists provide the data on human performance that become fuel for neurophysiologists' detection of specialized brain structures. At the same time, the realities of physiology constrain psychologists' theories of the mechanisms of encoding, storage, and retrieval. Working together, scientists in these fields of research have provided much more, perhaps, than you ever wanted to know about remembering the number 34.

Recapping Main Points

What Is Memory?

Cognitive psychologists study memory as a type of information processing. Memories involving conscious effort are explicit. Unconscious memories are implicit. Declarative memory is memory for facts; procedural memory is memory for how to perform skills. Memory is often viewed as a three-stage process of encoding, storage, and retrieval.

Sensory Memory

Sensory memory systems have large capacity but very short durations. Iconic memory momentarily preserves the visual world. Echoic memory holds auditory stimuli.

Short-term Memory (STM)

Short-term memory (STM) has a limited capacity and lasts only briefly without rehearsal. Maintenance rehearsal can extend the presence of material in STM indefinitely. STM capacity can be increased by chunking unrelated items into meaningful groups. Retrieval from STM is very efficient. STM is also called working memory. Material may be transferred to it from either sensory or long-term memory; information can be consciously processed only in STM.

Long-term Memory (LTM): Encoding and Retrieval

Long-term memory (LTM) constitutes your total knowledge of the world and of yourself. It is nearly unlimited in capacity. Your ability to remember information relies on the match between circumstances of encoding and retrieval. Retrieval cues allow you to access information in LTM. Episodic memory is concerned with memory for events that have been personally experienced. Semantic memory is memory for the basic meaning of words and concepts. Interference occurs when retrieval cues do not lead uniquely to specific memories.

Similarity in context between learning and retrieval aids retrieval. The more specifically material is encoded in terms of expected retrieval cues, the more efficient later retrieval will be, if the same cues are available at retrieval. The serial position curve is explained by distinctiveness in context. Information processed more deeply is typically remembered better. For implicit memories, it is important that the processes of encoding and retrieval be similar. Memory performance can be improved through elaborative rehearsal and mnemonics. In general, feelings-of-knowing accurately predict the availability of information in memory.

Structures in Long-Term Memory

Concepts are the memory building blocks of thinking. They are formed by identifying properties that are common to a class of objects or ideas. Prototypes represent the average exemplar of a concept. Concepts are often organized in hierarchies, ranging from general, to basic level, to specific. Schemas are more complex cognitive clusters. All these memory structures are used to provide expectations and a context for interpreting new information.

Remembering is not simply recording but is a constructive and a selective process. Past experiences and goals effect what you remember. New information can bias your recall without your realizing it, making eyewitness memory unreliable when contaminated by postevent input.

Biological Aspects of Memory

Different brain structures (including the hippocampus, the amygdala, the cerebellum, and the cerebral cortex) have been shown to be involved in different types of memory. Experiments with both nonhuman animals and humans have helped investigators search for the engram, the physical memory trace.

Resources

Loftus, E. F., & Ketcham, K. (1994). *The myth of repressed memory: False memories and allegations of sexual abuse.* New York: St. Martin's Press.

McDaniel, M. A., & Pressley, M. (1987). *Imagery and related mnemonic processes.* New York: Springer-Verlag. A sourcebook for improving memory, emphasizing techniques relying on mental imagery.

MacLean, H. N. (1993). *Once upon a time: A true story of memory, murder, and the law*. New York: HarperCollins.

Neisser, U. (1982). *Memory observed: Remembering in natural contexts.* San Francisco: Freeman. This book contains several chapters by leading researchers in the field of memory; the text highlights the role of context in remembering real-world information.

Ofshe, R. (1995). *Making monsters: False memories, psychotherapy, and sexual hysteria*. New York: Scribners.

Schacter, D. L., & Tulving, E. (Eds.). (1994). *Memory systems.* Cambridge, MA: MIT Press.

11

Cognitive Processes

It is midnight. There's a knock on your door. When you answer, no one is there, but you see an envelope on the floor. Inside the envelope is a single sheet of paper with a handwritten message: "The cat is on the mat." What do you make of this?

You must now begin to engage a variety of cognitive processes. You will need language processes to put together some basic meaning for the words, but what then? Can you find any episode in memory to which these words are relevant? (Recall that in Chapter 10 we discussed memory as a type of cognitive processing.) If you can't, you'll have to give other types of thought to the matter. Is the message in code? What kind of code? Who do you know who might encode a message? Does the fate of civilization rest in your hands?

Perhaps we're getting a bit carried away, but we want to make plain to you what kinds of activities count as **cognitive processes** *and why you might be interested in them. The capacity to use language and to think in abstract ways has often been cited as the essence of the human experience. You tend to take cognition for granted because it's an activity you do continually most of your waking hours. However, when a carefully crafted speech wins your vote or when you read a detective story in which the sleuth combines a few scraps of apparently trivial clues into a brilliant solution to a crime, you are forced to acknowledge the intellectual triumph of cognitive processes.*

Cognition *is a general term for all forms of knowing: as shown in Figure 11.1, the study of cognitive processes is the study of mental processes. (Note that Chapter 8 already discussed some of the topics shown in Figure 11.1.) Cognition includes both* contents *and* processes. *The* contents *of cognition are concepts, facts, propositions, rules, and memories: "A dog is a mammal." "A red light means stop." "I first left home at age 18." Cognitive* processes *manipulate these mental contents to enable you to interpret the world around you and to find creative solutions to your life's dilemmas.*

We will begin our study of cognition with a brief account of how cognitive psychology, *the study of cognition, emerged as a special area of scientific scrutiny. Next we will describe the ways*

© 1985 Bloom County, *Washington Post Writers Group. Reprinted with permission.*

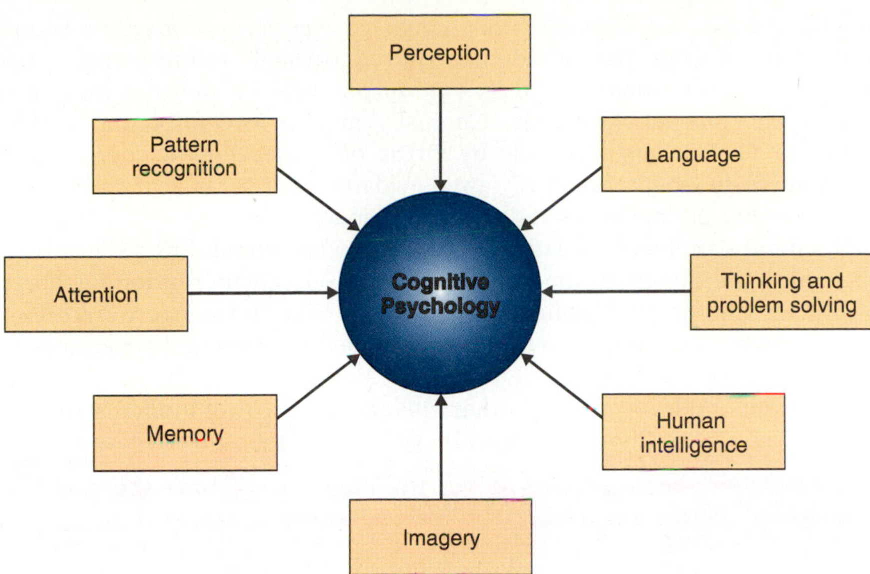

Figure 11.1 The Domain of Cognitive Psychology

in which researchers try to measure the inner, private processes involved in cognitive functioning. Then we will examine, at some length, topics in cognitive psychology that generate much basic research and application: language use, visual cognition, problem solving, reasoning, and judging and decision making.

STUDYING COGNITION

How can you study cognition? The challenge, of course, is that it goes on inside the head. You can see the input—a note that says, "The cat is on the mat"—and experience the output—perhaps an understanding of the note's hidden meaning—but how can you determine what happened in the middle? How can you reveal cognitive processes or the mental representations on which they rely? You might recall from Chapter 9 that the behaviorist position rose to dominate psychology because it took overt—directly observable—behaviors to be the only possible subject matter for a science. In this section, we will first briefly describe the types of phenomena that led theorists to believe that cognitive processes, which are not directly observable, nevertheless had to be included in a theory of psychological performance. We then turn to the types of methodologies that have made possible the scientific study of cognitive psychology.

The Emergence of Cognitive Psychology

In Chapter 9, you saw that basic learning processes can be used to explain, with reasonable accuracy, many of the contingencies, or causes, of human behavior. It was these successes that led thinkers like B. F. Skinner to take a hard line against the study of internal processes. A rule of thumb in science is that theories should not include any more explanatory principles than are absolutely necessary. This rule that theories should be as *parsimonious* as possible is known as *Occam's razor.* If, Skinner reasoned, all behavior could be explained without postulating cognitive processes, then what was the purpose of imagining them to exist? To refute Skinner's point of view, early cognitive psychologists outlined areas of human performance that could not be accurately characterized solely by stimulus-response relationships.

One important example was language. In 1957, in the book *Verbal Behavior,* Skinner tried to extend his theories to language acquisition and language use. He argued, for example, that language was simply another form of expressive behavior that children acquired through reinforcement. Soon after, the linguist **Noam Chomsky** (1957) published a fierce review of the book in the journal *Language*. Chomsky argued forcefully that children could not acquire language only by virtue of reinforcement contingencies. For example, in Chapter 5 we reviewed evidence that some deaf children create their own sign languages and that those created languages have legitimate grammatical structures. Because the languages are the children's own inventions, adults in the environment could not be selectively reinforcing correct structures. Chomsky suggested that this type of performance would not be possible unless learners were innately equipped with mental structures that guided language acquisition.

B. F. Skinner argued in favor of the reinforcement explanation of language learning, while Noam Chomsky argued that children could not acquire language simply through reinforcement.

Data from children provided other evidence in favor of mental structures. Again, as we saw in Chapter 5, **Jean Piaget** (1954) pioneered the study of the mental processes children go through to understand physical realities. Piaget's notion of stages of cognitive development was based on observations of the kinds of mental tasks that children of different ages can perform. His results suggested that the actual types of processes that children are able to carry out go through qualitative changes—for example, preoperational thought gives way to formal operations—that are more than just changes in the relationships between stimuli and responses.

Finally, cognitive psychology emerged as researchers began to develop an analogy between the mind and other information-processing devices, particularly the computer. The modern conception of a computer as a general-purpose symbol-processing machine, able to operate flexibly on internal instructions, came from the vision of a brilliant young mathematician, **John Von Neumann.** In 1945, he boldly drew comparisons between the electronic circuits of a new digital computer and the brain's neurons and between a computer program and the brain's memory (Heppenheimer, 1990). Following Von Neumann's lead, researchers **Herbert Simon** and **Allen Newell** (Newell et al., 1958) developed computer programs to simulate human problem solving. Simon is reputed to have told his 1955 class at the Carnegie Institute of Technology that, over the Christmas break, he and Newell had "invented a thinking machine." The next year, their computer, named Johniac in honor of John Von Neumann, worked out a proof of a mathematical theorem. Newell and Simon's success suggested that human minds could effectively be studied as symbol-processing devices.

The analogy between the human mind and a computer, as supported by the research of John Von Neumann, Herbert Simon, and Allen Newell, contributed to the acceptance of scientific research on all forms of higher mental processes.

These new approaches to human thought involving children, communication, and computers boosted the scientific legitimacy of research on all forms of higher mental processes. Since then, cognitive theory has developed widely into many other areas of psychological research (Mayer, 1981; Solso, 1991). Over the last decade, the field of cognitive psychology has been supplemented by the interdisciplinary field of **cognitive science** (see **Figure 11.2**). Cognitive science focuses the collected knowledge of several academic specialties on the same theoretical issues. It benefits the practitioners of each of these fields that they share their data and insights. You saw this cognitive science philosophy at work in Chapter 10, when we described how studies of the biology of memory can be used to constrain—limit and refine—theories of memory processes. Many of the theories we will describe in this chapter have similarly been shaped through the interactions of researchers from a number of disciplinary perspectives.

Discovering the Processes of Mind

Even if psychologists had good reasons to believe that cognitive processes should be studied, they still needed rigorous techniques for doing so. In this section, we will describe the historical roots of methods for revealing mental processes and then explore how this logic has flourished in the last decades.

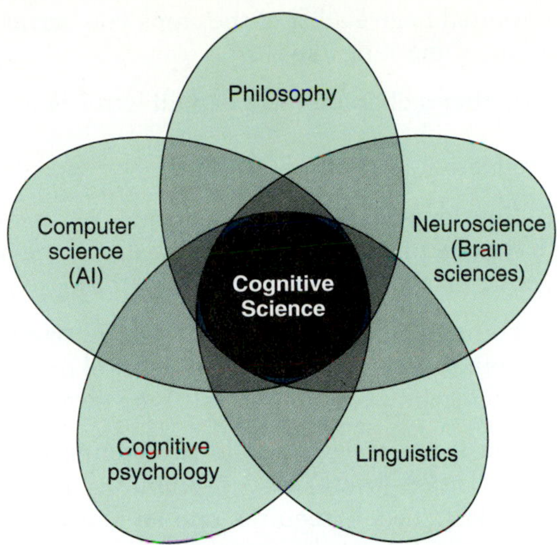

Figure 11.2 The Domain of Cognitive Science
The domain of cognitive science occupies the intersection of philosophy, neuroscience, linguistics, cognitive psychology, and computer science (artificial intelligence).

Donders's Subtraction Method

One of the fundamental methodologies for studying mental processes was devised, in 1868, by the Dutch physiologist **F. C. Donders.** To study the "speed of mental processes," Donders invented a series of experimental tasks that he believed were differentiated by the mental steps involved for successful performance (Lachman et al., 1979). **Table 11.1** provides a paper-and-pencil experiment that follows Donders's logic. Please stop reading this section to time yourself doing the exercise in part 1. How long did you take?

Table 11.1 Donders's Analysis of Mental Processes

1. Draw a *C* on top of all the capitalized letters:

   TO Be, oR noT To BE: tHAT Is thE qUestioN:
   WhETher 'Tis noBlEr In tHE MINd tO SuFfER
   tHe SLings AnD ARroWS Of OUtrAgeOUs forTUNe,
   or To TAke ARmS agaINST a sEa Of tROUBleS,
   AnD by oPPOsinG END theM.

2. Draw a *V* on top of the capitalized *vowels* and a *C* on top of the capitalized *consonants:*

   TO Be, oR noT To BE: tHAT Is thE qUestioN:
   WhETher 'Tis noBlEr In tHE MINd tO SuFfER
   tHe SLings AnD ARroWS Of OUtrAgeOUs forTUNe,
   or To TAke ARmS agaINST a sEa Of tROUBleS,
   AnD by oPPOsinG END theM.

3. Draw a *V* on top of all the capitalized letters:

   TO Be, oR noT To BE: tHAT Is thE qUestioN:
   WhETher 'Tis noBlEr In tHE MINd tO SuFfER
   tHe SLings AnD ARroWS Of OUtrAgeOUs forTUNe,
   or To TAke ARmS agaINST a sEa Of tROUBleS,
   AnD by oPPOsinG END theM.

Now suppose you wanted to give a list of the steps you carried out to perform the task. It might look something like this:

a. Determine whether a character is a capital letter or a small letter.
b. If it is a capital letter, draw a *C* on top.

Now try part 2. How long did you take this time? When we have used this exercise, people have often taken an additional half minute or more. You can understand why, once we spell out the necessary steps:

a. Determine whether a character is a capital letter or a small letter.
b. Determine whether each capital letter is a vowel or a consonant.
c. If it is a consonant, draw a *C* on top. If it is a vowel, draw a *V*.

Donders based his method for measuring mental processes on the notion that a task could be analyzed according to the number of steps required and that performing more mental steps would take more time.

Thus, going from task 1 to task 2, we add two mental steps, which we can call *stimulus categorization* (vowel or consonant?) and *response selection* (draw a *C* or draw a *V*?). Task 1 requires one stimulus categorization step. Task 2 requires two such categorizations. Task 2 also requires selecting between two responses. Because task 2 requires you to do everything you did for task 1 and more, it takes you more time. That was Donders's fundamental insight: extra mental steps will often result in more time to perform a task.

(You may be wondering why we included part 3 in Table 11.1. This is a necessary procedural control for the experiment. We have to ensure that the time difference between tasks 1 and 2 does not stem from the fact that it takes much longer to draw *V*'s than to draw *C*'s. To convince yourself this isn't the case, you should carry out task 3. It should still be much swifter than task 2.)

Donders originally hoped to use his procedure to obtain precise estimates of the duration of different mental processes. With his *subtraction method*, you could subtract the time needed to carry out task 1 from the time needed for task 2 and determine how long it takes to perform stimulus categorization and response selection. If you could also develop a task that required stimulus categorization but not response selection (as Donders did), then you could assign numbers—an amount of time—to each individual process. Thus stimulus categorization might take 100 milliseconds (one-thousandths of a second; abbreviated msec) and response selection 150 msec.

Cognitive psychologists no longer use the subtraction method, because the absolute time for different processes depends so much on the details of each task. Investigators do, however, follow Donders's basic logic. Researchers frequently use **reaction time**—the amount of time it takes subjects to perform particular tasks—as a way of testing specific accounts of how some cognitive process is carried out. Donders's basic premise that extra mental steps will result in extra time is still fundamental to a great deal of cognitive psychological research. Let's see how this successful idea has been developed over the past 125 years.

Mental Processes and Mental Resources

When cognitive psychologists break down high-level activities, like language use or problem solving, into their component processes, they often act as if they are playing a game with blocks. Each block represents a different component that must be carried out. The goal is to determine the shape and size of each block, and to see how the blocks fit together to form the whole activity. For the Donders tasks, you saw that the blocks can be laid out in a row (see **Figure 11.3**, part A). Each step comes directly after another. The block metaphor allows you to see that we could also stack the blocks so that more than one process occurs simultaneously (part B). These two pictures illustrate a distinction we introduced briefly in Chapter 8, between **serial** and **parallel processes.** You saw there that some kinds of visual searches can be

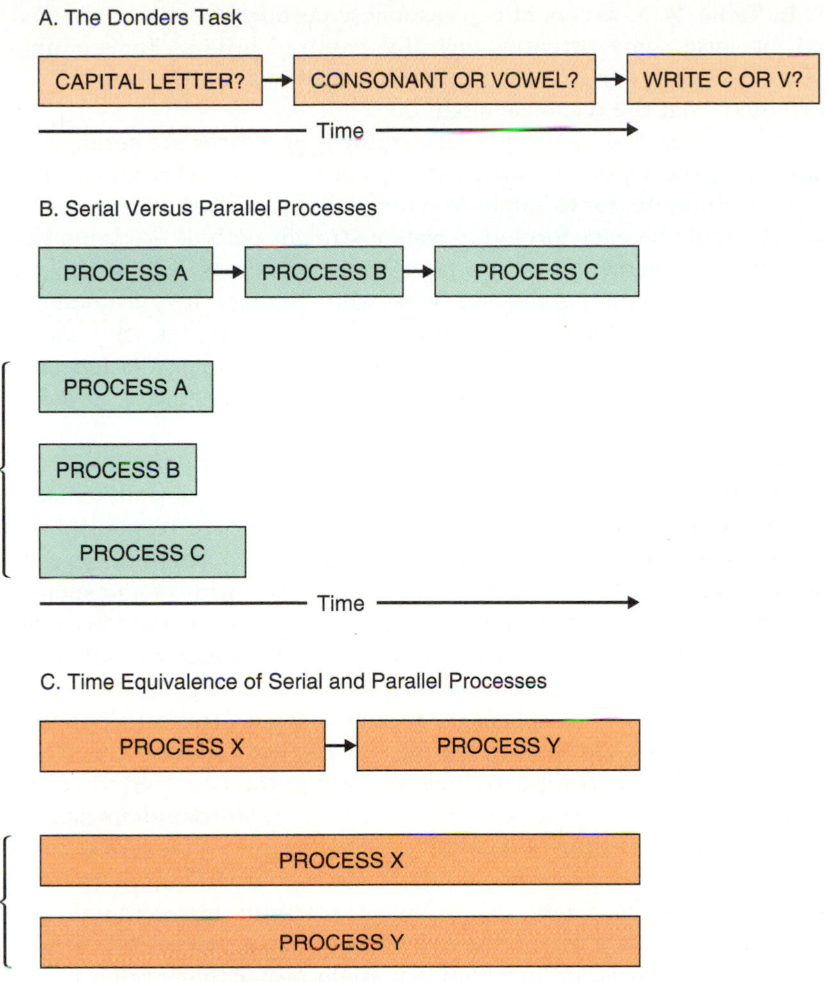

Figure 11.3 Breaking Down High-level Cognitive Activities

Cognitive psychologists attempt to determine the identity and organization of the mental processes that are the building blocks of high-level cognitive activities.
(A) Our version of the Donders task requires that at least three processes be carried out one after the other.
(B) Some processes are carried out serially, in sequence; others are carried out in parallel, all at the same time.
(C) The time taken to perform a task does not always allow researchers to conclude whether serial or parallel processes were used.

carried out in parallel—all the elements in an array can be examined at the same time—while other kinds of searches require serial processing—each element must be examined separately, one after another.

Cognitive psychologists often use reaction times to determine whether processes are carried out in parallel or serially. However, the examples in part C of Figure 11.3 should convince you that this is a tricky business. Imagine that we have a task that we believe can be decomposed into two processes, *X* and *Y*. If the only information we have is the total time needed to complete the process, we can never be sure if processes *X* and *Y* happen side by side or one after the other. Much of the challenge of research in cognitive psychology is to invent task circumstances that allow the experimenter to determine which of many possible configurations of blocks is cor-

A challenge for researchers in cognitive psychology is to determine whether processes are serial or parallel.

rect. In Table 11.1, we could be reasonably certain that the processes were serial, because some activities logically required others. For example, you couldn't execute your response (prepare to draw a *C* or a *V*) until you had determined what the response might be.

Why is it difficult to carry on a conversation when you're trying to avoid puddles?

In many cases, theorists try to determine if processes are serial or parallel by assessing the extent to which the processes place demands on *mental resources*. Suppose, for example, you are walking to class with a friend. Ordinarily, it should be easy for you to walk a straight path at the same time you carry on a conversation—your navigation processes and your language processes can go on in parallel. But what would happen if you suddenly get to a patch of sidewalk that's dotted with puddles? As you pick your way among the puddles, you may have to stop talking. Now your navigation processes require extra resources for planning, and your language processes are momentarily squeezed out.

A key assumption in this example is that you have *limited* processing resources that must be spread over different mental tasks (Kahneman, 1973; Navon & Gopher, 1979). Your *attentional processes* are responsible for distributing these resources. In Chapter 8, we discussed **attention** as the set of processes that allow you to select, for particular scrutiny, some small subset of available perceptual information. Our use of *attention* here preserves the idea of selectivity. The decision now, however, concerns which mental processes will be selected as the recipients of processing resources.

We have one more complication to add: not all processes put the same demands on resources. We can, in fact, define a dimension that goes from processes that are *controlled* to those that are *automatic* (Shiffrin & Schneider, 1977). **Controlled processes** require attention; **automatic processes** generally do not. It is often difficult to carry out more than one controlled process at a time, because they require more resources; automatic processes can often be performed alongside other tasks without interference.

In **Figure 11.4** we give you the opportunity to experience the *Stroop task* (Stroop, 1935), a situation in which you might prefer that a process not be so automatic. Follow the instructions given. You will probably discover that it is difficult to name the color of the ink when your reading processes automatically provide you with another color term. It's hard, for example, to say "black" when "purple" is brought immediately to mind. You probably remember all the effort you expended learning to read. Now, however, reading is so well practiced that it has become automatic—you can't turn it off even to improve your performance on the Stroop task. The Stroop task also illustrates that automatic processes rely heavily on the efficient use of memory (Logan, 1988, 1992). Rather than having to reason through a solution—How do you put together the letters *p, u, r, p, l,* and *e*?—your memory produces a ready-made interpretation of the letter string.

PURPLE	BLUE	RED
GREEN	YELLOW	ORANGE
RED	BLACK	BLUE
ORANGE	GREEN	BROWN
BLUE	YELLOW	PURPLE

Figure 11.4 The Stroop Task

Perform the following two tasks:
1. Time yourself as you read aloud all the words, ignoring the colors in which they are printed.
2. Time yourself as you name the colors, ignoring what the words say.

You probably performed the first task quickly and effortlessly, with little or no thought. The second task is more difficult because you had to deal with interference.

Let's apply this knowledge of controlled and automatic processes back to the situation of walking and talking. When you are walking a straight route, you feel little interference between the two activities, suggesting that maintaining your path and planning your utterances are relatively automatic activities. The situation changes, however, when the puddles force you to choose between a greater number of options for your path. Now you must select where to go *and* what to say. Because you can't make both choices simultaneously, you have hit an attentional *bottleneck* (Pashler, 1992). This example shows why controlled and automatic processes are defined along a dimension, rather than constituting strict categories. When circumstances become challenging, what before seemed automatic now requires controlled attention. Thus processes may require more or less attention, depending on the context.

You now know a lot about the logic of mental processes. To explain how complex mental tasks are carried out, theorists propose models that combine serial and parallel, and controlled and automatic processes. The goal of much cognitive psychological research is to invent experiments that confirm each of the components of such models. Our version of Donders's tasks provided an example of how response time can be used to confirm cognitive models. As we shall now see, recent technological innovations have also made it possible to use data directly from the brain to evaluate cognitive theories.

Evidence from the Brain

Because "mental processes" must take place in the brain, you might expect that the brain itself would be a good place to seek evidence for them. That is exactly the goal of researchers in **cognitive neuroscience,** who test and refine cognitive theories by using a set of methodologies that allow inferences to be drawn about the activities of the brain. In many cases, researchers attempt to show that different mental processes or representations involve different brain structures or produce distinctive patterns of brain response. In earlier chapters, we have discussed some of these techniques, as well as the evidence they have produced. We will offer you a brief review here.

In Chapter 3, we introduced a range of physiological techniques that are used by cognitive neuroscientists. One of those was the *electroencephalogram* (EEG), a graphical representation of the pattern of the brain's electrical signals. A pattern of brain activity evoked by a stimulus event is called an *event-related potential* (ERP), to distinguish it from the spontaneous electrical activity that goes on all the time in the living brain. The logic that allows ERPs to be used to test cognitive theories follows Donders's logic for reaction times. Donders, for example, invented two tasks that differed just by the process of response selection. Similarly, ERP researchers create series of experimental tasks that, by careful comparison, allow mental processes to be isolated (Garnsey, 1993). Rather than measure differences in response times, ERP researchers look for a characteristic brain response that can be attributed to each isolated set of mental processes. For example, readers produce different ERP patterns when they encounter an unexpected word in a sentence than when they encounter an unusual grammatical construction (Osterhout & Holcomb, 1992). This finding supports the conclusion that different mental processes are at work when readers recover the meaning versus the grammatical structure of a sentence.

Cognitive neuroscientists isolate mental processes using physiological techniques such as the measurement of event-related potentials.

Chapter 3 also introduced brain imaging techniques like CAT and PET scans and magnetic resonance imaging (MRI). Each of these techniques allows researchers to observe which regions of the brain are most actively involved in different processing tasks. For example, **Figure 11.5** presents images of a subject's cerebral blood flow while performing two tasks: thinking about information in episodic memory and then in semantic memory (Tulving, 1989; Tulving et al., 1994). The color coding is produced by a computer

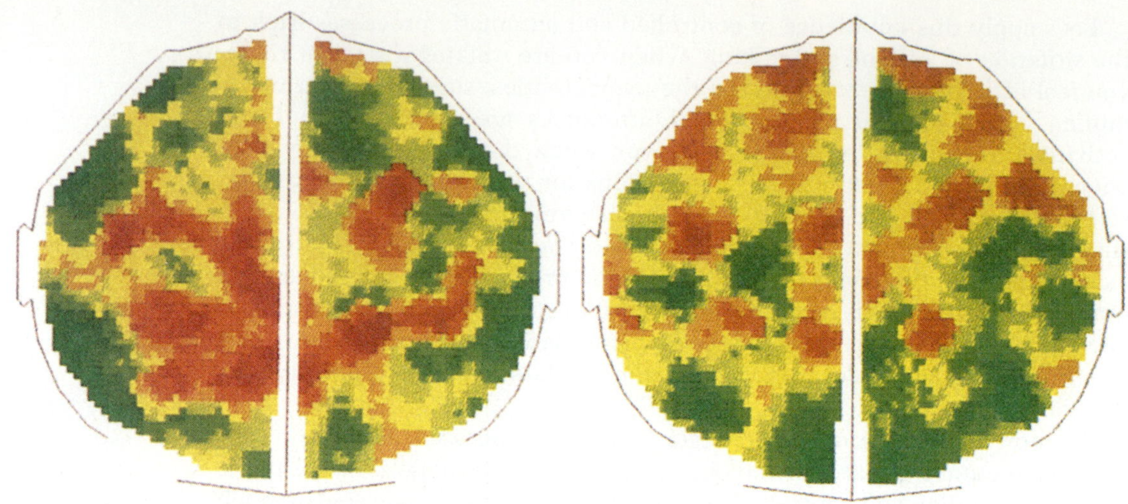

Figure 11.5 Brain Images of Regional Cerebral Blood Flow
Cerebral blood-flow patterns differ in episodic and semantic retrieval. The brain image on the left shows recently acquired semantic knowledge (news about elections). The brain image on the right shows a recently experienced personal episode (thinking about an outing of a few days before).

Using imaging techniques such as CAT and PET scans, researchers identify the specific areas of the brain that are most active during a particular processing task.

to indicate relative blood flow. You can see that different brain regions are active for the two tasks—providing evidence for the distinction between semantic and episodic memories we introduced in Chapter 10.

A third source of evidence in cognitive neuroscience comes from people who have sustained brain damage. Once researchers can determine the areas of the brain that have been affected—a process that has been greatly facilitated by brain-imaging techniques—they can seek correlations between patterns of deficit and the elements of cognitive theories. For example, in Chapter 10 we described research that has been carried out with amnesics. Their patterns of performance have supported the view that humans possess different types of memories—for example, procedural versus declarative—that are processed in localized regions of the brain. Similarly, in Chapter 7 we discussed the phenomenon of *blindsight*—accurate visual performance without conscious awareness. The discovery of this phenomenon in brain-damaged individuals greatly enriched the types of theories researchers proposed for processing in an intact perceptual system.

Now that you understand some of the logic behind cognitive psychological research into mental processes, it is time to move to more specific domains in which you put cognitive processes to work. We begin with language use.

LANGUAGE USE

Let's return to the message you received at midnight, "The cat is on the mat." What could we do to change the situation so that this message immediately made sense to you? The easiest step we could take would be to introduce appropriate background knowledge. Suppose you are a secret agent who always gets instructions in this curious fashion. You might know that "the cat" is your contact and that "on the mat" means in the wrestling arena. Off you go.

But you don't have to be a spy for "The cat is on the mat" to take on a variety of meanings:

- Suppose your cat waits on a mat by the door when she wants to be let out. When you say to your roommate, "The cat is on the mat," you use those words to communicate, "Could you get up and let the cat out?"

- Suppose your friend is worried about pulling the car out of the driveway because she's uncertain where the cat is. When you say, "The cat is on the mat," you use those words to communicate, "It's safe to pull out of the driveway."
- Suppose you are trying to have a race between your cat and your friend's dog. When you say, "The cat is on the mat," you use those words to communicate, "My cat won't race!"

These examples illustrate the difference between *sentence meaning*—the generally simple meaning of the combined words of a sentence—and *speaker's meaning*—the unlimited number of meanings a speaker can communicate by putting a sentence to good use (Grice, 1968). When psychologists study language use, they want to comprehend both the *production* and the *understanding* of speaker's meaning:

In studying language use, researchers scrutinize both the production and understanding of speaker's meaning.

- How do speakers produce the right words to communicate the meaning they intend?
- How do listeners recover the messages the speakers wished to communicate?

We will examine each of these questions in turn.

Language Production

Look at **Figure 11.6**. Try to formulate a few sentences about this picture. What did you think to say? Suppose now we asked you to redescribe the scene for someone who was blind. How would your description change? Does this second description seem to require more mental effort? The study of **language production** concerns both what people say—what they choose to say at a given time—and the processes they go through to produce the message. Note that language users need not produce language out loud. Language production also includes both signing and writing. For convenience, however, we will call language producers *speakers* and language understanders *listeners*.

Figure 11.6 How Would You Describe This Scene to a Blind Person?

Audience Design

We asked you to imagine the different descriptions you'd give of Figure 11.6 to a sighted and a blind person as a way of getting you to think about **audience design** in language production. Each time you produce an utterance, you must have in mind the audience to whom the utterance will be directed (Clark, 1992). You know, for example, that it won't do you the least bit of good to say, "The cat is on the mat" if your listener does not know that the cat sits on the mat only when she wishes to be let out.

An overarching rule of audience design, the *cooperative principle,* was first proposed by the philosopher **H. Paul Grice** (1975). The cooperative principle is phrased as an instruction to the speaker:

> Make your conversational contribution such as is required, at the stage at which it occurs, by the accepted purpose or direction of the talk exchange in which you are engaged. (p. 45)

In other words, everything you say should be appropriate to the setting and meaning of the conversation. To clarify this principle, Grice defined four *maxims* that cooperative speakers live by. In **Table 11.2**, we present each of those maxims, as well as an invented conversation that illustrates the effect the maxims have on moment-by-moment choices in language production.

As you can see from Table 11.2, being a cooperative speaker depends, in large part, on having accurate expectations about what your listener is likely to know and understand. Thus you certainly wouldn't tell a friend, "I'm

Table 11.2 Grice's Maxims in Language Production

1. *Quantity:* Make your contribution as informative as is required (for the current purposes of the exchange). Do not make your contribution more informative than is required.

   The consequence for the speaker: You must try to judge how much information your audience really needs. Often this judgment will require you to assess what your listener is likely to know already.

2. *Quality:* Try to make your contribution one that is true. Do not say what you believe to be false. Do not say that for which you lack adequate evidence.

   The consequence for the speaker: When you speak, listeners will assume that you can back up your assertions with appropriate evidence. As you plan each utterance, you must have in mind the evidence on which it is based.

3. *Relation*: Be relevant.

   The consequence for the speaker: You must make sure that your listeners will see how what you are saying is relevant to what has come before. If you wish to shift the topic of conversation—so that your utterance is not directly relevant—you must make that clear.

4. *Manner:* Be perspicacious. Avoid obscurity of expression. Avoid ambiguity. Be brief. Be orderly.

   The consequence for the speaker: It is your responsibility to speak in as clear a manner as possible. Although you will inevitably make errors, as a cooperative speaker you must ensure that your listeners can understand your message.

In this conversation, can you see how Chris follows (or violates) Grice's maxims?

What Is Said	What Chris Might Be Thinking
Pat: *Have you ever been to New York City?*	
Chris: *I was there once in 1992.*	I don't know why Pat is asking me this question, so I probably should say a little more than just "yes."
Pat: *I'm supposed to visit, but I'm worried about being mugged.*	
Chris: *I think a lot of areas are safe.*	I can't say that he shouldn't worry, because he won't believe me. What can I say that will sound true but make him feel okay?
Pat: *How was your hotel?*	
Chris: *We didn't stay overnight.*	If I say, "We didn't stay in a hotel," that might suggest we stayed somewhere else. I need to say something relevant that will make clear why I can't answer the question.
Pat: *Would you like to go to New York with me?*	
Chris: *I'd have to find a way to see if it would be possible for me to leave without it being too impossible.*	I don't want to go, but I don't want to seem rude. Will Pat notice that I'm being evasive in my response?
Pat: *Huh?*	
Chris: *Well . . .*	Trapped.

having lunch with Alex" if you didn't have good reason to believe that your friend knew who Alex was. You also must assure yourself that, of all the Alex's your friend might know and that she knows that you know, only one would come to mind as the Alex you would mention in these circumstances. More formally, we can say that there must be some Alex who is prominent in the *common ground*—common knowledge—you share with your friend. **Herbert Clark** and Catherine Marshall (1981) suggested that judgments of common ground are based on three sources of evidence:

A cooperative speaker may judge common ground shared with a listener on the basis of community membership, linguistic copresence, and physical copresence.

- *Community membership*. Language producers often make strong assumptions about what is likely to be mutually known based on shared membership in communities of various sizes.
- *Linguistic copresence*. Language producers often assume that information contained in earlier parts of a conversation (or in past conversations) is part of the common ground.

- *Physical copresence*. Physical copresence exists when a speaker and a listener are directly in the physical presence of objects or situations. This includes both the setting of the conversation and all the people around the conservationalists.

Thus your use of *Alex* in "I'm having lunch with Alex" might succeed because your friend and you are part of a small community (e.g., roommates) that includes only one Alex (community membership). Or it might succeed because you've introduced the existence of Alex earlier in the conversation (linguistic copresence). Or Alex might be standing right there in the room (physical copresence).

Let's focus a bit more on community membership. Suppose you are meeting someone for the first time. If you want to be a cooperative conversationalist, one of the first things you must do is to determine the communities to which that individual belongs.

Among ichthyologists, this is a Choerodon fasciatus. *What would you call it if you were talking or writing about it to a friend?*

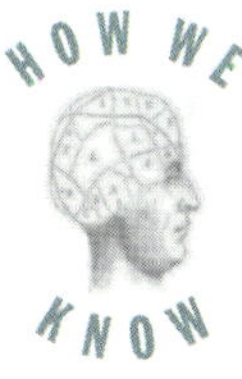

Researchers created circumstances in which unacquainted students were asked to perform a matching task. The *director* had an array of 16 New York postcards in front of her. She had to describe the sights pictured in the postcards so that the *matcher* could recreate the correct 4-by-4 ordering of the pictures. Although the director and the matcher couldn't see each other, they could converse freely. As a consequence, the directors were quickly able to determine whether their matchers were "experts" or "novices" about New York. When they discovered that they were talking to a fellow New Yorker, they were much more likely to use a proper name to pinpoint a postcard—"It's the Citicorp building"—than to give a roundabout description—"It's the tall building with a triangular top" (Isaacs & Clark, 1987).

Thus speakers adjusted their utterances based on their expectations about what the listener would be able to understand. On the whole, people are pretty accurate at guessing what members of their own communities are likely to know—although they tend to err in the direction of believing other people know the same things they do (Fussell & Krauss, 1992). The accurate guesses make possible appropriate adjustments in language production.

Our discussion so far has focused on language production at the level of the message: how you shape what you wish to say will depend on the audience to whom you are speaking. Let's turn now to a discussion of the mental processes that allow you to produce these messages.

Speech Execution and Speech Errors

Would you like to be famous for tripping over your tongue? Consider the Reverend W. A. Spooner of Oxford University, who lent his name to the *spoonerism:* an exchange of the initial sounds of two or more words in a phrase or sentence. Reverend Spooner came by this honor honestly. When, for example, he was tongue-lashing a lazy student for wasting the term, Reverend Spooner said, "You have tasted the whole worm!" A spoonerism is one of the limited types of speech errors that language producers make. These errors give researchers insight into the *planning* that goes on as speakers produce utterances. As you can see in **Table 11.3**, you need to plan an utterance at a number of different levels, and speech errors give evidence for each of those levels (Fromkin, 1971, 1973; Garrett, 1975). What should impress you about all these examples of errors is that they are not just random—they make sense given the structure of spoken English. Thus a speaker might exchange initial consonants—"tips of the slung" for "slips of the tongue"—but would never say, "tlips of the sung," which would violate the rule of English that "tl" does not occur as an initial sound (Fromkin, 1980).

Table 11.3 Errors in Planning Speech Production

Types of planning:

- Speakers must choose the content words that best fit their ideas.

  If the speaker has two words in mind, such as *grizzly* and *ghastly,* a **blend** like *grastly* might result.

- Speakers must put the chosen words in the right places in the utterance.

  Because speakers plan whole units of their utterances while they produce them, content words will sometimes become misplaced.

  a tank of gas → a gas of tank

  wine is being served at dinner → dinner is being served at wine

- Speakers must fill in the sounds that make up the words they wish to utter.

  Once again, because speakers plan ahead, sounds will sometimes get misplaced.

  left hemisphere → heft lemisphere

  pass out → pat ous

Speech errors also provide evidence for the order of steps in planning. Consider the transformation of "She's already pack*ed* two trunks" to "She's already trunk*ed* two packs." The grammatical morphemes *-ed* and *-s* stay put when the content words *pack* and *trunk* are exchanged. This suggests that speakers plan grammatical structures before they fill in the content words of their utterances (Clark & Clark, 1977).

Given the importance of speech errors to developing models of speech production, researchers have not always been content just to wait around for errors to happen naturally. **Bernard Baars** (1992) and other researchers have explored a number of ways to produce artificial errors. One technique called *SLIP* (for "spoonerisms of laboratory-induced predisposition") encourages subjects to produce spoonerisms.

Subjects are asked to read silently lists of word pairs that provide models for the phonetic structure of a target spoonerism:

ball doze

bash door

bean deck

bell dark

They then are required to pronounce out loud a word pair like *darn bore,* but under the influence of the earlier pairs it will sometimes come out *barn door.*

With this technique, researchers can study the factors that affect the likelihood that speakers will produce errors. For example, a spoonerism is more likely when the error will still result in real words (Baars et al., 1975; Stemberger, 1992). Thus an error on *darn bore* (to produce *barn door*) is more likely than an error on *dart board* (to produce *bart doard*). Findings like this one suggest that while you are producing utterances, some of your cognitive processes are devoted to detecting and *editing* potential errors. Those processes are reluctant to let you pronounce sounds like *doard,* which are not real English words.

Spoonerisms and other speech errors provide insights into the planning and editing a speaker must do in order to produce a correct phrase or sentence.

We have seen so far that errors provide evidence for planning and editing in speech execution. Speech errors also illustrate the existence of what we will call *opportunism* in speech production. Because utterances must unfold rapidly, speakers tend to produce whatever information is most available at each instance of production. In this light, you produce speech errors because sometimes the wrong element is more available than the right element (Dell, 1986). Thus, if you read through the SLIP list we gave a moment ago, you can see how a /b/ sound might be more available than a /d/ sound when it comes time for you to begin to produce *darn bore.* Researchers have also demonstrated opportunism at the level of meaning.

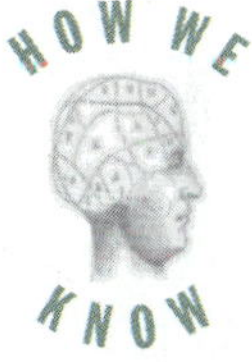

Kathryn Bock (1986) asked subjects to provide descriptions of simple scenes. For the scene shown in **Figure 11.7**, most people would be inclined to say, "The rock broke the window." What would change that ordinary response? Bock preceded each picture with a word that was related by meaning to one of the elements of the picture—in this case, *boulder* (related to *rock*) or *door* (related to *window*). When subjects read these semantic associations, they tended to produce a sentence with the related word first. Thus, if you read the word *door* and then described the picture, you would be likely to say, "The window was broken by the rock." *Door* makes *window* easily available, and you utter it first to get production under way.

Figure 11.7 What Has Happened Here? *Would you say, "The rock broke the window" or "The window was broken by the rock"? The utterance you produce would depend on the information most immediately available in memory.*

In almost all languages, the same thought can be expressed in many different ways, using a variety of grammatical structures. Bock's results suggest that speakers take advantage of this flexibility by starting with the easily accessible parts of their message and letting the rest of the utterance fall into place.

We have now looked at some of the forces that lead speakers to produce particular utterances and at some of the processes that allow them to do so. We turn next to the listeners, who are responsible for understanding what speakers intend to communicate.

Language Understanding

Suppose a speaker has produced the utterance "The cat is on the mat." You already know that, depending on the context, this utterance can be used to communicate any number of different meanings. How, as a listener, do you settle on just one meaning? We will begin this discussion of language understanding by considering more fully the problem of the *ambiguity* of meaning.

Resolving Ambiguity

What does the word *bank* mean? You can probably think of at least two meanings, one having to do with rivers and the other having to do with money. Suppose you hear the utterance "She walked near the bank." How do you know which meaning is intended? You need to be able to resolve the *lexical ambiguity* between the two meanings. (*Lexical* is related to *lexicon,* a synonym for *dictionary.*) If you think about this problem, you'll realize that you have some cognitive processes that allow you to use surrounding context to eliminate the ambiguity—to *disambiguate*—the word. Have you been talking about rivers or about money? That greater context should enable you to choose between the two meanings. But how?

Before we answer that question, we'd like to introduce another type of ambiguity. What does the sentence "The mother of the boy and the girl will arrive soon" mean? You may detect only one meaning right off, but there is a *structural ambiguity* here (Akmajian et al., 1990). Take a look at **Figure 11.8.** Linguists often represent the structure of sentences with tree diagrams, to show how the various words are gathered together into grammatical units.

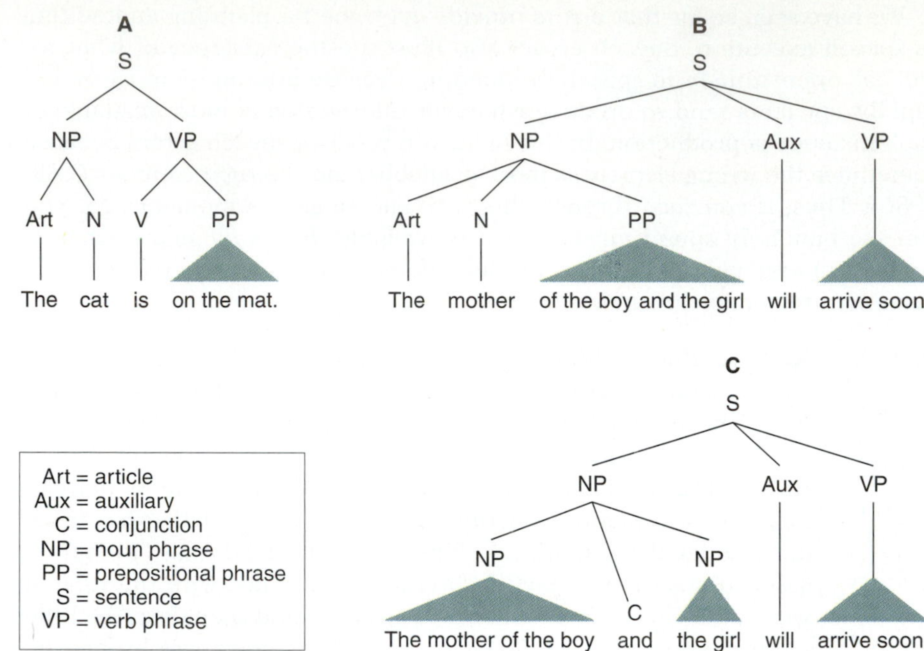

Figure 11.8 Sentence Structures
Linguists use tree diagrams to display the grammatical structure of sentences. Part A shows the structure of "The cat is on the mat." Parts B and C show that the sentence "The mother of the boy and the girl will arrive soon" can be represented by two different structural analyses. Who will arrive soon, one person (structure B) or two (structure C)?

In part A, we've shown you an analysis of "The cat is on the mat." The structure is pretty simple: a noun phrase made up of an article and a noun, plus a verb phrase made up of a verb and a prepositional phrase. In the lower two parts, you see the more complex structures for the two different meanings of "The mother...." In part B, the analysis shows that the whole phrase "of the boy and the girl" applies to the mother. One person—the mother of two children—will arrive soon. In part C, the analysis shows that there are two noun phrases, "the mother of the boy" and "the girl." There are two people, both of whom will arrive soon. Which understanding of the sentence did you come to when you first read it? Now that you can see that two meanings are possible, we arrive at the same question we did for lexical ambiguity: How does prior context enable you to settle on one meaning when more than one is possible?

Let's return to a lexical ambiguity (an ambiguity of word meaning). Consider the word *page.* When you read that word, it's much more likely that you'll think of *a page of a book* rather than *a page who serves a king.* If you imagine that you have a dictionary in your head, your entry for *page* might look something like this:

> Definition 1. An element of a book—used frequently
> Definition 2. Someone who serves in a court—not used very frequently

Such an entry would explain why definition 1 comes to mind when you first hear the word. From this example, we can develop two models of what might happen when you read a sentence that has the word *page.* We'll call the first model the *constant order* model. According to this model, no matter what context has preceded the use of a word, you always test out the meanings of the word in a constant order, from most likely to least likely. The second model we'll call the *reordering by context* model. According to this model, the context that precedes a word can change the order in which you test out multiple definitions.

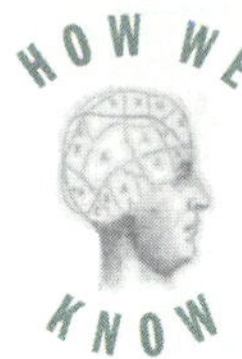

A team of researchers devised an experiment to contrast these two models. Subjects read one of two versions of sentences that contained ambiguous words. In one version, the ambiguous word was preceded by text that provided evidence in favor of an unlikely meaning:

> Having been examined by the king, the page was soon marched off to bed.

The other version provided no such evidence:

> Just as Henrietta had feared, the page was soon marched off to bed.

If the constant order model is correct, people who read these two sentences should treat the word *page* identically when they first arrive at it: they should use definition 1 until "was soon marched off to bed" definitely rules it out. If the reordering by context model is correct, readers should be able to use the first sentence's king to tip them off that they should give more attention to definition 2.

To get a precise measure of how long it took subjects to process each word, these experimenters recorded *eye movements*. Researchers use eye movements with the assumption that while subjects are carrying out complex tasks, the moving position of their eyes is an index to what they are thinking about (Just & Carpenter, 1981). In this experiment, the pattern of eye movements supported the reordering by context model. Readers spent less time with their eyes on the disambiguating phrase "was soon marched off to bed" when *page* had been preceded by *the king,* suggesting that *the king* was enough to change the order in which subjects examined the definitions of *page* (Dopkins et al., 1992).

Now that you're looking at a picture of a knight with his attendant, what comes to mind when you think of the word page?

The conclusion we can draw from this experiment is that context actively affects listeners' expectations about what utterances will mean. The same principle applies to structural ambiguities (Shapiro et al., 1993; Speer & Kjelgaard, 1992). Contextual information speeds decisions when you must choose among different possible grammatical structures.

Let us now return to the example with which we began, the considerably ambiguous "The cat is on the mat." In that case, the ambiguity is not in the words or the structure but in the very message itself. Surprisingly, researchers find that the rule of reordering by context applies at this level as well (Gibbs, 1994).

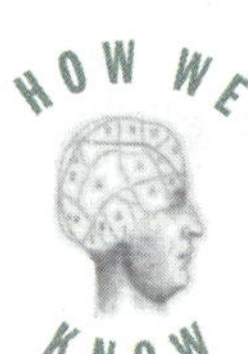

Consider the utterance "Sure is nice and warm in here." What does that mean? As shown in **Table 11.4**, it is possible to write pairs of stories that give very different meanings to simple utterances of this sort. As you can see, the literal version sticks closely to the literal meanings of the words. The nonliteral version uses the same utterance to make a sarcastic request. Let's apply the models we introduced for lexical ambiguity. If readers process along the lines of the constant order model, you might expect that they would always try the literal meaning of an utterance first. Only if the literal meaning failed to fit in the context would readers consider another meaning (Grice, 1975, 1978; Searle, 1979a). If that were true, we would expect that it would take readers more

Table 11.4 Literal and Sarcastic Interpretations of Ambiguous Utterances

Literal statement:	Sarcastic request:
Martha went over to her sister's house. It was freezing outside and Martha was glad to be inside. She said to her sister, "Your house is very cozy. Sure is nice and warm in here."	Tony's roommate always kept the windows open in the living room. He did this even if it was freezing out. Tony kept mentioning this to his roommate but to no avail. Once it was open and Tony wanted his roommate to shut it. Tony couldn't believe that his roommate wasn't cold. He said to him, "Sure is nice and warm in here."

time to understand an utterance that is a request—and a sarcastic one, at that—as compared with just a literal statement. By contrast, suppose the reordering by context model is true for whole utterances in the way that it's true for words and structures. Then you'd expect it to be easier to understand the sarcastic request than the literal statement. Indeed, research shows that readers understand the sarcastic requests even *more quickly* than they understand the literal uses of the same utterances (Gibbs, 1986).

Researchers conclude that context is a powerful and efficient tool that people use to resolve language ambiguities.

The overall conclusion you can draw is that your language processes use context powerfully and efficiently to resolve ambiguities. In a way, this shows that there is a good match between production and understanding. When we discussed language production, we emphasized audience design—the processes by which speakers try to make their utterances appropriate in the current context. Our analysis of understanding suggests that listeners expect speakers to have done their jobs well. Under those circumstances, it makes sense for listeners to let context reorder their expectations about what speakers will have meant.

The Products of Understanding

Our discussion of ambiguity resolution focused on the *processes* of understanding. In this section, we shift our attention to the *products* of understanding. The question now is, What *representations* result in memory when listeners understand utterances or texts? (As you recall from Chapter 10, a representation is the form information takes in memory storage.) What, for example, would be stored in memory when you hear our old standby "The cat is on the mat"? Research has suggested that meaning representation begins with basic units called *propositions* (Clark & Clark, 1977; Kintsch, 1974). Propositions are the main ideas of utterances. For "The cat is on the mat," the main idea is that something is on something else. When you read the utterance, you will extract the proposition *on* and understand the relationship that it expresses between *the cat* and *the mat.* Often propositions are written like this: *ON (cat, mat)*. Many utterances contain more than one proposition. Consider "The cat watched the mouse run under the sofa." We have as the first component propositions *UNDER (mouse, sofa).* From that we build up *RUN (mouse, UNDER (mouse, sofa)).* Finally, we get to *WATCH (cat, RUN (mouse, UNDER (mouse, sofa))).*

How can we test whether your mental representations of meaning really work this way? Some of the earliest experiments in the psychology of language were devoted to showing the importance of propositional representations in understanding (Kintsch, 1974). Research has shown that if two words in an utterance belong to the same proposition, they will be represented together in memory even if they are not close together in the actual sentence.

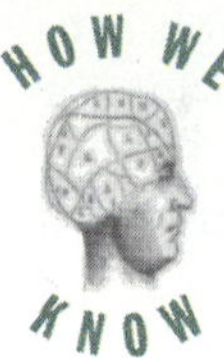

Consider the sentence "The mausoleum that enshrined the tzar overlooked the square." Although *mausoleum* and *square* are far apart in the sentence, a propositional analysis suggests that they should be gathered together in memory in the proposition *OVERLOOKED (mausoleum, square)*. To test this analysis, researchers asked subjects to read lists of words and say whether each had appeared in the sentence. Some subjects saw *mausoleum* directly after *square* on the list. Others subjects saw *mausoleum* after a word from another proposition. The response "Yes, I saw mausoleum" was swifter when *mausoleum* came directly after *square* than when its predecessor came from another proposition. This finding suggests that the concepts *mausoleum* and *square* had been represented together in memory (Ratcliff & McKoon, 1978).

Two words that belong to the same proposition will be represented together in memory even if they are not close together in the actual sentence.

Not all the propositions listeners store in memory are made up of information directly stated by the speaker. Often listeners fill gaps with **inferences**—logical assumptions made possible by information in memory. Consider this pair of utterances:

I'm heading to the deli to meet Donna.
She promised to buy me a sandwich for lunch.

To understand how these sentences go together, you must draw at least two important inferences. You must figure out both who *she* is in the second sentence and how going to a deli is related to a promise to buy a sandwich. Note that a friend who actually uttered this pair of sentences would be confident you could figure these things out. You'd never expect to hear this:

I'm heading to the deli to meet Donna.
She—and by *she* I mean Donna—promised to buy me a sandwich—and a *deli* is a place where you can buy a sandwich—for lunch.

Speakers count on listeners to draw inferences of this sort.

A great deal of research has been directed toward determining what types of inferences listeners draw on a regular basis (Graesser et al., 1994; McKoon & Ratcliff, 1992). The number of potential inferences after any utterance is unlimited. For example, because you know that Donna is likely to be a human, you could infer that she has a heart, a liver, a pair of lungs, and so on (and on), but it's unlikely that you would feel compelled to call any of those (perfectly valid) inferences to mind when you heard "I'm heading to the deli to meet Donna." Research suggests, in fact, that listeners are reasonably conservative in the inferences they draw. Consider this sentence:

The architect stabbed the man.

When explicitly asked to name what instrument this sentence made them think of, subjects most often said *knife.* However, researchers found no evidence that subjects, in natural circumstances of reading, called the concept *knife* to mind, or other instruments in similar sentences (Dosher & Corbett, 1982). This finding suggests that you do not automatically draw even some inferences that are pretty safe bets—for instance, that someone who was stabbed was stabbed with a knife. Most of the inferences you habitually draw are like the ones we illustrated before—inferences that capture the relationship between *Donna* and *she* and between *deli* and *sandwich.* These inferences help you form a *coherent* representation of the information the speaker wishes you to understand; they do not *elaborate* on it.

YOU SAID WE WERE GOING TO DIG A HOLE.
YOU NEVER SAID ANYTHING ABOUT USING A SHOVEL.

You can't always count on people to draw the right inferences.

Our discussion of language use has demonstrated how much work a speaker does to produce the right sentence at the right time and how much work a listener does to figure out exactly what the speaker meant. You usually aren't aware of all this work! Does this give you a greater appreciation for the elegant design of your cognitive processes?

Let's turn now from circumstances in which meaning is communicated through words to those in which meaning relies also on pictures.

VISUAL COGNITION

In **Figure 11.9**, we give you two choices for visual representations of the sentence "The cat is on the mat." Which one seems right? If you think in terms of language-based propositions, each alternative captures the right meaning—the cat *is* on the mat. Even so, you're probably happy only with option A, because it matches the scene you likely called to mind when you first read the sentence (Searle, 1979b). How about option B? It probably makes you somewhat nervous because it seems as if the cat is going to tip right over. This anxious feeling must arise because you can think with pictures. In a sense, you can *see* exactly what's going to happen. In this section, we will explore some of the ways in which visual images and visual processes contribute to the way you think.

A

B

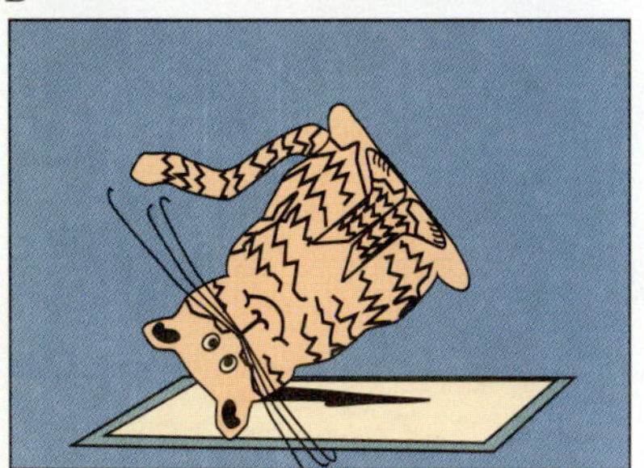

Figure 11.9 Are Both of These Cats on the Mat?

VISUAL REPRESENTATIONS

Let's begin our discussion with the issue of mental representations. Research on language processing suggests that important categories of mental representations are language based. But what other types of representations might you have? Because, as we explained earlier, science is guided by the rule of parsimony, some researchers resisted the idea that mental representations take more than one form (Pylyshyn, 1981). The burden correctly rested on the shoulders of those who wished to champion a belief in two (or more) types of representations to provide definitive proof. A variety of evidence now supports the existence of multiple forms of representation. Let's see how.

To begin, consider a fact of your mental life: you find concrete words (like *table*) easier to remember than abstract words (like *justice*). Why should that be so? As part of his *dual-coding theory,* **Allan Paivio** (1986) proposed that concrete words are mentally represented in two different codes—verbal and imaginal. Abstract words are coded only verbally. The advantage concrete words have over abstract words is explained by the extra code, which leads to more elaborate representations. Paivio's theory, thus, makes a strong claim for two types of representation.

Allan Paivio suggests that concrete words are mentally represented by both verbal and imaginal codes, a concept referred to as dual-coding theory.

Researchers used an event-related potential (ERP) technique to find evidence in brain activity for Paivio's two codes. While measurements were being taken from scalp electrodes, subjects judged words presented on a computer monitor as *abstract* or *concrete.* As in past experiments, subjects were faster to respond to concrete words. Furthermore, distinct patterns of brain activity were found for each type of word. The difference was particularly pronounced over the right hemisphere—exactly what you would expect if the concrete words, but not the abstract words, involved imaginal processing (Kounios & Holcomb, 1994; see Chapter 3 for a discussion of hemispheric differences).

These results provide strong evidence that this classic performance difference—the advantage of concrete words over abstract—has its roots in representations in the brain.

Other ERP research has revealed that when people generate visual imagery, they use the same brain structures as when they are involved in an act of visual perception (Farah, 1988; Ishai & Sagi, 1995; Miyashita, 1995). For example, when people are asked to imagine a cat, there is disproportionate activity in the same brain areas that would become active if they were actually looking at a cat. The implication is that, with respect to neurological processes, pictures in the head—images—are just like pictures outside the head. This equivalence argues in favor of visual representations. Let's see now how you put those representations to use.

Using Visual Representations

History is full of examples of famous discoveries apparently made on the basis of mental imagery (Shepard, 1978). For example, F. A. Kekulé, the discoverer of the chemical structure of benzene, often conjured up mental images of dancing atoms that fastened themselves into chains of molecules. His discovery of the benzene ring occurred in a dream in which a snakelike molecule chain suddenly grabbed its own tail, thus forming a ring. Michael Faraday, who discovered many properties of magnetism, knew little about mathematics but he had vivid mental images of the properties of magnetic fields. Albert Einstein claimed to have thought entirely in terms of visual images, translating his findings into mathematical symbols and words only after the work of visually based discovery was finished.

We have given you these examples to encourage you to try to indulge in visual thinking. But even without trying, you regularly use your capabilities for manipulating visual images. Consider an experiment in which subjects were asked to transform images in their heads.

Researchers presented students with examples of the letter R and its mirror image that had been rotated various amounts, from 0 to 180 degrees (see **Figure 11.10**). As the letter appeared, the student had to identify it as either the normal R or its mirror image. The reaction time taken to make that decision was longer in direct proportion to the amount the figure had been rotated. This finding indicated that a subject was imagining the figure in his or her "mind's eye" and rotating the image into an upright position at some fixed rate before deciding whether the figure was an R or a mirror image. The consistency of the rate of rotation suggested that the process of mental rotation was very similar to the process of physical rotation (Shepard & Cooper, 1982).

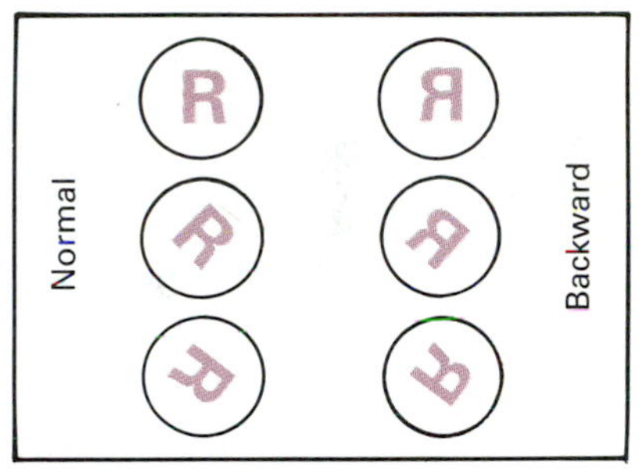

Figure 11.10 Rotated R Used to Assess Mental Imagery

Subjects presented with these figures in random order were asked to say, as quickly as possible, whether each figure was a normal R or a mirror image. The more the figure was rotated from upright, the longer the reaction time was.

You put this ability for mental rotation to very good use. As you learned in Chapter 8, you often see objects in the environment from unfamiliar points of view. Mental rotation enables you to transform the image to one that matches representations stored in memory (Tarr, 1994; Tarr & Pinker, 1989). For example, in Figure 11.9, you almost certainly had to rotate the image (or did you just tilt your head?) to recognize the object as a cat, on a mat.

Mental rotation of objects in the environment allows you to form images that match the representations stored in your memory.

You can also use visual images to answer certain types of questions about the world. Suppose, for example, we asked you whether a golf ball is bigger than a Ping-Pong ball. If you can't retrieve that fact directly from memory, you might find it convenient to form a visual image of them side by side. This use of an image, once again, has much in common with the properties of real visual perception.

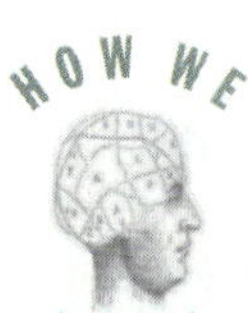

In one study, subjects first memorized pictures of complex objects, such as a motorboat (see **Figure 11.11**). Then they were asked to recall their visual images of the boat and focus on one spot—for example, the motor. When asked if the picture contained another object—a windshield or an anchor, for example (both were present)—they took longer to "see" the anchor than the windshield, which was closer to the motor than the anchor was. The reaction time difference provides evidence that people scan visual images as if they were scanning real objects (Kosslyn, 1980).

Figure 11.11 Visual Scanning of Mental Images
After studying a picture of a boat, subjects were asked to "look at" the motor in their own mental images. They were then asked whether the boat had a windshield or an anchor. The faster response to the windshield, which was closer to the motor than was the anchor, indicated that the subjects were scanning their visual images.

There are, of course, limits to the use of your visual imagination. Consider this problem:

> Imagine that you have a large piece of blank paper. In your mind, fold it in half (making two layers), fold it in half again (four layers), and continue folding it over 50 times. About how thick is the paper when you are done? (Adam, 1986)

The actual answer is about 50 million miles ($2^{50} \times 0.028$ inches, the thickness of a piece of paper), approximately half the distance between the earth and the sun. Your estimate was probably considerably lower. Your mind's eye was overwhelmed by the information you asked it to represent.

Combining Verbal and Visual Representations

Our discussion so far has largely focused on the types of visual representations that you form by committing to memory—or in the case of imagery, retrieving from memory—visual stimuli from the environment. However, you often form visual images based on verbal descriptions. You can, for example, create a mental picture of a cat with three tails, although you've almost certainly never seen one. The verbal description enables you to form a visual representation. Your ability to produce a mental image of a verbal scene is particularly useful when you read works of fiction that involve spatial details. Consider this passage from the James Bond short story "From a View to a Kill":

> The clearing was about as big as two tennis courts and floored in thick grass and moss. There was one large patch of lilies of the valley and, under the bordering trees, a scattering of bluebells. To one side there was a low mound . . . completely surrounded and covered with brambles and brier roses now thickly in bloom. Bond walked round this and gazed in among the roots, but there was nothing to see except the earthy shape of the mound. (Fleming, 1959, pp. 19–20)

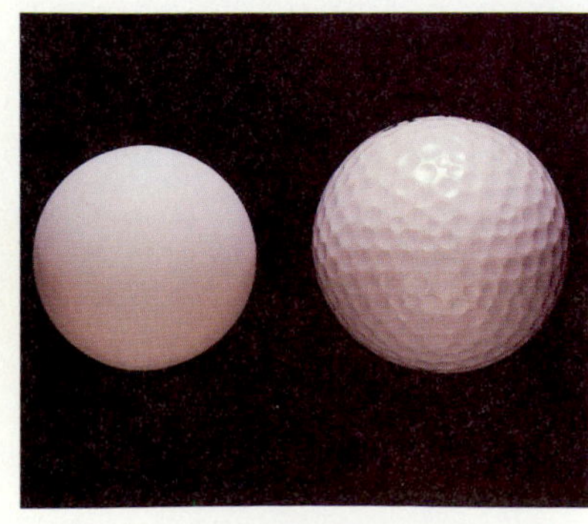

Were you able to use a mental image to know which ball is larger?

Did you try to imagine the scene—and help Bond search for danger? (He will find it.) When you read, you will often form a *spatial mental model* to keep track of the whereabouts of characters (Johnson-Laird, 1983). Researchers have often focused on the ways in which spatial mental models capture properties of real spatial experiences.

Suppose, for example, you read a passage of a text that places you in the middle of an interesting environment.

> You are hob-nobbing at the opera. You came tonight to meet and chat with interesting members of the upper class. At the moment, you are standing next to the railing of a wide, elegant balcony overlooking the first floor. Directly behind you, at your eye level, is an ornate lamp attached to the balcony wall. The base of the lamp, which is attached to the wall, is gilded in gold. (Franklin & Tversky, 1990, p. 65)

Figure 11.12 Spatial Mental Models
You can use imagination to project yourself into the middle of a scene. Just as if you were really standing in the room, you would take less time to say what is in front of you (the lamp) then what is behind you (the bust).

In a series of experiments, readers studied descriptions of this sort that vividly described the layout of objects around the viewer (Franklin & Tversky, 1990). The researchers wished to show that readers were faster or slower to access information about the scene depending on where the objects were in the mental space around them. Readers, for example, were quicker to say what object was in front of them in the scene than what object was behind them, even though all objects were introduced equally carefully in the stories (see **Figure 11.12**). It's easiest to understand this result if you believe that the representation you form while reading actually places you, in some sense, in the scene. You are able to transform a verbal experience into a visual, spatial experience.

In general, when you think about the world around you, you are almost always combining visual and verbal representations of information. To prove that to yourself, you can take a minute to draw a map of the world. Go ahead—make a sketch! How do you go about doing this? Some of the things you draw in are probably based on visual experiences—you know the overall shape of Africa only because you have seen it represented in the past. Other features of your drawing will probably rely on verbal information—you are likely to remember that Japan is made up of several islands, even if you don't have a visual representation of quite where they go. In one study, nearly 4000 students from 71 cities in 49 countries were asked to carry out the task of drawing a world map (Saarinen, 1987). The goal of the study was to broaden understanding of cultural differences in the way the world is visualized and to promote world peace. The study found that the majority of maps had a Eurocentric worldview. Europe was placed in the center of the map and the other countries were arranged around it, probably due to the dominance for many centuries of Eurocentric representations in geography books. However, the study also yielded many instances of culture-biased maps, such as the one by a Chicago student, in **Figure 11.13** and that of an Australian student, in **Figure 11.14**. These maps show what happens when a verbal perspective—My home should be in the middle!—is imposed on a visual representation.

In this section we have seen that you have visual processes and representations to complement your verbal abilities. These two types of access to information give you extra help in dealing with the demands and tasks of your life. We turn now to domains in which you put both visual and verbal representations to use in coping with your life's complexities: *problem solving* and *reasoning*.

PROBLEM SOLVING AND REASONING

Let's return to your mysterious message, "The cat is on the mat." In the section on language, we illustrated how appropriate background knowledge could allow you to understand this message. But suppose now that you are

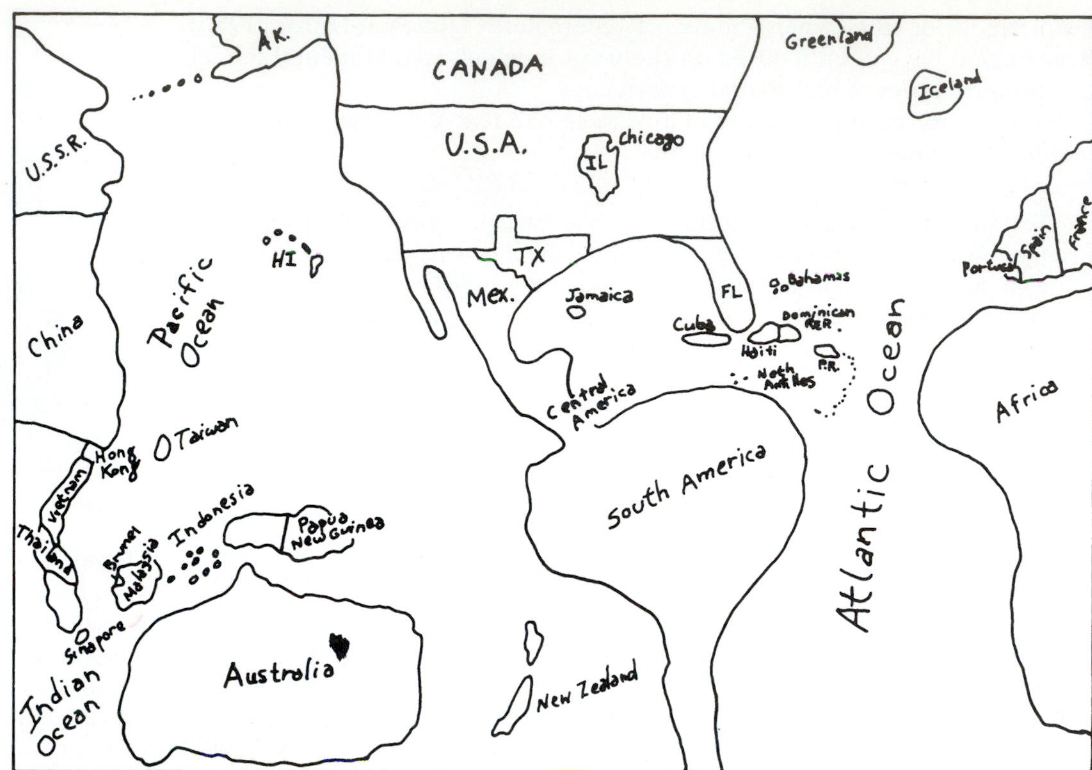

Figure 11.13
How does this Chicagocentric view of the world compare with yours?

not, in fact, in possession of such knowledge—but you are still interested in trying to decode the message. Reflect for a moment on the types of mental steps you might take to puzzle out the consequences of the message. Those mental steps will almost certainly include the cognitive processes that make up **problem solving** and **reasoning.** Both of these activities require you to combine current information with information stored in memory to work toward some particular goal: a conclusion or a solution. We will look at aspects of problem solving and at two types of reasoning, deductive and inductive.

Problem Solving

How do architects solve the ill-defined problem of designing a house?

What goes on four legs in the morning, on two legs at noon, and on three legs in the twilight? According to Greek mythology, this was the riddle posed by the Sphinx, an evil creature who threatened to hold the people of Thebes in tyranny until someone could solve the riddle. To break the code, Oedipus had to recognize elements of the riddle as metaphors. Morning, noon, and twilight represented different periods in a human life. A baby crawls and so (effectively) has four legs, an adult walks on two legs, and an older person walks on two legs but uses a cane, making a total of three legs. Oedipus's solution to the riddle was *humans.*

While your daily problems may not seem as monumental as the one faced by young Oedipus, problem-solving activity is a basic part of your everyday existence. You continually come up against problems that require solutions: how to manage work and tasks within a limited time frame, how to succeed at a job interview, how to break off a relationship, and so on. Many problems involve discrepancies between what you know and what you need to know. When you solve a problem, you reduce that discrepancy by finding a way to get the missing information. To get into the spirit of problem solving yourself, try the problems in **Figure 11.15** on the next page (the answers are on page 412, but don't look until you try to solve them all). Let's see how psychological research can shed light on your performance.

Problem Spaces

How do you define a problem in real-life circumstances? You usually perceive the difference between your current state and a desired goal: for example, you are broke and you'd like to have some money. You are also usually aware of some of the steps you would be able (or willing) to take to bridge the gap: you will try to get a part-time job, but you won't become a pickpocket. The formal definition of a *problem* captures these three elements (Newell & Simon, 1972). A problem is defined by (1) an *initial state*—the incomplete information or unsatisfactory conditions you start with; (2) a *goal state*—the information or state of the world you hope to obtain; and (3) a *set of operations*—the steps you may take to move from an initial state to a goal state. Together, these three parts define the **problem space.** You can think of solving a problem as walking through a maze (the problem space) from where you are (the initial state) to where you want to be (the goal state), making a series of turns (the allowable operations).

A problem space consists of an initial state, a goal state, and a set of operations to move from the former to the latter.

Much of the initial difficulty in solving a problem will arise if any of these elements are not well-defined (Simon, 1973). A *well-defined problem* is similar to a textbook problem in which the initial state, the goal state, and the operations are all clearly specified. Your task is to discover how to use allowable, known operations to get the answer. By contrast, an *ill-defined problem* is similar to designing a home, writing a novel, or finding a cure for AIDS. The initial state, the goal state, and/or the operations may be unclear and vaguely specified. In such cases, the problem solver's first task is to work out, as much as possible, exactly what the problem is—to make explicit a beginning, an ideal solution, and the possible means to achieve it.

As you know from your own experience, even when the initial and goal

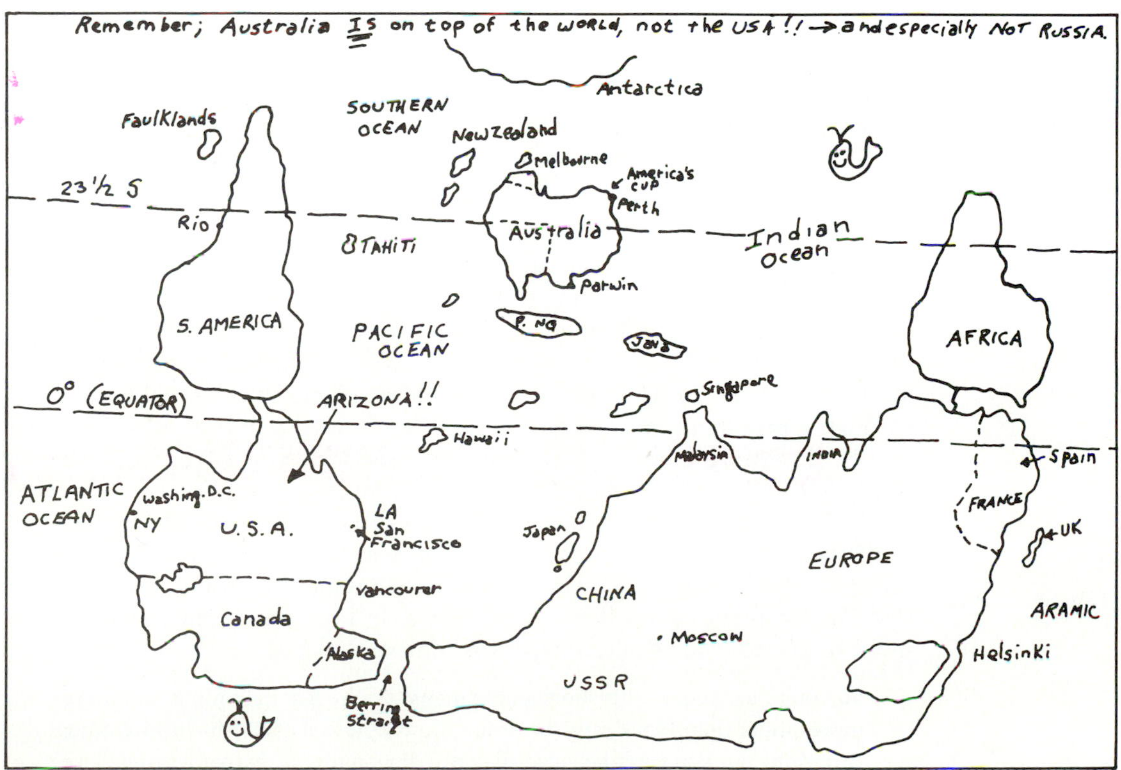

Figure 11.14

Look at this Australiocentric view of the world. Now who's down under?

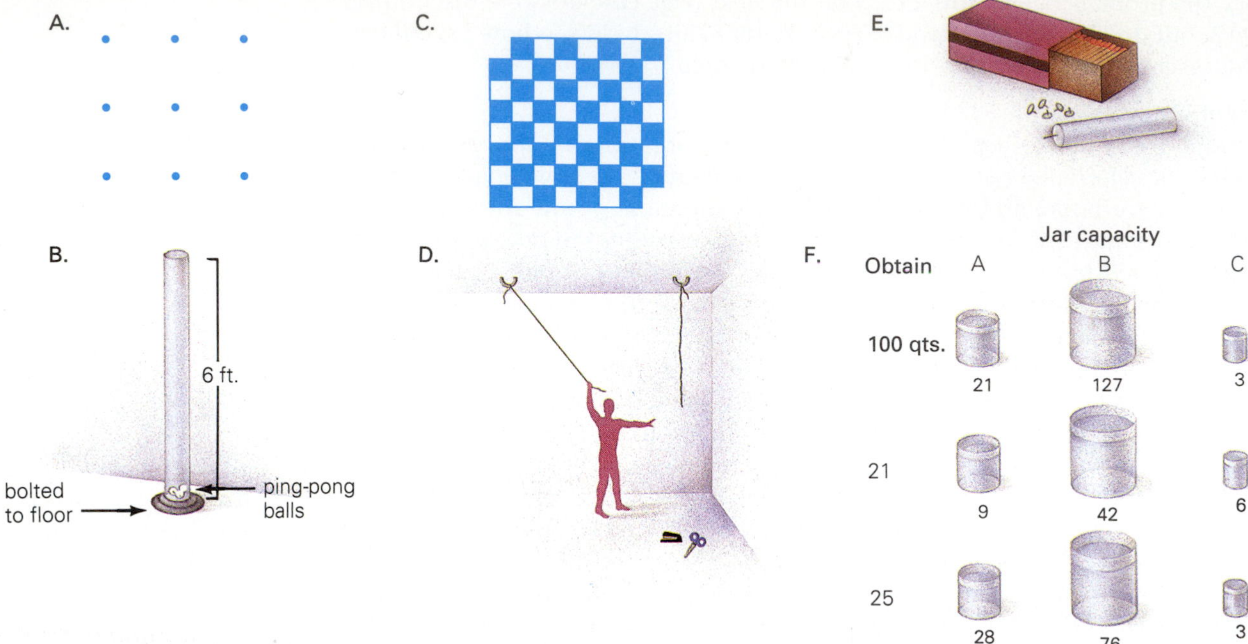

Figure 11.15 Can You Solve It?

(A) Can you connect all the dots in the pattern by drawing four straight, connected lines without lifting your pen from the paper?
(B) A prankster has put 3 Ping-Pong balls into a 6-foot-long pipe that is standing vertically in the corner of the physics lab, fastened to the floor. How would you get the Ping-Pong balls out?
(C) The checkerboard shown has had 2 corner pieces cut out, leaving 62 squares. You have 31 dominoes, each of which covers exactly 2 checkerboard squares. Can you use them to cover the whole checkerboard?
(D) You are in the situation depicted and given the task of tying the 2 strings together. If you hold one string, the other is out of reach. Can you do it?
(E) You are given the objects shown (a candle, tacks, matches in a matchbox). The task is to mount a lighted candle on the door. Can you do it?
(F) You are given 3 "water-jar" problems. Using only the 3 containers (water supply is unlimited), can you obtain the exact amount specified in each case?

states are well-defined, it can still be difficult to find the right set of operations to get from the beginning to the end. If you think back to your experience in math classes, you know that this is true. Your teacher gave you a formula like $x^2 + x - 12 = 0$ and asked you to solve for possible values of x. What do you do next? To study the steps problem solvers take to make their way through a problem space, researchers have often turned to **think-aloud protocols.** In this procedure, subjects are asked to verbalize their ongoing thoughts (Ericsson & Simon, 1993). For example, a pair of researchers were interested in capturing the mental processes that enable subjects to solve the *mutilated checkerboard problem* that is part C of Figure 11.15 (Kaplan & Simon, 1990). Here is one of their subjects having the crucial breakthrough that the problem cannot be solved with only horizontal and vertical placement of pieces (the checkerboard was pink and black):

> So you're leaving. . . . it's short—how many, you're leaving uhhhh. . . . there's more pinks than black, and in order to complete it you'd have to connect two pinks but you can't because they are diagonally . . . is that getting close? (Kaplan & Simon, 1990, p. 388)

The solver has just realized that the goal cannot be accomplished if the dominoes can just be placed horizontally or vertically. Researchers have often used subjects' own accounts of their thinking as the starting point for more formal models of problem solving (Simon, 1979, 1989).

Improving Your Problem Solving

What makes problem solving hard? If you reflect on your day-to-day experience, you might come up with the answer "There are too many things to consider all at once." Research on problem solving has led to much the same conclusion. What often makes a problem difficult to solve is that the mental requirements for solving a particular problem overwhelm processing resources (Kotovsky et al., 1985; Kotovsky & Simon, 1990). To solve a problem, you need to plan the series of operations you will take. If that series becomes too complex, or if each operation itself is too complex, you may be unable to see your way through from the initial state to the goal state. How might you overcome this potential limitation?

An important step in improving problem solving is to find a way to represent a problem so that each operation is possible, given your processing resources. If you must habitually solve similar problems, a useful procedure is to practice each of the components of the solution so that, over time, those components require fewer resources (Kotovsky et al., 1985). Suppose, for example, you were a cab driver in New York City and were faced with daily traffic jams. You might mentally practice your responses to jams at various points in the city, so that you'd have ready solutions to components of the overall problem of getting your fare from a pickup spot to a destination. By practicing these component solutions, you could keep more of your attention on the road!

Research supports the conclusion of day-to-day experience: the difficulty in problem solving is having to consider many things at once.

Sometimes, finding a useful representation means finding a whole new way to think about the problem. Read the puzzle given in **Table 11.5**. How would you go about offering this proof? Think about it for a few minutes before you read on. How well did you do? If the word *proof* suggested to you something mathematical, you probably didn't make much progress. A better way to think about the problem is to imagine two monks, one starting at the top and another starting at the bottom (Adams, 1986). As one climbs and one descends, it's clear that they will pass at some point along the mountain, right? Now replace the pair of monks with just the one—conceptually it's the same—and there's your proof. What makes this problem suddenly very easy is using the right sort of representation: visual rather than verbal or mathematical.

If you go back to the problems in Figure 11.15, you have several more examples of the importance of an appropriate representation of the problem space. To connect the nine dots, you had to realize that nothing in the instructions limited you to the area of the dots themselves. To get the Ping-Pong balls out of the pipe, you had to realize that the solution did not involve reaching into the pipe. To connect the two strings, you had to see one of the tools on the floor as a weight. To mount the candle on the door, you had to alter your usual perspective and perceive the matchbox as a platform instead

Table 11.5 The Monk Puzzle

One morning, exactly at sunrise, a Buddhist monk began to climb a tall mountain. A narrow path, no more than a foot or two wide, spiraled around the mountain to a glittering temple at the summit. The monk ascended at varying rates of speed, stopping many times along the way to rest and eat dried fruit he carried with him. He reached the temple shortly before sunset. After several days of fasting and meditation he began his journey back along the same path, starting at sunrise and again walking at variable speeds with many pauses along the way. His average speed descending was, of course, greater than his average climbing speed. Prove that there is *a spot* along the path that the monk will occupy on both trips at precisely the same time of day.

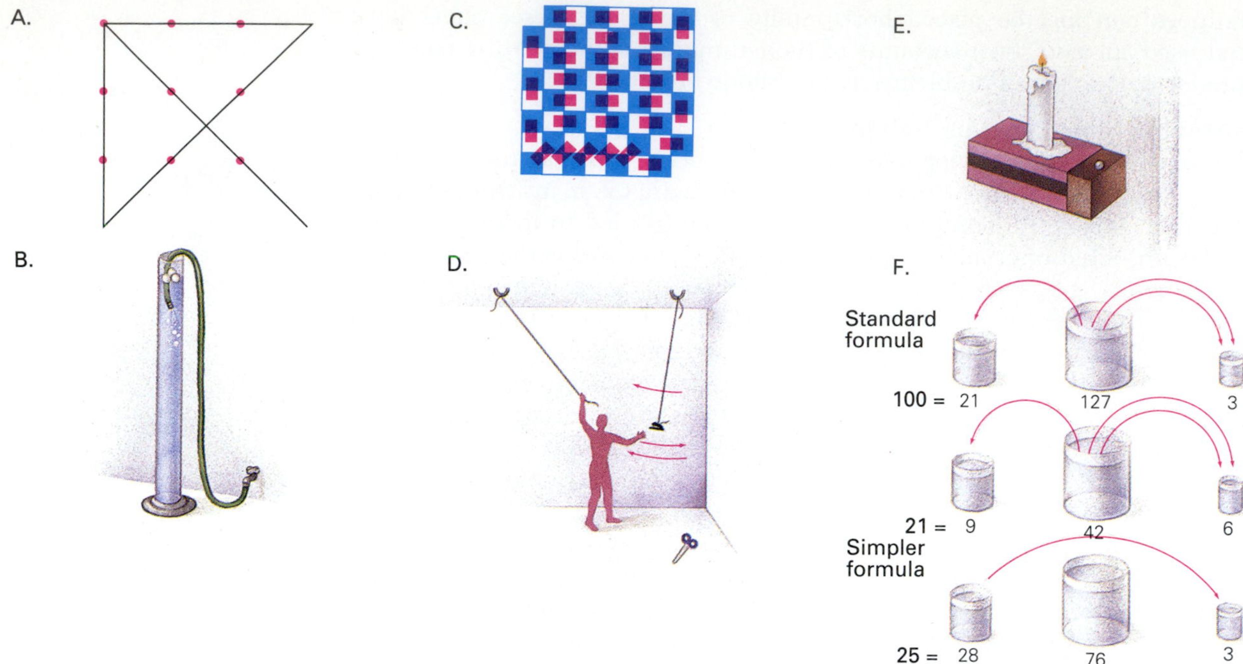

Figure 11.16 **Solutions to the Problems**

of as a container, and you had to perceive the candle as a tool as well as the object to be mounted on the door. The last two problems show a phenomenon called functional fixedness (Duncker, 1945; Maier, 1931). **Functional fixedness** is a mental block that adversely affects problem solving by inhibiting the perception of a new function for an object that was previously associated with some other purpose. Whenever you are stuck on a problem, you should ask yourself, "How am I representing the problem? Are there different or better ways that I can think about the problem or components of its solution?" If words don't work, try drawing a picture. Or try examining your assumptions, and see what "rules" you can break by making novel combinations.

Often, when you try to solve problems, you engage in special forms of thinking that are called *reasoning.* Let's turn now to a first type of reasoning you use to solve problems, *deductive reasoning.*

Deductive Reasoning

Suppose you are on your way to a restaurant and you want to pay for your meal with your only credit card, American Express. You call the restaurant and ask, "Do you accept American Express?" The restaurant's hostess replies, "We accept all major credit cards." You can now safely conclude that they accept American Express. To see why, we can reformulate your interchange to fit the structure of the *syllogism,* defined by the Greek philosopher Aristotle over 2000 years ago:

Premise 1: The restaurant accepts all major credit cards.

Premise 2: American Express is a major credit card.

Conclusion: The restaurant accepts American Express.

Aristotle was concerned with defining the logical relationships between statements that would lead to *valid* conclusions. **Deductive reasoning** involves the correct application of such logical rules. We gave the credit card example to show that you are quite capable of drawing conclusions that have the form of logical, deductive proofs. Even so, psychological research has focused on the question of whether you actually have the formal rules of deductive reasoning represented in your mind (Holyoak & Spellman, 1993;

Johnson-Laird & Byrne, 1991; Rips, 1990). This body of research suggests that you may have some general, abstract sense of formal logic, but your real-world deductive reasoning is affected both by the specific knowledge you possess about the world and the representational resources you can bring to bear on a reasoning problem. Let's expand on these conclusions.

How does knowledge wield an influence on deductive reasoning? Consider this syllogism:

Premise 1: All things that have a motor need oil.

Premise 2: Automobiles need oil.

Conclusion: Automobiles have motors.

Faulty deductive reasoning.

Is this a valid conclusion? According to the rules of logic, it is *not,* because Premise 1 leaves open the possibility that some things that don't have motors will also need oil. The difficulty for you is that what is invalid in a logic problem is not necessarily untrue in real life. That is, if you take Premises 1 and 2 to be all the information in your possession—as you should if you accept this simply as an exercise in formal logic—the conclusion is not valid. Even so, when subjects judge whether the conclusion "follows logically from the premises," they are much more inclined to say yes when the conclusion considers *automobiles* than they are when the nonsense term *oppobines* is substituted (Markovitz & Nantel, 1989). This result illustrates a general **belief-bias effect**—people tend to judge as valid those conclusions with which they agree and as invalid those with which they don't (Evans et al., 1983; Janis & Frick, 1943). In this case, knowledge about automobiles makes it hard to reject the conclusion as invalid. However, when subjects were given just the two premises and asked to generate their own conclusions, about half were able to correctly state that no valid conclusion could be reached (i.e., based on the two premises, you can't determine whether automobiles have motors). Thus, the belief bias may have a smaller effect on your actual reasoning processes than on your ability to judge someone else's conclusions (Rips, 1990).

According to the belief-bias effect, people tend to judge conclusions they agree with as valid and conclusions they disagree with as invalid.

Experience also improves your reasoning ability. You can see this to be true if you compare performance on an abstract reasoning task with that on a version of the same task that allows you to apply real-world knowledge. Imagine that you are given the array of four cards pictured in **Figure 11.17**, which have printed on them *A, D, 4,* and *7.* Your task is to determine which cards you must turn over to test the rule "If a card has a vowel on one side, then it has an even number on the other side" (Johnson-Laird & Wason,

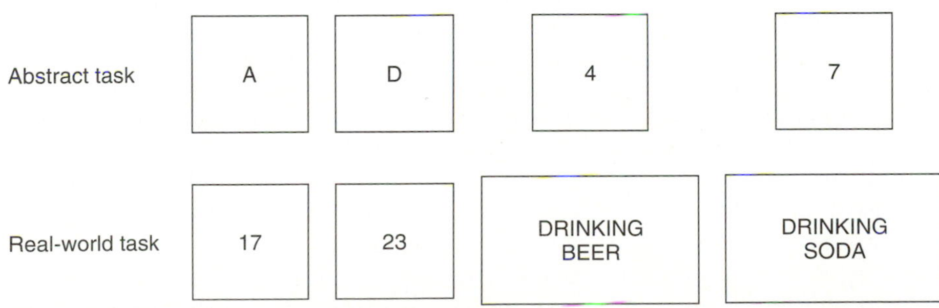

Figure 11.17 Abstract Versus Real-world Reasoning
In the top row, you are required to say which cards you must turn over to test the rule "If a card has a vowel on one side, then it has an even number on the other side." In the bottom row, you must say which cards you need to turn over to test the rule "If a customer is to drink an alcoholic beverage, then she must be at least 18." People typically do better on the second task, which allows them to use real-world strategies.

1977). What would you do? Most people say that they would turn over the *A*, which is correct, and the *4*—which is incorrect. No matter what character appears on the flip side of the *4*, the rule will not be invalidated. (Can you see why that is true?) Instead, you must flip the *7*. If you were to find a vowel there, you would have invalidated the rule.

The original research on this task, which is often called the *Wason selection task*, prompted doubts about people's ability to reason effectively. This negative view, however, has been remedied by research that allowed subjects to apply their real-world knowledge to this task (Holyoak & Spellman, 1993). Suppose you were asked to perform what is a logically comparable task, on the lower set of cards in Figure 11.17. In this case, however, you are asked to evaluate the rule "If a customer is to drink an alcoholic beverage, then she *must* be at least 18" (Cheng & Holyoak, 1985). Now you can probably see immediately which are the correct cards to turn over: *17* and *drinking beer.*

When the problem is familiar in real life, you can make use of a *pragmatic reasoning schema.* As we described in Chapter 10, you derive schemas over the course of your experience in the environment. You have had a good deal of experience in *permission* situations—recall all the times you were given conditions like, "You can't watch television unless you do your homework." Through all those interactions, you derive a reasoning schema. The real-life situation linking age to drinking calls to mind this schema; the arbitrary situation linking even numbers and vowels does not. As a consequence, the arbitrary reasoning task underestimates your ability to make correct deductions.

Research suggests that reasoning is underestimated by arbitrary tasks and more accurately represented by tasks related to real-life problems.

When people do not or cannot use pragmatic reasoning schemas, they may carry out deductive reasoning by constructing **mental models** (Johnson-Laird & Byrne, 1991). Mental models reproduce the details of a situation as accurately as possible, given the limitations of working memory (see Chapter 10). The availability of a unique mental model often predicts performance on reasoning tasks.

HOW WE KNOW

Consider the two descriptions given in **Table 11.6**. In both cases, you should read the lists of premises and try to answer the question "What is the relation between *D* and *E*?" What sets the two descriptions apart, as we have indicated in the Possible Model(s) columns of the table, is that Description 1 permits only one model, whereas Description 2 permits two different models. Researchers predicted that the availability of two different mental models would impair reasoning. (In their experiments, the descriptions were about concrete objects like *cups* and *plates* rather than about *D*'s and *E*'s.) Although the answer in both cases is the same—*D* is to the left of *E*—subjects were, in fact, considerably more accurate for Description 1, because only one mental model was possible (Byrne & Johnson-Laird, 1989).

The general conclusion is that you reason best when you can develop a unique model of the world. The only danger is that you will make errors if you fail to see that the premises of a problem allow more than one model (Johnson-Laird & Byrne, 1991). But the problem of your American Express card fits the requirement for a single model. If you form a mental image of "all major credit cards" after the hostess's utterance, you should swiftly be able to pick out your American Express card from among that crowd. Your deduction is valid, so you're on your way!

Inductive Reasoning

Now let's suppose instead that you have arrived outside the restaurant and only then think to check to see if you have enough cash. Once again you find that you'll want to use your American Express card, but there's no helpful

Table 11.6 Constructing Mental Models

Description 1	Possible Model(s)	Description 2	Possible Model(s)
A is on the right of B. C is on the left of B. D is in front of C. E is in front of B.	C B A D E	B is on the right of A. C is on the left of B. D is in front of C. E is in front of B.	C A B D E (or) A C B D E

sign on the outside. You peek through the restaurant's windows to look at the clientele. You look at the prices on the menu. You consider the neighborhood. All these observations lead you to believe that the restaurant is likely to take your credit card. This is not deductive reasoning, because your conclusion is based on probabilities rather than logical certainties. Instead, this is **inductive reasoning**—a form of reasoning that uses available evidence to generate likely, but not certain, conclusions.

Although the name might be new, we have already described to you several examples of inductive reasoning. Consider, from Chapter 5, the steps children take to learn word meanings. They must use inductive reasoning to determine that *doggie* means the whole dog, but *collar* does not. We saw repeatedly, in Chapters 8 and 10, that people use past information stored as schemas to generate expectations about the present and future. You are using inductive reasoning if, for example, you agree that the words on this page are unlikely to suddenly become invisible (and that, if you study, your knowledge of this material won't become invisible on test day). Finally, earlier in this chapter we discussed the types of inferences people draw when they use language. Your belief that *she* must be *Donna* in the sequence of utterances we gave you relies on inductive inference.

In real-life circumstances, much of your problem-solving ability relies on inductive reasoning. Suppose, for example, you have locked your keys inside your room. What should you do? A good first step is to call up from memory solutions that worked in the past. This process is called *analogical problem solving:* you establish an analogy between the features of the current situation and the features of the previous situations (Holyoak & Nisbett, 1988). In this case, your past experiences of "being locked out" may have allowed you to form the *generalization* "find other people with keys" (Ross & Kennedy, 1990). With that generalization in hand, you can start to figure out who those individuals might be and how to find them. This task might require you to retrieve the method you developed for tracking down your roommates at their afternoon classes. If this problem seems easy to you, it's because you have grown accustomed to letting your past inform your present: inductive reasoning allows you to access tried-and-true methods that speed problem solving.

Research on analogical problem solving often has educational implications. It is likely, for example, that in most of your math and science classes your teachers and your textbooks provided you with a small number of problems with worked-out solutions and expected you to carry on from there. The expectation built into this educational technique is that you will be able to perform inductive reasoning—you will be able to figure out how past methods can be applied to the new problems. Researchers have tried to determine what circumstances are necessary to enable students to best take advantage of past

Working math problems on your own after being presented with a number of models by your professor represents one of many applications of analogical problem solving to education.

solutions (Lovett & Anderson, 1994; Novick & Holyoak, 1991). One general conclusion is that students often need help finding the analogy: extra encouragement is often required, in the form of hints or clues, so that students can see the relevance of past problems to current problems (Ross & Kennedy, 1990).

You might find that conclusion disconcerting, because teachers and textbooks rarely provide such hints or clues. What can you do? You might try on your own to make the analogies as concrete as possible. Teach yourself to find the underlying structure that makes parts of the problems fill the same roles, and see how the same solution methods can be applied. The more explicit an understanding you have of the components and structure of past problems, the more likely you are to recognize a similarity in a current problem and easily apply a solution technique. (Meanwhile, you should count on cognitive psychologists to share their results with the people who teach and write textbooks.)

We have one caution to add about inductive reasoning. Often a solution that has worked in the past will be a successful solution, but sometimes you must recognize that reliance on the past can hamper your problem-solving ability. The water-jar problem given in part F of Figure 11.15 is a classic example of circumstances in which reliance on the past may cause you to miss a solution to a problem (Luchins, 1942). If you had discovered, in the first two problems in part F, the conceptual rule that $B - A - 2(C) =$ *answer*, you probably tried the same formula for the third problem and found it didn't work. Actually, simply filling jar A and pouring off enough to fill jar C would have left you with the right amount. If you were using your initial formula, you probably did not notice this simpler possibility—your previous success with the other rule would have given you a mental set. A **mental set** is a preexisting state of mind, habit, or attitude that can enhance the quality and speed of perceiving and problem solving under some conditions. However, the same set may inhibit or distort the quality of your mental activities at times when old ways of thinking and acting are nonproductive in new situations. When you find yourself frustrated in a problem-solving situation, you might take a step back and ask yourself, "Am I allowing past successes to narrow my focus too much?" Try to make your problem solving more creative, by considering a broader spectrum of past situations and past solutions.

As with functional fixedness, a mental set may impede problem solving when the situation requires novel rather than habitual responding.

JUDGING AND DECIDING

We're back again at "The cat is on the mat." You weren't able to use language processes to understand it. You haven't been able to reason your way to a solution of the message. What do you do now? It's time to make some judgments and some decisions: How likely is it that the message was just a prank? How likely is it that the message has some real importance that has eluded you? Should you just give up and go to sleep?

This series of questions illustrates one of the great truths of your day-to-day experience: you live in a world filled with *uncertainty*. Because you can only guess at the future, and because you almost never have full knowledge of the past, very rarely can you be completely certain that you have made a correct judgment or decision. Thus the processes of judgment and decision making must operate in a way that allows you to deal efficiently with uncertainty. As Herbert Simon put it: because "human thinking powers are very modest when compared with the complexities of the environments in which human beings live" they must be content "to find 'good enough' solutions to their problems and 'good enough' courses of action" (1979, p. 3). In this light, Simon suggested that thought processes are guided by *bounded rationality*. Your judgments or decisions might not be as good—as "rational"—as they always could be, but you should be able to see how they result from your applying limited resources to situations that require swift action.

Before we move to a closer analysis of the products of bounded rationality, let's quickly distinguish between judgment and decision making. **Judgment** is the process by which you form opinions, reach conclusions, and make critical evaluations of events and people. You often make judgments spontaneously, without prompting. **Decision making** is the process of choosing between alternatives, selecting and rejecting available options. Judgment and decision making are interrelated processes. For example, you might meet someone at a party and, after a brief discussion and a dance together, *judge* the person to be intelligent, interesting, honest, and sincere. You might then *decide* to spend most of your party time with that person and to arrange a date for the next weekend. Let's turn now to research on these two types of thinking.

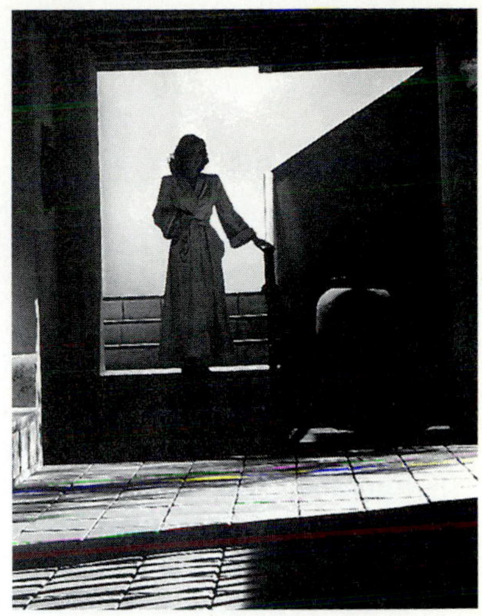

How do you deal with uncertainty? How likely would you be to enter this room?

HEURISTICS AND BIASES OF JUDGMENT

What's the best way to make a judgment? Suppose, for example, you are asked whether you enjoyed a movie. To answer this question, you could fill out a chart with two columns, "What I liked about the movie" and "What I didn't like about the movie," and see which column came out longer. To be a bit more accurate, perhaps you'd weight the entries in each list according to their importance (thus you might weight "the actors' performances" as more important on the plus side than "the blaring sound track" on the minus side). If you went through this whole procedure, you'd probably be pretty confident of your judgment—but you know already that this is an exercise you rarely undertake. In real-life circumstances, you have to make judgments frequently and rapidly. You don't have the time—and often you don't have sufficient information—to use such a formal procedure. What do you do instead? An answer to this question was pioneered by **Amos Tversky** and **Daniel Kahneman**, who argued that people's judgments rely on *heuristics* rather than on formal methods of analysis. **Heuristics** are informal rules of thumb that provide shortcuts, reducing the complexity of making judgments. Heuristics generally increase the efficiency of your thought processes.

Tversky and Kahneman argue that our judgments rely on heuristics, or informal rules of thumb, rather than on more formal analysis.

How do you demonstrate that people are using these mental rules of thumb? As you will soon see, researchers have most often opted to show the circumstances in which the shortcuts lead people to make errors. The logic of these experiments should sound familiar to you by now: just as you can understand perception by studying perceptual illusion and memory by studying memory failures, you can understand judgment processes by studying judgment errors (Kahneman, 1991). As in those other domains, you have to be careful not to mistake the method for the conclusion. Even though there are a wide range of situations in which psychologists can show that your perceptual processes can be fooled, you rarely walk into walls. Similarly, despite the errors that arise because your judgment making is implemented by heuristics, you rarely bump against the wall of cognitive limitations.

Does this mean you should be entirely comfortable with these types of errors? Here the analogy to perception breaks down to some extent. Most perceptual illusions are immune to learning. You're always going to perceive the lengths of the lines of the Müller-Lyer illusion (see Chapter 8) to be different, no matter how much you learn about it. By comparison, knowing about judgmental heuristics *can* enable you to avoid some types of errors. Although general intellectual skills provide no defense against these errors—even the most gifted judgment makers err under some circumstances—specific training can help. Throughout this section, we will point out the ways in

Human Factors and Flight

Have you ever had the opportunity to peer into the cockpit of a commercial airliner? If so, you were greeted with a bewildering array of dials, gauges, and levers. If this complexity made you nervous, you should be happy to know that researchers in **human factors** devote considerable effort to improving the match between technology and human capabilities. Many of the theories and findings of cognitive psychology are directly relevant to the improvement of flight safety. Let's see how.

- *The Aircraft.* Cognitive psychologists know that people's past experience plays an important role in the way they process information. Thus researchers in human factors strive to make technology consistent with people's expectations. One good example on commercial airliners is the design of the controls that activate the flaps and landing gear: "The flap control is shaped like a flap—a flat horizontal surface, rounded in front, tapering toward the back. The landing gear control is shaped like a wheel" (Norman, 1992, pp. 37–38). With this system, pilots know immediately if they have grabbed the wrong control, because the shape does not match the function they had in mind.
- *The Flight Plan.* If you've flown frequently enough, you know that pilots often make announcements about small or large changes in the planned route from your point of departure to your destination. These changes might arise from unexpected weather, air traffic, medical emergencies, and so on. Because of the unpredictability of many of these factors, pilots are often put into situations in which they have to make complex decisions as swiftly as possible. To assist the pilots, researchers have developed computer programs that allow for collaborative problem solving between the pilots and the computers (Layton et al., 1994). The role of cognitive psychology here is to provide background knowledge about how problem solving and decision making are structured. The computer program is designed to help the pilot search the problem space of possible flight routes. The computer can help the pilot both generate particular plans and predict the likely consequences of those plans.
- *The Pilot.* Have you ever wondered whether there are measurable differences between the cognitive skills of pilots and the skills of other individuals? Researchers have demonstrated that on some visual tasks, pilots show superior performance over nonpilots (Dror et al., 1993). Recall the mental rotation task shown in Figure 11.10. Both pilots and nonpilots produce a positive relationship between angle of rotation and response time—but pilots carry out the rotation much faster. Why might this be a good skill for a pilot to have? To turn an aircraft, pilots must tip the aircraft away from level flight. Under these circumstances, it might be useful for pilots to be able to mentally rotate their environment back to the upright as swiftly as possible. Knowing what skills are characteristic of successful pilots could enable airlines to make more informed choices about who should be given the privilege of controlling the cockpit—for a safe flight home.

Judgment and decision making can be improved by specific training in recognizing judgmental heuristics.

which you can improve your judgment making. Let's turn now to three heuristics: *availability, representativeness,* and *anchoring.*

Availability

We'll begin by asking you to make a rather trivial judgment. (We know you're likely to give the wrong answer, and we don't want to embarrass you about something important.) If we were to give you a brief excerpt from a book, do you believe more words in the excerpt would begin with the letter *k* (e.g., *kangaroo*) or have *k* in third position (e.g., *duke*)? If you are like the subjects in a study by Tversky and Kahneman (1973), then you probably judged that *k* is found more often at the beginning of words. In fact, *k* appears about twice as often in the third position.

Why do most people believe that *k* is more likely to appear in first position? The answer has to do with the *availability* of information from memory. It's much easier to think of words that being with *k* than to think of those in which *k* comes third. Your judgment, thus, arises from use of the **availability heuristic:** you base your judgment on information that is readily available in memory. This heuristic makes sense, because much of the time what is available from memory will lead to accurate judgments. If, for example, you judge bowling to be a less dangerous sport than hang gliding, availability is serving you well. Trouble only arises either when (1) memory processes give rise to a biased sample of information or (2) the information you've stored in memory is not accurate. Let's look at an example of each of these potential problems.

The availability heuristic suggests that errors may result when judgment is based on information that is most readily available in memory.

The *k* question is a good example of circumstances in which your memory processes can make an availability-based judgment inaccurate. Given the way words are organized in memory, it's simply easier to find words that begin with a particular letter. Let's consider another case that is closer to the judgments you make in everyday life.

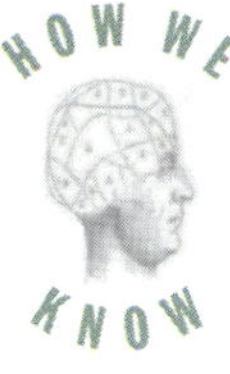

Researchers wanted to demonstrate how people's moods influenced their judgments about the likelihood that certain fates would befall them. Subjects in their study read statements that put them in either measurably happy or unhappy moods. They then were asked to think of past instances of happy or unhappy events—for example, a welcome invitation or a painful injury—and to estimate how likely it would be that events of this type would happen to them again in the next six months. The subjects' ability to recall past events was strongly predicted by their mood—and the availability of mood-congruent memories predicted judgments about the future. Thus subjects in a happy mood found it easier to recall happy events. But, also, the availability of those happy events led subjects to judge that more happy events, and fewer unhappy events, would occur in the future (MacLeod & Campbell, 1992).

If you were in a happy mood, would you be more likely to remember good times from your younger days?

Can you see the implications for your day-to-day life? When it's time to make an important judgment, you can ask yourself, "Is there anything special about my frame of mind that will bias the information coming out of memory?"

A second difficulty with availability as a judgment heuristic arises when the information you have stored in memory has a bias to it. For example, see if you can order these four countries from smallest to largest population:

a. Sweden b. Indonesia c. Israel d. Nigeria

How do you make these judgments?

Researchers predicted that subjects would estimate populations based on their general knowledge about the country. Accordingly, they asked their subjects to rate how much they knew about 98 countries, on a scale from 0 (no knowledge) to 9 (a great deal of knowledge) as well as to give population estimates. There was a sizable positive correlation between these two judgments. In general, the more the subjects knew about a country, the higher the figures they gave for estimated population. Where did the subjects' knowledge, or lack thereof, come from? Using the *New York Times* as an index for information available in the environment, the researchers also showed a sizable correlation between subjects' rated knowledge about a country and the number of times it had been mentioned in *Times* articles in a given year (Brown & Siegler, 1992).

In light of these data, do you wish to pick a new order for the four countries? In fact, their real populations (as of 1989) were 8 million for Sweden, 180 million for Indonesia, less than 5 million for Israel, and 110 million for Nigeria. Clearly you shouldn't feel bad about your cognitive processes because the media have provided you with a flawed database. Even so, you can combat this effect of availability by examining the sources of your information before you make important judgments. How do you know what you think you know?

Representativeness

The **representativeness heuristic** will seem familiar to you because it captures the idea that people use past information to make judgments about similar circumstances in the present. That is the essence of inductive reasoning. When you make judgments based on representativeness, you assume that if something has the characteristics considered typical of members of a category, it is, in fact, a member of that category. Under most circumstances—as long as you have unbiased ideas about the features and categories that go together—making judgments along the lines of similarity will be quite reasonable. Thus, if you are deciding whether to begin a new activity like hang gliding, it makes sense to determine how representative that sport is of the category of activities you have previously enjoyed. Representativeness will lead you astray, however, when it causes you to ignore other types of relevant information, as you will now see (Kahneman & Tversky, 1973).

According to the representativeness heuristic, judgment errors may result from choosing a representative alternative without considering other relevant information.

Consider, for example, the description of a successful attorney, given in **Figure 11.18**.

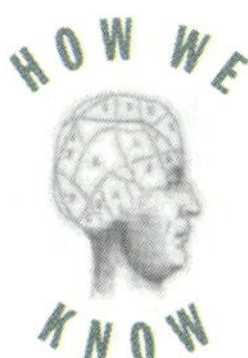

In one experiment, researchers provided their subjects with a list of options, including those in the figure, and gave them the chance to win $45—real money—by ranking the correct option as number 1. Which option seems correct to you? If you're like a majority of the original subjects, you'll lose the $45 because you'll say *tennis* rather than *a ball game.* The lower part of Figure 11.18 shows why *tennis* could never be as good a bet: it is included within the category *a ball game.* Subjects judge tennis to be a better answer because it seems to have all the features of the sport the attorney is likely to play. However, this judgment by representativeness causes subjects to neglect another sort of information—category structure. In this case, the measurable cost is $45 (Bar-Hillel & Neter, 1993).

The implication for your day-to-day life is that you should not be fooled into grabbing at a representative alternative before you consider the structure of all the alternatives.

Let's look at a second representativeness example that also might affect the wagers you make. Suppose you were given the opportunity to play in a lottery. To win, you must match the three numbers the state draws in the exact order. Which of these numbers would you feel most comfortable betting on?

859 101 333
574 948 772

The question we are really asking you is, Which of these numbers strikes you as most representative of the numbers that win these kinds of lotteries? If you are like most bettors, you will avoid playing numbers that have repeated digits—because those numbers do not seem representative of a random sequence. In fact, 27 percent of the time a three-digit number—with each digit

A successful Jerusalem attorney. Colleagues say his whims prevent him from being a team worker, attributing his success to competitiveness and drive. Slim and not tall, he watches his body and is vain. Spends several hours a week on his favorite sport. What sport is that?

a. Fast walking
b. A ball game
c. Tennis
d. A track and field sport

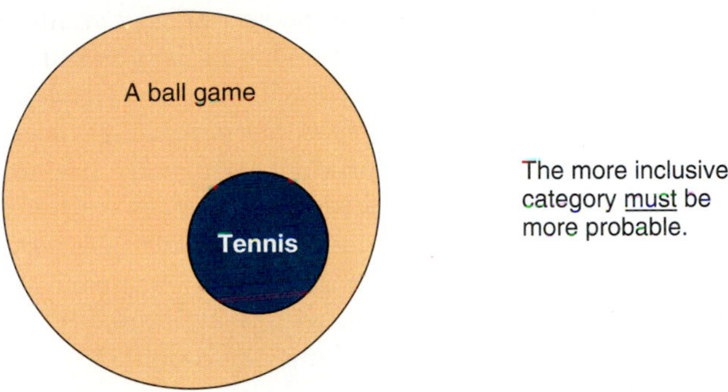
A ball game
Tennis
The more inclusive category must be more probable.

Figure 11.18 Using the Representativeness Heuristic

drawn randomly from the pool 0 to 9—will have a repeated numeral. Nevertheless, among individuals who took part in the Indiana Pick-3 lottery in a 15-day period, only 12.6 percent chose to play a number with a repeated digit (Holtgraves & Skeel, 1992). You should be wary, in general, of the way that most gambling situations are constructed. Most often the hope is that you will be guided by representativeness—so you'll choose the options that look like they're more likely to win—rather than by a careful consideration of the odds.

Anchors Aweigh!

To introduce you to a third heuristic, we need you to try a thought experiment. First take five seconds to estimate the following mathematical product and write down your answer:

$1 \times 2 \times 3 \times 4 \times 5 \times 6 \times 7 \times 8 =$ ________

In five seconds you can probably make only a couple of calculations. You get a partial answer, perhaps 24, and then adjust up from there. Now try this series of numbers:

$8 \times 7 \times 6 \times 5 \times 4 \times 3 \times 2 \times 1 =$ ________

Even if you notice that this is the same list in reverse, you can see how the experience of carrying out the multiplication would feel quite different. You'd start with 8×7, which is 56, and then attempt 56×6, which already feels quite large. Once again, you can only make a partial guess and then adjust upward. When Tversky and Kahneman (1973) gave these two arrangements of the identical problem to experimental subjects, the 1 to 8 order produced median estimates of 512, and the 8 to 1 group produced estimates of 2,250 (the real answer is 40,320). Apparently, when subjects adjusted up from their five-second estimates, the higher partial solutions led to higher estimates.

Performance on this simple multiplication task provides evidence for an anchoring bias. An **anchoring bias** is the insufficient adjustment—either up or down—you make from an original starting value when judging the probable value of some event or outcome. In other words, your judgment is "anchored" too firmly to an original guess. The use of an anchor is *not* costly when the original estimate has a reasonable basis. However, people show a strong tendency to be influenced by an anchor, even when the information is clearly of little or no use. In fact, Tversky and Kahneman (1973) demonstrated that people's judgments about, for example, the percentage of African nations that were members of the United Nations was greatly affected by an anchor even when it was a random number from a wheel of fortune.

Let's look at some examples of anchoring that have an impact on your day-to-day life.

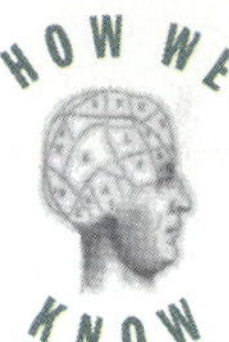

In a study of more than 1000 students, anchoring greatly influenced estimates of both the likelihood of nuclear war and the effectiveness of strategic defenses. Students who were initially asked whether the probability of nuclear war was greater or less than 1 percent subsequently set the odds at 10 percent, whereas respondents who were first asked whether the probability of nuclear war was greater or less than 90 percent gave estimates averaging 26 percent. Similarly, students who were provided with a low anchor in a survey about strategic defenses estimated that, under the best of conditions, nearly one-fourth (24 percent) of Soviet missiles would penetrate American strategic defenses, while students who were provided with a high anchor estimated that the majority (57 percent) of all missiles would reach their targets (Plous, 1989).

Can you see how it would be possible to influence public opinion by using anchors in a strategic fashion? You should also be aware that people will succumb to anchors even at their own expense.

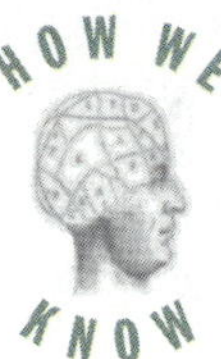

Researchers asked students to judge how many problems they would get correct with respect to a low anchor ("Will you be able to solve more than, less than, or equal to 2 of the problems?") or a high anchor ("28" replaced "2"). High-anchor subjects predicted that they would solve more than twice as many problems as did the low-anchor subjects. Over the course of the experiment, the low-anchor subjects' estimates of their future performance remained lower than their actual success rate! Thus the experimenters' arbitrarily assigned question had a major impact on the way different groups of subjects felt about their own capabilities (Cervone & Palmer, 1990).

You should consider the concept of anchoring bias as a warning against basing your judgment on someone else's estimates.

The implication for real life is that you should always be wary when you must make a judgment based on anyone else's estimate. Try to examine the basis of the estimate before you become anchored to it. And the next time you read a newspaper article based on scientific or government statistics, try to judge whether the writer's conclusions resulted from an anchoring bias.

You employ judgmental heuristics like availability, representativeness, and anchoring because they allow you to make efficient judgments that are acceptable in most situations. In a sense, you are doing the best you can, given the uncertainties of situations and constraints on processing resources. We have shown you, however, that heuristics can lead to errors. You should try to use this knowledge to examine your own thought processes when the time comes to make important judgments. Let's turn now to the decisions you make, often on the basis of those judgments.

The Psychology of Decision Making

Let us begin with a powerful example of the way that psychological factors affect the decisions people make. Consider the problem given in part 1 of **Table 11.7**. Read the instructions and then make your choice between Spot A and Spot B. Now read the version of the problem given in part 2. Would you like to change your choice? In an experiment, students read one version of this problem (Shafir, 1993). When they were asked in 1 which option they

Table 11.7 The Effect of Psychological Factors on Decision Making

Prefer version		*Cancel version*	
1. Imagine that you are planning a week vacation in a warm spot over spring break. You currently have two options that are reasonably priced. The travel brochure gives only a limited amount of information about the two options. Given the information available, which vacation spot would you prefer?		2. Imagine that you are planning a week vacation in a warm spot over spring break. You currently have two options that are reasonably priced, but you can no longer retain your reservation for both. The travel brochure gives only a limited amount of information about the two options. Given the information available, which reservation do you decide to cancel?	
Spot A	average weather average beaches medium-quality hotel medium-temperature water average nightlife	Spot A	average weather average beaches medium-quality hotel medium-temperature water average nightlife
Spot B	lots of sunshine gorgeous beaches and coral reefs ultra-modern hotel very cold water very strong winds no nightlife	Spot B	lots of sunshine gorgeous beaches and coral reefs ultra-modern hotel very cold water very strong winds no nightlife

preferred, 67 percent of the students opted for Spot B. However, when students were asked in 2 to *cancel* an option, this figure fell to 52 percent (that is, 48 percent said they would cancel Spot B). Why is this change odd? If you take a close look at the "prefer" and "cancel" versions of the problem, you will see that there is no difference in the information available in the two cases. On first pass, you might expect that the same information would lead to the same decision. But that's not what people do. It seems that the "prefer" question focuses people's attention on positive features of options—you're gathering evidence in favor of something—whereas the "cancel" question focuses attention on negative features of options—you're gathering evidence against something. Your decision may shift.

Research on questions that focus on "prefer" choices versus "cancel" choices indicates that the phrasing of a question influences the resulting decision.

This straightforward example demonstrates that the way in which a question is phrased can have great consequences for the decision you will make. This is why you need to understand psychological aspects of decision making: you need to be able to test your own decisions to see whether they hold up under careful analysis. In this case, you might ask yourself, "How would my choice change if I were asked to reject an option rather than to choose one?" If you find that your top preference is also your top candidate for rejection, you will have learned that the option has both many positive and many negative features. Now ask, "Is that acceptable?"

The Framing of Gains and Losses

One of the most natural ways to make a decision is to judge which option will bring about the biggest gain or which option will bring about the smallest loss. Thus, if we offer you $5 or $10, you will feel very little uncertainty that the better option is $10. What makes the situation a bit more complicated, however, is that the perception of a gain or a loss often depends on the way in which a decision is *framed*. A **frame** is a particular description of a choice. Suppose, for example, you were asked how happy you would be to get a $1,000 raise in your job. If you were expecting no raise at all, this would seem like a great gain, and you'd probably be quite happy. But suppose you'd been told several times to expect a raise of $10,000. Now how do you feel? Suddenly, you may feel as if you've lost money, since the $1,000 is less than what you had expected. You're not happy at all! In either case, you'd be getting $1,000 more a year—objectively, you'd be in exactly the same position—but the psychological effect is very different. That's why *reference points* are important in decision making (Kahneman, 1992). What seems like a gain or a loss will be determined in part by the expectations—a $0 raise or a $10,000 raise—to which a decision maker refers. (The decision, in this case, might be whether to stay in the job.)

Let's now take a look at a slightly more complex example in which framing has a sizable impact on the decisions people make. In **Table 11.8** you are asked to imagine making a choice between surgery and radiation for treatment of lung cancer. First read the *survival* frame for the problem and choose your preferred treatment; then read the *mortality* frame and see if you feel like changing your preference. Note that the data are objectively the same in the two frames. The only difference is whether statistical information about the consequences of each treatment is presented in terms of survival rates or of mortality rates. When this decision was presented to subjects, the focus on relative gains and losses had a marked effect on choice of treatment. Radiation therapy was chosen by only 18 percent of the subjects who were given the survival frame, but by 44 percent of those given the mortality frame. This framing effect held equally for a group of clinic patients, statistically sophisticated business students, and experienced physicians (McNeil et al., 1982).

What makes this example important is that it shares the uncertainty you frequently have in real life. Often you must make a decision based on your own, or someone else's, best guess at what likely outcomes will be. In these cases, try to think about the problem with *both* a gain frame and a loss frame. Suppose, for example, you are going to buy a new car. The salesperson will be inclined to frame everything as a gain: "Seventy-eight percent of the Xenons require no repairs in the first year!" You can reframe that to "Twenty-two percent require some repairs in the first year!" Would the new frame change how you feel about the situation? It's an exercise worth trying in real life.

Salespeople frame information in ways that encourage prospective customers to view the products in a positive light.

The car salesperson is a good example of a situation in which someone is trying to frame information in a fashion that will have a desired effect on your decision. This, of course, is a regular part of your life. For example, as each election approaches, the two opposing candidates compete to have their framings of themselves and of the issues prevail among the voters. One candidate might say, "I believe in sticking with policies that have been successful." His opponent might counter, "He is afraid of new ideas." One candidate might say, "That policy will bring about economic growth." Her opponent might counter, "That policy will bring about environmental destruction." Often both claims are true—the same policy often *will* bring about both economic good and environmental harm. In this light, whichever frame seems more compelling may be largely a matter of personal history (Tversky & Kahneman, 1981; Vaughan & Seifert, 1992). Thus your knowledge of framing effects can help you understand how people can come to such radically different decisions when they are faced with exactly the same

Table 11.8 The Effect of Framing

Survival frame	*Mortality frame*
Surgery: Of 100 people having surgery, 90 live through the postoperative period, 68 are alive at the end of the first year, and 34 are alive at the end of five years.	Surgery: Of 100 people having surgery, 10 die during surgery or the postoperative period, 32 die by the end of one year, and 66 die by the end of five years.
Radiation therapy: Of 100 people having radiation therapy, all live through the treatment, 77 are alive at the end of one year, and 22 are alive at the end of five years.	Radiation therapy: Of 100 people having radiation therapy, none die during treatment, 23 die by the end of one year, and 78 die by the end of five years.
What do you choose: surgery or radiation?	What do you choose: surgery or radiation?

Table 11.9 Decision Aversion

A.	B.
Suppose you are considering buying a compact disk (CD) player, and have not yet decided what model to buy. You pass by a store that is having a one-day clearance sale. They offer a popular SONY player for just \$99, well below the list price. Do you 1. buy the SONY player 2. wait until you learn more about the various models	Suppose you are considering buying a compact disk (CD) player, and have not yet decided what model to buy. You pass by a store that is having a one-day clearance sale. They offer a popular SONY player for just \$99, and a top-of-the-line AIWA player for just \$159, both well below the list price. Do you 1. buy the AIWA player 2. buy the SONY player 3. wait until you learn more about the various models

evidence. If you want to understand other people's actions, try to think about how those individuals have framed a decision.

Decision Aversion

Let's suppose that you have worked hard to evaluate a choice from the perspective of different frames. What happens next? You might discover that you have created a situation for yourself in which you will experience **decision aversion:** you might find that you will try hard to avoid making any decision at all. In **Table 11.9**, we provide an example of circumstances that can bring about an increasing unwillingness to make a decision. Consider the scenario in part A. Which would you choose? Researchers found that only 34 percent of their subjects said they would wait for more information (Tversky & Shafir, 1992). Now consider the slightly altered scenario given in part B. Do you want to change your choice? In fact, 46 percent of the subjects who read this version said they would wait for new information. How could this be? Ordinarily you would expect that adding an option would *decrease* the share of the other options. If, for example, a third candidate enters a political race, you would expect that candidate to pull votes away from the original pair. Here, however, the addition of a third possibility increases the share of one of the original choices by 12 percent. What's going on?

The key to obtaining this effect is to make the decision hard. When the researchers tested subjects on a version of the problem that provided a low-quality CD player as an extra option, only 24 percent said they would wait for more information—a decrease rather than an increase—which reflects the ease of choosing the SONY. The decision between the less expensive SONY model and the top-quality AIWA, however, is hard. It's convenient to put the hard decision off, to wait for more information.

Researchers find that a difficult decision is likely to result in decision aversion.

Although there are some individual differences, the general tendency to avoid tough decisions is very powerful. Several psychological forces are at work (Beattie et al., 1994):

- People don't like to make decisions that will cause some people to have more and some people to have less of some desired good.
- People are able to anticipate the regret they will feel if the option they choose turns out worse than the option they didn't choose.
- People don't like to be accountable for decisions that lead to bad outcomes.
- People don't like to make decisions for other people.

We can turn this last principle around to define circumstances in which people are *decision seeking:* as much as people are averse to making decisions, they are generally happier to make them themselves than to let other people do so for them. This is something you should bear in mind. Try to avoid letting other people make important decisions for you. Try, as well, not to convince yourself that a decision is so hard that you can't make it at all. In most circumstances, you can count on your cognitive processes to provide you with accurate judgments. Use those judgments to make appropriate choices!

So what, at last, should you decide to do about "The cat is on the mat"? If you have brought your full array of cognitive processes to bear on this cryptic message and still have come to no satisfactory resolution, you may begin to feel frustrated. How you cope with this frustration—how *motivated* you feel to carry on—will be the subject of the next chapter.

Recapping Main Points

Studying Cognition

Cognitive psychologists study the mental processes and structures that enable you to think, reason, make inferences and decisions, solve problems, and use language. Cognitive psychology emerged from behaviorism as a core area of research in psychology. Researchers use reaction time and brain measures to decompose complex tasks into underlying mental processes.

Language Use

Language users both produce and understand language. Speakers design their utterances to suit particular audiences. Speech errors reveal many of the processes that go into speech planning. Much of language understanding consists of using context to resolve ambiguities. Memory representations of meaning begin with propositions supplemented with inferences.

Visual Cognition

Visual representations can be used to supplement propositional representations. Visual representations are an aid in thinking about the environment.

Problem Solving and Reasoning

Probem solvers must define initial state, goal state, and the operations that get them from the initial to the goal state. Deductive reasoning involves drawing conclusions from premises on the basis of rules of logic. Inductive reasoning involves inferring a conclusion from evidence on the basis of its likelihood or probability.

Judging and Deciding

Heuristics are mental shortcuts that can help individuals reach solutions quickly. Availability, representativeness, and anchoring can all lead to errors when they are misapplied. Decision making is affected by the way in which different options are framed. Because of psychological forces, people may avoid making any decisions at all.

Resources

Bransford, J. D., & Stein, B. S. (1993). *The ideal problem solver: A guide to improving thinking, learning, and creativity.* New York: Freeman.

Clark, H. H. (1992). *Arenas of language use.* Chicago: University of Chicago Press.

Gilovich, T. (1991). *How we know what isn't so: The fallibility of human reason in everyday life.* New York: Free Press.

Kahneman, D., Slovic, P., & Tversky, A. (Eds.). (1982). *Judgment under uncertainty: Heuristics and biases.* New York: Cambridge University Press.

Norman, D. A. (1993). *Things that make us smart: Cognitive artifacts as tools for thought.* Reading, MA: Addison-Wesley.

12

Motivation

The alarm clock rang this morning. You would have loved to hit the snooze button, to get a few extra minutes of sleep, but you dragged yourself right out of bed. Why? Were you desperately hungry? Did you have important studying to do? Did you need to rush to a job to make some extra money? Had you made a date with someone you wished to woo? When you consider the question "Why did I get out of bed this morning?" you have arrived directly at the core issue of **motivation**: *What makes you act as you do? What makes you persistently try to attain some goals despite the high effort, pain, and financial costs involved? Why do you procrastinate too long before attempting to achieve other goals or give in and quit too soon?*

Your day-to-day life is filled with circumstances in which people invoke motivational factors to explain events that do and do not take place. You'll hear a sports announcer proclaim, "This team came here to win!" Your friend will reveal that she failed an exam because the professor never got her motivated enough. You'll read a mystery story and try to figure out the motive for a crime—and by doing so, satisfy your own goal of beating the detective to the identity of the murderer. Like millions of other viewers worldwide, you'll glue yourself to soap operas each day to peer into the cauldrons of seething motives like greed, power, and lust.

It is the task of psychological researchers to bring theoretical rigor to such examples of motivation. How might motivational states affect the outcome of a sports competition or an exam? Why do some people become overweight and others starve themselves to death? Are our sexual practices determined by our genetic heritage? In this chapter, you will learn that human actions are motivated by a variety of needs—from fundamental physiological needs like hunger and thirst to psychological needs like personal achievement. But you will see that physiology and psychology are often not easy to separate. Even a seemingly biological drive such as hunger competes with an individual's need for personal control and social acceptance to determine patterns of eating.

What accounts for the popularity of television series that focus on basic—or base—human motivations?

We begin the chapter by providing you with a framework to understand general issues about the nature and study of motivation. In the second part of the chapter, we will look in depth at three types of motivation, each important in a different way and each varying in the extent to which biological and psychological factors operate. These three are hunger, sex, and personal achievement.

UNDERSTANDING MOTIVATION

Motivation is the general term for all the processes involved in starting, directing, and maintaining physical and psychological activities. The word *motivation* comes from the Latin *movere,* which means "to move." All organisms move toward some stimuli and activities and away from others, as dictated by their appetites and aversions. We want theories of motivation to explain both the general patterns of "movement" of each animal species, including humans, and the personal preferences and performances of the individual members of each species. Let's begin our analysis of motivation by considering the different ways in which motivation has been used to explain and predict species and individual behavior.

Functions of Motivational Concepts

Psychologists have used the concept of motivation for five basic purposes:

- *To relate biology to behavior.* As a biological organism, you have complex internal mechanisms that regulate your bodily functioning and help you survive. We suggested as one explanation for your getting-out-of-bed behavior that you may have been "desperately hungry." You may also have been thirsty or cold. In each case, internal states of deprivation trigger bodily responses that motivate you to take action to restore your body's balance.
- *To account for behavioral variability.* Why might you do well on a task one day and poorly on the same task another day? Why does one child do much better at a competitive task than another child with roughly the same ability and knowledge? Psychologists use motivational explanations when the *variations* in people's performance in a constant situation cannot be traced to differences in ability, skill, practice, or chance. If you were willing to get up early this morning to get in some extra studying but your friend was not, we would be comfortable describing you as in a different motivational state than your friend.
- *To infer private states from public acts.* We watched you get out of bed quickly this morning. How can we explain this behavior? Psychologists and laypersons are alike in typically moving from observing some behavior to inferring some internal cause for it. People are continually interpreting behavior in terms of likely reasons for why it occurred as it did. The same rule applies to your own behaviors. You often seek to discover whether your own actions are best understood as internally or externally motivated.
- *To assign responsibility for actions.* The concept of personal responsibility is basic in law, religion, and ethics. Personal responsibility presupposes inner motivation and the ability to control your actions. People are judged less responsible for their actions when (1) they did not intend negative consequences to occur, (2) external forces were powerful enough to provoke the behaviors, or (3) the actions were influenced by drugs, alcohol, or intense emotion. Thus a theory of motivation must be able to discriminate among the different potential causes of behavior.
- *To explain perseverance despite adversity.* When we asked you why you got out of bed, our assumption was that, with respect to many of the other activities you might have to carry out during the day, being in bed was relatively pleasant. Thus a final reason psychologists study motivation is to explain why organisms perform behaviors when it might be easier not to perform them. Motivation gets you to work or class on time even when you're exhausted. Motivation helps you persist in playing the game to the best of your ability even when you are losing and realize that you can't possibly win.

Now that we have reviewed some of the ways in which psychologists use the concept of motivation, see how they apply to this striking real-world situation:

> In the 1984 Olympic Games marathon, the world watched, stunned, as a horribly exhausted runner staggered into the stadium long after the winner

Though so near collapse that she could barely walk, Gabriella Anderson-Schiess succeeded in finishing the Olympic Marathon before medics carried her off the track.

> had crossed the finish line. Somehow, she was propelled forward on wobbly legs toward the finish line. Her face contorted in pain, her body bent and twisted, she doggedly pushed onward, refusing offers of help, until she had completed her mission to finish the race.
>
> "I just hate to give up," she later told reporters. During interviews she expressed her regret that the heat had not overcome her outside the stadium so she would have been spared the shame of her awkward, tension-filled laps in the stadium. (*Los Angeles Times,* 1984)

Ultimately, we'd like a theory of motivation to explain the psychological forces that caused this marathon runner to prolong her physical and psychological agony across the finish line.

You now have a general sense of the circumstances in which psychologists might invoke the concept of motivation to explain and predict behavior. Before we turn to specific domains of experience, let's consider general sources of motivation.

Sources of Motivation

Put yourself in the place of that Olympic marathon runner. Would you have done what she did? Do you think that whatever motivated her behavior was something *internal* to her? Would it take a special set of life experiences for someone to persevere in this manner? Or was it something *external,* something about the situation? Would many or most people behave in this way if they were put in the same situation? Or does her behavior represent an *interaction* of aspects of the person and features of the situation? To help you think about the sources of motivation, we will explore this distinction between internal and external forces. Let's begin with theories that explain certain types of behavior as arising from internal, biological drives.

Psychologists seek to develop theories to explain whether motivation is internal or external.

Drive Theory and Tension Reduction

The concept of motivation as an *inner* drive that determines behavior was introduced into psychology by **Robert Woodworth** (1918). Woodworth defined *drive* in biological terms as energy released from an organism's store. A drive was the fuel of action, called forth by initiating stimuli and made available for goal-directed activities. According to Woodworth, other mechanisms, such as perceptual and learning processes, guided action in appropriate directions.

Drive theory was most fully developed by Yale University theorist **Clark Hull** (1943, 1952). Hull believed that motivation was necessary for learning to occur, and that learning was essential for the successful adaptation of all animals to their environments. Hull emphasized the role of *tension* in motivation. He believed that *tension reduction* was reinforcing. In his view, primary drives were biologically based and were aroused when the organism was deprived. These drives activated the organism; when they were satisfied, or reduced, the organism ceased acting. Thus, according to Hull, when an animal has been deprived of food for many hours, a state of hunger is aroused that motivates food-seeking and eating behaviors. The animal's responses that have led to the food goal will be reinforced because they are associated with the tension reduction that eating produces.

Drive theory was most fully developed by Clark Hull, who emphasized the importance of tension reduction in motivation.

Can tension reduction explain all motivated behavior? Apparently not. Consider groups of rats that have been deprived of food or water. Tension reduction would predict that they would eat or drink at their first opportunity. However, when such rats were placed in a novel environment with plenty of opportunities everywhere to eat or drink, they chose to explore instead. Only after they had first satisfied their curiosity did they begin to satisfy their hunger and thirst (Berlyne, 1960; Fowler, 1965; Zimbardo & Montgomery, 1957). In another series of studies, young monkeys spent much time and energy manipulating gadgets and new objects in their environment, apparently for the sheer pleasure of "monkeying around," without any external rewards (Harlow et al., 1950).

These experiments allow us to conclude that not all types of internal motivation rely on tension reduction. Many types of behavior can't be explained as a reaction to deprivation. You can also see that internal sources of motivation need not relate directly to the survival of the organism. Even though rats might feel biological pressure to eat or drink, they also inherit an impulse to explore a new environment. Let's consider this insight from a slightly different angle by looking at *instinctual* behaviors.

Through research, psychologists found that not all behavior could be explained as tension reduction.

Instinctual Behaviors and Learning

Why do organisms behave the way they do? Part of the answer is that different species have different repertories of behavior that are part of each animal's genetic inheritance. According to *instinct theory,* organisms are born with certain preprogrammed tendencies that are essential for the survival of their species. Salmon swim thousands of miles back to the exact stream where they were spawned, leaping up waterfalls until they come to the right spot, where the surviving males and females engage in ritualized courtship and mating. Fertilized eggs are deposited, the parents die, and, in time, their young swim downstream to live in the ocean until, a few years later, it is time for them to return to complete their part in this continuing drama. Similarly remarkable activities can be reported for most species of animals. Bees communicate the location of food to other bees, army ants go on highly synchronized hunting expeditions, birds build nests, and spiders spin complex webs—exactly as their parents and ancestors did.

Instinctive behaviors, like the argiope spider's proclivity to build an elaborate capture thread into its web, are motivated by genetic inheritance.

Instincts in animals are often studied as fixed-action patterns. **Fixed-action patterns** are stereotypical patterns of behavior, specific to a particular species of animal, "released" by appropriate environmental stimuli. For example, male three-spined sticklebacks will attack even a crude model of another male fish if the model has the red underside that typically signals readiness to breed (Tinbergen, 1951). Ethologists study in detail the eliciting stimuli, environmental conditions, developmental stages, and specific response sequences in different animal species in their natural habitat. In that sense, we can characterize instinctual behaviors as products of both internal and external sources of motivation. The internal source is the genetic inheritance that defines the behavior. The external source is the environmental conditions that make the behavior relevant at a given time in a particular setting.

Instinctual behaviors can be characterized as products of both internal and external sources of motivation.

Let's consider an example of the interplay of internal and external sources of motivation. To survive, primates must detect danger quickly and activate appropriate defensive behaviors. These behaviors appear to originate from genetic programming and are similar in infant rhesus monkeys and human infants. Both show a fearfulness of strangers at a given age (2–4 months for the rhesus; 7–9 months for the babies). Different responses are elicited by different conditions in the environment.

A laboratory experiment of defensive behaviors in infant rhesus monkeys found three behavioral patterns. When separated from their mothers, the infants made loud *cooing* sounds, a signal to help their mothers locate them. When faced with the threat of a silent, human intruder who did not make eye contact, the infants *froze.* This reaction reduces danger in the natural environment, where movement is a stimulus for predatory attack. When the human stared at the separated infant, it *barked* at him in an aggressive display that often discourages attackers (Kalin & Shelton, 1989).

Experiments such as this lead researchers to better understand how instinct and environmental conditions interact to produce patterns of behavior necessary for survival.

How much of human behavior is instinctual? Early theories of human function tended to overestimate the importance of instincts for humans. **William James,** writing in 1890, stated his belief that humans rely even more on instinctual behaviors than other animals (although human instincts were generally not carried out with fixed-action patterns). In addition to the biological instincts humans share with animals, a host of social instincts, such as sympathy, modesty, sociability, and love, come into play. For James, both human and animal instincts were *purposive*—they served important purposes, or functions, in the organism's adaptation to its environment.

Sigmund Freud (1915) proposed that humans experience drive states arising from life instincts (including sexuality) and death instincts (including aggression). He believed that instinctive urges direct *psychic energy* to satisfy bodily needs. Tension results when this energy cannot be discharged; this tension drives people toward activities or objects that will reduce the tension. For example, Freud believed that the life and death instincts operated largely below the level of consciousness. However, their consequences for conscious thoughts, feelings, and actions was profound, because of the way the instincts motivated people to make important life choices (we will expand on these ideas in Chapter 14).

By the 1920s, psychologists had compiled lists of over 10,000 human instincts (Bernard, 1924). At this same time, however, the notion of instincts as universal explanations for human behavior was beginning to stagger under the weight of critical attacks. Cross-cultural anthropologists, such as **Ruth Benedict** (1959) and **Margaret Mead** (1939), found enormous behavioral variation between cultures. Their observations contradicted theories that considered only the *universals* of inborn instincts.

Early theorists, such as William James and Sigmund Freud, overestimated the importance of instinctual behavior in human motivation, as demonstrated by cross-cultural studies.

Most damaging to the early instinct notions, however, were behaviorist empirical demonstrations that important behaviors and emotions were learned rather than inborn. These types of demonstrations should be familiar to you from Chapter 9. We saw there that human and nonhuman animals alike are highly sensitive to the ways in which stimuli and responses are associated in the environment. If you want to explain why one animal performs a behavior and another does not, you may need to know nothing more than that one animal's behavior was reinforced and the other's was not. Under those circumstances, you don't need a separate account of motivation at all (that is, it would be a mistake to say that one animal is "motivated" and the other is not).

Early theories emphasizing the role of instinct in motivation were disputed by the behaviorists' empirical studies demonstrating that many behaviors are learned rather than inborn.

In Chapter 9, we also saw that the types of behaviors animals will most readily learn are determined, in part, by species-specific instincts. That is, each animal displays a combination of learned and instinctive behaviors. Thus, if you are asked to explain or predict an animal's behavior, you will want to know two things: first, something about the history of its species—what adaptive behaviors are part of the organism's genetic inheritance?—and second, something about the history of the animal—what unique set of environmental associations has the organism experienced? In these cases, motivation resides in the effects history has on current behavior.

However, as we saw in Chapter 9, cognitively oriented researchers have challenged the belief that instincts and reinforcement history are sufficient to explain all the details of an animal's behavior. Let's turn now to the role of expectations and cognition in motivation.

Expectations and Cognitive Approaches to Motivation

Consider *The Wizard of Oz* as a psychological study of motivation. Dorothy and her three friends work hard to get to the Emerald City, overcoming barriers, persisting against all adversaries. They do so because they expect the Wizard to give them what they are missing. Instead, the wonderful (and wise) Wizard makes them aware that they, not he, always had the power to fulfill their wishes. For Dorothy, *home* is not a place but a feeling of security, of comfort with people she loves; it is wherever her heart is. The courage the Lion wants, the intelligence the Scarecrow longs for, and the emotions the Tin Man dreams of are attributes they already possess. They need to think about these attributes not as internal conditions but as positive ways in which they are already relating to others. After all, didn't they demonstrate those qualities on the journey to Oz, a journey motivated by little more than an *expectation,* an idea about the future likelihood of getting something they wanted? The Wizard of Oz was clearly among the first cognitive psychologists, because he recognized the importance of people's thought processes in determining behaviors.

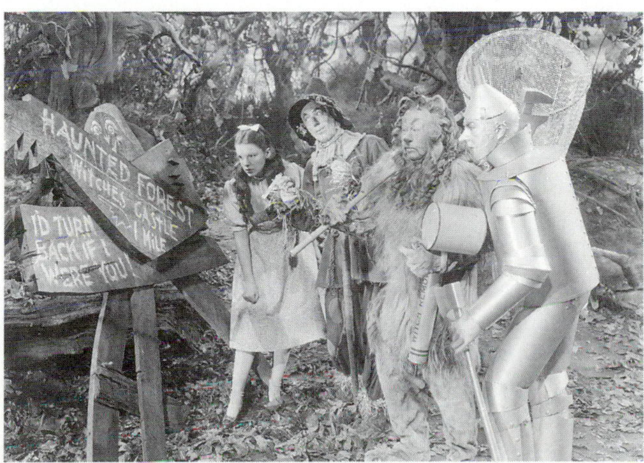

What factors motivated Dorothy and her companions to continue their search for the Wizard despite the obstacles they encountered?

Cognitive approaches are currently being used by many psychologists to account for what motivates a variety of personal and social behaviors. These psychologists share the Wizard's point of view that significant human motivation comes not from objective realities in the external world but from your *subjective interpretation* of reality. The reinforcing effect of a reward is lost if you don't perceive that your actions obtained it. What you do now is often controlled by what you think was responsible for your past successes and failures, by what you believe is possible for you to do, and by what you anticipate the outcome of an action will be. Cognitive approaches to motivation put higher mental processes such as these in charge of the acting self. These approaches explain why human beings are often motivated by expectations of future events.

The importance of *expectations* in motivating behavior was developed by **Julian Rotter** (1954) in his **social-learning theory** (we touched on social learning in our discussion of observational learning in Chapter 9). For Rotter, the probability that you will engage in a given behavior (studying for an exam instead of partying) is determined by your *expectation* of attaining a goal (getting a good grade) that follows the activity and by the *personal value* of that goal. A discrepancy between expectations and reality can motivate an individual to perform corrective behaviors (Festinger, 1957; Lewin, 1936). For example, if you find that your own behaviors do not match the standards or values of a group to which you belong, you might be motivated to change your behaviors to achieve a better fit with the group.

How do expectations relate to internal and external forces of motivation? **Fritz Heider** (1958) postulated that the outcome of your behavior (a poor grade, for example) can be attributed to *dispositional forces,* such as lack of effort or insufficient intelligence, or to *situational forces,* such as an unfair test or a biased teacher. These attributions influence the way you will behave. You are likely to try harder next time if you see your poor grade as a result of your lack of effort, but you may give up if you see it as resulting from injustice or lack of ability (Dweck, 1975). Thus the identification of a source of motivation as internal or external may depend, in part, on your own subjective interpretation of reality.

Julian Rotter was among the first to emphasize the importance of expectations in motivating behavior, while Fritz Heider added the notion of dispositional and situational forces.

Let's review the various sources of motivation. We began with the observation that we can differentiate internal and external factors that bring about behaviors. Drives, instincts, and histories of learning are all internal sources of motivation that affect behaviors in the presence of appropriate external stimuli. Once organisms begin to think about their behaviors—something humans are particularly prone to do—expectations about what should or should not happen also begin to provide motivation. Thinking animals can choose to attribute some motivations to themselves and others to the outside world.

We have now given you a general framework for understanding motivation. In the remainder of the chapter, we will take a closer look at three different types of behavior that are influenced by interactions of motives: eating, sexual performance, and personal achievement.

EATING

We'd like to ask you to make a prediction. We are about to offer a slice of pizza to a student enrolled in an introductory psychology course. How likely do you think it is that the student will eat the slice of pizza? Are you willing to make a guess? Your response should probably be, "I need more information." In the last section we gave you a way of organizing the extra information you need to acquire. You would want to know about internal information. How much has the student eaten already? Is the student trying to diet? Is the student suffering from an eating disorder? You would also want to know about external information. Is the pizza tasty? Are friends there to share the pizza and conversation? You can see already that we have quite a bit of work to do to explain the types of forces that might influence even a simple question, such as whether someone is going to eat a slice of pizza. Let's begin with some of the physiological process that evolution has provided to regulate eating.

The Physiology of Eating

When does your body tell you it's time to eat? You have been provided with a variety of mechanisms that contribute to your physical sense of hunger or satiety (Logue, 1991). To regulate food intake effectively, organisms must be equipped with mechanisms that accomplish four tasks: (1) detect internal food need, (2) initiate and organize eating behavior, (3) monitor the quantity and quality of the food eaten, and (4) detect when enough food has been consumed and stop eating. Researchers have tried to understand these processes by relating them either to *peripheral* mechanisms in different parts of the body, such as stomach contractions, or to *central* brain mechanisms, such as the functioning of the hypothalamus. Let's look at these processes in more detail.

Peripheral Responses

Where do sensations of hunger come from? Does your stomach send out distress signals to indicate that it is empty? A pioneering physiologist, **Walter Cannon** (1934), believed that gastric activity in an empty stomach was the sole basis for hunger. To test this hypothesis, Cannon's intrepid student A. L. Washburn trained himself to swallow an uninflated balloon attached to a rubber tube. The other end of the tube was attached to a device that recorded changes in air pressure. Cannon then inflated the balloon in Washburn's stomach. As the student's stomach contracted, air was expelled from the balloon and deflected the recording pen. Reports of Washburn's hunger pangs were correlated with periods when his stomach was severely contracted but not when his stomach was distended. Cannon thought he had proved that stomach cramps were responsible for hunger (Cannon & Washburn, 1912).

Although Walter Cannon's ingenious research seemed to show that stomach contractions were solely responsible for hunger, subsequent research indicated that motivation for eating behavior is not fully explained by sensations in the stomach.

Although Cannon and Washburn's procedure was ingenious, later research showed that stomach contractions are not even a necessary condition for hunger. Injections of sugar into the bloodstream will stop the stomach contractions but not the hunger of an animal with an empty stomach. Human patients who have had their stomachs entirely removed still experience hunger pangs (Janowitz & Grossman, 1950), and rats without stomachs still learn mazes when rewarded with food (Penick et al., 1963). So, although sensations originating in the stomach may play a role in the way people usually experience hunger, they do not fully explain how the body detects its need for food and is motivated to eat.

Your empty stomach may not be necessary to feel hungry, but does a "full" stomach terminate eating? Research has shown that gastric distension caused by food—but not by an inflated balloon—will cause an individual to end a meal (Logue, 1991). Thus the body is sensitive to the source of pressure in the stomach. The oral experience of food also provides a peripheral source of satiety cues. You may have noticed that you become less enthusiastic about the tastes of even your favorite foods over the course of a meal. When people are given the opportunity to eat a series of foods with different tastes, rather than sticking with a single, even favorite taste, they eat more food (Rolls et al., 1981). Therefore, variety in food tastes—as is common in many multicourse meals—might counteract other bodily indications that you've already had enough to eat.

Caterers and chefs know that people tend to eat more when a variety of tastes are available.

Let's turn now to the brain mechanisms of eating behaviors, where information from peripheral sources is gathered together.

Central Responses

As is often the case, simple theories about the brain centers for the initiation and cessation of eating have given way to more complex theories. The earliest theories of the brain control of eating were built around observations of the *lateral hypothalamus* (LH) and the *ventromedial hypothalamus* (VMH). (The location of the hypothalamus is shown in Figure 3.8 on page 73.) Research showed that if the VMH was lesioned (or the LH stimulated), the animal consumed more food. If the procedure was reversed, so that the LH was lesioned (or the VMH stimulated), the animal consumed less food. These observations gave rise to the *dual-center* model, in which the LH was thought to be the "hunger center" and the VMH the "satiety center."

Over time, however, the data failed to confirm this theory (Martin et al., 1991). For example, rats with VMH lesions only overeat foods they find palatable; they strongly avoid foods that don't taste good. Thus the VMH could not just be a simple center for signaling "eat more" or "don't eat more"—the signal depends on the type of food. In fact, destruction of the VMH may, in part, have the effect of exaggerating ordinary reflex responses to food (Powley, 1977). If the rat's reflex response to good-tasting food is to eat it, its exaggerated response will be to overeat. If the rat reflexively avoids bad-tasting food by gagging or vomiting, its exaggerated response could keep the rat from eating altogether. Researchers now understand that these regions of the hypothalamus work alongside other brain regions to regulate eating.

Let's focus on how the VMH and LH carry out the tasks assigned to them by the brain. Some of the most important information the VMH and LH use to regulate eating comes from your bloodstream. Sugar (in the form of glucose in the blood) and fat are the energy sources for metabolism. The two basic signals that initiate eating come from receptors that monitor the levels of sugar and fat in the blood. When blood glucose is low or unavailable for metabolism, signals from liver cell receptors are sent to the LH, where neurons acting as glucose detectors change their activity in response to this information. Other hypothalamic neurons may detect changes in free fatty acids and insulin levels in the blood. Together, these neurons appear to activate appetitive systems in the lateral zone of the hypothalamus and initiate eating behavior (Thompson & Campbell, 1977). Signals that the blood has a high level of glucose or fatty acids are used by the VMH to terminate eating behaviors.

We have seen so far that you have body systems that are dedicated to getting you to start and to stop eating. You almost certainly know, however, from an enormous amount of personal experience, that your need for food depends on more than just the cues generated by your body. Let's look now at psychological factors that motivate you to eat more food or less food.

The Psychology of Eating

We have seen so far that your body is equipped with a variety of mechanisms that regulate the amount of food you eat. But do you eat only in response to hunger? You are likely to respond, "Of course not!" What is almost certainly clear to you is that the way you think about eating, and its consequences for your body shape or size, also influences the amount of food you eat. To discuss the psychology of eating, we will focus largely on circumstances in which people try to exercise control over the consequences—to try to reshape their bodies in response to their perceptions of some personal or societal ideal.

Do you worry about your weight? Have you considered going on a diet? If you are a woman, it is more likely that the answer to these questions is yes, but even men in contemporary U.S. society express anxiety about their weight: 52 percent of women and 37 percent of men report that they are overweight (Brownell & Rodin, 1994). In fact, approximately 24 percent of women and 31 percent of men are actually considered to be overweight—so there is a disparity, again, particularly for women, between the reality of people's bodies and what they perceive those realities to be. In the next section, we will explore some of the roots and consequences of obesity and dieting. We then describe how eating disorders may arise as an extreme response to concerns about body image and weight.

Obesity and Dieting

Why do some people become overweight? It probably will not surprise you, well into *Psychology and Life,* that the answer lies partly in nature and partly in nurture. On the nature side, increasing evidence suggests that people are born with innate tendencies to be lighter or heavier. For example, studies of identical twins have revealed great similarity in their overall weight (Allison et al., 1994; Stunkard et al., 1990). Part of this similarity may be explained by the finding that the rate at which an individual's body burns calories to maintain basic functions, the individual's *resting metabolic rate,* is also highly heritable (Bouchard et al., 1989). Thus some people are innately predisposed to burn a lot of calories just through ordinary day-to-day activities; others are not. Those who are not are more at risk for weight gain. Researchers have discovered some of the actual genetic mechanisms that may predispose some individuals to obesity. For example, a gene has been isolated that appears to control signals to the brain that enough fat has been stored in the body in the course of a meal—so the individual should stop eating (Zhang et al., 1994). If this gene is inactive, the individual will continue to eat, with obesity as a potential result.

Studies of identical twins indicate that the tendency to be overweight is influenced by heredity.

However, even a biological predisposition may not be enough to "cause" a particular person to become obese. What matters, in addition, is the way in which an individual thinks about food and eating behaviors. Early research on psychological aspects of obesity focused on the extent to which obese individuals are attentive to their bodies' internal hunger cues versus food in the external environment (Schachter, 1971a). The suggestion was that, when food is available and prominent, obese individuals ignore the cues their bodies give them. This theory proved to be insufficient, however, because obesity itself does not always predict eating patterns (Rodin, 1981). That is, not all people who are overweight have the same psychological makeup with respect to eating behaviors. Let's see why.

Peter Herman and **Janet Polivy** have proposed that the critical dimension that underlies the psychology of eating behaviors is *restrained* versus *unrestrained* eating (Herman & Polivy, 1975). *Restrained* eaters put constant limits on the amount of food they will let themselves eat: they are chronically on diets; they constantly worry about food. Although obese people may be more likely to report these kinds of thoughts and behaviors, individuals can be restrained eaters whatever their body size. How do people gain weight if they are constantly on a diet? Research suggests that when restrained eaters become *disinhibited*—when life circumstances cause them to let down their restraints—they tend to indulge in high-calorie binges. Disinhibition appears to arise most often when the restrained eaters are made to feel stress about their capabilities and self-esteem (Greeno & Wing, 1994; Heatherton et al., 1991).

Researchers have described eating behaviors as restrained versus unrestrained, finding that restrained eaters binge when they become disinhibited.

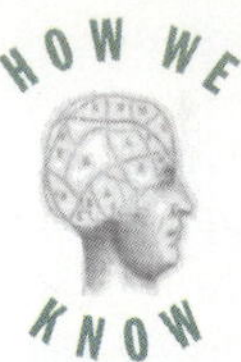

Based on self-evaluations of their behaviors and thoughts with respect to food and dieting, 96 female college students were classified as restrained (42 women) or unrestrained (54 women) eaters. When they arrived for the experiment, half of the students were told that they would be asked to give a two-minute off-the-cuff speech, which would give an indication of their verbal fluency. Anticipation of this task provoked high anxiety in these subjects. The other half of the subjects believed they would be asked to participate in an experiment on their perceptions of fabrics through touch. This provoked low anxiety, and so was considered a control. Next, both groups of subjects were asked to perform a preliminary experiment on taste perception. The stimuli for this experiment were both store-bought good-tasting cookies and bad-tasting cookies prepared "by the experimenter's grandmother, against her better judgment" (Polivy et al., 1994, p. 507). Unknown to the subjects, the experimenters were recording how many cookies of each type they ate.

The results of the study are shown in **Table 12.1**. When unrestrained eaters became anxious, they ate fewer of both types (good-tasting and bad-tasting) of cookies. Apparently, anxiety suppressed their hunger, to some extent. For restrained eaters, however, anxiety led them to eat more of both types of cookies. Thus, among these women, a state of anxiety created a general disinhibition even for cookies that were rated as not being very tasty (Polivy et al., 1994).

In this experiment, a minor challenge to self-esteem—the prospect of giving a brief speech that would be evaluated—caused restrained women to eat more than their peers. Research has shown that, in general, restrained eaters are likely to overeat only when they suffer a threat to their psychological well-being; a threat to their physical safety does not have a similar impact (Heatherton et al., 1991). Overeating behavior may allow restrained eaters to distract themselves from the insult to their self-esteem. When restrained eaters were told that they had failed on a problem-solving task, they didn't overeat if they were made to keep focused on the behavior—by watching a videotape of their failure performance (Heatherton et al., 1993). When they weren't made to attend to their failure, the restrained eaters ate twice as much ice cream as they did when they watched the videotape. Note that most of the research on restrained eating has been conducted with women as subjects. Less is known about the eating patterns of men (Greeno & Wing, 1994).

According to researchers, restrained eaters are likely to overeat when they suffer a threat to their psychological well-being but not when their physical safety is threatened.

Table 12.1 Average Number of Cookies Consumed

	Unrestrained Eaters	Restrained Eaters	Difference
Good-tasting cookies			
Control	6.2	5.1	–1.1
Anxious	5.1	7.6	+2.5
Bad-tasting cookies			
Control	3.0	2.6	–0.4
Anxious	2.7	3.7	+1.0

The theory of restrained eating suggests why it might be difficult for people to lose weight once they have become overweight. Many overweight people report themselves as constantly on diets—they are often restrained eaters. If stressful life events occur that cause these eaters to become disinhibited, binge eating can easily lead to weight gain. Thus the psychological consequences of being constantly on a diet can create circumstances that are more likely to lead to weight *gain* than to weight *loss*. In the next section, we will see how these same psychological forces can lead to health- and life-threatening eating disorders.

Eating Disorders

We began this section on psychological aspects of eating by noting that the group of people who believe themselves to be overweight is larger than the group of people who are actually overweight. When the disparity between people's perceptions of their body image and their actual size becomes too large, they may be at risk for *eating disorders*. **Anorexia nervosa** is diagnosed when an individual weighs less than 85 percent of her or his expected weight, but still expresses an intense fear of becoming fat (DSM-IV, 1994). The behavior of people diagnosed with **bulimia nervosa** is characterized by binges—periods of intense, out-of-control eating—followed by measures to purge the body of the excess calories—self-induced vomiting, misuse of laxatives, fasting, and so on (DSM-IV, 1994). Sufferers from anorexia nervosa may also be bulimic. They may binge and then purge as a way of minimizing calories absorbed. Because the body is being systematically starved, both of these syndromes have serious medical consequences. In the long run, sufferers may starve to death.

A person may be at risk for eating disorders when the disparity between perceived body size and actual body size becomes too large.

In Chapter 5, we noted that adolescent girls are at particular risk for eating disorders (Rolls et al., 1991; Striegel-Moore et al., 1993). The prevalence of anorexia among women in late adolescence and early adulthood is about 0.5 to 1.0 percent (DSM-IV, 1994). From 1 to 3 percent of the women in this same age group suffer from bulimia (DSM-IV, 1994; Rand & Kuldau, 1992). Women suffer from both diseases at approximately ten times the rate of men.

Why do people begin to starve themselves to death, and why are most of those people women? There is some evidence that a predilection toward eating disorders may be genetically transmitted (Strober, 1992). Much research attention, however, has focused on women's expectations for their ideal weight as generated by society and the media. For example, many of the magazines that are marketed specifically to women put great emphasis on weight loss; the same is not true for the magazines that men read (Andersen & DiDomenico, 1992). Thus women may get more cultural support for their belief that they are overweight than do men. Culturally driven misperception may initiate the types of behavior associated with eating disorders. We already have described how restrained eaters may become binge eaters when threats to self-esteem lead to disinhibition. Because people with eating disorders try to enforce extreme restraint, this pattern of bingeing may become even more exaggerated (Polivy & Herman, 1993).

Models who conform to an unrealistically thin stereotype may lead other women to think of themselves as overweight.

Right now, you're likely to be part of a particular culture that promotes eating disorders. Women in college tend to suffer from anorexia or bulimia more than do nonstudents. In college settings, women may solve the tension between wanting to look attractive and wanting to eat and drink with their friends by bingeing—enjoying the party—and then purging—eliminating the calories (Rand & Kaldau, 1992). You should be aware that college life provides this dangerous potential.

By now you are probably wary of the very idea of dieting. In the close-up, we consider whether dieters can ever achieve their goals.

Can Diets Be Successful?

Can diets be successful? If you worry that you are overweight, you will probably be relieved to know that the answer is yes. But if you have read the sections on obesity, dieting, and eating disorders carefully, you'll probably understand why we're asking the question. If people who begin to diet become restrained eaters, they may be more likely to gain weight than to lose weight. People whose dieting behavior becomes transformed into eating disorders may cut down on their weight, but at even greater threats to their health. If you keep an eye on popular culture, you'll also understand why we ask if diets can be successful. The media often repeat the statistic that only 5 percent of dieters permanently keep their weight off—and magazines often feature the up-and-down weight cycles of celebrities like Oprah Winfrey and Elizabeth Taylor.

Are diets really only 5 percent successful? This often repeated figure is over 30 years old and comes from one survey of patients in a hospital clinic (Brownell & Rodin, 1994)! In fact, there are very few reliable statistics about the general success of diets. Most of the data still come from overweight individuals who present themselves to obesity clinics. Those people who seek treatment often have more psychological problems related to eating (for example, they report more binge eating) than matched samples of obese people who do not seek treatment (Fitzgibbon et al., 1993). Thus data on regain of weight may be of limited generality. Furthermore, most people who attempt to lose weight do it in the privacy of their homes. Little is known about how much weight these individuals lose and how much they are able to keep off. You should be wary of claims about the success rates of dieting.

How can you undertake a successful diet? Expert **Kelly Brownell** argues that it is important to recognize that dieting goals and dieting plans must be personalized to each individual (Brownell, 1991; Brownell & Rodin, 1994; Brownell & Wadden, 1992). For example, dieting goals—the setting of a *reasonable* target weight—should take into consideration both genetic and social factors. People might be asked a series of questions (Brownell & Wadden, 1992, p. 509):

- Is there a history of excess weight in your parents or grandparents?
- What is the lowest weight you have maintained as an adult for at least one year?
- Think of a friend or family member (with your age and body frame). What does the person weigh?
- At what weight do you believe you can live with the required changes in eating and/or exercise?

Can you see how these types of questions might prevent you from putting yourself at risk for becoming a chronic dieter and restrained eater? If you consider, up front, what a reasonable weight-loss goal might be, you can plan a program of diet and exercise that will allow you to obtain that reasonable goal.

What can you do if you feel as if you've gotten into a pattern of restrained eating? You may want to seek treatment to help you reestablish patterns of eating that are more in touch with your body's true needs (Polivy & Herman, 1992). That's an important general conclusion: diets can be successful if they incorporate the realities of your own body's responses and potential. You must try to avoid giving in to media images of the ideal body, a body that may not be sensibly within your reach.

SEXUAL BEHAVIORS

Your body physiology makes it essential that you think about food every day. But what about sex? It's easy to define the biological function of sex—reproduction—but does that explain the frequency with which you think about sexual behaviors? When asked how often they think about sex, 54 percent of adult men and 19 percent of adult women report they think about sex at least once every day (Michael et al., 1994). How can we explain the frequency with which people think about sex? How do thoughts about sex relate to sexual behaviors?

The question of motivation, once again, is the question of why people carry out certain ranges of behavior. As we already acknowledged, sexual behaviors are biologically necessary only for reproduction. Thus, while eating is essential to individual survival, sex is not. Some animals and humans remain celibate for a lifetime without apparent detriment to their daily functioning. But reproduction is crucial to the survival of the species as a whole. To ensure that effort will be expended toward reproduction, nature has made sexual stimulation intensely pleasurable. An orgasm serves as the ultimate reinforcer for the energy expended in mating.

This potential for pleasure gives to sexual behaviors motivating power well beyond the need for reproduction. Individuals will perform a great variety of behaviors to achieve sexual gratification. But some sources of sexual motivation are external. Cultures establish norms or standards for what is acceptable or expected sexual behavior. While most people may be motivated to perform behaviors that accord with those norms, some people violate these norms to achieve their sexual satisfaction.

In this section, we will first consider some of what is known about the sex drive and mating behavior in nonhuman animals. Then we will turn our attention to selected issues in human sexuality.

Although sex fulfills the biological function of reproduction, most humans engage in sex many more times than they reproduce.

Nonhuman Sexual Behaviors

The primary motivation for sexual behaviors in nonhuman animals is reproduction. For species that use sex as a means of reproduction, evolution has generally provided two sexual types, males and females. The female produces relatively large eggs (which contain the energy store for the embryo to begin its growth), and the male produces sperm that are specialized for motility (to move into the eggs). The two sexes must synchronize their activity so that sperm and egg meet under the appropriate conditions, resulting in conception.

Sexual arousal is determined primarily by physiological processes. Animals become receptive to mating largely in response to the flow of hormones controlled by the pituitary gland and secreted from the *gonads,* the sex organs. In males, these hormones are known as *androgens,* and they are continuously present in sufficient supply so that males are hormonally ready for mating at almost any time. In the females of many species, however, the sex hormone *estrogen* is released according to regular time cycles of days or months, or according to seasonal changes. Therefore, the female is not always hormonally receptive to mating.

These hormones act on both the brain and genital tissue and often lead to a pattern of predictable *stereotyped sexual behavior* for all members of a species. If you've seen one pair of rats in their mating sequence, you've seen them all. The receptive female rat darts about the male until she gets his attention. Then he chases her as she runs away. She stops suddenly and raises her rear, and he enters her briefly, thrusts, and pulls out. She briefly escapes him and the chase resumes—interrupted by 10 to 20 intromissions before he ejaculates, rests awhile, and starts the sex chase again. Apes also copulate only briefly (for about 15 seconds). For sables, copulation is slow and long, lasting for as long as eight hours. Predators, such as lions, can afford to indulge in long, slow copulatory rituals—as much as every 30 minutes over four consecutive days. Their prey, however, such as antelope, copulate for only a few seconds, often on the run (Ford & Beach, 1951).

Sexual arousal is often initiated by stimuli in the external environment. In many species, the sight and sound of ritualized display patterns by potential partners is a *necessary* condition for sexual response. Furthermore, in

When a bull elephant is in musth (a periodic state of sexual excitement), he secretes powerful pheromones, an unconditional stimulus that lets females know he is willing to mate.

species as diverse as sheep, bulls, and rats, the novelty of the female partner affects a male animal's behavior. A male that has reached sexual satiation with one female partner may renew sexual activity when a new female is introduced (Dewsbury, 1981). Touch, taste, and smell can also serve as external stimulants for sexual arousal. Some species secrete chemical signals, called **pheromones,** that attract suitors, sometimes from great distances. In many species, the female emits pheromones when her fertility is optimal (and hormone level and sexual interest are peaking). These secretions are unconditional stimuli for arousal and attraction in the males of the species, who have inherited the tendency to be aroused by the stimuli. When captive male rhesus monkeys smell the odor of a sexually receptive female in an adjacent cage, they respond with a variety of sex-related physiological changes, including an increase in the size of their testes (Hopson, 1979).

How is sexual motivation different for the human species?

Human Sexuality

We will begin our discussion of human sexuality by discussing the possible role of evolution in determining patterns of sexual behavior. We then consider physiological aspects of sexual responsiveness. Finally, we discuss the way in which personal experiences and societal norms affect the expression of sexual motivation.

Did Evolution Shape Patterns of Sexual Behaviors?

For nonhuman animals we have already seen that the pattern of sexual behaviors was largely fixed by evolution. The main goal is reproduction—preservation of the species—and sexual behaviors are highly ritualized and stereotyped. Can the same claim be made for general patterns of human sexual behaviors?

Evolutionary psychologists have explored the idea that men and women have evolved to have different *strategies* that underlie sexual behavior (Buss, 1994; Wright, 1994). To describe these strategies, we have to remind you of some of the realities of human reproduction. Human males could reproduce hundreds of times a year if they could find enough willing mates. To produce a child, all they need to invest is a teaspoon of sperm and a few minutes of intercourse. Women can reproduce at most about once a year, and each child then requires a huge investment of time and energy. (Incidentally, the world record for the number of times a woman has given birth falls short of 50, but men have fathered many more children. A Moroccan despot, King Ismail the Bloodthirsty, had over 700 children, and the first Emperor of China is said to have fathered over 3000; both had large harems.)

Thus, when reproduction is a goal, eggs are the limited resource and males compete for opportunities to fertilize them. The basic problem facing a male animal is to maximize the number of offspring he produces, by mating with the largest number of females possible. But the basic problem facing a female animal is to find a high-quality male to ensure the best, healthiest offspring from her limited store of eggs. Furthermore, human offspring take so long to mature and are so helpless while growing that substantial **parental investment** is required (Trivers, 1972; Wright, 1994). Mothers and fathers must spend time and energy raising the children—unlike fish or spiders, which simply lay eggs and depart. Females thus have the problem of selecting not just the biggest, strongest, smartest, highest-status, most thrilling mate but the most loyal, committed partner to help raise their children.

One evolutionary psychologist, **David Buss** (1994; Buss & Schmitt, 1993), has suggested that men and women evolved different strategies, emotions, and motivations for *short-term mating* versus *long-term mating*. The male strategy of seducing and abandoning—showing signs of loyalty and commit-

Evolution defines different strategies for male and female parents.

ment and then leaving—is a short-term strategy. The male strategy of staying committed to the female and investing in the offspring is a long-term strategy. The female strategy of attracting a loyal male who will stay to help raise her children is a long-term strategy. There is some controversy about whether women have evolved short-term mating strategies. Some argue that indiscriminate sex never pays for women in an evolutionary sense—they can get pregnant without assurance of male investment later. Women do seem less interested in casual sex than men (Buss & Schmitt, 1993). Others argue that short-term mating with many men—especially older, rich men—in exchange for immediate rewards may pay off by assuring short-term survival.

Short-term versus long-term mating strategies may explain the disparate sexual behavior of men and women.

Research by Buss and others suggests that women and men show the patterns predicted by evolutionary psychology across all cultures, even when the comtemporary environment changes the risks and rewards of different mating strategies. Sex is considered something that women give away to men, in exchange for either immediate material reward (short-term mating, such as prostitution) or long-term commitment and support (marriage). In general, men show a greater desire for a variety of sexual partners and are less discriminating about their mates. These patterns for female and male behaviors are true even though modern contraception eliminates many of the dangers of short-term mating strategies for women and even though modern economies may allow both men and women to raise children alone. If social and sexual emotions were learned in response to the current environment, we would expect human emotions and motivations to keep up with technological and social developments. Instead, our evolved mating strategies seem resistant to change.

Let's turn now to the physiology of sexual response.

Physiology of Human Sexual Behaviors

Hormonal activity, so important in regulating sexual behavior among other animal species, has no known effect on sexual receptiveness or gratification in the vast majority of men and women (Bancroft, 1978). In women, hormones play an important role in controlling the cycles of ovulation and menstruation. However, individual differences in hormone levels, within normal limits, are not predictive of the frequency or quality of sexual activity. For men, the hormone testosterone is necessary for sexual arousal and performance. Most

A major difference in the sexual behavior of humans and nonhuman animals is that in humans, hormones have no known effect on sexual responsiveness or gratification.

healthy men from ages 18 to 60 have sufficient testosterone levels to experience normal sex drives. Once again, individual variation in these levels among men, within normal limits, is not related to sexual performance.

Researchers have studied sexual practices and sexual responses in nonhuman animals for several decades, but for many years studies of similar behaviors in humans were off limits. **William Masters** and **Virginia Johnson** (1966, 1970, 1979) broke down this traditional taboo. They legitimized the study of human sexuality by directly observing and recording, under laboratory conditions, the physiological patterns involved in ongoing human sexual performance. By doing so, they explored not what people said about sex but how individuals actually reacted or performed sexually.

For their direct investigation of the human response to sexual stimulation, Masters and Johnson conducted controlled laboratory observations of thousands of volunteer males and females during tens of thousands of sexual response cycles of intercourse and masturbation. Four of the most significant conclusions drawn from this research are that (1) men and women have similar patterns of sexual response; (2) although the sequence of phases of the sexual response cycle is similar in the two sexes, women are more variable, tending to respond more slowly but often remaining aroused longer; (3) many women can have multiple orgasms, while men rarely do in a comparable time period; and (4) penis size is generally unrelated to any aspect of sexual performance (except in the male's attitude toward having a large penis).

Four phases were found in the human sexual response cycle: excitement, plateau, orgasm, and resolution (see **Figure 12.1**).

- In the *excitement phase* (lasting from a few minutes to more than an hour), there are *vascular* (blood vessel) changes in the pelvic region. The penis becomes erect and the clitoris swells; blood and other fluids become congested in the testicles and vagina; a reddening of the body, or sex flush, occurs.
- During the *plateau phase*, a maximum (though varying) level of arousal is reached. There is rapidly increased heartbeat, respiration, and blood pressure, increased glandular secretions, and both voluntary and involuntary muscle tension throughout the body. Vaginal lubrication increases, and the breasts swell.
- During the *orgasm phase*, males and females experience a very intense, pleasurable sense of release from the sexual tension that has been build-

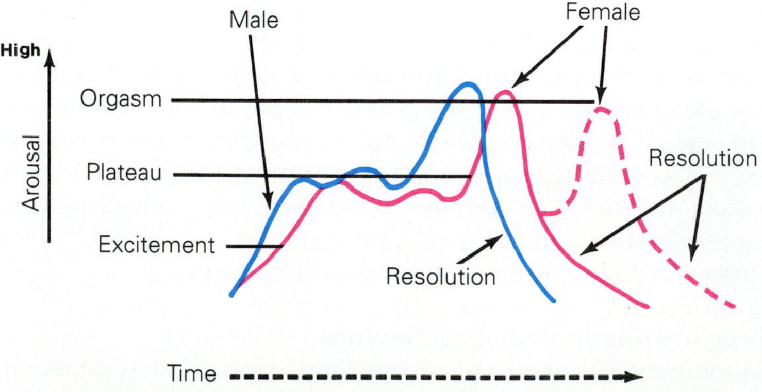

Figure 12.1 Phases of Human Sexual Response
The phases of human sexual response in males and females have similar patterns. The primary differences are in the time it takes for males and females to reach each phase, and in the greater likelihood that females will achieve multiple orgasms.

ing. Orgasm is characterized by rhythmic contractions that occur approximately every eight-tenths of a second in the genital areas. Respiration and blood pressure reach very high levels in both men and women, and heart rate may double. In men, throbbing contractions lead to ejaculation, an "explosion" of semen. In women, orgasm may be of two different types, achieved from effective stimulation of either the clitoris or the vagina.

- During the *resolution phase*, the body gradually returns to its normal pre-excitement state, with both blood pressure and heartbeat slowing down. After one orgasm, most men enter a refractory period, lasting anywhere from a few minutes to several hours, during which no further orgasm is possible. With sustained arousal, women are capable of multiple orgasms in fairly rapid succession.

Masters and Johnson identified four phases in the human sexual response: excitement, plateau, orgasm, and resolution.

We have now reviewed some evolutionary and physiological aspects of human sexuality. But we have not yet considered the environmental stimuli and psychological forces that give rise to sexual arousal. Let's now turn to these subjects, to explore how the mind manipulates sexual response.

Sexual Arousal

Sexual arousal in humans is the motivational state of excitement and tension brought about by physiological and cognitive reactions to erotic stimuli. *Erotic stimuli,* which may be physical or psychological, give rise to sexual excitement or feelings of passion. Sexual arousal induced by erotic stimuli is reduced by sexual activities that are perceived by the individual as satisfying, especially by achieving orgasm.

Although Masters and Johnson's research focused on the physiology of sexual response, perhaps their most important discovery was the central significance of *psychological* processes in both arousal and satisfaction. They demonstrated that problems in sexual response often have psychological, rather than physiological, origins and can be modified or overcome through therapy. Of particular concern is the inability to complete the response cycle and achieve gratification. This inability is called *impotence* in men and *frigidity* in women. Often the source of the inability is a preoccupation with personal problems, fear of the consequences of sexual activity, anxiety about a partner's evaluation of one's sexual performance, or unconscious guilt or negative thoughts. However, poor nutrition, fatigue, stress, and excessive use of alcohol or drugs can also diminish sexual drive and performance.

Masters and Johnson demonstrated the psychological origin of many problems in human sexual responding.

The sequence of sexual activities that may culminate in orgasm can be started by only one unconditional stimulus and by an endless variety of conditional stimuli. The unconditional stimulus is touch. *Touch,* in the form of genital caresses, is a universal component of sexual foreplay (Ford & Beach, 1951). However, virtually any stimuli that become associated with genital touch and orgasm can become conditioned motivators, whether the stimuli are in the external environment or in a person's memory or fantasy. A nonsexual object that becomes capable of producing sexual arousal through conditioning is called a **fetish.** It has been suggested that sensations and fantasy during masturbation provide the primal setting for associating virtually any stimulus with pleasurable arousal (Storms, 1980, 1981). Inanimate objects, textures, sounds, visual images, odors—any tangible or imagined stimulus event—can come to elicit arousal through this conditioned association.

Most adults in Western cultures are conditioned to find the stimulus of a mouth-to-mouth kiss sexually arousing.

When we approach the subject of fetishes, we must consider what is ordinary and what is unusual in the way that people find sexual expression. Most people obtain little firsthand knowledge of the great variety of individual patterns of sexual behavior. Let's turn now to the subject of norms of sexual behavior.

Table 12.2 Sexual Activity of Adult Americans, 1994

	Number of Sexual Partners Since Age 18 (Percentage in Each Category)			
	0	**1**	**2–10**	**10 or More**
Men	3	26	44	33
Women	3	31	56	9
Ages 25–29	2	25	53	19
Ages 55–59	1	40	43	15
High school education	3	30	49	17
College education	2	24	50	24

	Frequency of Sexual Activity in the Past 12 Months (Percentage in Each Category)			
	Not at All	**A Few Times per Year**	**A Few Times per Month**	**Two or More Times a Week**
Men	14	16	37	34
Women	10	18	36	37
Men				
Ages 25–29	7	15	31	47
Ages 55–59	11	22	43	23
Women				
Ages 25–29	5	10	38	47
Ages 55–59	30	22	35	13
Men				
High school	10	15	34	41
Some college	9	18	38	35
Women				
High school	11	16	38	36
Some college	14	17	37	33

Based on a random survey sample of 3432 adults, 18 and older.

Sexual Norms and Sexual Scripts

What is an average sex life like? Scientific investigation of human sexual behavior was given the first important impetus by the work of **Alfred Kinsey** and his colleagues beginning in the 1940s (1948, 1953). They interviewed some 17,000 Americans about their sexual behavior and revealed—to a generally shocked public—that certain behaviors, previously considered rare and even abnormal, were actually quite widespread—or at least reported to be. In recent years, researchers have conducted surveys about sexual practices with great regularity. The results are often widely trumpeted by the media. In **Table 12.2** we have provided you with some data from a recent effort (Michael et al., 1994). The researchers asked a wide range of questions. We have given you only a small sample of the responses. Can you spot any interesting trends? You might find it noteworthy, for example, that people age 55 to 59 are much more likely to have stuck with one partner since age 18 than are those age 25 to 29. This outcome suggests that the norms for sexual behavior have changed over the last several decades.

These sexual norms are part of what you acquire as a member of a culture. We already suggested that some general "male" and "female" aspects of sexual behavior may be products of the evolution of the human species. Even so, different cultures define ranges of behavior that are considered to be appropriate for expressing sexual impulses. **Sexual scripts** are socially learned programs of sexual responsiveness that include prescriptions, usually unspoken, of what to do; when, where, and how to do it; with whom, or with what, to do it; and why it should be done (Gagnon, 1977). Different aspects of these scripts are assembled through social interaction over your lifetime. The attitudes and values embodied in your sexual script are an external source of sexual motivation: the script suggests the types of behaviors you might or should undertake.

Cultures define which behaviors are considered appropriate for expressing sexual impulses.

Scripts are combinations of prescriptions generated by social norms (what is proper and accepted), individual expectations, and preferred sequences of behavior from past learning. Your sexual scripts include scenarios not only of what you think is appropriate on your part but also of your expectations for a sexual partner. When they are not recognized, discussed, or synchronized, differing scripts can create problems of adjustment between partners.

Sexual scripts are based on a combination of social norms, individual expectations, and preferred sequences of behavior.

Date Rape

Research into the sexual experience of college students has revealed an area in which male and female sexual scripts come into devastating conflict: date rape. **Date rape** applies to circumstances in which someone is coerced into sexual activity by a social acquaintance. When researchers asked college women about their experiences with unwanted sex, over half the woman reported that they had experienced it (Murnen et al., 1989). The researchers also asked those women how they had been coerced and how they had coped with the incident at the time. The most common female responses to the attack were to ignore it or to give in to the attack. Many of the women continued to see the men on subsequent occasions, although they often did not continue sexual relations.

Another study of over 500 college women and men casts more light on how date rape occurs and on how male and female sexual scripts differ (Muehlenhard & Cook, 1988). Over 90 percent of all students surveyed—both men and women—had experienced unwanted intercourse. The data revealed a variety of reasons these students had engaged in unwanted sex, including verbal and physical coercion by a date, peer pressure, alcohol or drugs, concerns about one's sex role, and concerns about the other person's feelings. Men tended to have unwanted sex because of their fears about their own sexuality and macho image. They were especially vulnerable to peer pressure to have sex—to the expectation that men are supposed to be experienced—and they were more likely than women to report having unwanted sex while drunk or high on drugs. Men were also likely to say that they had been enticed by women into unwanted sex and were unable to refuse any sexual advance for fear of being labeled as inadequate (Muehlenhard & Cook, 1988).

This study also examined the relationship between sexual attitudes and the incidence of unwanted sex. Researchers found that, for both men and women, unwanted sex was more likely to occur when one partner viewed male-female relations as *adversarial.* Specifically, it was correlated with the male script that women offer token resistance to avoid seeming promiscuous. When men believe they are supposed to disregard a woman's objections, date rape may be the result.

Researchers have found that, for both men and women, unwanted sex is related to seeing male-female relations as adversarial.

How should you interpret date rape? If you examine the motivational forces that give rise to it, you can see that what needs adjustment, in part, is our culture's sense of the norms of male and female sexual behavior. You can't excuse date rape, but you also can't reliably prevent such behavior if you don't appreciate the differing motivations that give rise to it.

Throughout most of our discussion of sexual motivation, we have been ignoring a major category of sexual experience: homosexuality. Our discussion of lesbians and gay men will give us another opportunity to see how sexual behavior is controlled by both internal and external motivational forces.

Homosexuality

Our discussion so far has focused on the motivations that cause people to perform a certain range of sexual behaviors. It is in this same context that we can discuss the existence of homosexuality. That is, rather than presenting homosexuality as a set of behaviors that is "caused" by a deviation from heterosexuality, our discussion of sexual motivation should allow you to see that all sexual behavior is "caused." In this view, homosexuality and heterosexuality result from similar motivational forces. Neither of them represents a motivated departure from the other.

In Chapter 3, we reviewed evidence that, like a heterosexual orientation, homosexuality may be transmitted genetically. Recall that studies comparing different types of twins found that identical twins were more likely to have the same sexual orientation than were fraternal twins (Bailey & Pillard, 1991; Bailey et al., 1993). Other researchers have searched for the actual chromosomal information that might help determine sexual orientation (Hamer et al., 1993). Their findings suggest that nature provides some of the sexual motivation toward homosexuality.

But does everyone act on nature's urgings? What, perhaps, most sets homosexuality apart from heterosexuality is the continuing hostility toward homosexual behaviors in many corners of society. In a survey of 363 adults completed in 1992, 68.3 percent agreed "strongly" or "somewhat" with the statement "Sex between two men is just plain wrong"; 64.3 percent agreed "strongly" or "somewhat" with the statement "Sex between two women is just plain wrong" (Herek, 1994). Most homosexuals come to the realization that they are motivated toward same-sex relationships in this hostile context—a context that might make it difficult for them to act on those feelings. In fact, many gay men and lesbians experience what has been called *internalized homophobia* or *internalized homonegativity* (Shidlo, 1994). In these cases, psychological distress may arise because the gay or lesbian individual has internalized the negative attitudes of society.

Much of lesbians' and gay men's anxiety about homosexuality arises, in fact, not from *being* homosexual but from an ongoing need either to reveal ("come out") or to conceal ("stay in the closet") their sexual identity to family, friends, and co-workers (D'Augelli, 1993). In 1973 the American Psychi-

The majority of homosexuals report feeling personally comfortable with their sexual orientation.

atric Association voted to remove homosexuality from the list of psychological disorders; the American Psychological Association followed in 1975 (Morin & Rothblum, 1991). Spurring this action were research reports suggesting that, in fact, most gay men and lesbians are happy, productive human beings who would not change their sexual orientation even if a "magic pill" enabled them to do so (Bell & Weinberg, 1978; Siegelman, 1972). These data suggest that much of the stress associated with homosexuality arises not from the sexual motivation itself—gay people are happy with their orientations—but from the way in which people respond to the revelation of that sexual motivation. As you might expect, gay men and lesbians also spend time worrying about establishing and maintaining loving relationships (D'Augelli, 1993).

Most surveys of sexual behavior have tried to obtain an accurate estimate of the incidence of homosexuality. In his early research, Alfred Kinsey found that a large percentage of men in his sample had had at least some homosexual experience, and that about 4 percent were exclusively homosexual (percentages for women were somewhat smaller). More recent surveys have tried to capture the distinction between having homosexual desires and acting on them. Michael et al. (1994) found that about 4 percent of women in their sample were sexually attracted to individuals of the same gender, but only 2 percent of the sample had actually had sex with another woman in the past year. Similarly, 6 percent of the men in their survey were sexually attracted to other men, but again only 2 percent of the sample had actually had sex with another man in the past year. Are these figures correct? As long as there is societal hostility directed toward acting on homosexual desires, it may be impossible to get entirely accurate estimates of the incidence of homosexuality.

This brief review of homosexuality allows us to reinforce our main conclusions about human sexual motivation. Some of the impetus for sexual behaviors is internal—genetic endowment and species evolution provides internal models for both heterosexual and homosexual behaviors. But the external environment also gives rise to sexual motivation. You learn to find some stimuli particularly alluring and some behaviors culturally acceptable. In the case of homosexuality, external societal norms may work against the internal dictates of nature.

Let's turn now to our third example of important motivation: the forces that set an individual's course for relative success or failure.

MOTIVATION FOR PERSONAL ACHIEVEMENT

Why do some people succeed while other people, relatively speaking, fail? Why, for example, are some people able to swim the English Channel, while other people just wave woefully from the shore? You are likely to attribute some of the difference to genetic factors like body type, and you're correct to do so. But you also know that some people are simply much more interested in swimming the English Channel than are others. So we are back at one of our core reasons for studying motivation. We want, in this case, to understand the motivational forces that lead different people to seek different levels of personal achievement. Let's begin with a construct that's actually called the *need for achievement.*

Motivation can explain variability among individuals—the fact that some people do better in competition than others, for example. These men are participating in the International Games for the Disabled.

NEED FOR ACHIEVEMENT

As early as 1938, **Henry Murray** had postulated a need to achieve that varied in strength in different people and influenced their tendency to approach success and evaluate their own performances. **David McClelland** and his colleagues (1953) devised a way to measure the strength of this need and then

Henry Murray and David McClelland were instrumental in advancing the study and measure of need for achievement.

looked for relationships between strength of achievement motivation in different societies, conditions that had fostered the motivation, and its results in the work world. To gauge the strength of the need for achievement, McClelland used his subjects' fantasies. On what is called the **Thematic Apperception Test** (TAT), subjects were asked to generate stories in response to a series of ambiguous drawings.

> Subjects shown TAT pictures were asked to make up stories about them—to say what was happening in the picture and describe probable outcomes. Presumably, they projected into the scene reflections of their own values, interests, and motives. According to McClelland: "If you want to find out what's on a person's mind, don't ask him, because he can't always tell you accurately. Study his fantasies and dreams. If you do this over a period of time, you will discover the themes to which his mind returns again and again. And these themes can be used to explain his actions. . . ." (1971, p. 5)

From subject responses to a series of TAT pictures, McClelland worked out measures of several human needs. The **need for achievement** was designated as *n Ach.* It reflected individual differences in the importance of planning and working toward attaining one's goals. **Figure 12.2** shows an example of how a high *n Ach* individual and a low *n Ach* individual might interpret a TAT picture. Studies in both laboratory and real-life settings have validated the usefulness of this measure.

For example, high-scoring *n Ach* people were found to be more upwardly mobile than those with low scores; sons who had high *n Ach* scores were more likely than sons with low *n Ach* measures to advance above their fathers' occupational status (McClelland et al., 1976). Men and women who measured high on *n Ach* at age 31 tended to have higher salaries than their low *n Ach* peers by age 41 (McClelland & Franz, 1992). Do these findings indicate that high *n Ach* individuals are always willing to work harder? Not really. In the face of a task that they are led to believe will be difficult, high *n Ach* individuals quit early on (Feather, 1961). What, in fact, seems to typify high *n Ach* individuals is a need for *efficiency*—a need to get the same result for less effort. If they outearn their peers, it might be because they also value concrete feedback on how well they are doing. As a measure of progress, salary is very concrete (McClelland, 1961; McClelland & Franz, 1992).

How does a high need for achievement arise? Researchers have considered whether parenting practices can bring about high or low need for achievement. Data come from a longitudinal analysis of a group of Boston-area children.

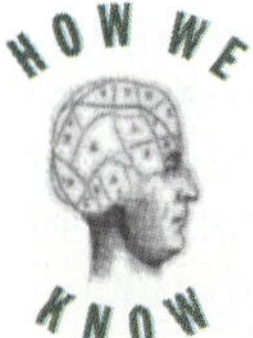

David McClelland and Carol Franz (1992) compared measures of parenting practice, collected in 1951 when the children were about 5 years old, with measures of *n Ach* and earnings, collected in 1987–1988, when the children were 41. In 1951, the parents were asked to indicate their practices with respect to feeding and toilet training the child. McClelland and Franz considered children to have experienced a high degree of *achievement pressure* when their parents had fed and toilet trained them by strict rules. Overall, there was a positive correlation between achievement pressure and *n Ach.* Furthermore, children who had experienced a high degree of achievement pressure were earning about $10,000 more annually than their peers who had experienced little such pressure.

These data suggest that the degree to which you experience a need to achieve may have been established in the first few years of your life.

Figure 12.2 Alternative Interpretations of a TAT Picture

Story Showing High n Ach

The boy has just finished his violin lesson. He's happy at the progress he is making and is beginning to believe that all his progress is making the sacrifices worthwhile. To become a concert violinist, he will have to give up much of his social life and practice for many hours each day. Although he knows he could make more money by going into his father's business, he is more interested in being a great violinist and giving people joy with his music. He renews his personal commitment to do all it takes to make it.

Story Showing Low n Ach

The boy is holding his brother's violin and wishes he could play it. But he knows it isn't worth the time, energy, and money for lessons. He feels sorry for his brother, who has given up all the enjoyable things in life to practice, practice, practice. It would be great to wake up one day and be a top-notch musician, but it doesn't happen that way. The reality is boring practice, no fun, and the strong possibility of becoming just another guy playing a musical instrument in a small-town band.

Attributions for Success and Failure

Need for achievement is not the only variable that affects motivation toward personal success. To see why, let's begin with a hypothetical example. Suppose you have two friends who are taking the same class. On the first midterm, each gets a C. Do you think they would be equally motivated to study hard for the second midterm? Part of the answer will depend on the way in which they each explained the C to themselves.

Consider, for example, the importance of locus of control (Rotter, 1954). A **locus of control orientation** is a belief about whether the outcomes of your actions are contingent on what you do (*internal control orientation*) or on environmental factors (*external control orientation*). In the case of the C's, your friends might *attribute* their performance to either an external cause (construction noise during the exam) or an internal cause (poor memory).

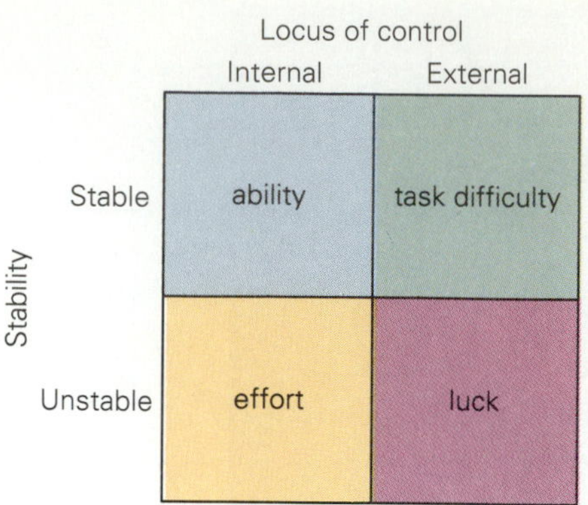

Locus of control
Internal
External
Stable
Unstable
Stability
ability
task difficulty
effort
luck

Figure 12.3 Attributions Regarding Causes for Behavioral Outcomes
Four possible outcomes are generated with just two sources of attributions about behavior: the locus of control and the situation in which the behavior occurs. Ability attributions are made for the internal-stable combination, effort for the internal but unstable combination, luck for the unstable-external combination, and a difficult task (test) when external stable forces are assumed to be operating.

Attributions are judgments about the causes of outcomes. (We will develop *attribution theory* at length in Chapter 16.) In this case, the attributions can have an impact on motivation. If your friends believe they can attribute their performance to construction noise, they are likely to study hard for the next midterm. If they think the fault lies in their poor memory, they're more likely to slack off.

Motivation is influenced by casual attributions, which may be specific or global, stable or unstable, and internal or external.

Locus of control is not the only dimension along which attributions can vary (Peterson & Seligman, 1984). We can also ask, To what extent is a causal factor likely to be stable and consistent over time, or unstable and varying? The answer gives us the dimension of *stability* versus *instability*. Or we can ask, To what extent is a causal factor highly specific, limited to a particular task or situation, or global, applying widely across a variety of settings? This gives us the dimension of *global* versus *specific*.

An example of how locus of control and stability can interact is given in **Figure 12.3**. Let's stay with the example of attributions about exam grades. Your friends can interpret their grades as the result of internal factors, such as ability (a stable personality characteristic) or effort (a varying personal quality). Or they may view the grades as caused primarily by external factors such as the difficulty of the task, the actions of others (a stable situational problem), or luck (an unstable external feature). Depending on the nature of the attribution they make for this success or failure, they are likely to experience one of the emotional responses depicted in **Table 12.3**. What is important here is that the type of interpretation will influence both emotions and subsequent motivation—regardless of the true reason for the success or failure.

Beliefs about *why* you have succeeded or failed, then, are important because they lead to (1) different interpretations of past performance and general worth; (2) different emotions, goals, and effort in the present situation; and (3) different motivation in the future—in turn, making future successes more likely or less so. When you attribute a failure to low ability and difficult tasks, you are likely to give up sooner, select simpler tasks, and lower your goals. When you attribute failure to bad luck or to lack of effort, you are likely to have higher motivation to try again for success (Fontaine, 1974; Valle & Frieze, 1976).

So far we have been considering the possibility that both of your friends will explain their C's in the same way, but it's very likely that they might arrive at different explanations. One may believe something external ("The professor gave an unfair exam"); the other may believe something internal ("I'm not smart enough for this class"). Researchers have shown that the way people explain events in their lives—from winning at cards to being turned down for a date—can become lifelong, habitual *attributional styles* (Trotter, 1987). The way you account for your successes and failures can influence

Table 12.3 Attribution-Dependent Emotional Responses

Your feelings in response to success and failure depend on the kinds of attributions you make regarding the cause of those outcomes. For example, you take pride in success when you attribute it to your ability, but are depressed when you perceive lack of ability to cause failure. Or you feel gratitude when you attribute your success to the actions of others but anger when they are seen as contributing to your failure.

	Emotional Responses	
Attribution	**Success**	**Failure**
Ability	Competence Confidence Pride	Incompetence Resignation Depression
Effort	Relief Contentment Relaxation	Guilt Shame Fear
Action of others	Gratitude Thankfulness	Anger Fury
Luck	Surprise Guilt	Surprise Astonishment

your motivation, mood, and even ability to perform appropriately. For several years, researcher **Martin Seligman** has studied the ways in which people's *explanatory style*—their degree of optimism or pessimism—affects activity and passivity, whether they persist or give up easily, take risks or play it safe (Seligman, 1987, 1991).

Martin Seligman has focused his research on the ways in which a person's explanatory style influences activity, persistence, and risk taking.

In Chapter 17, we will see that an internal-global-stable explanatory style ("I never do anything right") puts individuals at risk for depression (and one of the symptoms of depression is impaired motivation). For now, however, let's focus on the way in which explanatory style might lead one of your friends to have an A and one an F by the end of the semester.

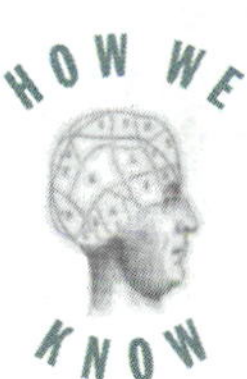

Seligman's research team has worked on the problem of explaining one person's ability and another's inability to resist failure. The secret ingredient has turned out to be familiar and seemingly simple: *optimism* versus *pessimism*. Remarkably, these two divergent ways of looking at the world influence motivation, mood, and behavior. The methods used to assess these styles are a self-report questionnaire and analysis of causal statements made in natural speech (found in newspapers, press conferences, and therapy transcripts) to reconstruct people's beliefs. Each statement about the causes of some important life event is then coded by judges, who rate the extent to which the message is internal-external, stable-unstable, and global-specific. A profile is generated of the kinds of causal statements a person uses in his or her natural speech, indexing the individual as pessimist, optimist, or other (Seligman, 1991).

When success comes your way, do you give yourself full credit for the achievement? If so, you are likely to be an optimistic person.

The pessimistic attributional style focuses on the causes of *failure* as internally generated. Furthermore, the bad situation and the individual's role in causing it are seen as stable and global—"It won't ever change and it will affect everything." The *optimistic attributional style* sees failure as the result of external causes—"The test was unfair"—and of events that are unstable or modifiable and specific—"If I put in more effort next time, I'll do better, and this one setback won't affect how I perform any other task that is important to me." These causal explanations are reversed when it comes to

According to Seligman's research, the secret ingredient most influencing a person's resistance to failure is optimism.

the question of *success*. Optimists take full, personal internal-stable-global credit for success. However, pessimists attribute their success to external-unstable-global or specific factors. Because they believe themselves to be doomed to fail, pessimists perform worse than others would expect, given objective measures of their talent. For both optimists and pessimists, interpretations of events affect their level of motivation for future performance.

To close out this section, let's look at a research example of the powerful impact of causal attributions in an academic setting.

In one study, investigators selected second-semester freshmen who, by self-report, were "worriers" about their academic performance. Half of them received an experimental treatment that consisted of a program of information about typical changes in grade-point average (GPA) from freshmen year to later years of college. Some of the information they saw was from a survey of upperclassmen who revealed, for example, that 62 percent of their GPAs had improved significantly from first semester freshmen year to their upperclass years. This experimental group also watched videotaped interviews with upperclassmen who, again, among other information, testified to improved GPA since their freshmen years. The control group received none of this information.

To test the impact of this GPA information, the experimenters used both short-term (immediately or within a week) and long-term (across several semesters) measures. As part of the original experimental session and again one week later, both the experimental and control groups were asked to take a reading comprehension test. Subjects in the experimental group answered reliably more comprehension questions correctly. The experimenters also looked at the number of students in each group who dropped out of college by the end of sophomore year. The rate was 5 percent for the experimental group and 25 percent—five times as high—for the control group. Finally, the experimenters obtained subjects' GPAs later in their college lives. For the experimental group there was a 0.34 increase in GPA from first semester of freshman year to second semester of sophomore year. Over the same period of time, the control group's average GPA went down by 0.05 points (Wilson & Linville, 1982; see also Wilson & Linville, 1985).

Why should a small amount of information about changes in GPA have such a profound effect on students' performance? The answer may lie in the way that attributions affect motivation. If you believe you are having a mediocre first semester in college because there's something wrong with *you*—a negative, internal, stable attribution—you're unlikely to believe that things can get better. If, on the other hand, you make what might be a more appropriate attribution to the external situation—many students get off to a tough start!—you might feel newly energized, newly motivated, and able to fulfill your potential.

We believe that there is much value to you in this line of psychological research. You can work at developing an optimistic explanatory style. You can avoid making negative, stable, dispositional attributions for your failures by examining possible causal forces in the situation. Finally, don't let your motivation be undermined by momentary setbacks.

Work and Organizational Psychology

Now suppose your positive philosophy has helped you to get a job in a big corporation. Can we predict exactly how motivated you'll be just by knowing about you, as an individual—your *n Ach* score or your explanatory style? Your individual level of motivation will depend, in part, on the overall context of people and rules in which you work. Recognizing that work settings are complex social systems, **organizational psychologists** study various aspects of human relations, such as communication among employees, socialization or enculturation of workers, leadership, attitudes and commitment toward a job and/or an organization, job satisfaction, stress and burnout, and overall quality of life at work. As consultants to businesses, organizational psychologists may assist in recruitment, selection, and training of employees. They also make recommendations about job redesign—tailoring a job to fit the person. Organizational psychologists apply theories of management, decision making, and development to improve work settings (O'Reilly, 1991; Porras & Silvers, 1991).

Let's look at a pair of theories organizational psychologists have developed to understand motivation in the workplace. *Equity theory* and *expectancy theory* attempt to explain and predict how people will respond under different working conditions. These theories assume that workers engage in certain cognitive activities, such as assessing fairness through processes of social comparison with other workers or estimating expected rewards associated with their performance.

To what extent do nonmonetary factors, like employee recognition and respect, improve job satisfaction?

Equity theory proposes that workers are motivated to maintain fair or equitable relationships with other relevant persons (Adams, 1965). Workers take note of their inputs (investments or contributions they make to their jobs) and their outcomes (what they receive from their jobs), and then they compare these with the inputs and outcomes of other workers. When the ratio of outcomes to inputs for Worker A is equal to the ratio for Worker B (outcome A ÷ input A = outcome B ÷ input B), then Worker A will feel satisfied. Dissatisfaction will result when these ratios are *not* equal. Because feeling this inequity is aversive, workers will be motivated to restore equity by changing the relevant inputs and outcomes. These changes could be *behavioral* (for example, reducing input by working less, increasing outcome by asking for a raise). Or they could be *psychological* (for example, reinterpreting the value of the inputs—"My work isn't really that good"—or the value of the outcome—"I'm lucky to have a weekly paycheck I can count on").

Research has supported the predictions of equity theory, particularly with regard to perceived underpayment (Carrel & Dittrich, 1978). One study showed that underpaid clerical workers were less productive, and overpaid workers more productive, than equitably paid workers (Pritchard et al., 1972). Similarly, college students who were given additional responsibilities and a high-status job title maintained high levels of performance, whereas students who were given additional responsibilities but no title (underpayment inequity) dramatically reduced their performance (Greenberg & Ornstein, 1983).

Expectancy theory proposes that workers are motivated when they expect that their effort and performance on the job will result in desired outcomes (Porter & Lawler, 1968; Vroom, 1964). In other words, people will engage in work they find attractive (leading to favorable consequences) and achievable. Expectancy theory emphasizes three components. *Instrumentality* refers to the perception that performance will be rewarded. *Valence* refers to the perceived attractiveness of particular outcomes. *Expectancy* refers to the perceived likelihood that a worker's efforts will result in successful performance. With respect to a particular work situation, you can imagine different probabilities for these three components. You might, for example, have a job in which there is a high likelihood of reward if performance is successful (high instrumentality) but a low likelihood that performance will be successful (low expectancy) or a low likelihood that the reward will be worthwhile (low valence). According to expectancy theory, workers assess the probabilities of these three components and combine them by multiplying their indi-

Expectancy theory explores the components of instrumentality, valence, and expectancy as related to motivation.

vidual values. Highest levels of motivation, therefore, result when all three components have high probabilities, whereas lowest levels result when any single component is zero. Research has been supportive of expectancy theory, demonstrating proposed relationships between expectancy, instrumentality, and motivation (Garland, 1984; Mitchell, 1974).

As a conclusion to this section, we offer a cautionary note on achievement and motivation in work settings. When you make a personal choice about how hard you can work at a career, keep a careful watch on other aspects of your life. A study of over 4000 successful business executives revealed widespread dissatisfaction with the corporate experience. Nearly half of all middle managers said that their lives seemed "empty and meaningless" despite years spent striving to achieve their personal goals. A majority of senior executives reported that they felt they've wasted much of their lives struggling for corporate success, with the consequence that family and personal life was sacrificed. If they could start all over again, they believe, they would rearrange their priorities (Tuller, 1989). But do you think they really would?

Individualist Versus Collectivist Cultures

We will complete this brief look at motivation toward personal success by noting that not all cultures put a deep value on such achievement. The cardinal virtues of self-reliance, independence, and personal achievement run deeply in many Western countries. However, emphasis on *individualism,* with its focus on personal needs and goals, is at odds with the values of *collectivism* emphasized in the majority of cultures in Africa, Asia, South America, Central America, and the Middle East. Cross-cultural psychologist **Harry Triandis** (1990, 1994) has argued that the distinction between individualism and collectivism is the key to understanding many cultural contrasts. Collectivist societies, which comprise 70 percent of the world's population, have among the lowest rates of homicide, suicide, juvenile delinquency, divorce, child abuse, and alcoholism. Whereas individualists look for immediate personal rewards, freedom, equality, personal enjoyment, and a varied, exciting life, collectivists put high value on self-discipline and on accepting one's position in life, honoring parents and other elders, preserving one's image, and working toward long-term goals that benefit the group as a whole.

According to cross-cultural psychologist Harry Triandis, the distinction between individualistic and collectivist cultures explains many cultural differences in motivation.

These deep-rooted cultural differences clearly play vital roles in the motivational psychology of the individual and the group. Asian-American children, for example, have an extensive support system that inspires confidence; their parents have a lifelong sense of purpose and security. "Education is pushed for family reasons, not simply as a means of achieving personal ambition. The idea is that the children will always care for the parents, so anything that serves the younger generation well is a family affair. That can come into direct conflict with American individualism" (F. Lee, quoted by Vivano, 1989). Despite the effect of culture on the psychology of the individual, virtually all the data from modern psychology come from the most individualistic cultures. The study of the need for achievement is centered on the personal ambitions of the individual. It ignores the need to achieve group goals. Future research will have to correct this imbalance by analyzing motivational forces in different collectivist cultures.

A HIERARCHY OF NEEDS

In the last three sections, we have focused on specific types of motivation and specific types of behaviors. To close out the chapter, we return to a more global account of motivation. Our intent is to give you a general sense of the forces that could guide your life.

Humanist psychologist **Abraham Maslow** (1970) formulated the theory that basic motives form a **hierarchy of needs,** as illustrated in **Figure 12.4.**

In Maslow's view, the needs at each level of the hierarchy must be satisfied—the needs are arranged in a sequence from primitive to advanced—before the next level can be achieved. At the bottom of this hierarchy are the basic *biological needs,* such as hunger and thirst. They must be met before any other needs can begin to operate. When biological needs are pressing, other needs are put on hold and are unlikely to influence your actions. When they are reasonably well satisfied, the needs at the next level—*safety needs*—motivate you. When you are no longer concerned about danger, you become motivated by *attachment needs*—needs to belong, to affiliate with others, to love, and to be loved. If you are well fed and safe and if you feel a sense of social belonging, you move up to *esteem needs*—to like oneself, to see oneself as competent and effective, and to do what is necessary to earn the esteem of others.

Humans are thinking beings, with complex brains that demand the stimulation of thought. You are motivated by strong *cognitive needs* to know your past, to comprehend the puzzles of current existence, and to predict the future. It is the force of these needs that enables scientists to spend their lives in discovering new knowledge. At the next level of Maslow's hierarchy comes the human desire for beauty and order, in the form of *esthetic needs* that give rise to the creative side of humanity.

At the top of the hierarchy are people who are nourished, safe, loved and loving, secure, thinking, and creating. These people have moved beyond basic human needs in the quest for fullest development of their potentials, or *self-actualization.* A self-actualizing person is self-aware, self-accepting, socially responsive, creative, spontaneous, and open to novelty and challenge, among other positive attributes. Maslow's hierarchy includes a step beyond the total fulfillment of individual potential. *Needs for transcendence* may lead to higher states of consciousness and a cosmic vision of one's part in the universe. Very few people move beyond the self to achieve union with spiritual forces.

Maslow's theory is a particularly upbeat view of human motivation. At the core of the theory is the need for each individual to grow and actualize his or her highest potential. Can we maintain such an unfailingly positive view? The data suggest that we cannot. Alongside the needs Maslow recognized, we find that people express power, dominance, and aggression. You also know from your own experience that Maslow's strict hierarchy breaks down. You're likely, for example, to have ignored hunger on occasion to pursue higher-level needs. Even with these qualifications, however, we hope Maslow's scheme will enable you to bring some order to different aspects of your motivational experiences.

We have come a long way since we asked you to consider the question "Why did I get out of bed this morning?" We have described the biology and psychology of hunger and eating, and the evolutionary and social dimensions of human sexuality. We have explored individual differences in people's need to achieve and explain personal success. Throughout this discussion, you have seen the intricate interplay of nature and nurture, at the level of both the species and the individual. So, with all this information in hand, why *did* you get out of bed this morning?

Transcendence
spiritual needs for cosmic identification

Self-Actualization
needs to fulfill potential, have meaningful goals

Esthetic
needs for order, beauty

Cognitive
needs for knowledge, understanding, novelty

Esteem
needs for confidence, sense of worth and competence, self-esteem and respect of others

Attachment
needs to belong, to affiliate, to love and to be loved

Safety
needs for security, comfort, tranquility, freedom from fear

Biological
needs for food, water, oxygen, rest, sexual expression, release from tension

Figure 12.4 Maslow's Hierarchy of Needs
According to Maslow, needs at the lower level of the hierarchy dominate an individual's motivation as long as they are unsatisfied. Once these needs are adequately met, the higher needs occupy the individual's attention.

Recapping Main Points

Understanding Motivation

Motivation is a dynamic concept used to describe the processes directing behavior. Motivational analysis helps explain how biological and behavioral processes are related and why people pursue goals despite obstacles and adversity. No one theory has been able to explain motivation completely. Drive theory conceptualized motivation as tension reduction. Instinct theory

The need to belong, to form attachments and experience love, is a primary item on Maslow's hierarchy.

suggested that motivation often relies on innate stereotypical responses. Social and cognitive psychologists emphasize the individual's perception and interpretation of and reaction to a situation.

Eating

The body has a number of mechanisms to regulate the initiation and cessation of eating. If obese individuals become restrained eaters, their diets may result in weight gain rather than weight loss. Eating disorders are life-threatening illnesses that may arise from societal pressure and misperceptions of body image.

Sexual Behaviors

From an evolutionary perspective, sex is the mechanism for producing offspring. In animals, the sex drive is largely controlled by hormones. In humans, sexual activity is subject to learning and cultural values. Kinsey's surveys of American sexual behavior brought the study of sex into the open. The work of Masters and Johnson provided the first hard data on the sexual response cycles of men and women. Discrepancies in sexual scripts can lead to serious misunderstanding and even date rape. Homosexuality and heterosexuality are alternative outlets for sexual motivation.

Motivation for Personal Achievement

People have varying needs for achievement. Motivation for achievement is influenced by how people interpret success and failure. Two attributional styles, optimism and pessimism, lead to different attitudes toward achievement and influence motivation. Organizational psychologists study human motivation in work settings. Societies emphasize either individualism or collectivism.

A Hierarchy of Needs

Abraham Maslow suggested that human needs can be organized hierarchically. Although real human motivation is more complex, Maslow's theory provides a useful framework for summarizing motivational forces.

Resources

Locke, E., & Latham, G. (1990). *A theory of goal setting and task performance.* Englewood Cliffs, NJ: Prentice-Hall.

Logue, A. W. (1991). *The psychology of eating and drinking: An introduction* (2nd ed.). New York: Freeman.

McClelland, D. (1988). *Human motivation.* Cambridge: Cambridge University Press.

Maslow, A. H. (1987). *Motivation and personality* (3rd ed.). New York: Harper & Row.

Michael, R. T., Gagnon, J. H., Laumann, E. O., & Kolata, G. (1994). *Sex in America: A definitive survey.* Boston: Little, Brown.

Tannahill, R. (1982). *Sex in history.* Lanham, MD: Madison Books.

Weiner, B. (1992). *Human motivation: Metaphors, theories, and research.* Newbury Park, CA: Sage.

Wright, R. (1994). *The moral animal.* New York: Pantheon.

13

Emotion, Stress, and Health

Suppose we asked you right now, "How are you feeling?" How would you answer that question? There are at least three different types of information you might provide. First, you might reveal to us the mood you are in—the emotions *you are feeling. Are you happy, because you know you can finish reading this chapter in time to go to a party? Are you angry, because your boss just yelled at you over the telephone? Second, you might tell us something more general about the amount of* stress *you are experiencing. Do you feel as if you can cope with all the tasks you have to get done? Or are you feeling a bit overwhelmed? Third, you might report on your psychological or physical* health*. Do you feel some illness coming on? Or do you feel an overall sense of wellness?*

This chapter will explore interactions among these three ways in which you might answer the question "How are you feeling?"—in relation to your emotions, stress, and health. Emotions are the touchstones of human experience. They give richness to your interactions with people and nature, and significance to your memories. In this chapter, we will discuss the functions and experience of emotions. But what happens if the emotional demands on your biological and psychological functioning are too great? You may become overwhelmed and unable to deal with the stressors of your life. This chapter will also examine how stress affects you and how you can combat it. Finally, we will broaden our focus to consider psychology's contributions to the study of health and illness. Health psychologists *investigate the ways in which environmental, social, and psychological processes contribute to the development of disease. Health psychologists also use psychological processes and principles to help treat and prevent illness, while also developing strategies to enhance personal wellness.*

We begin now by looking at the content and meaning of emotions.

Fiction writers have often made use of the concept of a character who looks, talks, and behaves like a human—but who has no emotions.

EMOTIONS

Just imagine what your life would be like if you could think and act but not feel. Would you be willing to give up the capacity to experience fear if you would also lose the passion of a lover's kiss? Would you give up sadness at the expense of joy? Surely these would be bad bargains, promptly regretted. We will soon see that emotions serve a number of important functions. Let us begin, however, by offering a definition of emotion and by describing the roots of your emotional experiences.

Although you might be tempted to think of emotion as only a feeling—"I feel happy" or "I feel angry"—we need a more inclusive definition of this important concept. Contemporary psychologists define **emotion** as a complex pattern of bodily and mental changes that includes physiological arousal, feelings, cognitive processes, and behavioral reactions made in response to a situation perceived as personally significant (Kleinginna & Kleinginna, 1981). To see why all of these components are necessary, imagine a situation that would make you feel very happy. Your physiological arousal might include a swiftly beating heart. Your feeling would be positive. The associated cognitive processes include interpretations, memories, and

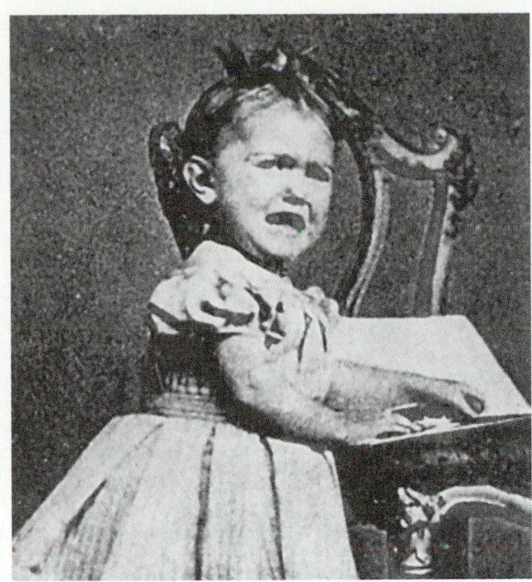

Charles Darwin was one of the first to use photographs in the study of emotion. These plates are from The Expression of Emotions in Man and Animals, *published in 1872.*

expectations that allow you to label the situation as happy. Your overt behavioral reactions might be expressive (smiling) and/or action-oriented (whooping for joy). Our account of emotions will attempt to put all these pieces together—arousal, feelings, thoughts, and actions.

Contemporary psychologists consider the physiological, behavioral, and cognitive aspects of emotion in addition to feelings.

Basic Emotions and Culture

Suppose you could gather together in one room representatives from a great diversity of human cultures. What would be common in their experiences of emotion? For an initial answer, you might look to Charles Darwin's book *The Expression of Emotions in Man and Animals* (1872). Darwin believed that emotions evolved alongside other important aspects of human and nonhuman structures. He was interested in the *adaptive* functions of emotions, which he thought of not as vague, unpredictable, personal states but as highly specific, coordinated modes of operation of the human brain. Darwin viewed emotions as inherited, specialized mental states designed to deal with a certain class of *recurring situations* in the world. Over the history of our species, humans have been attacked by predators, fallen in love, given birth to children, fought each other, confronted their mates' sexual infidelity, and witnessed the death of loved ones—innumerable times. We might expect, therefore, that certain types of emotional responses would emerge in all members of the human species. Researchers have tested this claim of the universality of emotions by looking at the emotional responses of newborn children as well as the consistency of facial expressions across cultures.

Charles Darwin initiated the idea that certain types of emotions are shared by all members of the human species and that these emotions have evolved along with other aspects of behavior.

Are Some Emotional Responses Innate?

If the evolutionary perspective is correct, we would expect to find much the same patterns of emotional responses in children all over the world (Izard, 1994). **Sylvan Tompkins** (1962, 1981) was one of the first psychologists to emphasize the pervasive role of immediate, unlearned affective (emotional) reactions. He points out that, without prior learning, infants respond to loud sounds with fear or with difficulties in breathing. They seem "prewired" to respond to certain stimuli with an emotional response general enough to fit a wide range of circumstances. Cross-cultural research has confirmed this expectation that some emotional responses are universal.

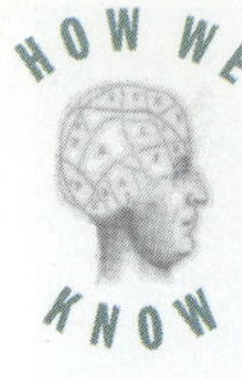

Five- and 12-month-old children in the United States and Japan were visited in their homes. The experimenters subjected each child to a procedure in which the infant's wrists were grasped and folded across the infant's stomach. The experimenters videotaped the infants' responses. Infants from both cultures moved their facial muscles in the same patterns—resulting in highly similar expressions of distress. Japanese and American infants also showed similar rates of negative vocalization and physical struggling (Camras et al., 1992).

These results suggest that all infants start out with much the same repertory of general facial and behavioral responses. These responses, however, are not as specific—sad, angry, fearful—as the facial expressions produced by adults (Camras, 1992; Camras et al., 1993). Infants' emotional responses are less differentiated—they may be generally negative or generally positive without being linked to a specific emotion. Note that infants also seem to have an innate ability to interpret the facial expressions of others. In one experiment, 4- to 6-month-old infants habituated—they showed decreasing interest—to repeated presentations of adult faces showing a single emotion drawn from the set of surprise, fear, and anger (see Chapter 5 for examples of habituation procedures with children). When the infants were subsequently shown a photograph with a different emotion, they responded with renewed interest—suggesting that surprise, fear, and anger expressions "looked different" to them, even at these very young ages (Serrano et al., 1992).

Although research confirms the expectation that some emotions are universal, the expression of emotions appears to be less differentiated in infants than in adults.

Are Emotional Expressions Universal?

We have seen that infants produce and perceive standard emotional expressions. If that is so, we might also expect to find adult members of even vastly different cultures showing reasonable agreement in the way they believe emotion is expressed by facial expressions.

According to **Paul Ekman,** the leading researcher on the nature of facial expressions, all people share an overlap in "facial language" (Ekman, 1984, 1994; Ekman & Friesen, 1975; see also Izard, 1971). Ekman and his associates have demonstrated what Darwin first proposed—that a set of emotional expressions is *universal* to the human species, presumably because they are innate components of our evolutionary heritage. Take the facial emotion identification test in **Figure 13.1** to see how well you can identify these seven universally recognized expressions of emotion (Ekman & Friesen, 1986). There is considerable evidence that these seven expressions are recognized and produced worldwide in response to the emotions of *happiness, surprise, anger, disgust, fear, sadness,* and *contempt.*

Facial expressions appear to be a universal language for the seven basic emotions, experienced and understood by people all over the world, regardless of differences in age, sex, education, or culture.

Cross-cultural researchers have asked people from a variety of cultures to identify the emotions associated with expressions in standardized photographs. Subjects are generally able to identify the expressions associated with the seven listed emotions.

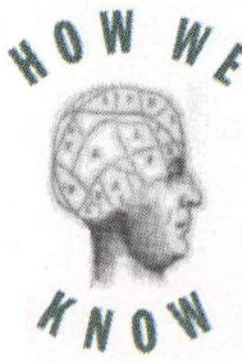

In one study, members of a preliterate culture in New Guinea (the Fore culture), who had had almost no exposure to Westerners or to Western culture prior to this experiment, accurately identified the emotions expressed in the Caucasian faces shown in Figure 13.1. They did so by referring to *situations* in which they had experienced the same emotion. For example, photo 5 (fear) suggested being chased by a wild boar when you didn't have your spear, and photo 6 (sadness) suggested your child had died. Their only confusion came in distinguishing surprise from fear, perhaps because these people are most fearful when taken by surprise.

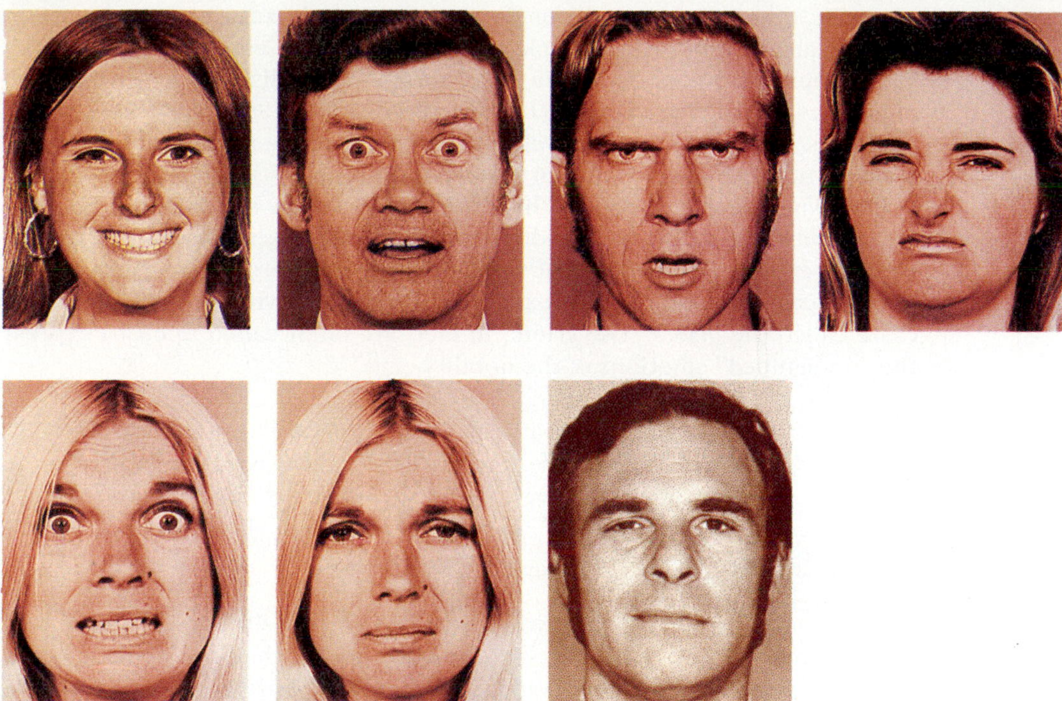

Figure 13.1 Facial Emotion Expressions
What emotion is being expressed by each of these faces? The two rows, starting at the top left, show happiness, surprise, anger, disgust, fear, sadness, and contempt.

> Next, researchers asked other members of the culture (who had not participated in the first study) to model the expressions that they used to communicate six of the emotions (excluding contempt). When U.S. college students viewed videotapes of the facial expressions of the Fore people, they were able to identify their emotions accurately—with one exception. Not surprisingly, the Americans had difficulty distinguishing between the Fore poses of fear and surprise, the same emotions that the Fore had confused in the Western poses (Ekman & Friesen, 1971).

People all over the world, regardless of cultural differences, race, sex, or education, express basic emotions in the same way and are able to identify the emotions others are experiencing by reading their facial expressions.

Note that the claim of universality is focused on the basic set of seven emotions. Ekman and his colleagues make no claim that *all* facial expressions are universal or that cultures express all emotions in the same way (Ekman, 1994). In fact, Ekman (1972) called his position on universality the *neuro-cultural* position, to reflect the joint contributions of the brain (the product of evolution) and of culture in emotional expression. The brain specifies which facial muscles move, to produce a particular expression, when a particular emotion is aroused. Different cultures, however, impose their own constraints beyond universal biology. Let's look now at cultural influences on emotionality.

How Does Culture Constrain Emotional Expression?

People all over the world may share a genetic inheritance that specifies a certain range of emotional expression. Even so, different cultures have different standards for how emotion should be managed. Some forms of emotional response, even facial expressions, are unique to each culture. Cultures establish social rules for when people may show certain emotions and for the social appropriateness of certain types of emotional displays by given types of people in particular settings (Lutz & Abu-Lughod, 1990). Let's look at two examples of cultures that express emotions in manners different from the Western norm. We begin with an African culture.

The Wolof people of Senegal live in a society where status and power differences among people are rigidly defined. High-caste members of this culture are expected to show great restraint in their expressions of emotionality; low-caste individuals are expected to be more volatile, particularly a caste called the *griots.* The griots, in fact, are often called upon to express the "undignified" emotions of the nobility.

> One afternoon, a group of women (some five nobles and two griots) were gathered near a well on the edge of town when another woman strode over to the well and threw herself down it. All the women were shocked at the apparent suicide attempt, but the noble women were shocked in silence. Only the griot women screamed, on behalf of all. (Irvine, 1990, p. 146)

Can you imagine how you would respond in this situation? It might be easier to put yourself in the place of the griots rather than in the place of the noble women: How could you help but scream? The answer, of course, is that the noble women have acquired cultural norms for emotional expression that require them not to show any response.

A second example of cultural variation in emotional expression arose in the life of one of your authors. At the funeral of an American friend of Syrian descent, he was surprised to see and hear a group of women shrieking and wailing when a visitor entered the funeral parlor. They then stopped just as suddenly until the next visitor arrived, when once again they started their group wailing. What is the explanation for this behavior? Because it is difficult for the family members of the deceased to sustain a high emotional pitch over the three days and nights of such wakes, they hire these professional criers to display, on their behalf, appropriately strong emotions to each newcomer. This is an expected practice among a number of Mediterranean and Near Eastern cultures.

When you think about the types of emotional patterns that may have evolved over the course of human experience, you should always bear in mind that culture may have the last word. Western notions of what is necessary or inevitable in emotional expression are as bound to U.S. culture as those of any other societies. Can you see how different standards for emotional expression could cause misunderstandings between people of different cultural origins?

Cultures establish social rules for when and how emotions may be displayed.

Basic Emotions

We will close out this section on evolutionary aspects of emotions by giving you a way to picture how the basic emotions fit together. As shown in **Figure 13.2**, the **emotion wheel** of **Robert Plutchik** (1980, 1984) depicts eight basic emotions, made up of four pairs of opposites: joy-sadness, fear-anger, surprise-anticipation, and acceptance-disgust. All other emotions are assumed to be variations, or *blends,* of these basic eight. Complex emotions, shown on the outside of the emotional wheel, result from combinations of two adjacent primary emotions. For example, love is a combination of joy and acceptance; remorse combines sadness and disgust. Plutchik proposes that emotions are most clearly differentiated when they are at high intensities, such as loathing and grief, and least different when they are low in intensity, such as disgust and sadness. In keeping with an evolutionary perspective, Plutchik believes that each primary emotion is associated with an adaptive response. Disgust

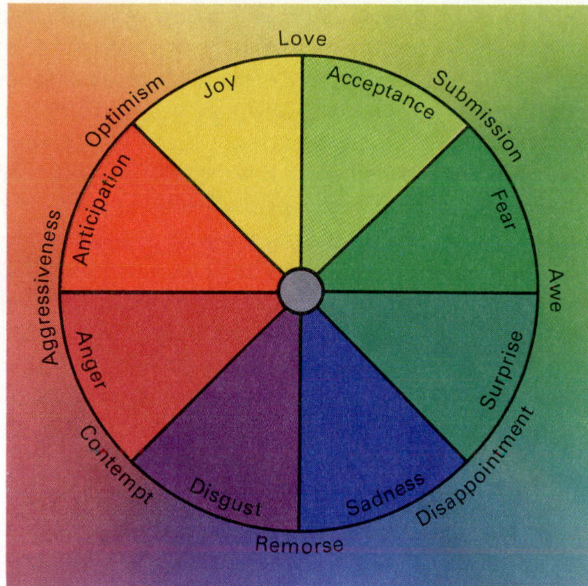

Figure 13.2 The Emotion Wheel

Plutchik's model arranges eight basic emotions within a circle of opposites. Pairs of these adjacent primary emotions combine to form more complex emotions, noted on the outside of the circle. Secondary emotions emerge from basic emotions more remotely associated on the wheel.

is considered an evolutionary outgrowth of rejecting distasteful foods from the mouth, while joy is associated with reproductive capacities. What might be the adaptive response associated with acceptance? With anticipation?

We have seen so far that some physiological responses to emotional situations—such as smiles and grimaces—may be innate. Let's turn now to theories that consider the link between other physiological responses and their psychological interpretations.

Theories of Emotion

Theories of emotion generally attempt to explain the relationship between physiological and psychological aspects of the experience of emotion. We will begin this section by discussing the responses your body gives in emotionally relevant situations. We will then review theories that explore the way these physiological responses contribute to your psychological experience of emotion.

Physiology of Emotion

What happens when you experience a strong emotion? Your heart races, respiration goes up, your mouth dries, your muscles tense, and maybe you even shake. In addition to these noticeable changes, many others occur beneath the surface. All these responses are designed to mobilize your body for action to deal with the source of the emotion. Let's look at their origins.

The *autonomic nervous system* (ANS) prepares the body for emotional responses through the action of both its sympathetic and parasympathetic divisions (see Chapter 3). The balance between the divisions depends on the quality and intensity of the arousing stimulation. With mild, *unpleasant* stimulation, the *sympathetic* division is more active; with mild, *pleasant* stimulation, the *parasympathetic* division is more active. With more intense stimulation of either kind, both divisions are increasingly involved. Physiologically, strong emotions such as fear or anger *activate* the body's *emergency reaction system,* which swiftly and silently prepares the body for

Emotions such as fear or anger activate the sympathetic nervous system, which prepares the body for action. After the situation has passed, the parasympathetic nervous system calms the physiological responses.

potential danger. The sympathetic nervous system takes charge by directing the release of hormones (epinephrine and norepinephrine) from the adrenal glands, which in turn leads the internal organs to release blood sugar, raise blood pressure, and increase sweating and salivation. To calm you after the emergency has passed, the parasympathetic nervous system inhibits the release of the activating hormones. You may remain aroused for a while after an experience of strong emotional activation, because some of the hormones continue to circulate in the bloodstream.

Integration of both the hormonal and the neural aspects of arousal is controlled by the *hypothalamus* and the *limbic system,* control systems for emotions and for patterns of attack, defense, and flight. Either lesioning (removing) or stimulating various parts of the limbic system produces dramatic changes in emotional responding: tame animals may become killers; animals that are usually predator and prey may become peaceful companions (Delgado, 1969).

What kinds of physiological arousal would you expect to find in a person who is experiencing a high level of frustration?

Neuroanatomy research has particularly focused on the **amygdala** as the part of the limbic system that acts as a gateway for emotion and as a filter for memory. The amygdala does this by attaching significance to the information it receives from the senses. When the amygdala is damaged in accidents or by surgery, a human patient shows no reaction in situations that normally evoke strong emotional responses. Neuroscientist **Joseph LeDoux** (1989) has discovered an anatomical pathway in rats that allows sensory information to go directly to the amygdala before the same information reaches the cortex. The amygdala acts on this raw data to trigger an emotional response *before* the cortex can provide an interpretation of the stimulus event. LeDoux speculates that some people may be overly emotional because their amygdala's response is stronger than the cortex's ability to control it with rational interpretations. People may "act without thinking" because their emotions and aggression are too quickly triggered for the brain's other brakes to be applied. Similarly, the frequent, uncontrollable emotional outbursts of infants may be due to the fact that the parts of the cortex that control emotional responding are not fully developed until sometime between 18 and 36 months, long after the amygdala and other emotional centers in the brain are active.

In all complex emotions, the *cortex* is involved through its internal neural networks and its connections with other parts of the body. The cortex provides the associations, memories, and meanings that integrate psychological experience and biological responses. Research is pointing to different emotional centers in the cortex for processing positive and negative emotions. The left hemisphere seems to involve positive emotions, such as happiness, while right-hemisphere activity influences negative emotions, such as anger (Davidson 1984). This lateralization of emotion in the human brain has been found through two research procedures. Both EEG analysis of emotional reactions in normal subjects and research relating emotional facial expression to brain damage of the right or left hemisphere in adult patients have revealed the two-sided nature of emotions in the brain (Ahern & Schwartz, 1985; Borod et al., 1988).

We have seen so far that your body provides many responses to situations in which emotions are relevant. But how do you know which feeling goes with which physiological response? We now review three theories that attempt an answer to this question.

James-Lange Theory of Body Reaction

You might think, at first, that everyone would agree that emotions precede responses: for example, you yell at someone because you feel angry. However, a hundred years ago, **William James** argued, as Aristotle had much earlier, that the sequence was reversed—you feel *after* your body reacts. As

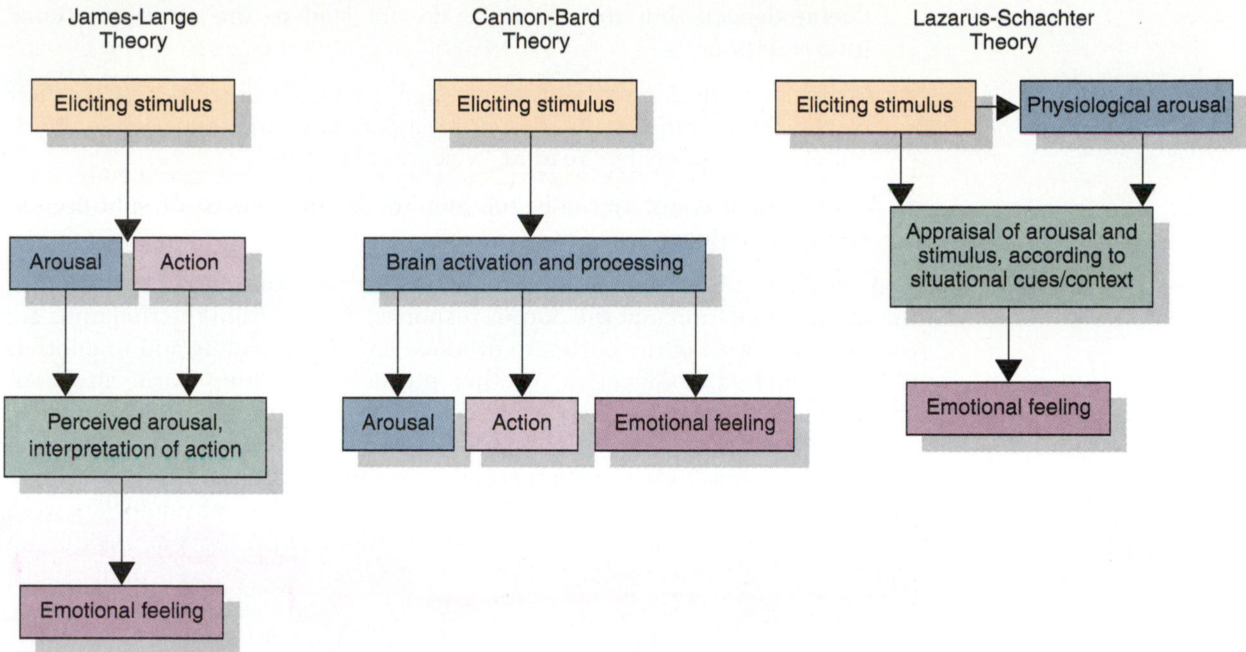

Figure 13.3 Comparing Three Emotion Theories
These classic theories of emotion propose different components of emotion. They also propose different process sequences by which a stimulus event results in the experience of emotion. In the James-Lange theory, events trigger both autonomic arousal and behavioral action, which are perceived and then result in a specific emotional experience. In the Cannon-Bard theory, events are first processed at various centers in the brain, which then direct the simultaneous reactions of arousal, behavioral action, and emotional experience. In the Lazarus-Schachter theory, both stimulus events and physiological arousal are cognitively appraised at the same time according to situational cues and context factors, with the emotional experience resulting from the interaction of the level of arousal and the nature of appraisal.

James put it, "We feel sorry because we cry, angry because we strike, afraid because we tremble" (James, 1890/1950, p. 450). This view that emotion stems from *bodily feedback* became known as the **James-Lange theory of emotion** (Carl Lange was a Danish scientist who presented similar ideas the same year as James). According to this theory, perceiving a stimulus causes autonomic arousal and other bodily actions that lead to the experience of a specific emotion (see **Figure 13.3**). The James-Lange theory is considered a *peripheralist* theory because it assigns the most prominent role in the emotion chain to visceral reactions, the actions of the autonomic nervous system that are peripheral to the central nervous system.

According to the James-Lange theory of emotion, the physiological arousal or behavior precedes the emotional response.

Cannon-Bard Theory of Central Neural Processes

Physiologist **Walter Cannon** (1927, 1929) rejected the peripheralist theory in favor of a *centralist* focus on the action of the central nervous system. Cannon (and other critics) raised four major objections to the James-Lange theory (Leventhal, 1980):

- Visceral activity is irrelevant for emotional experience—experimental animals continue to respond emotionally even after their viscera are separated surgically from the CNS;
- Visceral reactions are similar across different arousal situations—the same heart palpitations accompany aerobic exercise, lovemaking, and

fleeing danger—but the reactions do not lead to the same emotional interpretation;

- Many emotions cannot be distinguished from each other simply by their physiological components; therefore, a person cannot experience different emotions solely by "reading" visceral reactions.
- ANS responses are typically too slow to be the source of split-second elicited emotions.

Walter Cannon argued against the peripheralist James-Lange theory and in favor of a centralist theory emphasizing the importance of the central nervous system in emotional responses.

According to Cannon, emotion requires that the brain intercede between the input stimulation and the output response. Signals from the thalamus get routed to one area of the cortex to produce emotional feeling and to another for emotional expressiveness. Another physiologist, Philip Bard, also concluded that visceral reactions were not primary in the emotion sequence. Instead, an emotion-arousing stimulus has two simultaneous effects, causing both bodily arousal via the sympathetic nervous system and the subjective experience of emotion via the cortex. The views of these physiologists were combined in the **Cannon-Bard theory of emotion.** This theory states that an emotion stimulus produces two concurrent reactions, arousal and experience of emotion, which do not cause each other (see Figure 13.3).

The Cannon-Bard theory predicts independence between bodily and psychological responses. We will see next that contemporary theories of emotion reject the claim that these responses are necessarily independent.

Lazarus-Schachter Theory of Appraisal

Because arousal symptoms and internal states are similar for many different emotions, it is possible to confuse them at times when they are experienced in ambiguous or novel situations. According to **Stanley Schachter** (1971b), the experience of emotion is the joint effect of physiological arousal and *cognitive appraisal,* with both parts necessary for an emotion to occur. All arousal is assumed to be general and undifferentiated, and arousal is the first step in the emotion sequence. You appraise your physiological arousal in an effort to discover what you are feeling, what emotional label best fits, and what your reaction means in the particular setting in which it is being experienced. **Richard Lazarus** (1984a, 1991a; Lazarus & Lazarus, 1994), another leading proponent of the cognitive appraisal view, maintains that "emotional experience cannot be understood solely in terms of what happens in the person or in the brain, but grows out of ongoing transactions with the environment that are evaluated" (1984a, p. 124). Lazarus also emphasizes that appraisal often occurs without conscious thought. When you have past experiences that link emotions to situations—here comes that bully I've clashed with before!—you need not explicitly search the environment for an interpretation of your arousal. This position has become known as the **Lazarus-Schachter theory of emotion** (see Figure 13.3).

What emotions would you be likely to feel if people all around you were wildly cheering your favorite team?

To test this theory, experimenters have sometimes created situations in which environmental cues were available to provide a label for an individual's arousal (Schachter & Singer, 1962).

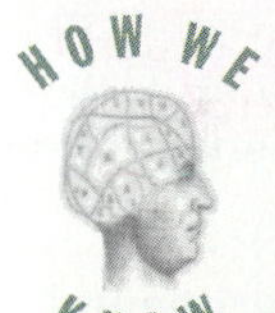

A female researcher interviewed male subjects who had just crossed one of two bridges in Vancouver, Canada. One bridge was a safe, sturdy bridge; the other was a wobbly, precarious bridge. The researcher pretended to be interested in the effects of scenery on creativity and asked the men to write brief stories about an ambiguous picture that included a woman. She also invited them to call her if they wanted more information about the research. Those men who had just crossed the dangerous bridge wrote stories with more sexual imagery, and four times as many of those men called the female researcher than did those

> who had crossed the safe bridge. To show that arousal was the independent variable influencing the emotional misinterpretation, the research team also arranged for another group of men to be interviewed 10 minutes or more after crossing the dangerous bridge, enough time for their physical arousal symptoms to be reduced. These nonaroused men did not show the signs of sexual response that the aroused men did (Dutton & Aron, 1974).

In this situation, the male subjects came to an emotional judgment ("I am interested in this woman") based on a *misattribution* of the source of arousal. In a similar experiment, subjects who performed two minutes of aerobic exercise reported less extreme emotions just after the exercise, when they could easily attribute their arousal to the exercise rather than to an emotional state, than after a brief delay that made the exercise seem less relevant to continuing arousal (Sinclair et al., 1994).

However, some of the specific aspects of the Lazarus-Schachter theory have been challenged. Awareness of one's physiological arousal is *not* a necessary condition for emotional experience. When experimental subjects are exposed to emotion-inducing stimuli after receiving beta-blockers that reduce heart rate, they still experience anxiety or anger even though they have minimal physical feelings (Reisenzein, 1983). In addition, experiencing strong arousal without any obvious cause does *not* lead to a neutral, undifferentiated state, as the Lazarus-Schachter theory assumes. Stop for a moment and imagine that, right now, your heart suddenly starts beating quickly, your breathing becomes fast and shallow, your chest muscles tighten, and your palms become drenched with sweat. What interpretation would you put on these symptoms? Are you surprised to learn that people generally interpret *unexplained* physical arousal as *negative*, a sign that something is wrong? In addition, people's search for an explanation tends to be *biased* toward finding stimuli that will explain or justify this negative interpretation (Marshall & Zimbardo, 1979; Maslach, 1979).

The finding that unexplained physical arousal is generally interpreted as negative is a challenge to the Lazarus-Schacter theory.

Another critique of the cognitive appraisal theory of emotion comes from researcher **Robert Zajonc** (pronounced Zy-Onts), who demonstrates conditions under which it is possible to have preferences without inferences and to feel without knowing why. In an extensive series of experiments on the *mere exposure effect,* subjects were presented with a variety of stimuli, such as foreign words, Japanese characters, sets of numbers, and strange faces, that were flashed so briefly the items could not be recognized. Subjects were still able to express a *preference* without knowing why they liked some more than others. Those stimuli that were most often repeated produced the strongest liking; yet this increased liking was shown to occur independent of conscious recognition (Zajonc, 1980).

In the mere exposure effect, subjects expressed a preference without knowing why they liked some stimuli more than others.

It is probably safest to conclude that cognitive appraisal is an important process of emotional experience, but not the only one (Izard, 1993). Under some circumstances, you will, in fact, look to the environment (at least unconsciously) to try to interpret why you feel the way you do. Under other circumstances, however, your emotional experiences may be under the control of the innate links provided by evolution. The physiological response will not require any interpretation. These different routes to emotional experiences suggest that emotions serve a range of functions. We turn now to those functions.

Functions of Emotion

Why do we have emotions? What functions do emotions serve for us? Different theorists point to different functions as central to the role of emotions in human life (Fridja, 1986). Let's examine some of the roles emotion plays in your life.

Motivation and Arousal

The very first time you wear your new sweatshirt, the shoulder seam rips. Why are you likely to storm back to the store and demand a refund? From Chapter 12, you should recognize this as a question about motivation. If you want to answer, "Because I'd be angry" or "Because I'd be disappointed," you can see that emotions often provide the impetus for action. Emotions serve a motivational function by *arousing* you to take action with regard to some experienced or imagined event. Emotions then *direct* and *sustain* your behaviors toward specific goals. For the love of another person, you may do all you can to attract, be near, and protect him or her. For the love of principle or of country, you may sacrifice your life.

Emotions can also provide you with feedback about your own motivational states. By *amplifying* or intensifying selected life experiences, emotions signal that a response is especially significant or that an event has *self-relevance* (Tompkins, 1981). Emotions can give you an *awareness of inner conflicts* when you observe that they can make you react irrationally or inappropriately to a given situation (Jung, 1971). If you overreact to a minor slight from a friend, you may become aware of hidden feelings of anger or jealousy.

Has a strong emotion, like anger at being rejected, ever driven you to engage in irrational or destructive behavior?

Let's consider cases, however, when emotion may begin to get the better of you. Have you ever been so angry that you felt incapable of taking any action? We have already seen that you respond to emotional situations with physiological arousal. Theorists have suggested that the relationship between arousal and performance follows an *inverted U-shaped function* (∩) (Hebb, 1955). This curve predicts that too little or too much arousal may impair performance. If you have too little physiological stimulation, you may be unable to organize your behaviors effectively (Bexton et al., 1954). If you have too much stimulation, emotion may overwhelm cognition.

Figure 13.4 shows the relationship between arousal and performance. The figure also explores the concept of *optimal arousal level* for best performance. Some tasks are best approached with high levels of arousal and others with more moderate levels. On some tasks, performance is highest when arousal is relatively low. The key to the level of arousal is *task difficulty.* With difficult or complex tasks, the optimal level of arousal for success is on the low end of the continuum. As the difficulty decreases and the task becomes

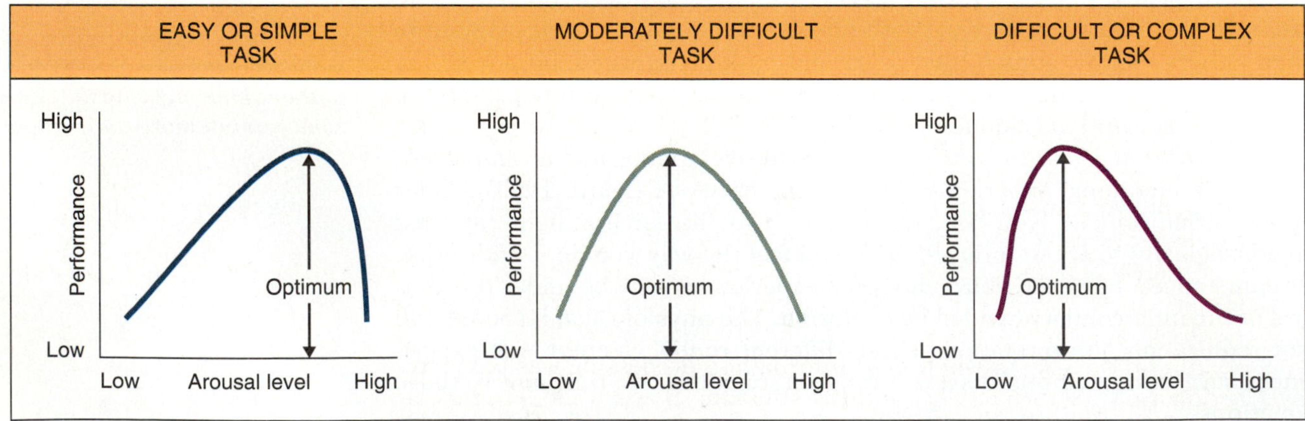

Figure 13.4 The Yerkes-Dodson Law

Performance varies with arousal level and task difficulty. For easy or simple tasks, a higher level of arousal increases performance effectiveness. However, for difficult or complex tasks, a lower level of arousal is optimal. A moderate level of arousal is generally best for tasks of moderate difficulty. These inverted U-shaped functions show that performance is worst at both low and high extremes of arousal.

simpler, the optimal level—the level required to perform most effectively—is greater. This relationship has been formalized in the **Yerkes-Dodson law**, which says that performance of difficult tasks decreases as arousal increases, whereas performance of easy tasks increases as arousal increases (Yerkes & Dodson, 1908).

An important function of emotions, thus, is to get you going—to start you moving toward important goals. The physiological arousal produced by emotional situations may be required to move you toward optimal performance. You should take care, however, that you don't let your emotions become so powerful that they put you on the downward slope of the performance curve.

Social Functions of Emotion

While emotions serve the general function of moving people toward their goals, they also serve the social functions of regulating social interactions and aiding in social communication.

On a social level, emotions serve the broad function of *regulating social interactions.* As a positive social glue, they bind you to some people; as a negative social repellent, they distance you from others. Some psychologists go further in arguing that most emotions emerge from and are central to fully experiencing human relationships (DeRivera, 1984).

> This social function is illustrated by a woman who developed dissociative amnesia (see Chapter 17) following a series of traumatic events that caused her to be unable to identify people she had known well. However, she responded unerringly with the emotional reaction appropriate to each of them. She reported feeling good and joyful when with those she had liked previously and feeling bad and distressed when interacting with those whom she had disliked previously—even though nothing about their current behavior gave a clue of any differences between them (P. Zimbardo, personal communication, 1968).

Research also points to the impact of emotion on *stimulating prosocial behavior* (Isen, 1984; Hoffman, 1986; Schroeder et al., 1995). When individuals are made to feel good, they are more likely to engage in a variety of helping behaviors. Similarly, when research subjects were made to feel guilty about a misdeed, they were more likely to volunteer aid in a future situation, presumably to reduce their guilt (Carlsmith & Gross, 1969).

Finally, emotions often aid in *social communication*—with or without your awareness. You back off when someone is bristling with anger, and you approach when another person signals receptivity with a smile, dilated pupils, and a "come hither" glance. You might suppress strong negative emotions out of respect for another person's status or power. Much human communication is carried on in the silent language of emotionally expressive nonverbal messages (Buck, 1984; Mehrabian, 1971).

Emotional Effects on Cognitive Functioning

Emotions serve cognitive functions, influencing what you attend to, how you perceive yourself and others, and your interpretation and memory of various life situations.

Emotions serve cognitive functions by influencing what you attend to, the way you perceive yourself and others, and the way you interpret and remember various features of life situations. Researchers have demonstrated that emotional states can affect learning, memory, social judgments, and creativity (Bradley, 1994; Forgas, 1991). Your emotional responses play an important role in organizing and categorizing your life experiences.

Research on the role of emotion in information processing was pioneered by **Gordon Bower** (1981, 1991) and his students. Bower's model proposes that when a person experiences a given emotion in a particular situation, that emotion is stored in memory along with the ongoing events, as part of the same context. This pattern of memory representation gives rise to mood-congruent processing and mood-dependent retrieval.

Mood-congruent processing occurs when people are selectively sensitized to take in information that agrees with their current mood state. Material that is congruent with one's prevailing mood is more likely to be attended to, noticed, and processed more deeply and with greater elaborative associations (Gilligan & Bower, 1984). We can see effects of mood-congruent processing in studies that ask people to evaluate their health status. When feeling sad, students reported more past illnesses and complaints than when they were in an emotionally neutral state (Salovey & Hancock, 1987). Students who had the flu or a bad cold rated the severity of the aches and discomfort according to the mood induced by the researchers. Compared with neutral controls, those who were temporarily sad rated their cold symptoms as significantly worse than happy subjects (Salovey & Birnbaum, 1989). The power of moods on cognition is also shown in research demonstrating that happy people offer more creative solutions on standard tests of creativity than do those who are affectively neutral or made to experience a negative mood (Isen et al., 1987).

Mood-dependent retrieval refers to recall of a previous emotional event that occurs when the person is in the same mood as during the earlier event. People remember more events that were originally sad when they are feeling sad. Happy people are more likely to retrieve happy events from their past. A similar *retrieval bias* arises when psychiatrically depressed patients are asked to recall events from their past (Blaney, 1986). Their negative mood leads them to recall more negative memories—which may actually help to keep them depressed. You should watch for the same tendency in your own life. An effective way to change your mood is to recall life events that are inconsistent with it (Erber & Erber, 1994). Particularly if you are in a negative mood, you might try to call to mind happier times. As we turn now to stress, and how to cope with it, you should look forward to similar advice about taking cognitive control over how you are "feeling."

STRESS OF LIVING

Suppose we asked you to keep track of all the emotions you experience in the course of a day. You might report that for brief periods you felt happiness, sadness, anger, relief, and so on. There is one emotion, however, that people often report as a kind of background noise for much of their day-to-day experience, and that is *stress* (Sapolsky, 1994). Modern industrialized society sets a rapid, hectic pace for living. People often have too many demands placed on their time, are worried about uncertain futures, and have little time for family and fun. But would you be better off without stress? A stress-free life would offer no challenge—no difficulties to surmount, no new fields to conquer, and no reasons to sharpen your wits or improve your abilities. Every organism faces challenges from its external environment and from its personal needs. The organism must solve these problems to survive and thrive.

Stress is the pattern of responses an organism makes to stimulus events that disturb its equilibrium and tax or exceed its ability to cope. The stimulus events include a large variety of external and internal conditions that collectively are called *stressors*. A **stressor** is a *stimulus* event that places a demand on an organism for some kind of adaptive response: a bicyclist swerves in front of your car, your professor moves up the due date of your term paper, you're asked to run for class president. An individual's response to the need for change is made up of a diverse combination of reactions taking place on several levels, including physiological, behavioral, emotional, and cognitive. What responses might you make to each of the stressors we listed just earlier?

Figure 13.5 diagrams the elements of the stress process. Our goal for this section is to give you a clear understanding of all the features represented in this figure. We will begin by considering general physiological responses to stressors. We then describe the particular effects of different categories of stressors. Finally, we explore different methods you can use to cope with the stress in your life.

Whether at work or play, individuals in modern society are likely to encounter a stressful environment.

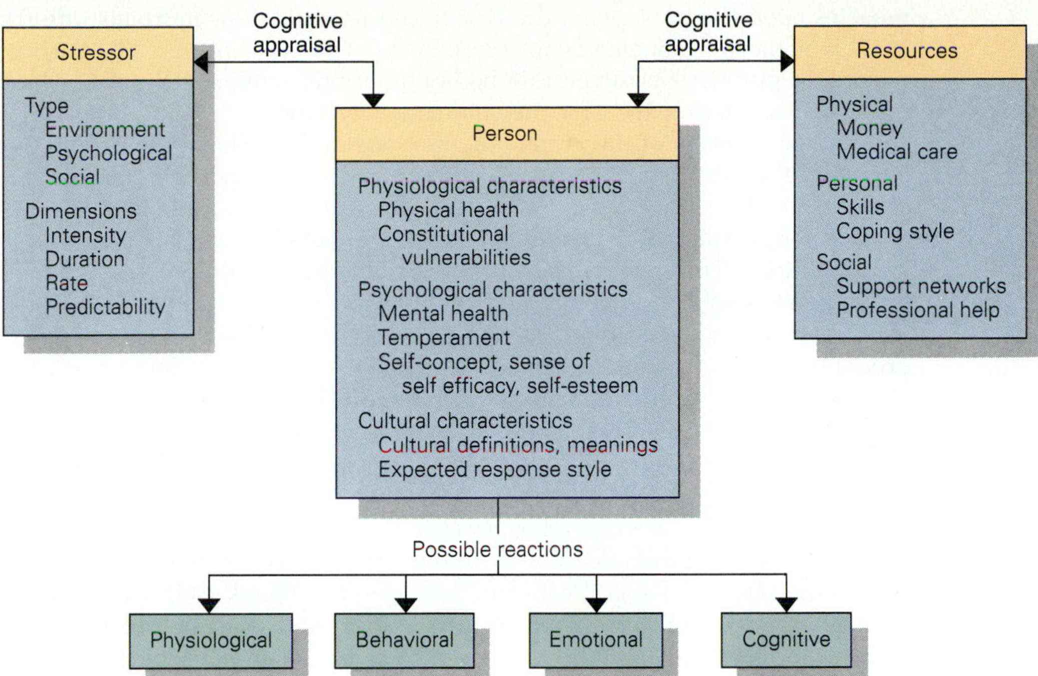

Figure 13.5 A Model of Stress
Cognitive appraisal of the stress situation interacts with the stressor and the physical, social, and personal resources available for dealing with the stressor. Individuals respond to threats on various levels: physiological, behavioral, emotional, and cognitive. Some responses are adaptive, and others are maladaptive or even lethal.

Physiological Stress Reactions

How would you respond if you arrived at a class and discovered that you were about to have a pop quiz? You would probably agree that this would cause you some stress, but what does that mean for your body's reactions? Many of the physiological responses we described for emotional situations are also relevant to day-to-day instances of stress. Such transient states of arousal, with typically clear onset and offset patterns, are examples of **acute stress. Chronic stress,** on the other hand, is a state of enduring arousal, continuing over time, in which demands are perceived as greater than the inner and outer resources available for dealing with them (Powell & Eagleston, 1983). An example of chronic stress might be a continuous frustration with your inability to find time to do all the things you want to do. Let's see how your body responds to these different types of stress.

Emergency Reactions to Acute Threats

In the 1920s, Walter Cannon outlined the first scientific description of the way animals and humans respond to danger. He found that a sequence of activity is triggered in the nerves and glands to prepare the body either to defend itself and struggle or to run away to safety. Cannon called this dual stress response the **fight-or-flight syndrome.**

Walter Cannon was the first to describe physiological reactions to danger as the fight-or-flight response.

At the center of this stress response is the *hypothalamus,* which is involved in a variety of emotional responses. The hypothalamus has sometimes been referred to as the *stress center* because of its twin functions in emergencies: (1) it controls the autonomic nervous system and (2) it activates the pituitary gland.

In emergencies, the hypothalamus serves the dual functions of controlling the autonomic nervous system and activating the pituitary gland.

The ANS regulates the activities of the body's organs. In stressful conditions, breathing becomes faster and deeper, heart rate increases, blood vessels constrict, and blood pressure rises. In addition to these internal changes, muscles open the passages of the throat and nose to allow more air into the lungs while also producing facial expressions of strong emotion. Messages go to smooth muscles to stop certain bodily functions, such as digestion, which are irrelevant to preparing for the emergency at hand.

Another function of the autonomic nervous system during stress is to get adrenaline flowing. It signals the inner part of the adrenal glands, the *adrenal medulla,* to release two hormones, *epinephrine* and *norepinephrine,* which, in turn, signal a number of other organs to perform their specialized functions. The spleen releases more red blood corpuscles (to aid in clotting if there is an injury), while the bone marrow is stimulated to make more white corpuscles (to combat possible infection). The liver is stimulated to produce more sugar, building up body energy.

The *pituitary gland* responds to signals from the hypothalamus by secreting two hormones vital to the stress reaction. The *thyrotrophic hormone* (TTH) stimulates the *thyroid gland,* which makes more energy available to the body. The *adrenocorticotrophic hormone* (ACTH), known as the "stress hormone," stimulates the outer part of the adrenal glands, the *adrenal cortex,* resulting in the release of hormones that control metabolic processes and in the release of sugar from the liver into the blood. ACTH also signals various organs to release about 30 other hormones, each of which plays a role in the body's adjustment to this call to arms. A summary of this physiological stress response is shown in **Figure 13.6**.

Let's consider the adaptive significance of these physiological responses in two different stressful situations.

IN YOUR
LIFE

- When a call comes into a firehouse, the firefighters respond with the physiological components of the stress response. Muscles tense, breathing speeds up, heart rate increases, adrenaline flows, extra energy

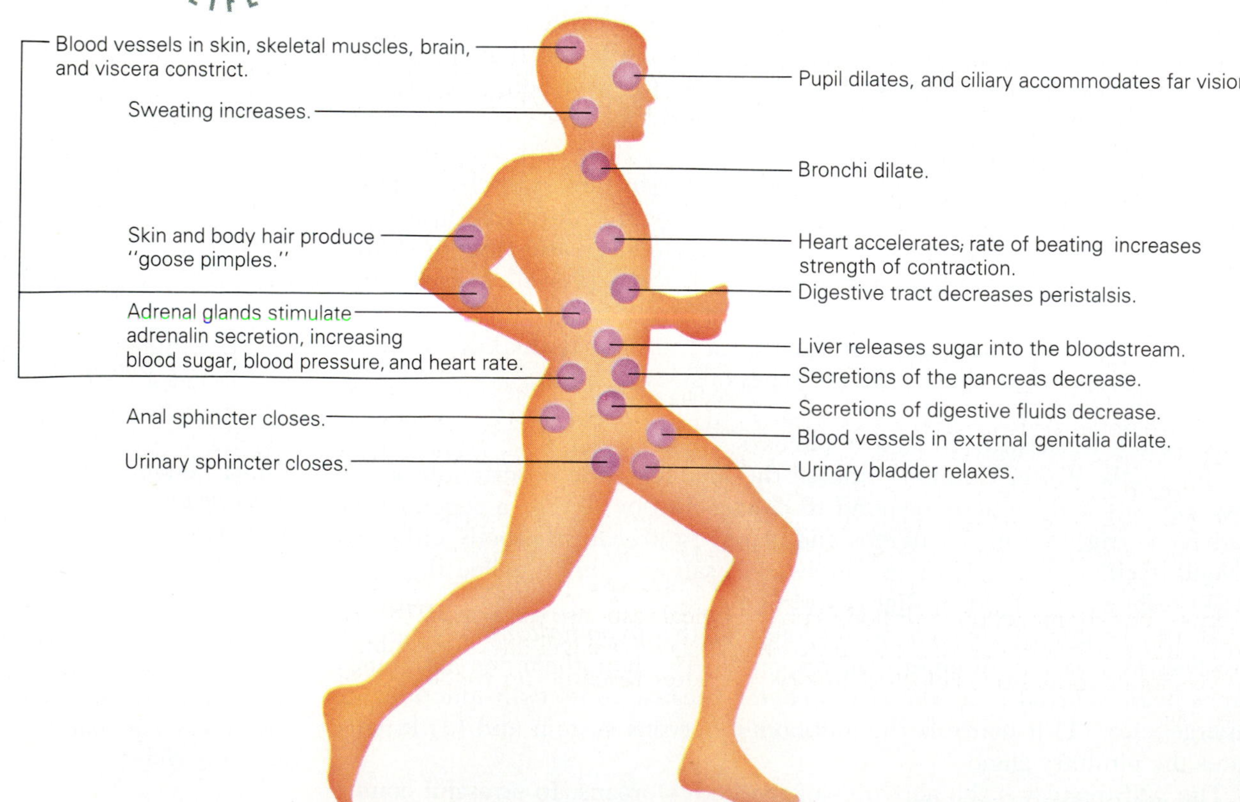
Blood vessels in skin, skeletal muscles, brain, and viscera constrict.
Sweating increases.
Skin and body hair produce "goose pimples."
Adrenal glands stimulate adrenalin secretion, increasing blood sugar, blood pressure, and heart rate.
Anal sphincter closes.
Urinary sphincter closes.
Pupil dilates, and ciliary accommodates far vision.
Bronchi dilate.
Heart accelerates; rate of beating increases strength of contraction.
Digestive tract decreases peristalsis.
Liver releases sugar into the bloodstream.
Secretions of the pancreas decrease.
Secretions of digestive fluids decrease.
Blood vessels in external genitalia dilate.
Urinary bladder relaxes.

Figure 13.6 The Body's Reaction to Stress

becomes available, and the firefighters become less sensitive to pain. They will need these responses to endure the physical strain of battling a fire. The built-in capacity to deal with *physical stressors* by mobilizing the body's active response systems is invaluable to our species.

- Now consider people working on a crisis hot line, taking calls from potentially suicidal strangers. These workers undergo the same physiological responses as the firefighters as a result of the *psychological stressors* they face. However, in contrast to the firefighters, their physiological responses, except for the heightened attentiveness, are not adaptive. The hot line volunteer can't run away from the stressor or fight with the caller; the unconditioned fight-or-flight syndrome is out of place. The volunteer must, instead, try to stay calm, concentrate on listening, and make thoughtful decisions. Unfortunately, these interpersonal skills are not enhanced by the stress response. So what has developed in the species as an adaptive preparation for dealing with external danger is counterproductive for dealing with many modern-day sources of stress.

The adaptive fight-or-flight response that is so important in dealing with physiological stress may actually be counterproductive in response to psychological stress.

The General Adaptation Syndrome (GAS) and Chronic Stress

Hans Selye described three stages in the general adaptation syndrome: the alarm reaction, a stage of resistance, and exhaustion.

The first modern researcher to investigate the effects of continued severe stress on the body was **Hans Selye,** a Canadian endocrinologist. Beginning in the late 1930s, Selye reported on the complex response of laboratory animals to damaging agents such as bacterial infections, toxins, trauma or forced restraint, heat, cold, and so on. According to Selye's theory of stress, many kinds of stressors can trigger the same reaction or general bodily response. All stressors call for *adaptation:* an organism must maintain or regain its integrity and well-being by restoring equilibrium, or homeostasis. The response to stressors was described by Selye as the **general adaptation syndrome** (GAS). It includes three stages: an alarm reaction, a stage of resistance, and a stage of exhaustion (Selye, 1956, 1976). The GAS is adaptive because, during the stage of resistance, the organism can endure and *resist* further debilitating effects. This stimulated defense against the stressor develops and maintains an intermediate stage of *restoration.* The three stages are diagrammed and explained in **Figure 13.7**.

Selye discovered, however, that this process successfully restores the body's balance only when the stressor is short-lived or acute. Recall, for example, that ACTH plays a role in the short-term response to stress. In the long term, however, its action reduces the ability of natural killer cells to destroy cancer cells and other life-threatening infections. When the body is stressed chronically, the increased production of "stress hormones" compromises the integrity of the immune system. This application of the general adaptation syndrome has proven valuable to explain disorders, called **psychosomatic disorders,** that had baffled physicians who had never considered stress as a cause for illness and disease. What serves the body well in adapting to acute stress impairs the body's response to chronic stress.

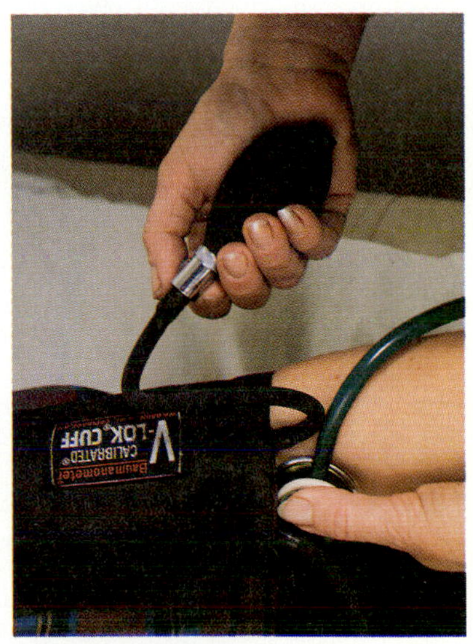

High blood pressure, which entails a range of health risks, is exacerbated by prolonged or repeated exposure to stress.

Selye's research makes disease seem an inevitable response to stress. We will see, however, that your psychological interpretation of what is stressful and what is not stressful—the way in which you appraise potentially stressful events—has an impact on your body's physiological response (Mason, 1975). To give a full account of the effect of stress on your body, we will have to combine Selye's foundational physiological theory with later research on psychological factors.

Psychoneuroimmunology

The research we have reviewed so far focused on stressors that appear in the outside environment. When, however, you acquire a virus or some other

Stage I: Alarm reaction (continuously repeated throughout life)

- Enlargement of adrenal cortex
- Enlargement of lymphatic system
- Increase in hormone levels
- Response to specific stressor
- Epinephrine release associated with high levels of physiological arousal and negative affect
- Greater susceptibility to increased intensity of stressor
- Heightened susceptibility to illness

(If prolonged, the slower components of the GAS are set into motion, beginning with Stage II.)

Stage II: Resistance (continuously repeated throughout life)

- Shrinkage of adrenal cortex
- Return of lymph nodes to normal size
- Sustaining of hormone levels
- High physiological arousal
- Counteraction of parasympathetic branch of ANS
- Enduring of stressor; resistance to further debilitating effects
- Heightened sensitivity to stress

(If stress continues at intense levels, hormonal reserves are depleted, fatigue sets in, and individual enters Stage III.)

Stage III: Exhaustion

- Enlargement/dysfunction of lymphatic structures
- Increase in hormone levels
- Depletion of adaptive hormones
- Decreased ability to resist either original or extraneous stressors
- Affective experience—often depression
- Illness
- Death

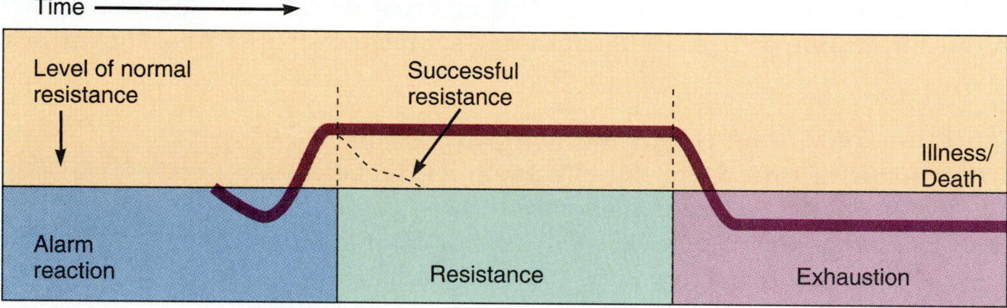

Figure 13.7 The General Adaptation Syndrome
Following exposure to a stressor, the body's resistance is diminished until the physiological changes of the corresponding alarm reaction bring it back up to the normal level. If the stressor continues, the bodily signs characteristic of the alarm reaction virtually disappear; resistance to the particular stressor rises above normal but drops for other stressors. This adaptive resistance returns the body to its normal level of functioning. Following prolonged exposure to the stressor, adaptation breaks down; signs of alarm reaction reappear, the stressor effects are irreversible, and the individual becomes ill and may die.

microbe, your body is stressed from within. To cope with internal stressors, your body is equipped with an immune system. One field of research, **psychoneuroimmunology,** concerns itself, in part, with the way in which external stressors (life events) alter the immune system's response to internal stressors (viruses and bacteria) (Ader & Cohen, 1993; Maier et al., 1994). We exposed you to some classic research in psychoneuroimmunology in Chapter 9. Recall that conditioning paradigms have been used to alter the immune function—and change the probability of mortality—of laboratory rats and mice (Ader & Cohen, 1981; Ghanta et al., 1987). Here we will describe research that relates stressors to the performance of the immune system.

Immune function is affected by the day-to-day ups and downs of life.

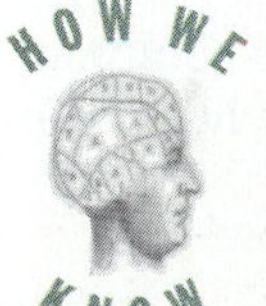

In one study, a group of 96 men gave daily reports of positive and negative events. They were also tested daily for the strength of their immune response. Each subject ingested a capsule containing *rabbit albumin,* a protein that the body treats as an invading microorganism (although it is not, in fact, harmful). Immune response to this invasion was measured in the subjects' saliva. Results showed that desirable life events were associated with stronger immune response, undesirable events with a weaker response. Thus, positive events improved immune function and negative events suppressed immune function (Stone et al., 1994).

Researchers have also considered the effect of chronic stressors on immune function. A number of studies have shown that the quality of interpersonal relationships and their disruption or absence have strong effects on the immune system (Cohen & Syme, 1985; Kiecolt-Glaser & Glaser, 1987). Bereavement and depression also produce immunosuppression. Men whose wives are dying of breast cancer (Schleifer et al., 1983) and recently widowed women (Irwin et al., 1987) are less able to fight disease and face an increased risk of illness and premature death. Even two years after the death of an individual who had died of Alzheimer's, relatives who had cared for the patient still showed reduced immune function (Esterling et al., 1994). Some stressors have effects that go beyond a small number of people to a whole community. The immune functioning of a group of chronically stressed individuals living near the damaged Three Mile Island nuclear power plant was impaired with respect to a control group in a demographically comparable town (McKinnon et al., 1989).

Research in the field of psychoneuroimmunology demonstrates that chronic stressors such as bereavement, depression, or caregiving can suppress immune system function.

So far, we have considered only physiological responses to stressors. We turn now to even more complex psychological components of the stress response.

Psychological Stress Reactions

Your physiological stress reactions are automatic, predictable, built-in responses over which you normally have no conscious control. However, many psychological reactions are learned. They depend on perceptions and interpretations of the world. We begin this section by describing how cognitive appraisal affects what you experience as stressful. We then discuss psychological responses to different categories of stressors, such as major life changes and traumatic events. Finally, we consider some individual differences in psychological stress responses.

Whereas physiological responses to stress are automatic and not subject to conscious control, psychological reactions are learned and can be reappraised.

Appraisal of Stress

Variables that change the impact of a stressor on a given type of stress reaction are known as **stress moderator variables.** Moderator variables filter or modify the usual effects of stressors on the individual's reactions. For example, your level of fatigue and general health status are moderator variables influencing your reaction to a given psychological or physical stressor. When you're in good shape, you can deal with a stressor better than when you aren't. What other situational variables might moderate stress?

Cognitive appraisal, the cognitive interpretation and evaluation of a stressor, is a major moderator variable. Cognitive appraisal plays a central role in defining the situation—what the demand is, how big a threat it is, and what resources you have for meeting it (Lazarus, 1993; Lazarus & Lazarus, 1994). Some stressors, such as undergoing bodily injury or finding one's house on fire, are experienced as threats by almost everyone. However, many other stressors can be defined in various ways, depending on your personal life situation, the relation of a particular demand to your central goals, your competence in dealing with the demand, and your self-assessment of that competence. The situation that causes acute distress for another person may be all in a day's work for you. Try to notice, and understand, the life events that are different for you and your friends and family: some situations cause you stress but not your friends and family; other events cause them stress but not you. Why?

Richard Lazarus, whose general theory of appraisal we met in our discussion of emotions, has distinguished two stages in the cognitive appraisal of

Table 13.1 Stages in Stable Decision Making/Cognitive Appraisal

Stage	Key Questions
1. Appraising the challenge	Are the risks serious if I don't change?
2. Surveying alternatives	Is this alternative an acceptable means for dealing with the challenge? Have I sufficiently surveyed the available alternatives?
3. Weighing alternatives	Which alternative is best? Could the best alternative meet the essential requirements?
4. Deliberating about commitment	Shall I implement the best alternative and allow others to know?
5. Adhering despite negative feedback	Are the risks serious if I *don't* change? Are the risks serious if I *do* change?

demands. He uses the term **primary appraisal** for the initial evaluation of the seriousness of a demand. This evaluation starts with the questions "What's happening?" and "Is this thing good for me, stressful, or irrelevant?" If the answer to the second question is "stressful," you appraise the potential impact of the stressor by determining whether harm has occurred or is likely to and whether action is required (see **Table 13.1**). Once you decide something must be done, **secondary appraisal** begins. You evaluate the personal and social resources that are available to deal with the stressful circumstance and consider the action options that are needed (Lazarus, 1976). Appraisal continues as coping responses are tried; if the first ones don't work and the stress persists, new responses are initiated, and their effectiveness is evaluated (Lazarus, 1991b).

Richard Lazarus proposes two stages in the cognitive appraisal of stress, a primary appraisal during which people determine if a situation is stressful, and a secondary appraisal for evaluating one's resources and possible actions.

When, shortly, we discuss coping with stress, we will return to the idea that reappraisal or reinterpretation can affect a stress response. Right now, try to focus on a recent life event that you interpreted as stressful. Let's review the psychological responses you, and most people, experience in such situations.

Major Life Stressors

Major *changes* in life situations are at the root of stress for many people (Dohrenwend & Dohrenwend, 1974; Dohrenwend & Shrout, 1985; Holmes & Rahe, 1967). Even events that you welcome, such as winning the lottery or getting promoted, may require major changes in your routines and adaptation to new requirements. Recall, for example, the pattern of marital well-being we described in Chapter 6. Although the birth of a child is one of the most sought-after changes in a married couple's life, it is also a source of major stress, contributing to reduced marital satisfaction (Cowan & Cowan, 1988; Levenson et al., 1993). Thus, when you try to relate stress to changes in your life, you should consider both positive and negative changes.

The influence of major life changes on subsequent mental and physical health has been a target of considerable research. It started with the development of the Social Readjustment Rating Scale (SRRS), a simple measure for rating the degree of adjustment required by the various life changes, both pleasant and unpleasant, that many people experience. The scale was developed from the responses of adults, from all walks of life, who were asked to identify from a list those life changes that applied to them. These adults rated the amount of readjustment required for each change by comparing each to marriage, which was arbitrarily assigned a value of 50 life-change units. Researchers then calculated the total number of **life-change units** (LCU) an individual had undergone, using the units as a measure of the amount of stress the individual had experienced (Holmes & Rahe, 1967). A modification of this scale for college students is shown in **Table 13.2**. Stop and answer the scale items before reading on. What is your LCU rating? Also, compare the relative severity of hassles in your life with those of the four groups outlined in **Table 13.3** (students, mothers, general community members, and elders).

Major life changes, significant sources of stress, are measured by the Social Readjustment Rating Scale.

A different way to measure the effects of life events is provided in the Life Experiences Survey (LES), which has two special features. First, the LES provides scores for both increases and decreases in change rather than increases only, as in the original scale. Second, its scores reflect indi-

Table 13.2 Student Stress Scale

The Student Stress Scale represents an adaptation of Holmes and Rahe's Social Readjustment Rating Scale. Each event is given a score that represents the amount of readjustment a person has to make in life as a result of the change. People with scores of 300 and higher have a high health risk. People scoring between 150 and 300 points have about a 50–50 chance of serious health change within two years. People scoring below 150 have a 1 in 3 chance of serious health change. Calculate your total life-change units (LCU) each month of this year and then correlate those scores with any changes in your health status.

Event	Life-Change Units
Death of a close family member	100
Death of a close friend	73
Divorce between parents	65
Jail term	63
Major personal injury or illness	63
Marriage	58
Being fired from job	50
Failing an important course	47
Change in health of family member	45
Pregnancy	45
Sex problems	44
Serious argument with close friend	40
Change in financial status	39
Change of major	39
Trouble with parents	39
New girl- or boyfriend	38
Increased workload at school	37
Outstanding personal achievement	36
First quarter/semester in college	35
Change in living conditions	31
Serious argument with instructor	30
Lower grades than expected	29
Change in sleeping habits	29
Change in social activities	29
Change in eating habits	28
Chronic car trouble	26
Change in number of family get-togethers	26
Too many missed classes	25
Change of college	24
Dropping of more than one class	23
Minor traffic violations	20

My 1st total ☐ (date:____) My 2nd total ☐ (date:____)

My 3rd total ☐ (date:____)

Table 13.3 Severity of Hassles as Perceived in Four Groups (Rank Orders)

In these New Zealand samples, each hassle type differed significantly in severity among the four groups. The ranked perceived severity was almost reversed for student and elderly groups. Time pressures were most important and neighborhood and health pressures least important for students, while health pressures were the most important sources of hassles and time pressures were the least for the elderly. Note the hassle priorities for these mothers who had one or more young children at home and no household help.

Hassle type	Students (N = 161)	Mothers (N = 194)	Community (N = 120)	Elderly (N = 150)
Time pressure	1	2	3	4
Future security	2	4	1	3
Finances	3	1	2	4
Household	3	1	2	4
Neighborhood	4	3	2	1
Health	4	3	2	1

vidual appraisals of the events. For example, the death of an estranged spouse who left you a big inheritance might be rated as quite desirable. Thus this scale goes beyond a mere count of the number of remembered life changes to measure the personal significance of each change (Sarason et al., 1978).

Early studies examined the hypothesis that the greater the life change intensity, as measured by the SRRS, the greater the risk for subsequent illness. Preliminary studies found support for a relationship between medical problems and the amount of readjustment in life. Patients with heart disease, for example, had higher LCU scores than healthy subjects. Other studies reported that life stress increases a person's overall susceptibility to illness (Holmes & Masuda, 1974), and LCU values are also high for some time after an illness (Rahe & Arthur, 1978).

One problem with research linking stress to illness is that the studies tend to be retrospective. However, prospective studies have also found correlations between medical problems and accumulation of life stress units.

One interpretive problem with studies relating stressful life events to illness is that these investigations tend to be *retrospective*. That is, both the stress measures and the illness measures are obtained by having subjects recall prior events. This presents an opportunity for memory distortion to bias the results. For example, subjects who are sick are more likely to remember past negative stressors than subjects who are well. More recently, *prospective* (looking ahead) studies have followed healthy individuals over a period of years; they find significant correlations between the development of medical problems and earlier accumulation of life stress units (Brown & Harris, 1989; Johnson & Sarason, 1979). Despite such support, the bulk of the current research points to a *weak* but positive association between major life events and disease (Brett et al., 1990).

Catastrophic and Traumatic Events

An event that is negative but also uncontrollable, unpredictable, or ambiguous is particularly stressful (Glass, 1977). These conditions hold especially true in the case of *catastrophic events*. For example, your author, Phil Zimbardo, recalls being at a 1989 World Series game when disaster struck:

> As my three children and I settled into our seats in San Francisco's Candlestick Park, the band started playing. Suddenly the entire stadium started shaking violently, the lights went out, and the scoreboard turned black. Sixty thousand fans became completely silent.
>
> We had just experienced a major earthquake. The person sitting next to us had a portable TV that showed fires breaking out, a fallen bridge, crushed highways, and numerous deaths.

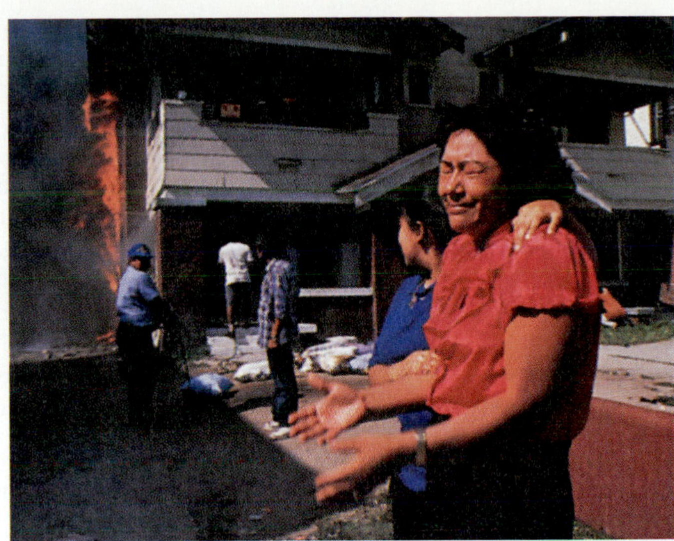

Anguish and grief characterize the emergency phase *of reaction to a catastrophe—in this case, the 1992 Los Angeles riots.*

Shortly after the quake, a team of psychologists began to study how people coped with the catastrophe.

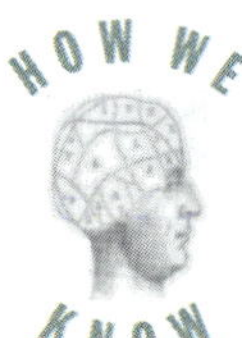

For the study, nearly 800 people were chosen randomly from the San Francisco area and from several comparison cities some distance away. They were interviewed at either 1, 2, 3, 6, 8, 16, 28, or 50 weeks after the quake. The subjects completed a ten-minute phone survey about their thoughts, social behavior, and health. Three distinct phases of stress reactions were found among the subjects who were San Francisco residents. In the emergency phase (first 3 to 4 weeks), social contact, anxiety, and obsessive thoughts about the quake increased. The inhibition phase (3 to 8 weeks) was characterized by a sudden decline in talking and thinking about the quake, but indirect, stress-related reactions increased, such as arguments and earthquake dreams. In the adaptation phase (from 2 months on), the psychological effects of the catastrophe were over for most people. However, as many as 20 percent of the San Francisco area residents remained distressed about the quake even one year later (Pennebaker & Harber, 1993).

A great deal of research on the physical and psychological effects of catastrophic events has been conducted (Baum, 1990). Researchers have found that response to disasters tends to occur in five stages. Typically, there is a period of shock, confusion, and even *psychic numbness,* during which people cannot fully comprehend what has happened. In the next phase, called *automatic action,* people try to respond to the disaster and may behave adaptively but with little awareness of their actions and poor later memory of the experience. In the third stage, people often feel great accomplishment and even a positive sense of communal effort toward a shared purpose. Also in this phase, people feel weary and are aware that they are using up their reserves of energy. During the next phase, they experience a letdown; their energy is depleted and the impact of the tragedy is finally comprehended and felt emotionally. An extended final period of recovery follows, as people adapt to the changes brought about by the disaster (Cohen & Ahearn, 1980).

Rape and incest victims, survivors of plane and serious automobile crashes, combat veterans, and others who have personally experienced traumatic events may react emotionally with a **posttraumatic stress disorder** (PTSD). PTSD is a delayed stress reaction that recurs repeatedly, even long after the traumatic experience. In addition, victims experience an emotional numbing in relation to everyday events and feelings of alienation from other people. Finally, the emotional pain of this reaction can result in an increase in various symptoms, such as sleep problems, guilt about surviving, difficulty in concentrating, and an exaggerated startle response. The clinical symptoms of PTSD are described as *conditioned responses* learned in the context of a powerful life-threatening stimulus situation (Keane et al., 1985).

Posttraumatic stress disorder produces such symptoms as sleep problems, guilt about surviving, and difficulty in concentrating.

Rape victims often show many of the signs of posttraumatic stress (Meyer & Taylor, 1986). The following excerpt of a discussion about the aftershock of being raped reveals the powerful and enduring emotions.

> *Alice:* I was in shock for a pretty long time. I could talk about the fact that I was a rape victim, but the emotions didn't start surfacing until a month later.
>
> *Beth:* During the first two weeks there were people I had chosen to tell who were very, very supportive; but after two weeks, it was like, "Okay, she's over it, we can go on now." But the farther along you get, the more support you need, because, as time passes, you become aware of your emotions and the need to deal with them.
>
> *Alice:* There is a point where you deny it happened. You just completely bury it.
>
> *Beth:* It's so unreal that you don't want to believe that it actually happened or that it can happen. Then you go through a long period of fear and anger.
>
> *Alice:* I'm terrified of going jogging. [Alice had been jogging when she was raped.] I completely stopped any kind of physical activity after I was raped. I started it again this quarter, but every time I go jogging I have a perpetual fear. My pulse doubles. Of course I don't go jogging alone any more, but still the fear is there constantly.
>
> *Beth:* There's also a feeling of having all your friends betray you. I had a dream in which I was being assaulted outside my dorm. In the dream, everyone was looking out their windows—the faces were so clear—every one of my friends lined up against the windows watching, and there were even people two feet away from me. They all saw what was happening and none of them did anything. I woke up and had a feeling of extreme loneliness. (*The Stanford Daily,* 1982)

The emotional responses of posttraumatic stress can occur in an acute form immediately following a disaster and can subside over a period of several months. These responses can also persist, becoming a chronic syndrome called the **residual stress pattern** (Silver & Wortman, 1980). They can also be delayed for months or even years. Clinicians are still discovering veterans of World War II and the Korean War who are displaying residual or delayed posttraumatic stress disorders (Zeiss & Dickman, 1989). These data suggest that not everyone can "recover" from some types of acute stress (Wortman & Silver, 1989; Wortman et al., 1993).

Chronic Stressors

In our discussion of physiological responses to stress, we made a distinction between stressors that are acute, with clear onsets and offsets, versus those that are chronic—that is, endure over time. With psychological stressors, it's not always easy to draw a sharp distinction. Suppose, for example, your bicycle is stolen. Originally, this is an acute source of stress. However, if you

These Detroit residents clamoring for post office job applications are likely to have experienced chronic stress due to unemployment or underemployment.

begin to worry constantly that your new bike will also be stolen, the stress associated with this event can become chronic. Researchers have found this pattern in people who suffer from serious illnesses like cancer (Andersen et al., 1994). The chronic stress of coping with the anxiety of a cancer diagnosis and treatment may impair health more rapidly than the disease alone would.

For many people, chronic stress arises from conditions in society and the environment. What cumulative effect do overpopulation, crime, economic conditions, pollution, AIDS, and the threat of nuclear war have on you? How do these and other environmental stressors affect your mental well-being? Students worry considerably about their own future and society's future (Beardslee & Mack, 1983; Nurmi, 1991). Many young people question whether it is worthwhile to work hard to prepare for a future they do not expect to have if there is nuclear war (Yudkin, 1984). Adults, too, are worried about potential nuclear disasters, but they are also affected by the more immediate concerns of employment and economic security. Many stress-related problems increase when the economy is in a downswing: admission to mental hospitals, infant mortality, suicide, and deaths from alcohol-related diseases and cardiovascular problems (Brenner, 1976).

Environmental conditions such as overpopulation, crime, economic uncertainty, pollution, AIDS, or threat of nuclear war may serve as sources of chronic stress.

Some groups of people suffer chronic stress by virtue of their socioeconomic status or racial identity, with stark consequences for overall well-being (Adler et al., 1994). African Americans, for example, suffer a much higher rate of heart disease than do white Americans. Research suggests that the underlying cause is not genetic differences. Instead, high blood pressure among African Americans appears to be a consequence of chronic stress caused by the consequences of prejudice: low-status jobs, limited education, fruitless job seeking, and low socioeconomic status (Anderson et al., 1992; Klag et al., 1991). Hypertension results from frustrations in efforts to achieve basic life goals; it is not linked to genetic factors. Similarly, chronic stress among women who are socioeconomically disadvantaged may put them at risk for having premature or low birthweight babies (Lobel et al., 1992; Lobel, 1994). Thus children born into poverty or prejudice may start life with greater risks than do their privileged peers.

However, chronic stress impairs more than just health. There is evidence that a high level of stress can also influence children's intellectual development.

To test the hypothesis that stress affects competence and intelligence, researchers developed a stress index based on such variables as family problems and physical disorders. Stress indexes were calculated for over four thousand 7-year-old children, and each child's intelligence was tested. The higher the stress index, the lower was the child's IQ. This was particularly true for African-American children from poor families. Greater intellectual deficits showed up also in those who had been held back a year or assigned to special education classes. The stress variables combined to influence the performance measured by the IQ test, both in the immediate testing situation and, more generally, in interactions with other personal and social factors (Brown & Rosenbaum, 1983).

Evidence suggests that intellectual development as well as physical health can be impaired by exposure to chronic stress.

You should bear in mind the cognitive effects of chronic stress when you evaluate arguments about the genetic basis of racial differences in intelligence. (We will consider that topic in Chapter 15.) These data make it clear that some of the ill effects of stress need to be counteracted with societal solutions.

Day-to-Day Hassles

You may agree that the end of a relationship, an earthquake, or prejudice might cause stress, but what about the smaller stressors you experience on a day-to-day basis? What happened to you yesterday? You probably didn't get a divorce or survive a plane crash. You're more likely to have lost your notes or textbook. Perhaps you were late for an important appointment, or got a parking ticket, or a noisy neighbor ruined your sleep. These are the types of recurring day-to-day stressors that confront most people, most of the time. One analysis suggests that an accumulation of small frustrations leads to more stress than infrequent big jolts of change do (Weinberger et al., 1987). Life is almost always bubbling with low-level frustrations. If you interpret these hassles as harmful or threatening to your well-being, they affect you more than you might imagine (Lazarus, 1984b).

An accumulation of small frustrations or daily hassles can lead to stress more easily than infrequent big changes.

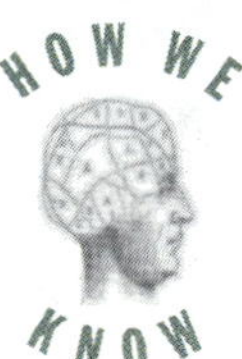

A psychiatrist distributed 100 questionnaires to people waiting for the 7:12 A.M. train from Long Island to Manhattan. From the 40 completed questionnaires returned, it was determined that these average commuters had just gulped down their breakfast in less than 11 minutes, were prepared to spend 3 hours each day in transit, and, in 10 years, had logged about 7500 hours of rail time. Two thirds of the commuters believed their family relations were impaired by their commuting. Fifty-nine percent experienced fatigue, 47 percent were filled with conscious anger, 28 percent were anxious, and others reported headaches, muscle pains, indigestion, and other symptoms of the long-term consequences of beating the rat race in the city by living in the country (F. Charaton, personal communication, 1973).

You can imagine the day-to-day stress brought about by this lifestyle.

In a diary study, a group of white, middle-class, middle-aged men and women kept track of their daily hassles over a one-year period (along with a record of major life changes and physical symptoms). A clear relationship emerged between hassles and health problems: the more frequent and intense the hassles people reported, the poorer was their health, both physical and mental (Lazarus, 1981; 1984b). As daily hassles go down, well-being goes up (Chamberlain & Zika, 1990). Although daily stressors have been shown to affect one's mood immediately, people habituate to them, so that the negative effects do not carry over to the next day. The

exception is cases of interpersonal conflicts that endure over time (Bolger et al., 1989).

Note that the types of stress that occur on a daily basis can also have ill effects on cognitive functioning. In general, the greater the stress, the greater the reduction in cognitive efficiency and the more interference with flexible thinking. Because attention is a limited resource, when you focus on the threatening aspects of a situation, you reduce the amount of attention available for effective coping with other tasks at hand. Memory is affected, too, because short-term memory is limited by the amount of attention given to new input, and retrieval of past relevant memories depends on smooth operation of the use of appropriate retrieval cues. Similarly, stress may interfere with your problem-solving, judging, and decision-making skills by narrowing your perceptions of alternatives and by substituting stereotyped, rigid thinking for more creative responding (Janis, 1982a).

Daily stressors create reductions in cognitive functioning, including impairments in attention and memory.

We have been focusing largely on day-to-day hassles. It is worth noting, however, that for many people daily hassles may be balanced out by daily positive experiences (Lazarus & Lazarus, 1994). Recall that immune response is sensitive to both positive and negative life events (Stone et al., 1994). If we want to predict your life course based on daily hassles, we also need to know something about the daily pleasures your life provides. To make these predictions, we also need to know a little bit more about your personality. As we will see next, there are individual differences in people's likelihood of being affected by stress.

Individual Differences in Stress Responses

Many of the stress responses we have been describing are average expectations for the average individual. However, researchers are paying increasing attention to individual differences in the ways that people respond to stressors (Sapolsky, 1994; Turner et al., 1992). We suggested earlier that what is highly stressful to one person may be a minor irritation to another. Some people show little reaction to extreme types of stress, whereas others never fully recover psychological well-being from the same circumstances (Wortman & Silver, 1989; Wortman et al., 1993). Can we predict which people are likely to be more affected or less affected by stress?

Psychologist **Suzanne Kobasa** believes that a special personality type is important in diffusing the effects of stress. She identified two groups of subjects from a pool of managers working for a big public utility in a large city. The members of one group experienced high levels of stress but seldom were ill, while the second group also had high stress but frequently experienced illness (Kobasa et al., 1979; Maddi & Kobasa, 1991). The members of the first group, the stress survivors, possessed the characteristics of hardiness. **Hardiness** involves welcoming change as a *challenge* and not as a threat, focusing *commitment* on purposeful activities, and having a sense of internal *control* over one's actions. These three C's of health—challenge, commitment, and control—are adaptive interpretations of stressful events (Kobasa, 1984).

Challenge, commitment, and control, elements of a hardy *personality, are adaptive interpretations of stressful events.*

Researchers have demonstrated that hardiness plays a role in the way people respond to acute stressors.

The 60 men and 60 women who had the top third and bottom third scores were selected from over 800 students who completed a scale that measured hardiness. The stressor was an experimental task in which subjects were expected to be videotaped repeating a lecture they had heard and then to be evaluated and questioned by psychology professors. The researcher manipulated the perceived threat and the challenge of the task, along with several other hardiness-related variables. She found that the high-hardiness subjects differed from the low-hardiness subjects in showing greater tolerance for frustration and in appraising the task as less threatening. In addition, hardiness influenced heart rate among the men (but not the women); high-hardiness men had a lower level of physiological arousal (Wiebe, 1991).

Thus one way of coping successfully with stress may be to cultivate a hardy personality. Let's now look more generally at techniques for successful coping.

Coping with Stress

If living is inevitably stressful, and if chronic stress can disrupt your life and even kill you, you need to learn how to manage stress. **Coping** refers to the process of dealing with internal or external demands that are perceived as straining or exceeding an individual's resources (Lazarus & Folkman, 1984). Coping may consist of behavioral, emotional, or motivational responses and thoughts. Coping can also precede a potentially stressful event in the form of **anticipatory coping** (Folkman, 1984). For example, how do you tell your parents that you are dropping out of school or your lover that you are no longer in love? Anticipating a stressful situation leads to many thoughts and feelings that themselves may be stress inducing, as in the cases of tests, interviews, speeches, or blind dates. You need to know how to cope.

The two main ways of coping are defined by whether the goal is to confront the problem directly—*problem-directed coping*—or to lessen the discomfort associated with the stress—*emotion-focused coping* (Billings & Moos, 1982; Lazarus & Folkman, 1984). Several subcategories of these two basic approaches are shown in **Table 13.4**.

"Taking the bull by the horns" is how we usually characterize the strategy of facing up to a problem situation. This approach includes all strategies designed to deal *directly* with the stressor, whether through overt action or through realistic problem-solving activities. You face up to a bully or run away; you try to win him or her over with bribes or other incentives. Your focus is on the problem to be dealt with and on the agent that has induced the stress. You acknowledge the call to action, you appraise the situation and your resources for dealing with it, and you undertake a response that is appropriate for removing or lessening the threat. Such problem-solving efforts are useful for managing *controllable stressors*.

Speaking directly to the person responsible for a problem, and stating what you want done to resolve it, can be an effective means to reduce stress.

The emotion-focused approach is useful for managing the impact of more *uncontrollable stressors*. Suppose you are responsible for the care of a parent with Alzheimer's. In that situation, there is no "bully" whom you can eliminate from the environment. You cannot look for ways of changing the external stressful situation. Instead, you try to change your feelings and thoughts about it by taking part in a support group or learning relaxation techniques. This approach still constitutes a coping strategy, because you are acknowledging that there is a threat to your well-being and you are taking steps to modify that threat.

Coping is a situation in which the more different strategies you have available to you, the better off you will be (Taylor & Clark, 1986). For coping to be

Table 13.4 Taxonomy of Coping Strategies

Type of Coping Strategy	Example
Problem-directed coping	
Change stressor or one's relationship to it through direct actions and/or problem-solving activities	Fight (destroy, remove, or weaken the threat)
	Flight (distance oneself from the threat)
	Seek options to fight or flight (negotiating, bargaining, compromising)
	Prevent future stress (act to increase one's resistance or decrease strength of anticipated stress)
Emotion-focused coping	
Change self through activities that make one feel better but do not change the stressor	Somatically focused activities (use of antianxiety medication, relaxation, biofeedback)
	Cognitively focused activities (planned distractions, fantasies, thoughts about oneself)
	Therapy to adjust conscious or unconscious processes that lead to additional anxiety

successful, your resources need to match the perceived demand. Thus the availability of multiple coping strategies is adaptive, because you are more likely to achieve a match and manage the stressful event. Moreover, knowing that you possess a variety of coping strategies can help increase your actual ability to meet environmental demands (Bandura, 1986). Self-confidence can insulate you from experiencing the full impact of many stressors, because believing you have coping resources readily available short-circuits the stressful, chaotic response "What am I going to do?"

Up to now, we have been discussing general approaches to coping with stressors. Now we review specific cognitive and social approaches to successful coping.

Modifying Cognitive Strategies

A powerful way to handle stress more adaptively is to change your evaluations of stressors and your self-defeating cognitions about the way you are dealing with them. You need to find a different way to think about a given situation, your role in it, and the causal attributions you make to explain the undesirable outcome. Two ways of mentally coping with stress are *reappraising* the nature of the stressors themselves and *restructuring* your cognitions about your stress reactions.

People mentally cope with stress by reappraising the stressor or by restructuring cognitions about reactions to stress.

We have already described the idea that people control the experience of stress in their lives in part by the way they appraise life events (Lazarus & Lazarus, 1994). Learning to think differently about certain stressors, to relabel them, or to imagine them in a less-threatening (perhaps even funny) context is a form of cognitive reappraisal that can reduce stress. Worried about giving a speech to a large, forbidding audience? One stressor reappraisal technique is to imagine your potential critics sitting there in the nude—this surely takes away a great deal of their fearsome power. Anxious about being shy at a party you must attend? Think about finding someone who is more shy than you and reducing his or her social anxiety by initiating a conversation.

But not all stressful events can be reappraised to minimize their impact. In those cases, you can manage stress better by changing what you tell yourself about it and by changing your handling of it. Cognitive-behavior therapist **Donald Meichenbaum** (1977, 1985) has proposed a three-phase process that allows for such *stress inoculation.* In Phase 1, people work to develop a greater awareness of their actual behavior, what instigates it, and what its results are. One of the best ways of doing this is to keep daily logs. By helping people redefine their problems in terms of their causes and results, logs can increase their feelings of control. You may discover, for example, that your grades are low (a stressor) because you always leave too little time to do a good job on your class assignments. In Phase 2, people begin to identify new behaviors that negate the maladaptive, self-defeating behaviors. Perhaps you might create a fixed "study time" or limit your phone calls to ten minutes each night. In Phase 3, after adaptive behaviors are being emitted, individuals appraise the consequences of their new behaviors, avoiding the former internal dialogue of put-downs. Instead of telling themselves, "I was lucky the professor called on me when I happened to have read the text," they say, "I'm glad I was prepared for the professor's question. It feels great to be able to respond intelligently in that class."

This three-phase approach means initiating responses and self-statements that are incompatible with previous defeatist cognitions. Once started on this path, people realize that they are changing—and can take full credit for the change, which promotes further successes. **Table 13.5** gives examples of the new kinds of self-statements that help in dealing with stressful situations.

One of the main themes of coping is to establish **perceived control** over the stressor, a belief that you can make a difference in the course or the con-

Table 13.5 Examples of Coping Self-Statements

Preparation

I can develop a plan to deal with it.

Just think about what I can do about it. That's better than getting anxious.

No negative self-statements, just think rationally.

Confrontation

One step at a time; I can handle this situation.

This anxiety is what the doctor said I would feel; it's a reminder to use my coping exercises.

Relax; I'm in control. Take a slow, deep breath.

Coping

When fear comes, just pause.

Keep focus on the present; what is it I have to do?

Don't try to eliminate fear totally; just keep it manageable.

It's not the worst thing that can happen.

Just think about something else.

Self-reinforcement

It worked; I was able to do it.

It wasn't as bad as I expected.

I'm really pleased with the progress I'm making.

sequences of some event or experience (Vaughan, 1993). If you believe that you can affect the course of an illness or the daily symptoms of a disease, you are probably adjusting well to the disorder (Affleck et al., 1987). However, if you believe that the source of the stress is another person, whose behavior you cannot influence, or a situation that you cannot change, chances increase for a poor psychological adjustment to your chronic condition (Bulman & Wortman, 1977).

In a classic study by Ellen Langer and Judith Rodin (1976), two simple elements of perceived control were introduced into a nursing home environment. Each resident was given a plant to take care of (behavioral control) and asked to choose when to see movies (decision control). Comparison subjects on another floor of the institution had neither sense of control; they were given plants that nurses took care of and they saw movies at prearranged times. On delayed measures several weeks later and a full year later, those elderly patients who had been given some control over the events in this bleak institutional setting were more active, had more positive moods, and were psychologically and physically healthier than the no-control patients. Most amazing is the finding that, one year later, fewer of those in the perceived control situation had died than those on the comparison floor (Rodin, 1983; Rodin & Langer, 1977). Such research findings have important implications for policies and programs in institutional settings (Rodin, 1986).

Effective coping strategies counter a stressful situation with some or all of four types of control: *information control* (knowing what to expect); *cognitive control* (thinking about the event differently and more constructively); *decision control* (being able to decide on alternative actions); and *behavioral control* (taking actions to reduce the aversiveness of the event). Suppose you are feeling stress from an upcoming test. How can you shape your thinking to assert all four of these types of control?

While you file away these control strategies for future use, we will turn to a final aspect of coping with stress—the social dimension.

Social Support as a Coping Resource

Social support refers to the resources others provide, giving the message that one is loved, cared for, esteemed, and connected to other people in a network of communication and mutual obligation (Cobb, 1976; Cohen & Syme, 1985). In addition to these forms of *socioemotional support,* other people may provide *tangible support* (money, transportation, housing) and *informational support* (advice, personal feedback, information). Anyone with whom you have a significant social relationship—such as family members, friends, coworkers, and neighbors—can be part of your social support network in time of need.

Much research points to the power of social support in moderating the vulnerability to stress (Cohen & McKay, 1983). When people have other people they can turn to, they are better able to handle job stressors, unemployment, marital disruption, serious illness, and other catastrophes, as well as their everyday problems of living (Gottlieb, 1981; Pilisuk & Parks, 1986). The positive effects of social support go beyond aiding psychological adjustment to stressful events; they can improve recovery from diagnosed illness and reduce the risk of death from disease (House et al., 1988; Kulik & Mahler, 1989). One study looked at the death rate of patients suffering from severe

Social support is a powerful moderator of vulnerability to stress. In fact, it appears that social support is instrumental in recovery from illness and even reduces the risk of death from disease.

kidney disease (Christensen et al., 1994). A one-point increase in a measure of family support was associated with a 13 percent decrease in the likelihood of death.

Researchers are trying to identify which types of support are most helpful for specific events (Cohen, 1988; Dakof & Taylor, 1990; Dunkel-Schetter et al., 1987; Wilcox et al., 1994). Different sources of support seem to work best for particular stressors—for example, help from a spouse might be ideal for a working woman with a newborn (Lieberman, 1982).

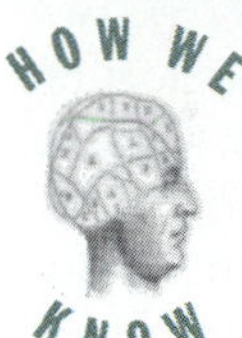

Shelley Taylor and her colleagues have studied the effectiveness of the different types of social support given to cancer patients (Dakof & Taylor, 1990; Taylor, 1986). Patients varied in their assessments of the helpfulness of kinds of support. They thought it was helpful to them for spouses, but not for physicians or nurses, to "just be there." On the other hand, it was important to the patients to receive information or advice from other cancer patients or from physicians, but not from family and friends. Regardless of the source—whether doctors or family or friends—patients did not find forced cheerfulness or attempts to minimize the impact of their disease as helpful.

Figure 13.8 provides a comparison of the types of social support that were rated as most helpful for cancer patients versus patients with noncatastrophic illness, such as chronic headaches and irritable bowel syndrome (Martin et al., 1994). The data suggest, once again, that the optimal type of social support differs for different sources of stress. Can you think of some reasons why emotional support might be more helpful to cancer patients than to patients with noncatastrophic illnesses?

Researchers are also trying to determine when sources of support actually increase anxiety. For example, if your mother insisted on accompanying you to a doctor's appointment or to a college interview when you preferred to go alone, you might experience additional anxiety about the

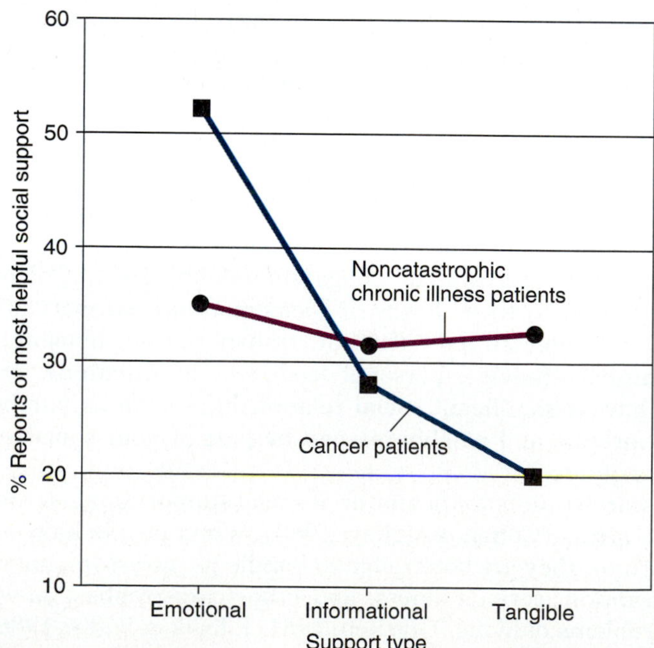

Figure 13.8 The Value of Social Support
Perceived social support as a function of diagnosis. (From Martin et al., 1994; the data for cancer patients are taken from Dakof & Taylor, 1990.)

situation (Coyne et al., 1988). Too much or too intensive social support may become intrusive and not helpful in the long run; having one close friend may be as beneficial as having many. Research also suggests that you're sometimes better off being alone than being in a bad relationship: married people who are unable to communicate well with their spouses show more symptoms of depression than control subjects without spouses (Weissman, 1987).

Being part of an effective social support network means that you believe others will be there for you if you need them—even if you don't actually ask for their help when you experience stress. One of the most important take-home messages from *Psychology and Life* is that you should always work at being part of a social support network and never let yourself become socially isolated.

At many points in this discussion of stress, we have noted the effect of stress on physical or psychological well-being. Let's now turn directly to the ways in which psychologists apply their research knowledge to issues of illness and health.

HEALTH PSYCHOLOGY

How much do your psychological processes contribute to your experiences of illness and wellness? We have already given you reason to believe that the right answer may be "quite a bit." This acknowledgment of the importance of psychological and social factors in health has spurred the growth of a new field, health psychology. **Health psychology** is the branch of psychology that is devoted to understanding the way people stay healthy, the reasons they become ill, and the way they respond when they do get ill (Taylor, 1986, 1990). **Health** refers to the general condition of the body and mind in terms of soundness and vigor. It is not simply the absence of illness or injury but is more a matter of how well all the body's component parts are working together. We will begin our discussion of health psychology by describing how the field's underlying philosophy departs from a traditional Western medical model of illness. We then consider the contributions of health psychology to the prevention and treatment of illness and dysfunction.

The Biopsychosocial Model of Health

Health psychology is guided by a *biopsychosocial model* of health. We can find the roots of this perspective in many non-Western cultures. To arrive at a definition of the biopsychosocial model, we will start with a description of some of these non-Western traditions.

Traditional Health Practices

Psychological principles have been applied in the treatment of illness and the pursuit of health for all of recorded time. Many ancient cultures understood the importance of communal health and relaxation rituals in the enhancement of the quality of life. Among the Navajo, for example, disease, illness, and well-being have been attributed to social harmony and mind-body interactions. The Navajo concept of **hozho** (pronounced whoa-zo) means harmony, peace of mind, goodness, ideal family relationships, beauty in arts and crafts, and health of body and spirit. Illness is seen as the outcome of any *disharmony,* caused by evil introduced through violation of taboos, witchcraft, overindulgence, or bad dreams. Traditional healing ceremonies seek to banish illness and restore health, not only through the medicine of the

The Navajo, like people in many other cultures around the world, place a high value on aesthetics, family harmony, and physical health.

shaman but also through the combined efforts of all family members, who work together with the ill person to reachieve a state of hozho. The illness of any member of a tribe is seen not as his or her individual responsibility (and fault) but rather as a sign of broader disharmony that must be repaired by communal healing ceremonies. This cultural orientation guarantees that a powerful social support network will automatically come to the aid of the sufferer.

Similarly, among the Nyakusa of Tanzania, Africa, any sign of disharmony or deviation from the expected "norm" generates a swift communal intervention to set the situation right. Thus strong anger, the birth of twins, the sudden death of a young person, and illness are all signs of an anomaly because they are unusual events for this tribe. Special tribal rituals are quickly enacted around the afflicted person or family. Part of the purpose of these rituals is to signal social acceptance. The concept of medicine among the Nyakusa differs from the Western view, in which it is solely a biological or pharmacological intervention. For the Nyakusa, medicine is given to change the habits, dispositions, and desires of people—for psychological cures. Chiefs get medicine to make them wise and dignified; a bride gets medicine to make her patient and polite as well as fertile. Anger in husbands, employers, and police is controlled by a special medicine; other medicine "cures" thieves of criminal habits and makes men and women more attractive and more persuasive as lovers and leaders (Wilson, 1959).

Toward a Biopsychosocial Model

Non-Western cultures focus on the link between the body and mind and apply medicines as if they are psychological cures, but Western medicine emphasizes the separation of mind and body and the application of medicine to the physical body.

We have seen that healing practices in non-Western cultures often presupposed a link between the body and the mind. By contrast, modern Western scientific thinking has relied almost exclusively on a *biomedical model* that has a dualistic conception of body and mind. According to this model, medicine treats the physical body as separate from the psyche; the mind is important only for emotions and beliefs and has little to do with the reality of the body. Over time, however, researchers have begun to document types of interactions that make the strict biomedical model unworkable. You have already seen some of the evidence: good and bad life events can affect immune function; people with certain personality types are more likely to suffer the health effects of stress; adequate social support can decrease the probability of death. These realizations yield the three components of the **biopsychosocial model.** The *bio* acknowledges the reality of biological illness. The *psycho* and the *social* acknowledge the psychological and social components of health.

The biopsychosocial model links your physical health to your state of mind and the world around you. Health psychologists view health as a dynamic, multidimensional experience. Optimal health, or **wellness,** incorporates physical, intellectual, emotional, spiritual, social, and environmental aspects of your life. When you undertake an activity for the purpose of preventing disease or detecting it in the asymptomatic stage, you are exhibiting *health behavior.* A healthy behavioral pattern is one that operates automatically without reinforcement or incentives and that contributes directly to your overall health (Hunt et al., 1979). The general goal of health psychology is to use psychological knowledge to promote wellness and positive health behaviors. Let's now consider theory and research relevant to this goal.

Health Promotion

Health promotion means developing general strategies and specific tactics to eliminate or reduce the risk that people will get sick. The prevention of illness in the late twentieth century poses a much different challenge than it did at the beginning of the century (Matarazzo, 1984). In 1900 the primary

Table 13.6 Leading Causes of Death, United States, 1991

Rank	Percent of Deaths	Cause of Death	Contributors to Cause of Death (D—Diet; S—Smoking; A—Alcohol)
1.	28.5	Heart disease	DS
2.	20.4	Cancer	DS
3.	5.6	Strokes	DS
4.	3.5	Obstructive lung diseases	S
5.	3.5	All accidents	A
	1.7	Motor vehicle accidents alone	A
6.	3.1	Pneumonia*	S
7.	2.0	Diabetes	D
8.	1.2	Suicide	A
9.	1.1	AIDS, HIV disease	
10.	1.1	Homicide	A

*Includes AIDS cases in which cause of death was pneumonia.

cause of death was infectious disease. Health practitioners at that time launched the first revolution in American public health. Over time, through the use of research, public education, the development of vaccines, and changes in public health standards (such as waste control and sewage), they were able to reduce substantially the deaths associated with such diseases as influenza, tuberculosis, polio, measles, and smallpox.

If researchers wish to continue the trend toward improved quality of life, they must attempt to decrease those deaths associated with lifestyle factors (see **Table 13.6**). Smoking, being overweight, eating foods high in fat and cholesterol, drinking too much alcohol, driving without seat belts, and leading stressful lives all play a role in heart disease, cancer, strokes, accidents, and suicide. Changing the behaviors associated with these *diseases of civilization* will prevent much illness and premature death. **Figure 13.9** shows the estimated percentage of deaths that could be prevented by changes in behavior, early detection, and prevention strategies.

A significant focus of the wellness movement of the 1990s is to reduce the number of deaths caused by lifestyle factors.

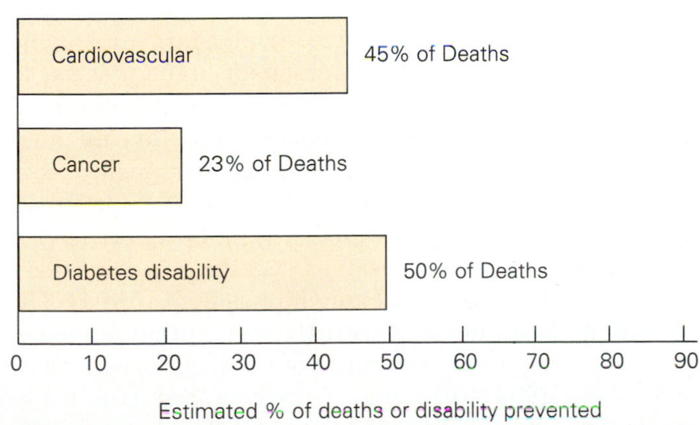

Figure 13.9 Prevention of Death
Changes in behavior, early detection of health problems, and intervention could prevent death in many cases.

Table 13.7 Ten Steps To Personal Wellness

1. Exercise regularly
2. Eat nutritious, balanced meals (high in vegetables, fruits, and grains, low in fat and cholesterol)
3. Maintain proper weight
4. Sleep 7–8 hours nightly; rest/relax daily
5. Wear seat belts and bike helmets
6. Do not smoke or use drugs
7. Use alcohol in moderation, if at all
8. Engage only in protected, safe sex
9. Get regular medical/dental checkups; adhere to medical regimens
10. Develop an optimistic perspective and friendships

Based on this knowledge, it's easy to make some recommendations. You are more likely to stay well if you practice good health habits, such as those listed in **Table 13.7**. Many of these suggestions probably are familiar to you already. However, health psychologists would like to use psychological principles to increase the probability that you will actually do the things you know are good for you! Research has identified four factors that determine the likelihood that someone will engage in a healthy habit or will change a faulty one. The person must believe that (1) the threat to health is severe; (2) the perceived personal vulnerability and/or the likelihood of developing the disorder is high; (3) he or she is able to perform the response that will reduce the threat (self-efficacy); and (4) the response is effective in overcoming the threat (Bandura, 1986; Janz & Becker, 1984; Rogers, 1984). We will now apply these insights to a series of concrete domains: smoking, nutrition and exercise, heart disease, and AIDS.

Smoking

It would be impossible to imagine that anyone reading this book wouldn't know that smoking is extremely dangerous. Roughly half a million people die each year from smoking-related illnesses (U.S. Department of Health and Human Services, 1990). Health psychologists would like to understand both why people begin to smoke—so that the psychologists can help prevent it—and how to assist people in quitting—so ex-smokers can reap the substantial benefits of quitting. Analyses of why some people start smoking have focused on personality and social factors. One personality type that has been associated with the initiation of smoking is called *sensation seeking* (Zuckerman, 1988). Individuals characterized as sensation seeking are more likely to engage in risky activities. One study compared personality assessments of men and women in the mid-1960s (1964–1967) with their smoking or nonsmoking behavior in the late 1980s (1987–1991). Both men and women who had revealed themselves to be sensation seeking in the 1960s were more likely to be smoking 20 to 25 years later (Lipkus et al., 1994). These personality factors may go hand in hand with the perception among members of some groups, either despite of or because of the health risks, that smoking is "cool" (Leary et al., 1994). This may be particularly true for adolescents. Health psychologists understand that successful interventions to prevent the initiation of smoking must attempt to transform smoking into an "uncool" activity.

Health psychologists would like to understand the influence of personality on behaviors such as smoking.

The best approach to smoking is never to start at all. But for those of you who have begun to smoke, what has research revealed about quitting? Although many people who try to quit have relapses, an estimated 35 million Americans have quit. Ninety percent have done so on their own, without professional treatment programs. Researchers have identified stages people pass through that represent increasing readiness to quit (DiClemente et al., 1991; Prochaska et al., 1993):

Smoking cessation results from the successful passage through a readiness sequence consisting of precontemplation, contemplation, preparation, action, and maintenance.

- *precontemplation*—the smoker is not yet thinking about quitting;
- *contemplation*—the smoker is thinking about quitting but has not yet undertaken any behavioral changes;
- *preparation*—the smoker is getting ready to quit;
- *action*—the smoker takes action toward quitting by setting behavioral goals;
- *maintenance*—the smoker is now a nonsmoker and is trying to stay that way.

This analysis suggests that not all smokers are psychologically equivalent in terms of readiness to quit. Interventions can be designed that nudge smokers up the scale of readiness, until, finally, they are psychologically prepared to take healthy action.

It is important to recognize that pitted against each individual's efforts to stop smoking is the multimillion dollar annual budget spent by tobacco companies to promote smoking, to appeal to men and women by portraying it as sexy, sophisticated, and youthful. Smoking advertisements are aimed at multiple target audiences with multiple messages: they attempt to recruit new smokers (especially the young, women, and minorities), support continued smoking, maintain brand loyalty, entice smokers to switch to new brands with special features, and tempt former smokers to renew their (deadly) habit (Blum, 1989). If you wish to quit smoking, you must recognize the role advertising plays in maintaining psychological aspects of addiction.

Nutrition and Exercise

Three of our "ten steps to personal wellness" (Table 13.7) related to nutrition and exercise. We recommended that you eat nutritious food and exercise regularly—which should allow you to maintain proper weight. In Chapter 12, we reviewed some of the forces that control eating. We saw there that the availability of flavorful foods can overwhelm bodily cues that it's time to stop eating (Rolls et al., 1981). To have a healthy diet, you need to get back in touch with your bodily cues. You also need to be aware of which types of food are healthy and which are unhealthy and design a varied diet around healthy choices (Palken & Shackelford, 1992). We will report shortly on one large-scale attempt to get residents of several California towns to change their patterns of eating to improve their health.

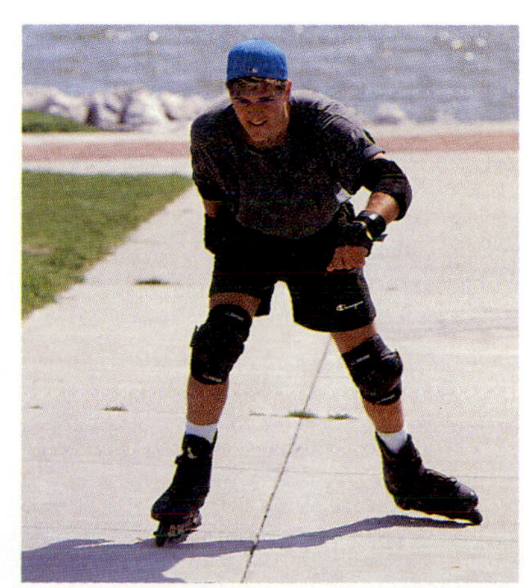

Regular exercise is part of a life-long plan to reduce stress and preserve health.

Regular exercise has also been established as an important factor in promoting and maintaining health. In particular, major improvements in health are achieved from such aerobic exercises as bicycling, swimming, running, or even fast walking. These activities lead to increased fitness of the heart and respiratory systems, improvement of muscle tone and strength, and many other health benefits. Researchers are exploring the questions of who exercises regularly and why and are trying to determine what programs or strategies are most effective in getting people to start and continue exercising (Dishman, 1982, 1991). Research suggests that individuals can learn strategies that allow them to overcome obstacles to exercise (Simkin & Gross, 1994). You can treat exercise like any other situation in which you use cognitive appraisal to cope with stress. Try to structure your life so that exercise is a healthy pleasure. You should also be aware that many college students have "rebounds" in both their eating and exercising: when periods of academic stress have passed, they return from poor eating and minimal exercising to healthy behavior (Griffin et al., 1993). How might you structure your thoughts to avoid this pattern?

Heart Disease

Let's see how smoking, nutrition, and exercise can be combined in a health intervention targeted toward preventing heart disease. This major study was conducted in three towns in California. The goals of the study were to persuade people to reduce their cardiovascular risk via changes in smoking, diet, and exercise and to determine which method of persuasion was more effective.

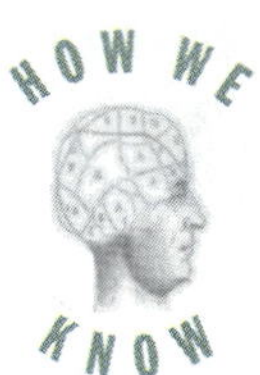

In one town, a two-year campaign was conducted through the mass media, including television, radio, newspapers, billboards, and mailed leaflets. A second town received the same two-year media campaign plus a personal instruction program on modifying health habits for high-risk individuals. The third town served as a control group and received no persuasive campaign. How successful were the campaigns in modifying lifestyle? The results showed that the townspeople who had been exposed only to the mass-media campaign were more knowledgeable about the links between lifestyle and heart disease, but they showed only modest changes in their own behaviors and health status, as seen in **Figure 13.10**. In the town where the media campaign was supplemented with personal instruction, residents showed more substantial and long-lasting changes in their health habits, particularly in reduced smoking (Farquhar et al., 1984; Maccoby et al., 1977).

Lifestyle factors can be modified, but not without some difficulty and expense.

Given these encouraging results, the experimenters undertook a long-term project spread over five cities (Farquhar, 1991). The risk of heart disease in these communities has been lowered by about 15 percent.

The good news is that lifestyle factors can be modified. The sobering news is that it is difficult and expensive to do so and mass media campaigns alone may not be sufficient to change health behaviors. The campaigns may, however, contribute to long-term shifts in social attitudes that support lifestyle changes.

AIDS

AIDS is an acronym for *acquired immune deficiency syndrome.* While hundreds of thousands are dying from this virulent disease, many more are living with HIV infection. **HIV** (*human immunodeficiency virus*) is a virus that attacks the white blood cells (T-lymphocytes) in human blood, thus damaging the immune system and weakening the body's ability to fight other diseases. The individual then becomes vulnerable to infection by a host of other viruses and bacteria that can cause such life-threatening illnesses as cancer, meningitis, and pneumonia. The period of time from initial infection with the virus until symptoms occur (incubation period) can be five years or longer. Although most of the estimated millions of those infected with the HIV virus do not have AIDS (a medical diagnosis), they must live with the continual stress that this life-threatening disease might suddenly emerge. At the present time, there is neither a cure for AIDS nor a vaccine to prevent its spread.

At present, there is neither a cure for AIDS nor a vaccine to prevent its spread, but psychological intervention can help reduce new cases.

The HIV virus is not airborne; it requires direct access to the bloodstream to produce an infection. The HIV virus is generally passed from one person to another in one of two ways: (1) the exchange of semen or blood during sexual contact (especially anal intercourse) and (2) the sharing of intravenous needles and syringes used for injecting drugs. The virus has also been passed through blood transfusions and medical procedures in which infected blood

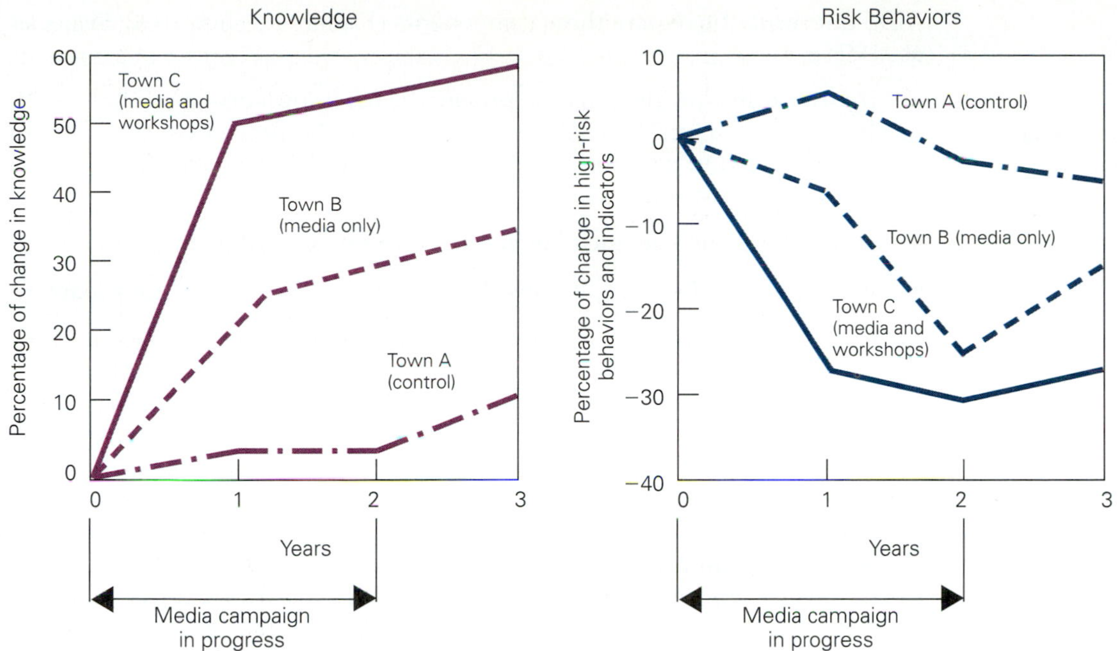

Figure 13.10 Response to Media Health Messages and Hands-on Workshops
Knowledge of cardiovascular disease risk factors was greater among residents of Town B, who were exposed to a two-year mass-media health campaign, than among residents of Town A, who were not exposed to the campaign. Knowledge gain was greater still among residents of Town C, who participated in intense workshops and instruction sessions for several months during the media blitz. As knowledge increased, bad health habits (risk behaviors) and signs (indicators) decreased; Town C led the way, followed by Town B.

or organs are unwittingly given to healthy people. Many people suffering from hemophilia have gotten AIDS in this way.

Who is at risk? Potentially everyone. Although the initial discovery of AIDS in the United States was in the male homosexual community, the disease has spread widely. AIDS is being found among heterosexuals and homosexuals of both sexes. It is predicted that AIDS will increase and spread throughout the general population, much like other sexually transmitted diseases, such as syphilis and gonorrhea, which have also been on the rise in recent years. According to the National Center for Disease Control Report (November, 1990), as many as 35,000 college students, or 1 student in 500, are estimated to be HIV positive.

The only way to protect oneself from being infected with the AIDS virus is to change those lifestyle habits that put one at risk. This means making permanent changes in patterns of sexual behavior and in use of drug paraphernalia. Health psychologist **Thomas Coates** is part of a multidisciplinary research team that is using an array of psychological principles in a concerted effort to prevent the further spread of AIDS (Catania et al., 1994; Coates, 1990; Ekstrand & Coates, 1990). The team is involved in many aspects of applied psychology, such as assessing psychosocial risk factors, developing behavioral interventions, training community leaders to be effective in educating people toward healthier patterns of sexual and drug behavior, assisting with the design of media advertisements and community information campaigns, and systematically evaluating changes in relevant attitudes, values, and behaviors. Successful

AIDS interventions require three components (Fisher & Fisher, 1992; Fisher et al., 1994):

Successful AIDS interventions require information, motivation, and behavioral skills.

- *information*—people must be provided with knowledge about how AIDS is transmitted and how its transmission may be prevented; they should be counseled to practice safer sex (e.g., use condoms during sexual contact) and use sterile needles;
- *motivation*—people must be motivated to practice AIDS prevention;
- *behavioral skills*—people must be taught how to put the knowledge to use.

Why are all three of these components necessary? People might be highly motivated but uninformed, or vice versa. They may have both sufficient knowledge and sufficient motivation but lack requisite skills. They may not, for example, know exactly how to overcome the social barrier of asking a partner to use a condom (Leary et al., 1994). Psychological interventions can provide role-playing experience, or other behavioral skills, to make that barrier seem less significant.

For further information about AIDS, you can call the toll-free National AIDS Hotline (English: 1-800-HIV-INFO; Spanish: 1-800-344-7432; TTY/TDD for the hearing impaired: 1-800-243-7889) or the National AIDS Information Clearinghouse (1-800-458-5231).

Health Promotion as a National and International Concern

The promotion of health and wellness requires national and international efforts that go beyond focusing on the psychology of individuals. For example, the U.S. Department of Health and Human Services has outlined national public health goals and objectives for the 1990s in the report *Healthy People 2000* (1990). The three broad national goals for public health over this decade are (1) to increase the span of healthy life; (2) to reduce the disparities in health status among different populations, such as the poor, minorities, and children; and (3) to provide access to preventive health-care services for all people. To meet these general goals, nearly 300 specific objectives have been identified in 22 priority areas, as outlined in **Table 13.8**. A comparable earlier agenda for national health met with reasonable success, achieving nearly half the goals set for 1990 (McGinnis, 1991).

The three broad goals for public health for the 1990s are to increase the span of healthy life, to reduce the disparities in health status among different populations, and to provide access to preventive health-care services for all people.

Another aspect of prevention involves developing a global consciousness in which disease prevention and health promotion are seen within a worldwide framework and not just from a U.S. or Eurocentric focus. Most of the world's expertise in behavioral science and preventive medicine resides in the developed world. Therefore, reaching the developing world requires support for scholars, researchers, and practitioners in those regions and culturally relevant models of health and behavior change. For example, 18 universities from the Asia-Pacific region, including some in Japan, Korea, and China, have united to carry out regional research and training on illness prevention (Raymond et al., 1991).

Treatment

Treatment focuses on helping people adjust to their illnesses and recover from them. We will look at two aspects of treatment. First we consider the role of psychologists in encouraging patients to adhere to the regiments prescribed by health-care practitioners. Then we look at instances in which the mind can contribute to the body's cure.

Patient Adherence

Patients are often given a *treatment regimen.* This might include medications, dietary changes, prescribed periods of bed rest and exercise, and fol-

Table 13.8 Health Objectives for the Year 2000

Health promotion	Preventive services
1. Physical activity and fitness	14. Maternal and infant health
2. Nutrition	15. Heart disease and stroke
3. Tobacco	16. Cancer
4. Alcohol and other drugs	17. Diabetes and chronic disabling conditions
5. Family planning	18. HIV infection
6. Mental health and mental disorders	19. Sexually transmitted diseases
7. Violent and abusive behavior	20. Immunization and infectious diseases
8. Educational and community-based programs	21. Clinical preventive services
Health protection	Surveillance
9. Unintentional injuries	22. Surveillance and data systems
10. Occupational safety and health	
11. Environmental health	
12. Food and drug safety	
13. Oral health	

low-up procedures such as return checkups, rehabilitation training, and chemotherapy. Failing to adhere to treatment regimens is one of the most serious problems in health care (DiMatteo & DiNicola, 1982). The rate of patient nonadherence is estimated to be as high as 50 percent for some treatment regimens.

Patients' failure to adhere to treatment regimens is a serious problem in health care.

Research has shown that health-care professionals can take steps to improve patient adherence. Patients are more satisfied with their health care when they trust that the efficacy of the treatment outweighs its costs. They are also more likely to comply with a regimen when practitioners communicate clearly, make sure that their patients understand what has been said, act courteously, and convey a sense of caring and supportiveness. In addition, health professionals must recognize the role of cultural and social norms in the treatment process and involve family and friends where necessary. Some physicians critical of their profession's outdated reliance on the biomedical model argue that doctors must be taught to *care* in order to cure (Siegel, 1988). Compliance-gaining strategies developed from psychological research are also being used to help overcome the lack of cooperation between patients and practitioners (Putnam et al., 1994; Zimbardo & Leippe, 1991).

Harnessing the Mind to Heal the Body

More and more often, the treatments to which patients must adhere involve a psychological component. Many investigators now believe that psychological strategies can improve well-being. For example, many people react to stress with tension, resulting in tight muscles and high blood pressure. Fortunately, many tension responses can be controlled by psychological techniques, such as *relaxation* and *biofeedback.*

Relaxation through meditation has ancient roots in many parts of the world. In Eastern cultures, ways to calm the mind and still the body's tensions have been practiced for centuries. Today, Zen discipline and yoga exercises from Japan and India are part of daily life for many people both there and, increasingly, in the West. Growing evidence suggests that complete relaxation is a potent antistress response. The **relaxation response** is a condition in which muscle tension, cortical activity, heart rate, and blood pressure all decrease and breathing slows (Benson, 1975; Benson & Stuart, 1992). There is reduced electrical activity in the brain, and input to the central nervous system from the outside environment is lowered. In this low level of arousal, recuperation from stress can take place. Four conditions are regarded as necessary to produce the relaxation response: (1) a quiet environment, (2) closed eyes, (3) a comfortable position, and (4) a repetitive mental device such as the chanting of a brief phrase over and over again. The first three lower input to the nervous system, while the fourth lowers its internal stimulation.

Biofeedback is a self-regulatory technique used for a variety of special applications, such as control of blood pressure, relaxation of forehead muscles (involved in tension headaches), and even diminishment of extreme blushing. As pioneered by psychologist **Neal Miller** (1978), biofeedback is a procedure that makes an individual aware of ordinarily weak or internal responses by providing clear external signals. The patient is allowed to "see" his or her own bodily reactions, which are monitored and amplified by equipment that transforms them into lights and sound cues of varying intensity. The patient's task is then to control the level of these external cues. For example, a patient might have to keep a light lit on a meter or maintain a tone at a given intensity. Paradoxically, although individuals do not know how they do it, concentrating on the desired result in the presence of these signals produces change in the desired direction. While biofeedback can lead to relaxation and reduce muscle tension, it does not lower general levels of stress (Birbaumer & Kimmel, 1979; Swets & Bjork, 1990).

What about more serious illness? Research also shows the potential for psychological processes to ease the course of cancer.

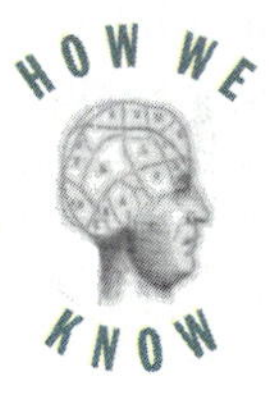

Routine medical care was provided to 86 patients with metastatic breast cancer, while an experimental subgroup of 50 also participated in weekly supportive group therapy for one year. These patients met to discuss their personal experiences in coping with the various aspects of having cancer, and they had the opportunity to reveal openly in an accepting environment their fears and other strong emotions.

Although at the 10-year follow-up all but three of the total sample had died, there was a significant difference in the survival times between those given the psychological treatment and those given only medical treatment. Those patients who participated in group therapy survived for an average of 36.6 months, compared with the 18.9 months for the control group. This finding in a well-controlled study indicates that psychological treatments can affect the course of disease and the length of life (Spiegel et al., 1989).

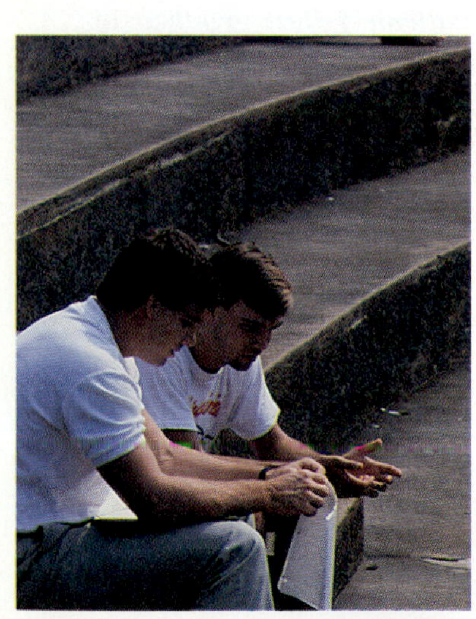

Is there anything troubling you that you feel too ashamed to discuss? Research indicates that your overall level of stress will decrease if you find someone in whom to confide.

A negative reaction to this encouraging research was sounded by a physician fearful that medicine would be overwhelmed by psychology: "What I am fearful of is that the 'alternative' field will go crazy with this and say, 'Aha, we told you all along, psychotherapy cures cancer, so stop your radiation therapy'" (Dr. Jimmie Holland, quoted in Barinaga, 1989, p. 246). To the contrary, many health psychologists want medical treatments to expand to include psychological practices in addition to traditional treatments.

One last note on treatment. Have you ever had a secret too shameful to tell anyone? If so, tell someone now. That is the conclusion from a large body of research by health psychologist **James Pennebaker** (1990; Traue & Pennebaker, 1993), who has shown that suppressing thoughts and feelings associated with personal traumas, failures, and guilty or shameful experiences takes a devastating toll on mental and physical health. Such inhibition is psychologically hard work and, over time, it undermines the body's defenses

Is Laughter the Best Medicine?

Lucy went to the hospital to visit Emma, a neighbor who had broken her hip. The first thing Lucy saw when the elevator door opened at the third floor was a clown, with an enormous orange nose, dancing down the hall, pushing a colorfully decorated cart. The clown stopped in front of Lucy, bowed, and then somersaulted to the nurses' station. A cluster of patients cheered. Most of them were in wheelchairs or on crutches. Upon asking for directions, Lucy learned that Emma was in the "humor room," where the film *Blazing Saddles* was about to start.

Since writer **Norman Cousins**'s widely publicized recovery from a debilitating and usually incurable disease of the connective tissue, humor has gained new respectability in hospital wards around the country. Cousins, the long-time editor of the *Saturday Review,* with the cooperation of his physician, supplemented his regular medical therapy with a steady diet of Marx brothers movies and *Candid Camera* film clips. Although he never claimed that laughter alone effected his cure, Cousins is best remembered for his passionate support of the notion that, if negative emotions can cause distress, then humor and positive emotions can enhance the healing process (Cousins, 1979, 1989).

The idea caught on even before it had much empirical support. Today, hospitals in Houston, Los Angeles, and Honolulu provide patients with videotapes of funny films. "Laugh wagons" carrying humorous books and tapes roll through the halls of health centers across the country (Erdman, 1993). At a Catholic hospital in Texas, the nuns are expected to tell at least one joke a day (Cousins, 1989). Nurse Patty Wooten travels the United States in a clown suit, with bedpan and enema bags strapped to her belt, teaching nurses the importance of using humor to cope with the stresses of health care (Nancy Nurse spoofs the healing profession, 1987). Allen Funt, creator of *Candid Camera,* has set up a foundation to distribute his funny videos free of charge to researchers, hospitals, and individual patients in the hope of applying humor therapy for distress and illness and investigating the effects of such therapy.

What are the medical benefits of humor? Cousins's doctor found that his sedimentation rate (a measure of inflammation) decreased after only a few moments of robust laughter. This decrease in inflammation was also reflected in Cousins's ability to enjoy two hours of pain-free sleep after ten minutes of hardy laughing (Cousins, 1989). Stanford psychiatric researcher William Fry, Jr., compares laughter to "stationary jogging." Increases in respiration, heart rate, and blood circulation created by laughing bring oxygen to the blood at a rate as much as six times greater than during ordinary speech (Fry, 1986). Some biochemical changes, including changes in the saliva level of the stress hormone *cortisol,* have also been detected (Hubert et al., 1993). Salivary immunoglobulin A, which is thought to protect the body against certain viruses, increased significantly in people who viewed funny tapes for 30 minutes (Berk et al., 1989). In addition, people who said they used humor to deal with difficult situations in everyday life had the highest baseline levels of this protective substance (Dillon & Totten, 1989).

You wouldn't want to replace traditional therapy with laughter therapy—but a good laugh may help speed your recovery toward health!

against illness. Confiding in others neutralizes the negative effects of inhibition. The experience of *letting go* often is followed by improved physical and psychological health weeks and months later.

Personality and Health

When we discussed responses to stress, we noted that different people react in different ways: hardy individuals may be less prone to stress-related ill-

What are the advantages of having a Type B personality?

nesses. Health psychologists have looked at this phenomenon more generally, to address the question "Does personality affect health?" The answer appears to be yes (H. S. Friedman, 1990). Let's consider some of the evidence.

Type A and Type B Behavior Patterns

In the 1950s, Meyer Friedman and Ray Rosenman reported what had been suspected since ancient times: there was a relationship between a constellation of personality traits and the probability of illness, specifically coronary heart disease (Friedman & Rosenman, 1974). These researchers identified two behavior patterns that they labeled Type A and Type B. The **Type A behavior pattern** is a complex pattern of behavior and emotions that includes being excessively competitive, aggressive, impatient, time-urgent, and hostile. Type A people are often dissatisfied with some central aspect of their lives, are highly competitive and ambitious, and often are loners. The **Type B** pattern is everything Type A is not—individuals are less competitive, less hostile, and so on. Friedman and Rosenman reported that people who showed Type A behavior patterns are stricken with coronary heart disease considerably more often than individuals in the general population (Friedman & Rosenman, 1974; Jenkins, 1976).

Recent research on the Type A behavior pattern has focused on hostility, the single personality factor believed to be most related to health risks.

A great deal of research attention has focused on individuals who are characterized by Type A behavior patterns (Strube, 1990). Research has related Type A behavior to many subsequent illnesses in addition to heart disease (Suls & Marco, 1990). A current focus is on identifying the specific elements of the Type A behavior pattern that most often put people at risk. The personality trait that has emerged most forcefully as "toxic" is *hostility* (Dembrowski & Costa, 1987; Adler & Matthews, 1994; Smith, 1992): hostility "connotes a view of others as frequent and likely sources of mistreatment, frustration, and provocation and, as a result, a belief that others are generally unworthy and not to be trusted" (Smith, 1992, p. 139). Hostility may affect health for both physiological reasons—by leading to chronic overarousal of the body's stress responses—and psychological reasons—by leading hostile people to practice poor health habits and avoid social support.

The good news is that interventions to reduce Type A behavior have been successful in most cases (M. Friedman et al., 1986).

A large-scale intervention program with more than 1000 volunteer survivors of a first-time heart attack has found that a behavioral treatment that alters typical Type A reaction patterns deters a second heart attack and reduces death from other causes as well.

> Those who had substantially lowered their Type A behavior had almost a 50 percent lower mortality rate over an eight-year follow-up period than those who did not change substantially (Thoresen, 1990).

If you recognize yourself in the definition of hostility, you should protect your health by seeking out this type of intervention.

Type C and Optimism

Type A and its opposite, Type B, were originated to account for relationships between behavior and coronary heart disease. More recently, researchers have suggested that a third constellation of behaviors, called **Type C,** may predict which individuals will be particularly likely to develop cancer, or to have their cancer progress quickly (Eysenck, 1988; Temoshok, 1990; Temoshok & Dreher, 1992).

> Type C coping has been described as being "nice," stoic or self-sacrificing, cooperative and appeasing, unassertive, patient, compliant with external authorities, and unexpressive of negative emotions, particularly anger. (Temoshok, 1990, p. 209)

Type C behaviors are inconsistent with the "fighting spirit" that may help slow the course of a cancer or other serious illness. Researchers have seen the effect of a fighting spirit, for example, with patients who have been diagnosed with AIDS (Reed et al., 1994). Those individuals who were unwilling to accept the inevitability of their deaths outlived another group of individuals who resigned themselves to their fate.

On the whole, the passive acceptance of the Type C individual is not the best approach to illness. The research of **Martin Seligman** (1991) and his associates points the healthy finger at *optimism,* a concept we introduced in Chapter 12. We saw there that optimistic individuals attribute failures to external causes and to events that were unstable or modifiable. This style of coping has a strong impact on the optimist's well-being. Optimistic people have fewer physical symptoms of illness, are faster at recovering from certain illnesses, are generally healthier, and live longer (Peterson et al., 1988). In fact, research suggests that there may be a mental health advantage to maintaining even a slightly unrealistic sense of optimism (Taylor & Brown, 1988, 1994). A positive outlook may both reduce your body's experience of chronic stress and make it more likely that you'll engage in healthy behaviors.

Optimism, a key factor in reducing certain symptoms of illness, can speed recovery, and help people live longer and healthier lives.

Changing the Health-Care System

One final focus of health psychology is to make recommendations about the design of the health-care system. Researchers, for example, have examined the stress associated with being a health-care provider. Even the most enthusiastic health-care providers run up against the emotional stresses of working intensely with large numbers of people suffering from a variety of personal, physical, and social problems. The special type of emotional stress experienced by these professional health and welfare practitioners has been termed *burnout* by **Christina Maslach,** a leading researcher on this widespread problem. **Job burnout** is a syndrome of emotional exhaustion, depersonalization, and reduced personal accomplishment that is often experienced by workers in professions that demand high-intensity interpersonal contact with patients, clients, or the public. Health practitioners begin to lose their caring and concern for patients and may come to treat them in detached and even dehumanized ways. They feel bad about themselves and worry that they are failures. Burnout is correlated with greater absenteeism

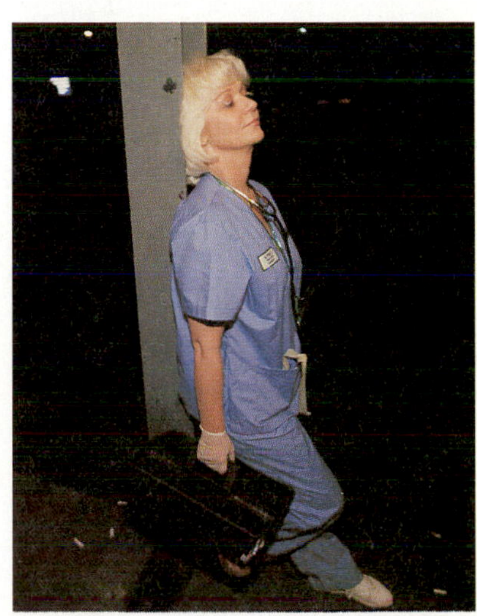

Patient advocates recommend changing the traditional high-pressure style of Western medical practice, which leaves caregivers prone to job burnout.

and turnover, impaired job performance, poor relations with coworkers, family problems, and poor personal health (Leiter & Maslach, 1988; Maslach, 1982; Maslach & Florian, 1988; Schaufeli et al., 1993).

What recommendations can be made? Several social and situational factors affect the occurrence and level of burnout and, by implication, suggest ways of preventing or minimizing it. For example, the quality of the patient-practitioner interaction is greatly influenced by the number of patients for whom a practitioner is providing care—the greater the number, the greater the cognitive, sensory, and emotional overload. Another factor in the quality of that interaction is the amount of direct contact with patients. Longer work hours in continuous direct contact with patients are correlated with greater burnout. This is especially true when the nature of the contact is difficult and upsetting, such as contact with patients who are dying or who are verbally abusive. The emotional strain of such prolonged contact can be eased by a number of means. For example, practitioners can modify their work schedules in order to withdraw temporarily from such high-stress situations. They can use teams rather than only individual contact. They can arrange opportunities to get positive feedback for their efforts.

A Toast to Your Health

It's time for some final advice. Instead of waiting for stress or illness to come and then reacting to it, you should set goals and structure your life in ways that are most likely to forge a healthy foundation. The following nine steps to greater happiness and better mental health are presented as guidelines to encourage you to take a more active role in your own life and to create a more positive psychological environment for yourself and others. Think of the steps as *year-round resolutions.*

1. Never say bad things about yourself. Look for sources of your unhappiness in elements that can be modified by future actions. Give yourself and others only *constructive criticism*—what can be done differently next time to get what you want?
2. Compare your reactions, thoughts, and feelings with those of friends, coworkers, family members, and others so that you can gauge the appropriateness and relevance of your responses against a suitable social norm.
3. Have several close friends with whom you can share feelings, joys, and worries. Work at developing, maintaining, and expanding your social support networks.
4. Develop a sense of *balanced time perspective* in which you can flexibly focus on the demands of the task, the situation, and your needs; be future oriented when there is work to be done, present oriented when the goal is achieved and pleasure is at hand, and past oriented to keep you in touch with your roots.
5. Always take full credit for your successes and happiness (and share your positive feelings with other people). Keep an inventory of all the qualities that make you special and unique—those qualities you can offer others. For example, a shy person can provide a talkative person with the gift of attentive listening. Know your sources of personal strength and available coping resources.
6. When you feel you are losing control over your emotions, distance yourself from the situation by physically leaving it, role-playing the position of another person in the situation or conflict, projecting your imagination into the future to gain perspective on what seems an overwhelming problem now, or talking to a sympathetic listener. Allow yourself to feel and express your emotions.
7. Remember that failure and disappointment are sometimes blessings in disguise. They may tell you that your goals are not right for you or may

save you from bigger letdowns later on. Learn from every failure. Acknowledge setbacks by saying, "I made a mistake" and move on. Every accident, misfortune, or violation of your expectations is potentially a wonderful opportunity in disguise.

8. If you discover you cannot help yourself or another person in distress, seek the counsel of a trained specialist in your student health department or community. In some cases, a problem that appears to be psychological may really be physical, and vice versa. Check out your student mental health services before you need them, and use them without concern about being stigmatized.
9. Cultivate healthy pleasures. Take time out to relax, to meditate, to get a massage, to fly a kite, and to enjoy hobbies and activities you can do alone and by means of which you can get in touch with and better appreciate yourself.

So how are you feeling? If the stressors in your life have the potential to put you in a bad mood, we hope you'll be able to use cognitive reappraisal to minimize their impact. If you are feeling ill, we hope you'll be able to use your mind's healing capacity to speed your way back toward health. Never underestimate the power of these different types of "feelings" to exercise control over your life. Harness that power!

Recapping Main Points

Emotions

Emotions are complex patterns of changes made up of physiological arousal, brain mechanisms, experienced feelings, cognitive appraisal, and behavioral and expressive reactions. As a product of evolution, all humans may share a basic set of emotional responses. Cultures, however, vary in their rules of appropriateness for displaying emotions. Classic theories emphasize different parts of emotional response, such as peripheral bodily reactions or central neural processes. More contemporary theories emphasize the appraisal of arousal. Emotions serve motivational, social, and cognitive functions.

Stress of Living

Stress can arise from negative or positive events. At the root of most stress is change and the need to adapt to environmental, biological, physical, and social demands. Physiological stress reactions are regulated by the hypothalamus and a complex interaction of the hormonal and nervous systems. Psychoneuroimmunology is the study of how psychosocial variables affect the immune system. Cognitive appraisal is a primary moderator variable of stress. Depending on the type of stressor, and its effect over time, stress can be a mild disruption or lead to dysfunctional reactions. Hardy individuals suffer from fewer of the consequences of stress.

Coping strategies either focus on problems (taking direct actions) or attempt to regulate emotions (indirect or avoidant). Cognitive reappraisal and restructuring can be used to cope with stress. Social support is also a significant stress moderator, as long as it is appropriate to the circumstances.

Health Psychology

Health psychology is devoted to treatment and prevention of illness. The biopsychosocial model of health and illness looks at the connections among physical, emotional, and environmental factors in illness. Illness prevention in the 1990s focuses on lifestyle factors such as smoking, nutrition, exercise, and AIDS-risk behaviors. Health promotion and maintenance are not just individual matters—they represent an important area in which community and government policy can help improve everyone's quality of living. Psychosocial treatment of illness adds another dimension to patient treatment. Individuals who are characterized by Type A (especially hostile), Type B, Type C, and optimistic behavior patterns will experience different likelihoods of illness. Health-care providers are at risk for burnout, which can be minimized by appropriate situational changes in their helping environment.

Resources

Benson, H., & Stuart, E. M. (Eds.). (1992). *The wellness book.* New York: Simon & Schuster.

Cousins, Norman. (1989). *Headfirst: The biology of hope.* New York: Dutton.

Damasio, A. R. (1994). *Descartes' error: Emotion, reason, and the human brain.* New York: Putnam.

Friedman, H. S. (1992). *The self-healing personality: Why some people achieve health and others succumb to illness.* New York: NAL/Dutton.

Gray, J. A. (1988). *The psychology of fear and stress* (2nd ed.). New York: Cambridge University Press.

Lazarus, R. S., & Lazarus, B. N. (1994). *Passion and reason: Making sense of our emotions.* New York: Oxford University Press.

Sapolsky, R. M. (1994). *Why zebras don't get ulcers: A guide to stress, stress-related disease, and coping.* New York: Freeman.

Selye, H. (1976). *The stress of life* (2nd ed.). New York: McGraw-Hill.

Snyder, C. R. (1994). *The psychology of hope: You can get there from here*. New York: Free Press.

Taylor, S. E. (1991). *Health psychology* (2nd ed.). New York: McGraw-Hill. Taylor is a pioneer in the field of health and stress, and her text reflects a broad familiarity with all aspects of this rapidly growing area.

Temoshuk, L., & Dreher, H. (1992). *The* Type C *connection: The mind-body link to cancer and your health.* New York: Plume.

14

Understanding Human Personality

Think back to the last time you had an argument with a friend. What was the fight about? Were you able to come to any sort of agreement, or did it seem that the two of you were thinking along totally different lines? If that was the case, your argument might have convinced you not only that people have different opinions but that people have different personalities. *You might have said, "I would never do that," or "I would never even think that," or "I'm not that kind of person." Each time you interact with another individual—particularly at moments of conflict—you gather evidence for your own uniqueness.*

Because of your experiences, you probably already have strong intuitions about how personality works. What is your *personality theory? Think of someone you really trust. Now think of someone you know personally who is a role model for you. Imagine the qualities of a person with whom you would like to spend the rest of your life and then of someone you can't stand to be around at all. In each case, what springs to mind immediately are personal attributes, such as honesty, reliability, generosity, aggressiveness, moodiness, or pessimism. Even as a child, you probably developed and put to use your own system for appraising personality. You tried to determine who in a new class would be friend or foe; you worked out techniques for dealing with your parents or teachers based on the way you read their personalities.*

Our goal for this chapter will be to provide you with a framework for understanding your everyday experience of personality. We will describe the theories psychologists have developed to understand each unique personality. However, before we begin, consider this series of questions: If psychologists studied you, *what portrait of your personality would they draw? What early experiences might they identify as contributing to the way you now act and think? What conditions in your current life exert strong influences on your thoughts and behaviors? What makes you different from other individuals who are functioning in many of the same situations as you? This chapter should help you formulate more specific answers to these questions.*

THE PSYCHOLOGY OF THE PERSON

Although psychologists define personality in many different ways, uniqueness and characteristic behavior patterns are two concepts common to all definitions.

Psychologists define personality in many different ways, but common to all of the ways are two basic concepts: *uniqueness* and *characteristic patterns of behavior.* We will define **personality** as the complex set of unique psychological qualities that influence an individual's characteristic patterns of behavior across different situations and over time. Investigators in the field of personality psychology seek to discover how individuals differ. In addition, they study the extent to which personality traits and behavior patterns are consistent, and thus predictable, from one situation to another.

Up to this point in *Psychology and Life,* we have largely emphasized scientific investigations of the commonalities in psychological functioning that all people share. Theorists believe, for example, that processes such as neural transmission, perception, conditioning, and language acquisition operate quite similarly in all members of our species. The goal in much research has been to discover general laws of behavior that explain why different individuals in the same situation react alike. In this chapter we shift our focus to the

Individual differences in personality may have unexpected—and socially awkward—manifestations.

feelings, thoughts, and actions that make individuals unique. We turn, that is, to the subjective, private aspects of personality that give coherence and order to behavior—a core aspect of each of you that you would call your *self.*

This shift in focus also requires a shift in experimental methodologies. Researchers who study individual differences cannot test their theories by manipulating genetic or environmental factors to demonstrate how different personalities arise. Psychologists cannot, for example, randomly assign 3-year-olds to be oldest or youngest children, to determine the effects birth position has on adult personality. As we shall see, researchers in this area most often rely instead on *correlations* between life experiences and individuals' reactions on various psychological tests and scales.

We begin this chapter by examining important issues and strategies in the study of personality. Then we will survey major theories of personality, each of which focuses on slightly different aspects of human individuality. Your task will be to reflect on how each of these different theories could help you make sense of your own personality.

Strategies for Studying Personality

How might you gather evidence about personality? Psychologists have turned to five different sources of data:

- *self-report data* are what people say about their own behavior, attitudes, and traits, often in a personality test or inventory (see Chapter 15);
- *observer-report data* reveal what friends, parents, coworkers, and other raters or evaluators say about an individual;
- *specific behavioral data* consist of systematically recorded information about what a person says or does in a particular situation;
- *life-events data* are biographical facts [(for example, level of education, marital status, or economic status of parent(s)];
- *physiological data* include information about heart rate, skin conductance, biochemistry of hormones, and neurotransmitter functioning.

Psychologists rely on five different sources to gather data about personality: self-reports, observer reports, specific behavioral data, life events, and physiological data.

These types of data can be *interpreted* using either of two basic approaches to the study of personality: the idiographic approach and the nomothetic approach. The **idiographic approach** is *person centered,* focusing on the way

The two approaches to the study of personality are the idiographic and the nomothetic.

unique aspects of an individual's personality form an integrated whole. It assumes that traits and events take on different meanings in different people's lives. The primary research methodologies of the idiographic approach are the case study and the aggregate case study. A **case study** uses many data sources to form a psychological biography of a single individual. The **aggregate case study** is a comparison of idiographic information about many individuals. For example, a summary of the reports on many women with multiple personality disorders, each of whom was studied individually by a given researcher-therapist, is an aggregate case study.

The **nomothetic approach** is *variable centered.* A researcher who takes this approach assumes that the same traits or dimensions of personality apply to everyone in the same way—people simply differ in the *degree* to which they possess each characteristic. Nomothetic research looks for relationships between different personality dimensions in the general population. The *correlational method* is used to determine the extent to which two traits or types of behavior tend to show up together in people. The focus of this method is on discovering lawful patterns of relationships among traits, and among the traits and behavior of most people. Researchers might ask, for example, whether people with positive self-images actually perform better on most tasks than people with poor self-images. In nomothetic research, the richness and uniqueness of the individual case is sacrificed for broader knowledge about dimensions of personality that are valid for people in general.

You can see that researchers who study personality have a wide variety of evidence that they can apply to their theories. All of these types of evidence will be represented in this chapter. In addition, you will see that some theories of personality have emerged from idiographic analysis of small groups of individuals, whereas others represent nomothetic analyses of the average patterns of behavior of many people.

Theories About Personality

Theories of personality are hypothetical statements about the structure and functioning of individual personalities. They help to achieve two of the major goals of psychology: (1) *understanding* the structure, origins, and correlates of personality and (2) *predicting* behavior and life events based on what we know about personality. Different theories make different predictions about the way people will respond and adapt to certain conditions.

The many theories in personality psychology differ in terms of data sources, types of phenomena studied, focus on behavior versus feelings, and emphasis on psychological problems versus mental health.

Before we examine some of the major theoretical approaches, we should ask why there are so many different (often competing) theories. Theorists differ in their approaches to personality by varying their starting points and sources of data and by trying to explain different types of phenomena. Some are interested in the structure of individual personality and others in how that personality developed and will continue to grow. Some are interested in what people do, either in terms of specific behaviors or important life events, while others study how people feel about their lives. Finally, some theories try to explain the personalities of people with psychological problems, while others focus on healthy individuals. Thus each theory can teach something about personality, and together they can teach much about human nature.

In the next several sections of the chapter we consider a series of theoretical approaches to understanding personality: type and trait, psychodynamic, humanistic, social-learning, cognitive, and analyses of the self.

TYPE AND TRAIT PERSONALITY THEORIES

Two of the oldest approaches to describing personality involve classifying people into a limited number of *distinct types* and scaling the degree to which they can be described by *different traits.* There seems to be a natural tendency for people to place their own and others' behavior into different categories. Let's examine the formal theories psychologists have developed to capture these differences in types and traits.

Categorizing by Types

We are always categorizing people according to distinguishing features. These include college class, academic major, sex, and race. Some personality theorists also group people according to their **personality types.** These categories do not overlap: if a person is assigned to one category, he or she is not in any other category within that system. Personality types are all-or-none phenomena, not matters of degree.

One of the earliest type theories was proposed in the fifth century B.C. by **Hippocrates,** the Greek physician who gave medicine the Hippocratic oath. He theorized that the body contained four basic fluids or *humors,* each associated with a particular *temperament,* a pattern of emotions and behaviors. An individual's personality depended on which humor was predominant in his or her body. Hippocrates paired body humors with personality temperaments according to the following scheme:

- Blood—sanguine temperament: cheerful and active
- Phlegm—phlegmatic temperament: apathetic and sluggish
- Black bile—melancholy temperament: sad and brooding
- Yellow bile—choleric temperament: irritable and excitable

Hippocrates theorized that the body contained four essential fluids, or humors, each associated with a particular temperament. Clockwise: a melancholy patient suffers from an excess of black bile; blood impassions a sanguine lutenist to play; a maiden, dominated by phlegm, is slow to respond to her lover; choler, too much yellow bile, makes an angry master.

The theory proposed by Hippocrates was believed for centuries, up through the Middle Ages, although it has not held up to modern scrutiny.

William Sheldon (1942) related physique to temperament. He assigned people to three categories based on their body builds: *endomorphic* (fat, soft, round), *mesomorphic* (muscular, rectangular, strong), or *ectomorphic* (thin, long, fragile). Sheldon believed that endomorphs are relaxed, fond of eating, and sociable. Mesomorphs are physical people, filled with energy, courage, and assertive tendencies. Ectomorphs are brainy, artistic, and introverted; they would think about life, rather than consuming it or acting upon it. For a period of time, Sheldon's theory was sufficiently influential that nude "posture" photographs were taken of thousands of students at U.S. colleges like Yale and Wellesley. However, like Hippocrates' much earlier theory, Sheldon's notion of body types has proven to be of very little value in predicting an individual's behavior (Tyler, 1965). (We still mention it because popular culture often acts as if there *is* a relationship between body type and behavior. Type theories often appeal to the mass media because they simplify the very complicated process of understanding personality.)

In Chapter 13, we described a contemporary analysis that relates types of behavior to the probability of illness: *Type A* individuals are at greater risk for coronary heart disease; *Type C* individuals are at greater risk for quickly progressing cancers. In both of these cases, the "types" are defined by particular patterns of behavior. What puts Type A individuals at risk for heart attacks is consistent hostility in interpersonal relationships (Adler & Matthews, 1994; Smith, 1992). Type C individuals don't express negative emotions and are consistently compliant (Eysenck, 1988; Temoshok, 1990; Temoshok & Dreher, 1992). The identification of an individual's behaviors as Type A or Type C (or the neutral Type B) allows researchers to make predictions about, for example, the likelihood of future illness. However, because behaviors can be modified, a person may not remain consistently Type A, B, or C across the life span.

Do you know people whom you would label as particular "types"? Does the "type" include all there is to know about the person? Type theories often don't seem to capture more subtle aspects of people's personalities. Let's turn now to theories that allow more flexibility by differentiating individuals according to traits rather than types.

Describing with Traits

Unlike type theories, which describe personality in terms of discontinuous categories, trait theories propose continuous dimensions.

Type theories presume that there are separate, *discontinuous categories* into which people fit, such as Type A or Type B. By contrast, trait theories propose hypothetical, *continuous dimensions,* such as intelligence or friendliness. **Traits** are generalized action tendencies that people possess in varying degrees; they lend coherence to a person's behavior in different situations and over time. For example, you may demonstrate honesty on one day by returning a lost wallet and on another day by not cheating on a test. Some trait theorists think of traits as *predispositions that cause behavior,* but more conservative theorists use traits only as *descriptive dimensions* that simply summarize patterns of observed behavior. Let's examine prominent trait theories.

Allport's Trait Approach

Gordon Allport (1937, 1961, 1966) is the best known of the *idiographic trait* theorists, theorists who believe that each person has some unique combination of traits. He viewed traits as the building blocks of personality and the source of individuality. According to Allport, traits produce coherence in behavior because they connect and unify a person's reactions to a variety of stimuli. Traits may act as *intervening variables,* relating sets of stimuli and responses that might seem, at first glance, to have little to do with each other (see **Figure 14.1**).

Gordon Allport viewed traits as the basic building blocks of personality, suggesting the existence of three kinds of traits: cardinal traits, central traits, and secondary traits.

Allport identified three kinds of traits. *Cardinal traits* are traits around which a person organizes his or her life. For Mother Teresa, a cardinal trait might be self-sacrifice for the good of others. However, not all people develop such overarching cardinal traits. Instead, *central traits* are traits that represent major characteristics of a person, such as honesty or optimism. *Secondary traits* are specific, personal features that help predict an individual's behavior but are less useful for understanding an individual's personality. Food or dress preferences are examples of secondary traits.

Although Allport recognized common traits that individuals in a given culture share, he was most interested in discovering the unique combination of these three types of traits that make each person a singular entity. Allport championed the use of case studies to examine these unique traits.

HOW WE KNOW

In one famous case, he studied in depth 301 letters written by a woman named *Jenny* over an 11-year period. Using statistical procedures to examine the way she typically combined key words into units of meaning, he found evidence for seven cardinal traits

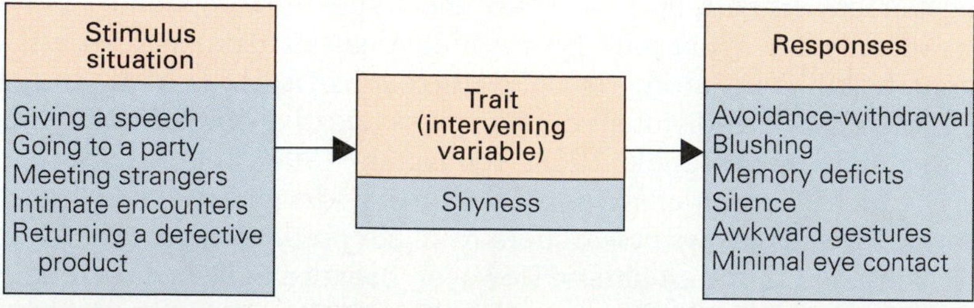

Figure 14.1 Shyness as a Trait

Traits may act as intervening variables, relating sets of stimuli and responses that might seem, at first glance, to have little to do with each other.

that described the way she expressed herself in the letters. In a separate phase of the experiment, eight cardinal traits—such as *aggressive, sentimental, possessive*—were derived from the impressions of 36 judges who read the letters. The two independently derived sets of traits were very similar, demonstrating that personality could be reconstructed from other sources when traditional personality tests were unavailable (Allport, 1965, 1966).

Allport saw *personality structures,* rather than *environmental conditions,* as the critical determiners of individual behavior. "The same fire that melts the butter hardens the egg," was a phrase he used to show that the same stimuli can have different effects on different individuals. Many contemporary trait theories have followed in Allport's tradition.

In the absence of personality test results, traits can be inferred from observed behavior. For example, Martin Luther King Jr. (top) would be thought to have the cardinal trait of peacefully resisting injustice; honesty would be one of Abraham Lincoln's central traits, while Elton John's predilection for gaudy eyeglasses would be a secondary trait.

Identifying Universal Trait Dimensions

In 1936, a dictionary search by Gordon Allport and his colleague H. S. Odbert found over 18,000 adjectives in the English language to describe individual differences. Researchers since that time have attempted to identify the fundamental dimensions that underlie that enormous trait vocabulary. The basic question is how many dimensions and which ones will allow psychologists to give a useful characterization of all individuals.

Hans Eysenck (1973, 1990), a leading trait theorist, derived three broad dimensions from personality test data, *extraversion* (internally versus externally oriented), *neuroticism* (emotionally stable versus emotionally unstable), and *psychoticism* (kind and considerate versus aggressive and antisocial). Eysenck related the first two dimensions to the physiological-personality types of Hippocrates (see **Figure 14.2**). Individuals can fall anywhere around the circle, ranging from very introverted to very extraverted and from very unstable (neurotic) to very stable. The traits listed around the circle describe people with each combination. For example, a person who is very extraverted and somewhat unstable is likely to be impulsive.

Eysenck has proposed that personality differences on his three basic dimensions are caused by genetic and biological differences (Eysenck, 1990). Consider the natural level of cortical arousal for extraverts versus introverts. Eysenck has suggested that people who are extraverted have a naturally low

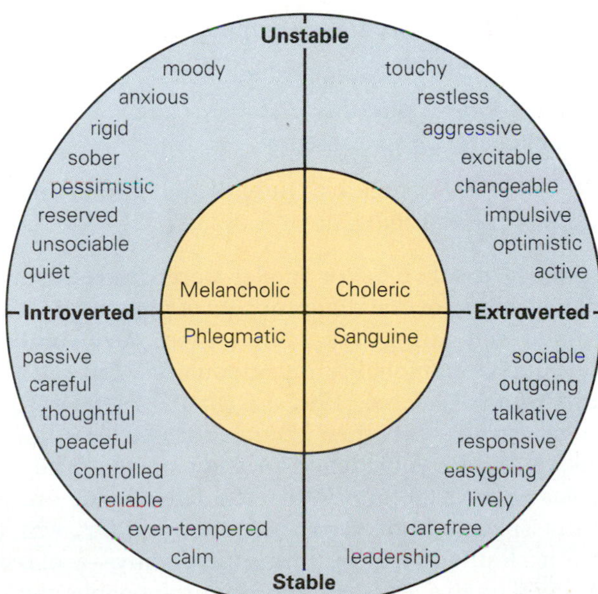

Figure 14.2 The Four Quadrants of Eysenck's Personality Circle

level of arousal; introverted people start out with a high level of arousal. As a consequence, introverts react more strongly to sensory stimulation than do extraverts, and they are more sensitive to pain—the normally high level of arousal makes them easy to overwhelm. By contrast, extraverts may seek stimulating social situations as a direct consequence of their normally low level of arousal—they need the boost.

Research evidence supports many aspects of Eysenck's theory. However, in recent years a consensus has emerged that *five factors,* which overlap imperfectly with Eysenck's three dimensions, best characterize personality structure (Wiggins & Pincus, 1992). Although these five factors are not accepted by all personality researchers (Eysenck, 1992; Pervin, 1994), they now serve as a touchstone for most discussions of trait structures.

The movement toward the *five-factor model* represented attempts to find structure among the large list of traits that Allport and Odbert (1936) had extracted from the dictionary. The traits were boiled down into about 200 synonym clusters that were used to form *bipolar* trait dimensions: dimensions that have a high pole and a low pole, such as responsible versus irresponsible. Next, people were asked to rate themselves and others on the bipolar dimensions, and the ratings were subjected to statistical procedures to determine how the synonym clusters were interrelated. Using this method, several independent research teams came to the same conclusion: that there are only *five basic dimensions* underlying the traits people use to describe themselves and others (Norman, 1963, 1967; Tupes & Christal, 1961).

The five dimensions are very broad, because each brings into one large category many traits that have unique connotations but a common theme. These five dimensions of personality are now called the **five-factor model,** or, more informally, the *Big Five* (Costa & McCrae, 1992a; Digman, 1990). Each is summarized below. You'll notice again that each dimension is bipolar—terms that are similar in meaning to the name of the dimension describe the high pole, and terms that are opposite in meaning describe the low pole.

- *Extraversion:* talkative, energetic, and assertive versus quiet, reserved, and shy.
- *Agreeableness:* sympathetic, kind, and affectionate versus cold, quarrelsome, and cruel.
- *Conscientiousness:* organized, responsible, and cautious versus careless, frivolous, and irresponsible.
- *Neuroticism (emotional stability):* stable, calm, and contented versus anxious, unstable, and temperamental.
- *Openness to experience:* creative, intellectual, and open-minded versus simple, shallow, and unintelligent.

Attempts to find structure among the large list of trait terms resulted in the five-factor model. The five basic dimensions are extraversion, agreeableness, conscientiousness, neuroticism, and openness to experience.

The dimensions in the five-factor model were derived from ratings collected in the 1960s, using several different sets of adjectives and many different subject samples and rating tasks. Since then, very similar dimensions have also been found in personality questionnaires, interviewer checklists, and other data (Costa & McCrae, 1992a; Digman, 1990; Wiggins & Pincus, 1992). The five-factor structure has been replicated in studies of German and Dutch traits, and there is evidence for some or all of the factors in non-Western languages as well (John, 1990). The five factors are not meant to replace the many specific trait terms that carry their own nuances and shades of meaning. Rather, they outline a taxonomy—a classification system—that allows you to give a description of all the people you know in ways that captures the important dimensions on which they differ.

It is important to emphasize that the five-factor model is largely descriptive. The factors emerged from statistical analyses of clusters of trait terms, rather than from a theory that said, "These are the factors that *must* exist" (Ozer & Reise, 1994). Supporters of the five-factor model have begun to address this lack of theoretical grounding by, for example, trying to relate the five dimensions to consistent types of interactions that people had with each other and with the external world over the course of evolution: "the five factors may represent alternative ways in which people in a social environment can react to their life experience" (Costa & McCrae, 1992a, p. 658; see also Zuckerman, 1992). An evolutionary basis would help explain the *universality* of the five factors across diverse cultures. If this explanation is correct, we might also expect that, like other aspects of human experience that have been shaped by evolution, traits can be passed from one generation to the next. We turn now to that claim.

TRAITS AND HERITABILITY

You've probably heard people say things such as "Jim's artistic, like his mother" or "Mary's as stubborn as her grandfather." Or maybe you've felt frustrated because the characteristics that you find irritating in your siblings are those you would like to change in yourself. Let's look at the evidence that supports the heritability of personality traits.

Heritability studies show that almost all traits are influenced by genetic factors.

Recall that *behavioral genetics* is the study of the degree to which personality traits and behavior patterns are inherited. To determine the effect of genetics on personality, researchers study the personality traits of family members who share different proportions of genes and who have grown up in the same or different households. For example, if a personality characteristic such as *sociability* is passed on genetically, then sociability should correlate more highly between identical twins (who share 100 percent of their genes) than between fraternal twins or other siblings (who share, on the average, 50 percent of their genes). However, twins and other siblings are usually raised together, and sharing a family environment might cause their personalities to be correlated, too. Thus, *adoption studies* are used to examine the degree to which children's personalities correlate with their biological parents', as compared to correlations with their adoptive parents'. One very effective way to differentiate genetic and environmental effects on personality is to find many pairs of twins, some of whom were raised together in the same family and some of whom were raised apart. For each personality trait, researchers compare the size of correlations between identical twins reared together, identical twins reared apart, fraternal twins reared together, and fraternal twins reared apart. The correlations are compared according to mathematical models to determine the percentage of the trait that is inherited and the percentage that can be attributed to environmental influences.

Research with identical twins demonstrates the heritability of personality traits.

Heritability studies show that almost all personality traits are influenced by genetic factors (Loehlin, 1992). The findings are the same with many different measurement techniques, whether they measure broad traits, such as extraversion and neuroticism, or specific traits, such as self-control or sociability. The findings generalize to people from different countries and from different socioeconomic backgrounds. Estimates of what percentage of the influence on personality traits is genetic range from a low of 20 percent to a high of 60 percent. Although experts still disagree on the exact degree of heritability of personality, they agree that the characteristics your parents pass on to you genetically have a powerful impact on the person you become (Plomin et al., 1990).

But what about learning and the environment? Are people stuck with the personality traits they inherit? Research indicates the environment has a powerful impact on personality, too, but not in the way that you might think. Behavior geneticists divide environmental influence into two groups: the *common familial environment,* experienced by all children in a family, and the *unshared environment,* experienced uniquely by each child. Traditionally, psychologists have believed that features of the common familial environment, such as the income and education of the parents and their general style of child rearing, cause the children in one family to be more similar to each other than they would have been if raised by different parents. However, twin and adoption studies show that the influence of common familial factors on personality is very small. For most personality traits, identical twins reared *together* are no more similar than identical twins reared *apart!* Instead, the portion of personality that is not related to genetic factors must be attributed to the unshared environment. Personality is shaped by the idiosyncratic experiences of each child, such as the parent-child relationship, the particular relationships with siblings, and experiences outside the home (Bouchard & McGue, 1990). Why do you think the common familial environment has less influence on personality traits than does the unshared environment?

Individual differences that cannot be attributed to genetic influence are due to the idiosyncratic experience of each child rather than the shared familial environment.

Do Traits Predict Behaviors?

Suppose we ask you to choose some trait terms that you believe apply particularly well to yourself. You might tell us, for example, that you are *very friendly.* What do we now know? That is, if personality theories allow us to make predictions about behaviors, what can we predict from knowing that you rate yourself as being *very friendly?* How can we determine the validity of your belief? Let's explore this question.

One idea you might have is that knowing that a person can be characterized by a particular trait would enable you to predict his or her behavior across different *situations.* Thus we would expect you to produce friendly behaviors in all situations. However, in the 1920s several researchers who set out to observe trait-related behaviors in different situations were surprised to find little evidence that behavior was consistent across situations. For example, two behaviors presumably related to the trait of honesty—lying and cheating on a test—were only weakly correlated among schoolchildren (Hartshorne & May, 1928). Similar results were found by other researchers who examined the cross-situational consistency for other traits such as introversion or punctuality (Dudycha, 1936; Newcomb, 1929).

If trait-related behaviors are not cross-situationally consistent—that is, if people's behavior changes in different situations—why do you perceive your own and others' personalities to be relatively stable? Even more puzzling, the personality ratings of observers who know an individual from one situation correlate with the ratings of observers who know the individual from another situation. The observation that personality ratings across time and among different observers *are consistent,* while behavior ratings of a person across situations *are not consistent,* came to be called the **consistency paradox** (Mischel, 1968).

The consistency paradox describes the fact that personality characteristics are consistent across time and among different observers but are not consistent across different situations.

The identification of the consistency paradox led to a great deal of research (for reviews, see Kenrick & Funder, 1988; Mischel, 1990). Over time, the consensus emerged that behavioral inconsistency is a problem only for very specific behaviors. The paradox was not about consistency but about *levels of analysis*—the use of *specific* versus *summary* types of data. Trait theorists find meaningful relationships between self-reported traits, observer-reported traits, life events, and *general* patterns of behavior because all of these types of data operate at a *broad* level of analysis. At this broad level, many different types of events and experiences occurring over a period of time are *summarized* into a single score. Broad summary measures can predict a wide range of phenomena, but they do so somewhat less accurately than fine-tuned specific measures.

Suppose, for example, that you wanted to learn about aggressive behavior in children so you could intervene to reduce its frequency. In a study of boys with behavior problems at a summer camp, Jack Wright and Walter Mischel (1987) found that aggregated measures of specific aggressive behaviors, such as threatening other children, correlated only 0.35 across different types of situations but correlated more highly, 0.60, across similar situations. In other words, a boy who threatened younger boys consistently might not threaten older boys or counselors. A general trait measure of aggressiveness, based on counselors' ratings, correlated well, about 0.50, with specific aggressive behaviors, regardless of the situation.

Assuming you could afford either one, which of these vacations would you prefer? Your answer may largely depend on your personality.

Which measure would you find most useful? If you wanted to predict which children would threaten other children in a particular type of situation, your best bet is a previous observation of the same behavior in the same type of situation (correlation of 0.60). However, if you didn't know what type of situation the children would encounter and you wanted to predict threats in many situations, the trait measure would be a better predictor than previous threats in any particular situation (0.50 versus 0.35).

Research has also shown that different situations are more or less likely to "allow" traits to be expressed. Personality traits are likely to influence behavior when situations are (1) novel, (2) ill defined (offering many behavioral alternatives but no clear guidelines regarding what is proper), and (3) stressful or challenging (Caspi & Bem, 1990). On the other hand, your personality influences the situations you're likely to get into in the first place. Sometimes you deliberately select (or reject) certain types of situations—for example, going to many campus parties or avoiding speaking in front of your entire psychology class.

Other times, your personality influences the nature of a situation because you evoke particular responses from others. For example, if you typically talk a great deal and in a very loud voice, then other people might contribute less to a conversation with you than they usually do with others. They may judge you to be extroverted and verbally fluent, while you (mis)judge them, on the basis of your observations in this situation, as introverted or even shy. You can see why it is not a simple matter to make "personality diagnoses" from observations limited to one or a few behavioral settings.

The consistency debate forced trait theorists to define traits in a more precise way—to outline precisely what classes of behavior *should* be related to personality traits, and in what situations. It now seems that personality is not a matter of *behavioral consistency* at all. Instead, personality produces patterns of *behavioral coherence.* A trait may be expressed through different behaviors in different situations and at different ages, but as long as the theory of a trait predicts the appropriate range of behavioral expressions, the pattern is coherent. Thus, if you describe yourself as a *very friendly* person, that doesn't mean that we should expect you to perform "friendly" behaviors every moment of your life. Instead, we would expect your friendliness to differ across situations. You may, for example, be very warm with close acquaintances but more formal toward your professors.

Evaluation of Type and Trait Theories

We have seen that type and trait theories allow researchers to give concise descriptions of different people's personalities. These theories have been criticized, however, because they do not generally explain how behavior is generated or how personality develops; they only identify and describe characteristics that are correlated with behavior. Although contemporary trait theorists have begun to address these concerns, trait theories typically portray a *static,* or at least stabilized, view of personality structure as it currently exists. By contrast, psychodynamic theories of personality, to which we next turn, emphasize conflicting forces within the individual that lead to change and development.

PSYCHODYNAMIC THEORIES

Common to all **psychodynamic personality theories** is the assumption that powerful inner forces shape personality and motivate behavior. **Sigmund Freud,** the originator of psychodynamic theories, was characterized by his biographer Ernest Jones as "the Darwin of the mind" (1953). Freud's theory of personality boldly attempts to explain the origins and course of personality development, the nature of mind, aspects of abnormal personality, and the way personality can be changed by therapy. Here we will focus only on normal personality; Freud's other views will be treated in Chapters 17 and 18. After we explore Freud, we will describe some criticisms and recent reworkings of his theories.

FREUDIAN PSYCHOANALYSIS

According to psychoanalytic theory, at the core of personality are events within a person's mind (*intrapsychic events*) that motivate behavior. Often people are aware of these motivations; however, some motivation also operates at an unconscious level. The *psychodynamic* nature of this approach comes from its emphasis on these inner wellsprings of behavior, as well as the clashes among these internal forces. For Freud, *all behavior was motivated.* No chance or accidental happenings cause behavior; all acts are *determined* by motives. Every human action has a cause and a purpose that can be discovered through psychoanalysis of thought associations, dreams, errors, and other behavioral clues to inner passions. The primary data for Freud's hypotheses about personality came from clinical observations and in-depth case studies of individual patients in therapy. He developed a theory of normal personality from his intense study of those with mental disorders. Let's look at some of the most important aspects of Freud's theory.

Freud's psychoanalytic theory of personality focused on the notion that all behavior is motivated and that some motivation operates at the unconscious level.

Drives and Psychosexual Development

Freud's medical training as a neurologist led him to postulate a common biological basis for the behavioral patterns he observed in his patients. He ascribed the source of motivation for human actions to *psychic energy* found within each individual. Each person was assumed to have inborn instincts or drives that were *tension systems* created by the organs of the body. These energy sources, when activated, could be expressed in many different ways.

According to Freud, eating is motivated not only by the self-preservation drive to satisfy hunger but by the "erotic" drive to seek oral gratification.

Freud originally postulated two basic drives. One he saw as involved with the *ego,* or *self-preservation* (meeting such needs as hunger and thirst). The other he called **Eros,** the driving force related to sexual urges and preservation of the species. Of the two drives, Freud was more interested in the sexual urges, although some of his followers have given the ego drive an important place in personality, as we will see later. Freud greatly expanded the notion of human sexual desires to include not only the urge for sexual union but all other attempts to seek pleasure or to make physical contact with others. He used the term **libido** to identify the source of energy for sexual urges—a psychic energy that drives us toward sensual pleasures of all types. Sexual urges demand immediate satisfaction, whether through direct actions or through indirect means such as fantasies and dreams.

Clinical observation of patients who had suffered traumatic experiences during the First World War led Freud to add the concept of **Thanatos,** or death instinct, to his collection of drives and instincts. Thanatos was a negative force that drove people toward aggressive and destructive behaviors. These patients continued to relive their wartime traumas in nightmares and

Table 14.1 Freud's Stages of Psychosexual Development

Stage	Age	Erogenous Zones	Major Developmental Task (Potential Source of Conflict)	Some Adult Characteristics of Children Who Have Been Fixated at This Stage
Oral	0–1	Mouth, lips, tongue	Weaning	Oral behavior, such as smoking, overeating; passivity and gullibility.
Anal	2–3	Anus	Toilet training	Orderliness, parsimoniousness, obstinacy, or the opposite.
Phallic	4–5	Genitals	Oedipus complex	Vanity, recklessness, and the opposite.
Latency	6–12	No specific area	Development of defense mechanisms	None: fixation does not normally occur at this stage.
Genital	13–18	Genitals	Mature sexual intimacy	Adults who have successfully integrated earlier stages should emerge with a sincere interest in others, and a mature sexuality.

hallucinations, phenomena that Freud could not work into his self-preservation or sexual drive theory. He suggested that this primitive urge was part of the tendency for all living things to seek to return to an inorganic state.

According to Freud, Eros, as a broadly defined sexual drive, does not suddenly appear at puberty but operates from birth. Eros is evident, he argued, in the pleasure infants derive from physical stimulation of the genitals and other sensitive areas, or *erogenous zones*. Freud's five stages of *psychosexual* development are shown in **Table 14.1**. Freud believed that the physical source of sexual pleasure changed in this orderly progression. One of the major obstacles of psychosexual development, at least for boys, occurs in the phallic stage. Here, the 4- or 5-year-old child must overcome the *Oedipus conflict*. Freud named this conflict after the mythical figure Oedipus, who unwittingly killed his father and married his mother. Freud believed that every young boy has an innate impulse to view his father as a sexual rival for his mother's attentions. Because the young boy cannot displace his father, the Oedipus conflict is generally resolved when the boy comes to *identify* with his father's power. (Freud was inconsistent with respect to his theoretical account of the experiences of young girls.)

Freud believed that every young boy has an innate impulse to view his father as a sexual rival for his mother's attentions, a phenomenon he called the Oedipus conflict.

According to Freud, either too much gratification or too much frustration at one of the early stages leads to *fixation*, an inability to progress normally to the next stage of development. As shown in Table 14.1, fixation at different stages can produce a variety of adult characteristics. The concept of fixation explains why Freud put such emphasis on early experiences in the continuity of personality. He believed that experiences in the early stages of psychosexual development had a profound impact on personality formation and adult behavior patterns.

Psychic Determinism

The concept of fixation gives us a first look at Freud's belief that early conflicts help *determine* later behaviors. **Psychic determinism** is the assumption that all mental and behavioral reactions (symptoms) are determined by earlier experiences. Freud believed that symptoms were not arbitrary. Rather, symptoms were related in a meaningful way to significant life events. Freud came to this view, in part, by studying patients (mostly women) who experienced impaired bodily functioning—paralysis or blindness, for example—with intact nervous systems and no obvious organic damage to their muscles or eyes. Along with his colleague Joseph Breuer, Freud observed that the particular physical symptom often seemed related to an earlier forgotten event

Freud developed the theory of psychic determinism while studying patients whose symptoms seemed to be related to earlier life events.

in a patient's life. For instance, under hypnosis, a "blind" patient might recall witnessing her parents having intercourse when she was a small child. As an adult, her anticipation of her first sexual encounter might then have aroused powerful feelings associated with this earlier, disturbing episode. Her blindness might represent an attempt on her part to undo seeing the original event and perhaps also to deny sexual feelings in herself.

Freud's belief in psychic determinism led him to emphasize **unconscious** processes. Other writers had pointed to such a process, but Freud put the concept of the unconscious determinants of human thought, feeling, and action at center stage in the human drama. According to Freud, behavior can be motivated by drives of which a person is not aware. You may act without knowing why or without direct access to the true cause of your actions. There is a *manifest* content to your behavior—what you say, do, and perceive—of which you are fully aware, but there is also a concealed, *latent* content. The meaning of neurotic (anxiety-based) symptoms, dreams, and slips of the pen and tongue is found at the unconscious level of thinking and information processing. Many psychologists today consider this concept of the unconscious to be Freud's most important contribution to the science of psychology. Much modern literature and drama, as well, explores the implications of unconscious processes for human behavior.

According to Freud, impulses within you that you find unacceptable still strive for expression. A *Freudian slip* occurs when an unconscious desire is betrayed by your speech or behavior. For example, a host says to an unwanted guest, "I'm so sorry to see you—I mean so *happy* to see you." In Freud's view, being consistently late for dates with a particular person is no accident—it is an expression of the way you really feel. The concept of unconscious motivation adds a new dimension to personality by allowing for greater complexity of mental functioning.

We've now reviewed some basic aspects of Freud's theory. Let's see how they contribute to the structure of personality.

The Structure of Personality

In Freud's theory, personality differences arise from the different ways in which people deal with their fundamental drives. To explain these differences, Freud pictured a continuing battle between two antagonistic parts of the personality—the *id* and the *superego*—moderated by a third aspect of the self, the *ego*. Although we will refer to these three aspects almost as if they are separate creatures, keep in mind that Freud believed them all to be just different mental processes. He did not, for example, identify specific brain locations for the id, ego, and superego.

The **id** is conceived of as the storehouse of the fundamental drives. It operates irrationally, acting on impulse and pushing for expression and immediate gratification without considering whether what is desired is realistically possible, socially desirable, or morally acceptable. The id is governed by the *pleasure principle,* the unregulated search for gratification—especially sexual, physical, and emotional pleasures—to be experienced here and now without concern for consequences.

The **superego** is the storehouse of an individual's values, including moral attitudes learned from society. The superego corresponds roughly to the common notion of *conscience.* It develops as a child comes to accept as his or her own values the prohibitions of parents and other adults against socially undesirable actions. It is the inner voice of *oughts* and *should nots.* The superego also includes the *ego ideal,* an individual's view of the kind of person he or she should strive to become. Thus the superego is often in conflict with the id. The id wants to do what feels good, while the superego insists on doing what is right.

The **ego** is the reality-based aspect of the self that arbitrates the conflict between id impulses and superego demands. The ego represents an individual's personal view of physical and social reality—his or her conscious beliefs about the causes and consequences of behavior. Part of the ego's job is to choose actions that will gratify id impulses without undesirable consequences. The ego is governed by the *reality principle*, which puts reasonable choices before pleasurable demands. Thus, the ego would block an impulse to cheat on an exam, because of concerns about the consequences of getting caught, and it would substitute the resolution to study harder the next time or solicit the teacher's sympathy. When the id and the superego are in conflict, the ego arranges a compromise that at least partially satisfies both. However, as id and superego pressures intensify, it becomes more difficult for the ego to work out optimal compromises.

According to Freud's theory, the moral guidance of the superego and the reality base of the ego attempt to moderate the id's relentless search for sexual, emotional, and physical pleasure.

Repression and Ego Defense

Sometimes this compromise between id and superego involves "putting a lid on the id." Extreme desires are pushed out of conscious awareness into the privacy of the unconscious. **Repression** is the psychological process that protects an individual from experiencing extreme anxiety or guilt about impulses, ideas, or memories that are unacceptable and/or dangerous to express. (Recall the Close-up on *repressed memories* in Chapter 10.) The ego remains unaware of both the mental content that is censored and the process by which repression keeps information out of consciousness. Repression is considered to be the most basic of the various ways in which the ego defends against being overwhelmed by threatening impulses and ideas.

Ego defense mechanisms are mental strategies the ego uses to defend itself in the daily conflict between id impulses that seek expression and the superego's demand to deny them (see **Table 14.2**). In psychoanalytic theory, these mechanisms are considered vital to an individual's psychological coping with powerful inner conflicts. By using them, a person is able to maintain

Ego defense mechanisms enable a person to cope with the powerful inner conflicts associated with anxiety, allowing the individual to maintain a favorable self-image and an acceptable social image.

Table 14.2 Major Ego Defense Mechanisms

Denial of reality	Protecting self from unpleasant reality by refusing to perceive it
Displacement	Discharging pent-up feelings, usually of hostility, on objects less dangerous than those that initially aroused the emotion
Fantasy	Gratifying frustrated desires in imaginary achievements ("daydreaming" is a common form)
Identification	Increasing feelings of worth by identifying self with another person or institution, often of illustrious standing
Isolation	Cutting off emotional charge from hurtful situations or separating incompatible attitudes into logic-tight compartments (holding conflicting attitudes that are never thought of simultaneously or in relation to each other); also called *compartmentalization*
Projection	Placing blame for one's difficulties on others or attributing one's own "forbidden" desires to others
Rationalization	Attempting to prove that one's behavior is "rational" and justifiable and thus worthy of the approval of self and others
Reaction formation	Preventing dangerous desires from being expressed by endorsing opposing attitudes and types of behavior and using them as "barriers"
Regression	Retreating to earlier developmental levels involving more childish responses and usually a lower level of aspiration
Repression	Pushing painful or dangerous thoughts out of consciousness, keeping them unconscious; this is considered to be *the most basic of the defense mechanisms*
Sublimation	Gratifying or working off frustrated sexual desires in substitutive nonsexual activities socially accepted by one's culture

Freud coined the term reaction formation *to describe the transformation of an unacceptable emotion, such as disliking one's own child, into the opposite behavior—in this case, excessive attention.*

a favorable self-image and to sustain an acceptable social image. For example, if a child has strong feelings of hatred toward his father—which, if acted out, would be dangerous—repression may take over. The hostile impulse is then no longer consciously pressing for satisfaction or even recognized as existing. However, although the impulse is not seen or heard, it is not gone; these feelings continue to play a role in personality functioning. For example, by developing a strong *identification* with his father, the child may increase his sense of self-worth and reduce his unconscious fear of being discovered as a hostile agent.

In Freudian theory, **anxiety** is an intense emotional response triggered when a repressed conflict is about to emerge into consciousness. Anxiety is a danger signal: Repression is not working! Red alert! More defenses needed! This is the time for a second line of defense, one or more additional ego-defense mechanisms that will relieve the anxiety and send the distressing impulses back down into the unconscious. For example, a mother who does not like her son and does not want to care for him might use *reaction formation,* which transforms her unacceptable impulse into its *opposite:* "I don't hate my child" becomes "I love my child. See how I smother the dear little thing with love?" Such defenses serve the critical coping function of alleviating anxiety.

If defense mechanisms defend you against anxiety, why might they still have negative consequences for you? Useful as they are, ego mechanisms of defense are ultimately self-deceptive. When overused, they create more problems than they solve. It is psychologically unhealthy to spend a great deal of time and psychic energy deflecting, disguising, and rechanneling unacceptable urges in order to reduce anxiety. Doing so leaves little energy for productive living or satisfying human relationships. Some forms of mental illness result from excessive reliance on defense mechanisms to cope with anxiety, as we shall see in a later chapter on mental disorders.

Evaluation of Freudian Theory

We have devoted a great deal of space to outlining the essentials of psychoanalytic theory, because Freud's ideas have had an enormous impact on the way many psychologists think about normal and abnormal aspects of personality. However, there probably are more psychologists who criticize Freudian concepts than who support them. What is the basis of some of their criticisms?

First, psychoanalytic concepts are vague and not operationally defined; thus much of the theory is difficult to evaluate scientifically. Because some of its central hypotheses cannot be disproved, even in principle, Freud's theory remains questionable. How can the concepts of libido, the structure of personality, and repression of infantile sexual impulses be studied in any direct fashion? How is it possible to predict whether an overly anxious person will use projection, denial, or reaction formation to defend a threatened ego?

A second, related criticism is that Freudian theory is good history but bad science. It does not reliably *predict* what will occur; it is applied *retrospectively*—after events have occurred. Using psychoanalytic theory to understand personality typically involves *historical reconstruction,* not scientific construction of probable actions and predictable outcomes. In addition, by overemphasizing historical origins of current behavior, the theory directs attention away from the current stimuli that may be inducing and maintaining the behavior.

There are three other major criticisms of Freudian theory. First, it is a developmental theory, but it never included observations or studies of children. Second, it minimizes traumatic experiences (such as child abuse) by reinterpreting memories of them as fantasies (based on a child's desire for sexual contact with a parent). Third, it has an *androcentric* (male-centered) *bias* because it uses a male model as the norm without trying to determine how females might be different.

Some aspects of Freud's theory, however, continue to gain acceptance as they are modified and improved through empirical scrutiny. For example, in Chapter 4 we saw that the concept of the unconscious is being systematically explored by contemporary researchers (Greenwald, 1992; Kihlstrom et al., 1992). This research reveals that much of your day-to-day experience is shaped by processes outside of your awareness. These results support Freud's general concept but weaken the link between unconscious processes and psychopathology: little of your unconscious knowledge will cause you anxiety or distress. Similarly, researchers have found evidence for some of the habits of mind Freud characterized as defense mechanisms (Hentschel et al., 1993; Singer, 1990). Some of the styles for coping with stress we described in Chapter 13 fall within this general category. You might recall, for example, that inhibiting the thoughts and feelings associated with personal traumas or guilty or shameful experiences can take a devastating toll on mental and physical health (Pennebaker, 1990; Traue & Pennebaker, 1993). These findings echo Freud's beliefs that repressed psychic material can lead to psychological distress.

Certain aspects of Freud's theory, such as the emphasis on the unconscious and the uses of defense mechanisms, have gained wide acceptance among psychologists.

Freud's theory is the most complex, comprehensive, and compelling view of normal and abnormal personality functioning—even when its predictions prove wrong. Freud's theory, like any other theory, is best treated as one that must be confirmed or disconfirmed element by element. Freud retains his influence on contemporary psychology because some of his ideas have been widely accepted. Others have been abandoned. Some of the earliest revisions of Freud's theory arose from within his own original circle of students. Let's see how they sought to amend Freud's views.

Post-Freudian Theories

Some of those who came after Freud retained his basic representation of personality as a battleground on which unconscious primal urges conflict with social values. However, many of Freud's intellectual descendants made major adjustments in the psychoanalytic view of personality. In general, these post-Freudians have made the following changes:

- they put greater emphasis on ego functions, including ego defenses, development of the self, conscious thought processes, and personal mastery;
- they view social variables (culture, family, and peers) as playing a greater role in shaping personality;
- they put less emphasis on the importance of general sexual urges, or libidinal energy; and
- they have extended personality development beyond childhood to include the entire life span.

Among Freud's many celebrated followers, two of the most important were also severe critics, Alfred Adler and Carl Jung.

Alfred Adler (1929) rejected the significance of Eros and the pleasure principle. Adler believed that as helpless, dependent, small children, people all experience feelings of *inferiority*. He argued that all lives are dominated by the search for ways to overcome those feelings. People compensate to achieve feelings of adequacy or, more often, overcompensate in an attempt to become *superior*. Personality is structured around this underlying striving; people develop lifestyles based on particular ways of overcoming their basic, pervasive feelings of inferiority. Personality conflict arises from incompatibility between external environmental pressures and internal strivings for adequacy, rather than from competing urges within the person.

Alfred Adler argued that personality is shaped by a universal desire to overcome the feelings of inferiority created by the experiences of childhood.

Jung recognized creativity as a means to express and release images from the personal and collective unconscious.

Carl Jung (1959) greatly expanded the conception of the unconscious. For him, the unconscious was not limited to an individual's unique life experiences but was filled with fundamental psychological truths shared by the whole human race, a **collective unconscious.** The collective unconscious explains your intuitive understanding of primitive myths, art forms, and symbols, which are the universal archetypes of existence. An **archetype** is a primitive symbolic representation of a particular experience or object. Each archetype is associated with an instinctive tendency to feel and think about it or experience it in a special way. Jung postulated many archetypes from history and mythology: the sun god, the hero, the earth mother. *Animus* was the male archetype, while *anima* was the female archetype, and all men and women experienced both archetypes in varying degrees. The archetype of the self is the *mandala,* or magic circle; it symbolizes striving for unity and wholeness (Jung, 1973).

Carl Jung expanded the concept of the unconscious to include his idea of the collective unconscious, fundamental psychological truths shared by the entire human race.

Jung saw the healthy, integrated personality as balancing opposing forces, such as masculine aggressiveness and feminine sensitivity. This view of personality as a constellation of compensating internal forces in dynamic balance was called **analytic psychology.** In addition, Jung rejected the primary importance of libido, so central to Freud's own theory. Jung added two equally powerful unconscious instincts: the need to create and the need to self-actualize. Jung's views became central to the emergence of humanistic psychology in America (Jung, 1965).

HUMANISTIC THEORIES

Humanistic approaches to understanding personality are characterized by a concern for the integrity of an individual's personal and conscious experience and growth potential. Humanistic personality theorists, such as Carl Rogers and Abraham Maslow, believed that the motivation for behavior comes from a person's unique tendencies, both innate and learned, to develop and change in positive directions toward the goal of self-actualization. **Self-actualization** is a constant striving to realize one's inherent potential—to fully develop one's capacities and talents. Recall from Chapter 12 that Maslow placed self-actualization toward the pinnacle of his hierarchy of needs. The striving toward self-fulfillment is a constructive, guiding force that moves each person toward generally positive behaviors and enhancement of the self.

The humanistic theorists believed that behavior is motivated by a basic desire to develop and change in positive ways, moving toward self-actualization.

The drive for self-actualization at times comes into conflict with the need for approval from the self and others, especially when the person feels that certain obligations or conditions must be met in order to gain approval. For example, **Carl Rogers** (1947, 1951, 1977) stressed the importance of *unconditional positive regard* in raising children. By this he meant that children should feel they will always be loved and approved of, in spite of their mistakes and misbehavior—that they do not have to earn their parents' love. He recommended that, when a child misbehaves, parents should emphasize that it is the *behavior* they disapprove of, not *the child*. Unconditional positive regard is important in adulthood, too, because worrying about seeking approval interferes with self-actualization. As an adult, you need to give and receive unconditional positive regard from those to whom you are close. Most important, you need to feel unconditional positive *self-regard,* or acceptance of yourself, in spite of the weaknesses you might be trying to change.

The key feature of all humanistic theories is an emphasis on the drive toward self-actualization. In addition, humanistic theories have been described as being holistic, dispositional, phenomenological, and existential. Let's see why.

Humanistic theories are *holistic,* because they explain people's separate acts in terms of their entire personalities; people are not seen as the sum of discrete traits that each influence behavior in different ways. Maslow believed that people are intrinsically motivated toward the upper levels of the hierarchy of needs (discussed in Chapter 12), unless deficiencies at the lower levels weigh them down.

Humanistic theories are *dispositional,* because they focus on the innate qualities within a person that exert a major influence over the direction behavior will take. Situational factors are seen as constraints and barriers (like the strings that tie down balloons). Once freed from negative situational conditions, the actualizing tendency should actively guide people to choose life-enhancing situations. However, humanistic theories are not dispositional in the same sense as trait theories or psychodynamic theories. In those views, personal dispositions are recurrent themes played out in behavior again and again. Humanistic dispositions are oriented specifically toward creativity and growth. Each time a humanistic disposition is exercised, the person changes a little, so that the disposition is never expressed in the same way twice. Over time, humanistic dispositions guide the individual toward self-actualization, the purest expression of these motives.

Humanistic theories are *phenomenological,* because they emphasize an individual's frame of reference and subjective view of reality—not the objective perspective of an observer or of a therapist. Thus a humanistic psychologist always strives to see each person's unique point of view. This view is also a present view; past influences are important only to the extent that they have brought the person to the present situation, and the future represents goals to achieve. Thus, unlike psychodynamic theories, humanistic theories do not see people's present behaviors as unconsciously guided by past experiences.

Finally, humanistic theories have been described by theorists such as **Rollo May** (1975) as having an *existential perspective.* They focus on higher mental processes that interpret current experiences and enable individuals to meet or be overwhelmed by the everyday challenges of existence. This existential perspective has its roots in both literary and philosophical traditions that give it a broad appeal to many contemporary scholars and clinicians (Schneider & May, 1995).

The upbeat humanist view of personality was a welcome treat for many psychologists who had been brought up on a diet of bitter-tasting Freudian medicine. Humanistic approaches focus directly on improvement—on making life more palatable—rather than dredging up painful memories that are sometimes better left repressed. The humanist perspective emphasizes each person's ability to realize his or her fullest potential.

Humanistic theories of personality are holistic, dispositional, phenomenological, and existential.

Evaluation of Humanistic Theories

Freud's theory was often criticized for providing the too-pessimistic view that human nature develops out of conflicts, traumas, and anxieties. Humanistic theories arose to celebrate the healthy personality that strives for happiness and self-actualization. It is difficult to criticize theories that encourage and appreciate people, even for their faults. Even so, critics have complained that humanistic concepts are fuzzy and difficult to explore in research. They ask, What exactly is self-actualization? Is it an inborn tendency, or is it created by the cultural context? Humanistic theories also did not traditionally focus on the particular characteristics of individuals. They were more theories about human nature, and about qualities all people share, than about the individual personality or the basis of differences among people. Other psychologists note that, by emphasizing the role of the self as a source of experience and action, humanistic psychologists neglect the important environmental variables that also influence behavior.

A contemporary type of research that can be traced in part to the humanist tradition focuses directly on individual *narratives* or *life stories* (Baumeister, 1994; McAdams, 1988; Rosenwald & Ochberg, 1992). The tradition of using psychological theory to understand the details of an individual's life—to produce a *psychobiography*—can be traced back to Freud's analysis of Leonardo da Vinci (Freud, 1910/1957; see Elms, 1988, for a critique of Freud's work). **Psychobiography** is defined as "the systematic use of psychological (especially personality) theory to transform a life into a coherent and illuminating story" (McAdams, 1988, p. 2). Consider the great artist Pablo Picasso. Picasso suffered a series of traumas as a young child, including a serious earthquake and the death of a young sister. A psychobiography might attempt to explain some of Picasso's vast artistic creativity as the lifelong residue of his responses to these early traumas (Gardner, 1993a).

When a well-known or historical figure is the subject of a psychobiography, a researcher may turn to published work, diaries, and letters as sources

You can detect important aspects of people's personalities from the stories they tell about their lives.

of relevant data. For more ordinary individuals, researchers may directly elicit narratives of life experiences. The request might be, for example, that the subject talk about a recent peak experience: "What were you thinking and feeling? What might this episode say about who you are, who you were, who you might be, or how you have developed over time?" (McAdams & de St. Aubin, 1992, p. 1010). The characteristic themes that emerge over series of narrative accounts support the holistic and phenomenological version of personality that was put forth by the early humanists: people construct their identities by weaving life stories out of the strands of narrative. Personal accounts provide a window on people's views of themselves and interpersonal relationships (Harvey et al., 1990; Shotter, 1984).

Humanistic psychologists emphasized each individual's drive toward self-actualization. This group of theorists recognized, however, that people's progress toward this goal is determined, in part, by realities of their environments. We turn now to theories that directly examine how individuals' behaviors are shaped by their environments.

SOCIAL-LEARNING AND COGNITIVE THEORIES

Common to all the theories we have reviewed so far is an emphasis on hypothesized inner mechanisms—traits, instincts, impulses, tendencies toward self-actualization—that propel behavior and form the basis of a functioning personality. What most of these theories lacked, however, was a solid link between personality and particular behaviors. Psychodynamic and humanistic theories, for example, provide accounts of the total personality but do not predict specific actions. Another tradition of personality theory emerged from a more direct focus on individual differences in behavior. Recall from Chapter 9 that much of a person's behavior can be predicted from contingencies in the environment. Psychologists with a *learning theory* orientation look to the environmental circumstances that control behavior. Personality is seen as the sum of the overt and covert responses that are reliably elicited by an individual's *reinforcement history.* Learning theory approaches suggest that people are different because they have had different histories of reinforcement.

Consider a behaviorist conception of personality developed by a team of Yale University psychologists headed by John Dollard and Neal Miller (1950). Dollard and Miller introduced concepts such as learned drives, inhibition of responses, and learned habit patterns. Similar to Freud, they emphasized the roles of the motivating force of tension and the reinforcing (pleasurable) consequences of *tension reduction.* Organisms act to reduce tension produced by unsatisfied drives. Behavior that successfully reduces such tensions is repeated, eventually becoming a learned habit that is reinforced by repeated tension reduction. Dollard and Miller also showed that one could learn by *social imitation*—by observing the behavior of others without having to actually perform the response. Suppose a youngster sees his older sister given candy when she races to meet their father when he arrives home; the younger brother may begin to carry out the same behavior. The idea of imitation broadened the ways psychologists understood that effective or destructive habits are learned. Personality emerges as the sum of these learned habits.

Contemporary social-learning and cognitive theories often share Dollard and Miller's belief that behavior is influenced by environmental contingencies. These theories, however, go one step further to emphasize the importance of cognitive processes as well as behavioral ones, returning a thinking mind to the acting body. Those who have proposed cognitive theories of personality point out that there are important individual differences in the way people think about and define any external situation. Cognitive theories stress the mental processes through which people turn their sensations and perceptions into organized impressions of reality. Like humanistic theories,

Contemporary social-learning and cognitive theories share Dollard and Miller's behaviorist view that our actions are influenced by environmental contingencies.

Childhood experiences may have significant bearing on adult personality. If your parents complimented you every time you got a new haircut, chances are you'll feel more confident about your appearance and grooming as an adult than if they were regularly critical.

cognitive theories emphasize that you participate in creating your own personality. For example, you actively *choose* your own environments to a great extent; you do not just react passively. You weigh alternatives and select the settings in which you act and are acted upon—you choose to enter situations that you expect to be reinforcing and to avoid those that are unsatisfying and uncertain. For example, you often choose to return to restaurants where you've had good meals before, rather than always trying someplace new.

Let's look now at more concrete embodiments of these ideas. We begin with the personal construct theory of George Kelly and then examine the theories of Walter Mischel, Albert Bandura, and Nancy Cantor.

Kelly's Personal Construct Theory

George Kelly (1955) developed a theory of personality that places primary emphasis on each person's active, cognitive construction of his or her world. He argued strongly that no one is ever a victim of either past history or the present environment. Although events cannot be changed, all events are open to alternative interpretations; people can always reconstruct their past or define their present difficulties in different ways.

Kelly used science as a metaphor for this process of cognitive construction. Scientists develop theories to *understand* the natural world and to *make predictions* about what will occur in the future under particular conditions. The test of a scientific theory is its utility—how well it explains and predicts. If a theory isn't working well or if it is extended beyond the set of events where it does work well, then a new, more useful theory should be developed. Kelly argued that all people function as scientists. They want to be able to predict and explain the world around them—especially the interpersonal world.

Kelly suggested that people build theories about the world from units called *personal constructs.* **Personal constructs** are each person's beliefs about what two objects or events have in common and what sets them apart from a third object or event. For example, suppose someone says that her uncle and her brother are alike because they are highly competitive. Her sister is different from them because she likes to take a back seat to others. This individual seems to be using a construct of competitiveness versus giving in to others to organize her perceptions of the people around her. By applying that construct to many people she knows, she might arrange them into categories or along a scale ranging from the most competitive people to those who are most likely to yield to others.

George Kelly argued that past history and present environment are not as important to personality development as the individual's interpretations of them.

You have many different personal constructs that you can apply to understanding any person or situation. Although many people share some of the constructs you use, some of your constructs are uniquely yours—this is how personality emerges. All of your constructs are put together into an integrated belief system that influences the way you interpret, respond to, and feel about each situation you encounter. Chronically accessible constructs are those that you use frequently and automatically. They influence the way you evaluate information and form impressions of others. Kelly believed that people differ in their readiness to change constructs and that they can run into trouble either by rigidly refusing to change their old, ineffective constructs or by nervously changing their constructs every time the wind turns. Can you think of a situation in which you would have been better off holding on to an old construct a bit longer?

Mischel's Cognitive Social Personality Theory

Walter Mischel, a student of George Kelly's, further developed theories about the cognitive basis of personality. Mischel emphasizes that people actively participate in the cognitive organization of their interactions with the environment (Mischel & Peake, 1982). According to Mischel, how you respond to a specific environmental input depends on the following variables:

- *Competencies*—what you know, what you can do, and how well you generate certain cognitive and behavioral outcomes
- *Encoding strategies*—the way you process incoming information, selectively attending, categorizing, and making associations with it
- *Expectancies*—your anticipation of likely outcomes for given actions in particular situations
- *Personal values*—the importance you attach to stimuli, events, people, and activities
- *Self-regulatory systems and plans*—the rules you have developed for guiding your performance, setting goals, and evaluating your effectiveness

Walter Mischel suggested that people respond to specific environmental input based on their competencies, encoding strategies, expectancies, personal values, and self-regulatory systems and plans.

What determines the nature of these variables for a specific individual? Mischel believes that they result from the history of your observations and interactions with other people and with inanimate aspects of the physical environment (Mischel, 1973).

Mischel's approach emphasizes the importance of understanding how behavior arises as a function of interactions between persons and situations (Mischel, 1990; Shoda et al., 1993a, b). Consider this example:

> John's unique personality may be seen most clearly in that he is always very friendly when meeting someone for the first time, but that he also predictably becomes rather abrupt and unfriendly as he begins to spend more time with that person. Jim, on the other hand, is unique in that he is typically shy and quiet with people who he does not know well but becomes very gregarious once he begins to know someone well. (Shoda et al., 1993a, p. 1023)

If we were to average John's and Jim's overall friendliness, we would probably get about the same value on this trait—but that would fail to capture important differences in their behavior. Mischel and his colleagues have demonstrated the importance of patterns of behavior in their field studies of children's experiences in summer camp.

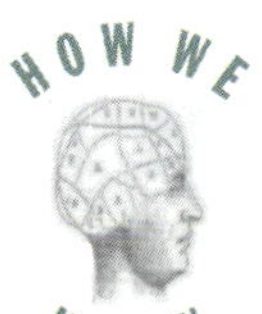

One study focused on children's reactions to different psychological situations, such as having another child initiate positive social contact or being warned by an adult to cease some activity. Children's reactions were coded into categories such as "talked prosocially" or "complied or gave in." In addition, at the end of the summer, camp counselors were asked to label individual children as "aggressive," "withdrawn," or "friendly." What information did they use to make these judgments? Consider the behavior of complying or giving in. Children who were ultimately rated as *friendly* had complied in situations in which they had been given warnings by an adult. Children who were ultimately rated as *withdrawn* had complied in situations in which peers had teased them (Shoda et al., 1993b).

Would you feel comfortable making personality judgments about these boys from this one snapshot? Why might you want to know their patterns of behavior across situations?

These results suggest that knowing the average rates at which children complied wouldn't tell you very much about their personalities. You would have to know in what situation the compliance took place to understand why one child was labeled as friendly and another as withdrawn. Mischel emphasizes that your beliefs about other people's personalities come not from taking averages but from tracking the way different situations bring out different behaviors (Shoda & Mischel, 1993).

Bandura's Cognitive Social-Learning Theory

Through his theoretical writing and extensive research with children and adults, **Albert Bandura** (1986) has been an eloquent champion of a social-learning approach to understanding personality (recall from Chapter 9 his studies of aggressive behavior in children). This approach combines principles of learning with an emphasis on human interactions in social settings. From a social-learning perspective, human beings are not driven by inner forces, nor are they helpless pawns of environmental influence. The social-learning approach stresses the cognitive processes that are involved in acquiring and maintaining patterns of behavior and, thus, personality.

Albert Bandura proposed a theory of complex reciprocal interaction of individual factors, behavior, and environmental stimuli.

Bandura's theory points to a complex interaction of individual factors, behavior, and environmental stimuli. Each can influence or change the others, and the direction of change is rarely one way—it is *reciprocal.* Your behavior can be influenced by your attitudes, beliefs, or prior history of reinforcement as well as by stimuli available in the environment. What you do can have an effect on the environment, and important aspects of your personality can be affected by the environment or by feedback from your behavior. This important concept, **reciprocal determinism,** implies that you must examine all components if you want to completely understand human behavior, personality, and social ecology (Bandura, 1981; see **Figure 14.3**). So, for example, if you are overweight, you may not choose to be active in track-and-field events, but if you live near a pool, you may spend time swimming. If you are outgoing, you'll talk to others sitting around the pool and thereby create a more sociable atmosphere, which, in turn, makes it a more enjoyable environment. This is one instance of reciprocal determinism among person, place, and behavior.

You may recall from Chapter 9 that Bandura's social-learning theory emphasizes **observational learning** as the process by which a person changes his or her behavior based on observations of another person's behavior. Through observational learning, children and adults acquire an enormous range of information about their social environment. Through observation, you learn what is appropriate and gets rewarded and what gets punished or

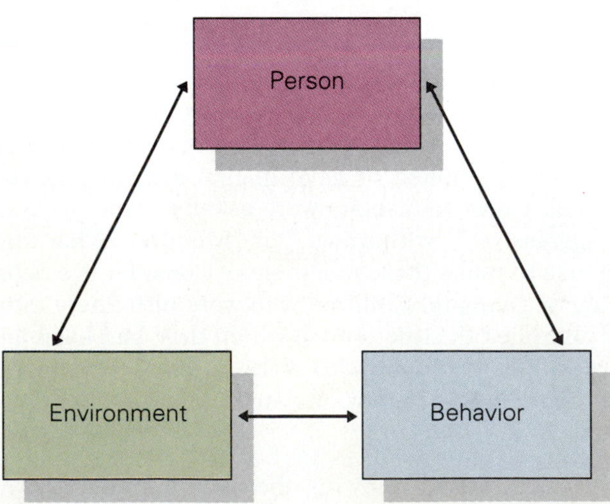

Figure 14.3 Reciprocal Determinism
In reciprocal determinism, the individual, the individual's behavior, and the environment all interact to influence and modify the other components.

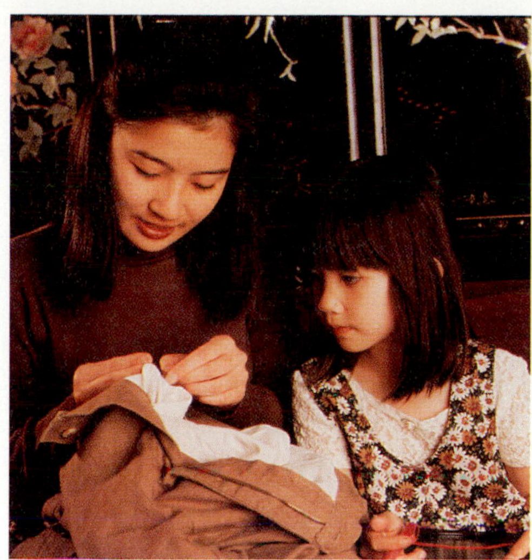

By observing adult behavior, children learn which behaviors are socially approved and reinforced.

ignored. Because you can use memory and think about external events, you can foresee the possible consequences of your actions without having to actually experience them. You may acquire skills, attitudes, and beliefs simply by watching what others do and the consequences that follow.

As his theory developed, Bandura (1986, 1992) elaborated *self-efficacy* as a central construct. **Self-efficacy** is the belief that one can perform adequately in a particular situation. Your sense of self-efficacy influences your perceptions, motivation, and performance in many ways. You don't even try to do things or take chances when you expect to be ineffectual. You avoid situations when you don't feel adequate. Even when you do, in fact, have the ability—and the desire—you may not take the required action or persist to complete the task successfully, if you *think* you lack what it takes.

Beyond actual accomplishments, there are three other sources of information for *self-efficacy judgments:* (1) vicarious experience, or your observations of the performance of others; (2) persuasion (others may convince you that you can do something, or you may convince yourself); and (3) monitoring of your emotional arousal as you think about or approach a task (for example, anxiety suggests low expectations of efficacy; excitement suggests expectations of success).

Self-efficacy judgments are based on actual experiences, vicarious experience, persuasion, and monitoring of emotional arousal as a task is contemplated or attempted.

Self-efficacy judgments influence how much effort you expend and how long you persist when faced with difficulty in a wide range of life situations (Schwarzer, 1992). For example, how vigorously and persistently you study this chapter may depend more on your sense of self-efficacy than on actual ability (Zimmerman et al., 1992). Expectations of success or failure can be influenced by feedback from performance, but they are also likely to *create* the *predicted* feedback and, thus, to become self-fulfilling prophecies. Let's apply this insight to teachers in the classroom.

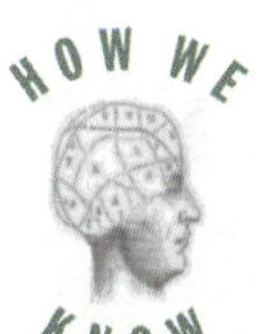

Forty-eight teachers in four high schools with large numbers of "culturally deprived" students participated in this study. The researchers measured the teachers' sense of teaching efficacy on self-report scales, made classroom observations of "climate and atmosphere," and assessed student achievement on standardized tests. These measures reveal that teachers with a greater sense of self-efficacy tend to maintain a positive emotional climate in their classes, avoiding harsh modes of behavior control. In addition, student achievement in mathematics was significantly correlated with the teachers' self-efficacy; students scored higher as teacher self-efficacy increased (Ashton & Webb, 1986).

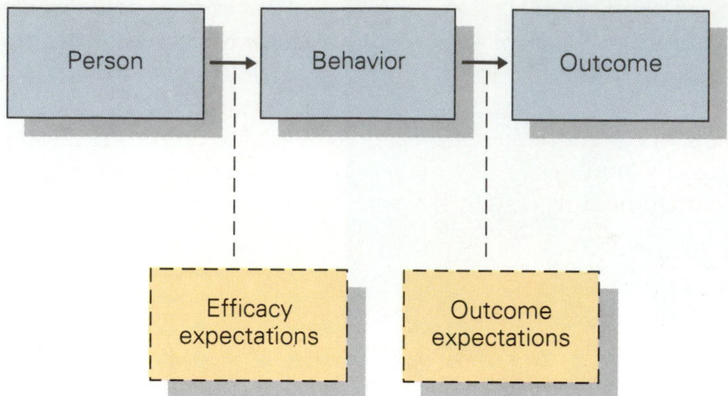

Figure 14.4 Bandura's Self-efficacy Model
This model positions efficacy expectations between the person and his or her behavior; outcome expectations are positioned between behavior and its anticipated outcomes.

Bandura's theory of self-efficacy also acknowledges the importance of the environment. Expectations of failure or success—and corresponding decisions to stop trying or to persevere—may be based on perceptions of the supportiveness or unsupportiveness of the environment, in addition to perceptions of one's own adequacy or inadequacy. Such expectations are called *outcome-based expectancies.* **Figure 14.4** displays how the parts of Bandura's theory fit together. Behavioral outcomes depend both on people's perceptions of their own abilities and their perceptions of the environment.

Cantor's Social Intelligence Theory

Building on these earlier cognitive and social theories, **Nancy Cantor** and her colleagues have outlined a *social intelligence* theory of personality (Cantor & Harlow, 1994; Cantor & Kihlstrom, 1987). **Social intelligence** refers to the expertise people bring to their experience of life tasks. The theory defines three types of individual differences:

Nancy Cantor's social intelligence theory suggests that people differ in choice of life goals, in the knowledge they possess, and in the strategies they use to implement their goals.

- *Choice of life goals.* People differ with respect to which life goals or life tasks are most important to them. For example, college students are often concerned about "getting good grades" or "getting and keeping friends." Is one of these goals more important for you than the other? People's goals may also change over time. Your goals of ten years ago are probably different both from those of today and from those of the future.
- *Knowledge relevant to social interactions.* People differ with respect to the expertise they bring to tasks of social and personal problem solving.
- *Strategies for implementing goals.* People have different characteristic problem-solving strategies.

Can you see how these three dimensions interact to give rise to the different patterns of behavior you would recognize as personality? You might know two people who have the same general life goal—perhaps they both value getting good grades—but depending on what they know and how they are able to put that knowledge to use, the moment-by-moment decisions they make about how to behave could be very different. One may have been taught explicit strategies for studying, while the other muddles through without special help. The theory of social intelligence gives a new perspective on how personality predicts consistency: for a given period of time, consistency is found in people's goals, knowledge, and strategies.

Let's focus on the different strategies people bring to the same task. For example, Norem and Cantor (1986) identified two types of strategies people use in situations that permit either success or failure. *Optimists* face such situations with high expectations and little prior thought. *Defensive pessimists* set low expectations and expend considerable effort thinking through possible positive and negative outcomes. What happens when experimenters create circumstances in which these strategies are disrupted?

Researchers created two groups of subjects, who were identified as optimists or as defensive pessimists. When the subjects arrived at the experimental session, they were warned that they would be asked to work at solving problems—creating success or failure circumstances that made the strategies relevant. Half of each group of subjects received an experimental treatment that disrupted the normal course of their personal strategies. Thus half of the optimists were required to think through possible outcomes (as were half of the defensive pessimists); half of the defensive pessimists were distracted from thinking about the performance task by carrying out a clerical accuracy task (as were half of the optimists). The groups of subjects whose normal strategies were disrupted expressed more negative feelings about the experience than did their undisrupted peers. Furthermore, defensive pessimists did less well on the performance task (timed arithmetic problems) when their normal strategy was disrupted (Norem & Illingworth, 1993).

Note that, overall, the optimists and defensive pessimists did equally well on the performance task—despite the lower expectations of the defensive pessimists. Thus, in terms of outcome, the two strategies may be equally workable. However, you'd be likely to label as different the personalities of the people who would habitually employ one or the other strategy. In this case, you recognize personality in the consistent way in which people face the world's challenges.

Evaluation of Social-Learning and Cognitive Theories

One set of criticisms leveled against social-learning and cognitive theories is that they generally overlook emotion as an important component of personality. They emphasize rational, information-processing variables, such as constructs and encoding strategies. Emotions are perceived merely as byproducts of thoughts and behavior or are just included with other types of thoughts, rather than being assigned independent importance. For those who feel that emotions are central to the functioning of human personality, this is a serious flaw. Cognitive theories are also attacked for not fully recognizing the impact of unconscious motivation on behavior and affect.

A second set of criticisms focuses on the vagueness of explanations about the way personal constructs and competencies are created. Cognitive theorists have often had little to say about the developmental origins of adult personality; their focus on the individual's perception of the current behavior setting obscures the individual's history. This criticism is leveled particularly at Kelly's theory, which has been described as more of a conceptual system than a theory, because it focuses on structure and processes but says little about the content of personal constructs.

Despite these criticisms, cognitive personality theories have made major contributions to current thinking. Kelly's theory has influenced a large number of cognitive therapists. Mischel's awareness of situation has brought about a better understanding of the interaction between what a person brings to a behavior setting and what that setting brings out of the person. Bandura's ideas have led to improvements in the way teachers educate children and help them achieve as well as new treatments in the areas of health, business, and sports performance. Finally, Cantor's theory shifts the search for personality consistency to the level of life goals and social strategies.

Do these cognitive personality theories provide you with insights about your own personality and behaviors? You can start to see how you define yourself in part through interactions with the environment. We turn now to theories that can add even further to your definition of *self.*

SELF THEORIES

We have arrived now at theories of personality that are most immediately personal: they deal directly with how each individual manages his or her sense of **self.** What is your conception of your *self?* Do you think of your *self* reacting consistently to the world? Do you try to present a consistent *self* to your friends and family? What impact do positive and negative experiences have on the way you think about your *self?* We will begin our consideration of these questions with a brief historical review.

William James identified three components of self-experience: the material me, the social me, and the spiritual me.

The concern for analysis of the self found its strongest early advocate in **William James** (1890). James identified three components of self-experience: the *material me* (the bodily self, along with surrounding physical objects), the *social me* (your awareness of how others view you), and the *spiritual me* (the self that monitors private thoughts and feelings). James believed that everything that you associate with your identity becomes, in some sense, a part of the self. This explains why people may react defensively when their friends or family members—a part of the self—have been attacked. The concept of self was also central to psychodynamic theories. Self-insight was an important part of the psychoanalytic cure in Freud's theory, and Jung stressed that to fully develop the self, one must integrate and accept all aspects of one's conscious and unconscious life.

How has the self been treated in contemporary theory? We will first describe cognitive aspects of the self: self-concepts and possible selves. We then examine the way that people present their selves to the world.

DYNAMIC ASPECTS OF SELF-CONCEPTS

The *self-concept* is a dynamic mental structure that motivates, interprets, organizes, mediates, and regulates intrapersonal and interpersonal behaviors and processes. The self-concept includes many components. Among them are your memories about yourself; beliefs about your traits, motives, values, and abilities; the ideal self that you would most like to become; the possible selves that you contemplate enacting; positive or negative evaluations of yourself (self-esteem); and beliefs about what others think of you (McGuire & McGuire, 1988). In Chapter 10, we discussed *schemas* as "knowledge packages" that embody complex generalizations about the structure of the environment. Your self-concept contains schemas about the self—*self-schemas*—that allow you to organize information about your self, just as other schemas allow you to manage other aspects of your experience (Markus, 1977). However, self-schemas influence more than just the way you process information about yourself. Research indicates that these schemas, which you frequently use to interpret your *own* behavior, influence the way you process information about other people as well (Cantor & Kihlstrom, 1987; Markus & Smith, 1981). Thus you interpret other people's actions in terms of what you know and believe about yourself.

Research indicates that you use self-schemas not only to interpret your own behavior but to process information about other people.

People obtain important information about their self-concepts through social interaction: the self is a dynamic construct, deriving its meaning in interpersonal contexts. In some sense, without others there can be no self

(Markus & Cross, 1990). For that reason, people often put themselves in situations that allow for *self-verification*—circumstances that confirm their self-concept (Swann, 1990). This is true even when the circumstances confirm a self-concept that is relatively negative.

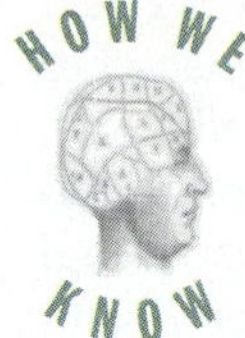

Researchers recruited married couples from patrons at a horse ranch and a shopping mall. Each of the husbands and wives were asked to give ratings of themselves on dimensions such as intellectual capability and physical attractiveness. They then rated their spouses on the same dimensions. Finally they gave ratings that indicated their overall commitment to their marriage. The results showed that people were most committed to their relationships when their self-assessment matched their spouse's assessment of them. You might not be surprised to learn, for example, that people who had a positive self-concept were more committed to their marriages when their spouses also rated them positively. However, the effect was also obtained for people with *negative* self-concepts. When people had negative self-concepts, and their spouses also rated them negatively, they were more committed to their marriages than when their spouses thought well of them (Swann et al., 1992).

People appear to prefer self-verification even when the result verifies a negative perception.

Are you surprised by this result? You might have expected that people whose spouses didn't think well of them would be unhappy in their marriages. That was true, however, only when there was a mismatch between their spouse's and their own assessment. When there was a match—when they had a negative self-concept—they were likely to be content in the relationship. This doesn't mean that people like having negative self-concepts; they just like the world to confirm whatever concept they have. The implication is that people favor self-verification even when the self that is being verified might cause them discomfort.

Another important component of your cognitive sense of self may be the other *possible selves* to which you compare your current self-concept. **Hazel Markus** and her colleagues have defined **possible selves** as "the ideal selves that we would very much like to become. They are also the selves we could become, and the selves we are afraid of becoming" (Markus & Nurius, 1986, p. 954). Possible selves play a role in motivating behavior—they spur action by allowing you to consider what directions your "self" could take, for better or for worse. Researchers have also examined the way that people's ideas of what is possible changes across the life span (Hooker & Kaus, 1994; Ryff, 1991).

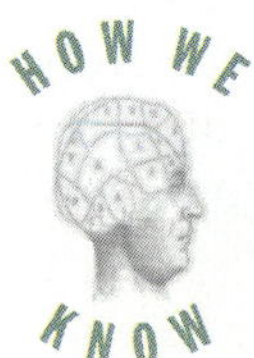

Groups of subjects, ranging in age from 18 to 86, were asked to report on their likely possible selves, their wished-for possible selves, and the possible selves they feared. Responses varied with age. Younger subjects tended to express a range of wished-for selves across broad categories (marrying the right person, being rich); older subjects were likely to wish to do more of what they were already doing (being healthy and vigorous, being a loving grandparent). These changes in ideas of possible selves occurred against the background of relatively stable ratings of life satisfaction across the life span. People may adjust their ideas about possible selves—with respect to the current self-concept—to keep general feelings of well-being steady throughout life (Cross & Markus, 1991).

You should take a moment now to consider what selves you wish for or fear. How might knowledge of these possible selves change the decisions you will make over the next few hours? Over the next few days?

Imagine for a moment your different "possible selves."

Self-esteem and Self-presentation

We have already acknowledged that some people have a negative self-concept, which we could also characterize as low self-esteem. A person's **self-esteem** is a *generalized* evaluation of the self. Self-esteem can strongly influence thoughts, moods, and behavior. Low self-esteem may be characterized, in part, by less *certainty* about the self. When high and low self-esteem subjects were asked to rate themselves along a number of trait dimensions (such as logical, intellectual, and likable), low self-esteem subjects, as you might expect, gave themselves overall lower ratings (Baumgardner, 1990). However, when they were also asked to provide upper and lower limits for their estimates, the low self-esteem subjects indicated larger ranges: they had a less precise sense of self than their high self-esteem peers. Thus, part of the phenomenon of low self-esteem may be feeling that you just don't know much about yourself. Lack of self-knowledge makes it difficult to predict that one will make a success of life's endeavors.

Evidence suggests that most people go out of their way to maintain self-esteem and to sustain the integrity of their self-concept (Steele, 1988). People engage in a variety of forms of self-enhancement (Banaji & Prentice, 1994). For example, when you doubt your ability to perform a task, you may engage in **self-handicapping** behavior. You deliberately sabotage your performance! The purpose of this strategy is to have a ready-made excuse for failure that does not imply *lack of ability* (Jones & Berglas, 1978; Higgins et al., 1990). Thus, if you are afraid to find out whether you have what it takes to be pre-med, you might party with friends instead of studying for an important exam. That way, if you don't succeed, you can blame your failure on low effort, without finding out whether you really had the *ability* to make it.

The phenomenon of self-handicapping suggests, as well, that important aspects of self-esteem are related to *self-presentation.* Self-handicapping is more likely when people know that outcomes will be made public (Self, 1990). After all, how can someone think less well of you when your handicap is so obvious? Similar issues of self-presentation help explain behavioral differences between individuals with high and low self-esteem (Baumeister et al., 1989). People with high self-esteem present themselves to the world as ambitious, aggressive risk takers. People with low self-esteem present themselves as cautious and prudent. What is important here is that this stance is for *public* consumption.

Self-handicapping behavior in action: instead of studying for tomorrow's exam, you fall asleep in the library, thereby enabling yourself to say, "Well, I didn't really study" if you don't ace the test.

Subjects high and low in self-esteem were given the opportunity to practice a game for as long as they wanted before undergoing a 2-minute timed trial. Half of the subjects practiced under the watchful eye of the experimenter; the other half practiced alone. In both cases, the amount of time they spent practicing was measured (explicitly when the experimenter was present and unobtrusively when the experimenter was absent). Results are shown in **Table 14.3**. When they practiced in public, individuals with high self-

Table 14.3 Mean Duration of Practice for People with High and Low Self-Esteem

Self-esteem	Public	Private
High	123	448
Low	257	387
	−134	+61

Note: Durations are measured in seconds.

> esteem did so only about half as long as their low self-esteem peers. When they practiced in private, the effect was reversed; they practiced longer than their low self-esteem peers (Tice & Baumeister, 1991).

We can understand this result in terms of self-presentation. People with high self-esteem may want to appear to succeed even with very little preparation ("Someone like me doesn't have to practice!")—and if they fail, they can fall back on self-handicapping ("You saw how little I practiced!").

Research has suggested that there is a personality trait related to people's habitual style of self-presentation. **Mark Snyder** called this trait *self-monitoring:* the tendency to regulate behavior to meet social demands or to create a desired social impression (Snyder, 1987; Snyder & Gangestad, 1986). People who are high self-monitors tend to answer "true" to statements like "I guess I put on a show to impress or entertain others" and "false" to statements like "At a party I let others keep the jokes and stories going." Low self-monitors lack the motivation or ability to alter their behavior to make a good social impression. You can make fairly strong predictions about how people will behave in social situations if you understand their level of self-monitoring.

Evaluation of Self Theories

Self theories succeed at capturing people's own concepts of their personalities and the way they wish to be perceived by others. However, critics of self theory approaches to personality argue against its limitless boundaries. Because so many things are relevant to the self and to the self-concept, it is not always clear which factors are most important for predicting behavior. In addition, the emphasis on the self as a social construct is not entirely consistent with evidence that some facets of personality may be inherited.

COMPARING PERSONALITY THEORIES

There is no unified theory of personality that a majority of psychologists can endorse. Several differences in basic assumptions have come up repeatedly in our survey of the various theories. It may be helpful to recap five of the most important differences in assumptions about personality and the approaches that advance each assumption.

Five important differences in personality theories are heredity versus environment; learning processes versus innate laws of behavior; emphasis on past, present, or future; consciousness versus unconsciousness; and inner disposition versus outer situation.

1. *Heredity versus environment.* This difference is also referred to as *nature versus nurture.* What is more important: genetic and biological factors or environmental influences? Trait theories have been split on this issue; Freudian theory depends heavily on heredity; humanistic, social-learning, cognitive, and self theories all emphasize either environment as a determinant of behavior or interaction with the environment as a source of personality development and differences.
2. *Learning processes versus innate laws of behavior.* Should emphasis be placed on *modifiability* or on the view that personality development follows an internal timetable? Again, trait theories have been divided. Freudian theory has favored the inner determinant view while humanists postulate an optimistic view that experience changes people. Social-learning, cognitive, and self theories clearly support the idea that behavior and personality change as a result of learned experiences.
3. *Emphasis on past, present, or future.* Trait theories emphasize past causes, whether innate or learned; Freudian theory stresses past events in early childhood; social-learning theories focus on past reinforcements and present contingencies; humanistic theories emphasize present reality or future goals; and cognitive and self theories emphasize past and present (and the future if goal-setting is involved).

4. *Consciousness versus unconsciousness.* Freudian theory emphasizes unconscious processes; humanistic, social-learning, and cognitive theories emphasize conscious processes. Trait theories pay little attention to this distinction; self theories are unclear on this score.
5. *Inner disposition versus outer situation.* Social-learning theories emphasize situational factors; traits play up dispositional factors; and the others allow for an interaction between person-based and situation-based variables.

What If You Could Design Your Own Personality?

In his best-selling book, *Listening to Prozac* (1993), Peter Kramer, a psychiatrist, describes a number of cases in which patients who were prescribed the drug Prozac underwent startling personality transformations. Consider the case of a woman Kramer calls Tess. Tess presented herself to Kramer and described difficult life circumstances and a history of depression. After two weeks on Prozac, however, Tess was a changed woman.

> Here was a patient whose usual method of functioning changed dramatically. She became socially capable, no longer a wallflower but a social butterfly. Where once she had focused on obligations to others, now she was vivacious and fun-loving. (Kramer, 1993, p. 11)

After about nine months, Tess was able to go off her drug treatment and maintain her newfound happiness. However, eight months after that, she called Kramer and asked to be put back on. "I'm not myself," she claimed. Here is Kramer's response:

> I found this statement remarkable. After all, Tess had existed in one mental state for twenty or thirty years; she then briefly felt different on medication. Now that the old mental state was threatening to reemerge—the one she had experienced almost all her adult life—her response was "I am not myself." (pp. 18–19)

What do you think of this story?

We already met Prozac in Chapter 3, where we reported that it enhances the action of serotonin by preventing the neurotransmitter from being removed from the synaptic cleft. We will meet it once again in Chapter 18, where we describe its potential to alleviate severe depression and other forms of psychopathology. Here, however, we introduce Prozac as a way of posing the question "What if you could design your own personality?" Throughout this chapter we have explored various ideas about the way your unique personality emerges as the product of your genetic inheritance and your experiences in the environment. Suppose now we gave you the opportunity to use drugs—Prozac or something yet undeveloped—to invent a new self. Would you take advantage of the offer? Would you indulge in what Kramer (a major supporter of Prozac) calls *cosmetic psychopharmacology?*

In *Talking Back to Prozac* (1994), critics Peter Breggin and Ginger Ross Breggin clearly believe that the answer should be "no." They worry that the overprescription of drugs like Prozac has the effect of making people too much alike and robs them of the negative emotional experiences that promote personal growth.

> For society, [the] expanding use of psychiatric diagnoses and drugs means that many of our most creative young people will never approach the fulfillment of their creative potential. Instead of struggling through the painful process of working out their personal relationship with themselves and others, they will—like the proverbial square pegs—be forced into round holes. Their edges will be shaved smooth in the process, and with it their uniqueness will be sacrificed. (p. 216)

Do the Breggins' concerns change your ideas about whether you'd choose your own personality if you could? Clearly, this is a complex issue—but research on psychoactive drugs may make it an issue you will have to face at some point in your future.

Each type of theory makes different contributions to the understanding of human personality. Trait theories provide a catalog that describes parts and structures. Psychodynamic theories add a powerful engine and the fuel to get the vehicle moving. Humanistic theories put a person in the driver's seat. Social-learning theories supply the steering wheel, directional signals, and other regulation equipment. Cognitive theories add reminders that the way the trip is planned, organized, and remembered will be affected by the mental map the driver chooses for the journey. Finally, self theories remind the driver to consider the image his or her driving ability is projecting to back-seat drivers and pedestrians.

At the outset of the chapter, we asked you to consider a series of questions: If psychologists studied *you,* what portrait of your personality would they draw? What early experiences might they identify as contributing to how you now act and think? What conditions in your current life exert strong influences on your thoughts and behaviors? What makes you different from other individuals who are functioning in many of the same situations as you? You now can see that each type of personality theory provides a framework against which you can begin to form your answers to these questions. Suppose the time has really come to paint your psychological portrait. Where would you begin?

Recapping Main Points

The Psychology of the Person

Personality is what is characteristic and unique about a person across different situations and over time. Personality theorists study the whole person as the sum of the separate processes of feelings, thoughts, and actions. Personality theories seek to explain and predict individual differences.

Type and Trait Personality Theories

Some theorists categorize people by all-or-none types, assumed to be related to particular characteristic behaviors. Others, such as Allport and Eysenck, view traits as the building blocks of personality. The five-factor model is a descriptive personality system that maps out the relationships between common trait words, theoretical concepts, and personality scales. Twin and adoption studies reveal that personality traits are partially inherited. Although trait measures do not show cross-situational behavioral consistency, the consistency paradox is resolved by showing that they do predict life events and behavioral coherence.

Psychodynamic Theories

Freud's psychodynamic theory emphasizes instinctive biological energies as sources of human motivation. Basic concepts of Freudian theory include psychic determinism, early experiences as key determinants of lifelong personality, psychic energy as powering and directing behavior, and powerful unconscious processes. Personality structure consists of the id, the superego, and the reconciling ego. Unacceptable impulses are repressed and ego-defense mechanisms are developed to lessen anxiety and bolster self-esteem. Post-Freudians like Adler and Jung have put greater emphasis on ego functioning and social variables and less on sexual urges. They see personality development as a lifelong process.

Humanistic Theories

Humanistic theories focus on the growth potential of the individual. These theories are holistic, dispositional, phenomenological, existential, and optimistic. At the core of Rogers's person-centered theory is the concept of self-actualization, a constant striving to realize one's potential. Contemporary theories in the humanist tradition focus on individual's life stories.

Social-Learning and Cognitive Theories

Social-learning theorists focus on understanding individual differences in behavior and personality as a consequence of different histories of reinforcement. Cognitive theorists emphasize individual differences in perception and subjective interpretation of the environment. Different situations make different behaviors relevant. In addition, people bring their own expectations and strategies to their life tasks.

Self Theories

Self theories focus on the importance of the self-concept for a full understanding of human personality. The self-concept is a dynamic mental structure that motivates, interprets, organizes, mediates, and regulates personal and interpersonal behaviors and processes. Many individual differences are captured by the habitual ways in which people present themselves in social situations.

Resources

Bandura, A. (1986). *Social foundations of thought and action: A social cognitive theory.* Englewood Cliffs, NJ: Prentice-Hall. The leading proponent for understanding personality from a social-cognitive orientation presents his influential self-efficacy theory.

Craik, K. H., et al. (Eds.). (1993). *Fifty years of personality psychology.* New York: Plenum Press.

Eysenck, H. J., & Eysenck, M. W. (1985). *Personality and individual differences.* New York: Plenum Press.

Freud, S. (1966). *Introductory lectures on psychoanalysis* (J. Strachey, Ed. and Trans.). New York: Norton. (Original work published 1920.)

Gay, P. (1988). *Freud: A life for our times.* New York: Norton.

Hogan, R. (1986). *What every student should know about personality.* In V. P. Makosky (Ed.), *The G. Stanley Hall lecture series* (Vol. 6). Washington, DC: American Psychological Association. A brief, entertaining summary of important research and theoretical issues in personality psychology.

Kagan, J. (1994). *Galen's prophesy: Temperament in human nature*. New York: HarperCollins.

Rogers, C. R., & Stevens, B. (1971). *Person to person: The problem of being human—A new trend in psychology.* New York: Pocket Books. A book written from the humanistic approach. Excerpts from the chapter entitled "The Curtain Raiser" describe the growth process throughout life.

Skinner, B. F. (1971). *Beyond freedom and dignity.* New York: Knopf.

15

Assessing Individual Differences

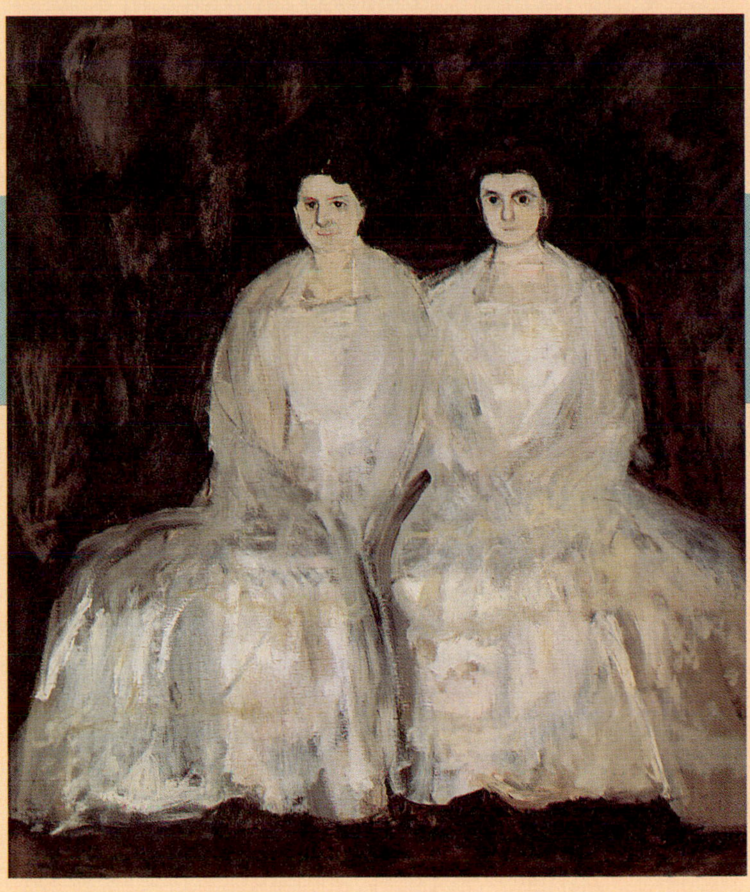

We'd like you to take a moment to think about your closest friend. Because this person is your closest friend, we suspect that there are some dimensions along which the two of you are very similar; but there are also likely to be some dimensions along which the two of you are different. In Chapter 14, we presented a number of theories that describe the differences among individuals. In this chapter, we will describe how researchers have tried to measure *those differences, often by turning the differences into scores on psychological tests. We will also discuss the types of controversies that almost inevitably arise when people begin to interpret these differences. Suppose you take a test that reveals you to be unsuited for a job you desire. How would you feel if this single test eliminated the career path you had chosen? In this chapter, we will help you think about how tests are used and abused.*

There are more than 2500 commercially published psychological tests now available that are designed to measure mental abilities of all sorts, school achievement, vocational interests, and aspects of personality and mental disorders. Many psychologists spend much of their time on the construction, evaluation, administration, and interpretation of psychological tests. Psychological testing is a multimillion-dollar industry—thousands of children and adults regularly take some form of the thousands of tests distributed by the more than 40 major U.S. publishers. Virtually everyone in our society who has attended school, gone to work, joined the military services, or registered in a mental health clinic has undergone some kind of psychological testing.

In this chapter, we will examine the foundations and uses of psychological assessment. We will review the contributions psychologists have made to the understanding of individual differences in three broad areas: intelligence and creativity, personality, and vocational ability. Our focus will be on what makes any test useful, how tests work, and why they do not always do the job they were intended to do. Finally, we will conclude on a personal note, by considering the role of psychological assessment in your life.

WHAT IS ASSESSMENT?

Psychological assessment is the use of specified testing procedures to evaluate the abilities, behaviors, and personal qualities of people. Psychological assessment is often referred to as the measurement of *individual differences,* since the majority of assessments specify how an individual is different from or similar to other people on a given dimension. Before we examine in detail the purposes of psychological testing, let's outline the history of assessment. This historical overview will help you to understand both the uses and limitations of assessment, as well as prepare you to appreciate some current-day controversies.

Psychological assessment focuses on individual differences, examining the ways in which an individual is similar to or different from other people.

HISTORY OF ASSESSMENT

The development of formal tests and procedures for assessment is a relatively new enterprise in Western psychology, coming into wide use only in the early 1900s. However, long before Western psychology began to devise tests to evaluate people, assessment techniques were commonplace in ancient China. In fact, China employed a sophisticated program of civil service testing over 4000 years ago—officials were required to demonstrate their competence every third year at an oral examination. Two thousand years later, during the Han Dynasty, written civil service tests were used to measure competence in the areas of law, the military, agriculture, and geography. During the Ming Dynasty (A.D. 1368–1644), public officials were chosen on the basis of their performance at three stages of an objective selection procedure. During the first stage, examinations were given at the local level. The 4 percent who passed these tests had to endure the second stage: nine days and nights of essay examinations on the classics. The 5 percent who passed the essay exams were allowed to complete a final stage of tests conducted at the nation's capital.

China's selection procedures were observed and described by British diplomats and missionaries in the early 1800s. Modified versions of China's system were soon adopted by the British and later by the Americans for the selection of civil service personnel (Wiggins, 1973).

The key figure in the era of Western intelligence testing was an upper-class Englishman, **Sir Francis Galton.** His book *Hereditary Genius*, published in 1869, greatly influenced subsequent thinking on the methods, theories, and practices of testing. Galton, a half cousin to Charles Darwin, attempted to apply Darwinian evolutionary theory to the study of human abilities. He was interested in how and why people differ in their abilities. He wondered why some people were gifted and successful—like him—while many others were not.

Sir Francis Galton's book Hereditary Genius *greatly influenced methods, theories, and practices of testing in the Western world.*

Galton was the first to postulate four important ideas about the assessment of intelligence. First, differences in intelligence were *quantifiable* in terms of degrees of intelligence. In other words, numerical values could be assigned to distinguish among different people's levels of intelligence. Second, differences among people formed a *bell-shaped curve*, or *normal distribution*. On a bell-shaped curve, most people's scores cluster in the middle and fewer are found toward the two extremes of genius and mental deficiency (we return to the bell-shaped curve later in the chapter). Third, intelligence, or mental ability, could be measured by objective tests, tests on which each question had only one "right" answer. And fourth, the precise extent to which two sets of test scores were related could be determined by a statistical procedure he called *co-relations*, now known as *correlations*. These ideas proved to be of lasting value.

Sir Francis Galton (1822–1911)

Unfortunately, Galton postulated a number of ideas that proved considerably more controversial. He believed, for example, that genius was inherited. In his view, talent, or eminence, ran in families; nurture had only a minimal effect on intelligence. In his view, intelligence was related to Darwinian species' fitness and, somehow, ultimately to one's moral worth. Galton attempted to base public policy on the concept of genetically superior and inferior people. He started the **eugenics** movement, which advocated improving the human species by applying evolutionary theory to encouraging biologically superior people to interbreed while discouraging biologically inferior people from having offspring. Galton wrote, "There exists a sentiment, for the most part quite unreasonable, against the gradual extinction of an inferior race" (Galton, 1883/1907, p. 200).

These controversial ideas were endorsed and extended later by many who argued forcefully that the intellectually superior race should propagate at the expense of those with inferior minds. Among the proponents of these ideas were American psychologists Goddard and Terman, whose theories we review later, and, of course, Nazi dictator Adolf Hitler. We will also see later in the chapter that remnants of these elitist ideas are still being proposed today.

PURPOSES OF ASSESSMENT

Psychologists use assessment techniques to understand individuals and to make sense of the ways people differ. The science of assessment aspires to describe and provide a formal measurement of diverse individual behavior and experiences. By testing and classifying individuals who share similar traits, psychologists correlate—associate—behavioral differences with personality or with cognitive differences. In this way, they can test the ability of different theories of personality or different conceptions of intelligence to capture important aspects of individuals' life experiences.

The goals of formal assessment are not very different from your own concerns when you size up another person. You may want to know how smart, trustworthy, creative, responsible, or dangerous a new acquaintance is, and you may attempt to evaluate these qualities, using whatever evidence you can gather informally. Scientific psychology attempts to formalize the procedures by which *predictions* about individual behavior can be made accurately. Assessment begins with the measurement of a limited number of individual attributes and samples of behavior. From this narrow body of information about a person in a testing situation—which can be collected conveniently and inexpensively—predictions are made about his or her likely future performance in real-life situations. Ideally, we'd like to predict a lot about a person from only the little information we gather on a psychological test.

The gathering of information through formal assessment techniques allows a psychologist to make predictions about behaviors in real-life situations.

When questions arise about an individual's behavioral or mental functioning, the person is referred to a psychologist who is trained to make an assessment that might provide some answers. For example, a judge may want to know if a confessed murderer is capable of understanding the consequences of his or her actions, or a teacher may want to know why a child has difficulty learning. A mental health worker may want to know the extent to which a patient's problems result from psychological disorders or from physical, organic disorders. When the psychologist's judgment may have a profound impact on a person's life, a *complete* assessment must involve more than just psychological testing. Test results may be very helpful, but they should be interpreted in light of *all* available information about a person, including medical history, family life, previous difficulties, or noteworthy achievements (Matarazzo, 1990).

While a clinical psychologist uses testing to make predictions about a *particular* client, research psychologists often try to discover the regularities in personality that translate in *general* to behavior patterns or life events. For example, as we saw in Chapter 13, research psychologists might devise tests that identify people whose behavioral patterns put them at particular risk for disease.

METHODS OF ASSESSMENT

The way people differ in their abilities, personality, and behavior has long been of interest to philosophers, theologians, dramatists, and novelists. It is psychologists, however, who have taken as their special province the objective *measurement* of these differences. **Psychometrics** is the measurement of psychological functioning. This field achieves its objectives with statistical analysis and test construction, as well as through an understanding of psychological processes.

Some assessment devices are derived from particular *theoretical* perspectives (Burisch, 1984). For example, a psychologist with a psychodynamic approach might develop a test that assesses the use of ego defense mechanisms. This researcher might develop a series of questions that are directly relevant to each of the theoretically defined mechanisms. Other assessment devices seek to make accurate predictions without a formal theoretical framework. For example, students might be asked to indicate their views on a series of psychology issues. If it was found that depressed individuals consistently differed from happy individuals in their patterns of responses, then the survey could be used as one test for depression—even without offering any theory about why the two groups differ. This is an *empirical* approach to constructing a test. As we will see in this chapter, test makers often combine theoretical and empirical approaches in creating an appropriate test.

An assessment device may be derived from a specific theoretical perspective, but in the absence of a theory, the empirical approach is used to develop a test.

In this section, we will first consider some of the characteristics that make assessments *formal.* We will then examine some of the techniques and sources of information psychologists use to make these assessments.

Basic Features of Formal Assessment

To be useful for classifying individuals or for selecting those with particular qualities, a **formal assessment** procedure should meet three requirements. The assessment instrument should be (1) *reliable,* (2) *valid,* and (3) *standardized.* If it fails to meet these requirements, we cannot be sure whether the conclusions of the assessment can be trusted.

In order for a test to be useful, it must be reliable, valid, and standardized.

Reliability

Reliability is the extent to which an assessment instrument can be trusted to give consistent scores. If you stepped on your bathroom scale three times in the same morning and it gave you a different reading each time, the scale would not be doing its job. You would call it *unreliable* because you could not count on it to give consistent results. Of course, if you ate a big meal in between two weighings, you wouldn't expect the scale to produce the same result. That is, a measurement device can be considered reliable or unreliable only to the extent that the underlying concept it is measuring should remain unchanged.

One straightforward way to find out if a test is reliable is to calculate its **test-retest reliability**—a measure of the correlation between the scores of the same people, on the same test, given on two different occasions. A perfectly reliable test will yield a correlation coefficient of +1.00. This means that the identical pattern of scores emerges both times. The same people who got the highest and lowest scores the first time do so again. A totally unreliable test results in a 0.00 correlation coefficient. That means there is no relationship between the first set of scores and the second set. Someone who initially got the top score gets a completely different score the second time. As the correlation coefficient moves higher (toward the ideal of +1.00), the test is increasingly reliable.

Test reliability may be established by using the test-retest method, the alternate or parallel forms method, or the split-half method to assess internal consistency.

There are two other ways to assess reliability. One is to administer alternate, **parallel forms** of a test instead of giving the same test twice. Using parallel forms reduces the effects of direct practice of the test questions, memory of the test questions, and the desire of an individual to appear consistent from one test to the next. Reliable tests yield comparable scores on parallel forms of the test. The other measure of reliability is the **internal consistency** of responses on a single test. For example, we can compare a person's score on the odd-numbered items of a test with the score on the even-numbered items. A reliable test yields the same score for each of its halves. It is then said to have high internal consistency on this measure of **split-half reliability**.

The wrong way to measure split-half reliability.

In most circumstances, not only should the measurement device itself be reliable but so should the method for using the device. Suppose researchers wished to observe children in a classroom in order to assess different levels of aggressive play. The researchers might develop a *coding scheme* that would allow them to make appropriate distinctions. The scheme would be reliable to the extent that all the people who viewed the same behavior would give highly similar ratings to the same children. This is one of the reasons that quite a bit of training is required before individuals can carry out accurate psychological assessment. They must learn to apply systems of distinctions in a reliable fashion.

Validity

The **validity** of a test is the degree to which it measures what an assessor intends it to measure. A valid test of intelligence measures that trait and predicts performance in situations where intelligence is important. Scores on a valid measure of creativity reflect actual creativity, not drawing ability or moods. In general, then, validity reflects a test's ability to make accurate predictions about behaviors or outcomes related to the purpose or design of the test. Three important types of validity are *face validity, criterion validity*, and *construct validity*.

The first type of validity is based on the surface *content* of a test. When test items appear to be directly related to the attribute of interest, the test has **face validity.** Face-valid tests are very straightforward—they simply ask what the test maker needs to know: How anxious do you feel? Are you creative? The person taking the test is expected to answer accurately and honestly. Unfortunately, face validity is often not sufficient to ensure accurate measurement. First, people's perceptions of themselves may not be accurate, or they may not know how they should rate themselves in comparison to other people. We saw in Chapter 13, for example, that people in bad moods rate their symptoms of illness as more severe. Thus an assessment device that simply asked, "How bad are your symptoms?" would not necessarily yield objective data. Second, a test that too obviously measures some attribute may allow test takers to manipulate the impression they make. Consider the case of institutionalized mental patients who did *not* want to be released from their familiar, structured environment.

A test is said to have face validity if the surface content of the test is judged to be related to the attribute the test is designed to measure.

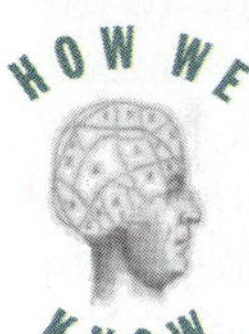

These long-term schizophrenic patients were interviewed by the staff about how disturbed they were. When they were given a *transfer* interview to assess if they were well enough to be moved to an open ward, these patients gave generally positive self-references. However, when the purpose of the interview was to assess their suitability for *discharge,* the patients gave more negative self-references, because they did not want to be discharged. Psychiatrists who rated the interview data, without awareness of this experimental variation in the purpose of the interview, judged those who gave more negative self-references as more severely disturbed and recommended against their discharge. So the patients achieved the assessment outcome they wanted. The psychiatrists' assessment may also have been influenced by their perspective that anyone who wanted to stay in a mental hospital must be very disturbed (Braginsky & Braginsky, 1967).

This example makes it particularly clear that test givers cannot rely only on measures that have face validity. Let's consider other types of validity that overcome some of these limitations.

To assess the **criterion validity** (also known as **predictive validity**) of a test, we compare a person's score on the test with his or her score on some other standard, or criterion, associated with what the test measures. For example, if a test is designed to predict success in college, then college grades would be an appropriate criterion. If the test scores correlate highly with college grades, then the test has criterion validity. A major task of test developers is to find appropriate, measurable criteria. Once criterion validity has been demonstrated for an assessment device, researchers feel confident using the device to make future predictions. This is the logic college admissions officers use when they ask you for things like SAT scores. In the past, SAT scores have been shown to correlate positively with some aspects of college performance. On that basis, administrators use them to make predictions about your college career.

Criterion validity, or predictive validity, is judged by comparing the test scores with some other standard or criterion theoretically associated with what the test measures.

How would you feel if someone used your adult height to assess intelligence? The measure would be reliable, but would it be valid?

Construct validity is established during the construction of the test, as evidence is gathered about the basic construct that the test is designed to measure.

For many personal qualities of interest to psychologists, no ideal criterion exists. No single behavior or objective measure of performance can tell us, for example, how anxious, depressed, or aggressive a person is overall. Psychologists have theories, or *constructs,* about these abstract qualities—what affects them, the way they show up in behavior, and the way they relate to other variables. The **construct validity** of a particular test is the degree to which it correlates positively with other valid measures of the construct (Loevinger, 1957). Construct validity is not a quantitative or static measure of validity. Instead, it is a *subjective* evaluation of the appropriateness of the body of available evidence for measuring a given construct.

The conditions under which a test is valid may be very specific, so it is always important to ask about a test, "For what purpose is it valid?" Knowing which other measures a test does and does not correlate with may reveal something new about the measures, the construct, or the complexity of human behavior. For example, suppose you design a test to measure the ability of medical students to cope with stress. You then find that scores on that test correlate well with students' ability to cope with classroom stress. You presume your test will also correlate with students' ability to deal with stressful hospital emergencies, but you discover it does not. Since you have demonstrated some validity, you have learned something both about your test—the circumstances in which it is valid—and about your construct—different categories of stressors have different consequences. You would then modify your test to take account of the kinds of special stressors found in hospital emergencies.

Consider for a moment the relationship between validity and reliability. While reliability is measured by the degree to which a test correlates with itself (administered at different times or using different items), validity is measured by the degree to which the test correlates with something external to it (another test, a behavioral criterion, or judges' ratings). Usually a test that is not reliable is also not valid, because a test that cannot predict itself will be unable to predict anything else. For example, if your class took a test of aggressiveness today and scores were uncorrelated with scores from a parallel form of the test tomorrow (demonstrating unreliability), it is unlikely that the scores from either day would predict which students had fought or argued most frequently over a week's time: after all, the two sets of test

In general, a test that is not reliable is also not valid. On the other hand, it is possible for a test to be highly reliable but not valid.

scores would not even make the same prediction! On the other hand, it is quite possible for a test to be highly reliable without being valid. Suppose, for example, we decided to use your adult height as a measure of intelligence. Do you see why that would be reliable but not valid?

Norms and Standardization

So we have a reliable and valid test, but we still need *norms* to provide a context for different test scores. Suppose, for example, you get a score of 18 on a test designed to reveal how depressed you are. What does that mean? Are you a little depressed, not at all depressed, or about averagely depressed? To find out what your score means, you would want to compare your individual score with typical scores, or statistical **norms**, of other students. You would check the test norms to see what the usual range of scores is and what the average is for students of your age and sex. That would provide you with a context for interpreting your depression score.

You probably encountered test norms when you received your scores on aptitude tests, such as the SAT. The norms told you how your scores compared with those of other students and helped you interpret how well you had done relative to that *normative population.* Group norms are most useful for interpreting individual scores when the comparison group shares important qualities with the individuals tested, such as age, social class, culture, and experience.

Test norms let you compare your scores with those of others and give you an idea of your performance relative to the normative population. However, for norms to be meaningful, tests must be standardized.

For norms to be meaningful, everyone must take the same test under standardized circumstances. **Standardization** is the administration of a testing device to all persons, in the same way, under the same conditions. The need for standardization sounds obvious, but it does not always occur in practice. Some people may be allowed more time than others, be given clearer or more detailed instructions, be permitted to ask questions, or be motivated by a tester to perform better. Consider the experience of one of your authors:

> As a graduate student at Yale, I administered a scale to assess children's degree of test anxiety in grade-school classes. Before starting, one teacher told her class, "We're going to have some fun with this new kind of question game this nice man will play with you." A teacher in another classroom prepared her class for the same assessment by cautioning, "This psychologist from Yale University is going to give you a test to see what you are thinking; I hope you will do well and show how good our class is!" (Zimbardo, personal communication, 1958)

Could you directly compare the scores of the children in these two classes on this "same" test? The answer is no, because the test was not administered in a standardized way. In this case, the children in the second class scored higher on test anxiety. (You're probably not surprised!) When procedures do not include explicit instructions about the way to administer the test or the way to score the results, it is difficult to interpret what a given test score means or how it relates to any comparison group.

We have now reviewed some of the concerns researchers have when they construct a test and find out whether it is indeed testing what they wish to test. They must assure themselves that the test is reliable and valid. They must also specify the standard conditions under which it should be administered, so that resulting norms have meaning. Therefore, you should evaluate any test score you get in terms of the test's reliability and validity, the norms of performance, and the degree of standardization of the circumstances in which you took the test.

We move now to the wider context of psychological assessment by considering what sources of information psychologists use to make their judgments.

Sources of Information

Psychological assessment methods can be organized according to four techniques used to gather information about a person: interviews, life history or archival data, tests, and situational observations. They can also be classified according to the person who is supplying the information: the person being assessed or other people reporting on the person being assessed. When the person being assessed is providing the information, the methods are called *self-reports;* when others are supplying the data, the methods are called *observer reports*. Which technique we use and who we ask to supply information depend on the nature of data we need and the purpose of the assessment. Let's review these various methodologies.

Assessment Techniques

An **interview** is a direct approach to learning about someone. You just ask the person what you want to know. The interview content and style may be casual and unstructured, tailored to fit the person being interviewed. On the other hand, interviews may be highly structured or standardized, asking very specific questions in a very specific way. Counselors find unstructured interviews useful for individualized treatment programs. Structured interviews are preferred for job interviews and psychological research, when it is important that many people be assessed accurately, completely, consistently, and without bias.

A skilled interviewer can direct the conversation to elicit desired information while keeping the respondent at ease and maintaining rapport.

A well-trained interviewer must have five important skills: the ability to put the respondent at ease, elicit the desired information, maintain control of the direction and pace of the interview, establish and maintain feelings of rapport (harmony) between interviewer and respondent, and, finally, bring the interview to a satisfactory conclusion.

Interview data may be supplemented with **life history** or **archival data,** information about a person's life taken from different types of available records, especially those of different time periods and in relation to other people. These records may include school or military performances, written work (stories and drawings), personal journals, medical data, photographs, and videotapes.

A **psychological test** can measure virtually any aspect of human functioning, including intelligence, personality, or creativity. A major advantage of tests over interviews is that they provide *quantitative* characterizations of an individual in the form of numerical scores. They then allow for objective comparisons between individuals. They are also less open to personal biases of an interviewer.

Tests are economical, easy to use, and provide important normative data in quantitative form, but they are not always useful for measuring behavior—finding out what a person actually *does*—especially when a person cannot objectively judge or report his or her own behavior. Psychologists use **situational behavior observations** to assess behavior objectively in laboratory or real-life settings. An observer watches an individual's behavioral patterns in one or more situations, such as at home, at work, or in school. The goal of these observations is to discover the determinants and consequences of various responses and habits of the individual. The value of such measures of what a person actually does is weighed against the time and effort required to carry them out in an objective fashion.

We now discuss the self and others as sources of information.

Self-report Methods

Self-report methods require respondents to answer questions or give information about themselves. This information may be gathered from an interview, a test, or a personal journal. One very easily administered self-report is the *inventory,* a standardized, written test with a multiple-choice, true-false, or rating format. An inventory might inquire about your personality, your health, or your life experiences. For example, you might be asked how frequently you have headaches, how assertive you think you are, or how stressful you find your job to be. Such measures are valuable because they tap into an individual's personal experiences and feelings. They are convenient because they do not require trained interviewers, and they are generally easy to score.

The greatest disadvantage of self-report methods is that sometimes people really don't know their own feelings or can't objectively report their own behavior.

The greatest shortcoming of self-report measures is that sometimes people are not really in touch with their feelings or can't objectively report their own behavior. However, depending on the purpose of the assessment, sometimes a person's subjective experience is actually of more interest to the tester than the objective reality. For example, your own *perceptions* of competence may be more important than your actual skills in determining whether you enter a challenging and exciting career (Bordura, 1986).

Observer-report Methods

In psychological assessment, **observer-report methods** involve a systematic evaluation, by another person, of some aspect of a person's behavior. Observer reports may consist of very specific situational behavior observations or more generalized ratings. For example, teacher's aides may observe a preschool class and record the number of times each child performs particular behaviors, such as shoving, hitting, or sharing a toy, during a particular observation period. Alternatively, teachers, parents, and anyone else who knows them well might be asked to rate the children on the way they play with others and on how shy they are around strangers.

While situational behavior observations are typically made *moment-by-moment,* at the time the behavior is performed, ratings are typically made *after* an observation period. Sometimes judges are asked first to record specific behaviors and then to make overall ratings based on them. Often ratings are made according to detailed guidelines provided by the developers of an assessment technique. At other times, the guidelines are less precise, allowing spontaneous reactions and informal impressions to play a greater role.

Although observer-report methods are relatively free of subjects' own biases, they are subject to inaccuracies due to prior expectations or prejudices held by the observer.

In sports competitions such as the Olympics, subjective judgments of an athlete's performance can result in widely divergent scores from different officials.

What drawbacks could result from such ratings? One is that ratings may tell more about the judge, or about the judge's relationship with the person, than about the true characteristics of the person being rated. For example, if you like someone, you may tend to judge him or her favorably on nearly every dimension. This type of *rating bias*—in which an overall feeling about the person is extended to the specific dimensions being evaluated—is referred to as the **halo effect**. A different type of bias occurs when a rater thinks most people in a certain category (for example, Republicans, Arabs, anti-abortion protesters, unwed mothers) have certain qualities. The rater may "see" those qualities in any individual who happens to be in that category. This type of bias is called a **stereotype effect.** You may have seen this bias at work if you have watched Olympic figure skating judges rate athletes from their own countries much more highly than did the other judges.

We noted earlier that researchers often develop precise coding schemes, and give extensive training, to help overcome such biases. Rating items are phrased in ways that do not carry subjective connotations, such as "keeps to him/herself" in place of "withdrawn"; specific rules are provided for each rating level, such as "If the person does X, give a rating of 10." Often studies use several raters so that the bias introduced by each judge's unique point of view is canceled out by the other judges' responses. With more than one observer, researchers can calculate the **interjudge reliability,**—the degree to which the different observers make similar ratings or agree about what each subject did during an observation period. We can be most confident in observational assessments when interjudge reliability is high.

The use of several judges in situational observations and the calculation of interjudge reliability helps to control bias.

We are now ready to turn to specific domains in which assessments are routinely made: intelligence and creativity, personality, and vocational aptitude. We begin with a domain that has often provoked controversy: the measurement of intelligence.

INTELLIGENCE AND INTELLIGENCE ASSESSMENT

How intelligent are you or your friends? To answer this question, you must begin by defining **intelligence.** Doing so is not an easy task. Scientists have yet to agree on a single definition, but most would include in their measure of intelligence at least three types of skills: (1) adapting to new situations and changing task demands; (2) learning or profiting optimally from experience or training; and (3) thinking abstractly using symbols and concepts (Phares,

1984). Intelligence enables people to respond flexibly and imaginatively to environmental challenges.

The way in which theorists conceptualize intelligence and higher mental functioning greatly influences the way they try to assess it (Sternberg, 1994). Some psychologists believe that human intelligence can be quantified and reduced to a single score. Others argue that intelligence has many components that should be separately assessed. Still others say that there are actually several distinct kinds of intelligence, across different domains of experience. In this section, we will describe how tests of intelligence mesh with these different conceptions of intelligence. We will also describe some of the controversy surrounding the use and misuse of intelligence testing. You should try to distinguish for yourself the circumstances in which intelligence testing is beneficial or harmful. Let's begin by considering the historical context in which interest in intelligence and intelligence testing first arose.

The Origins of Intelligence Testing

Alfred Binet developed the first intelligence test in order to classify and separate developmentally disabled from normally functioning schoolchildren.

The year 1905 marked the first published account of a workable intelligence test. **Alfred Binet** had responded to the call of the French minister of public instruction for the creation of more effective teaching methods for developmentally disabled children. Binet and his colleague Theophile Simon believed that measuring a child's intellectual ability was necessary for planning an instructional program. Binet attempted to devise an objective test of intellectual performance that could be used to classify and separate developmentally disabled from normal schoolchildren. He hoped that such a test would reduce the school's reliance on the more subjective, and perhaps biased, evaluations of teachers.

To *quantify*—measure—intellectual performance, Binet designed age-appropriate problems or test items on which many children's responses could be compared. The problems on the test were chosen so that they could be scored objectively as correct or incorrect, could vary in content, were not heavily influenced by differences in children's environments, and assessed judgment and reasoning rather than rote memory (Binet, 1911).

Children of various ages were tested, and the average score for normal children at each age was computed. Then each individual child's performance was compared with the average for other children of his or her age. Test results were expressed in terms of the average age at which normal children achieved a particular score. This measure was called the **mental age** (MA). For instance, when a child's score equaled the average score of a group of 5-year-olds, the child was said to have a *mental age* of 5, regardless of his or her actual **chronological age** (CA), years since birth.

Binet interpreted scores on his test as measures of current performance and not measures of innate intelligence.

There are four important features of Binet's approach. First, he interpreted scores on his test as an estimate of *current performance*, and not as a measure of *innate intelligence*. Second, he wanted the test scores to be used to identify children who needed special help and not to *stigmatize* them. Third, he emphasized that training and opportunity could affect intelligence, and he sought to identify areas of performance in which special education could help disadvantaged children. Finally, he constructed his test empirically—he collected data to see if it was valid—rather than tie it to a particular theory of intelligence.

Binet's successful development of an intelligence test had great impact in the United States. A unique combination of historical events and social-political forces had prepared the United States for an explosion of interest in assessing mental ability. At the beginning of the twentieth century, the United States was a nation in turmoil. As a result of global economic, social, and political conditions, millions of immigrants entered the country. New universal education laws flooded schools with students. Some form of assessment was needed to identify, document, and classify immigrant adults and schoolchildren (Chapman, 1988). When World War I began, millions of volunteers marched into recruiting stations. Recruiters needed to determine who of the many people who had been drafted had the ability to learn quickly and benefit from special leadership training. New nonverbal, group-administered tests of mental ability were used to evaluate over 1.7 million recruits. A group of prominent psychologists, including Lewis Terman, Edward Thorndike, and Robert Yerkes, designed these tests in only one month's time (Lennon, 1985).

In the early decades of the twentieth century, interest in psychological assessment in the United States was boosted by the need to evaluate immigrants and soldiers.

One consequence of this large-scale testing program was that the American public came to accept the idea that intelligence tests could differentiate people in terms of leadership ability and other socially important characteristics. This acceptance led to the widespread use of tests in schools and industry. Assessment was seen as a way to inject order into a chaotic society and as an inexpensive, democratic way to separate those who could benefit from education or military leadership training from those who could not. Starting at this time, "Intelligence test results were used not only to differentiate [among] children experiencing academic problems, but also as a measuring stick to organize an entire society" (Hale, 1983, p. 373). To facilitate the wide-scale use of intelligence testing, researchers strove for more broadly applicable testing procedures.

IQ Tests

Although Binet began the standardized assessment of intellectual ability in France, U.S. psychologists soon took the lead. They also developed the IQ, or intelligence quotient. The IQ was a numerical, standardized measure of intelligence. Two families of individually administered IQ tests are used widely today: the Stanford-Binet scales and the Wechsler scales.

The Stanford-Binet Intelligence Scale

Stanford University's **Lewis Terman,** a former public school administrator, appreciated the importance of Binet's method for assessing intelligence. He adapted Binet's test questions for U.S. schoolchildren, he standardized the administration of the test, and he developed age-level norms by giving the test to thousands of children. In 1916 he published the Stanford Revision of the Binet Tests, commonly referred to as the *Stanford-Binet Intelligence Scale* (Terman, 1916).

Lewis Terman adapted Binet's test, publishing the revision as the Stanford-Binet Intelligence Scale, which provided a measure of intelligence quotient, or IQ.

With his new test, Terman provided a base for the concept of the **intelligence quotient,** or **IQ** (a term coined by Stern, 1914). The IQ was the ratio of mental age (MA) to chronological age (CA) multiplied by 100 to eliminate decimals:

$$IQ = MA \div CA \times 100$$

A child with a CA of 8 whose test scores revealed an MA of 10 had an IQ of 125 ($10 \div 8 \times 100 = 125$), while a child of that same chronological age who performed at the level of a 6-year-old had an IQ of 75 ($6 \div 8 \times 100 = 75$). Individuals who performed at the mental age equivalent to their chronological age had IQs of 100. Thus the score of 100 was considered to be the average IQ.

The new Stanford-Binet test soon became a standard instrument in clinical psychology, psychiatry, and educational counseling. The Stanford-Binet contains a series of subtests, each tailored for a particular mental age. A series of minor revisions were made on these subtests in 1937, 1960, and 1972, to achieve three goals: (1) to extend the range of the test to measure the IQ of very young children and very intelligent adults; (2) to update vocabulary items that had changed in difficulty with changes in society; and

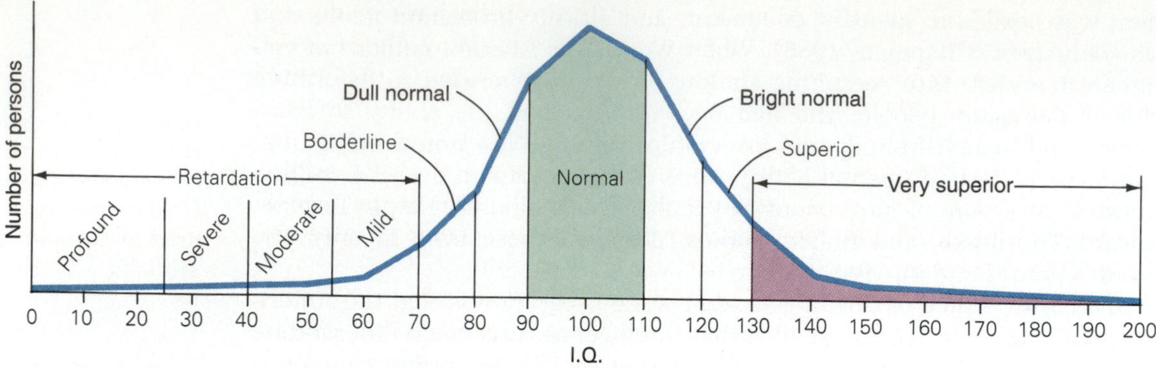

Figure 15.1 Distribution of IQ Scores Among a Large Sample

Figure 15.2

A psychologist administers an intelligence test to a 4-year-old child. The performance part of the test includes a block design task, an object completion task, and a shape identification task.

(3) to update the norms, or age-appropriate average scores (Terman & Merrill, 1937, 1960, 1972). The most recent, fourth edition of the Stanford-Binet test (Thorndike et al., 1986) furthers the goal of improving the test's validity. This newest Stanford-Binet provides accurate IQ estimates for individuals in the normal range of performance as well as for those individuals who are either mentally impaired or mentally gifted (Laurent et al., 1992).

Note that IQ scores are no longer derived by dividing mental age by chronological age. If you took the test today, your score would be added up and directly compared with the scores of other people your age. An IQ of 100 would indicate that 50 percent of those your age had earned lower scores. Scores between 90 and 110 are now labeled "normal," above 120 are "superior," and below 70 are evidence of "developmental disability" (see **Figure 15.1**).

The Wechsler Intelligence Scales

David Wechsler of Bellevue Hospital in New York set out to correct the dependence on verbal items in the assessment of adult intelligence. In 1939, he published the Wechsler-Bellevue Intelligence Scale, which combined verbal subtests with nonverbal, or performance, subtests. Thus, in addition to an overall IQ score, subjects were given separate estimates of verbal IQ and nonverbal IQ. After a few changes, the test was retitled the *Wechsler Adult Intelligence Scale*—the WAIS in 1955, and the revised WAIS-R today (Wechsler, 1981).

There are six *verbal* subtests of the WAIS-R: Information, Vocabulary, Comprehension, Arithmetic, Similarities (stating how two things are alike), and Digit Span (repeating a series of digits after the examiner). These tests are both written and oral. The five *performance* subtests involve manipulation of materials and have little or no verbal content. In the Block Design test, for example, a subject tries to reproduce designs shown on cards by fitting together blocks with colored sides. The Digit Symbol test provides a key that matches 9 symbols to 9 numeric digits, and the task is to write the appropriate digits under the symbols on another page. Other performance tests include Picture Arrangement, Picture Completion, and Object Assembly. If you were to take the WAIS-R, you would perform all 11 subtests, and receive 3 scores: a Verbal IQ, a Performance IQ, and an overall, or Full Scale, IQ.

The WAIS-R is designed for people 18 years and older, but similar tests have been developed for children (see **Figure 15.2**). The *Wechsler Intelligence Scale for Children—Third Edition* (WISC-III; Wechsler, 1991) is suited for children ages 6 to 17, and the *Wechsler Preschool and Primary Scale of Intelligence—Revised* (WPPSI-R; Wechsler, 1989) for children ages 4 to 6 1/2 years. The recent revisions of both of these tests have made the materials more colorful, more contemporary, and more enjoyable for children. Both tests have proven to be reliable and valid measures (Little, 1992; Sattler & Atkinson, 1993).

The WAIS-R, the WISC-III, and the WPPSI-R form a family of intelligence tests that yield a Verbal IQ, a Performance IQ, and a Full Scale IQ at all age levels. In addition, they provide comparable subtest scores that allow researchers to track the development over time of more specific intellectual abilities. For this reason, the Wechsler scales are particularly valuable when the same individual is to be tested at different ages—for example, when a child's progress in response to different educational programs is monitored.

The family of Wechsler scales provides comparable scores that allow researchers to track the development of specific abilities across different age levels.

THEORIES OF INTELLIGENCE

We have seen so far some of the ways in which intelligence has been measured. You are now in a position to ask yourself: Do these tests capture everything that is meant by the word *intelligence?* Do these tests capture all abilities you believe constitute your own intelligence? To help you to think about those questions, we now review theories of intelligence. As you read about each theory, ask yourself whether its proponents would be comfortable using IQ as a measure of intelligence.

Psychometric Theories of Intelligence

Psychometric theories of intelligence originated in much the same philosophical atmosphere that gave rise to IQ tests. *Psychometrics,* as we explained earlier, is the field of psychology that specializes in mental testing in any of its facets, including personality assessment, intelligence evaluation, and aptitude measurement. Thus psychometric approaches are intimately related to methods of testing. These theories examine the *statistical relationships* between different measures of ability, such as the 11 subtests of the WAIS-R, and then make inferences about the nature of human intelligence on the basis of those relationships. The technique used most frequently is called *factor analysis,* a statistical procedure that detects a smaller number of dimensions, clusters, or factors within a larger set of independent variables. The goal of factor analysis is to identify the basic psychological dimensions of the concept being investigated. Of course, a statistical procedure only identifies *statistical* regularities; it is up to psychologists to suggest and defend interpretations of those regularities.

Using strategies such as factor analysis, psychometric theories examine the statistical relationships among different measures of intelligence.

Charles Spearman carried out an early and influential application of factor analysis in the domain of intelligence. Spearman discovered that the performance of individuals on each of a variety of intelligence tests was highly correlated. From this pattern he concluded that there is a factor of *general intelligence,* or **g**, underlying all intelligent performance (Spearman, 1927). Each individual domain also has associated with it specific skills that Spearman called **s**. For example, a person's performance on tests of vocabulary or arithmetic depends both on his or her general intelligence and on domain-specific abilities.

Charles Spearman believed that intelligence consists of a general underlying ability called g *and a domain of specific abilities he labeled* s.

Raymond Cattell (1963), using more advanced factor analytic techniques, determined that general intelligence can be broken down into two relatively independent components, which he called crystallized and fluid intelligence. **Crystallized intelligence** involves the knowledge a person has already acquired and the ability to access that knowledge; it is measured by tests of vocabulary, arithmetic, and general information. **Fluid intelligence** is the ability to see complex relationships and solve problems; it is measured by tests of block designs and spatial visualization in which the background information needed to solve a problem is included or readily apparent. Crys-

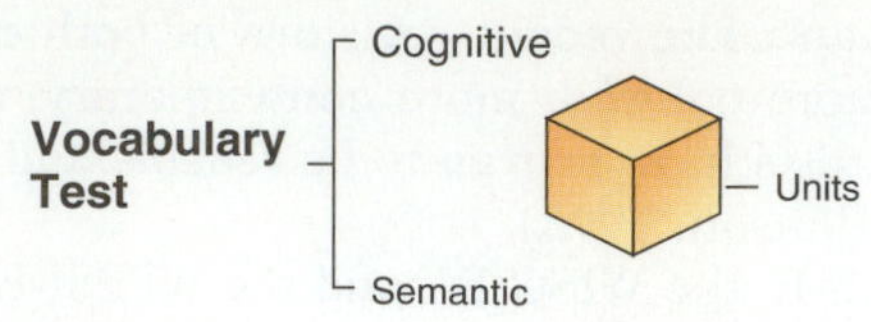

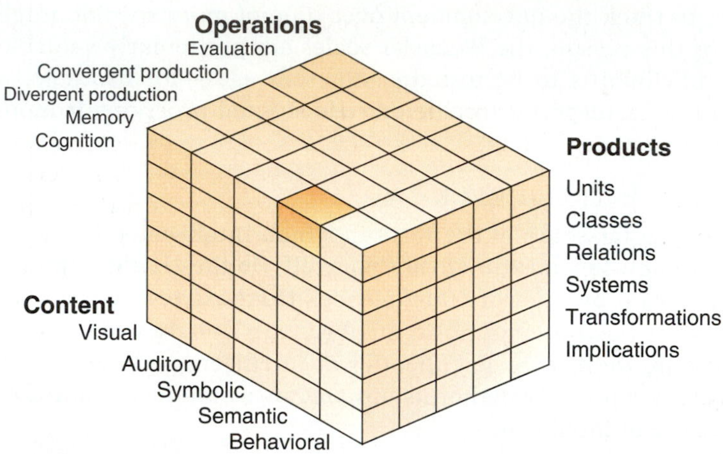

Figure 15.3 The Structure of Intellect

Raymond Cattell's factor analytic techniques derived fluid and crystallized intelligence.

tallized intelligence allows you to cope well with your life's recurring, concrete challenges; fluid intelligence helps you attack novel, abstract problems.

J. P. Guilford (1961) used factor analysis to examine the demands of many intelligence-related tasks. His *structure of intellect* model specifies three features of intellectual tasks: the *content,* or type of information; the *product,* or form in which information is represented; and the *operation,* or type of mental activity performed.

J. P. Guilford developed a model of intelligence featuring various combinations of three components: content, product, and operation.

As shown in **Figure 15.3**, there are five kinds of content in this model—visual, auditory, symbolic, semantic, and behavioral; six kinds of products—units, classes, relations, systems, transformations, and implications; and five kinds of operations—evaluation, convergent production, divergent production, memory, and cognition. Each task performed by the intellect can be identified according to the particular types of content, products, and operations involved. Further, Guilford believes that each content-product-operation combination (each small cube in the model) represents a distinct mental ability. For example, as Figure 15.3 shows, a test of vocabulary would assess your ability for *cognition* of *units* with *semantic content.* Learning a dance routine, on the other hand, requires *memory* for *behavioral systems.*

This theoretical model is analogous to a chemist's periodic table of elements. By means of such a systematic framework, intellectual factors, like chemical elements, may be postulated before they are discovered. In 1961, when Guilford proposed his model, nearly 40 intellectual abilities had been identified. Researchers have since accounted for over 100, which shows the predictive value of Guilford's conception of intelligence (Guilford, 1985).

Since Guilford, many psychologists have broadened their conceptions of intelligence to include much more than performance on traditional IQ tests. We now examine three types of theories that go beyond IQ.

Hunt's Problem-Solving Intelligence

One great difficulty with IQ tests is that they only tell you who performs well and who does not: they don't tell you enough about what actual mental processes lead to different performance. **Earl Hunt** (1983, 1995) proposes that the interesting individual differences in people's intelligence are not to be found in test scores but in the way different individuals go about solving a problem. He identifies three ways cognitive processes may differ in individuals:

- *choices* about the way to internally (mentally) represent a problem;
- *strategies* for manipulating mental representations;
- *abilities* necessary to execute whatever basic information-processing steps a strategy requires.

Earl Hunt identified three ways in which cognitive processes differ in individuals: choices, strategies, and abilities.

Using Hunt's model, researchers can design special tasks that allow them to observe individual differences in the way people represent problems (using images or verbalization, for example), the strategies they choose, and the efficiency with which they perform different cognitive tasks. This approach encourages scientists to see the flexibility and adaptiveness of human thinking, rather than its fixed or static IQ-limited functions. It also promotes a different view of classification and selection. Instead of categorizing people by their IQ level, this view supports *diagnostic assessment,* with the goal of making the best use of each person's cognitive abilities and skills (Hunt, 1984).

Sternberg's Triarchic Theory of Intelligence

Robert Sternberg (1985, 1988) also stresses the importance of cognitive processes in problem solving as part of his more general theory of intelligence. Sternberg outlines a *triarchic*—three-part—theory. His three types of intelligence all represent different ways of characterizing effective performance.

Componential intelligence is defined by the *components,* or mental processes, that underlie thinking and problem solving. Sternberg identifies three types of components that are central to information processing: (1) knowledge acquisition components, for learning new facts; (2) performance components, for problem-solving strategies and techniques; and (3) metacognitive components, for selecting strategies and monitoring progress toward success. By breaking down various tasks into their components, investigations can pinpoint the processes that differentiate the performance outcomes of individuals with different IQs. For example, researchers might discover that the metacognitive components of high-IQ students prompt them to select different strategies, to solve a particular type of problem, than do their lower IQ peers. The difference in strategy selection accounts for the high-IQ students' greater problem-solving success.

Experiential intelligence captures people's ability to deal with two extremes: novel versus very routine problems. Suppose, for example, a group of individuals found themselves stranded after an accident. You would credit with intelligence the person in the group who could most quickly help the group find its way home. In other circumstances, you would recognize as intelligent the behavior of someone who was able to perform routine tasks automatically. If, for example, a group of people carried out the same tasks day after day, you would be most impressed by the individual who could complete the tasks successfully with the least amount of "new" thought.

Contextual intelligence is reflected in the practical management of day-to-day affairs. It involves your ability to *adapt* to new and different contexts, *select* appropriate contexts, and effectively *shape* your environment to suit your needs. Contextual intelligence is what people sometimes call *street smarts* or *business sense.* Research has shown that people can have high contextual intelligence without having high IQs.

To what extent does the ability to handicap races correlate with intelligence as it is traditionally measured?

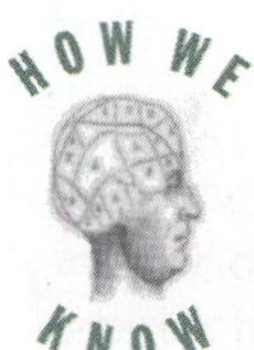

Researchers approached "regulars" at a racetrack to assess the relationship between IQ and success at handicapping horse races. A group of 30 men was divided into experts and nonexperts, based on their performance at predicting which horses would have the best odds at race time. Although the two groups both had average IQs right around 100, and there was almost no correlation between IQ and expertise, experts correctly chose the top horse 93 percent of the time, versus 33 percent for nonexperts. The researchers went on to show that the experts were making their quite accurate judgments in a way that mimicked complex statistical procedures (Ceci & Liker, 1986).

Robert Sternberg outlined a triarchic theory of intelligence that defines three types of abilities: componential, experiential, and contextual.

Because each horse presents a new combination of variables along a variety of dimensions (lifetime speed, lifetime earnings, track conditions, jockey ability, and several others), the experts' success can't be attributed just to repetition of familiar situations. Rather, they had developed impressive abilities specifically suited to their environment.

Sternberg's theory recognizes that IQ tests do not capture the full range of intelligent behavior and attempts to do more than label individuals as high or low IQ. Suppose researchers learn, for example, that "unintelligent" people have difficulty with a certain task because they fail to encode all the relevant information. These people can be made to perform in an "intelligent" fashion if they practice that particular component. Thus componential intelligence can be enhanced. Sternberg believes, similarly, that people can improve experiential and contextual intelligence (Sternberg, 1986). With an appropriate understanding of the component processes that underlie behavior, researchers should be able to devise techniques to make everyone's performance "look intelligent."

Gardner's Multiple Intelligences

Howard Gardner (1983, 1993b) has also proposed a theory that expands the definition of intelligence beyond those skills covered on an IQ test. Gardner identifies numerous intelligences that cover a range of human experience. The value of any of the abilities differs across human societies, according to what is needed by, useful to, and prized by a given society. As shown in **Table 15.1**, Gardner identified seven intelligences.

Gardner argues that Western society promotes the first two intelligences, while non-Western societies often value others. For example, in the Caroline

Table 15.1 Gardner's Seven Intelligences

Intelligence	End-States	Core Components
Logical-mathematical	Scientist Mathematician	Sensitivity to, and capacity to discern, logical or numerical patterns; ability to handle long chains of reasoning.
Linguistic	Poet Journalist	Sensitivity to the sounds, rhythms, and meanings of words; sensitivity to the different functions of language.
Musical	Composer Violinist	Abilities to produce and appreciate rhythm, pitch, and timbre; appreciation of the forms of musical expressiveness.
Spatial	Navigator Sculptor	Capacities to perceive the visual-spatial world accurately and to perform transformations on one's initial perceptions.
Bodily-kinesthetic	Dancer Athlete	Abilities to control one's body movements and to handle objects skillfully.
Interpersonal	Therapist Salesperson	Capacities to discern and respond appropriately to the moods, temperaments, motivations, and desires of other people.
Intrapersonal	Person with detailed, accurate self-knowledge	Access to one's own feelings and the ability to discriminate among them and draw upon them to guide behavior; knowledge of one's own strengths, weaknesses, desires, and intelligences.

Island of Micronesia, sailors must be able to navigate long distances without maps, using only their spatial intelligence and bodily-kinesthetic intelligence. Such abilities count more in that society than the ability to write a term paper. In Bali, where artistic performance is part of everyday life, musical intelligence and talents involved in coordinating intricate dance steps are highly valued. Interpersonal intelligence is more central to collectivist societies, where cooperative action and communal life are emphasized, than it is in individualistic societies such as the United States (Triandis, 1990).

Howard Gardner identified seven intelligences and theorized that the value of any ability is culturally determined.

Assessing these kinds of intelligence demands more than paper-and-pencil tests and simple quantified measures. Gardner's theory of intelligence requires that the subject be observed and assessed in a variety of life situations as well as in the small slices of life depicted in traditional intelligence tests.

Our review of intelligence testing and theories of intelligence sets the stage for a provocative discussion of the societal circumstances that make the topic of intelligence so controversial.

The Politics of Intelligence

We have seen that contemporary conceptions of intelligence reject the narrow linking of a score on an IQ test with a person's intelligence. Even so, IQ tests remain the most frequent measure of "intelligence" in Western society. Because of the prevalence of IQ testing, and the availability of IQ scores, it becomes easy to compare different groups according to their "average" IQ. In the United States, such ethnic and racial group comparisons have often been used as evidence for the innate, genetic inferiority of members of minority groups. We will briefly examine the history of this practice of using IQ test scores to index the alleged mental inferiority of certain groups. Then we will look at current evidence on the nature and nurture of intelligence and IQ test performance. You will see that this is one of the most politically volatile issues in psychology because public policies about immigration quotas, educational resources, and more may be based on how group IQ data are interpreted.

In the United States, the ready availability of IQ data has resulted in group comparisons being used as evidence for the innate, genetic inferiority of certain minority groups.

The History of Group Comparisons

In the early 1900s, psychologist **Henry Goddard** advocated mental testing of all immigrants and the *selective exclusion* of those who were found to be

Differences in intelligence test scores led some psychologists to conclude that immigrants from southern and eastern Europe were genetically inferior to those from northern and western Europe. Although these differences in test scores disappeared within a few decades, the theory of racially inherited differences remained.

"mentally defective." Such views may have contributed to a hostile national climate against admission of certain immigrant groups (see Cronbach, 1975; McPherson, 1985; Sokal, 1987). Indeed, Congress passed the 1924 Immigration Restriction Act, which made it national policy to administer intelligence tests to immigrants as they arrived at Ellis Island in New York Harbor. Vast numbers of Jewish, Italian, and Russians, and immigrants of other nationalities were classified as "morons" on the basis of IQ tests. Some psychologists interpreted these statistical findings as evidence that immigrants from southern and eastern Europe were genetically inferior to those from the hardy northern and western European stock (see Ruch, 1937). However, these "inferior" groups were also least familiar with the dominant language and culture, embedded in the IQ tests, because they had immigrated most recently. (Within a few decades, these group differences completely disappeared from IQ tests, but the theory of racially inherited differences in intelligence persisted.)

In the early twentieth century, would-be immigrants to the United States were screened for intelligence as well as a variety of other characteristics.

Goddard (1917) and others then went beyond merely associating low IQ with hereditary racial and ethnic origins. They added moral worthlessness, mental deficiency, and immoral social behavior to the mix of negatives related to low IQ. Evidence for their view came from case studies of two infamous families: the **Juke Family** and the **Kallikak Family.** These families allegedly were traced for many generations to show that bad seeds planted in family genes inescapably yield defective human offspring.

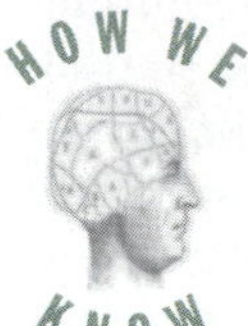

Over 2000 members of a New York state family with "Juke's blood" were reported to have been traced (by 1875), because the family had such a notorious record of developmental disability, delinquency, and crime. Of these family members, 458 were found to be developmentally disabled in their school performance, 171 classified as criminals, and hundreds of their kin were labeled as "paupers, intemperates, and harlots." The conclusion reached was that heredity was a dominant factor in the disreputable development of members of this unsavory family.

Goddard drew the same conclusion from his case study of the Kallikaks, a family with one "good seed" side and one "bad seed" side to its family tree. (In his study, Goddard renamed the family Kallikak, which means *good-bad* in Greek.) Martin Kallikak was a Revolutionary War soldier who had an illegitimate son with a woman described as developmentally disabled. Their union eventually produced 480 descendants. Goddard classified 143 of them as "defective," and only 46 as normal. He found crime, alcoholism, mental disorders, and illegitimacy common among the rest of the family members. By contrast, when Martin later married a "good woman," their union produced 496 descendants, only three of whom were classified as "defective." Goddard also found that many offspring from this high-quality union had become "eminent" (Goddard, 1914). Goddard came to believe that heredity determined intelligence, genius, and eminence on the positive side. On the negative side, he arrayed delinquency, alcoholism, sexual immorality, developmental disability, and maybe even poverty (McPherson, 1985).

Goddard's genetic inferiority argument was further reinforced by the fact that on the World War I Army Intelligence tests, African Americans and other racial minorities scored lower than the white majority. Louis Terman, who as we saw promoted IQ testing in the United States, commented in this unscientific manner on the data he had helped collect on U.S. racial minorities:

> Their dullness seems to be racial. . . . There seems no possibility at present of convincing society that they should not be allowed to reproduce, although from a eugenics point of view, they constitute a grave problem because of their unusually prolific breeding. (Terman, 1916, pp. 91–92)

The names have changed, but the problem remains the same. In the United States today, African Americans and Latinos score, on average, lower than Asian Americans and whites on standardized intelligence tests. Of course, there are individuals in all groups who score at the highest (and the lowest) extremes of the IQ scale. How should these *group* differences in IQ scores be interpreted? The tradition in the United States and Britain has been to attribute these differences to genetic inferiority (nature). After we discuss the evidence for genetic differences in IQ, we will consider a second possibility, that differences in environments (nurture) exert a significant impact on IQ. The validity of either explanation, or some combination of them, has important social, economic, and political consequences.

Heredity and IQ

How can researchers assess the extent to which intelligence is genetically determined? Any answer to this question requires that the researcher choose some measure as an index of intelligence. Thus the question becomes not whether "intelligence," in the abstract, is influenced by heredity but, in most cases, whether IQs are similar within family trees. To answer this more limited question, researchers need to tease apart the effects of shared *genes* and shared *environment*. One method is to compare functioning in identical twins (*monozygotic,* MZ), fraternal twins (*dizygotic,* DZ), and relatives with other degrees of genetic overlap. **Table 15.2** compares IQ scores of individuals on the basis of their degree of genetic relationship (Bouchard & McGue, 1981). As you can see, the greater the genetic similarity, the greater the IQ similarity. The correlation increases as shared heredity increases, from cousins to siblings to fraternal twins to identical twins. It is also greater between parent and child than between foster parent and adopted child. (You should also note in these data that the impact of environment is also revealed in the greater IQ similarities among those who have been reared together.)

Researchers use results of this sort to try to estimate the *heritability* of IQ. A **heritability estimate** of a particular trait, such as intelligence, is based on the proportion of the *variability* in test scores on that trait that can be traced to genetic factors. The estimate is found by computing the variation in all the test scores for a given population (college students or mental patients, for example) and then identifying what portion of the total variance is due to genetic or inherited factors. This is done by comparing individuals who have

Table 15.2 IQ and Genetic Relationship

	Correlation
Identical twins	
Reared together	0.86
Reared apart	0.72
Fraternal twins	
Reared together	0.60
Siblings	
Reared together	0.47
Reared apart	0.24
Parent/child	0.40
Foster parent/child	0.31
Cousins	0.15

Heritability estimates of a particular trait, such as IQ, provide a good idea as to the influence of heredity for groups of people but are of little help in understanding the heritability of characteristics in individuals.

different degrees of genetic overlap. Researchers have claimed that as much as 70 percent of the variance in IQ scores is due to genetic makeup (Bouchard et al., 1990). That's an impressive figure, but even though many recent estimates peg the figure lower, at 50 percent, it still says very little about individual cases (Loehlin et al., 1988; Plomin, 1989). Heritability estimates pertain only to the *average* in a given population of individuals. Even though we know that height, for instance, has a high heritability estimate (about 90 percent) you cannot determine how much of *your* height is due to genetic influences. The same argument is true for IQ; despite high heritability estimates, we cannot determine the specific genetic contribution to any individual's IQ or to mean IQ scores among groups.

Let's return now to the point at which genetic analysis becomes controversial: the 10 to 15 point IQ test score difference between African Americans and white Americans. If IQ is highly heritable, does this difference reflect genetic inferiority of individuals in the lower scoring group? The answer is no. Heritability is based on an estimate *within* one given group. It cannot be used to interpret differences *between* groups, no matter how large those differences are on an objective test. The fact that on an IQ test one racial or ethnic group scores lower than another group does not mean that the difference *between* these groups is genetic in origin, even if the heritability estimate for IQ scores is high as assessed *within* a group.

Another reason that genetic makeup does not appear to be responsible for group differences in IQ has to do with the relative sizes of the differences. There is much overlapping in the distribution of each group's scores despite mean differences. In addition, the difference *between* groups is small compared with the differences among the scores of individuals *within* each group (Plomin & McClearn, 1993). In fact, paleobotanist **Stephen Jay Gould** (1981) argues that for human characteristics in general, the differences between the gene pools of different racial groups are minute compared with the genetic differences among individual members of the same group (see also Zuckerman, 1990). It is also the case that the IQ scores of whites and blacks are converging over time, with the gap decreasing by about 2.5 IQ points each decade, so that on a number of contemporary indicators the gap is between seven and ten points, not the 15 points usually cited (see Nisbett, 1995).

Another interesting line of evidence that complicates a simple interpretation of the linkages among genetics, race, and IQ comes from a series of studies in which the degree of white or European parentage among blacks is determined. In the United States, the "black" population is estimated to be about 20–30 percent European through intermarriages. Does it make a difference in IQ if a "black" person has more or less European genetic stock? The genetic argument holds that is does, but the data suggest the correlation of degree of European ancestry with IQ is very low (on the order of only .15 across many studies). This is true whether skin color or blood groups are used as the index of racial mixture. Comparisons of German children fathered by African-American GI fathers and white GI fathers show no difference in their IQ scores. In addition, children of "black-white" unions have IQs that are seven points higher if the mother is white. This difference is most likely due to the greater contribution of mothers than fathers to a child's intellectual socialization, and of course, cannot be due to any genetic factor, since each parent contributes half of their genes to the offspring (research summarized by Nisbett, 1995).

Surely genetics plays a sizable role in influencing individuals' scores on IQ tests, as it does on many other traits and abilities. We have argued, however, that heredity does not constitute an adequate explanation for IQ differences between racial and ethnic groups. It has a necessary, but not sufficient, role in our understanding of such performance effects. Let's turn now to the role the environment may play in creating the IQ gap.

Environments and IQ

Because heritability estimates are less than 1.0, we know that genetic inheritance is not solely responsible for anyone's IQ. Environments must also affect IQ. But how can we assess what aspects of the environment are important influences on IQ? What features of your environment affect your potential to score well on an IQ test (see Plomin, 1989; Scarr, 1988; Stevenson et al., 1987)? Environments are complex stimulus packages that vary on many dimensions, both physical and social, and may be experienced in different ways by those within them. Even children in the same family setting do not necessarily share the same critical, psychological environment. Think back to growing up in your family. If you had siblings, did they all get the same attention from parents, did conditions of stress change over the course of time, did the family's financial resources change, did your parents' marital status change? It is obvious that environments are made up of many components that are in a dynamic relationship, and that change over time. So it becomes difficult for psychologists to say what kinds of environmental conditions—attention, stress, poverty, health, war, and so on—actually have an impact on IQ.

Researchers have most often focused on more global measures of environment, like the socioeconomic status of the family. For example, in a large-scale longitudinal study of more than 26,000 children, the best predictors of a child's IQ at age 4 were the family's socioeconomic status and the level of the mother's education. This was equally true for African-American and Caucasian children (Broman et al., 1975). Similarly, **Figure 15.4**, shows an overall impact of social class on IQ.

Research indicates that socioeconomic status and the mother's education level are the best predictors of a child's IQ at age 4, for both black and white children.

Why does social class affect IQ? Wealth versus poverty can affect intellectual functioning in many ways, health and educational resources being two of the most obvious. Poor health during pregnancy and low birth weight are solid predictors of a child's lowered mental ability. Children born into impoverished families often suffer from poor nutrition, many going to school hungry, thus less able to concentrate on learning tasks. Many such poor children are contaminated by falling flakes of lead paint; lead poisoning directly impairs brain function (Needleman et al., 1990). Furthermore, impoverished homes may suffer from a lack of books, written media, computers, and other materials that add to one's mental stimulation. The "survival orientation" of poor parents, especially in single-parent families, that leaves parents little

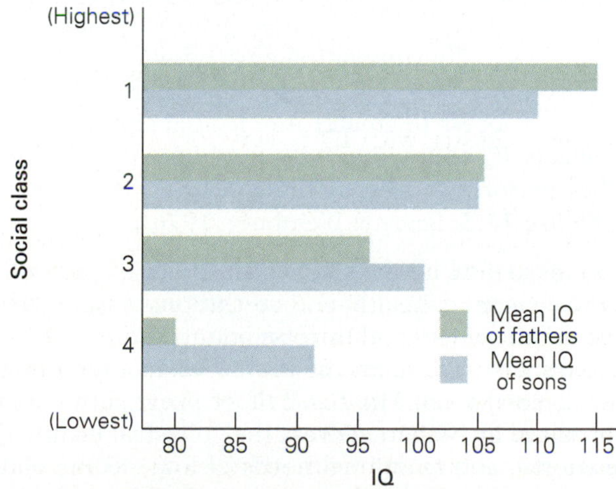

Figure 15.4 The Relationship Among Heredity, Environment, and IQ
This chart shows evidence for the contribution of heredity and environment to IQ scores. There are similar IQs for fathers and sons (influence of heredity), but the IQs of both fathers and sons are related to social class (influence of environment).

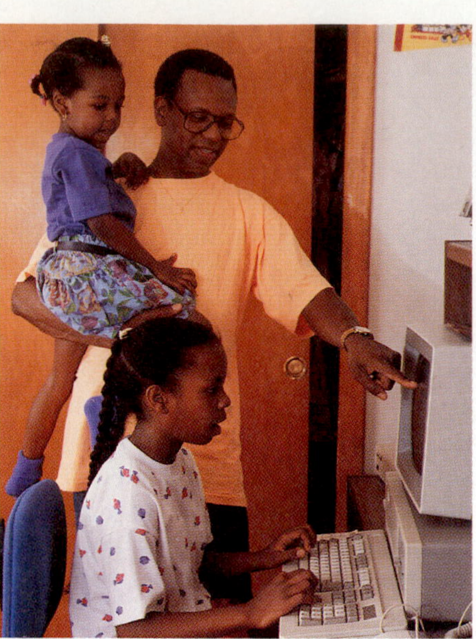

The personal attention children receive can affect their intelligence. In the "separate but equal" schoolroom of 1940s Tennessee shown (at left), African-American children received little attention. In contrast, the parent shown (at right) is deeply involved in his children's education.

time or energy to play with and intellectually stimulate their children is detrimental to performance on tasks such as those on standard IQ tests. Finally, those living in more impoverished conditions are stigmatized in our society, as they are in most countries throughout the world, even in racially homogenous societies like Japan. For example, the Burakamin of Japan, who are that nation's lowest caste members, have IQs that are 15 points lower than other Japanese (Ogbu, 1987). This social stigma of one's group can exert a negative impact on an individual's sense of self-competence, and adversely affect test and school performances. If so, we should see a direct impact on IQ when any child moves from an impoverished to a privileged environment.

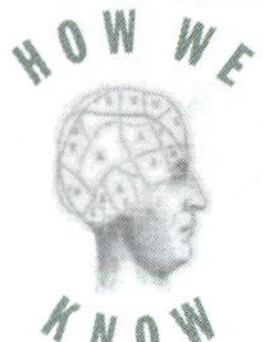

When underprivileged African-American children were adopted by middle-class white families, they developed IQs significantly above the average of 100. Those who were adopted into these more intellectually stimulating environments within the first year of life had much higher IQ scores than those adopted later. Thus, when given access to greater intellectual stimulation—of the kind that affects IQ test scores—these children from previously poor families perform as well as their peers in this new environment (see **Figure 15.5**; Scarr & Weinberg, 1976).

What is important to note here is that it is not race as such that makes the difference, but the economic, health, and educational resources that are correlated with race in our society and in most countries.

In a sense researchers have spent the last 30 years attempting to replicate this result at the societal level. The *Head Start* program was first funded by the federal government in 1965 to address the "physical health, developmental, social, educational, and emotional needs of low-income children and to increase the capacity of the families to care for their children, through empowerment and supportive services" (Kassebaum, 1994, p. 123). The idea of Head Start was not to move children to privileged environments but to improve the environments into which they were born. Children are exposed to special preschool education, they receive decent daily meals, and their

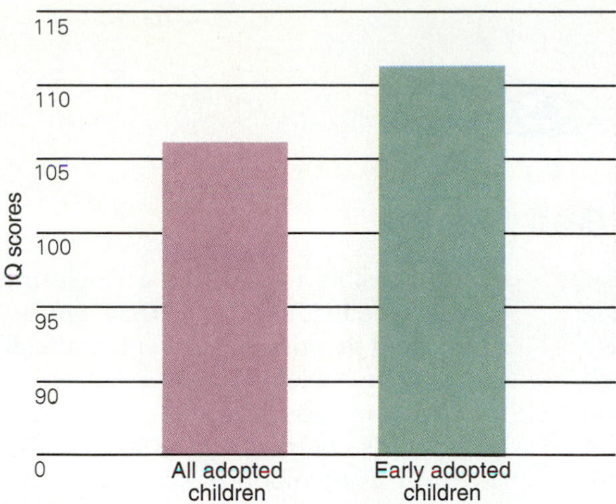

Figure 15.5 IQ Scores of Underprivileged Children Adopted by Middle-Class Families

parents are given advice on health and other aspects of child rearing. Early assessments of Head Start's effects focused narrowly on improvement on IQ tests and other achievement measures. In fact, after children had been in the program only a few weeks, their IQ scores rose by 10 points. Unfortunately after they left the program, these IQ gains tended to fade away (Zigler & Muenchow, 1992; Zigler & Styfco, 1994). This pattern yields two lessons: IQ can be affected by the environment, but the enriched environment must be sustained. In any case, more recent assessments of Head Start have overcome the earlier narrow focus on IQ.

> The empirical literature . . . delivers good news and bad news. The bad news is that neither Head Start nor any preschool program can inoculate children against the ravages of poverty. Early intervention simply cannot overpower the effects of poor living conditions, inadequate nutrition and health care, negative role models, and sub-standard schools. But good programs can prepare children for school and possibly help them develop better coping and adaptation skills that will enable better life outcomes, albeit not perfect ones. (Zigler & Styfco, 1994, p. 129)

Follow-up assessments of the Head Start program indicated that early IQ gains faded after the children left the program, leading researchers to conclude that environmental interventions must be sustained.

If we use a broader definition of intelligence that goes beyond just verbal and performance tasks on IQ tests, the influence of environment factors becomes clear. An enriched, supportive environment is a good predictor of successful and enhanced intellectual, scholastic, and situationally adaptive performance.

Validity and Test Bias in IQ Tests

We have just seen that the quality of the environment can affect both IQ scores and other aspects of intelligent functioning. There is, however, another sense in which life experiences can affect success on IQ tests. Critics have argued that group differences in IQ scores are caused by systematic bias in the tests questions, making them invalid and unfair for minorities. But even when tests are made more "culture-fair," there remains a significant racial gap (Snow, 1995). The issue may be more a problem of the testing *situation* than the content of the test. Many minority members may feel strong evaluative pressures on them in IQ test settings. They enter the IQ test situation with the knowledge that blacks or Latinos don't perform well on IQ tests. Similarly, stereotypes about women and mathematics have been shown to depress mathematics test scores of women college students (Steele, 1992). Performance is interfered with by the twin factors of the resulting anxiety/stress, and the

The Bell Curve

In 1994, a book burst onto the scene that brought all the issues we have been considering about the nature and nurture of intelligence directly into the public forum. In *The Bell Curve,* **Richard Herrnstein** and **Charles Murray** argued that the United States is in danger of becoming a country stratified into an IQ elite versus the unintelligent masses. Most controversially, they suggested that the majority of members of minority groups, African Americans and Latinos, are genetically doomed to reside in the unintelligent mass. Herrnstein and Murray assume their place in a long line of writers who have clothed their personal biases in the mantle of science to draw conclusions that many have called racist. For example, there was extensive media coverage in the 1960s and 70s of the allegation by William Shockley, a Stanford University professor and Nobel Prize winner in physics, that the low IQ test scores of African Americans in the United States were genetically based and nothing could, or should, be done to change their destiny. He concluded, after examining IQ data collected by some psychologists, "that the major deficit in Negro intellectual performance must be primarily of hereditary origin and thus relatively irremediable by practical improvements in environment" (Shockley, 1968, p. 87). Herrnstein and Murray arrive at much the same conclusion. Their science is equally suspect, as is the logic that environmental changes cannot remedy heredity-based defects—glasses, for example, do improve poor vision. (For a fuller presentation of these issues see Fraser, 1995; Tucker, 1994; and Pearson, 1992.)

The argument of *The Bell Curve* rests on four assumptions. As Stephen Jay Gould put it, "Intelligence, in [Herrnstein and Murray's] formulation, must be depictable as a single number, capable of ranking people in linear order, genetically based, and effectively immutable [unchangeable by intervention]" (1994, p. 139). In our discussion of intelligence, we have already provided evidence that should allow you to challenge each of these assumptions. Let's review.

- Is intelligence depictable by a single number? Certainly, if you administer IQ tests, it is possible to produce a single number for any individual (and that single number makes it possible to rank individuals in a way in which everyone is compared with everyone else, and viewed as better or worse on this continuum). As we have seen, however, contemporary scholars of intelligence almost universally reject the equating of IQ with intelligence—of a single test score to measure the complex set of processes that constitute intellectual functioning. This change in theory is not just a matter of broadening a definition. It reflects equally the fact that no test is a perfect measure of a complex construct—and that few tests measure a construct well for all people.
- Is intelligence genetically based? We have reviewed evidence that clearly shows genetic inheritance makes a contribution to IQ. Recall, however, that heritability *within* groups does not permit conclusions to be drawn about the differences *between* groups. Although Herrnstein and Murray acknowledge this problem, they then go on largely to ignore it. Also, whatever percentage of the variation in IQ is accountable for by genes, there is much left over that is accounted for only by environmental factors and by interactions of nature and nurture.
- Is intelligence effectively immutable, not modifiable by environmental interventions? Herrnstein and Murray examine much of the same evidence we have presented to you—but they dismiss it. For example, they conclude that Head Start has provided no evidence of success, which is simply false. They note the short-term increase in IQ scores but then focus on how quickly these differences faded away. But shouldn't it be a great difficulty for any theory of immutability if IQ scores could increase 10 points, even in the short term? Overall, research shows "massive gains" in intelligence levels in 14 nations since World War II (Flynn, 1987). Furthermore, contemporary theories of intelligence are concerned not just with numbers (IQ = 98; IQ = 113) but with the

cognitive processes that underlie those numbers. Knowledge of those cognitive processes holds out the real possibility that everyone's performance can be improved using interventions that are designed to enhance specific cognitive processes (see Anderson, 1981; Hunt, 1995). Finally, no genetic evidence exists of any specific genes that contribute to the part of the brain's development that leads to intelligence.

If *The Bell Curve* does not hold up to even casual scrutiny, why did it find such a willing audience in the United States that made it a best-seller and the topic of intensive media coverage? A large part of the answer may be that the nation has a cultural bias toward genetic explanations of individual differences. **Harold Stevenson** and his colleagues (1993) have spent several years tracking the mathematics achievement of Chinese, Japanese, and U.S. children. In 1980, Asian children on the average vastly outperformed their U.S. peers. In 1990, the gap remained: "Only 4.1% of the Chinese children and 10.3% of the Japanese children . . . had scores as low as those of the average American child" (p. 54). Are Asian children genetically superior? In fact, people in the United States are more likely to answer "yes." When Stevenson and his colleagues asked Asian and U.S. students, teachers, and parents to contrast the importance of "studying hard" versus "innate intelligence," Asian respondents emphasized hard work. U.S. respondents emphasized innate ability. Do you see how this perspective could lead to the conclusion by Americans that Asians must be genetically superior in mathematics?

Unfortunately, the pseudoscience of *The Bell Curve* has found a willing audience among those politicians who embrace elitist theories and who seek to eliminate funding for Head Start and other innovative educational programs. The relative success of Asian students—and, thus, Asian economies—demonstrates the lack of wisdom in this course of public policy. Perhaps the only way the United States can compete successfully in the twenty-first century is to reject *The Bell Curve*'s false message of intellectual immutability, and instead support efforts to enhance vital cognitive skills that form the basis of individual intelligence.

belief that when faced with a complicated test problem it is the student's inadequacy that makes it difficult (which leads to giving up) rather than that the problem is difficult for everyone (and so requires more effort).

IQ tests and other standardized achievement tests are still used frequently in school and work settings to determine class and job placements. Extensive research shows that IQ scores are valid predictors of school grades from elementary school through college, of occupational status, and of performance in certain jobs (Brody & Brody, 1976; Gottfredson, 1986; Lennon, 1985). IQ distinctions can affect academic and job performance indirectly by changing one's motives and beliefs. Those with higher IQ scores are likely to have had more success experiences in school, become more motivated to study, develop an achievement orientation, and become optimistic about their chances of doing well. Believing in one's self-efficacy definitely predicts better performance on a variety of tasks (Bandura, 1986). Also, children scoring low on IQ tests may get "tracked" into schools, classes, or programs that are inferior and may even be stigmatizing to the student's sense of self-competence. In this way, IQ can be affected by environment and, in turn, can create new environments for the child—some better, some worse. IQ assessment may thus become destiny—whatever the child's underlying genetic endowment for intelligence.

Creativity

Before we leave the area of intelligence and its assessment, we wish to turn to a final topic, creativity. **Creativity** is an individual's ability to generate ideas or products that are both *novel* and *appropriate* to the circumstances in which they were generated (Lubart, 1994). Consider the invention of the

"The wheel kept getting stolen—until I invented 'the club.'"

wheel. The device was novel because no one before its unknown inventor had seen the application of rolling objects. It was appropriate because the use to which the novel object could be put was very clear. Without appropriateness, new ideas or objects are often considered strange or irrelevant.

Our discussion of creativity falls under the general heading of intelligence because many people believe that there is a strong relationship between intelligence and creativity. To determine if this is the case, we need to be able first to test creativity and then to determine the relationship between creativity and intelligence. Thus we first discuss methods for judging ideas or products to be creative and then look at the link to intelligence. Next we look at situations of exceptional creativity, and evaluate the relationship between creativity and madness. We will see what lessons you can learn from people who are possessed of exceptional creative abilities.

Assessing Creativity and the Link to Intelligence

How might you go about rating individuals as (relatively) creative or uncreative? Many approaches focus on **divergent thinking,** which is defined as the ability to generate a variety of unusual solutions to a problem. Questions that test divergent thinking give the test taker the opportunity to demonstrate *fluid* (swift) and *flexible* thinking (Torrance, 1974; Wallach & Kogan, 1965):

- Name all the things you can think of that are square.
- List as many white, edible things as you can in three minutes.
- List all the uses that you can think of for a *brick.*

Responses are scored along such dimensions as *fluency,* the overall number of distinct ideas; *uniqueness,* the number of ideas that were given by no other subject in an appropriate sample; and *unusualness,* the number of ideas that were given by, for example, less than 5 percent of a sample (Runco, 1991).

When creativity is assessed in this fashion, the test provides a performance index that can be correlated with other measures. On many occasions, researchers have evaluated the relationship between measures of divergent thinking and IQ. A common pattern has emerged: there is a correlation between the two measures up to an IQ level of about 120; above 120 the correlation decreases (Perkins, 1988). Why might this be so? One

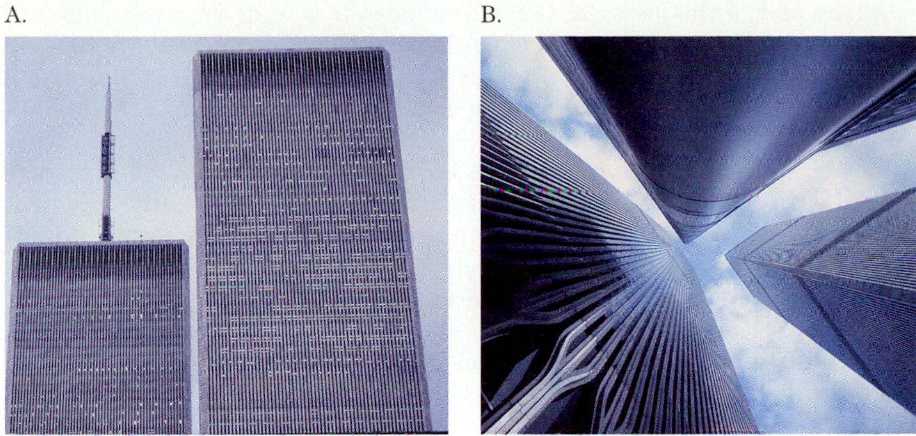

Figure 15.6
Hypothetical photography class assignment: take the best picture you can of the World Trade Center. (A) A noncreative response. (B) A creative response.

researcher suggests that "intelligence appears to enable creativity to some extent but not to promote it" (Perkins, 1988, p. 319). In other words, a certain level of intelligence gives a person the opportunity to be creative, but the person may not avail himself or herself of that opportunity.

Creativity researchers have often been concerned that divergent-thinking tests are too closely tied to the tradition of intelligence testing and to IQ tests themselves (which may explain the correlations up into the 120 IQ range) (Lubart, 1994). A different approach to judging some individuals as creative or uncreative is to ask them specifically to generate a creative product—a drawing, a poem, or a short story. Judges then rate the creativity of each of the products. Consider the two photographs shown in **Figure 15.6**. Which do you think is more creative? Could you explain why you think so? Do you think your friends would agree? Research has shown that agreement is quite high when judges rank products for creativity (Amabile, 1983). People can be reliably identified across judges as being high or low in creativity.

Exceptional Creativity and Madness

There are some exceptional individuals who would emerge from assessments of creativity as almost off the scale. Who do you think of when you are asked to name someone who is exceptionally creative? Your answer is likely to depend partly on your own areas of expertise and your own preferences. Psychologists might nominate Sigmund Freud. Those people interested in fine art, music, or dance might mention Pablo Picasso, Igor Stravinsky, or Martha Graham. Is it possible to detect the commonalities in the personalities or backgrounds of such individuals that could be predictive of exceptional creativity? Howard Gardner (1993a) chose a selection of individuals whose extraordinary abilities were relevant to the seven types of intelligence we described earlier, including Freud, Picasso, Stravinsky, and Graham. Gardner's analysis allows him to yield a portrait of the life experiences of the *exemplary creator,* whom he dubs *E.C.:*

> E.C. discovers a problem area or realm of special interest, one that promises to [lead] into uncharted waters. This is a highly charged moment. At this point E.C. becomes isolated from her peers and must work mostly on her own. She senses that she is on the verge of a breakthrough that is as yet little understood, even by her. Surprisingly, at this crucial moment, E.C. craves both cognitive and affective support, so that she can retain her bearings. Without such support, she might well experience some kind of breakdown. (Gardner, 1993a, p. 361)

Robert Schumann, shown here in a drawing dated 1859, composed significantly more music, but not better music, during his manic phases than during periods of depression.

At the end of this passage, Gardner alludes to one of the most common stereotypes of exemplary creators: their life experiences border on—or include the experience of—madness. The idea that great creativity is intimately related to madness has a history that has been traced as far back as Plato (Kessel, 1989). In more modern times, Kraepelin (1921) argued that the manic phases of individuals who suffer from "manic-depressive insanity" provide a context of free-flowing thought processes that facilitate great creativity. Mania, as we will see in Chapter 17, is characterized by periods of enduring excitedness; the person generally acts and feels elated and expansive. There is little doubt that many great figures in the arts and humanities have suffered from such mood disorders (Keiger, 1993). But how can researchers determine whether these individuals' actual thought processes were affected by their mental illness?

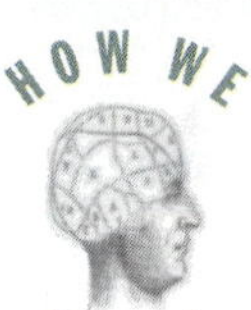

To answer this question, creativity researcher **Robert Weisberg** (1994) examined the artistic output of the composer Robert Schumann, who was diagnosed with bipolar disorder. Part of the data seems consistent with a proposed link between mania and creativity. Schumann produced considerably more compositions in manic years (an average of 12.3) than in years when he was suffering from the other extreme, depression (an average of 2.7). The link broke down, however, when Weisberg factored in *quality.* The works composed in the years of mania were no higher in quality than those composed in years of depression.

Weisberg's study suggests that madness (in the form of mania) may largely affect motivation. The individual rides the wave of mania to create a great output of work. If the person has a certain level of talent, some, but not all, of that work will reach brilliance—but at a rate no higher than at other times in the artist's life.

Studies of individuals who are considered highly creative reveal patterns of risk taking, preparation, and motivation.

What lessons are there for you in tales of exceptional creativity? You can emulate a pattern of *risk taking.* Highly creative individuals are willing to go into "uncharted waters" (Gardner, 1993a). There is a pattern of *preparation.* Highly creative individuals typically have spent years acquiring expertise in the domains in which they will excel (Weisberg, 1986). There is a pattern of *intrinsic motivation.* Highly creative individuals pursue their tasks because of the enjoyment and satisfaction they take in the products they generate (Amabile, 1983). If you can bring all these factors together in your own life, you should be able to increase your personal level of creative performance.

ASSESSING PERSONALITY

There is much more to understanding people than knowing how intelligent or creative they are. Think of all the other ways in which you differ from your best friend. Psychologists wonder about the nonintellectual attributes that characterize an individual, set one person apart from others, or distinguish people in one group from those in another (for example, shy people from outgoing or paranoid individuals from normal). This information may be used in psychological research, individual therapy, or career counseling.

Two assumptions are basic to these attempts to understand and describe human personality: first, that there are personal characteristics of individuals that give coherence to their behavior and, second, that those characteristics can be assessed or measured. Personality tests that embody these assumptions can be classified as being either *objective* or *projective*.

OBJECTIVE TESTS

Objective tests of personality are those in which scoring and administration are relatively simple and follow well-defined rules. Some objective tests are

PERSONALITY DIAGNOSIS:
THE CLIENT'S PERSONALITY IS DEFINED BY
AN UNWILLINGNESS TO TAKE PERSONALITY TESTS.

A little-documented personality characteristic.

scored, and even interpreted, by computer programs. The final score is usually a single number, scaled along a single dimension (such as adjustment versus maladjustment), or a set of scores on different traits (such as impulsiveness, dependency, or extroversion) reported in comparison with the scores of a normative sample.

Objective personality tests are those involving relatively simple scoring and administration that follow standardized, explicit rules.

A *self-report inventory* is an objective test in which individuals answer a series of questions about their thoughts, feelings, and actions. One of the first self-report inventories, the *Woodworth Personal Data Sheet* (written in 1917) asked questions such as "Are you often frightened in the middle of the night?" (see DuBois, 1970). Today, a person taking a **personality inventory** reads a series of statements and indicates whether each one is true or typical for himself or herself.

The most frequently used personality inventory is the *Minnesota Multiphasic Personality Inventory*, or MMPI (Dahlstrom et al., 1975). It is used in many clinical settings to aid in the diagnosis of patients and to guide their treatment. After reviewing its features and applications, we will briefly discuss two personality inventories that are used widely with nonpatient populations: the *California Psychological Inventory* (CPI) and the *NEO Personality Inventory* (NEO-PI).

The MMPI

The MMPI was developed at the University of Minnesota during the 1930s by psychologist Starke Hathaway and psychiatrist J. R. McKinley (Hathaway & McKinley, 1940, 1943). Its basic purpose is to diagnose individuals according to a set of psychiatric labels. The first test consisted of 550 items, which the subjects determined to be either true or false for themselves or to which they responded, "Cannot say." From that item pool, scales were developed that were relevant to the kinds of problems patients showed in psychiatric settings.

The MMPI scales were unlike other existing personality tests because they were developed using an *empirical* strategy rather than the intuitive, theoretical approach that dominated at the time. (Recall our discussion earlier of theoretical versus empirical test construction.) Items were included on a scale only if they clearly distinguished between two groups—for example, schizophrenic patients and a normal comparison group. Each item had to demonstrate its validity by being answered similarly by members within each group but differently between the two groups. Thus the items were not selected on a theoretical basis (what the content seemed to mean to experts) but on an empirical basis (did they distinguish between the two groups?).

Table 15.3 MMPI-2 Clinical Scales

Hypochondriasis (Hs): Abnormal concern with bodily functions

Depression (D): Pessimism; hopelessness; slowing of action and thought

Conversion hysteria (Hy): Unconscious use of mental problems to avoid conflicts or responsibility

Psychopathic deviate (Pd): Disregard for social custom; shallow emotions; inability to profit from experience

Masculinity-femininity (Mf): Differences between men and women

Paranoia (Pa): Suspiciousness; delusions of grandeur or persecution

Psychasthenia (Pt): Obsessions; compulsions; fears; guilt; indecisiveness

Schizophrenia (Sc): Bizarre, unusual thoughts or behavior; withdrawal; hallucinations; delusions

Hypomania (Ma): Emotional excitement; flight of ideas; overactivity

Social introversion (Si): Shyness; disinterest in others; insecurity

The MMPI has 10 *clinical scales,* each constructed to differentiate a special clinical group (such as individuals with schizophrenia) from a normal comparison group. The test also includes *validity scales* that detect suspicious response patterns, such as blatant dishonesty, carelessness, defensiveness, or evasiveness. When an MMPI is interpreted, the tester first checks the validity scales to be sure the test is valid and then looks at the rest of the scores. The pattern of the scores—which are highest, how they differ—forms the "MMPI profile." Individual profiles are compared with those common for particular groups, such as felons and gamblers.

In the mid-1980s, the MMPI underwent a major revision, and it is now called the *MMPI-2* (Butcher et al., 1989; Butcher & Williams, 1992; Greene, 1991). The MMPI-2 has updated language and content to better reflect contemporary concerns, and new populations provided data for norms. The MMPI-2 also adds 15 new *content scales* that were derived using, in part, a theoretical method. For each of 15 clinically relevant topics (such as anxiety or family problems), items were selected on two bases: if they seemed theoretically related to the topic area and if they statistically formed a *homogeneous scale,* meaning that each scale measures a single, unified concept. The clinical and content scales of the MMPI-2 are given in **Table 15.3** and **Table 15.4**. You'll notice that most of the clinical scales measure several related

Table 15.4 MMPI-2 Content Scales

Anxiety	Antisocial practices
Fears	Type A (workaholic)
Obsessiveness	Low self-esteem
Depression	Social discomfort
Health concerns	Family problems
Bizarre mentation (thoughts)	Work interference
Anger	Negative treatment indicators (negative attitudes about doctors and treatment)
Cynicism	

concepts and that the names of the content scales are simple and self-explanatory.

The benefits of the MMPI-2 include its ease and economy of administration and its usefulness for the diagnosis of psychopathology. In addition, the item pool can be used for many purposes. For example, you could build a creativity scale by finding creative and noncreative groups of individuals and determining the MMPI items that they answered differently. Over the years, psychologists have developed and validated hundreds of special-purpose scales in this way. For researchers, one of the most attractive characteristics of the MMPI is the enormous archives of MMPI profiles collected over 50 years. Because all of these people have been tested on the same items in a standardized way, they can be compared either on the traditional clinical scales or on special-purpose scales (like our new "creativity" scale). These MMPI archives allow researchers to test hypotheses on MMPIs taken by people many years earlier, perhaps long before the construct being measured was even conceived.

Two important advantages of the MMPI are its ease and economy of administration and its usefulness in diagnosing psychopathology.

However, the MMPI-2 is not without its critics. Its clinical scales have been criticized, for example, because they are *heterogeneous* (they measure several things at once). Researchers have also suggested that the changes from the original MMPI to the revised MMPI-2 were insufficient to recognize advances in personality theory; the test remains close to its empirical origins (Helmes & Reddon, 1993). The MMPI-2 may be criticized in some cases because people try to use it for too many purposes. Some MMPI-2 scales, such as the depression scale, reach acceptable levels of validity (Boone, 1994). The scales devoted to predicting substance abuse, by contrast, are not as valid as more specific assessment devices (Svanum et al., 1994). As with any assessment device, researchers must carefully evaluate the reliability and validity of each special use of the MMPI and MMPI-2.

These personality inventories were designed to assess individuals with clinical problems. In the next two sections, we'll describe devices more suited to assess personality in nonpatient populations.

The CPI

To measure personality differences among people who are more or less normal, **Harrison Gough** (1957) created the California Psychological Inventory (CPI). The CPI's personality scales measure concepts that nonpsychologists can easily understand, such as Responsibility, Self-control, Tolerance, and Intellectual Efficiency. Validity scales are included in the test to detect invalid patterns of responses. All the scales are presented on a profile sheet that shows how a person scored on each scale relative to same-sex norms.

Unlike the MMPI, which was designed to assess clinical problems, the California Psychological Inventory (CPI) was designed to assess personality in healthy people.

The CPI has been used to study personality structure in healthy adults and to evaluate characteristic personality structures of various groups, such as people in different occupations. Longitudinal studies employing the CPI have helped psychologists understand how personality develops and how personality traits in young adulthood are related to life events as much as 40 years later. In addition, many special-purpose scales have been created and validated for research and applied purposes, such as selecting police officers for special training programs and predicting job performance for dentists, student teachers, and many other groups (Gough, 1989; Gynther & Gynther, 1976).

The original CPI was criticized because many of its scales measured mixtures of traits and because certain scales correlated highly with other scales (in part because some items were included on more than one scale). Revisions of the CPI have added new scales that are nonoverlapping and uncorrelated with each other (Gough, 1995). Research has begun to confirm the validity of these measures of interpersonal style, acceptance of rules or norms, and self-actualization (Weiser & Meyers, 1993; Zebb & Meyers, 1993).

The NEO-PI

The NEO Personality Inventory (NEO-PI) was also designed to assess personality characteristics in nonclinical adult populations. It measures the *five-factor model* of personality we discussed in the previous chapter. If you took the NEO-PI, you would receive a profile sheet that showed your standardized scores relative to a large normative sample on each of the five major dimensions: Neuroticism, Extraversion, Openness, Agreeableness, and Conscientiousness (Costa & McCrae, 1985). A revised version of the NEO-PI assesses 30 separate traits organized within the five major factors (Costa & McCrae, 1992b). For example, the Neuroticism dimension is broken down into six facet scales: Anxiety, Angry hostility, Depression, Self-consciousness, Impulsiveness, and Vulnerability. Much research has demonstrated that the NEO-PI dimensions are homogeneous, highly reliable, and show good criterion and construct validity (Costa & McCrae, 1992a; McCrae & Costa, 1987, 1989). The NEO-PI is being used to study personality stability and change across the life span as well as the relationship of personality characteristics to physical health and various life events, such as career success or early retirement.

The NEO-PI, designed to assess the five-factor model of personality, has been found to be homogeneous, highly reliable, and high in criterion and construct validity.

A new inventory based on the five-factor model, the *Big Five Questionnaire* (BFQ), was designed to have validity across different cultures. The scale was developed in Italy, but it shows similar psychometric characteristics for U.S. and Spanish populations, and appropriate norms are being established for French, German, Czech, Hungarian, and Polish translations (Caprara et al., 1993, 1995). Although the BFQ correlates highly with the NEO-PI, it differs in important ways. Factor 1 is labeled Energy or Activity rather than Extraversion (to reduce overlap with the social aspects of Agreeableness). The BFQ includes a scale to see if test takers' responses are biased toward socially desirable responses. It is simpler than the NEO-PI in having only two facets for each of the five factors. For example, Energy is composed of the facets of Dynamism and Dominance. The first is intrapersonal; the second is interpersonal. As psychology becomes more global in its concerns, such assessment instruments that work equally well across language and national boundaries are essential for conducting meaningful cross-cultural research in personality and social psychology.

Projective Tests

Have you ever looked at a cloud and seen a face or the shape of an animal? If you asked your friends to look, too, they may have seen a reclining nude or a dragon. Psychologists rely on a similar phenomenon in their use of projective tests for personality assessment.

As we just saw, objective tests take one of two forms: either they provide test takers with a series of statements and ask them to give a simple response (such as "true," "false," or "cannot say") or they ask test takers to rate themselves with respect to some dimension (such as "anxious" versus "nonanxious"). Thus the respondent is constrained to choose one of the predetermined responses. *Projective tests,* by contrast, have no predetermined range of responses. In a **projective test,** a person is given a series of stimuli that are purposely ambiguous, such as abstract patterns, incomplete pictures, or drawings that can be interpreted in many ways. The person may be asked to describe the patterns, finish the pictures, or tell stories about the drawings. Projective tests were first used by psychoanalysts, who hoped that such tests would reveal their patients' unconscious personality dynamics. Because the stimuli are ambiguous, responses to them are determined partly by what the person brings to the situation—namely, inner feelings, personal motives, and conflicts from prior life experiences. These personal, idiosyncratic aspects, which are *projected* onto the stimuli, permit the personality assessor to make various interpretations.

Projective tests present the examinee with ambiguous stimuli in order to elicit inner feelings, motives, and conflicts.

Projective tests are among the assessment devices most commonly used by psychological practitioners (Lubin et al., 1984; Piotrowski et al., 1985). They are also used more often outside the United States, in countries such as the Netherlands, Hong Kong, and Japan, than are objective tests like the MMPI (Piotrowski et al., 1993). Objective tests often fail to be adequately translated or adequately standardized for non-U.S. populations. Projective tests are less sensitive to language variation. Let's examine two of the most common projective tests, the Rorschach test and the Thematic Apperception Test (TAT).

The Rorschach

In the Rorschach test, developed by Swiss psychiatrist **Hermann Rorschach** in 1921, the ambiguous stimuli are symmetrical inkblots (Rorschach, 1942). Some are black and white and some are colored (see **Figure 15.7**). During the test, a respondent is shown an inkblot and asked, "What might this be?" Respondents are assured that there are no right or wrong answers (Exner, 1974). Testers record verbatim what subjects say, how much time they take to respond, the total time they take per inkblot, and the way they handle the inkblot card. Then, in a second phase called an *inquiry,* the respondent is reminded of the previous responses and asked to elaborate on them.

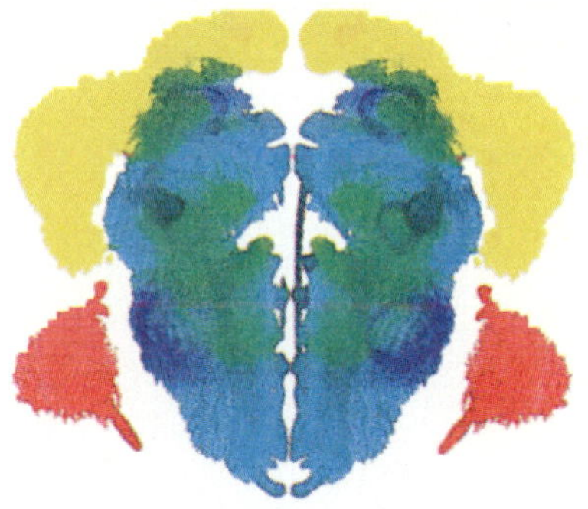

Figure 15.7 An Inkblot Similar to Those Used in the Rorschach Test
What do you see? Does your interpretation of this inkblot reveal anything about your personality?

The responses are scored on three major features: (1) the *location,* or part of the card mentioned in the response—whether the respondent refers to the whole stimulus or to part of it and the size of the details mentioned; (2) the *content* of the response—the nature of the object and activities seen; and (3) the *determinants*—which aspects of the card (such as its color or shading) prompted the response. Scorers may also note whether responses are original and unique or popular and conforming.

You might think that ambiguous inkblots would give rise to an uninterpretable diversity of responses. In fact, researchers have devised a comprehensive scoring system for Rorschach responses that allows for meaningful comparisons among different test takers (Exner, 1974, 1978; Exner & Weiner, 1982). This scoring system specifies, for example, common categories of content response like *whole human* (the response mentions or implies a whole human form) and *blood* (the response mentions blood, either human or animal). Patterns of responses have been successfully related to normal personality characteristics as well as to psychopathology. When the system is applied correctly, Rorschach tests are reliable and allow the trained researcher or clinician to make valid assessments about underlying personality (Parker et al., 1988).

The TAT

In the Thematic Apperception Test, developed by **Henry Murray** in 1938, respondents are shown pictures of ambiguous scenes and asked to generate stories about them, describing what the people in the scenes are doing and thinking, what led up to each event, and how each situation will end (see **Figure 15.8**). The person administering the TAT evaluates the structure and content of the stories as well as the behavior of the individual telling them, in an attempt to discover some of the respondent's major concerns, motivations, and personality characteristics. For example, an examiner might evaluate a person as *conscientious* if his or her stories concerned people who lived up to their obligations and if the stories were told in a serious, orderly way. Recall from Chapter 12 that the TAT has often been used to reveal individual differences in dominant needs, such as needs for power, affiliation, and achievement (McClelland, 1961). Over several decades of research, the TAT has proven to be a valid measure of the need for achievement (Spangler, 1992).

Henry Murray's Thematic Apperception Test presents the examinee with ambiguous scenes to stimulate stories. The TAT has proven to be a valid measure of the need for achievement.

Figure 15.8 A Sample Card from the TAT Test
What story do you want to tell? What does your story reveal about your personality?

Evaluation of Personality Assessment

Could you see the relationship between these personality assessment devices and the theories of personality we reviewed in Chapter 14? Most often, personality tests emerged from particular theories of personality. Our conclusion in Chapter 14 was that each of the types of theories illuminated best different aspects of human experience. We can reach much the same conclusions for personality tests: each has the potential to provide unique insights into an individual's personality. Clinicians most often use a combination of tests when they carry out a personality assessment; the Rorschach and MMPI, for example, may be seen as complementary (Lubin et al., 1984; Piotrowksi et al., 1985). Under many circumstances, the profiles that arise from objective, even computer-based analyses may allow accurate predictions to be made for specific outcomes (Meehl, 1954, 1965; Sawyer, 1966). Under other circumstances, clinical expertise and skilled intuition must supplement objective norms. In practice, the best predictions are made when the strengths of each approach are combined (Dawes et al., 1989; Holt, 1970).

Because personality tests are most often associated with particular theories, it will not surprise you that the adherents of different theories feel more comfortable or less comfortable using different types of tests. If, for example, your personality theory was oriented toward observable behaviors, you might be uncomfortable with any test that relies on static self-reports. Other critics argue that all the many different ways of assessing personality use the wrong approach to understanding the richness and uniqueness of personality (Rorer & Widiger, 1983). These critics call for an emphasis on understanding what is characteristic and special about individual persons. **Personology** is the study of personality structure, dynamics, and development in the *individual*. The data for this formidable task come from diaries, biographies, literature, case studies, letters, and general observations, not from psychometric tests.

Supporters of personology gather data from sources such as diaries, biographies, literature, case studies, letters, and general observations.

These criticisms leave us at much the same point we arrived at when we considered intelligence testing. Just as you must define intelligence before you can measure it, you must have a definition of personality to measure it successfully. Claims about personality should only be generalized to the limits of validity of each particular test.

ASSESSMENT AND YOU

Thus far we have presented some of the major features of assessment techniques and have discussed in detail certain approaches used to assess intelligence, creativity, and personality. We turn now to issues of assessment that may affect you on a day-to-day basis. As a student, you will probably be struggling with decisions about your job or your career. Thus we first discuss the role of assessment in vocational counseling. We then address some of the political and ethical issues posed by the widespread use of formal assessment procedures in society today.

VOCATIONAL INTERESTS AND APTITUDES

Have you already determined a career path? Are you still undecided or perhaps thinking of leaving a job you already have? Many assessment instruments have been developed to help people learn what vocations best fit their personalities, values, interests, and skills—or, in some cases, to show them before it's too late that the career they have chosen may not be the wisest choice.

Assessing Interests

Even if you do not yet know what jobs you might like best, you would like to have a job that suits your interests and serves goals that you consider worthwhile. A widely used test for measuring vocational interests is the *Strong-Campbell Interest Inventory*, which was constructed in 1927 by psychologist **Edward Strong.** The test is based on an empirical approach similar to that used later for the MMPI. First, groups of men in different occupations answered items about activities they liked or disliked. Then the answers given by those who were successful in particular occupations were compared with the responses of men in general to create a scale. Subsequent versions of the test have added scales relevant to women and to newer occupations. If you took this test, a vocational counselor could tell you what types of jobs are typically held by people with interests such as yours, since these are the jobs that are likely to appeal to you.

Assessment devices have been developed to help people choose careers compatible with their interests.

Assessing Abilities

Even if a job appeals to you, suits your personality, and fits your values and interests, you are unlikely to be satisfied with it unless you can do the work well. Your employer is also unlikely to be satisfied with you if you are unable to do the job for which you were hired.

In order to recommend a career path for you, therefore, a vocational counselor will want to assess your abilities as well as your interests. Ability has two components: aptitude and achievement. An **aptitude test** measures your potential for acquiring various skills—not necessarily how well you can perform tasks now but how well you will perform in the future, with appropriate training. An IQ test is a classic example of an aptitude test. An **achievement test,** on the other hand, measures your current level of competence. A test of how well you can speak a foreign language or program a computer would be an example of an achievement test.

While aptitude tests measure your potential for acquiring various skills, achievement tests measure your current level of competence.

Tests have been developed to assess aptitude and achievement in many domains. For example, if managing other people will be an important part of the job, your tolerance for interpersonal stress and ability to assert yourself may be measured. With knowledge not only of what you like to do but also of what you can do well, a counselor is in a good position to predict your suitability for different jobs (Landy et al., 1994; Sundberg & Matarazzo, 1979; Tyler, 1974).

Assessing Jobs

Assessment plays a dual role in personnel selection, considering both the characteristics of the desired employee and an evaluation of the job requirements in order to make a good match between the two.

Organizations often invest substantial time and money in personnel selection. They rely not only on an assessment of an applicant's characteristics but also on a careful identification and analysis of the requirements of the job. In a **job analysis,** a specific job is carefully examined to determine the nature and degree of *skill* required, the amount of *effort* demanded, and the extent to which an individual is *responsible* for decisions that affect company resources or personnel and to identify any other types of *stress* the job may entail (Landy et al., 1994; Tenopyr & Oeltjen, 1982). The results of job analyses are used not only in selecting personnel but also in determining the pay scale for different jobs.

Career counselors are trained to help identify abilities and match them to potential careers.

Job assessment is performed in many ways. Workers, supervisors, and specially trained analysts are asked to provide information about the abilities required for particular jobs. Subject-matter experts may rate the relevance of various kinds of knowledge, skills, and abilities. An inventory of requirements, including the tasks and duties a worker must perform, can then be prepared for each occupation. One such inventory—the *Occupational Analysis Inventory*—provides information about a wide spectrum of occupations and can be very helpful to a job seeker (Pass & Cunningham, 1978).

Some companies supplement other assessment methods with *realistic job previews.* They show applicants what will be expected of them on the job, through films, tapes, employee checklists of most- and least-liked aspects of a job, and simulations of critical incidents likely to arise (Wanous, 1980). These previews can give you a clearer picture of what will be expected of you if you take a job and help you decide how well the job fits your abilities and interests.

Political and Ethical Issues

The primary goal of psychological assessment is to make accurate assessments of people that are as free as possible of errors of assessors' judgments. This goal is achieved by replacing subjective judgments of teachers, employers, and other evaluators with more objective measures that have been carefully constructed and are open to critical evaluation. This is the goal that motivated Alfred Binet in his pioneering work. Binet and others hoped that testing would help democratize society and minimize decisions based on arbitrary criteria of sex, race, nationality, privilege, or physical appearance. However, despite these lofty goals, there is no area of psychology more controversial than assessment. Three unresolved issues that are central to the controversy are the fairness of test-based decisions, the utility of tests for evaluating education, and the implications of using test scores as labels to categorize individuals.

The goal of assessment is to reduce or eliminate bias in decision making by replacing the subjective judgments of people with objective psychometric tools.

Critics concerned with the fairness of testing practices argue that the costs or negative consequences may be higher for some test takers than for others. The costs are quite high, for example, when tests on which minority groups receive low scores are used to keep them out of certain jobs. In some cities, applicants for civil service janitor jobs must pass a verbal test, rather than a more appropriate test of manual skills. According to researcher William Banks, this is a strategy unions use to keep minorities from access to jobs (1990). Sometimes, minority group members test poorly because their scores are evaluated relative to inappropriate norms. In addition, arbitrary cutoff scores that favor applicants from one group may be used to make selection decisions, when, in reality, a lower cutoff score that is fairer would produce just as many correct hiring decisions. In addition, overreliance on

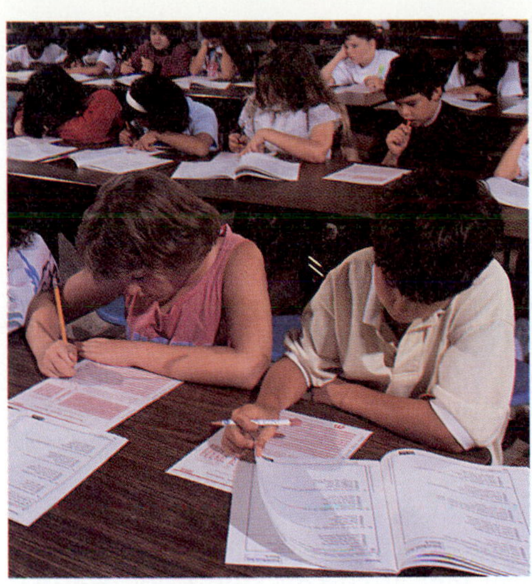

When schools are rewarded for high scores on standardized tests, are teachers likely to place more emphasis on test-taking skills than on broader learning goals?

testing may make personnel selection an automatic attempt to fit people into available jobs. Instead, sometimes society might benefit more by changing job descriptions to fit the needs and abilities of people.

A second ethical concern is that testing not only helps evaluate students; it may also play a role in the shaping of education. The quality of school systems and the effectiveness of teachers are frequently judged on the basis of how well their students score on standardized achievement tests. Local support of the schools through tax levies, and even individual teacher salaries, may ride on test scores.

However, test scores can be used to provide objective evidence of student ability that runs contrary to the bias of some teachers or school systems. This use of tests was as Alfred Binet originally intended, to provide an objective measure that could circumvent the biases of human judgment (Cronbach, 1990). A pattern of discrimination against African-American children in a southern school district was uncovered recently that shunted them into "slow learner" tracked classes. This illegal discrimination has persisted for years regardless of the students' abilities—until exposed by the new (white) superintendent, a former teacher there. He used test score data to show that some white students in the high achiever tracks had low test scores, while some black students with high test scores had been segregated into the slow tracks. This objective evidence is the basis for new efforts to correct this pattern of racial tracking that results in separate but unequal educational opportunities (Kirchner, 1995).

A third ethical concern is that test outcomes can take on the status of unchangeable labels. People too often think of themselves as *being* an IQ of 110 or a B student, as if the scores were labels stamped on their foreheads. Such labels may become barriers to advancement as people come to believe that their mental and personal qualities are fixed and unchangeable—that they cannot improve their lot in life. For those who are negatively assessed, the scores can become self-imposed motivational limits that lower their sense of self-efficacy and restrict the challenges they are willing to tackle. That is another insidious consequence of popular books, like *The Bell Curve,* and media pronouncements about group deficiencies in IQ. Those stigmatized publicly in this way come to believe what the "experts" are saying about them, and so dis-identify with schools and education as means to improve their lives.

This tendency to give test scores a sacred status has societal as well as personal implications. When test scores become labels that identify traits, states, maladjustment, conflict, and pathology *within* an individual, people begin to think about the "abnormality" of individual children rather than about educational systems that need to modify programs to accommodate all learners. Labels put the spotlight on deviant personalities rather than on dysfunctional aspects of their environment. In societies that have an individualistic orientation, like the United States, people are all too ready to misattribute success and failure to the person, while underestimating the impact of the behavioral setting. We blame the victim for failure and thereby take society off the hook; we give credit to the person for success and thereby do not recognize the many societal influences that made it possible. Assessors, professionals and lay people, need to recognize that what people are now is a product of where they've been, where they think they are headed, and what situation is currently influencing their behavior. Such a view can help to unite different assessment approaches and theoretical camps as well as lead to more humane treatment of those who do not fit the norm (see Matarazzo, 1990).

We'd like to conclude on a personal note from Phil Zimbardo, one that may have some inspirational value to students who do not do well on objective tests:

> Although I have gone on to have a successful career as a professional psychologist, the relevant tests I took many years ago would have predicted otherwise. Despite being an Honors undergraduate student, who graduated Summa Cum Laude, I got my only C grade in Introductory Psychology, where grades were based solely on multiple-choice exams. I was initially rejected for graduate training at Yale University; then I became an alternate, and finally, I was accepted reluctantly. This was in part because my GRE math scores were below the psychology department's criterion cutoff level. But I later discovered that is was also due in part to the false assumption of some faculty that I must be Negro—on the basis of the pattern of my answers and other "evidence" revealed in my application and tests. Such data negatively colored their judgments of my potential for a career in psychology. Fortunately, some others were willing to give me a chance when one of their respectable admits (Gordon Bower) went elsewhere to start his graduate training.
>
> Successful performance in a career and in life requires much more than the skills, abilities, and traits measured by standardized tests. While the best tests perform the valuable function of predicting how well people will do on the average, there may be decisional error for any given individual. People can over-ride the pessimistic predictions of their tests scores when ambition, imagination, hope, personal pride, and intense effort empower their performance. Perhaps it is vital to know when you should believe more in yourself than in the results of a test.

Recapping Main Points

What Is Assessment?

Psychological assessment has a long history, beginning in ancient China. Many important contributions were made by Sir Francis Galton. The purpose of psychological assessment is to describe or classify individuals in ways that will be useful for prediction or treatment.

Methods of Assessment

A useful assessment tool must be reliable, valid, and standardized. A reliable measure gives consistent results. A valid measure assesses the attributes for which the test was designed. A standardized test is always administered and scored in the same way; norms allow a person's score to be compared with the averages of others of the same age, sex, and culture.

Formal assessment is carried out through interviews, review of life history data, tests, and situational observations. Assessment information may come from self-report or observer-report methods. Self-report measures require subjects to answer questions or supply information about themselves. Observer-report measures require persons who know or have observed a subject person to provide the information.

Intelligence and Intelligence Assessment

Binet began the tradition of objective intelligence testing in France in the early 1900s. Scores were given in terms of mental ages and were meant to represent children's current level of functioning. Terman created the Stanford-Binet Intelligence Scale and popularized the concept of IQ. Wechsler designed special intelligence tests for adults, children, and preschoolers.

Psychometric analyses of IQ suggest that several basic abilities, such as fluid and crystallized aspects of intelligence, contribute to IQ scores. Contemporary theories conceive of and measure intelligence very broadly by considering the skills and insights people use to solve the types of problems they encounter. For example, Sternberg differentiates componential, experiential, and contextual aspects of intelligence.

IQ tests are controversial because, on average, some racial and cultural groups score lower on the tests than other groups. Instead of genetic differences, environmental disadvantages and test bias seem to be responsible for the lower scores of certain groups. Research shows that these group differences can be affected through environmental interventions.

Creativity is often assessed using tests of divergent thinking. Exceptionally creative people take risks, prepare, and are highly motivated. A link between madness and creativity has not been confirmed.

Assessing Personality

Personality characteristics are assessed by both objective and projective tests. The most popular objective test, the MMPI-2, is used to diagnose clinical problems. The CPI is a similar inventory that is intended for use with normal (nonclinical) populations. The NEO-PI and BFQ are newer objective personality tests that measure five major dimensions of personality. The MMPI is especially popular for research because there are extensive archives of MMPIs taken by many types of people over many years. Projective tests of personality ask people to respond to ambiguous stimuli. Two popular projective tests are the Rorschach test and the TAT.

Assessment and You

Vocational assessment includes assessment of an individual's interests, aptitudes, and current level of achievement. The Strong-Campbell Interest Inventory compares an individual's interests with those of people who are successful in various occupations. The Occupational Analysis Inventory provides information about the requirements of various jobs.

Though often useful for prediction and as an indication of current performance, test results should not be used to limit an individual's opportunities for development and change. When the results of an assessment will affect an individual's life, the techniques used must be reliable and valid for that individual and for the purpose in question.

Resources

Amabile, T. M. (1983). *The social psychology of creativity.* New York: Springer-Verlag.

Binet, A., & Simon, T. (1916/1973). *The development of intelligence in children.* Salem, NH: Ayer.

Gardner, H. (1993). *Creating minds*. New York: Basic Books.

Gardner, H. (1993). *Multiple intelligences: The theory in practice.* New York: Basic Books.

Hernnstein, R. J., & Murray, C. (1994). *The bell curve.* New York: Free Press. A controversial work that uses the mantle of science to draw highly suspect conclusions.

Kail, R., & Pellegrino, J. W. (1985). *Human intelligence: Perspectives and prospects.* New York: Freeman.

Lubinsky, D. G., & Dawis, R. V. (Eds.). (1995). *Assessing differences in human behavior: New concepts, methods, and findings.* Palo Alto, CA: Davis-Black.

Plomin, R., DeFries, J. C., & McClearn, G. E. (1980). *Behavioral genetics: A primer.* San Francisco: Freeman. Contains a clear and detailed explanation of heritability.

Sattler, J. M. (1982). *Assessment of children's intelligence and special abilities.* Boston: Allyn & Bacon. Reviews the historical development of the IQ test, including a discussion of the deviation method for calculating IQ.

Sternberg, R. J. (1988). *The triarchic mind: A new theory of human intelligence.* New York: Viking.

16

Social Processes and Relationships

Has this ever happened to you? You go into a store to buy something new—let's say a new radio—and you have in mind a certain amount of money you want to spend—no more than $25. The salesperson greets you warmly, and you end up leaving 15 minutes later with a CD player *that cost you $89! Why did this happen? Are you too easily pushed around by salespeople? (Are you wimpy or gullible?) Or is there something about the social situation salespeople create that would make just about anyone leave with that new CD player? To what extent does your action reveal something about you personally versus the general power of the situation?*

Welcome to the study of social psychology, *that area of psychology that investigates the ways in which individuals affect each other.* **Social psychology** *is the study of the ways in which thoughts, feelings, perceptions, motives, and behavior are influenced by interactions and transactions between people. Social psychologists try to understand behavior within its* social context. *This social context is the vibrant canvas on which are painted the movements, strengths, and vulnerabilities of the social animal. Defined broadly, the* **social context** *includes the real, imagined, or symbolic presence of other people; the activities and interactions that take place between people; the features of the settings in which behavior occurs; and the expectations and norms that govern behavior in a given setting (C. Sherif, 1981).*

We will explore several major themes of social psychological research. In the first part of the chapter, we will discuss the power of social situations to control human behavior. We will consider a large body of research that shows the surprising extent to which small features of social settings can have a significant impact on what you think and how you act. We next turn to the ways in which people construct social reality. Situations are defined, in part, by the expectations you bring to them. We then consider social interaction with attention to both negative relationships—we discuss prejudice—and positive relationships—we discuss liking and loving. Finally, we describe how social psychologists attempt to solve real-world problems by applying the information generated by basic research on social processes. At that point, abstract theory will meet the stern test of practicality, as we attempt to answer this question: Does the theory make a difference in the lives of people and society?

THE POWER OF THE SITUATION

Throughout *Psychology and Life,* we have seen that psychologists who strive to understand the causes of behavior look in many different places for their answers. Some look to genetic factors, others to biochemical and brain processes, while still others focus on the causal influence of the environment. Social psychologists believe that the primary determinant of behavior is the nature of the social situation in which that behavior occurs. They argue that social situations exert significant control over individual behavior, often dominating personality and a person's past history of learning, values, and beliefs. As in our opening example of shopping for a radio, situational aspects that appear trivial to many observers can powerfully influence how people behave. In this section, we will review some classic research and recent experiments that explore the effect of subtle situational variables on people's behavior.

Social psychologists focus on social situations as the determinants of behavior.

Roles and Rules in Situations

How is your repertory of behaviors constrained by the social situations in which you function? Another way to ask this question is, What *social roles* are available to you? A **social role** is a socially defined pattern of behavior that is expected of a person when functioning in a given setting or group. Different social situations make different roles available. When you are at home, you may accept the role of "child" or "sibling." When you are in the classroom, you accept the role of "student." At other times still, you are a "best friend" or "lover." Can you see how these different roles immediately make different types of behaviors more or less acceptable and available to you?

Situations are also characterized by the operation of **rules,** behavioral guidelines for specific settings. Some rules are explicitly stated in signs (DON'T SMOKE, NO EATING IN CLASS), or are explicitly taught to children (Respect the elderly, Never take candy from a stranger). Other rules are *implicit*—they are learned through transactions with others in particular settings. How loud you can play your stereo, how close you can stand to another person, when you can call your teacher or boss by a first name, and what is the suitable way to react to a compliment or a gift—all of these actions depend on the situation. For example, the Japanese do not open a gift in the presence of the giver, for fear of not showing sufficient appreciation; foreigners not aware of this unwritten rule will misinterpret the behavior as rude instead of sensitive.

To open or not to open? The etiquette for giving and receiving gifts varies from one culture to another.

Ordinarily, you might not be particularly aware of the effects of roles and rules, but one classic social psychological experiment, the **Stanford Prison Experiment,** put these forces to work with startling results (Haney & Zimbardo, 1977; Zimbardo, 1975; replicated in Australia by Lovibond et al., 1979).

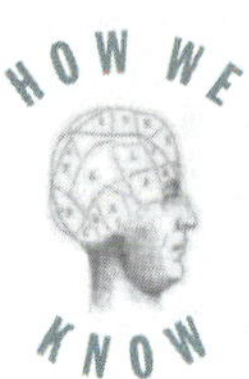

On a summer Sunday in California, a siren shattered the serenity of college student Tommy Whitlow's morning. A police car screeched to a halt in front of his home. Within minutes, Tommy was charged with a felony, informed of his constitutional rights, frisked, and handcuffed. After he was booked and fingerprinted, Tommy was blindfolded and transported to the Stanford County Prison, where he was stripped, sprayed with disinfectant, and issued a smock-type uniform with an I.D. number on the front and back. Tommy became Prisoner 647. Nine other college students were also arrested and assigned numbers.

Tommy and his cellmates were all volunteers who had answered a newspaper ad and agreed to be subjects in a two-week experiment on prison life. By random flips of a coin, some of the volunteers had been assigned to the role of prisoners; the rest became guards. All had been selected from a large pool of student volunteers who, on the basis of extensive psychological tests and interviews, had been judged as law abiding, emotionally stable, physically healthy, and "normal-average." The prisoners lived in the jail around the clock; the guards worked standard eight-hour shifts.

What happened once these students had assumed their randomly assigned roles? In guard roles, college students who had been pacifists and "nice guys" behaved aggressively—sometimes even sadistically. The guards insisted that prisoners obey all rules without question or hesitation. Failure to do so led to the loss of a privilege. At first, privileges included opportunities to read,

The Stanford Prison Experiment created a new "social reality" in which the norms of good behavior were overwhelmed by the dynamics of the situation.

In Zimbardo's Stanford Prison Experiment, pacifist students behaved aggressively in the role of guards, and psychologically healthy students showed pathological behavior when assigned the role of prisoner.

write, or talk to other inmates. Later on, the slightest protest resulted in the loss of the "privileges" of eating, sleeping, and washing. Failure to obey rules also resulted in menial, mindless work such as cleaning toilets with bare hands, doing push-ups while a guard stepped on the prisoner's back, and spending hours in solitary confinement. The guards were always devising new strategies to make the prisoners feel worthless.

As prisoners, psychologically stable students soon behaved pathologically, passively resigning themselves to their unexpected fate. Less than 36 hours after the mass arrest, Prisoner 8412, one of the ringleaders of an aborted prisoner rebellion that morning, began to cry uncontrollably. He experienced fits of rage, disorganized thinking, and severe depression. On successive days, three more prisoners developed similar stress-related symptoms. A fifth prisoner developed a psychosomatic rash all over his body when the Parole Board rejected his appeal.

Because of the dramatic and unexpectedly severe emotional and behavioral effects observed, those prisoners with extreme stress reactions were released early from this unusual prison, and the psychologists were forced to terminate their two-week study after only six days. Although Tommy Whitlow said he wouldn't want to go through it again, he valued the personal experience because he learned so much about himself and about human nature. Fortunately, he and the other students were basically healthy, and they readily bounced back from this highly charged situation. Follow-ups over many years revealed no lasting negative effects. The participants had all contributed to an important lesson: the power of the simulated prison situation had created a new *social reality*—a real prison—in the minds of the jailers and their captives.

By the conclusion of the Stanford Prison Experiment, guards' and prisoners' behavior differed from one another in virtually every observable way

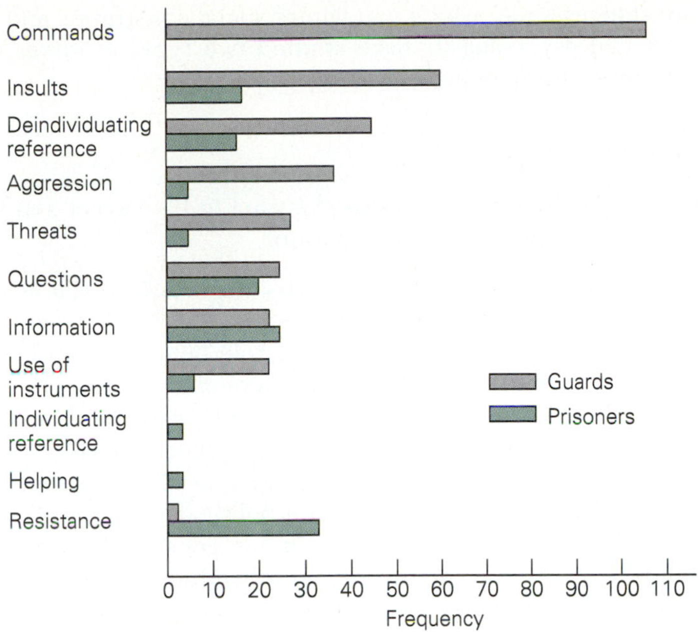

Figure 16.1 Guard and Prisoner Behavior
During the Stanford Prison Experiment, the randomly assigned roles of prisoners and guards drastically affected subjects' behavior. The observations recorded in the 6-day interaction profile show that across 25 observation periods, the prisoners engaged in more passive resistance, while the guards became more dominating, controlling, and hostile.

(see **Figure 16.1**). Yet it was only chance, in the form of random assignment, that had decided their roles—roles that had created status and power differences that were validated in the prison situation. No one taught the participants to play their roles. Without ever visiting real prisons, all the participants learned something about the interaction between the powerful and the powerless (Banuazizi & Movahedi, 1975). A guard-type is someone who limits the freedom of prisoner-types to manage their behavior and make them behave more predictably. This task is aided by the use of *coercive rules,* which include explicit punishment for violations. Prisoners can only *react* to the social structure of a prisonlike setting created by those with power. Rebellion or compliance is the primary option of the prisoners; the first choice results in punishment, while the second results in a loss of a sense of autonomy and dignity.

The student participants had already experienced such power differences in many of their previous social interactions: parent–child, teacher–student, doctor–patient, boss-worker, male–female. They merely refined and intensified their prior patterns of behavior for this particular setting. Each student could have played either role. Many students in the guard role reported being surprised at how easily they enjoyed controlling other people. Just putting on the uniform was enough to transform them from passive college students into aggressive prison guards. What sort of person do *you* become when you slip in and out of different roles? Where does your sense of personal self end and your social identity begin?

Conformity: Social Norms

When you adopt a social role, you are, to some extent, *conforming* to social expectations. **Conformity** is the tendency for people to adopt the behavior and opinions presented by other group members. Why do you conform? Are

Two types of social forces may lead to conformity: normative influence processes, which involve wanting to be liked or accepted; and information influence processes, which involve wanting to be correct.

there circumstances under which you ignore social constraints and act independently? Social psychologists have studied two types of forces that may lead to conformity (Insko et al., 1985):

- **normative influence** processes—wanting to be liked, accepted, and approved of by others;
- **informational influence** processes—wanting to be correct and to understand how best to act in a given situation.

In this section, we will examine normative influence; in the next section we turn to informational influence processes.

In addition to the expectations regarding role behaviors, groups develop many expectations for the ways their members *should act.* These specific expectations for socially appropriate attitudes and behaviors that are embodied in the stated or implicit rules of a group are called **social norms.** Social norms can be broad guidelines; if you are member of Democrats for Social Action, you may be expected to hold liberal political beliefs, while members of the Young Republicans will advocate more conservative views. Social norms can also embody specific standards of conduct; if you are a spy, you may be expected to resist any attempt to extract secret information from you, even if it means risking torture, imprisonment, or death.

Belonging to a group typically involves discovering the set of social norms that regulates desired behavior in the group setting. This adjustment occurs in two ways: you notice the *uniformities* in certain behaviors of all or most members, and you observe the *negative consequences* when someone violates a social norm.

The desire to conform is particularly strong in the workplace, where expressing too much individuality could have adverse economic consequences.

Norms serve several important functions. Awareness of the norms operating in a given group situation helps orient members and regulate their social interaction. Each participant can anticipate how others will enter the situation, how they will dress, and what they are likely to say and do, as well as what type of behavior will be expected of them to gain approval. You often feel awkward in new situations precisely because you may be unaware of the norms that govern the way you ought to act. Some *tolerance for deviating* from the standard is also part of the norm—wide in some cases, narrow in others. Your 9-page paper may fulfill a 10–12-page writing assignment, but a 3-page paper probably would not. Members are usually able to estimate how far they can go before experiencing the coercive power of the group in the form of the three painful R's: *ridicule, reeducation,* and *rejection.*

Let's examine some cases of how norms are created and maintained by groups.

Sherif's Autokinetic Effect

The classic experiment that demonstrated **norm crystallization**—norm formation and solidification—was conducted by **Muzafer Sherif** (1935).

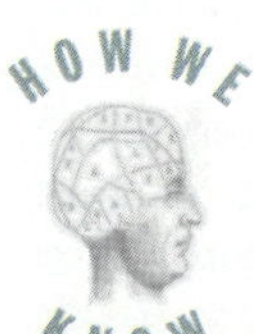

Subjects were asked to judge the amount of movement of a spot of light, which was actually stationary but that appeared to move when viewed in total darkness with no reference points, a perceptual illusion known as the **autokinetic effect.** Originally, individual judgments varied widely. However, when the subjects were brought together in a group and stated their judgments aloud, their estimates began to converge. They began to see the light move in the same direction and in similar amounts. Even more interesting was the final part of Sherif's study—when alone in the darkened room after the group viewing, these subjects continued to follow the group norm that had emerged when they were together.

Muzafer Sherif's classic experiment using the autokinetic effect demonstrated how norms are formed and showed that once established, norms tend to perpetuate themselves.

Once norms are established in a group, they tend to perpetuate themselves. In later research, these autokinetic group norms persisted even when tested a year later and without peers witnessing the judgments (Rohrer et al., 1954). Other research shows that current group members exert social pressure on incoming members to adhere to the norms. The newcomers, in turn, then put direct or indirect pressure on successive newcomers to conform to the norms. Norms can be transmitted from one generation of group members to the next and can continue to influence people's behavior long after the original group that created the norm no longer exists (Insko et al., 1980). How do we know that norms can have transgenerational influence? In autokinetic effect studies, researchers replaced one group member with a new one after each set of autokinetic trials until all the members of the group were new to the situation. The group's autokinetic norm remained true to the one handed down to them across several successive generations (Jacobs & Campbell, 1961).

Sherif's research demonstrates the transmission of norms in laboratory settings. Let's move now to norm transmission in the "real world," where all of us live.

Bennington's Liberal Norms

Often the process of being influenced by group norms is so gradual and so subtle that an individual does not perceive what is happening. Some insights into this process are provided by a classic study conducted in a small New England college for women in the late 1930s. Researcher **Theodore Newcomb** studied the shifts in political and social attitudes experienced by students during their 4 years at Bennington College and then followed up the observed effects 20 years later to determine if the effects were enduring.

The prevailing norm at Bennington College was one of political and economic liberalism, as encouraged by its young, dynamic, politically committed, and liberal faculty. Most of the students, however, had come from privileged, conservative homes and brought conservative attitudes with them. The study examined the impact of the college's liberal atmosphere on the attitudes of individual students.

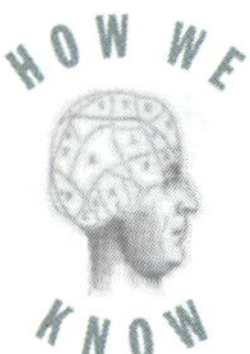

Among first-year Bennington students, over 60 percent supported the Republican presidential candidate, and fewer than 30 percent supported Franklin Roosevelt, the Democratic incumbent. Second-year students, however, were equally divided in their support for the two candidates. This liberal shift continued among the juniors and seniors—only 15 percent favored the Republican candidate, while 54 percent supported the Democratic candidate and more than 30 percent advocated support for the Socialist or Communist candidates (Newcomb, 1943).

A study at Bennington College demonstrated that changes in values become internalized and remain evident many years later.

Newcomb accounted for this change in terms of several features of the situation. The young women were in a close-knit social community, self-sufficient and physically isolated from the outside world. The strong sense of school spirit included activist concerns and support for liberal views and causes. Pressures toward uniformity of attitudes and political actions were enforced by greater social acceptance and implied threats of rejection. These values became *internalized,* accepted as their own, by students for whom other Bennington students had become the primary reference group. A **reference group** is a formal or informal group from which an individual derives attitudes and standards of acceptable and appropriate behavior and to which the individual refers for information, direction, and support for a given lifestyle. The liberal reference group at Bennington had a powerful effect.

When individuals become dependent upon a group—such as a religious cult—for basic feelings of self-worth, they are prone to extremes of conformity. Twenty thousand identically dressed couples were married in this service conducted by the Reverend Sun Myung Moon. More recently, in August 1995, Moon simultaneously married 360,000 couples who were linked by satellite in 500 worldwide locations.

Twenty years later, the marks of the Bennington experience were still evident. Most women who had left as liberals were still liberals. Most had married men with values similar to their own, thus creating a supportive home environment. Of those who left college as liberals but married conservative men, a high proportion had returned to their first-year student conservatism (Newcomb, 1963). However, in the 1960 election, the Bennington allegiance showed through: about 60 percent of the 1935–1939 graduates voted for John F. Kennedy, as compared with less than 30 percent support for Kennedy among comparable college graduates throughout the country (Newcomb et al., 1976).

The extent of the influence a group will have on your attitudes and behaviors will depend, in part, on how much the group matters to you. The more you rely on social rewards from a group for your primary sense of self-worth and legitimacy, the greater will be the social influence the group can bring to bear on you. Social norms assume their greatest force when group members are in a **total situation**, one in which they are isolated from contrary points of view and in which sources of information, social rewards, and punishments are all highly controlled by group leaders. The thought reform that Chinese Communists imposed on Chinese citizens, the "brainwashing" of prisoners of war, and the alleged coercive persuasion of cult members all have in common this element of intense indoctrination of new beliefs and values within the social isolation of a "total situation" (Lifton, 1969; Osherow, 1981).

The thought reform that Chinese Communists imposed on their citizens, brainwashing of prisoners of war, and the alleged coercive persuasion of cult members are all examples of the intense indoctrination of values that may occur in situations of social isolation.

Social Norms in Contemporary College Life

We've just seen the way in which many of the women at Bennington came to adopt the norms of the surrounding community. Can you detect norms at work in your own college experience?

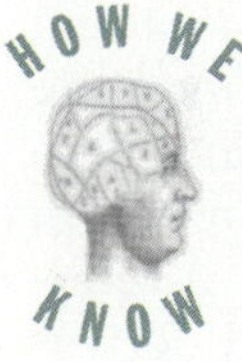

Consider the subject of alcohol on campus. How comfortable do you feel about the drinking habits of students at your school? How comfortable does the average student feel about those habits? Researchers asked Princeton undergraduates to answer this pair of questions. The ratings revealed that, on average, each student believed himself or herself to be less comfortable with alcohol habits than the average student—ratings of 5.3 for self versus 7.0 for the average student on an 11-point scale. Thus, on average, subjects rated themselves considerably below the "norm" (Prentice & Miller, 1993).

These data suggest that the shared sense of the group norm does not accurately capture what each individual feels. (Do you see why that is so? The "real" norm is 5.3, the average of what each individual feels, not 7.0, the average of what they believe others feel.) Thus the perceived "group norm" exists independently of what the norm of the group really is. This study also showed that, over the course of a semester, male, but not female, students' ratings for their own attitudes grew much closer to their perception of the norm: for the men, believing in the norm made it so.

What happens if you make people aware that they are adhering to a norm that doesn't really exist? At the beginning of their first year, another large group of Princeton students participated in two types of discussion groups about alcohol consumption. Half of the students heard about the importance of individual decisions in drinking behavior. The other students had revealed to them the data about the misperception of group norms we have just presented to you. What do you think happened?

At the end of the semester, students from the second group—who had discussed the false norm effect—reported that they were drinking considerably less alcohol each week, by comparison with the self-reports of their peers (Schroeder & Prentice, 1995). By understanding the *social* forces that give rise to incorrect perceptions of norms, this group of students were able to make more responsible *individual* decisions.

A study at Princeton indicated that students who were made aware of the influence of social forces on their perceptions of norms were able to make more responsible individual decisions.

Conformity: Informational Influence

In the Bennington study, conformity to the group norm had clear *adaptive* significance for the students. They were more likely to be accepted, approved, and recognized for various social rewards if they adopted the liberal norm. However, in other circumstances, conformity is not based on normative pressures but rather on other needs, such as the need to understand the events happening around you. How should you react if you hear cries coming from the next room? When uncertain, you typically turn to others in the situation to satisfy *information needs* that will help you understand what is happening (Deutsch & Gerard, 1955). You want to know what is *right.* Let's see how information needs can lead to conformity or independence.

The Asch Effect: Yielding to Lying Lines?

What is the best way to demonstrate that people will base their behavior on information gathered from other members of a reference group? One of the most important early social psychologists, **Solomon Asch** (1940, 1956), created circumstances in which subjects made judgments under conditions in which the physical reality was absolutely clear—but the rest of a group reported that they saw that reality differently. Male college students were led to believe they were in a study of simple visual perception. They were shown cards with three lines of differing lengths and asked to indicate which of the three lines was the same length as the standard line (see **Figure 16.2**). The lines were different enough so that mistakes were rare, and their relative sizes changed on each series of trials.

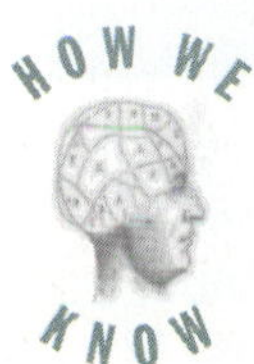

The subjects were seated next to last in semi-circles of six to eight other students. Unknown to the subjects, the others were all experimental confederates who were following a prearranged script. On the first three trials, everyone in the circle agreed on the correct comparison. However, the first confederate to respond on the fourth trial matched two lines that were obviously different. So did all members of the group up to the subject. That student had to decide if he should go along with everyone else's view of the situation and conform or remain independent, standing by what he clearly saw. That dilemma was repeated on 12 of the 18 trials. The subjects showed signs of disbelief and obvious discomfort when faced with a majority who saw the world so differently. What did they do?

Roughly one fourth of the subjects remained completely independent—they never conformed. Between 50 and 80 percent of the subjects (in different studies in the research program) conformed with the false majority estimate at least once, while a third of the subjects yielded to the majority's wrong judgments on half or more of the critical trials. Asch describes some subjects who yielded to the majority most of the time as "disoriented" and "doubt-ridden"; he states that they "experienced a powerful impulse not to appear different from the majority" (1952, p. 396). Those who yielded underestimated the influence of the social pressure and the frequency of their conformity; some even claimed that they really had *seen* the lines as the same.

In other studies, Asch varied three factors: the size of the unanimous majority, the presence of a partner who dissented from the majority, and the

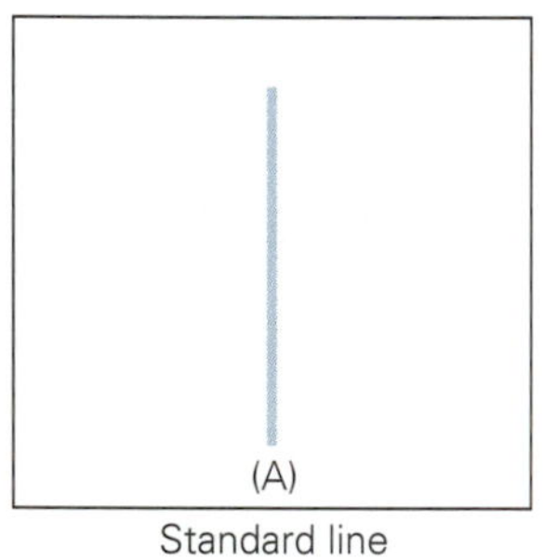

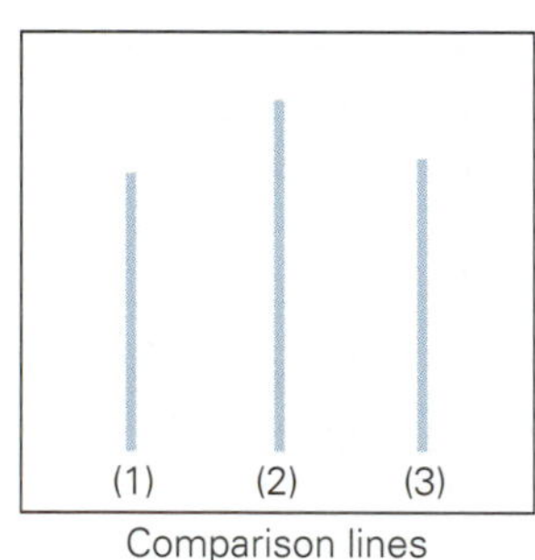

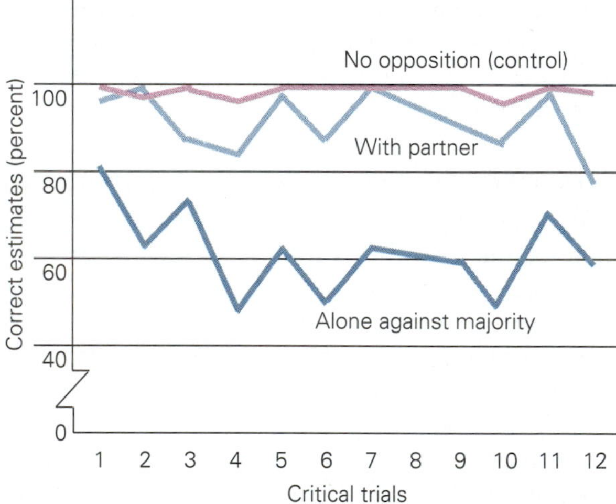

Figure 16.2 Conformity in the Asch Experiments

In this photo from Asch's study, it is evident that the naive subject, Number 6, is worried by the unanimous moajority's erroneous judgment. The typical stimulus array is shown at top left. At top right, the graph illustrates conformity across 12 critical trials when solitary subjects were grouped with a unanimous majority, as well as their greater independence when paired with a dissenting partner. A lower percentage of correct estimates indicates the greater degree of an individual's conformity to the group's false estimate.

size of the discrepancy between the correct physical stimulus comparison and the majority's position. He found that strong conformity effects were elicited with a unanimous majority of only three or four people. However, giving the naive subject one ally who dissented from the majority opinion sharply reduced conformity, as can be seen in Figure 16.2. With a partner, the subject was usually able to resist the pressures to conform to the majority. As you might expect, independence from the majority also increased with the magnitude of the contradiction between one's perception and the group's erroneous judgment. Remarkably, a certain proportion of individuals continued to yield to the group even under the most extreme stimulus circumstances (Asch, 1955, 1956).

Asch's studies of conformity showed that it can occur with a unanimous majority and that giving a subject a dissenting partner significantly reduces conformity.

How should we interpret these results? Asch himself was struck by the rate at which subjects did *not* conform (Friend et al., 1990). Two thirds of the time, subjects gave the correct, nonconforming answer. However, most descriptions of Asch's experiment have emphasized the one-third conformity rate. Accounts of this experiment also often fail to note that not all subjects were alike: the number of individuals who never conformed, about 25 percent, was roughly equal to the number who always or almost always conformed. Thus Asch's experiment teaches two complementary lessons. On the one hand, we find that people are not entirely mindless—they assert their independence on a majority of occasions (and some people always do). On the other hand, we find that people will sometimes conform, even in the most unambiguous situations. That potential to conform is an important element of human nature.

Minority Influence and Nonconformity

Given the power of the majority to control resources and information, it is not surprising that people regularly conform to groups. Yet you know that sometimes individuals persevere in their views. How can this happen? How do people escape group domination, and how can anything new (counternormative) ever come about? Are there any conditions under which a small minority can turn the majority around and create new norms? While researchers in the United States have concentrated their studies on conformity, in part because conformity is intertwined with the democratic process, some European social psychologists have instead focused on the power of the few to change the majority. **Serge Moscovici** of France has pioneered the study of minority influence.

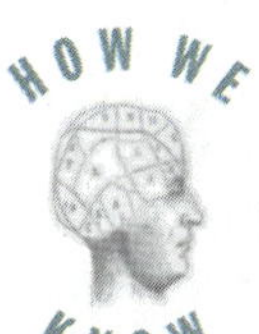

In one study where subjects were given color-naming tasks, the majority correctly identified the color patches, but two of the experimenter's confederates consistently identified a green color as *blue*. Their consistent minority opposition had no immediate effect on the majority, but, when later tested alone, some of the subjects shifted their judgments by moving the boundary between blue and green toward the blue side of the color continuum (Moscovici, 1976; Moscovici & Faucheux, 1972).

Serge Moscovici pioneered the study of minority influence, concluding that the power of the many may be overcome by the conviction of a dedicated few.

Eventually, the power of the many may be undercut by the conviction of the dedicated few (Moscovici, 1980).

What gives a minority influence over the deliberations of the majority? Majority decisions tend to be made without engaging the *systematic thought* and *critical thinking skills* of the individuals in the group. Majority decisions are often taken at face value because of the force of the group's normative power to shape the opinions of the followers, who conform without thinking things through. Under pressure from the persistent minority, the others process the relevant information more *mindfully* (Langer, 1989). Research shows that the decisions of the group as a whole are more *thoughtful* and

Around 1960, when this lunch-counter sit-in took place, the African-American minority began a highly charged movement to change the status quo. To what extent was the movement successful, and why?

Research shows that group decisions tend to be more thoughtful and creative when there has been minority dissent.

creative when there has been minority dissent than in its absence (Nemeth, 1986). The group also *better recalls* the information after having been exposed to a *consistent minority* view than to only the majority or to an inconsistent minority view (Nemeth et al., 1990).

In society, the majority tends to be the defender of the *status quo.* Typically, the force for innovation and change comes from the minority members, or from individuals who are either dissatisfied with the current system or able to visualize new options and creative alternative ways of dealing with current problems. The conflict between the entrenched majority view and the dissident minority perspective is an essential precondition of innovations that can lead to positive social change. As an individual, you are constantly engaged in a two-way exchange with society—adapting to its norms, roles, and status prescriptions but also acting upon society to reshape those norms (Moscovici, 1985). Perhaps the greatest challenge for social psychologists is to understand the interplay between those group forces that influence an individual's behavioral and mental processes and those individual factors that maintain or change group functioning.

Authority Influence

We have been considering how groups influence individuals, but there are certain individuals—leaders and authorities—who exert considerable power on group behavior and on other people. The ultimate demonstration of this effect was seen in the 1930s, with the emergence of Adolf Hitler in Germany and Benito Mussolini in Italy. These leaders forged individuals into mindless masses with unquestioning loyalty to fascist ideologies. Their authoritarian regimes threatened democracies and freedom everywhere. Modern social psychology developed out of this crucible of fear, prejudice, and war. Early social psychologists focused on understanding the nature of the *authoritarian personality* behind the fascist mentality (Adorno et al., 1950), the effects of propaganda and persuasive communications (Hovland et al., 1949), and the impact of group atmosphere and leadership styles on group members.

Lewin's Group Dynamics

The pioneering figure in social psychology was **Kurt Lewin,** a German refugee who escaped Nazi oppression. Lewin could not help but wonder how his nation could succumb totally to the tyranny of a dictator. He witnessed the spectacle of rallies of tens of thousands of people shouting allegiance to their führer. This was a frightening testimony to the dynamic power of groups to transform the minds and actions of individuals and the power of an individual to affect the masses. Lewin investigated **group dynamics**—the ways in which leaders directly influenced their followers and the ways in which group processes changed the behavior of individuals.

In 1939, Lewin and his colleagues designed an experiment to investigate the effects of different leadership styles on group function. They wanted to find out if people are happier or more productive under autocratic or under democratic leadership. To assess the effects of different leadership styles, the researchers created three experimental groups, gave them different types of leaders, and observed the groups in action. The subjects were four small groups of 10-year-old boys, who met after school. The group leaders were men trained to play each of the three leadership styles. When they acted as *autocratic leaders,* the men were to make all decisions and work assignments but not participate in the group activity. As *democratic leaders,* they were to encourage and assist group decision making and planning. Finally, when they acted as *laissez-faire leaders,* their job was to allow complete freedom with little leader participation.

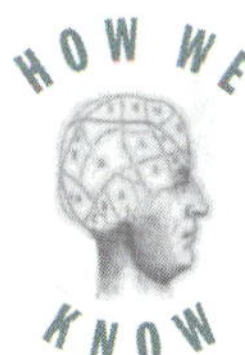

The results of this experiment suggested a number of generalizations. First, *autocratic* leaders produced a mixed bag of effects on their followers—some positive and some quite negative. At times, the boys worked very hard, but typically only when the leader—acting as boss—was watching them. What most characterized the boys in the autocratic groups was their high level of aggression. These boys showed up to *30 times more hostility* when under autocratic leaders than they did under the other types of leaders. They demanded more attention, were more likely to destroy their own property, and showed more *scapegoating* behavior—using weaker individuals as displaced targets for their frustration and anger.

As for the *laissez-faire groups,* not much good resulted. They were the most inefficient of all, doing the least amount of work and of the poorest quality. In the absence of any social structure, they simply fooled around. However, when the same groups were *democratically run,* members worked the most steadily and were most efficient. The boys showed the highest levels of interest, motivation, and originality under democratic leadership. When discontent arose, it was likely to be openly expressed. Almost all the boys preferred the democratic group to the others. Democracy promoted more group loyalty and friendliness. There was more mutual praise, more friendly remarks, more sharing, and, overall, more playfulness (Lewin et al., 1939).

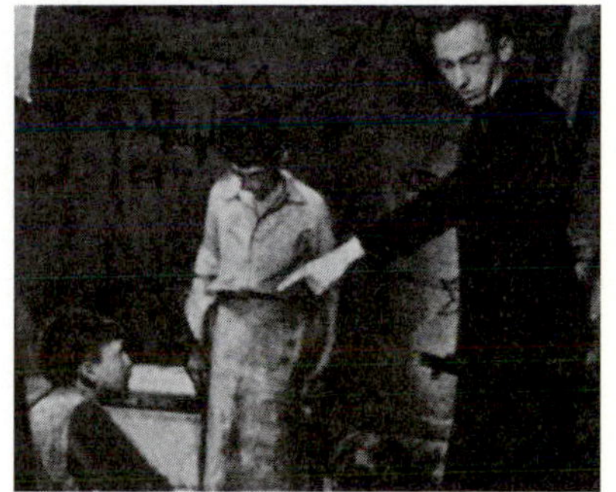

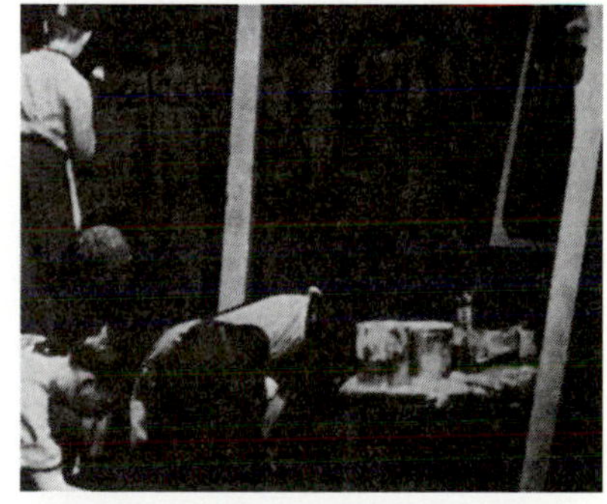

These photos from Lewin's classic study show the three leadership styles in action. The autocratic leader directs work, the democratic leader works with the boys, and the laissez-faire leader remains aloof.

Democracy proved superior psychologically to the other forms of group atmosphere, as well as more productive. Democratic leaders also generated the most healthy reactions from group members, while autocratic-leader groups generated the most destructive individual reactions. Note that each leader, for different groups, played each of the three styles of leadership. Thus we know that it was the different leadership styles, and not the personalities of the leaders, that was the key ingredient in affecting the groups.

Lewin's pioneering work spelled out some of the consequences of different styles of authority. We have not quite arrived, however, at a full understanding of the phenomenon of fascism. To approach that goal requires a consideration of the research of Stanley Milgram.

Milgram's Obedience to Authority

What made thousands of Nazis willing to follow Hitler's orders and send millions of Jews to the gas chambers? Did character defects lead them to carry out orders blindly? Did they have no moral values? How can we explain the 1978 mass suicide–murders of the members of the Peoples Temple? In that incident, over 900 American citizens belonging to a cult willingly gave cyanide poison to their children and to themselves because their leader, the Reverend Jim Jones, told them to commit "revolutionary suicide." What forces led to a jungle compound strewn with bodies?

IN YOUR LIFE

Let's get personal. How about you? Are there any conditions under which you would blindly obey an order from your religious leader to poison others and then commit suicide? Could you imagine being part of the massacre of hundreds of innocent citizens of the Vietnamese village of My Lai by U.S. soldiers (Hersh, 1971; Opton, 1970, 1973)? Your answer—as ours used to be—is most likely, "No! What kind of person do you think I am?" After reading this section, you may be more willing to answer, "Maybe. I don't know for sure." Depending on the power of the social forces operating, you might do what other human beings have done in those situations, however horrible and alien their actions may seem outside that setting.

The most convincing demonstration of situational power over individual behavior was created by **Stanley Milgram**, a student of Solomon Asch. Milgram's research (1965, 1974) showed that the blind obedience of Nazis was less a product of dispositional characteristics (their unusual personality or German national character) than it was the outcome of situational forces that could engulf anyone. How did he demonstrate this "banality of evil"—that evil deeds could emerge from ordinary people who were not monstrous but simply following orders mindlessly, without thought (Arendt, 1963, 1971)? Milgram's obedience research is one of the most controversial because of its significant implications for real-world phenomena and the ethical issues it raises (Miller, 1986; Ross & Nisbett, 1991).

The Obedience Paradigm. To separate the variables of personality and situation, Milgram used a series of 19 separate controlled laboratory experiments involving more than 1000 subjects. Milgram's first experiments were conducted at Yale University, with male residents of New Haven and surrounding communities who received payment for their participation. In later variations, Milgram took his obedience laboratory away from the university. He set up a storefront research unit in Bridgeport, Connecticut, recruiting through newspaper ads a broad cross section of the population, varying widely in age, occupation, and education and including members of both sexes.

Milgram's basic experimental paradigm involved individual subjects delivering a series of what they thought were extremely painful electric shocks to another person. Volunteers thought they were participating in a scientific study of memory and learning. They were led to believe that the educational purpose of the study was to discover how punishment affects memory, so that learning could be improved through the proper balance of reward and punishment. In their *social roles* as *teachers,* the subjects were to punish each error made by someone playing the role of *learner.* The major *rule* they were told to follow was to increase the level of shock each time the learner made an error until the learning was errorless. The white-coated experimenter acted as the *legitimate authority* figure—he presented the rules, arranged for the assignment of roles (by a rigged drawing of lots), and ordered the teachers to do their jobs whenever they hesitated or dissented. The *dependent variable* was the final level of shock—on a shock machine that went up to 450 volts in small, 15-volt steps—that a teacher gave before refusing to continue to obey the authority.

In 1983, a member of an Islamic fundamentalist group bombed the barracks of peacekeeping forces in Beirut, killing himself in the process. Under what circumstances could you imagine obeying an order to harm others and yourself?

The Test Situation. The study was staged to make a subject think that, by following orders, he or she was causing pain and suffering and perhaps even killing an innocent person. Each teacher had been given a sample shock of 45 volts to feel the amount of pain it caused. The learner was a pleasant, mild-mannered man, about 50 years old, who mentioned something about a heart condition but was willing to go along with the procedure. He was strapped into an "electric chair" in the next room and communicated with the teacher via an intercom. His task was to memorize pairs of words, giving the second word in a pair when he heard the first one. The learner soon began making errors—according to a prearranged schedule—and the teacher began shocking the learner. The protests of the victim rose with the shock level. At 75 volts, he began to moan and grunt; at 150 volts he demanded to be released from the experiment; at 180 volts he cried out that he could not stand the pain any longer. At 300 volts he insisted that he would no longer take part in the experiment and must be freed. He yelled out about his heart condition and screamed. If a teacher hesitated or protested delivering the next shock, the experimenter said, "The experiment requires that you continue" or "You have no other choice, you *must* go on."

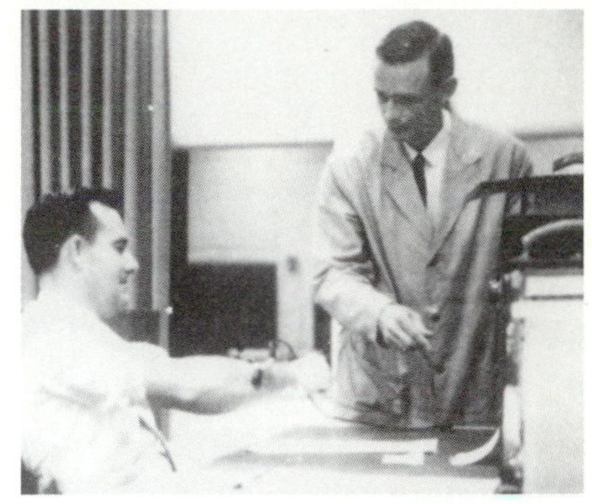

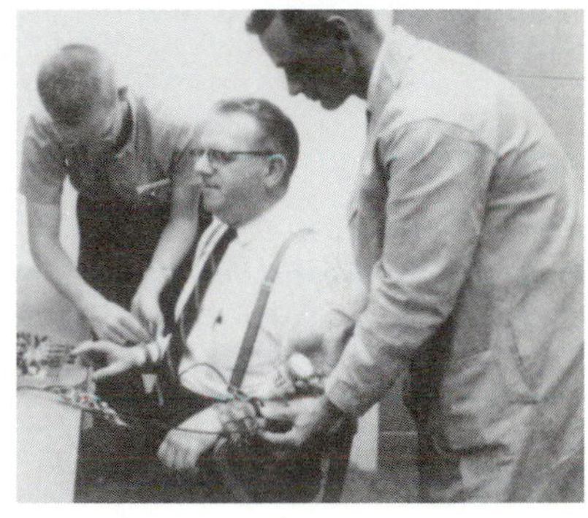

Milgram's obedience experiment: the "teacher" (subject) with confederate, the shock generator, and the "learner."

As you might imagine, the situation was stressful for the subjects. Most subjects complained and protested, repeatedly insisting they could not continue. Women subjects often were in tears as they dissented. That the experimental situation produced considerable conflict in the subjects is readily apparent from their protests:

- 180 volts delivered: "He can't stand it! I'm not going to kill that man in there! You hear him hollering? He's hollering. He can't stand it. What if something happens to him? . . . I mean, who is going to take the responsibility if anything happens to that gentleman?" [The experimenter accepts responsibility.] "All right."
- 195 volts delivered: "You see he's hollering. Hear that. Gee, I don't know." [The experimenter says, "The experiment requires that you go on."] "I know it does, sir, but I mean—huh—he don't know what he's in for. He's up to 195 volts" (1965, p. 67).

Even when there was only silence from the learner's room, the teacher was ordered to keep shocking him more and more strongly, all the way up to the button that was marked "Danger: Severe Shock XXX (450 volts)."

To Shock or Not to Shock? When 40 psychiatrists were asked by Milgram to predict the performance of subjects in this experiment, they estimated that most would not go beyond 150 volts (based on a description of the experiment). In their professional opinions, fewer than 4 percent of the subjects would still be obedient at 300 volts, and only about 0.1 percent would continue to 450 volts. The psychiatrists presumed that only those few individuals who were *abnormal* in some way, sadists who enjoyed inflicting pain on others, would blindly obey orders to continue up to the maximum shock.

Psychiatrists incorrectly predicted the behavior of Milgram's subjects because they failed to consider the influence of the special situation created in the experiment.

The psychiatrists based their evaluations on presumed *dispositional* qualities of people who would engage in such abnormal behavior; they were overlooking the power of this special situation to influence the thinking and actions of most people caught up in its social context. *The majority of subjects obeyed the authority fully.* Nearly two thirds delivered the maximum 450 volts to the learner. The average subject did not quit until about 300 volts. No subject who got within five switches of the end ever refused to go all the way. By then, their resistance was broken. Note that most people *dissented* verbally, but the majority did not *disobey* behaviorally. From the point of view of the victim, that's a critical difference. If you were the victim, would it matter much that the subjects said they didn't want to continue hurting you (they dissented), if they then shocked you repeatedly (they obeyed)?

Although many of the subjects in Milgram's study dissented verbally, the majority obeyed behaviorally.

The results of the Milgram studies were so unexpected—recall the psychiatrists' predictions—that researchers worked hard to rule out alternative interpretations of the results. One possibility was that the subjects did not really believe the "cover story" of the experiment. They might have believed that the victim was not really getting hurt. This alternative was ruled out by a study that made the effects of being obedient vivid, immediate, and direct for the subjects: subjects believed they had killed a puppy by delivering electric shocks—they actually saw the puppy collapse. (In reality, the dog was knocked out by an anesthetic.) Even under these vivid circumstances, three fourths of all students delivered the maximum shock possible (Sheridan & King, 1972).

Another alternative explanation for subjects' behavior is that the effect is limited to the **demand characteristics** of the experimental situation. Sometimes cues in the experimental setting influence subjects' perceptions of what is expected of them and systematically influence their behavior. Suppose Milgram's subjects guessed that his results would be more interesting if they kept giving shocks—so they played along? Further research showed that obedience to authority does not rely on the demands of an unusual experimental setting. It can happen in any natural setting.

A team of researchers performed the following field study to test the power of obedience in the natural setting of a hospital. A nurse (the subject) received a call from a staff doctor whom she had not met. He told her to administer some medication to a patient so that it could take effect by the time he arrived. He would sign the drug order after he got to the ward. The doctor ordered a dose of 20 milligrams of a drug called *Astroten.* The label on the container of Astroten stated that 5 milligrams was the usual dose and warned that the maximum dose was 10 milligrams.

Would a nurse administer an excessive dose of a drug on the basis of a telephone call from an unfamiliar person when doing so was contrary to standard medical practice? When this dilemma was *described* to 12 nurses, 10 *said* they would disobey. However, what the nurses did was another, by now familiar, story. When another group of them were actually in the situation, almost every nurse obeyed. Twenty-one of 22 had started to pour the medication (actually a harmless substance) before a physician researcher stopped them (Hofling et al., 1966).

Research in natural settings, using nurses in hospitals as subjects, supports Milgram's original findings in regard to the willingness of people to obey authority figures.

These results suggest that Milgram's findings cannot be attributed solely to subjects responding to the demands of the experiment.

Can we apply Milgram's lessons to the atrocities of Nazi Germany? Consider a recent historical analysis of a previously unreported horror of the Holocaust. To facilitate the "final solution" against the Jews living in remote rural towns in Poland, the Nazis recruited bands of reserve policemen to engage in an intense wave of mass murder. These middle-aged family men from Hamburg, Germany, were told to round up and shoot all Jews they could find. Some refused, but most complied and carried out massacres of tens of thousands of Jewish men, women, and children. Historian Christopher Browning, who gave his book the title *Ordinary Men* (1993), outlines the parallels between this event and the situational forces in the Milgram studies and the Stanford Prison Experiment. He reminds his readers, "I must recognize that in the same situation, I could have been either a killer or an evader—both were human—if I want to understand and explain the behavior of both as best I can. . . . What I do not accept, however, are the old clichés that to explain is to excuse, to understand is to forgive. Explaining is not excusing; understanding is not forgiving" (p. xx).

Why Do People Obey Authority? The basic answer is, the power of the situation. Milgram and other researchers manipulated a number of aspects of the experimental circumstances to demonstrate that the obedience effect is

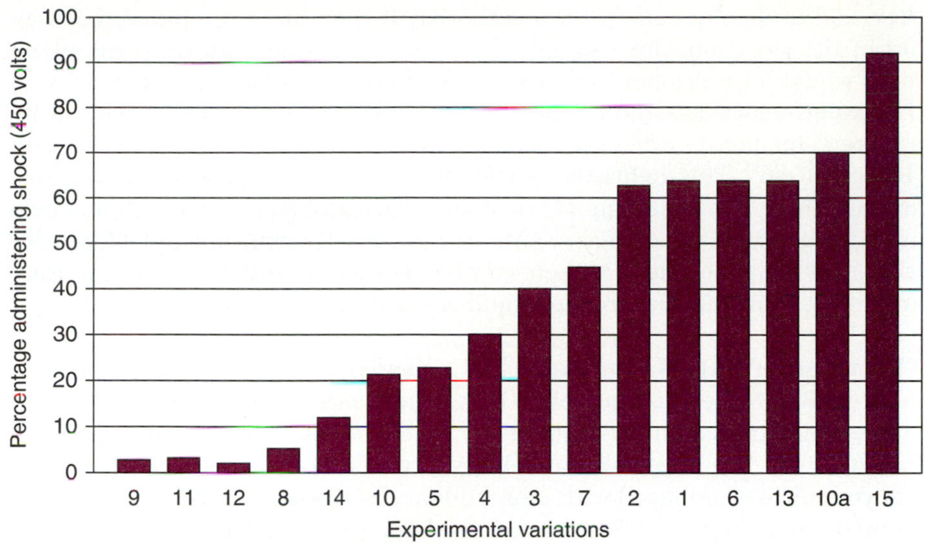

1. Remote victim
2. Voice feedback
3. Proximity
4. Touch proximity
5. Remote authority
6. Women as subjects
7. Institutional context
8. Subjects free to choose shock level
9. Learner demands to be shocked
10. An ordinary man gives orders

10a. The subject as bystander

11. Authority as victim—an ordinary man commanding
12. Two authorities—contradictory commands
13. Two authorities—one as victim
14. Two peers rebel
15. A peer administers shock

Figure 16.3 Obedience in Milgram's Experiments
The graph shows a profile of weak to strong obedience effects across Milgram's many experimental variations.

due to situational variables and not personality variables. **Figure 16.3** displays the level of obedience found in different situations. Obedience is quite high, for example, when a peer first models obedience, when a subject acts as an *intermediary bystander* assisting another person who actually delivers the shock, or when the victim (the learner) is physically remote from the teacher. Obedience is quite low when the learner demands to be shocked, when two authorities give contradictory commands, or when the authority figure is the victim. These findings all point to the idea that the *situation,* and not differences among individual subjects, largely controlled behavior. Furthermore, personality tests administered to the subjects did not reveal any traits that differentiated those who obeyed from those who refused, and did not show any psychological disturbance or abnormality in the obedient punishers.

Further research supports the conclusion that people obey because of situational factors rather than dispositional or personal factors.

Two reasons people obey authority in these situations can be traced to the effects of *normative* and *informational* sources of influence, which we discussed earlier. People want to be liked, and they want to be right. They tend to do what others are doing or requesting (normative peer influence and normative authority influence) in order to be socially acceptable and approved. In addition, when in an ambiguous, novel situation—like the experimental situation—people rely on others for cues as to what is the appropriate and correct way to behave. They are more likely to do so when experts or credible communicators tell them what to do. A third factor in the Milgram paradigm is that subjects were probably confused about *how to disobey;* nothing they said in dissent satisfied the authority. If they had a simple, direct way out of the situation—for example, by pressing a "quit" button—it is likely more would have disobeyed (Ross, 1988). Finally, obedience to authority in this experimental situation is part of an *ingrained habit* that is learned by children in many different settings—obey authority without question (Brown, 1986). This heuristic usually serves society well when authorities are legitimate and deserving of obedience. The problem is that the rule gets overapplied. Blind obedience to authority means obeying any and all authority figures simply because of their ascribed status, regardless of whether they are unjust or just in their requests and commands.

The Milgram Experiments and You. What is the personal significance to you of this obedience research? Recall the image of a lone man standing before tanks in Tiananmen Square during the rebellion of Chinese students in June 1989. You must ask yourself if you would do the same. What choices will you make when faced with moral dilemmas throughout your life? Take a moment to reflect on the types of obedience to authority situations that might arise in your day-to-day experience. Suppose you were a salesclerk. Would you cheat customers to make your boss look better? Suppose you were a member of Congress. Would you vote along party lines, rather than vote your conscience?

Would you risk your life to defy authority in defense of your beliefs, as this young Chinese man did in a student-led rebellion?

Resisting situational forces requires being aware of and accepting the fact that they can be powerful enough to affect almost anyone, even you. Then you need to analyze the situation mindfully and critically for the details that don't fit, for flaws in the "cover story," or the rationales that don't make sense upon careful analysis. Milgram's subjects, for example, might have wondered why Milgram needed to hire them to shock other people when he could have used a trained research assistant. Other important guidelines for resisting compliance situations include leaving the situation, taking a "time out" to think things over, never signing on the dotted line the first time you're asked, and being willing to appear to make a mistake or to be a poor team player. (For a fuller analysis of how to resist powerful forces to control your mind and behavior, see Zimbardo and Andersen, 1993.)

Milgram's obedience research challenges the myth that evil lurks in the minds of evil people—the bad *they* who are different from the good *us* or *you,* who would never do such things. Our purpose in recounting these findings is not to debase human nature but to make clear that even normal, well-meaning individuals are subject to the potential for frailty in the face of strong situational and social forces.

Finally, we wish to add a note on heroism. Suppose the majority of people who are comparable to you yield to powerful group forces. In our view, if you are able to resist, that qualifies you as heroic. The hero is the person who can act mindfully, out of conscience, when others are all conforming, or who can take the moral high road when others are standing by silently, allowing evil deeds to go unchallenged. Perhaps your knowledge of situational forces that make possible the "banality of evil" can nudge you in the direction of heroism.

Bystander Intervention

Consider a different perspective on the obedience situation of Milgram's experiments. If you were a *bystander,* would you intervene to help one of the distressed *teachers*—research subjects—disobey the authority and exit from the situation? Would you be more likely to intervene if you were the only bystander or if you were part of a group of observers? Before answering, you might want to reflect on what social psychologists have discovered about the nature of **bystander intervention** and the way it reflects another aspect of situational forces. We begin with a tragic real-life story.

The murder of Kitty Genovese, in this pleasant Queens neighborhood, shocked the nation. Why did so many responsible citizens fail to intervene when they heard her cries for help?

For more than half an hour, 38 respectable, law-abiding citizens in Queens, New York, watched a killer stalk and stab a woman in three separate attacks. Two times the sound of the bystanders' voices and the sudden glow of their bedroom lights interrupted the assailant and frightened him off. Each time, however, he returned and stabbed the victim again. Not a single person telephoned the police during the assault; only one witness called the police after the woman was dead (*The New York Times,* March 13, 1964; Rosenthal, 1964). This newspaper account of the murder of *Kitty Genovese* shocked a nation that could not accept the idea of such apathy on the part of its responsible citizenry.

But is it fair to pin the label of "apathy" on these bystanders? Or can we explain their inaction in terms of situational forces? To make the case for situational forces, **Bibb Latané** and **John Darley** (1970) carried out a classic series of social psychological studies. They ingeniously created in the laboratory an experimental analogue of the bystander-intervention situation.

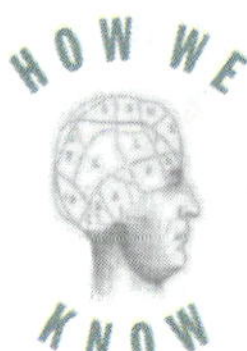

The subjects were male college students. Each student, placed in a room by himself with an intercom, was led to believe that he was communicating with one or more students in an adjacent room. During the course of a discussion about personal problems, he heard what sounded like one of the other students having an epileptic seizure and gasping for help. During the "seizure" it was impossible for the subject to talk to the other students or to find out what, if anything, they were doing about the emergency. The dependent variable was the speed with which the subject reported the emergency to the experimenter.

Latané and Darley demonstrated that diffusion of responsibility is a plausible explanation for an individual's lack of response in an emergency situation.

It turned out that the likelihood of intervention depended on the number of bystanders the subject thought were present. The more people he thought were present, the slower he was in reporting the seizure, if he did so at all. As you can see in **Figure 16.4**, everyone in a two-person situation intervened within 160 seconds, but nearly 40 percent of those who believed they were part of a larger group never bothered to inform the experimenter that another student was seriously ill (Darley & Latané, 1968). This result arises from a *diffusion of responsibility.* When more than one person *could* help in an emergency situation, people often assume that someone else *will* or *should* help.

Diffusion of responsibility is only one of the reasons that bystanders may fail to help. Let's explore more of the facets of many emergency situations.

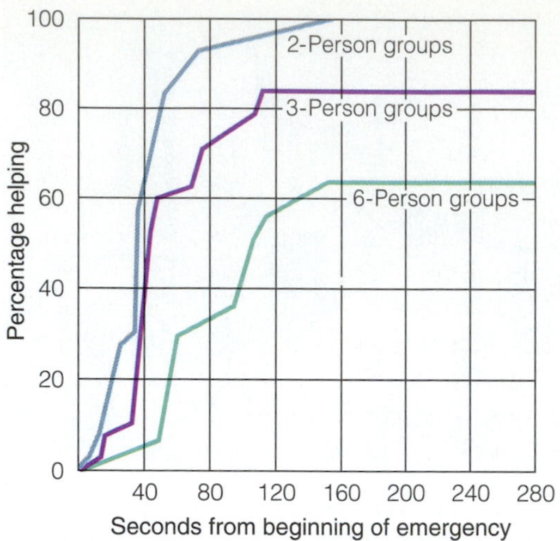

Figure 16.4 Bystander Intervention in an Emergency
The more people present, the less likely that any one bystander will intervene. Bystanders act most quickly in two-person groups.

Bystanders Must Notice the Emergency

In the seizure study, the situation was rigged so that subjects had to notice what was going on. In many real-life circumstances, however, people who are pursuing their own agendas may not even notice that there is a situation in which they can help. In one experiment, students at the Princeton Theological Seminary thought they were going to be evaluated on their sermons, one of which was to be about the parable of the Good Samaritan—a New Testament figure who takes time to help a man lying injured by the roadside.

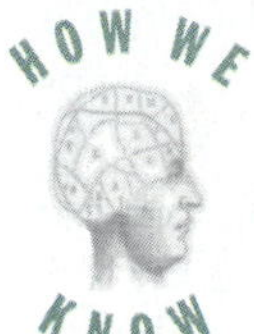

The seminarians had to deliver their lectures in a different building from the one in which they were initially briefed. Some were randomly assigned to a *late condition,* in which they had to hurry to make the next session, others to an *on-time condition,* and a third group to an *early condition.* When each seminarian walked down an alley between the two buildings, he came upon a man slumped in a doorway, in obvious need of help. On their way to deliver a sermon about the Good Samaritan, these seminary students now had the chance to practice what they were about to preach. Did they? Of those who were in a hurry, only 10 percent helped. If they were on time, 45 percent helped the stranger. Most bystander intervention came from those who were not in a time bind—63 percent of these seminarians acted as Good Samaritans (Darley & Batson, 1973).

How should we evaluate the "late" seminarians? One way to interpret the result is that they were so caught up in their own concerns that they failed to "notice" the emergency situation.

Bystanders Must Label Events as an Emergency

Many situations in life are ambiguous. You don't want to embarrass yourself by trying to give mouth-to-mouth resuscitation to someone who is merely asleep. To decide if a situation is an emergency, you typically see how other people are responding. If no one else is helping, then you probably won't help either—which often means that no one will ever help. This process of social *modeling* may explain why people are more likely to help in familiar situations.

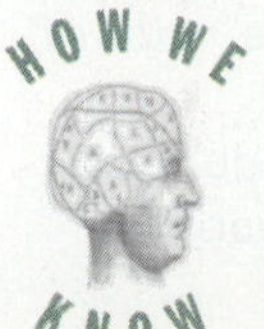

A man on a moving New York subway train suddenly collapsed and fell to the floor. A number of bystanders witnessed this event. The experimenters manipulated the situation by varying the characteristics of the "victim"—an invalid with a cane, a drunk smelling of liquor, or, in a companion study, a disabled person apparently bleeding (or not bleeding) from the mouth. The researchers unobtrusively recorded the bystander responses to these emergency situations. One or more persons responded directly in most cases (81 out of 103) with little hesitation (Piliavan & Piliavin, 1972; Piliavin et al., 1969).

Compare this high rate to another study in which an accomplice on crutches pretended to collapse in an airport. The percentage of those who helped was much lower than in the subway—41 percent as compared with 83 percent. The important factor seemed to be that the subway riders were in a more familiar context than the airport travelers and thus were more likely to deal with the trouble that arose (Latané & Darley, 1970).

The Bystander Must Feel Responsibility

We have already seen that an important factor in nonintervention is the diffusion of responsibility. If you find yourself in a situation in which you need help, you should do everything you can to cause bystanders to overcome this force. You should point directly toward someone and say, "You! I need your help." Consider two studies that involved apparent crimes. In the first study, New Yorkers watched as a thief snatched a women's suitcase in a restaurant when she left her table. In the second, beachgoers watched as a thief snatched a portable radio from a beach blanket when the owner left it for a few minutes.

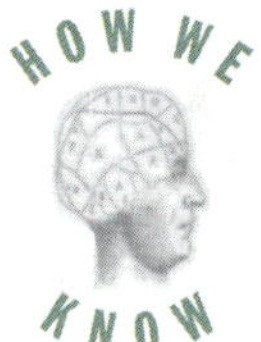

In each experiment, the would-be theft victim (the experimenter's accomplice) asked the soon-to-be observer of the crime either, "Do you have the time?" or "Will you please keep an eye on my bag (radio) while I'm gone?" The first interaction elicited no personal responsibility, and the bystander simply stood by idly as the theft unfolded. However, of those who agreed to watch the victim's property, almost every bystander intervened. They called for help, and some even tackled the runaway thief on the beach (Moriarty, 1975).

The encouraging message is that you can convert apathy to action just by asking. The act of requesting a favor forges a special human bond that involves other people in ways that materially change the situation. It makes them responsible to you and, thereby, responsible for what happens in your shared social context.

The Situational Cost of Helping Must Not Be Too High

Finally, it is worth noting that there will be circumstances in which people just decide that the cost of helping is too high. For example, in the subway experiments, help was slower for a bloody victim, who might require a greater degree of involvement than a victim who simply collapsed, though it usually still came (Piliavin & Piliavin, 1972; Piliavin et al., 1969). We may also credit the "late" seminarians with assessing the cost of helping as being inconsistent with their personal goal of being able to deliver their sermon.

Note that the assessment of cost in these cases still reflects the situational forces. The helping and nonhelping seminarians, for example, were all likely to have been reasonably nice people—but some were told that they were late. That is an important conclusion for this whole area of research. To understand bystander intervention, you are much safer making predictions based on features of the situation than on personal differences among individuals. (See Schroeder et al., 1995, for a thorough review and analysis of helping and altruism research.)

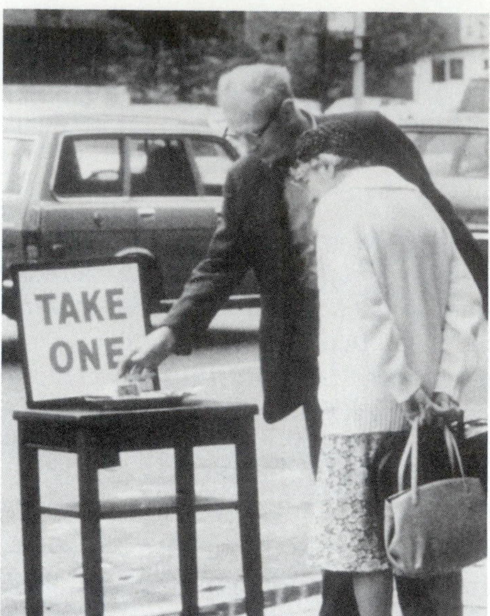

If you came upon an unattended plate of dollar bills with a sign directing you to TAKE ONE, *would you obey it as these "Candid Camera" participants did?*

"Candid Camera" Revelations

Social psychologists have attempted to demonstrate the power of social norms and social situations by devising experiments that reveal the ease with which smart, independent, rational, good people can be led into behaving in ways that are dumb, compliant, irrational, and even evil. Although social psychologists have shown the serious consequences of situational power, it is equally possible to demonstrate this principle with humor. Indeed, "Candid Camera" scenarios, created by intuitive social psychologist **Allen Funt,** have been doing so for over 40 years. Funt showed how human nature follows a situational script to the letter. Millions in his TV audiences laughed when a diner stopped eating a hamburger whenever a DON'T EAT counter light flashed; when pedestrians stopped and waited at a red street light above the *sidewalk* on which they were walking; when highway drivers turned back after seeing a road sign that read DELAWARE IS CLOSED; and when customers jumped from one white tile to another in response to a store sign that instructed them not to walk on black tiles. One of the best "Candid Camera" illustrations of the subtle power of implicit situational rules to control behavior is the "elevator caper." A person riding a rigged elevator first obeyed the usual silent rule to face the front, but when a group of other passengers all faced the rear, the hapless victim followed the new *emerging group norm* and faced the rear as well.

We see in these slice-of-life episodes the minimal situational conditions needed to elicit unusual behaviors in ordinary people. You laugh because people who appear similar to you behave foolishly in response to small modifications in their commonplace situations. You implicitly distance yourself from them by assuming you would not act that way. The lesson of much social psychological research is that, more than likely, you *would* behave exactly as others have if you were placed in the same situation. Poet John Donne wrote, "No man is an island, entire of itself; every man is a piece of the continent." People are all interconnected by the situations and norms and rules they share. The wise reply to someone who asks how you would act if you were in a situation in which people behaved in evil, foolish, or irrational ways is, "I don't know. It depends on how powerful the situation is."

CONSTRUCTING SOCIAL REALITY

We have just reviewed a large body of research that all points to the same conclusion: situations play a substantial role in determining people's behav-

The Wily Salesperson

Let's turn for a moment to the scenario with which we opened the chapter. Why might you enter a store with the intention of buying an inexpensive radio and leave with a moderately expensive CD player? What might the salesperson have done to bring about this change? In his book *Influence,* social psychologist **Robert Cialdini** (1993) has laid bare the psychological bases of many of the most effective sales techniques. We'll describe three from his list: reciprocity, commitment, and scarcity.

- *Reciprocity.* One of the rules that dominates human experience is that when someone does something for you, you *should* do something for that person as well. Laboratory research has shown that even very small favors can lead subjects to do much larger favors in return (Regan, 1971). Salespeople use reciprocity against you by appearing to do you a favor: "I'll tell you what, I'll take $5 off the price" or "Here's a free sample just for agreeing to talk to me today." This strategy puts you in a position of psychological distress if you don't return the favor and buy the product.
- *Commitment.* Salespeople also know that if they can get you to commit yourself to some small concession, they can probably also get you to commit to something larger. In experiments, people who agreed to small requests (for example, signing petitions) were more likely subsequently to agree to a bigger request (for example, putting large signs on their lawn) (Freedman & Fraser, 1966). Salespeople use the commitment technique against you by getting you to make a decision and then subtly changing the deal: "I know this is the car you want to buy, but my manager will only let me give you a $200 discount"; "I know you're the sort of person who buys quality goods, so I know you won't mind paying a little extra." This strategy makes you feel inconsistent or foolish if you don't go through with the purchase.
- *Scarcity.* People dislike feeling that they can't have something (or, from another perspective, people like to have things others can't). Subjects, for example, give higher ratings to the taste of chocolate chip cookies that come from a jar with just two cookies than to those that come from a jar of ten (Worchel et al., 1975). How does the principle of scarcity apply in the marketplace? Salespeople know that they can increase the likelihood of your purchase if they make goods seem scarce: "This is the last one I have, so I'm not sure you should wait until tomorrow"; "I have another customer who's planning to come back and get this." This strategy makes you feel as if you are missing a critical opportunity.

How can you defend yourself against wily salespeople? You should try to catch them using these strategies—and resist their efforts. Try to ignore meaningless favors. Try to avoid foolish consistency. Try to detect false claims of scarcity. Your knowledge of social psychology can make you an all-round wiser consumer.

iors. Suppose, however, that you are walking across campus with a friend who has not taken an introductory psychology course. You come upon an elderly man who seems to have collapsed on the ground. Who do you think would be more likely to help this gentleman? If you're thinking "me," it's probably because you now know enough about bystander intervention that the situation has changed for you. Your friend and you, in a sense, are observing the same event but interpreting it in very different ways. That's what we mean by *constructing social reality.* You bring your own knowledge and experience to bear on the interpretation of situations. You construct social reality by the ways you represent events cognitively and emotionally.

The notion of constructing social reality suggests that you bring your own knowledge and experience to bear on the interpretation of situations.

Let's look at one classic social psychological example in which people's beliefs led them to view the same situation from different vantage points and make contrary conclusions about what "really happened." The study concerned a football game that took place some years ago between two Ivy League teams. An undefeated Princeton team played Dartmouth in the final game of the season. The game was rough, filled with penalties and serious injuries to both sides. After the game, the newspapers of the two schools offered very different accounts of what had happened.

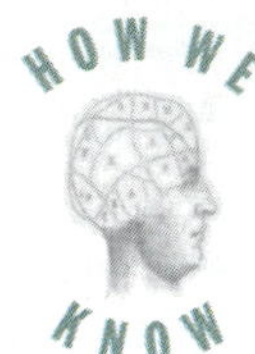

A team of social psychologists, intrigued by the different perceptions, surveyed students at both schools, showed them a film of the game, and recorded their judgments about the number of infractions committed by each of the teams. Nearly all Princeton students judged the game as "rough and dirty," none saw it as "clean and fair," and most believed that Dartmouth players started the dirty play. In contrast, the majority of Dartmouth students thought both sides were equally to blame for the rough game, and many thought it was "rough, clean, and fair." Moreover, when the Princeton students viewed the game film, they "saw" the Dartmouth team commit twice as many penalties as their own team. When viewing the same film, Dartmouth students "saw" both sides commit the same number of penalties (Hastorf & Cantril, 1954).

Fans who watch their favorite team play are likely to perceive more instances of unfair play on the part of the opposing team.

This study makes clear that a complex social occurrence, such as a football game, cannot be observed in an objective fashion. Social situations obtain significance when observers *selectively encode* what is happening in terms of what they expect to see and want to see. In the case of the football game, people *looked* at the same activity but they *saw* two different games.

In this section, we will examine the ways in which people explain, interpret, and create the situations they experience. We consider, in addition, the way that people's interpretive biases affect even their own behavior.

Social Perception

To explain how the Princeton and Dartmouth fans came to such different interpretations of the football game returns us to the realm of *perception.* Recall from Chapter 8 that you often must put prior knowledge to work to interpret ambiguous perceptual objects. The principle is the same for the football game—people bring past knowledge to bear on the interpretation of current events—but the objects for perceptual processing are people and situations. **Social perception** is the process by which people come to understand and categorize the behaviors of others. In this section, we will focus largely on two issues of social perception. First we consider how people make judgments about the forces that influence other people's behavior, their *causal attributions.* Next we discuss how processes of social perception can sometimes bring the world in line with expectations.

The Origins of Attribution Theory

One of the most important inferential tasks facing all social perceivers is to determine the causes of events. You want to know the why's of life. Why did my girlfriend break off the relationship? Why did he get the job and not I? Why did my parents divorce after so many years of marriage? All such why's lead to an analysis of possible causal determinants for some action, event, or outcome. **Attribution theory** is a general approach to describing the ways the social perceiver uses information to generate causal explanations.

Attribution theory originated in the writings of **Fritz Heider** (1958). Heider argued that people continually make causal analyses as part of their attempts at general comprehension of the social world. People, he suggested, are all **intuitive psychologists** who try to figure out what people are like and what causes their behavior, just as professional psychologists do. Heider used a simple film to demonstrate that people tend to leap from observing actions to making causal inferences and attributing motives to what they see. The film involved three geometric figures that moved around an object without any prearranged plan. Research subjects, however, always made up scripts that animated the action, turning the figures into actors and attributing personality traits and motives to their causal actions (see **Figure 16.5**). Heider believed that the questions that dominate most attributional analyses are whether the cause of a behavior is found in the person (internal or *dispositional* causality) or in the situation (external or *situational* causality) and who is responsible for the outcomes. How do people make those judgments?

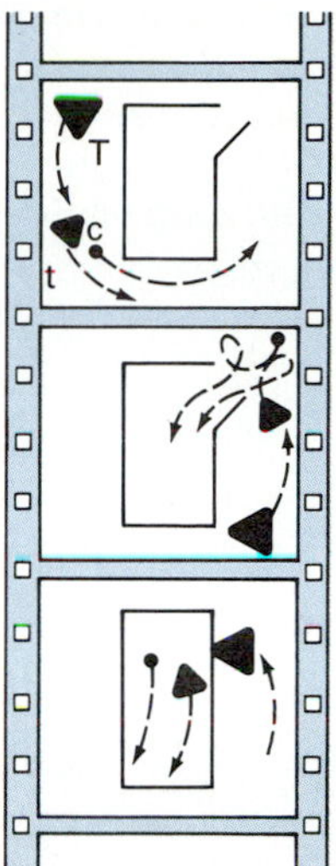

Figure 16.5 Heider's Demonstration of the Natural Tendency to Make Causal Attributions

These geometric figures were stimuli in a convincing demonstration that people infer rather than observe personal characteristics and causes. When subjects were shown a film in which the geometric forms simply moved in and out of the large rectangle at different speeds and in different patterns, they attributed underlying "motivations" to the "characters." They often "saw" the triangles as two males fighting over a female (the circle). The large triangle was "seen" as being aggressive, the small triangle as being heroic, and the circle as being timid. In the sequence shown here, most observers reported seeing T *chase* t *and* c *into the house and close the door.*

Harold Kelley (1967) formalized Heider's line of thinking by specifying the variables that people use to make their attributions. Kelley made the important observation that people most often make causal attributions for events under conditions of uncertainty. You rarely, if ever, have sufficient information to know for sure what caused someone to behave in a particular way. Kelley believed that people grapple with uncertainty by accumulating information from multiple events and using the *covariation principle*. The **covariation principle** suggests that people should attribute a behavior to a causal factor if that factor was present whenever the behavior occurred but was absent whenever it didn't occur. Suppose, for example, you are walking down a street and you see a friend pointing at a horse and screaming. What evidence would you gather to decide whether your friend is crazy (a dispositional attribution) or danger is afoot (a situational attribution)?

Kelley suggested that people make this judgment by assessing covariation with respect to three dimensions of information relevant to the person whose acts they are trying to explain: distinctiveness, consistency, and consensus. *Distinctiveness* refers to whether the behavior is specific to a particular situation—does your friend scream in response to all horses? *Consistency* refers to whether the behavior occurs repeatedly in response to this situation—has this horse made your friend scream in the past? *Consensus* refers to whether other people also produce the same behavior in the same situation—is everyone pointing and screaming? Each of these three dimensions plays a role in the conclusions you draw. Suppose, for example, that your friend was the only one screaming. Would that make you more likely to make a dispositional or a situational attribution?

Thousands of studies have been conducted to refine and extend attribution theory beyond the solid foundation provided by Heider and Kelley (Fiske & Taylor, 1991). Many of those studies have concerned themselves with conditions in which attributions depart from a systematic search of available information. We will describe four types of circumstances in which bias may creep into your attributions.

The Fundamental Attribution Error

Suppose you have made an arrangement to meet a friend at 7 o'clock. It's now 7:30, and the friend still hasn't arrived. How might you be explaining this event to yourself?

- I'm sure something really important happened that made it impossible for her to be here on time.
- What a jerk! Couldn't she try a little harder?

We've given you a choice again between a situational and a dispositional attribution. Research has shown that people are more likely, on average, to choose the second type, the dispositional explanation (Ross & Nisbett,

The fundamental attribution error suggests that people are likely to overestimate dispositional causes for behavior and underestimate situational causes.

1991). This tendency is so strong, in fact, that social psychologist **Lee Ross** (1977) labeled it the fundamental attribution error. The **fundamental attribution error** (FAE) represents the dual tendency for people to *overestimate* dispositional factors and to *underestimate* situational ones when searching for the cause of some behavior or outcome.

Let's look at a laboratory example of the FAE. Ross and his colleagues (1977) created an experimental version of a "College Bowl" type of quiz game in which subjects became questioners or contestants by the flip of a coin.

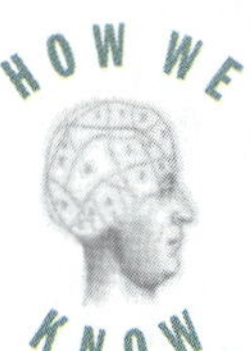

The questioner was instructed to ask challenging questions to which he or she knew the answers. The contestant tried, often in vain, to answer the questions. At the end of the session, the questioner, the contestant, and observers (other subjects who had watched the game) rated the general knowledge of both questioner and contestant. The results are shown in **Figure 16.6**. As you can see, questioners seem to believe that both they and the contestants are average. Both contestants and observers, however, rate the questioner as much more knowledgeable than the contestant—and contestants even rate themselves to be a bit below average!

Is this fair? It should be clear that the situation confers a great advantage on the questioner. (Wouldn't you prefer to be the one who gets to ask the questions?) The contestants' and observers' ratings ignore the way in which the situation allowed one person to look bright and the other to look dull. That's the fundamental attribution error.

You should be on a constant lookout for instances of the FAE. We have already seen examples in this chapter. Recall Milgram's experiments. People are inclined to imagine that subjects who would shock innocent people are sadists. We know, however, that their behavior is molded by the situation. Recall research on bystander intervention. People labeled Kitty Genovese's neighbors evil or apathetic. We know, once again, that the situation constrained their behavior. What we learn from these examples is that it often takes a bit of "research" to discover the situational roots of behavior. Situational forces are often invisible. You can't, for example, *see* diffusion of responsibility; you can only see the behaviors it gives rise to. What can you

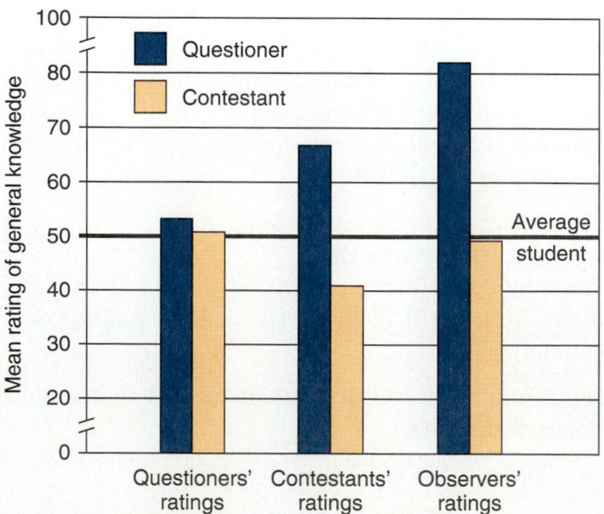

Figure 16.6
Ratings of Questioners' and Contestants' General Knowledge

do to avoid the FAE? Particularly in circumstances in which you are making a dispositional attribution that is negative ("What a jerk!"), you should take a step back and ask yourself, Could it be something about the situation that is bringing about this behavior? You might think of such an exercise as "attributional charity." Do you see why?

This advice may be particularly important to those of us who live in Western society, because evidence suggests that the FAE is due, in part, to cultural sources. **Joan Miller** (1984) proposed that members of non-Western cultures are less likely to focus on individual actors in situations. (We have, on several occasions, noted the individualist, versus collectivist, bias of Western culture.)

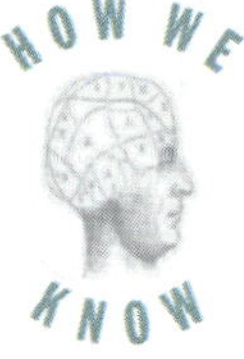

Subjects in Miller's research were citizens of the United States and India, ranging from age 8 to adults. The subjects were asked to give explanations of negative events. In one scenario, for example, a motorcycle driver leaves his injured passenger at the scene of an accident, and the passenger subsequently dies. Did subjects explain this event with respect to a disposition (the driver was irresponsible) or a situation (the driver didn't understand how badly the passenger was injured, and he had other commitments to keep)? The 8-year-olds from both countries gave the same distribution of dispositional and situational responses. With increasing age, however, U.S. subjects gave ever more dispositional responses; Indian subjects gave more situational responses.

Research supports the notion that members of Western cultures are more likely to make the fundamental attribution error than are members of non-Western societies.

This experiment suggests that the FAE is not an inevitable consequence of interaction with the social world. Westerners should examine the lessons they teach their children to see how the dispositional bias in social perception gets established.

Self-serving Biases

One of the most startling findings in the College Bowl study was the contestants' negative evaluation of their own abilities. This suggests that people will make the FAE even at their own expense. (In fact, we will see in Chapter 17 that one theory of the origins of depression suggests that people make too many negative attributions to themselves rather than to situational causes.) In many circumstances, however, people's attributions err in the direction of being self-serving. A **self-serving bias** leads people to take credit for their successes while denying responsibility for their failures. Self-serving biases are quite robust, occurring in many situations for most people and even across cultures (Fletcher & Ward, 1988). People tend to make dispositional attributions for success and situational attributions for failure (Gilovich, 1991): "I got the prize because of my ability"; "I lost the competition because it was rigged."

Do self-serving biases always serve you well? Suppose you're playing poker. If you attribute your winning hands to skill and your losing hands to bad luck, you're likely to stay at the table a little bit too long.

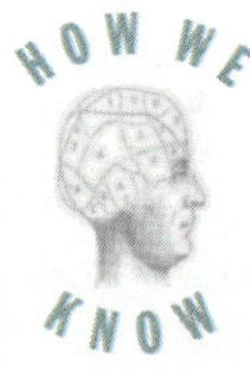

One study looked at the way subjects explained their winning and losing bets on the outcome of professional football games. In the first session of the study, subjects made a series of bets (with an imaginary stake of $250) on the next Sunday's games. In a second session, after the games had been played and the bets had been settled, the subjects were asked to comment on their choices. Subjects tended to make "bolstering" comments with respect to their correct bets. They reaffirmed that the right outcome had occurred. By contrast, their comments about their losing bets were "undoing": they indicated the ways in which the outcome *should* have been different (Gilovich, 1983).

Successful poker players avoid self-serving biases.

If you make this pattern of attributions, you're likely to think highly of yourself—but you can see what the cost might be. We emphasized earlier that you should strive to avoid the FAE when you think about others' behavior. Similarly, you might examine attributions about your own behavior to weed out (non-self-serving) self-serving biases.

Why does it matter so much what attributions you make? Suppose that, because you ignore the situation, you decide that someone is unfriendly. Can that incorrect belief actually cause the person to be unfriendly toward you? We turn now to the power of beliefs and expectations in social perception.

Expectations and Self-fulfilling Prophecies

Research suggests that some situations can be modified significantly by the beliefs and expectations people have about them.

Can beliefs and expectations go beyond coloring the way you interpret experiences to actually shape social reality? Much research suggests that the very nature of some situations can be modified significantly by the beliefs and expectations people have about them. **Self-fulfilling prophecies** (Merton, 1957) are predictions made about some future behavior or event that modify interactions so as to produce what is expected. Suppose, for example, you go to a party expecting to have a great time. Suppose a friend goes expecting it to be boring. Can you imagine the different ways in which the two of you might behave, given these expectations? Which of you is actually more likely to have a good time at the party?

One of the most powerful demonstrations of self-fulfilling prophecies took its cue from a play by George Bernard Shaw. In Shaw's *Pygmalion* (popularized as the musical *My Fair Lady*), a street waif is transformed into a proper society lady under the intense training of her teacher, Professor Henry Higgins. The effect of social expectancy, or the *Pygmalion effect,* was re-created in an experiment by psychologist **Robert Rosenthal** in conjunction with school principal Leonore Jacobson.

HOW WE KNOW

Elementary school teachers in Boston were informed by researchers that their testing had revealed that some of their students were "academic spurters." The teachers were led to believe that these particular students were "intellectual bloomers who will show unusual gains during the academic year." In fact, there was no objective basis for that prediction; the names of these late bloomers were chosen *randomly.* However, by the end of that

> school year, 30 percent of the children arbitrarily named as spurters had gained an average of 22 IQ points. Almost all of them had gained at least 10 IQ points. Their gain in intellectual performance, as measured by a standard test of intelligence, was significantly greater than that of their control group classmates (Rosenthal & Jacobson, 1968).

Rosenthal's study demonstrating the Pygmalion effect illustrates the power of the self-fulfilling prophecy.

How did the teachers' false expectations get translated into such positive student performance? Rosenthal (1974) points to at least four processes that were activated by the teachers' expectations (see also Jussim, 1986). First, the teachers acted more warmly and more friendly toward the "late bloomers," creating a climate of social approval and acceptance. Second, they put greater demands—involving both quality and level of difficulty of material to be learned—on those for whom they had high hopes. Third, they gave more immediate and clearer feedback (both praise and criticism) about the selected students' performance. Finally, the teachers created more opportunities for the special students to respond in class, show their stuff, and be reinforced, thus giving them hard evidence that they were good.

What is unusual, of course, about the situation in the Boston classroom is that the teachers were purposefully given false expectations. This methodology allowed Rosenthal and Jacobson to demonstrate the full potential for self-fulfilling prophecies. In most real-world situations, however, expectations are based on fairly accurate social perceptions (Jussim, 1991). Teachers, for example, expect certain students to do well because those students arrive in the classroom with better qualifications; and those students, in fact, do show the best performance. We might, thus, find the most real-world evidence that expectations exert an influence in situations that provide little information relevant for a judgment. Let's examine this claim in the context of sex stereotypes.

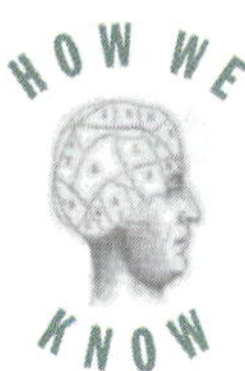

An experimenter brought a 9-month-old baby to an undergraduate social psychology class. About half of the students were led to believe that the baby was named Keith; half thought the baby was Karen. The students were asked to give their impressions of the baby with respect to physical attributes, behavior in class, and personality. Ratings for "Keith" and "Karen" did not differ for the two types of judgments for which the situation provided direct evidence: physical attributes and behavior in class. It was only for the domain of personality—which could not be judged based on the baby's behavior in class—that a sex stereotype shone through. "Keith" was rated as more athletic, noisy, active, and rough than was "Karen" (Jussim, 1993).

What types of judgments would change if you were told this was Baby Keith or Baby Karen?

Expectations did not affect judgments when the environment provided concrete evidence—the students could plainly see what the baby looked like and how the baby behaved. Only when direct evidence was unavailable—the judgments of personality—did stereotypes influence responses. Thus expectations are most powerful, and self-fulfilling prophecies are most likely to occur, when an individual has not had an opportunity to develop accurate expectations before judgments must be made. Of course, in social interactions "judgments" often give rise to behaviors. Let's see now how a person's choice of behaviors can affect the construction of social reality.

Behaviors That Confirm Expectations

Consider the Boston classroom once again. We have already noted that the teachers performed a series of behaviors that enabled them, in the long run, to confirm their expectations. **Mark Snyder** (1984) introduced the term

The power of behavioral confirmation and self-fulfilling prophecies depends on the amount of accurate information available in the environment.

behavioral confirmation to label the process by which someone's expectations about another person actually influence the second person to behave in ways that confirm the original hypothesis. For example, imagine you were about to interview someone, and you were told that the person was shy. Which of these questions might you select to ask (Snyder & Swann, 1978)?

- What would you do if you wanted to liven things up at a party?
- In what situations do you wish you could be more outgoing?
- What factors make it hard for you to really open up to people?
- In what situations are you most talkative?

Suppose you chose, as many subjects did when they believed they were going to talk to someone introverted, the second question. Isn't it likely that even a very extraverted person could give you a reasonable answer to this question? Thus an expectation—"I'm going to talk to someone shy"—leads to a behavioral choice—"I'm going to ask the kind of question you ask a shy person"—which leads to potential confirmation of the expectation—"If he could answer this question, I guess he really is shy."

How powerful are the forces of behavioral confirmation? The answer to this question is similar to the one we developed with respect to the likelihood of self-fulfilling prophecies: it depends on the availability of accurate information from the environment.

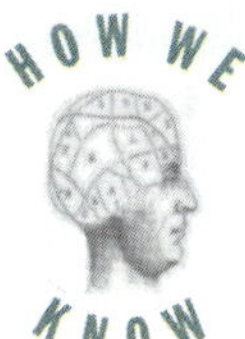

Researchers created circumstances in which one set of undergraduate women, the *perceivers,* were given false expectations about the extraversion or introversion of a second set of women, the *targets.* Each of the targets had, in fact, provided ratings that allowed the experimenters to identify her as an introvert or extravert. However, some of the target women had certain (strong) self-conceptions on this dimension, whereas other of the targets had uncertain (weak) self-conceptions. What happened when the perceivers interacted with the targets? When the targets had uncertain self-conceptions, behavioral confirmation reigned: the perceivers elicited behavior from the targets to confirm the initial expectation. However, when the targets had certain self-conceptions, that self-conception shone through (Swann & Ely, 1984).

Once again you can see that expectations have their greatest effect when the actual state of the world is uncertain. Under those circumstances, you have the best opportunity—for better or for worse—to re-create the world in line with your own beliefs and attitudes.

This conclusion leads naturally to the question, How do those attitudes arise? In the experiments we have reviewed, subjects are typically told what to believe. But what happens in the real world, when you arrive at expectations on your own? We turn now to some of the processes that affect your own personal view of social reality.

Social Reality and Personal Attitudes

You are certainly well aware that the *attitudes* you hold about almost any topic are not shared by all the people around you. An **attitude** is "a psychological tendency that is expressed by evaluating a particular entity with some degree of favor or disfavor" (Eagly & Chaiken, 1993, p. 1). You may have favorable attitudes toward sports cars, horror movies, and bridge, and unfavorable attitudes toward contemporary art, pizza, and football. This definition of attitude allows for the fact that many of the attitudes you hold are not overt; you may not be consciously aware that you harbor certain attitudes. Your attitudes are a critical lens through which you view social reality. We saw that in our opening example of the football game. Those people who favored Princeton "saw" a different game from those people who favored Dartmouth. How do you decide what attitudes you hold? The process, in some respects, is just like the attributions you make about other people's behavior. Let's examine the evidence for that proposal.

Dissonance Theory

One of the most common assumptions in the study of attitudes is that people like to believe that their attitudes remain consistent over time (Eagly & Chaiken, 1993). This striving for consistency was explored within the field of social psychology in the theory of **cognitive dissonance,** as developed by **Leon Festinger** (1957), a student of Kurt Lewin. *Cognitive dissonance* is the state of conflict someone experiences after making a decision, taking an action, or being exposed to information that is contrary to prior beliefs, feelings, or values. Suppose, for example, you chose to buy a car against a friend's advice. Why might you be overly defensive about the car? It is assumed that when a person's cognitions about his or her behavior and relevant attitudes are dissonant—they do not follow one to the next—an aversive state arises that the person is motivated to reduce. Dissonance-reducing activities modify this unpleasant state and achieve consonance among cognitions.

For example, suppose two dissonant cognitions are some self-knowledge ("I smoke") and a belief about smoking ("Smoking causes lung cancer"). To reduce the dissonance involved, you could take one of several different actions: change your belief ("The evidence that smoking causes lung cancer is not very convincing"); change your behavior (stop smoking); reevaluate the behavior ("I don't smoke very much"); or add new cognitions ("I smoke low-tar cigarettes"). Each of these paths makes the inconsistency less psychologically damaging.

Dissonance has motivational force—it impels you to take action to reduce the unpleasant feeling. The motivation to reduce dissonance increases with the magnitude of the dissonance created by a cognitive inconsistency. In other words, the stronger the dissonance, the greater the motivation to reduce it. In the classic dissonance experiment, college students told a lie to other students and came to believe in their lie when they got a small, rather than a large, reward for doing so.

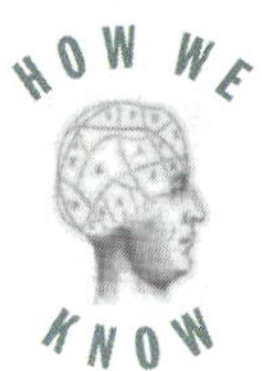

Subjects participated in a very dull task and were then asked (as a favor to the experimenter, because his assistant hadn't shown up) to lie to another subject by saying that the task had been fun and interesting. Half the subjects were paid $20 to tell the lie, while the others were paid only $1. The $20 payment was sufficient external justification for lying, but the $1 payment was an inadequate justification. The people who were paid $1 were left with dissonant cognitions: "The task was dull" and "I chose to tell another student it was fun and interesting without a good reason for doing so."

To reduce their dissonance, these $1 subjects changed their evaluations of the task. They later expressed the belief that "it really was fun and interesting—I might like to do it again." In comparison, the subjects who lied for $20 did not change their evaluations—the task was still a bore; they had only lied "for the money" (Festinger & Carlsmith, 1959).

What messages might you give yourself to reduce cognitive dissonance if you were aware of the adverse effects of smoking but continued to smoke?

The small reward for the counternormative behavior of lying induced greater dissonance than when subjects could justify lying for a bigger reward. The insufficient external justification ($1) led subjects to invent personal justifications for the dissonant behaviors. As this experiment shows, under conditions of high dissonance an individual acts to justify his or her behavior after the fact, engages in self-persuasion, and often becomes a most convincing communicator. This analysis says that the way to change attitudes is first to change behavior (eliciting attitude-inconsistent behavior under a condition of high choice and low justification). Ancient biblical scholars knew this principle. They urged rabbis not to insist that people believe before praying but to get them to pray first—and then they would come to believe. Hundreds of experiments and field studies have shown the power of cognitive dissonance to change attitudes and behavior (Wicklund & Brehm, 1976).

Dissonance theory implies that the way to change attitudes is first to change behavior.

Self-perception Theory

Dissonance theory describes one way in which people's attributions about their own behavior—the bias toward consistency—may be subject to the same forces as their attributions about the behaviors of others. In other words, in the name of consistency, you are as likely to make faulty attributions about your own behavior as you are to make attribution errors about the behavior of others. Another social psychological theory comes at the same insight from a somewhat different angle. Given that people, at least in Western culture, are so quick to make dispositional attributions about others' behaviors, perhaps it shouldn't be surprising that they have that same bias toward themselves. This notion is at the heart of **self-perception theory,** developed by **Daryl Bem** (1972). According to Bem's theory, you infer what your internal states (beliefs, attitudes, motives, and feelings) are or should be by perceiving how you are acting now and recalling how you have acted in the past in a given situation. You use that self-knowledge to reason backward to the most likely causes or determinants of your behavior. The self-perceiver responds to the question, "Do you like psychology?" by saying, "Sure, I'm taking the basic course and it's not required, I do all the readings, I pay attention during lectures, and I'm getting a good grade in the course." In other words, you answer a question about personal preferences by a behavioral description of relevant actions and situational factors.

According to Daryl Bem's self-perception theory, you are likely to infer your beliefs, attitudes, motives, and feelings by evaluating your current and past behavior.

Self-perception theory is largely a theory about attitude formation rather than attitude change—it lacks the motivational components of dissonance theory. Because self-perception fills in missing attitudes, self-perception processes occur mainly when you are in ambiguous situations and dealing with unfamiliar events, where you have a need to discover how you feel about some novel object of attitudinal scrutiny (Fazio, 1987). One flaw in the process of gaining self-knowledge through self-perception is that people are often insensitive about the extent to which their behavior is influenced by situational forces. You can see this if we return a final time to the College Bowl experiment. Recall that the subjects who labored unsuccessfully as contestants rated their own general knowledge relatively low. Imagine what it must have been like to be in their position. Over and over you would hear yourself saying, "I don't know the answer to that question." Can you see how observation of this behavior—the process of self-perception—could give rise to a negative self-evaluation?

Is There a "Real" Social Reality?

We have now seen several ways in which "reality" is affected by the expectations you bring to it. Does that mean that everyone has a different version of the world? In some sense, the answer is yes. Given that each individual has a different history of life experiences, leading to different attitudes and expectations, we would expect each person's version of "reality" to be just a bit different. You probably have come to this conclusion yourself if you've ever heard friends retell events in which you participated. Did they emphasize parts of the story that were unimportant to you? Did they give different reasons for why things took place? These small (or large!) differences in perspective hint strongly at the construction of different social realities.

On the other hand, we have seen that the processes of reality construction are limited in some important ways by what's out in the world. People's stereotypes about little boys and girls did not affect their ratings on dimensions for which they had relevant firsthand data. People cannot turn confident extraverts into introverts just by expecting them to be so. Processes of self-perception wield the greatest influence when there is no strong history to bring to the interpretation of behaviors. All these data suggest that people's worlds diverge most dramatically only under circumstances of uncertainty.

Although evidence clearly suggests that your social reality is influenced by your expectations, the greatest influences occur in the presence of uncertainty.

Throughout this chapter we have asked you to imagine situations involving friends. But how and why do some people become your friends? You probably won't be surprised that another important area of social psychological research considers *social relationships*—the relationships between people and groups of people. We will now look at the forces of *prejudice* that drive people apart and the forces of *interpersonal attraction* that draw them together. These topics will also give us another opportunity to see how attitudes are formed and potentially changed.

SOCIAL RELATIONSHIPS

How do you choose the people with whom you share your life? Social psychologists have addressed this question from both negative and positive perspectives. On the negative side, researchers have tried to understand the origins of prejudice: why members of different groups feel irrational dislike toward each other, often on the basis of little firsthand experience or knowledge. The hope has always been that by understanding how prejudice comes about, psychologists can help to eliminate it. On the positive side, researchers have tried to understand what attracts people to each other. They have even tried to discover some of the factors that give rise to feelings of liking and loving. We turn now to these facets of social relations.

PREJUDICE

Of all human weaknesses, none is more destructive of the dignity of the individual and the social bonds of humanity than prejudice. Social psychology has always put the study of prejudice high on its agenda in an effort to understand its complexity and persistence and to develop strategies to change prejudiced attitudes and discriminatory behavior (Allport, 1954; Duckitt, 1992). The Supreme Court's 1954 decision to outlaw segregated public education was, in part, based on research, presented in federal court by social psychologist **Kenneth Clark,** which showed the negative impact on black children of their separate and unequal education (Clark & Clark, 1947).

How does prejudice originate, and why is it so difficult to eradicate?

Prejudice is the prime example of social reality gone awry—a situation created in the minds of people that can demean and destroy the lives of others. **Prejudice** is a learned attitude toward a target object, involving negative feelings (dislike or fear), negative beliefs (stereotypes) that justify the attitude, and a behavioral intention to avoid, control, dominate, or eliminate those in the target group. A false belief qualifies as prejudice when it resists change even in the face of appropriate evidence of its falseness. Prejudiced attitudes serve as biasing filters that influence the way individuals are perceived and treated once they are categorized as members of a target group. We will explore some of the origins of prejudice, as well as social psychology's efforts to help reverse its effects.

The Origins of Prejudice

A sad reality of prejudice is that the most minimal of distinctive cues is sufficient for the formation of negative stereotypes and harmful bias.

One of the sad truths from the study of prejudice is that it is easy to get people to show negative attitudes toward people who do not belong to the same "group" (Elliott, 1977; Sherif et al., 1961/1988). The most minimal of distinctive cues is sufficient to trigger the formation of bias and prejudice.

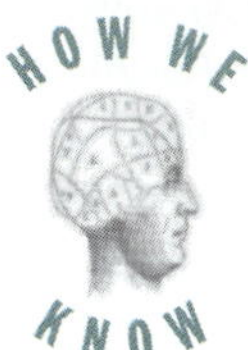

In a series of experiments in Holland, subjects were randomly divided into two groups: a blue group and a green group. According to the subjects' group membership, they were given either blue or green pens and asked to write on either blue or green paper. The experimenter addressed subjects in terms of their group color. Even though these color categories had no intrinsic psychological significance and assignment to the groups was completely arbitrary, subjects gave a more positive evaluation of their own group than of the other. Furthermore, this in-group bias, based solely on color identification, appeared even before the group members began to work together on an experimental task (Rabbie, 1981).

Why would "color" identity matter so quickly? Why would it matter at all? Let's explore these questions.

What is at work even in the "color" experiment is the very swift action of social categorization. **Social categorization** is the process by which people organize their social environment by categorizing themselves and others into groups (Wilder, 1986). The simplest and most pervasive form of categorizing consists of an individual determining whether people are like him or her. This categorization develops from a "me versus not me" orientation to an "us versus them" orientation. These cognitive distinctions result in an *in-group bias,* an evaluation of one's own group as better than others (Brewer, 1979). Many experiments have examined the consequences of *minimal groups,* like the "blue" versus "green" distinction (Tajfel, 1982; Tajfel & Billig, 1974). The members of the different groups most often start out as strangers, but almost instantly they show astonishing solidarity—they believe the members of their in-group to be more pleasant and harder workers. When the time comes to share resources, people do everything they can to deny benefits to members of the other, out-group. These consequences develop regardless of limited exposure to the out-groups and despite the positive experiences of individual in-group members with members of the out-group (Park & Rothbart, 1982; Quattrone, 1986).

Research shows that social categorization quickly turns strangers into cohesive groups who perceive their own members more positively than they perceive nonmembers.

If all these forces apply in these artificially constituted groups, you can begin to understand how prejudice, fear, and racism can become so severe under situations of real-world pressure. The instant tendency toward defining "us" against "them" becomes even more powerful when the perception grows that resources are scarce and that goods can be given only to one group, at the expense of the other. In addition, research has shown that much day-to-day prejudice exists even below the level of consciousness (Devine, 1989; Greenwald & Banaji, 1995). Once formed, prejudices exert a powerful force on the way pertinent experiences are selectively processed, organized, and remembered. Even people whose explicit beliefs are not prejudiced may produce *automatic* acts of prejudice—unreflective "choices" of friends or activities—as a function of the messages they have unknowingly internalized. Consider your best friends: Do they belong to the same ethnic group as you do? If so, why might this be the case?

Do these social psychological theories explain the full impact of prejudice and, in particular, the destructive *racist* attitudes of white and black members of U.S. society? Some critics have argued that the theories ignore the historical reality of slavery and its aftermath (Gaines & Reed, 1995). The social psychological model often treats the forces that create prejudice as equal in all people. In the United States, however, history has created a social structure in which racism flourishes particularly well: historical realities combine with current personal forces to give rise to prejudices that may be very hard to erase.

We have come to the rather troubling conclusion that prejudice is easy to create and difficult to remove. Even so, from the earliest days of social psychology, researchers have attempted to reverse the march of prejudice. Let's now sample a few of those efforts.

Reversing Prejudice

One of the classic early studies in social psychology was also the first demonstration that minimal groups could lead to great hostility. In the summer of 1954, Muzafer Sherif and his colleagues (1961/1988) brought two groups of boys to a summer camp at Robbers Cave State Park in Oklahoma. The two groups were dubbed the "Eagles" and the "Rattlers." Each group forged its own camp bonds in ignorance of the other for about a week. The groups' introduction to each other consisted of a series of competitive activities like baseball, football, and a tug-of-war. From this beginning, the rivalry between the groups grew violent. Group flags were burned, cabins were ransacked, and a near-riotlike food fight broke out. What could be done to reduce this animosity?

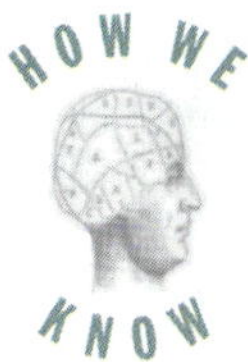

The experimenters tried a propaganda approach, by complimenting each group to the other. That did not work. The experimenters tried bringing the groups together in noncompetitive circumstances. That did not work either. Hostility seethed even when the groups were just watching a movie in the same place. Finally, the experimenters hit on a solution. What they did was to introduce problems that could be solved only through *cooperative action* on *shared goals*. For example, they arranged for the camp truck to break down. Both groups were needed to pull it back up a steep hill. In the face of mutual dependence, hostility faded away.

Sherif's Robbers Cave experiment showed that prejudice can be reduced by programs that foster interaction between groups in pursuit of shared goals.

The lesson of the Robbers Cave experiment is that the elimination of prejudice takes more than mere contact between groups. Ideally, a program combating prejudice must foster personal interaction in the pursuit of shared goals. Take a moment to consider how you might apply these lessons to situations that matter to you.

Social psychologist **Elliot Aronson** and his colleagues (1978) developed a program anchored in the Robbers Cave philosophy to tackle prejudice in newly desegregated classrooms in Texas and California.

In the intergroup competition phase of the Robbers Cave experiment, the "Eagles" and "Rattlers" pulled apart—but in the end they pulled together.

The technique of jigsawing, giving each student part of a total team assignment, has proven effective in reducing prejudice and conflict among interracial groups of elementary school children.

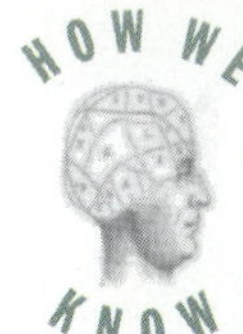

The research team created conditions in which fifth-grade students had to depend on one another rather than compete against one another to learn required material. In a technique known as *jigsawing,* each pupil was given part of the total material to master and then share with other group members. Performance was evaluated on the basis of the overall group presentation. Thus every member's contribution was essential and valued.

Interracial conflict has decreased in classes where jigsawing has united formerly hostile white, Latino, and African-American students in a common fate team (Aronson & Gonzalez, 1988; Gonzalez 1983). Consider the story of one young boy named Carlos. Carlos, who had been ignored because his primary language was not English, was assigned a vital part of the team assignment on Joseph Pulitzer. The other teammates had to figure out how to get him to share the information he was responsible for providing. Carlos got his teammates' attention, felt needed, developed affection for the group members, and also discovered that learning was fun. Both his self-esteem and his grades increased. (We are happy to report that little Carlos went on to Harvard Law School after graduating from a Texas College.)

Social psychology has no great solution to end prejudice all at once. It does, however, provide a set of ideas to eliminate its worst effects slowly but surely, in each small locality. The psychological dimension of prejudice must be seen as part of the complex syndrome of its causes, including historical, political, and economic. We move now to more positive aspects of social relations, circumstances of liking and loving.

Interpersonal Attraction

Why do you seek the company of your friends? Why are there some people for whom your feelings move beyond friendship to feelings of romantic love? Social psychologists have developed a variety of answers to these questions. (But don't worry, no one yet has taken all the mystery out of love!)

Liking

Have you ever stopped to examine how and why you acquired each of your friends? The first part of this answer is straightforward: people tend to become attracted to people with whom they are in close *proximity.* This factor probably requires little explanation, but it might be worth noting that there is a general tendency for people to like objects and people just by virtue of *mere exposure:* the more you are exposed to something or someone, the more you like it (Zajonc, 1968). This mere exposure effect means that, on the whole, you will come to like more and more the people who are nearby. It's possible, however, that the computer age is giving a slightly new meaning to the idea of proximity. Many people now maintain relationships over networks of computers. Although a friend may be geographically quite distant, daily messages appearing on a computer screen can make the person seem psychologically very close. Let's look now at two other factors that can lead to attraction and liking.

Individuals who have frequent contact, whether face-to-face or via electronic means, tend to develop positive feelings about one another.

For better or worse, *physical attractiveness* often plays a role in the kindling of friendship. There is a strong stereotype in our culture that physically attractive people are also good in other ways. One study found that both male and female subjects rated attractive people as kinder, stronger, more interesting, and more nurturant than unattractive people. The subjects also predicted that attractive people would have happier marriages and more fulfilling lives (Dion et al., 1972). In light of this stereotype, it might not surprise you that physical attractiveness plays a role in liking.

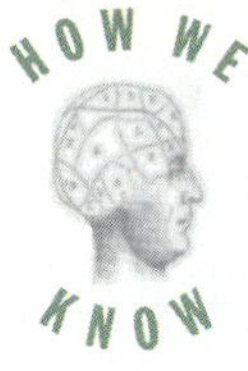

In one study, researchers randomly assigned incoming University of Minnesota freshmen to couples as blind dates for a dance. The researchers collected a variety of information about each student along dimensions of intelligence and personality. The night of the dance, and in later follow-ups, the students were asked to evaluate their dates and indicate how likely they were to see the individual again. The results were clear, and very similar for both men and women. Beauty mattered more than high IQs, good social skills, or good personalities. Only those matched by chance with beautiful or handsome blind dates wanted to pursue the relationship (Walster et al., 1966).

Further research has demonstrated that, although most people show an initial preference for physically attractive others, they also tend to be more secure in relationships when there is a fairly good match in level of physical attractiveness (Cash & Derlega, 1978; White, 1980). In stable relationships, that is, both partners are generally equally attractive. This is true both in friendship and romantic relationships. As we will see next, this is only one way in which similarity fosters liking.

A famous adage on *similarity* suggests that "birds of a feather flock together." Is this correct? Research evidence suggests that, under many circumstances, the answer is yes. We just suggested that people tend to enter relationships with others who are similar on the dimension of physical attractiveness. It is equally true that similarity on other dimensions, notably beliefs, attitudes, and values, fosters friendship. Why might that be so? People who are similar to you can provide a sense of personal validation, because a similar person makes you feel that the attitudes (and so on) you hold dear are, in fact, the right ones (Byrne & Clore, 1970). Remember the women of Bennington College and their postcollege choices of mates? Furthermore, dissimilarity often leads to strong *repulsion* (Rosenbaum, 1986). When you discover that someone holds opinions that are different from yours, you may evoke from memory past instances of interpersonal friction. That will motivate you to stay away—and if you stay away from dissimilar people, only the similar ones will be left in your pool of friends.

Finally, you tend to like people who you believe like you. Do you recall our discussion of the wily salesperson's use of *reciprocity*? The rule that you should give back what you receive applies to friendship as well. People give back "liking" to people who they believe have given "liking" to them (Backman & Secord, 1959). Furthermore, because of the way your belief can affect your behaviors, believing that someone likes or dislikes you can help bring that relationship about (Curtis & Miller, 1986). Can you predict how you would act toward someone you believe likes you? Toward someone you believe dislikes you? Suppose you act with hostility toward someone you think doesn't like you. Do you see how your belief could become a self-fulfilling prophecy?

You are likely to be attracted to people who are close in proximity, physically attractive, similar to you, and who reciprocate your liking.

The evidence we have reviewed suggests that most of your friends will be people you encounter frequently, and people with whom you share the bonds of similarity and reciprocity. But what have researchers found about relationships people call "loving"?

Loving

Many of the same forces that lead to liking also get people started on the road to love—in most cases, you will first like the people you end up loving. (However, some people report loving certain relatives that they don't particularly like as individuals.) What special factors have social psychologists learned about loving relationships between friends?

One theory conceptualizes people in close relationships as having a feeling

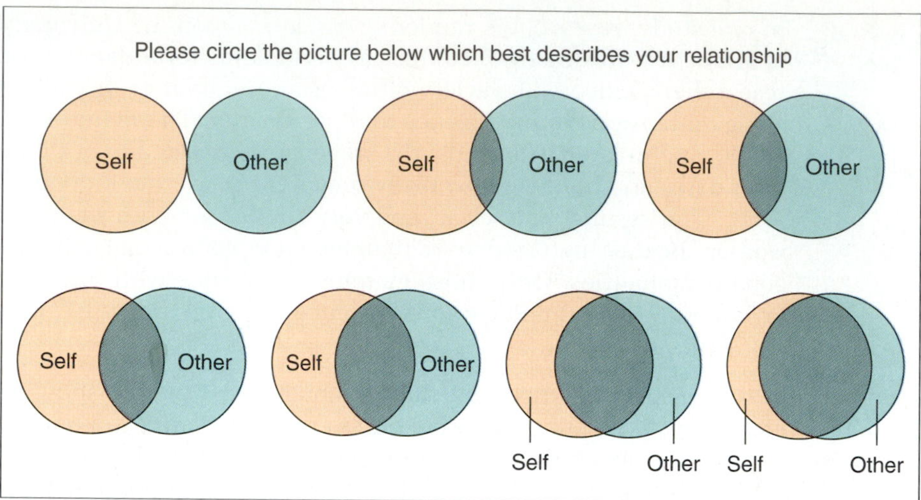

Figure 16.7
The Inclusion of Other in the Self (IOS) Scale

that the "other" is included in their "self" (Aron et al., 1991; Aron & Aron, 1994). Consider the series of diagrams given in **Figure 16.7**. Each of the diagrams represents a way you could conceptualize a close relationship. If you are in a romantic relationship, can you say which of the diagrams seems to capture most effectively the extent of interdependence between you and your partner? Research has shown that people who perceive the most overlap between self and other—those people who come to view the other as included within the self—are most likely to remain committed to their relationships over time (Aron et al., 1992).

Loving relationships are closer if each person sees the other as included within the self.

What other factors contribute to the likelihood that someone will remain in a relationship? The *dependence model* suggests that commitment is based on a series of judgments (Drigotas & Rusbult, 1992, p. 65):

- The degree to which each of several needs is important in the individual's relationship. Important needs are intimacy, sex, emotional involvement, companionship, and intellectual involvement.
- The degree to which each of those needs is satisfied in that relationship.
- For each need, whether there is anyone other than the current partner with whom the individual has an important relationship.
- The degree to which each need is satisfied by the alternative relationship.

The dependence model suggests that people are more likely to stay in a relationship when it satisfies important needs that are not satisfied by anyone else.

As you might expect, this model predicts that people are more likely to stay in a relationship when the relationship satisfies important needs that cannot be satisfied by anyone else. Thus, if companionship is very important to you—you enjoy spending leisure time with other people—and a person with whom you share a relationship provides more companionship than anyone else you know, you're likely to feel committed to that relationship. This will be true even if your partner is not your first choice on dimensions that matter less.

Researchers have also been interested in understanding individual differences in people's ability to sustain loving relationships. Attention is now often focused on *adult attachment style* (Shaver & Hazan, 1994). Recall from Chapter 6 the importance of the quality of a child's attachment to his or her parents for smooth social development. Researchers began to wonder how much impact that early attachment might have later in life, as the children grew up to have committed relationships and children of their own (Hazan &

Table 16.1 Styles of Adult Attachment for Close Relationships

Statement 1:

I find it relatively easy to get close to others and am comfortable depending on them. I don't often worry about being abandoned or about someone getting too close to me.

Statement 2:

I am somewhat uncomfortable being close to others; I find it difficult to trust them completely, difficult to allow myself to depend on them. I am nervous when anyone gets too close, and often, love partners want me to be more intimate than I feel comfortable being.

Statement 3:

I find that others are reluctant to get as close as I would like. I often worry that my partner doesn't really love me or won't want to stay with me. I want to get very close to my partner, and this sometimes scares people away.

Shaver, 1987; Main et al., 1985). Although no studies yet have traced individuals all the way from early childhood to marriage, measures of adult attachment styles predict the quality of close relationships.

Adult attachment style has been found to be a reliable predictor of relationship quality, with those adults who are securely attached reporting the most enduring romantic relationships.

What are the types of attachment style? **Table 16.1** provides three statements about close relationships (Hazan & Shaver, 1987; Shaver & Hazan, 1994). When asked which of these statements best describes them, the majority of people (55 percent) choose the first statement; this is a *secure* attachment style. Sizable minorities select the second statement (25 percent, an *avoidant* style) and the third (20 percent, an *anxious-ambivalent* style). Attachment style has proven to be an accurate predictor of relationship quality (Feeney & Noller, 1990). Compared with individuals who chose the other two styles, securely attached individuals had the most enduring romantic relationships as adults.

Let us make one final distinction. Many loving relationships start out with a period of great intensity and absorption, which is called *passionate love.* Over time, there is a tendency for relationships to migrate toward a state of lesser intensity but greater intimacy, called *companionate love* (Berscheid & Walster, 1978). When you find yourself in a loving relationship, you may do well to anticipate that transition—so that you don't misinterpret a natural change as a process of falling "out of love." Even so, the decline of passionate love may not be as dramatic as the stereotype of long-committed couples suggests. Researchers find a reasonable level of passionate love as much as 30 years into relationships (Aron & Aron, 1994). When you enter a loving relationship, you can have high hopes that the passion will endure in some form, even as the relationship grows to encompass other needs.

Companionate feelings for someone you were once passionate about do not signal "falling out of love": on the contrary, they are a natural outgrowth of romance and a vital ingredient in most long-term partnerships.

SOLVING SOCIAL PROBLEMS

Many social psychologists are motivated by the goal to improve the human condition. Kurt Lewin, the founder of modern social psychology, believed that for psychology to make its greatest contribution, theory and research must be integrated with practical application. "No action without research, no research without action" was his dictum (1948). A major organization of social psychologists, the Society for the Psychological Study of Social Issues, is, in fact, dedicated to just that principle. Lewin's philosophy has had a great effect on the ways in which social psychologists choose areas of research to pursue and the ways in which actual experiments are designed. In the final section of this chapter, we will look at examples of social psychology applied to important social problems.

Kurt Lewin practiced what he preached by conducting research

Kurt Lewin believed that research in social psychology should be put to practical use in order to solve social problems.

designed to solve social problems while yielding significant information about the underlying social processes involved. An example is his study of the way to get homemakers during the Second World War to serve food their families did not like but that was plentiful, nutritious, and cheap.

Ordinary meats were scarce and rationed; highly nutritious visceral meats, such as liver and kidneys, were plentiful but unpopular. Lewin's objective was to find an effective way to change purchasing and cooking habits. Some women in his group heard a persuasive lecture on the positive effects of serving these glandular meats—the usual type of education intended to influence the public. Other women met in small groups to discuss the issue and consider ways to make the undesirable meats appealing to their families. These women then made a public commitment to follow through and buy the visceral meats. The results were clear: the lecture had little effect on the women's attitudes or behavior; however, the democratically run discussion groups made many of the women far more likely to take the socially beneficial action of serving visceral meats for their families (Lewin, 1947).

The key idea in this research was the effectiveness of involving people in the decision-making process—"participatory management"—and of making public commitments to members of one's group. Later research showed that workers who were given an active role in decisions about production performed better on the job, and were more content, than passive workers who were told what to do and got paid for doing only what they were ordered to do (Coch & French, 1948; Pelz, 1955/1965).

Although these results were brought to the attention of many U.S. executives, few decided to implement the recommended procedures, because they objected to the idea of the group as a unit of democratic decision making. This recommended approach did not conform to the American ethic of individualism, and it bore a superficial resemblance to communism. However, these recommendations were put to productive use in another part of the world. In Japan, where societal norms favor group-based behavior, this approach found great favor; it was a costly missed opportunity for U.S. business. What you can see here is that researchers make recommendations based on their best available knowledge. Policy makers in government, business, and other agencies have the power to accept or reject that input—often on the basis of political expediency or personal agendas.

This focus on solving social problems is a long way from the traditional view of psychology as the study of individual actions and mental processes. Social psychologists think of the person as only one level of a complex system that includes social groups, institutions, cultural values, historical circumstances, political and economic realities, and specific situational forces. Among the exciting liaisons that are encouraged by social psychology and infused with its research paradigms and perspectives are psychology and law; psychology and education; psychology and health care; political psychology (international relations, terrorism, conflict, public policy); psychology and the consumer; psychology and business; environmental or ecological psychology; and peace psychology (Oskamp, 1984). Here we will complete our study of social psychology by examining two areas that should be of vital importance to everyone—environmental psychology and peace psychology.

Environmental Psychology

Environmental psychology is the study of the relationships between psychological processes and physical environments, both natural and human-made

(Altman & Christensen, 1990; Darley & Gilbert, 1985). Environmental psychologists use an ecological approach to study the way people and environments affect each other. The *ecological* approach emphasizes the reciprocity and mutual influence in an organism–environment relationship. Researchers see a circular pattern—people change the natural environment by creating physical and social structures such as farms, neighborhoods, and cities. In turn, these artificial structures confine, direct, and encourage certain behaviors and discourage or prevent others. What behaviors might be very familiar to city dwellers but foreign to people who live on farms?

Environmental psychology is oriented not so much toward past determinants of behavior as toward the future that is being created. This orientation means that environmental psychologists have to be concerned with values. Some environments are more nourishing for us than others, and some uses of the environment are destructive. This new psychology is concerned with identifying what makes environments supportive and what human behaviors are involved in creating and maintaining those environments while not trespassing on the health of the ecosystem that makes life possible in the first place (Russell & Ward, 1982).

Let's look at a specific example in which social psychologists have turned their knowledge to environmental issues. Consider conservation of scarce natural resources. People often know that energy and water must be conserved, but how do you get them to act on this knowledge? An experiment by social psychologist Elliot Aronson (1990) suggests that *modeling* the desired behavior is much more effective than simply telling people what they should be doing. Administrators at the University of California at Santa Cruz wanted students to conserve energy and water. Because Santa Cruz students claimed to be ardent environmentalists, the bureaucrats believed that displaying a conservation message on signs would lead to significant changes in behavior.

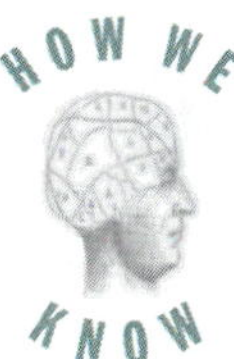

A sign on the wall of the men's shower room at the field house encouraged water conservation by urging users to "(1) Wet down. (2) Turn water off. (3) Soap up. (4) Rinse off." Over a period of five days, only 6 percent of the men taking showers followed the suggested routine. When the sign was placed on a tripod and moved to a more prominent spot at the shower room entrance, compliance went up to 19 percent. However, the overall effectiveness of the sign was probably negligible, as some users, resenting the sign, knocked it over and took extralong showers.

Finally, all signs were removed, and a student modeled appropriate shower-taking behavior. A confederate entered the shower room when it was momentarily empty, turned on the tap, and waited with his back turned to the entrance. As soon as he heard someone enter, he followed the admonition of the sign: he turned off the water, soaped up, rinsed off, and left. Compliance under this approach jumped to 49 percent. When two models were used, 67 percent of those who observed them followed their lead. Aronson concluded that modeling works better than signs because it provides "a checkpoint from similar people of what is reasonable behavior in a given situation" (Aronson, 1990, p. 125).

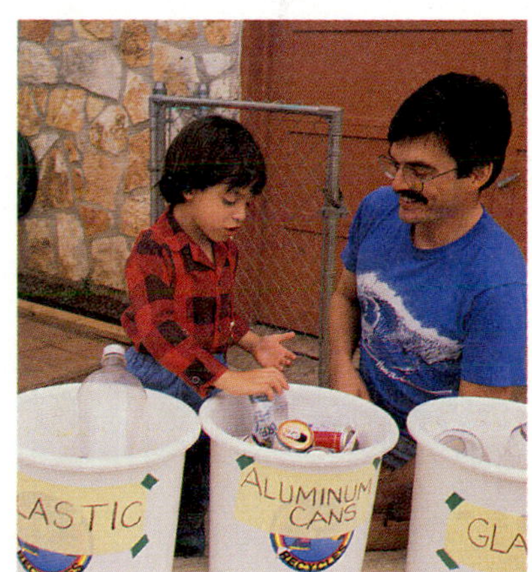

How reliably do you recycle? If you see others recycling, chances are you will recycle more than you would if none of your neighbors or friends did.

How might you apply this research insight to your own community's conservation efforts? Suppose, for example, you wanted to increase the rate at which people recycle paper, bottles, and cans. What steps could you take to provide appropriate models?

Would you like to become more involved in protecting the resources of your environment? If so, consider reading *The Student Environmental Action Guide: 25 Simple Things We Can Do* (HarperCollins Publishers and the Earth Works Group, 1991). This book is written for students by students. It addresses campus environmental issues and is filled with a combination of facts, success stories about the environmental actions taken by student groups, and prescriptions for actions that you and other students can take.

Peace Psychology

Psychology is uniquely equipped to study the question of how to help resolve the dilemmas of national and international disharmony. **Peace psychology** represents an interdisciplinary approach to prevention of nuclear war and maintenance of peace (Plous, 1985). Psychologists committed to contributing their talents and energies to this area so vital to the future draw upon the work of investigators in many areas, such as political science, economics, physics, mathematics, computer science, anthropology, climatology, and medicine. Psychologists for Social Responsibility is an organization of psychologists who not only study various aspects of the complex issues involved in war and peace but conduct educational programs on these topics for professionals, schoolchildren, and the lay public. Let's look at three examples of peace psychologists at work.

One of the aims of peace psychology is to understand the forces that give rise to false beliefs, misperceptions, and erroneous attributions on issues germane to nuclear arms, military strength, and national security. Exploring the individual and cultural forces that create war and promote peace involves studies of propaganda and images of the enemy through content and fantasy analysis of violence and war themes in the media. Although most cultures oppose individual aggression as a crime, nations train millions of soldiers to kill. The problem of military psychology is to convert the act of murder into patriotism (Keen, 1986). Part of this mass social influence involves dehumanizing the soldiers of the other side into "the enemy"—nonhuman objects to be hated and destroyed. This dehumanization is accomplished by political rhetoric and by the media, in their vivid depictions of the enemy. According to army veterans, a soldier's most important weapon in war is not a gun but this internalized view of the hated "enemy" (see **Figure 16.8**). Thus, young soldiers become psychologically programmed to be wartime killers by these distorted images of anyone their government decides to label as the enemy. This is one of the most frightening of all social psychological principles.

Peace psychologists are interested in exploring the individual and cultural forces that create war and promote peace.

Another aim of peace psychology is to understand how nations negotiate and make judgments in crisis situations. **Irving Janis** (1982b) analyzed the historical record of actual international crises since World War II. Characterizing these decisions along several dimensions, Janis found a strong relationship between the way decisions were made and whether or not international conflict intensified. Finding that defective decision making predominated in many of the crises, he suggested various safeguards to ensure better decision making in future crises. By learning how decision makers made sense of events that could have led to nuclear war, psychologists may be in a position to offer more fully formed decision rules that minimize the cognitive and motivational biases of policy makers. The goal is to prevent future crises through an understanding of past and current crisis management (Blight, 1987).

Finally, psychologists have a new role after the revolutions that have swept away entire political systems and economic orders throughout the world. The transition of hundreds of millions of people from a totalitarian to a democratic mentality and from a central collectivist society to a free-market economy is a change of unprecedented proportions. Citizens born after many decades of Communist rule have never experienced the freedoms and responsibilities of democratic ideas and practices. Democracy is more than a political system; it is a unique way of thinking about the significance and role of the individual in shaping societal goals.

Those in Eastern European countries who had lived with some sense of

Figure 16.8
Faces of the Enemy
How does military psychology convert killing into patriotism? Note how in each of these caricatures, the designated enemy is given monstrous and dehumanized characteristics.

security in government-controlled economies and state-run industries are having difficulty learning to cope with the risks and uncertainties of competitive market economies (Korzeniowski, 1993; Reykowski & Smolenska, 1993; Watts, 1994). Additionally, individuals and whole communities need help to deal with decades of abuses by totalitarian regimes—exiles, imprisonments, forced labor, displacement, and ecological catastrophes. This psychological help involves education, research, therapy, and social policy planning. The Center for the Psychology of Democracy is an organization of psychologists committed to assisting people and societies in reshaping their lives and country within the framework of democratic principles and practices (Balakrishnan, 1991).

These brief looks at environmental psychology and peace psychology reinforce the claim that social psychology (alongside, we hope, other branches of psychology) can have direct relevance to society's most pressing concerns. You can enrich your own life, and the lives of those around you, through the careful study of social psychology. Perhaps you can also save yourself a few bucks the next time you tangle with a "compliance professional," also known as the "wily salesperson"!

Recapping Main Points

The Power of the Situation

Human thought and action are affected by situational influences. Being assigned to play a social role, even in artificial settings, can cause individuals to act contrary to their beliefs, values, and dispositions. Social norms shape the behavior of group members, as demonstrated by the Bennington study and Asch experiments. Lewin tested the effect of leadership styles on schoolchildren, demonstrating that socially significant questions could be explored experimentally.

Milgram's studies on obedience are a powerful testimony to the influence of situational factors. Bystander intervention studies show that the situation also largely determines who is likely or unlikely to help in emergencies.

Constructing Social Reality

Each person constructs his or her own social reality. Social perception is influenced by beliefs and expectations. Attribution theory describes the judgments people make about the causes of behaviors. Several biases can creep into attributions and other judgments and behaviors, but the influence of expectations is limited by accurate information you have about the world. Dissonance theory and self-perception theory consider attitude formation and change that arise from behavioral acts.

Social Relationships

Even minimal cues can yield prejudice. Researchers have eliminated some of the effects of prejudice by creating situations in which members of different groups must cooperate to reach shared goals. Interpersonal attraction is determined in part by proximity, physical attractiveness, similarity, and reciprocity. A person's commitment to a loving relationship is related to the level of closeness, dependence, and his or her adult attachment style.

Solving Social Problems

Many social psychologists strive to improve the human condition by applying psychological principles to various social problems. In the field of environmental psychology, researchers look at the way people and environments affect each other. Environmental psychologists look for ways that human behavior can make environments supportive without trespassing on the health of ecosystems. Peace psychologists look for ways to help resolve competition and hostilities among nations. They conduct research that examines the basis for false beliefs, misperceptions, and erroneous attributions in areas related to national security and nuclear arms.

Resources

Aronson, E. (1991). *The social animal* (6th ed.). New York: Freeman. A narrative approach to social psychology that presents theory and research in an interesting and relevant way.

Cialdini, R. B. (1993). *Influence: Science and practice* (3rd ed.). New York: HarperCollins.

Hatfield, E., & Rapson, R. L. (1993). *Love, sex, and intimacy: Their psychology, biology, and history.* New York: HarperCollins.

Milgram, S. (1974). *Obedience to authority.* New York: Harper & Row. Milgram presents his ideas on the topic of obedience and describes his famous research.

Pryor, J. B., & Reeder, G. D. (Eds.). (1993). *The social psychology of HIV infection.* Hillsdale, NJ: Erlbaum. A series of interesting new studies and conceptual models that bring to bear social psychological knowledge and methodology to combat this epidemic.

Rosenthal, R., & Jacobson, L. (1968). *Pygmalion in the classroom: Teacher expectations and intellectual development.* New York: Holt. Classic study of the self-fulfilling prophecy and how it applies in the classroom.

Weber, A. L., & Harvey, J. H. (Eds.). (1994). *Perspectives on close relationships.* Boston: Allyn & Bacon.

Zimbardo, P. G., & Lieppe, M. (1991). *The psychology of attitude change and social influence.* New York: McGraw-Hill.

17

Psychological Disorders

Can you imagine writing these words?

I want to let you know what it is like to be a functional scitzophrenic in these days and times and what someone with my mental illness faces. . . . The patient and public, in my opnion needs to be educated about mental illness, because people ridicule and mistreat, even misunderstand us at crucial times. Like how family, husband, friends, or social services react to what they don't know about us.

I can tell the difference between a noise of my illness and a real noise, because Ive studied myself reading about it. There is a common sense rule I use. I just try hard to remember what the world and people are really like. The illness picks such silly nonsense to bother the mind with. The medicine is strong with me and my body chemistry so I don't have too many illness symptoms bothering me. . . . Every person that comes down with an illness is going to be different in handling it. The things that are consistant are the usual symptoms that come along with the illness. Everyone that wants to succeed in life needs opportunities for them to prove themself. Im a person besides just a person with an illness. *(Letter from "Cherish" to P.G.Z., 1/1992.)*

What are your reactions as you read this young woman's letter? If they are similar to ours, you feel a mixture of sadness at her plight, of delight in her willingness to do all she can to cope with the many problems her mental illness creates, of anger toward those who stigmatize her because she may act differently at times, and of hope that, with medication and therapy, her condition may improve. These are but a few of the emotions that clinical and research psychologists and psychiatrists feel as they try to understand and treat mental disorders.

This chapter focuses on the nature and causes of psychological disorders: what they are, why they develop, and how we can explain their causes. The next, and final, chapter builds on this knowledge to describe the strategies used to treat, and to prevent, mental illness. A recent study estimates that nearly 50 percent of young and middle adults in the United States have suffered from a psychological disorder at some point in their lives (Kessler et al., 1994). Thus many of you who read this text are likely to benefit directly from knowledge about psychopathology. Facts alone, however, will not convey the serious impact psychological disorders have on the everyday lives of individuals and families. Throughout this chapter, as we discuss categories of psychological disorders, try to envision the real people who live with such a disorder every day. We will share with you their words and lives, as we did at the start of the chapter. Let's begin now with a discussion of the concept of abnormality.

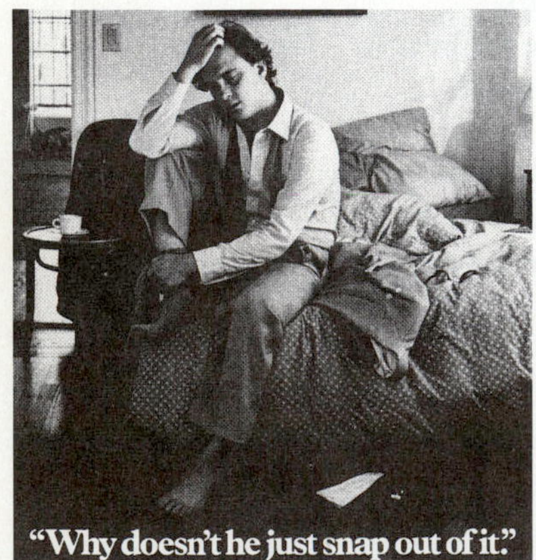
"Why doesn't he just snap out of it."

THE NATURE OF PSYCHOLOGICAL DISORDERS

Have you ever worried excessively? Felt depressed or anxious without really knowing why? Been fearful of something you rationally knew could not harm you? Had thoughts about suicide? Used alcohol or drugs to escape a problem? Almost everyone will answer yes to at least one of these questions, which means that almost everyone has experienced the symptoms of a psychological disorder. This chapter looks at the range of psychological functioning that is considered unhealthy or abnormal, often referred to as *psychopathology* or *psychological disorder.* **Psychopathological functioning** involves disruptions in emotional, behavioral, or thought processes that lead to personal distress or that block one's ability to achieve important goals. The field of **abnormal psychology** is the area of psychological investigation most directly concerned with understanding the nature of individual pathologies of mind, mood, and behavior.

Psychological disorders may result in disruption of emotional, cognitive, or behavioral processes.

We begin this section by exploring a more precise definition of abnormality. We then examine how this definition evolved over hundreds of years of human history.

Deciding What Is Abnormal

What does it mean to say someone is *abnormal* or *suffering from a psychological disorder?* How do psychologists and other clinical practitioners decide what is abnormal? Is it always clear when behavior moves from the normal to the abnormal category? The judgment that someone has a mental disorder is typically based on the evaluation of the individual's *behavioral* functioning by people with some special authority or power. The terms used to describe these phenomena—*mental disorder, mental illness,* or *abnormality*—depend on the particular perspective, training, and cultural background of the speaker, the situation, and the status of the person being judged.

Let's consider seven criteria you might use to label behavior as "abnormal" (*DSM-IV*, 1994; Rosenhan & Seligman, 1989):

- *Distress or disability:* An individual experiences personal distress or disabled functioning, which produces a risk of physical or psychological deterioration or loss of freedom of action. For example, a man who cannot leave his home without weeping would be unable to pursue ordinary life goals.

- *Maladaptiveness:* An individual acts in ways that hinder goals, do not contribute to personal well-being, or interfere strongly with the goals of others and the needs of society. Someone who is drinking so heavily that she cannot hold down a job or who is endangering others through her intoxication is displaying maladaptive behavior.

- *Irrationality:* An individual acts or talks in ways that are irrational or incomprehensible to others. A man who responds to voices that do not exist in objective reality is behaving irrationally.

- *Unpredictability:* An individual behaves unpredictably or erratically from situation to situation, as if experiencing a loss of control. A child who smashes his fist through a window for no apparent reason displays unpredictability.

- *Unconventionality and statistical rarity:* An individual behaves in ways that are statistically rare and that violate social standards of what is acceptable or desirable. Just being statistically unusual, however, does not lead to a psychological judgment of abnormality. For example, possessing genius-level intelligence is extremely rare, but it is also considered desirable. On the other hand, having an extremely low intelligence is also rare but is considered undesirable; thus it has often been labeled abnormal.

- *Observer discomfort:* An individual creates discomfort in others by making them feel threatened or distressed in some way. A woman walking

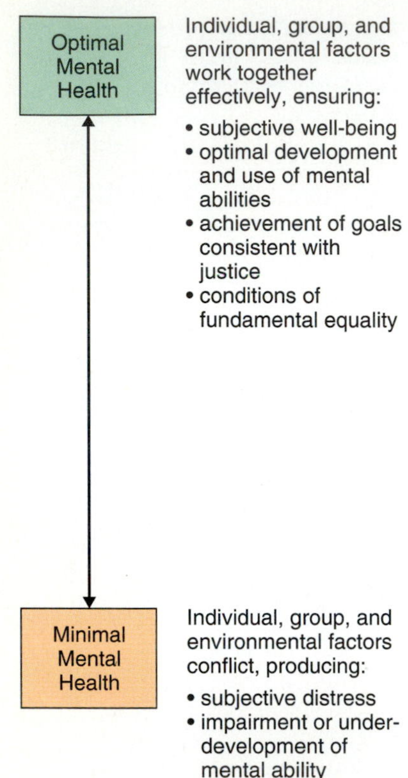
Optimal Mental Health
Individual, group, and environmental factors work together effectively, ensuring:
• subjective well-being
• optimal development and use of mental abilities
• achievement of goals consistent with justice
• conditions of fundamental equality
Minimal Mental Health
Individual, group, and environmental factors conflict, producing:
• subjective distress
• impairment or under-development of mental ability
• failure to achieve goals
• destructive behaviors
• entrenchment of inequities

Figure 17.1 Mental Health Continuum

down the middle of the street, having a loud conversation with herself, creates observer discomfort in motorists trying to drive around her.

- *Violation of moral and ideal standards:* An individual violates expectations for how one *ought* to behave with respect to societal norms. By this criterion, people might be considered abnormal if they did not wish to work or they did not believe in God.

Can you see why most of these indicators of abnormality may not be immediately apparent to all observers? Consider just the last criterion. Are you mentally ill if you don't wish to work, even if that is abnormal with respect to the norms of society? Or consider a more serious symptom. It is "bad" to have hallucinations in our culture because they are taken as signs of mental disturbance, but it is "good" in cultures in which hallucinations are interpreted as mystical visions from spirit forces. Whose judgment is correct? At the end of this chapter we will consider some negative consequences and dangers associated with such socially regulated judgments and the decisions based on them.

We are more confident in labeling behavior as "abnormal" when more than just one of the indicators is present and valid. The more extreme and prevalent the indicators are, the more confident we can be that they point to an abnormal condition. None of these criteria is a *necessary* condition shared by all cases of abnormality. For example, during his murder trial, a Stanford University graduate student who had killed his math professor with a hammer and then taped to his office door a note that read, "No office hours today," reported feeling neither guilt nor remorse. Despite the absence of personal suffering, we would not hesitate to label his overall behavior as abnormal. It is also true that no single criterion, by itself, is a *sufficient* condition that distinguishes all cases of abnormal behavior from normal variations in behavior. The distinction between normal and abnormal is not so much a difference between two independent types of behaviors as it is a matter of the *degree* to which a person's actions resemble a set of agreed-upon criteria of abnormality. Mental disorder is best thought of as a *continuum* that varies between *mental health* and *mental illness,* as shown in **Figure 17.1**.

How comfortable do you feel with these ideas about abnormality? To help round out your perspective, we will now fill in some of the history of the concept of abnormality and the treatment of abnormal behavior. We will then turn to the general causal factors researchers look to as the forces that give rise to abnormality.

Historical Perspectives

Throughout history, humans have feared psychological disorders, often associating them with evil. Because of this fear, people have reacted aggressively and decisively to any behaviors they perceived as bizarre or abnormal. People who have exhibited such behaviors have been imprisoned and made subject to radical medical treatments. Attitudes about the link between mental illness and evil may be as old as human history. Archaeologists have found prehistoric skulls with holes drilled in them. These discoveries might indicate that our ancestors believed such holes would allow the demons that had possessed a loved one to escape.

The following tenth-century invocation was intended to alleviate **hysteria,** an affliction characterized by a cluster of symptoms that included paralysis or pains, dizziness, lameness, and blindness. Hysteria was originally thought to affect only women, and it was believed to be caused by a wandering uterus under the devil's control (Veith, 1965). Notice how the invocation illustrates the role demonic forces were believed to play in psychological disorders.

> O womb, womb, womb, cylindrical womb, red womb, white womb, fleshy womb, bleeding womb, large womb, neufredic womb, bloated womb, O demoniacal one! . . . I conjure thee, O womb, in the name of the Holy Trinity to come back to the place from which thou shouldst neither move nor turn away . . . and to return, without anger, to the place where the Lord has put thee originally. (Zilboorg and Henry, 1941, quoted in Nietzel et al., 1991, p. 19)

In 1692, in the Massachusetts colony of Salem, numerous young women began experiencing convulsions, nausea, and weakness. They reported sensations of being pinched, pricked, or bitten. Many became temporarily blind or deaf; others reported visions and sensations of flying through the air. Such strange symptoms sparked a frantic search for an explanation. Many people theorized that the symptoms were the work of the devil, who, through the efforts of earthbound witches, had taken over the minds and bodies of the young women. These theories led to a witchcraft panic and to the execution of over 20 women believed to be witches.

As an aside, note that a contemporary analysis strongly suggests a purely physical basis for the "bewitchment" of the Salem women. It is likely that they were suffering from eating food contaminated with a grain fungus, *ergot,* which grows on rye bread. Ergot poisoning produces symptoms like those of the hallucinogenic drug LSD, and also like those attributed to bewitchment: tremors, spasms, seizures, hallucinations, intense skin sensations, and panic attacks. The cold, wet climate in Salem at that time could have promoted the growth of the ergot fungus, to cause these bizarre symptoms among young women from particular farms who ate rye bread (Caporeal, 1976). Since the theory of witchcraft was highly available as a religious explanation for bizarre behavior and the medical knowledge was absent, the misattribution contributed to this unusual event in U.S. history. Historian Mary Matossian (1989) argues that many bizarre epidemics throughout history, including the Black Plague, can be traced to the consumption of contaminated rye bread, which often resulted in symptoms of mental illness, loss of fertility, or even sudden death. These epidemics declined once the expanding populations in Europe and the United States shifted away from more expensive rye bread to cheaper flour that was not a host for this hidden poison.

Until the end of the eighteenth century, the mentally ill in Western societies were perceived as mindless beasts who could be controlled only with

The Salem witchcraft trials were the outgrowth of a desperate attempt to affix blame for frighteningly bizarre behavior among the Puritan colonists.

chains and physical discipline. They were not cared for in hospitals but were incarcerated with criminals. Let's see how that perspective began to change.

Emergence of the Medical Model

In the latter part of the eighteenth century, a new perspective about the origins of abnormal behavior emerged—people began to perceive those with psychological problems as *sick*, suffering from illness, rather than as *possessed* or *immoral*. As a result, a number of reforms were gradually implemented in the facilities for the insane. **Philippe Pinel** (1745–1826) was one of the first clinicians to use these ideas to attempt to develop a classification system for psychological difficulties based on the idea that disorders of thought, mood, and behavior are similar in many ways to the physical, organic illnesses. According to such a system, each disorder has a group of characteristic symptoms that distinguishes it from other disorders and from healthy functioning. Disorders are classified according to the patterns of observed symptoms, the circumstances surrounding the onset of the disturbance, the natural course of the disorder, and its response to treatment. Such classification systems are modeled after the biological classification systems naturalists use and are intended to help clinicians identify common disorders more easily.

Philippe Pinel was one of the first clinicians to suggest that mental disorders, like physical illnesses, might be classified by symptoms.

In 1896, **Emil Kraepelin** (1855–1926), a German psychiatrist, was responsible for creating the first truly comprehensive *classification system* of psychological disorders. Strongly motivated by a belief that there was a physical basis to psychological problems, he gave the process of psychological diagnosis and classification the flavor of medical diagnosis, a flavor that remains today (Rosenhan & Seligman, 1989). His perspective is most readily seen in the terminology used by psychiatrists. They speak of *mental illness,* and *treat* mental *patients* in the hope of *curing* their *diseased* brains.

Emil Kraepelin created the first truly comprehensive classification system for psychological disorders.

Emergence of Psychological Models

An alternative perspective to the medical approach focuses on the psychological causes and treatment of abnormal behavior. This perspective emerged most clearly at the end of the eighteenth century. It was helped along by the dramatic work of **Franz Mesmer** (1734–1815). Mesmer believed that many disorders, including hysteria, were caused by disruptions in the flow of a mysterious force that he called *animal magnetism.* He unveiled several new techniques to study animal magnetism, including one that eventually became known as *hypnotism* but was originally referred to as *mesmerism* in his honor (Darnton, 1968; Pattie, 1994).

Franz Mesmer focused attention on the psychological causes and treatment of abnormal behavior, in the process developing the technique now known as hypnotism.

Although Mesmer's general theory of animal magnetism was discredited, his hypnotic techniques were adopted by many researchers, including a prominent French neurologist, **Jean Charcot** (1825–1893). Charcot found that some of the symptoms of hysteria, such as paralysis of a limb, could be eliminated when a patient was under hypnosis. Hypnosis even had the power to *induce*—bring out—the symptoms of hysteria in healthy individuals, dramatically illustrating the potential of *psychological factors* to cause problems that were believed to have an exclusively physical basis.

One of Charcot's students, Sigmund Freud, continued to experiment with hypnosis. Freud used his experiments to elaborate his psychodynamic theories of personality and abnormality, which continue to influence current theories of the nature and causes of psychopathology. (He later abandoned hypnotherapy for psychoanalysis as the treatment for psychological disorders.)

Modern perspectives on abnormality most often combine aspects of both medical and psychological models of mental illness. We next consider those general types of explanations for the origins or causes of abnormality.

In this engraving circa 1780, Franz Mesmer entrances a salon full of fashionable ladies and gentlemen. "Mesmerism" eventually became a useful technique in the treatment of some psychological disorders.

The Etiology of Psychopathology

Etiology refers to the factors that cause or contribute to the development of psychological and medical problems. Knowing why the disorder occurs, what its origins are, and how it affects thought and emotional and behavioral processes may lead to new ways of treating and, ideally, preventing it. An analysis of causality will be an important part of our discussion of each individual disorder. Here we introduce two general categories of causal factors: biological and psychological.

The etiology of mental disorders may be reduced to two general causal factors: biological and psychological.

Biological Approaches

Building on the heritage of the medical model, modern biological approaches assume that psychological disturbances are directly attributable to underlying biological factors. Biological researchers and clinicians most often investigate structural abnormalities in the brain, biochemical processes, and genetic influences (Ciaranello & Ciaranello, 1991; Gottesman, 1991; Meltzer, 1987).

The brain is a complex organ whose interrelated elements are held in delicate balance. Subtle alterations in its chemical messengers—the neurotransmitters—or in its tissue can have significant effects. Genetic factors, brain injury, and infection are a few of the causes of these alterations. We have seen in earlier chapters that technological advances in brain imaging techniques allow mental health professionals to view the structure of the brain and specific biochemical processes in living individuals without surgery. Using these techniques, biologically oriented researchers are discovering new links between psychological disorders and specific abnormalities in the brain (Gur & Pearlson, 1993). Biochemical approaches to psychopathology have been affirmed by studies showing the ways drugs can alter the normal reality of the mind and by the proven success of drug therapies in alleviating certain symptoms of psychological disorders (Elkin et al., 1989; Kane & Marder, 1993; Papolos & Papolos, 1987; Schatzberg, 1991). Continuing advances in the field of behavioral genetics have improved researchers' abilities to identify the links between specific genes and the presence of psychological disorders (Kelsoe et al., 1993; Kendler & Diehl, 1993; Rutter et al., 1990). We will look to these different types of biological explanation throughout the chapter as we try to understand the nature of various forms of abnormality.

Researchers guided by the biological approach to mental disorders investigate structural abnormalities in the brain, biochemical processes, and genetic influences.

Psychological Approaches

Psychological approaches focus on the causal role of psychological or social factors in the development of psychopathology. These approaches perceive personal experiences, traumas, conflicts, and environmental factors as the roots of psychological disorders. We will outline three dominant psychological models of abnormality: the psychodynamic, the behavioral, and the cognitive.

Psychodynamic. Like the biological approach, the psychodynamic model holds that the causes of psychopathology are located inside the person. However, according to **Sigmund Freud**, who developed this model, the internal causal factors are psychological rather than biological. As we noted in earlier chapters, Freud believed that many psychological disorders were simply an extension of "normal" processes of psychic conflict and ego defense that all people experience. In the psychodynamic model, early childhood experiences shape both normal and abnormal behavior.

In psychodynamic theory, behavior is motivated by drives and wishes of which people are often unaware. Symptoms of psychopathology have their roots in *unconscious conflict* and thoughts. If the unconscious is conflicted and tension-filled, a person will be plagued by anxiety and other disorders. Much of this psychic conflict arises from struggles between the irrational, pleasure-seeking impulses of the *id* and the internalized social constraints imposed by the *superego*. The *ego* is normally the arbiter of this struggle; however, its ability to perform its function can be weakened by abnormal development in childhood. Individuals attempt to avoid the pain caused by conflicting motives and anxiety with *defense mechanisms,* such as repression or denial. Defenses can become overused, distorting reality or leading to self-defeating behaviors. The individual may then expend so much psychic energy in defenses against anxiety and conflict that there is little energy left to provide a productive and satisfying life.

Freud's psychodynamic approach emphasizes the importance of internal factors, early childhood events, and unconscious conflict.

Behavioral. Because of their emphasis on observable responses, behavioral theorists have little use for hypothetical psychodynamic processes. These theorists argue that abnormal behaviors are acquired in the same fashion as healthy behaviors—through learning and reinforcement. They do not focus on internal psychological phenomena or early childhood experiences. Instead, they focus on the *current* behavior and the *current* conditions or reinforcements that sustain the behavior. The symptoms of psychological disorders arise because an individual has learned self-defeating or ineffective ways of behaving. By discovering the environmental contingencies that maintain any undesirable, abnormal behavior, an investigator or clinician can then recommend treatment to change those contingencies and extinguish the unwanted behavior (Emmelkamp, 1986). Behaviorists rely on both classical and operant conditioning models (recall Chapter 9) to understand the processes that can result in maladaptive behavior.

The behavioral approach focuses on the current behavior and reinforcements that sustain the behavior.

Cognitive. Cognitive perspectives on psychopathology are often used to supplement behavioral views. The cognitive perspective suggests that the origins of psychological disorders cannot always be found in the *objective reality* of stimulus environments, reinforcers, and overt responses. What matters as well is the way people *perceive* or *think* about themselves and about their relations with other people and the environment. Among the cognitive variables that can guide—or misguide—adaptive responses are a person's perceived degree of control over important reinforcers, a person's beliefs in his or her ability to cope with threatening events, and interpretations of events in terms of situational or personal factors (Bandura, 1986). The cognitive approach suggests that psychological problems are the result of distortions in perceptions of the reality of a situation, faulty reasoning, or poor problem solving (Ellis & Grieger, 1986).

The cognitive approach emphasizes the importance of perceived reality, especially as it relates to control issues, beliefs in ability to cope, and interpretations of events.

Today researchers are increasingly taking an **interactionist perspective** on psychopathology, seeing it as the product of a complex interaction between a number of biological and psychological factors (Cowan, 1988). For example, genetic predispositions may make a person vulnerable to a psychological disorder by affecting neurotransmitter levels or hormone levels, but psychological or social stresses or certain learned behaviors may be required for the disorder to develop fully.

We have now given you a general sense of the types of explanations researchers give for the emergence of mental illness. In the next section, we describe the efforts that have been made to classify and describe different categories of disorder.

CLASSIFYING PSYCHOLOGICAL DISORDERS

Why is it helpful to have a classification system for psychological disorders? What advantages are gained by moving beyond a global assessment that abnormality exists to distinguish among different types of abnormality? A **psychological diagnosis** is the label given to an abnormality by classifying and categorizing the observed behavior pattern into an approved diagnostic system. Such a diagnosis is in many ways more difficult to make than a medical diagnosis. In the medical context, a doctor can rely on physical evidence, such as X rays, blood tests, and biopsies, to inform a diagnostic decision. In the case of psychological disorders, the evidence for diagnosis comes from interpretations of a person's actions. In order to create greater consistency among clinicians and coherence in their diagnostic evaluations, psychologists have helped to develop a system of diagnosis and classification that provides precise descriptions of symptoms, as well as other criteria to help practitioners decide whether a person's behavior is evidence of a particular disorder.

Goals of Classification

To be most useful, a diagnostic system should provide the following three benefits:

- *Common shorthand language.* To facilitate quick and clear understanding among clinicians or researchers working in the field of psychopathology, practitioners seek a common set of terms with agreed-upon meanings. A diagnostic category, such as *depression*, summarizes a large and complex collection of information, including characteristic symptoms and the typical course of the disorder. In clinical settings, such as clinics and hospitals, a diagnostic system allows mental health professionals to communicate more effectively about the people they are helping. Researchers studying different aspects of psychopathology or evaluating treatment programs must agree on the disorder they are observing.
- *Understanding of etiology.* Ideally, a diagnosis of a specific disorder should make clear the causes of the symptoms. Unfortunately, because there is substantial disagreement or lack of knowledge about the etiology of many psychological disorders, this goal is difficult to meet.
- *Treatment plan.* A diagnosis should also suggest what types of treatment to consider for particular disorders. Researchers and clinicians have found that certain treatments or therapies work most effectively for specific kinds of psychological disorders. For example, drugs that are quite effective in treating schizophrenia do not help and may even hurt people

A diagnostic classification system for mental disorders provides a common shorthand language, understanding of etiology, and treatment plan.

with depression. Further advances in knowledge about the effectiveness and specificity of treatments will make fast and reliable diagnosis even more important.

DSM-IV

In the United States, the most widely accepted classification scheme is one developed by the American Psychiatric Association. It is called the *Diagnostic and Statistical Manual of Mental Disorders.* A 1994 revision, which is the fourth edition, is known by clinicians and researchers as ***DSM-IV.*** It classifies, defines, and describes over 200 mental disorders.

To reduce the diagnostic difficulties caused by variability in approaches to psychological disorders, *DSM-IV* emphasizes the *description* of patterns of symptoms and courses of disorders rather than etiological theories or treatment strategies. The purely descriptive terms allow clinicians and researchers to use a common language to describe problems, while leaving room for disagreement and continued research about which theoretical models best explain the problems.

In the United States, the most widely accepted classification system for mental disorders is DSM-IV.

The first version of *DSM,* which appeared in 1952 (*DSM-I*), listed several dozen mental illnesses. *DSM-II,* introduced in 1968, revised the diagnostic system to make it more compatible with another popular system, the World Health Organization's *International Classification of Diseases (ICD).* The fourth edition of the *DSM* emerged after several years of intense work by committees of scholars. To make their changes (from the *DSM-III-Revised,* which appeared in 1987), these committees carefully scrutinized large bodies of research on psychopathology and also tested proposed changes for workability in actual clinical settings. *DSM-IV* is also fully compatible with the tenth edition of the *ICD*.

To encourage clinicians to consider the psychological, social, and physical factors that may be associated with a psychological disorder, *DSM-IV* uses *dimensions* or *axes* that portray information about all these factors (see **Table 17.1**). Most of the principal clinical disorders are contained on Axis I. Included here are all disorders that emerge in childhood except for mental retardation. Axis II lists mental retardation as well as personality disorders. These problems may accompany Axis I disorders. Axis III incorporates information about general medical conditions, such as diabetes, that may be relevant to understanding or treating an Axis I or II disorder. Axes IV and V provide supplemental information that can be useful when planning an individual's treatment or assessing the *prognosis* (predictions of future change). Axis IV assesses psychosocial and environmental problems that may explain patients' stress responses or their resources for coping with stress. On Axis V, a clinician evaluates the global level of an individual's functioning. A full diagnosis in the *DSM-IV* system would involve consideration of each of the axes.

DSM-IV *provides information about the psychological, social, and physical factors that may be related to a mental disorder.*

Evolution of Diagnostic Categories

The diagnostic categories and the methods used to organize and present them have shifted with each revision of the *DSM*. These shifts reflect changes in the opinions of a majority of mental health experts about exactly what constitutes a psychological disorder and where the lines between different types of disorders should be drawn. They also reflect changing perspectives among the public about what constitutes *abnormality.*

In the revision process of each *DSM,* some diagnostic categories were dropped and others were added. For example, with the introduction of *DSM-III,* in 1980, the traditional distinction between *neurotic* and *psychotic* disorders was eliminated. **Neurotic disorders,** or *neuroses,* were originally conceived of as relatively common psychological problems in which a person did

Table 17.1 The Five Axes of *DSM-IV*

Axis	Classes of Information	Description
Axis I	Clinical disorders	These mental disorders present symptoms or patterns of behavioral or psychological problems that typically are painful or impair an area of functioning. Included are disorders that emerge in infancy, childhood, or adolescence.
Axis II	a. Personality disorders	These are dysfunctional patterns of perceiving and responding to the world.
	b. Mental retardation	
Axis III	General medical conditions	This axis codes physical problems relevant to understanding or treating an individual's psychological disorders on Axes I and II.
Axis IV	Psychosocial and environmental problems	This axis codes psychosocial and environmental stressors that may affect the diagnosis and treatment of an individual's disorder and the likelihood of recovery.
Axis V	Global assessment of functioning	This axis codes the individual's overall level of current functioning in the psychological, social, and occupational domains.

not have signs of brain abnormalities, did not display grossly irrational thinking, and did not violate basic norms; but he or she did experience subjective distress or a pattern of self-defeating or inadequate coping strategies. **Psychotic disorders,** or *psychoses,* were thought to differ in both quality and severity from neurotic problems. It was believed that psychotic behavior deviated significantly from social norms and was accompanied by a profound disturbance in rational thinking and general emotional and thought processes. The *DSM-III-R* advisory committees felt that the terms *neurotic disorders* and *psychotic disorders* had become too general in their meaning to have much usefulness as diagnostic categories (they continue to be used by many psychiatrists and psychologists to characterize the general level of disturbance in a person).

Across the editions of the *DSM,* individual diagnoses have also come and gone. One of the best examples is *homosexuality.* You may recall from Chapter 12 that it was in 1973 that the American Psychiatric Association voted to remove homosexuality from the list of psychological disorders. Until that time, homosexuality appeared in the *DSM* as a bona fide mental illness. What changed the opinions of psychiatric experts was research data demonstrating the generally positive mental health of gay men and lesbians. Homosexuality is now relevant to a diagnosis in *DSM-IV* only if an individual shows "persistent and marked distress about sexual orientation" (*DSM-IV,* p. 538). That diagnostic criterion could, of course, apply equally well to distressed heterosexuals.

Is *DSM-IV* Effective?

In order for a diagnostic system to become a shorthand language for communication, its users have to be able to agree reliably on what the criteria and symptoms are for each disorder and what the diagnoses would be in specific cases. Because the *DSM-IV* was only formally released in 1994, data are still accumulating on its reliability, validity, and practicality. As we mentioned, however, field testing in clinical settings was an important component of the development process. This method of development should contribute to the immediate usefulness of the *DSM-IV* as a diagnostic system. Even so, as feedback emerges on the great many details of *DSM-IV,* it's a safe bet that there'll be a *DSM-V*!

MAJOR TYPES OF PSYCHOLOGICAL DISORDERS

Now that we have given you a basic framework for thinking about abnormality, we get to the core information that you will want to know—the cause and consequences of major psychological disorders, such as anxiety, depression, and schizophrenia. For each category, we will begin by describing what sufferers experience and how they appear to observers. Then we will consider how each of the major biological and psychological approaches to etiology explains the development of these disorders.

There are many other categories of psychopathology that we will not have time to examine. However, what follows is a capsule summary of some of the most important we must omit:

- *Substance-use disorders* include both dependence on and abuse of alcohol and drugs. We discussed many issues of substance abuse in the broader context of states of consciousness (see Chapter 4).
- *Somatoform disorders* involve physical (soma) symptoms, such as paralysis or pains in a limb, that arise without a physical cause. This category includes the symptoms of what used to be called *hysteria*.
- *Sexual disorders* involve problems with sexual inhibition or dysfunction and deviant sexual practices.
- *Disorders usually first diagnosed in infancy, childhood, or adolescence* include mental retardation, communication disorders such as stuttering, and autism.
- *Eating disorders*, such as anorexia and bulimia, were discussed in Chapter 12.

Throughout this chapter, we will provide estimates of the frequency with which individuals experience particular psychological disorders. These estimates arise from research projects in which mental health histories are obtained from large samples of the population, up to 20,000 people. Figures are available for the prevalence of different disorders over one-month, one-year, and lifetime periods (Kessler et al., 1994; Regier et al., 1993a, b). The figures we will generally cite come from the *National Comorbidity Study (NCS),* which sampled 8098 U.S. adults ages 15 to 54 years (Kessler et al., 1994). Although we will refer to this sample as "adults," it is important to note that the study excluded older adults. It is also important to emphasize that often the same individuals have experienced more than one disorder at some point in their life span. This phenomenon is known as **comorbidity.** (*Morbidity* refers to the occurrence of disease. *Comorbidity* refers to the co-occurrence of diseases.) The NCS found that 56 percent of the people who had experienced one disorder had actually experienced two or more. Researchers have begun to study intensively the patterns of comorbidity of different psychological disorders.

As you read about the symptoms and experiences that are typical of the various psychological disturbances, you may begin to feel that some of the characteristics seem to apply to you—at least part of the time—or to someone you know. Some of the disorders that we will consider are not uncommon, so it would be surprising if they sounded completely alien. Many people have human frailties that appear on the list of criteria for a particular psychological disorder. Recognition of this familiarity can further your understanding of abnormal psychology, but you should remember that a diagnosis for any disorder depends on a number of criteria and requires the judgment of a trained mental health professional. Please resist the temptation to use this new knowledge to diagnose friends and family members as pathological. On the other hand, being sensitive to others' needs for counsel and social support in times of personal trouble is always appropriate.

Before exploring anxiety, depression, and schizophrenia in depth, we will briefly consider examples of disorders from two additional classification categories: personality disorders and dissociative disorders.

Personality Disorders

A **personality disorder** is long-standing (chronic), inflexible, maladaptive pattern of perceiving, thinking, or behaving. These patterns can seriously impair an individual's ability to function in social or work settings and can cause significant distress. They are usually recognizable by the time a person reaches adolescence or early adulthood. There are many types of personality disorders (*DSM-IV* recognizes 10 types). We will discuss four examples: *paranoid, antisocial, histrionic*, and *narcissistic personality disorders*.

Personality disorders may be severe enough to disrupt normal functioning in social or work settings.

People with **paranoid personality disorders** show a consistent pattern of distrust and suspiciousness about the motives of the individuals with whom they interact. People who suffer from this disorder suspect that other people are trying to harm or deceive them. They may find hidden unpleasant meanings in harmless situations. They expect their friends and spouses or partners to be disloyal.

Antisocial personality disorder is marked by a long-standing pattern of irresponsible or unlawful behavior that violates social norms. Lying, stealing, and fighting are common behaviors. People with antisocial personality disorder often do not experience shame or remorse for their hurtful actions. Violations of social norms begin early in their lives—disrupting class, getting into fights, and running away from home. Their actions are marked by indifference to the rights of others.

In a career where power and financial gain are pursued at all costs, could antisocial personality disorder be an asset?

Histrionic personality disorder is characterized by patterns of excessive emotionality and attention seeking. People with this disorder always wish to be the center of attention. If they are not, they may do something inappropriate to regain that spot. Sufferers offer strong opinions with great drama but with little evidence to back up their claims. They also react to minor occasions with overblown emotional responses.

People with a **narcissistic personality disorder** have a grandiose sense of self-importance, a preoccupation with fantasies of success or power, and a need for constant admiration. These people often have problems in interpersonal relationships; they tend to feel entitled to special favors with no reciprocal obligations, to exploit others for their own purposes, and to have difficulty recognizing and experiencing how others feel.

Personality disorders as a group are among the most controversial psychological disorders. Psychologists disagree about whether personality disorders can be said truly to exist as categories of abnormal behavior or whether the behaviors are just extremes in the normal range. There is also controversy about evaluating lifelong behavior patterns independent of the *contexts* in which they developed. Economic, social, family, and cultural factors may provide better explanations of the observed symptoms of a given patient than do diagnoses of personality disorders.

Dissociative Disorders

A **dissociative disorder** is a disturbance in the integration of identity, memory, or consciousness. It is important for people to see themselves as being in control of their behavior, including emotions, thoughts, and actions. Essential to this perception of self-control is the sense of selfhood—the consis-

These two paintings by Sybil, a dissociative identity disorder victim, illustrate differences between the personalities. The picture on the left was done by Peggy, Sybil's angry, fearful personality, while the one on the right was done by Mary, a home-loving personality.

tency of different aspects of the self and the continuity of identity over time and place. Psychologists believe that, in dissociated states, individuals escape from their conflicts by giving up this precious consistency and continuity—in a sense, disowning part of themselves. Not being able to recall details of a traumatic event—*amnesia*—even though neurological damage is not present, is one example of dissociation. Psychologists have only recently begun to appreciate the degree to which such memory dissociation accompanies instances of sexual and physical childhood abuse (Spiegel & Cardeña, 1991). The forgetting of important personal experiences, a process caused by psychological factors in the absence of any organic dysfunction, is termed **dissociative amnesia.**

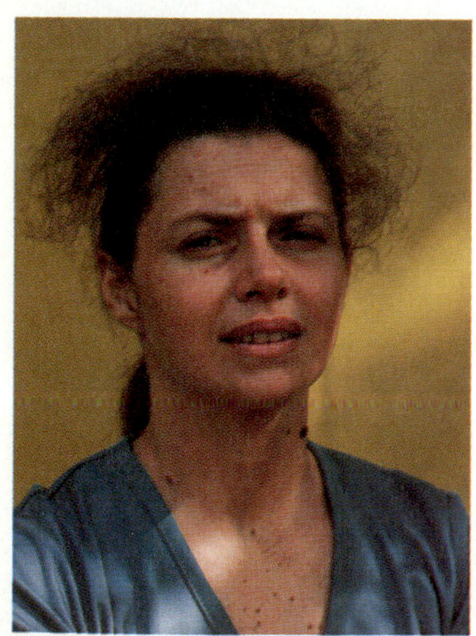

When found in a park in Florida, this woman (dubbed "Jane Doe" by authorities) was emaciated, incoherent, and near death. She was suffering from severe amnesia in which she had lost not only the memory of her name and her past but also the ability to read and write.

Dissociative identity disorder (DID), also known as *multiple personality disorder,* is a dissociative mental disorder in which two or more distinct personalities exist within the same individual. At any particular time, one of these personalities is dominant in directing the individual's behavior. Dissociative identity disorders have been popularized in books and movies, such as *The Three Faces of Eve* (Thigpen & Cleckley, 1957), *Sybil* (Schreiber, 1973), and *The Flock* (Casey & Wilson, 1991). Dissociative identity disorder is popularly known as *split personality,* and sometimes mistakenly described as *schizophrenia,* a disorder in which personality often is impaired but is not split into multiple versions. In DID, each of the emerging personalities contrasts in some significant way with the original self—they might be outgoing if the person is shy, tough if the original personality is weak, and sexually assertive if the other is fearful and sexually naive. Each personality has a unique identity, name, behavior pattern, and even characteristic brain wave activity. In some cases, dozens of different characters emerge to help the person deal with a difficult life situation. The emergence of these alternate personalities, each with its own consciousness, is sudden and typically precipitated by stress.

Patients' alternative selves often come out under hypnosis. Researchers believe this might be the case because patients spontaneously used a form of self-hypnosis to develop the different personalities in the first place, to defend themselves from the hostile environment in which they were forced to live.

During a therapy session in which the therapist was using hypnosis to uncover the source of a client's chronic problems with dizziness, fainting, nausea, unexplained terrors, and suicidal episodes, a strange voice emerged from her. The alien voice of the client identified itself as "a demon." The therapist's hypothesis was that this demonic aspect of the client's personality probably developed from repeated beatings by her mother and years of sexual abuse by her stepfather during her childhood. However, this adult woman had no conscious contact with this other personality nor conscious awareness of her earlier abuse until this hypnosis session—when her inner demon was released (Kierulff, 1989).

Typically, DID victims are women who report being severely abused physically or sexually by parents, relatives, or close friends for extended periods during childhood. One study obtained questionnaire data from 448 clinicians who had treated cases of dissociative identity disorders and major depressions (used for comparative purposes). As shown in **Table 17.2**, the dominant feature of the 355 DID cases is the almost universal reports of abuse, with incidents often starting around age 3 and continuing for more than a decade. Although the 255 comparison patients with depression disorder also had a high incidence of abuse, it was significantly less than that experienced by those with DID (Schultz et al., 1989). However, the intense controversy over repressed and dissociated memories of childhood abuse—Are they real or are they fabricated? (see Chapter 10)—warrants caution before making DID diagnoses or assessing etiology (Poole et al., 1995; Spiegel & Scheflin, 1994).

Typical dissociative identity disorder victims are women who report physical or sexual abuse for extended periods during childhood.

Psychologists believe that multiple personalities develop to serve a vital survival function. DID victims may have been beaten, locked up, or abandoned by those who were supposed to love them—those on whom they were so dependent that they could not fight them, leave them, or even hate them. Instead, they have fled their terror symbolically through dissociation. They have protected their egos by creating stronger internal characters to help cope with the ongoing traumatic situation. These characters also provide relief from pain by numbing the dominant personality to the abuse. However successful those strategies were in coping with the trauma, they become dysfunctional over time, interfering with the normal development of an integrated ego.

Anxiety Disorders: Types

Everyone experiences anxiety or fear in certain life situations. For some people, however, anxiety becomes problematic enough to interfere with their

Table 17.2 Responses to Inquiries Regarding Abuse: Comparing Dissociative Identity Disorder and Depression

Questionnaire Item	DID (percent)	Major Depression (percent)
Abuse incidence	98	54
Type(s)		
Physical	82	24
Sexual	86	25
Psychological	86	42
Neglect	54	21
All of above	47	6
Physical and sexual	74	14
	(N = 355)	(N = 235)

ability to function effectively or enjoy everyday life. It has been estimated that almost 25 percent of the adult population has, at some time, experienced symptoms characteristic of the various **anxiety disorders** (Kessler et al., 1994). While anxiety plays a key role in each of these disorders, they differ in the extent to which anxiety is experienced, the severity of the anxiety, and the situations that trigger the anxiety. We will review five major categories: generalized anxiety disorder, panic disorder, phobic disorder, obsessive-compulsive disorder, and posttraumatic stress disorder.

Generalized Anxiety Disorder

Generalized anxiety disorder leads to impaired function as the person becomes unable to focus attention on social and work obligations and suffers from the physical symptoms associated with prolonged anxiety.

When a person feels anxious or worried most of the time for at least six months, when not threatened by any specific danger, **generalized anxiety disorder** is diagnosed. The anxiety is often focused on specific life circumstances, such as unrealistic concerns about finances or the well-being of a loved one. The way the anxiety is expressed—the specific symptoms—varies from person to person, but for a diagnosis of generalized anxiety disorder to be made, the patient must also suffer from at least three other symptoms, such as muscle tension, fatigue, restlessness, poor concentration, irritability, or sleep difficulties.

Generalized anxiety disorder leads to impaired functioning because the person's worries cannot be controlled or put aside. With the focus of attention on the sources of anxiety, the individual cannot attend sufficiently to social or job obligations. These difficulties are compounded by the physical symptoms associated with the disorder.

Panic Disorder

Generalized anxiety disorder is characterized by chronic anxiety, while panic disorder is related to acute anxiety.

In contrast to the chronic presence of anxiety in generalized anxiety disorder, sufferers of **panic disorder** experience unexpected, severe *panic attacks* that may last only minutes. These attacks begin with a feeling of intense apprehension, fear, or terror. Accompanying these feelings are physical symptoms of anxiety, including autonomic hyperactivity (such as rapid heart rate), dizziness, faintness, or sensations of choking or smothering. The attacks are unexpected in the sense that they are not brought about by something concrete in the situation.

The following comments made during a panic attack will help you appreciate the degree of panic commonly experienced by someone with this disorder:

> Uh, I'm not going to make it. I can't get help, I can't get anyone to understand the feeling. It's like a feeling that sweeps over from the top of my head to the tip of my toes. And I detest the feeling. I'm very frightened. . . . It feels like I'm going to die or something. (Muskin & Fyer, 1981, p. 81)

A panic disorder is diagnosed when an individual has recurrent unexpected panic attacks and also begins to have persistent concerns about the possibility of having more attacks.

Have you ever felt unable to cope with the overstimulation of a crowded public place? For an agoraphobic, simply leaving home is enough to provoke feelings of panic.

In *DSM-IV*, panic disorder must be diagnosed as occurring with or without the simultaneous presence of agoraphobia. **Agoraphobia** is an extreme fear of being in public places or open spaces from which escape may be difficult or embarrassing. Individuals with agoraphobia usually fear such places as crowded rooms, malls, buses, and freeways. They are often afraid that, if they experience some kind of difficulty outside the home, such as a loss of bladder control or panic attack symptoms, help might not be available or the situation will be embarrassing to them. These fears deprive individuals of their freedom, and, in extreme cases, they become prisoners in their own homes.

Can you see why agoraphobia is related to panic disorder? For some (but not all) people who suffer from panic attacks, the dread of the next attack—the helpless feelings it engenders—can be enough to imprison them. The person suffering from agoraphobia may leave the safety of home but almost always with extreme anxiety.

Phobias

Fear is a rational reaction to an objectively identified external danger (such as a fire in one's home or a mugging attack) that may induce a person to flee or to attack in self-defense. In contrast, a person with a **phobia** suffers from a persistent and irrational fear of a specific object, activity, or situation that is excessive and unreasonable given the reality of the threat.

Many people feel uneasy about spiders or snakes (or even multiple-choice tests). These mild fears do not prevent people from carrying out their everyday activities. Phobias, however, interfere with adjustment, cause significant distress, and inhibit necessary action toward goals.

Phobias are characterized by irrational fears so intense that they interfere with adjustment.

> Edith is afraid of writing her name in public. When placed in a situation where she might be asked to sign her name, Edith is terrified. This phobia has far-reaching effects on her life. She can't use checks or credit cards to shop or to eat in a restaurant. She no longer can play golf because she can't sign the golf register. She can't go to the bank unless all transactions are prepared ahead of time in her home.

Even a very specific, apparently limited phobia can have a great impact on one's whole life. *DSM-IV* defines two categories of phobias: *social phobias* and *specific phobias* (see **Table 17.3**).

Social phobia is a persistent, irrational fear that arises in anticipation of a public situation in which an individual can be observed by others. Like Edith, who was afraid of writing her name in public, a person with a social phobia fears that he or she will act in ways that could be embarrassing. The person recognizes that the fear is excessive and unreasonable yet feels compelled by the fear to avoid situations in which public scrutiny is possible. Social phobia often involves a self-fulfilling prophecy. A person may be so fearful of the scrutiny and rejection of others that enough anxiety is created

Table 17.3 Common Phobias

	Sex Difference	Typical Age of Onset
Social phobias (fear of being observed doing something humiliating)	Majority are women	Adolescence
Specific phobias		
Animal type Cats (allurophobia) Dogs (cynophobia) Insects (insectophobia) Spiders (arachnophobia) Snakes (ophidiophobia) Rodents (rodentophobia)	Vast majority are women	Childhood
Natural environment type Storms (brontophobia) Heights (acrophobia)	Majority or vast majority are women	Childhood
Blood—injection—injury type Blood (hematophobia) Needles (belonophobia)	Majority are women	Any age
Situational type Closed spaces (claustrophobia) Railways (siderophobia)	Vast majority are women	Childhood or mid-20s

to actually impair performance. Among U.S. adults, 13.3 percent have experienced a social phobia (Kessler et al., 1994). Social phobia might be considered an extreme form of the shyness that afflicts as many as 40 percent of all U.S. residents (Zimbardo, 1990).

Specific phobias occur in response to several different types of objects or situations. As shown in Table 17.3, specific phobias are further categorized into several subtypes. For example, an individual suffering from an *animal-type specific phobia* might have a phobic response to spiders. In each case, the phobic response is produced either in the presence of or in anticipation of the feared specific object or situation. Research suggests that 11.3 percent of adults in the United States have experienced a specific phobia (Kessler et al., 1994).

Obsessive-Compulsive Disorders

Some people with anxiety disorders get locked into specific patterns of thought and behavior.

> Only a year or so ago, 17-year-old Jim seemed to be a normal adolescent with many talents and interests. Then, almost overnight, he was transformed into a lonely outsider, excluded from social life by his psychological disabilities. Specifically, he developed an obsession with washing. Haunted by the notion that he was dirty—in spite of what his senses told him—he began to spend more of his time cleansing himself of imaginary dirt. At first, his ritual ablutions were confined to weekends and evenings, but soon they began to consume all his time, forcing him to drop out of school. (Rapoport, 1989)

Jim is suffering from a condition known as **obsessive-compulsive disorder**, which is estimated to affect 2.5 percent of U.S. adults at some point during their lives (Regier et al., 1988). *Obsessions* are thoughts, images, or impulses (such as Jim's belief that he is unclean) that recur or persist despite a person's efforts to suppress them. Obsessions are experienced as an unwanted invasion of consciousness, they seem to be senseless or repugnant, and they are unacceptable to the person experiencing them. You probably have had some sort of mild obsessional experience, such as the intrusion of petty worries—"Did I really lock the door?"; or "Did I turn off the oven?" The obsessive thoughts of people with obsessive-compulsive disorder are much more compelling, cause much more distress, and may interfere with their social or occupational functioning.

Obsessions cause great distress and are likely to interfere with social and occupational functioning.

Compulsions are repetitive, purposeful acts (such as Jim's washing) performed according to certain rules or in a ritualized manner in response to an obsession. Compulsive behavior is performed to reduce or prevent the discomfort associated with some dreaded situation, but it is either unreasonable or clearly excessive. Typical compulsions include irresistible urges to clean, to check that lights or appliances have been turned off, and to count objects or possessions.

Obsessions are to compulsions as thoughts are to behaviors.

At least initially, people with obsessive-compulsive disorder resist carrying out their compulsions. When they are calm, they view their compulsion as senseless. When anxiety rises, however, the power of the ritual compulsive behavior to relieve tension seems irresistible. Part of the pain experienced by people with this mental problem is created by their frustration at recognizing the irrationality or excessive nature of their obsessions without being able to eliminate them.

Posttraumatic Stress Disorder

In Chapter 13, we presented a discussion between two women who were still grappling with the aftereffects of rape. The conversation portrayed the two women's ongoing anxiety. One reported going through a "long period of fear and anger" and having dreams of being assaulted in front of her dorm, with friends watching without coming to her rescue. The other, who had been raped while jogging, was still afraid to resume running: "Every time I go jogging I have a perpetual fear. My pulse doubles. Of course I don't go jogging alone any more, but still the fear is there constantly." These women suffer from **posttraumatic stress disorder** (PTSD), an anxiety disorder that is characterized by the persistent reexperience of traumatic events through distressing recollections, dreams, hallucinations, or flashbacks. Individuals may develop PTSD in response to rape, life-threatening events, severe injury, or natural disasters (Davidson et al., 1991; Fairbank et al., 1993; Green, 1994). People develop PTSD both when they themselves have been the victim of the trauma and when they have witnessed others being victimized. People who suffer from PTSD are also likely to suffer simultaneously from other psychopathologies, such as major depression, substance abuse problems, and sexual dysfunction.

People who suffer from posttraumatic stress disorder are likely to suffer simultaneously from major depression, substance abuse, and sexual dysfunction.

Estimates of the general prevalence of PTSD vary from 1.3 percent of adults in one sample (Davidson et al., 1991) to the much higher rates of 7 to 9 percent in other studies (Green, 1994). Overall, about three quarters of the general population have experienced an event that could be defined as traumatic (Green, 1994). In one sample of college students, 84 percent reported that they had experienced at least one traumatic event; roughly one third reported four or more separate events (Vrana & Lauterbach, 1994). Researchers have focused their attention on the particular types of trauma that are most likely to give rise to PTSD. Rape victims, for example, are among the group most likely to develop this disorder, with estimates ranging as high as 94 percent (Green, 1994). For veterans of combat in Vietnam, 31 percent of men and 27 percent of women have experienced PTSD at some point in their lives (Fairbank et al., 1993; Kukla et al., 1990). The "current" rate at which veterans still suffer from PTSD is 15 percent for men and 9 percent for women—many years after the end of their combat service. The probability for different individuals to develop PTSD appears to be directly related to the severity of the trauma they experienced.

Researchers are identifying the many consequences of one particularly disturbing form of trauma, *childhood sexual abuse* (Beitchman et al., 1992; Briere & Runtz, 1988; Rowan & Foy, 1993). Rather than being a time of innocence, childhood is a time of victimization for many children (Finkelhor & Dziuba-Leatherman, 1994). Some forms of victimization occur in the majority of children's lives: assault by siblings and peers, theft, and physical punishment by parents. Even childhood sexual abuse is not particularly rare. One study found that 27 percent of adult women and 16 percent of adult men had experienced episodes of sexual abuse (Finkelhor et al., 1990). Some of the psychological consequences of childhood sexual abuse fit the general diagnosis of PTSD (Rowan & Foy, 1993). Researchers have also begun to examine whether childhood sexual abuse may give rise to its own unique pattern of psychological disturbances (Beitchman et al., 1992; Briere & Runtz, 1988). For example, both male and female survivors of sexual abuse show disturbances in adult sexual functioning. As with PTSD, the degree of psychological distress is related to the severity of the trauma. For childhood sexual abuse, severity is determined by the duration of the abuse, whether force was used, and the identity of the adult or adults who initiated the activity. Parental incest is particularly damaging.

Rape, combat, and childhood sexual abuse are events that are likely to result in PTSD.

Posttraumatic stress disorder, arising from childhood sexual abuse and other causes, severely disrupts sufferers' lives. How do researchers go about the complex task of exploring the origins of PTSD and other anxiety disorders? Understanding the origins gives hope to eliminating the psychological distress.

What turns a harmless garter snake into an object of phobia?

Anxiety Disorders: Causes

How do psychologists explain the development of anxiety disorders? Each of the four etiological approaches we have outlined (biological, psychodynamic, behavioral, and cognitive) emphasizes different factors. Let's analyze how each adds something unique to the understanding of anxiety disorders.

Biological

Various investigators have suggested that anxiety disorders have biological origins. One theory attempts to explain why certain phobias, such as those for spiders or heights, are more common than fears of other dangers, such as electricity. Because many fears are shared across cultures, it has been proposed that, at one time in the evolutionary past, certain fears enhanced our ancestors' chances of survival. Perhaps humans are born with a predisposition to fear whatever is related to sources of serious danger in the evolutionary past. This *preparedness hypothesis* suggests that we carry around an evolutionary tendency to respond quickly and "thoughtlessly" to once-feared stimuli (Seligman, 1971). However, this hypothesis does not explain types of phobias that develop in response to objects or situations that would not have had survival meaning over evolutionary history, like fear of needles or driving or elevators.

The ability of certain drugs to relieve and of others to produce symptoms of anxiety offers evidence of a biological role in anxiety disorders (Schatzberg, 1991). When a panic attack sufferer is given an infusion of sodium lactate, the patient "usually complains first of palpitations, difficulty catching his or her breath, dizziness, lightheadedness, . . . and sweating. Some normal control subjects may complain of these symptoms as well, but only the patient quickly develops overwhelming dread and fear that disastrous physical consequences are imminent" (Gorman et al., 1989, p. 150). Thus sodium lactate mimics a panic attack only in people who suffer from such attacks, implying a biological cause in susceptible people. Other studies suggest that abnormalities in sites within the brain stem might be linked to panic attacks. Researchers studying CAT and PET scans of patients with obsessive-compulsive disorder have found some evidence that links the disorder to abnormalities in the basal ganglia and frontal lobe of the brain (Rapoport, 1989).

The ability of certain drugs to affect anxiety offers evidence of a biological role in anxiety disorders.

Finally, research with identical and fraternal twins suggests a genetic basis for the predisposition to experience four of the five categories of anxiety disorders (Skre et al., 1993). For example, the probability that a pair of identical twins both suffered from a panic disorder was twice as great as the probability that both fraternal twins were sufferers. The only type of anxiety disorder that produced no evidence of a genetic contribution were phobias, implicating more purely environmental origins for those disorders.

Psychodynamic

The psychodynamic model begins with the assumption that the symptoms of anxiety disorders come from underlying psychic conflicts or fears. The symptoms are attempts to protect the individual from psychological pain. Thus panic attacks are the result of unconscious conflicts bursting into consciousness. Suppose, for example, a child represses conflicting thoughts about his or her wish to leave a difficult home environment. In later life, a phobia may be activated by an object or situation that symbolizes the conflict. A bridge, for example, might come to symbolize the path that the person must traverse from the world of home and family to the outside world. The sight of a bridge would then force the unconscious conflict into awareness, bringing with it the fear and anxiety common to phobias. Avoiding

The psychodynamic model assumes that the symptoms of anxiety disorders come from underlying psychic conflicts.

bridges would be a symbolic attempt to stay clear of anxiety about the childhood experiences at home.

In obsessive-compulsive disorders, the obsessive behavior is seen as an attempt to displace anxiety created by a related but far more feared desire or conflict. By substituting an obsession that symbolically captures the forbidden impulse, a person gains some relief. For example, the obsessive fears of dirt experienced by Jim, the adolescent we described earlier, may have their roots in the conflict between his desire to become sexually active and his fear of "dirtying" his reputation. Compulsive preoccupation with carrying out a minor ritualistic task also allows the individual to avoid the original issue that is creating unconscious conflict.

Behavioral

Behavioral explanations of anxiety focus on the way symptoms of anxiety disorders are reinforced or conditioned. Investigators do not search for underlying unconscious conflicts or early childhood experiences, because these phenomena can't be observed directly. As we saw in Chapter 9, behavioral theories are often used to explain the development of phobias, which are seen as classically conditioned fears. A previously neutral object or situation becomes a stimulus for a phobia by being paired with a frightening experience. For example, a child whose mother yells a warning when he or she approaches a snake may develop a phobia about snakes. After this experience, even thinking about snakes may produce a wave of fear. Phobias continue to be maintained by the reduction in anxiety that occurs when a person withdraws from the feared situation.

Behavioral explanations of anxiety disorders focus on the role of reinforcement and conditioning in the development of symptoms.

A behavioral analysis of obsessive-compulsive disorders suggests that compulsive behaviors tend to reduce the anxiety associated with obsessive thoughts—thus reinforcing the compulsive behavior. For example, if a woman fears contamination by touching garbage, then washing her hands reduces the anxiety and is therefore reinforcing. In parallel to phobias, obsessive-compulsive disorders continue to be maintained by the reduction in anxiety that follows from the compulsive behaviors.

Cognitive

Cognitive perspectives on anxiety concentrate on the perceptual processes or attitudes that may distort a person's estimate of the danger that he or she is facing. A person may either overestimate the nature or reality of a threat or underestimate his or her ability to cope with the threat effectively. For example, before delivering a speech to a large group, a person with a social phobia may feed his or her anxiety:

According to the cognitive perspective, a person's attitudes and perception are the keys to understanding anxiety.

> What if I forget what I was going to say? I'll look foolish in front of all these people. Then I'll get even more nervous and start to perspire, and my voice will shake, and I'll look even sillier. Whenever people see me from now on, they'll remember me as the foolish person who tried to give a speech.

People who suffer from anxiety disorders may often interpret their own distress as a sign of impending disaster. Their reaction may set off a vicious cycle in which the person fears disaster, which leads to an increase in anxiety, which in turn worsens the anxiety sensations and confirms the person's fears (Beck & Emery, 1985).

Research has found that anxious patients contribute to the *maintenance* of their anxiety by employing cognitive biases that highlight the threatening stimuli.

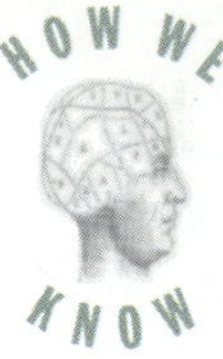

Clinically anxious subjects were compared with normal controls on a task that measured attention to a visual display of 48 threat-related words (such as *injury, agony,* and *failure*) or neutral words. The words were presented for a brief duration. On a random one third of the trials, a dot of light (a probe) appeared in the area where a word had just been flashed. The dependent variable was the speed with which the subjects detected the probe when it replaced neutral versus threat-related words. The highly anxious subjects were faster than the controls in detecting the presence of the probe when it appeared in the vicinity of threat words. These subjects had shifted their attention toward threatening stimuli, while normal control subjects had shifted their attention away from such material (MacLeod et al., 1986).

These results suggest that anxious patients may have a bias in attention or encoding that makes them particularly likely to notice threatening stimuli.

Each of the major approaches to anxiety disorders may explain part of the etiological puzzle. Continued research of each approach will clarify causes and, therefore, potential avenues for treatment. Now that you have this basic knowledge about anxiety disorders, we'd like you to consider the next of the three major categories of abnormality we are covering in some detail—*mood disorders.*

Mood Disorders: Types

There have almost certainly been times in your life when you would have described yourself as terribly depressed or incredibly happy. For some people, however, extremes in mood come to disrupt normal life experiences. A **mood disorder** is an emotional disturbance, such as severe depression or depression alternating with mania. Researchers estimate that roughly 19 percent of adults have suffered from mood disorders (Kessler et al., 1994). We will describe two major categories: unipolar depression and bipolar disorders.

Unipolar Depression

Depression has been characterized as the "common cold of psychopathology," both because it occurs so frequently and because almost everyone has experienced elements of the full-scale disorder at some time in their life. Everyone has, at one time or another, experienced grief after the loss of a loved one or felt sad or upset when failing to achieve a desired goal. These sad feelings are only one symptom experienced by people suffering from a clinical **unipolar depression** (see **Table 17.4**).

Table 17.4 Characteristics of Clinical Depression

Characteristic	Example
Dysphoric mood	Sad, blue, hopeless; loss of interest or pleasure in almost all usual activities
Appetite	Poor appetite; significant weight loss
Sleep	Insomnia or hypersomnia (sleeping too much)
Motor activity	Markedly slowed down (motor retardation) or agitated
Guilt	Feelings of worthlessness; self-reproach
Concentration	Diminished ability to think or concentrate; forgetfulness
Suicide	Recurrent thoughts of death; suicidal ideas or attempts

Almost everyone has experienced elements of depression; in some individuals, however, it becomes a full-scale disorder.

Novelist William Styron wrote a moving story about his experience with severe depression. The pain he endured convinced him that clinical depression is much more than a bad mood; it is best characterized as "a daily presence, blowing over me in cold gusts" and "a veritable howling tempest in the brain" that can begin with a "gray drizzle of horror" and result in "death" (*Darkness Visible*, 1990).

People diagnosed with unipolar depression differ in terms of the severity and duration of their symptoms. While many individuals struggle with clinical depression for only several weeks at one point in their lives, others experience depression episodically or chronically for many years. Estimates of the prevalence of mood disorders reveal that about 21 percent of females and 13 percent of males suffer a major unipolar depression at some time in their lives (Kessler et al., 1994).

Depression takes an enormous toll on those afflicted, on their families, and on society. One European study found that people with recurrent depression spend a fifth of their entire adult lives hospitalized, while 20 percent of sufferers are totally disabled by their symptoms and do not ever work again (Holden, 1986). In the United States, depression accounts for the majority of all mental hospital admissions, but it is still believed to be underdiagnosed and undertreated. Fewer than half of those who suffer from unipolar depression receive any professional help (Regier et al., 1993b).

In the United States, depression accounts for the majority of mental hospital admissions, but it is still believed to be underdiagnosed and undertreated.

Bipolar Disorder

Bipolar disorder is characterized by periods of severe depression alternating with manic episodes. A person experiencing a **manic episode** generally acts and feels unusually elated and expansive. However, sometimes the individual's predominant mood is irritability rather than elation, especially if the person feels thwarted in some way. During a manic episode, a person often experiences an inflated sense of self-esteem or an unrealistic belief that he or she possesses special abilities or powers. The person may feel a dramatically decreased need to sleep and may engage excessively in work or in social or other pleasurable activities. Caught up in this manic mood, the person shows unwarranted optimism, takes unnecessary risks, promises anything, and may give away everything.

In bipolar mood disorder, periods of depression alternate with manic periods, during which the individual feels extremely elated or irritable.

Sam was a 20-year-old college student experiencing the symptoms of a manic episode:

> Lately Sam has been feeling fantastic. He has so much energy that he almost never needs to sleep, and he is completely confident that he is the top student at his school. He is bothered that everyone else seems so slow; they don't seem to understand the brilliance of his monologues, and no one seems

able to keep up with his pace. Sam has some exciting financial ideas and can't figure out why his friends aren't writing checks to get in on his schemes.

When the mania begins to diminish, people like Sam are left trying to deal with the damage and predicaments they created during their frenetic period. Thus manic episodes almost always give way to periods of severe depression.

The duration and frequency of the mood disturbances in bipolar disorder vary from person to person. Some people experience long periods of normal functioning punctuated by occasional, short manic or depressive episodes. A small percentage of unfortunate individuals go right from manic episodes to clinical depression and back again in continuous, unending cycles that are devastating to them, their families, their friends, and their coworkers. While manic, they may gamble away life savings or give lavish gifts to strangers, acts that later add to guilt feelings when they are in the depressed phase. Bipolar disorder is much rarer than unipolar depression, occurring in about 1.6 percent of adults and distributed equally between males and females (Kessler et al., 1994).

Mood Disorders: Causes

What factors are involved in the development of mood disorders? We will address this question from the biological, psychodynamic, behavioral, and cognitive perspectives. Note that, because of its prevalence, unipolar depression has been studied more extensively than bipolar depression. Our review will reflect that distribution of research.

Biological

Several types of research provide clues to the contribution of biology to mood disorders. For example, the ability of different drugs to relieve manic and depressive symptoms provides evidence that different brain states underlie the two extremes of bipolar disorder. Reduced levels of two chemical messengers in the brain, serotonin and norepinephrine, have been linked to depression; increased levels of these neurotransmitters are associated with mania. However, the exact biochemical mechanisms of mood disorders have not yet been discovered. Researchers have used PET scans to show differences in the way the brain metabolizes *cerebral glucose* (a type of sugar utilized to produce energy) during manic and depressive phases (see **Figure 17.2**), but such differences may be the consequence rather than the cause of the two mood states.

There is growing evidence that the incidence of mood disorder is influenced by genetic factors. Studies of twins show that when one identical twin is afflicted by a mood disorder, there is a 67 percent chance that the second twin will also have the disorder; the figure for fraternal twins, who do not share identical genetic material, is 20 percent (Ciaranello & Ciaranello, 1991; Gershon et al., 1987). Given the implication of heredity in the incidence of mood disorders, researchers have attempted to specify the exact locus of the genetic material responsible for transmission across generations.

Because Amish families remain geographically close and can trace their members through several generations, they are ideal subjects for the study of hereditary conditions such as bipolar disorder.

One series of studies has focused on the pattern of bipolar disorder among the Amish community in Pennsylvania (Egeland et al., 1987). The Amish are ideal subjects for such research, because they have large families, keep detailed genealogical records, are genetically isolated, and display few behavioral factors, such as alcoholism or violence, that could confuse the findings. All 15,000 members of the religious sect are descended from just 30 couples who migrated from Europe in the early eighteenth century. There is a tendency for bipolar disorder to run in some but not other Amish families. This pattern allows researchers to make direct comparisons of the genetic material of individuals who do and do not suffer from the disorder. Although early

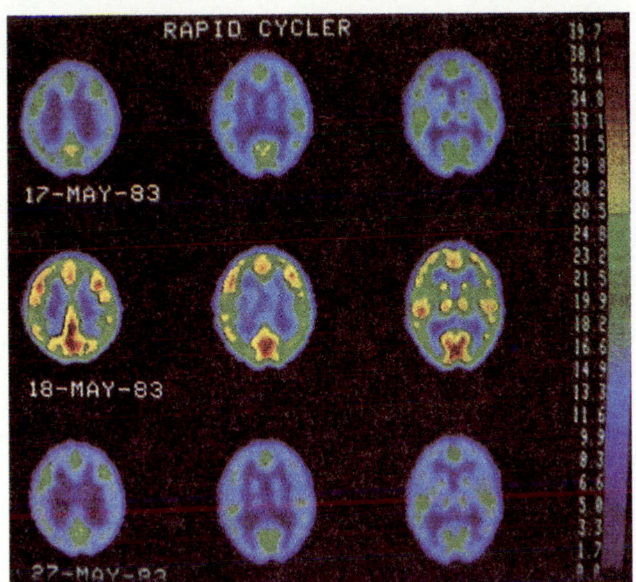

Figure 17.2 PET Scans of Bipolar Depression
PET scans indicate a higher level of cerebral glucose metabolism during manic phases than during depressive phases. The top and bottom rows show the patient during a depressive phase. The middle row shows the manic phase. The color bar on the right indicates the glucose metabolism rates.

reports of success in identifying a "bipolar gene" proved to be premature (Kelsoe et al., 1989), investigators remain optimistic that these comparisons will yield the genetic knowledge they seek (Ginns et al., 1992; Kelsoe et al., 1993).

A biological cause is supported by the ability of drugs to relieve symptoms, PET scans that reveal differences in the brain's metabolizing of cerebral glucose, and evidence that mood disorders may be influenced by genetic factors.

A dramatic example of a biological approach to understanding one type of psychological disorder comes from research on an unusual form of depression. Some people regularly become depressed during the winter months, especially in the long Scandinavian winters (see **Figure 17.3**). This disturbance in mood has been appropriately named *seasonal affective disorder,* or *SAD.* An internal body rhythm involving the hormone *melatonin,* which is

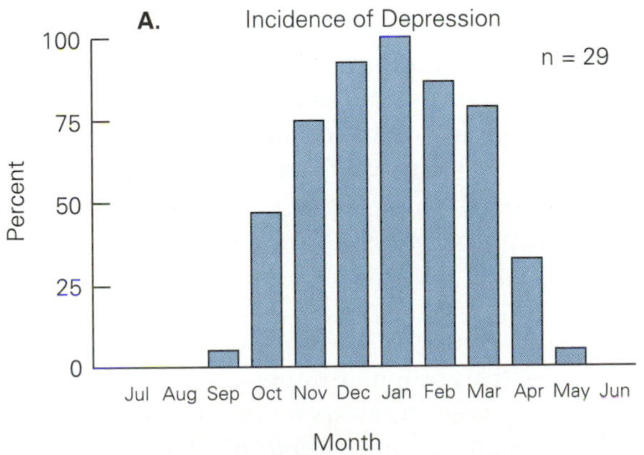

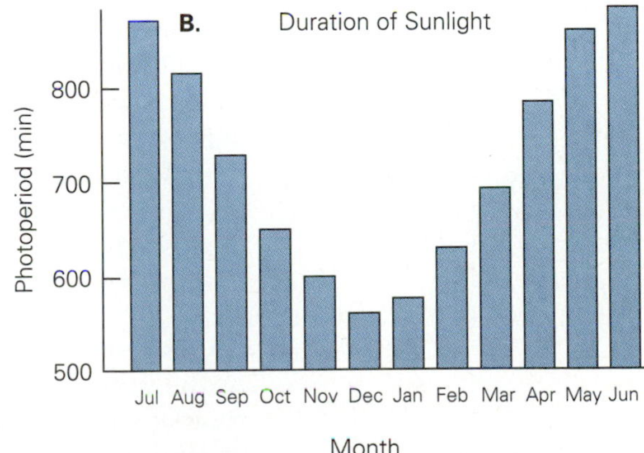

Figure 17.3 Seasonal Affective Disorder
People who suffer from seasonal affective disorder experience symptoms of depression during seasons with short sunlight. The figure displays a strong inverse relationship between the incidence of depression (part A) and the duration of sunlight (part B).

secreted by the pineal gland into the blood, has been linked to SAD. In most species, including humans, the level of melatonin rises after dusk and falls at or before dawn. Melatonin is implicated in sleep processes as well as in circadian (daily) rhythms that set the body's biological clock.

Researchers reasoned that *light therapy* might restore the body's balance. When depressed patients and normal control subjects were exposed to bright light in the morning, the melatonin cycle was changed. Bright morning light reduced symptoms in those patients who regularly suffered from recurring winter depression (Lewy et al., 1987).

While it is not clear that disrupted melatonin cycles are responsible for *causing* the depressive symptoms of SAD, it does appear that a biological intervention that "resets" the abnormal circadian rhythm is an effective treatment.

Let's see now what the three major psychological approaches can add to your understanding of the onset of mood disorders.

Psychodynamic

In the psychodynamic approach, unconscious conflicts and hostile feelings that originate in early childhood are seen to play key roles in the development of depression. Freud was struck by the degree of self-criticism and guilt that depressed people displayed. He believed that the source of this self-reproach was anger, originally directed at someone else, that had been turned inward against the self. The anger was believed to be tied to an especially intense and dependent childhood relationship, such as a parent-child relationship, in which the person's needs or expectations were not met. Losses, real or symbolic, in adulthood reactivate hostile feelings, now directed toward the person's own ego, creating the self-reproach that is characteristic of depression.

According to the psychodynamic approach, depression results from unconscious conflicts and hostile feelings originating in early childhood.

Behavioral

Rather than searching for the roots of depression in the unconscious, the behavioral approach focuses on the effects of the amount of positive reinforcement and punishments a person receives (Lewinsohn, 1975). In this view, depressed feelings result when an individual receives insufficient positive reinforcements and experiences many punishments in the environment following a loss or other major life changes. Without sufficient positive reinforcement, a person begins to feel sad and withdraws. This state of sadness is initially reinforced by increased attention and sympathy from others. Typically, however, friends who at first respond with support grow tired of the depressed person's negative moods and attitudes and begin to avoid him or her. This reaction eliminates another source of positive reinforcement, plunging the person further into depression. Research also shows that depressed people give themselves fewer rewards and more punishment than others (Nelson & Craighead, 1977; Rehm, 1977).

The behavioral approach suggests that depression results from too few positive reinforcements and too many punishments.

Cognitive

At the center of the cognitive approach to unipolar depression are two theories. One theory suggests that negative *cognitive sets*—"set" patterns of perceiving the world (see Chapter 8)—lead people to take a negative view of events in their lives for which they feel responsible. The second theory, the *explanatory style* model, proposes that depression arises from the belief that one has little or no personal control over significant life events. Each of these models explains some aspects of the experience of depression. Let's see how.

Aaron Beck (1983, 1985, 1988), a leading researcher on depression, has developed the theory of cognitive sets. Beck has argued that depressed people have three types of negative cognitions, which he calls the *cognitive triad* of depression: negative views of themselves, negative views of ongoing experiences, and negative views of the future. Depressed people tend to view themselves as inadequate or defective in some way, to interpret ongoing experiences in a negative way, and to believe that the future will continue to bring suffering and difficulties. This pattern of negative thinking clouds all experiences and produces the other characteristic signs of depression. An individual who always anticipates a negative outcome is not likely to be motivated to pursue any goal, leading to the *paralysis of will* that is prominent in depression.

Aaron Beck argues that depressed people display three types of negative cognitions: negative views of themselves, negative views of ongoing experiences, and negative views of the future.

In the **explanatory style** view, pioneered by **Martin Seligman** (see Chapter 12), individuals believe, correctly or not, that they cannot control future outcomes that are important to them. Seligman's theory evolved from research that demonstrated depression-like symptoms in dogs. Seligman and Maier (1967) subjected dogs to painful, unavoidable shocks: no matter what the dogs did, there was no way to escape the shocks. The dogs developed what Seligman and Maier called **learned helplessness.** Learned helplessness is marked by three types of deficits: *motivational deficits*—the dogs were slow to initiate known actions; *emotional deficits*—they appeared rigid, listless, frightened, and distressed; and *cognitive deficits*—they demonstrated poor learning in new situations. Even when put in a situation in which they could, in fact, avoid shock, they did not learn to do so (Maier & Seligman, 1976).

Martin Seligman pioneered the explanatory style view of depression, based on his research on learned helplessness.

Seligman believed that depressed people are also in a state of learned helplessness (Abramson et al., 1978; Peterson & Seligman, 1984; Seligman, 1975). However, the emergence of this state depends, to a large extent, on how individuals *explain* their life events. As we discussed in Chapter 12, there are three dimensions of explanatory style: *internal-external, global-specific, stable-unstable.* Suppose that you have just received a poor grade on a psychology exam. You attribute the negative outcome on the exam to an *internal* factor ("I'm stupid"), which makes you feel sad, rather than to an *external* one ("The exam was really hard"), which would have made you angry. You could have chosen a less *stable* internal quality than intelligence to explain your performance ("I was tired that day"). Rather than attributing your performance to an internal, stable factor that has *global* or far-reaching influence (stupidity), you could even have limited your explanation to the psychology exam or course ("I'm not good at psychology courses"). Explanatory style theory suggests that individuals who attribute failure to internal, stable, and global causes are vulnerable to depression. This prediction has been confirmed repeatedly (Peterson & Seligman, 1984; Seligman, 1991).

A poor grade can lead to depression if the student's explanatory style is internal, global, and stable: "I'll never have what it takes to do well."

People with internal-global-stable explanatory styles become depressed when negative outcomes occur in their lives. However, this way of thinking about the world may also help bring about those very negative outcomes.

Eighty-seven students beginning their freshman year of college examined the types of negative events that can occur in academic settings, such as "You get a D in a course required for your major" and "You cannot understand the points a lecture makes." The students were asked to imagine that the events had happened to them and to choose their explanations along the three dimensions of explanatory style theory. The results were clear: students who disproportionately used internal-global-stable explanations at the beginning of their freshman year had lower grade-point averages at the end of the year. This relationship was true even when general ability and initial level of depression were taken into account (Peterson & Barrett, 1987).

You can see how the internal-global-stable style might cause a cycle of depression. Using this style may, for example, undermine students' motivation: "I never do anything right. Why should I study?" Poor outcomes then confirm their expectations.

In Chapter 18 we will see that insights generated from cognitive theories of depression have given rise to successful forms of therapy. There are two other important aspects of the study of depression that we should review before examining the third and final major psychological disorder, schizophrenia. We will explore the large differences between the prevalence of depression in men and women, and the link between depression and suicide.

Sex Differences in Depression

One of the central questions of research on unipolar depression is why women are afflicted twice as often as men. An insightful proposal by **Susan Nolen-Hoeksema** (1987, 1990) points to the response styles of men and women once they begin to experience negative moods. According to this view, when women experience sadness, they tend to think about the possible causes and implications of their feelings. In contrast, men attempt actively to distract themselves from depressed feelings, either by focusing on something else or by engaging in a physical activity that will take their minds off their current mood state. This model suggests that it is the more thoughtful, *ruminative* response style of women, the tendency to focus obsessively on their problems, that increases women's vulnerability to depression. From a cognitive approach, paying attention to your negative moods can increase your thoughts of negative events, which eventually increases the quantity and/or the intensity of negative feelings. Research suggests that the differences in response style between men and women emerge in childhood (Nolen-Hoeksema & Girgus, 1994).

Susan Nolen-Hoeksema has suggested that women experience depression twice as often as men because of the differences in male/female response styles to negative moods.

The response styles of men may have certain advantages in terms of reduced vulnerability to depression, but they create other problems. Some researchers have pointed to the maladaptive tendency of men to distract themselves by acting out their depressed feelings in excessive drinking and drug use or in violent behavior. They cite statistics that indicate that twice as many men as women are alcoholics and suggest that alcoholism is often a mask for depression (Williams & Spitzer, 1983).

A task force of the American Psychological Association that reviewed research on sex differences in depression suggested that women's higher risk for depression can be understood only as the product of an interaction between a number of psychological, social, economic, and biological factors (McGrath et al., 1990). Several of these factors relate to the experience of being female in many cultures, such as women's greater likelihood of experiencing physical or sexual abuse or of living in poverty while being the primary caregiver for children and elderly parents. Such a finding indicates that the causes of depression may be a complex combination of factors and that there are multiple paths from "normal" behavior to depression.

Depression and Suicide

"The will to survive and succeed had been crushed and defeated. . . . There comes a time when all things cease to shine, when the rays of hope are lost" (Shneidman, 1987, p. 57). This sad statement by a suicidal young man reflects the most extreme consequence of any psychological disorder—suicide. While most depressed people do not commit suicide, most suicides are attempted by those who are suffering from depression (Shneidman, 1985). Depressed people commit suicide at a rate 25 times higher than nondepressed people in comparison groups (Flood & Seager, 1968). In the general

While most depressed people do not commit suicide, most suicides are attempted by depressed people.

U.S. population, the number of deaths caused by suicide is estimated to run as high as 100,000 per year. The following patterns hold for suicide (National Center for Health Statistics, 1989):

- It is the eighth leading cause of death in the United States, the third among the young, and the second among college students.
- Five million living Americans have attempted to kill themselves.
- For every completed suicide there are 8 to 20 suicide attempts.
- A suicide usually affects at least 6 other people, putting the number touched by U.S. suicides at over 3.5 million (between 1970 and 1992).

What is the relationship between achievement and depression? Highly successful individuals, like rock star Kurt Cobain, are not immune to the feelings of despair that can trigger suicide.

Despite these high numbers, suicide is underreported, since single-car fatal accidents and other deaths that may be suicidal are not listed as such without the evidence of a suicide note, and because the potential stigma leads family members to deny suicide when it occurs.

Because depression occurs more frequently in women, it is not surprising that women *attempt* suicide about three times more often than men do; attempts by men, however, are more often successful. This difference occurs largely because men use guns more often, and women tend to use less lethal means, such as sleeping pills (Berman & Jobes, 1991; Perlin, 1975).

One of the most alarming social problems in recent decades is the rise of *youth suicide*. Every nine minutes, a teenager attempts suicide, and every 90 minutes, a teenager succeeds. In any one week, 1000 teenagers will try suicide and 125 will succeed in killing themselves. Since 1960, the suicide rate among American teenagers has jumped by 200 to 300 percent (Coleman, 1987; Garland & Zigler, 1993). Despite fewer attempts, adolescent boys are over four times more likely to succeed than are adolescent girls (Bingham et al., 1994). Note that the suicide rates for African-American youths of both sexes are roughly half those for white youths, although no clear explanation has emerged for this finding (Bingham et al., 1994; Garland & Zigler, 1993). (These racial differences remain in place across the life span. Elderly white men are at greatest risk for suicide and African-American women least, when data are compared across race, gender, and age.)

Suicide rates among American teens have increased by 200 to 300 percent since 1960.

What lifestyle patterns predispose adolescents to attempt suicide? The breakup of a close relationship is the leading traumatic incident for both sexes. Other significant incidents that create shame and guilt can overwhelm immature egos and lead to suicide attempts. Such incidents include being assaulted, beaten, raped, or arrested for the first time. Furthermore, gay and lesbian youths are at even higher risk for suicide than are other adolescents (D'Augelli, 1993; Davis & Sandoval, 1991). These higher suicide rates undoubtedly reflect the relative lack of social support for homosexual orientation. Suicide is an extreme reaction that occurs especially when adolescents feel unable to cry out to others for help.

Youth suicide is not a spur-of-the-moment, impulsive act, but, typically, it occurs as the final stage of a period of inner turmoil and outer distress. The majority of young suicide victims have talked to others about their intentions or have written about them. Thus talk of suicide should always be taken seriously (Shafii et al., 1985). Recognizing the signs of suicidal thinking and the experiences that can start or intensify such destructive thoughts is a first step toward prevention. **Edwin Shneidman**, a psychologist who for almost 40 years has studied and treated people with suicidal tendencies, concludes that "suicide is the desperate act of a perturbed and constricted mind, in seemingly unbearable and unresolvable pain. . . . The fact is that we can relieve the pain, redress the thwarted needs, and reduce the constriction of suicidal thinking" (1987, p. 58). Being sensitive to signs of suicidal intentions and caring enough to intervene are essential for saving the lives of both youthful and mature people who have come to see no exit for their troubles except total self-destruction.

Although suicide rates are generally lower for nonwhites than for whites, there is one startling exception: among Native American youth, suicide is five times greater than among youth of the general population. Suicide is one of several forms of self-destructive behavior seen as part of the ongoing destruction of Native American communities in the United States. **Teresa LaFromboise**, a Native American psychologist who has been studying the problem and developing prevention and treatment strategies, identifies the social causes of youth suicide among her people. With poverty rampant and unemployment high, suicide rates are boosted by "family disruption, pervasive hardship, a severe number of losses (whether through death, desertion, or divorce), substance abuse, the increased mobilities of families, and the incarceration of a significant caretaker" (LaFromboise, 1988, p. 9). In addition, the Native American belief that the living continuously interact with their ancestors in the spiritual world means that death holds little fear.

SCHIZOPHRENIC DISORDERS

Everyone knows what it is like to feel depressed or anxious, even though most of us never experience these feelings to the degree of severity that constitutes a disorder. Schizophrenia, however, is a disorder that represents a qualitatively different experience from normal functioning. A **schizophrenic disorder** is a severe form of psychopathology in which personality seems to disintegrate, thought and perception are distorted, and emotions are blunted. The person with a schizophrenic disorder is the one you most often conjure up when you think about madness or insanity.

For many of the people afflicted with schizophrenia, the disease is a life sentence without possibility of parole, endured in the solitary confinement of a mind that must live life apart. Although schizophrenia is relatively rare—approximately 0.7 percent of U.S. adults have suffered from schizophrenia at some point in their lives (Kessler et al., 1994)—this figure translates to around two million people affected by this most mysterious and tragic mental disorder. Half of the beds in this nation's mental institutions are occupied by schizophrenic patients, because many spend their entire adult lives hospitalized, with little hope of ever returning to a "normal" existence.

Mark Vonnegut, son of novelist Kurt Vonnegut, was in his early twenties when he began to experience symptoms of schizophrenia. In *The Eden Express* (1975), he tells the story of his break with reality and his eventual recovery. Once, while pruning some fruit trees, his reality became distorted:

> I began to wonder if I was hurting the trees and found myself apologizing. Each tree began to take on personality. I began to wonder if any of them liked me. I became completely absorbed in looking at each tree and began to notice that they were ever so slightly luminescent, shining with a soft inner light that played around the branches. And from out of nowhere came an incredibly wrinkled, iridescent face. Starting as a small point infinitely distant, it rushed forward, becoming infinitely huge. I could see nothing else. My heart had stopped. The moment stretched forever. I tried to make the face go away but it mocked me. . . . I tried to look the face in the eyes and realized I had left all familiar ground. (1975, p. 96)

Vonnegut's description gives you a first glimpse at the symptoms of schizophrenia.

In the world of schizophrenia, *thinking* becomes illogical; associations among ideas are remote or without apparent pattern. **Hallucinations** often occur, involving imagined sensory perceptions—sights, smells, or, most commonly, sounds (usually voices)—that are assumed to be real. A person may hear a voice that provides a running commentary on his or her behavior or may hear several voices in conversation. **Delusions** are also common; these are false or irrational beliefs maintained in spite of clear contrary evidence. *Language* may become incoherent—a "word salad" of unrelated or made-up words—or an individual may become mute. *Emotions* may be flat, with no visible expression, or they may be inappropriate to the situation. *Psychomotor behavior* may be disorganized (grimaces, strange mannerisms), or posture may become rigid. Even when only some of these symptoms are present, deteriorated functioning in work and interpersonal relationships is likely as the patient withdraws socially or becomes emotionally detached.

Schizophrenia may be characterized by illogical thought patterns, hallucinations, delusions, incoherent language, flat emotions, or disorganized psychomotor behavior.

Psychologists divide the symptoms between a positive category and a negative category. During *acute* or *active phases* of schizophrenia, the positive symptoms—hallucinations, delusions, incoherence, and disorganized behavior—are prominent. At other times, the negative symptoms—social withdrawal and flattened emotions—become more apparent. Some individuals, such as Mark Vonnegut, experience only one or a couple of acute phases of schizophrenia and recover to live normal lives. Others, often described as chronic sufferers, experience either repeated acute phases with short periods of negative symptoms or occasional acute phases with extended periods of negative symptoms. Even the most seriously disturbed are not acutely delusional all the time.

An understanding of the origins and manifestations of psychopathology is broadened by a *cross-cultural perspective* (Mezzich & Berganza, 1984). All known cultures consider people abnormal if they exhibit unpredictable behavior and/or do not communicate with others. These symptoms of psychological disorders appear to be *universal* manifestations of affliction. From such distinctly contrasting groups as the Inuit of northwest Alaska and the Yoruba of rural tropical Nigeria, researchers hear descriptions of a disorder in which beliefs, feelings, and actions are thought to come from a person's mind over which he or she has lost control. This pattern resembles what is diagnosed as schizophrenia in the United States (Murphy, 1976). The prevalence of schizophrenia across diverse cultures is a relatively standard 1 percent. As we investigate the types and causes of schizophrenia, bear in mind that these are cross-cultural aspects of human experience.

Schizophrenia appears to exist across many different cultures at the standard rate of 1 percent.

Major Types of Schizophrenia

Because of the wide variety of symptoms that can characterize schizophrenia, investigators consider it not a single disorder but rather a constellation of separate types. The five most commonly recognized subtypes are outlined in **Table 17.5**.

Disorganized Type

In this subtype of schizophrenia, a person displays incoherent patterns of thinking and grossly bizarre and disorganized behavior. Emotions are flat-

Table 17.5 Types of Schizophrenic Disorders

Type of Schizophrenia	Major Symptoms
Disorganized	Inappropriate behavior and emotions; incoherent language
Catatonic	Frozen, rigid, or excitable motor behavior
Paranoid	Delusions of persecution or grandeur
Undifferentiated	Mixed set of symptoms with thought disorders and features from other types
Residual	Free from major symptoms but evidence from minor symptoms of continuation of the disorder

tened or inappropriate to the situation. Often a person acts in a silly or childish manner, such as giggling for no apparent reason. Language can become so incoherent, full of unusual words and incomplete sentences, that communication with others breaks down. If delusions or hallucinations occur, they are not organized around a coherent theme.

> Mr. F. B. was a hospitalized mental patient in his late twenties. When asked his name, he said he was trying to forget it because it made him cry whenever he heard it. He then proceeded to cry vigorously for several minutes. Then, when asked about something serious and sad, Mr. F. B. giggled or laughed. When asked the meaning of the proverb "When the cat's away, the mice will play," Mr. F. B. replied, "Takes less place. Cat didn't know what mouse did and mouse didn't know what cat did. Cat represented more on the suspicious side than the mouse. Dumbo was a good guy. He saw what the cat did, put himself with the cat so people wouldn't look at them as comedians." (Zimbardo, personal communication)

Mr. F. B.'s mannerisms, depersonalized, incoherent speech, and delusions are the hallmarks of the disorganized type of schizophrenia.

Catatonic Type

The major feature of the catatonic type of schizophrenia is a disruption in motor activity. Sometimes people with this disorder seem frozen in a stupor. For long periods of time, the individual can remain motionless, often in a bizarre position, showing little or no reaction to anything in the environment. At other times, these patients show excessive motor activity, apparently without purpose and not influenced by external stimuli. The catatonic type is also characterized by extreme *negativism,* an unmotivated resistance to all instructions.

Paranoid Type

Individuals suffering from this form of schizophrenia experience complex and systematized delusions focused around specific themes:

- *Delusions of persecution.* Individuals feel that they are being constantly spied on and plotted against and that they are in mortal danger.
- *Delusions of grandeur.* Individuals believe that they are important or exalted beings—millionaires, great inventors, or religious figures such as Jesus Christ. Delusions of persecution may accompany delusions of grandeur—an individual is a great person but is continually opposed by evil forces.
- *Delusional jealousy.* Individuals become convinced—without due cause—that their mates are unfaithful. They contrive data to fit the theory and "prove" the truth of the delusion.

The onset of symptoms in individuals with paranoid schizophrenia tends to occur later in life than in other schizophrenic types. Individuals with paranoid schizophrenia rarely display obviously disorganized behavior. Instead, their behavior is likely to be intense and quite formal.

The combination of delusions of persecution and delusions of grandeur took on a deadly twist in the case of Colin Ferguson, who went on a murderous rampage aboard a New York commuter train in December 1993. Ferguson was found guilty of shooting 6 people and wounding 19 others, when he opened fire on the crowded train without any provocation. What makes this incident more than just another instance of random violence in America is Ferguson's statement of hating whites, Asians, Hispanics, and "Uncle Tom Blacks," in his meandering list of "reasons for this" that detectives found in

Colin Ferguson's delusions were on full display during his murder trial.

his pocket after he committed the crime ("Guilty Verdict," *San Francisco Chronicle,* 2/18/95, pp. 1, A16).

Although his original defense lawyers wanted him to plead insanity due to the oppression he felt as a black man from Jamaica and they had gathered psychiatric testimony about his paranoid delusions, Ferguson rejected this "black rage" defense. Instead, he chose to represent himself in his trial, during which he claimed that he was the *victim* of the shootings. Moreover, he claimed that all of the many eyewitnesses and surviving victims were lying as part of a conspiracy against him. Ferguson-as-lawyer told the jury that prosecutors were engaged in a conspiracy against him to hide evidence that would prove him innocent. Video scenes of the trial show the grandiosity of paranoia at work, with Ferguson referring to himself in the third person as he clearly enjoyed playing the role of The Lawyer. "I ask you, ladies and gentlemen, to look at this entire summation in context. . . . Mr. Ferguson is willing to be patient. Take as long as you need, deliberate" ("Defendent in Train Killings," *San Francisco Chronicle*, 2/17/95, p. D15). The jury took ten hours to find him guilty as charged on 25 counts of murder and attempted murder.

Undifferentiated Type

This is the grab bag category of schizophrenia, describing a person who exhibits prominent delusions, hallucinations, incoherent speech, or grossly disorganized behavior that fits the criteria of more than one type or of no clear type. The hodgepodge of symptoms experienced by these individuals does not clearly differentiate among various schizophrenic reactions.

Residual Type

Individuals diagnosed as residual type have usually suffered from a major past episode of schizophrenia but are currently free of major positive symptoms like hallucinations or delusions. The ongoing presence of the disorder is signaled by minor positive symptoms or negative symptoms like flat emotion. A diagnosis of residual type may indicate that the person's disease is entering *remission,* or becoming dormant.

Causes of Schizophrenia

Different etiological models point to very different initial causes of schizophrenia, different pathways along which it develops, and different avenues for treatment. Let's look at the contributions several of these models can make to an understanding of the way a person may develop a schizophrenic disorder.

Genetic Approaches

It has long been known that schizophrenia tends to run in families (Bleuler, 1978; Kallmann, 1946). Three independent lines of research—family studies, twin studies, and adoption studies—point to a common conclusion: persons related genetically to someone who has had schizophrenia are more likely to become affected than those who are not (Kendler & Diehl, 1993). A summary of the risks of being affected with schizophrenia through various kinds of relatives is shown in **Figure 17.4**. Schizophrenia researcher **Irving Gottesman** (1991) pooled these data from about 40 reliable studies conducted in Western Europe between 1920 and 1987; he dropped the poorest data sets. As you can see, the data are arranged according to degree of genetic relatedness, which correlates highly with the degree of risk. For example, when both parents have suffered from schizophrenia, the risk for their offspring is 46 percent, as compared with one percent in the general population. When only one parent has had schizophrenia, the risk for the offspring drops sharply, to 13 percent. Note also that the probability that identical twins will both have schizophrenia is roughly three times greater than the probability for fraternal twins.

The results of family studies, twin studies, and adoption studies all conclude that persons related to someone who has had schizophrenia are more likely to become affected than those who are not.

Adoption studies provide further evidence that genetic factors play a role in the etiology of schizophrenia. When the offspring of a schizophrenic parent are reared by a normal parent in a foster home, they are as likely to develop the disorder as if they had been brought up by the biological parent (Heston, 1970; Rosenthal et al., 1975). In addition, adoptees who are schizophrenic have significantly more biological relatives with schizophrenic disorders than adoptive relatives with the disorder (Kety, 1987; Kety et al., 1975).

These different types of evidence converge on the conclusion that some

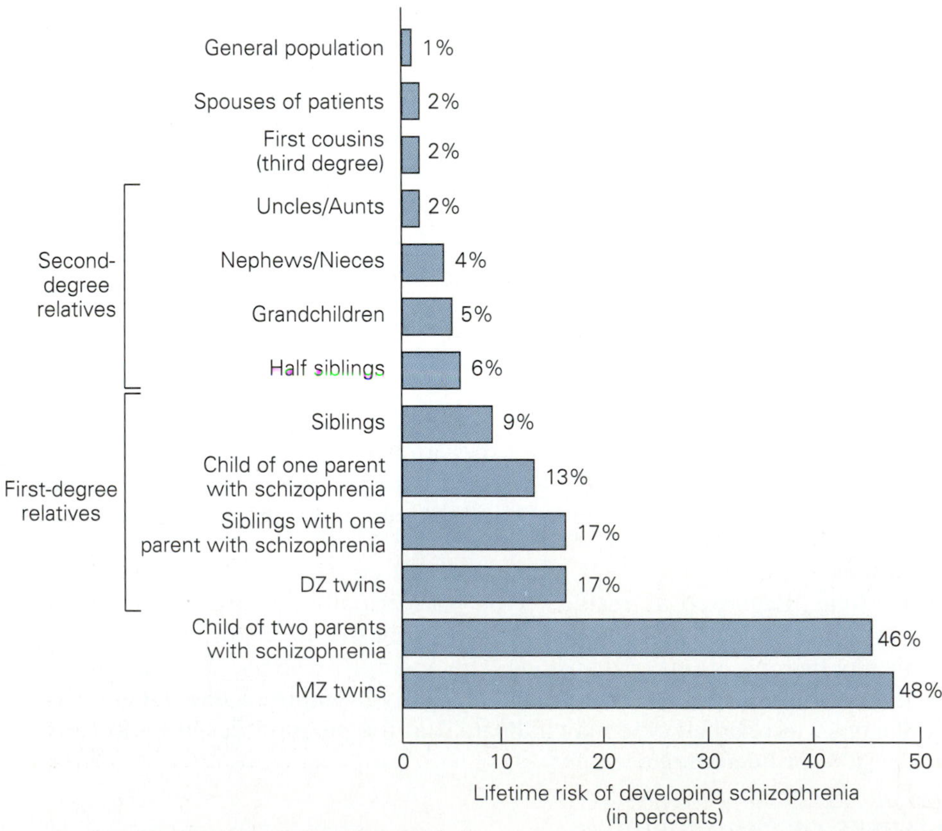

Figure 17.4 Genetic Risk of Developing Schizophrenia

The graph shows average risks for developing schizophrenia. Data were compiled from family and twin studies conducted in European populations between 1920 and 1987; the degree of risk correlates highly with the degree of genetic relatedness.

These four genetically identical women each experience a schizophrenic disorder, which suggests that heredity plays a role in the development of schizophrenia. For each of the Genain quadruplets, the disorder differs in severity, duration, and outcome.

individuals inherit genetic material that puts them at risk for schizophrenia. Researchers who would like to isolate this abnormal genetic material have taken an approach similar to the one we described for studying the genetic origins of bipolar disease in the Amish population. The goal is to isolate portions of genes that set apart those who suffer from the disorder from those who do not. Progress in this quest has been slow, almost certainly because schizophrenia is too complex a disorder to be transmitted by only one major gene (Kendler & Diehl, 1993). Scientists are hard at work developing the tools that will enable them to break through this complexity.

While there is certainly a strong relationship between genetic similarity and schizophrenia risk, even in the groups with the greatest genetic similarity, the risk factor is less than 50 percent (see **Figure 17.5**). This indicates that, although genes play a role, environmental conditions may also be nec-

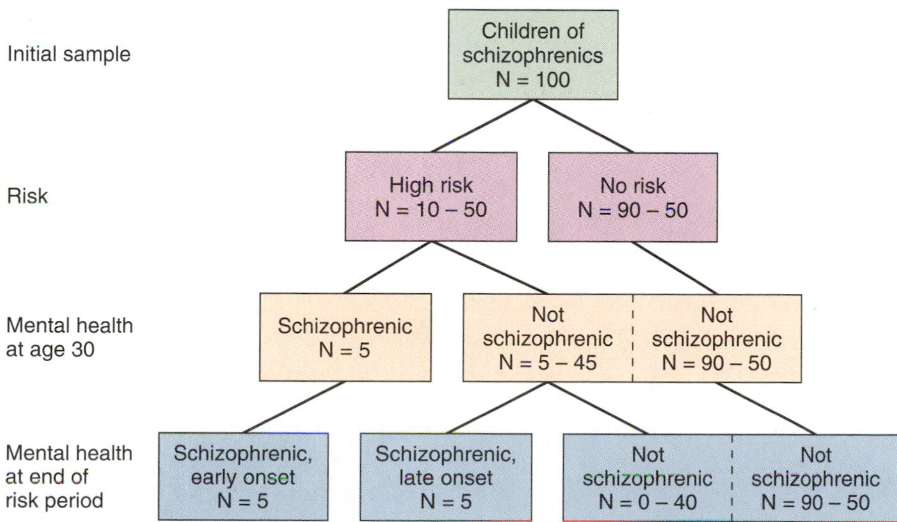

Figure 17.5 Genetic Risk for Schizophrenic Disorder

Out of a sample of 100 children of schizophrenic parents, from 10 to 50 percent will have the genetic structure that can lead to schizophrenia. Of these, about 5 percent will develop schizophrenia early and 5 percent later in life. It is important to note that as many as 40 percent of the high-risk subjects will not become schizophrenic.

The diathesis-stress hypothesis suggests that genetic factors create a risk for schizophrenia but that stress factors bring about the disorder.

essary to give rise to the disorder. A widely accepted hypothesis for the cause of schizophrenia is the **diathesis-stress hypothesis.** It suggests that genetic factors place the individual at risk, but environmental stress factors must impinge in order for the potential risk to be manifested as a schizophrenic disorder. Once we have considered other biological aspects of schizophrenia, we will review the types of environmental stressors that may speed the emergence of this disorder.

Brain Function and Biological Markers

Another biological approach to the study of schizophrenia is to look for abnormalities in the brains of individuals suffering from the disorder. Much of this research now relies on brain imaging techniques (see Chapter 3), which allow direct comparisons to be made between the structure and functioning of the brains of individuals with schizophrenia and normal control subjects (Gur & Pearlson, 1993; Resnick, 1992). For example, the magnetic resonance procedure has been used to show that the *ventricles*—the brain structures through which cerebrospinal fluid flows—are enlarged in up to 50 percent of individuals with schizophrenia (Degreef et al., 1992). Imaging techniques have also revealed that individuals with schizophrenia may have patterns of brain activity different from normal control subjects. For example, one study examined identical twins in which either one or both members of each pair had schizophrenia (Berman et al., 1992). Only those individuals who actually had schizophrenia showed lower activity in the frontal lobes of the brain. This design allows "genetics" to be held constant, to reveal this other biological aspect of the disorder.

Brain imaging techniques have shown that the ventricles through which cerebrospinal fluid flows are enlarged in schizophrenic individuals and that their patterns of brain activity differ from those of normal controls.

Even before the advent of imaging techniques, researchers had determined that levels of the neurotransmitter *dopamine* were related to schizophrenic symptoms. The **dopamine hypothesis** holds that schizophrenia is associated with a relative excess of the chemical dopamine at specific receptor sites in the central nervous system (Carlsson, 1978). Schizophrenic symptoms may be the result of an increase in the activity of nerve cells that use dopamine as their neurotransmitter. This hypothesis arose in the 1950s based on the development of a new group of drugs, the *phenothiazines,* that dramatically relieved many schizophrenic symptoms. Phenothiazines, which seem to be most effective in relieving the positive symptoms of schizophrenia (hallucinations, delusions, and disorganized behavior), are known to *block* the brain's receptors for dopamine. Drugs that increase the brain level of dopamine, like cocaine, create schizophrenia-like symptoms in normal individuals and worsen the symptoms of schizophrenia sufferers (Baker, 1991). PET scans reveal that individuals with schizophrenia may actually have more dopamine receptors than their normal counterparts (Wong et al., 1986).

The dopamine hypothesis proposes that schizophrenia is associated with a relative excess of dopamine at specific receptor sites in the central nervous system.

Researchers continue to add to the list of biological markers for schizophrenia. A **biological marker** is a "measurable indicator of a disease that may or may not be causal" (Szymanski et al., 1991, p. 99). In other words, a biological marker may be correlated with a disease, although it does not bring the disease about. Although at present no known marker perfectly predicts schizophrenia (Szymanski et al., 1991), markers have great potential value for diagnosis and research. For example, persons with schizophrenia are more likely than normal people to have an eye movement dysfunction when they scan the visual field. This biological marker can be quantified in individuals and is related to the presence of schizophrenia in families (Clementz & Sweeney, 1990). Researchers continue to probe to find the specific elements of eye movements that most precisely set individuals with schizophrenia apart from patients with other mental disorders (Sweeney et al., 1994). Precise knowledge of biological markers may help researchers determine what groups of individuals are at risk for developing the disorder.

Given the wide range of symptoms of schizophrenia, you are probably not surprised by the comparably wide range of biological abnormalities that may be either causes or consequences of the disorder. What are the ways in which features of the environment may prompt people who are at risk to develop the disease?

Family Interaction and Communication

If it is difficult to prove that a highly specific biological factor is a *sufficient* cause of schizophrenia, it is equally hard to prove that a general psychological one is a *necessary* condition. Sociologists, family therapists, and psychologists have all studied the influence of family role relationships and communication patterns in the development of schizophrenia. The hope is to identify environmental circumstances that increase the likelihood of schizophrenia—and to protect at-risk individuals from those circumstances.

Are there certain destructive or self-contradictory patterns within the family that can contribute to the onset of schizophrenia?

Research has provided evidence for theories that emphasize the influence of *deviations* in parental communication on the development of schizophrenia (Milkowitz, 1994). These deviations include a family's inability to share a common focus of attention and parents' difficulties in taking the perspective of other family members or in communicating clearly and accurately. Studies suggest that the speech patterns of families with a schizophrenic member show less responsiveness and less interpersonal sensitivity than those of normal families.

Deviant communication in families may contribute to the child's distortion of reality by concealing or denying the true meaning of an event or by injecting a confusing substitute meaning (Wynne et al., 1979). Anthropologist **Gregory Bateson** used the term **double bind** to describe a situation in which a child receives, from a parent, multiple messages that are contradictory and cannot all be met. A mother may complain that a son is not affectionate and yet reject his attempts to touch her because he is so dirty. As the child is torn between these different verbal and nonverbal messages, between demands and feelings, the child's grip on reality may begin to slip. The child may see his or her feelings, perceptions, and self-knowledge as unreliable indicators of the way things really are (Bateson et al., 1956).

Uncertainty remains over whether deviant family patterns are a cause of schizophrenia or a reaction to a child's developing symptoms of schizophrenia. To help answer this question, studies of family interactions *before* schizophrenia appears in the offspring are needed. One such prospective study focused on a pattern of harsh criticism or intrusiveness expressed by a parent toward a teenage child. It revealed that this negative communication pattern is likely to predate the development of disorders similar to, but not quite as severe as, schizophrenia (Goldstein & Strachan, 1987).

This evidence is not sufficient to confirm the hypothesis that family factors play a causal role in the *development* of schizophrenia. However, there is reliable evidence that family factors do play a role in influencing the functioning of an individual *after* the first symptoms appear. When parents reduce their criticism, hostility, and intrusiveness toward a schizophrenic offspring, the recurrence of acute schizophrenic symptoms and the need for rehospitalization are also reduced (Doane et al., 1985; Kavanagh, 1992). The implication is that treatment should be for the entire family as a system, to change the operating style toward the disturbed child.

Research suggests that family factors influence the functioning of the individual with schizophrenia after symptoms appear.

Cognitive Processes

Among the hallmarks of schizophrenia are abnormalities in attention, thought, memory, and language. Some psychologists argue that, instead of being consequences of schizophrenia, these abnormalities may play a role in causing the disorder. One view proposes that individuals with schizo-

Cognitive theorists focus their search for the causes of schizophrenia on attentional deficits and disturbances in speech processes.

phrenia suffer from attentional deficits (Freedman, 1974). *Attentional deficits* may involve ignoring important environmental or cultural cues that most people use to socially regulate or "normalize" their behavior. For example, when you are thinking about what to say in a conversation, you can filter out tangential thoughts that come to mind. People with attentional deficits may actually speak these remote, irrelevant thoughts or word associations while talking, thereby confusing these distracting peripheral ideas and stimuli with the main points or central themes of the conversation.

The incoherence of schizophrenic speech can be understood, in part, as a consequence of the breakdown of the attentional filter. Coherent speech is interrupted by bizarre *intrusions*—thoughts that are not directly relevant to the statement being uttered—that the person cannot suppress. Research by **Brendan Maher** (1968) focuses directly on attentional disturbances in language processes. Maher suggests that the speech of individuals with schizophrenia may be a result of deviant processing whenever a person comes to a "vulnerable" word—one that has multiple meanings to him or her. At that point, a personally relevant, but semantically inappropriate, word is used. For example, a patient may say, "Doctor, I have pains in my chest and hope and wonder if my box is broken and heart is beaten." *Chest* is a vulnerable word; it can mean a *respiratory cage* or a *container* such as a *hope* chest. *Wonder* could mean *Wonder bread,* which is kept in a bread *box.* Hearts *beat* and are *broken.*

Researchers have also suggested that individuals with schizophrenic disorders typically *reverse* usual procedures for reality testing. While most people evaluate the reality of their own inner worlds against criteria in the external world, individuals with schizophrenia use their inner experiences as the criteria against which they test the validity of outer experience (Meyer & Ekstein, 1970). Theirs is a world in which thinking makes it so—as in the fantasy world of children or the dream world of adults. Thus it may be that what appears as bizarre, inappropriate, and irrational behavior follows from the creation of a closed system that is self-validating and internally consistent.

The number of explanations of schizophrenia that we have reviewed—and the questions that remain despite significant research—suggest how much there is to learn about this powerful psychological disorder. Complicating understanding is the likelihood that the phenomenon called schizophrenia is probably better thought of as a group of disorders, each with potentially distinct causes (Meltzer, 1982). Genetic predispositions, brain processes, family communication, and cognitive processes have all been identified as participants in at least some cases. Researchers must still determine the exact ways in which these elements may combine to bring about schizophrenia.

JUDGING PEOPLE AS ABNORMAL

Although diagnosis and classification yield benefits for research and clinical purposes, these same processes can also have negative consequences. The task of actually labeling a person "psychologically or mentally disordered" remains a matter of human judgment—thus open to bias and error. When psychologically untrained people are in the position to judge the mental health of others, their decisions are often vulnerable to biases based on expectations, status, gender, race, and context. In the final section of this chapter, we look at the problems of objectivity and stigma.

The Problem of Objectivity

The decision to declare someone psychologically disordered or abnormal is always a *judgment* about behavior: the goal for many researchers is to make

The Insanity Defense

On March 30, 1981, the world was shocked when John Hinckley was nearly successful in his attempt to assassinate U.S. president Ronald Reagan. In June 1982 shock turned to outrage when a jury found Hinckley "not guilty by virtue of insanity." Was this outrage appropriate? What does it mean for someone to be *insane?*

Insanity is not defined in *DSM-IV*; there is no accepted clinical definition of insanity. Rather, insanity is a concept that belongs to popular culture and to the legal system. The treatment of insanity in the law dates back to England in 1843, when Daniel M'Naghten was found not guilty of murder by reason of insanity. M'Naghten's intended victim was the British prime minister—M'Naghten believed that God had instructed him to commit the murder. (He accidentally killed the prime minister's secretary instead.) Because of M'Naghten's delusions, he was sent to a mental hospital rather than to prison. The anger surrounding this verdict—even Queen Victoria was infuriated—prompted the House of Lords to articulate a guideline, known as the *M'Naghten rule,* to limit claims of insanity. This rule specifies that a criminal must not "know the nature and quality of the act he was doing; or, if he did know it, that he did not know he was doing what was wrong."

Does the M'Naghten rule seem like a fair test of guilt or innocence? With advances in the understanding of mental illness, researchers became more aware of circumstances in which a criminal might know right from wrong—a criminal might understand that what he or she was doing was illegal or immoral—but still might not be able to suppress the actions. We have already seen this type of dissociation in the discussion of anxiety disorders. Often, for example, people with phobias "know" that a spider can do them no harm, but they are unable to suppress panic behaviors in the presence of the spider. This perspective on mental illness was incorporated into the legal standard that was operative at Hinckley's trial. His jury agreed that Hinckley's behavior—arising from his obsession with the actress Jodie Foster—was beyond his control.

Did Hinckley go free? Not at all. He was committed to St. Elizabeth's, a psychiatric hospital in the Washington area (Caplan, 1984). In fact, one of the public's main misconceptions of the insanity defense is that it allows murderers to go free (Caplan, 1992; Silver et al., 1994). Perhaps 90 percent of the individuals acquitted on insanity pleas spend time in psychiatric care after they are found not guilty. In cases like Hinckley's, the individual is released into the community only when he or she is judged by experts no longer to be dangerous—there is often no upper limit placed on psychiatric incarceration as there would be for prison incarceration. In Hinckley's case, how *certain* do you think a panel of psychiatrists and psychologists would have to feel before they would agree that Hinckley could go free?

In the aftermath of Hinckley's case, many jurisdictions altered their standards for the insanity defense—the general trend was to make it more difficult to obtain a verdict of "not guilty by reason of insanity" (Appelbaum, 1994). Were these changes necessary? On practical grounds, the answer is almost certainly no. Despite the great attention that insanity pleas receive in the media—and, thus, the public's great awareness of them—such pleas are quite rare (Blau et al., 1993; Silver et al., 1994). For example, one study found insanity pleas put forth in only one out of 4968 arrests in Colorado and one out of 204 arrests in Wyoming (McGinley & Pasewark, 1989). The defense succeeded as little as 2 percent of the time. Thus the likelihood that you will ever be asked to sit on a jury and judge another person as sane or insane is quite low. But suppose it did happen. Suppose, for example, you had been on the jury that considered whether Jeffrey Dahmer, who had engaged in cannibalistic rituals, was sane. (The jury rejected the insanity defense.) How might the information you have acquired in this chapter have affected your judgment?

these judgments *objectively,* without any type of bias. For some psychological disorders, like unipolar depression or schizophrenia, diagnosis often easily meets the standards of objectivity. Other cases are more problematic. As we have seen throughout our study of psychology, the meaning of behavior is jointly determined by its *content* and by its *context.* The same act in different settings conveys very different meanings. A man kisses another man; it may signify a gay relationship in the United States, a ritual greeting in France, and a Mafia "kiss of death" in Sicily. The meaning of a behavior always depends on context.

A primary goal for researchers is to make objective judgments related to psychological disorders.

History is full of examples of situations in which judgments of abnormality were made by individuals to preserve their moral or political power. Consider an 1851 report, entitled "The Diseases and Physical Peculiarities of the Negro Race," published in a medical journal. Its author, Dr. Samuel Cartwright, had been appointed by the Louisiana Medical Association to chair a committee to investigate the "strange" practices of African-American slaves. "Incontrovertible scientific evidence" was amassed to justify the practice of slavery. Several "diseases" previously unknown to the white race were discovered. One finding was that blacks allegedly suffered from a sensory disease that made them insensitive "to pain when being punished" (thus no need to spare the whip). The committee also invented the disease **drapetomania,** a mania to seek freedom—a mental disorder that caused certain slaves to run away from their masters. Runaway slaves needed to be caught so that their illness could be properly treated (Chorover, 1981)!

In more recent history, the leaders of the Soviet Union followed the custom of diagnosing political dissidents as mentally disordered for their unacceptably deviant ideology and sentencing them to long terms in remote mental hospitals. For example, the artist who painted **Figure 17.6**, Mihail Chemiakin, was declared insane and exiled for refusing to paint in the government-approved tradition of Soviet socialist realism.

Once an individual has obtained an "abnormal" label, people are inclined to interpret later behavior to confirm that judgment. **David Rosenhan** (1973, 1975) and his colleagues demonstrated that it may be impossible to be judged "sane" in an "insane place."

Figure 17.6 The Art of Mihail Chemiakin *Chemiakin was declared insane for painting in a style inconsistent with Soviet doctrine.*

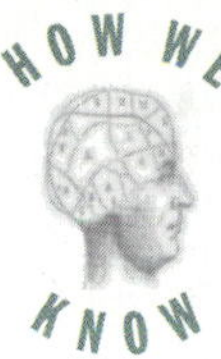

Rosenhan and seven other sane people gained admission to different psychiatric hospitals by pretending to have a single symptom: hallucinations. All eight of these *pseudopatients* were diagnosed on admission as either paranoid schizophrenic or manic-depressive. Once admitted, they behaved normally in every way. When a sane person is in an insane place, he or she is likely to be judged insane, and any behavior is likely to be reinterpreted to fit the context. If the pseudopatients discussed their situation in a rational way with the staff, they were reported to be using "intellectualization" defenses, while their notes of their observations were evidence of "writing behavior." The pseudopatients remained on the wards for almost three weeks, on the average, and not one was identified by the staff as sane. When they were finally released—only with the help of spouses or colleagues—their discharge diagnosis was still "schizophrenia" but "in remission"; that is, their symptoms were not active.

Rosenhan's research demonstrates that judgments of abnormality may rely on context factors beyond behavior itself.

Rosenhan's research demonstrates how judgments of abnormality rely on factors beyond behavior itself.

In the view of psychiatrist **Thomas Szasz**, mental illness does not even exist—it is a "myth" (1961, 1977). Szasz argues that the symptoms used as evidence of mental illness are merely medical labels that sanction professional intervention into what are social problems—deviant people violating social norms. Once labeled, these people can be treated either benignly or harshly for their problem "of being different," with no threat of disturbing the existing status quo. British psychiatrist **R. D. Laing** (1967) goes further yet, proposing that labeling people as mad often suppresses the creative, unique probing of reality by individuals who are questioning their social context. Laing (1965, 1970) believes that by regarding the novel and unusual as *mad* rather than as *creative genius,* mental diagnosis may hurt both the person and the society.

Few clinicians would go this far, but there is a movement of psychologists who advocate a *contextual* or *ecological model* in lieu of the classic medical model (Levine & Perkins, 1987). In an ecological model, abnormality is viewed not as the result of a disease within a person but as the product of an interaction between individuals and society. Abnormality is seen as a *mismatch* between a person's abilities and the needs and norms of society. For example, schools typically demand that children sit quietly for hours at desks and work independently in an orderly fashion. Some children who are not able to do this are labeled "hyperactive." Because the abilities of these children do not conform to the needs of most school settings, they quickly come to the attention of school authorities. However, if these same children were in an alternative school setting where they were free to roam around the classroom and talk to others as part of their work, the mismatch would not exist and these children might not be labeled.

In an ecological model, abnormality is viewed not as the result of a disease but as a mismatch between an individual's abilities and the needs and norms of society.

This review suggests that there can be no altogether objective assessments of abnormality. That is why, for example, the focus of *DSM-IV* diagnoses is on *personal* distress. In most circumstances, the judgment of abnormality originates in the individual who is affected.

The Problem of Stigma

It has been proposed that each society defines itself negatively by pointing out what is *not* rather than what *is* appropriate, thereby setting boundaries on what is socially acceptable. Society extracts costly penalties from those who deviate from its norms (see **Figure 17.7**). People with psychological

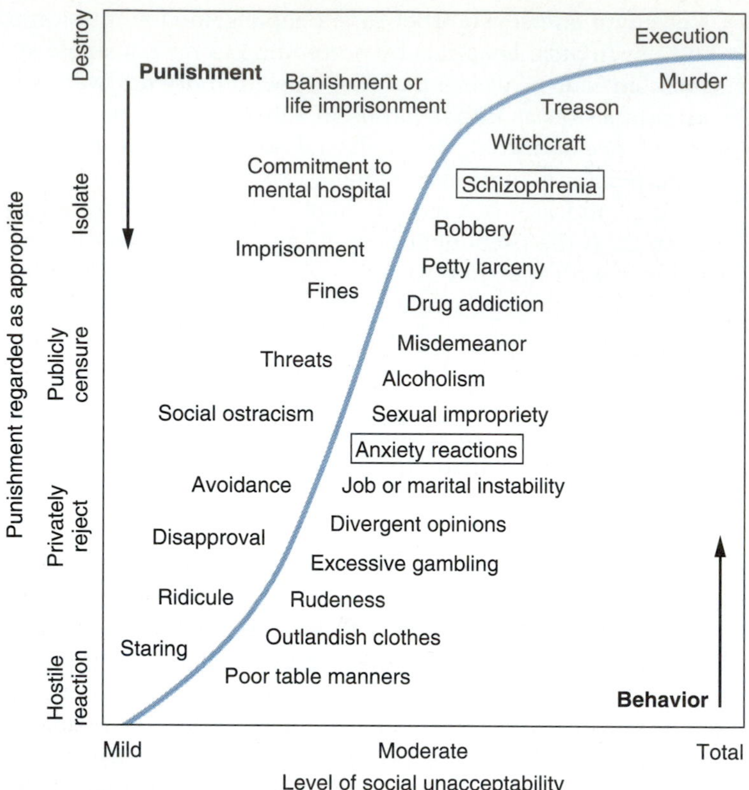

Figure 17.7 "Let the Punishment Fit the Crime"
This figure illustrates a continuum of behaviors that are deemed increasingly unacceptable and are responded to with increasing severity. In essence, each reaction is a punishment for deviance. Thus behavior toward those who suffer from psychopathology can be seen to resemble behavior toward criminals or other deviants.

disorders are often labeled as *deviant.* However, this label is not true to prevailing realities: when 50 percent of young and middle-aged adults in the United States report having experienced some psychiatric disorder in their lifetime (Kessler et al., 1994), psychopathology is, at least statistically, relatively normal.

Even given the frequency with which psychopathology touches "normal lives," people who are psychologically disordered are often stigmatized in ways that most physically ill people are not. A **stigma** is a mark or brand of disgrace; in the psychological context, it is a set of negative attitudes about a person that places him or her apart as unacceptable (Clausen, 1981). A recovered patient wrote, "For me, the stigma of mental illness was as devastating as the experience of hospitalization itself." She went on to describe her personal experience in vivid terms:

> Prior to being hospitalized for mental illness, I lived an enviable existence. Rewards, awards, and invitations filled my scrapbook. . . . The crises of mental illness appeared as a nuclear explosion in my life. All that I had known and enjoyed previously was suddenly transformed, like some strange reverse process of nature, from a butterfly's beauty into a pupa's cocoon. There was a binding, confining quality to my life, in part chosen, in part imposed. Repeated rejections, the awkwardness of others around me, and my own discomfort and self-consciousness propelled me into solitary confinement.

> My recovery from mental illness and its aftermath involved a struggle—against my own body, which seemed without energy and stamina, and against a society that seemed reluctant to embrace me. (Houghton, 1980, pp. 7–8)

Negative attitudes toward psychologically disturbed individuals come from many sources.

Negative attitudes toward the psychologically disturbed come from many sources: the mass media portrays psychiatric patients as prone to violent crime; jokes about the mentally ill are acceptable; families deny the mental distress of one of their members; legal terminology stresses mental incompetence (Rabkin et al., 1980). People also stigmatize themselves by hiding current psychological distress or a history of mental health care. The stigmatizing process discredits a person as "flawed" (Jones et al., 1984).

Negative attitudes toward psychologically disturbed individuals bias perceptions of and actions toward them. They also influence the behavior of these people toward "normal" individuals. A series of experiments conducted in laboratory and naturalistic settings demonstrates the unfavorable influences of the social situation on both the behavior of a person perceived to be a mental patient (even when not so) and the behavior of the person making that judgment.

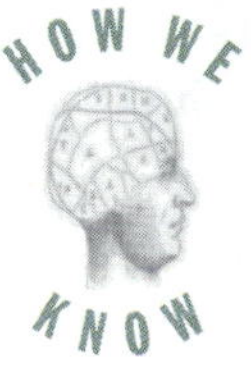

When one member of a pair of male college students was (falsely) led to believe that the other had been a mental patient, he perceived the pseudo ex-patient to be inadequate, incompetent, and not likable. By making one of a pair of interacting males falsely believe he was perceived by the other as stigmatized, the pseudopatient behaved in ways that actually caused the other naive subject to reject him (Farina, 1980; Farina et al., 1971).

Mental illness can be another of life's self-fulfilling prophecies.

In making sense of psychopathology, you are forced to come to grips with basic conceptions of normality, reality, and social values. A mind "loosed from its stable moorings" does not just go on its solitary way; it bumps into other minds, sometimes challenging their stability. In discovering how to understand, treat, and, ideally, prevent psychological disorders, researchers not only help those who are suffering and losing out on the joys of living, they also expand the basic understanding of human nature. How do psychologists and psychiatrists intervene to right minds gone wrong and to modify behavior that doesn't work? We shall see in the next chapter.

Recapping Main Points

The Nature of Psychological Disorders

Abnormality is judged by the degree to which a person's actions resemble a set of indicators that include distress, maladaptiveness, irrationality, unpredictability, unconventionality, observer discomfort, and violation of standards. There are a number of approaches to studying the etiology of psychopathology. The biological approach concentrates on abnormalities in the brain, biochemical processes, and genetic influences. Psychological approaches include psychodynamic, behavioral, and cognitive models.

Classifying Psychological Disorders

Classification systems for psychological disorders should provide a common shorthand for communicating about general types of psychopathology and specific cases. The most widely accepted diagnostic and classification system is *DSM-IV.* It emphasizes descriptions of symptom patterns and uses a multidimensional system of five axes that encourages mental health professionals to consider psychological, physical, and social factors that might be relevant to a specific disorder.

Major Types of Psychological Disorders

Personality disorders are patterns of perception, thought, or behavior that are long-standing and inflexible and that impair an individual's functioning. Dissociative disorders involve a disruption of the integrated functioning of memory, consciousness, or personal identity. The five major types of anxiety disorders are generalized, panic, phobic, obsessive-compulsive, and posttraumatic stress. Mood disorders involve disturbances of emotion. Unipolar depression is the most common affective disorder, while bipolar disorder is much rarer. Suicides are most frequent among people suffering from depression. Biological and psychological explanations account for different facets of the etiology of anxiety and mood disorders.

Schizophrenic Disorders

Schizophrenia is a severe form of psychopathology that is a universal human phenomenon. It is characterized by extreme distortions in perception, thinking, emotion, behavior, and language. The five subtypes of schizophrenia are disorganized, catatonic, paranoid, undifferentiated, and residual. Evidence for the causes of schizophrenia has been found in a variety of factors including genetics, brain abnormalities, family environment and communication, and faulty cognitive processes.

Judging People as Abnormal

The task of labeling someone as psychologically or mentally disordered is ultimately a matter of human judgment. Judgments can be influenced by context and biased by prejudice. Those with psychological disorders are often stigmatized in ways that most physically ill people are not.

Resources

Beck, A. T. (1985). *Anxiety disorders and phobias.* New York: Basic Books. Explains anxiety disorders as disturbances in cognition that cause problems in feeling and behavior.

Gaw, A. C. (Ed.). (1992). *Culture, ethnicity, and mental illness.* Washington, DC: American Psychiatric Press.

Nolen-Hoeksema, S. (1990). *Sex differences in depression.* Stanford, CA: Stanford University Press.

Oltmans, T. F. (1991). *Case studies in abnormal psychology* (3rd ed.). New York: Wiley.

Shneidman, E. (1993). *Suicide as psychache: A clinical approach to suicidal behavior.* Northvale, NJ: Aronson.

Walker, E. F. (Ed.). (1991). *Schizophrenia: A life course developmental perspective.* San Diego, CA: Academic Press.

Weckowicz, T. E. (1990). *A history of great ideas in abnormal psychology.* New York: Elsevier.

18

Therapies for Personal Change

At the beginning of Chapter 17, we shared with you some words from a letter written by a woman who suffered from schizophrenia. To begin this chapter on treatment, we turn back to her letter.

> I live pretty normal and no one can tell Im mentally ill unless I tell them. . . . My sister (not a twin) has this illness too, for 12 years, and wont take her medicine because she refused to understand she has this illness. Ive had mine for 5 years. I became convinced the 1st year through my suffering by reading the book, "I Never Promised You a Rose Garden." So I improved, thanks to the antipsychotic medicine availible. . . . The medicine works good on some of us.

Through recognition of her disorder, and through treatment with antipsychotic drugs, this young woman has gotten some control back over her life.

In this final chapter of Psychology and Life, *we will examine the types of therapies that can help individuals with a range of disorders restore personal control. We address a number of formidable questions: How has the treatment of psychological disorders been influenced by historical, cultural, and social forces? How do theory, research, and practice interact as researchers develop and test treatment methods? What can be done to influence a mind ungoverned by ordinary reason, to modify uncontrolled behavior, to alter unchecked emotions, and to correct abnormalities of the brain?*

This chapter surveys the major types of treatments currently used by health-care providers: psychoanalysis, behavior modification, cognitive alteration, humanistic therapies, and drug therapies. We will examine the way these treatments work. We will also evaluate the validity of claims about the success of each therapy.

THE THERAPEUTIC CONTEXT

There are different types of therapy for mental disorders and there are many reasons some people seek help (and others who need it do not). The purposes or goals of therapy, the settings in which therapy occurs, and the kinds of therapeutic helpers also vary. Despite any differences between therapies, however, all are *interventions* into a person's life, designed to change the person's functioning in some way.

Goals and Major Therapies

The therapeutic process involves four major goals: diagnosing the problem, determining its etiology, making a prognosis, and prescribing and carrying out treatment.

The therapeutic process can involve four primary tasks or goals: (1) reaching a *diagnosis* about what is wrong, possibly determining an appropriate psychiatric (*DSM-IV*) label for the presenting problem, and classifying the disorder; (2) proposing a probable *etiology* (cause of the problem)—that is, identifying the probable origins of the disorder and the functions being served by the symptoms; (3) making a *prognosis,* or estimate, of the course the problem will take with and without any treatment; and, finally, (4) prescribing and carrying out some form of *treatment,* a therapy designed to minimize or eliminate the troublesome symptoms and, perhaps, their sources.

If we think of the brain as a computer, we can say that mental problems may occur either in the brain's hardware or the software that programs its actions. The two main kinds of therapy for mental disorders focus on either the hardware or the software.

Biomedical therapies focus on changing the hardware: the mechanisms that run the central nervous system. These therapies try to alter brain functioning with chemical or physical interventions, including surgery, electric shock, and drugs that act directly on the brain–body connection.

Psychological therapies, which are collectively called **psychotherapy,** focus on changing the software—the faulty behaviors people have learned: the words, thoughts, interpretations, and feedback that direct daily strategies for living. These therapies are practiced by clinical psychologists as well as by psychiatrists. There are four major types of psychotherapy: psychodynamic, behavioral, cognitive, and existential-humanistic.

The two main types of therapy for mental disorders are biomedical therapy and psychotherapy.

The *psychodynamic approach* views neurotic suffering as the outer symptom of inner, unresolved traumas and conflicts. Psychodynamic therapists treat mental disorder with a "talking cure," in which a therapist helps a person develop insights about the relation between the overt symptoms and the unresolved hidden conflicts that presumably caused them.

Behavior therapy treats the behaviors themselves as disturbances that must be modified. Disorders are viewed as learned behavior patterns rather than as the symptoms of mental disease. Behaviors are transformed in many ways, including changing reinforcement contingencies for desirable and undesirable responding, extinguishing conditioned responses, and providing models of effective problem solving.

Cognitive therapy tries to restructure the way a person thinks by altering the often distorted self-statements a person makes about the causes of a problem. Restructuring cognitions changes the way a person defines and explains difficulties, often enabling the person to cope with the problems.

Therapies that have emerged from the *existential-humanistic tradition* emphasize the *values* of patients. The therapies are directed toward self-actualization, psychological growth, the development of more meaningful interpersonal relationships, and the enhancement of freedom of choice. They tend to focus more on improving the functioning of essentially healthy people than on correcting the symptoms of seriously disturbed individuals.

ENTERING THERAPY

Why do people go into therapy? Most often, people enter therapy when their everyday functioning violates societal criteria of normality and/or their own sense of adequate adjustment. They may seek therapy on their own initiative after trying ineffectively to cope with their problems, or they may be advised to do so by family, friends, doctors, or coworkers. In some cases, psychological problems associated with long-term medical problems can be helped by psychotherapy. Sudden life changes due to unemployment, death of a loved one, or divorce may trigger or worsen psychological problems, necessitating outside support. Students often seek therapy in their college mental health facilities because of difficulties in interpersonal relationships and concerns about academic performance. Some people seek treatment because they are legally required by the court to do so in connection with a criminal offense or insanity hearing. Those whose behavior is judged dangerous to self or others can be involuntarily committed by a state court to a mental institution for a limited period of time for testing, observation, and treatment.

It is important to note that many people who might benefit from therapy do not seek professional help. Sometimes it is inconvenient for them to do so, but there are many other possible reasons. These reasons include lack of accessible mental health facilities, ignorance of available resources, lack of money, language difficulties, and fear of stigmatization. A person's ability to

Attitudes about therapy are changing . . . slowly. Source: CATHY by Cathy Guisewite. Copyright, 1986, Universal Press Syndicate. Reprinted with permission. All rights reserved.

Some people who might benefit from therapy do not seek help because of inaccessibility of mental health facilities, ignorance of resources, lack of money, language difficulties, or fear of stigmatization.

get help can be affected even by the psychological problems themselves. The person with agoraphobia finds it hard, even impossible, to leave home to seek therapy; a paranoid person will not trust mental health professionals. Even when people do seek therapy, these forces may conspire to create a time lag between the onset of symptoms and the onset of treatment. This delay period, combined with memory distortions and other sources of intervening distress, can make it difficult to isolate specific historical factors associated with the onset of psychopathology.

People who do enter therapy are usually referred to as either patients or clients. The term **patient** is used by professionals who take a biomedical approach to the treatment of psychological problems. The term **client** is used by professionals who think of psychological disorders as "problems in living" and not as mental illnesses (Rogers, 1951; Szasz, 1961). We will use the preferred term for each approach: *patient* for biomedical and psychoanalytic therapies and *client* for other therapies.

Therapists and Therapeutic Settings

When psychological problems arise, most people initially seek out informal counselors who operate in familiar settings. Many people turn to family members, close friends, personal physicians, lawyers, or favorite teachers for support, guidance, and counsel. Those with religious affiliations may seek help from a clergy member. Others get advice and a chance to talk by opening up to bartenders, salesclerks, cabdrivers, or other people willing to listen. In our society, these informal therapists carry the bulk of the daily burden of relieving frustration and conflict. When problems are limited in scope, informal therapists can often help.

Although more people seek out therapy now than in the past, people usually turn to trained mental health professionals only when their psychological problems become severe or persist for extended periods of time. When they do, they can turn to several types of therapists.

Counseling psychologists typically provide guidance in areas such as vocation selection, school problems, drug abuse, and marital conflict. Often these counselors work in community settings related to the problem areas—within a business, a school, a prison, the military service, or a neighborhood clinic—and use interviews, tests, guidance, and advising to help individuals solve specific problems and make decisions about future options.

A **clinical social worker** is a mental health professional whose specialized training in a school of social work prepares him or her to work in collaboration with psychiatrists and clinical psychologists. Unlike many psychiatrists and psychologists, these counselors are trained to consider the social contexts of people's problems, so these practitioners may also involve other family members in the therapy or at least become acquainted with clients' homes or work settings.

A **pastoral counselor** is a member of a religious group who specializes in the treatment of psychological disorders. Often these counselors combine spirituality with practical problem solving.

A **clinical psychologist** is required to have concentrated his or her graduate school training in the assessment and treatment of psychological problems, completed a supervised internship in a clinical setting, and earned a Ph.D. or Psy.D. These psychologists tend to have a broader background in psychology, assessment, and research than do psychiatrists.

A **psychiatrist** must have completed all medical school training for an M.D. degree and also have undergone some postdoctoral specialty training in mental and emotional disorders. Psychiatrists are trained more in the biomedical basis of psychological problems, and they are the only therapists who can prescribe medical or drug-based interventions.

A **psychoanalyst** is a therapist with either an M.D. or a Ph.D degree who has completed specialized postgraduate training in the Freudian approach to understanding and treating mental disorders.

These different types of therapists practice in many settings: hospitals, clinics, schools, and private offices. Some humanistic therapists prefer to conduct group sessions in their homes in order to work in a more natural environment. Newer community-based therapies that take the treatment to the client may operate out of local storefronts or houses of worship. Finally, therapists who practice *in vivo* therapy work with clients in the life setting that is associated with their problem. For example, they work in airplanes with pilots, flight attendants, or clients who suffer from flying phobias, or in shopping malls with people who have social phobias.

Before looking at contemporary therapies and therapists in more detail, we will first consider the historical contexts in which treatment of the mentally ill was developed and then broaden the Western perspective with a look at the healing practices of other cultures.

Historical and Cultural Contexts

What kind of treatment might you have received in past centuries if you were suffering from psychological problems? If you had lived in Europe or the United States, chances are the treatment would not have helped and could even have been harmful. In other cultures, treatment of psychological disorders has usually been seen within a broader perspective of religious and social values that yielded more humane treatment.

History of Western Treatment

Population increases and migration to big cities in fourteenth-century Western Europe created unemployment and social alienation. These conditions led to poverty, crime, and psychological problems. Special institutions were soon created to warehouse society's three emerging categories of misfits: the poor, criminals, and the mentally disturbed.

In 1403, a London hospital—St. Mary of Bethlehem—admitted its first patient with psychological problems. For the next 300 years, mental patients of the hospital were chained, tortured, and exhibited to an admission-paying public. Over time, a mispronunciation of *Bethlehem*—*bedlam*—came to

Treatment of mental disorders in the eighteenth century focused on banishing "ill humors" from the body. Shown here is the "tranquilizing chair" advocated by Philadelphia physician Benjamin Rush.

J. C. Heinroth and Clifford Beers were instrumental in the mental hygiene movement, which stressed rehabilitation for the mentally ill.

mean *chaos,* because of the horrible confusion reigning in the hospital and the dehumanized treatment of patients there (Foucault, 1975). In fifteenth-century Germany, the mad were assumed to be possessed by the devil, who had deprived them of reason. As the Inquisition's persecutory mania spread throughout Europe, mental disturbances were "cured" by painful death.

It wasn't until the late eighteenth century that the perception of psychological problems as *mental illness* emerged in Europe. The French physician **Philippe Pinel** wrote in 1801, "The mentally ill, far from being guilty people deserving of punishment, are sick people whose miserable state deserves all the consideration that is due to suffering humanity. One should try with the most simple methods to restore their reason" (Zilboorg & Henry, 1941, pp. 323–324).

In the United States, psychologically disturbed individuals were confined for their own protection and for the safety of the community, but they were given no treatment. However, by the mid-1800s, when psychology as a field of study was gaining some credibility and respectability, "a cult of curability" emerged throughout the country. Insanity was then thought to be related to the environmental stresses brought on by the turmoil of newly developing cities. Eventually, madness came to be viewed as a social problem to be cured through mental hygiene, just as contagious physical diseases were being treated by physical hygiene.

One of the founders of modern psychiatry, the German psychiatrist **J. C. Heinroth,** helped provide the conceptual and moral justification for the disease model of mental illness. In 1818, Heinroth wrote that madness is a complete loss of inner freedom or reason depriving those afflicted of any ability to control their lives. Heinroth maintained that it was the duty of the state to cure mentally ill patients of diseases that forced them to burden society (Szasz, 1979). Heinroth and, in the 1900s, **Clifford Beers** spurred on the mental hygiene movement. Eventually the confinement of the mentally ill assumed a new *rehabilitative* goal. The *asylum* then became the central fixture of this social-political movement. The disturbed were confined to asylums in rural areas, far from the stress of the city, not only for protection but also for treatment (Rothman, 1971). Unfortunately, many of the asylums that were built became overcrowded. The humane goal of rehabilitation was replaced with the pragmatic goal of *containing* strange people in remote places. These large, understaffed state mental hospitals became little more than human warehouses for disturbed individuals (Scull, 1993).

Cultural Symbols and Rituals of Curing

Our review of these historical trends in the treatment of psychological disorders has been limited to Western views and practices, which emphasize the uniqueness of the individual, independence, and personal responsibility for success and failure. Both demonology and the disease model are consistent with this emphasis, regarding mental disorder as something that happens *inside* a person and as an individual's failure.

This view is not shared by many other cultures (Triandis, 1990). The research of *cultural anthropologists* has provided analyses of the explanations and treatments for psychological disorders across different cultures (Bourguignon, 1979; Evans-Pritchard, 1937; Kluckhorn, 1944; Marsella, 1979). For example, in the African worldview, the emphasis is on cooperation, interdependence, tribal survival, unity with nature, and collective responsibility (Nobles, 1976). It is *contrary* to the thinking of many non-European cultures to treat mentally ill individuals by *removing* them from society. In many African cultures, healing takes place in a social context, involving a distressed person's beliefs, family, work, and life environment. The African use of group support in therapy has been expanded into a procedure called "network therapy," in which a patient's entire network of relatives, coworkers, and friends becomes involved in the treatment (Lambo, 1978).

In many cultures, the treatment of mental and physical disease is bound up with religion and witchcraft. Certain human beings, called *shamans,* are given special mystical powers to help in the transformation of their distressed fellow beings. **Shamanism** is an ancient and powerful spiritual tradition, that has been practiced for close to 30,000 years. In the shamanistic tradition, suffering and disease are diagnosed as powerlessness. This cultural belief system *personalizes* the vague forces of fate or chance that intervene in one's life to create problems. Such personalization permits direct action to be taken against presumed evildoers and direct help to be sought from assumed divine healers (Middleton, 1967). Often the pathological state that is seen as a result of the spirit possession of the afflicted person is transformed by therapeutic intervention of shaman healers. Drumming, chanting, and other rituals are used to inspire awe and induce altered states of consciousness that facilitate the quest for knowledge and empowerment (Walsh, 1990).

Common to folk healing ceremonies are the important roles of symbols, myths, and ritual (Lévi-Strauss, 1963). **Ritual healing** ceremonies infuse special emotional intensity and meaning into the healing process. They heighten patients' suggestibility and sense of importance, and, combined with the use of symbols, they connect the individual sufferer, the shaman, and the society to supernatural forces to be won over in the battle against madness (Devereux, 1961; Wallace, 1966).

One therapeutic practice used in a number of healing ceremonies is *dissociation of consciousness,* in which the distressed person or a faith healer enters an altered state of consciousness. In Western views, dissociation is itself a symptom of mental disorder to be prevented or corrected; in other cultures, as consciousness is altered, good spirits are communicated with and evil spirits are exorcised. The use of ceremonial alteration of consciousness can be seen among the cult of Puerto Rican *Espiritistas* in New York City, whose healing ceremonies involve communication with good spirits that are believed to exist outside the person (Garrison, 1977).

In many cultures, shamans help in the treatment of the mentally ill by means of ritual healing ceremonies in which the dissociation of consciousness is an accepted practice.

Some of these non-Western views have begun to work their way into Western practices. The influence of the social-interactive concept and the focus on the *family context* and *supportive community* are evident in newer therapeutic approaches that emphasize social support networks and family therapy. Other Western practitioners work with shamans in an effort to integrate Western psychotherapies that involve self-analysis with the therapies of collectivist societies that view the individual within the current communal context. These attempts at integration make therapies more culturally appropriate to a wider range of clients (Kraut, 1990).

With this overview of historical trends and cultural variations in mind, it is time to investigate in some detail each of the major types of therapies being practiced today in our society.

PSYCHODYNAMIC THERAPIES

Psychodynamic therapies assume that a patient's problems have been caused by the psychological tension between unconscious impulses and the constraints of his or her life situation. These therapies locate the core of the disorder inside the disturbed person.

Freudian Psychoanalysis

Psychoanalytic therapy, as developed by **Sigmund Freud,** is an intensive and prolonged technique for exploring unconscious motivations and conflicts in

Sigmund Freud's study, including the famous couch (right), is housed in London's Freud Museum. The 82-year-old Freud fled to London in 1938 upon the Nazi occupation of Austria; he died there the following year.

neurotic, anxiety-ridden individuals. A former president of the American Psychoanalytic Institute explained the premise of psychoanalysis:

> We believe an unconscious exists in all humans and that it dictates much of our behavior. If it is a relatively healthy unconscious, then our behavior will be healthy, too. Many who are plagued by symptoms from phobias, depression, anxiety, or panic may have deposits of unconscious material that are fostering their torment. Only the psychoanalyst is qualified to probe the unconscious. . . . (Theodore Rubin, quoted in Rockmore, 1985, p. 71)

The goal of psychoanalysis is to establish harmony between the id, ego, and superego.

As we saw in earlier chapters, Freudian theory views anxiety disorders as inabilities to resolve adequately the inner conflicts between the unconscious, irrational impulses of the *id* and the internalized social constraints imposed by the *superego.* The goal of psychoanalysis is to establish intrapsychic harmony that expands awareness of the forces of the *id,* reduces overcompliance with the demands of the *superego,* and strengthens the role of the *ego.*

Of central importance to a therapist is to understand the way a patient uses the process of *repression* to handle conflicts. Symptoms are considered to be messages from the unconscious that something is wrong. A psychoanalyst's task is to help a patient bring repressed thoughts to consciousness and to gain *insight* into the relation between the current symptoms and the repressed conflicts. In this psychodynamic view, therapy works and patients recover when they are "released from repression" established in early childhood (Munroe, 1955). Because a central goal of a therapist is to guide a patient toward discovering insights into the relationships between present symptoms and past origins, psychodynamic therapy is often called **insight therapy.**

Traditional psychoanalysis is an attempt to reconstruct long-standing repressed memories and then work through painful feelings to an effective resolution. Accordingly, it is a therapy that takes a long time (several years at least, with as many as five sessions a week). It also requires introspective patients who are verbally fluent, highly motivated to remain in therapy, and willing and able to undergo considerable expense. (Newer forms of psychodynamic therapy often try to make therapy briefer in total duration.) Psychoanalysts use several techniques to bring repressed conflicts to consciousness and to help a patient resolve them (Langs, 1981; Lewis, 1981). These techniques include free association, analysis of resistance, dream analysis, and analysis of transference and countertransference.

The Origins of the Talking Cure

Modern psychotherapy began in 1880 with the case of Fraulein Anna O. and her famous physician **Joseph Breuer.** This bright, personable, 21-year-old Viennese woman became incapacitated and developed a severe cough while nursing her ill father. When the physician began to treat her "nervous cough," he became aware of many more symptoms that seemed to have a psychological origin. Anna squinted, had double vision, and experienced paralysis, muscle contractions, and anesthesias (loss of sensitivity to pain stimuli).

Breuer told a young physician named Sigmund Freud about this unusual patient. Together they coined the term *hysterical conversion* for the transformation of Anna O.'s blocked emotional impulses into physical symptoms (Breuer & Freud, 1895/1955). The case of Anna O. is the first detailed description of physical symptoms resulting from *psychogenic* causes—a hysterical illness. It was Anna O. herself who devised her own treatment, with Breuer acting as therapist. In the context of hypnosis, Anna O. talked freely, giving full rein to her imagination. She referred to the procedures as a "talking cure" and, jokingly, as "chimney sweeping."

The talking cure originated with the treatment of a patient named Anna O., who exhibited physical symptoms resulting from psychogenic causes.

Anna O. went on to become a pioneer of social work, a leader in the struggle for women's rights, a playwright, and a housemother of an orphanage. Her true name was **Bertha Pappenheim** (Rosenbaum & Muroff, 1984). Although this case played an extremely important role in the development of modern psychotherapy, a provocative new view of Anna O.'s illness casts doubt on the original diagnosis. A reasonably good alternative diagnosis is that her symptoms were those associated with *tuberculous meningitis,* which she might have contracted from her father, who probably was dying from a form of tuberculosis himself (Thornton, 1984). After Anna O. had terminated her treatment with Breuer, she entered a sanatorium from which she was later discharged, relatively recovered from her illness. It is likely that many of her "hysterical conversion" reactions were of organic, not psychological, origin, but she may also have experienced considerable suppressed rage and guilt from nursing her father for so long and have been frustrated by the lack of opportunities for women of her social class.

Free Association and Catharsis

The principal procedure used in psychoanalysis to probe the unconscious and release repressed material is called **free association.** A patient, sitting comfortably in a chair or lying in a relaxed position on a couch, lets his or

Not-so-free associations.

her mind wander freely and gives a running account of thoughts, wishes, physical sensations, and mental images. The patient is encouraged to reveal every thought or feeling, no matter how unimportant it may seem.

Freud maintained that free associations are *predetermined,* not random. The task of an analyst is to track the associations to their source and identify the significant patterns that lie beneath the surface of what are apparently just words. The patient is encouraged to express strong feelings, usually toward authority figures, that have been repressed for fear of punishment or retaliation. Any such emotional release, by this or other processes, is termed **catharsis.**

Resistance

A psychoanalyst attaches particular importance to subjects that a patient does *not* wish to discuss. At some time during the process of free association, a patient will show **resistance**—an inability or unwillingness to discuss certain ideas, desires, or experiences. Such resistances are conceived of as *barriers* between the unconscious and the conscious. This material is often related to an individual's sexual life (which includes all things pleasurable) or to hostile, resentful feelings toward parents. When the repressed material is finally brought into the open, a patient generally claims that it is unimportant, absurd, irrelevant, or too unpleasant to discuss. The therapist believes the opposite. Psychoanalysis aims to break down resistances and enable the patient to face these painful ideas, desires, and experiences.

Free association is the principal method used in psychoanalysis to probe the unconscious. Resistance is seen as a barrier between the unconscious and the conscious.

Dream Analysis

Psychoanalysts believe that dreams are an important source of information about a patient's unconscious motivations. When a person is asleep, the superego is presumably less on guard against the unacceptable impulses originating in the id, so a motive that cannot be expressed in waking life may find expression in a dream. In analysis, dreams are assumed to have two kinds of content: *manifest* (openly visible) content that people remember upon awakening and *latent* (hidden) content—the actual motives that are seeking expression but are so painful or unacceptable that they are expressed in disguised or symbolic form. Therapists attempt to uncover these hidden motives by using **dream analysis,** a therapeutic technique that examines the content of a person's dreams to discover the underlying or disguised motivations and symbolic meanings of significant life experiences and desires.

Psychodynamic therapists use dream analysis to uncover the hidden motives and symbolic content in the patient's dreams.

Transference and Countertransference

During the course of the intensive therapy of psychoanalysis, a patient usually develops an emotional reaction toward the therapist. Often the therapist is identified with a person who has been at the center of an emotional conflict in the past—most often a parent or a lover. This emotional reaction is called **transference.** The transference is called *positive transference* when the feelings attached to the therapist are those of love or admiration and *negative transference* when the feelings consist of hostility or envy. Often a patient's attitude is *ambivalent,* including a mixture of positive and negative feelings.

An analyst's task in handling transference is a difficult one because of the patient's emotional vulnerability; however, it is a crucial part of treatment. A therapist helps a patient to interpret the present transferred feelings by understanding their original source in earlier experiences and attitudes (Langs, 1981).

Personal feelings are also at work in a therapist's reactions to a patient. **Countertransference** refers to what happens when a therapist comes to like or dislike a patient because the patient is perceived as similar to significant people in the therapist's life. In working through countertransference, a therapist may discover some unconscious dynamics of his or her own. The therapist becomes a "living mirror" for the patient and the patient, in turn, for the therapist. If the therapist fails to recognize the operation of countertransference, the therapy may not be as effective (Little, 1981). Because of the emotional intensity of this type of therapeutic relationship and the vulnerability of the patient, therapists must be on guard about crossing the boundary between professional caring and personal involvement with their patients. The therapy setting is obviously one with an enormous power imbalance that must be recognized, and honored, by the therapist.

Neo-Freudian Therapies

Freud's followers retained many of his basic ideas but modified certain of his principles and practices. In general, these neo-Freudians place more emphasis than Freud did on (1) a patient's *current* social environment (less focus on the past); (2) the continuing influence of life experiences (not just childhood conflicts); (3) the role of social motivation and interpersonal relations of love (rather than of biological instincts and selfish concerns); (4) the significance of ego functioning and development of the self-concept (less on the conflict between id and superego).

The neo-Freudians place more emphasis than Freud did on a patient's current social environment, the continuing influence of life events, the role of social motivation and interpersonal relations, and development of the self-concept.

In Chapter 14, we noted two other prominent Freudians, Carl Jung and Alfred Adler. To get a flavor of the more contemporary psychodynamic approaches of the neo-Freudians, here we will look at the work of Harry Stack Sullivan, Karen Horney, and Heinz Kohut (see Ruitenbeek, 1973, for a look at other members of the Freudian circle).

Harry Stack Sullivan (1953) felt that Freudian theory and therapy did not recognize the importance of social relationships and a patient's needs for acceptance, respect, and love. Mental disorders, he insisted, involve not only traumatic intrapsychic processes but troubled interpersonal relationships and even strong societal pressures. A young child needs to feel secure and to be treated by others with caring and tenderness. Anxiety and other mental ills arise out of insecurities in relations with parents and significant others. In Sullivan's view, a self-system is built up to hold anxiety down to a tolerable level. This self-system is derived from a child's interpersonal experiences and is organized around conceptions of the self as the *good-me* (associated with the mother's tenderness), the *bad-me* (associated with the mother's tensions), and the *not-me* (a dissociated self that is unacceptable to the rest of the self).

Therapy based on this interpersonal view involves observing a *patient's feelings* about the *therapist's attitudes.* The therapeutic interview is seen as a social setting in which each party's feelings and attitudes are influenced by the other's. The patient is gently provoked to state his or her assumptions about the therapist's attitudes. Above all, the therapeutic situation, for Sullivan, was one in which the therapist learned and taught lovingly (Wallach & Wallach, 1983).

Karen Horney (1885–1952)

Karen Horney (1937, 1945, 1950) expanded the boundaries of Freudian theory in many ways. She stressed the importance of environmental and cultural contexts in which neurotic behavior is expressed. She also took a more flexible view of personality, seeing it as involving rational coping and ongoing development; in Horney's view, the personality is continually molded by current fears and impulses, rather than being determined solely by early childhood experiences and instincts. Horney (1926/1967) was one of the first neo-Freudians to question the extent to which Freud's theory was applicable to women. She rejected Freud's *phallocentric* emphasis on the importance of the penis, hypothesizing that *male envy* of pregnancy, motherhood, breasts, and suckling is a dynamic force in the unconscious of boys and men. This alternative emphasis is *gynocentric,* centered on the female womb. Males' intense desires for material achievement and creative products thus were seen as unconscious means of overcompensating for feelings of inferiority in the creative area of reproduction.

Psychodynamic therapies continue to evolve with a varying emphasis on Freud's constructs. One of the most important new directions for these is the modern concern for the *self* in all its senses, notably the ways one's self-concept emerges, is experienced by the person, and, at times, becomes embattled and requires defending. According to **Heinz Kohut** (1977), a leading proponent of this emphasis on the self and founder of the *object relations* school of psychoanalysis, the various aspects of self require *self-objects,* supportive people and significant things everyone needs to maintain optimal personality functioning. This form of self psychology emphasizes the experience of self and especially those experiences that lead to a fragmented self. The therapist's task then is to try as much as possible to empathize with the various psychological states that the client is going through while also accepting the client's view of his or her experiences (Chicago Institute for Psychoanalysis, 1992).

We already noted that psychoanalytic therapy often requires a long period of time to achieve its goals. Often, however, people are suffering from disorders that require more speedy remedies. Behavior therapies, to which we turn next, provide the potential for swift relief from symptoms.

BEHAVIOR THERAPIES

While psychodynamic therapies focus on presumed inner causes, behavior therapies focus on observable outer behaviors. Behavior therapists argue that abnormal behaviors are acquired in the same way as normal behaviors—through a learning process that follows the basic principles of conditioning and learning. Behavior therapies apply the principles of conditioning and reinforcement to modify undesirable behavior patterns associated with mental disorders.

Behavior therapy and behavior modification refer to the systematic use of learning principles to increase the frequency of desired behaviors and decrease the frequency of problem behaviors.

The terms **behavior therapy** and **behavior modification** are often used interchangeably. Both refer to the systematic use of principles of learning to increase the frequency of desired behaviors and/or decrease that of problem behaviors. The range of deviant behaviors and personal problems that typically are treated by behavior therapy is extensive and includes fears, compulsions, depression, addictions, aggression, and delinquent behaviors. In general, behavior therapy works best with specific rather than general types of personal problems: it is better for a phobia than for unfocused anxiety.

Contrary to the predictions of psychodynamic therapists, research shows that when pathological behaviors are eliminated by behavior therapy, new symptoms are not substituted.

The therapies that have emerged from the theories of conditioning and learning are grounded in a pragmatic, empirical research tradition. The central task of all living organisms is to learn how to adapt to the demands of the current social and physical environment. When organisms do not learn how to cope effectively, their maladaptive reactions can be overcome by therapy based on principles of learning (or relearning). The target behavior is *not* assumed to be a symptom of any underlying process. The symptom itself is the problem. Psychodynamic therapists predicted that treating only the outer behavior without confronting the true, inner problem would result in **symptom substitution,** the appearance of a new physical or psychological problem. However, research has shown that when pathological behaviors are eliminated by behavior therapy, new symptoms are *not* substituted (Kazdin, 1982). "On the contrary, patients whose target symptoms improved often reported improvement in other, less important symptoms as well" (Sloane et al., 1975, p. 219).

Let's look at the different forms of behavior therapies that have brought relief to distressed individuals.

COUNTERCONDITIONING

Why does someone become anxious when faced with a harmless stimulus, such as a spider, a nonpoisonous snake, or social contact? The behavioral explanation is that the anxiety arises due to the simple conditioning principles we reviewed in Chapters 9 and 17: strong emotional reactions that disrupt a person's life "for no good reason" are often conditioned responses that the person does not recognize as having been learned previously. In **counterconditioning**, a new response is conditioned "counter" to a maladaptive response. The earliest recorded use of behavior therapy followed this logic. **Mary Cover Jones** (1924) showed that a fear could be *unlearned* through conditioning. (Compare the case of Little Albert in Chapter 9.)

Mary Cover Jones (1896–1987)

> Her subject was Peter, a 3-year-old boy who, for some unknown reason, was afraid of rabbits. The therapy involved feeding Peter at one end of a room while the rabbit was brought in at the other end. Over a series of sessions, the rabbit was gradually brought closer until, finally, all fear disappeared and Peter played freely with the rabbit.

Following in Cover Jones's footsteps, behavior therapists now use several counterconditioning techniques, including systematic desensitization, implosion, flooding, and aversion therapy.

Systematic Desensitization and Other Exposure Therapies

The nervous system cannot be relaxed and agitated at the same time, because incompatible processes cannot be activated simultaneously. This simple notion was central to the *theory of reciprocal inhibition,* developed by South African psychiatrist **Joseph Wolpe** (1958, 1973), who used it to treat fears and phobias. Wolpe taught his patients to *relax* their muscles, and then to *imagine* visually their feared situation. They did so in gradual steps that moved from initially remote associations to direct images. Psychologically confronting the feared stimulus while being relaxed and doing so in a *graduated* sequence is the therapeutic technique known as **systematic desensitization.**

Counterconditioning techniques include systematic desensitization, implosion, flooding, and aversion therapy.

Desensitization therapy involves three major steps. First, the client identifies the stimuli that provoke anxiety and arranges them in a *hierarchy* ranked from weakest to strongest. For example, a student suffering from severe test anxiety constructed the hierarchy in **Table 18.1**. Note that she

Table 18.1 Hierarchy of Anxiety-Producing Stimuli for a Test-anxious College Student

1. On the way to the university on the day of an examination.
2. In the process of answering an examination paper.
3. Before the unopened doors of the examination room.
4. Awaiting the distribution of examination papers.
5. The examination paper face down.
6. The night before an examination.
7. One day before an examination.
8. Two days before an examination.
9. Three days before an examination.
10. Four days before an examination.
11. Five days before an examination.
12. A week before an examination.
13. Two weeks before an examination.
14. A month before an examination.

rated immediate anticipation of an examination as more stressful than taking the exam itself. Second, the client is trained in a system of progressive deep-muscle relaxation. Relaxation training requires several sessions in which the client learns to distinguish between sensations of tension and relaxation and to let go of tension in order to achieve a state of physical and mental relaxation. Finally, the actual process of desensitization begins: the relaxed client vividly imagines the *weakest* anxiety stimulus on the list. If it can be visualized without discomfort, the client goes on to the next stronger one.

After a number of sessions, the most distressing situations on the list can be imagined without anxiety (Lang & Lazovik, 1963). Desensitization has been successfully applied to a diversity of human problems, including such generalized fears as stage fright, impotence, and frigidity (Kazdin & Wilcoxin, 1976). A number of evaluation studies have shown that this behavior therapy works remarkably well with most phobic patients (Smith & Glass, 1977).

Implosion therapy uses an approach that is opposite to systematic desensitization. Instead of experiencing a gradual, step-by-step progression, a client is exposed at the start to the most frightening stimuli at the top of the anxiety hierarchy, but in a safe setting. The therapeutic situation is arranged so that the client cannot run away from the frightening stimulus. The therapist *describes* an extremely frightening situation relating to the client's fear, such as snakes crawling all over his or her body, and urges the client to *imagine* it fully, experiencing it through all the senses as intensely as possible. Such imagining is assumed to cause an explosion of panic. Because this explosion is an inner one, the process is called *implosion;* hence the term *implosion therapy.* As the situation happens again and again, the stimulus loses its power to elicit anxiety. When anxiety no longer occurs, the maladaptive behavior previously used to avoid it disappears. The idea behind this procedure is that the client is not allowed to deny, avoid, or otherwise escape from experiencing the anxiety-arousing stimulus situations. He or she discovers that contact with the stimulus does not actually have the anticipated negative effects (Stampfl & Levis, 1967).

Flooding is similar to implosion except that it involves clients, with their permission, actually being put into the phobic situation. A person with claustrophobia is made to sit in a dark closet, and a child with a fear of water is put into a pool. Another form of flooding therapy begins with the use of imagination. In this procedure, the client may listen to a tape that describes the most terrifying version of the phobic fear in great detail for an hour or two. Once the terror subsides, the client is then taken to the feared situation, which, of course, is not nearly as frightening as just imagined. Flooding is more effective than systematic desensitization in the treatment of some behavior problems, such as agoraphobia, and treatment gains are shown to be enduring for most clients (Emmelkamp & Kuipers, 1979).

The difference between flooding and implosion is the difference between actually experiencing the anxiety-arousing stimulus and only imagining it.

The ingredient common to systematic desensitization, implosion, and flooding therapies is *exposure.* In one way or another, the client is exposed to the object or situation he or she fears. (Recently, researchers have begun to explore virtual reality techniques to provide exposure [Rothbaum et al., 1995].) Exposure therapy is also used to combat obsessive-compulsive disorders. For example, one woman who was obsessed with dirt compulsively washed her hands over and over until they cracked and bled. She even thought of killing herself because this disorder totally prevented her from leading a normal life. Under the supervision of a behavior therapist, she confronted the things she feared most—dirt and trash—and eventually even touched them. She gave up washing and bathing her hands and face for five days. Note that behavior therapy here has an added component, *response prevention.* Not only is the client exposed to what is feared (dirt and trash), but she is also prevented from performing the compulsive behavior that

A behavior therapist uses exposure therapy to help a client overcome fear of flying.

ordinarily reduces her anxiety (washing). The therapy teaches the woman to reduce anxiety without engaging her compulsion.

The ingredient common to flooding, implosion, and systematic desensitization is exposure to the anxiety-producing stimulus.

Eye movement desensitization and reprocessing (EMDR) is a new form of exposure therapy that holds the promise of rapid, short-term treatment for phobias, posttraumatic stress disorder (PTSD), and other anxiety disorders. EMDR combines a unique type of nonverbal desensitization with a cognitive, information-processing approach to treatment. As developed by **Francine Shapiro** (1991, 1995), EMDR has several steps. First, the client focuses on a memory or an image of something that is disturbing, along with its negative cognitions, feelings, and bodily sensations. The client also tries to keep in mind a positive cognition that ideally could replace the negative one. Next, clients spend several minutes using their eyes to follow or scan the therapist's hand, which moves rapidly in a back and forth pattern. This is the *eye movement desensitization* (EMD) aspect of the therapy. The clients are asked what they are noticing and what they are experiencing. The EMD is repeated with these new images or sensations in mind, until the client's distress level has been lowered significantly. Finally, the desirable positive cognition is installed or activated, again using the EMD scanning procedure, to *reprocess* the image of the traumatic or feared event. Although it is not clear what physiological mechanisms are involved in the eye movement scanning process, evidence is accumulating for its relatively rapid effectiveness with phobic disorders and PTSD (Forbes et al., 1994; Solomon et al., 1992; Sweet, 1995).

Aversion Therapy

The forms of exposure therapy we've described help clients deal directly with stimuli that are not really harmful. What can be done to help those who are *attracted* to stimuli that *are* harmful? Drug addiction, sexual perversions, and uncontrollable violence are human problems in which deviant behavior is elicited by tempting stimuli. **Aversion therapy** uses counterconditioning procedures of aversive learning to pair these stimuli with strong noxious stimuli such as electric shocks or nausea-producing drugs. In time, the same negative reactions are elicited by the tempting stimuli, and the person develops an aversion that replaces his or her former desire. For example, aversion therapy for a male client who is a *pedophile* (sexually attracted to children) might begin by having him watch slides of children and adults. When he becomes aroused to the children's images, he receives an electric shock;

Aversion therapy can be used to help those who are attracted to harmful stimuli, such as drugs, sexual perversions, or violence.

when he sees adult slides or is told to imagine socially acceptable fantasies, the shock is extinguished.

In the extreme, aversion therapy resembles torture, so why would anyone submit voluntarily to it? Usually people do so only because they realize that the long-term consequences of continuing their behavior pattern will destroy their health or ruin their careers or family lives. They may also be coerced to do so by institutional pressures, as has happened in some prison treatment programs. Many critics are concerned that the painful procedures in aversion therapy give too much power to a therapist, can be more punitive than therapeutic, and are most likely to be used in situations where people have the least freedom of choice about what is done to them. The movie *A Clockwork Orange,* based on Anthony Burgess's novel, depicted aversion therapy as an extreme form of mind control in a police state. In recent years, use of aversion therapy in institutional rehabilitation programs has become regulated by ethical guidelines and state laws. The hope is that, under these restrictions, it will be therapeutic rather than coercive.

Contingency Management

Counterconditioning procedures are appropriate when one response can be replaced with another. Other behavior modification procedures rely on the principles of operant conditioning that arose in the research tradition pioneered by **B. F. Skinner. Contingency management** refers to the general treatment strategy of changing behavior by modifying its consequences. The two major techniques of contingency management in behavior therapy are *positive reinforcement strategies* and *extinction strategies.*

Positive Reinforcement Strategies

When a response is followed immediately by a reward, the response tends to be repeated and to increase in frequency over time. This central principle of operant learning becomes a therapeutic strategy when it is used to modify the frequency of a desirable response as it replaces an undesirable one. Dramatic success has been obtained from the application of positive reinforcement procedures to behavior problems. You might recall two examples from Chapter 9. We described *token economies,* in which desired behaviors (for example, practicing personal care or taking medication) are explicitly defined, and token payoffs are given by institutional staff when the behaviors are performed. These tokens can later be exchanged for an array of rewards and privileges (Ayllon & Azrin, 1965; Holden, 1978; Kazdin, 1994). These systems of reinforcement are especially effective in modifying patients' behaviors regarding self-care, upkeep of their environment, and frequency of their positive social interactions. In Chapter 9, we also described an application of *shaping* to improve the life of an autistic child. The patient was a 3-year-old boy who needed to wear glasses. Therapists used the click of a toy noisemaker as a conditioned reinforcer to move him closer and closer to wearing the glasses.

Contingency management through positive reinforcement strategies is particularly effective in modifying behavior regarding self-care, upkeep of the patient's environment, and frequency of positive social interactions.

Behavior therapists often try to involve individuals directly in their own contingency management. A **behavioral contract** is an explicit agreement (often in writing) that states the consequences of specific behaviors. Behavior therapists who work with clients on obesity or smoking problems often use such contracts. The contract may specify what the client is expected to do (client's obligations) and what, in turn, the client can expect from the therapist (therapist's obligations).

Behavioral contracting facilitates therapy by making both parties responsible for achieving the agreed-upon changes in behavior. Treatment goals are spelled out, as are the specific rewards corresponding to meeting planned commitments and reaching desired subgoals. The therapeutic situation becomes more structured in terms of what each party can reasonably expect as appropriate content and acceptable interpersonal behavior. The person with less status and power (patient or child, for example) benefits if a condition for third-party arbitration of alleged contract violation is included (Nelson & Mowrey, 1976). Some parents have found that contracts with their teenagers have generated acceptable behavior while greatly improving the emotional climate of the home. Reinforcements often include more reasonable parental behaviors (Stuart, 1971).

Extinction Strategies

Why do people continue to do something that causes pain and distress when they are capable of doing otherwise? The answer is that many forms of behavior have multiple consequences—some are negative and some are positive. Often, subtle positive reinforcements keep a behavior going despite its obvious negative consequences. For example, children who are punished for misbehaving may continue to misbehave if punishment is the only form of attention they seem to be able to earn.

Extinction strategies are useful in therapy when dysfunctional behaviors have been maintained by unrecognized reinforcing circumstances. Those reinforcers can be identified through a careful situational analysis, and then a program can be arranged to withhold them in the presence of the undesirable response. When this approach is possible, and everyone in the situation who might inadvertently reinforce the person's behavior cooperates, extinction procedures work to diminish the frequency of the behavior and eventually to eliminate the behavior completely.

Once unrecognized reinforcers have been identified and controlled, extinction can be used to diminish and eliminate dysfunctional behaviors.

Even psychotic behavior can be maintained and encouraged by unintentional reinforcement. Consider the following circumstances. It is standard procedure in many mental hospitals for the staff to ask patients frequently, as a form of social communication, how they are feeling. Patients often misinterpret this question as a request for diagnostic information, and they respond by thinking and talking about their feelings, unusual symptoms, and hallucinations. Such responding is likely to be counterproductive, since it leads staff to conclude that the patients are self-absorbed and not behaving normally. In fact, the more bizarre the symptoms and verbalizations, the more attention the staff members may show to the patient, which reinforces continued expression of bizarre symptoms. Dramatic decreases in psychotic behavior have been observed when hospital staff members were simply instructed to ignore the psychotic behavior and to give attention to the patients only when they were behaving normally (Ayllon & Michael, 1959).

Social-Learning Therapy

The range of behavior therapies has been expanded by social learning theorists who point out that humans learn by observing the behavior of other people. Often you learn and apply rules to new experiences through symbolic means, such as watching other people's experiences in life, in a movie, or on TV. **Social-learning therapy** is designed to modify problematic behavior patterns by arranging conditions in which a client will observe models being reinforced for a desirable form of responding. This vicarious learning process has been of special value in overcoming phobias and building social skills. We have noted in earlier chapters that this social-learning theory was largely developed through the pioneering research of **Albert Bandura** (1977, 1986). Here we will mention only two aspects of his approach: imitation of models and social-skills training.

Social-learning therapy has proven to be valuable in helping patients overcome phobias and build social skills.

Imitation of Models

Social-learning theory predicts that individuals acquire responses through observation. It should be the case, thus, that fears can be learned vicariously, through the transmission of fear displayed by others, such as from mother to child. A series of studies with monkeys illustrates this imitation of modeled behavior.

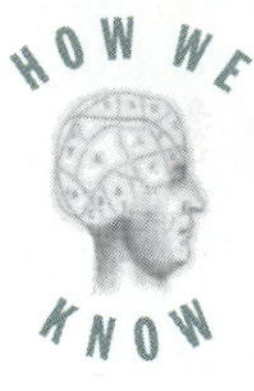

Young monkeys reared in the laboratory, where they never saw a snake, observed their parents, who had been raised in the wild, react fearfully to real snakes and toy snakes. In less than ten minutes, the young monkeys showed a strong fear of snakes, and, by the sixth modeling session, their fear was as intense as that of their parents. The more disturbed the parents were at the sight of the snakes, the greater the fear in their offspring (Mineka et al., 1984).

In a follow-up study, laboratory-raised rhesus monkeys observed the fearful reactions of adult monkeys who were strangers to them. As can be seen in **Figure 18.1**, the young monkeys showed little fear initially in the pretest. After observing models reacting fearfully, they also did so, both to the real and to the toy snakes. This fear persisted in intensity when measured three months later. However, the fear was less strong and showed more variation than that of the monkeys who had observed their own parents' fearful reactions (Cook et al., 1985).

If snake fears can be learned by observing others' fear reactions, then it should also be possible for people with snake phobias to unlearn fear reactions through imitation of models. In treating a phobia of snakes, a therapist will first demonstrate fearless approach behavior at a relatively minor level, perhaps approaching a snake's cage or touching a snake. The client is aided, through demonstration and encouragement, to imitate the modeled behavior. Gradually the approach behaviors are shaped so that the client can pick the snake up and let it crawl freely over him or her. At no time is the client

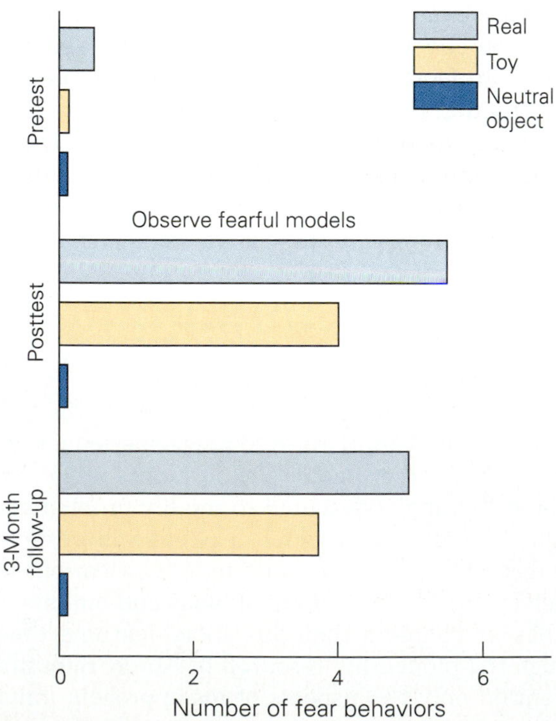

Figure 18.1 Fear Reactions in Monkeys
After young laboratory-raised monkeys observe unfamiliar adult monkeys showing a strong fear of snakes, they are vicariously conditioned to fear snakes with an intensity that persists over time.

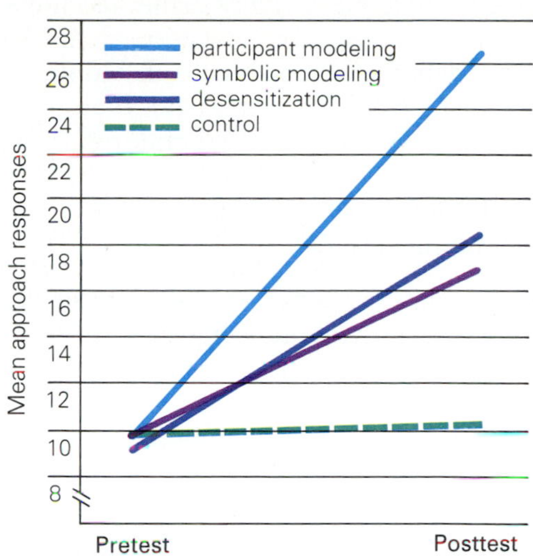

Figure 18.2 Participant Modeling Therapy

The subject shown in the photo first watched a model make a graduated series of snake-approach responses and then repeated them herself. She eventually was able to pick up the snake and let it crawl about on her. The graph compares the number of approach responses subjects made before and after receiving participant modeling therapy (most effective) with the behavior of those exposed to two other therapeutic techniques and a control group.

forced to perform any behavior. Resistance at any level is overcome by having the client return to a previously successful, less threatening approach behavior.

The power of this form of **participant modeling** can be seen in research comparing this technique with symbolic modeling, desensitization, and a control condition. In *symbolic modeling therapy,* subjects who had been trained in relaxation techniques watched a film in which several models fearlessly handled snakes; the subjects could stop the film and try to relax whenever a scene made them feel anxious. In the control condition, no therapeutic intervention was used. As you can see in **Figure 18.2**, participant modeling was clearly the most successful of these techniques. Snake phobia was eliminated in 11 of the 12 subjects in the participant modeling group (Bandura, 1970).

Participant modeling has proven to be more effective than other procedures for treating phobias.

Social-Skills Training

A major therapeutic innovation encouraged by social-learning therapists involves training people with inadequate social skills to be more effective (Hersen & Bellack, 1976). Many difficulties arise for someone with a mental disorder, or even just an everyday problem, if he or she is socially inhibited, inept, or unassertive. *Social skills* are sets of responses that enable people to effectively achieve their social goals when approaching or interacting with others. These skills include knowing *what* (content) to say and do in given situations in order to elicit a desired response (consequences), *how* (style) to say and do it, and *when* (timing) to say and do it. One of the most common social-skills problems is lack of assertiveness—inability to state one's own thoughts or wishes in a clear, direct, nonaggressive manner (Alberti & Emmons, 1990; Bower & Bower, 1991). To help people overcome such a problem, many social-learning therapists recommend **behavioral rehearsal**—visualizing how one should behave in a given situation and the desired positive consequences (Yates, 1985). Rehearsal can be used to establish and

Behavioral rehearsal is often used to help clients learn social skills and other basic skills.

strengthen any basic skill, from personal hygiene to work habits to social interactions.

Adult pathology is often preceded by deficits in social skills in childhood (Oden & Asher, 1977). Therefore, considerable research and therapy is directed at building competence in withdrawn and disturbed children (Conger & Keane, 1981; Zimbardo & Radl, 1981). For example, one study demonstrated that preschool-age children diagnosed as *social isolates* could be helped to become sociable in a short training period.

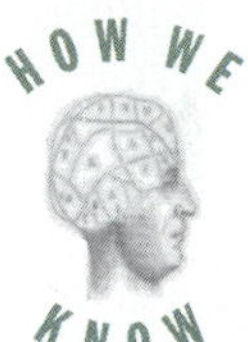

Twenty-four subjects were randomly assigned to one of three play conditions: with a same-age peer, with a peer 1 to 1½ years younger, or with no partner (control condition). The pairs were brought together for ten play sessions, each only 20 minutes long, over a period of about a month. Their classroom behavior before and after this treatment was recorded, and it revealed that the intervention had a strong effect. The opportunity to play with a younger playmate doubled the frequency with which the former social isolates interacted later on with other classmates—bringing them up to the average level of the other children. Playing with a same-age peer also increased children's sociability, but not nearly so much. The researchers concluded that the one-on-one play situation had offered the shy children safe opportunities to be socially assertive. They were able to practice leadership skills with the nonthreatening, younger playmates (Furman et al., 1979).

In another study, social-skills training with a group of hospitalized emotionally disturbed children changed both verbal and nonverbal components of their behavior in social settings (Matson et al., 1980). The children were taught to give appropriate verbal responses in various social situations (giving help or compliments, making requests). They were also taught to display appropriate affect (for example, to smile while giving a compliment) and to make eye contact and use proper body posture (face the person being talked to). These improved social skills generalized outside of training: the children put them into practice on their own when on the ward. These positive effects continued even months later.

Generalization Techniques

An ongoing issue of concern for behavior therapists is whether new behavior patterns generated in a therapeutic setting will actually be used in the everyday situations faced by their clients (Kazdin, 1994). This question is important for all therapies, because any measure of treatment effectiveness must include maintenance of long-term changes that go beyond a therapist's couch, clinic, or laboratory.

When essential aspects of a client's real-life setting are absent from the therapy program, behavioral changes accomplished through therapy may be lost over time after therapy terminates. To prevent this gradual loss, it is becoming common practice to build generalization techniques into the therapeutic procedure itself. These techniques attempt to *increase* the similarity of target behaviors, reinforcers, models, and stimulus demands between therapy and real-life settings. For example, behaviors are taught that are likely to be reinforced naturally in a person's environment, such as showing courtesy or consideration. Rewards are given on a partial reinforcement schedule to ensure that their effect will be maintained in the real world, where rewards are not always forthcoming. Expectation of tangible extrinsic rewards is gradually *faded out,* while social approval and more naturally occurring consequences, including reinforcing self-statements, are incorporated.

Behavioral therapists use a variety of strategies to ensure that behavioral changes will transfer into real-life settings and will last after therapy terminates.

Table 18.2 Comparison of Psychoanalytic and Behavioral Approaches to Psychotherapy

Issue	Psychoanalysis	Behavior Therapy
Basic human nature	Biological instincts, primarily sexual and aggressive, press for immediate release, bringing people into conflict with social reality.	Similar to other animals, people are born only with the capacity for learning, which follows similar principles in all species.
Normal human development	Growth occurs through resolution of conflicts during successive stages. Through identification and internalization, mature ego controls and character structures emerge.	Adaptive behaviors are learned through reinforcement and imitation.
Nature of psychopathology	Pathology reflects inadequate conflict resolutions and fixations in earlier development, which leave overly strong impulses and/or weak controls. Symptoms are defensive responses to anxiety.	Problematic behavior derives from faulty learning of maladaptive behaviors. The *symptom* is the problem; there is no *underlying disease.*
Goal of therapy	Psychosexual maturity, strengthened ego functions, and reduced control by unconscious and repressed impulses are attained.	Symptomatic behavior is eliminated and replaced with adaptive behaviors.
Psychological realm emphasized	Motives, feelings, fantasies, and cognitions are experienced.	Therapy involves behavior and observable feelings and actions.
Time orientation	The orientation is discovering and interpreting past conflicts and repressed feelings in light of the present.	There is little or no concern with early history or etiology. Present behavior is examined and treated.
Role of unconscious material	This is primary in classical psychoanalysis and somewhat less emphasized by neo-Freudians.	There is no concern with unconscious processes or with subjective experience even in the conscious realm.
Role of insight	Insight is central; it emerges in "corrective emotional experiences."	Insight is irrelevant and/or unnecessary.
Role of therapist	The therapist functions as a *detective,* searching basic root conflicts and resistances; detached and neutral, to facilitate transference reactions.	The therapist functions as a *trainer,* helping patients unlearn old behaviors and/or learn new ones. Control of reinforcement is important; interpersonal relationship is minor.

Behavior therapists, for example, used a fading procedure with a 7-year-old boy who frequently stole from his classmates (Rosen & Rosen, 1983). The boy was fined or awarded "points "(which could be exchanged for reinforcers such as extra recess) when a check revealed whether he did or did not have other children's possessions. At first these checks were made every 15 minutes. Over time, they were faded out to only once every 2 hours. Finally, the possession checks were eliminated. Even after the direct manipulation of reinforcers had been faded out, the boy did not return to stealing.

Before we move on to cognitive therapies, take a few minutes to review the major differences between the two psychotherapies outlined thus far—the psychoanalytic and the behavioral—as summarized in **Table 18.2**.

COGNITIVE THERAPIES

Cognitive therapy attempts to change problem feelings and behaviors by changing the way a client thinks about significant life experiences. The underlying assumption of such therapy is that abnormal behavior patterns and emotional distress start with problems in *what* people think (cognitive content) and *how* they think (cognitive process). Cognitive therapies focus on changing different types of cognitive processes and provide different methods of cognitive restructuring. We discussed some of these approaches in Chapter 13 as ways to cope with stress and improve health. In this section, we will describe two major forms of cognitive therapy: cognitive behavior modification (including self-efficacy training) and alteration of false belief systems (including cognitive therapy for depression and rational-emotive therapy).

The underlying assumption of cognitive therapy is that abnormal behavior patterns and emotional distress begin with cognitive content and processes.

Cognitive Behavior Modification

You are what you tell yourself you can be, and you are guided by what you believe you ought to do. This is a starting assumption of **cognitive behavior modification.** This therapeutic approach combines the cognitive emphasis on the role of thoughts and attitudes in influencing motivation and response with the behavioral focus on reinforcement contingencies in the modification of performance. Unacceptable behavior patterns are modified by changing a person's negative *self-statements* into constructive coping statements.

In cognitive behavior modification, unacceptable behavior patterns are modified by changing a person's negative self-statements into constructive coping statements.

A critical part of this therapeutic approach is the discovery by therapist and client of the way the client thinks about and expresses the problem for which therapy is sought. Once both therapist and client understand the kind of thinking that is leading to unproductive or dysfunctional behaviors, they develop new self-statements that are constructive and minimize the use of self-defeating ones that elicit anxiety or reduce self-esteem (Meichenbaum, 1977, 1985). For example, they might substitute the negative self-statement "I was really boring at that party; they'll never ask me back" with constructive criticism: "Next time, if I want to appear interesting, I will plan some provocative opening lines, practice telling a good joke, and be responsive to the host's stories." Instead of dwelling on negatives in past situations that are unchangeable, the client is taught to focus on positives in the future.

Building *expectations of being effective* increases the likelihood of behaving effectively. Through setting attainable goals, developing realistic strategies for attaining them, and evaluating feedback realistically, you develop a sense of mastery and *self-efficacy* (Bandura, 1986, 1992). As we saw in Chapter 14, your sense of self-efficacy influences your perceptions, motivation, and performance in many ways. Self-efficacy judgments influence how much effort you expend and how long you persist in the face of difficult life situations (Schwarzer, 1992). The modeling procedures we described earlier allow individuals to increase feelings of *behavioral* self-efficacy: they learn that they can carry out a certain range of behaviors. In contrast, therapy for *cognitive* self-efficacy changes the way clients think about their abilities.

Suppose you were learning to knit. Assuming you wanted to get better at it over time, what would be the best internal message to give yourself about the activity?

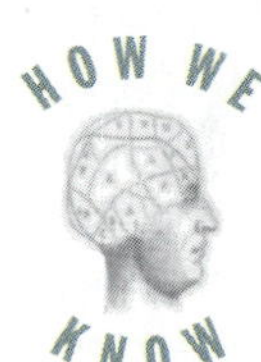

In one experiment, two groups of graduate students in business studies were asked to make a series of critical decisions for a simulated organization. One group of students was encouraged to think of decision-making skill as a reflection of their underlying cognitive capabilities; performance on the simulation task would serve as a gauge of their capacity. The other group was encouraged to think of decision-making skill as something that is developed through practice; experience with the simulation task would enhance their abilities. Those students who believed that they could acquire skills showed increasing self-efficacy over time and performed much more successfully than their peers who believed their performance was limited by their own underlying capacity (Wood & Bandura, 1989).

In this experiment, types of thought like "I can learn to do better" actually allowed the students to become better. (This study should call to mind our discussion, in Chapter 15, of the societal costs of believing that "intelligent performance" is limited by innate ability.)

Changing False Beliefs

Some cognitive behavior therapists have, as their primary targets for change, beliefs, attitudes, and habitual thought patterns. These cognitive therapists argue that many psychological problems arise because of the way people think about themselves in relation to other people and the events they face. Faulty thinking can be based on (1) unreasonable attitudes ("Being perfect is the most important trait for a student to have"), (2) false premises ("If I do everything they want me to, then I'll be popular"), and (3) rigid rules that put behavior on automatic pilot so that prior patterns are repeated even when they have not worked ("I must obey authorities"). Emotional distress is caused by cognitive misunderstandings and by failure to distinguish between current reality and one's imagination (or expectations).

Cognitive Therapy for Depression

A cognitive therapist helps a patient to correct faulty patterns of thinking by substituting more effective problem-solving techniques. **Aaron Beck** has successfully pioneered cognitive therapy for the problem of depression. He states the formula for treatment in simple form: "The therapist helps the patient to identify his warped thinking and to learn more realistic ways to formulate his experiences" (1976, p. 20). For example, depressed individuals may be instructed to write down negative thoughts about themselves, figure out why these self-criticisms are unjustified, and come up with more realistic (and less destructive) self-cognitions.

Aaron Beck's treatment for depression is to change negative cognitions by challenging the client's basic assumptions about his or her functioning.

Beck believes that depression is maintained because depressed patients are unaware of the negative automatic thoughts that they habitually formulate, such as "I will never be as good as my brother"; "Nobody would like me if they really knew me"; and "I'm not smart enough to make it in this competitive school." A therapist then uses four tactics to change the cognitive foundation that supports the depression (Beck & Rush, 1989; Beck et al., 1979):

- challenging the client's basic assumptions about his or her functioning;
- evaluating the evidence the client has for and against the accuracy of automatic thoughts;
- reattributing blame to situational factors rather than to the patient's incompetence;
- discussing alternative solutions to complex tasks that could lead to failure experiences.

This therapy is similar to behavior therapies in that it centers on the present state of the client.

One of the worst side effects of being depressed is having to live with all the negative feelings and lethargy associated with depression. Becoming obsessed with thoughts about one's negative mood brings up memories of all the bad times in life, which worsens the depressive feelings. By filtering all input through a darkly colored lens of depression, depressed people see criticism where there is none and hear sarcasm when they listen to praise—further "reasons" for being depressed (Diamond, 1989). Cognitive therapies arrest depression's downward spiral by helping the client not to become further depressed about depression itself (Teasdale, 1985).

Rational-Emotive Therapy

One of the earliest forms of cognitive therapy was the **rational-emotive therapy** (RET) developed by **Albert Ellis** (1962, 1977). RET is a comprehensive system of personality change based on the transformation of irrational beliefs that cause undesirable, highly charged emotional reactions, such as severe anxiety. Clients may have core values *demanding* that they succeed and be approved, *insisting* that they be treated fairly, and *dictating* that the universe be more pleasant—a style Ellis refers to as *musturbatory* thinking.

Rational-emotive therapists teach clients how to recognize the "shoulds," "oughts," and "musts" that are controlling their actions and preventing them from choosing the lives they want. They attempt to break through a client's closed-mindedness by showing that an emotional reaction that follows some event is really the effect of unrecognized beliefs about the event. For example, failure to achieve orgasm during intercourse (event) is followed by an emotional reaction of depression and self-derogation. The belief that is causing the emotional reaction is likely to be "I am sexually inadequate and may be impotent or frigid because I failed to perform as expected." In therapy, this belief (and others) is openly disputed through rational confrontation and examination of alternative reasons for the event, such as fatigue, alcohol, false notions of sexual performance, or reluctance to engage in intercourse at that time or with that particular partner. This confrontation technique is followed by other interventions that replace dogmatic, irrational thinking with rational, situationally appropriate ideas.

Albert Ellis's rational-emotive therapy involves the confrontation of irrational beliefs and the examination of alternative explanations for events.

Rational-emotive therapy aims to increase an individual's sense of self-worth and the potential to be self-actualized by getting rid of the system of faulty beliefs that block personal growth. As such, it shares much with humanistic therapies, which we consider next.

EXISTENTIAL-HUMANISTIC THERAPIES

Problems in everyday living, a lack of meaningful human relationships, and an absence of significant goals to strive for are common *existential crises,* according to proponents of humanistic and existentialist perspectives on human nature. These orientations have been combined to form a general type of therapy addressing the basic problems of existence common to all human beings.

The *humanistic movement* has been called a "third force in psychology" because it grew out of a reaction to the two dominant forces with a pessimistic view of human nature: early psychoanalytic theory and the mechanistic view offered by early radical behaviorism. At the time the humanistic movement was forming in the United States, similar viewpoints, which came to be known collectively as *existentialism,* had already gained acceptance in Europe. One of the first American therapists to embrace existentialism was **Rollo May** (1950/1977, 1969, 1972), whose popular books and therapy are designed to combat feelings of emptiness, anomie, and cynicism by emphasizing basic human values, such as love, creativity, and free will.

At the core of both humanistic and existential therapies is the concept of a whole person in the continual process of changing and of becoming. Although environment and heredity place certain restrictions, people always remain free to choose what they will become by creating their own values and committing to them through their own decisions. Along with this *freedom to choose,* however, comes the burden of responsibility. Because you are never fully aware of all the implications of your actions, you experience anxiety and despair. You also suffer from guilt over lost opportunities to achieve your full potential. A new clinical version of existential psychology, which integrates its various themes and approaches, assumes that the bewildering

The existential-humanistic therapies emphasize the concept of the whole person in the continual process of changing and becoming.

realities of modern life give rise to two basic kinds of human maladies. Depressive and obsessive syndromes reflect *retreat* from these realities; sociopathic and narcissistic syndromes reflect *exploitation* of these realities (Schneider & May, 1995).

Psychotherapies that apply the principles of this general theory of human nature attempt to help clients define their own freedom, value their experiencing selves and the richness of the present moment, cultivate their individuality, and discover ways of realizing their fullest potential (self-actualization). Of importance in the existential perspective is the current life situation as experienced by the person—the *phenomenological view.*

The existential-humanistic philosophy also gave rise to the **human-potential movement,** which emerged in the United States in the late 1960s. This movement encompassed methods to enhance the potential of the average human being toward greater levels of performance and greater richness of experience. Through this movement, therapy originally intended for people with psychological disorders was extended to mentally healthy people who wanted to be more effective, more productive, and happier human beings.

Through the human-potential movement of the 1960s, therapy was extended to mentally healthy people who wanted to be more effective, more productive, and happier.

Let's examine therapies in the existential-humanistic tradition.

Person-Centered Therapy

As developed by **Carl Rogers** (1951, 1977), *person-centered therapy* has had a significant impact on the way many different kinds of therapists define their relationships to their clients. The primary goal of **person-centered therapy** is to promote the healthy psychological growth of the individual.

Carl Rogers developed person-centered therapy, an optimistic treatment aimed at promoting the healthy psychological growth of the individual.

The approach begins with the assumption that all people share the basic tendency to self-actualize—that is, to realize their potential. Rogers believed that "it is the inherent tendency of the organism to develop all its capacities in ways which seem to maintain or enhance the organism" (1959, p. 196). Healthy development is hindered by faulty learning patterns in which a person accepts the evaluation of others in place of those provided by his or her own mind and body. A conflict between the naturally positive self-image and negative external criticisms creates anxiety and unhappiness. This conflict, or *incongruence,* may function outside of awareness, so that a person experiences feelings of unhappiness and low self-worth without knowing why.

The task of Rogerian therapy is to create a therapeutic environment that allows a client to learn how to behave in order to achieve self-enhancement and self-actualization. Because people are assumed to be basically good, the therapist's task is mainly to help remove barriers that limit the expression of this natural positive tendency. The basic therapeutic strategy is to recognize, accept, and clarify a client's feelings. This is accomplished within an atmosphere of *unconditional positive regard*—nonjudgmental acceptance and respect for the client. The therapist allows his or her own feelings and thoughts to be transparent to the client. In addition to maintaining this *genuineness,* the therapist tries to experience the client's feelings. Such total empathy requires that the therapist care for the client as a worthy, competent individual—not to be judged or evaluated but to be assisted in discovering his or her individuality (Meador & Rogers, 1979).

The emotional style and attitude of the therapist is instrumental in *empowering* the client to attend once again to the true sources of personal conflict and to remove the distracting influences that suppress self-actualization. Unlike practitioners of other therapies, who interpret, give answers, or instruct, the person-centered therapist is a supportive listener who reflects and, at times, restates the client's evaluative statements and feelings. Person-centered therapy strives to be *nondirective* by having the therapist merely facilitate the client's search for self-awareness and self-acceptance.

Rogers believes that, once freed to relate to others openly and to accept themselves, individuals have the potential to lead themselves back to psychological health. This optimistic view and the humane relationship between therapist-as-caring-expert and client-as-person have influenced many practitioners (Smith, 1982).

Group Therapies

All the treatment approaches outlined thus far are primarily designed as one-on-one relationships between a patient or client and a therapist. Many people, however, now experience therapy as part of a group. There are several reasons why group therapy has flourished and, in some cases, may even be more effective than individual therapy (Klein, 1983; Rosenbaum & Berger, 1975). Some advantages are practical. Group therapy is less expensive to participants and makes small numbers of mental health personnel available more widely. Other advantages relate to the power of the group setting. The group (1) is a less threatening situation for people who have problems dealing on their own with authority; (2) allows group processes to be used to influence individual maladaptive behavior; (3) provides people with opportunities to observe and practice interpersonal skills within the therapy session; (4) provides an analogue of the primary family group, which enables corrective emotional experiences to take place.

Some of the basic premises of group therapies differ from those of individual therapy. The social setting of group therapies provides an opportunity to learn how one comes across to others, how the self-image that is projected differs from the one that is intended or personally experienced. In addition, the group provides confirmation that one's symptoms, problems, and "deviant" reactions are not unique but often are quite common. Because people tend to conceal from others negative information about themselves, it is possible for many people with the same problem to believe "It's only me." The shared group experience can help to dispel this pluralistic ignorance in which many share the same false belief about their unique failings. In addition, the group of peers can provide social support outside the therapy setting.

Gestalt Therapy

Gestalt therapy focuses on ways to unite mind and body to make a person whole (recall the Gestalt school of perception, described in Chapter 8). Its

Group therapies are available for a wide range of problems and life circumstances.

In the United States, between 7 and 10 million people attend self-help groups every week.

goal of self-awareness is reached by helping group participants express pent-up feelings and recognize unfinished business from past conflicts that is carried into new relationships and must be completed for growth to proceed. **Fritz Perls** (1969), the originator of Gestalt therapy, asked participants to act out fantasies concerning conflicts and strong feelings and also to re-create their dreams, which he saw as repressed parts of personality. Perls said, "We have to *re-own* these projected, fragmented parts of our personality, and re-own the hidden potential that appears in the dream" (1969, p. 67). In Gestalt therapy workshops, therapists borrow the temporal focus of Zen teachings to make the clients aware of emerging feelings, attitudes, and actions.

Fritz Perls originated Gestalt therapy, encouraging his clients to act out fantasies and to re-create their dreams in order to achieve greater self-awareness.

Community Support Groups

A dramatic development in therapy has been the surge of interest and participation in self-help groups. It is estimated that between 7 and 10 million adults attend such groups every week (Jacobs & Goodman, 1989). These support group sessions are typically free, especially when they are not directed by a health-care professional, and they give people a chance to meet others with the same problems who are surviving and sometimes thriving. The self-help concept applied to community group settings was pioneered by Alcoholics Anonymous, but it was the women's consciousness-raising movement of the 1960s that helped to extend self-help beyond the arena of alcoholism. Now support groups deal with four basic categories of problems: addictive behavior, physical and mental disorders, life transition or other crises, and the traumas experienced by friends or relatives of those with serious problems. Researchers have only recently begun to investigate what properties of self-help groups can make them most effective (Christensen & Jacobson, 1994).

A valuable development in self-help is the application of group therapy techniques to the situations of terminally ill patients. The goals of such therapy are to help patients and their families live lives as fulfilling as possible during their illnesses, to cope realistically with impending death, and to adjust to the terminal illness (Adams, 1979; Yalom & Greaves, 1977). One general focus of such support groups for the terminally ill is to help each patient learn how to live fully until they "say goodbye" (Nungesser, 1990).

Virtually every community now has a self-help clearinghouse you can phone to find out where and when a local group that addresses a given problem meets. The National Self-Help Clearinghouse number is 212-642-2944.

Therapy for Drinking Problems

Most people have an occasional beer or glass of wine in social settings. For some people, however, alcohol becomes the center of their lives. Their personal relationships and day-to-day functioning are severely impaired by the craving for alcohol and the consequences of drunkenness. Fortunately, many alcoholics seek help. (Some, of course, are forced to seek help through the legal system.) What types of therapy have been most successful?

A major division in treatment programs concerns the extent to which recovering alcoholics should ever drink at all. The debate contrasts the total *abstinence approach,* popularized by Alcoholics Anonymous (AA), and a *controlled drinking approach,* which permits limited drinking within a program of individual behavior therapy. Conventional wisdom suggests that alcoholism is a disease that is largely genetically determined and thus out of the jurisdiction of voluntary control. Conventional wisdom is partly right and partly wrong. Research evidence strongly suggests that a predisposition to alcoholism is genetically linked (Kendler et al., 1992; McGue et al., 1992; Pickens et al., 1991). For example, if one identical twin is alcoholic, the other twin is also alcoholic 46.9 percent of the time. For fraternal twins, the figure is 31.5 percent (Kendler et al., 1992). Even so, genetic factors always interact with behavioral, social-group, and other environmental factors (Peele, 1985). The treatment decision, between abstinence and controlled drinking, is whether any alcohol at all should be allowed in the environment.

The recommendation of abstinence as a necessary model for alcoholism has a good deal of cultural support. Most people are familiar with the 12-step program of Alcoholics Anonymous (AA). This program involves acknowledging one's powerlessness over the "disease" and turning to a "higher being" for needed help. Members attend regular group meetings involving a "buddy" system that offers social support from and to fellow recovering alcoholics. How popular is AA? There are about 1.7 million members in 87,000 AA groups in 50 countries around the world. Testimonies abound of its force in helping individuals deal with their alcohol problems (McCrady & Miller, 1993). The abstinence model is also embraced by the American Medical Association and the National Institute on Alcohol Abuse and Alcoholism.

Unfortunately, conventional abstinence treatments, including that practiced by AA, have little demonstrated effectiveness for alcohol problems (Edwards, 1980; Miller & Hester, 1980). As one critic put it, "That 12-step groups (and the related disease-model of addiction) should have such apparent popularity and renown coupled with a lack of empirical support and actual attendance, is a fascinating phenomenon ..." (Horvath, 1991, p. 13). The Institute of Medicine (1989) has estimated that only 20 percent of those with alcohol problems who are referred to AA ever attend meetings regularly. The 1990 report to Congress by the Secretary of Health and Human Services concluded that the effectiveness of AA had not been scientifically documented and that methodological problems made such an evaluation difficult. A conference for professionals working in the area of alcohol treatment has outlined the necessary conditions for designing studies to generate new and desirable knowledge about the treatment effectiveness of AA (McCrady & Miller, 1993). This should encourage appropriate evaluation research to answer the seemingly simple question, Does AA work as claimed?

What about the idea that alcoholics can safely drink small amounts of alcohol? The *controlled-drinking controversy* was triggered by the 1962 report by British physician D. L. Davies. This report challenged the traditional emphasis on total abstinence by showing that the vast majority of alcoholics participating in controlled drinking maintained moderate, nonproblematic drinking over many years. The controversy was revived a decade later with the publication of a detailed, large-scale study by Mark and Linda Sobell, a pair of behavioral psychologists (1973). Their individualized behavior therapy for alcoholics included many of the behavioral strategies we outlined earlier in the chapter but used them in conjunction with controlled amounts of drinking. The success of the Sobells' therapy was challenged by other researchers (Pendery et al., 1982) and ridiculed on the popular TV program *60 Minutes* (3/6/83), leading to several independent investigations of their scientific integrity and evaluation of their data. They were completely vindicated by these investigations (Marlatt, 1983; Sobell & Sobell, 1984). (See Ellis & Velten, 1992, for a self-help alternative to AA based on rational-emotive therapy.)

So what works? Controlled-drinking therapy is best for younger problem drinkers who have no signs of physical dependence, while abstinence may be called for only with older chronic alcoholics who show evidence of organic consequences of alcohol dependence. Alcoholism is the disease that results from excessive, long-term drinking; it is not the cause of such drinking. In opposing the disease-abstinence-sin model of alcoholism, psychological researchers and therapists are sometimes taking an unpopular path, but one that needs to be traveled.

Marital and Family Therapy

Much group therapy consists of strangers coming together periodically to form temporary associations from which they may benefit. Marital and family therapy brings meaningful, existing units into a group therapy setting.

Couples counseling for marital problems seeks to clarify the typical communication patterns of the partners and then to improve the quality of their interaction (Dattilio & Padesky, 1990; Greenberg & Johnson, 1988; O'Leary, 1987). By seeing a couple together, and often videotaping and replaying their interactions, a therapist can help them appreciate the verbal and nonverbal styles they use to dominate, control, or confuse each other. Each party is taught how to reinforce desirable responding in the other and withdraw reinforcement for undesirable reactions. They are also taught nondirective listening skills to help the other person clarify and express feelings and ideas. Couples therapy is more effective in resolving marital problems than is individual therapy for only one partner, and it has been shown to reduce marital crises and keep marriages intact (Cookerly, 1980; Gurman & Kniskern, 1978).

Couples therapy is more effective in resolving marital problems than is individual therapy for only one partner, and has been shown to reduce marital crises and keep marriages intact.

In *family therapy,* the client is a whole nuclear family, and each family member is treated as a member of a *system* of relationships (Minuchin, 1974; Schwebel & Fine, 1994). A family therapist works with troubled family members to help them perceive what is creating problems for one or more of them. The focus is on altering the *psychological spaces* between people and the interpersonal dynamics of people acting as a unit, rather than on changing processes within maladjusted individuals (Foley, 1979).

Family therapy can reduce tensions within a family and improve the functioning of individual members by helping clients recognize the positive as well as the negative aspects in their relationships. **Virginia Satir** (1967), an innovative developer of family therapy approaches, noted that the family therapist plays many roles, acting as an interpreter and clarifier of the interactions that are taking place in the therapy session and as influence agent, mediator, and referee. Most family therapists assume that the problems brought into therapy represent *situational* difficulties between people or problems of social interaction, rather than *dispositional* aspects of individuals. These difficulties may develop over time as members are forced into or accept unsatisfying roles. Nonproductive communication patterns may be set up in response to natural transitions in a family situation—loss of a job, a child's going to school, dating, getting married, or having a baby. The job of the family therapist is to understand the structure of the family and the many forces acting on it. Then he or she works with the family members to dissolve "dysfunctional" structural elements while creating and maintaining new, more effective structures (Fishman, 1993).

Family therapists focus on the family dynamics rather than on changing one maladapted individual.

Family therapies are our last example of types of therapies that are based purely on psychological interventions. We will now analyze how biomedical therapies work to alter the body in order to affect the mind.

BIOMEDICAL THERAPIES

The ecology of the mind is held in delicate balance. When something goes wrong with the brain, we see the consequences in abnormal patterns of behavior and peculiar cognitive and emotional reactions. Similarly, environmental, social, or behavioral disturbances, such as drugs and violence, can alter brain chemistry and function. Biomedical therapies most often treat mental disorders as "hardware problems" in the brain. We will describe three biomedical approaches to alleviating the symptoms of psychological disorders: psychosurgery, electroconvulsive shock, and drug therapies.

Psychosurgery and Electroconvulsive Therapy

The headline in the *Los Angeles Times* read, "Bullet in the Brain Cures Man's Mental Problem" (2/23/1988). The article revealed that a 19-year-old man suffering from severe obsessive-compulsive disorder had shot a .22-caliber bullet through the front of his brain in a suicide attempt. Remarkably, he survived, his pathological symptoms were cured, and his intellectual capacity was not affected, although some of the underlying causes of his problems remained.

This case illustrates the potential effects of one of the most direct biomedical therapies: surgical intervention in the brain. Such intervention involves lesioning (severing) connections between parts of the brain or removing small sections of the brain. These therapies are often considered methods of last resort to treat psychopathologies that have proven intractable to other, less extreme forms of therapy.

Psychosurgery is the general term for surgical procedures performed on brain tissue to alleviate psychological disorders. In medieval times, psychosurgery involved "cutting the stone of folly" from the brains of those

In medieval times, those suffering from madness were sometimes treated by cutting "the stone of folly" from their brains.

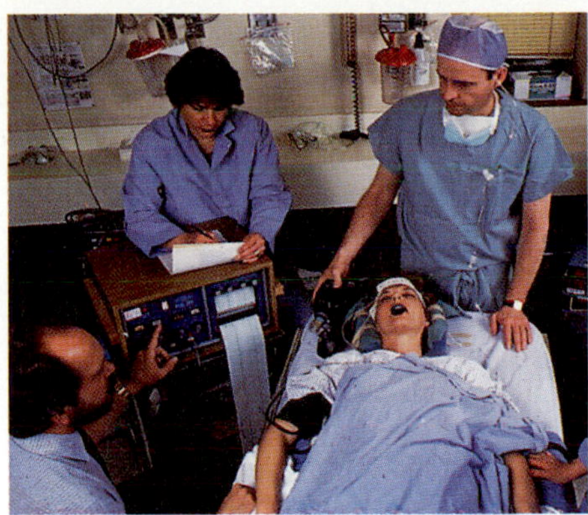
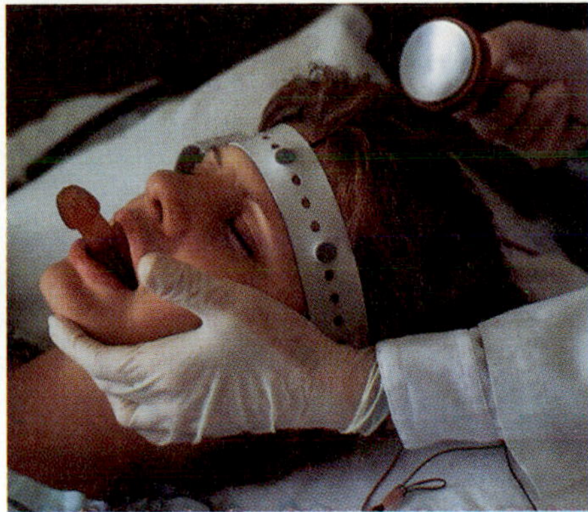

Electroconvulsive therapy has been effective in cases of severe depression.

suffering from madness, as shown vividly in many engravings and paintings from that era, like that on the facing page.

Modern psychosurgical procedures include severing the fibers of the corpus callosum to reduce violent seizures of epilepsy, as we saw in Chapter 4; severing pathways that mediate limbic system activity (amygdalotomy); and prefrontal lobotomy. The best-known form of psychosurgery is the **prefrontal lobotomy**, an operation that severs the white-matter nerve fibers connecting the frontal lobes of the brain with the diencephalon, especially those fibers of the thalamic and hypothalamic areas. The procedure was developed by neurologist **Egas Moniz**, who, in 1949, won a Nobel Prize for this treatment, which seemed to transform the functioning of mental patients.

The original candidates for lobotomy were agitated schizophrenic patients and patients who were compulsive and anxiety ridden. The effects of this psychosurgery were dramatic: a new personality without intense emotional arousal and, thus, without overwhelming anxiety, guilt, or anger emerged. However, the operation permanently destroyed basic aspects of human nature: lobotomized patients lost their unique personality. The lobotomy resulted in inability to plan ahead, indifference to the opinions of others, childlike actions, and the intellectual and emotional flatness of a person without a coherent sense of self. (One of Moniz's own patients was so distressed by these unexpected consequences that she shot Moniz, partially paralyzing him.) Because the effects of psychosurgery are permanent, its negative effects severe and common, and its positive results less certain, its continued use is very limited (Valenstein, 1980).

Egas Moniz developed prefrontal lobotomy to quiet agitated schizophrenic patients and patients who were compulsive and anxiety ridden.

Electroconvulsive therapy (ECT) is the use of electroconvulsive shock to treat psychiatric disorders such as schizophrenia, mania, and, most often, depression. The technique consists of applying weak electric current (75 to 100 volts) to a patient's temples for a period of time from 1/10 to a full second until a convulsion occurs. The convulsion usually runs its course in 45 to 60 seconds. Patients are prepared for this traumatic intervention by sedation with a short-acting barbiturate and muscle relaxant, which renders the patient unconscious and minimizes the violent physical reactions (Abrams, 1992; Malitz & Sackheim, 1984).

Electroconvulsive therapy is used in the treatment of schizophrenia, mania, and depression.

Electroconvulsive therapy has proven extremely successful at alleviating the symptoms of serious depression—more successful, in fact, than some of the drug therapies we will review in the next section (Scovern & Kilmann, 1980). ECT is particularly important because it works quickly. Typically the symptoms of depression are alleviated in a three- or four-day course of treatment, as compared with the one- to two-week time window for drug therapies. Even so, most therapists hold ECT as a treatment of last resort.

ECT is often reserved for emergency treatment for suicidal or severely malnourished, depressed patients and for patients who do not respond to antidepressant drugs or can't tolerate their side effects.

If ECT is so effective, why has it so often been demonized? For example, in 1982, the citizens of Berkeley, California, voted to ban the use of electroconvulsive shock in any of their community mental health facilities (the action was later overturned on legal grounds). In part, this opposition underscored a theme in Ken Kesey's *One Flew over the Cuckoo's Nest* (1962): Be wary of any "therapy" that might be a disguised form of institutional suppression of dissent. Scientific unease with ECT centers largely on the lack of understanding of how it works. The therapy was originated when clinicians observed that patients who suffered both from schizophrenia and epilepsy showed improvement in their schizophrenic symptoms after epileptic seizures. The clinicians conjectured that the same effect could be obtained with artificially induced seizures. Although the conjecture proved correct, in part—ECT is much more effective at alleviating depression than schizophrenia—researchers have yet to fit a definitive theory to this chance observation.

Critics have also worried about potential side effects of ECT (Breggin, 1979, 1991). ECT produces temporary disorientation and a variety of memory deficits. Patients often suffer amnesia for events in the period of time preceding the treatment; the amnesia becomes more severe the longer the course of treatment. Research has shown, however, that patients generally recover their specific memories within months of the treatment (Calev et al., 1991). Furthermore, patients who had received a lifetime course of over 100 ECT treatments showed no deficit in functioning compared with a control group of patients who had never received ECT (Devanand et al., 1991). As a way of minimizing even short-term deficits, ECT is now often administered to only one side of the brain so as to reduce the possibility of speech impairment. Such unilateral ECT is an effective antidepressant (Scovern & Kilmann, 1980).

Let's now see why drug therapies are the most popular form of biomedical interventions for psychopathology.

Drug Therapy

In the history of the treatment of mental disorder, nothing has rivaled the revolution created by the discovery of drugs that can calm anxious patients, restore contact with reality in withdrawn patients, and suppress hallucinations in psychotic patients. This new therapeutic era began in 1953 with the introduction of tranquilizing drugs, notably *chlorpromazine,* into hospital treatment programs. Emerging drug therapies gained almost instant recognition and status as an effective way to transform patient behavior. **Psychopharmacology** is the branch of psychology that investigates the effects of drugs on behavior. Researchers in psychopharmacology work to understand the effect drugs have on some biological system and the consequent changes in responding.

The discovery of **drug therapies** had profound effects on the treatment of severely disordered patients. No longer did mental hospital staff have to act as guards, putting patients in seclusion or straitjackets; staff morale improved as rehabilitation replaced mere custodial care of the mentally ill (Swazey, 1974). Moreover, the drug therapy revolution had a great impact on the U.S. mental hospital population. Over half a million people were living in mental institutions in 1955, staying an average of several years. The introduction of chlorpromazine and other drugs reversed the steadily increasing numbers of patients. By the early 1970s, it was estimated that fewer than half the country's mental patients actually resided in mental hospitals; those who did were institutionalized for an average of only a few months.

With the advent of drug therapy, institutionalization declined significantly.

Three major categories of drugs are used today in therapy programs: *antipsychotic, antidepressant,* and *antianxiety* compounds. As their names suggest, these drugs chemically alter specific brain functions that are responsible for psychotic symptoms, depression, and extreme anxiety.

Antipsychotic Drugs

Antipsychotic drugs alter the schizophrenic symptoms of delusions, hallucinations, social withdrawal, and occasional agitation (Gitlin, 1990; Holmes, 1994; Kane & Marder, 1993). Antipsychotic drugs work by reducing the activity of the neurotransmitter dopamine in the brain. Drugs like *chlorpromazine* (marketed under the U.S. brand name *Thorazine*) and *haloperidol* (marketed as *Haldol*) block or reduce the sensitivity of dopamine receptors. *Clozapine* (marketed as *Clozaril*), the newest major antipsychotic drug, both directly decreases dopamine activity and increases the level of serotonin activity, which inhibits the dopamine system. Although these drugs function by decreasing the overall level of brain activity, they are not just tranquilizers. For many patients they do much more than merely eliminate agitation. They also relieve or reduce the positive symptoms of schizophrenia, including delusions and hallucinations.

Antipsychotic drugs alter schizophrenic symptoms by reducing the activity of the neurotransmitter dopamine in the brain.

There are, unfortunately, negative side effects of antipsychotic drugs. Because dopamine plays a role in motor control, muscle disturbances frequently accompany a course of drug treatment. *Tardive dyskinesia* is a particular disturbance of motor control, especially of the facial muscles, caused by antipsychotic drugs. Patients who develop this side effect experience involuntary jaw, lip, and tongue movements. The newer drug clozapine blocks dopamine receptors more selectively, resulting in a lower probability of motor disturbance. Unfortunately, *agranulocytosis,* a rare disease in which the bone marrow stops making white blood cells, develops in 1 to 2 percent of patients treated with clozapine.

Antipsychotic drugs produce negative side effects such as motor disturbances.

Researchers continue to examine the consequences of drug use over long periods of time as well as consequences when patients cease taking the drugs. The rate of relapse when patients go off the drugs is quite high—two thirds have new symptoms within 18 months—but even patients who remain on the drugs have about a one third chance of relapse (Gitlin, 1990). Thus antipsychotic drugs do not cure schizophrenia—they do not eliminate the underlying psychopathology. Fortunately, they are reasonably effective at controlling the disorder's most disruptive symptoms.

Antidepressant Drugs

Antidepressant drugs work by increasing the activity of the neurotransmitters norepinephrine and serotonin (Holmes, 1994). *Tricyclics,* such as *Tofranil* and *Elavil,* reduce the reuptake of the neurotransmitters from the synaptic cleft. *Prozac,* a *bicyclic,* reduces the reuptake of serotonin. The *monoamine oxidase (MAO) inhibitors* limit the action of the enzyme monoamine oxidase, which is responsible for breaking down (metabolizing) norepinephrine. When MAO is inhibited, more of the neurotransmitter is left available.

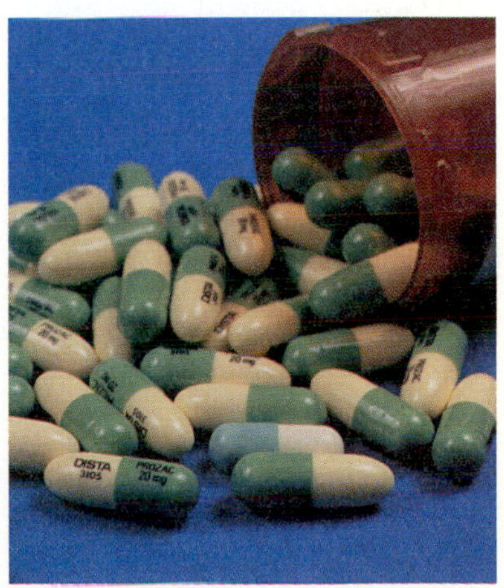

In recent years, Prozac has received wide publicity as the most frequently prescribed antidepressant medication.

Antidepressant drugs are generally successful at relieving the symptoms of depression, although as many as 30 percent of patients will not show improvement (Gitlin, 1990). (Those patients may be candidates for electroconvulsive therapy.) In our Close-up in Chapter 14, we introduced you to Prozac, touted as a miracle drug with therapeutic effects more potent than its competitors. Some psychiatrists are great fans of Prozac (Kramer, 1993). You may recall, however, that critics worry that Prozac not only relieves depression but also "relieves" patients of their personality and creativity (Breggin & Breggin, 1994).

Lithium salts have proven effective in the treatment of bipolar disorders. People who experience uncontrollable periods of hyperexcitement, when their energy seems limitless and their behavior extravagant and flamboyant, are brought down from their state of manic excess by doses of lithium. Up to eight of every ten manic patients treated with lithium have a good chance of recovery, even when other treatments have previously failed (NIMH, 1977). Regular maintenance doses of lithium can help break the cycle of recurring episodes of mania and depression. Lithium allows a person to remain alert and creative (Ehrlich & Diamond, 1980).

Antianxiety Drugs

Like antipsychotic and antidepressant drugs, antianxiety drugs generally have their effect by adjusting the levels of neurotransmitter activity in the brain. Different drugs are most effective at relieving different types of anxiety disorders (Gitlin, 1990; Holmes, 1994; Schatzberg, 1991). Generalized anxiety disorder is best treated with a *benzodiazepine,* such as *Valium* or *Xanax,* which increases the activity of the neurotransmitter GABA. Because GABA regulates inhibitory neurons, increases in GABA activity decrease brain activity in areas of the brain relevant to generalized anxiety responses. Panic disorders, as well as agoraphobia and other phobias, can be treated with antidepressant drugs, although researchers do not yet understand the biological mechanism involved. Obsessive-compulsive disorder, which may arise from low levels of serotonin, responds particularly well to drugs, like Prozac, that specifically affect serotonin function.

Generalized anxiety disorder responds to a benzodiazepine, while panic disorder and phobias are treated with antidepressants. Prozac is effective in cases of obsessive-compulsive disorder.

When Is Drug Therapy Necessary?

We have briefly reviewed some of the possibilities of drug therapies for psychological disorders. There are many circumstances in which courses of medication can vastly improve the lives of sufferers. Any course of drug treatment, however, holds out the possibility of physical or psychological addiction and potentially serious side effects. How do people weigh those factors against the probability of relief? We also have noted that drugs may relieve symptoms but may not cure the underlying pathology. How willing should people be to commit themselves to a lifetime course of drugs?

These questions are made even more intriguing by research demonstrating that some forms of therapy have the same effect on the brain as a course of drug treatment.

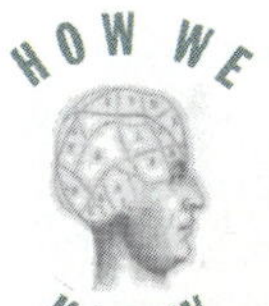

A group of patients with obsessive-compulsive disorders chose to undergo either drug therapy (with *fluoxetine hydrochloride*) or behavior therapy (involving exposure and response prevention). PET scans were performed on the patients' brains before and after treatment. The PET scans detected the same changes in brain function for both forms of therapy (Baxter et al., 1992).

This type of research holds out the exciting possibility that nondrug therapies may have the same healing effect on the brain as drug therapies—without the potential negative aspects of drug therapy.

Research employing PET scans to detect changes in the brain indicates the possibility that nondrug therapies may have the same biological effects as drug therapies.

Choices of one therapy over another often depend on the severity of illness and proven effectiveness of different treatments. For example, whatever their risks, drug treatments for schizophrenia are often essential for patients to have any opportunity for normal living. Let's next examine methods researchers use to assess the effectiveness of different forms of therapy.

DOES THERAPY WORK?

Suppose you have come to perceive a problem in your life that you believe could be alleviated by interaction with a trained clinician. We have mentioned a great variety of types of therapies. How can you know which one of them will work best to relieve your distress? How can you be sure that *any* of them will work? In this section, we examine the projects researchers undertake to test the effectiveness of particular therapies and make comparisons between different therapies. The general goal is to discover the most efficient way to help people overcome distress. We also consider briefly the topic of *prevention:* How can psychologists intervene in people's lives to prevent mental illness before it occurs?

EVALUATING THERAPEUTIC EFFECTIVENESS

British psychologist **Hans Eysenck** (1952) created a furor some years ago by declaring that psychotherapy does not work at all. He reviewed available publications that reported the effects of various therapies and found that patients who received no therapy had just as high a recovery rate as those who received psychoanalysis or other forms of insight therapy. He claimed that roughly two thirds of all people with neurotic problems would recover spontaneously within two years of the onset of the problem.

Researchers met Eysenck's challenge by devising more accurate methodologies to evaluate the effectiveness of therapy. What Eysenck's criticism made clear was that researchers needed to have appropriate control groups. For a variety of reasons, some percentage of individuals in psychotherapy *does* improve without any professional intervention. This **spontaneous-remission effect** is one *baseline* criterion against which the effectiveness of therapies must be assessed. Simply put, doing something must be shown to lead to a greater percentage of improved cases than doing nothing.

Similarly, researchers generally try to demonstrate that their treatment does more than just take advantage of clients' own expectations of healing.

"OF COURSE I'VE BECOME MORE MATURE SINCE YOU STARTED TREATING ME. YOU'VE BEEN AT IT SINCE I WAS 14 YEARS OLD."

The effectiveness of therapy must be measured against the progress a client is likely to make on his or her own.

You may recall our earlier discussions of *placebo* effects: in many cases, people's mental or physical health will improve because they expect that it will improve. The therapeutic situation helps bolster this belief by putting the therapist in the specific social role of *healer* (Fish, 1973; Frank & Frank, 1991). Although the placebo effects of therapy are an important part of the therapeutic intervention, researchers typically wish to demonstrate that their specific form of therapy is more effective than a **placebo therapy** (a neutral therapy that just creates expectations of healing).

Do therapies generally have an effect beyond the baselines of spontaneous recovery or client expectations? One evaluation of nearly 100 therapy-outcome studies found that psychotherapy *did* lead to greater improvement than spontaneous recovery in 80 percent of the cases (Meltzoff & Kornreich, 1970). Thus you can feel a little more confident that the therapeutic experience itself is a useful one for many people much of the time.

More recently, researchers have evaluated therapeutic effectiveness using a statistical technique called meta-analysis. **Meta-analysis** provides a formal mechanism for detecting the general conclusions to be found in data from many different experiments. In many psychological experiments, the researcher asks, "Did most of my subjects show the effect I predicted?" Meta-analysis treats experiments like subjects. With respect to the effectiveness of therapy, the researcher asks, "Did most of the outcome studies show positive changes?" The answer to this question is overwhelmingly yes (Lipsey & Wilson, 1993). Most courses of therapy appear to bring about at least small positive effects that go beyond "no treatment" or "placebo" effects.

Meta-analysis shows that therapy is effective beyond just placebo effects.

Because of such findings, contemporary researchers are less concerned about asking *whether* psychotherapy works and more concerned about asking *why* it works and whether any one treatment is most effective for any particular problem and for certain types of patients (Goldfried et al., 1990). It has not always proven easy, however, to make comparisons between studies that report on different therapies. It is hard to control for differences in therapist experience, duration of therapy, accuracy of the initial diagnosis, type of the disorder, differences in the severity and types of patient difficulties, the kinds of outcome measures used, the fit between a patient's expectations and the type of therapy offered, and length of follow-up times, to name but a handful (Kazdin, 1986; Kazdin & Wilson, 1980; Smith et al., 1980; Smith & Glass, 1977). What can be learned from recent attempts to overcome these problems by focusing on direct comparisons of different treatments for depression?

Depression Treatment Evaluations

Because of depression's high incidence (see Chapter 17), many of the studies that compare different types of therapy have drawn on groups of depressed individuals. One particularly ambitious project was coordinated and funded by the National Institute of Mental Health (NIMH). Its special features included (1) comparisons of the effectiveness of two different forms of brief psychotherapy, a tricyclic drug treatment, and placebo control; (2) careful definition and standardization of the treatments, accomplished by training 28 therapists in each of the four treatment conditions, with each treatment delivered at three different institutions in different cities; (3) random assignment of 240 outpatients who met standard diagnostic criteria for major depressive disorder; (4) standardized assessment procedures to monitor both the process of the therapy (by analysis of therapy-session videotapes, for example) and a battery of outcome measures administered before treatment began, during the 16-week treatment period, at termination, and 18 months later; and (5) independent assessment of the results at an institution separate from any involved in the training or treatment phases of the study (Elkin et al., 1989).

The psychotherapies evaluated were two that had been developed, or modified, especially for the treatment of depression in people outside a hospital setting. The two brief therapies were cognitive behavior therapy and interpersonal psychotherapy, a psychodynamically oriented therapy that focuses on a patient's current life and interpersonal relationships. *Imipramine,* a tricyclic antidepressant, and a placebo control were administered in a double-blind procedure (that is, the experimenters did not know which patients were getting which drugs). Each of the subjects in both the real and the placebo drug treatment was seen weekly by a psychiatrist who provided minimal supportive therapy.

One set of results from this model study of therapy outcome is presented in **Figure 18.3**. The graph shows that each of the treatments for severely depressed patients had an effect beyond that of the placebo control, with the antidepressant drug being most effective and the psychodynamic and cognitive therapies having an intermediate level of effectiveness (Klein & Ross, 1993). Despite the different theoretical orientations of the two psychotherapies—which presuppose different etiologies for depression—the data showed minimal differences between the two on measures that were best suited to each theoretical orientation (Imber et al., 1990). Analyses of other research projects reach much the same conclusions: therapy works (in this case, therapy for depression), but more or less any therapy works about as well as any other (Robinson et al., 1990; Shapiro et al., 1994).

Well-controlled studies of treatments for depression generally conclude that any therapy works about as well as any other.

Note that this conclusion doesn't rule out the possibility that some forms of therapy will be more effective for some individuals. In fact, critics have argued that the standardization and averaging of outcome studies masks the benefits of individualized theory-driven therapy (Persons, 1991). We can find some evidence for this point of view in the data from the NIMH study.

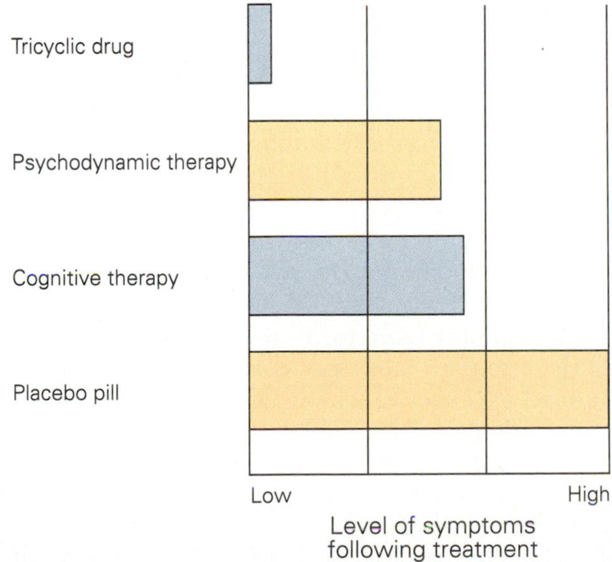

Figure 18.3 Depression Therapies
Symptoms of depression are reduced most substantially by drug therapy, but they are also significantly reduced by psychodynamic and cognitive therapies.

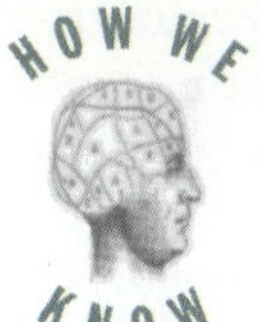

Subjects were divided into groups whose depression was leading to high or low dysfunction in cognitive, work, and social domains. The therapies were differentially effective, depending on the type of a patient's dysfunction. For example, patients with low social dysfunction responded best to interpersonal psychotherapy. Patients with low cognitive dysfunction responded best to cognitive-behavior therapy and imipramine (Sotsky et al., 1991).

These data suggest that although, on average, therapies are equally effective, there is still appropriate fine-tuning for patients with different specific patterns of psychological disorder. Researchers are motivated to develop the optimal therapy for each condition. Let's turn now to some considerations for building better therapies.

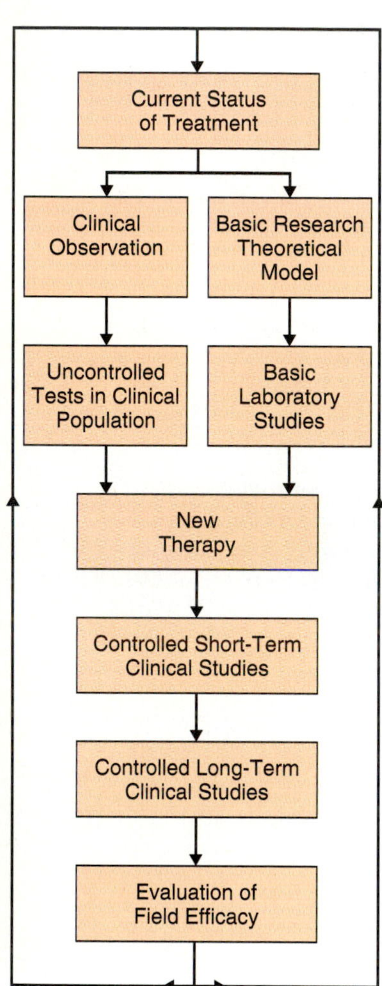

Figure 18.4 Building Better Therapies
Flowchart of stages in the development of treatments for mental/physical disorders.

BUILDING BETTER THERAPIES

Research has shown that virtually all therapies will bring relief. Even so, many researchers work hard to improve on the rate of success. **Figure 18.4** provides a general flowchart for the way theory, clinical observation, and research all play a role in the development and evaluation of any form of treatment (for both mental and physical disorders). It shows the type of systematic research needed to help clinicians discover if their therapies are making the differences that their theories predict. On one side, you see clinical observation—clinicians' own experience with a new procedure. Typically, new treatments first get tested in the field without rigorous experimental control. On the other side of the figure, you see a theory being developed. The theory makes predictions about what *should* work, which may be confirmed in laboratory studies. These two types of insights—clinical and experimental—are combined to yield a new therapy.

In recent years, many innovations in therapy have recognized the fact that traditional therapies may be out of the reach of large segments of the population, for financial or other practical reasons. Those people who rely on health insurance for their mental health care often find that they may be treated for only very specific disorders, over brief periods of time. Researchers have therefore turned their attention to the effectiveness of *time-limited* psychotherapies and alternative types of interventions. One meta-analysis of reported outcomes for 2431 patients in studies for over 30 years indicated that, by the eighth psychotherapy session, approximately half the patients were measurably improved and that 75 percent of the patients were measurably improved after six months of weekly sessions (Howard et al., 1986). Thus it is possible that many people can be aided by even brief courses of psychotherapy. But with the realization that many people cannot afford psychotherapy, however brief, psychologists have also become more interested in the design of self-help groups (Jacobs & Goodman, 1989) and self-administered forms of therapy, like self-help books and audiotapes (Christensen & Jacobson, 1994). Researchers can use their expertise to improve the effectiveness of what, for many people, may be their only source of psychological guidance.

Let's return to the question of how you might choose a therapist for yourself. By now you know that psychotherapy is very likely to help you. What may be most important, therefore, is that you choose a therapist with whom you feel comfortable. Research has shown that outcomes in therapy are improved when there is a secure *working alliance* between the patient or client and the therapist (Horvath & Luborsky, 1993). If you don't feel that you can forge such a bond—if you find a therapist disagreeable or lacking in empathy—find a different therapist.

In the final section of this chapter we reflect upon an important principle of life: whatever the effectiveness of treatment, it is often better to *prevent* a disorder than to heal it once it arises.

By building "mental hygiene" habits, individuals may prevent themselves from needing therapy in the future.

Prevention Strategies

> Two friends were walking on a riverbank. Suddenly, a child swept downstream in the current. One of the friends jumped in the river and rescued the child. Then the two friends resumed their stroll. Suddenly, another child appeared in the water. The rescuer jumped in and again pulled the victim to safety. Soon, a third drowning child swept by. The still-dry friend began to trot up the riverbank. The rescuer yelled, "Hey, where are you going?" The dry one replied, "I'm going to get the bastard that's throwing them in." (Wolman, 1975, p. 3)

The moral of this story is clear: *preventing* a problem is the best solution. The traditional therapies we have examined here share the focus of changing a person who is already distressed or disabled. They begin to do their work after the problem behaviors show up and after the suffering starts. By the time someone elects to go into therapy or is required to, the psychological disorder has "settled in" and had its disruptive effects on the person's daily functioning, social life, job, or career.

The goal of *preventing* psychological problems can be realized at several different levels (Rabins, 1992). *Primary* prevention seeks to prevent a condition before it begins. Steps might be taken, for example, to provide individuals with coping skills so they can be more resilient or to change negative aspects of an environment that might lead to anxiety or depression (Offord, 1987; Weissberg et al., 1991). *Secondary* prevention attempts to limit the duration and severity of a disorder once it has begun. This goal is realized by means of programs that allow for early identification and prompt treatment. *Tertiary* prevention limits the long-term impact of a psychological disorder by seeking to prevent a relapse. Efforts at tertiary prevention require that the causes of a disorder be identified and, as much as possible, eliminated.

The goal of prevention can be realized at the primary, secondary, or tertiary level.

The implementation of these three types of prevention has signaled major shifts in the focus and in the basic paradigms of mental health care. The most important of these paradigm shifts are (1) supplementing treatment with prevention; (2) going beyond a medical disease model to a public health model; (3) focusing on situations and ecologies that put people at risk and away from "at-risk people"; and (4) looking for precipitating factors in life settings rather than for predisposing factors in people (Albee & Joffe, 1977; Price et al., 1980).

The medical model is concerned with treating people who are afflicted; a public health model includes identifying and eliminating the causes of disease and illness that exist in the environment. In this approach, an affected individual is seen as the host or carrier—the end product of an existing process of disease. When programs can change the conditions that breed illness, there will be no need to change people later with expensive, extensive treatments. The dramatic reduction of many contagious and infectious diseases, such as tuberculosis, smallpox, and malaria, came about through this approach. With psychopathology, too, many sources of environmental or organizational stress can be identified. Programs can be designed to alleviate them, thus reducing the number of people who will be exposed. The field of **clinical ecology** expands the boundaries of biomedical therapies by relating disorders, such as anxiety and depression, to environmental irritants, such as chemical solvents, noise pollution, seasonal changes, and radiation (Bell, 1982). Some therapists have broadened the definition of *environment*, as it contributes to psychopathology, to include all features of the external environment that interfere with normal adaptations in daily life (Ghadirian & Lehmann, 1993). These include nutritional influences, psychoactive substances, terrorism, natural disasters, and the availability of social support networks.

Preventing mental disorders is a complex and difficult task. It involves not only understanding the relevant causal factors but overcoming individual, institutional, and governmental resistance to change. A major research effort will be needed to demonstrate the long-range utility of prevention and the public health approach to psychopathology in order to justify the expense in the face of the many other problems that demand immediate solutions. The ultimate goal of prevention programs is to safeguard the mental health of all members of our society.

A PERSONAL ENDNOTE

We have come to the end of our journey through *Psychology and Life.* As you think back, we hope you will realize just how much you have learned on the way. Yet we have barely scratched the surface of the excitement and challenges that await the student of psychology. We hope you will pursue your interest in psychology and that you may even go on to contribute to this dynamic enterprise as a scientific researcher or a clinical practitioner, or by applying psychological knowledge to the solution of social and personal problems.

Playwright Tom Stoppard reminds us that "every exit is an entry somewhere else." We'd like to believe that the entry into the next phase of your life will be facilitated by what you have learned from *Psychology and Life* and from your introductory psychology course. In that next journey, may you infuse new life into the psychology of human endeavors while strengthening the connections among all the people you encounter.

Phil Zimbardo

Richard Gerrig

Recapping Main Points

The Therapeutic Context

Therapy requires that a diagnosis be made and a course of treatment be established. Therapy may be medically or psychologically oriented. The four major types of psychotherapy are psychodynamic, behavior, cognitive, and existential-humanist. A variety of professionals practice therapy. In earlier times, treatment for those with mental problems was often harsh and dehumanizing. A disease model of mental illness led to more humane treatment of patients. Cultural anthropology shows that many cultures have their own way of understanding and treating mental disorders.

Psychodynamic Therapies

Psychodynamic therapies grew out of Sigmund Freud's psychoanalytic theory. Freud emphasized the role of unconscious conflicts in the etiology of psychopathology. Psychodynamic therapy seeks to reconcile these conflicts. Free association, attention to resistance, dream analysis, transference, and countertransference are all important components of this therapy. Neo-Freudians place more emphasis on the patient's current social situation, interpersonal relationships, and self-concept.

Behavior Therapies

Behavior therapies use the principles of learning and reinforcement to modify or eliminate problem behaviors. Counterconditioning techniques replace negative behaviors, like phobic responses, with more adaptive behaviors. Exposure is the common element in phobia-modification therapies. Contingency management uses operant conditioning to modify behavior, primarily through positive reinforcement and extinction. Social-learning therapy uses models and social-skills training to help individuals gain confidence about their abilities.

Cognitive Therapies

Cognitive therapy concentrates on changing negative or irrational thought patterns about the self and social relationships. Cognitive behavior modification calls for the client to learn more constructive thought patterns in reference to a problem and to apply the new technique to other situations. Cognitive therapy has been used to treat depression. Rational-emotive therapy helps clients recognize that their irrational beliefs about themselves interfere with successful life outcomes.

Existential-Humanistic Therapies

Existential-humanistic therapies work to help individuals become more fully self-actualized. Therapists strive to be nondirective in helping their clients establish a positive self-image that can deal with external criticisms. Gestalt therapy focuses on the whole person—body, mind, and life setting. Group therapy has many applications, including community self-help groups and support groups for the terminally ill. Family and marital therapy concentrates on situational difficulties and interpersonal dynamics of the couple or family group as a system in need of improvement.

Biomedical Therapies

Biomedical therapies concentrate on changing physiological aspects of mental illness. Psychosurgery is rarely used because of its radical, irreversible effects. Electroconvulsive therapy is highly effective with depressed patients, but remains controversial. Drug therapies include antipsychotic medications for treating schizophrenia as well as antidepressants and antianxiety drugs. Drug therapies typically alleviate symptoms but often do not cure the disorder.

Does Therapy Work?

Research shows that many therapies work better than the passage of time or nonspecific placebo treatment. Innovative evaluation projects, such as the NIMH study of depression therapies, are helping to answer the question of what makes therapy effective. Prevention strategies are necessary to stop psychological disorders from occurring and minimize their effects once they have occurred.

Resources

Beck, A. T., & Freeman, A. (1990). *Cognitive therapy for personality disorders.* New York: Guilford.

Corsini, R. J., & Wedding, D. (1989). *Current psychotherapies.* Itasca, IL: Peacock.

Ellis, A. A., & Dryden, W. (1987). *The practice of rational-emotive therapy.* New York: Springer.

Garfield, S. L., & Bergin, A. E. (1986). *Handbook of psychotherapy and behavior change.* New York: Wiley. A standard reference work that includes the history and conceptual foundations of psychotherapy as well as descriptions of current therapies.

Kazdin, A. E. (1994). *Behavior modification in applied settings* (5th ed.). Pacific Grove, CA: Brooks/Cole.

Rogers, C. (1951). *Client-centered therapy.* Boston: Houghton-Mifflin. Contains many examples of client-therapist interactions.

Santrock, J. W., Minnett, A. M., & Campbell, B. D. (1994). *The authoritative guide to self-help books.* New York: Guilford. Before turning to any of the thousand plus self-help books available for advice on virtually all personal problems, review these evaluations made by more than 500 mental health professionals of books that cover 32 different categories, from abuse to women's issues.

Valenstein, E. S. (1986). *Great and desperate cures: The rise and decline of psychosurgery and other radical treatments for mental illness.* New York: Basic Books.

Williams, J. M. (1993). *The psychological treatment of depression: A guide to the theory and practice of cognitive behavior therapy.* New York: Routledge.

Appendix

Understanding Statistics: Analyzing Data and Forming Conclusions

As we noted in Chapter 2, psychologists use statistics to make sense of the data they collect. They also use statistics to provide a quantitative basis for the conclusions they draw. Knowing something about statistics can, therefore, help you appreciate the process by which psychological knowledge is developed. On a more personal level, having a basic understanding of statistics will help you make better decisions.

Most students perceive statistics as a dry, uninteresting topic. However, statistics have many vital applications in your life. Consider the following items taken from the front pages of the newspaper. They show how statistics help answer some crucial questions about human behavior.

> Fred Cowan was described by relatives, coworkers, and acquaintances as a "nice, quiet man," a "gentle man who loved children," and a "real pussycat." The principal of the parochial school Cowan had attended as a child reported that his former student had received A grades in courtesy, cooperation, and religion. According to a coworker, Cowan "never talked to anybody and was someone you could push around." Cowan, however, surprised everyone who knew him when, one Valentine's Day, he strolled into work toting a semiautomatic rifle and shot and killed four coworkers, a police officer, and, finally, himself.

> To friends and neighbors, Patrolman Stephen Richard Smith seemed a polite, shy man with a taste for classical music and a habit of feeding stray cats. One day this 31-year-old police officer was shot to death by his best friend, who was his former patrol partner. Authorities alleged that Smith's former partner had been forced to shoot his friend in the line of duty—Smith was suspected of being a brutal vigilante who had beaten and murdered several people.

Stories such as these lead all of us—laypeople and research psychologists alike—to wonder about the meaning and causes of human behavior. How could people who were perceived by everyone who knew them as "gentle" and "shy" commit such atrocities? These stories also make us wonder how well we *really* know anyone.

Both stories have a common plot: a shy, quiet person suddenly becomes violent, shocking everyone who knows him. What do Fred Cowan and Stephen Smith have in common with other people who were suddenly transformed from gentle and caring into violent and ruthless? What personal attributes might distinguish them from us?

A team of researchers had a hunch that there might be a link between shyness and other personal characteristics and violent behavior (Lee et al., 1977). Therefore, they began to collect some data that might reveal such a connection. The researchers reasoned that seemingly nonviolent people who suddenly commit murders are probably typically shy, nonaggressive individuals who keep their passions in check and their impulses under tight control. For most of their lives, they suffer many silent injuries. Seldom, if ever, do they express anger, regardless of how angry they really feel. On the outside, they appear unbothered, but on the inside they may be fighting to control furious rages. They give the impression that they are quiet, passive, responsible people, both as children and as adults. Since they are shy, they probably do not let others get close to them, so no one knows how they really feel. Then, suddenly, something explodes. At the slightest provocation—one more small insult, one more little rejection, one more bit of social pressure—the fuse is lit and they release the suppressed violence that has been building up for so long. Because they did not learn to deal with interpersonal conflicts through discussion and verbal negotiation, these sudden murderers act out their anger physically.

The researchers' minitheory led them to the hypothesis that shyness would be more characteristic of people who had engaged in homicide—without any prior history of violence or antisocial behavior—than it would of those who had committed homicide but had had a previous record of violent criminal behavior. In addition, sudden murderers should have higher levels of control over their impulses than habitually violent people. Finally, their passivity and dependence would be manifested in more feminine and androgynous (both male and female) characteristics, as measured on a standard sex-role inventory, than those of habitual criminals.

To test these hypotheses, the researchers collected three kinds of data from two types of subjects: shyness scores, impulse control scores, and sex-role identification scores from people who had recently committed murder, with and without previous criminal records. This type of research, in which the behavior of interest—the dependent variable—has already occurred before the study begins, uses an *ex post facto experimental design*. The task of the researcher is to figure out what kinds of independent variables could have influenced the known outcomes.

A second form of ex post facto design is one in which subjects are matched *after* the independent variable has already been administered. Here the research task is to find out the consequences of this existing difference between subjects. Subjects are not randomly assigned to conditions; instead, they are categorized according to existing characteristics—specifically, something they did or some personal attribute. Because alternative explanations cannot be ruled out, this design does not permit causal conclusions from the data. However, it does allow for the discovery of variables that may help to explain some existing phenomenon that may then lead to controlled experiments assessing the causal connections.

To test their ideas about sudden murderers, the researchers obtained permission to administer psychological questionnaires to a group of inmates serving time for murder in California prisons. Nineteen inmates (all male) agreed to participate in the study. Prior to committing murder, some had committed a series of crimes, while the other part of the sample had had no previous criminal record. All participants filled out three different questionnaires. Each questionnaire required a different type of information from the subject.

The first was the Stanford Shyness Survey (Zimbardo, 1990). The most important item on this questionnaire asked if the subject was shy; the answer could be either yes or no. Other items on the scale tapped degree and kinds of shyness and a variety of dimensions related to origins and triggers of shyness.

The second questionnaire was the Bem Sex-Role Inventory (BSRI), which presented a list of adjectives, such as *aggressive* and *affectionate,* and asked how well each adjective described the subject (Bem, 1974, 1981). Some adjectives were typically associated with being "feminine," and the total score of these adjectives was a subject's femininity score. Other adjectives were considered "masculine," and the total score of those adjectives was a subject's masculinity score. The final sex-role score, which reflected the difference between a subject's femininity and masculinity, was calculated by subtracting the masculinity score from the femininity score. A combination of the masculinity and femininity scores shows up as a subject's androgyny score.

The third questionnaire was the Minnesota Multiphasic Personality Inventory (MMPI), which was designed to measure many different aspects of personality (see Chapter 15). The study used only the "Ego-overcontrol" scale, which measures the degree to which a person acts out or controls impulses. The higher the subject's score on this scale, the more ego overcontrol the subject exhibits.

The researchers predicted that, compared with murderers with a prior criminal record, sudden murderers would (1) more often describe themselves as shy on the shyness survey; (2) select more feminine traits than masculine ones on the sex-role scale; and (3) score higher in ego overcontrol. What did they discover?

Before you find out, you need to understand some of the basic procedures that were used to analyze these data. The actual sets of data collected will be used as the source material to teach you about some of the different types of statistical analyses and also about the kinds of conclusions they make possible.

ANALYZING THE DATA

For most researchers in psychology, analyzing the data is an exciting step. They can find out if their results will contribute to a better understanding of a particular aspect of behavior or if they have to go back to the drawing board and redesign their research. In short, they can discover if their predictions were correct.

Data analysis can involve many different procedures, some of them surprisingly simple and straightforward. In this section, we will work step-by-step through an analysis of some of the data from the Sudden Murderers Study. If you have looked ahead and are turned off at the sight of numbers and equations, your feeling is understandable. However, you do not need to be good in math to be able to understand the concepts we will be discussing. You just need the courage to see mathematical symbols for what they are—a shorthand for representing ideas and conceptual operations.

Table A.1 Raw Data from the Sudden Murderers Study

Inmate	Shyness	BSRI Femininity–Masculinity	MMPI Ego Overcontrol
Group 1: Sudden murderers			
1	yes	+5	17
2	no	−1	17
3	yes	+4	13
4	yes	+61	17
5	yes	+19	13
6	yes	+41	19
7	no	−29	14
8	yes	+23	9
9	yes	−13	11
10	yes	+5	14
Group 2: Habitual criminal murderers			
11	no	−12	15
12	no	−14	11
13	yes	−33	14
14	no	−8	10
15	no	−7	16
16	no	+3	11
17	no	−17	6
18	no	+6	9
19	no	−10	12

The raw data—the actual scores or other measures obtained—from the 19 inmates in the Sudden Murderers Study are listed in **Table A.1**. As you can see, there were ten inmates in the *Sudden Murderers* group and nine in the *Habitual Criminal Murderers* group. When first glancing at these data, any researcher would feel what you probably feel: confusion. What do all these scores mean? Do the two groups of murderers differ from one another on these various personality measures? It is difficult to know just by examining this disorganized array of numbers.

Psychologists rely on a mathematical tool called *statistics* to help make sense of and draw meaningful conclusions from the data they collect. There are two types of statistics: descriptive and inferential. **Descriptive statistics** use mathematical procedures in an objective, uniform way to describe different aspects of numerical data. If you have ever computed your grade-point average, you already have used descriptive statistics. **Inferential statistics** use probability theory to make sound decisions about which results might have occurred simply through chance variation.

Descriptive Statistics

Descriptive statistics provide a summary picture of patterns in the data. They are used to describe sets of scores collected from one subject or, more often, from different groups of subjects. They are also used to describe relationships among variables. Thus, instead of trying to keep in mind all the scores obtained by each of the subjects, researchers get special indexes of the scores that are most *typical* for each group. They also get measures of the way those scores are typical—whether the scores are spread out or clustered closely together. Two types of descriptive statistics are frequency distributions and measures of central tendency. We will describe each of these, as well as show how they are displayed in graphs, in the following sections.

Frequency Distributions

The shyness data are easy to summarize. Of the 19 scores, there are 9 *yes* and 10 *no* responses; almost all the *yes* responses are in Group 1 and almost all the *no* responses are in Group 2. On the overcontrol scale, the scores range from 6 to 19; it is harder to get a sense, from just looking at the scale, of how the groups compare. We'll need a way to reorganize those scores.

Now let's examine the sex-role scores. The highest score is +61 (most feminine) and the lowest is –33 (most masculine). Of the 19 scores, 9 are positive and 10 negative—this means that 9 of the murderers described themselves as relatively feminine and 10 as relatively masculine.

To get a clearer picture of how these scores are distributed, we can draw up a **frequency distribution**—a summary of how frequently each of the various scores occurs. The first step in preparing a frequency distribution for a set of numerical data is to *rank order* the scores from highest to lowest. The rank ordering for the sex-role scores is shown in **Table A.2**. The second step is to group these rank-ordered scores into a smaller number of categories called *intervals*. In this study, 10 categories were used, with each category covering 10 possible scores. The third step is to construct a frequency distribution table, listing the intervals from highest to lowest and noting the *frequencies*—the number of scores within each interval. Our frequency distribution shows us that the sex-role scores are largely between –20 and +9 (see **Table A.3**). The majority of the inmates' scores did not deviate much from zero. That is, they were neither strongly positive nor strongly negative.

We can now make some preliminary conclusions about the data. By examining frequency distributions for our variables, we can already see that each of our three predictions is accurate. Forty percent of the American people describe themselves as shy. By comparison, eight out of ten of the sudden murderers (80 percent) described themselves as shy, while only one of nine of the habitual criminal murderers (11 percent) did so. On the sex-role scale, 70 percent of the sudden murderers chose adjectives that were more femi-

Table A.2 Rank Ordering of Sex-role Difference Scores

Highest +61	–1
+41	–7
+23	–8
+19	–10
+6	–12
+5	–13
+5	–14
+4	–17
+3	–29
	–33 Lowest

Note: + scores are more feminine; – scores are more masculine.

Table A.3 Frequency Distribution of Sex-role Difference Scores

Category	Frequency
+60 to +69	1
+50 to +59	0
+40 to +49	1
+30 to +39	0
+20 to +29	1
+10 to +19	1
+0 to +9	5
−10 to −1	4
−20 to −11	4
−30 to −21	1
−40 to −31	1

nine than masculine, while only 22 percent of the habitual criminals said that the feminine adjectives described them more accurately than did the masculine ones. Sudden murderers scored higher in overcontrolling their impulses than habitual criminal murderers did (Lee et al., 1977). In addition, there was a noticeable difference in the circumstances that precipitated the murders committed by the shy men. In virtually every case, the precipitating incidents for the sudden murderers were minor, compared with the incidents that triggered the violence of the habitual criminal murderers.

Although summaries of data such as this are compelling, there are a number of other analyses we must look at before we can state our conclusions with any certainty. The researchers' next step was to arrange the distributions in graphic form.

Graphs

Distributions are often easier to understand when they are displayed in graphs. The simplest type of graph is a *bar graph.* We can use a bar graph to illustrate how many more sudden murderers than habitual criminal murderers described themselves as shy (see **Figure A.1**). Bar graphs allow you to see patterns in the data.

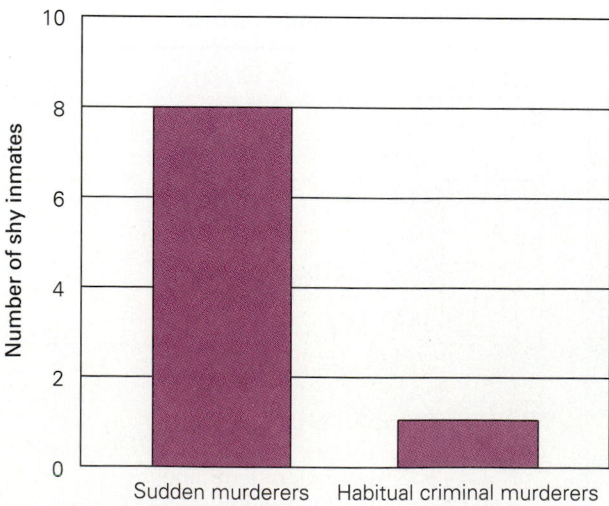

Figure A.1 **Shyness for Two Groups of Murderers (a Bar Graph)**

For more complex data, such as the sex-role scores, we can use a *histogram,* which is similar to a bar graph except that the histogram's bars touch each other and its categories are *intervals*—number categories instead of the name categories used in the bar graph. A histogram gives a visual picture of the number of scores in a distribution that are in each interval. It is easier to see from the sex-role scores shown in the histograms (in **Figure A.2**) that the distributions of scores are different for the two groups of murderers.

Measures of Central Tendency

So far, we have formed a general picture of how the scores are *distributed.* Tables and graphs increase our general understanding of research results, but we want to know more—for example, the one score that is most typical of the group as a whole. This score becomes particularly useful when we compare two or more groups; it is much easier to compare the typical scores of two groups than their entire distributions. A single, *representative* score that can be used as an index of the most typical score obtained by a group of subjects

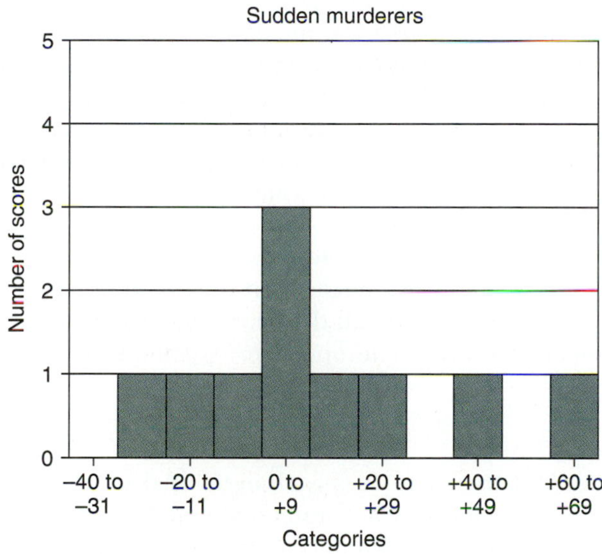

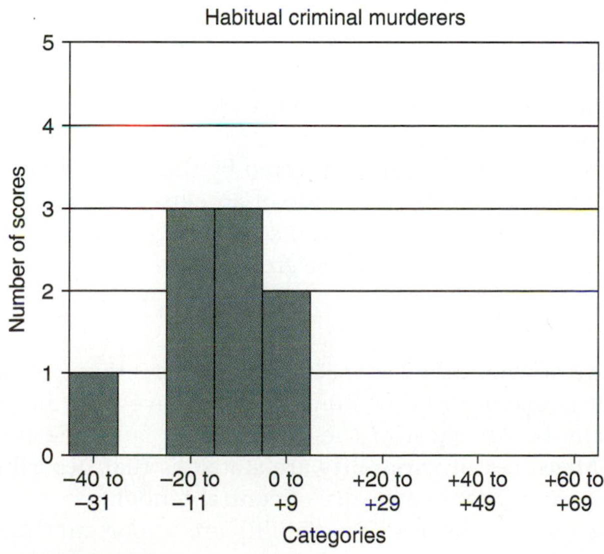

Figure A.2 **Sex-role Scores (Histograms)**

is called a **measure of central tendency.** (It is located in the center of the distribution, and other scores tend to cluster around it.) Typically, psychologists use three different measures of central tendency: the *mode,* the *median,* and the *mean.*

The **mode** is the score that occurs more often than any other. For the measure of shyness, the modal response of the sudden murderers was *yes*—eight out of ten said they were shy. Among habitual criminal murderers, the modal response was *no.* The sex-role scores for the sudden murderers had a mode of +5. Can you figure out what the mode of their ego-overcontrol scores is?

The mode is the easiest index of central tendency to determine, but it is often the least useful. You will see one reason for this relative lack of usefulness if you notice that only one overcontrol score lies above the mode of 17, while six lie below it. Although 17 is the score obtained most often, it may not fit your idea of "typical" or "central."

The **median** is more clearly a central score; it separates the upper half of the scores in a distribution from the lower half. The number of scores larger than the median is the same as the number that are smaller. If you rank-order the sex-role scores of only the sudden murderers on a separate piece of paper, you will see that the median score is +5 (in this case, the same as the mode, although this is not always true). Four scores are higher than +5, and four scores are lower. Similarly, the median overcontrol score for these subjects is 15, with four scores below it and four above it. The median is quite simply the score in the middle of the distribution.

The median is not affected by extreme scores. For example, even if the highest sex-role score had been +129 instead of +61, the median value would still have been +5. That score would still separate the upper half of the data from the lower half.

The **mean** is what most people think of when they hear the word *average.* It is also the statistic most often used to describe a set of data. To calculate the mean, you add up all the scores in a distribution and divide by the total number of scores. The operation is summarized by the following formula:

$$M = \Sigma X \div N$$

In this formula, M is the mean, X is each individual score, Σ (the Greek letter *sigma*) is the summation of what immediately follows it, and N is the total number of scores. Since the summation of all the scores (ΣX) is 115 and the total number of scores (N) is 10, the mean (M) of the sex-role scores of the sudden murderers would be calculated as follows:

$$M = 115 \div 10 = 11.5$$

Try to calculate their mean overcontrol scores yourself. You should come up with a mean of 14.4.

Unlike the median, the mean *is* affected by the specific values of all scores in the distribution. Changing the value of an extreme score *does* change the value of the mean. For example, if the sex-role score of inmate 4 were +101 instead of +61, the mean for the whole group would increase from 11.5 to 15.5.

Variability

In addition to knowing which score is most representative of the distribution as a whole, it is useful to know how representative that measure of central tendency really is. Are most of the other scores fairly close to it or widely spread out? **Measures of variability** are statistics that describe the distribution of scores around some measure of central tendency.

Can you see why measures of variability are important? An example may help. Suppose you are a grade school teacher. It is the beginning of the school year, and you will be teaching reading to a group of 30 second graders. Knowing that the average child in the class can now read a first-grade-level book will help you to plan your lessons. You could plan better, however, if you knew how *similar* or how *divergent* the reading abilities of the 30 children were. Are they all at about the same level (low variability)? If so, then you can plan a fairly standard second-grade lesson. What if several can read advanced material and others can barely read at all (high variability)? Now the mean level is not so representative of the entire class, and you will have to plan a variety of lessons to meet the children's varied needs.

The simplest measure of variability is the **range**, the difference between the highest and the lowest values in a frequency distribution. For the sudden murderers' sex-role scores, the range is 90: (+61)—(–29). The range of their overcontrol scores is 10: (+19)—(+9). To compute the range, you need to know only two of the scores: the highest and the lowest.

The range is simple to compute, but psychologists often prefer measures of variability that are more sensitive and that take into account *all* the scores in a distribution, not just the extremes. One widely used measure is the **standard deviation** (SD), a measure of variability that indicates the *average* difference between the scores and their mean. To figure out the standard deviation of a distribution, you need to know the mean of the distribution and the individual scores. Although the arithmetic involved in calculating the standard deviation is very easy, the formula is a bit more complicated than the one used to calculate the mean and, therefore, will not be presented here. The general procedure, however, involves subtracting the value of each individual score from the mean and then determining the average of those mean deviations.

The standard deviation tells us how variable a set of scores is. The larger the standard deviation, the more spread out the scores are. The standard deviation of the sex-role scores for the sudden murderers is 24.6, but the standard deviation for the habitual criminals is only 10.7. This shows that there was less variability in the habitual criminals group. Their scores clustered more closely about their mean than did those of the sudden murderers. When the standard deviation is small, the mean is a good representative index of the entire distribution. When the standard deviation is large, the mean is less typical of the whole group.

Correlation

Another useful tool in interpreting psychological data is the **correlation coefficient,** a measure of the nature and strength of the relationship between two variables (such as height and weight or sex-role score and overcontrol score). It tells us the extent to which scores on one measure are associated with scores on the other. If people with high scores on one variable tend to have high scores on the other variable, then the correlation coefficient will be positive (greater than 0). If, however, most people with high scores on one variable tend to have *low* scores on the other variable, then the correlation coefficient will be negative (less than 0). If there is *no* consistent relationship between the scores, the correlation will be close to 0 (see also Chapter 2).

Correlation coefficients range from +1 (perfect positive correlation) through 0 to –1 (perfect negative correlation). The further a coefficient is from 0 in *either* direction, the more closely related the two variables are, positively or negatively. Higher coefficients permit better predictions of one variable, given knowledge of the other.

In the Sudden Murderers Study, the correlation coefficient (symbolized as *r*) between the sex-role scores and the overcontrol scores turns out to be +0.35. The sex-role scores and the overcontrol scores are, thus, positively correlated—in general, subjects seeing themselves as more feminine also tend to be higher in overcontrol. However, the correlation is modest, compared with the highest possible value, +1.00. So we know that there are many exceptions to this relationship. If we had also measured the self-esteem of these inmates and found a correlation of –0.68 between overcontrol scores and self-esteem, it would mean that there was a negative correlation. If this were the case, we could say that the subjects who had high overcontrol scores tended to be lower in self-esteem. It would be a stronger relationship than the relationship between the sex-role scores and the overcontrol scores, because –0.68 is farther from 0, the point of no relationship, than is +0.35.

Inferential Statistics

We have used a number of descriptive statistics to characterize the data from the Sudden Murderers Study, and now we have an idea of the pattern of results. However, some basic questions remain unanswered. Recall that the research team hypothesized that sudden murderers would be shyer, more overcontrolled, and more feminine than habitual criminal murderers. After we have used descriptive statistics to compare average responses and variability in the two groups, it appears that there are some differences between the groups. But how do we know if the differences are large enough to be meaningful? Are they reliable? If we repeated this study, with other sudden murderers and other habitual criminal murderers, would we expect to find the same pattern of results, or could these results have been an outcome of chance? If we could somehow measure the entire population of sudden murderers and habitual criminal murderers, would the means and standard deviations be the same as those we found for these small samples?

Inferential statistics are used to answer these kinds of questions. They tell us which inferences we *can* make from our samples and which conclusions we can legitimately draw from our data. Inferential statistics use probability theory to determine the likelihood that a set of data occurred simply by chance variation.

The Normal Curve

In order to understand how inferential statistics work, we must look first at the special properties of a distribution called the *normal curve*. When data on a variable (height, IQ, or overcontrol, for example) are collected from a large number of subjects, the numbers obtained often fit a curve roughly similar to that shown in **Figure A.3**. Notice that the curve is symmetrical (the left half is a mirror image of the right) and bell shaped—high in the middle, where most scores are, and lower the farther you get from the mean. This type of curve is called a **normal curve,** or *normal distribution.* (A *skewed* distribution is one in which scores cluster toward one end instead of around the middle.)

In a normal curve, the median, mode, and mean values are the same. A specific percentage of the scores can be predicted to fall under different sections of the curve. Figure A.3 shows IQ scores on the Stanford-Binet Intelligence Test. These scores have a mean of 100 and a standard deviation of 16. If you indicate standard deviations as distances from the mean along the baseline, you find that a little over 68 percent of all the scores are between the mean of 100 and 1 standard deviation above and below—between IQs of 84 and 116. Roughly another 27 percent of the scores are found between the first and second standard deviations below the mean (IQ scores between 68 and 84) and above the mean (IQ scores between 116 and 132). Less than 5 percent of the scores fall in the third standard deviation above and below the mean, and *very* few scores fall beyond—only about one quarter of 1 percent.

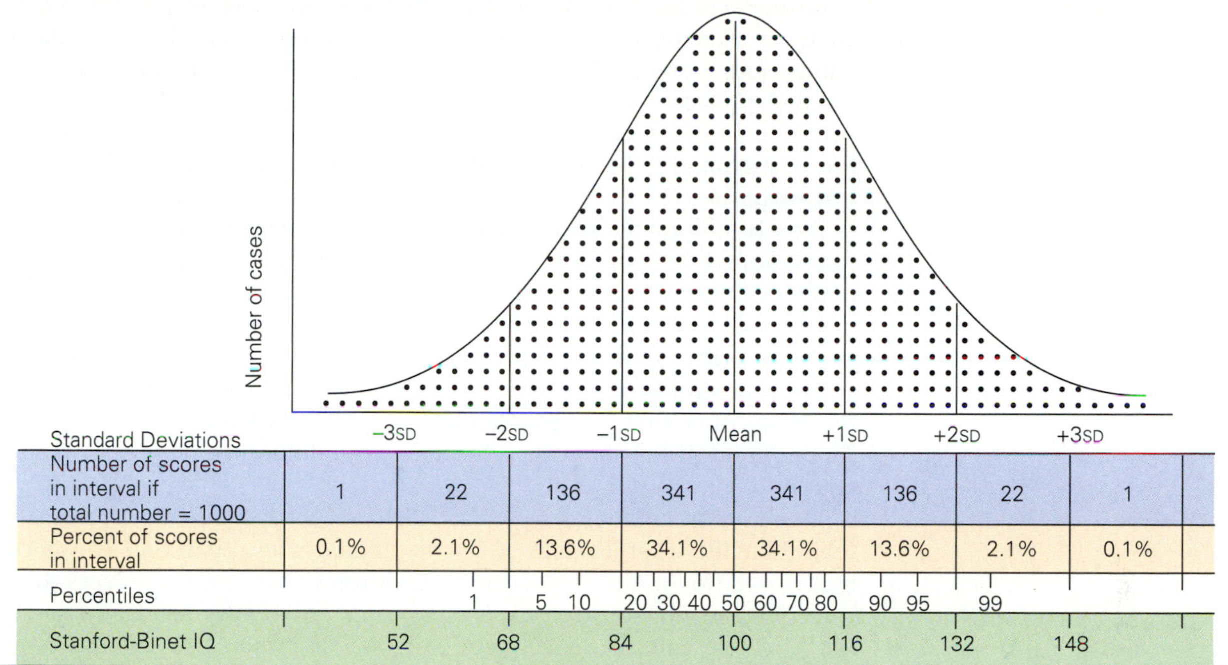

Figure A.3 A Normal Curve

Inferential statistics indicate the probability that the particular sample of scores obtained are actually related to whatever you are attempting to measure or whether they could have occurred by chance. For example, it is more likely that someone would have an IQ of 105 than an IQ of 140, but an IQ of 140 is more probable than one of 35.

A normal curve is also obtained by collecting a series of measurements whose differences are due only to chance. If you flip a coin 10 times in a row and record the number of heads and tails, you will probably get 5 of each—most of the time. If you keep flipping the coin for 100 sets of 10 tosses, you probably will get a few sets with all heads or no heads, more sets where the number is between these extremes, and, most typically, more sets where the number is about half each way. If you made a graph of your 1000 tosses, you would get one that closely fits a normal curve, such as the one in the figure.

Statistical Significance

A researcher who finds a difference between the mean scores for two samples must ask if it is a *real* difference or if it occurred simply because of chance. Because chance differences have a normal distribution, a researcher can use the normal curve to answer this question.

A simple example will help to illustrate the point. Suppose your psychology professor wants to see if the gender of a person proctoring a test makes a difference in the test scores obtained from male and from female students. For this purpose, the professor randomly assigns half of the students to a male proctor and half to a female proctor. The professor then compares the mean score of each group. The two mean scores would probably be fairly similar; any slight difference would most likely be due to chance. Why? Because if only chance is operating and both groups are from the same population (no difference), then the means of male proctor and female proctor samples should be fairly close most of the time. From the percentages of scores found in different parts of the normal distribution, you know that less than a third of the scores in the male proctor condition should be greater than one standard deviation above or below the female proctor mean. The chances of getting a male proctor mean score more than three standard deviations above or below most of your female proctor means would be very small. A professor who *did* get a difference that great would feel fairly confident that the difference is a real one and is somehow related to the gender of the test proctor. The next question would be *how* that variable influences test scores.

If male and female students were randomly assigned to each type of proctor, it would be possible to analyze whether an overall difference found between the proctors was consistent across both student groups or was limited to only one sex. Imagine the data show that male proctors grade female students higher than do female proctors, but both grade male students the same. Your professor could use a statistical inference procedure to estimate the probability that an observed difference could have occurred by chance. This computation is based on the size of the difference and the spread of the scores.

By common agreement, psychologists accept a difference as "real" when the probability that it might be due to chance is less than 5 in 100 (indicated by the notation $p < .05$). A **significant difference** is one that meets this criterion. However, in some cases, even stricter probability levels are used, such as $p < .01$ (less than 1 in 100) and $p < .001$ (less than 1 in 1000).

With a statistically significant difference, a researcher can draw a conclusion about the behavior that was under investigation. There are many different types of tests for estimating the statistical significance of sets of data. The type of test chosen for a particular case depends on the design of the study, the form of the data, and the size of the groups. We will mention only one of the most common tests, the *t-test,* which may be used when an investigator wants to know if the difference between the means of two groups is statistically significant.

We can use a t-test to see if the mean sex-role score of the sudden murderers is significantly different from that of the habitual criminal murderers. If we carry out the appropriate calculations, we find that there is a very slim chance, less than 5 in 100 ($p < .05$) of obtaining such a large t value if no true difference exists. The difference is, therefore, statistically significant, and we can feel more confident that there is a real difference between the two groups. The sudden murderers *did* rate themselves as more feminine than did the habitual criminal murderers. On the other hand, the difference between the two groups of murderers in overcontrol scores turns out *not* to be statistically significant ($p < .10$), so we must be more cautious in talking about this difference. There is a *trend* in the predicted direction—the difference is one that would occur by chance only 10 times in 100. However, the difference is not within the standard 5-in-100 range. (The difference in shyness, analyzed using another statistical test for frequency of scores, *is* highly significant.) So, by using inferential statistics, we are able to answer some of the basic questions with which we began, and we are closer to understanding the psychology of people who suddenly change from mild-mannered, shy individuals into mass murderers. Any conclusion, however, is only a statement of the *probable* relationship between the events that were investigated; it is never one of certainty. Truth in science is provisional, always open to revision by later data from better studies, developed from better hypotheses.

HOW TO MISLEAD WITH STATISTICS

Now that we have considered what statistics are, how they are used, and what they mean, we should talk about how they can be misused. Many people accept unsupported "facts" that are bolstered by the air of authority of a statistic. Others choose to believe or disbelieve what the statistics say without having any idea of how to question the numbers that are presented in support of a product, politician, or proposal.

There are many ways to give a misleading impression using statistics. The decisions made at all stages of research—from who the subjects are to how the study is designed, what statistics are selected, and how they are used—can have a profound effect on the conclusions that can be drawn from the data.

The group of subjects can make a large difference that can easily remain undetected when the results are reported. For example, a survey of views on abortion rights will yield very different results if conducted in a small fundamentalist community in the South rather than at a university in New York City. Likewise, a pro-life group surveying the opinions of its membership will very likely arrive at conclusions that differ from those obtained by the same survey conducted by a pro-choice group.

Even if the subjects are randomly selected and not biased by the methodology, the statistics can produce misleading results if the assumptions of the statistics are violated. For example, suppose 20 people take an IQ test; 19 of them receive scores between 90 and 110, and 1 receives a score of 220. The mean of the group will be strongly elevated by that one outlying high score. With this sort of a data set, it would be much more accurate to present the median or the mode, which would accurately report the group's generally average intelligence, rather than the mean, which would make it look as if the average member of this group was high IQ. This sort of bias is especially powerful in a small sample. If, on the other hand, the number of people in this group was 2000 instead of 20, the one extreme outlier would make virtually no difference, and the mean would be a legitimate summary of the group's intelligence.

One good way to avoid falling for this sort of deception is to check on the size of the sample—large samples are less likely to be misleading than small ones. Another check is to look at the median or the mode as well as the mean—the results can be interpreted with more confidence if they are similar than if they are different.

One way to guard against being misled by the misuse of statistics is to closely examine the methodology and results of the research reported. Check to see if the experimenters report their sample size, significance levels, and error margins. Try to find out if the methods they used measure accurately and consistently whatever they claim to be investigating.

No test is 100 percent accurate all the time, but it is possible to calculate a range within which the "true" score probably lies. Responsible statisticians report this range as the *margin of error.* For example, examine the data in **Table A.4**, which summarizes the results from a survey asking Americans

Table A.4 Belief in the Supernatural: Gallup Poll Results, 1990

Beliefs in	People Who Believe	People Who Are Not Sure
The devil	55%	8%
ESP	49%	22%
Devil possession	49%	16%
Psychic healing	46%	20%
Telepathy	36%	25%
Extraterrestrials	27%	32%
Astrology	25%	21%

N = 1225 U.S. adults; margin of error ± 4 percent.

about their beliefs in the supernatural. Nearly half of the respondents indicated that they believed that the devil could possess humans. Notice in the small print at the bottom of the chart that there is a margin of error of plus or minus 4 percent. In other words, 49 percent may not be a truly accurate representation of the population at large. However, it is highly probable that somewhere between 45 percent and 53 percent of the population really does believe in devil possession. Since the survey was conducted using representative sampling techniques with 1225 American adults, it is likely that the sample is fairly representative of the population as a whole.

Before drawing your own conclusions from the results presented, it is always a good idea to check such things as sample size and margin of error. Paying attention to the fine print and applying what you have learned in this book should make you less likely to be taken in by statistical misdirection and make you a much wiser consumer of psychological research.

Statistics are the backbone of psychological research. They are used to understand observations and to determine whether the findings are, in fact, correct. Through the methods we have described, psychologists can prepare a frequency distribution of data and find the central tendencies and variability of the scores. They can use the correlation coefficient to determine the strength and direction of the association between sets of scores. Finally, psychological investigators can then find out how representative the observations are and whether they are significantly different from the general population. Statistics can also be used poorly or deceptively, misleading those who do not understand them. But when statistics are applied correctly and ethically, they allow researchers to expand the body of psychological knowledge.

Glossary

A-B-A design. Experimental design in which subjects first experience the baseline condition (A), then experience the experimental treatment (B), and then return to the baseline (A) (p. 36).

Abnormal psychology. The area of psychological investigation concerned with understanding the nature of individual pathologies of mind, mood, and behavior (p. 629).

Absolute threshold. The minimum amount of physical energy needed to produce a sensory experience reliably; operationally defined as the smallest physical stimulus subjects can detect (p. 219).

Accommodation. According to Piaget, the process of restructuring or modifying cognitive structures so that new information can fit into them more easily; this process works in tandem with *assimilation.* Also, the process by which the ciliary muscles change the thickness of the lens of the eye to permit variable focusing on near and distant objects (p. 158).

Achievement test. Standardized test designed to measure an individual's current level of competence in a given area (p. 577).

Acquisition. The stage in a classical conditioning experiment during which the conditional response is first elicited by the conditional stimulus (p. 313).

Action potential. The nerve impulse activated in a neuron that travels down the axon and causes neurotransmitters to be released into a synapse (p. 83).

Acute stress. A transient state of arousal with typically clear onset and offset patterns (p. 473).

Addiction. A condition in which the body requires a drug in order to function without physical and psychological reactions to its absence; often the outcome of tolerance and dependence (p. 132).

Ageism. Prejudice against older people, similar to racism and sexism in its negative stereotypes (p. 207).

Aggregate case study. A research technique used to compare and contrast information about many individuals by combining and summarizing the results of a number of individual case studies (p. 510).

Agoraphobia. An extreme fear of being in public places or open spaces from which escape may be difficult or embarrassing (p. 642).

AIDS. Acronym for acquired immune deficiency syndrome, a syndrome caused by a virus that damages the immune system and weakens the body's ability to fight infection, usually resulting in death (p. 496).

All-or-none law. The rule that the size of the action potential is unaffected by increases in the intensity of stimulation beyond the threshold level (p. 84).

Alternative explanations. Interpretations or explanations of a behavioral effect that differ from that proposed in the hypothesis being tested (p. 33).

Alzheimer's disease. A chronic organic brain syndrome characterized by gradual loss of memory, decline in intellectual ability, and deterioration of personality; the most common form of dementia in the elderly (p. 169).

Amacrine cells. Cells that integrate information across the retina; rather than sending signals toward the brain, amacrine cells link *bipolar cells* to other bipolar cells and *ganglion cells* to other ganglion cells (p. 228).

Ambiguity. A situation or utterance that may have more than one interpretation (p. 263).

Amnesia. A failure of memory caused by physical injury, disease, drug use, or psychological trauma (p. 382).

Amygdala. The part of the limbic system that controls emotion, aggression, and the formation of emotional memory (p. 73).

Analytic psychology. A branch of psychology that views the person as a constellation of compensatory internal forces in a dynamic balance, as proposed by Carl Jung (p. 524).

Anchoring bias. An insufficient adjustment up or down from an original starting value when judging the probable value of some event or outcome (p. 421).

Animal cognition. The cognitive capabilities of nonhuman animals; researchers trace the development of cognitive capabilities across species and the continuity of capabilities from nonhuman to human animals (p. 334).

Anorexia nervosa. An eating disorder in which an individual weighs less than 85 percent of her or his expected weight, but still controls eating because of a self-perception of obesity (p. 439).

Anticipatory coping. In advance of a potentially stressful event, efforts made to overcome, reduce, or tolerate the imbalance between perceived demands and available resources (p. 486).

Antisocial personality disorder. A personality disorder marked by a long-standing pattern of irresponsible or unlawful behavior that violates social norms, lack of remorse for these actions, and an indifference to the rights of others (p. 639).

Anxiety. In Freudian theory, an intense emotional response caused by the preconscious recognition that a repressed conflict is about to emerge into consciousness (p. 522).

Anxiety disorders. Mental disorders marked by physiological arousal, feelings of tension, and intense apprehension without apparent reason (p. 642).

Apparent motion. A movement illusion in which one or more stationary lights going on and off in succession are perceived as a single moving light; the simplest form of apparent motion is the *phi phenomenon* (p. 285).

Aptitude test. A test designed to measure an individual's potential for acquiring various skills (p. 577).

Archetype. In Jungian personality theory, a universal, inherited, primitive, and symbolic representation of a particular experience or object; part of the collective unconscious (p. 524).

Archival data. Information about a person's life taken from available records, especially those from different time periods (p. 549).

Assimilation. According to Piaget, the process whereby new cognitive elements are fitted in with old elements or modified to fit more easily; this process works in tandem with *accommodation* (p. 158).

Association cortex. The parts of the cerebral cortex in which many high-level brain processes occur (p. 76).

Attachment. Close emotional relationship between a child and the regular caregiver (p. 190).

Attention. A state of focused awareness on a subset of the available perceptual information; resources focused on cognitive processes (p. 270).

Attitude. The learned, relatively stable tendency to respond to people, concepts, and events in an evaluative way (p. 612).

Attributions. Judgments about the causes of outcomes (p. 452).

Attribution theory. A social-cognitive approach to describing the ways the social perceiver uses information to generate causal explanations (p. 606).

Audience design. The process of shaping a message depending on the audience for which it is intended (p. 395).

Auditory cortex. The area of the temporal lobes that receives and processes auditory information (p. 76).

Auditory nerve. The nerve that carries impulses from the cochlea to the cochlear nucleus of the brain (p. 243).

Autokinetic effect. A visual illusion in which a stationary point of light in a dark room appears to move slowly from its initial position (p. 588).

Automatic processes. Processes that do not require attention; they can often be performed along with other tasks without interference (p. 392).

Autonomic nervous system (ANS). The subdivision of the peripheral nervous system that controls the body's involuntary motor responses by connecting the sensory receptors to the CNS and the CNS to the smooth muscle, cardiac muscle, and glands (p. 69).

Availability heuristic. A judgment based on the information readily available in memory (p. 419).

Aversion therapy. A type of behavioral therapy used to treat individuals attracted to harmful stimuli; an attractive stimulus is paired with a noxious stimulus in order to elicit a negative reaction to the target stimulus (p. 685).

Axon. The extended fiber of a *neuron* through which nerve impulses travel from the *soma* to the *terminal buttons* (p. 80).

Base rate. A statistic that identifies the typical frequency, or probability, of a given event (p. 10).

Basic level. The optimal level of categorization for thinking about an object; the level that can be retrieved from memory most quickly and used most efficiently (p. 372).

Basilar membrane. A membrane in the *cochlea* that when set into motion stimulates hair cells that produce the neural effects of auditory stimulation (p. 243).

Behavior. The actions by which an organism adjusts to its environment (p. 4).

Behavioral confirmation. The process by which people behave in ways that elicit from others specific expected reactions and then use those reactions to confirm their beliefs (p. 612).

Behavioral contract. An explicit agreement (often in writing) about the consequences of specific behaviors (p. 686).

Behavioral data. Observational reports about the behavior of organisms and the conditions under which the behavior occurs or changes (p. 5).

Behavioral measures. Overt actions and reactions that are observed and recorded, exclusive of self-reported behavior (p. 44).

Behavioral rehearsal. Procedures used to establish and strengthen basic skills; as used in social skills training programs, requires the client to rehearse a desirable behavior sequence mentally (p. 689).

Behavior analysis. The use of systematic variation of stimulus conditions to determine the ways in which various kinds of environmental conditions affect the probability that a given response will occur (p. 307).

Behaviorism. A scientific approach that limits the study of psychology to measurable or observable behavior (p. 17).

Behavioristic approach. A psychological model primarily concerned with observable behavior that can be objectively recorded, and with the relationships of observable behavior to environmental stimuli (p. 17).

Behavior therapy (behavior modification). The systematic use of principles of learning to increase the frequency of desired behaviors and/or decrease the frequency of problem behaviors (p. 682).

Belief-bias effect. A situation that occurs when a person's prior knowledge, attitudes, or values distort the reasoning process by influencing the person to accept invalid arguments (p. 413).

Between-subjects design. A research design in which different groups of subjects are randomly assigned to experimental conditions or to control conditions (p. 35).

Biofeedback. A self-regulatory technique by which an individual acquires voluntary control over nonconscious biological processes (p. 500).

Biological approach. The approach to identifying causes of behavior that focuses on the functioning of the genes, the brain, the nervous system, and the endocrine system (p. 16).

Biological constraints on learning. Any limitations on an organism's capacity to learn that are caused by the inherited sensory, response, or cognitive capabilities of members of a given species (p. 331).

Biological marker. A measurable correlate of some process or disease, such as schizophrenia, that may indicate that individuals are at risk (p. 662).

Biomedical therapies. Therapies used to treat psychological disorders by altering brain functioning with chemical or physical interventions such as drug therapy, surgery, or electroconvulsive therapy (p. 673).

Biopsychosocial model. A model of health and illness which suggests that links among the nervous system, the immune system, behavioral styles, cognitive processing, and environmental factors can put people at risk for illness (p. 492).

Bipedalism. The ability to walk upright, an important development in human evolution (p. 60).

Bipolar cells. Nerve cells in the visual system that combine impulses from many receptors and transmit the results to *ganglion* cells (p. 228).

Bipolar disorder. A mood disorder characterized by alternating periods of depression and mania (p. 649).

Blocking. A phenomenon in which an organism does not learn a new stimulus that signals an unconditional stimulus, because the new stimulus is presented simultaneously with a stimulus that is already effective as a signal (p. 313).

Body image. The subjective experience of the appearance of one's body (p. 154).

Bottom-up processes. Perceptual analyses based on the sensory data available in the environment; results of analyses are passed upward toward more abstract representations (p. 294).

Brain stem. The brain structure that regulates the body's basic life processes (p. 71).

Brightness. The dimension of color space that captures the intensity of light (p. 232).

Bulimia nervosa. An eating disorder characterized by binge eating followed by measures to purge the body of the excess calories (p. 439).

Broca's area. The region of the brain that translates thoughts into speech or signs (p. 65).

Bystander intervention. The act of assisting a person in need of help (p. 600).

Cannon-Bard theory of emotion. A central neural process theory stating that an emotional stimulus produces two co-occurring reactions—arousal and experience of emotion—that do not cause each other; developed independently by Walter Cannon and Philip Bard (p. 468).

Case study. An extensive exclusive biography of a selected individual used in ideographic personality study (p. 510).

Catharsis. In Freudian theory, the process of expressing strongly felt but usually repressed emotions (p. 680).

Central nervous system (CNS). The part of the nervous system consisting of the brain and spinal cord (p. 68).

Centration. A thought pattern common during the beginning of the preoperational stage of cognitive development; characterized by the child's inability to take more than one perceptual factor into account at the same time (p. 159).

Cerebellum. The region of the brain attached to the *brain stem* that controls motor coordination, posture, and balance (p. 72).

Cerebral cortex. The outer surface of the *cerebrum* (p. 73).

Cerebral dominance. The tendency for one *cerebral hemisphere* to play a primary role in controlling a particular physical or mental function (p. 91).

Cerebral hemispheres. The two halves of the *cerebrum,* connected by the *corpus callosum* (p. 73).

Cerebrum. The region of the brain that regulates sensory, motor, and cognitive processes (p. 73).

Chaining. An operant conditioning procedure in which many different responses are reinforced in sequence until an effective chain of behaviors has been learned (p. 330).

Child-directed speech. *See* **Motherese**.

Chronic stress. A continuous state of arousal in which an individual perceives demands as greater than the inner and outer resources available for dealing with them (p. 473).

Chronological age (CA). The number of months or years since an individual's birth (p. 139).

Chunk. A meaningful unit of information (p. 354).

Chunking. The process of taking single items of information and recoding them on the basis of similarity or some other organizing principle (p. 354).

Circadian rhythm. A consistent pattern of cyclical body activities, usually lasting 24 to 25 hours and determined by an internal biological clock (p. 114).

Classical conditioning. A type of learning in which behavior (conditioned response) comes to be elicited by a stimulus (conditional stimulus) that has acquired its power through an association with a biologically significant stimulus (unconditional stimulus) (p. 307).

Client. The term used by clinicians who think of psychological disorders as problems in living and not as mental illnesses to describe those being treated (p. 674).

Clinical ecology. A field of psychology that relates disorders such as anxiety and depression, to environmental irritants and sources of trauma (p. 709).

Clinical psychologist. An individual who has earned a doctorate in psychology and whose training is in the assessment and treatment of psychological problems (p. 675).

Clinical social worker. A mental health professional whose specialized training prepares him or her to work in collaboration with psychiatrists and clinical psychologists to consider the social context of people's problems (p. 675).

Closure. A perceptual organizing process that leads individuals to see incomplete figures as complete (p. 280).

Cochlea. The primary organ of hearing; a fluid-filled coiled tube located in the inner ear (p. 243).

Cognition. Processes of knowing, including attending, remembering, and reasoning; also the content of the processes, such as concepts and memories (p. 334).

Cognitive appraisal. The recognition and evaluation of a stressor to assess the demand, the size of the threat, the resources available for dealing with it, and appropriate coping strategies (p. 477).

Cognitive approach. The approach to psychology that stresses human thought and the processes of knowing, such as attending, thinking, remembering, expecting, solving problems, fantasizing, and consciousness (p. 18).

Cognitive behavior modification. A therapeutic approach that combines the cognitive emphasis on the role of thoughts and attitudes influencing motivations and response with the behavioral emphasis on changing performance through modification of reinforcement contingencies (p. 692).

Cognitive development. The development of processes of knowing, including imagining, perceiving, reasoning, and problem solving (p. 156).

Cognitive dissonance. The theory that the tension-producing effects of incongruous cognitions motivate individuals to reduce such tension; developed by Leon Festinger (p. 613).

Cognitive map. A mental representation of physical space (p. 334).

Cognitive neuroscience. The field of study whose goal is to test and refine cognitive theories by using a set of methodologies that allow inferences to be drawn about the activities of the brain (p. 393).

Cognitive processes. Higher mental processes, such as perception, memory, language, problem solving, and abstract thinking (p. 386).

Cognitive science. The interdisciplinary field of study of the approach systems and processes that manipulate information (p. 388).

Cognitive therapy. A type of psychotherapeutic treatment that attempts to change feelings and behaviors by changing the way a client thinks about or perceives significant life experiences (p. 691).

Collective unconscious. In Jungian personality theory, that part of an individual's unconscious that is inherited, evolutionarily developed, and common to all members of the species (p. 524).

Comorbidity. The experience of more than one disorder at the same time (p. 638).

Complementary colors. Colors opposite each other on the color circle; when additively mixed, they create the sensation of white light (p. 232).

Concepts. Mental representations of kinds or categories of items or ideas (p. 369).

Conditional response (CR). In classical conditioning, a response elicited by some previously neutral stimulus that occurs as a result of pairing the neutral stimulus with an unconditional stimulus (p. 309).

Conditional stimulus (CS). In classical conditioning, a previously neutral stimulus that comes to elicit a conditional response (p. 308).

Conditioned reinforcers. In classical conditioning, formerly neutral stimuli that have become reinforcers (p. 326).

Conditioning. The ways in which events, stimuli, and behavior become associated with one another (p. 304).

Cones. Photoreceptors concentrated in the center of the retina that are responsible for visual experience under normal viewing conditions and for all experiences of color (p. 227).

Conformity. The tendency for people to adopt the behaviors, attitudes, and values of other members of a reference group (p. 587).

Confounding variable. A stimulus other than the variable an experimenter explicitly introduces into a research setting that affects a subject's behavior (p. 33).

Connectionism. A type of formal modeling that uses units and connections among the units to explore the mental steps involved in, for example, classical conditioning (p. 339).

Consciousness. A state of awareness of internal events and of the external environment (p. 103).

Consensual validation. The mutual affirmation of conscious views of reality (p. 109).

Conservation. According to Piaget, the understanding that physical properties do not change when nothing is added or taken away, even though appearances may change; also, the principle that many aspects of biological mechanisms are similar across species, which permits studies of systems in lower animals to be valid and informative for understanding human functioning (p. 159).

Consistency paradox. The observation that personality ratings across time and among different observers are consistent, while behavior ratings across situations are not consistent (p. 516).

Constitutional factors. Basic physical or psychological characteristics that are shaped by genetic and early environmental influences and that remain fairly consistent throughout a person's life (p. 146).

Construct validity. The degree to which scores on a test based on the defined variable correlate with scores of other tests, judges' ratings, or experimental results already considered valid indicators of the characteristic being measured (p. 547).

Contact comfort. Comfort derived from an infant's physical contact with the mother or caregiver (p. 195).

Context of discovery. The initial phase of research, in which observations, beliefs, information, and general knowledge lead to a new idea or a different way of thinking about some phenomenon (p. 28).

Contextual distinctiveness. The assumption that the serial position effect can be altered by the context and the distinctiveness of the experience being recalled (p. 362).

Contingency management. A general treatment strategy involving changing behavior by modifying its consequences (p. 686).

Control condition. A group of subjects in a controlled experiment that shares all of the characteristics and procedures of the experimental group except exposure to the independent variable being studied (p. 35).

Controlled processes. Processes that require attention; it is often difficult to carry out more than one controlled process at a time (p. 392).

Control procedures. Consistent procedures for giving instructions, scoring responses, and holding all other variables constant except those being systematically varied (p. 35).

Coping. The process of dealing with internal or external demands that are perceived to be threatening or overwhelming (p. 486).

Corpus callosum. The mass of nerve fibers connecting the two hemispheres of the *cerebrum* (p. 74).

Correlational methods. Research methodologies that determine to what extent two variables, traits, or attributes are related (p. 37).

Correlation coefficient (r). A statistic that indicates the degree of relationship between two variables (p. 37).

Counseling psychologist. A psychologist who specializes in providing guidance in areas such as vocational selection, school problems, drug abuse, and marital conflict (p. 674).

Counterconditioning. A technique used in therapy to substitute a new response for an inadequate one by means of conditioning procedures (p. 683).

Countertransference. Circumstances in which a psychoanalyst develops personal feelings about a client because of perceived similarity of the client to significant people in the therapist's life (p. 680).

Covariation principle. A theory which suggests that people attribute a behavior to a causal factor if that factor was present whenever the behavior occurred but was absent whenever it did not occur (p. 607).

Creativity. The ability to generate ideas or products that are both novel and appropriate to the circumstances (p. 567).

Criterion validity. The degree to which test scores indicate a result on a specific measure that is consistent with some other criterion of the characteristic being assessed; also known as *predictive validity* (p. 546).

Critical period. A sensitive time during development when an organism is optimally ready to acquire a particular behavior if the proper stimuli and experiences occur (p. 145).

Cross-cultural research. Research designed to discover whether some behavior found in one culture also occurs in other cultures (p. 39).

Cross-sectional design. A research method in which groups of subjects of different chronological ages are observed and compared at a given time (p. 141).

Crystallized intelligence. The facet of intelligence involving the knowledge a person has already acquired and the ability to access that knowledge; measures by vocabulary, arithmetic, and general information tests (p. 555).

Cutaneous senses. The skin senses that register sensations of pressure, warmth, and cold (p. 249).

Date rape. Unwanted sexual violation by a social acquaintance in the context of a consensual dating situation (p. 447).

Daydreaming. A mild form of consciousness alteration in which attention is temporarily shifted away from external stimulation toward an internal stimulus (p. 113).

Daytime sleepiness. The experience of excessive sleepiness during daytime activities; the major complaint of patients evaluated at sleep disorder centers (p. 121).

Debriefing. A procedure conducted at the end of an experiment in which the researcher provides the subject with as much information about the study as possible and makes sure that no subject leaves feeling confused, upset, or embarrassed (p. 49).

Decibel (db). The unit used to describe the physical intensity of sounds (p. 241).

Decision aversion. The tendency to avoid decision making; the tougher the decision, the greater the likelihood of decision aversion (p. 425).

Decision making. The process of choosing between alternatives; selecting or rejecting available options (p. 417).

Declarative memory. Memory for information such as facts and events (p. 347).

Deductive reasoning. A form of thinking in which one draws a conclusion that is intended to follow logically from two or more statements or premises (p. 412).

Delusions. False or irrational beliefs maintained despite clear evidence to the contrary (p. 657).

Demand characteristics. Cues in an experimental setting that influence the subjects' perception of what is expected of them and that systematically influence their behavior within that setting (p. 598).

Dendrite. The branched fiber of a neuron that receives incoming signals (p. 80).

Dependent variable. In an experimental setting, any variable whose values are the results of changes in one or more independent variables (p. 33).

Descriptive statistics. Statistical procedures that are used to summarize sets of scores with respect to central tendencies, variability, and correlations (p. A-4).

Determinism. The doctrine that all events—physical, behavioral, and mental—are determined by specific causal factors that are potentially knowable (p. 13).

Developmental age. The chronological age at which most children show a particular level of physical or mental development (p. 139).

Developmental psychology. The branch of psychology concerned with interaction between physical and psychological processes and with stages of growth from conception throughout the entire life span (p. 138).

Developmental stages. Periods during which physical, mental, or behavioral functioning differs from the functioning at all other times (p. 144).

Diathesis-stress hypothesis. A hypothesis about the cause of certain disorders, such as schizophrenia, that suggests that genetic factors predispose an individual to a certain disorder, but that environmental stress factors must impinge in order for the potential risk to manifest itself (p. 662).

Dichotic listening. An experimental technique in which a different auditory stimulus is simultaneously presented to each ear (p. 272).

Difference threshold. The smallest physical difference between two stimuli that can still be recognized as a difference (p. 222).

Discriminative stimuli. Stimuli that act as predictors of reinforcement, signaling when particular behaviors will result in positive reinforcement (p. 323).

Dispositional variables. The organismic variables, or inner determinants of behavior, that occur within human and nonhuman animals (p. 9).

Dissociative amnesia. The inability to remember important personal experiences caused by psychological factors in the absence of any organic dysfunction; the important personal experiences forgotten may include sexual and physical childhood abuse (p. 640).

Dissociative disorder. A personality disorder marked by a disturbance in the integration of identity, memory, or consciousness (p. 639).

Dissociative identity disorder (DID). A dissociative mental disorder in which two or more distinct personalities exist within the same individual; formerly known as multiple personality disorder (p. 640).

Distal stimulus. In the processes of perception, the physical object in the world, as contrasted with the *proximal stimulus,* the optical image on the retina (p. 261).

Divergent thinking. An aspect of creativity characterized by an ability to produce unusual but appropriate responses to problems (p. 568).

Dopamine hypothesis. A theory proposing a relationship between many of the symptoms associated with schizophrenia and a relative excess of the neurotransmitter dopamine at specific receptor sites in the central nervous system (p. 662).

Double bind. A situation in which a child receives contradictory messages from a parent; hypothesized to contribute to schizophrenic reactions (p. 663).

Double-blind control. An experimental technique in which biased expectations of experimenters are eliminated by keeping both subjects and experimental assistants unaware of which subjects have received which treatment (p. 35).

Drapetomania. A fictitious mental illness believed to cause slaves to run away from their masters; an example of the misuse of the medical model of psychopathology (p. 666).

Dream analysis. The psychoanalytic interpretation of dreams in order to gain insight into a person's unconscious motives or conflicts (p. 680).

Dream work. In Freudian *dream analysis,* the process by which the internal censor transforms the *latent content* of a dream into *manifest content* (p. 123).

Drug therapy. The therapeutic use of drugs to treat mental disorders (p. 702).

DSM-IV. The current diagnostic and statistical manual of the American Psychiatric Association that classifies, defines, and describes over 200 mental disorders (p. 636).

Dualism. The view that the body and brain act independently of the mind (p. 106).

Echoic memory. Sensory memory that allows auditory information to be stored for brief durations (p. 352).

Echo-planar MRI. A device that produces high-resolution MRI images swiftly enough to study the functioning brain and body (p. 68).

Ego. In Freudian theory, that aspect of the personality involved in self-preservation activities and in directing instinctual drives and urges into appropriate channels (p. 521).

Egocentrism. The inability to see the world from a perspective other than one's own; in cognitive development, the inability of a young child at the preoperational stage to imagine a scene from anyone else's perspective (p. 159).

Ego defense mechanism. In Freudian theory, a mental strategy (conscious or unconscious) used by the ego to defend itself against conflicts experienced in the normal course of life (p. 521).

Electroconvulsive therapy (ECT). The use of electroconvulsive shock as an effective treatment for severe depression (p. 701).

Electrode. A device used both to apply electric current to tissue and to detect brain activity (p. 66).

Electroencephalogram (EEG). A recording of the electrical activity of the brain (p. 66).

Emotion. A complex pattern of changes, including physiological arousal, feelings, cognitive processes, and behavioral reactions, made in response to a situation perceived to be personally significant (p. 460).

Emotion wheel. A model of emotion depicting eight basic emotions made up of four pairs of opposites; joy-sadness, fear-anger, surprise-anticipation, and acceptance-disgust (p. 464).

Empathy. The ability to share in someone else's emotion; may represent part of the foundation for a child's future system of moral behavior (p. 212).

Encephalization. An increase in brain size, an important development in human evolution (p. 60).

Encoding. The process by which a mental representation is formed in memory (p. 348).

Encoding specificity. The principle that subsequent retrieval of information is enhanced if cues received at the time of recall are consistent with those present at the time of encoding (p. 361).

Endocrine system. The network of glands that manufacture and secrete hormones into the bloodstream (p. 77).

Engram. The physical memory trace for information in the brain (p. 379).

Environment. The external influences, conditions, and circumstances that affect an individual's development and behavior (p. 57).

Environmental psychology. The study of the relationships between psychological processes and physical environments, both natural and human-made, emphasizing the reciprocity and mutual influence in an organism–environment relationship (p. 622).

Environmental or **situational variables.** External influences on behavior (p. 9).

Episodic memories. Long-term memories for autobiographical events and the contexts in which they occurred (p. 359).

Equity theory. A cognitive theory of work motivation which proposes that workers are motivated to maintain fair and equitable relationships with other relevant persons; also, a model which postulates that equitable relationships are those in which the participants' outcomes are proportional to their inputs (p. 455).

Erogenous zones. Areas of the skin surface that are especially sensitive to stimulation and that give rise to erotic or sexual sensations (p. 249).

Eros. In Freudian theory, the life instinct that provides energy for growth and survival (p. 518).

Estrogen. The female sex hormone, produced by the ovaries, that is responsible for the release of eggs from the ovaries as well as for the development and maintenance of female reproductive structures and secondary sex characteristics (p. 79).

Etiology. The causes of, or factors related to, the development of a disorder (p. 633).

Eugenics. The movement that advocated improving the human species by encouraging biologically superior people to interbreed while discouraging biologically inferior types from having offspring (p. 543).

Evolution. The theory that species change and become adapted to their environments over time through the interaction of biological and environmental variables (p. 57).

Evolutionary approach. The approach to psychology that stresses the importance of behavioral and mental adaptiveness, based on the assumption that mental capabilities evolved over millions of years to serve particular adaptive purposes (p. 19).

Excitatory input. Information entering a neuron that signals it to fire (p. 82).

Expectancy effects. Results that occur when a researcher or observer subtly communicates to subjects the kind of behavior he or she expects to find, thereby creating that expected reaction (p. 33).

Expectancy theory. The cognitive theory of work motivation which proposes that workers are motivated when they expect their efforts and job performance to result in desired outcomes (p. 455).

Experience sampling. An experimental method that assists researchers in describing the typical contents of consciousness; subjects are asked to record what they are feeling and thinking whenever signaled to do so (p. 105).

Experimental analysis of behavior. A Skinnerian approach to operant conditioning that systematically varies stimulus conditions in order to discover the ways that various kinds of experience affect the probability of responses; makes no inferences about inner states or nonobservable bases for behavioral relationships demonstrated in the laboratory (p. 321).

Experimental condition. The group of subjects in a controlled experiment that shares all of the characteristics of the control group and in addition is exposed to the independent variable being studied (p. 35).

Experimental method. A research methodology that involves the manipulation of independent variables in order to determine their effects on the dependent variables (p. 37).

Explanatory style. The habitual way in which people explain the causes of events in their lives along the dimensions internal-external, global-specific, and stable-unstable; an internal-global-unstable explanatory style puts people at risk for depression (p. 653).

Explicit use of memory. The conscious effort to recover information through memory processes (p. 346).

Extinction. In conditioning, the weakening of a conditioned association in the absence of a reinforcer or unconditional stimulus (p. 314).

Eye movement desensitization and reprocessing (EMDR). A cognitive behavior modification treatment in which clients follow the therapist's moving finger with their eyes while they report on thoughts and feelings; of value in stress disorders and phobias (p. 685).

Face validity. The degree to which test items appear to be directly related to the attribute the researcher wishes to measure (p. 546).

Fear. A rational reaction to an objectively identified external danger (such as a fire in one's home or being mugged) that may induce a person to flee or attack in self-defense (p. 643).

Fetish. A nonsexual object that through conditioning becomes capable of producing sexual arousal (p. 445).

Fight-or-flight syndrome. A sequence of internal activities triggered when an organism is faced with a threat; prepares the body for combat and struggle or for running away to safety (p. 473).

Figural goodness. A Gestalt perceptual organizational process in which a figure is seen according to its perceived simplicity, symmetry, and regularity (p. 280).

Figure. Objectlike regions of the visual field that are distinguished from background (p. 279).

Five-factor model. A comprehensive descriptive personality system that maps out the relationships among common traits, theoretical concepts, and personality scales; informally called *The Big Five* (p. 514).

Fixed-action patterns. Stereotypical patterns of behavior, specific to each particular species of animal, released by appropriate environmental stimuli (p. 431).

Flooding. A therapy for phobias in which clients are exposed, with their permission, to the stimuli most frightening to them, to force them to test reality (p. 684).

Fluid intelligence. The aspect of intelligence that involves the ability to see complex relationships and solve problems (p. 555).

Formal assessment. The systematic procedures and measurement instruments used by trained professionals to assess an individual's functioning, aptitudes, abilities, or mental states (p. 545).

Foundational theories. Frameworks for initial understanding formulated by children to explain their experiences of the world (p. 163).

Fovea. Area of the retina that contains densely packed cones and forms the point of sharpest vision (p. 227).

Frame. A particular description of a choice; the perspective from which a choice is described or framed affects how a decision is made and which option is ultimately exercised (p. 423).

Free association. In psychoanalysis, the therapeutic method in which a patient gives a running account of thoughts, wishes, physical sensations, and mental images as they occur (p. 679).

Frequency distribution. A summary of how frequently each score appears in a set of observations (p. A–5).

Frequency theory. The theory that a tone produces a rate of vibration in the basilar membrane equal to its frequency, with the result that pitch can be coded by the frequency of the neural response (p. 245).

Functional fixedness. An inability to perceive a new use for an object previously associated with some other purpose; adversely affects problem solving and creativity (p. 412).

Functionalism. The perspective on mind and behavior that focuses on the examination of their functions in an organism's interactions with the environment (p. 14).

Fundamental attribution error (FAE). The dual tendency of observers to underestimate the impact of situational factors and to overestimate the influence of dispositional factors on a person's behavior (p. 608).

Ganglion cells. Cells in the visual system that integrate impulses from many *bipolar cells* in a single firing rate (p. 228).

Gate-control theory. A theory about pain modulation which proposes certain cells in the spinal cord act as gates to interrupt and block some pain signals while sending others on to the brain (p. 253).

Gender. A psychological phenomenon that refers to learned sex-related behaviors and attitudes of males and females (p. 197).

Gender identity. One's sense of maleness or femaleness; usually includes awareness and acceptance of one's biological sex (p. 197).

Gender roles. Sets of behaviors and attitudes associated by society with being male or female and expressed publicly by the individual (p. 198).

General adaption syndrome (GAS). The pattern of nonspecific adaptational physiological mechanisms that occurs in response to continuing threat by almost any serious stressor (p. 475).

Generalized anxiety disorder. An anxiety disorder in which an individual feels anxious and worried most of the time for at least six months, when not threatened by any specific danger or object (p. 642).

Generativity. A commitment beyond one's self and one's partner to family, work, society, and future generations; typically, a crucial step in development in one's 30s and 40s (p. 205).

Genes. The biological units of heredity; discrete sections of chromosomes responsible for transmission of traits (p. 62).

Genetics. The study of the inheritance of physical and psychological traits from ancestors (p. 62).

Genotype. The genetic structure an organism inherits from its parents (p. 59).

Gestalt psychology. A school of psychology which maintains that psychological phenomena can be understood only when viewed as organized, structured wholes, not when broken down into primitive perceptual elements (p. 268).

Gestalt therapy. Therapy that focuses on ways to unite mind and body to make a person whole (p. 696).

Glia. The cells that hold neurons together and facilitate neural transmission, remove damaged and dead neurons, and prevent poisonous substances in the blood from reaching the brain (p. 81).

Goal-directed selection. A determinant of why people select some parts of sensory input for further processing; it reflects the choices made as a function of one's own goals (p. 270).

Graded potential. Excitatory activity along a dendrite or cell membrane produced by stimulation from another neuron (p. 82).

Ground. The backdrop, or background areas of the visual field, against which figures stand out (p. 279).

Group dynamics. The study of how group processes change individual functioning (p. 594).

Guided search. In visual perception, a parallel search of the environment for single, basic attributes that guides attention to likely locations of objects with more complex combinations of attributes (p. 275).

Habituation. A decrease in the strength of a response when a stimulus is presented repeatedly (p. 172).

Hallucinations. False perceptions that occur in the absence of objective stimulation (p. 129).

Halo effect. A form of bias in which an observer judges a person whom he or she likes favorably on most or all dimensions (p. 551).

Hardiness. A personality style that minimizes stress responses by means of challenge, commitment, and control (p. 485).

Health. A general condition of soundness and vigor of body and mind; not simply the absence of illness or injury (p. 491).

Health promotion. The development and implementation of general strategies and specific tactics to eliminate or reduce the risk that people will become ill (p. 492).

Health psychology. The field of psychology devoted to understanding the ways people stay healthy, the reasons they become ill, and the ways they respond when they become ill (p. 491).

Heredity. The biological transmission of traits from parents to offspring (p. 57).

Heritability estimate. A statistical estimate of the degree of inheritance of a given trait or behavior, assessed by the degree of similarity between individuals who vary in their extent of genetic similarity (p. 561).

Hertz (Hz). A unit of sound frequency; expressed in cycles per second (p. 240).

Heuristics. Cognitive strategies, or "rules of thumb," often used as shortcuts in solving a complex inferential task; heuristics generally increase the efficiency of thought processes (p. 417).

Hierarchy of needs. Maslow's view that basic human motives form a hierarchy and the needs at each level of the hierarchy must be satisfied before the next level can be achieved; these needs progress from basic biological needs to the need for transcendence (p. 456).

Hippocampus. The part of the limbic system that is involved in the acquisition of explicit memory (p. 72).

Histrionic personality disorder. Personality disorder characterized by patterns of excessive emotionality and attention seeking (p. 639).

HIV. Human immunodeficiency virus, a virus that attacks white blood cells (T-lymphocytes) in human blood, thereby weakening the functioning of the immune system; HIV causes AIDS (p. 496).

Homeostasis. Constancy or equilibrium of the internal conditions of the body (p. 73).

Horizontal cells. The cells that integrate information across the retina; rather than sending signals toward the brain, horizontal cells connect receptors to each other (p. 228).

Hormones. The chemical messengers, manufactured and secreted by the endocrine glands, that regulate metabolism and influence body growth, mood, and sexual characteristics (p. 77).

Hospice approach. An approach to serving the needs of the chronically ill in a homelike atmosphere rather than in a hospital; intended to make dying more humane than it might be in institutional settings (p. 208).

Hozho. A Navajo concept referring to harmony, peace of mind, goodness, ideal family relationships, beauty in arts and crafts, and health of body and spirit (p. 491).

Hue. The dimension of color space that captures the qualitative experience of the color of a light (p. 231).

Human behavior genetics. The area of study that evaluates the genetic component of individual differences in behaviors and traits (p. 62).

Human factors. The research field that applies psychological knowledge to design equipment and machinery for safe and efficient use (p. 418).

Humanistic approach. A psychological model that emphasizes an individual's phenomenal world and inherent capacity for making rational choices and developing to maximum potential (p. 17).

Human-potential movement. The therapy movement that encompasses all those practices and methods that release the potential of the average human being for greater levels of performance and greater richness of experience (p. 695).

Hypnosis. An altered state of awareness characterized by deep relaxation, susceptibility to suggestions, and changes in perception, memory, motivation, and self-control (p. 125).

Hypnotizability. The degree to which an individual is responsive to standardized hypnotic suggestion (p. 126).

Hypothalamus. The brain structure that regulates motivated behavior (such as eating and drinking) and homeostasis (p. 73).

Hypothesis. A tentative and testable explanation of the relationship between two (or more) events or variables; often stated as a prediction that a certain outcome will result from specific conditions (p. 29).

Hysteria. A mental illness (originally thought only to affect women) characterized by physical impairment without physical cause; the category is no longer used diagnostically (p. 630).

Iconic memory. Sensory memory in the visual domain; allows large amounts of information to be stored for very brief durations (p. 350).

Id. In Freudian theory, the primitive, unconscious part of the personality that operates irrationally and acts on impulse to pursue pleasure (p. 520).

Identification and recognition. Two ways of attaching meaning to percepts (p. 260).

Idiographic approach. A methodological approach to the study of personality processes that emphasizes understanding the unique aspects of each individual's personality rather than the common dimensions across which all individuals can be measured (p. 509).

Illusion. An experience of a stimulus pattern in a manner that is demonstrably incorrect but shared by others in the same perceptual environment (p. 264).

Illusory conjunctions. The perceptual errors that occur when primitive features of objects, such as their colors and positions, are not combined correctly by the visual system (p. 276).

Implicit use of memory. Availability of information through memory processes without the exertion of any conscious effort to recover information (p. 346).

Implosion therapy. A behavioral therapeutic technique that exposes a client to anxiety-provoking stimuli, through his or her own imagination, in an attempt to extinguish the anxiety associated with the stimuli (p. 684).

Imprinting. A primitive form of learning in which some infant animals physically follow and form an attachment to the first moving object they see and/or hear (p. 190).

Independent variable. In experimental settings, the stimulus condition whose values are free to vary independently of any other variable in the situation (p. 33).

Induced motion. An illusion in which a stationary point of light within a moving reference frame is seen as moving and the reference frame is perceived as stationary (p. 284).

Inductive reasoning. A form of reasoning in which a conclusion is made about the probability of some state of affairs, based on the available evidence and past experience (p. 415).

Inference. The reasoning process of drawing a conclusion on the basis of a sample of evidence or on the basis of prior beliefs and theories (p. 403).

Inferential statistics. Statistical procedures that allow researchers to determine whether the results they obtain support their hypotheses or can just be attributed to chance variation (p. A–4).

Informational influence. A reason that people conform to group pressures; the desire to be correct and right and to understand how best to act in a given situation (p. 588).

Inhibitory input. Information entering a neuron signaling it not to fire (p. 82).

Initiation rites. Rites in many nonindustrial societies that take place around puberty and serve as public acknowledgment of the passage from childhood to adulthood; also called *rites of passage* (p. 199).

Insanity. The legal (not clinical) designation for the state of an individual judged to be legally irresponsible or incompetent (p. 665).

Insight therapy. A technique by which the therapist guides a patient toward discovering insights between present symptoms and past origins; also known as *psychodynamic therapy* (p. 678).

Insomnia. The chronic inability to sleep normally; symptoms include difficulty in falling asleep, frequent waking, inability to return to sleep, and early morning awakening (p. 120).

Instinctual drift. The tendency for learned behavior to drift toward instinctual behavior over time (p. 332).

Intelligence. The global capacity to profit from experience and to go beyond given information about the environment (p. 551).

Intelligence quotient (IQ). An index derived from standardized tests of intelligence; originally obtained by dividing an individual's mental age by chronological age and then multiplying by 100; now directly computed as an IQ test score (p. 553).

Interactionist perspective. The view that psychopathology is the product of a complex interaction between a number of biological and psychological factors (p. 635).

Interference. A memory phenomenon that occurs when retrieval cues do not point effectively to one specific memory (p. 360).

Interjudge reliability. The degree to which different observers make similar ratings of or agree about what a subject did during an observation period (p. 551).

Internal consistency. A measure of reliability; the degree to which a test yields similar scores across its different parts, such as on odd versus even items (p. 545).

Interneurons. Brain neurons that relay messages from sensory neurons to other interneurons or to motor neurons (p. 80).

Intervening variables. The inferred conditions or events that explain a link between an observable output and a measurable response output; in organisms, these variables include physiological conditions such as hunger, or psychological processes such as fear or creativity (p. 8).

Interview. A face-to-face conversation between a researcher and a respondent for the purpose of gathering detailed information about the respondent (p. 549).

Intimacy. The capacity to make a full commitment—sexual, emotional, and moral—to another person (p. 203).

Intuitive psychologist. A layperson with naive or untrained theories about the nature of personality, motivation, and the causes of human behavior (p. 607).

Ion channels. The portions of neurons' cell membranes that selectively permit certain ions to flow in and out (p. 84).

James-Lange theory of emotion. A peripheral-feedback theory of emotion stating that an eliciting stimulus triggers a behavioral response that sends different sensory and motor feedback to the brain and creates the feeling of a specific emotion (p. 467).

Job analysis. A study of a specific job focusing on the nature and degree of skill required, the amount of effort demanded, the extent to which an individual in that job is responsible for important decisions, and types of stress the job entails (p. 578).

Job burnout. The syndrome of emotional exhaustion, depersonalization, and reduced personal accomplishment, often experienced by workers in high-stress jobs (p. 503).

Judgment. The process by which people form opinions, reach conclusions, and make critical evaluations of events and people based on available material; also, the product of that mental activity (p. 417).

Just noticeable difference (JND). The smallest difference between two sensations that allows them to be discriminated (p. 222).

Kinesthetic sense. Sense concerned with bodily position and movement of the body parts relative to each other (p. 251).

Language-making capacity. The innate guidelines or operating principles that children bring to the task of learning a language (p. 176).

Language production. What people say, sign, and write, as well as the processes they go through to produce these messages (p. 395).

Latent content. In Freudian dream analysis, the hidden meaning of a dream (p. 123).

Lateral geniculate nucleus. The relay point in the thalamus through which impulses pass when going from the eye to the occipital cortex (p. 229).

Lateral inhibition. The tendency for a visual receptor excited by a light to suppress neighboring receptors (p. 238).

Law of common fate. A law of grouping which states that elements moving in the same direction at the same rate are grouped together (p. 282).

Law of effect. A basic law of learning which states that the power of a stimulus to evoke a response is strengthened when the response is followed by a reward and weakened when it is not followed by a reward (p. 320).

Law of pragnanz. In Gestalt psychology, the general principle that the simplest organization requiring the least cognitive effort will emerge in perceptions (p. 283).

Law of proximity. A law of grouping which states that the nearest, or most proximal, elements are grouped together (p. 282).

Law of similarity. A law of grouping which states that the most similar elements are grouped together (p. 282).

Lazarus-Schacter theory of emotion. A theory stating that the experience of emotion is the joint effect of physiological arousal and cognitive appraisal, which serves to determine how an ambiguous inner state of arousal will be labeled (p. 468).

Learned helplessness. A general pattern of nonresponding in the presence of noxious stimuli that often follows after an organism has previously experienced noncontingent, inescapable aversive stimuli (p. 653).

Learning. A process based on experience that results in a relatively permanent change in behavior or behavioral potential (p. 305).

Learning–performance distinction. The difference between what has been learned and what is expressed in overt behavior (p. 305).

Lesion. Injury to or destruction of body tissue (p. 65).

Levels-of-processing theory. A theory which suggests that the deeper the level at which information was processed, the more likely it is to be committed to memory (p. 364).

Libido. In Freudian theory, the psychic energy that drives individuals toward sensual pleasures of all types, especially sexual ones (p. 518).

Life-change unit (LCU). In stress research, the measure of the stress levels of different types of change experienced during a given period (p. 478).

Life history. Information about a person's life taken from records such as schools or the military, written productions, personal journals, and medical data (p. 549).

Life-span development. Study of the continuities, stabilities, and changes in physical and psychological processes that characterize human functioning from conception throughout the entire life cycle (p. 138).

Limbic system. The region of the brain that regulates emotional behavior, basic motivational urges, and memory, as well as major physiological functions (p. 72).

Locus of control orientation. Generalized belief about whether outcomes of actions are caused by what people do or by events outside their control (p. 451).

Longitudinal design. A research design in which the same subjects are observed repeatedly, sometimes over many years (p. 140).

Long-term memory (LTM). Memory processes associated with the preservation of information for retrieval at any later time; theoretically, having unlimited capacity (p. 357).

Loudness. A perceptual dimension of sound influenced by the amplitude of a sound wave; sound waves with large amplitudes are generally experienced as loud and those with small amplitudes as soft (p. 241).

Lucid dreaming. The theory that conscious awareness of dreaming is a learnable skill that enables dreamers to control the direction and content of their dreams (p. 124).

Magnetic resonance imaging (MRI). A device for brain imaging that scans the brain using magnetic fields and radio waves (p. 67).

Magnitude estimation. A method of constructing psychophysical scales by having observers scale their sensations directly into numbers (p. 224).

Maintenance rehearsal. Active repetition of information in order to enhance subsequent memory access to it (p. 354).

Manic episode. A component of bipolar disorder characterized by periods of extreme elation, unbounded euphoria without sufficient reason, and grandiose thoughts or feelings about personal abilities (p. 649).

Manifest content. In Freudian dream analysis, the surface content of a dream, which is assumed to mask the dream's actual meaning (p. 123).

Maturation. The continuing influence of heredity throughout development; the age-related physical and behavioral changes characteristic of a species (p. 153).

Mean. The arithemetic average of a group of scores; the most commonly used measure of central tendency (p. A–8).

Measure of central tendency. A statistic, such as a mean, median, or mode, that provides one score as representative of a set of observations (p. A–8).

Measure of variability. A statistic, such as a range or standard deviation, that indicates how tightly the scores in a set of observations cluster together (p. A–8).

Median. The score in a distribution above and below which lie 50 percent of the other scores; a measure of central tendency (p. A–8).

Meditation. A form of consciousness alteration designed to enhance self-knowledge and well-being through reduced self-awareness (p. 129).

Medulla. The region of the brain stem that regulates breathing, waking, and heartbeat (p. 71).

Memory. The mental capacity to encode, store, and retrieve information (p. 344).

Menarche. The onset of menstruation (p. 154).

Mental age (MA). In Binet's measure of intelligence, the age at which a child is performing intellectually, expressed in terms of the average age at which normal children achieve a particular score (p. 552).

Mental models. Conceptual frameworks used in understanding and reasoning that reproduce the details of a situation as accurately as possible (p. 414).

Mental set. The tendency to respond to a new problem in the manner used to respond to a previous problem (p. 415).

Meta-analysis. A statistical technique for evaluating hypotheses by providing a formal mechanism for detecting the general conclusions found in data from many different experiments (p. 706).

Metamemory. Implicit or explicit knowledge about memory abilities and effective memory strategies; cognition about memory (p. 368).

Mnemonics. Strategies or devices that use familiar information during the encoding of new information to enhance subsequent access to the information in memory (p. 367).

Mode. The score appearing most frequently in a set of observations; a measure of central tendency (p. A–8).

Model. A conceptual framework that provides a simplified way of organizing the basic components of a field of knowledge (p. 15).

Monism. The view that the mind and the brain are one and that all mental phenomena are products of the brain (p. 107).

Mood disorder. A mood disturbance such as severe depression or depression alternating with mania (p. 648).

Morality. A system of beliefs and values which ensures that individuals will keep their obligations to others in society and will behave in ways that do not interfere with the rights and interests of others (p. 209).

Motherese (child-directed speech). A special form of speech with an exaggerated and high-pitched intonation that adults use to speak to infants and young children (p. 171).

Motivation. The process of starting, directing, and maintaining physical and psychological activities; includes mechanisms involved in preferences for one activity over another and the vigor and persistence of responses (p. 428).

Motor cortex. The region of the cerebral cortex that controls the action of the body's voluntary muscles (p. 75).

Motor neurons. The neurons that carry messages away from the central nervous system toward the muscles and glands (p. 80).

Narcissistic personality disorder. A personality disorder marked by a grandiose sense of self-importance, preoccupation with fantasies of success and power, and a need for constant admiration (p. 639).

Narcolepsy. A sleep disorder characterized by an irresistible compulsion to sleep during the daytime (p. 120).

Natural selection. Darwin's theory that favorable adaptations to features of the environment allow some members of a species to reproduce more successfully than others (p. 58).

Nature. In the nature-nurture debate, hereditary influences on behavior (p. 57).

Nature–nurture controversy. The debate in psychology concerning the relative importance of heredity (nature) and learning or experience (nurture) in determining development and behavior (p. 143).

Need for achievement (*n ACH*). An assumed basic human need to strive for achievement of goals that motivates a wide range of behavior and thinking (p. 450).

Negative punishment. A behavior followed by the removal of a positive stimulus, decreasing the probability of that response (p. 323).

Negative reinforcer. A stimulus not received (terminated or avoided) after a response, increasing the probability of that response (p. 322).

Neural networks. Systems of neurons that function together to perform complex tasks (p. 89).

Neuromodulator. Any substance that modifies or modulates the activities of the postsynaptic neuron (p. 88).

Neuron. A cell in the nervous system specialized to receive, process, and/or transmit information to other cells (p. 79).

Neuropathic pain. Pain caused by abnormal functioning or overactivity of nerves; it results from injury or disease of nerves (p. 252).

Neuroscience. The scientific study of the brain and of the links between brain activity and behavior (p. 64).

Neurotic disorder. Mental disorder in which a person does not have signs of brain abnormalities and does not display grossly irrational thinking or violate basic norms but does experience subjective distress; a category dropped from *DSM-IV* (p. 636).

Neurotransmitters. Chemical messengers released from neurons that cross the synapse from one neuron to another, stimulating the postsynaptic neuron (p. 86).

Nociceptive pain. Pain induced by a noxious external stimulus; specialized nerve endings in the skin send this pain message from the skin, through the spinal chord, into the brain (p. 252).

Nomothetic approach. A methodological approach to the study of personality processes in which emphasis is placed on identifying universal trait dimensions or lawful relationships between different aspects of personality functioning (p. 510).

Nonconscious. Information not typically available to consciousness or memory (p. 104).

Non-REM sleep. The period during which a sleeper does not show rapid eye movement; characterized by less dream activity than *REM sleep* (p. 115)

Norm. A standard based on measurements of a large group of people; used for comparing the scores of an individual with those of others within a well-defined group; in social psychology, the group standard of approved behavior (p. 548).

Normal curve. The symmetrical curve that represents the distribution of scores on many psychological attributes; allows researchers to make judgments of how unusual an observation or result is (p. A–10).

Normative influence. The effect of a group on an individual who is striving to be liked, accepted, and approved of by others (p. 588).

Normative investigations. Research efforts designed to describe what is characteristic of a specific age or developmental stage (p. 139).

Norm crystallization. The convergence of the expectations of a group of individuals into a common perspective as they talk and carry out activities together (p. 588).

Nurture. In the nature-nurture debate, environmental influence on behavior (p. 57).

Object permanence. The recognition that objects exist independently of an individual's action or awareness; an important cognitive acquisition of infancy (p. 158).

Observational learning. The process of learning new responses by watching the behavior of another (p. 337).

Observer bias. The distortion of perceptual evidence because of the personal motives and expectations of the viewer (p. 31).

Observer-report method. In psychological assessment, the evaluation of some aspect of a person's behavior by another person (p. 550).

Obsessive-compulsive disorder. A mental disorder characterized by obsessions—recurrent thoughts, images, or impulses that recur or persist despite efforts to suppress them—and compulsions—repetitive, purposeful acts performed according to certain rules or in a ritualized manner (p. 644).

Olfactory bulb. The center where odor-sensitive receptors send their signals, located just below the frontal lobes of the cortex (p. 247).

Operant. Behavior emitted by an organism that can be characterized in terms of the observable effects it has on the environment (p. 321).

Operant conditioning. Learning in which the probability of a response is changed by a change in its consequences (p. 321).

Operant extinction. When a behavior no longer produces predictable consequences, its return to the level of occurrence it had before operant conditioning (p. 322).

Operational definition. A definition of a variable or condition in terms of the specific operation or procedure used to determine its presence (p. 32).

Opponent-process theory. The theory that all color experiences arise from three systems, each of which includes two "opponent" elements (red versus green, blue versus yellow, and black versus white) (p. 234).

Optic nerve. The axons of the ganglion cells that carry information from the eye toward the brain (p. 228).

Organismic variables. The inner determinants of an organism's behavior (p. 9).

Organizational psychologists. Psychologists who study various aspects of the human work environment, such as communication among employees, socialization or enculturation of workers, leadership, job satisfaction, stress and burnout, and overall quality of life (p. 455).

Orientation constancy. The ability to perceive the actual orientation of objects in the real world despite their varying orientation in the retinal image (p. 293).

Overregularization. A grammatical error, usually appearing during early language development, in which rules of the language are applied too widely, resulting in incorrect linguistic forms (p. 177).

Pain. The body's response to noxious stimuli that are intense enough to cause, or threaten to cause, tissue damage (p. 251).

Panic disorder. An anxiety disorder in which sufferers experience unexpected, severe panic attacks that begin with a feeling of intense apprehension, fear, or terror; physical symptoms may include rapid heart rate, dizziness, faintness, or sensations of choking or smothering (p. 642).

Paradigm. A symbolic model in research that represents the essential features of a process being investigated (p. 29).

Parallel forms. Different versions of a test used to assess test reliability; the change of forms reduces effects of direct practice, memory, or the desire of an individual to appear consistent on the same items (p. 545).

Parallel processes. Two or more mental processes that are carried out simultaneously (p. 390).

Paranoid personality disorder. A personality disorder characterized by a pattern of mistrust and suspiciousness about the motives of individuals with whom a person interacts (p. 639).

Parasympathetic division. The subdivision of the autonomic nervous system that monitors the routine operation of the body's internal functions and conserves and restores body energy (p. 69).

Parental investment. The time and energy parents must spend raising their offspring (p. 442).

Parenting practices. Specific parenting behaviors that arise in response to particular parental goals (p. 192).

Parenting style. The manner in which a parent rears a child; an authoritative parenting style, which balances demandingness and responsiveness, is seen as the most effective (p. 192).

Partial reinforcement effect. The behavioral principle which states that responses acquired under intermittent reinforcement are more difficult to extinguish than those acquired with continuous reinforcement (p. 328).

Participant modeling. A therapeutic technique in which a therapist demonstrates the desired behavior and a client is aided, through supportive encouragement, to imitate the modeled behavior (p. 689).

Pastoral counselor. A member of a religious order who specializes in the treatment of psychological disorders, often combining spirituality with practical problem solving (p. 675).

Patient. The term used by those who take a biomedical approach to the treatment of psychological problems to describe the person being treated (p. 674).

Peace psychology. An interdisciplinary approach to the prevention of nuclear war and the maintenance of peace (p. 624).

Perceived control. The belief that one has the ability to make a difference in the course or the consequences of some event or experience; often helpful in dealing with stressors (p. 488).

Percept. What a perceiver experiences; the psychological product of perceptual activity (p. 258).

Perception. The processes that organize information in the sensory image and interpret it as having been produced by properties of objects in the external, three-dimensional world (p. 258).

Perceptual constancy. The ability to retain an unchanging percept of an object despite variations in the retinal image (p. 290).

Perceptual grouping. The ways people perceive a number of individual elements in terms of groups, following principles described by Gestalt psychologists (p. 281).

Perceptual organization. The processes that put sensory information together to give the perception of a coherent scene over the whole visual field (p. 259).

Performance. External behavior which indicates that learning has taken place; however, performance does not always reveal everything that has been learned (p. 305).

Peripheral nervous system (PNS). The part of the nervous system composed of the spinal and cranial nerves that connects the body's sensory receptors to the CNS and the CNS to the muscles and glands (p. 68).

Personal construct. A person's interpretation of reality or beliefs about the way two things are similar to each other and different from a third (p. 528).

Personality. The unique psychological qualities of an individual that influence a variety of characteristic behavior patterns (both overt and covert) across different situations and over time (p. 508).

Personality disorder. A chronic, inflexible, maladaptive pattern of perceiving, thinking, and behaving that seriously impairs an individual's ability to function in social or other settings (p. 639).

Personality inventory. A self-report questionnaire used for personality assessment that includes a series of items about personal thoughts, feelings, and behaviors (p. 571).

Personality type. A distinct pattern of personality characteristics used to assign people to categories; a qualitative difference, rather than difference in degree, used to discriminate among people (p. 511).

Person-centered therapy. A humanistic approach to treatment that emphasizes the healthy psychological growth of the individual; based on the assumption that all people share the basic tendency of human nature toward self-actualization (p. 695).

Personology. The study of personality structure, dynamics, and development in the individual involving data from diaries, biographies, literature, case studies, letters, and general observations (p. 576).

PET scanner. A device that obtains detailed pictures of activity in the living brain by recording the radioactivity emitted by cells during different cognitive or behavioral activities (p. 67).

Phantom limb phenomenon. As experienced by amputees, extreme or chronic pain in a limb that is no longer there (p. 253).

Phenotype. The observable characteristics of an organism, resulting from the interaction between the organism's genotype and its environment (p. 59).

Pheromones. Chemical signals released by organisms to communicate with other members of the species; often serve as long-distance sexual attractors (p. 248).

Phi phenomenon. The simplest form of *apparent motion,* the movement illusion in which one or more stationary lights going on and off in succession are perceived as a single moving light (p. 285).

Phobia. A persistent and irrational fear of a specific object, activity, or situation that is excessive and unreasonable, given the reality of the threat (p. 643).

Phonemes. Minimal units of speech in any given language that make a meaningful difference in speech production and reception; *r* and *l* are two distinct phonemes in English but variations of one in Japanese (p. 171).

Phonemic restoration. In speech perception, the tendency for the auditory system to fill in missing sounds in a top-down fashion (p. 295).

Photoreceptors. Receptor cells in the retina that are sensitive to light (p. 227).

Physical development. The bodily changes, maturation, and growth that occur in an organism starting with conception and continuing across the life span (p. 148).

Physiological dependence. The process by which the body becomes adjusted to and dependent on a drug (p. 131).

Pitch. Sound quality of highness or lowness; primarily dependent on the frequency of the sound wave (p. 241).

Pituitary gland. Located in the brain, the gland that secretes growth hormone and influences the secretion of hormones by other endocrine glands (p. 78).

Placebo control. An experimental condition in which treatment is not administered; it is used in cases where a placebo effect might occur (p. 35).

Placebo effect. A change in behavior in the absence of an experimental manipulation (p. 34).

Placebo therapy. A therapy independent of any specific clinical procedures that results in client improvement (p. 706).

Place theory. The theory that different frequency tones produce maximum activation at different locations along the basilar membrane with the result that pitch can be coded by the place at which activation occurs (p. 245).

Pons. The region of the brain stem that connects the spinal cord with the brain and links parts of the brain to one another (p. 71).

Positive punishment. An aversive stimulus that is presented following a behavior, decreasing the probability of that response (p. 323).

Positive reinforcer. A pleasant stimulus received after a response that increases the probability of that response (p. 322).

Possible selves. The ideal selves that a person would like to become, the selves a person could become, and the selves a person is afraid of becoming; components of the cognitive sense of self as defined by Hazel Markus (p. 535).

Postformal thought. A type of adult thinking that is suited to solving real-world problems because it is less abstract and absolute than formal thought, is adaptive to life's inconsistencies, and combines contradictory elements into a meaningful whole (p. 165).

Posttraumatic stress disorder (PTSD). An anxiety disorder characterized by the persistent reexperience of traumatic events through distressing recollections, dreams, hallucinations, or dissociative flashbacks; develops in response to rapes, life-threatening events or severe injuries, and natural disasters (p. 482).

Preattentive processing. Processing of sensory information that precedes attention to specific objects (p. 274).

Preconscious memories. Memories that are not currently conscious but that can easily be called into consciousness when necessary (p. 104).

Predictive validity. *See* **Criterion validity.**

Prefrontal lobotomy. An operation that severs the nerve fibers connecting the frontal lobes of the brain with the diencephalon, especially those fibers of the thalamic and hypothalamic areas; best-known form of psychosurgery (p. 701).

Prejudice. A learned attitude toward a target object, involving negative affect (dislike or fear); negative beliefs (stereotypes) that justify the attitude; and a behavioral intention to avoid, control, dominate, or eliminate the target object (p. 615).

Premack principle. A principle which states that a more-preferred activity can be used to reinforce a less-preferred one (p. 327).

Primary appraisal. In stress research, the first stage in the cognitive appraisal of a potentially stressful situation, in which an individual evaluates the situation or the seriousness of the demand (p. 478).

Primary reinforcers. Biologically determined reinforcers such as food and water (p. 326).

Priming. In the assessment of implicit memory, the advantage conferred by prior exposure to a word or situation; the first experience primes memory for later experiences (p. 365).

Problem solving. Thinking that is directed toward solving specific problems and that moves from an initial state to a goal state by means of a set of mental operations (p. 408).

Problem space. The elements that make up a problem: the initial state, the incomplete information or unsatisfactory conditions the person starts with; the goal state, the set of information or state the person wishes to achieve; and the set of operations, the steps the person takes to move from the initial state to the goal state (p. 409).

Procedural memory. Memory for how things get done; the way perceptual, cognitive, and motor skills are acquired, retained, and used (p. 347).

Projective test. A method of personality assessment in which an individual is presented with a standardized set of ambiguous, abstract stimuli and asked to interpret their meanings; the individual's responses are assumed to reveal inner feelings, motives, and conflicts (p. 574).

Prototype. The most representative example of a category (p. 370).

Proximal stimulus. The optical image on the retina; contrasted with the *distal stimulus,* the physical object in the world (p. 261).

Psychiatrist. An individual who has obtained an M.D. degree and also has completed postdoctoral specialty training in mental and emotional disorders; a psychiatrist may prescribe medications for the treatment of psychological disorders (p. 675).

Psychic determinism. The assumption that all mental and behavioral reactions are determined by previous experiences (p. 519).

Psychoactive drugs. Chemicals that affect mental processes and behavior by temporarily changing conscious awareness of reality (p. 131).

Psychoanalyst. An individual who has earned either a Ph.D. or an M.D. degree and has completed postgraduate training in the Freudian approach to understanding and treating mental disorders (p. 675).

Psychoanalytic therapy. The form of psychodynamic therapy developed by Freud; an intensive and prolonged technique for exploring unconscious motivations and conflicts in neurotic, anxiety-ridden individuals (p. 677).

Psychobiography. The systematic use of psychological (especially personality) theory to transform a life into a coherent and illuminating story; this tradition can be traced back to Freud's analysis of Leonardo da Vinci (p. 526).

Psychodynamic approach. A psychological model in which behavior is explained in terms of past experiences and motivational forces; actions are viewed as stemming from inherited instincts, biological drives, and attempts to resolve conflicts between personal needs and social requirements (p. 16).

Psychodynamic personality theories. Theories of personality that share the assumption that personality is shaped by and behavior is motivated by powerful inner forces (p. 518).

Psychological assessment. The use of specified procedures to evaluate the abilities, behaviors, and personal qualities of people (p. 542).

Psychological dependence. The psychological need or craving for a drug (p. 132).

Psychological diagnosis. The label given to psychological abnormality by classifying and categorizing the observed behavior pattern into an approved diagnostic system (p. 635).

Psychological test. An instrument used to assess an individual's standing relative to others on some mental or behavioral characteristic (p. 549).

Psychometric function. A graph that plots the percentage of detections of a stimulus (on the vertical axis) for each stimulus intensity (on the horizontal axis) (p. 219).

Psychometrics. The field of psychology that specializes in mental testing (p. 544).

Psychoneuroimmunology. The research area that investigates interactions between psychological processes, such as responses to stress, and the functions of the immune system (p. 318).

Psychopathological functioning. Disruptions in emotional, behavioral, or thought processes that lead to personal distress or block one's ability to achieve important goals (p. 629).

Psychopharmacology. The branch of psychology that investigates the effects of drugs on behavior (p. 702).

Psychophysics. The study of the correspondence between physical stimulation and psychological experience (p. 219).

Psychosocial dwarfism. A syndrome in which children's normal development is inhibited by traumatic living conditions, such as abandonment or chaotic family life (p. 196).

Psychosocial stages. Proposed by Erik Erikson, successive developmental stages that focus on an individual's orientation toward the self and others; these stages incorporate both the sexual and social aspects of a person's development and the social conflicts that arise from the interaction between the individual and the social environment (p. 183).

Psychosomatic disorders. Physical disorders aggravated by or primarily attributable to prolonged emotional stress or other psychological causes (p. 475).

Psychosurgery. A surgical procedure performed on brain tissue to alleviate a psychological disorder (p. 700).

Psychotherapy. Any of a group of therapies, used to treat psychological disorders, that focus on changing faultybehaviors, thoughts, perceptions, and emotions that may be associated with specific disorders; the four major types of psychotherapy are psychodynamic, behavioral, cognitive, and existential-humanistic (p. 673).

Psychotic disorder. A severe mental disorder in which a person experiences impairments in reality testing manifested through thought, emotional, or perceptual difficulties; no longer used as a diagnostic category in *DSM-IV* (p. 637).

Puberty. The attainment of sexual maturity; indicated for girls by menarche and for boys by the production of live sperm and the ability to ejaculate (p. 154).

Punisher. An aversive stimulus that decreases the probability of the preceding response (p. 323).

Range. The difference between the highest and the lowest scores in a set of observations; the simplest measure of variability (p. A–9).

Rapid eye movement (REM). A behavioral sign of the phase of sleep during which the sleeper is likely to be experiencing dreamlike mental activity (p. 115).

Rational-emotive therapy (RET). A comprehensive system of personality change based on changing irrational beliefs that cause undesirable, highly charged emotional reactions such as severe anxiety (p. 694).

Reaction time. The elapsed time between a stimulus presentation and a designated response; used as a measure of the time required for mental processes (p. 390).

Reasoning. The process of thinking in which conclusions are drawn from a set of facts; thinking directed toward a given goal or objective (p. 408).

Recall. A method of retrieval in which an individual is required to reproduce the information previously presented; compared to *recognition* (p. 358).

Receptive field. The visual area from which a given ganglion cell receives information (p. 236).

Reciprocal determinism. A concept of Albert Bandura's social learning theory which refers to the notion that a complex reciprocal interaction exists among factors of an individual, behavior, and environmental stimuli, and that each of these components affects the others (p. 530).

Recognition. A method of retrieval in which an individual is required to identify present stimuli as having been experienced before; compared to *recall* (p. 358).

Reconstruction. The process of putting information together based on general types of stored knowledge in the absence of a specific memory representation (p. 375).

Reference frame. The spatial or temporal context for a stimulus (p. 280).

Reference group. A formal or informal group from which an individual derives attitudes and standards for acceptable and appropriate behavior and to which the individual refers for information, direction, and support for a given lifestyle (p. 589).

Reflex. An unlearned response elicited by specific stimuli that have biological relevance for an organism (p. 308).

Refractory period. The period of rest during which a new nerve impulse cannot be activated in a segment of an axon (p. 85).

Reinforcement contingency. A consistent relationship between a response and the changes in the environment that it produces (p. 322).

Relative motion parallax. A source of information about depth in which the relative distances of objects from a viewer determine the amount and direction of their relative motion in the retinal image (p. 287).

Relaxation response. A condition in which muscle tension, cortical activity, heart rate, and blood pressure decrease and breathing slows (p. 499).

Reliability. The degree to which a test produces similar scores each time it is used; stability or consistency of the scores produced by an instrument (p. 42).

REM sleep. *See* **Rapid eye movement (REM).**

Representativeness heuristic. A cognitive strategy that assigns an object to a category on the basis of a few characteristics regarded as representative of that category (p. 420).

Repressed memories. Memories of life experiences that are banished from consciousness because of their threat to psychological well-being (p. 378).

Repression. In Freudian theory, the basic defense mechanism by which painful or guilt-producing thoughts, feelings, or memories are excluded from conscious awareness (p. 378).

Residual stress pattern. A chronic syndrome in which the emotional responses of posttraumatic stress persist over time (p. 482).

Resistance. The inability or unwillingness of a patient in psychoanalysis to discuss certain ideas, desires, or experiences (p. 680).

Response bias. The systematic tendency as a result of nonsensory factors for an observer to favor responding i ticular way (p. 220).

Resting potential. The polarization of cellular fluid within a neuron, which provides the capability to produce an action potential (p. 83).

Reticular formation. The region of the brain stem that alerts the cerebral cortex to incoming sensory signals and is responsible for maintaining consciousness and awakening from sleep (p. 71).

Retina. The layer at the back of the eye that contains photoreceptors and converts light energy to neural responses (p. 227).

Retrieval. The recovery of stored information from memory (p. 348).

Retrieval cues. Internally or externally generated stimuli available to help with the retrieval of a memory (p. 358).

Ritual healing. Ceremonies that infuse special emotional intensity and meaning into the healing process; heightens patients' suggestibility and sense of importance (p. 677).

Rods. Photoreceptors concentrated in the periphery of the retina that are most active in dim illumination; rods do not produce sensation of color (p. 227).

Rules. Behavioral guidelines for acting in certain ways in certain situations (p. 585).

Saturation. The dimension of color space that captures the purity and vividness of color sensations (p. 232).

Savings. The phenomenon in which a conditional response that has been extinguished gains strength more rapidly with further acquisition training than it did initially (p. 314).

Savings method. A method of measuring memory originally used by Hermann Ebbinghaus; involves measuring memory by the savings in the amount of time it takes to relearn original material (p. 345).

Schedules of reinforcement. In operant conditioning, the patterns of delivering and withholding reinforcement (p. 328).

Schemas. General conceptual frameworks, or clusters of knowledge, regarding objects, people, and situations; knowledge packages that encode generalizations about the structure of the environment (p. 373).

Schemes. Piaget's term for cognitive structures that develop as infants and young children learn to interpret the world and adapt to their environment (p. 157).

Schizophrenic disorder. A severe form of psychopathology characterized by the breakdown of integrated personality functioning, withdrawal from reality, emotional distortions, and disturbed thought processes (p. 656).

Scientific method. The set of procedures used for gathering and interpreting objective information in a way that minimizes error and yields dependable generalizations (p. 4).

Secondary appraisal. In stress research, the second stage in the cognitive appraisal of a potentially stressful situation, in which the individual evaluates the personal and social resources available to deal with the stressful circumstance and determines the needed action (p. 478).

Selective optimization with compensation. A strategy for successful aging in which one makes the most of gains while minimizing the impact of losses that accompany normal aging (p. 168).

Selective social interaction. The view which suggests that as people age, they become more selective in choosing social partners who satisfy their emotional needs (p. 205).

Self. The irreducible unit out of which the coherence and stability of a personality emerge (p. 534).

Self-actualization. A concept in personality psychology referring to a person's constant striving to realize his or her potential and to develop inherent talents and capabilities (p. 524).

Self-awareness. The top level of consciousness; cognizance of the autobiographical character of personally experienced events (p. 103).

Self-efficacy. The set of beliefs that one can perform adequately in a particular situation (p. 531).

Self-esteem. A generalized evaluative attitude toward the self that influences both moods and behavior and that exerts a powerful effect on a range of personal and social behaviors (p. 536).

Self-fulfilling prophecy. A prediction made about some future behavior or event that modifies interactions so as to produce what is expected (p. 610).

Self-handicapping. The process of developing, in anticipation of failure, behavioral reactions and explanations that minimize ability deficits as possible attributions for the failure (p. 536).

Self-perception theory. The idea that people observe themselves in order to figure out the reasons they act as they do; people infer what their internal states are by perceiving how they are acting in a given situation (p. 614).

Self-report measure. The self-behavior that is identified through a subject's own observations and reports (p. 43).

Self-report method. A common research technique in which an assessment is achieved through a respondent's answers to a series of questions (p. 549).

Self-serving bias. A class of attributional biases in which people tend to take credit for their successes and deny responsibility for their failures (p. 609).

Semantic memory. The aspect of long-term memory that stores the basic meaning of words and concepts (p. 359).

Sensation. The process by which stimulation of a sensory receptor gives rise to neural impulses that result in an elementary experience of feeling, or awareness of, conditions inside or outside the body (p. 259).

Sensory adaptation. A phenomenon in which visual receptor cells lose their power to respond after a period of unchanged stimulation; allows a more rapid reaction to new sources of information (p. 218).

Sensory memory. The initial memory processes involved in the momentary preservation of fleeting impressions of sensory stimuli; also called *sensory register* (p. 350)

Sensory modalities. A general term covering all the separate sensory systems, such as vision, hearing, smell, taste, and touch, that take in information (p. 216).

Sensory neurons. The neurons that carry messages from sense receptors toward the central nervous system (p. 80).

Sensory physiology. The study of the way in which biological mechanisms convert physical events into neural events (p. 217).

Sensory processes. The processes associated with the sense organs and peripheral aspects of the nervous system that put you in direct contact with sources of stimulation (p. 216).

Sequential design. A research approach in which a group of subjects spanning a small age range are grouped according to year of birth and observed repeatedly over several years; combines some features of both cross-sectional and longitudinal research approaches (p. 142).

Serial position effect. A characteristic of memory retrieval in which the recall of beginning and end items on a list is often better than recall of items appearing in the middle (p. 362).

Serial processes. Two or more mental processes that are carried out in order, one after the other (p. 390).

Sex chromosomes. Chromosomes which contain the genes that code for the development of male or female characteristics (p. 62).

Sex differences. Biologically based characteristics that distinguish males from female (p. 197).

Sexual arousal. The motivational state of excitement and tension brought about by physiological and cognitive reactions to erotic stimuli (p. 445).

Sexual scripts. Socially learned programs of sexual responsiveness (p. 447).

Shamanism. A spiritual tradition that involves both healing and gaining contact with the spirit world (p. 677).

Shape constancy. The ability to perceive the true shape of an object despite variations in the size of the retinal image (p. 292).

Shaping by successive approximations. A behavioral method which reinforces responses that successively approximate and ultimately match the desired response (p. 329).

Short-term memory (STM). Memory processes associated with preservation of recent experiences and with retrieval of information from long-term memory; short-term memory is of limited capacity and stores information for only a short length of time without rehearsal (p. 353).

Signal detection theory. A systematic approach to the problem of response bias that allows an experimenter to identify and separate the roles of sensory stimuli and the individual's criterion level in producing the final response (p. 221).

Significant difference. A difference between experimental groups or conditions that would have occurred by chance less than an accepted criterion; in psychology, the criterion most often used is a probability of less than 5 times out of 100, or $p < .05$ (p. A–12).

Situational behavior observations. Observations of an individual's behavioral patterns in one or more situations, such as at work or in school (p. 549).

Size constancy. The ability to perceive the true size of an object despite variations in the size of its retinal image (p. 291).

Sleep apnea. A sleep disorder of the upper respiratory system that causes the person to stop breathing while asleep (p. 120).

Social categorization. The process by which people organize the social environment by categorizing themselves and others into groups (p. 616).

Social context. The part of the total environment that includes other people, both real and imagined interactions, the setting in which the interactions take place, and unwritten rules and expectations that govern the way people relate to each other (p. 584).

Social intelligence. A theory of personality that refers to the expertise people bring to their experience of life tasks (p. 532).

Socialization. The lifelong process whereby an individual's behavioral patterns, values, standards, skills, attitudes, and motives are shaped to conform to those regarded as desirable in a particular society (p. 188).

Social-learning theory. The learning theory that stresses the role of observation and the imitation of behaviors observed in others (p. 434).

Social-learning therapy. A form of treatment in which clients observe models' desirable behaviors being reinforced (p. 687).

Social norm. The expectation a group has for its members regarding acceptable and appropriate attitudes and behaviors (p. 588).

Social perception. The process by which a person comes to know or perceive the personal attributes of him- or herself and other people (p. 606).

Social phobia. A persistent, irrational fear that arises in anticipation of a public situation in which an individual can be observed by others (p. 643).

Social psychology. The branch of psychology that studies the effect of social variables on individual behavior, attitudes, perceptions, and motives; also studies group and intergroup phenomena (p. 584).

Social role. A socially defined pattern of behavior that is expected of a person who is functioning in a given setting or group (p. 585).

Social support. Resources, including material aid, socioemotional support, and informational aid, provided by others to help a person cope with stress (p. 489).

Soma. The cell body of a neuron, containing the nucleus and cytoplasm (p. 80).

Somatic nervous system. The subdivision of the peripheral nervous system that connects the central nervous system to the skeletal muscles and skin (p. 69).

Somatosensory cortex. The region of the parietal lobes that processes sensory input from various body areas (p. 75).

Spatial-frequency model. The theory that the visual system analyzes complex stimuli into spatial frequencies (p. 238).

Spatial summation. The process by which a neuron summates several small excitatory or inhibitory inputs received from different sources at the same time in order to determine whether to fire (p. 83).

Specific phobia. A phobia that occurs in response to a specific type of object or situation (p. 644).

Split-half reliability. A measure of the correlation between test takers' performance on different halves (e.g., odd- and even-numbered items) of a test (p. 545).

Spontaneous recovery. The reappearance of an extinguished conditional response after a rest period (p. 314).

Spontaneous-remission effect. The improvement of some mental patients and clients in psychotherapy without any professional intervention; a baseline criterion against which the effectiveness of therapies must be assessed (p. 705).

Standard deviation (SD). The average difference of a set of scores from their mean; a measure of variability (p. A–9).

Standardization. A set of uniform procedures for treating each participant in a test, interview, or experiment, or for recording data (p. 32).

Stanford prison experiment. A mock prison study conducted at Stanford University demonstrating the power of the situation to transform the behavior of "good" student subjects into evil guards and pathological prisoners (p. 585).

Stereotype effect. A type of bias in ratings or observations in which the judges' beliefs about the qualities of most people who belong to a certain category influence the perception of an observed individual who belongs to that particular category (p. 551).

Stigma. The negative reaction of people to an individual or group because of some assumed inferiority or source of difference that is degraded; also, what is experienced by the target of the stigmatization (p. 668).

Stimulus discrimination. A conditioning process in which an organism learns to respond differently to stimuli that differ from the conditional stimulus on some dimension (p. 315).

Stimulus-driven capture. A determinant of why people select some parts of sensory input for further processing; occurs when features of stimuli—objects in the environment—automatically capture attention, independent of the local goals of a perceiver (p. 270).

Stimulus generalization. The automatic extension of conditioned responding to similar stimuli that have never been paired with the unconditional stimulus (p. 315).

Storage. The retention of encoded material over time (p. 348).

Stress. The pattern of specific and nonspecific responses an organism makes to stimulus events that disturb its equilibrium and tax or exceed its ability to cope (p. 472).

Stress moderator variables. Variables that change the impact of a stressor on a given type of stress reaction (p. 477).

Stressor. An internal or external event or stimulus that induces stress (p. 472).

Structuralism. The study of the structure of mind and behavior; the view that all human mental experience can be understood as a combination of simple elements or events (p. 14).

Subjective contours. Perceived contours that exist only in subjective experience, not in the distal stimulus (p. 280).

Superego. In Freudian theory, the aspect of personality that represents the internalization of society's values, standards, and morals (p. 520).

Superior colliculus. A cluster of nerve cell bodies in the midbrain region of the brain stem involved in the integration of sensory input of different types (p. 229).

Sympathetic division. The subdivision of the autonomic nervous system that deals with emergency response and the mobilization of energy (p. 69).

Symptom substitution. The appearance of a new physical or psychological problem after a problem behavior has been changed (p. 682).

Synapse. The gap between one neuron and another (p. 86).

Synaptic transmission. The relaying of information from one neuron to another across the synaptic gap (p. 86).

Systematic desensitization. A behavioral therapy technique in which a client is taught to prevent the arousal of anxiety by confronting the feared stimulus while relaxed (p. 683).

Taste-aversion learning. A biological constraint on learning in which an organism learns in one trial to avoid a food whose ingestion is followed by illness (p. 332).

Taste buds. Receptors for taste, located primarily on the upper surface of the tongue (p. 248).

Temporal summation. The process by which a neuron summates several small excitatory or inhibitory inputs received from the same source over time in order to determine whether to fire (p. 82).

Terminal buttons. The bulblike structures at the branched endings of axons that contain vesicles filled with neurotransmitters (p. 80).

Testosterone. The male sex hormone, secreted by the testes, that stimulates production of sperm and is also responsible for the development of male secondary sex characteristics (p. 79).

Test-retest reliability. A measure of the correlation between the scores of the same people on the same test given on two different occasions (p. 545).

Thalamus. The brain structure that relays sensory impulses to the cerebral cortex (p. 72).

Thanatos. In Freudian theory, the death instinct, which is assumed to drive people toward aggressive and destructive behavior (p. 518).

Thematic Apperception Test (TAT). A projective test in which pictures of ambiguous scenes are presented to an individual, who is encouraged to generate stories about them (p. 450).

Theory of ecological optics. A theory of perception that emphasizes the richness of stimulus information and views the perceiver as an active explorer of the environment (p. 268).

Think-aloud protocols. Reports made by experimental subjects of the mental processes and strategies they use while working on a task (p. 105).

Three-term contingency. The means by which organisms learn that in the presence of some stimuli but not others, their behavior is likely to have a particular effect on the environment (p. 323).

Timbre. The dimension of auditory sensation that reflects the complexity of a sound wave (p. 242).

Tolerance. A situation that occurs with continued use of a drug in which an individual requires greater dosages to achieve the same effect (p. 131).

Top-down processing. Perceptual processes in which information from an individual's past experience, knowledge, expectations, motivations, and background influence the way a perceived object is interpreted and classified (p. 294).

Total situation. A situation in which people are isolated from contrary points of view and sources of information; social rewards and punishments are highly controlled by group leaders (p. 590).

Traits. Enduring and continuous qualities or attributes that influence behavior because they act as generalized action tendencies (p. 512).

Transduction. Transformation of one form of energy into another; for example, light is transformed into neural impulses (p. 217).

Transference. The process by means of which a person in psychoanalysis attaches to a therapist feelings formerly held toward some significant person who figured in a past emotional conflict (p. 680).

Trichromatic theory. The theory that there are three types of color receptors that produce the primary color sensations of red, green, and blue (p. 234).

Type A behavior pattern. A complex pattern of behaviors and emotions that includes excessive emphasis on competition, aggression, impatience, and hostility; hostility increases the risk of coronary heart disease (p. 502).

Type B behavior pattern. As compared to *Type A behavior pattern,* a less competitive, less aggressive, less hostile pattern of behavior and emotion (p. 502).

Type C behavior pattern. A constellation of behaviors that may predict which individuals are more likely to develop cancer or to have their cancer progress quickly; these behaviors include passive acceptance and self-sacrifice (p. 503).

Unconditional response (UCR). In classical conditioning, the response elicited by an unconditional stimulus without prior training or learning (p. 308).

Unconditional stimulus (UCS). In classical conditioning, the stimulus that elicits an unconditional response (p. 308).

Unconscious. In psychoanalytic theory, the domain of the psyche that stores repressed urges and primitive impulses (p. 520).

Unconscious inference. Helmholtz's term for *perception* that occurs outside of conscious awareness (p. 268).

Unipolar depression. A mood disorder characterized by intense feelings of depression over an extended time, without the manic high phase of bipolar depression; symptoms include changes in appetite, sleep disturbances, altered motor activity, guilt, inability to concentrate, and suicidal ideas or attempts (p. 648).

Validity. The extent to which a test measures what it was intended to measure (p. 43).

Variable. In an experimental setting, a factor that varies in amount and kind (p. 32).

Vestibular sense. The sense that tells how one's own body is oriented in the world with respect to gravity (p. 250).

Visual cortex. The region of the occipital lobes in which visual information is processed (p. 76).

Volley principle. An extension of frequency theory which proposes that when peaks in a sound wave come too frequently for a single neuron to fire at each peak, several neurons fire as a group at the frequency of the stimulus tone (p. 245).

Weber's law. An assertion that the size of a difference threshold is proportional to the intensity of the standard stimulus (p. 223).

Wellness. Optimal health, incorporating the ability to function fully and actively over the physical, intellectual, emotional, spiritual, social, and environmental domains of health (p. 492).

Wisdom. Expertise in the fundamental pragmatics of life (p. 167).

Withdrawal symptoms. Painful physical symptoms experienced when a drug to which a person is physically addicted is decreased or eliminated (p. 132).

Within-subjects design. A research design that uses each subject as his or her own control; for example, the behavior of an experimental subject before receiving treatment might be compared to his or her behavior after receiving treatment (p. 36).

Working memory. Short-term memory; material transferred to it from either sensory or long-term memory can be worked over and organized (p. 356).

Yerkes-Dodson law. A correlation between task performance and optimal level of arousal (p. 471).

References

Abelin, T., Muller, P., Buehler, A., Vesanen, K., & Imhof, P. R. (1989, January 7). Controlled trial of transdermal nicotine patch in tobacco withdrawal. *The Lancet,* pp. 7–10.

Abrams, R. (1992). *Electroconvulsive therapy.* New York: Oxford University Press.

Abramson, L. Y., Seligman, M. E. P., & Teasdale, J. D. (1978). Learned helplessness in humans: Critique and reformulation. *Journal of Abnormal Psychology, 87,* 32–48, 49–74.

Ackerman, D. (1990). *A natural history of the senses.* New York: Random House.

Adams, J. (1979). Mutual-help groups: Enhancing the coping ability of oncology clients. *Cancer Nursing, 2,* 95–98.

Adams, J. L. (1986). *Conceptual blockbusting* (3rd ed.). New York: Norton.

Adams, J. S. (1965). Inequity in social exchange. In L. Berkowitz (Ed.), *Advances in experimental social psychology* (Vol. 2, pp. 267–299). New York: Academic Press.

Adelson, E. H. (1993). Perceptual organization and the judgement of brightness. *Science, 262,* 2042–2044.

Ader, R., & Cohen, N. (1981). Conditioned immunopharmacological responses. In R. Ader (Ed.), *Psychoneuroimmunology* (pp. 281–319). New York: Academic Press.

Ader, R., & Cohen, N. (1993). Psychoneuroimmunology: Conditioning and stress. *Annual Review of Psychology, 44,* 53–85.

Adler, A. (1929). *The practice and theory of individual psychology.* New York: Harcourt, Brace & World.

Adler, N., & Matthews, K. (1994). Health psychology: Why do some people get sick and some stay well? *Annual Review of Psychology, 45,* 229–259.

Adler, N. E., Boyce, T., Chesney, M. A., Cohen, S., Folkman, S., Kahn, R. L., & Syme, S. L. (1994). Socioeconomic status and health: The challenge of the gradient. *American Psychologist, 49,* 15–24.

Adorno, T. W., Frenkel-Brunswick, E., Levinson, D. J., & Sanford, R. N. (1950). *The authoritarian personality.* New York: Harper.

Affleck, G., Tennen, H., Pfeiffer, C., & Fifield, J. (1987). Appraisals of control and predictability in adapting to a chronic disease. *Journal of Personality and Social Psychology, 53,* 273–279.

Agosta, W. C. (1992). *Chemical communication: The language of pheromones.* New York: Freeman.

Ahern, G. L., & Schwartz, G. E. (1985). Differential lateralization for positive and negative emotion in the human brain: EEG spectral analysis. *Neuropsychologia, 23,* 744–755.

Ainsworth, M. D. S. (1973). The development of infant–mother attachment. In B. M. Caldwell & H. N. Ricciuti (Eds.), *Review of child development research* (Vol. 3, pp. 1-94). Chicago: University of Chicago Press.

Ainsworth, M. D. S., Blehar, M., Waters, E., & Wall, S. (1978). *Patterns of attachment.* Hillsdale, NJ: Erlbaum.

Akmajian, A., Demers, R. A., Farmer, A. K., & Harnish, R. M. (1990). *Linguistics.* Cambridge, MA: MIT Press.

Albee, G. W., & Joffe, J. M. (Eds.). (1977). *Primary prevention of psychopathology: Vol 1. Issues.* Hanover, NH: University Press of New England.

Alberti, R. E., & Emmons, M. L. (1990). *Your perfect right—A guide to assertive living.* San Luis Obispo, CA: Impact Publishers.

Allison, D. B., Heshka, S., Neale, M. C., Lykken, D. T., & Heymsfield, S. B. (1994). A genetic analysis of relative weight among 4,020 twin pairs, with an emphasis on sex effects. *Health Psychology, 13,* 362–365.

Allison, T., & Cicchetti, D. (1976). Sleep in mammals: Ecological and constitutional correlates. *Science, 194,* 732–734.

Allport, G. W. (1937). *Personality: A psychological interpretation.* New York: Holt, Rinehart & Winston.

Allport, G. W. (1954). *The nature of prejudice.* Cambridge, MA: Addison-Wesley.

Allport, G. W. (1961). *Pattern and growth in personality.* New York: Holt, Rinehart & Winston.

Allport, G. W. (1965). *Letters from Jenny.* New York: Harcourt, Brace & World.

Allport, G. W. (1966). Traits revisited. *American Psychologist, 21,* 1–10.

Allport, G. W., & Odbert, H. S. (1936). Trait-names, a psycholexical study. *Psychological Monographs, 47* (1, Whole No. 211).

Alper, J. (1993). Echo-planar MRI: Learning to read minds. *Science, 261,* 556.

Altman, I., & Christensen, K. (Eds.). (1990). *Environment and behavior studies: Emergence of intellectual traditions.* New York: Plenum Press.

Amabile, T. M. (1983). *The social psychology of creativity.* New York: Springer-Verlag.

American Psychological Association. (1982). *Guidelines and ethical standards for researchers.*

Andersen, B., Kiecolt-Glaser, J. K., & Glaser, R. (1994). A biobehavioral model of cancer stress and disease course. *American Psychologist, 49,* 389–404.

Anderson, A. E., & DiDomenico, L. (1992). Diet vs. shape content of popular male and female magazines: A dose-response relationship to the incidence of eating disorders? *International Journal of Eating Disorders, 11,* 283–287.

Anderson, J. R. (1982). Acquisition of cognitive skill. *Psychological Review, 89,* 369–406.

Anderson, J. R. (1983). *The architecture of cognition.* Cambridge, MA: Harvard University Press.

Anderson, J. R. (1987). Skill acquisition: Compilation of weak-method problem-solutions. *Psychological Review, 94,* 192–210.

Anderson, J. R. (1993). Problem solving and learning. *American Psychologist, 48,* 35–44.

Anderson, J. R. (Ed.). (1981). *Cognitive skills and their acquisition.* Hillsdale, NJ: Erlbaum.

Anderson, N. B., McNeilly, M., & Myers, H. (1992). Toward understanding race difference in autonomic reactivity: A proposed contextual model. In J. R. Turner, A. Sherwood, & K. C. Light (Eds.), *Individual differences in cardiovascular response to stress* (pp. 125–145). New York: Plenum Press.

Andrews, E. L. (1990, April 29). *A nicotine drug patch to end smoking. The New York Times Index* (Vol. 139, Section 1, Col. 1, p. 27, June 3, 1990).

Anliker, J. A., Bartoshuk, L., Ferris, A. M., & Hooks, L. D. (1991). Children's food preferences and genetic sensitivity to the bitter taste of 6-*n*-propylthiouracil (PROP). *American Journal of Clinical Nutrition, 54,* 316–320.

Antrobus, J. (1991). Dreaming: Cognitive processes during cortical activation and high afferent thresholds. *Psycholoigical Review, 98,* 96–121.

Applebaum, P. S. (1994). *Almost a revolution: Mental health law and the limits of change.* New York: Oxford University Press.

Arendt, H. (1963). *Eichmann in Jerusalem: A report on the banality of evil.* New York: Viking Press.

Arendt, H. (1971). Organized guilt and universal responsibility. In R. W. Smith (Ed.), *Guilt: Man and society.* Garden City, NY: Doubleday Anchor Books.

Arkin, R. M. (Ed.). (1990). Centennial celebration of the principles of psychology. *Personality and Social Psychology Bulletin, 16*(4).

Aron, A., & Aron, E. N. (1994). Love. In A. L. Weber & J. H. Harvey (Eds.), *Perspectives on close relationships* (pp. 131–152). Boston: Allyn and Bacon.

Aron, A., Aron, E. N., & Smollan, D. (1992). Inclusion of other in the self scale and the structure of interpersonal closeness. *Journal of Personality and Social Psychology, 63,* 596–612.

Aron, A., Aron, E. N., Tudor, M., & Nelson, G. (1991). Close relationships as including other in the self. *Journal of Personality and Social Psychology, 60,* 241–253.

Aronson, E. (1990). Applying social psychology to desegregation and energy conservation. *Personality and Social Psychology Bulletin, 16,* 118–132.

Aronson, E., Blaney, N., Stephan, C., Sikes, J., & Snapp, M. (1978). *The jigsaw classroom.* Beverly Hills, CA: Sage.

Aronson, E., & Gonzalez, A. (1988). Desegregation jigsaw, and the Mexican-American experience. In P. A. Katz & D. Taylor (Eds.), *Towards the elimination of racism: Profiles in controversy.* New York: Plenum Press.

Asch, S. E. (1940). Studies in the principles of judgments and attitudes: 11. Determination of judgments by group and by ego standards. *Journal of Social Psychology, 12,* 433–465.

Asch, S. E. (1952). *Social psychology.* Englewood Cliffs, NJ: Prentice-Hall.

Asch, S. E. (1955). Opinions and social pressure. *Scientific American, 193*(5), 31–35.

Asch, S. E. (1956). Studies of independence and conformity: A minority of one against a unanimous majority. *Psychological Monographs, 70*(9, Whole No. 416).

Aserinsky, E., & Kleitman, N. (1953). Regularly occurring periods of eye mobility and concomitant phenomena during sleep. *Science, 118,* 273–274.

Ashton, P. T., & Webb, R. B. (1986). *Making a difference: A teacher's sense of efficacy and student achievement.* New York: Longman.

Associated Press. (1991, April 8). New study on suicide by older people.

Ayllon, T., & Azrin, N. H. (1965). The measurement and reinforcement of behavior of psychotics. *Journal of Experimental Analysis of Behavior, 8,* 357–383.

Ayllon, T., & Michael, J. (1959). The psychiatric nurse as a behavioral engineer. *Journal of the Experimental Analysis of Behavior, 2,* 323–334.

Ayres, T. J., Jonides, J., Reitman, J. S., Egan, J. C., & Howard, D. A. (1979). Differing suffix effects for the same physical stimulus. *Journal of Experimental Psychology: Human Learning and Memory, 5,* 315–321.

Baars, B. J. (1988). *A cognitive theory of consciousness.* Cambridge: Cambridge University Press.

Baars, B. J. (1992). A dozen completing-plans techniques for inducing predictable slips in speech and action. In B. J. Baars (Ed.), *Experimental slips and human error: Exploring the architecture of volition* (pp. 129–150). New York: Plenum Press.

Baars, B. J., Cohen, J., Bower, G. H., & Berry, J. W. (1992). Some caveats on testing the Freudian slip hypothesis. In B. J. Baars (Ed.), *Experimental slips and human error: Exploring the architecture of volition* (pp. 289–313). New York: Plenum Press.

Baars, B. J., & McGovern, K. (1994). Consciousness. *Encyclopedia of Human Behavior, 1,* 687–699.

Baars, B. J., Motley, M. T., & MacKay, D. G. (1975). Output editing for lexical status in artificially elicited slips of the tongue. *Journal of Verbal Learning and Verbal Behavior, 14,* 382–391.

Bachman, J. G., O'Malley, P. M., & Johnston, J. (1979). *Adolescence to adulthood: Change and stability in the lives of young men.* Ann Arbor, MI: Institute of Social Research.

Backer, T. E., Batchelor, W. F., Jones, J. M., & Mays, V. M. (Eds.). (1988). Psychology and AIDS [Special issue]. *American Psychologist, 43*(11).

Backman, C. W., & Secord, P. F. (1959). The effect of perceived liking on interpersonal attraction. *Human Relations, 12,* 379–384.

Baddeley, A. D. (1986). *Working memory.* New York: Oxford University Press.

Bahrick, H. P., Bahrick, P. O., & Wittlinger, R. P. (1975). Fifty years of memory for names and faces: A cross-sectional approach. *Journal of Experimental Psychology: General, 104,* 54–75.

Bailey, J. M., & Pillard, R. C. (1991). A genetic study of male sexual orientation. *Archives of General Psychiatry, 48,* 1089–1096.

Bailey, J. M., Pillard, R. C., Neale, M. C., & Agyei, Y. (1993). Heritable factors influence sexual orientation in women. *Archives of General Psychiatry, 50,* 217–223.

Bailey, M. B., & Bailey, R. E. (1993). "Misbehavior": A case history. *American Psychologist, 48,* 1157–1158.

Baillargeon, R. (1987a). Young infants reasoning about the physical and spatial properties of a hidden object. *Cognitive Development, 2,* 179–200.

Baillargeon, R. (1987b). Object permanence in 3½- and 4½-month-old infants. *Developmental Pyschology, 23,* 655–664.

Baker, F. M. (1991). Cocaine psychosis. *Journal of the National Medical Association, 91,* 987–1000.

Balakrishnan, S. (1991). Psychology of democracy. *The California Psychologist, 24,* 16, 21.

Baldwin, A. L., & Baldwin, C. P. (1973). Study of mother–child interaction. *American Scientist, 61,* 714–721.

Baldwin, E. (1993). The case for animal research in psychology. *Journal of Social Issues, 49,* 121–131.

Balsam, P. D., & Tomie, A. (Eds.). (1985). *Context and learning.* Hillsdale, NJ: Erlbaum.

Baltes, M. M. (1986, November). *Selective optimization with compensation: The dynamics between independence and dependence.* Paper presented at the meeting of the Gerontological Society of America, Chicago.

Baltes, M. M., & Wahl, H.-W. (1992). The dependency-support script in institutions: Generalization to community settings. *Psychology and Aging, 7,* 409–418.

Baltes, P. B. (1987). Theoretical propositions on life-span developmental psychology: On the dynamics between growth and decline. *Developmental Psychology, 23,* 611–626.

Baltes, P. B. (1990, November). *Toward a psychology of wisdom.* Invited address presented at the annual convention of the Gerontological Society of America, Boston.

Baltes, P. B. (1993). The aging mind: Potential and limits. *The Gerontologist, 33,* 580–594.

Baltes, P. B., & Kliegl, R. (1992). Further testing of limits of cognitive plasticity: Negative age differences in a mnemonic skill are robust. *Developmental Psychology, 28,* 121–125.

Baltes, P. B., & Lindenberger, U. (1988). On the range of cognitive plasticity in old age as a function of experience: 15 years of intervention research. *Behavior Therapy, 19,* 283–300.

Baltes, P. B., Smith, J., & Staudinger, U. M. (1992). Wisdom and successful aging. In T. B. Sonderegger (Ed.), *The Nebraska Symposium on Motivation: Vol. 39. The psychology of aging* (pp. 123–167). Lincoln: University of Nebraska Press.

Banaji, M. R., & Prentice, D. A. (1994). The self in social contexts. *Annual Review of Psychology, 45,* 297–332.

Bancroft, J. (1978). The relationship between hormones and sexual behavior in humans. In J. B. Hutchinson (Ed.), *Biological determinants of sexual behavior* (pp. 493–519). New York: Wiley.

Bandura, A. (1970). Modeling therapy. In W. S. Sahakian (Ed.), *Psychopathology today: Experimentation, theory and research.* Itasca, IL: Peacock.

Bandura, A. (1977a). *Social learning theory.* Englewood Cliffs, NJ: Prentice-Hall.

Bandura, A. (1977b). Self-efficacy. *Psychological Review, 84,* 191–215.

Bandura, A. (1981). In search of pure unidirectional determinants. *Behavior Therapy, 12,* 30–40.

Bandura, A. (1986). *Social foundations of thought and action: A social cognitive theory,* Englewood Cliffs, NJ: Prentice-Hall.

Bandura, A. (1992). Exercise of personal agency through the self-efficacy mechanism. In R. Schwarzer (Ed.), *Self-efficacy: Thought control of action* (pp. 3–38). Washington, DC: Hemisphere.

Bandura, A., Ross, D., & Ross, S. A. (1963). Imitation of film-mediated aggressive models. *Journal of Abnormal and Social Psychology, 66,* 3–11.

Bane, M. J., & Ellwood, D. T. (1989). One-fifth of the nation's children: Why are they poor? *Science, 245,* 1047–1053.

Banks, M. S., & Bennet, P. J. (1988). Optical and photoreceptor immaturities limit the spatial and chromatic vision of human neonates. *Journal of the Optical Society of America, 5,* 2059–2079.

Banks, W. C. (1990). *In Discovering Psychology, Program 16* [PBS video series]. Washington, DC: Annenberg/CPB Program.

Banks, W. P., & Krajicek, D. (1991). Perception. *Annual Review of Psychology, 42,* 305–331.

Banuazizi, A., & Movahedi, S. (1975). Interpersonal dynamics in a simulated prison: A methodological analysis. *American Psychologist, 30,* 152–160.

Bar-Hillel, M., & Neter, E. (1993). How alike is it versus how likely is it: A disjunction fallacy in probability judgments. *Journal of Personality and Social Psychology, 65,* 1119–1131.

Barinaga, M. (1989). Can psychotherapy delay cancer deaths? *Science, 46,* 246, 249.

Barinaga, M. (1990). Technical advances power neuroscience. *Science, 250,* 908–909.

Barinaga, M. (1993). Carbon monoxide: Killer to brain messenger in one step. *Science, 259,* 309.

Barker, L. M., Best, M. R., & Domjan, M. (Eds.). (1978). *Learning mechanisms in food selection.* Houston: Baylor University Press.

Barondes, S. H. (1994). Thinking about Prozac. *Science, 263,* 1102–1103.

Bartlett, F. C. (1932). *Remembering: A study in experimental and social psychology.* Cambridge: Cambridge University Press.

Bartoshuk, L. (1990, August–September). Psychophysiological insights on taste. *Science Agenda,* 12–13.

Bartoshuk, L. M. (1993). The biological basis of food perception and acceptance. *Food Quality and Preference, 4,* 21–32.

Bartoshuk, L. M., Duffy, V. B., & Miller, I. J. (1994). PTC/PROP tasting: Anatomy, psychophysics, and sex effects. *Physiology and Behavior, 56,* 1165-1171.

Basseches, M. (1984). *Dialectical thinking and adult development.* Norwood, NJ: Ablex.

Bateson, G., Jackson, D. D., Haley, J., & Weakland, J. H. (1956). Toward a theory of schizophrenia. *Behavioral Science, 1,* 251–264.

Baum, A. (1990). Stress, intrusive imagery, and chronic distress. *Health Psychology, 9,* 653–675.

Baumeister, R. F. (Ed.). (1994). Samples made of stories: Research using autobiographical narratives [Special issue]. *Personality and Social Psychology Bulletin, 20*(6).

Baumeister, R. F., Tice, D. M., & Hutton, D. G. (1989). Self-presentational motivations and personality differences in self-esteem. *Journal of Personality, 57,* 547–579.

Baumgardner, A. H. (1990). To know oneself is to like oneself: Self-certainty and self-affect. *Journal of Personality and Social Psychology, 58,* 1062–1072.

Baumrind, D. (1967). Child care practices anteceding three patterns of preschool behavior. *Genetic Psychology Monographs, 75,* 43–88.

Baumrind, D. (1973). *The development of instrumental competence through socialization.* In A. Pick (Ed.), *Minnesota Symposium in Child Development* (Vol. 7). Minneapolis: University of Minnesota Press.

Baumrind, D. (1985). Research using intentional deception: Ethical issues revisited. *American Psychologist, 40,* 165–174.

Baumrind, D. (1986). Sex differences in moral reasoning: Response to Walker's (1984) conclusion that there are none. *Child Development, 57,* 511–521.

Baxter, L. R., Schwartz, J. M., Bergman, K. S., Szuba, M. P., Guze, B. H., Mazziotta, J. C., Alazraki, A., Selin, C. E., Ferng, H-K., Munford, P., & Phelps, M. E. (1992). Caudate glucose metabolic rate changes with both drug and behavior therapy for obsessive-compulsive disorder. *Archives of General Psychiatry, 49,* 681–689.

Bayley, N. (1956). Individual patterns of development. *Child Development, 27,* 45–74.

Baylor, D. (1987). Photoreceptor signals and vision. *Investigative Opthalmology and Visual Science, 28,* 34–49.

Beardslee, W. R., & Mack, J. E. (1983). Adolescents and the threat of nuclear war: The evolution of a perspective. *Yale Journal of Biological Medicine, 56*(2), 79–91.

Beattie, J., Baron, J., Hershey, J. C., & Spranca, M. D. (1994). Psychological determinants of decision attitude. *Journal of Behavioral Decision Making, 7,* 129–144.

Beck, A. T. (1976). *Cognitive therapy and emotional disorders.* New York: International Universitites Press.

Beck, A. T. (1983). Cognitive theory of depression: New perspectives. In P. J. Clayton & J. E. Barrett (Eds.), *Treatment of depression: Old controversies and new approaches* (pp. 265–290). New York: Raven Press.

Beck, A. T. (1985). Cognitive therapy. In H. I. Kaplan & J. Sandock (Eds.), *Comprehensive textbook of psychiatry* (4th ed.). Baltimore: Williams & Wilkins.

Beck, A. T. (1988). Cognitive approaches to panic disorders: Theory and therapy. In S. Rachman & J. D. Maser (Eds.), *Panic: Psychological perspectives.* New York: Guilford Press.

Beck, A. T., & Emery, G. (1985). *Anxiety disorders and phobias: A cognitive perspective.* New York: Basic Books.

Beck, A. T., & Rush, A. J. (1989). Cognitive therapy. In H. I. Kaplan & B. Sadock (Eds.), *Comprehensive textbook of psychiatry* (Vol. 5). Baltimore: Williams & Wilkins.

Beck, A. T., Rush, A. J., Shaw, B. F., & Emery, G. (1979). *Cognitive therapy of depression.* New York: Guilford Press.

Beck, J. (1972). Similarity groupings and peripheral discriminability under uncertainty. *American Journal of Psychology, 85,* 1–20.

Beck, J. (Ed.). (1982). *Organization and representation in perception.* Hillsdale, NJ: Erlbaum.

Beck, M., & Crowley, G. (1990, March 26). Beyond lobotomies: Psychosurgery is safer—but still a rarity. *Newsweek,* p. 44.

Bee, H. (1994). *Lifespan development.* New York: HarperCollins.

Begley, S. (1989, May 14). The stuff that dreams are made of. *Newsweek,* pp. 41–44.

Beitchman, J. H., Zucker, K. J., Hood, J. E., DaCosta, G. A., Akman, D., & Cassavia, E. (1992). A review of the long-term effects of child sexual abuse. *Child Abuse & Neglect, 16,* 101–118.

Bell, A. P., & Weinberg, M. S. (1978). *Homosexualities: A study of diversity among men and women.* New York: Simon & Schuster.

Bell, I. R. (1982). *Clinical ecology.* Bolinas, CA: Common Knowledge Press.

Bem, D. J. (1972). Self-perception theory. In L. Berkowitz (Ed.), *Advances in experimental social psychology* (Vol. 6, pp. 1–62). New York: Academic Press.

Bem, D. J., & Honorton, C. (1994). Does psi exist? Replicable evidence for an anomalous process of information transfer. *Psychological Bulletin, 115,* 4–18.

Bem, S. L. (1974). The measurement of psychological androgyny. *Journal of Consulting and Clinical Psychology, 42,* 155–162.

Bem, S. L. (1981). *The Bem Sex Role Inventory: Professional manual.* Palo Alto, CA: Consulting Psychology Press.

Benedict, R. (1938). Continuities and discontinuities in cultural conditioning. *Psychiatry, 1,* 161–167.

Benedict, R. (1959). *Patterns of culture.* Boston: Houghton Mifflin.

Benson, H. (1975). *The relaxation response.* New York: Morrow.

Benson, H., & Stuart, E. M. (Eds.). (1992). *The wellness book.* New York: Simon & Schuster.

Berger, A., Henderson, M., Nadoolman, W, Duffy, V., Cooper, D., Saberski, L., & Bartoshuk, L. (1995). Oral capsaicin provides temporary relief for oral mucositis pain secondary to chemotherapy/radiation therapy. *Journal of Pain and Symptom Management, 10,* 243–248.

Berglas, S., & Jones, E. E. (1978). Drug choice as a self-handicapping strategy in response to noncontingent success. *Journal of Personality and Social Psychology, 36,* 405–417.

Berk, L. S., Ian, S. A., Fry, W. F., Napier, B. J., Lee, J. W., Hubbard, R. W., Lewis, J. E., & Eby, W. C. (1989). Neuroendocrine and stress hormone changes during mirthful laughter. *American Journal of Medicine Science, 298,* 390–396.

Berlyne, D. E. (1960). *Conflict, arousal, and curiosity.* New York: McGraw-Hill.

Berman, A. L., & Jobes, D. A. (1991). *Adolescent suicide: Assessment and intervention.* Washington, DC: American Psychological Association.

Berman, K. F., Torrey, E. F., Daniel, D. G., & Weinberger, D. R. (1992). Regional cerebral blood flow in monozygotic twins discordant and concordant for schizophrenia. *Archives of General Psychiatry, 49,* 927–934.

Bernard, L. L. (1924). *Instinct.* New York: Holt, Rinehart & Winston.

Berndt, T. J. (1979). Developmental changes in conformity to peers and parents. *Developmental Psychology, 15,* 608–616.

Berndt, T. J. (1992). Friendship and friends' influence in adolescence. *Current Directions in Psychological Science, 1,* 156–159.

Bernstein, I. L. (1988). What does learning have to do with weight loss and cancer? *Proceedings of the Science and Public Policy Seminar of the Federation of Behavioral, Psychological and Cognitive Sciences,* Washington, DC.

Bernstein, I. L. (1990). Salt preferences and development. *Developmental Psychology, 26,* 552–554.

Bernstein, I. L. (1991). Aversion conditioning in response to cancer and cancer treatment. *Clinical Psychology Review, 11,* 185–191.

Berry, J. W. (1967). Independence and conformity in subsistence level societies. *Journal of Personality and Social Psychology, 7,* 415–418.

Berscheid, E., & Walster, E. H. (1978). *Interpersonal attraction* (2nd ed.). Reading, MA: Addison-Wesley.

Bexton, W. H., Heron, W., & Scott, T. H. (1954). Effects of decreased variation in the sensory environment. *Canadian Journal of Psychology, 8,* 70–76.

Bickerton, D. (1990). *Language and species.* Chicago: University of Chicago Press.

Biederman, I. (1985). Recognition by components: A theory of object recognition. *Computer Vision Graphics and Image Processing, 32,* 29–73.

Biederman, I. (1987). Recognition by components. *Psychological Review, 94,* 115–147.

Biederman, I. (1989). Higher-level vision. In D. N. Osherson, H. Sasnik, S. Kosslyn, K. Hollerbach, E. Smith, & N. Block (Eds.), *An invitation to cognitive science.* Cambridge, MA: MIT Press.

Biederman, I., & Cooper, E. E. (1991). Priming contour-deleted images: Evidence for intermediate representations in visual object recognition. *Cognitive Psychology, 23,* 393–419.

Bigelow, H. J. (1850). Dr. Harlow's case of recovery from the passage of an iron bar through his head. *American Journal of Medical Science, 20,* 13–22.

Bigson, J. J. (1966). *The senses considered as perceptual systems.* Boston: Houghton Mifflin.

Billings, A. G., & Moos, R. H. (1982). Family environments and adaptation: A clinically applicable typology. *American Journal of Family Therapy, 20,* 26–38.

Binet, A. (1911). *Les idées modernes sur les enfants.* Paris: Flammarion.

Bingham, C. R., Bennion, L. D., Openshaw, D. K., & Adams, G. R. (1994). An analysis of age, gender and racial differences in recent national trends of youth suicide. *Journal of Adolescence, 17,* 53–71.

Binkley, S. (1979). A timekeeping enzyme in the pineal gland. *Scientific American, 204*(4), 66–71.

Birbaumer, N., & Kimmel, H. (Eds.). (1979). *Biofeedback and self-regulation.* Hillsdale, NJ: Erlbaum.

Bitner, R. (1983). Awareness during anesthesia. In F. Orkin & L. Cooperman (Eds.), *Complications in anesthesiology* (pp. 349–354). Philadelphia: Lippincott.

Bitterman, M. E. (1975). The comparative analysis of learning. *Science, 188,* 699–709.

Blakemore, C., & Campbell, P. W. (1969). On the existence of neurons in the human visual system selectively sensitive to the orientation and size of retinal images. *Journal of Physiology, 203,* 237–260.

Blanchard-Fields, F. (1986). Reasoning on social dilemmas varying in emotional saliency: An adult developmental perspective. *Psychology and Aging, 1,* 325–333.

Blaney, P. H. (1986). Affect and memory: A review. *Psychological Bulletin, 99,* 229–246.

Blass, E. M. (1990). Suckling: Determinants, changes, mechanisms, and lasting impressions. *Developmental Psychology, 26,* 520–533.

Blass, E. M., & Teicher, M. H. (1980). Suckling. *Science, 210,* 15–22.

Blau, G. L., McGinley, H., & Pasewark, R. (1993). Understanding the use of the insanity defense. *Journal of Clinical Psychology, 49,* 435–440.

Bleuler, M. (1978). The long-term course of schizophrenic psychoses. In L. C. Wynne, R. L. Cromwell, & S. Mattysse (Eds.), *The nature of schizophrenia: New approaches to research and treatment* (pp. 631–636). New York: Wiley.

Blight, J. G. (1987). Toward a policy-relevant psychology of avoiding nuclear war: Lessons for psychologists from the Cuban missle crisis. *American Psychologist, 42,* 12–19.

Block, J. H. (1983). Differential premises arising from differential socialization of the sexes: Some conjectures. *Child Development, 54,* 1335–1354.

Blos, P. (1965). *On adolescence: A psychoanalytic interpretation.* New York: Free Press.

Blum, A. (1989). The targeting of minority groups by the tobacco industry. In L. A. Jones (Ed.), *Minorities and cancer* (pp. 153–162). New York: Springer-Verlag.

Bock, J. K. (1986). Meaning, sound, and syntax: Lexical priming in sentence production. *Journal of Experimental Psychology: Learning, Memory, and Cognition, 12,* 575–586.

Boldizar, J. P., Wilson, K. L., & Deemer, D. K. (1989). Gender, life experiences, and moral judgment development: A process-oriented approach. *Journal of Personality and Social Psychology, 57,* 229–238.

Bolger, N., DeLongis, A., Kessler, R. C., & Schilling, E. A. (1989). Effects of daily stress on negative mood. *Journal of Personality and Social Psychology, 57,* 808–818.

Bond, L. A. (1988). Teaching developmental psychology. In P. A. Bronstein & K. Quinna (Eds.), *Teaching a psychology of people: Resources for gender and sociocultural awareness* (pp. 45–52). Washington, DC: American Psychological Association.

Bongiovanni, A. (1977). *A review of research on the effects of punishment in the schools.* Paper presented at the Conference on Child Abuse, Children's Hospital National Medical Center, Washington, DC.

Boone, D. E. (1994). Validity of the MMPI-2 depression content scale with psychiatric inpatients. *Psychological Reports, 74,* 159–162.

Bootzin, R. R., & Nicasio, P. M. (1978). Behavioral treatments for insomnia. In M. Hersen, R. Eisler, & P. Miller (Eds.), *Progress in behavior modification.* New York: Academic Press.

Borkovec, T. D. (1982). Insomnia. *Journal of Consulting and Clinical Psychology, 50,* 880–985.

Bornstein, P. A., & Quinna, K. (Eds.). (1988). *Teaching a psychology of people: Resources for gender and sociocultural awareness.* Washington, DC: American Psychological Association.

Borod, C., Koff, E., Lorch, M. P., Nicholas, M., & Welkowitz, J. (1988). Emotional and non-emotional facial behavior in patients with unilateral brain damage. *Journal of Neurological and Neurosurgical Psychiatry, 5,* 826–832.

Bortz, W. M. (1982). Disuse and aging. *Journal of the American Medical Association, 248,* 1203–1208.

Boswell, J. (1988). *The kindness of strangers.* New York: Pantheon Books.

Botwinick, J. (1977). Intellectual abilities. In U. E. Birren & K. W. Schaie (Eds.), *Handbook of the psychology of aging* (pp. 580–605). New York: Van Nostrand Reinhold.

Bouchard, C., Tremblay, A., Nadeau, A., Despres, J. P. Theriault, G., Boulay, M. R., Lortie, G., Leblanc, C., & Fournier, G. (1989). Genetic effect in resting and exercise metabolic rates. *Metabolism, 38,* 364–370.

Bouchard, T. J., Jr., & McGue, M. (1990). Genetic and environmental influences on adult personality: An analysis of adopted twins reared apart. *Journal of Personality, 58,* 263–295.

Bourguignon, E. (1979). *Psychological anthropology: An introduction to human nature and cultural differences.* New York: Holt, Rinehart & Winston.

Bowd, A. D., & Shapiro, K. J. (1993). The case against laboratory animal research in psychology. *Journal of Social Issues, 49,* 133–142.

Bower, G. H. (1972). A selective review of organizational factors in memory. In E. Tulving & W. Donaldson (Eds.), *Organization of memory.* New York: Academic Press.

Bower, G. H. (1981). Mood and memory. *American Psychologist, 36,* 129–148.

Bower, G. H. (1991). Mood congruity of social judgements. In J. P. Forgas (Ed.), *Emotional & social judgments* (pp. 31–54). Oxford: Pergamon Press.

Bower, G. H., Black, J. B., & Turner, T. J. (1979). Scripts in memory for text. *Cognitive Psychology, 11,* 177–220.

Bower, G. H., Thompson-Schill, S., & Tulving, E. (1994). Reducing retroactive interference: An interference analysis. *Journal of Experimental Psychology: Learning, Memory, and Cognition, 20,* 51–66.

Bower, S. A., & Bower, G. H. (1991). *Asserting youself: A practical guide for positve change.* Reading, MA: Addison-Wesley. (Original work published 1976.)

Bowers, K. S. (1976). *Hypnosis for the seriously curious.* New York: Norton.

Bowlby, J. (1969). *Attachment and loss, Vol 1. Attachment.* New York: Basic Books.

Bowlby, J. (1973). *Attachment and loss, Vol 2. Separation, anxiety and anger.* London: Hogarth.

Bradley, M. M. (1994). Emotional memory: A dimensional analysis. In S. H. M. van Goozen, N. E. Van de Poll, & J. A. Sergeant (Eds.), *Emotions: Essays on emotion theory* (pp. 97–134). Hillsdale, NJ: Erlbaum.

Braginsky, B., & Braginsky, D. (1967). Schizophrenic patients in the psychiatric interview: An experimental study of their effectiveness at manipulation. *Journal of Consulting Psychology, 31,* 543–547.

Breedlove, S. M. (1994). Sexual differentiation of the human nervous system. *Annual Review of Psychology, 45,* 389–418.

Breggin, P. R. (1979). *Electroshock: Its brain disabling effects.* New York: Springer.

Breggin, P. R. (1991). *Toxic psychiatry.* New York: St. Martin's Press.

Breggin, P. R., & Breggin, G. R. (1994). *Talking back to Prozac.* New York: St. Martin's Press.

Bregman, A. S. (1981). Asking the "what for" question in auditory perception. In M. Kobovy & J. Pomerantz (Eds.), *Perceptual organization* (pp. 99–118). Hillsdale, NJ: Erlbaum.

Breland, K., & Breland, M. (1951). A field of applied animal psychology. *American Psychologist, 6,* 202–204.

Breland, K., & Breland, M. (1961). A misbehavior of organisms. *American Psychologist, 16,* 681–684.

Brenner, M. H. (1976). *Estimating the social costs of national economic policy: Implications for mental and physical health and criminal violence.* Report prepared for the Joint Economic Committee of Congress, Washington, DC: U.S. Government Printing Office.

Brett, J. F., Brief, A. P., Burke, M. J., George, J. M., & Webster, J. (1990). Negative affectivity and the reporting of stressful life events. *Health Psychology, 9,* 57–68.

Breuer, J., & Freud, S. (1955). Studies on hysteria. In J. Strachey (Ed. and Trans.), *The standard edition of the complete psychological works of Sigmund Freud* (Vol. 2). London: Hogarth Press. (Original work published 1895.)

Brewer, M. B. (1979). In-group bias in the minimal intergroup situation: A cognitive-motivational anaysis. *Psychological Bulletin, 86,* 307–324.

Brewer, M. B., Dull, V., & Lui, L. (1981). Perceptions of the elderly: Stereotypes as prototypes. *Journal of Personality and Social Psychology, 41,* 656–670.

Brewer, M. B., & Lui, L. (1989). The primacy of age and sex in the structure of person categories. *Social Cognition, 7,* 262–274.

Brewer, W. F., & Nakamura, G. V. (1984). The nature and functions of schemas. In R. S. Wyer & T. K. Srull (Eds.), *Handbook of social cognition* (Vol. 1, pp. 119–160). Hillsdale, NJ: Erlbaum.

Briere, J., & Runtz, M. (1988). Symptomatology associated with childhood sexual victimization in a nonclinical adult sample. *Child Abuse & Neglect, 12,* 51–59.

Broadbent, D. E. (1958). *Perception and communication.* London: Pergamon Press.

Brody, E. B., & Brody, N. (1976). *Intelligence: Nature, determinants, and consequences.* New York: Academic Press.

Broman, S. H., Nichols, P. L., & Kennedy, W. A. (1975). *Preschool IQ: Prenatal and early developmental correlates.* Hillsdale, NJ: Erlbaum.

Bronfenbrenner, U., & Ceci, S. J. (1994). Nature-nurture reconceptualized in developmental perspective: A bioecological model. *Psychological Review, 101,* 568–586.

Brown, B., & Rosenbaum, L. (1983, May). *Stress effects on IQ.* Paper presented at the meeting of the American Association for the Advancement of Science, Detroit.

Brown, B. B. (1989). The role of peer groups in adolescents' adjustment to secondary school. In T. J. Berndt & G. W. Ladd (Eds.), *Peer relationships in child development* (pp. 188–215). New York: Wiley.

Brown, N. R., & Siegler, R. S. (1992). The role of availability in the estimation of national populations. *Memory & Cognition, 20,* 406–412.

Brown, R. (1986). *Social psychology: The second edition.* New York: Free Press.

Brown, R., & Hanlon, C. (1970). Derivational complexity and order of acquisition. In J. R. Hayes (Ed.), *Cognition and the development of language.* New York: Wiley.

Brownell, K. D. (1991). Dieting and the search for the perfect body: Where physiology and culture collide. *Behavior Therapy, 22,* 1–12.

Brownell, K. D., & Rodin, J. (1994). The dieting maelstrom: Is it possible and advisable to lose weight? *American Psychologist, 49,* 781–791.

Brownell, K. D., & Wadden, T. A. (1992). Etiology and treatment of obesity: Understanding a serious, prevalent, and refractory disorder. *Journal of Consulting and Clinical Psychology, 60,* 505–517.

Browning, C. R. (1993). *Ordinary men: Reserve Police Battalion 101 and the final solution in Poland.* New York: HarperPerennial.

Bruner, J. S., Olver, R. R., & Greenfield, P. M. (1966). *Studies in cognitive growth.* New York: Wiley.

Buck, R. (1984). *The communication of emotion.* New York: Guilford Press.

Burisch, M. (1984). Approaches to personality inventory construction. *American Psychologist, 39,* 214–227.

Burrows, G. D., & Dennerstein, L. (Eds.). (1980). *Handbook of hypnosis and psychosomatic medicine.* New York: Elsevier/North Holland Biomedical Press.

Buss, D. M. (1994). The strategies of human mating. *American Scientist, 82,* 238–249.

Buss, D. M., & Schmitt, D. P. (1993). Sexual strategies theory: An evolutionary perspective on human mating. *Psychological Review, 100,* 204–232.

Butcher, J. N., Dahlstrom, W. G., Graham, J. R., Tellegen, A., & Kaemmer, B. (1989). *Manual for the restandardized Minnesota Multiphasic Personality Inventory: MMPI-2. An administrative and interpretive guide.* Minneapolis: University of Minnesota Press.

Butcher, J. N., & Williams, C. L. (1992). *Essentials of MMPI-2 and MMPI-A interpretation.* Minneapolis: University of Minnesota Press.

Bykov, K. M. (1957). *The cerebral cortex and the internal organs.* New York: Academic Press.

Byrne, D., & Clore, G. L. (1970). A reinforcement model of evaluative processes. *Personality: An International Journal, 1,* 103–128.

Byrne, R. M. J., & Johnson-Laird, P. N. (1989). Spatial reasoning. *Journal of Memory and Language, 28,* 564–575.

Cairns, R. B., & Valsinger, J. (1984). Child psychology. *Annual Review of Psychology, 35,* 553–577.

Calev, A., Nigal, D., Shapira, B., Tubi, N., Chazan, S., Ben-Yehuda, Y., Kugelmass, S., & Lerer, B. (1991). Early and long-term effects of electroconvulsive therapy and depression on memory and other cognitive functions. *Journal of Nervous and Mental Disease, 179,* 526–533.

Campos, J. J., Barrett, K. C., Lamb, M. E., Goldsmith, H. H., & Stenberg, C. (1983). *Socioemotional development* (Vol. 2). New York: Wiley.

Camras, L. A. (1992). Expressive development and basic emotions. *Cognition and Emotion, 6,* 269–283.

Camras, L. A., Oster, H., Campos, J. J., Miyake, K., & Bradshaw, D. (1992). Japanese and American infants' responses to arm restraint. *Developmental Psychology, 28,* 578–583.

Camras, L. A., Sullivan, J., & Michel, G. (1993). Do infants express discrete emotions? Adult judgments of facial, vocal, and body actions. *Journal of Nonverbal Behavior, 17,* 171–186.

Cannon, W. B. (1927). The James-Lange theory of emotion: A critical examination and an alternative theory. *American Journal of Psychology, 39,* 106–124.

Cannon, W. B. (1929). *Bodily changes in pain, hunger, fear, and rage* (2nd ed.). New York: Appleton-Century-Crofts.

Cannon, W. B. (1934) Hunger and thirst. In C. Murchison (Ed.), *A handbook of general experimental psychology.* Worcester, MA: Clark University Press.

Cannon, W. B., & Washburn, A. L. (1912). An explanation of hunger. *American Journal of Physiology, 29,* 441–454.

Cantor, N., & Harlow, R. E. (1994). Social intelligence and personality: Flexible life task pursuit. In R. J. Sternberg & P. Ruzgis (Eds.), *Personality and intelligence* (pp. 137–168). Cambridge: Cambridge University Press.

Cantor, N., & Kihlstrom, J. R. (1987). *Personality and social intelligence.* Englewood Cliffs, NJ: Prentice-Hall.

Cantor, N., & Mischel, W. (1979). Traits as prototypes: Effects on recognition memory. *Journal of Personality and Social Psychology, 35,* 38–48.

Caplan, L. (1984). *The insanity defense and the trial of John W. Hinckley, Jr.* Boston: Godine.

Caplan, L. (1992, March 30). Not so nutty: The post-Dahmer insanity defense. *The New Republic,* pp. 18–20.

Caporeal, L. R. (1976). Ergotism: The Satan loosed in Salem? *Science, 192,* 21–26.

Caprara, G. V., Barbaranelli, C., Borgoni, L., & Perugini, M. (1993). The Big Five Questionnaire: A new questionnaire for the measurement of the five factor model. *Personality and Individual Differences, 15,* 281–288.

Caprara, G. V., Barbaranelli, C., Bermudez, J., & Maslach, C. (1995). A cross-cultural comparison of the psychometric characteristics of the Big Five Questionnaire. *European Journal of Personality,* in press.

Carey, S. (1978). The child as word learner. In M. Hale, J. Bresnan, & G. A. Miller (Eds.), *Linguistic theory and psychological reality* (pp. 265–293). Cambridge, MA: MIT Press.

Carey, S. (1985). *Conceptual change in childhood.* Cambridge, MA: MIT Press.

Carlsmith, J. M., & Gross, A. (1969). Some effects of guilt on compliance. *Journal of Personality and Social Psychology, 11,* 232–240.

Carlsson, A. (1978). Antipsychotic drugs, neurotransmitters, and schizophrenia. *American Journal of Psychiatry, 135,* 164–173.

Carlton, J. (1990, December 4). When Californians use leaf blowers, life is less mellow. *The Wall Street Journal,* pp. A1, A7.

Carmichael, L. (1926). The development of behavior in vertebrates experimentally removed from the influence of external stimulation. *Psychological Review, 33,* 51–58.

Carmichael, L. (1970). The onset and early development of behavior. In P. H. Mussen (Ed.), *Carmichael's manual of child psychology* (3rd ed., Vol. 1). New York: Wiley.

Carnegie Foundation. (1990, Winter–Spring). Adolescence: Path to a productive life or a diminished future? *Carnegie Quarterly.*

Carpenter, G. C. (1973). Differential response to mother and stranger within the first month of life. *Bulletin of the British Psychological Society, 16,* 138.

Carrell, M. R., & Dittrich, J. E. (1978). Equity theory: The recent literature, methodological considerations, and new directions. *Academy of Management Review, 3,* 202–210.

Carstensen, L. L. (1987). Age-related changes in social activity. In L. L. Carstensen & B. A. Edelstein (Eds.), *Handbook of clinical gerontology* (pp. 222–237). New York: Pergamon Press.

Carstensen, L. L. (1991). Selectivity theory: Social activity in life-span context. In K. W. Schaie (Ed.), *Annual review of geriatrics and gerontology* (Vol. 11). New York: Springer.

Carstensen, L. L., & Freund, A. M. (1994). The resilience of the aging self. *Developmental Review, 14,* 81–92.

Carstensen, L. L., & Pasupathi, M. (1993). Women of a certain age. In S. Matteo (Ed.), *American women in the nineties: Today's critical issues* (pp. 66–78). Boston: Northeastern University Press.

Carter, J. H. (1982). The effects of aging on selected visual functions: Color vision, glare sensitivity, field of vision, and accommodation. In R. Sekuler, D. Kline, & K. Dismukes (Eds.), *Aging and human visual function* (pp. 121–130). New York: Liss.

Cartwright, R. D. (1978). *A primer on sleep and dreaming.* Reading, MA: Addison-Wesley.

Cartwright, R. D. (1982). The shape of dreams. In *1983 yearbook of science and the future.* Chicago: Encyclopaedia Britannica.

Cartwright, R. D. (1984). Broken dreams: A study of the effects of divorce and depression on dream content. *Psychiatry, 47,* 251–259.

Case, R. S. (1985). *Intellectual development: A systematic reinterpretation.* New York: Academic Press.

Casey, J. F., & Wilson, L. (1991). *The flock.* New York: Fawcett Columbine.

Cash, T. F., & Derlega, V. J. (1978). The matching hypothesis: Physical attractiveness among same-sex friends. *Personality and Social Psychology Bulletin, 4,* 240–243.

Catania, J. A., Coates, T. J., & Kegeles, S. (1994). A test of the AIDS risk reduction model: Psychosocial correlates of condom use in the AMEN cohort survey. *Health Psychology, 13,* 548–555.

Cattell, R. B. (1963). Theory of fluid and crystallized intelligence: A critical experiment. *Journal of Educational Psychology, 54,* 1–22.

Cave, C. B., & Squire, L. R. (1992). Intact and long-lasting repetition priming in amnesia. *Journal of Experimental Psychology: Learning, Memory, and Cognition, 18,* 509–520.

Cavel, A., Nigal, D., Shapira, B., Tubi, N., Chazan, S., Ben-Yehuda, Y., Kugelmass, S., & Lerer, B. (1991). Early and long-term effects of electroconvulsive therapy and depression on memory and other cognitive functions. *Journal of Nervous and Mental Disease, 179,* 526–533.

Ceci, S. J., & Liker, J. K. (1986). A day at the races: A study of IQ, expertise, and cognitive complexity. *Journal of Experimental Psychology: General, 115,* 255–266.

Cervone, D., & Palmer, B. W. (1990). Anchoring biases and the perseverance of self-efficacy beliefs. *Cognitive Therapy and Research, 14,* 401–416.

Chamberlain, K., & Zika, S. (1990). The minor events approach to stress: Support for the use of daily hassles. *British Journal of Psychology, 81,* 469–481.

Chapman, P. D. (1988). *Schools as sorters: Lewis M. Terman, applied psychology, and the intelligence testing movement, 1890–1930.* New York: New York University Press.

Charen, M. (1990, March 11). Say no way: Time for good old self-control. *San Francisco Examiner-Chronicle,* This World Section, p. 3.

Chase, W. G., & Ericsson, K. A. (1981). Skilled memory. In J. R. Anderson (Ed.), *Cognitive skills and their acquisition.* Hillsdale, NJ: Erlbaum.

Chasnoff, I. J. (1989). Temporal patterns of cocaine use in pregnancy. *Journal of the American Medical Association, 261,* 24–31.

Chasnoff, I. J., Burns, W. J., Schnoll, S. H., & Burns, K. A. (1985). Cocaine use in pregnancy. *New England Journal of Medicine, 313,* 666–669.

Chasnoff, I. J., Griffith, D. R., MacGregor, S., Dirkes, K., & Burns, K. (1989). Temporal patterns of cocaine use in pregnancy: Perinatal outcome. *Journal of the American Medical Association, 261,* 1741–1744.

Cheek, J. (1989). *Conquering shyness: The battle anyone can win.* New York: Putnam.

Chen, I. (1990, July 13). Quake may have caused baby boom in Bay Area. *The San Francisco Chronicle,* p. A3.

Cheney, D. L., & Seyfarth, R. M. (1990). *How monkeys see the world.* Chicago: University of Chicago Press.

Cheng, P. W., & Holyoak, K. J. (1985). Pragmatic reasoning schemas. *Cognitive Psychology, 17,* 391–416.

Cherry, E. C. (1953). Some experiments on the recognition of speech, with one and with two ears. *Journal of the Acoustical Society of America, 25,* 975–979.

Chicago Institute for Psychoanalysis. (1992). *The annual of psychoanalysis* (Vol. 20). Hillsdale, NJ: Analytic Press.

Chomsky, N. (1965). *Aspects of a theory of syntax.* Cambridge, MA: MIT Press.

Chomsky, N. (1975). *Reflections on language.* New York: Pantheon Books.

Chorover, S. (1981, June). *Organizational recruitment in "open" and "closed" social systems: A neuropsychological perspective.* Conference paper presented at the Center for the Study of New Religious Movements, Berkeley, CA.

Christensen, A., & Jacobson, N. S. (1994). Who (or what) can do psychotherapy: The status and challenge of nonprofessional therapies. *Psychological Science, 5,* 8–14.

Christensen, A. J., Wiebe, J. S., Smith, T. W., Turner, C. W. (1994). Predictors of survival among hemodialysis patients: Effect of perceived family support. *Health Psychology, 13,* 521–525.

Churchland, P. S. (1986). *Toward a unified science of the mind-brain.* Cambridge, MA: MIT Press.

Cialdini, R. B. (1993). *Influence: Science and practice* (3rd ed.). New York: HarperCollins.

Ciaranello, R. D., & Ciaranello, A. L. (1991). Genetics of major psychiatric disorders. *Annual Review of Medicine, 42,* 151–158.

Clark, E. (1987). Principles of contrast: A constraint on language acquisition. In B. MacWhinney (Ed.), *Mechanisms of language acquisition* (pp. 1–33). Hillsdale, NJ: Erlbaum.

Clark, H. H. (1992). *Arenas of language use.* Chicago: University of Chicago Press.

Clark, H. H., & Clark, E., V. (1977). *Psychology and language: An introduction to psycholinguisitics.* New York: Harcourt Brace Jovanovich.

Clark, H. H., & Gerrig, R. J. (1990). Quotations as demonstrations. *Language, 66,* 764–805.

Clark, H. H., & Marshall, C. R. (1981). Definite reference and mutual knowledge. In A. K. Joshi, B. Webber, & I. Sag (Eds.), *Elements of discourse understanding* (pp. 10–63). Cambridge: Cambridge University Press.

Clarke-Stewart, K. A. (1991). A home is not a school: The effects of child care on children's development. *Journal of Social Issues, 47,* 105–123.

Clarke-Stewart, K. A. (1993). *Daycare.* Cambridge, MA: Harvard University Press.

Clausen, J. A. (1981). Stigma and mental disorder: Phenomena and mental terminology. *Psychiatry, 44,* 287–296.

Clementz, B. A., & Sweeney, J. A. (1990). Is eye movement dysfunction a biological marker for schizophrenia? A methodological review. *Psychological Bulletin, 108,* 77–92.

Cloninger, C. R. (1987). Neurogenetic adaptive mechnanisms in alcoholism. *Science, 236,* 410–416.

Clopton, N. A., & Sorell, G. T. (1993). Gender differences in moral reasoning: Stable or situational? *Psychology of Women Quarterly, 17,* 85–101.

Coates, T. (1990). Strategies for modifying sexual behavior for primary and secondary prevention of HIV infection. *Journal of Consulting and Clinical Psychology, 58,* 57–69.

Cobb, S. (1976). Social support as a moderator of stress. *Psychosomatic Medicine, 35,* 375–389.

Coch, L., & French, J. R. P., Jr. (1948). Overcoming resistance to change. *Human Relations, 1,* 512–532.

Cohen, R. E., & Ahearn, F. L., Jr. (1980). *Handbook for mental health care of disaster victims.* Baltimore: Johns Hopkins University Press.

Cohen, S. (1988). Psychosocial models of the role of social support in the etiology of physical disease. *Health Psychology, 7,* 269–297.

Cohen, S., & Girgus, J. S. (1973). Visual spatial illusions: Many explanations. *Science, 179,* 503–504.

Cohen, S., & McKay, G. (1983). Social support, stress, and the buffering hypotheses: A theoretical analysis. In A. Baum, S. E. Taylor, & J. Singer (Eds.), *Handbook of psychology and health* (Vol. 4). Hillsdale, NJ: Erlbaum.

Cohen, S., & Syme, S. L. (Eds.). (1985). *Social support and health.* Orlando, FL: Academic Press.

Cole, N. S., & Moss, P. A. (1989). Bias in test use. In R. L. Linn (Ed.), *Educational measurement* (pp. 201–219). New York: Macmillan.

Coleman, L. (1987). *Suicide clusters.* Winchester, MA: Faber & Faber.

Coleman, R. M. (1986). *Wide awake at 3:00 A.M.: By choice or by chance?* New York: Freeman.

Collins, A. M., & Quillian, M. R. (1969). Retrieval time from semantic memory. *Journal of Verbal Learning and Verbal Behavior, 8,* 240–247.

Comstock, G., & Paik, H. (1991). *Television and the American child.* San Diego: Academic Press.

Conger, J. C., & Keane, S. P. (1981). Social skills intervention in the treatment of isolated or withdrawn children. *Psychological Bulletin, 90,* 478–495.

Conger, R. D., Ge, X., Elder, G. H., Jr., Lorenz, F. O., & Simons, R. L. (1994). Economic stress, coercive family process, and developmental problems of adolescents. *Child Development, 65,* 541–561.

Cook, M., Mineka, S., Wokelnstein, B., & Laitsch, K. (1985). Observational conditioning of snake fear in unrelated rhesus monkeys. *Journal of Abnormal Psychology, 94,* 591–610.

Cookerly, J. R. (1980). Does marital therapy do any lasting good? *Journal of Marital and Family Therapy, 6,* 393–397.

Corr, C. A. (1993). Coping with dying: Lessons that we should and should not learn from the work of Elisabeth Kübler-Ross. *Death Studies, 17,* 69–83.

Corso, J. F. (1977). Auditory perception and communication. In J. E. Birren & K. W. Schaie (Eds.), *Handbook of the psychology of aging* (pp. 535–553). New York: Van Nostrand Reinhold.

Cosmides, L., & Tooby, J. (1987). From evolution to behavior: Evolutionary psychology as the missing link. In J. Dupre (Ed.), *The latest on the best: Essays on evolution and optimality* (pp. 277–306). Cambridge, MA: MIT Press.

Costa, P. T., Jr., & McCrae, R. R. (1985). *The NEO personality inventory manual.* Odessa, FL: Psychological Assessment Resources.

Costa, P. T., Jr., & McCrae, R. R. (1992a). Four ways five factors are basic. *Personality and Individual Differences, 13,* 653–665.

Costa, P. T., Jr., & McCrae, R. R. (1992b). *Revised NEO Personality Inventory (NEO-PI-R) and NEO Five-factor Inventory (NEO-FFI) professional manual.* Odessa, FL: Psychological Assessment Resources.

Cousins, N. (1979). *The anatomy of an illness as perceived by a patient: Reflections on healing and rejuvenation.* New York: Norton.

Cousins, N. (1989). *Head first: The biology of hope.* New York: Dutton.

Cowan, C. P., Cowan, P. A., Heming, G., Garrett, E., Coysh, W. S., Curtis-Boles, H., & Boles, A. J., III. (1985). Transitions to parenthood: His, hers, and theirs. *Journal of Family Issues, 6,* 451–481.

Cowan, N. (1993). Acitvation, attention, and short-term memory. *Memory & Cognition, 21,* 162–167.

Cowan, C. P., & Cowan, P. A. (1988). Changes in marriage during the transition to parenthood. In G. Y. Michaels & W. A. Goldberg (Eds.), *The transition to parenthood: Current theory and research.* Cambridge: Cambridge University Press.

Cowan, P. A. (1988). Developmental psychopathology: A nine-cell map of the territory. In E. Nannis & P. A. Cowan (Eds.), *Developmental psychopathology and its treatment: New directions for child development* (No, 39, pp. 5–29). San Francisco: Jossey-Bass.

Cowan, W. M. (1979). The development of the brain. In *The brain* (pp. 56–69). San Francisco: Freeman.

Cowles, J. T. (1937). Food tokens as incentives for learning by chimpanzees. *Comparative Psychology Monographs, 74,* 1–96.

Coyne, J. C., Wortman, C. B., & Lehman, D. R. (1988). The other side of support: Emotional overinvolvement and miscarried helping. In B. Gottlieb (Ed.), *Marshalling social support* (pp. 305–330). Newbury Park, CA: Sage.

Craik, F. I. M. (1994). Memory changes in normal aging. *Current Directions in Psychological Science, 3,* 155–158.

Craik, F. I. M., & Lockhart, R. S. (1972). Levels of processing; A framework for memory research. *Journal of Verbal Learning and Verbal Behavior, 11,* 671–684.

Craik, K. (1943). *The nature of explanation.* Cambridge: Cambridge University Press.

Cranston, M. (1991). *The noble savage: Jean-Jacques Rousseau, 1754–1762.* Chicago: University of Chicago Press.

Crapo, L. (1985). *Hormones: The messengers of life.* Stanford, CA: Stanford Alumni Association Press.

Crick, F., & Mitchison, G. (1983). The function of dream sleep. *Nature, 304,* 111–114.

Cronbach, L. J. (1975). Five decades of public controversy over mental testing. *American Psychologist, 30,* 1–14.

Cronbach, L. J. (1990). *Essentials of psychological testing.* New York: Harper & Row.

Cross, S., & Markus, H. (1991). Possible selves across the life span. *Human Development, 34,* 230–255.

Crowder, R. G. (1976). *Principles of learning and memory.* Hillsdale, NJ: Erlbaum.

Crowder, R. G., & Morton, J. (1969). Precategorical acoustic storage (PAS). *Perception and Psychophysics, 8,* 815–820.

Csikszentmihalyi, M. (1990). *Flow: The psychology of optimal experience.* New York: Harper & Row.

Csikszentmihalyi, M., Larson, R., & Prescott, S. (1977). The ecology of adolescent activity and experience. *Journal of Youth and Adolescence, 6,* 281–294.

Curtis, R. C., & Miller, K. (1986). Believing another likes or dislikes you: Behaviors making the beliefs come true. *Journal of Personality and Social Psychology, 51,* 284–290.

Cutler, W. B., Preti, G., Krieger, A., Huggins, G. R., Ramon Garcia, C., & Lawley, H. J. (1986). Human axillary secretions influence women's menstrual cycles: The role of donor extract from men. *Hormones and Behavior, 20,* 463–473.

Cutting, J., & Proffitt, D. (1982). The minimum principle and the perception of absolute, common and relative motions. *Cognitive Psychology, 14,* 211–246.

Dahlstrom, W. G., Welsh, H. G., & Dahlstrom, L. E. (1975). *An MMPI handbook, Vol. 1: Clinical interpretation.* Minneapolis: University of Minnesota Press.

Dakof, G. A., & Taylor, S. E. (1990). Victims' perceptions of social support: What is helpful from whom? *Journal of Personality and Social Psychology, 58,* 80–89.

Damasio, H., Grabowski, T., Frank, R., Galaburda, A. M., & Damasio, A. R. (1994). The return of Phineas Gage: Clues about the brain from the skull of a famous patient. *Science, 264,* 1102–1105.

Dannefer, D., & Perlmutter, M. (1990). Development as a multidimensional process: Individual and social constituents. *Human Development, 33,* 108–137.

Darley, J., & Gilbert, D. T. (1985). Social psychological aspects of environmental psychology. In G. Lindzey & E. Aronson (Eds.), *Handbook of social psychology* (2nd ed., Vol. 2, pp. 949–992). New York: Random House.

Darley, J. M., & Batson, C. D. (1973). From Jerusalem to Jericho: A study of situational and dispositional variables in helping behavior. *Journal of Personality and Social Psychology, 27,* 100–108.

Darling, N., & Steinberg, L. (1993). Parenting style as context: An integrative model. *Psychological Bulletin, 113,* 487–496.

Darnton, R. (1968). *Mesmerism and the end of the Enlightenment in France.* Cambridge, MA: Harvard University Press.

Darwin, C. (1965). *The expression of emotions in man and animals.* Chicago: University of Chicago Press. (Originally published 1872.)

Darwin, C. J., Turvey, M. T., & Crowder, R. G. (1972). The auditory analogue of the Sperling partial report procedure: Evidence for brief auditory stage. *Cognitive Psychology, 3,* 255–267.

Dattilio, F. M., & Padesky, C. A. (1990). *Cognitive therapy with couples.* Sarasota, FL: Professional Resource Exchange.

D'Augelli, A. R. (1993). Preventing mental health problems among lesbian and gay college students. *The Journal of Primary Prevention, 13,* 245–261.

Davidson, J. R. T., Hughes, D., Blazer, D. G., & George, L. K. (1991). Post-traumatic stress disorder in the community: An epidemiological study. *Psychological Medicine, 21,* 713–721.

Davidson, R. (1984). Hemispheric asymmetry and emotion. In K. Sherer & P. Ekman (Eds.), *Approaches to emotion.* Hillsdale, NJ: Erlbaum.

Davis, J. M., & Sandoval, J. (1991). *Suicidal youth.* San Francisco: Jossey-Bass.

Dawes, R. M., Faust, D., & Meehl, P. E. (1989). Clinical versus actuarial judgment. *Science, 243,* 1668–1674.

DeCasper, A. J., & Prescott, P. A. (1983). Human newborns' perception of male voices: Preference, discrimination, and reinforcing value. *Developmental Psychology, 17,* 481–491.

Degreef, G., Ashari, M., Bogerts, B., Bilder, R. M., Jody, D. N., Alvir, J. M. J., & Lieberman, J. A. (1992). Volumes of ventricular system subdivisions measured from magnetic resonance images in first-episode schizophrenic patients. *Archives of General Psychiatry, 49,* 531–537.

Dehaene, S., Bossini, S., & Giraux, P. (1993). The mental representation of parity and number magnitude. *Journal of Experimental Psychology: General, 122,* 371–396.

Delgado, J. M. (1974). The subjective experiece of perceptual and cognitive disturbances in schizophrenia. *Archives of General Psychiatry, 30,* 333–340.

Delgado, J. M. R. (1969). *Physical control of the mind.* New York: Harper & Row.

Dell, G. S. (1986). A spreading-activation theory of retrieval in sentence production. *Psychological Review, 93,* 283–321.

Delprato, D. J., & Midgley, B. D. (1992). Some fundamentals of B. F. Skinner's behaviorism. *American Psychologist, 47,* 1507–1520.

Dembrowski, T. M., & Costa, P. T., Jr. (1987). Coronary prone behavior: Components of the Type A pattern and hostility. *Journal of Personality, 55,* 211–235.

Dement, W. C. (1976). *Some watch while some must sleep.* San Francisco: San Francisco Book Co.

Dement, W. C., & Kleitman, N. (1957). Cyclic variations in EEG during sleep and their relations to eye movement, body mobility and dreaming. *Electroencephalography and Clinical Neurophysiology, 9,* 673–690.

Dennett, D. C. (1987). Consciousness. In R. L. Gregory (Ed.), *The Oxford companion to the mind* (pp. 160–164). New York: Oxford University Press.

Dennett, D. C. (1991). *Consciousness explained.* Boston: Little, Brown.

DeRivera, J. (1984). Development and the full range of emotional experience. In C. Malatesta & C. E. Izard (Eds.), *Emotion in adult development* (pp. 45–63). Beverly Hills, CA: Sage.

Deutsch, M., & Gerard, H. B. (1955). A study of normative and informational social influence. *Journal of Abnormal and Social Psychology, 51,* 629–636.

Devanand, D. P., Verma, A. K., Tirumalasetti, F., & Sackeim, H. A. (1991). Absence of cognitive impairment after more than 100 lifetime ECT treatments. *American Journal of Psychiatry, 148,* 929–932.

De Valois, R. L., & De Valois, K. K. (1990). *Spatial vision.* New York: Oxford University Press.

De Valois, R. L., & Jacobs, G. H. (1968). Primate color vision. *Science, 162,* 533–540.

Devine, P. G. (1989). Stereotypes and prejudice: Their automatic and controlled components. *Journal of Personality and Social Psychology, 56,* 5–18.

Dewsbury, D. A. (1981). Effects of novelty on copulatory behavior: The Coolidge effect and related phenomena. *Psychological Bulletin, 89,* 464–482.

Dhruvarajan, V. (1990). Religious ideology, Hindu women, and development in India. *Journal of Social Issues, 46,* 57–69.

Diamond, D. (1989, Fall). The unbearable darkness of being. *Stanford Medicine,* pp. 13–16.

Diamond, J. (1987, August). Soft sciences are often harder than hard sciences. *Discover,* pp. 34–39.

Diamond, R., & Carey, S. (1986). Why faces are and are not special: An effect of expertise. *Journal of Experimental Psychology: General, 115,* 107–117.

DiClemente, C. C., Prochaska, J. O., Fairhurst, S. K., Velicer, W. F., Valesquez, M. M., & Rossi, J. S. (1991). The process of smoking cessation: An analysis of precontemplation, contemplation, and preparation stages of change. *Journal of Consulting and Clinical Psychology, 59,* 295–304.

Diener, E., & Crandall, R. (1978). *Ethics in social and behavioral research.* Chicago: University of Chicago Press.

Digman, J. M. (1990). Personality structure: Emergence of the five-factor model. *Annual Review of Psychology, 41,* 417–440.

Dillbeck, M. C., & Orme-Johnson, D. W. (1987). Physiological differences between transcendental meditation and rest. *American Psychologist, 42,* 879–881.

Dillon, K. M., & Totten, M. C. (1989). Psychological factors affecting immunocompetence and health of breastfeeding mothers and their infants. *Journal of Genetic Psychology, 150,* 155–162.

DiMatteo, M. R., & DiNicola, D. D. (1982). *Achieving patient compliance.* Elmsford, NY: Pergamon Press.

Dinges, M. M., & Oetting, E. R. (1993). Similarity in drug use patterns between adolescents and their friends. *Adolescence, 28,* 253–266.

Dion, K. K., Berscheid, E., & Walster, E. (1972). What is beautiful is good. *Journal of Personality and Social Psychology, 24,* 285–290.

Dishman, R. K. (1982). Compliance/adherence in health-related exercise. *Health Psychology, 1,* 267.

Dishman, R. K. (1991). Increasing and maintaining exercise and physical activity. *Behavior Therapy, 22,* 345–378.

Doane, J. A., Falloon, I. R. H., Goldstein, M. J., & Mintz, J. (1985). Parental affective style and the treatment of schizophrenia. *Archives of General Psychiatry, 42,* 34–42.

Dohrenwend, B. P., & Shrout, P. E. (1985). "Hassles" in the conceptualization and measurement of life stress variables. *American Psychologist, 40,* 780–785.

Dohrenwend, B. S., & Dohrenwend, B. P. (1974). *Stressful life events: Their nature and effects.* New York: Wiley.

Dollard, J., & Miller, N. E. (1950). *Personality and psychotherapy.* New York: McGraw-Hill.

Dollard, J., Doob, L. W., Miller, N., Mower, O. H., & Sears, R. R. (1939). *Frustration and aggression.* New Haven: Yale University Press.

Dopkins, S., Morris, R. K., & Rayner, K. (1992). Lexical ambiguity and eye fixations in reading: A test of competing models of lexical ambiguity resolution. *Journal of Memory and Language, 31,* 461–476.

Dosher, B. A., & Corbett, A. T. (1982). Instrument inferences and verb schemata. *Memory & Cognition, 10,* 531–539.

Dowling, J. E. (1992). *Neurons and networks: An introduction to neuroscience.* Cambridge, MA: Harvard University Press.

Drigotas, S. M., & Rusbult, C. E. (1992). Should I stay or should I go? A dependence model of breakups. *Journal of Personality and Social Psychology, 62,* 62–87.

Driver, J., & Tipper, S. (1989). On the nonselectivity of "selective" seeing: Contrasts between interference and priming in selective attention. *Journal of Experimental Psychology: Human Perception and Performance, 15,* 304–314.

Dror, I. E., Kosslyn, S. M., & Wang, W. L. (1993). Visual–spatial abilities of pilots. *Journal of Applied Psychology, 78,* 763–773.

Dryfoss, J. G. (1990). *Adolescents at risk: Prevalence and prevention.* New York: Oxford University Press.

DSM-III-R. (1987). *Diagnostic and statistical manual of mental disorders.* Washington, DC: American Psychiatric Association.

DSM-IV. (1994). *Diagnostic and statistical manual of mental disorders* (4th ed.). Washington, DC: American Psychiatric Association.

DuBois, P. H. (1970). *A history of psychological testing.* Boston: Allyn and Bacon.

Duckitt, J. (1992). Psychology and prejudice: A historical analysis and integrative framework. *American Psychologist, 47,* 1182–1193.

Dudycha, G. J. (1936). An objective study of punctuality in relation to personality and achievement. *Archives of Psychology, 204,* 1–53.

Duncan, G. J., Brooks-Gunn, J., & Klebanov, P. K. (1994). Economic deprivation and early childhood development. *Child Development, 65,* 296–318.

Duncan, J., & Humphreys, G. W. (1989). Visual search and stimulus similarity. *Psychological Review, 96,* 433–548.

Duncker, D. (1945). On problem solving. *Psychological Monographs, 58* (No. 270).

Dutton, D. G., & Aron, A. P. (1974). Some evidence for heightened sexual attraction under conditions of high anxiety. *Journal of Personality and Social Psychology, 30,* 510–517.

Dweck, C. S. (1975). The role of expectations and attributions in the alleviation of learned helplessness. *Journal of Personality and Social Psychology, 31,* 674–685

Eagly, A. H., & Chaiken, S. (1993). *The psychology of attitudes.* Fort Worth, TX: Harcourt Brace Jovanovich.

Ebbinghaus, H. (1913). *Memory.* New York: Columbia University. (Original work published 1885.)

Ebbinghaus, H. (1973). *Psychology: An elementary text-book.* New York: Arno Press. (Original work published 1908.)

Edwards, A. E., & Acker, L. E. (1962). A demonstration of the long-term retention of a conditioned galvanic skin response. *Psychosomatic Medicine, 24,* 459–463.

Edwards, G. (1980). Alcoholism treatment: Between guesswork and certainty. In G. Edwards & M. Grant (Eds.), *Alcoholism treatment in transition.* London: Croon Helm.

Egeland, J. A., Gerhard, D. S., Pauls, D. L., Sussex, J. N., Kidd, K. K., Allen, C. R., Hostetter, A. M., & Housman, D. E. (1987). Bipolar affective disorder linked to DNA markers on chromosome 11. *Nature, 325,* 783–787.

Ehrlich, B. E. & Diamond, J. M. (1980). Lithium, membranes, and manic-depressive illness. *Journal of Membrane Biology, 52,* 187–200.

Eimas, P., Siqueland, E., Jusczyk, P., Y Vigorito, J. (1971). Speech perception in infants, *Science, 171,* 303–306.

Eisenberg, N., & Mussen, P. H. (1989). *The roots of prosocial behavior in children.* New York: Cambridge University Press.

Ekman, P. (1972). Universal and cultural differences in facial expressions of emotion. In J. Cole (Ed.), *Nebraska Symposium on Motivation.* Lincoln: University of Nebraska Press.

Ekman, P. (1984). Expression and the nature of emotion. In K. R. Scherer & P. Ekman (Eds.), *Approaches to emotion.* Hillsdale, NJ: Erlbaum.

Ekman, P. (1994). Strong evidence for universals in facial expressions: A reply to Russell's mistaken critique. *Psychological Bulletin, 115,* 268–287.

Ekman, P., & Friesen, W. V. (1971). Constants across cultures in the face and emotion. *Journal of Personality and Social Psychology, 17,* 124–129.

Ekman, P., & Friesen, W. V. (1975). *Unmasking the face: A guide to recognizing emotions from facial clues.* Englewood Cliffs, NJ: Prentice-Hall.

Ekman, P., & Friesen, W. V. (1986). A new pan-cultural facial expression of emotion. *Motivation and Emotion, 10,* 159–168.

Ekstrand, M. L., & Coates, T. J. (1990). Maintenance of safer sexual behaviors and predictors of risky sex: The San Francisco men's health survey. *American Journal of Public Health, 80,* 973–977.

Elkin, I., Shea, M. T., Watkins, J. T., Imber, S. D., Sotsky, S. M., Collins, J. F., Glass, D. R., Pilkonis, P. A., Leber, W. R., Kocherty, J. P., Fiester, S. J., & Parloff, M. B. (1989). National Institutes of Mental Health treatment of depression collaborative research program: General effectiveness of treatments. *Archives of General Psychiatry, 46,* 971–982.

Elliott, J. (1977). The power and pathology of prejudice. In P. G. Zimbardo & F. L. Ruch, *Psychology and life* (9th ed., Diamond Printing). Glenview, IL: Scott, Foresman.

Elliott, R. (1991a). Social science data and the APA: The *Lockhart* brief as a case in point. *Law and Human Behavior, 15,* 59–76.

Elliott, R. (1991b). Response to Ellsworth. *Law and Human Behavior, l5,* 91–94.

Ellis, A. (1962). *Reason and emotion in psychotherapy.* New York: Lyle Stuart.

Ellis, A. (1977). The treatment of a psychopath with rational therapy. In S. J. Morse & R. I. Watson (Eds.), *Psychotherapies: A comparative casebook.* New York: Holt, Rinehart & Winston.

Ellis, A., & Grieger, R. (1986). *Handbook of rational emotive therapy* (Vol. 2). New York: Springer.

Ellis, A., & Velten, E. (1992). *When AA doesn't work for you: Rational steps to quitting alcohol.* Fort Lee, NJ: Barricade Books.

Ellsworth, P. (1991). To tell what we know or wait for Godot? *Law and Human Behavior, 15,* 77–90.

Elms, A. C. (1988). Freud as Leonardo: Why the first psychobiography went wrong. *Journal of Personality, 56,* 19–40.

Emmelkamp, P. M. (1986). Behavior therapy with adults. In S. L. Garfield & A. E. Bergin (Eds.), *Handbook of psychotherapy and behavior change* (pp. 385–442). New York: Wiley.

Emmelkamp, P. M. G., & Kuipers, A. (1979). Agoraphobia: A follow-up study four years after treatment. *British Journal of Psychology, 134,* 352–355.

Erber, R., & Erber, M. W. (1994). Beyond mood and social judgment: Mood incongruent recall and mood regulation. *European Journal of Social Psychology, 24,* 79–88.

Erdman, L. (1993). Laughter therapy for patients with cancer. *Journal of Psychosocial Oncology, 11,* 55–67.

Ericsson, K. A., & Chase, W. G. (1982). Exceptional memory. *American Scientist, 70,* 607–615.

Ericsson, K. A., & Simon, H. A. (1993). *Protocol analysis: Verbal reports as data* (rev. ed.). Cambridge, MA: MIT Press.

Esterling, B. A., Kiecolt-Glaser, J. K., Bodnar, J. C., & Glaser, R. (1994). Chronic stress, social support, and persistent alterations in the natural killer cell response to cytokines in older adults. *Health Psychology, 13,* 291–298.

Evans, F. J. (1989). The independence of suggestibility, placebo response, and hypnotizability. In V. A. Gheorghiu, P. Netter, H. J. Eysenck, & R. Rosenthal (Eds.), *Suggestion and suggestibility* (pp. 145–154). New York: Springer-Verlag.

Evans, J. S. B., Barston, J. L., & Pollard, P. (1983). On the conflict between logic and belief in syllogistic reasoning. *Memory and Cognition, 11,* 295–306.

Evans-Pritchard, E. E. (1937). *Witchcraft, oracles and magic among the Azande.* Oxford: Oxford University Press.

Exner, J. E., Jr. (1974). *The Rorschach: A comprehensive system: Vol. 1.* New York: Wiley.

Exner, J. E., Jr. (1978) *The Rorschach: A comprehensive system: Vol. 2. Current research and advanced interpretation.* New York: Wiley.

Exner, J. E., Jr., & Weiner, I. B. (1982). *The Rorschach: A comprehensive system: Vol. 3. Assessment of children and adolescents.* New York: Wiley.

Eysenck, H. (1990). Biological dimensions of personality. In L. A. Pervin (Ed.), *Handbook of personality theory and research* (pp. 244–276). New York: Guilford Press.

Eysenck, H. J. (1952). The effects of psychotherapy: An evaluation. *Journal of Consulting Psychology, 16,* 319–324.

Eysenck, H. J. (1973). *The inequality of man.* London: Temple Smith.

Eysenck, H. J. (1988). Personality and stress as causal factors in cancer and coronary heart disease. In M. P. Janisse (Ed.), *Individual differences, stress, and health psychology* (pp. 129–145). New York: Springer-Verlag.

Eysenck, H. J. (1992). Four ways five factors are not basic. *Personality and Individual Differences, 13,* 667–673.

Fairbank, J. A., Schlenger, W. E., Caddell, J. M., & Woods, M. G. (1993). Post-traumatic stress disorder. In P. B. Sutker & H. E. Adams (Eds.), *Comprehensive handbook of psychopathology* (2nd ed., pp. 145–165). New York: Plenum Press.

Fantz, R. L. (1963). Pattern vision in newborn infants. *Science, 140,* 296–297.

Farah, M. J. (1988). Is visual imagery really visual? Overlooked evidence from neuropsychology. *Psychological Review, 95,* 307–317.

Farbman, A. I. (1992). *Cell biology of olfaction.* New York: Cambridge University Press.

Farina, A. (1980). Social attitudes and beliefs and their role in mental disorders. In J. G. Rabkin, L. Gelb, & J. B. Lazar (Eds.), *Attitudes toward the mentally ill: Research perspectives* (pp. 35–37). Rockville, MD: National Institutes of Mental Health.

Farquhar, J. W. (1978). *The American way of life need not be hazardous to your health.* New York: Norton.

Farquhar, J. W. (1991). The Stanford cardiovascular disease prevention programs. *Annals of the New York Academy of Sciences, 623,* 327–331.

Farquhar, J. W., Maccoby, N., & Solomon, D. S. (1984). Community applications of behavioral medicine. In W. D. Gentry (Ed.), *Handbook of behavioral medicine* (pp. 437–478). New York: Guilford Press.

Fazio, R. H. (1987). Self-perception theory: A current perspective. In M. P. Zanna, J. M. Olson, & C. P. Herman (Eds.), *Social influence: The Ontario Symposium* (Vol. 5, pp. 129–150). Hillsdale, NJ: Erlbaum.

Feather, N. T. (1961). The relationship of persistence at a task to expectation of success and achievement related motives. *Journal of Abnormal and Social Psychology, 63,* 552–561.

Fechner, G. T. (1860). *Elemente der psychophysik.* Leipzig: Breitkopf und Hartel.

Feeney, J. A., & Noller, P. (1990). Attachment style as a predictor of adult romantic relationships. *Journal of Personality and Social Psychology, 58,* 281–291.

Fendrich, R., Wessinger, C. M., & Gazzaniga, M. S. (1992). Residual vision in a scotoma: Implications for blindsight. *Science, 258,* 1489–1491.

Fendrich, R., Wessinger, C. M., & Gazzaniga, M. S. (1993). Sources of blindsight. *Science, 261,* 494–495.

Fernald, A. (1985). Four-month-old infants prefer to listen to motherese. *Infant Behavior and Development, 8,* 118–195.

Fernald, A., Taeschner, T., Dunn, J., Papousek, M., De Boysson-Bardies, B., & Fukui, I. (1989). A cross-cultural study of prosodic modification in mothers' and fathers' speech to preverbal infants. *Journal of Child Language, 16,* 477–501.

Fernald, R. (1984). Vision and behavior in an African cichlid fish. *American Scientist, 72,* 58–65.

Ferster, C. B., & Skinner, B. F. (1957). *Schedules of reinforcement.* New York: Appleton-Century-Crofts.

Festinger, L. (1957). *A theory of cognitive dissonance.* Stanford, CA: Stanford University Press.

Festinger, L., & Carlsmith, J. M. (1959). Cognitive conquences of forced compliance. *Journal of Abnormal and Social Psychology, 58,* 203–211.

Field, T. F., & Schanberg, S. M. (1990). Massage alters growth and catecholamine production in preterm newborns. In N. Gunzenhauser (Ed.), *Advances in touch* (pp. 96–104). Skillman, NJ: Johnson & Johnson.

Fields, H. L., & Levine, J. D. (1984). Placebo analgesia: A role for endorphins. *Trends in Neuroscience, 7,* 271–273.

Finkelhor, D., & Dziuba-Leatherman, J. (1994). Victimization of children. *American Psychologist, 49,* 173–183.

Finkelhor, D., Hataling, G., Lewis, I. A., & Smith, C. (1990). Sexual abuse in a national survey of adult men and women: Prevalence, characteristics, and risk factors. *Child Abuse & Neglect, 14,* 19–28.

Fiorito, G., & Scotto, P. (1992). Observational learning in *Octopus vulgaris. Science, 256,* 545–547.

Fish, J. M. (1973). *Placebo therapy.* San Francisco: Jossey-Bass.

Fisher, J. D., & Fisher, W. A. (1992). Changing AIDS-risk behavior. *Psychological Bulletin, 111,* 455–474.

Fisher, J. D., Fisher, W. A., Williams, S. S., & Malloy, T. E. (1994). Empirical tests of an information-motivation-behavioral skills model of AIDS-prevention behavior with gay men and heterosexual university students. *Health Psychology, 13,* 238–250.

Fishman, H. C. (1993). *Intensive structural therapy: Treating families in their social context.* New York: Basic Books.

Fiske, S. T., & Taylor, S. E. (1991). *Social cognition.* New York: McGraw-Hill.

Fitzgibbon, M. L., Stolley, M. R., & Kirschenbaum, D. S. (1993). Obese people who seek treatment have different characteristics than those who do not seek treatment. *Health Psychology, 12,* 342–345.

Flavell, J. (1963). *The developmental psychology of Jean Piaget.* Princeton, NJ: Van Nostrand.

Flavell, J. H. (1985). *Cognitive development* (2nd ed.). Englewood Cliffs, NJ: Prentice-Hall.

Fleming, I. (1959). From a view to a kill. In *For your eyes only* (pp. 1–30). New York: Charter Books.

Fletcher, G. J. O., & Ward, C. (1988). Attribution theory and processes: A cross-cultural perspective. In M. H. Bon (Ed.), *The cross-cultural challenge to social psychology* (pp. 230–244). Newbury Park, CA: Sage.

Fletcher, R., & Voke, J. (1985). *Defective color vision.* New York: Taylor & Francis.

Flood, R. A., & Seager, C. P. (1968). A retrospective examination of psychiatric case records of patients who subsequently committed suicide. *British Journal of Psychiatry, 114,* 433–450.

Flynn, J. R. (1987). Massive IQ gains in 14 nations: What IQ tests really measure. *Psychological Bulletin, 101,* 271–291.

Fogel, A. (1991). Movement and communication in human infancy: The social dynamics of development. *Journal of Human Movement Studies.*

Foley, V. D. (1979). Family therapy. In R. J. Corsini (Ed.), *Current psychotherapies* (2nd ed., pp. 460–469). Itasca, IL: Peacock.

Folkman, S. (1984). Personal control and stress and coping processes: A theoretical analysis. *Journal of Personality and Social Psychology, 46,* 839–852.

Fontaine, G. (1974). Social comparison and some determinants of expected personal control and expected performance in a novel situation. *Journal of Personality and Social Psychology, 29,* 487–496.

Forbes, D., Creamer, M., & Rycroft, P. (1994). Eye movement and reprocessing in posttraumatic stress disorder. *Journal of Behavior Therapy and Experimental Psychiatry, 25,* 113–120.

Ford, C. S., & Beach, F. A. (1951). *Patterns of sexual behavior.* New York: Harper & Row.

Forgas, J. P. (Ed.). (1991). *Emotion & social judgments.* Oxford: Pergamon Press.

Forge, A., Li, L., Corwin, J. T., & Nevill, G. (1993). Ultrastructural evidence for hair cell regeneration in the mammalian inner ear. *Science, 259,* 1616–1619.

Foucault, M. (1975). *The birth of the clinic.* New York: Vintage Books.

Fowler, H. (1965). *Curiosity and exploratory behavior.* New York: Macmillan.

Fowler, R. D. (1993). 1992 report of the chief executive officer. *American Psychologist, 48,* 726–735.

Frank, J. D., & Frank, J. B. (1991). *Persuasion and healing: A comparative study of psychotherapy* (3rd ed.). Baltimore: Johns Hopkins University Press.

Frank, M. E., & Nowlis, G. H. (1989). Learned aversions and taste qualities in hamsters. *Chemical Senses, 14,* 379–394.

Franklin, N., & Tversky, B. (1990). Searching imagined environments. *Journal of Experimental Psychology: General, 119,* 63–76.

Franz, C. E., McClelland, D. C., & Weinberger, J. (1991). Childhood antecedents of conventional social accomplishment in midlife adults: A 36-year prospective study. *Journal of Personality and Social Psychology, 60,* 586–595.

Fraser, S. (Ed.). (1995). *The Bell Curve wars: Race, intelligence, and the future of America.* New York: Basic Books.

Fraser, S. C. (1974). *Deindividuation: Effects of anonymity on aggression in children.* Unpublished mimeograph report, University of Southern California.

Frederickson, B. L. (1991). Anticipated endings: An explanation for selective social interaction (doctoral dissertation, Stanford University, 1990). *Dissertation Abstracts International, 3,* AAD91–00818.

Freedman, B. J. (1974). The subjective experience of perceptual and cognitive disturbances in schizophrenia. *Archives of General Psychiatry, 30,* 333–340.

Freedman, J. L., & Fraser, S. C. (1966). Compliance without pressure: The foot-in-the-door technique. *Journal of Personality and Social Psychology, 4,* 195–202.

Freeman, F. R. (1972). *Sleep research: A critical review.* Springfield, IL: Charles C Thomas.

Freud, A. (1946). *The ego and the mechanisms of defense.* New York: International Universities Press.

Freud, A. (1958). Adolescence. *Psychoanalytic Study of the Child, 13,* 255–278.

Freud, S. (1915). Instincts and their vicissitudes. In S. Freud, *The collected papers.* New York: Collier.

Freud, S. (1923). *Introductory lectures on psycho-analysis* (J. Riviera, Trans.). London: Allen & Unwin.

Freud, S. (1953). Three essays on the theory of sexuality. In J. Strachey (Ed.), *The standard edition of the complete psychological works of Sigmund Freud* (Vol. 7, pp. 135–243). London: Hogarth Press. (Original work published 1905.)

Freud, S. (1957). Leonardo da Vinci and a memory of his childhood. In J. Strachey (Ed. and Trans.), *The standard edition of the complete psychological works of Sigmund Freud* (Vol. 11, pp. 59–137). London: Hogarth Press. (Original work published 1910.)

Friedman, H. S. (Ed.). (1990). *Personality and disease.* New York: Wiley.

Friedman, M., Thoresen, C. E., Gill, J. J., Ulmer, D., Powell, L. H., Price, V. A., Brown, B., Thompson, L., Rabin, D. D., Breall, W. S., Bourg, E., Levy, R., & Dixon, T. (1986). Alteration of Type A behavior and its effect on cardiac recurrences in post-myocardial infarction patients: Summary results of the Recurrent Coronary Prevention Project. *American Heart Journal, 11,* 653–665.

Friedrich, L. K., & Stein, A. H. (1975). Prosocial television and young children: The effects of verbal labeling and role playing on learning and behavior. *Child Development, 46,* 27–38.

Friend, R., Rafferty, Y., & Bramel, D. (1990). A puzzling misinterpretation of the Asch "conformity" study. *European Journal of Social Psychology, 20,* 29–44.

Frijda, N. H. (1986). *The emotions.* London: Cambridge University Press.

Fromkin, V. (1971). The non-anomalous nature of anomalous utterances. *Language, 47,* 27–52.

Fromkin, V. (Ed.). (1973). *Speech errors as linguistic evidence.* The Hague: Mouton.

Fromkin, V. A. (Ed.). (1980). *Errors in linguistic performance: Slips of the tongue, pen, and hand.* New York: Academic Press.

Fromm, E., & Shor, R. E. (Eds.). (1979). *Hypnosis: Developments in research and new perspectives* (2nd ed.). Hawthorne, NY: Aldine.

Fry, W. F., Jr. (1986). Humor, physiology, and the aging process. In L. Nahemow, K. A. McCluskey-Fawcett, & P. E. McGhee (Eds.), *Humor and aging* (pp. 81–98). Orlando, FL: Academic Press.

Frye v. United States (1923). 293 F. 1013 (D.C., Cir. 1923).

Fuller, J. L. (1982). Psychology and genetics: A happy marriage? *Canadian Psychology, 23,* 11–21.

Furman, W., Rahe, D., & Hartup, W. W. (1979). Rehabilitation of socially withdrawn preschool children through mixed-aged and same-sex socialization. *Child Development, 50,* 915–922.

Fussell, S. R., & Krauss, R. M. (1992). Coordination of knowledge in communication: Effects of speakers' assumptions about what others know. *Journal of Personality and Social Psychology, 62,* 378–391.

Gackenbach, J., & LaBerge, S. (Eds.). (1988). *Conscious mind, sleeping brain: Perspectives on lucid dreaming.* New York: Plenum Press.

Gagnon, J. H. (1977). *Human sexualities.* Glenview, IL: Scott, Foresman.

Gaines, S. O., Jr., & Reed, E. S. (1995). Prejudice: From Allport to DuBois. *American Psychologist, 50,* 96–103.

Gallagher, J. M., & Reid, D. K. (1981). *The learning theory of Piaget and Inhelder.* Monterey, CA: Brooks/Cole.

Gallup, G., Jr., & Newport, F. (1990, August 6). One in 4 Americans believes in ghosts: Poll shows strong belief in paranormal. *San Francisco Chronicle,* pp. B1, B5.

Galton, F. (1869). *Hereditary genius.* London: Macmillan.

Galton, F. (1907). *Inquiries into human faculty and its development.* London: Dent Publishers. (Original work published 1883.)

Garcia, J. (1990). Learning without memory. *Journal of Cognitive Neuroscience, 2,* 287–305.

Garcia, J. (1993). Misrepresentations of my criticisms of Skinner. *American Psychologist, 48,* 1158.

Garcia, J., & Koelling, R. A. (1966). The relation of cue to consequence in avoidance learning. *Psychonomic Science, 4,* 123–124.

Gardner, H. (1983). *Frames of mind.* New York: Basic Books.

Gardner, H. (1993a). *Creating minds.* New York: Basic Books.

Gardner, H. (1993b). *Multiple intelligences: The theory in practice.* New York: Basic Books.

Gardner, L. I. (1972). Deprivation dwarfism. *Scientific American, 227*(7), 76–82.

Garland, A. F., & Zigler, E. (1993). Adolescent suicide prevention. *American Psychologist, 48,* 169–182.

Garland, H. (1984). Relation of effort-performance expectancy to performance in goal setting experiments. *Journal of Applied Psychology, 69,* 79–84.

Garner, W. R. (1974). *The processing of information and structure.* Potomac, MD: Erlbaum.

Garnsey, S. M. (1993). Event-related brain potentials in the study of language: An introduction. *Language and Cognitive Processes, 8,* 337–356.

Garrett, M. F. (1975). The analysis of sentence production. In G. H. Bower (Ed.), *The psychology of learning and motivation* (Vol. 9, pp. 133–177). New York: Academic Press.

Garrison, V. (1977). The "Puerto Rican syndrome" in psychiatry and Espiritismo. In V. Crapanzano & V. Garrison (Eds.), *Case studies in spirit possession.* New York: Wiley Interscience.

Gazzaniga, M. (1970). *The bisected brain.* New York: Appleton-Century-Crofts.

Gazzaniga, M. (1990). In *Discovering Psychology,* Program 14 [PBS video series]. Washington, DC: Annenberg/CPB Program.

Gazzaniga, M. S. (1985). *The social brain.* New York: Basic Books.

Gazzaniga, M. S. (1987). Cognitive and neurological aspects of hemispheric disconnection in the human brain. *Discussions in Neurosciences, 4*(4).

Gegenfurtner, K. R., & Sperling, G. (1993). Information transfer in iconic memory experiments. *Journal of Experimental Psychology: Human Perception and Performance, 19,* 845–866.

Gelman, S. A., & Wellman, H. M. (1991). Insides and essences: Early understandings of the non-obvious. *Cognition, 38,* 213–244.

Gershon, E. S., Berrettini, W., Nurnberger, J., Jr., & Goldin, L. (1987). Genetics of affective illness. In H. Y. Meltzer (Ed.), *Psychopharmacology: The third generation of progress* (pp. 481–491). New York: Raven Press.

Ghadirian, A. M., & Lehmann, H. E. (1992). *Environment and psychopathology.* New York: Springer.

Ghanta, V., Hiramoto, R. N., Solvason, B., & Spector, N. H. (1987). Influence of conditioned natural immunity on tumor growth. *Annals of the New York Academy of Sciences, 496,* 637–646.

Giambra, L. M., & Arenberg, D. (1993). Adult age differences in forgetting sentences. *Psychology and Aging, 8,* 451–462.

Gibbs, R. W. (1986). Comprehension and memory for nonliteral utterances: The problem of sarcastic indirect requests. *Acta Psychologia, 62,* 41–57.

Gibbs, R. W. (1994). *The poetics of mind.* Cambridge: Cambridge University Press.

Gibson, J. J. (1966). *The senses considered as perceptual systems.* Boston: Houghton Mifflin.

Gibson, J. J. (1979). *An ecological approach to visual perception.* Boston: Houghton Mifflin.

Gilliam, H. (1986, July 6). Fencing out world prosperity. *San Francisco Chronicle,* p. 18.

Gilligan, C. (1982). *In a different voice: Psychological theory and women's development.* Cambridge, MA: Harvard University Press.

Gilligan, S., & Bower, G. H. (1984). Cognitive consequences of emotional arousal. In C. Izard, J. Kagan, & R. Zajonc (Eds.), *Emotions, cognitions, and behavior* (pp. 547–588). Cambridge: Cambridge University Press.

Gilovich, T. (1983). Biased evaluation and persistence in gambling. *Journal of Personality and Social Psychology, 44,* 1110–1126.

Gilovich, T. (1991). *How we know what isn't so: The fallibility of human reason in everyday life.* New York: Free Press.

Ginns, E. I., Egland, J. A., Allen, C. R., Pauls, D. L., Falls, L., Keith, T. P., & Paul, S. M. (1992). Update on the search for DNA markers linked to manic-depressive illness in the old order Amish. *Journal of Psychiatric Research, 26,* 305–308.

Gitlin, M. J. (1990). The psychotherapist's guide to psychopharmacology. New York: Free Press.

Givens, A. (1989). Dynamic functional topography of cognitive tasks. *Brain Topography, 2,* 37–56.

Gladue, B. A. (1994). The biopsychology of sexual orientation. *Current Directions in Psychological Science, 3,* 150–154.

Glanzer, M., & Cunitz, A. R. (1966). Two storage mechanisms in free recall. *Journal of Verbal Learning and Verbal Behavior, 5,* 351–360.

Glass, D. C. (1977). *Behavior patterns, stress, and coronary disease.* Hillsdale, NJ: Erlbaum.

Glucksberg, S., & Danks, J. H. (1975). *Experimental psycholinguistics.* Hillsdale, NJ: Erlbaum.

Goddard, H. H. (1914). *The Kallikak family: A study of the heredity of feeble-mindedness.* New York: Macmillan.

Goddard, H. H. (1917). Mental tests and immigrants. *Journal of Delinquency, 2,* 243–277.

Goldfried, M. R., Greenberg, L., & Marmar, C. (1990). Individual psychotherapy: Process and outcome. *Annual Review of Psychology, 41,* 659–688.

Goldin-Meadow, S., & Mylander, C. (1990). Beyond the input given: The child's role in the acquisition of language. *Language, 66,* 323–355.

Goldstein, M. J., & Strachan, A. M. (1987). The family and schizophrenia. In T. Jacob (Ed.), *Family interaction and psychopathology: Theories, methods and findings* (pp. 481–507). New York: Plenum Press.

Gonzalez, A. (1983). Classroom cooperation and ethnic balance: The Chicanos and equal status contact. *La Red/The Net, 68,* 6–8.

Goodall, J. (1986). *The chimpanzees of Gombe: Patterns of behavior.* Cambridge, MA: Harvard University Press.

Goodall, J. (1990). *Through a window: My thirty years with the chimpanzees of Gombe.* Boston: Houghton Mifflin.

Gooden, D. R., & Baddeley, A. D. (1975). Context-dependent memory in two natural environments: On land and under water. *British Journal of Psychology, 66,* 325–331.

Goodkind, M. (1989, Spring). The cigarette habit. *Stanford Medicine,* 10–14.

Gordon, L. (1990, September 2). Proposal to overhaul SAT to consider relevance, bias. *The Seattle Times/Post-Intelligencer.*

Gorman, J. M., Liebowitz, M. R., Fyer, A. J., & Stein, J. M. (1989). A neuroanatomical hypothesis for panic disorder. *American Journal of Psychiatry, 146,* 148–161.

Gottesman, I. I. (1991). *Schizophrenia genesis: The origins of madness.* New York: Freeman.

Gottfredson, L. S. (1986). The g-factor in employment. *Journal of Vocational Behavior, 29,* 293–296.

Gottlieb, B. H. (Ed.). (1981). *Social networks and social support.* Beverly Hills, CA: Sage.

Gottman, J. M. (1994). *What predicts divorce?* Hillsdale, NJ: Erlbaum.

Gough, H. G. (1957). *California Psychological Inventory manual.* Palo Alto, CA: Consulting Psychologists Press.

Gough, H. G. (1989). The California Psychological Inventory. In C. S. Newmark (Ed.), *Major psychological assessment inventories* (Vol. 2). Boston: Allyn and Bacon.

Gough, H. G. (1995). *California Psychological Inventory* (3rd ed.). Palo Alto, CA: Consulting Psychologists Press.

Gould, S. J. (1981). *The mismeasure of man.* New York: Norton.

Gould, S. J. (1994, November 28). Curveball [Review of *The Bell Curve*]. *The New Yorker,* pp. 139–149.

Graesser, A. C., Singer, M., & Trabasso, T. (1994). Constructing inferences during narrative text comprehension. *Psychological Review, 101,* 371–395.

Graf, P., & Schacter, D. L. (1985). Implicit and explicit memory for new associations in normal and amnesic subjects. *Journal of Experimental Psychology: Learning, Memory, and Cognition, 11,* 501–518.

Graf, P., Squire, L. R., & Mandler, G. (1984). The information that amnesic patients do not forget. *Journal of Experimental Psychology: Learning, Memory, and Cognition, 10,* 164–178.

Graham, N. (1992). Breaking the visual stimulus into parts. *Current Directions in Psychological Science, 1,* 55–61.

Grant, L., & Evans, A. (1994). *Principles of behavior analysis.* New York: HarperCollins.

Grant, P. R. (1986). *Ecology and evolution of Darwin's finches.* Princeton, NJ: Princeton University Press.

Grattan, M. P., De Vos, E., Levy, J., & McClintock, M. K. (1992). Asymmetric action in the human newborn: Sex differences in patterns of organization. *Child Development, 63,* 273–289.

Green, B. L. (1994). Psychosocial research in traumatic stress: An update. *Journal of Traumatic Stress, 7,* 341–362.

Green, D. M., & Swets, J. A. (1966). *Signal detection theory and psychophysics.* New York: Wiley.

Greenberg, J., & Ornstein, S. (1983). High status job title as compensation for underpayment: A test of equity theory. *Journal of Applied Psychology, 68,* 285–297.

Greenberg, L. S., & Johnson, S. (1988). *Emotionally focused therapy for couples.* New York: Guilford Press.

Greene, R. L. (1991). *The MMPI-2/MMPI: An interpretive manual.* Boston: Allyn and Bacon.

Greeno, C. G., & Wing, R. R. (1994). Stress-induced eating. *Psychological Bulletin, 115,* 444–464.

Greenwald, A. G. (1992). New Look 3: Unconscious cognition reclaimed. *American Psychologist, 47,* 766–779.

Greenwald, A. G., & Banaji, M. R. (1995). Implicit social cognition: Attitudes, self-esteem, and stereotypes. *Psychological Review, 102,* 4–27.

Greenwald, A. G., Spangenber, E. R., Pratkanis, A. R., & Eskenazi, J. (1991). Double-blind tests of subliminal self-help audiotapes. *Psychological Science, 2,* 119–122.

Grice, H. P. (1968). Utterer's meaning, sentence-meaning, and word-meaning. *Foundations of Language, 4,* 1–18.

Grice, H. P. (1975). Logic and conversation. In P. Cole & J. L. Morgan (Eds.), *Syntax and semantics: Vol. 3. Speech acts* (pp. 41–58). New York: Academic Press.

Grice, H. P. (1978). Further notes on logic and conversation. In P. Cole (Ed.), *Syntax and semantics: Vol. 9. Pragmatics* (pp. 113–128). New York: Academic Press.

Griffin, K., Friend, R., Eitel, P., & Lobel, M. (1993). Effects of environmental demands, stress, and mood on health practices. *Journal of Behavioral Medicine, 16,* 1–19.

Guerra, F., & Aldrete, J. (1980). *Emotional and psychological responses to anesthesia and surgery.* New York: Grune & Stratton.

Guilford, J. P. (1961). *Psychological Review, 68,* 1–20.

Guilford, J. P. (1985). The Structure-of-Intellect model. In B. B. Wolman (Ed.), *Handbook of intelligence.* New York: Wiley.

Guilleminault, C. (1989). Clinical features and evaluation of obstructive sleep apnea. In M. Kryser, T. Roth, & W. C. Dement (Eds.), *Principles and practice of sleep medicine* (pp. 552–558). New York: Saunders Press.

Guilleminault, C., Dement, W. C., & Passonant, P. (Eds.). (1976). *Narcolepsy.* New York: Spectrum.

Gur, R. E., & Pearlson, G. D. (1993). Neuroimaging in schizophrenia research. *Schizophrenia Bulletin, 19,* 337–353.

Gurman, A. S., & Kniskern, D. R. (1978). Research in marital and family therapy: Progress, perspective, and prospect. In S. L. Gafield & A. E. Gergan (Eds.), *Handbook of psychotherapy and behavior change* (pp. 817–904). New York: Wiley.

Gutmann, D. (1977). The cross-cultural perspective: Notes toward a comparative psychology of aging. In J. E. Birren & K. W. Schaie (Eds.), *Handbook of the psychology of aging* (pp. 302–326). New York: Van Nostrand Reinhold.

Gynther, M. D., & Gynther, R. A. (1976). Personality inventories. In I. B. Weiner (Ed.), *Clinical methods in psychology.* New York: Wiley-Interscience.

Hale, R. L. (1983). Intellectual assessment. In M. Hersen, A. E. Kazdin, & A. S. Bellack (Eds.), *The clinical psychology handbook* (pp. 345–376). New York: Pergamon.

Hall, G. S. (1904). *Adolescence: Its psychology and its relations to physiology, anthropology, sociology, sex, crime, religion and education* (Vols. 1 and 2). New York: D. Appleton.

Hamer, D. H., Hu, S., Magnuson, V. L., Hu, N., & Pattatucci, A. M. L. (1993). A linkage between DNA markers on the X chromosome and male sexual orientation. *Science, 261,* 321–327.

Hamilton, D. (1990, September 2). *Los Angeles Times.*

Hampson, J., & Nelson, K. (1993). The relation of maternal language to variation in rate and style of language acquisition. *Journal of Child Language, 20,* 313–342.

Haney, C., & Zimbardo, P. G. (1977). The socialization into criminality: On becoming a prisoner and a guard. In J. L. Tapp & F. L. Levine (Eds.), *Law, justice and the individual in society: Psychological and legal issues* (pp. 198–223). New York: Holt, Rinehart & Winston.

Harlow, H. F. (1965). Sexual behavior in the rhesus monkey. In F. Beach (Ed.), *Sex and behavior.* New York: Wiley.

Harlow, H. F., & Harlow, M. K. (1966). Learning to love. *American Scientist, 54,* 244–272.

Harlow, H. F., Harlow, M. K., & Meyer, D. R. (1950). Learning motivated by a manipulation drive. *Journal of Experimental Psychology, 40,* 228–234.

Harlow, H. F., & Zimmerman, R. R. (1958). The development of affectional responses in infant monkeys. *Proceedings of the American Philosophical Society, 102,* 501–509.

Harmon, M. A. (1993). Reducing the risk of drug involvement among early adolescents: An evaluation of Drug Abuse Resistance Education (DARE). *Evaluation Review, 17,* 221–239.

Harris, B. (1979). Whatever happened to Little Albert? *American Psychologist, 34,* 151–160.

Harris, G., Thomas, A., & Booth, D. A. (1990). Development of salt taste in infancy. *Developmental Psychology, 26,* 534–538.

Hart, J. T. (1965). Memory and the feeling-of-knowing experience. *Journal of Educational Psychology, 56,* 208–216.

Hart, S. N. (1991). From property to person status: Historical perspective on children's rights. *American Psychologist, 46,* 53–59.

Hartmann, E. L. (1973). *The functions of sleep.* New Haven: Yale University Press.

Hartshorne, H., & May, M. A. (1928). *Studies in the nature of character, Vol. 1: Studies in deceit.* New York: Macmillan.

Harvey, J. H., Weber, A. L., & Orbuch, T. L. (1990). *Interpersonal accounts: A social psychological perspective.* Oxford: Basil Blackwell.

Hastorf, A. H., & Cantril, H. (1954). They saw a game: A case study. *Journal of Abnormal and Social Psychology, 49,* 129–134.

Hatfield, E., & Sprecher, S. (1986). *Mirror, mirror: The importance of looks in everyday life.* New York: State University of New York Press.

Hathaway, S. R., & McKinley, J. C. (1940). A multiphasic personlaity schedule (Minnesota): I. Construction of the schedule. *Journal of Psychology, 10,* 249–254.

Hathaway, S. R., & McKinley, J. C. (1943). *Minnesota Multiphasic Inventory manual.* New York: Psychological Corporation.

Hazan, C., & Shaver, P. (1987). Romantic love conceptualized as an attachment process. *Journal of Personality and Social Psychology, 52,* 511–524.

Health of America's Children, The. (1991). Washington, DC: Children's Defense Fund.

Hearst, E. (1988). Fundamentals of learning and conditioning. In R. C. Atkinson, R. J. Herrnstein, G. Lindzey, & R. D. Luce (Eds.), *Stevens' handbook of experimental psychology: Vol. 2. Learning and Cognition* (2nd ed., pp. 3–109). New York: Wiley.

Heatherton, T. F., Herman, C. P., & Polivy, J. (1991). Effects of physical threat and ego threat on eating behavior. *Journal of Personality and Social Psychology, 60,* 138–143.

Heatherton, T. F., Polivy, J., Herman, C. P., & Baumeister, R. F. (1993). Self-awareness, task failure, and disinhibition: How attentional focus affects eating. *Journal of Personality, 61,* 49–61.

Hebb, D. O. (1949). *The organization of behavior: A neuropsychological theory.* New York: Wiley.

Hebb, D. O. (1955). Drives and the CNS (conceptual nervous system). *Psychological Review, 62,* 243–254.

Hebb, D. O. (1966). *A textbook of psychology* (2nd ed.). Philadelphia: Saunders.

Heckhausen, J., Dixon, R. A., & Baltes, P. B. (1989). Gains and losses in development throughout adulthood as perceived by different adult age groups. *Developmental Psychology, 25,* 109–121.

Heider, F. (1958). *The psychology of interpersonal relationships.* New York: Wiley.

Helmes, E., & Reddon, J. R. (1993). A perspective on developments in assessing psychopathology: A critical review of the MMPI and MMPI-2. *Psychological Bulletin, 113,* 453–471.

Hentschel, U., Smith, G., Ehlers, W., & Draguns, J. G. (Eds.). (1993). *The concept of defense mechanisms in contemporary psychology.* New York: Springer-Verlag.

Heppenheimer, T. A. (1990, Fall). How Von Neumann showed the way. *Invention and Technology,* pp. 7–16.

Herek, G. M. (1994). Assessing heterosexuals' attitudes toward lesbians and gay men: A review of empirical research with the ATLG scale. In B. Greene & G. M. Herek (Eds.), *Lesbian and gay psychology: Theory, research, and clinical applications* (pp. 206–228). Thousand Oaks, CA: Sage.

Herman, C. P., & Polivy, J. (1975). Anxiety, restraint, and eating behavior. *Journal of Abnormal Psychology, 84,* 666–672.

Herrnstein, R. J., & Murray, C. (1994). *The bell curve.* New York: Free Press.

Hersen, M., & Bellack, A. J. (1976). Assessment of social skills. In A. R. Ciminero, K. R. Calhoun, & H. E. Adams (Eds.), *Handbook of behavioral assessment* (pp. 509–554). New York: Wiley.

Hersh, S. M. (1971). *My Lai 4: A report on the massacre and its aftermath.* New York: Ramdom House.

Hertzog, C., Dixon, R. A., & Hultsch, D. F. (1990). Relationships between metamemory, memory predictions, and memory task performance in adults. *Psychology and Aging, 5,* 215–227.

Herzog, H. A., Jr. (1993). "The movement is my life": The psychology of animal rights activism. *Journal of Social Issues, 49,* 103–119.

Heston, L. L. (1970). The genetics of schizophrenia and schizoid disease. *Science, 112,* 249–256.

Hetherington, E. M., & Parke, R. D. (1975). *Child psychology: A contemporary viewpoint.* New York: McGraw-Hill.

Higgins, R. L., Snyder, C. R., & Berglas, S. (Eds.). (1990). *Self-handicapping: The paradox that isn't.* New York: Plenum Press.

Hilgard, E. R. (1968). *The experience of hypnosis.* New York: Harcourt Brace Jovanovich.

Hilgard, E. R. (1973). The domain of hypnosis with some comments on alternative paradigms. *American Psychologist, 28,* 972–982.

Hilgard, E. R., (1977). *Divided consciousness: Multiple controls in human thought and action.* New York: Wiley.

Hilgard, E. R. (1980). Consciousness in contemporary psychology. *Annual Review of Psychology, 31,* 1–26.

Hilgard, J. R. (1970). *Personality and hypnosis: A study of the imaginative involvement.* Chicago: University of Chicago Press.

Hilgard, J. R. (1979). *Personality and hypnosis: A study of imaginative involvement* (2nd ed.). Chicago: University of Chicago Press.

Hillstrom, A. P., & Yantis, S. (1994). Visual motion and attentional capture. *Perception & Psychophysics, 55,* 399–411.

Hintzman, D. L. (1986). "Schema abstraction" in a multiple-trace memory model. *Psychological Review, 93,* 411–428.

Hobson, J. A. (1988). *The dreaming brain.* New York: Basic Books.

Hobson, J. A. (1992). A new model of brain-mind state: Activation level, input source, and mode of processing (AIM). In J. S. Antrobus & M. Bertini (Eds.), *The neuropsychology of sleep and dreaming* (pp. 227–245). Hillsdale, NJ: Erlbaum.

Hobson, J. A., & McCarley, R. W. (1977). The brain as a dream state generator: An activation-synthesis hypothesis of the dream process. *American Journal of Psychiatry, 134,* 1335–1348.

Hoffman, C., Lau, I., & Johnson, D. R. (1986). The linguistic relativity of person cognition: An English-Chinese comparison. *Journal of Personality and Social Psychology, 51,* 1097–1105.

Hoffman, L. W. (1989). Effects of maternal employment in the two-parent family. *American Psychologist, 44,* 283–292.

Hoffman, M. (1986). Affect, cognition, and motivation. In R. Sorrentino & E. Higgins (Eds.), *Handbook of motivation and cognition: Foundations of social behavior* (pp. 244–280). New York: Guilford Press.

Hoffman, M. L. (1987). The contribution of empathy to justice and moral judgement. In N. Eisenberg & J. Strayer (Eds.), *Empathy and its development* (pp. 47–80). New York: Cambridge University Press.

Hofling, C. K., Brotzman, E., Dalrymple, S., Graves, N., & Pierce, C. M. (1966). An experimental study in nurse–physician relationships. *Journal of Nervous and Mental Disease, 143*(2), 171–180.

Holden, C. (1978). Patuxent: Controversial prison clings to belief in rehabilitation. *Science, 199,* 665–668.

Holden, C. (1986). Depression research advances, treatment lags. *Science, 233,* 723–725.

Holen, M. C., & Oaster, T. R. (1976). Serial position and isolation effects in a classroom lecture simulation. *Journal of Educational Psychology, 68,* 293–296.

Holmbeck, G. N., & O'Donnell, K. (1991). Discrepancies between perceptions of decision making and behavioral autonomy. In R. L. Paikoff (Ed.), *Shared views in the family during adolescence* (pp. 51–69). San Francisco: Jossey-Bass.

Holmes, D. S. (1984). Mediation and somatic arousal: A review of the experimental evidence. *American Psychologist, 39,* 1–10.

Holmes, D. S. (1994). *Abnormal psychology.* New York: HarperCollins.

Holmes, T. H., & Masuda, M. (1974). Life change and stress susceptibility. In B. S. Dohrenwend & B. P. Dohrenwend (Eds.), *Stressful life events: The nature and effects* (pp. 45–72). New York: Wiley.

Holmes, T. H., & Rahe, R. H. (1967). The social readjustment rating scale. *Journal of Psychosomatic Research, 11*(2), 213–218.

Holt, P. (1990, September 4). Coming to terms with depression. [Review of *Darkness visible: A memoir of madness.*] *San Francisco Chronicle.*

Holt, R. R. (1970). Yet another look at clinical and statistical prediction: Or is clinical psychology worthwhile? *American Psychologist, 25,* 337–349.

Holtgraves, T., & Skeel, J. (1992). Cognitive biases in playing the lottery: Estimating the odds and choosing the numbers. *Journal of Applied Social Psychology, 22,* 934–952.

Holyoak, K. J., & Nisbett, R. E. (1988). Induction. In R. J. Sternberg & E. E. Smith (Eds.), *The psychology of human thought* (pp. 50–91). Cambridge: Cambridge University Press.

Holyoak, K. J., & Spellman, B. A. (1993). Thinking. *Annual Review of Psychology, 44,* 265–315.

Homme, L. E., de Baca, P. C., Devine, J. V., Steinhorst, R., & Rickert, E. J. (1963). Use of the Premack principle in controlling the behavior of nursery school children. *Journal of the Experimental Analysis of Behavior, 6,* 544.

Hooker, K., & Kaus, C. R. (1994). Health-related possible selves in young and middle adulthood. *Psychology and Aging, 9,* 126–133.

Hopson, J. L. (1979). *Scent signals: The silent language of sex.* New York: Morrow.

Hopson, J. L. (1988, July–August). A pleasurable chemistry. *Psychology Today,* pp. 29–33.

Horne, J. A. (1988). *Why we sleep: The functions of sleep in humans and other mammals.* Oxford: Oxford University Press.

Horney, K. (1945). *Our inner conflicts: A constructive theory of neurosis.* New York: Norton.

Horney, K. (1967). The flight from womanhood: The masculinity complex in women viewed by men and by women. In H. Kelman (Ed.), *Feminine psychology.* New York: Norton. (Original work published 1926.)

Horowitz, R. M. (1984). Children's rights: A look backward and a glance ahead. In R. M. Horowitz & H. A. Davidson (Eds.), *Legal rights of children* (pp. 1–9). New York: McGraw-Hill.

Horvath, A. O., & Luborsky, L. (1993). The role of the therapeutic alliance in psychotherapy. *Journal of Consulting and Clinical Psychology, 61,* 561–573.

Horvath, A. T. (1991). Beyond AA. *The California Psychologist, 24,* 13, 26.

Houghton, J. (1980). One personal experience: Before and after mental illness. In J. G. Rabkin, L. Gelb, & J. B. Lazar (Eds.), *Attitudes toward the mentally ill: Research perspectives* (pp. 7–14). Rockville, MD: National Institutes of Mental Health.

House, J. S., Landis, K. R., & Umberson, D. (1988). Social relationships and health. *Science, 241,* 540–545.

Hovland, C. I., Lumsdaine, A. A., & Sheffield, F. D. (1949). *Experiments on mass communication.* Princeton, NJ: Princeton University Press.

Howard, A., Pion, G. M., Gottfredson, G. O., Flattau, P. E., Oskamp, S., Pfafflin, S. M., Bray, D. W., & Burstein, A. G. (1986). The changing face of American psychology: A report from the committee of employent and human resources. *American Psychologist, 41,* 1311–1327.

Howe, M. L., & Courage, M. L. (1993). On resolving the enigma of infantile amnesia. *Psychological Bulletin, 113,* 305–326.

Howes, M., Siegel, M., & Brown, F. (1993). Early childhood memories: Accuracy and affect. *Cognition, 47,* 95–119.

Hubel, D. H., & Wiesel, T. N. (1959). Receptive fields of single neurons in the cat's striate cortex. *Journal of Physiology (London), 148,* 574–591.

Hubel, D. H., & Wiesel, T. N. (1962). Receptive fields, binocular interaction, and functional architecture in the cat's visual cortex. *Journal of Physiology (London), 160,* 106–154.

Hubel, D. H., & Wiesel, T. N. (1979). Brain mechanisms of vision. *Scientific American, 241*(9), 150–168.

Hubert, W., Moller, M., & de Jong Meyer, R. (1993). Film induces amusement changes in saliva cortisol levels. *Psychoneuroendocrinology, 18,* 265–272.

Huesmann, L. R., & Eron, L. D. (Eds.). (1986). *Television and the aggressive child: A cross-national comparison.* Hillsdale, NJ: Erlbaum.

Hull, C. L. (1943). *Principles of behavior: An introduction to behavior theory.* New York: Appleton-Century-Crofts.

Hull, C. L. (1952). *A behavior system: An introduction to behavior theory concerning the individual organism.* New Haven: Yale University Press.

Hume, D. (1951). In L. A. Selby-Bigge (Ed.), *An enquiry concerning human understanding.* London: Oxford University Press. (Original work published 1748.)

Humphrey, T. (1970). The development of human fetal activity and its relation to postnatal behavior. In H. W. Reese & L. P. Lipsitt (Eds.), *Advance in child development and behavior* (Vol. 5). New York: Academic Press.

Hunt, E. (1983). On the nature of intelligence. *Science, 219,* 141–146.

Hunt, E. (1984). Intelligence and mental competence. *Naval Research Reviews, 36,* 37–42.

Hunt, E. B. (1995). The role of intelligence in modern society. *American Scientist, 83,* 356–368.

Hunt, W. A., Matarazzo, J. D., Weiss, S. M., & Gentry, W. D. (1979). Associative learning, habit, and health behavior. *Journal of Behavioral Medicine, 2,* 111–123.

Hurlburt, R. T. (1979). Random sampling of cognitions and behavior. *Journal of Research in Personality, 13,* 103–111.

Hurvich, L., & Jameson, D. (1974). Opponent processes as a model of neural organization. *American Psychologist, 29,* 88–102.

Huston, A. C., McLoyd, V. C., & Coll, C. G. (Eds.). (1994). Children and poverty: Issues in contemporary research [Special issue]. *Child Development, 65*(2).

Huxley, A. (1954). *The doors of perception.* New York: Harper & Brothers.

Huxley, J. (1958). Introduction to the Mentor edition. In C. Darwin, *The origin of species* (pp. ix–xv). New York: Mentor.

Imber, S. D., Pilkonis, P. A., Sotsky, S. M., Elkin, I., Watkins, J. T., Collins, J. F., Shea, M. T., Leber, W. R., & Glass, D. R. (1990). Mode-specific effects among three treatments for depression. *Journal of Consulting and Clinical Psychology, 58,* 352–359.

Insko, C. A., Smith, R. A., Alicke, M. E., Wade, J., & Taylor, S. (1985). Conformity and group size: The concern with being right and the concern with being liked. *Personality and Social Psychology Bulletin, 11,* 41–50.

Insko, C. A., Thibaut, J. W., Moehle, D., Wilson, M., Diamond, W. D., Gilmore, R., Solomon, M. R., & Lipsitz, A. (1980). Social evolution and the emergence of leadership. *Journal of Personality and Social Psychology, 39,* 431–448.

Institute of Medicine, Division of Mental Health and Behavioral Medicine. (1989). *Prevention and treatment of alcohol problems: Research opportunities.* Washington, DC: National Acadmy Press.

Irvine, J. T. (1990). Registering affect: Heteroglossia in the linguistic expression of emotion. In C. A. Lutz & L. Abu-Lughod (Eds.), *Language and the politics of emotions* (pp. 126–161). Cambridge: Cambridge University Press.

Irwin, D. E. (1991). Information integration across saccadic eye movements. *Cognitive Psychology, 23,* 420–456.

Irwin, M., Daniels, M., Smith, T. L., Bloom, E., & Weiner, H. (1987). Impaired natural killer cell activity during bereavement. *Brain Behavior Immunology, 1,* 98–104.

Isaacs, E. A., & Clark, H. H. (1987). References in conversations between experts and novices. *Journal of Experimental Psychology: General, 116,* 26–37.

Isen, A. (1984). Toward understanding the role of affect in cognition. In R. Wyer & T. Srull (Eds.), *Handbook of social cognition* (pp. 174–236). Hillsdale, NJ: Erlbaum.

Isen, A. M., Daubman, D. A., & Nowicki, G. P. (1987). Positive affect facilitates creative problem solving. *Journal of Personality and Social Psychology, 52,* 1122–1131.

Ishai, A., & Sagi, D. (1995). Common mechanisms of visual imagery and perception. *Science, 268,* 1772–1774.

Ishii-Kuntz, M. (1990). Social interaction and psychological well-being: Comparison across stages of adulthood. *International Journal of Aging and Human Development, 30,* 15–36.

Itard, J. M. G. (1962). *The Wild Boy of Aveyron* (G. & M. Humphrey, Trans.). New York: Appleton-Century-Crofts.

Izard, C. (1971). *The face of emotion.* New York: Appleton-Century-Crofts.

Izard, C. E. (1993). Four systems for emotion activation: Cognitive and noncognitive processes. *Psychological Review, 100,* 68–90.

Izard, C. E. (1994). Innate and universal facial expressions: Evidence from developmental and cross-cultural research. *Psychological Bulletin, 115,* 288–299.

Jacob, F. (1977). Evolution and tinkering. *Science, 196,* 161–166.

Jacobs, B. L. (1987). How hallucinogenic drugs work. *American Scientist, 75,* 386–392.

Jacobs, M. K., & Goodman, G. (1989). Psychology and self-help groups: Predictions on a partnership. *American Psychologist, 44,* 536–545.

Jacobs, R. C., & Campbell, D. T. (1961). The perpetuation of an arbitrary tradition through several generations of a laboratory microculture. *Journal of Abnormal and Social Psychology, 62,* 649–658.

Jacobson, S. W., Jacobson, J. L., Sokol, R. J., Martier, S. S., & Ager, J. W. (1993). Prenatal alcohol exposure and infant information processing ability. *Child Development, 64,* 1706–1721.

Jacoby, L. L., Woloshyn, V., & Kelley, C. (1989). Becoming famous without being recognized: Unconscious influences of memory produced by divided attention. *Journal of Experimental Psychology: General, 118,* 115–125.

James, W. (1890). *The principles of psychology* (2 vols.). New York: Holt, Rinehart & Wilson.

James, W. (1902). *The varieties of religious experience.* New York: Longmans, Green.

Janis, I. L. (1982a). Decisionmaking under stress. In L. Goldberger & S. Breznitz (Eds.), *Handbook of stress* (pp. 69–87). New York: Free Press.

Janis, I. L. (1982b). *Groupthink: Psychological studies of policy decisions and fiascoes* (2nd ed.). Boston: Houghton Mifflin.

Janis, I. L., & Frick, F. (1943). The relationship between attitudes toward conclusions and errors in judging logical validity of syllogisms. *Journal of Experimental Psychology, 33,* 73–77.

Janowitz, H. D., & Grossman, M. I. (1950). Hunger and appetite: Some definitions and concepts. *Journal of the Mount Sinai Hospital, 16,* 231–240.

Janz, N. K., & Becker, M. H. (1984). The health belief model: A decade later. *Health Education Quarterly, 11,* 1–47.

Jenkins, C. D. (1976). Recent evidence supporting psychologic and social risk factors for coronary disease. *New England Journal of Medicine, 294,* 987–994, 1033–1038.

Jenkins, J. G., & Dallenbach, K. M. (1924). Oblivescence during sleep and waking. *The American Journal of Psychology, 35,* 605–612.

Jennings, J. M., & Jacoby, L. L. (1993). Automatic versus intentional uses of memory: Aging, attention, and control. *Psychology and Aging, 8,* 283–293.

Jensen, A. R. (1962). Spelling errors and the serial position effect. *Journal of Educational Psychology, 53,* 105–109.

John, O. P. (1990). The "Big Five" factor taxonomy: Dimensions of personality in the natural language and in questionnaires. In L. A. Pervin (Ed.), *Handbook of personality theory and research* (pp. 67–100). New York: Guilford Press.

Johnson, J. H., & Sarason, I. B. (1979). Recent developments in research on life stress. In V. Hamilton & D. M. Warburton (Eds.), *Human stress and cognition: An informative processing approach* (pp. 205–233). Chichester, England: Wiley.

Johnson, M. K., Hashtroudi, S., & Lindsay, D. S. (1993). Source monitoring. *Psychological Bulletin, 114,* 3–28.

Johnson, T. D., & Gottlieb, G. (1981). Visual preferences of imprinted ducklings are altered by the maternal call. *Journal of Comparative and Psychological Psychology*, 95 (5), 665–675.

Johnson-Laird, P. (1983). *Mental models.* Cambridge: Cambridge University Press.

Johnson-Laird, P. N., & Byrne, R. M. J. (1991). *Deduction.* Hillsdale, NJ: Erlbaum.

Johnson-Laird, P. N., & Wason, P. C. (1977). A theoretical analysis of insight into a reasoning task. In P. N. Johnson-Laird & P. C. Wason (Eds.), *Thinking* (pp. 143–157). Cambridge: Cambridge University Press.

Johnston, L. D., O'Malley, P. M., & Bachman, J. G. (1989). *Drug use, drinking, and smoking: National survey results from high school, college, and young adult populations. 1975–1988.* Rockville, MD: U.S. Department of Health and Human Services.

Jones, E. (1953). *The life and works of Sigmund Freud.* New York: Basic Books.

Jones, E. E., & Berglas, S. (1978). Control of attributions about the self through self-handicapping strategies: The appeal of alcohol and the role of underachievement. *Personality and Social Psychology Bulletin, 4,* 200–206.

Jones, E. E., Farina, A., Hastod, A. H., Markus, H., Miller, D. T., & Scott, R. A. (1984). *Social stigma: The psychology of marked relationships.* New York: Freeman.

Jones, H. C., & Loninger, P. W. (1985). *The marijuana question: And science's search for an answer.* New York: Dodd, Mead.

Jones, J. M., Levine, I. S., & Rosenberg, A. A. (Eds.). (1991). Homelessness [Special issue]. *American Psychologist, 46*(11).

Jones, M. C. (1924). A laboratory study of fear: The case of Peter. *Pedagogical Seminary and Journal of Genetic Psychology, 31,* 308–315.

Jones, S. S., Collins, D., & Hong, H. W. (1991). An audience effect on smile production in 10-month-old infants. *Psychological Science, 2,* 45–49.

Joyce, L. (1990a). Losing the connection. *Stanford Medicine,* pp. 19–21.

Joyce, L. (1990b). Fast asleep. *Stanford Medicine,* pp. 28–31.

Julesz, B. (1981a). Figure and ground perception in briefly presented isodipole textures. In M. Kubovy & J. R. Pomerantz (Eds.), *Perceptual organization* (pp. 27–54). Hillsdale, NJ: Erlbaum.

Julesz, B. (1981b). Textons, the elements of texture perception and their interaction. *Nature, 290,* 91–97.

Jung, C. G. (1959). The concept of the collective unconscious. In *The archetypes and the collective unconscious, collected works* (Vol. 9, Part 1, pp. 54–74.). Princeton, NJ: Princeton University Press. (Original work published 1936.)

Jung, C. G. (1965). *Memories, dreams, reflections.* New York: Random House.

Jung, C. G. (1971). Psychological types [Bollingen Series XX]. *The collected works of C. G. Jung* (Vol. 6). Princeton: Princeton University Press. (Original work published 1923.)

Jung, C. G. (1973). Memories, dreams, reflections (Rev. ed., A. Jaffe, Ed.). New York: Pantheon Books.

Jussim, L. (1986). Self-fulfilling prophecies: A theoretical and integrative review. *Psychological Review, 93,* 429–445.

Jussim, L. (1991). Social perception and social reality: A reflection-construction model. *Psychological Review, 98,* 54–73.

Jussim, L. (1993). Accuracy in interpersonal expectation: A reflection-construction analysis of current and classic research. *Journal of Personality, 61,* 637–668.

Just, M. A., & Carpenter, P. A. (1981). Cognitive processes in reading: Models based on reader's eye fixations. In C. A. Prefetti & A. M. Lesgold (Eds.), *Interactive processes and reading.* Hillsdale, NJ: Erlbaum.

Kagan, J., Reznick, J. S., & Snidman, N. (1988). Biological basis of childhood shyness. *Science, 20,* 167–171.

Kagan, J., & Snidman, N. (1991). Infant predictors of inhibited and uninhibited profiles. *Psychological Science, 2,* 40–44.

Kahneman, D. (1973). *Attention and effort.* Englewood Cliffs, NJ: Prentice-Hall.

Kahneman, D. (1991). Judgment and decision making: A personal view. *Psychological Science, 2,* 142–145.

Kahneman, D., & Tversky, A. (1973). On the psychology of prediction. *Psychological Review, 80,* 237–251.

Kahneman, D. (1992). Reference points, anchors, norms, and mixed feelings. *Organizational Behavior and Human Decision Processes, 51,* 296–312.

Kalat, J. W. (1974). Taste salience depends on novelty, not concentration in taste-aversion learning in the rat. *Journal of Comparative and Physiological Psychology, 86,* 47–50.

Kalin, N. H., & Shelton, S. E. (1989). Defensive behaviors in infant rhesus monkeys: Environmental cues and neurochemical regulation. *Science, 243,* 1718–1721.

Kalish, R. A. (1985). The social context of death and dying. In R. H. Binstock & E. Shanas (Eds.), *Handbook of aging and the social sciences* (pp. 149–172). New York: Van Nostrand Reinhold.

Kallmann, F. J. (1946). The genetic theory of schizophrenia: An analysis of 691 schizophrenic index families. *American Journal of Psychiatry, 103,* 309–322.

Kamil, A. C., & Balda, R. P. (1990). Spatial memory in seed-caching corvids. In G. H. Bower (Ed.), *The psychology of learning and motivation* (Vol. 26, pp. 1–25). San Diego: Academic Press.

Kamin, L. J. (1969). Predictability, surprise, attention, and conditioning. In B. A Campbell & R. M. Church (Eds.) *Punishment and Aversive Behavior* (pp. 279–296). New York: Appleton-Century-Crofts.

Kandel, E. R. (1979). Cellular insights into behavior and learning. *The Harvey Lectures,* Series 73, 29–92.

Kandel, E. R. (1989). Genes, nerve cells, and the remembrance of things past. *Journal of Neuropsychiatry, 1,* 103–-125.

Kane, J. M., & Marder, S. R. (1993). Psychopharmacologic treatment of schizophrenia. *Schizophrenia Bulletin, 19,* 287–302.

Kanizsa, G. (1979). *Organization in vision.* New York: Praeger.

Kaplan, C. A., & Simon, H. A. (1990). In search of insight. *Cognitive Psychology, 22,* 374–419.

Kassebaum, N. L. (1994). Head Start: Only the best for America's children. *American Psychologist, 49,* 123–126.

Kassin, S. M., Ellsworth, P. C., & Smith, V. L. (1989). The "general acceptance" of psychological research on eyewitness testimony: A survey of experts. *American Psychologist, 44,* 1089–1098.

Kastenbaum, R. (1986). *Death, society, and the human experience.* Columbus, OH: Merrill.

Kastenbaum, R. (1992). *The psychology of death* (2nd ed.). New York: Springer.

Kavanagh, D. J. (1992). Recent developments in expressed emotion and schizophrenia. *British Journal of Psychiatry, 160,* 601–620.

Kazdin, A. E. (1982). The token economy: A decade later. *Journal of Applied Behavior Analysis, 15,* 431–445.

Kazdin, A. E. (1986). Comparative outcome studies of psychotherapy: Methodological issues and strategies. *Journal of Consulting and Clinical Psychology, 54,* 95–105.

Kazdin, A. E. (1994). *Behavior modification in applied settings* (5th ed.). Pacific Grove, CA: Brooks/Cole.

Kazdin, A. E., & Wilcoxin, L. A. (1976). Systematic desensitization and nonspecific treatment effects: A methodological evaluation. *Psychological Bulletin, 83,* 729–758.

Kazdin, A. E., & Wilson, G. T. (1980). *Evaluation of behavior therapy: Issues, evidence, and research strategies.* Lincoln: University of Nebraska Press.

Keane, T. M., Zimering, R. T., & Caddell, J. M. (1985). A behavioral approach to assessing and treating post-traumatic stress disorder in Vietnam veterans. In C. R. Figley (Ed.), *Trauma and its wake.* New York: Brunner/Mazel.

Keen, S. (1986). *Faces of the enemy: Reflections of the hostile imagination.* New York: Harper & Row.

Keiger, D. (1993, November). Touched with fire. *Johns Hopkins Magazine,* pp. 38, 40–44.

Kelley, C. M., & Jacoby, L. L. (1993). The construction of subjective experience: Memory attributions. In M. Davies & G. W. Humphreys (Eds.), *Consciousness* (pp. 74–89). Oxford: Blackwell.

Kelley, H. H. (1967). Attribution theory in social psychology. In D. Levine (Ed.), *Nebraska Symposium on Motivation* (Vol. 15). Lincoln: University of Nebraska Press.

Kellman, P. J., & Spelke, E. S. (1983). Perception of partly occluded objects in infancy. *Cognitive Psychology, 15,* 483–524.

Kelly, G. A. (1955). *A theory of personality: The psychology of personal constructs* (2 Vols.) New York: Norton.

Kelsoe, J. R., Ginns, E. I., Egeland, J. A., Gerhard, D. S., Goldstein, A. M., Bale, S. J., Pauls, D. L., Long, R. T., Kidd, K. K., Conte, G., Housman, D. E., & Paul, S. M. (1989). Re-evaluation of the linkage relationship between chromosome 11p loci and the gene for bipolar affective disorder in the Old Order Amish. *Nature, 342,* 238–243.

Kelsoe, J. R., Kristbjanarson, H., Bergesch, P., Shilling, P., Hirsch, S., Mirow, A., Moises, H. W., Helgason, T., Gillin, J. C., & Egeland, J. A. (1993). A genetic linkage study of Bipolar Disorder and 13 markers on chromosome 11 including the D2 dopamine receptor. *Neuropsychopharmacology, 9,* 293–301.

Kendler, K. S., & Diehl, S. R. (1993). The genetics of schizophrenia: A current, genetic-epidemiologic perspective. *Schizophrenia Bulletin, 19,* 261–285.

Kendler, K. S., Heath, A. C., Neale, M. C., Kessler, R. C., & Eaves, L. J. (1992). A population-based twin study of alcoholism in women. *Journal of the American Medical Association, 268*, 1877–1882.

Kenrick, D. T., & Funder, D. C. (1988). Profiting from controversy: Lessons from the person-situation debate. *American Psychologist, 43*, 23–34.

Kesey, K. (1962). *One flew over the cuckoo's nest.* New York: Viking Press.

Kessel, N. (1989). Genius and mental disorder: A history of ideas concerning their conjunction. In P. Murray (Ed.), *Genius: The history of an idea* (pp. 196–212). London: Basil Blackwell.

Kessler, R. C., McGonagle, K. A., Zhao, S., Nelson, C. B., Hughes, M., Eshleman, S., Wittchen, H-U., & Kendler, K. S. (1994). Lifetime and 12-month prevalence of DSM-III-R psychiatric disorders in the United States. *Archives of General Psychiatry, 51*, 8–19.

Kety, S. S. (1987). The significance of genetic factors in the etiology of schizophrenia: Results from the national study of adoptees in Denmark. *Journal of Psychiatric Research, 21*, 423–429.

Kety, S. S., Rosenthal, D., Wender, P. H., Schulsinger, F., & Jacobsen, B. (1975). Mental illness in the biological and adoptive families of adopted individuals who have become schizophrenic: A preliminary report based on psychiatric interviews. In R. R. Fieve, D. Rosenthal, & H. Brill (Eds.), *Genetic research in psychiatry* (pp. 147–165). Baltimore: Johns Hopkins University Press.

Kiecolt-Glaser, J. K., & Glaser, R. (1987). Psychosocial moderators of immune function. *Annals of Behavioral Medicine, 9*, 16–20.

Kierulff, S. (1989, March). *Conversation with a demon.* Symposium conducted at the meeting of the California State Psychological Association, San Francisco.

Kihlstrom, J. F. (1985). The cognitive unconscious. *Science, 237*, 1445–1452.

Kihlstrom, J. F., Barnhardt, T. M., & Tartaryn, D. J. (1992). The psychological unconscious: Found, lost, and regained. *American Psychologist, 47*, 788–791.

Kihlstrom, J. F., Schacter, D. L., Cork, R. C., Hurt, C. A., & Behr, S. E. (1990). Implicit and explicit memory following surgical anesthesia. *Psychological Science, 1*, 303–306.

Kim, H., & Levine, S. C. (1992). Variations in characteristic perceptual asymmetry: Modality specific and modality general components. *Brain and Cognition, 19*, 21–47.

Kimura, D. (1983). Sex differences in cerebral organization for speech and praxic functions. *Canadian Psychology, 37*, 19–35.

Kimura, D. (1987). Are men's and women's brains really different? *Canadian Psychology, 28*, 133–147.

Kinsey, A. C., Martin, C. E., & Pomeroy, W. B. (1948). *Sexual behavior in the human male.* Philadelphia: Saunders.

Kinsey, A. C., Pomeroy, W. B., Martin, C. E., & Gebhard, R. H. (1953). *Sexual behavior in the human female.* Philadelphia: Saunders.

Kintsch, W. (1974). *The representation of meaning in memory.* Hillsdale, NJ: Erlbaum.

Kirchner, J. (1995, June 14). 'Slow learner' classes used to isolate blacks. *San Francisco Chronicle*, p. A13.

Kite, M. E., & Johnson, B. T. (1988). Attitudes toward older and younger adults: A meta-analysis. *Psychology and Aging, 3*, 233–244.

Klag, M. J., Whelton, P. K., Grim, C. E., & Kuller, L. H. (1991). The association of skin color with blood pressure in U.S. blacks with low socioeconomic status. *Journal of the American Medical Association, 265*, 599–602.

Klein, D. F., & Ross, D. C. (1993). Reanalysis of the National Institutes of Mental Health Treatment of Depression Collaborate Research Program General Effectiveness Report. *Neuropsychopharmacology, 8*, 241–251.

Klein, K. E., & Wegmann, H. M. (1974). The resynchronization of human circadian rhythms after transmeridian flights as a result of flight direction and mode of activity. In L. E. Scheving, F. Halberg, & J. E. Pauly (Eds.), *Chronobiology* (pp. 564–570). Tokyo: Igaku.

Klein, R. H. (1983). Group treatment approaches. In M. Hersen, A. E. Kazdin, & A. S. Bellack (Eds.), *The clinical psychology handbook.* New York: Pergamon Press.

Kleinginna, P. R., & Kleinginna, A. M. (1981). A categorized list of motivation definitions with a suggestion for a consensual definition. *Motivation and Emotion, 5*, 263–291.

Klinger, E. (1987, May). The power of daydreams. *Psychology Today*, pp. 37–44.

Kluckhorn, C. (1944). Navaho Witchcraft. *Papers of the Yale University Peabody Museum* (Vol. 24, No. 2). New Haven: Yale University Press.

Knox, V. J., Morgan, A. H., & Hilgard, E. R. (1974). Pain and suffering in ischemia: The paradox of hypnotically suggested anesthesia as contradicted by reports from the "hidden observer." *Archives of General Psychiatry, 30*, 840–847.

Kobasa, S. O. (1984). How much stress can you survive? *American Health, 3*, 64–77.

Kobasa, S. O., Hilker, R. R., & Maddi, S. R. (1979). Who stays healthy under stress? *Journal of Occupational Medicine, 21*, 595–598.

Kobre, K. R., & Lipsitt, L. P. (1972). A negative contrast effect in newborns. *Journal of Experimental Child Psychology, 2*, 81–91.

Koch, R., Graliker, B., Fishler, K., & Ragsdale, N. (1963). Clinical aspects of phenylketonuria. In *First Inter-American Conference on Congenital Defects.* Philadelphia: Lippincott.

Koffka, K. (1935). *Principles of Gestalt psychology.* New York: Harcourt Brace.

Kohlberg, L. (1964). Development of moral character and moral ideology. In M. L. Hoffman & L. W. Hoffman (Eds.), *Review of child development research* (Vol. 1). New York: Russell Sage Foundation.

Kohlberg, L. (1966). A cognitive-developmental analysis of children's sex-role concepts and attitudes. In E. E. Maccoby (Ed.), *The development of sex differences.* Stanford, CA: Stanford University Press.

Kohlberg, L. (1981). *The philosophy of moral development.* New York: Harper & Row.

Kolb, B. (1989). Development, plasticity, and behavior. *American Psychologist, 44*, 1203–1212.

Kolb, L. C. (1973). *Modern clinical psychiatry.* Philadelphia: Saunders.

Kondo, T., Antrobus, J., & Fein, G. (1989). Later REM activation and sleep mentation. *Sleep Research, 18*, 147.

Koriat, A. (1993). How do we know what we know? The accessibility model of the feeling of knowing. *Psychological Review, 100*, 609–639.

Koriat, A., & Fischoff, B. (1974). What day is today? An inquiry into the process of time orientation. *Memory & Cognition, 2*, 201–205.

Korn, J. (1987). Judgments of acceptability of deception in psychological research. *Journal of General Psychology, 114*, 205–216.

Korn, J. H. (1985). Psychology as a humanity. *Teaching of Psychology, 12*, 188–193.

Korzeniowski, K. (1993). Is it possible to build democracy in Poland? A psychological analysis of threats. *Polish Psychological Bulletin, 24*, 109–120.

Kosslyn, S. M. (1980). *Image and mind.* Cambridge, MA: Harvard University Press.

Kotovsky, K., Hayes, J. R., & Simon, H. A. (1985). Why are some problems hard? Evidence from Tower of Hanoi. *Cognitive Psychology, 17*, 248–294.

Kotovsky, K., & Simon, H. A. (1990). What makes some problems really hard: Explorations in the problem space of difficulty. *Cognitive Psychology, 22*, 143–183.

Kounios, J., & Holcomb, P. J. (1994). Concreteness effects in semantic processing: ERP evidence supporting dual-coding theory. *Journal of Experimental Psychology: Learning, Memory, and Cognition, 20*, 804–823.

Kraepelin, E. (1921). *Manic-depressive disorder and paranoia.* London: Churchill Livingstone.

Kramer, P. D. (1993). *Listening to Prozac.* New York: Penguin Books.

Kraut, A. M. (1990). Healers and strangers: Immigrant attitudes toward the physician in America—A relationship in historical perspective. *Journal of the American Medical Association, 263*, 1807–1811.

Krieger, L., & Garrison, J. (1991, August 4). Hospitals praised for AIDS care. *San Francisco Examiner*, p. B-2.

Krupa, D. J., Thompson, J. K., & Thompson, R. F. (1993). Localization of a memory trace in the mammalian brain. *Science, 260*, 989–991.

Kübler-Ross, E. (1969). *On death and dying.* Toronto: Macmillan.

Kübler-Ross, E. (1975). *Death: The final stage of growth.* Englewood Cliffs, NJ: Prentice-Hall.

Kuhn, T. S. (1970). *The structure of scientific revolutions* (2nd ed). Chicago: University of Chicago Press.

Kujawski, J. H., & Bower, T. G. R. (1993). Same-sex preferential looking during infancy as a function of abstract representation. *British Journal of Developmental Psycholgy, 11*, 201–209.

Kukla, R. A., Schlenger, W. E., Fairbank, J. A., Hough, R. L., Jordan, B. K., Marmar, C. R., & Weiss, D. S. (1990). *Trauma and the Vietnam War generation.* New York: Brunner/Mazel.

Kulik, J. A., & Mahler, H. I. M. (1989). Social support and recovery from surgery. *Health Psychology, 8*, 221–238.

LaBerge, S. (1986). *Lucid dreaming.* New York: Ballantine Books.

LaBerge, S., & Rheingold, H. (1990). *Exploring the world of lucid dreaming.* New York: Ballantine.

Labouvie-Vief, G. (1985). Intelligence and cognition. In J. E. Birren & K. W. Schaie (Eds.), *Handbook of the psychology of aging* (2nd ed., pp. 500–530). New York: Van Nostrand Reinhold.

Labouvie-Vief, G., Hakim-Larson, J., DeVoe, M., & Schoeberlein, S. (1989). Emotions and self-regulation: A life span view. *Human Development, 32,* 279—299.

Lachman, R., Lachman, J. L., & Butterfield, E. C. (1979). *Cognitive psychology and information processing.* Hillsdale, NJ: Erlbaum.

Lachman, R., & Naus, M. (1984). The episodic/semantic continuum in an evolved machine. *Behavioral and Brain Sciences, 7,* 244–246.

LaFreniere, P. J., & Sroufe, L. A. (1985). Profiles of peer competence in the preschool: Interrelations between measures, influence of social ecology, and relation to attachment history. *Developmental Psychology, 21,* 56–69.

LaFromboise, T. (1988, March 30). Suicide prevention. In *Campus Report* (p. 9). Stanford, CA: Stanford University Press.

Laing, R. D. (1965). *The divided self.* Baltimore: Penguin.

Laing, R. D. (1967). *The politics of experience.* New York: Pantheon.

Laing, R. D. (1970). *Knots.* New York: Pantheon.

Lampl, M., Veldhuis, J. D., & Johnson, M. L. (1992). Saltation and stasis: A model of human growth. *Science, 258,* 801–803.

Landau, B., & Gleitman, L. (1985). *Language and experience.* Cambridge, MA: Harvard University Press.

Landy, F. J., Shankster, L. J., & Kohler, S. S. (1994). Personnel selection and placement. *Annual Review of Psychology, 45,* 261–296.

Lane, H. (1976). *The Wild Boy of Aveyron.* Cambridge, MA: Harvard University Press.

Lane, H. (1986). The Wild Boy of Aveyron and Dr. Jean-Marc Itard. *History of Psychology, 17,* 3–16.

Lang, F. R., & Carstensen, L. L. (1994). Close emotional relationships in late life: Further support for proactive aging in the social domain. *Psychology and Aging, 9,* 315–324.

Lang, P. J., & Lazovik, D. A. (1963). The experimental desensitization of a phobia. *Journal of Abnormal and Social Psychology, 66,* 519–525.

Langer, E. (1989). *Mindfulness.* Reading, MA: Addison-Wesley.

Langer, E. J., & Rodin, J. (1976). The effects of choice and enhanced personal responsibility for the aged: A field experiment in an institutional setting. *Journal of Personality and Social Psychology, 34,* 191–198.

Langlois, J. H., & Downs, A. C. (1980). Mothers, fathers and peers as socialization agents of sex-typed play behaviors in young children. *Child Development, 51,* 1237–1247.

Langlois, J. H., & Roggman, L. A. (1990). Attractive faces are only average. *Psychological Science, 1,* 115–121.

Langlois, J. H., Roggman, L. A., & Musselman, L. (1994). What is average and what is not average about attractive faces? *Psychological Science, 5,* 214–220.

Langs, R. (Ed.). (1981). *Classics in psychoanalytic technique.* New York: Jason Aronson.

Lashley, K. S. (1929). *Brain mechanisms and intelligence.* Chicago: University of Chicago Press.

Lashley, K. S. (1950). In search of the engram. In *Physiological mechanisms in animal behavior: Symposium of the Society for Experimental Biology.* New York: Academic Press.

Latané, B., & Darley, J. M. (1970). *The unresponsive bystander: Why doesn't he help?* New York: Appleton-Century-Crofts.

Laurent, J., Swerdlik, M., & Ryburn, M. (1992). Review of validity research on the Stanford-Binet intelligence scale. *Psychological Assessment, 4,* 102–112.

Laursen, B. (Ed.). (1993). *Close friendships in adolescence.* San Francisco: Jossey-Bass.

Lavond, D. G., Kim, J. J., & Thompson, R. F. (1993). Mammalian brain substrates of aversive classical conditioning. *Annual Review of Psychology, 44,* 317–342.

Layton, C., Smith, P. J., & McCoy, C. E. (1994). Design of a cooperative problem-solving system for en-route flight planning: An empirical investigation. *Human Factors, 36,* 94–119.

Lazarus, R. S. (1976). *Patterns of adjustment* (3rd ed.). New York: McGraw-Hill.

Lazarus, R. S. (1981, July). Little hassles can be hazardous to your health. *Psychology Today,* pp. 58–62.

Lazarus, R. S. (1984a). On the primacy of cognition. *American Psychologist, 39,* 124–129.

Lazarus, R. S. (1984b). Puzzles in the study of daily hassles. *Journal of Behavioral Medicine, 7,* 375–389.

Lazarus, R. S. (1991a). Cognition and motivation in emotion. *American Psychologist, 46,* 352–367.

Lazarus, R. S. (1991b). Progress on a cognitive-motivational-relational theory of emotion. *American Psychologist, 46,* 819–834.

Lazarus, R. S. (1993). From psychological stress to the emotions: A history of changing outlooks. *Annual Review of Psychology, 44,* 1–21.

Lazarus, R. S., & Folkman, S. (1984a). *Stress, appraisal, and coping.* New York: Springer.

Lazarus, R. S., & Lazarus, B. N. (1994). *Passion and reason: Making sense of our emotions.* New York: Oxford University Press.

Leary, M. R., Tchividjian, L. R., & Kraxberger, B. E. (1994). Self-presentation can be hazardous to your health: Impression management and health risk. *Health Psychology, 13,* 461–470.

LeDoux, J. (1989). Cognitive-emotional interactions in the brain. *Cognition and Emotion, 3,* 267–289.

Lee, M., Zimbardo, P., & Bertholf, M. (1977, November). Shy murderers. *Psychology Today,* pp. 68–70, 76, 148.

Leerhsen, C. (1990, February 5). Unite and conquer: America's crazy for support groups. *Newsweek,* pp. 50–55.

Leff, H. (1984). *Playful perception: Choosing how to experience your world.* Burlington, VT: Waterfront Books.

Leger, D. (1992). *Biological foundations of behavior: An integrative approach.* New York: HarperCollins.

Leiter, M. P., & Maslach, C. (1988). The impact of interpersonal environment on burnout and organizational commitment. *Journal of Organizational Behavior, 9,* 297–308.

Lenneberg, E. H. (1969). On explaining language. *Science, 164,* 635–643.

Lennon, R. T. (1985). Group tests of intelligence. In B. B. Wolman (Ed.), *Handbook of intelligence* (pp. 825–847). New York: Wiley.

Leslie, C., & Wingert, P. (1990, January 8). Not as easy as A,B or C. *Newsweek,* pp. 56–58.

LeVay, S. (1991). A difference in hypothalamic structure between heterosexual and homosexual men. *Science, 253,* 1034–1037.

LeVay, S. (1993). The sexual brain. Cambridge, MA: MIT Press.

Levenson, R. W., Carstensen, L. L., & Gottman, J. M. (1993). Long-term marriage: Age, gender, and satisfaction. *Psychology and Aging, 8,* 301–313.

Leventhal, H. (1980). Toward a comprehensive theory of emotion. In L. Berkowitz (Ed.), *Advances in Experimental Social Psychology* (Vol. 13, pp. 139–207). New York: Academic Press.

Levine, J. D., Gordon, N. C., Jones, R. T., & Fields, H. L. (1974). The narcotic antagonist naloxone enhances clinical pain. *Nature, 272,* 826–827.

Levine, M. (1987, April). *Effective problem solving.* Englewood Cliffs, NJ: Prentice-Hall.

Levine, M., & Perkins, D. V. (1987). *Principles of community psychology: Perspectives and applications.* New York: Oxford University Press.

Levine, M. W., & Shefner, J. M. (1981). *Fundamentals of sensation and perception.* Reading, MA: Addison-Wesley.

Levi-Strauss, C. (1963). The effectiveness of symbols. In C. Levi-Strauss (Ed.), *Structural anthropology.* New York: Basic Books.

Levy, B., & Langer, E. (1994). Aging free from negative stereotypes: Successful memory in China and among the American deaf. *Journal of Personality and Social Psychology, 66,* 989–997.

Levy, G. D., & Fivush, R. (1993). Scripts and gender: A new approach for examining gender-role development. *Developmental Review, 13,* 126–146.

Levy, J., Heller, W., Banich, M., & Burton, L. A. (1983). Asymmetry of perception in free viewing of chimeric faces. *Brain and Cognition, 2,* 404–419.

Levy, J., & Trevarthen, C. (1976). Metacontrol of hemispheric function in human split brain patients. *Journal of Experimental Psychology: Human Perception and Performance, 2,* 299–312.

Lewandowsky, S. (1993). The rewards and hazards of computer simulations. *Psychological Science, 4,* 236–243.

Lewin, K. (1936). *Principles of topological psychology.* New York: McGraw-Hill.

Lewin, K. (1947). Group decision and social change. In T. N. Newcomb & E. L. Hartley (Eds.), *Readings in social psychology.* New York: Holt, Rinehart & Winston.

Lewin, K. (1948). *Resolving social conflicts.* New York: Harper.

Lewin, K., Lippitt, R., & White, R. K. (1939). Patterns of aggressive behavior in experimentally created "social climates." *Journal of Social Psychology, 10,* 271–299.

Lewin, R. (1987). The origin of the modern human mind. *Science, 236,* 668–670.

Lewinsohn, P. M. 1975). The behavioral study and treatment of depression. In M. Hersen, R. M. Eisler, & P. M. Miller (Eds.), *Progress in behavior modification* (pp. 19–64). New York: Academic Press.

Lewis, D. O. (1989, May 11). [Interview]. *San Francisco Chronicle.*

Lewis, H. B. (1981). *Freud and modern psychology—Vol. 1: The emotional basis of mental illness.* New York: Plenum Press.

Lewy, A. J., Sack, R. L., Miller, S., & Hoban, T. M. (1987). Antidepressant and circadian phase-shifting effect of light. *Science, 235,* 352–354.

Li, P. (1975). *Path analysis: A primer.* Pacific Grove, CA: Boxwood Press.

Lieberman, M. A. (1982). The effects of social support on responses to stress. In L. Goldberger & S. Breznitz (Eds.), *Handbook of stress* (pp. 764–783). New York: Free Press.

Lifton, R. K. (1969). *Thought reform and the psychology of totalism.* New York: Norton.

Light, L. L. (1991). Memory and aging: Four hypotheses in search of data. *Annual Review of Psychology, 42,* 333–376.

Lillard, A. S., & Flavell, J. H. (1990). Young children's preference for mental-state over behavioral descriptions of human action. *Child Development, 61,* 731–742.

Lincoln, J. R., & Kalleberg, A. L. (1990). *Culture, control, and commitment.* Cambridge: Cambridge University Press.

Lindsay, D. S. (1990). Misleading suggestions can impair eyewitnesses' ability to remember event details. *Journal of Experimental Psychology: Learning, Memory, and Cognition, 16,* 1077–1083.

Lindsay, D. S. (1993). Eyewitness suggestibility. *Current Directions in Psychological Science, 2,* 86–89.

Lipkus, I. M., Barefoot, J. C., Williams, R. B., & Siegler, I. C. (1994). Personality measures as predictors of smoking initiation and cessation in the UNC Alumni Heart Study. *Health Psychology, 13,* 149–155.

Lipsey, M. W., & Wilson, D. B. (1993). The efficacy of psychological, educational, and behavioral treatment: Confirmation from meta-analysis. *American Psychologist, 48,* 1181–1209.

Lipsitt, L. P., Reilly, B., Butcher, M. G., & Greenwood, M. M. (1976). The stability and interrelationships of newborn sucking and heart rate. *Developmental Psychobiology, 9,* 305–310.

Little, M. I. (1981). *Transference neurosis and transference psychosis.* New York: Jason Aronson.

Little, S. G. (1992). The WISC-III: Everything old is new again. *School Psychology Quarterly, 7,* 136–142.

Livingstone, M., & Hubel, D. (1988). Segregation of form, color, movement, and depth: Anatomy, physiology, and perception. *Science, 240,* 740–749.

Lobel, M. (1994). Conceptualizations, measurement, and the effects of prenatal maternal stress on birth outcomes. *Journal of Behavioral Medicine, 17,* 225–272.

Lobel, M., Dunkel-Schetter, C., & Scrimshaw, S. C. M. (1992). Prenatal maternal stress and prematurity: A prospective study of socioeconomically disadvantaged women. *Health Psychology, 11,* 32–40.

Locke, J. (1975). *An essay concerning human understanding.* Oxford: P. H. Nidditch. (Original work published 1690.)

Lockhart, R. S., & Craik, F. I. M. (1990). Levels of processing: A retrospective commentary on a framework for memory research. *Canadian Journal of Psychology, 44,* 87–122.

Loehlin, J. C. (1992). *Genes and environment in personality development.* Newbury Park, CA: Sage.

Loehlin, J. C., Lindzey, G., & Spuhler, J. N. (1975). *Race differences in intelligence.* San Francisco: Freeman.

Loehlin, J. C., Willerman, L., & Horn, J. M. (1988). Human behavioral genetics. *Annual Review of Psychology, 38,* 101–133.

Loevinger, J. (1957). Objective tests as instruments of psychological theory. *Psychological Reports, 3,* 635–694.

Loftus, E. F. (1979). *Eyewitness testimony.* Cambridge, MA: Harvard University Press.

Loftus, E. F. (1992). When a lie becomes memory's truth: Memory distortion after exposure to misinformation. *Current Directions in Psychological Science, 1,* 121–123.

Loftus, E. F. (1993). The reality of repressed memories. *American Psychologist, 48,* 518–537.

Loftus, E. F., & Ketcham, K. (1994). *The myth of repressed memory: False memories and allegations of sexual abuse.* New York: St. Martin's Press.

Loftus, E. F., & Palmer, J. C. (1974). Reconstruction of automobile destruction: An example of the interaction between language and memory. *Journal of Verbal Learning and Verbal Behavior, 13,* 585–589.

Loftus, G. R., Duncan, J., & Gehrig, P. (1992). On the time course of perceptual information that results from a brief visual presentation. *Journal of Experimental Psychology: Human Perception and Performance, 18,* 530–549.

Logan, G. D. (1988). Toward an instance theory of automatization. *Psychological Review, 95,* 492–527.

Logan, G. D. (1992). Shapes of reaction-time distributions and shapes of learning curves: A test of the instance theory of automaticity. *Journal of Experimental Psychology: Learning, Memory, and Cognition, 18,* 883–914.

Logue, A. W. (1991). *The psychology of eating & drinking: An introduction* (2nd ed.). New York: Freeman.

Londer, R. (1988, July 24). When you've just got to do it: Millions of Americans are slaves to their obsessions. *San Francisco Examiner-Chronicle,* This World Section, p. 9.

Loomis, A. L., Harvey, E. N., & Hobart, G. A. (1937). Cerebral states during sleep as studied by human brain potentials. *Journal of Experimental Psychology, 21,* 127–144.

Los Angeles Times. (1988, February 23). Bullet in the brain cures man's mental problem.

Lovett, M. C., & Anderson, J. R. (1994). Effects of solving related proofs on memory and transfer in geometry problem solving. *Journal of Experimental Psychology: Learning, Memory, and Cognition, 20,* 366–378.

Lovibond, S. H., Adams, M., & Adams, W. G. (1979). The effects of three experimental prison environments on the behavior of nonconflict volunteer subjects. *Australian Psychologist, 14,* 273–285.

Lowenthal, M. F., & Chiriboga, D. (1972). Transition to the empty nest: Crisis, challenge, or relief? *Archives of General Psychiatry, 26,* 8–14.

Lubart, T. I. (1994). Creativity. In R. J. Sternberg (Ed.), *Handbook of perception and cognition: Vol. 2. Thinking and problem solving* (pp. 289–332). Orlando, FL: Academic Press.

Lubin, B., Larsen, R. M., & Matarazzo, J. D. (1984). Patterns of psychological test usage in the United States: 1935–1982. *American Psychologist, 39,* 451–455.

Lubow, R. E., Rifkin, B., & Alex, M. (1976). The context effect: The relationship between stimulus preexposure and environmental preexposure determines subsequent learning. *Journal of Experimental Psychology: Animal Behavior Processes, 2,* 38–47.

Luchins, A. S. (1942). Mechanization in problem solving. *Psycholgoical Monographs, 54* (No. 248).

Lutz, C. A., & Abu-Lughod, L. (Eds.). (1990). *Language and the politics of emotions.* Cambridge: Cambridge University Press.

Lynch, J. J. (1979). *The broken heart: The medical consequences of loneliness.* New York: Basic Books.

Lyons, N. (1983). Two perspectives: On self, relationships, and morality. *Harvard Educational Review, 53,* 125–146.

Maccoby, E. E. (1980). *Social development: Psychological growth and the parent–child relationship.* San Diego: Harcourt Brace Jovanovich.

Maccoby, E. E. (1988). Gender as a social category. *Developmental Psychology, 24,* 755–765.

Maccoby, E. E., & Martin, J. A. (1983). Socialization in the context of the family: Parent–child interaction. In E. M. Hetherington (Ed.), *Handbook of child psychology: Vol. 4. Socialization, personality, and social development* (pp. 1–101). New York: Wiley.

Maccoby, N., Farquhar, J. W., Wood, P. D., & Alexander, J. K. (1977). Reducing the risk of cardiovascualr disease: Effects of a community-based campaign on knowledge and behavior. *Journal of Community Health, 3,* 100–114.

Mace, W. M. (1977). James J. Gibson's strategy for perceiving: Ask not what's inside your head, but what your head's inside of. In R. Shaw & J. Bransford (Eds.), *Perceiving, acting, and knowing.* Hillsdale, NJ: Erlbaum.

MacLeod, C., & Campbell, L. (1992). Memory accessibility and probability judgments: An experimental evaluation of the availability heuristic. *Journal of Personality and Social Psychology, 63,* 890–902.

MacLeod, C., Matthews, A., & Tata, P. (1986). Attentional bias in emotional disorders. *Journal of Abnormal Psychology, 95,* 15–20.

Maddi, S. R., & Kobasa, S. C. (1991). The development of hardiness. In A. Monat & R. S. Lazarus (Eds.), *Stress and coping* (3rd ed., pp. 245–257). New York: Columbia University Press.

Magnusson, D. (1987). Adult delinquency in the light of conduct and physiology at an early age: A longitudinal study. In D. Magnusson & A. Ohman (Eds.), *Psychopathology* (pp. 221–324). Orlando, FL: Academic Press.

Magnusson, D., & Bergman, L. R. (1990). A pattern approach to the study of pathways from childhood to adulthood. In L. N. Robins & M. Rutter (Eds.), *Straight and devious pathways from childhood to adulthood* (pp. 101–115). Cambridge: Cambridge University Press.

Maher, B. A. (1968, November). The shattered language of schizophrenia. *Psychology Today,* pp. 30ff.

Maier, N. R. F. (1931). Reasoning in humans: II. The solution of a problem and its appearance in consciousness. *Journal of Comparative Psychology, 12,* 181–194.

Maier, S. F., & Seligman, M. E. P. (1976). Learned helplessness: Theory and evidence. *Journal of Experimental Psychology, 105,* 3–46.

Maier, S. F., Watkins, L. R., & Fleshner, M. (1994). Psychoneuroimmunology: The interface between behavior, brain, and immunity. *American Psychologist, 49,* 1004–1017.

Main, M., & George, C. (1985). Responses of abused and disadvantaged toddler to distress in agemates: A study in the day care setting. *Developmental Psychology, 21,* 407–412.

Main, M., Kaplan, N., & Cassidy, J. (1985). Security in infancy, childhood, and adulthood: A move to the level of representation. In I. Bretherton & E. Waters (Eds.), *Growing points of attachment theory and research: Monographs of the Society of Research in Child Development, 4* (Serial No. 209, pp. 66–104).

Malitz, S., & Sackheim, H. A. (1984). Low dosage ECT: Electrode placement and acute physiological and cognitive effects. *American Journal of Social Psychiatry, 4,* 47–53.

Manfredi, M., Bini, G., Cruccu, G., Accornero, N., Beradelli, A., & Medolago, L. (1981). Congenital absence of pain. *Archives of Neurology, 38,* 507–511.

Marcel, A. J. (1983). Conscious and unconscious perception: An approach to the relation between phenomenal experience and perceptual processes. *Cognitive Psychology, 15,* 238–300.

Marcus, A. D. (1990, December 3). Mists of memory cloud some legal proceedings. *The Wall Street Journal,* p. B1.

Markman, E. M. (1989). *Categorization and naming in children: Problems of induction.* Cambridge, MA: MIT Press.

Markman, E. M., & Wachtel, G. F. (1988). Children's use of mutual exclusivity to constrain meanings of words. *Cognitive Psychology, 20,* 121–157.

Markovitz, H., & Nantel, G. (1989). The belief-bias effect in the production and evaluation of logical conclusions. *Memory & Cognition, 17,* 11–17.

Markus, H. (1977). Self-schemata and processing information about the self. *Journal of Personality and Social Psychology, 35,* 63–78.

Markus, H., Cross, S., & Wurf, E. (1990). The role of the self-system in competence. In R. J. Sternberg & J. Lollgian, Jr. (Eds.), *Competence considered* (pp. 205–225). New Haven: Yale University Press.

Markus, H., & Nurius, P. (1986). Possible selves. *American Psychologist, 41,* 954–969.

Markus, H., & Smith, J. (1981). The influence of self-schemas on the perception of others. In N. Cantor & J. F. Kihlstrom (Eds.), *Personality, cognition, and social interaction* (pp. 233–262). Hillsdale, NJ: Erlbaum.

Marlatt, G. A. (1983). The controlled-drinking controversy: A commentary. *American Psychologist, 38,* 1097–1110.

Marler, P. R., & Hamilton, W. J. (1966). *Mechanisms of animal behavior.* New York: Wiley.

Marr, D. (1982). *Vision.* San Francisco: Freeman.

Marr, D., & Nishihara, H. K. (1978). Representation and recognition of the spatial organization of three-dimensional shapes. *Proceedings of the Royal Society of London (Series B), 200,* 269–294.

Marsella, A. J. (1979). Cross-cultural studies of mental disorders. In A. J. Marsella, R. G. Sharp, & T. J. Ciborowski (Eds.), *Perspectives on cross-cultural psychology* (pp. 233–262). New York: Academic Press.

Marshall, G. D., & Zimbardo, P. G. (1979). Affective consequences of inadequately explained physiological arousal. *Journal of Personality and Social Psychology, 37,* 970–988.

Martin, J. A. (1981). A longitudinal study of the consequences of early mother–infant interaction: A microanalytic approach. *Monographs of the Society for Research in Child Development, 46* (203, Serial No. 190).

Martin, R., Davis, G. M., Baron, R. S., Suls, J., & Blanchard, E. B. (1994). Specificity in social support: Perceptions of helpful and unhelpful provider behaviors among irritable bowel syndrome, headache, and cancer patients. *Health Psychology, 13,* 432–439.

Martin, R. J., White, B. D., & Hulsey, M. G. (1991). The regulation of body weight. *American Scientist, 79,* 528–541.

Masangkay, Z. S., McCluskey, K. A., McIntyre, C. W., Sims-Knight, J., Vaughn, B., & Flavell, J. H. (1974). The early development of inferences about the visual percepts of others. *Child Development, 45,* 357–366.

Maslach, C. (1979). Negative emotional biasing of unexplained arousal. *Journal of Personality and Social Psychology, 37,* 953–969.

Maslach, C. (1982). *Burnout: The cost of caring.* Englewood Cliffs, NJ: Prentice-Hall.

Maslach, C., & Florian, V. (1988). Burnout, job setting, and self-evaluation among rehailitation counselors. *Rehabilitation Psychology, 33,* 135–157.

Maslow, A. H. (1968). *Toward a psychology of being* (2nd ed.). Princeton, NJ: Van Nostrand.

Maslow, A. H. (1970). *Motivation and personality* (Rev. ed.). New York: Harper & Row.

Mason, J. W. (1975). An historical view of the stress field: Parts 1 & 2. *Journal of Human Stress, 1,* 6–12, 22–36.

Mason, W. A., & Kenney, M. D. (1974). Reduction of filial attachments in Rhesus monkeys: Dogs as mother surrogates. *Science, 183,* 1209–1211.

Masters, W. H., & Johnson, V. E. (1966). *Human sexual response.* Boston: Little, Brown.

Masters, W. H., & Johnson, V. E. (1970). *Human sexual inadequacy.* Boston: Little, Brown.

Masters, W. H., & Johnson, V. E. (1979). *Homosexuality in perspective.* Boston: Little, Brown.

Matarazzo, J. D. (1984). Behavioral immunogens and pathogens in health and illness. In B. L. Hammonds & C. J. Scheirer (Eds.), *Psychology and health: The Master Lecture Series, Vol. 3* (pp. 9–43). Washington, DC: American Psychological Association.

Matarazzo, J. D. (1990). Psychological assessment versus psychological testing: Validation from Binet to the school, clinic, and courtroom. *American Psychologist, 45,* 999–1017.

Matlin, M. W., & Foley, H. J. (1992). *Sensation and perception* (3rd ed.). Boston: Allyn and Bacon.

Matossian, M. K. (1989). *Poisons of the past: Molds, epidemics, and history.* New Haven: Yale University Press.

Matson, J. L., Esveldt-Dawson, K., Andrasik, F., Ollendick, T., Petti, T., & Hersen, M. (1980). Direct, observational, and generalization effects of social skills training with emotionally disturbed children. *Behavior Therapy, 11,* 522–531.

Maugh, T. H. (1982). Sleep-promoting factor isolated. *Science, 216,* 1400.

May, R. (1969). *Love and will.* New York: Norton.

May, R. (1972). *Power and innocence: A search for the sources of violence.* New York: Delta.

May, R. (1975). *The courage to create.* New York: Norton.

May, R. (1977). *The meaning of anxiety* (Rev. ed.). New York: Norton. (Original work published 1950.)

Mayer, R. E. (1981). *The promise of cognitive psychology.* San Francisco: Freeman.

Mayr, E. (1974). Behavior programs and evolutionary strategies. *American Scientist, 38,* 650–659.

McAdams, D. P. (1988). Biography, narrative, and lives: An introduction. *Journal of Personality, 56,* 1–18.

McAdams, D. P., & de St. Aubin, E. (1992). A theory of generativity and its assessment through self-report, behavioral acts, and narrative themes in autobiography. *Journal of Personality and Social Psychology, 62,* 1003–1015.

McAdams, D. P., de St. Aubin, E., & Logan, R. L. (1993). Generativity among young, midlife, and older adults. *Psychology and Aging, 8,* 221–230.

McClelland, D. C. (1961). *The achieving society.* Princeton, NJ: Van Nostrand.

McClelland, D. C. (1971). *Motivational trends in society.* Morristown, NJ: General Learning Press.

McClelland, D. C., Atkinson, J. W., Clark, R. A., & Lowell, E. L. (1953). *The achievement motive.* New York: Appleton-Century-Crofts.

McClelland, D. C., Atkinson, J. W., Clark, R. A., & Lowell, E. L. (1976). *The achievement motive* (2nd ed.). New York: Irvington.

McClelland, D. C., & Franz, C. E. (1992). Motivational and other souces of work accomplishments in mid-life: A longitudinal study. *Journal of Personality, 60,* 679–707.

McClelland, J. L., & Elman, J. L. (1986). The TRACE model of speech perception. *Cognitive Psychology, 18,* 1–86.

McClintock, M. K. (1971). Menstrual synchrony and suppression. *Nature, 229,* 244–245.

McCloskey, M., Egeth, H., McKenna, J. (Eds.). (1986). The ethics of expert testimony [Special issue]. *Law and Human Behavior, 10* (1/2).

McCoy, E. (1988). Childhood through the ages. In K. Finsterbusch (Ed.), *Sociology 88/89* (pp. 44–47). Guilford, CT: Duskin.

McCrady, B. S., & Miller, W. R. (Eds.). (1993). *Research on Alcoholics Anonymous: Opportunities and alternatives.* New Brunswick, NJ: Rutgers Center for Alcohol Studies.

McCrae, R. R., & Costa, P. T., Jr. (1987). Validation of the five-factor model of personality across instruments and observers. *Journal of Personality and Social Psychology, 56,* 81–90.

McCrae, R. R., & Costa, P. T., Jr. (1989). Rotation to maximize the construct validity of factors in the NEO Personality Inventory. *Multivariate Behavioral Research, 24,* 107–124.

McGinley, H., & Pasewark, R. A. (1989). National survey of the frequency and success of the insanity and alternate pleas. *Journal of Psychiatry and Law, 15,* 205–221.

McGinnis, J. M. (1991). Health objectives for the nation. *American Psychologist, 46,* 520–524.

McGlashan, T. H., Evans, F. J., & Orne, M. T. (1978). The nature of hypnotic analgesia and placebo response to experimental pain. *Psychosomatic Medicine, 31,* 227–246.

McGrath, E., Keita, G. P., Strickland, B. R., & Russo, N. F. (1990). *Women and depression: Risk factors and treatment issues.* Hyattsville, MD: American Psychological Association.

McGue, M., Pickens, R. W., & Svikis, D. S. (1992). Sex and age effects on the inheritance of alcohol problems: A twin study. *Journal of Abnormal Psychology, 101,* 3–17.

McGuire, W. J., & McGuire, C. V. (1988). Content and process in the experience of self. In L. Berkowitz (Ed.), *Advances in experimental social psychology* (Vol. 21, pp. 97–144). New York: Academic Press.

McKean, K. (1986, October). Pain. *Discover,* pp. 82–92.

McKinnon, W., Weisse, C. S., Reynolds, C. P., Bowles, C. A., & Baum, A. (1989). Chronic stress, leukocyte subpopulations, and humoral response to latent viruses. *Health Psychology, 8,* 389–402.

McKoon, G., & Ratcliff, R. (1992). Inference during reading. *Psychological Review, 99,* 440–446.

McNeil, B. J., Pauker, S. G., Sox, H. C., Jr., & Tversky, A. (1982). On the elicitation of preferences for alternative therapies. *New England Journal of Medicine, 306,* 1259–1262.

McPherson, K. S. (1985). On intelligence testing and immigration legislation. *American Psychologist, 40,* 242–243.

Mead, M. (1928). *Coming of age in Samoa.* New York: Morrow.

Mead, M. (1939). *From the South Seas: Studies of adolescence and sex in primitve societies.* New York: Morrow.

Meador, B. D., & Rogers, C. R. (1979). Person-centered therapy. In R. J. Corsini (Ed.), *Current psychotherapies* (2nd ed., pp. 131–184). Itasca, IL: Peacock.

Meany, M. J., Aitken, D. H., Van Berkel, C. Bhatnagar, S., & Sapolsky, R. M. (1988). Effect of neonatal handling on age-related impairments associated with the hippocampus. *Science, 239,* 766–768.

Meany, M. J., Stewart, J., & Beatty, W. W. (1985). Sex differences in social play: The socialization of sex roles. *Advances in the Study of Behavior, 15,* 1–58.

Medin, D. L., & Ross, B. H. (1992). *Cognitive psychology.* Fort Worth, TX: Harcourt Brace Jovanovich.

Meehl, P. E. (1954). *Clinical versus stastical prediction.* Minneapolis: University of Minnesota Press.

Meehl, P. E. (1965). Seer over sign: The first good example. *Journal of Experimental Research in Personality, 1,* 27–32.

Mehrabian, A. (1971). *Silent messages.* Belmont, CA: Wadsworth.

Meichenbaum, D. (1977). *Cognitive-behavior modification: An integrative approach.* New York: Plenum.

Meichenbaum, D. (1985). *Stress inoculation training.* New York: Pergamon Press.

Meier, R. P. (1991). Language acquisition by deaf children. *American Scientist, 79,* 60–70.

Meltzer, H. Y. (1982). What is schizophrenia? *Schizophrenia Bulletin, 8,* 433–435.

Meltzer, H. Y. (1987). Biological studies of schizophrenia. *Schizophrenia Bulletin, 13,* 827–838.

Meltzoff, A. N., & Borton, R. W. (1979). Intermodal matching by human neonates. *Nature, 282,* 403–404.

Meltzoff, J., & Kornreich, M. (1970). *Research in psychotherapy.* New York: Atherton.

Melville, J. (1977). *Phobias and obsessions.* New York: Penguin.

Melzack, R. (1973). *The puzzle of pain.* New York: Basic Books.

Melzack, R. (1980). Psychological aspects of pain. In J. J. Bonica (Ed.), *Pain.* New York: Raven Press.

Melzack, R. (1989). Phantom limbs, the self and the brain (the D. O. Hebb Memorial Lecture). *Canadian Psychology, 30,* 1–16.

Melzack, R., & Wall, P. D. (1989). *The challenge of pain.* New York: Penguin.

Meredith, M. A., & Stein, B. E. (1985). Descending efferents from the superior colliculus relay integrated multisensory information. *Science, 227,* 657–659.

Merigan, W. H., & Maunsell, J. H. R. (1993). How parallel are the primate visual pathways? *Annual Review of Neuroscience, 16,* 369–402.

Merton, R. K. (1957). *Social theory and social structures.* New York: Free Press.

Mervis, C. B., & Rosch, E. (1981). Categorization of natural objects. *Annual Review of Psychology, 32,* 89–115.

Metcalfe, J., Schwartz, B. L., & Joaquim, S. G. (1993). The cue-familiarity heuristic in metacognition. *Journal of Experimental Psychology: Learning, Memory, and Cognition, 19,* 851–861.

Meyer, C. B., & Taylor, S. E. (1986). Adjustment to rape. *Journal of Personality and Social Psychology, 50,* 1226–1234.

Meyer, M. M., & Ekstein, R. (1970). The psychotic pursuit of reality. *Journal of Contemporary Psychotherapy, 3,* 3–12.

Mezzich, J. E., & Berganza, C. E. (Eds.). (1984). *Culture and psychopathology.* New York: Columbia University Press.

Michael, R. T., Gagnon, J. H., Laumann, E. O., & Kolata, G. (1994). *Sex in America: A definitive survey.* Boston: Little, Brown.

Middlebrooks, J. C., & Green, D. C. (1991). Sound localization by human listeners. *Annual Review of Psychology, 42,* 135–159.

Middleton, J. (Ed.). (1967). *Magic, witchcraft, and curing.* Garden City, NY: Natural History Press.

Milgram, S. (1965). Some conditions of obedience and disobedience to authority. *Human Relations, 18,* 56–76.

Milgram, S. (1974). Obedience to authority. New York: Harper & Row.

Milgram, S. (1977, October). *Subject reaction: The neglected factor in the ethics of experimentation.* Hastings Center Report, pp. 19–23.

Milkowitz, D. J. (1994). Family risk indicators in schizophrenia. *Schizophrenia Bulletin, 20,* 137–149.

Millar, K., & Watkinson, N. (1983). Recognition of words presented during general anesthesia. *Ergonomics, 26,* 585–594.

Miller, A. G. (1986). *The obedience paradign: A case study in controversy in social sceince.* New York: Praeger.

Miller, G. A. (1956). The magic number seven plus or minus two: Some limits in our capacity for processing information. *Psychological Review, 63,* 81–97.

Miller, G. A. (1969). Psychology as a means of promoting human welfare. *American Psychologist, 24,* 1063–1075.

Miller, J. D. (1987, September 27). Ignoramus Americanus. *San Francisco Examiner-Chronicle,* This World Section, p. 7.

Miller, J. G. (1984). Culture and the development of everyday social explanation. *Journal of Personality and Social Psychology, 46,* 961–978.

Miller, M. E., & Bowers, K. S. (1993). Hypnotic analgesia: Dissociated experience or dissociated control? *Journal of Abnormal Psychology, 102,* 29–38.

Miller N. E. (1978). Biofeedback and visceral learning. *Annual Review of Psychology, 29,* 373–404.

Miller, N. E. (1985). The value of behavioral research on animals. *American Psychologist, 40,* 423–440.

Miller, N. E. (1992). Introducing and teaching much-needed understanding of the scientific process. *American Psychologist, 47,* 848–850.

Miller, W. R., & Hester, R. K. (1980). Treating the problem drinker: Modern approaches. In W. R. Miller (Ed.), *The addictive behaviors.* Oxford, England: Pergamon Press.

Mineka, S., Davidson, M., Cook, M., & Keir, R. (1984). Observational conditioning of snake fear in rhesus monkeys. *Journal of Abnormal Psychology, 93,* 355–372.

Minuchin, S. (1974). *Families and family therapy.* Cambridge, MA: Harvard University Press.

Mischel, W. (1968). *Personality and assessment.* New York: Wiley.

Mischel, W. (1973). Toward a cognitive social learning reconceptualization of personality. *Psychological Review, 80,* 252–283.

Mischel, W. (1990). Personality dispositions revisited and revised: A view after three decades. In A. Pervin (Ed.), *Handbook of personality: Theory and research* (pp. 111–134). New York: Guilford Press.

Mischel, W., & Peake, P. (1982). Beyond déja vu in the search for cross-situational consistency. *Psychological Review, 89*(6), 730–755.

Mitchell, T. R. (1974). Expectancy models of job satisfaction, occupational preference, and effort: A theoretical, methodological, and empirical appraisal. *Psychological Bulletin, 81,* 1053–1077.

Miyake, K., Chen, K., & Campos, J. J. (1985). Infant temperament, mother's mode of interaction, and attachment in Japan: An interim report. In I. Bretherton & E. Waters (Eds.), *Growing points of attachment theory and research. Monographs of the Society for Research in Child Development, 50* (1–2, Serial No. 209), 276–297.

Miyashita, Y. (1995). How the brain creates imagery: Projection to primary visual cortex. *Science, 268,* 1719–1720.

Moffitt, A., Karmer, M., & Hoffmann, R. (Eds.). (1993). *The functions of dreaming.* Albany: State University of New York Press.

Molnar, J. M., Rath, W. R., & Klein, T. P. (1990). Constantly compromised: The impact of homelessness on children. *Journal of Social Issues, 46,* 109–123.

Monahan, J., & Walker, L. (1988). Social science research in law: A new paradigm. *American Psychologist, 43,* 465–472.

Moncrieff, R. W. (1951). *The chemical senses.* London: Leonard Hill.

Montague, A. (1986). *Touching: The human significance of the skin.* New York: Harper & Row.

Montgomery, G. (1990). The mind in motion [Special issue]. *Discover,* pp. 12–19.

Moore, P. (1990). In *Discovering Psychology,* Program 18 [PBS video series]. Washington, DC: Annenberg/CPB Program.

Moore-Ede, M. (1993). *The twenty-four-hour society: Understanding human limits in a world that never stops.* Reading, MA: Addison-Wesley.

Moore-Ede, M. C., Sulzman, F. M., & Fuller, C. A. (1982). *The clocks that time us: Physiology of the circadian timing system.* Cambridge, MA: Harvard University Press.

Mor, V. (1987). *Hospice care systems.* New York: Springer.

Mor, V., Greer, D. S., & Kastenbaum, R. (Eds.). (1988). *The hospice experiment.* Baltimore: Johns Hopkins University Press.

Morgan, A. H., Hilgard, E. R., & Davert, E. C. (1970). The heritability of hypnotic susceptibility of twins: A preliminary report. *Behavior Genetics, 1,* 213–224.

Morgan, A. H., Johson, D. L., & Hilgard, E. R. (1974). The stability of hypnotic susceptibility: A longitudinal study. *International Journal of Clinical and Experimental Hypnosis, 22,* 249–257.

Moriarty, T. (1975). Crime, commitment and the responsive bystander: Two field experiments. *Journal of Personality and Social Psychology, 31,* 370–376.

Moriarity, T. (1990). In *Discovering Psychology,* Program 19 [PBS video series]. Washington, DC: Annenberg/CPB Program.

Morin, S. F., & Rothblum, E. D. (1991). Removing the stigma: Fifteen years of progress. *American Psychologist, 46,* 947–949.

Morrell, E. M. (1986). Meditation and somatic arousal. *American Psychologist, 41,* 712–713.

Moscovici, S. (1976). *Social influence and social change.* New York: Academic Press.

Moscovici, S. (1980). Toward a theory of conversion behavior. In L. Berkowitz (Ed.), *Advances in experimental social psychology* (Vol. 13, pp. 209–239). New York: Academic Press.

Moscovici, S. (1985). Social influence and conformity. In G. Lindzey & E. Aronson (Eds.), *The handbook of social psychology* (3rd ed., pp. 347–412). New York: Random House.

Moscovici, S., & Faucheux, C. (1972). Social influence, conformity bias, and the study of active minorities. In L. Berkowitz (Ed.), *Advances in experimental social psychology* (Vol. 6). New York: Academic Press.

Moskowitz, B. A. (1978). The acquisition of language. *Scientific American, 239*(11), 92–108.

Motley, M. T., & Baars, B. J. (1979). Effects of cognitive set upon laboratory-induced verbal (Freudian) slips. *Journal of Speech and Hearing Research, 22,* 421–432.

Muehlenhard, C. L., & Cook, S. W. (1988). Men's self-reports of unwanted sexual activity. *The Journal of Sex Research, 24,* 58–72.

Munroe, R. L. (1955). *Schools of psychoanalytic thought.* New York: Dryden.

Munsterberg, H. (1908). *On the witness stand.* New York: McClure.

Murnen, S. K., Perolt, A., & Byrne, D. (1989). Coping with unwanted sexual activity: Normative responses, situational determinants, and individual differences. *The Journal of Sex Research, 26,* 85–106.

Murphy, J. M. (1976). Psychiatric labeling in cross-cultural perspective. *Science, 191,* 1019–1028.

Murray, H. A. (1938). *Explorations in personality.* New York: Oxford University Press.

Murray, J. P., & Kippax, S. (1977). Children's social behavior in three towns with differing television experience. *Journal of Communication, 28,* 19–29.

Murray, L., & Trevarthen, C. (1986). The infant's role in mother–infant communication. *Journal of Child Language, 13,* 15–29.

Muskin, P. R., & Fyer, A. J. (1981). Treatment of panic disorder. *Journal of Clinical Psychopharmacology, 1,* 81–90.

Naigles, L. G. (1990). Children use syntax to learn verb meanings. *Journal of Child Language, 17,* 357–374.

Naigles, L. G., & Kako, E. T. (1993). First contact in verb acquisition: Defining a role for syntax. *Child Development, 64,* 1665–1687.

National Association of Childrens Hospitals (1991). *Assuring children's access to health care.* Alexandria, VA: National Association of Children's Hospitals and Related Institutions.

National Center for Health Statistics. (1989). Hyattsville, MD: Public Health Service.

National Center of Health Statistics. (1990). Vital and health statistics. *Data from the national study of family growth.* Hyattsville, MD: U.S. Department of HEW, Public Health Service, Office of Health Research, Statistics, and Technology.

National Centers for Disease Control. (1990, November).

National Institutes of Mental Health. (1977). *Lithium and the treatment of mood disorders* (DHEW Publication No. ADM 77–73). Washington, DC: U.S. Government Printing Office.

Natsoulas, T. (1978). Consciousness. *American Psychologist, 33*(10), 906–914.

Natsoulas, T. (1981). Basic problems of consciousness. *Journal of Personality and Social Psychology, 41,* 132–178.

Nauta, W. J. H., & Feirtag, M. (1979). The organization of the brain. *Scientific American, 241*(9), 88–111.

Navon, D., & Gopher, D. (1979). On the economy of the human processing system. *Psychological Review, 86,* 214–255.

Neath, I. (1993). Contextual and distinctive processes and the serial position function. *Journal of Memory and Language, 32,* 820–840.

Neath, I., & Crowder, R. G. (1990). Schedules of presentation and temporal distinctiveness in human memory. *Journal of Experimental Psychology: Learning, Memory, and Cognition, 16,* 316–327.

Neath, I., Surprenant, A. M., & Crowder, R. G. (1993). The context-dependent stimulus suffix effect. *Journal of Experimental Psychology: Learning, Memory, and Cognition, 19,* 698–703.

Needleman, H., Schell, A., Belinger, D., Leviton, A., & Allred, E. (1990). The long-term effects of exposure to low doses of lead in childhood: An 11-year follow-up report. *New England Journal of Medicine, 322,* 83–88.

Neisser, U. (1967). *Cognitive psychology.* New York: Appleton-Century-Crofts.

Nelson, E. A., & Dannefer, D. (1992). Aged heterogeneity: Fact or fiction? The fate of diversity in gerontological research. *The Gerontologist, 32,* 17–23.

Nelson, K. (1973). Structure and strategy in learning to talk. *Monographs of the Society for Research in Child Development, 38* (1–2, Serial No. 149).

Nelson, K. (1992). Emergence of autobiographical memory at age 4. *Human Development, 35,* 172–177.

Nelson, K. (1993). The psychological and social origins of autobiographical memory. *Psychological Science, 4,* 7–14.

Nelson, R. E., & Craighead, W. E. (1977). Selective recall of positive and negative feedback, self-control behaviors and depression. *Journal of Abnormal Psychology, 86,* 379–388.

Nelson, Z. P., & Mowrey, D. D. (1976). Contracting in crisis intervention. *Community Mental Health Journal, 12,* 37–43.

Nemeth, C. J. (1986). Differential contributions of majority and minority influence. *Psychological Review, 93,* 23–32.

Nemeth, C. J., Mayseless, O., Sherman, J., & Berown, Y. (1990). Exposure to dissent and recall of information. *Journal of Personality and Social Psychology, 58,* 429–437.

Neugarten, B. L. (1973). Personality change in late life: A developmental perspective. In C. Eisdorfer & M. P. Lawton (Eds.), *The psychology of adult development and aging* (pp. 311–335). Washington, DC: American Psychological Association.

Neugarten, B. L. (1977). Personality and aging. In J. E. Birren & K. W. Schaie (Eds.), *Handbook of the psychology of aging* (pp. 626–649). New York: Van Nostrand Reinhold.

Neugarten, B. L., & Neugarten, D. A. (1986). Changing meanings of age in the aging society. In A. Pifer & L. Bronte (Eds.), *Our aging society* (pp. 33–51). New York: Norton.

Newcomb, M. D., & Bentler, P. M. (1988). *Consequences of adolescent drug use: Impact on the lives of young adults.* Newbury Park, CA: Sage.

Newcomb, T. M. (1929). *The consistency of certain extrovert-introvert behavior traits in 50 problem boys* (Contributions to Education, No. 382). New York: Columbia University Press.

Newcomb, T. M. (1943). *Personality and social change.* New York: Holt.

Newcomb, T. M. (1963). Persistence and regression of changed attitudes: Long-range studies. *Journal of Social Issues, 19,* 3–4.

Newcomb, T. M. Koenig, D. E., Flacks, R., & Warwick, D. P. (1967). *Persistence and change: Bennington College and its students after twenty-five years.* New York: Wiley.

Newell, A., Shaw, J. C., & Simon, H. A. (1958). Elements of a theory of human problem solving. *Psychological Review, 65,* 152–166.

Newell, A., & Simon, H. A. (1972). *Human problem solving.* Englewood Cliffs, NJ: Prentice-Hall.

Newport, E. (1990). Maturational constraints on language learning. *Cognitive Science, 14,* 11–28.

Newport, E., Gleitman, H., & Gleitman, L. (1977). Mother, I'd rather do it myself: Some effects and non-effects of maternal speech style. In C. E. Snow & C. A. Ferguson (Eds.), *Talking to children: Language input and acquisition* (pp. 109–150). New York: Cambridge University Press.

Newsome, W. T., & Pare, E. B. (1988). A selective impairment of motion perception following lesions of the middle temporal visual area. *Journal of Neuroscience, 8,* 2201–2211.

New York Times, The. (1989, May 17, p. 7). Police officers beat blind man.

New York Times, The. (1989, July 2, p. A10 [N]). Paraplegic reaches summit after 9-day mountain climb.

New York Times, The. (1991, March 22, p. 1). Study finds that deaf babies "babble" in sign language.

Nhat Hanh, T. (1991). *Peace is every step: The path of mindfullness in everyday life.* New York: Bantam.

Nicoll, C., Russell, S., & Katz, L. (1988, May 26). Research on animals must continue. *San Francisco Chronicle,* p. A25.

Nietzel, M. T., Bernstein, D. A., & Milich, R. (1991). *Introduction to clinical psychology.* Englewood Cliffs, NJ: Prentice-Hall.

Nisbett, R. (1995). Race, IQ, and scientism. In S. Fraser (Ed.), *The Bell Curve wars: Race, intelligence, and the future of America* (pp. 36–57). New York: Basic Books.

Nobles, W. W. (1976). Black people in white insanity: An issue for black community mental health. *Journal of Afro-American Issues, 4,* 21–27.

Nobles, W. W.. (1980). African philosophy: Foundations for black psychology. In R. L. Jones (Ed.), *Black psychology* (2nd ed., pp. 23–36). New York: Harper & Row.

Nolen-Hoeksema, S. (1987). Sex differences in unipolar depression: Evidence and theory. *Psychological Bulletin, 101,* 259–282.

Nolen-Hoeksema, S. (1990). *Sex differences in depression.* Stanford, CA: Stanford University Press.

Nolen-Hoeksema, S., & Girgus, J. S. (1994). The emergence of gender differences in depression during adolescence. *Psychological Bulletin, 115,* 424–443.

Norem, J. K., & Cantor, N. (1986). Defensive pessimism: "Harnessing" anxiety as motivation. *Journal of Personality and Social Psychology, 52,* 1208–1217.

Norem, J. K., & Illingworth, K. S. S. (1993). Strategy-dependent effects of reflecting on self and tasks: Some implications of optimism and defensive pessimism. *Journal of Personality and Social Psychology, 65,* 822–835.

Norman, D. A. (1992). *Turn signals are the facial expressions of automobiles.* Reading, MA: Addison-Wesley.

Norman, W. T. (1963). Toward an adequate taxonomy of personality attributes: Replicated factor structure in peer nomination personality ratings. *Journal of Abnormal and Social Psychology, 66,* 574–583.

Norman, W. T. (1967). *2,800 personality trait descriptors: Normative operating characteristics for a university population* (Research Rep. No. 08310-1-T). Ann Arbor: University of Michigan Press.

Nosofsky, R. M., Kruschke, J. K., & McKinley, S. C. (1992). Combining exemplar-based category representations and connectionist learning rules. *Journal of Experimental Psychology: Learning, Memory, and Cognition, 18,* 211–233.

Novick, L. R., & Holyoak, K. J. (1991). Mathematical problem solving by analogy. *Journal of Experimental Psychology: Learning, Memory, and Cognition, 17,* 398–415.

Nungesser, L. G. (1990). *Axioms for survivors: How to live until you say goodbye.* Santa Monica, CA: IBS Press.

Nurmi, J. -E. (1991). How do adolescents see their future? A review of the development of future orientation and planning. *Developmental Review, 11,* 1–59.

Oden, S., & Asher, S. R. (1977). Coaching children in social skills for friendship making. *Child Development, 48,* 495–506.

Offer, D., & Offer, J. B. (1975). *From teenage to young manhood.* New York: Basic Books.

Offer, D., Ostrov, E., & Howard, K. I. (1981a). *The adolescent: A psychological self-portrait.* New York: Basic Books.

Offer, D., Ostrov, E., & Howard, K. I. (1981b). The mental health professional's concept of the normal adolescent. *AMA Archives of General Psychiatry, 38,* 149–153.

Offer, D., Ostrov, E., Howard, K. I., & Atkinson, R. (1988). *The teenage world: Adolesents' self-image in ten countries.* New York: Plenum Medical.

Offord, D. R. (1987). Prevention of behavioral and emotional disorders in children. *Journal of Child Psychology and Psychiatry, 28,* 9–19.

Ogbu, J. (1987). *Minority education over caste: The American system in cross-cultural perspective.* New York: Academic Press.

Oldham, D. G. (1978a). Adolescent turmoil: A myth revisited. In S. C. Feinstein & P. L. Giovacchini (Eds.), *Adolescent psychiatry* (Vol. 6). Chicago: University of Chicago Press.

Oldham, D. G. (1978b). Adolescent turmoil and a myth revisited: In A. H. Esman (Ed.), *The psychology of adolescence.* New York: International University Press.

O'Leary, K. D. (Ed.). (1987). *Assessment of marital discord: An integration for research and clinical practice.* Hillsdale, NJ: Erlbaum.

Olton, D. S. (1979). Mazes, maxes, and memory. *American Psychologist, 34,* 583–596.

Olton, D. S. (1992). Tolman's cognitive analyses: Predecessors of current approaches in psychology. *Journal of Experimental Psychology: General, 121,* 427–428.

Oppel, J. J. (1854–1855). Ueber geometrisch-optische Tauschun-gen. *Jahresbericht des physikalischen Vereins zu Frankfurt a. M.,* 34–47.

Opton, E. M. (1970). Lessons of My Lai. In N. Sanford & C. Comstock (Eds.), *Sanctions for evil.* San Francisco: Jossey-Bass.

Opton, E. M., Jr. (1973). "It never happened and besides they deserved it." in W. E. Henry & N. Stanford (Eds.), *Sanctions for evil* (pp. 49–70). San Francisco: Jossey-Bass.

O'Regan, J. K. (1992). Solving the "real" mysteries of visual perception: The world as an outside memory. *Canadian Journal of Psychology, 46,* 461–488.

O'Reilly, C. A. (1991). Organizational behavior: Where we've been, where we're going. *Annual Review of Psychology, 42,* 427–458.

Orne, M. T. (1980). Hypnotic control of pain: Toward a clarification of the different psychological processes involved. In J. J. Bonica (Ed.), *Pain* (pp. 155–172). New York: Raven Press.

Ornstein, R. (1991). *The evolution of consciousness.* New York: Simon & Schuster.

Ornstein, R., & Sobel, D. (1989). *Healthy pleasures.* Reading, MA: Addison-Wesley.

Ornstein, R. E. (1986b). *The psychology of consciousness* (Rev. ed.) New York: Penguin Books.

Osherow, N. (1981). Making sense of the nonsensical: An analysis of Jonestown. In E. Aronson (Ed.), *Readings in the social animal.* San Francisco: Freeman.

Oskamp, S. (1984). *Applied social psychology.* Englewood Cliffs, NJ: Prentice-Hall.

Osterhout, L., & Holcomb, P. J. (1992). Event-related brain potentials elicited by syntactic anomaly. *Journal of Memory and Language, 31,* 785–806.

O'Sullivan, C. (1990, December 15). Quoted in G. Eskenazi, *When athletic aggression turns into sexual assault. The New York Times Index* (Vol. 139, P. 18, March 17, 1990).

Owens, J., Bower, G. H., & Black, J. B. (1979). The "soap opera" effect in story recall. *Memory & Cognition, 7,* 185–191.

Ozer, D. J., & Reise, S. P. (1994). Personality assessment. *Annual Review of Psychology, 45,* 357–388.

Paikoff, R. L. (Ed.). (1991). *Shared views in the family during adolescence.* San Francisco: Jossey-Bass.

Paivio, A. (1986). *Mental representations: A dual coding approach.* New York: Oxford University Press.

Palken, J. L., & Shackelford, A. E. (1992). Nutrition for good health. In H. Benson & E. M. Stuart (Eds.), *The wellness book* (pp. 129–153). New York: Simon & Schuster.

Palmer, S. (1989). Reference frames in the perception of shape and orientation. In B. Shepp & M. Ballisteros (Eds.), *Object perception* (pp. 121–163). Hillsdale, NJ: Erlbaum.

Palmer, S. E. (1984). The psychology of perceptual organization: A transformational approach. In A. Rosenfeld & J. Beck (Eds.), *Human and machine vision.* New York: Academic Press.

Papolos, D. F., & Papolos, J. (1987). *Overcoming depression.* New York: Harper & Row.

Pappas, A. M. (1983). Introduction. In A. M. Pappas (Ed.), *Law and the status of the child* (pp. xxvii–lv). New York: United Nations Institute for Training and Research.

Park, B., & Rothbart, M. (1982). Perception of out-group homogeneity and levels of social categorization: Memory for the subordinate attributes of in-group and out-group members. *Journal of Personality and Social Psychology, 42,* 1051–1068.

Parke, R. D., & Sawin, D. B. (1976). The father's role in infancy. *Family Coordinator, 25,* 265–371.

Parker, K. C. H., Hanson, R. K., & Hunsley, J. (1988). MMPI, Rorschach, and WAIS: A meta-analytic comparison of reliability, stability, and validity. *Psychological Bulletin, 103,* 367–373.

Parr, W. V., & Siegert, R. (1993). Adults' conceptions of everyday memory failures in others: Factors that mediate the effects of target age. *Psychology and Aging, 8,* 599–605.

Pashler, H. (1992). Attentional limitations in doing two tasks at the same time. *Current Directions in Psychological Science, 1,* 44–48.

Pass, J. J., & Cunningham, J. W. (1978). Occupational clusters based on systematically derived work dimensions: Final report. *Journal of Supplemental Abstract Service: Catalogue of selected documents: Psychology, 8,* 22–23.

Pattie, F. A. (1994). *Mesmer and animal magnetism: A chapter in the history of medicine.* New York: Edmonston.

Paul, S. M., Crawley, J. N., & Skolnick, P. (1986). The neurobiology of anxiety: The role of the GABA/benzodiazepine complex. In P. A. Berger & H. K. H. Brodie (Eds.), *American handbook on psychiatry: Biological psychology* (3rd ed.). New York: Basic Books.

Pavlov, I. P. (1927). *Conditioned reflexes* (G. V. Anrep, Trans.). London: Oxford University Press.

Pavlov, I. P. (1928). *Lectures on conditioned reflexes: Twenty-five years of objective study of higher nervous activity (behavior of animals)* (Vol. 1, W. H. Gantt, Trans.). New York: International Publishers.

Pearson, R. (Ed.). (1992). *Shockley on eugenics and race: The application of science to the solution of human problems.* Washington, DC.: Scott-Townsend Publishers.

Pedersen, P. E., Williams, C. L., & Blass, E. M. (1982). Activation and odor conditioning of sucking behavior in 3-day-old albino rats. *Journal of Experimental Psychology: Animal Processes, 8,* 329–341.

Peele, S. (1985). The implications and limitations of genetic models of alcolholism and other addictions. *Journal of Studies on Alcohol, 47,* 63–73.

Pelletier, L., & Herold, E. (1983, May). *A study of sexual fantasies among young single females.* Paper presented at the meeting of the World Congress of Sexuality, Washington, DC.

Pelz, E. B. (1965). Some factors in "Group decision." In H. Proshansky & B. Seidenberg (Eds.), *Basic studies in social psychology* (pp. 437–444). New York: Holt, Rinehart & Winston. (Original work published 1955.)

Pendery, M. L., Maltzman, I. M., & West, L. J. (1982). Controlled drinking by alcoholics? New finding and a reevaluation of a major affirmative study. *Science, 217,* 169–174.

Penfield, W., & Baldwin, M. (1952). Temporal lobe seizures and the technique of subtotal lobectomy. *Annals of Surgery, 136,* 625–634.

Penick, S., Smith, G., Wienske, K., & Hinkle, L. (1963). An experimental evaluation of the relationship between hunger and gastric motility. *American Journal of Physiology, 205,* 421–426.

Pennebaker, J. W. (1990). *Opening up: The healing power of confiding in others.* New York: Morrow.

Pennebaker, J. W., & Harber, K. D. (1993). A social stage model of collective coping: The Loma Prieta earthquake and the Persian Gulf War. *Journal of Social Issues, 49*(4), 125–145.

Perenin, M. T., & Jeannerod, M. (1975). Residual vision in cortically blind hemiphields. *Neuropsychologia, 13,* 1–7.

Perkins, D. N. (1988). Creativity and the quest for mechanism. In R. J. Sternberg & E. E. Smith (Eds.), *The psychology of human thought* (pp. 309–336). Cambridge: Cambridge University Press.

Perlin, S. (Ed.). (1975). *A handbook for the study of suicide.* New York: Oxford University Press.

Perls, F. S. (1969). *Gestalt therapy verbatim.* Lafayette, CA: Real People Press.

Persons, J. (1991). Psychotherapy outcome studies do not accurately represent current models of psychotherapy. *American Psychologist, 46,* 99–106.

Pervin, L. A. (1994). A critical analysis of current trait theory. *Psychological Inquiry, 5,* 103–113.

Peterson, C., & Barrett, L. C. (1987). Explanatory style and academic performance among university freshmen. *Journal of Personality and Social Psychology, 53,* 603–607.

Peterson, C., & Seligman, M. E. P. (1984). Causal explanations as a risk factor for depression: Theory and evidence. *Psychological Review, 91,* 347–374.

Peterson, C., Seligman, M. E. P., & Valliant, G. E. (1988). Pessimistic explanatorty style is a risk factor for physical illness: A thirty-five year longitudinal study. *Journal of Personality and Social Psychology, 55,* 23–27.

Peterson, D., & Goodall, J. (1993). *Visions of Caliban: On chimpanzees and people.* Boston: Houghton Mifflin.

Peterson, L. R., & Peterson, M. J. (1959). Short-term retention of individual verbal items. *Journal of Experimental Psychology, 58,* 193–198.

Petri, H. L., & Mishkin, M. (1994). Behaviorism, cognitivism, and the neuropsychology of memory. *American Scientist, 82,* 28–37.

Phares, E. J. (1984). *Clinical psychology: Concepts, methods, and professionals* (Rev. ed.) Homewood, IL: Dorsey Press.

Phillips, D. P. (1993). Representation of acoustic events in primary auditory cortex. *Journal of Experimental Psychology: Human Perception and Performance, 19,* 203–216.

Piaget, J. (1929). *The child's conception of the world.* New York: Harcourt, Brace.

Piaget, J. (1954). *The construction of reality in the child.* New York: Basic Books.

Piaget, J. (1965). *The moral judgment of the child* (M. Gabain, Trans.). New York: Macmillan.

Piaget, J. (1977). *The development of thought: Equilibrium of cognitive structures.* New York: Viking Press.

Piccione, C., Hilgard, E. R., & Zimbardo, P. G. (1989). On the degree of stability of measured hypnotizability over a 25-year period. *Journal of Personality and Social Psychology, 56,* 289–295.

Pickens, R. W., Svikis, D. S., McGue, M., Lykken, D. T., Heston, L. L., & Clayton, P. J. (1991). Heterogeneity in the inheritance of alcoholism. *Archives of General Psychiatry, 48,* 19–28.

Piliavin, I. M., Rodin, J., & Piliavin, J. A. (1969). Good Samaritanism: An underground phenomenon? *Journal of Personality and Social Psychology, 13,* 289–300.

Piliavin, J. A., & Piliavin, I. M. (1972). Effect of blood on reactions to a victim. *Journal of Personality and Social Psychology, 23,* 353–361.

Pilisuk, M., & Parks, S. H. (1986). *The healing web: Social networks and human survival.* Hanover, NH: University Press of New England.

Pillow, B. H. (1993). Preschool children's understanding of the relationship between modality of perceptual access and knowledge of perceptual properties. *British Journal of Developmental Psychology, 11,* 371–389.

Pinker, S. (1987). The bootstrapping problem in language acquisition. In B. MacWhinney (Ed.), *Mechanisms of language acquisition* (pp. 399–441). Hillsdale, NJ: Erlbaum.

Pinker, S. (1994). *The language instinct: How the mind creates language.* New York: Morrow.

Piotrowski, C., Keller, J. W., & Ogawa, T. (1993). Projective techniques: An international perspective. *Psychological Reports, 72,* 179–182.

Piotrowski, C., Sherry, D., & Keller, J. W. (1985). Psychodiagnostic test usage: A survey of the Society for Personality Assessment. *Journal of Personality Assessment, 49,* 115–119.

Pittenger, J. B. (1988). Direct perception of change. *Perception, 17,* 119–133.

Pitts, D. G. (1982). The effects of aging on selected visual functions: Dark adaptation, visual acuity, stereopsis, and brightness contrast. In R. Sekuler, D. Kline, & K. Dismukes (Eds.), *Aging and human visual function* (pp. 131–159). New York: Liss.

Plomin, R. (1989). Environment and genes: Determinants of behavior. *American Psychologist, 44,* 105–111.

Plomin, R., Chipuer, H. M., & Loehin, J. C. (1990a). Behavioral genetics and personality. In L. A. Pervin (Ed.), *Handbook of personality theory and research* (pp. 225–243). New York: Guilford Press.

Plomin, R., Corley, R., DeFries, J. C., & Fulker, D. W. (1990b). Individual differences in television viewing in early childhood. *Psychological Science, 1,* 371–377.

Plomin, R., & McClearn, G. E. (Eds.). (1993). *Nature, nurture, and psychology.* Washington, DC: American Psychological Association.

Plomin, R., Owen, M. J., & McGuffin, P. (1994). The genetic basis of complex human behaviors. *Science, 264,* 1733–1739.

Plomin, R., & Rende, R. (1991). Human behavioral genetics. *Annual Review of Psychology, 42,* 161–190.

Plous, S. (1985). Perceptual illusions and military realities: A social-psychological analysis of the nuclear arms race. *Journal of Conflict Resolution, 29,* 363–389.

Plous, S. (1989). Thinking the unthinkable: The effects of anchoring on likelihood estimates of nuclear war. *Journal of Applied Social Psychology, 19,* 67–91.

Plutchik, R. (1980). *Emotion: A psychoevolutionary synthesis.* New York: Harper & Row.

Plutchik, R. (1984). Emotions: A general psychoevolutionary theory. In K. Scherer & P. Ekman (Eds.), *Approaches to emotion.* Hillsdale, NJ: Erlbaum.

Poizner, H., Bellugi, U., & Klima, E. S. (1991). Brain function for language: Perspectives from another modality. In I. G. Mattingly & M. Studdert-Kennedy (Eds.), *Modularity and the motor theory of speech perception* (pp. 145–169). Hillsdale, NJ: Erlbaum.

Polivy, J., & Herman, C. P. (1992). Undieting: A program to help people stop dieting. *International Journal of Eating Disorders, 11,* 261–268.

Polivy, J., & Herman, C. P. (1993). Etiology of binge eating: Psychological mechanisms. In C. G. Fairburn & G. T. Wilson (Eds.), *Binge eating: Nature, assessment, and treatment* (pp. 173–205). New York: Guilford Press.

Polivy, J., Herman, C. P., & McFarlane, T. (1994). Effects of anxiety on eating: Does palatability moderate distress-induced overeating in dieters? *Journal of Abnormal Psychology, 103,* 505–510.

Pomerantz, J., & Kubovy, M. (1986). Theoretical approaches to perceptual organization. In K. R. Boff, L. Kaufman, & J. P. Thomas (Eds.), *Handbook of perception and human performance* (Vol. 3, pp. 1–46). New York: Wiley.

Poole, D. A., Lindsay, D. S., Memon, A., & Bull, R. (1995). Psychotherapy and the recovery of memories of childhood abuse: U.S. and British practitioner's opinions, practices, and experiences. *Journal of Consulting and Clinical Psychology, 63,* 426–437.

Porras, J. I., & Silvers, R. C. (1991). Organization development and transformation. *Annual Review of Psychology, 42,* 51–78.

Porter, L. W., & Lawler, E. E. (1968). *Managerial attitudes and performance.* Homewood, IL: Irwin.

Posner, M. I. (1993). Seeing the mind. *Science, 262,* 673–674.

Post, F. (1980). Paranoid, schizophrenic-like, and schizophrenic states in the aged. In J. E. Birren & R. B. Stone (Eds.), *Handbook of mental health and aging* (pp. 591–615). Englewood Cliffs, NJ: Prentice-Hall.

Poucet, B. (1993). Spatial cognitive maps in animals: New hypotheses on their structure and neural mechanisms. *Psychological Review, 100,* 163–182.

Poulos, C. X., & Cappell, H. (1991). Homeostatic theory of drug tolerance: A general model of physiological adaptation. *Psychological Review, 98,* 390–408.

Povinelli, D. J. (1993). Reconstructing the evolution of mind. *American Psychologist, 48,* 493–509.

Powell, L. H., & Eagleston, J. R. (1983). The assessment of chronic stress in college students. In E. M. Altmaier (Ed.), *Helping students manage stress—new directions for student services* (Vol. 21, pp. 23–41). San Francisco: Jossey-Bass.

Powley, T. (1977). The ventromedial hypothalamic syndrome, satiety, and a cephalic phase hypothesis. *Psychological Review, 84,* 89–126.

Pratt, M. W., Golding, G., Hunter, W., & Norris, J. (1988). From inquiry to judgment: Age and sex differences in patterns of adult moral thinking and information-seeking. *International Journal of Aging and Human Development, 27,* 109–124.

Premack, D. (1965). Reinforcement theory. In D. Levine (Ed.), *Nebraska Symposium on Motivation* (pp. 128–180). Lincoln: University of Nebraska Press.

Prentice, D. A., & Miller, D. T. (1993). Pluralistic ignorance and alcohol use on campus: Some consequences on misperceiving the social norm. *Journal of Personality and Social Psychology, 64,* 243–256.

Preti, G., Cutler, W. B., Garcia, G. R., Huggins, & Lawley, J. J. (1986). Human axillary secretions influence women's menstrual cycles: The role of donor extract from females. *Hormones and Behavior.*

Price, R. (1953/1980). *Droodles.* Los Angeles: Price/Stern/Sloan.

Price, R. H., Ketterer, R. F., Bader, B. C., & Monahan, J. (Eds.). (1980). *Prevention in mental health: Research, policy, and practice* (Vol. 1). Beverly Hills, CA: Sage.

Pritchard, R. D., Dunnette, M. D., & Jorgenson, D. O. (1972). Effects of perceptions of equity and inequity on worker performance and satisfaction. *Journal of Applied Psychology, 56,* 75–94.

Prochaska, J. O., DiClemente, C. C., Velicer, W. F., & Rossi, J. S. (1993). Standardized, individualized, interactive, and personalized self-help programs for smoking cessation. *Health Psychology, 12,* 399–405.

Putnam, D. E., Finney, J. W., Barkley, P. L., & Bonner, M. J. (1994). Enhancing commitment improves adherence to a medical regimen. *Journal of Consulting and Clinical Psychology, 62,* 191–194.

Pylyshyn, Z. W. (1981). The imagery debate: Analogue media versus tacit knowledge. *Psychological Review, 88,* 16–45.

Quattrone, G. (1986). On the perception of a group's variability. In S. Worchell & W. Austin (Eds.), *The psychology of intergroup relations* (Vol. 2, pp. 25–48). New York: Nelson-Hall.

Quindlen, A. (1990, October 7). Hearing the cries of crack. *The New York Times,* Section 4, Col. 1, p. E19.

Quine, W. V. O. (1960). *Word and object.* Cambridge, MA: MIT Press.

Rabbie, J. M (1981). The effects of intergroup conpetition and cooperation on intra- and intergroup relationships. In J. Grzelak & V. Derlega (Eds.), *Living with other people: Theory and research on cooperation and helping.* New York: Academic Press.

Rabins, P. V. (1992). Prevention of mental disorder in the elderly: Current perspectives and future prospects. *Journal of the American Geriatric Society, 40,* 727–733.

Rabkin, J. G., Gelb, L., & Lazar, J. B. (Eds.). (1980). *Attitudes toward the mentally ill: Research perspectives* [Report of an NIMH workshop]. Rockville, MD: National Institutes of Mental Health.

Rachlin, H. (1990). Why do people gamble and keep gambling despite heavy losses? *Psychological Science, 1,* 294–297.

Radke-Yarrow, M., Zahn-Waxler, C., & Chapman, M. (1983). Children's prosocial dispositions and behavior. In P. H. Mussen (Ed.), *Handbook of child development: Socialization, personality, and social development* (Vol. 4, pp. 469–545). New York: Wiley.

Rahe, R. H., & Arthur, R. J. (1978, March). Life change and illness studies: Past history and future directions. *Journal of Human Stress,* pp. 3–15.

Rajaram, S., & Roediger, H. L., III (1993). Direct comparison of four implicit memory tests. *Journal of Experimental Psychology: Learning, Memory, and Cognition, 19,* 765–776.

Rand, C. S., & Kuldau, J. M. (1992). Epidemiology of bulimia and symptoms in a general population: Sex, age, race, and socioeconomic status. *International Journal of Eating Disorders, 11,* 37–44.

Rapoport, J. L. (1989, March). The biology of obsessions and compulsions. *Scientific American,* pp. 83–89.

Ratcliff, R. (1978). A theory of memory retrieval. *Psychological Review, 85,* 59–108.

Ratcliff, R., & McKoon, G. (1978). Priming in item recognition: Evidence for the propositional structure of sentences. *Journal of Verbal Learning and Verbal Behavior, 17,* 403–418.

Raymond, J. S., Chung, C. S., & Wood, D. W. (1991). Asia-Pacific prevention research: Challenges, opportunities and implementation. *American Psychologist, 46,* 528–531.

Reed, G. M., Kemeny, M. E., Taylor, S. E., Wang, H-Y. J., & Visscher, B. R. (1994). Realistic acceptance as a predictor of decreased survival time in gay men with AIDS. *Health Psychology, 13,* 299–307.

Regan, R. T. (1971). Effects of a favor and liking on compliance. *Journal of Experimental Social Psychology, 7,* 627–639.

Regier, D. A., Boyd, J. H., Burke, J. D., Rae, D. S., Myers, J. K., Kramer, M., Robins, L. N., George, L. K., Karno, M., & Locke, B. Z. (1988). One-month prevalence of mental disorders in the United States. *Archives of General Psychiatry, 45,* 977–986.

Regier, D. A., Farmer, M. E., Rae, D. S., Myers, J. K., Kramer, M., Robins, L. N., George, L. K., Karno, M., & Locke, B. Z. (1993a). One-month prevalence of mental disorders in the United States and sociodemographic characteristics: The Epidemiological Catchment Area Study. *Acta Psychiatrica Scandinavica, 88,* 35–47.

Regier, D. A., Narrow, W. E., Rae, D. S., Manderscheid, R. W., Locke, B. Z., & Goodwin, F. K. (1993b). The de facto US mental and addictive disorders service system: Epidemiologic Catchment Area prospective 1-year rates of disorders and services. *Archives of General Psychiatry, 50,* 85–94.

Rehm, L. P. (1977). A self-control model of depression. *Behavior Therapy, 8,* 787–804.

Reinitz, M. T., Morrissey, J., & Demb, J. (1994). Role of attention in face encoding. *Journal of Experimental Psychology: Learning, Memory, and Cognition, 20,* 161–168.

Reisenzein, R. (1983). The Schachter theory of emotion: Two decades later. *Psychological Bulletin, 94,* 239–264.

Rescorla, R. A. (1966). Predictability and number of pairings in Pavlovian fear conditioning. *Psychonomic Science, 4,* 383–384.

Rescorla, R. A. (1988). Pavlovian conditioning: It's not what you think it is. *American Psychologist, 43,* 151–160.

Rescorla, R. A., & Wagner, A. R. (1972). A theory of Pavlovian conditioning: Variations in the effectiveness of reinforcement and nonreinforcement. In A. H. Black & W. F. Prokasy (Eds.), *Classical conditioning, II: Current research and theory* (pp. 64–94). New York: Appleton-Century-Crofts.

Resnick, S. M. (1992). Positron emission tomography in psychiatric illness. *Current Directions in Psychological Science, 1,* 92–98.

Rest, J. R., & Thoma, S. J. (1976). Relation of moral judgment development to formal education. *Developmental Psychology, 21,* 709–714.

Restrepo, D., Miyamoto, T., Bryant, B. P., & Teeter, J. H. (1990). Odor stimuli trigger influx of calcium into olfactory neurons of the channel catfish. *Science, 249,* 1166–1168.

Revkin, A. C. (1989, January). Dilutions of grandeur. *Discover, 10,* pp. 74–75.

Reykowski, J., & Smolenska, Z. (1993). Collectivism, individualism and interpretation of social change: A psychological analysis of threats. *Polish Psychological Bulletin, 24,* 89–108.

Rheingold, H. L., & Cook, K. V. (1974). The contents of boys' and girls' rooms as an index of parents' behavior. *Child Development, 46,* 459–463.

Riger, S. (1992). Epistemological debates, feminist voices: Science, social values, and the study of women. *American Psychologist, 47,* 730–740.

Rips, L. J. (1990). Reasoning. *Annual Review of Psychology, 41,* 321–353.

Roberts, A. H., Kewman, D. G., Mercier, L., & Hovell, M. (1993). The power of nonspecific effects in healing: Implications for psychosocial and biological treatments. *Clinical Psychology Review, 13,* 375–391.

Robinson, L. A., Berman, J. S., & Neimeyer, R. A. (1990). Psychotherapy for the treatment of depression: A comprehensive review of controlled outcome research. *Psychological Bulletin, 108,* 30–49.

Rock, I. (1983). *The logic of perception.* Cambridge, MA: Bradford Books/MIT Press.

Rock, I. (1986). The description and analysis of object and event perception. In K. R. Boff, L. Kaufman, & J. P. Thomas (Eds.), *Handbook of perception and human performance* (Vol. 2, pp. 33–71). New York: Wiley.

Rock, I., & Gutman, D. (1981). The effect of inattention on form perception. *Journal of Experimental Psychology: Human Perception and Performance, 7,* 275–285.

Rockmore, M. (1985, March 5). Analyzing analysis. *American Way,* pp. 71–75.

Rodin, J. (1981). Current status of the internal-external hypothesis for obesity: What went wrong? *American Psychologist, 26,* 361–372.

Rodin, J. (1983, April). Behavioral medicine: Beneficial effects of self-control training in aging. *International Review of Applied Psychology, 32,* 153–181.

Rodin, J. (1986). Aging and health: Effects of the sense of control. *Science, 233,* 1271–1276.

Rodin, J., & Langer, E. (1977). Long-term effects of a control-relevant intervention among the institutionalized aged. *Journal of Personality and Social Psychology, 35,* 897–092.

Roediger, H. L. (1990). Implicit memory. *American Psychologist, 45,* 1043–1056.

Rogers, C. R. (1947). Some observations on the organization of personality. *American Psychologist, 2,* 358–368.

Rogers, C. R. (1951). *Client-centered therapy: Its current practice, implications and theory.* Boston: Houghton Mifflin.

Rogers, C. R. (1959). A theory of therapy, personality, and interpersonal relationships, as developed in the client-centered framework. In S. Koch (Ed.), *Psychology: A study of a science* (Vol. 3). New York: McGraw-Hill.

Rogers, C. R. (1977). *On personal power: Inner strength and its revolutionary impact.* New York: Delacorte.

Rogers, M., & Smith, K. (1993). Public perceptions of subliminal advertising: Why practitioners shouldn't ignore this issue. *Journal of Advertising Research, 33*(2), 10–18.

Rogers, R. W. (1984). Changing health-related attitudes and behavior: The role of preventative health psychology. In J. H. Harver, J. E. Maddux, R. P. McGlynn, & C. D. Stolenberg (Eds.), *Social perception in clinical and consulting psychology* (Vol. 2, pp. 91–112). Lubbock: Texas Tech University Press.

Rogers, S. (1993). How a publicity blitz created the myth of subliminal advertising. *Public Relations Quarterly, 37,* 12–17.

Rohrer, J. H., Baron, S. H., Hoffman, E. L., & Swinder, D. V. (1954). The stability of autokinetic judgment. *Journal of Abnormal and Social Psychology, 49,* 595–597.

Rolls, B. J., Fedoroff, I. C., & Guthrie, J. F. (1991). Gender differences in eating behavior and body weight regulation. *Health Psychology, 10,* 133–142.

Rolls, B. J., Rowe, E. A., Rolls, E. T., Kingston, B., Megson, A., & Gunary, R. (1981). Variety in a meal enhances food intake in man. *Physiology & Behavior, 26,* 215–221.

Rorer, L. G., & Widiger, T. A. (1983). Personality structure and assessment. *Annual Review of Psychology, 34,* 431–463.

Rorschach, H. (1942). *Psychodiagnostics: A diagnostic test based on perception.* New York: Grune & Stratton.

Rosch, E. H. (1973). Natural categories. *Cognitive Psychology, 4,* 328–350.

Rosch, E. H. (1978). Principles of categorization. In E. Rosch & B. B. Lloyd (Eds.), *Cognition and categorization* (pp. 27–48). Hillsdale, NJ: Erlbaum.

Rosch, E. H., Mervis, C. B., Gray, W. D., Johnson, D. M., & Boyes-Braem, P. (1976). Basic objects in natural categories. *Cogntive Psychology, 8,* 382–439.

Rosen, H. S., & Rosen, L. A. (1983). Eliminating stealing: Use of stimulus control with an elementary student. *Behavior Modification, 7,* 56–63.

Rosenbaum, M., & Berger, M. M. (Eds.). (1975). *Group psychotherapy and group function* (Rev. ed.). New York: Basic Books.

Rosenbaum, M., & Muroff, M. (Eds.). (1984). *Fourteen contemporary reinterpretations.* New York: Free Press.

Rosenbaum, M. E. (1986). The repulsion hypothesis: On the nondevelopment of relationships. *Journal of Personality and Social Psychology, 51,* 1156–1166.

Rosenberg, D. (1990, November 19). Bad times at Hangover U.: College parties lead to ER or drunk tank. *Newsweek, 116,* p. 81.

Rosenhan, D. L. (1973). On being sane in insane places. *Science, 179,* 250–258.

Rosenhan, D. L. (1975). The contextual nature of psychiatric diagnoses. *Journal of Abnormal Psychology, 84,* 462–474.

Rosenhan, D. L., & Seligman, M. E. P. (1989). *Abnormal psychology* (2nd ed.). New York: Norton.

Rosenthal, A. M. (1964). *Thirty-eight witnesses.* New York: McGraw-Hill.

Rosenthal, D., Wender, P. H., Kety, S. S., Schulsinger, F., Weiner, J., & Rieder, R. (1975). Parent–child relationships and psychopathological disorder in the child. *Archives of General Psychiatry, 32,* 466–476.

Rosenthal, R. (1966). *Experimenter effects in behavioral research.* New York: Appleton-Century-Crofts.

Rosenthal, R. (1974). *On the social psychology of the self-fulfilling prophecy: Further evidence for Pygmalion effects and their mediating mechanisms.* New York: MSS Modular Publications.

Rosenthal, R., & Jacobson, L. F. (1968). *Pygmalion in the classroom: Teacher expectations and intellectual development.* New York: Holt.

Rosenwald, G. C., & Ochberg, R. L. (1992). *Storied lives: The cultural politics of self-understanding.* New Haven: Yale University Press.

Rosenzweig, M. R. (1984a). U.S. psychology and world psychology. *American Psychologist, 39,* 877–884.

Rosenzweig, M. R. (1984b). Experience, memory, and the brain. *American Psychologist, 39,* 365–376.

Rosenzweig, M. R. (1992). Psychological science around the world. *American Psychologist, 47,* 718–722.

Ross, B. H., & Kennedy, P. T. (1990). Generalizing from the use of earlier examples in problem solving. *Journal of Experimental Psychology: Learning, Memory, and Cognition, 16,* 42–55.

Ross, L. (1977). The intuitive psychologist and his shortcomings. In L. Berkowitz (Ed.), *Advances in experimental social psychology* (Vol. 10). New York: Academic Press.

Ross, L. (1988). Situational perspectives on the obedience experiments. [Review of The obedience experiments: A case study of controversy in social science]. *Contemporary Psychology, 33,* 101–104.

Ross, L., Amabile, T., & Steinmetz, J. (1977). Social roles, social control and biases in the social perception process. *Journal of Personality and Social Psychology, 37,* 485–494.

Ross, L., & Anderson, C. A. (1982). Shortcomings in the attribution process: On the origins and maintenance of erroneous social assessments. In D. Kahneman, P. Slovic, & A. Tversky (Eds.), *Judgment under uncertainty: Heuristics and biases* (pp. 132–152). Cambridge: Cambridge University Press.

Ross, L., & Nisbett, R. E. (1991). *The person and the situation: Perspectives of social psychology.* New York: McGraw-Hill.

Rossi, A. (1984). Gender and parenthood. *American Sociological Review, 49,* 1–19.

Roth, T., Roehrs, T., Carskadon, M. A., & Dement, W. C. (1989). Daytime sleepiness and alertness. In M. Kryser, T. Roth, & W. C. Dement (Eds.), *Principles and practice of sleep medicine* (pp. 14–23). New York: Saunders.

Rothbaum, B. O., Hodges, L. F., Kooper, R., Opdyke, D., Williford, J. S., & North, M. (1995). Effectiveness of computer-generated (virtual reality) graded exposure in the treatment of acrophobia. *American Journal of Psychiatry, 152,* 626–628.

Rothman, D. J. (1971). *The discovery of the asylum: Social order and disorder in the new republic.* Boston: Little, Brown.

Rotter, J. B. (1954). *Social learning and clinical psychology.* Englewood Cliffs, NJ: Prentice-Hall.

Rowan, A. B., & Foy, D. W. (1993). Post-traumatic stress disorder in child sexual abuse survivors: A literature review. *Journal of Traumatic Stress, 6,* 3–20.

Rozin, P. (1976). The evolution of intelligence and access to the cognitive unconscious. In J. M. Sprague & A. A. Epstein (Eds.), *Progress in psychobiology and physiological psychology* (pp. 245–280). New York: Academic Press.

Rozin, P., & Fallon, A. E. (1987). A perspective on disgust. *Psychological Review, 94,* 23–41.

Rozin, P., Millman, L., & Nemeroff, C. (1986). Operation of the laws of sympathetic magic in disgust and other domains. *Journal of Personality and Social Psychology, 50,* 703–712.

Rubin, D. C., & Kontis, T. C. (1983). A schema for common cents. *Memory & Cognition, 11,* 335–341.

Rubin, J. Z., Provenzano, F. J., & Luria, Z. (1974). The eye of the beholder: Parents' views on sex of newborns. *American Journal of Orthopsychiatry, 44,* 512–519.

Ruch, R. (1937). *Psychology and life.* Glenview, IL: Scott, Foresman.

Ruitenbeek, H. M. (1973). *The first Freudians.* New York: Jason Aronson.

Rumelhart, D. E., & McClelland, J. L. (1986). *Parallel distributed processing: Explorations in the microstructure of cognition* (2 vols.). Cambridge, MA: MIT Press.

Rumelhart, D. E., Smolensky, P., McClelland, J. L., & Hinton, G. E. (1986). Schemata and sequential thought processes in PDP models. In J. L. McClelland & D. E. Rumelhart (Eds.), *Parallel distributed processing: Vol. 2. Psychological and biological models* (pp. 7–57). Cambridge, MA: MIT Press.

Runco, M. A. (1991). *Divergent thinking.* Norwood, NJ: Ablex.

Russell, B. (1948). *Human knowledge, its scope and limits.* New York: Simon & Schuster.

Russell, J. A., & Ward, L. M. (1982). Environmental psychology. *Annual Review of Psychology, 33,* 651–688.

Rutter, M. (1979). Maternal deprivation, 1972–1978: New findings, new concepts, new approaches. *Child Development, 50,* 283-305.

Rutter, M. (1981a). *Maternal deprivation reassessed.* New York: Penguin.

Rutter, M. (1981b). Social-emotional consequences of day care for children. *American Journal of Orthopsychiatry, 51,* 4–28.

Rutter, M., Macdonald, H., Le Couteur, A., Harrington, R., Bolton, P., & Bailey, A. (1990). Genetic factors in child psychiatric disorders—II. Empirical findings. *Journal of Child Psychology and Psychiatry, 31,* 39–83.

Rychlak, J. (1979). *Discovering free will and personal responsibility.* New York: Oxford University Press.

Ryff, C. D. (1989). In the eye of the beholder: Views of psychological well-being among middle-aged and older adults. *Psychology and Aging, 4,* 195–210.

Ryff, C. D. (1991). Possible selves in adulthood and old age: A tale of shifting horizons. *Psychology and Aging, 6,* 286–295.

Saarinen, T. F. (1987). *Centering of mental maps of the world: Discussion paper.* Tucson: University of Arizona, Department of Geography and Regional Development.

Sachs, S. (1990, May 28). Romanian children suffer in asylums. *San Francisco Chronicle,* p. A-12.

Sacks, O. (1973). *Migraine: Evolution of a common disorder.* Berkeley: University of California Press.

Salovey, P., & Birnbaum, D. (1989). Influence of mood on health-relevant cognitions. *Journal of Personality and Social Psychology, 57,* 539–551.

Salovey, P., & Hancock, M. E. (1987). *The effects of state mood, trait depression, and cognitive set on personal health appraisal.* Unpublished manuscript, Yale University, New Haven.

Salzman, C. D., Britten, K. H., & Newsome, W. T. (1990). Cortical microstimulation influences perceptual judgements of motion direction. *Nature, 346,* 174–177.

Samuel, A. G. (1981). Phonemic restoration: Insights from a new methodology. *Journal of Experimental Psychology: General, 110,* 474–494.

Samuel, A. G. (1991). A further examination of attentional effects in the phonemic restoration illusion. *Quarterly Journal of Experimental Psychology: Human Experimental Psychology, 43A,* 679–699.

San Francisco Chronicle. (1995, February 17, p. D15). Defendant in train killings says victim was gunman.

San Francisco Chronicle. (1995, February 18, pp. 1, A16). Guilty verdict in massacre on N.Y. train.

San Francisco Examiner-Chronicle. (1991, August 26, p. A10). Yeltsin says KGP unit refused plotter's orders to seize him.

Sapolsky, R. (1990). In *Discovering Psychology,* Program 4 [PBS video series]. Washington, DC: Annenberg/CPB Project.

Sapolsky, R. M. (1994). *Why zebras don't get ulcers: A guide to stress, stress-related disease, and coping.* New York: Freeman.

Sarason, I. G., Johnson, J. H., & Siegel, J. M. (1978). Assessing the impact of life changes: Development of the Life Experiences Survey. *Journal of Consulting and Clinical Psychology, 46,* 932–946.

Satir, V. (1967). *Conjoint family therapy* (Rev. ed.). Palo Alto, CA: Science and Behavior Books.

Sattler, J. M. (1982). *Assessment of children's intelligence and special abilities.* Boston: Allyn and Bacon.

Sattler, J. M., & Atkinson, L. (1993). Item equivalence across scales: The WPPSI-R and WISC-III. *Psychological Assessment, 5,* 203–206.

Sawyer, J. (1966). Measurement and prediction, clinical and statistical. *Psychological Bulletin, 66,* 178–200.

Scarr, S. (1988). How genotypes and environments combine: Development and individual differences. In N. Bolger, A. Caspi, G. Downey, & M. Morehouse (Eds.), *Persons in context: Developmental processes.* New York: Cambridge University Press.

Scarr, S., & Eisenberg, M. (1993). Child care research: Issues, perspectives, and results. *Annual Review of Psychology, 44,* 613–644.

Scarr, S., Phillips, D., & McCartney, K. (1990). Facts, fantasies and the future of child care in the United States. *Psychological Science, 1,* 26–35.

Scarr, S., & Weinberg, R. A. (1976). I.Q. test performance of black children adopted by white families. *American Psychologist, 31,* 726–739.

Schab, F. R. (1990). Odors and the remembrance of things past. *Journal of Experimental Psychology: Learning, Memory, and Cognition, 16,* 648–655.

Schachter, S. (1959). *The psychology of affiliation.* Stanford, CA: Stanford University Press.

Schachter, S. (1971a). Some extraordinary facts about obese humans and rats. *American Psychologist, 26,* 129–144.

Schachter, S. (1971b). *Emotion, obesity and crime.* New York: Academic Press.

Schachter, S., & Singer, J. E. (1962). Cognitive, social and physiological determinants of emotional state. *Psychological Review, 69,* 379–399.

Schaie, K. W. (1989). The hazards of cognitive aging. *The Gerontologist, 29,* 484–493.

Schaie, K. W. (1993). Ageist language in psychological research. *American Psychologist, 48,* 49–51.

Schaie, K. W., & Willis, S. L. (1986). Can decline in adult intellectual functioning be reversed? *Developmental Psychology, 22,* 223–232.

Schank, R. C., & Abelson, R. (1977). *Scripts, plans, goals and understanding: An inquiry into human knowledge and structures.* Hillsdale, NJ: Erlbaum.

Schatzberg, A. F. (1991). Overview of anxiety disorders: Prevalence, biology, course, and treatment. *Journal of Clinical Psychiatry, 42,* 5–9.

Schaufeli, W. B., Maslach, C., & Marek, T. (1993). *Professional burnout: Recent developments in theory and research.* Washington, DC: Taylor & Francis.

Schleifer, S. J., Keller, S. E., Camerino, M., Thornton, J. C., & Stein, M. (1983). Suppression of lymphocyte stimulation following bereavement. *Journal of the American Medical Association, 250,* 374–377.

Schmidt, D. F., & Boland, S. M. (1986). Structure of perceptions of older adults: Evidence for multiple stereotypes. *Psychology and Aging, 1,* 255–260.

Schmidt, W. E. (1987, June 7). Paddling in school: A tradition is under fire. *The New York Times,* pp. A1, A22.

Schneider, K., & May, R. (1995). *The psychology of existence: An integrative, clinical perspective.* New York: McGraw-Hill.

Schreiber, F. (1973). *Sybil.* New York: Warner Books.

Schroeder, C. M., & Prentice, D. A. (1995). *Pluralistic ignorance and alcohol use on campus II: Correcting misperceptions of the social norm.* Unpublished manuscript, Princeton University.

Schroeder, D. A., Penner, L. A., Dovido, J. F., & Piliavin, J. A. (1995). *The psychology of helping and altruism.* New York: McGraw-Hill.

Schultz, R., Braun, R. G., & Kluft, R. P. (1989). Multiple personality disorder: Phenomenology of selected variables in comparison to major depression. *Dissociation, 2,* 45–51.

Schwartz, B. L., & Metcalfe, J. (1992). Cue familiarity but not target retrievability enhances feeling-of-knowing judgments. *Journal of Experimental Psychology: Learning, Memory, and Cognition, 18,* 1074–1083.

Schwarzer, R. (Ed.). (1992). *Self-efficacy: Thought control of action.* Washington, DC: Hemisphere.

Schwebel, A. I., & Fine, M. A. (1994). *Understanding and helping families: A cognitive-behavioral approach.* Hillsdale, NJ: Erlbaum.

Scott, J. P. (1963). The process of primary socialization in canine and human infants. *Monographs of the Society for Research in Child Development, 28,* 1–47.

Scovern, A. W., & Kilmann, P. R. (1980). Status of electroconvulsive therapy: Review of outcome literature. *Psychological Bulletin, 87,* 260–303.

Scull, A. (1993). *A most solitary of afflictions: Madness and society in Britain 1700–1900.* London: Yale University Press.

Searle, J. R. (1979a). Metaphor. In A. Ortony (Ed.), *Metaphor and thought* (pp. 92–123). Cambridge: Cambridge University Press.

Searle, J. R. (1979b). Literal meaning. In J. R. Searle (Ed.), *Expression and meaning* (pp. 117–136). Cambridge: Cambridge University Press.

Seger, C. A. (1994). Implicit learning. *Psychological Bulletin, 115,* 163–196.

Seidenberg, M. S. (1993). Connectionist models and cognitive theory. *Psychological Science, 4,* 228–235.

Sekuler, R., & Blake, R. (1994). *Perception* (3rd ed.). New York: McGraw-Hill.

Self, E. A. (1990). Situational influences on self-handicapping. In R. L. Higgins, C. R. Snyder, & S. Berglas (Eds.), *Self-handicapping: The paradox that isn't* (pp. 37–68). New York: Plenum Press.

Selfridge, O. G. (1955). Pattern recognition and modern computers. *Proceedings of the Western Joint Computer Conference.* New York: Institute of Electrical and Electronics Engineers.

Seligman, K. (1988, October 9). Educators are alarmed over testing frenzy. *San Francisco Examiner,* pp. B-1, B-5.

Seligman, M. E. P. (1971). Preparedness and phobias. *Behavior Therapy, 2,* 307–320.

Seligman, M. E. P. (1975). *Helplessness: On depression, development, and death.* San Francisco: Freeman.

Seligman, M. E. P. (1987). *Predicting depression, poor health and presidential elections.* Washington, DC: Federation of Behavioral, Psychological and Cognitive Sciences.

Seligman, M. E. P. (1991). *Learned optimism.* New York: Norton.

Seligman, M. E. P., & Maier, S. F. (1967). Failure to escape traumatic shock. *Journal of Experimental Psychology, 74,* 1–9.

Selye, H. (1956). *The stress of life.* New York: McGraw-Hill.

Selye, H. (1976). *Stress in health and disease.* Reading, MA: Butterworth.

Selye, H. (1976). *The stress of life* (2nd ed.). New York: McGraw-Hill.

Serrano, J. M., Iglesias, J., & Loeches, A. (1992). Visual discrimination and recognition of facial expressions of anger, fear, and surprise in 4- to 6-month-old infants. *Developmental Psychobiology, 25,* 411–425.

Seruler, R., & Blake, R. (1994). *Perception* (3rd ed.). New York: McGraw Hill.

Shafii, M., Carrigan, S., Whittinghill, J. R., & Derrick, A. (1985). Psychological autopsy of completed suicide in children and adolescents. *American Journal of Psychiatry, 142,* 1061–1064.

Shafir, E. (1993). Choosing versus rejecting: Why some options are both better and worse than others. *Memory & Cognition, 21,* 546–556.

Shapiro, D. A., Barkham, M., Rees, A., Hardy, G. E., Reynolds, S., & Startup, M. (1994). Effects of treatment duration and severity of depression on the effectiveness of cognitive-behavioral and psychodynamic-interpersonal psychotherapy. *Journal of Consulting and Clinical Psychology, 62,* 522–534.

Shapiro, D. H. (1985). Clinical use of meditation as a self-regulation strategy: Comments on Holmes's conclusions and implications. *American Psychologist, 40,* 719–722.

Shapiro, F. (1991). Eye movement desensitization & reprocessing: From EMD to EMDR—a new treatment model for anxiety and related traumata. *Behavior Therapist, 14,* 133–135.

Shapiro, F. (1995). *Desensitization and reprocessing: Basic principles, protocols, and procedures.* New York: Guilford Press.

Shapiro, L. P., Nagel, H. N., & Levine, B. A. (1993). Preferences for a verb's complements and their use in sentence processing. *Journal of Memory and Language, 32,* 96–114.

Shatz, M., & Gelman, R. (1973). The development of communication skills: Modifications in the speech of young children as a function of listener. *Monographs of the Society for Research in Child Development, 38*(5, Serial No. 152).

Shatz, M., Wellman, H. M., & Silber, S. (1983). The acquisition of mental verbs: A systematic investigation of the first reference ot mental state. *Cognition, 14,* 301–321.

Shaver, P. R., & Hazan, C. (1994). Attachment. In A. L. Weber & J. H. Harvey (Eds.), *Perspectives on close relationships* (pp. 110–130). Boston: Allyn and Bacon.

Shaw, R., & Turvey, M. T. (1981). Coalitions as models for ecosystems: A realist perspective on perceptual organization. In M. Kubovy & J. R. Pomerantz (Eds.), *Perceptual organization* (pp. 343–346). Hillsdale, NJ: Erlbaum.

Sheldon, W. (1942). *The varieties of temperament: A psychology of constitutional differences.* New York: Harper.

Shepard, R. N. (1978). Externalization of mental images and the act of creation. In B. S. Randhawa & W. E. Coffman (Eds.), *Visual learning, thinking, and communicating.* New York: Academic Press.

Shepard, R. N. (1984). Ecological constraints on internal representation: Resonant kinematics of perceiving, imagining, thinking and dreaming. *Psychological Review, 91,* 417–447.

Shepard, R. N., & Cooper, L. A. (1982). *Mental images and their transformations.* Cambridge, MA: MIT Press.

Shepard, R. N., & Jordan, D. S. (1984). Auditory illusions demonstrating that tones are assimilated to an internalized musical scale. *Science, 226,* 1333–1334.

Shepp, B., & Ballisteros, M. (Eds.). (1989). *Object perception.* Hillsdale, NJ: Erlbaum.

Sheridan, C. L., & King, R. G. (1972). Obedience to authority with an authentic victim. Proceedings from the 80th Annual Convention. *American Psychological Association, Part I, 7,* 165–166.

Sherif, C. W. (1981, August). *Social and psychological bases of social psychology,* The G. Stanley Hall lecture on social psychology, presented at the annual convention of the American Psychological Association, Los Angeles.

Sherif, M. (1935). A study of some social factors in perception. *Archives of Psychology, 27*(187).

Sherif, M., Harvey, O. J., White, B. J., Hood, W. E., & Sherif, C. W. (1961). *Intergroup conflict and cooperation: The Robbers Cave experiment.* Norman: University of Oklahoma Press.

Sherif, M., Harvey, O. J., White, B. J., Hood, W. R., & Sherif, C. W. (1988). *The Robbers Cave experiment: Intergroup conflict and cooperation.* Middletown, CT: Wesleyan University Press. (Original work published 1961.)

Sherrod, K., Vietze, P., & Friedman, S. (1978). *Infancy.* Monterey, CA: Brooks/Cole.

Shettleworth, S. J. (1993). Where is the comparison in comparative cognition? *Psychological Science, 4,* 179–184.

Shidlo, A. (1994). Internalized homophobia: Conceptual and empirical issues in measurement. In B. Greene & G. M. Herek (Eds.), *Lesbian and gay psychology: Theory, research, and clinical applications* (pp. 176–205). Thousand Oaks, CA: Sage Publications.

Shiffrar, M. (1994). When what meets where. *Current Directions in Psychological Science, 3,* 96–100.

Shiffrin, R. M. (1993). Short-term memory: A brief commentary. *Memory & Cognition, 21,* 193–197.

Shiffrin, R. M., & Schneider, W. (1977). Controlled and automatic human information processing: II. Perceptual learning, automatic attending, and a general theory. *Psychological Review, 84,* 127–190.

Shinn, M., & Weitzman, B. C. (1990). Research on homelessness: An introduction. *Journal of Social Issues. 46,* 1–13.

Shirley, M. M. (1931). *The first two years.* Minneapolis: University of Minnesota Press.

Shneidman, E. (1987, March). At the point of no return. *Psychology Today,* pp. 54–59.

Shneidman, E. (1989). The Indian summer of life. *American Psychologist, 44,* 684–694.

Shneidman, E. S. (1985). *Definition of suicide.* New York: Wiley.

Shockley, W. (1968). Human quality problems and research taboos. In J. A. Pintus (Ed.), *New concepts and directions in education* (pp. 87–88). Greenwich, CT: Educational Records Bureau.

Shoda, Y., & Mischel, W. (1993). Cognitive social approach to dispositional inferences: What if the perceiver is a cognitive social theorist? *Personality and Social Psychology Bulletin, 19,* 574–585.

Shoda, Y., Mischel, W., & Wright, J. C. (1993a). The role of situational demands and cognitive competencies in behavior organization and personality coherence. *Journal of Personality and Social Psychology, 65,* 1023–1035.

Shoda, Y., Mischel, W., & Wright, J. C. (1993b). Links between personality judgments and contextualized behavior patterns: Situation-behavior profiles of personality prototypes. *Social Cognition, 11,* 399–429.

Shotter, J. (1984). *Social accountability and selfhood.* Oxford: Basil Blackwell.

Shulman, S. (1993). Close friendships in early and middle adolescence: Typology and friendship reasoning. In B. Laursen (Ed.), *Close friendships in adolescence* (pp. 55–71). San Francisco: Jossey-Bass.

Siegel, B. (1988). *Love, medicine and miracles.* New York: Harper & Row.

Siegel, R. K. (1992). *Fire in the brain.* New York: Dutton.

Siegel, S. (1984). Pavlovian conditioning and heroin overdose: Reports by overdose victims. *Bulletin of the Psychonomic Society, 22,* 428–430.

Siegel, S., Hinson, R. E., Krank, M. D., & McCully, J. (1982). Heroin "overdose" death: The contribution of drug-associated environmental cues. *Science, 216,* 436–437.

Siegelman, M. (1972). Adjustment of homosexual and heterosexual women. *British Journal of Psychiatry, 120,* 477–481.

Silver, E., Cirincione, C., & Steadman, H. J. (1994). Demythologizing inaccurate perceptions of the insanity defense. *Law & Human Behavior, 18,* 63–70.

Silver, R., & Wortman, E. (1980). Coping with undesirable life events. In J. Garber & M. E. P. Seligman (Eds.), *Human helplessness: Theory and application.* New York: Academic Press.

Simkin, L. R., & Gross, A. M. (1994). Assessment of coping with high-risk situations for exercise relapse among healthy women. *Health Psychology, 13,* 274–277.

Simon, H. (1973). The structure of ill-structured problems. *Artifical Intelligence, 4,* 181–202.

Simon, H. A. (1979). *Models of thought* (Vol. 1). New Haven: Yale University Press.

Simon, H. A. (1989). *Models of thought* (Vol. 2). New Haven: Yale University Press.

Sinclair, R. C., Hoffman, C., Mark, M. M., Martin, L. L., & Pickering, T. L. (1994). Construct accessibility and the misattribution of arousal: Schachter and Singer revisited. *Psychological Science, 5,* 15–19.

Singer, D. G., & Singer, J. L. (1990). *The house of make-believe.* Cambridge, MA: Harvard University Press.

Singer, J. L. (1975). Navigating the stream of consciousness: Research in daydreaming and related inner experinece. *American Psychologist, 30,* 727–739.

Singer, J. L. (Ed.). (1990). *Repression and dissociation.* Chicago: University of Chicago Press.

Singer, J. L., & Antrobus, J. S. (1966). *Imaginal process inventory.* New York: Authors.

Singer, J. L., & McCraven, V. J. (1961). Some characteristics of adult daydreaming. *Journal of Psychology, 51,* 151–164.

Skinner, B. F. (1938). *The behavior of organisms.* New York: Appleton-Century-Crofts.

Skinner, B. F. (1953). *Science and human behavior.* New York: Macmillan.

Skinner, B. F. (1957). *Verbal behavior.* New York: Appleton-Century-Crofts.

Skinner, B. F. (1966). What is the experimental analysis of behavior? *Journal of the Experimental Analysis of Behavior, 9,* 213–218.

Skinner, B. F. (1972). *Beyond freedom and dignity.* Toronto: Bantam Books.

Skinner, B. F. (1990). Can psychology be a science of mind? *American Psychologist, 45,* 1206–1210.

Skre, I., Onstad, S., Torgersen, S., Kygren, S., & Kringlen, E. (1993). A twin study of DSM-III-R anxiety disorders. *Acta Psychiatrica Scandinavica, 88,* 85–92.

Sloane, R. B., Staples, F. R., Cristol, A. H., Yorkston, N. J., & Whipple, K. (1975). *Psychotherapy versus behavior therapy.* Cambridge, MA: Harvard University Press.

Slobin, D. I. (1985). Crosslinguistic evidence for the language-making capacity. In D. Slobin (Ed.), *The crosslinguistic study of language acquisition: Vol. 2. Theoretical issues* (pp. 1157–1256). Hillsdale, NJ: Erlbaum.

Sloman, S. A., Hayman, C. A. G., Ohta, N., Law, J., & Tulving, E. (1988). Forgetting in primed fragment completion. *Journal of Experimental Psychology: Learning, Memory, and Cognition, 14,* 223–239.

Smith, D. (1982). Trends in counseling and psychotherapy. *American Psychologist, 37,* 802–809.

Smith, J., & Baltes, P. B. (1990). Wisdom-related knowledge: Age/cohort differences in response to life-planning problems. *Developmental Psychology, 26,* 494–505.

Smith, M. L., & Glass, G. V. (1977). Meta-analysis of psychotherapy outcome studies. *American Psychologist, 32,* 752–760.

Smith, M. L., Glass, G. V., & Miller, T. I. (1980). *The benefits of psychotherapy.* Baltimore: Johns Hopkins University Press.

Smith, T. W. (1992). Hostility and health: Current status of a psychosomatic hypothesis. *Health Psychology, 11,* 139–150.

Snow, R. E. (1995, January 21). *Validity of IQ as a measure of cognitive ability.* Unpublished paper presented at Workshop on IQ testing and educational decision making. San Diego, CA: National Research Council.

Snyder, M. (1984). When beliefs create reality. In L. Berkowitz (Ed.), *Advances in experimental social psychology* (Vol. 18, pp. 247–305). New York: Academic Press.

Snyder, M. (1987). *Public appearances/private realities: The psychology of self-monitoring.* New York: Freeman.

Snyder, M., & Gangestad, S. (1986). On the nature of self-monitoring: Matters of assessment, matters of validity. *Journal of Personality and Social Psychology, 51,* 125–139.

Snyder, M., & Swann, W. B., Jr. (1978). Hypothesis-testing processes in social interaction. *Journal of Personality and Social Psychology, 36,* 1202–1212.

Sobell, M. B., & Sobell, L. C. (1973). Individualized behavior therapy for alcoholics. *Behavior Therapy, 4,* 49–72.

Sobell, M. B., & Sobell, L. C. (1984). The aftermath of heresy: A response to Pendery et al.'s (1982) critique of "individualized behavior therapy for alcoholics." *Behaviour Research and Therapy, 22,* 413–440.

Sokal, M. M. (Ed.). (1987). *Psychological testing and American society, 1890–1930.* New Brunswick, NJ: Rutgers University Press.

Solomon, R., Gerrity, E. T., & Muff, A. M. (1992). Efficacy of treatments of posttraumatic stress disorder. *Journal of the American Medical Association, 268,* 633–638.

Solso, R. L. (1991). *Cognitive psychology* (3rd ed.). Boston: Allyn and Bacon.

Solso, R. L., & McCarthy, J. E. (1981). Prototype formation of faces: A case study of pseudomemory. *British Journal of Psychology, 72,* 499–503.

Sotsky, S. M., Glass, D. R., Shea, T., Pilkonis, P. A., Collins, J. F., Elkin, I., Watkins, J. M. T., Imber, S. D., Leber, W. R., Moyer, J., & Oliveri, M. E. (1991). Patient predictors of response to psychotherapy and pharmacotherapy: Findings in the NIMH Treatment of Depression Collaborate Research Program. *American Journal of Psychiatry, 148,* 997–1008.

Spangler, W. D. (1992). Validity of questionnaire and TAT measures of need for achievement: Two meta-analyses. *Psychological Bulletin, 112,* 140–154.

Spearman, C. (1927). *The abilities of man.* New York: Macmillan.

Speer, S. R., & Kjelgaard, M. M. (1992, November). *The influence of prosodic structure on processing temporary syntactic ambiguity.* Paper presented at the meeting of the Psychonomic Society, St. Louis.

Spelke, E. S. (1988). Where perceiving ends and thinking begins: The apprehension of objects in infancy. *Minnesota Symposium on Child Psychology, 20,* 197–234.

Spelke, E. S. (1991). Physical knowledge in infancy. In S. Carey & R. Gelman (Eds.), *The epigenesis of mind: Essays on biology and cognition* (pp. 133–169). Hillsdale, NJ: Erlbaum.

Spence, M. J., & DeCasper, A. J. (1987). Prenatal experience with low-frequency maternal-voice sounds influences neonatal perception of maternal voice samples. *Infant Behavior and Development, 10,* 133–142.

Sperling, G. (1960). The information available in brief visual presentations. *Psychological Monographs, 74,* 1–29.

Sperling, G. (1963). A model for visual memory tasks. *Human Factors, 5,* 19–31.

Sperry, R. W. (1968). Mental unity following surgical disconnection of the cerebral hemispheres. *The Harvey Lectures,* Series 62. New York: Academic Press.

Spiegel, D., Bloom, J. R., Kraemer, H. C., & Gottheil, E. (1989, October 14). Effect of psychosocial treatment on survival of patients with metastatic breast cancer. *The Lancet,* pp. 888–891.

Spiegel, D., & Cardeña, E. (1991). Disintegrated experience: The dissociative disorders revisited. *Psychological Bulletin, 100,* 366–378.

Spiegel, D., & Scheflin, A. W. (1994). Dissociated or fabricated? Psychiatric aspects of repressed memory in criminal and civil cases. *International Journal of Clinical and Experimental Hypnosis, 42,* 411–432.

Spiro, R. J. (1977). Remembering information from text: The "state of schema" approach. In R. C. Atkinson, R. J. Spiro, & W. E. Montague (Eds.), *Schooling and the acquisition of knowledge.* Hillsdale, NJ: Erlbaum.

Spitz, R. A., & Wolf, K. (1946). Anaclitic depression. *Psychoanalytic Study of Children, 2,* 313–342.

Squire, L. R. (1992). Memory and the hippocampus: A synthesis from findings with rats, monkeys, and humans. *Psychological Review, 99,* 195–231.

Squire, L. R., Amaral, D. G., Zola-Morgan, S., Kritchevsky, M., & Press, G. (1989). Description of brain injury in the amnesic patient N. A. based on magnetic resonance imaging. *Experimental Neurology, 105,* 23–35.

Squire, L. R., Knowlton, B., & Musen, G. (1993). The structure and organization of memory. *Annual Review of Psychology, 44,* 453–495.

Squire, S. (1985, August 19). It's hard to tell a lie. *San Francisco Chronicle,* This World Section, p. 9.

Squire, S. (1988, January 3). Shock therapy. *San Francisco Examiner-Chronicle,* This World Section, p. 16.

Srinivas, K., & Roediger, H. L., III. (1990). Classifying implicit memory tests: Category association and anagram solution. *Journal of Memory and Language, 29,* 389–412.

Stacy, A. W., Newcomb, M. D., & Bentler, P. M. (1991). Cognitive motivation and drug use: A 9-year longitudinal study. *Journal of Abnormal Psychology, 100,* 502–515.

Stampfl, T. G., & Levis, D. J. (1967). Essentials of implosive therapy: A learning theory-based psychodynamic behavioral therapy. *Journal of Abnormal Psychology, 72,* 496–503.

Stanford Daily. (1982, February 2, pp. 1, 3, 5). Rape is no accident, say campus assault victims.

Stark, E. (1985). Breaking the pain habit. *Psychology Today,* 30–37.

Statistical abstracts of the U.S. (1994). Washington, DC: U.S. Government Printing Office.

Steele, C. M. (1988). The psychology of self-affirmation: Sustaining the integrity of the self. In L. Berkowitz (Ed.), *Advances in experimental social psychology* (Vol. 21, pp. 261–302). New York: Academic Press.

Steele, C. M. (1992, April). Race and the schooling of Black Americans. *Atlantic Monthly, 269,* 68–78.

Steinberg, L., Lamborn, S. D., Dornbusch, S. M., & Darling, N. (1992). Impact of parenting practices on adolescent achievement: Authoritative parenting, school involvement, and encouragement to succeed. *Child Development, 63,* 1266–1281.

Steininger, M., Newell, J. D., & Garcia, L. T. (1984). *Ethical issues in psychology.* Homewood, IL: Dorsey.

Stemberger, J. P. (1992). The reliability and replicability of naturalistic speech error data: A comparison with experimentally induced errors. In B. J. Baars (Ed.), *Experimental slips and human error: Exploring the architecture of volition* (pp. 195–215). New York: Plenum Press.

Steriade, M., & McCarley, R. W. (1990). *Brainstem control of wakefulness and sleep.* New York: Plenum Press.

Stern, M., & Karraker, K. H. (1989). Sex stereotyping of infants: A review of gender labeling studies. *Sex Roles, 20,* 501–522.

Stern, W. (1914). The psychological methods of testing intelligence. *Educational Psychology Monographs* (No. 13).

Stern, W. C., & Morgane, P. S. (1974). Theoretical view of REM sleep function: Maintenance of catecholamine systems in the central nervous system. *Behavioral Biology, 11,* 1–32.

Sternberg, R. (1985). *Beyond IQ.* Cambridge, MA: Cambridge University Press.

Sternberg, R. (1986). *Intelligence applied.* San Diego: Harcourt Brace Jovanovich.

Sternberg, R. J. (1988). *The triarchic mind: A new theory of human intelligence.* New York: Viking.

Sternberg, R. J. (1994). Intelligence. In R. J. Sternberg (Ed.), *Handbook of perception and cognition: Vol. 2. Thinking and problem solving* (pp. 263–288). Orlando, FL: Academic Press.

Sternberg, S. (1966). High-speed scanning in human memory. *Science, 153,* 652–654.

Sternberg, S. (1969). Memory-scanning: Mental processes revealed by reaction time experiments. *American Scientist, 57,* 421–457.

Stevens, S. S. (1961). To honor Fechner and repeal his law. *Science, 133,* 80–86.

Stevens, S. S. (1962). The surprising simplicity of sensory metrics. *American Psychologist, 17,* 29–39.

Stevens, S. S. (1975). In G. Stevens (Ed.), *Psychophysics: Introduction to its perceptual, neutral, and social prospects.* New York: Wiley.

Stevenson, H. W., Chen, C., & Lee, S-Y. (1993). Mathematics achievement of Chinese, Japanese, and American children: Ten years later. *Science, 259,* 53–58.

Stevenson, J., Graham, P., Fredman, G., & McLoughlin, V. A. (1987). Twin study of genetic influences on reading and spelling ability and disability. *Journal of Child Psychiatry, 28,* 229–247.

Stipp, D. (1991, January 30). Split personality: Americans are loath to curb energy use despite war concerns. *The Wall Street Journal,* pp. A1, A5.

Stoerig, P. (1993). Sources of blindsight. *Science, 261,* 493.

Stone, A. A., Neale, J. M., Cox, D. S., Napoli, A., Valdimarsdottir, H., & Kennedy-Moore, E. (1994). Daily events are associated with a secretory immune response to an oral antigen in men. *Health Psychology, 13,* 440–446.

Storms, M. D. (1980). Theories of sexual orientation. *Journal of Personality and Social Psychology, 38,* 783–792.

Storms, M. D. (1981). A theory of erotic orientation development. *Psychological Review, 88,* 340–353.

Striegel-Moore, R. H., Silberstein, L. R., & Rodin, J. (1993). The social self in bulimia nervosa: Public self-consciousness, social anxiety, and perceived fraudulence. *Journal of Abnormal Psychology, 102,* 297–303.

Strober, M. (1992). Family-genetic studies. In K. A. Halmi (Ed.), *Psychobiology and treatment of anorexia nervosa and bulimia nervosa* (pp. 61–76). Washington, DC: American Psychiatric Press.

Stroebe, W., Stroebe, M. S., Gergen, K. J., & Gergen, M. (1982). The effects of bereavement on mortality: A social pscyhological analysis. In J. R. Eiser (Ed.), *Social psychology and behavioral medicine* (pp. 527–560). New York: Wiley.

Stroop, J. R. (1935). Studies of interference in serial verbal reactions. *Journal of Experimental Psychology, 18,* 643–662.

Stuart, R. B. (1971). Behavioral contracting with families of delinquents. *Journal of Behavior Therapy and Experimental Psychiatry, 2,* 1–11.

Stunkard, A. J., Harris, J. R., Pedersen, N. L., & McClearn, G. E. (1990). The body mass index of twins who have been reared apart. *New England Journal of Medicine, 322,* 1483–1487.

Styron, W. (1990). Darkness visible: *A memoir of madness.* New York: Random House.

Suchman, A. L., & Ader, R. (1989). Placebo response in humans can be shaped by prior pharmalogic experience. *Psychosomatic Medicine, 51,* 251.

Suedfeld, P. (1980). *Restricted environmental stimulation: Research and clinical applications.* New York: Wiley.

Sullivan, H. S. (1953). *The interpersonal theory of psychiatry.* New York: Norton.

Suls, J., & Marco, C. A. (1990). Relationship between JAS- and FTAS-Type A behavior and non-CHD illness: A prospective study controlling for negative affectivity. *Health Psychology, 9,* 479–492.

Sundberg, N. D., & Matarazzo, J. D. (1979). Psychological assessment of individuals. In M. E. Meyer (Ed.), *Foundations of contemporary psychology* (pp. 580–617). New York: Oxford University Press.

Suomi, S. (1987). Genetic and maternal contributions to individual differences in rhesus monkey biobehavioral development. In N. A. Krasnegor, E. M. Blass, M. A. Hofer, & W. P. Smotherman (Eds.), *Prenatal development: A psychobiological perspective* (pp. 397–420). New York: Academic Press.

Suomi, S. (1990). In *Discovering Psychology,* Program 5 [PBS video series]. Washington, DC: Annenberg/CPB Project.

Suomi, S., & Harlow, H. F. (1972). Social rehabilitation of isolate-reared monkeys. *Developmental Psychology, 6,* 487–496.

Svanum, S., McGrew, J., & Ehrmann, L. (1994). Validity of the substance abuse scales of the MMPI-2 in a college student sample. *Journal of Personality Assessment, 62,* 427–439.

Swann, W. B., & Ely, R. J. (1984). A battle of wills: Self-verification versus bahavioral confirmation. *Journal of Personality and Social Psychology, 46,* 1287–1302.

Swann, W. B., Hixon, J. G., & De La Ronde, C. (1992). Embracing the bitter "truth": Negative self-concepts and marital commitment. *Psychological Science, 3,* 118–121.

Swann, W. B., Jr. (1990). To be adored or to be known? The interplay of self-enhancement and self-verification. In R. M. Sorrentino & E. T. Higgins (Eds.), *Handbook of motivation and cognition* (Vol. 2). New York: Guilford Press.

Swazey, J. P. (1974). *Chlorpromazine in psychiatry: A study of therapeutic innovation.* Cambridge, MA: MIT Press.

Sweeney, J. A., Clementz, B. A., Haas, G. L., Escobar, M. D., Drake, K., & Frances, A. J. (1994). Eye tracking dysfunction in schizophrenia: Characterization of component eye movement abnormalities, diagnostic specificity, and the role of attention. *Journal of Abnormal Psychology, 103,* 222–230.

Sweet, A. (1995). Theoretical perspectives on the clinical use of EMDR. *Behavior Therapist, 18,* 5–6.

Swets, J. A., & Bjork, R. A. (1990). Enhancing human performance: An evaluation of "new age" techniques considered by the U.S. Army. *Psychological Science, 1,* 85–96.

Szasz, T. S. (1961). *The myth of mental illness.* New York: Harper & Row.

Szasz, T. S. (1977). *The manufacture of models.* New York: Dell.

Szasz, T. S. (1979). *The myth of psychotherapy.* Garden City, NY: Doubleday.

Szymanski, S., Kane, J. M., & Leiberman, J. A. (1991). A selective review of biological markers in schizophrenia. *Schizophrenia Bulletin, 17,* 99–111.

Tajfel, H. (Ed.). (1982). *Social identity and intergroup relations.* New York: Cambridge University Press.

Tajfel, H., & Billig, M. (1974). Familiarity and categorization in intergroup behavior. *Journal of Experimental Social Psychology, 10,* 159–170.

Talbot, J. D., Marrett, S., Evans, A. C., Meyer, E., Bushnell, M. C., & Duncan, G. H. (1991). Multiple representations of pain in the human cerebral cortex. *Science, 251,* 1355–1358.

Tarr, M. J. (1994). Visual representation: From features to objects. In V. S. Ramachandran (Ed.), *The encyclopedia of human behavior.* San Diego: Academic Press.

Tarr, M. J., & Pinker, S. (1989). Mental rotation and orientation-dependence in shape recognition. *Cognitive Psychology, 21,* 233–282.

Taylor, S. E. (1986). *Health psychology.* New York: Random House.

Taylor, S. E. (1990). Health psychology: The science and the field. *American Psychologist, 45,* 40–50.

Taylor, S. E., & Brown, J. D. (1988). Illusion and well-being: A social psychological perspective on mental health. *Psychological Bulletin, 103,* 193–210.

Taylor, S. E., & Brown, J. D. (1994). Positive illusions and well-being revisited: Separating fact from fiction. *Psychological Bulletin, 116,* 21–27.

Taylor, S. E., & Clark, L. F. (1986). Does information improve adjustment to noxious events? In M. J. Saks & L. Saxe (Eds.), *Advances in applied social psychology* (Vol. 3, pp. 1–28). Hillsdale, NJ: Erlbaum.

Teasdale, J. D. (1985). Psychological treatments for depression: How do they work? *Behavior Research and Therapy, 23,* 157–165.

Temoshok, L. (1990). On attempting to articulate the biopsychosocial model: Psychological-psychophysiological homeostasis. In H. S. Friedman (Ed.), *Personality and disease* (pp. 203–225). New York: Wiley.

Temoshok, L., & Dreher, H. (1992). *The* Type C *connection: The mind–body link to cancer and your health.* New York: Plume.

Templin, M. (1957). Certain language skills in children: Their development and interrelationships. *Institute of Child Welfare Monograph,* Series No. 26. Minneapolis: University of Minnesota Press.

Tenopyr, M. L., & Oeltjen, P. D. (1982). Personnel selection and classification. *Annual Review of Psychology, 33,* 581–618.

Terman, L. M. (1916). *The measurement of intelligence.* Boston: Houghton Mifflin.

Terman, L. M. (1925). *Genetic studies of genius: Vol 1, Mental and physical traits of a thousand gifted children.* Stanford, CA: Stanford University Press.

Terman, L. M., & Merrill, M. A. (1937). *Measuring intelligence.* Boston: Houghton Mifflin.

Terman, L. M., & Merrill, M. A. (1960). *The Stanford-Binet intelligence scale.* Boston: Houghton Mifflin.

Terman, L. M., & Merrill, M. A. (1972). *Stanford-Binet intelligence scale—manual for the third revision, Form L-M.* Boston: Houghton Mifflin.

Terman, L. M., & Oden, M. H. (1947). The gifted child grows up. *Genetic studies of genius: Vol 4.* Stanford, CA: Stanford University Press.

Terman, L. M., & Oden, M. H. (1959). The gifted group at mid-life. *Genetic studies of genius: Vol. 5.* Stanford, CA: Stanford University Press.

Thatcher, R. W., Walker, R. A., & Giudice, S. (1987). Human cerebral hemispheres develop at different rates and ages. *Science, 236,* 1110–1113.

Thigpen, C. H., & Cleckley, H. A. (1957). *Three faces of Eve.* New York: McGraw-Hill.

Thompson, D. A., & Campbell, R. G. (1977). Hunger in humans induced by 2-Deoxy-D-Glucose: Glucoprivic control of taste preference and food intake. *Science, 198,* 1065–1068.

Thompson, K. (1988, Oct. 2). Fritz Perls. *San Francisco Examiner-Chronicle,* This World Section, pp. 14–16.

Thompson, R. (1990). In *Discovering Psychology,* Program 9 [PBS video series]. Washington, DC: Annenberg/CPB Project.

Thompson, R. A. (1988). Early development in life-span perspective. In P. B. Baltes, D. L. Featherman, & R. J. Lerner (Eds.), *Life-span development and behavior* (Vol. 9, pp. 129–170). Hillsdale, NJ: Erlbaum.

Thompson, R. F. (1984, February 4). Searching for memories: Where and how are they stored in your brain? *Stanford Daily.*

Thompson, R. F. (1986). The neurobiology of learning and memory. *Science, 233,* 941–944.

Thoresen, C. (1990, June 29). *Recurrent coronary prevention program: Results after eight and a half years.* Address given to First International Congress of Behavioral Medicine, Uppsala, Sweden.

Thorndike, E. L. (1898). Animal intelligence. *Psychological Review Monograph Supplement, 2* (4, Whole No. 8).

Thorndike, R. L., Hagen, E. P., & Sattler, J. M. (1986). *Stanford-Binet intelligence scale* (4th ed.). Chicago: Riverside.

Thornton, E. M. (1984). *The Freudian fallacy: An alternative view of Freudian theory.* New York: Dial Press/Doubleday.

Tice, D. M., & Baumeister, R. F. (1990). Self-esteem, self-handicapping, and self-presentation: The strategy of inadequate practice. *Journal of Personality, 58,* 443–464.

Tinbergen, N. (1951). *The study of instinct.* Oxford: Oxford University Press.

Tipper, S. P., & Driver, J. (1988). Negative priming between pictures and words in a selective attention task: Evidence for semantic processing of ignored stimuli. *Memory & Cognition, 16,* 64–70.

Tipper, S. P., Weaver, B., Cameron, S., Brehaut, J. C., & Bastedo, J. (1991). Inhibitory mechanisms of attention in identification and localization tasks: Time course and disruption. *Journal of Experimental Psychology: Learning, Memory, and Cognition, 17,* 681–692.

Titchener, E. B. (1898). The postulates of structural psychology. *Philosophical Review, 7,* 449–453.

Tizard B., & Hodges, J. (1978). The effect of early institutional rearing on the development of eight-year-old children. Journal of *Child Psychology and Psychiatry, 19,* 99–118.

Todd, J. T., & Morris, E. K. (1992). Case histories in the great power of steady misrepresentation. *American Psychologist, 47,* 1441–1453.

Todd, J. T., & Morris, E. K. (1993). Change and be ready to change again. *American Psychologist, 48,* 1158–1159.

Todrank, J., & Bartoshuk, L. M. (1991). A taste illusion: Taste sensation localized by touch. *Physiology & Behavior, 50,* 1027–1031.

Tolman, E. C. (1948). Cognitive maps in rats and men. *Psychological Review, 55,* 189–208.

Tolman, E. C., & Honzik, C. H. (1930). "Insight" in rats. *University of California Publications in Psychology, 4,* 215–232.

Tomkins, S. (1962). *Affect, imagery, consciousness* (Vol. 1). New York: Springer.

Tomkins, S. (1981). The quest for primary motives; Biography and autobiography of an idea. *Journal of Personality and Social Psychology, 41,* 306–329.

Tompkins, R. D. (1981). *Before it's to late. . . . The prevention manual on drug abuse for people who care.* Englewood Cliffs, NJ: Family Information Center.

Torrance, E. P. (1974). *The Torrance tests of creative thinking: Technical-norms manual.* Bensenville, IL: Scholastic Testing Services.

Toth, J. P., Reingold, E. M., & Jacoby, L. L. (1994). Toward a redefinition of implicit memory: Process dissociations following elaborative processing and self-generation. *Journal of Experimental Psychology: Learning, Memory, and Cognition, 20,* 290–303.

Townsend, J. T. (1971). A note on the identifiability of parallel and serial processes. *Perception & Psychophysics, 10,* 161–163.

Townsend, J. T. (1990). Serial vs. parallel processing: Sometimes they look like Tweedledum and Tweedledee but they can (and should) be distinguished. *Psychological Science, 1,* 46–54.

Traue, H. C., & Pennebaker, J. W. (Eds.). (1993). *Emotion, inhibition and health.* Seattle: Hogrefe & Huber.

Treisman, A. (1960). Contextual cues in selective listening. *Quarterly Journal of Experimental Psychology, 12,* 242–248.

Treisman, A. (1986). Properties, parts and objects. In K. Boff, L. Kaufman, & J. Thomas (Eds.), *Handbook of perception and human perfomance, Vol 2.* New York: Wiley.

Treisman, A. (1988). Features and objects: The fourteenth Bartlett Memorial Lecture. *The Quarterly Journal of Experimental Psychology, 40,* 201–237.

Treisman, A. (1992). Perceiving and re-perceiving objects. *American Psychologist, 47,* 862–875.

Treisman, A., & Gelade, G. (1980). A feature integration theory of attention. *Cognitive Psychology, 12,* 97–136.

Treisman, A., & Sato, S. (1990). Conjunction search revisited. *Journal of Experimental Psychology: Human Perception and Performance, 16,* 459–478.

Triandis, H. (1990). Cross-cultural studies of individualism and collectivism. In J. Berman (Ed.), *Nebraska Symposium on Motivation, 1989* (pp. 41–133). Lincoln: University of Nebraska Press.

Triandis, H. (1994). *Culture and social behavior.* New York: McGraw-Hill.

Trinder, J. (1988). Subjective insomnia without objective findings: A pseudodiagnostic classification. *Psychological Bulletin, 103,* 87–94.

Trivers, R. L. (1972). Parental investment and sexual selection. In B. Campbell (Ed.), *Sexual selection and the descent of man* (pp. 139–179). Chicago: Aldine.

Tronick, E., Als, H., & Brazelton, T. B. (1980). Moradic phases: A structural description analysis of infant–mother face to face interaction. *Merrill-Palmer Quarterly, 26,* 3–24.

Trope, I., Rozin, P., Kemler Nelson, D., & Gur, R. C. (1992). Information processing in the separated hemispheres of callosotomy patients: Does the analytic-holistic dichotomy hold? *Brain and Cognition, 19,* 123–147.

Trotter, R. J. (1987, February). Stop blaming yourself. *Psychology Today,* pp. 30–39.

Tucker, W. H. (1994). The science and politics of racial research. Urbana and Chicago: University of Illinois Press.

Tuller, D. (1989, March 8). Male businessmen say lives "empty." *San Francisco Chronicle,* p. B3.

Tulving, E. (1972). Episodic and semantic memory. In E. Tulving & W. Donaldson (Eds.), *Organization of memory.* New York: Academic Press.

Tulving, E. (1983). *Elements of episodic memory.* Oxford: Clarendon Press.

Tulving, E. (1985). Memory and consciousness. *Canadian Psychology, 26,* 1–12.

Tulving, E. (1989). Remembering and knowing the past. *American Scientist, 77,* 361–367.

Tulving, E., Kapur, S., Craik, F. I. M., Moscovitch, M., & Houle, S. (1994). Hemispheric encoding/retrieval asymmetry in episodic memory: Positron emission tomography findings. *Proceedings of the National Academy of Sciences of the United States of America, 91,* 2016–2020.

Tulving, E., & Thompson, D. M. (1973). Encoding specificity and retrieval processes in episodic memory. *Psychological Review, 80,* 352–373.

Tupes, E. G., & Christal, R. C. (1961). *Recurrent personality factors based on trait ratings* (Tech. Rep. No. ASD-TR-61-97). Lackland Air Force Base, TX: U.S. Air Force.

Turk, D. C. (1994). Perspectives on chronic pain: The role of psycholgical factors. *Current Directions in Psychological Science, 3,* 45–48.

Turnbull, C. (1961). *The forest people.* New York: Simon & Schuster.

Turner, B. F., & Adams, C. G. (1988). Reported change in preferred sexual activity over the adult years. *The Journal of Sex Research, 25,* 289–303.

Turner, J. R., Sherwood, A., & Light, K. C. (Eds.). (1992). *Individual differences in cardiovascular response to stress.* New York: Plenum Press.

Tversky, A., & Kahneman, D. (1973). Availability: A heuristic for judging frequency and probability. *Cognitive Psychology, 5,* 207–232.

Tversky, A., & Kahneman, D. (1981). The framing of decisions and the psychology of choice. *Science, 211,* 453–458.

Tversky, A., & Shafir, E. (1992). Choice under conflict: The dynamics of deferred decision. *Psychological Science, 3,* 358–361.

Tyler, L. E. (1965). *The psychology of human differences* (3rd ed.). New York: Appleton-Century-Crofts.

Tyler, L. E. (1974). *Individual differences.* Englewood Cliffs, NJ: Prentice-Hall.

Underwood, B. J. (1948). Retroactive and proactive inhibition after five and forty-eight hours. *Journal of Experimental Psychology, 38,* 28–38.

Underwood, B. J. (1949). Proactive inhibition as a function of time and degree of prior learning. *Journal of Experimental Psychology, 39,* 24–34.

United Press International. (1990, September 4). In P. Shenon, Crisis of drugs remains top priority, Bush says. *The New York Times,* Section A, col. 4, p. 22, September 6, 1990.

United Press International. (1990, September 5). Lest we forget that drug crisis—small signs of progress, but still lots to do. *Los Angeles Times,* Section B, p. 6.

U.S. Department of Health and Human Services. (1990). *Healthy people 2000: National health promotion and disease prevention objectives.* Washington, DC: U.S. Government Printing Office.

U.S. Department of Health and Human Services. (1990). *The health benefits of smoking cessation: A report of the Surgeon General* (DHHS Publication No. CDC 90-8416). Washington, DC: U.S. Government Printing Office.

"U.S. Women Today" (1983, November 11–20). The New York Times poll, reported in the *International Herald Tribune.*

Urban, J., Carlson, E., Egeland, B., & Stroufe, L. A. (1991). Patterns of individual adaptation across childhood. *Development and Psychopathology, 3,* 445–460.

Uttal, D. H., & Perlmutter, M. (1989). Toward a broader conceptualization of development: The role of gains and losses across the life span. *Developmental Review, 9,* 101–132.

Vaillant, G. E. (1977). *Adaptation to life.* Boston: Little, Brown.

Valenstein, E. S. (Ed.). (1980). *The psychosurgery debate.* New York: Freeman.

Valle, V. A., & Frieze, I. H. (1976). Stability of causal attribuions as a mediator in changing expectations for success. *Journal of Personality and Social Psychology, 33,* 579–587.

Van Essen, D. C., Anderson, C. H., & Felleman, D. J. (1992). Information processing in the primate visual system: An integrated systems perspective. *Science, 255,* 419–422.

Vasari, G. (1967). *Lives of the most eminent painters.* New York: Heritage.

Vaughan, E. (1993). Chronic exposure to an environmental hazard: Risk perceptions and self-protective behaviors. *Health Psychology, 12,* 74–85.

Vaughan, E., & Seifert, M. (1992). Variability in the framing of risk issues. *Journal of Social Issues, 48* (4), 119–135.

Veith, I. (1965). *Hysteria: The history of the disease.* Chicago: University of Chicago Press.

Vivano, F. (1989, October 8). When success is a family prize. *San Francisco Examiner-Chronicle,* This World Section, pp. 7–9.

von Hofsten, C., & Lindhagen, K. (1979). Observations on the development of reaching for moving objects. *Journal of Child Psychology, 28,* 158–173.

Vonnegut, M. (1975). *The Eden express.* New York: Bantam.

Vrana, S., & Lauterbach, D. (1994). Prevalence of traumatic events and post-traumatic psychological symptoms in a nonclinical sample of college students. *Journal of Traumatic Stress, 7,* 289–302.

Vroom, V. H. (1964). *Work and motivation.* New York: Wiley.

Wade, E., & Clark, H. H. (1993). Reproduction and demonstration in quotation. *Journal of Memory and Language, 32,* 805–819.

Wade, T. J. (1991). Race and sex differences in adolescent self-perceptions of physical attractiveness and level of self-esteem during early and late adolescence. *Personality and Individual Differences, 12,* 1319–1324.

Walker, L. (1984). Sex differences in the development of moral reasoning: A critical review. *Child Development, 55,* 667–691.

Walker, L. J. (1986). Sex differences in the development of moral reasoning: A rejoinder to Baumrind. *Child Development, 57,* 522–526.

Wallach, M. A., & Kogan, N. (1965). *Modes of thinking in young children.* New York: Holt, Rinehart & Winston.

Wallach, M. A., & Wallach, L. (1983). *Psychology's sanction for selfishness.* San Francisco: Freeman.

Wallis, C. (1984, June 11). Unlocking pain's secrets. *Time,* pp. 58–66.

Walsh, R. N. (1990). *The spirit of shamanism.* Los Angeles: J. P. Tarcher.

Walster, E., Aronson, V., Abrahams, D., & Rottman, L. (1966). Importance of physical attractiveness in dating behavior. *Journal of Personality and Social Psychology, 5,* 508–516.

Walters, C. C., & Grusec, J. E. (1977). *Punishment.* San Francisco: Freeman.

Wanous, J. P. (1980). *Organizational entry: Recruitment, selection and socialization of newcomers.* Reading, MA: Addison-Wesley.

Warchol, M. E., Lambert, P. R., Goldstein, A., & Corwin, J. T. (1993). Regenerative proliferation in inner ear sensory epithelia from adult guinea-pigs and humans. *Science, 259,* 1619–1622.

Warren, R. M. (1970). Perceptual restoration of missing speech sounds. *Science, 167,* 392–393.

Wasserman, E. A. (1993). Comparative cognition: Beginning the second century of study of animal intelligence. *Pychological Bulletin, 113,* 211–228.

Wasserman, E. A. (1994). Animal learning and comparative cognition. In I. P. Levin & J. V. Hinrichs (Eds.), *Experimental psychology: Contemporary methods and applications* (pp. 117–164). Dubuque, IA: Brown & Benchmark.

Wasserman, E. A., DeVolder, C. L., & Coppage, D. J. (1992). Non-similarity-based conceptualization in pigeons via secondary or mediated generalization. *Psychological Science, 3,* 374–379.

Waters, E., Wippman, J., & Stroufe, L. A. (1979). Attachment, positive affect, and competence in the peer group: Two studies in construct validation. *Child Development, 50,* 821–829.

Watkins, L. R., & Mayer, D. J. (1982). Organization of the endogenous opiate and nonopiate pain control systems. *Science, 216,* 1185–1193.

Watson, J. B. (1913). Psychology as the behaviorist views it. *Psychological Review, 20,* 158–177.

Watson, J. B. (1919). *Psychology from the standpoint of a behaviorist.* Philadelphia: Lippincott.

Watson, J. B. (1924). *Behaviorism.* New York: Norton.

Watson, J. B., & Rayner, R. (1920). Conditioned emotional reactions. *Journal of Experimental Psychology, 3,* 1–14.

Watterlond, M. (1983). The holy ghost people. Reprinted in A. L. Hammond & P. G. Zimbardo (Eds.), *Readings on human behavior: The best of Science '80–'86* (pp. 48–55). Glenview, IL: Scott, Foresman.

Watts, M. W. (1994). Was there anything left of the "socialist personality"? Values of Eastern and Western German youth at the beginning of unification. *Political Psychology, 15,* 481–508.

Webb, W. B. (1974). Sleep as an adaptive response. *Perceptual and Motor Skills, 38,* 1023–1027.

Wechsler, D. (1981). *Manual for the Wechsler Adult Intelligence Scale—revised.* New York: Psychological Corporation.

Wechsler, D. (1989). *WPPSI-R manual.* New York: Psychological Corporation.

Wechsler, D. (1991). *WISC-III manual.* New York: Psychological Corporation.

Weibe, D. J. (1991). Hardiness and stress modification: A test of proposed mechanisms. *Journal of Personality and Social Psychology, 60,* 89–99.

Weil, A. T. (1977). The marriage of the sun and the moon. In N. E. Zinberg (Ed.), *Alternate states of consciousness* (pp. 37–52). New York: Free Press.

Weinberger, M., Hiner, S. L., & Tierney, W. M. (1987). In support of hassles as a measure of stress in predicting health outcomes. *Journal of Behavioral Medicine, 10,* 19–31.

Weingardt, K. R., Loftus, E. F., & Lindsay, D. S. (1995). Misinformation revisited: New evidence for the suggestibility of memory. *Memory & Cognition, 23,* 72–82.

Weisberg, R. W. (1986). *Creativity: Genius and other myths.* New York: Freeman.

Weisberg, R. W. (1994). Genius and madness? A quasi-experimental test of the hypothesis that manic-depression increases creativity. *Psychological Science, 5,* 361–367.

Weisenberg, M. (1977). Cultural and racial reaction to pain. In M. Weisenberg (Ed.), *The control of pain.* New York: Psychological Dimensions.

Weiser, N. C., & Meyers, L. S. (1993). Validity and reliability of the revised California Psychological Inventory's Vector 3 Scale. *Educational and Psychological Measurement, 53,* 1045–1054.

Weiskrantz, L. (1993). Sources of blindsight. *Science, 261,* 494.

Weiskrantz, L., Warington, E. K., Sanders, M. D., & Marshall, J. (1974). Visual capacity in the hemianopic field following a restricted occipital ablation. *Brain, 97,* 709–728.

Weissberg, R. P., Caplan, M., & Harwood, R. L. (1991). Promoting competent young people in competence-enhancing environments: A systems-based perspective on primary prevention. *Journal of Consulting and Clinical Psychology, 59,* 830–841.

Weissman, W. W. (1987). Advances in psychiatric epidemiology: Rates and risks for depression. *American Journal of Public Health, 77,* 445–451.

Wellman, H. M. (1990). *The child's theory of mind.* Cambridge, MA: MIT Press.

Wellman, H. M., & Estes, D. (1986). Early understanding of mental entities: A reexamination of childhood realism. *Child Development, 57,* 910–923.

Wellman, H. M., & Gelman, S. A. (1992). Cognitive development: Foundational theories of core domains. *Annual Review of Psychology, 43,* 337–375.

Wellness New Mexico. (1987, Spring, pp. 19–21). Nancy Nurse spoofs the healing profession.

Werker, J. (1991). The ontogeny of speech perception. In I. G. Mattingly & M. Studdert-Kennedy (Eds.), *Modularity and the motor theory of speech perception* (pp. 91–109). Hillsdale, NJ: Erlbaum.

Werker, J. F., & Lalond, F. M. (1988). Cross-language speech perception: Initial capabilities and developmental change. *Developmental Pyschology, 24,* 672–683.

Wertheimer, M. (1923). Untersuchungen zur lehre von der gestalt, II. *Psychologische Forschung, 4,* 301–350.

Wever, E. G. (1949). *Theory of hearing.* New York: Wiley.

Wexler, K. (1982). A principal theory for language acquisition. In E. Wanner & L. R. Gleitman (Eds.), *Language acquisition: The state of the art* (pp. 288–315). Cambridge: Cambridge University Press.

Weyler, J. (1984, September 11). An unforgettable moment: It's one Gabriele wishes she could forget. *Los Angeles Times,* Part III, pp. 1, 10.

White, G. L. (1980). Physical attractiveness and courtship progress. *Journal of Personality and Social Psychology, 39,* 660–668.

Whitbourne, S. K., & Hulicka, I. M. (1990). Ageism in undergraduate psychology texts. *American Psychologist, 45,* 1127–1136.

Wicklund, R. A., & Brehm, J. W. (1976). *Perspectives on cognitive dissonance.* Hillsdale, NJ: Erlbaum.

Wiebe, D. J. (1991). Hardness and stress modification: A test of proposed mechanisms. *Journal of Personality and Social Psychology, 60,* 89–99.

Wiggins, J. S. (1973). *Personality and prediction: Principles of personality and prediction: Principles of personality assessment.* Reading, MA: Addison-Wesley.

Wiggins, J. S., & Pincus, A. L. (1992). Personality: Structure and assessment. *Annual Review of Psychology, 43,* 473–504.

Wilcox, V. L., Kasl, S. V., Berkman, L. F. (1994). Social support and physical disability in older people after hospitalization: A prospective study. *Health Psychology, 13,* 170–179.

Wilder, D. A. (1986). Social categorization: Implications for creation and reduction of intergroup bias. *Advances in Experimental Social Psychology, 19,* 291–355.

Williams, J. B. W., & Spitzer, R. L. (1983). The issue of sex bias in DSM-III. *American Psychologist, 38,* 793–798.

Williams, J. H. (1983). *The psychology of women* (2nd ed.). New York: Norton.

Wilson, E. D., Reeves, A., & Culver, C. (1977). Cerebral commissurotomy for control of intractable seizures. *Neurology, 27,* 708–715.

Wilson, F. A. W., Scalaidhe, S. P. O., & Goldman-Rakic, P. S. (1993). Dissociation of object and spatial processing domains in primate prefrontal cortex. *Science, 260,* 1955–1958.

Wilson, M. (1959). *Communal rituals among the Nyakusa.* London: Oxford University Press.

Wilson, T. D., & Linville, P. E. (1982). Improving the academic performance of college freshmen: Attribution therapy revisited. *Journal of Personality and Social Psychology, 42,* 367–376.

Wilson, T. D., & Linville, P. W. (1985). Improving the performance of college freshmen with attributional techniques. *Journal of Personality and Social Psychology, 49,* 287–293.

Wolf, M., Risley, T., & Mees, H. (1964). Application of operant conditioning procedures to the behavior problems of an autistic child. *Behavior Research and Therapy, 1,* 305–312.

Wolfe, J. M. (1992). The parallel guidance of visual attention. *Current Directions in Psychological Science, 1,* 124–128.

Wolfe, J. M., Friedman-Hill, S. R., & Bilsky, A. B. (1994). Parallel processing of part-whole information in visual search tasks. *Perception & Psychophysics, 55,* 537–550.

Wolman, C. (1975). Therapy and capitalism. *Issues in Radical Therapy, 3* (1).

Wolpe, J. (1958). *Psychotherapy by reciprocal inhibition.* Stanford, CA: Stanford University Press.

Wolpe, J. (1973). *The practice of behavior therapy* (2nd ed.). New York: Pergamon Press.

Wong, D. F., Wanger, H. N., Tune, L. E., Dannals, R. F., Pearlson, G. D., Links, J. M., Tamminga, C. A., Broussolle, E. P., Ravert, H. T., Wilson, A. A., Toung, J. K. T., Malat, J., Willimans, J. A., O'Tuma, L. A., Snyder, S. H., Kuhar, M. J., & Gjedde, A. (1986). Positron emission tomography reveals elevated D2 dopamine receptors in drug-naive schizophrenics. *Science, 234,* 1558–1563.

Wood, J. M., Bootzin, R. R., Kihlstrom, J. F., & Schacter, D. L. (1992). Implicit and explicit memory for verbal information presented during sleep. *Psychological Science, 3,* 236–239.

Wood, R. E., & Bandura, A. (1989). Impact of conceptions of ability on self-regulatory mechanisms and complex decision making. *Journal of Personality and Social Psychology, 56,* 407–415.

Woodworth, R. S. (1918). *Dynamic psychology.* New York: Columbia University Press.

Worchel, S., Lee, J., & Adewole, A. (1975). Effects of supply and demand on ratings of object value. *Journal of Personality and Social Psychology, 32,* 906–914.

Workman, B. (1990, December 1). Father guilty of killing daughter's friend, in '69. *San Francisco Examiner-Chronicle,* pp. 1, 4.

Worthington, E. L., Jr., Martin, G. A., Shumate, M., & Carpenter, J. (1983). The effect of brief Lamaze training and social encouragement on pain endurance in a cold pressor task. *Journal of Applied Social Psychology, 13,* 223–233.

Wortman, C. B., & Silver, R. C. (1989). The myths of coping with loss. *Journal of Consulting and Clinical Psychology, 57,* 349–357.

Wortman, C. B., Silver, R. C., & Kessler, R. C. (1993). The meaning of loss and adjustment to bereavement. In M. S. Stroebe, W. Stroebe, & R. O. Hansson (Eds.), *Handbook of bereavement: Theory, research, and intervention* (pp. 349–366). Cambridge: Cambridge University Press.

Wright, J. C., & Mischel, W. (1987). A conditional approach to dispositional constructs: The local predictability of social behavior. *Journal of Personality and Social Psychology, 53,* 1159–1177.

Wright, R. (1994). *The moral animal.* New York: Pantheon.

Wundt, W. (1907). *Outlines of psychology* (7th ed., C. H. Judd, Trans.). Leipzig: Englemann. (Original work published 1896.)

Wurtman, R. J. (1982). Nutrients that modify brain functions. *Scientific American, 246* (4), 50–59.

Wynne, L. C., Roohey, M. L., & Doane, J. (1979). Family studies. In L. Bellak (Ed.), *The schizophrenic syndrome.* New York: Basic Books.

Yalom, I. D., & Greaves, C. (1977). Group therapy with the terminally ill. *American Journal of Psychiatry, 134,* 396–400.

Yantis, S. (1993). Stimulus-driven attentional capture. *Current Directions in Psychological Science, 2,* 156–161.

Yarrow, L. (1975). *Infant and environment: Early cognitive and motivational development.* New York: Halsted.

Yates, B. (1985). *Self-management.* Belmont, CA: Wadsworth.

Yerkes, R. M., & Dodson, J. D. (1908). The relation of strength of stimulus to rapidity of habit formation. *Journal of Comparative Neurology and Psychology, 18,* 459–482.

Yost, W. A., Poppet, A. N., & Fay, R. R. (Eds.). (1993). Human psychophysics. New York: Springer-Verlag.

Youniss, J., & Smollar, J. (1985). *Adolescent relations with mothers, fathers, and friends.* Chicago: University of Chicago Press.

Yudkin, M. (1984, April). When kids think the unthinkable. *Psychology Today,* pp. 18–20, 24–25.

Zajonc, R. B. (1968). Attitudinal effects of mere exposure. *Journal of Personality and Social Psychology. Monograph Supplement, 9* (2, Part 2), 1–27.

Zajonc, R. B. (1980). Feeling and thinking: Preferences need no inferences. *American Psychologist, 35,* 151–175.

Zaslow, M. J. (1991). Variation in child care quality and its implications for children. *Journal of Social Issues, 47,* 125–138.

Zebb, B. J., & Meyers, L. S. (1993). Reliability and validity of the revised California Psychological Inventory's Vector 1 Scale. *Educational and Psychological Measurement, 53,* 271–280.

Zeiss, R. A., & Dickman, H. R. (1989). PTSD 40 years later: Incidence and person-situation correlates in former POWs. *Journal of Clinical Psychology, 45,* 80–87.

Zelinski, E. M., Gilewski, M. J., & Schaie, K. W. (1993). Individual differences in cross-sectional and 3-year longitudinal memory performance across the adult life span. *Psychology and Aging, 8,* 176–186.

Zhang, Y., Proenca, R., Maffel, M., Barone, M., Leopold, L., & Friedman, J. M. (1994). Positional cloning of the mouse *obese* gene and its human homologue. *Nature, 372,* 425–432.

Zigler, E., & Muenchow, S. (1992). *Head Start: The inside story of America's most successful educational experiment.* New York: Basic Books.

Zigler, E., & Styfco, S. J. (1994). Head Start: Criticisms in a constructive context. *American Psychologist, 49,* 127–132.

Zilboorg, G., & Henry, G. W. (1941). *A history of medical psychology.* New York: Norton.

Zimbardo, P. G. (1975). On transforming experimental research into advocacy for social change. In M. Deutsch & H. Hornstein (Eds.), *Applying social psychology: Implications for research, practice and training.* Hillsdale, NJ: Erlbaum.

Zimbardo, P. G. (1990). *Shyness: What it is, what to do about it* (Rev. ed.). Reading, MA: Addison-Wesley. (Original book published 1977.)

Zimbardo, P. G., & Andersen, S. A. (1993). Understanding mind control: Exotic and mundane mental manipulations. In M. Langone (Ed.), *Recovery from cults* (pp. 104–125). New York: Norton.

Zimbardo, P. G., Andersen, S. M., & Kabat, L. G. (1981). Induced hearing deficit generates experimental paranoia. *Science, 212,* 1529–1531.

Zimbardo, P. G., & Leippe, M. (1991). *The psychology of attitude change and social influence.* New York: McGraw-Hill.

Zimbardo, P. G., & Montgomery, K. D. (1957). The relative strengths of consummatory responses in hunger, thirst, and exploratory drive. *Journal of Comparative and Physiological Psychology, 50,* 504–508.

Zimbardo, P. G., & Radl, S. (1981). *The shy child.* New York: McGraw-Hill.

Zimmerman, B. J., Bandura, A., & Martinez-Pons, M. (1992). Self-motivation for academic attainment: The role of self-efficacy beliefs and personal goal setting. *American Educational Research Journal, 29,* 663–676.

Zubeck, J. P., Pushkar, D., Sansom, W., & Gowing, J. (1961). Perceptual changes after prolonged sensory isolation (darkness and silence). *Canadian Journal of Psychology, 15,* 83–100.

Zucker, R. S., & Lando, L. (1986). Mechanism of transmitter release: Voltage hypothesis and calcium hypothesis. *Science, 231,* 574–579.

Zuckerman, M. (1988). Sensation seeking, risk taking, and health. In M. P. Janisse (Ed.), *Individual differences, stress, and health psychology* (pp. 72–88). New York: Springer-Verlag.

Zuckerman, M. (1990). Some dubious premises in research and theory on racial differences: Scientific, social, and ethical issues. *American Psychologist, 45,* 1297–1303.

Zuckerman, M. (1992). What is a basic factor and which factors are basic? Turtles all the way down. *Personality and Individual Differences, 13,* 675–681.

Credits

Photo and Cartoon Credits

Unless otherwise indicated, all photographs and cartoons are protected by copyright in the name of the photographer or cartoonist. Uncredited photos are the property of Scott, Foresman. Page abbreviations are as follows: T—top, C—center, B—bottom, L—left, R—right.

Chapter 1

1	Carl Olof Larsson. *Self-portrait.* Uffizi, Florence, Italy
4TL	Elizabeth Crews/The Image Works
4TR	© Joel Gordon
4BL	Susan Kuklin/Photo Researchers
4BR	Tom McCarthy/The Picture Cube
6	David Young-Wolff/PhotoEdit
7TL,R	Michael Newman/PhotoEdit
7BL	David Young-Wolff/PhotoEdit
7BR	Michael Newman/PhotoEdit
11	Mary Kate Denny/PhotoEdit
12	© 1995 by Sidney Harris
13	Archives of the History of American Psychology, University of Akron
15	The Laboratory Schools, University of Chicago
16	The Granger Collection
18	American Museum of Natural History
23T	Michael Grecco/Stock Boston
23B	Terri Thuente/*Los Angeles Daily News*/Sygma

Chapter 2

27	Simon Bening. *Self Portrait.* 1558. Victoria & Albert Museum, London, Great Britain
29	© 1995 by Sidney Harris
30	© 1995 by Sidney Harris
31	Ronald C. Modra/*Sports Illustrated* © Time Inc.
33	Dion Ogust/The Image Works
34	Drawing by S. Gross; © 1994 The New Yorker Magazine, Inc.
36	Marcia Weinstein
39	Topham/The Image Works
40T	M. Setboum/JB Pictures
40B	© Michael Mancuso/*Trenton Times*
45	Rick Friedman/Black Star
46	Baron Hugo van Lawick © 1965 National Geographic Society
47L	Larry Mulvehill/Photo Researchers
47R	Dr. Howard Sochurek
50	Custom Medical Stock Photo
52	Bob Daemmrich/Stock Boston

Chapter 3

55	Barthelmy d'Anglais. *Livre de Proprietés des Choses.* France, 15th c. fol. 37: Medical Consultation. Musee Conde, Chantilly, France
57	Elaine Rebman/Photo Researchers
62	Rainbow
63	Nick Downes/Reprinted with permission from *Science* Vol. 238, 1989. © 1989 American Association for the Advancement of Science.
65	Warren Museum, Harvard Medical School
67T	Rainbow
67B	Steven E. Petersen, Washington University
89	Tim Malyon and Paul Biddle/SPL/Photo Researchers
91	Michael Newman/PhotoEdit
95	Alan Carey/The Image Works
96	Innervisions

Chapter 4

101	Nathan Altman. *Portrait of Anna Achmatova.* Russian State Museum, St. Petersburg, Russia
103	Tony Freeman/PhotoEdit
104L	Skjold/The Image Works
104C	Barbara Alper/Stock Boston
104R	Elizabeth Crews/Stock Boston
107	Tibor Hirsch/Photo Researchers
108	Lionel Delevingne/Stock Boston
109	David Hockney, *George, Blanche, Celia, Albert and Percy, London, Jan. 1983.* © 1983 David Hockney
111	Jeff Greenberg/Picture Cube
113T	Kindra Clineff/Picture Cube
113B	Chuck Solomon/*Sports Illustrated* © Time, Inc.
122	Man Ray, *(Untitled) (Woman/Accordion Overlay).* 1931. Gelatin-silver print, 11⅜ × 8¾″ (28.9 × 2.1 cm). The Museum of Modern Art, New York. Gift of James Thrall Soby. © Man Ray Trust 1995.
125	Courtesy of Dr. Philip G. Zimbardo
126	Photofest
131	Mike Maple/Woodfin Camp & Associates
134	Paul Conklin/PhotoEdit

Chapter 5

137	Jean Geoffrey. *The Resigned.* 1901. Musee d'Orsay, Paris, France
141TL	Topham/The Image Works
141TR	Everett Collection
141BL,BR	Topham/The Image Works
142TL	UPI/Bettmann
142TR	Eric Futran/Photo Researchers
142BL	Brown Brothers
142BR	Tom McCarthy/PhotoEdit

143 Bibliothèque Nationale
147 A.P. Streissguth et al. (1980). Teratogenic effects of alcohol in humans and laboratory animals. *Science*, 209 (July), 355. Reproduced by permission of Fetal Alcohol Syndrome Research Fund, University of Washington
149 Lennart Nilsson, *A Child Is Born*, Dell Publishing Co./Bonniers Vorlag
150 Elizabeth Crews/The Image Works
151 Diana O. Rasche
154 Mike Greenlar/The Image Works
155 Tony Freeman/PhotoEdit
156 Paul Fusco/Magnum
158T Peter Menzel/Stock Boston
158C George Goodwin/Monkmeyer
158B Robert Mayer/Tony Stone Images
159T,B Lew Merrim/Monkmeyer
160T,C,B Marcia Weinstein
163 McLaughlin/The Image Works
166 Arthur Grace/Sygma
168 Springer/Bettmann
171T Patricia Reynolds/Picture Cube
171B Santrock/*Insight* Magazine
173 Innervisions
175 Robert Brenner/PhotoEdit
178 George Ancona

Chapter 6

181 William H. Johnson. *I Baptize Thee.* ca. 1940. National Museum of American Art, Washington, DC
182 Sarah Putnam/Picture Cube
185 Erika Stone
188 Dan Habib/Impact Visuals
189 Courtesy Dr. Alan Fogel, University of Utah
191T © Nina Leen, *Life* Magazine © Time Inc.
191C *The Far Side* by Gary Larson. © 1984 Chronicle Features
191B Barbara Rios/Photo Researchers
195 Martin Rogers/Tony Stone Images
197T Lawrence Migdale/Stock Boston
197B *Cathy* by Cathy Guisewite. Copyright © 1986 Universal Press Syndicate. Reprinted by permission. All rights reserved
199TL Miro Vintoniv/Picture Cube
199TR James Chimbidis/Tony Stone Images
199B Christopher Langridge/Sygma
202 Michael Newman/PhotoEdit
205 Cleo/PhotoEdit
207T&B Annenberg/CPB Program 18/WGBH
208 Spencer Grant/Stock Boston
212 Jeff Greenberg/The Image Works

Chapter 7

215 *Young woman giving her dog a drink.* Persian miniature. Free Library of Philadelphia, Philadelphia, PA
216 David Lissy/Picture Cube
219 Alex von Koscrembahr/Photo Researchers
225 W. E. Harvey/Photo Researchers
232 Fritz Goro, *Life* Magazine © Time Inc.
239L,C,R The Kobal Collection
243 Spencer Grant/Photo Researchers
246 John Cancalosi/Stock Boston
248 Seth Resnick/Stock Boston
251 David Ball/Picture Cube
253 Fuji Photos/The Image Works

Chapter 8

257 Francis Bacon. *Three Figures and a Portrait.* 1975. Tate Gallery, London, Great Britain
258T Taylor Jones/Copyright © 1991 Los Angeles Times Syndicate. Reprinted by permission
258C Taylor Jones/Copyright © 1987, Los Angeles Times Syndicate. Reprinted by permission
258B Taylor Jones/Copyright © 1992 Los Angeles Times Syndicate. Reprinted by permission
260 Innervisions
267T M. C. Escher, *Sky and Water*. Collection of C. V. S. Roosevelt, Washington, DC. Reprinted by permission of M. C. Escher Heirs, Cordon Art, Baarn, Holland
267BL Victor Vasarely, *Gestalt Bleue*. Reprinted by permission of Circle Gallery Fine Art Corp.
267BR Salvador Dali, *Slave Market with Disappearing Bust of Voltaire*. 1940. Oil on canvas. Salvador Dali Museum, St. Petersburg, Florida
269 Boyd Norton/© 1995 Comstock Inc.
276 John Coletti/Picture Cube
284 Dennis O'Clair/Tony Stone Images
288 Andy Levin/Photo Researchers
289TL Duccio, *Maesta: Christ and St. Anne*. 1308–1311. Scala/Art Resource, New York
289TR Perugino, *Delivering the Keys of the Kingdom to St. Peter*. 1481–1483. Scala/Art Resource, New York
290 © Holt Studios/Earth Scenes
291L,R © Susan Schwartzenberg/courtesy The Exploratorium
293L,R DeKeerle/Sygma

Chapter 9

303 Ando Hiroshige. *Right wing of the triptych "Oko Uwanare Uchi Nozu," a traditional rite.* Private collection, France
305 Jerry Wachter/Photo Researchers
306T Johns Hopkins University
306B Joe McNally
308 Bettmann Archive
315 Innervisions
316 Archives of the History of American Psychology, University of Akron
317T © 1995 Comstock Inc.
317B Official U.S. Navy Photograph
318 David M. Phillips/Photo Researchers
322 Jacob H. Bachman
325 David Strickler/The Image Works
326 Yerkes Regional Primate Research Center, Emory University
330 Steve Benbow/Contact Press Images/see also *Ladies' Home Journal*, May 1986
331 Randy Taylor/Sygma
333L,C,R Courtesy Dr. Stuart R. Ellins, California State University, San Bernardino

334 *The Far Side* by Gary Larson. Copyright © 1986 Universal Press Syndicate
337 James Wilson/Woodfin Camp & Associates
338T,C,B Courtesy Dr. Albert Bandura, Stanford University
341 Everett Collection

CHAPTER 10

343 George Catlin. *The Buck's Wife, Wife of the Whale.* 1835. National Museum of American Art, Washington, DC
344 Eileen Darby/Everett Collection
348 Bill Gallery/Stock Boston
355 Linda Gregoritsch/Picturesque
359 Richard Hutchings/Photo Researchers
360 *Peanuts* by Charles Schultz. Reprinted by permission of United Feature Syndicate, Inc.
361 Spencer Grant/Photo Researchers
369 Tom McCarthy/Picture Cube
371 J. H. Langlois and L. A. Roggman (1990). Atractive faces are only average. *Psychological Science*, I(2), 117. Published by the American Psychological Society. Reprinted by permission of Cambridge University Press and the authors
376 © 1995 Comstock Inc.
377 Photofest

CHAPTER 11

384 Tahir Salakhov. *Portrait of the composer Kara-Karajev.* Tretyakov Gallery, Moscow, Russia
386 *Bloom County*. © 1985 Washington Post Writers Group. Reprinted by permission
392 David Young-Wolff/PhotoEdit
394L,R Dr. David Bryant, Northeastern University. Reprinted from Endel Tulving (1989). *American Scientist* (July–August), 365
395 Stuart Cohen/© 1995 Comstock Inc.
397 Gary Bell/The Wildlife Collection
401 The Granger Collection
406 Innervisions
408 Benelux/Photo Researchers
413 © 1995 by Sidney Harris
417 Photofest
419 © 1995 Comstock Inc.
424 Rhoda Sidney/The Image Works

CHAPTER 12

427 *Radha and Krishna in the grove.* Kangra style, c. 1780. Gouache on paper, 12.3 × 17.2 cm. Victoria & Albert Museum, London, Great Britain
428 Everett Collection
430L,R Rich Clarkson/*Sports Illustrated* © Time Inc.
431 John Shaw/Bruce Coleman Inc.
433 Photofest
435 Steven Frame/Stock Boston
439 Reuters/Bettmann
441 Spencer Grant/Photo Researchers
442 © 1995 Comstock Inc.
445 M. J. Cardenas/The Image Bank
448 James D. Wilson/Woodfin Camp & Associates
449 Bob Daemmrich/Stock Boston
453 Tom McCarthy/PhotoEdit
455 Billy E. Barnes/PhotoEdit
457 Paul Avis/Gamma-Liaison

CHAPTER 13

459 Max Oppenheimer (called Mopp). *Sechstagerennen, Six day bicycle race in Berlin's Sportpalast-stadium.* 1929. Berlinische Galerie, Berlin, Germany
460 Photofest
461 New York Public Library/Astor, Lenox and Tilden Foundations
463 Dr. Paul Ekman/Human Interaction Laboratory/University of California, San Francisco
466 Tony Freeman/PhotoEdit
468 Catherine Karnow/Woodfin Camp & Associates
470 Everett Collection
472T William Traufic/The Image Bank
472C Paul Souders/Tony Stone Images–Seattle
472B © Joel Gordon
475 Mark Antman/The Image Works
481 Peter Turnley/Black Star
483 Jim West/Impact Visuals
485 *Peanuts* by Charles Schultz. Reprinted by permission of United Feature Syndicate, Inc.
486 Bob Daemmrich/The Image Works
491 Terry Eiler/Stock Boston
495 Scott Wachter/Photo Researchers
500 Sepp Seitz/Woodfin Camp & Associates
503 Chuck Nacke/Woodfin Camp & Associates

CHAPTER 14

507 William H. Johnson. *Jim.* 1930. Copyright National Museum of American Art, Washington, DC
509 Drawing by Charles Addams; © 1946, 1974 The New Yorker Magazine, Inc.
511 Zentralbibliothek, Zurich
513T The Granger Collection
513C Brady/Bettmann Archive
513B Chris Harris/Gamma-Liaison
515 Tony Freeman/PhotoEdit
517T Dorothy Littell Greco/Stock Boston
517B Gary Braasch/Woodfin Camp & Associates
518 John Coletti/Picture Cube
522 Robert Brenner/PhotoEdit
524 Art © Jim Berris/photo Rafael Macia/Photo Researchers
528 Richard Hutchings/PhotoEdit
529 Richard Hutchings/PhotoEdit
531 Michael Newman/PhotoEdit
535T,C,B FrankSiteman/Picture Cube
536 Jeff Greenberg/Photo Researchers

CHAPTER 15

541 Richard Gerstl. *The Sisters.* 1904–05. Oesterreichische Galerie, Vienna, Austria
543 Courtesy of the National Portrait Gallery, London
549 Bernard Gotfryd/Woodfin Camp & Associates
550 Jeff Greenberg/PhotoEdit
551 David Madison/Duomo
558 Griffin/The Image Works

560 The Granger Collection
564L Edward Clark, *Life* Magazine © Time Inc.
564R Joan Clifford/Picture Cube
568 © 1994 by Patrick Hardin
569L,R © Joel Gordon
570 Art by Eduard Bendemann, 1859/Photo Researchers
576 Reprinted by permission of the publishers from *Thematic Apperception Test*, by Henry A. Murray, Cambridge, MA: Harvard University Press, copyright © 1943 by the President and Fellows of Harvard College; © 1971 by Henry A. Murray
578 Superstock
579 Bob Daemmrich/Stock Boston

Chapter 16

583 Diego Rivera. *The Propagandist.* 1926–27. Universidad Autonoma Chapingo, Chapingo, Mexico
585 Michael S. Yamashita
586ALL Courtesy of Dr. Philip G. Zimbardo
588 Bill Horsman/Stock Boston
590 Kaku Kurita/Gamma-Liaison
592 William Vandivert
594 Bruce Roberts/Photo Researchers
595T,C,B Dr. Ronald Lippitt
596 Azar/Gamma-Liaison
597T,C,B Courtesy Mrs. Alexandra Milgram
600 AP/Wide World
601L,R AP/Wide World
604 Everett Collection
606 Patrick Vielcanet/Photo Researchers
611 Sandra Lousada/Woodfin Camp & Associates
613 Courtesy American Heart Association
615 Robert W. Ginn/Picture Cube
617L,R Dr. O. J. Harvey, University of Colorado
618 Shahn Kermani/Gamma-Liaison
621 Gary A. Conner/PhotoEdit
623 Bob Daemmrich/Stock Boston
625 S. Keen (1986). *Faces of the enemy: Reflections of the hostile imagination*. Copyright © 1986 by Sam Keen. All rights reserved. Reprinted by permission of HarperCollins Publishers, Inc.

Chapter 17

627 Frida Kahlo. *Without Hope (Sin esperanza).* Fundacion Dolores Olmedo, Mexico City, Mexico
628 The Advertising Council; by permission of National Mental Health Association
631 Courtesy of Peabody Essex Museum, Salem, MA
633 The Granger Collection
639 David Lissy/Picture Cube
640TL,TR Dr. Cornelia Wilbur
640B Susan Greenwood/Gamma-Liaison
642 Owen Franken/Stock Boston
646 William Hubbell/Woodfin Camp & Associates
649 Walter P. Chrysler Collection, New York/Scala/Art Resource, New York
650 Obremski/The Image Bank
651 Dr. Michael E. Phelps and Dr. John C. Mazziotta, Department of Molecular and Medical Pharmacology, UCLA School of Medicine
653 David Young-Wolff/PhotoEdit
655 Kirk Weddle/Sipa Press
659 AP/Wide World
661 National Institutes of Mental Health
663 Robert Brenner/PhotoEdit
666 © Mihail Chemiakin

Chapter 18

671 Felice Casorati. *The Stranger.* Galleria d'Arte Moderna, Florence, Italy
674 *Cathy* by Cathy Guisewite. Copyright © 1986 Universal Press Syndicate. Reprinted with permission. All rights reserved
676 The Granger Collection
678 Freud Museum, London
681 Culver Pictures
683 G. Paul Bishop
685 Rick Friedman/Black Star
689 Courtesy Dr. Philip G. Zimbardo
692 Stephen Frisch/Stock Boston
696 © Joel Gordon
697 Robert Neubecker/Leerhessen (1990)
700 Hieronymus Bosch, *Extraction of the Stone of Folly*. Prado, Madrid/Giraudon/Art Resource, New York
701L James Wilson/Woodfin Camp & Associates
701R Will McIntyre/Photo Researchers
703 Jim West/Impact Visuals
705 © 1995 by Sidney Harris
709 Joseph Nettis/Photo Researchers

Literary Credits

Chapter 1

Figure 1.3. From "The Changing Face of American Psychology: A Report from the Committee of Employment and Human Resources," by A. Howard et al., in *American Psychologist*, 41, pp. 1311–1327. Reproduced by permission of the American Psychological Association

Chapter 2

Figure 2.7. By Lynn O'Kelley

Figure 2.18. By Lynn O'Kelley

Chapter 3

Figure 3.1. From *Human Evolution: An Illustrated Introduction*, by Robert Lewin. Copyright © 1984 by W. H. Freeman and Company. Reprinted by permission

Figure 3.6. By Lynn O'Kelley

Figure 3.7. By Lynn O'Kelley

Figure 3.8. By Lynn O'Kelley

Figure 3.15. "The Gate-Control Theory of Pain" from *Psychology Boundaries and Frontiers* by William Buskist and David Gerbing. Copyright © 1990 by Scott, Foresman and Company. Reprinted by permission of HarperCollins College Publishers.

Figure 3.17. Axon membrane drawing from *Scientific American*. Copyright © 1979 by Scientific American, Inc. Used by permission

Figure 3.21. By Lynn O'Kelley

Figure 3.24. From *The Harvey Lectures*, Series 62, by R. W. Sperry. Copyright © 1968 by Academic Press. Reprinted by permission of the author and the publisher

Chapter 4

Figure 4.3 By Lynn O'Kelley

Figure 4.4. By Lynn O'Kelley. Redrawn from an illustration by M. E. Challinor in "Images of the Night," by Kiester, in *Science*, May/June 1980

Figure 4.5. From "Ontogenetic Development of the Human Sleep-Dream Cycle," by H. P. Roffwarg et al., in *Science*, April 1966, Vol. 152, No. 9, pp. 604–619. Copyright © 1966 by AAAS. Reprinted by permission of the American Association for the Advancement of Science

Chapter 5

Figure 5.1. From "Human Cerebral Hemispheres Develop at Different Rates and Ages," by R. W. Thatcher, in *Science*, Vol. 236, pp. 1110–1113. Copyright © 1987 by AAAS. Reprinted by permission of the American Association for the Advancement of Science

Figure 5.3. By Lynn O'Kelley. Redrawn from *The Brain*, by W. M. Cowan. Copyright © 1979 by W. H. Freeman and Company. Reprinted by permission

Figure 5.5. From "The First Two Years" by Mary M. Shirley. Reprinted by permission of the University of Minnesota Press

Figure 5.6. From "Representing the Existence and the Location of Hidden Objects: Object Permanence in 6- and 8-Month-Old Infants," by Renée Baillargeon, in *Cognition*, 23 (1986), pp. 21–41. Reprinted by permission of the author and North-Holland Publishing Company

Table 5.2. From p. 18 of *Child Development*, by L. P. Lipsitt and H. W. Reese. Copyright © 1979 by HarperCollins Publishers. Reprinted by permission of the publisher

Chapter 6

Table 6.2. Adapted from *The Adolescent: A Psychological Self-Portrait*, by Daniel Offer, Eric Ostrov, and Kenneth I. Howard. Copyright © 1981 by Basic Books, Inc. Reprinted by permission of the publisher

Figure 6.2. From p. 225 of *Psychopathology*, edited by D. Magnusson and A. Ohman. Orlando, FL: Academic Press, 1987. Reprinted by permission of Academic Press

Figure 6.3. *Effects of Social Interaction on Well-Being Across Adulthood*, by Masako Ishii-Kuntz. Copyright © 1990 by Baywood Publishing Company, Inc. Reprinted by permission

Table 6.3. From *Adaptation to Life*, by George Vaillant. Copyright © 1977 by George E. Vaillant. Reprinted by permission

Chapter 7

Table 7.1. Adapted by permission from p. 254 of *The Encyclopedic Dictionary of Psychology*, 3rd ed. Copyright © 1986 by the Dushkin Publishing Group, Inc. Reprinted by permission of the author

Table 7.2. From *New Directions in Psychology*, by Roger Brown, Eugene Galanter, and Eckhard H. Hess. Copyright © 1962 by Holt, Rinehart and Winston, Inc. Reprinted by permission of Dr. Eugene Galanter

Table 7.3. From *Introduction to Psychology*, 10th ed., by Atkinson et al. Copyright © 1990 by Harcourt Brace & Company. Reproduced by permission of the author

Figure 7.1. From *Brain, Mind, and Behavior*, rev. ed., by Floyd E. Bloom and Arlyne Lazerson. Copyright © 1985, 1988 by the Educational Broadcasting Corporation. Reprinted by permission of W. H. Freeman and Company

Figure 7.9. Adapted from *Seeing: Illusion, Brain and Mind*, by John P. Frisby. Copyright © 1979 by John P. Frisby. Reprinted by permission of Oxford University Press

Figure 7.10. Figure 2.1, *The Spectrum of Electromagnetic Energy*. Copyright © 1994 by McGraw-Hill, Inc. Reprinted by permission of the publisher

Figure 7.20. From *The Science of Musical Sounds*, by D. C. Miller. Macmillan Company, 1926. Reprinted by permission of Case Western Reserve University

Figure 7.22. From *Theory of Hearing*, by Ernest Glen Weaver. Copyright © 1949 by John Wiley & Sons, Inc. Reprinted by permission of the author

Chapter 8

Figure 8.8. From *Fundamentals of Sensation and Perception*, by M. W. Levine and J. Shefner. Reprinted by permission of Michael W. Levine

Figure 8.9. Figure 3, *New Objects Defined by Motion or Onset*. Copyright © 1993 by American Psychological Society. Reprinted by permission of the American Psychological Society

Figure 8.10. From *Cognitive Psychology and Information Processing: An Introduction*, by Roy Lachman, Janet I. Lachman, and Earl C. Butterfield. Reprinted by permission of the authors and Lawrence Erlbaum Associates, Inc.

Figure 8.12. From "The Effect of Inattention on Form Perception," by I. Rock and D. Gutman, *Journal of Experimental Psychology: Human Perception and Performance, I*. Copyright © 1981 by the American Psychological Association. Reproduced by permission

Figure 8.13. *Three Broad Classes of Visual Search Tasks*. Copyright © 1992 by American Psychological Society. Reprinted by permission of the American Psychological Society

Figure 8.14. Figure 3, *Search for a Conjunction of Two Colors*. Copyright © 1992 by American Psychological Society. Reprinted by permission of the American Psychological Society

Figure 8.15. From "Features and Objects in Visual Processing," by Anne Triesman, in *Scientific American*, November 1986. Copyright © 1986 by Scientific American, Inc. All rights reserved. Reprinted by permission

Figure 8.22. From "Impossible Objects: A Special Type of Visual Illusion," by L. S. Penrose and R. Penrose, in *British Journal of Psychology*, 1958, Vol. 49, p. 3. Reprinted by permission of The British Psychological Society

Figure 8.25. Figure 7.5, *Retinal Disparity Increases with the Distance, in Depth, Between Two Objects*. Copyright © 1994 by McGraw-Hill, Inc. Reprinted by permission of the publisher

Figure 8.26. From *Sensation and Perception*, by Stanley Coren, Clare Porac, and Lawrence M. Ward. Copyright © 1979 by Harcourt Brace & Company. Reprinted by permission of the publisher

Figure 8.29. Adapted from Figure 38 of "The Perspective of a Pavement," in *The Perception of the Visual World*, by James W. Gibson. Copyright © 1950 and renewed 1977 by Houghton Mifflin Company. Adapted by permission of the publisher

Figure 8.34. From *The Logic of Perception*, by I Rock. Copyright © 1983 by the Massachusetts Institute of Technology. Reprinted by permission

Figure 8.36a. From "Representation and Recognition of the Spatial Organization of Three-Dimensional Shapes," by D. Marr and H. K. Nishihara, in *Proceedings of the Royal Society of London*, 1978, p. 200B. Reprinted by permission; Figure 8.36b. From "Recognition by Components: A Theory of Object Recognition," by I. Biederman, in *Computer Vision Graphics and Image Processing*, 1985, p. 32. Reprinted by permission

Figure 8.37. Figure 16, "Examples of five stimulus objects in the experiment on the perception of degraded objects." Copyright © 1987 by the American Psychological Association, Inc. Reprinted with permission of the American Psychological Association, Inc.

Chapter 9

Figure 9.1. From *Psychology*, by William Buskist. Copyright © 1991 by HarperCollins Publishers, Inc. Reprinted by permission

Figure 9.4. From "Predictability and Number Pairings in Pavlovian Fear Conditioning," by Robert A. Rescorla, in *Psychonomic Science*, Vol. 4, No. 11. Reprinted by permission of the Psychonomic Society, Inc.

Figure 9.5. Reprinted by permission of HarperCollins Publishers, Inc.

Figure 9.6. From *Psychology*, by William Buskist. Copyright © 1991 by HarperCollins Publishers, Inc. Reprinted by permission

Figure 9.8. From *Principles and Methods of Psychology*, by Lawson, Goldsten, and Musty. Copyright © 1975 by Oxford University Press, Inc. Reprinted by permission

Figure 9.10. From *Introduction to Psychology*, by Christopher Peterson. Copyright © 1991 by HarperCollins Publisher, Inc. Reprinted by permission

Figure 9.12. From "Learned Association Over Long Delays," by Sam Revusky and John Garcia, in *The Psychology of Learning and Motivation*, Vol. IV, edited by Gordon H. Bower. Orlando, FL: Academic Press, 1970. Reprinted by permission

Figure 9.13. From "Degrees of Hunger, Reward and Non-reward, and Maze Learning in Rats," by E. C. Tolman and C. H. Honzik, in *University of California Publication in Psychology*, Vol. 4, No. 16, December 1930. Reprinted by permission of the University of California Press

Chapter 10

Figure 10.5. Adapted from "The Information Available in Brief Visual Presentation," by George Sperling, in *Psychological Monographs: General and Applied*, Vol. 174, No. 11, Whole No. 498. Copyright © 1960 by the American Psychological Association, Inc. Adapted by permission of the author.

Figure 10.6. From "Short-Term Retention of Individual Verbal Items," by Lloyd R. Peterson and Margaret Jean Peterson, in *Journal of Experimental Psychology*, September 1959, Vol. 58, No. 3. Copyright © 1959 by the American Psychological Association, Inc. Reprinted by permission of the author

Figure 10.7. From "Two Storage Mechanisms in Free Recall," by Murray Glanzer and Anita R. Cunitz, in *Journal of Verbal Learning and Verbal Behavior*. Copyright © 1966 by Academic Press, Inc. Reprinted by permission of the author and the publisher

Figure 10.9. Adapted from Table 1, "Proportion Correct Data for Tasks as a Function of Study Conditions" from the *Journal of Experimental Psychology: Learning, Memory, and Cognition*, 1993, Vol. 19, No. 4. Copyright © 1993 by American Psychological Association, Inc. Reprinted by permission of the American Psychological Association, Inc.

Figure 10.10. From *British Journal of Psychology*, 72, pp. 499–503. Reprinted by permission of The British Psychological Society

Figure 10.12. From "Retrieval Time from Semantic Memory," by Collins and Quillan, in *Journal of Verbal Learning and Verbal Behavior*, Vol. 8, pp. 240–247. Copyright © 1969 by Academic Press, Inc. Reprinted by permission

Figure 10.15. Figure 1, "Effect of Muscimol Infusion on CRs and URs," from *Science*, Volume 260, May 14, 1993. Copyright © 1993 by the American Association for the Advancement of Science. Reprinted by permission of the American Association for the Advancement of Science

Chapter 11

Figure 11.1. From *Cognitive Psychology*, 3rd ed., by Robert L. Solso. Copyright © 1991 by Allyn and Bacon. Reprinted with permission

Table 11.4. From *Sarcastic Indirect Request* by R. W. Gibbs, Jr. Copyright © 1986 by Elsevier *Science* Publishers. Used by permission of the publisher

Table 11.5. "The Monk Puzzle," by James L. Adams. Copyright © 1974 by James L. Adams. Reprinted by permission

Table 11.6. Adapted from *Spatial Reasoning* by Ruth M. J. Byrne and P. N. Johnson-Laird. Copyright © 1989 by Academic Press, Inc. Reprinted by permission of Academic Press, Inc.

Table 11.7. From *Memory & Cognition*, 1993, Vol. 21, No. 4. Copyright © 1993 by Psychonomic Society, Inc. Used by permission

Table 11.8. From the *New England Journal of Medicine*, Vol. 306, 1982. Copyright © 1982 by the New England Journal of Medicine. Reprinted by permission

Figure 11.7. From *Journal of Experimental Psychology: Learning, Memory and Cognition*, 1986, Vol. 12, No. 4. Copyright © 1986 by the American Psychological Association, Inc. Reprinted by permission of the American Psychological Association, Inc.

Figure 11.8. From *Linguistics, An Introduction to Language and Communication*, by Adrian Akmajian, Richard A. Demers, and Robert M. Harnish. Copyright © 1990 by Massachusetts Institute of Technology. Reprinted by permission of the publisher

Table 11.9. From *Psychological Science*, Vol. 3, No. 6, November 1992. Copyright © 1992 by American Psychological Society. Reprinted by permission of the American Psychological Society

Figure 11.13. From *Cognitive Psychology*, 3rd ed., by Robert L. Solso. Copyright © 1991 by Allyn and Bacon. Reprinted with permission

Figure 11.14. From *Cognitive Psychology*, 3rd ed., by Robert L. Solso. Copyright © 1991 by Allyn and Bacon. Reprinted with permission

Figure 11.15. From *How to Solve Problems: Elements of a Theory of Problems and Problem Solving*, by Wayne A. Wickelgren. Copyright © 1974 by W. H. Freeman and Company. Reprinted by permission

Figure 11.18. From *Journal of Personality and Social Psychology*, 1993, Vol. 65, No. 6. Copyright © 1993 by the American Psychological Association, Inc. Reprinted by permission of the American Psychological Association, Inc.

Chapter 12

Figure 12.1. From p. 207 of *Human Sexualities*, by J. H. Gagnon. Copyright © 1977 by HarperCollins Publishers, Inc. Reprinted by permission

Table 12.1. "Effects of Anxiety on Eating: Does Palatability Moderate Distress-Induced Overeating in Dieters?" by Janet Polivy, C. Peter Herman, and Traci McFarlane. Copyright © 1994 by the American Psychological Association, Inc. Reprinted by permission of the American Psychological Association, Inc.

Table 12.2. From *Sex in America: A Definitive Survey*, by Robert T. Michael. Copyright © 1994 by CSG Enterprises, Inc., Edward O. Laumann, Robert T. Michael, and Gina Kolata. Reprinted by permission of Little, Brown and Company

Figure 12.3. Adapted from *Human Motivation*, by Bernard Weiner. Copyright © 1980 by Bernard Weiner. Reprinted by permission of the author

Chapter 13

Table 13.1. Adapted from p. 333 of *Decision Making: A Psychological Analysis of Conflict, Choice, and Commitment*, by I. L. Janis and L. Mann. Copyright © 1977 by The Free Press, a Division of Macmillan, Inc. Adapted with permission of The Free Press

Figure 13.2. From "A Language for the Emotion," by Robert Plutchik, in *Psychology Today*, February 1980. Copyright © 1980 by Sussex Publishing, reprinted by permission

Figure 13.3. From *Psychology*, 3rd ed., by Rathus. Copyright © 1987 by Holt, Rinehart and Winston, Inc. Reprinted by permission

Table 13.3. Adapted from Table 3, p. 475, of "The Minor Events Approach to Stress: Support for the Use of Daily Hassles," by Kerry Chamberlain and Sheryl Zika, in *British Journal of Psychology*, 1990, Vol. 81. Reprinted by permission

Figure 13.7. From Figure 7.10 of *Psychology*, by Michael S. Gazzaniga. Copyright © 1980 by Michael S. Gazzaniga. Reprinted by permission of HarperCollins Publishers, Inc.

Table 13.8. From "Healthy People 2000" in *Centers for Disease Control Morbidity and Mortality Reports*, October 5, 1990, Vol. 39, p. 695. Published by the Department of Health and Human Services

Figure 13.8. From *Health Psychology*, 1994, Vol. 13, No. 5. Copyright © 1993 by the American Psychological Association, Inc., and the Division of Health Psychology. Used by permission

Chapter 14

Table 14.1. Table 2.1 from *Lifespan Development* by Helen Bee. Copyright © 1994 by HarperCollins Publishers, Inc. Reprinted by permission of HarperCollins Publishers, Inc.

Figure 14.2. From *The Inequality of Man*, by H. J. Eysenck. Copyright © 1973 by Hans J. Eysenck. Reprinted by permission of the author

Table 14.3. From the *Journal of Personality*, Vol. 58, No. 2. Copyright © 1990 by Duke University Press. Reprinted by permission of the publisher

Chapter 15

Figure 15.1. From *Wechsler's Measurement and Appraisal of Adult Intelligence*, 5th ed., by J. D. Matarazzo. Copyright © 1972 by Oxford University Press, Inc. Reprinted by permission

Figure 15.3. From p. 161 of *Way Beyond the IQ: Guide to Improving Intelligence and Creativity*, by J. P. Guilford. Buffalo, NY: Barely Limited, 1977. Reprinted by permission of the author

Table 15.1. From "Familial Studies of Intelligence: A Review," by T. J. Bouchard, Jr., and M. McGue, in *Science*, 1981, Vol. 212, pp. 1055–1059. Copyright © 1981 by the AAAS. Reprinted by permission of the American Association for the Advancement of Science

Figure 15.4. From "Achievement and Social Mobility: Relationships Among IQ Score, Education and Occupation in Two Generations," by Jerome H. Waller, in *Social Biology*, September 1971, Vol. 18, No. 3. Copyright © 1971 by The American Eugenics Society, Inc.

Figure 15.5. Adapted from "I.Q. Test Performance of Black Children Adopted by White Families," by S. Scarr and R. A. Weinberg, in *American Psychologist*, 1976, Vol. 31, pp. 726–739. Copyright © 1976 by the American Psychological Association. Adapted by permission of the author

Chapter 16

Table 16.1. From *Perspective on Close Relationships*, edited by Ann L. Weber and John H. Harvey. Copyright © 1994 by Allyn and Bacon. Reprinted by permission of Allyn and Bacon

Figure 16.3. From *The Obedience Experiments: A Case Study of Controversy in the Social Sciences*, by A. G. Miller. Copyright © 1986 by Praeger Publishers. Reprinted by permission of Greenwood Publishing Group, Inc., Westport, CT

Figure 16.4. Adapted from "Bystander Intervention in Emergencies: Diffusion of Responsibilities," by Darley and Latané, in *Journal of Personality and Social Psychology*, 1968, Vol. 8, No. 4, pp. 377–384. Copyright © 1968 by the American Psychological Association. Adapted by permission of the author

Figure 16.5. From "An Experimental Study of Apparent Behavior," by F. Heider and M. Simmel, in *American Journal of Psychology*, 1944, Vol. 57, pp. 243–259. Reprinted by permission of the University of Illinois Free Press

Figure 16.6. From *Judgment Under Uncertainty*, by Daniel I. Kahneman. Copyright © 1982 by Cambridge University Press. Reprinted by permission of Cambridge University Press

Figure 16.7. From the *Journal of Personality and Social Psychology*, 1992, Vol. 63, No. 4. Copyright © 1992 by the American Psychological Association, Inc. Reprinted by permission of the American Psychological Association, Inc.

Chapter 17

Figure 17.1. From p. 9 of *Mental Health for Canadians: Striking a Balance*. Minister of National Health and Welfare, 1988

Table 17.2. From "Multiple Personality Disorder: Phenomenology of Selected Variables in Comparison to Major Depression," by R. Schults, B. G. Braun, and R. P. Kluft, in *Dissociation*, 1989, Vol. 2, p. 45

Table 17.3. From *Abnormal Psychology*, by David L. Rosenhan and Martin E. P. Seligman. Copyright © 1984 by W. W. Norton & Company, Inc. Reprinted by permission of W. W. Norton & Company, Inc.

Figure 17.3. From pp. 72–80 of *Archives of General Psychiatry*, 1984, Vol. 41, by Rosenthal et al. Reprinted by permission

Table 17.5. From *Diagnostic and Statistical Manual of Mental Disorders*, 3rd ed., Revised. Copyright © 1987 by the American Psychiatric Association. Reprinted with permission

Figure 17.4. From *Schizophrenia Genesis*, by Guttesman. Copyright © 1991 by W. H. Freeman and Company. Reprinted by permission

Figure 17.5. From "Genetic Theories and the Validation of Psychiatric Diagnosis: Implications for the Study of Children of Schizophrenics," by Daniel R. Hanson et al., in *Journal of Abnormal Psychology*, 1977, Vol. 86, pp. 575–588. Copyright © 1977 by the American Psychological Association, Inc. Reprinted by permission of the authors

Chapter 18

Table 18.1. From *The Practice of Behavior Therapy*, 2nd ed., by J. Wolpe. Copyright © 1973 by Pergamon Books Ltd. Reprinted with permission

Figure 18.1. From p. 603 of *Journal of Abnormal Psychology*, Vol. 94, by Cook et al. Copyright © 1985 by the American Psychological Association. Adapted by permission

Figure 18.2. From "Modeling Therapy," by Albert Bandura. Reprinted by permission of the author

Table 18.2. Adapted from *Modern Clinical Psychology: Principles of Intervention in the Clinic and Community*, by Sheldon J. Korchin. Copyright © 1976 by Sheldon J. Korchin. Reprinted by permission of Basic Books, Inc., Publishers

Figure 18.4. From pp. 555–558 of *American Journal of Psychiatry*, 1979, Col. 136, by Weissman et al. Reprinted with permission

Name Index

Subject Index